Global Business Law

Global Business Law

Principles and Practice

David Frisch

Professor of Law
Widener University, Wilmington, Delaware

Raj Bhala

Professor of Law
The George Washington University
Washington, D.C.

Carolina Academic Press
Durham, North Carolina

Library of Congress Cataloging-in-Publication Data

Frisch, David.
    Global business law : principles and practice / David Frisch, Raj Bhala.
       p.   cm.
    Includes index.
    ISBN 0-89089-683-6
    1. Export sales contracts — Cases.   2. Commercial law — Cases.
    3. International business enterprises — Law and legislation — Cases.
    I. Bhala, Raj, 1962– . II. Title. III. Series.
    K1030.3.B48   1999
    346.07 — dc21   99-22352
                                              CIP

Carolina Academic Press
700 Kent Street
Durham, North Carolina 27701
Telephone (919) 489-7486
Facsimile (919) 493-5668
E-mail: cap@cap-press.com
www. cap-press.com

Printed in the United States of America.

To Xandy and Julianna, my daughters, with love.

D.J.F.

*To Dad, with an admiration and respect that
even this wordsmith cannot describe.*

R.K.B.

Contents

PART III REGULATORY CHALLENGES

Chapter 9 Regulating Foreign Direct Investment

Chapter 10 Regulating Multinational Corporate Conduct

Table of Cases

Preface to the First Edition

Perhaps it will come as a surprise to admit that I took on this book project with an impending sense of doom, and that my excellent co-author and dear friend, Professor David Frisch, and I complete it with a sense of failure.

Global Business Law, and the accompanying *Documents Supplement* and *Teacher's Manual*, are designed for what is now a standard course in the curriculum of American, and indeed many overseas, law schools: "International Business Transactions" (frequently abbreviated as "IBT"), which sometimes is called "International Business Law." The rubric is of no consequence. The real problem is that after teaching the course two or three times, every professor should realize that it is an impossible one. Not even the best of professors with the most gifted of students can cover all aspects of international business law in one semester. There is no clear way to determine what topics should be covered, and what should be omitted. There is no obvious way to focus the course. There is no one best way to organize the voluminous subject matter. In short, teaching a second or third year law student, or LL.M. candidate, the transactional, legal, and policy aspects of global business in one semester is about as easy as explaining to a foreign guest what America is like in one hour.

Given the inherent impossibility of the course, why should I have enlisted Dave, and why should we together have started what is possibly a march of folly? We offer five reasons.

First, because we believe that whatever topics are covered, wherever the emphasis is placed, whichever organizational framework is used, the course can "globalize" law students and professors alike. In other words, as "impossible" as an IBT course is, we believe there is no simpler, more efficient, or more practical alternative. The course can make the second or third year law student, or LL.M. candidate, more conscious of the global dimensions of legal practice. She can become better able to "spot" cross-border issues, and thus be better prepared for the global economy of the 21st Century. In this respect, the course makes the notoriously parochial American legal curriculum just a little less so. That is a good thing.

In turn, this introductory survey course in international business course can provide the necessary foundation for advanced courses in the specialty areas of international business law, which ought—both in a positive and normative sense—to be offered with increasing frequency in American law schools in the New Millennium. Such courses include International Trade Law, International Dispute Resolution, and International Tax Law. (Indeed, I use *Global Business Law* in my IBT course. This course is followed by International Trade Law, in which I use *International Trade Law: Cases and Materials* (published by Lexis Law Publishing).) Using *Global Business Law* in an IBT course also can provide the foundation for advanced classes, sometimes offered as seminars, in Foreign Direct Investment, International Banking Law, International Commercial Law, and International Negotiations.

Second, because while we believe that there are excellent course books available for use in the course, we believe we offer a distinct and attractive alternative. We very much believe in "letting 100 flowers bloom." A large number of books in a legal field bespeaks the growing importance and continued maturation of that field. Indeed, we submit that any author of any worthwhile work who claims to be content with the *status quo* is either lying or engaged in self-deception. Each of us in the legal academy is motivated to write a law review article, treatise, or casebook, in part because we are profoundly dissatisfied with some of the "flowers." That dissatisfaction is healthy, because it forms part of the basis for our passion to create, to contribute to scholarship and pedagogy, and most of all, to help.

Professor Frisch and I have enormous respect for the courageous scholars who have gone before us down the treacherous path on which we now find ourselves. But, we put ourselves on this path because we are not complacent about many of the extant course books. Many try to be all things to all readers. Many are characterized by a very large number of very short excerpts on an uncontrollably wide array of topics. Many lack vision. As regards personal finance, you would be right to invest your savings with a financial consultant who (among other virtues) has a clear perspective on global capital flows and market movements. Why be less demanding when it comes to your international business law education? You would be right to expect a book that prioritizes subject matter coverage based on a keen and articulated sense of what will be important in global business in the New Millennium. Mindful of the law and economics movement, we are idealistic (naive?) enough to believe that at least as much rational planning ought to be put into decisions about human capital growth as household wealth accumulation!

Yes, the IBT course is supposed to be a survey. But, the law student and, dare we admit, law professor ought not be left as confused as she is stimulated, as frustrated as she is enthusiastic. As lawyers, we yearn for depth, to know more and more, and thus rarely are we happy with "snippets." Moreover, as international business lawyers, we must have a thorough understanding not only of relevant law and policy, but also—indeed first—of how the transaction at hand "works," and what potential risks are involved. Indeed, so important are risks in particular that we would be prepared to defend the proposition that much of the practice of international business law consists of the effective identification of risks and management thereof.

We would also be prepared to defend the proposition that the multinational corporations (MNCs) are as—if not more—important actors in the global economy than all but a handful of sovereign national governments. The stark fact is that of the top 100 economies in the world, 51 are MNCs. The size of the Ford Motor Company, for example, is larger than the economy of either Saudi Arabia or Norway (both of which are major oil producing countries). You would not go to a Green Bay Packer football game to watch the food and beverage vendors (unless you were participating in a sociological experiment!). Why would you select a casebook that does not emphasize risks and risk management in the conduct of multinational corporate affairs, and that fails to grapple with the possible relationship of MNCs to corruption, human rights abuses, and environmental degradation? Put differently, in the New Millennium, understanding how the MNC is destroying traditional distinctions between business and legal judgments, and between public and private international law, is crucial—and, therefore, a theme that resonates in this Casebook.

Professor Frisch and I, therefore, have tried to prepare *Global Business Law* with the "big game" in mind. We endeavor to cover a still-impressive array of topics, but not at the expense of depth. We strive to choose excerpts in *Global Business Law* that convey the range of legal and policy problems, and risk issues, in global business, but then edit them in a way that allows the reader to get as complete a picture as possible about these problems. Thus, we have a smaller number of challenging readings, but the average length of each reading is longer, than most other course books. We make no apologies, in particular, for not trying to teach International Trade Law, International Dispute Resolution, or substantial chunks of International Tax Law through this Casebook. Those specialties are far too rich to capture in a few weeks. Better to leave them to a full course of its own, and target *Global Business Law* on the principles and practice of the most important types of wealth-generating, wealth-spreading transactions known to the global economy. Whatever trade, dispute resolution, or tax issues the student of *Global Business Law* misses, she certainly makes up for with a profound knowledge — and thus a keen ability to "issue spot" — with respect to exporting, foreign direct investment, and attendant regulatory matters.

Third, and closely related to the second, because we believe that exporting and foreign direct investment (FDI) are the essential foundations of contemporary international business. Here, then, is the vision: the most essential global business transactions a law student must understand are exporting and FDI. These two transactions are the "big game" in global business (excluding finance). Indeed, they reflect the life-cycle of many companies. A firm begins to sell its product or offer its services in a domestic market, and thereafter realizes there are ready, willing, and able buyers in overseas locations. Indeed, many prospective consumers are likely to be in newly industrializing and less developed countries of the non-western world. So, the company commences exporting. Later, the exporter finds that making its goods in overseas locations, or offering its services with a base in those locations, is desirable for an array of economic, political, and cultural reasons. Therefore, the exporter sets up operations in one or more other countries, hence becoming an MNC.

Exporting — if it is to be understood thoroughly — entails an array of contract, carriage, and payments issues. Thus, Part I (the first four Chapters) of *Global Business Law* are dedicated to exporting. The FDI transaction — again, if it is to be understood thoroughly — entails an array of negotiating and structuring, financing, political risk, and currency risk issues. Thus, Part II (the subsequent four Chapters) of *Global Business Law* are dedicated to FDI. Both exporting and FDI raise many cross-border regulatory challenges. Thus, Part III (the last four Chapters) of *Global Business Law* cover the regulation of FDI flows, the new social responsibilities of MNCs, technology transfer, countertrade, government procurement, telecommunications, and antitrust. The learning experience is cumulative, not *ad hoc*, *i.e.*, each Part, and each Chapter of each Part, builds on its predecessor in a logical fashion.

Fourth, because we believe our alternative is user-friendly. As just suggested, there are three Parts to *Global Business Law*, each with four Chapters. Most law school academic semesters are fourteen weeks. We have constructed *Global Business Law* so that most of the Chapters are of roughly equal length and difficulty, and thus can be covered in one week's worth of classes (*i.e.*, assuming a three-credit course, two 75 minute classes, or three 50-minute classes, per week). This plan leaves two weeks, to be used at the discretion of the professor. One possibility is to spend an extra week on the longer chapters — namely, Chapter 3, on Cross-Border Payments, Chapter 10, on Regulating Multinational Corporate Conduct, and Chapter 12, on International Antitrust Issues. Another possibility is to spend an extra week on one of the longer Chapters, and the final week of the semester on review sessions. Still another possibility is for the instructor to spend either or both of the extra weeks covering material she finds interesting that is not covered in *Global Business Law*.

Of course, there is more to being user-friendly than organizing a casebook in a way that fits naturally with the academic calendar. We — and our friends at Carolina

Academic Press—have done our best to minimize errors, which obviously annoy us all and, to a certain degree, are inevitable. But, we also have taken a few editing liberties to make the excerpts in *Global Business Law* and the accompanying *Documents Supplement* easier on the eye to read. It is a wonder what **bold**, *italics*, and SMALL CAPS can do for the naked eye, especially late the night before class. Tab sets, indenting, and centering also can be a fillip that enhances learning simply by clarifying a text, and we have used these devices when appropriate.

Fifth, because we believe our alternative is a uniquely cosmopolitan one. The word "global" in the title of this Casebook is no accident. This is not simply a book for Americans who are interested in "going international," any more than it is a book for a law student—or again, dare we say, law professor—who does not want to take the time to read learn about exporting, FDI, and related regulatory issues in depth. *Global Business Law* aims at the present or aspiring *world* citizens who are going to practice, and *world* law professors who are going to teach, in an increasingly borderless business world. There are, for example, cases and case abstracts in *Global Business Law* from all over the world. Moreover, *Global Business Law* tries to probe differences across legal cultures without providing the reader with a false sense of certainty. To the contrary, perhaps the most valuable pedagogical contribution *Global Business Law* can make is to leave the student and teach alike with a higher level of comfort with, and a greater understanding of, uncertainty.

Thus, while many of the "classics" are found between the covers of *Global Business Law*, throughout the casebook, readings—often from overseas sources—challenge conventional wisdom and reflect non-American perspectives. In this (and other) respects, the Casebook is not easy. We want to challenge the sophisticated student and professor who already has traveled widely abroad. At the same time, we seek to stimulate in the reader who has not yet done that sense of adventure that compels her to get her passport and get on a plane the day after the exam.

So, if, for these five reasons, we believe sincerely in the course and are proud of the alternative we offer you, then why do we confess a sense of failure? Because we know from researching and writing *Global Business Law* how vast international business law is, how there is no end to detail, and—most importantly—how there are legitimate competing visions. There are always those readings not included, those organizational frameworks not selected, and those themes not highlighted, that give us pause, indeed doubt, about our own work. In brief, we know that our choices are not necessarily "right," and that in truth it is impossible for anyone to get it "right." The more we learn, the more we realize that there are no right—much less easy—answers, only hard questions that cry out for exploration. Thus, we commend *Global Business Law* to you with intellectual humility.

Because we know there is room for improvement, we look to you to help us through your comments and suggestions. Please direct them anytime to me at the co-ordinates below. With all good wishes.

Raj Bhala
Professor of Law
August 1999

Law School, The George Washington University
2000 H Street, N.W., Washington, D.C. 20052
Tel. 202-994-2266 / Fax. 202-994-9446

Acknowledgments

We would like to express our thanks to the publishers listed below for their kind willingness to allow us to reprint materials originally published by them on which they hold the copyright:

Eric E. Bersten and Anthony J. Miller, *The Remedy of Reduction of Price*, 27 AM. J. COMP. L. 255, — (1979). Reprinted by permission.

Raj Bhala, *Risk Trade-Offs in the Foreign Exchange Spot, Forward and Derivative Markets*, 1 THE FINANCIER 34-49 (August 1994). Reprinted with permission (www.the-financier.com).

Michael Joachim Bonell, *The UNIDROIT Principles of International Commerical Contracts: Why? What? How?* originally published in 69 TUL. L. REV. 1121-1147 (1995). Reprinted with permission of the Tulane Law Review, which holds the copyright. All rights reserved.

Eric M. Burt, *Developing Countries and the Framework for Negotiations on Foreign Direct Investment in the World Trade Organization*, 12 AMERICAN UNIVERSITY JOURNAL OF INTERNATIONAL LAW AND PUBLIC POLICY 1015, 1040-49 (1997). Reprinted by permission.

Francesco Caramazza and Jahangir Aziz, *Fixed or Flexible?* 1-11, 13 (International Monetary Fund 1998). Reprinted by permission.

Robert C. Ciricillo et al., International Negotiations: A Cultural Perprective, in *The ABA Guide to International Business Negotiations* 5, 7-14 (James R. Silkenat & Jeffrey M. Aresty Eds. 1994). Reprinted by permission.

Bernardo M. Cremades and Steven Plehn, *The New Lex Mercatoria and the Harmonization of the Laws of International Commercial Transaction*, 2 B.U. INT'L L.J. 317, 318-20, 324 (1984). Reprinted by permission.

Peter V. Darrow, et al., *Financing Infrastructure Projects in the International Capital Markets: The Trisbasa Toll Road Trust*, 1 THE FINANCIER 9-19 (August 1994). Reprinted by permission.

Joshua P. Eaton, *The Nigerian Tragedy, Environmental Regulation of Transnational Corporations, and the Human Right to a Healthy Environment*, 15 BOSTON UNIVERSITY INTERNATIONAL LAW JOURNAL 262, 264-71, 292-303 (Spring 1997). Reprinted by permission.

Robert H. Edwards and Simon N. Lester, *Towards a More Comprehensive World Trade Organization Agreement on Trade Related Investment Measures*, 33 STANFORD JOURNAL OF INTERNATIONAL LAW 169, 170-80, 187, 195-97, 199, 201-04, 206-13 (1997). Reprinted with permission of the STANFORD JOURNAL OF INTERNATIONAL LAW. Copyright © 1997 by the Board of Trustees of the Leland Stanford Junior University.

Kimberly Ann Elliott, *Corruption as an International Policy Problem: Overview and Recommendations, in Corruption and the Global Economy*, 175, 177-190, 192-200, 216-24 (Kimberly Ann Elliott Ed. June 1997). Reprinted by permission.

Robert J. Fowler, *International Environmental Standards for Transnational Corporations*, 25 ENVIRONMENTAL LAW 1-4, 8-30 (1995). Reprinted by permission.

William F. Fox, Jr., *International Commercial Agreements* 154, 159-64, 177-82 (2nd ed. 1992). Reprinted with kind permission from Kluwer Law International.

Sir Joseph Gold, *The IMF's Article VIII, Section 2(b) and Scrupulosity, in Yearbook of International Financial & Economic Law*, 25-27, 45-51 (Joseph J. Norton, Ed.) (1998). Reprinted with kind permission from Kluwer Law International.

Edward F. Greene et al., *Hegemony or Deference: U.S. Disclosure Requirement in the International Capital Markets*, 50 THE BUSINESS LAWYER 413-21, 423-43 (February 1995). Reprinted by permission.

Claudio Grossman and Daniel D. Bradlow, *Are We Being Propelled Towards a People-Centered Transnational Legal Order?* 9 AMERICAN UNIVERSITY JOURNAL OF INTERNATIONAL LAW AND POLICY 1, 2-9, 11-13, 22-25 (1993). Reprinted by permission.

Joongi Kim and Jong B. Kim, *Cultural Differences in the Crusade Against International Bribery: Rice-Cake Expenses in Korea and the Foreign Corrupt Practices Act*, 6 PACIFIC RIM LAW & POLICY JOURNAL 549, 561-70 (1997). Reprinted by permission.

Boris Kozolchyk, *The Immunization of Fradulently Procured Letter of Credit Acceptances: All Services Exportacao, Importacao Comercio, S.A. v. Banco Bamerindus Do Brazil, S.A. and First Commercial v. Gotham Originals*, 58 BROOKLYN LAW REVIEW 369, 380-85 (1992).

Boris Kozolchyk, *The Emerging Law of Standby Letters of Credit and Bank Guarantees*, 24 ARIZONA LAW REVIEW 319, 320-30 (1982). Copyright © 1982 by the Arizona Board of Regents. Reprinted by permission.

William H. Meyer, *Human Rights and MNCs: Theory Versus Quantitative Analysis*, 18 HUMAN RIGHTS QUARTERLY 368, 375-82, 386-94, 396-97 (1996). Copyright © 1996. The Johns Hopkins University Press.

Peter Muchlinski, *Multinational Enterprises and the Law* 425-47, 449 (1995)

James C. Nobles, Jr. and Johannes Lang, *The UNCITRAL Legal Guide on International Countertrade Transactions: The Foundation for a New Era in Countertrade?* 30 INTERNATIONAL LAWYER 739-54 (Winter 1996).

Joseph M. Perillo, *UNIDROIT Principles of International Commerical Contracts: The Black Letter Text and a Review*, 63 FORDHAM L. REV. 281, 313-14 (1997). Reprinted by permission.

R. Edward Price, *Foreign Blocking Statutes and the GATT: State Sovereignty and the Enforcement of U.S. Economic Law Abroad*, 23 GEORGE WASHINGTON JOURNAL OF INTERNATIONAL LAW AND ECONOMICS 315, 322-31 (1995). Reprinted with permission of *The George Washington Journal of International Law and Economics*.

David Reid, *Foreign Exchange Controls and Repatriation, in Negotiating and Structuring International Commercial Transactions* 67-79 (Shelly P. Battram & David N. Goldsweig Eds., 1991). Reprinted by permission.

Otto Sandrock, *"Handcuffs" Clauses in International Contracts: Basic Reflections on the Autonomy of the Parties to Choose the Proper Law for Their Contracts*, 31 INTERNATIONAL LAWYER 1105 (1997). Reprinted by permission.

John A. Spanogle, *Incoterms and UCC Article 2 - Conflicts and Confusions*, 31 INTERNATIONAL LAWYER 111, 116-124 (1997). Reprinted by permission.

Raymond Vernon, *Where are the Multinationals Head? in Foreign Direct Investments* 57-77 (Kenneth A. Froot Ed. 1993). Reprinted with permission from The University of Chicago Press.

David A. Victor, Cross-Cultural Awareness, in *The ABA Guide to International Business Negotiations* 15, 19-21 (James R. Silkenat & Jeffrey M. Aresty Eds. 1994). Reprinted by permission.

Throughout *Global Business Law*, we have endeavored to ensure that the excerpted material appears as it was originally published. However, we have taken the editorial liberty of making minor typographical, spelling, and punctuation corrections, and occasionally putting special titles (particularly those of international agreements conventions) in *italics* (*e.g.*, the *Agreement on Trade-Related Investment Measures*). Also, in some cases we have altered slightly the format (*e.g.*, tab spaces, centering, and indents, and the use of **bold**, *italics*, or SMALL CAPS) of headings and sub-headings. These changes are designed only to make the text as readable as possible. In no way do they alter the substantive content of the material.

We have, like most casebook authors, omitted virtually all of the footnotes from the material we excerpt, preserving only those citations that seem to have a strong pedagogical value. Some of the Notes prepared for *Global Business Law* do have footnotes, which may provide useful information for further study and research.

We are indebted to Ms. Winifred Hercules of The George Washington University Law School, and to the Faculty Support Center at the William & Mary School of Law (particularly Ms. Della Harris and Ms. Felicia Burton), for their tireless efforts and cheerful demeanor in preparing Professor Bhala's manuscript chapters. Thanks also are due to Julianna Frisch, who taught Professor Frisch all he knows about computers, and thus was indispensable. Doug Dziak, Esq., Greg Logerfo, Esq., Chris Matteson, Esq., Scott McBride, Esq. provided critical help in preparing questions and answers for the *Teacher's Manual*. The support of these fine people shows just how much of a team effort a massive undertaking like this one really is.

Finally, the wise and mature counsel of our publisher, Keith Sipe, cannot go unmentioned. Always available, always empathetic, always flexible, always creative, always fun, Keith stimulates us to challenge ourselves to be better scholars and teachers. We hope we have not disappointed him.

Global Business Law

Part I

Exporting

Chapter 1

Formation of the Export Contract

I. Introduction

Documents Supplement References:

1. *United Nations Convention on Contracts for the International Sale of Goods (CISG).*
2. *UNIDROIT International Principles of CommercialContracts.*
3. *Uniform Commercial Code Article 2 (Sales).*

NOTE ON INTERNATIONAL CONTRACTS

It should be obvious to anyone who thinks about international sales, even for a brief moment, that the typical export-import contract involves risks far different in degree and substance from those encountered by parties to a domestic sales transaction. For one thing, the risk that either the buyer or the seller might be dishonest or otherwise fail to perform is exacerbated by the fact that international trading partners are frequently far removed from one another. If, for example, the buyer wrongfully refuses to pay or the seller wrongfully refuses to deliver, the aggrieved may be faced with the vagaries, uncertainties, and delays of foreign litigation. For another thing, the goods must usually travel relatively long distances under a separate contract of carriage with an independent third-party carrier. Inherent in such an arrangement are various transportation risks such as the risk that the goods will be damaged or lost while still in transit. Finally, because the goods must necessarily cross national boundaries, risks of governmental intervention abound: necessary licenses may be revoked, transfer of foreign exchange may be prohibited, and relevant borders may be closed.

Given these and other risks, the practical problem for each contracting party is to shape the transaction so that the burdens and risks are allocated in a manner acceptable to each. In order to do this effectively, it is absolutely essential that the parties have a basic understanding of the law applicable to the contract. When trading domestically, such comprehension is not difficult. Even an inexperienced attorney will know that a contract involving a New York seller of goods and a Texas buyer is governed primarily by the Uniform Commercial Code, regardless of where a lawsuit might be brought. Even if the attorney's understanding of the relevant rules is uncertain, the source of law is not. She need only consult Article 2 to discover those rules and the extent to which they may be modified by the parties' agreement. Knowing the source of law is, therefore, more important in the first instance than knowing the law itself; without a grasp of the former one cannot hope to know the latter.

Next, consider an American seller who wishes to sell goods to a German buyer. What is the applicable source of law? An answer may not be possible until the competent forum is established. That is, this very same contract may well be subject to the law of the United States or the law of Germany, depending on the conflict of laws rules of the forum chosen. Moreover, one must ascertain whether the law to be applied is the domestic law of the chosen state (*e.g.*, the U.C.C.) or rules of law reserved for international trade. Fortunately, much progress has been made in recent years to remedy the defects in international trade generally and, specifically, to reduce the impact of national boundaries in the important area of sales law.

Aside from the particular details of the chosen technique, the harmonization of transnational commerce has assumed two basic forms. One can be described as international legislation. This would include supranational legislation, international conventions, and model laws. An example is the United Nations Convention on Contracts for the International Sale of Goods (CISG), which is arguably the single greatest legislative achievement aimed at harmonizing the law of sales. The CISG is currently in force in a total of 47 countries, and the United Nations maintains a "hotline" for up-to-date information on the state of ratifications. The number is (212) 963-5047.

Another convention of importance and one which supplements the CISG is the Convention on the Limitation Period in the International Sale of Goods, June 14, 1974, U.N. Doc. A/Conf.63/15, and an amending Protocol, April 10, 1980, U.N. Doc. A/Conf.97/18. The United States became a party on January 1, 1988, and the Convention and Protocol both entered into force August 1, 1988.

The other form of harmonization is international commercial custom in its broadest sense. This presupposes, of course, a certain degree of uniformity with regard to matters such as commercial usages, standard clauses, contracts, and contractual rules. What follows is an overview of the basic components of each form of harmonization as they relate to contracts for the sale of goods.

A. The CISG and Its Background

Franco Ferrari, Uniform Interpretation of the 1980 Uniform Sales Law
24 Georgia Journal of International and Comparative Law
183, 189-195 (1994)

[A]t the end of the 1920's, Ernst Rabel suggested to the Governing Council for the International Institute for the Unification of Private law (UNIDROIT) that it start with the work for the unification of the law of international sales of goods. Upon this suggestion, UNIDROIT decided to undertake the necessary preparatory studies that consequently led to the appointment of a commission entrusted with the elaboration of a uniform law and, in 1935, to the first draft of a uniform law on the sale of goods....

Work had to be interrupted as a result of World War II, but resumed in 1951 with a conference at the Hague where a new draft uniform law was presented. Other drafts followed this, the last of which formed the subject of the Diplomatic Conference held at the Hague from the first to the twenty-fifth of April, 1964. Twenty-eight States participated and approved two conventions, creating respectively the Uniform Law on the International Sale of Goods (ULIS) and the Uniform Law on the Formation of Contracts for the International Sale of Goods (ULF).

These laws, even thought they constituted the most important point of reference for the discipline of international trade in that era, were not as successful as expected. Indeed, they were given force in only nine countries, only one-third of the states which participated in the Hague Conference. Such failure can in part be attributed to the scarce role that both Socialist and the Third World countries played in the elaboration and compilation of the aforementioned Conventions, and which resulted in these countries' refusal to enact the 1964 Hague Conventions which they considered as being modeled on the sole exigencies of the industrialized nations.

The continuing dissatisfaction produced by the forgoing laws was manifested not only in the already-noted scarce number of contracting states, but also in the refusal on the part of other states, such as the United States and France, to ratify those conventions. This led, still before their enactment in 1972, the United Nations Commission on International Trade Law (UNICITRAL), established by the United Nations in 1966 with the task of promoting the progressive harmonization and unification of the law of international trade by promoting wider participation in existing international conventions and wider acceptance of existing model and uniform laws, to attempt the revision of the Hague Uniform Laws. However, when it became apparent that such uniform laws would not be accepted without substantial alterations, "[a] fourteen-member Working Group was established to begin drafting a new text."

In the following years, UNICITRAL proposed various drafts, the last of which-dating back to 1978-was the draft upon which the General Assembly of the United Nations authorized the convening of a diplomatic conference, held from March 10 to April 11, 1980 in Vienna. At the end of the conference, which was attended by representatives of 62 States, after the Convention had been voted upon in Plenary article by article, it was, as a whole, submitted to a roll-call vote and was approved unanimously. The Convention, which is officially known as the "United Nations Convention on Contracts for the International Sale of Goods," came into force January 1, 1988.

Today, this example of a so-called self-executing treaty, is in force in more than thirty States, among which are some of the major commercial partners of the United States, such as China, France, Germany, and Italy.

B. International Commercial Custom (The New Lex Mercatoria)

Bernado M. Cremades & Steven L. Plehn,
The New Lex Mercatoria and the Harmonization of the Laws of International Commercial Transactions,
2 Boston University International Law Journal 317, 318-20, 324 (1984)

The inchoate nation-state system which characterized Western European *medieval* society was conductive to the development of an autonomous merchant law. Feudal society was tightly-knit, tied to the land and isolated. The medieval merchant, however, was geographically dynamic, and encountered a host of different and conflicting lawmaking authorities.

Sovereigns throughout the European continent and England adopted a laissez-faire approach toward the merchant class because of the increased tax revenues and access to foreign goods provided by the merchant class. Merchants were permitted to regulate their own affairs provided they did not infringe upon local concerns. In addition, sovereigns established special commercial courts for merchants to settle their disputes. The merchant judges presiding at these courts acted much like modern arbitrators; they relied on norms of commercial behavior and their familiarity with the needs of commerce to resolve conflicts. These norms reflected the need for flexibility and trust within a dynamic environment. Because of their familiarity with the needs of commerce, these merchants applied a law differing from that applied by local adjudicators who were bound by regional needs and a static feudal society. In the merchant courts the crucial principles of good faith dealing and the binding nature of agreements helped to produce more specific rules and determine the growth of new commercial instruments. This evolution of rules and instruments facilitating trade is exemplified by this abandonment of contractual formalities, the legal recognition given to bearer bills of exchange, and the protection of good faith purchasers from the claims of original owners. The law evolving from the merchant courts is what we now call the *Lex Mercatoria*.

The *Lex Mercatoria* was largely self-enforcing; a party who refused to comply with a merchant court's decision risked his reputation and could be excluded from trading at the all-important fairs where the merchant courts were located. Parties to a dispute rarely needed the aid of the local sovereign to enforce a merchant court's decision. The ability of the merchant class to both generate and enforce its own norms of behavior allowed it to achieve a large degree of independence from these local sovereigns.

As the modern nation-state developed during the sixteenth century, rulers of sovereign states began to regard the autonomous *Lex Mercatoria* as an external threat to internal cohesiveness. In an attempt to subject all citizens to a single national law, the privileged status afforded merchants during the medieval era was terminated. Merchant courts were merged into national court systems at the same time. However, the innovations of the *Lex Mercatoria* were not ignored; rather, they were assimilated into national law to the extent that they were compatible with national policies. Unfortunately, the assimilation of the *Lex Mercatoria* into separate legal systems rendered it subject to the idiosyncrasies of each nation-state. The *Lex Mercatoria* ceased to exist as a homogeneous and autonomous body of law.

Centuries later, the disintegration of the European empires after World War II produced a plethora of independent nations with unique laws, courts, and procedures for regulation of commercial transactions. The post-war global fragmentation contrasts sharply with the increasingly international character of the world's economy. Multinational enterprises, the vehicles of much of the world's commerce, are normally associated with particular countries, but are essentially international in character. They are analogous to the medieval merchants whose activities were superimposed on a patchwork of local sovereignties and were hardly amenable to local regulation. Not surprisingly, this environment has fostered the development of a New *Lex Mercatoria*.

NOTE ON MANIFESTATIONS OF THE NEW *LEX MERCATORIA*

The application of the new "law merchant" or international commercial custom has taken place in the context of international arbitration where arbitrators are aware of general commercial principles and practices and utilize them in rendering their decisions. One also sees the New *Lex Mercatoria* at work in the promulgation of standard contracts and conditions by trade associations whose members are actively engaged in international commerce. For example, there are the standard contract forms sponsored by the Grain and Feed Trade Association (GAFTA, London) and the Federation of Oil, Seed and Fats Association (FOSFA, London). Commercial understandings reflected in the contract practices of international traders have also served as the basis for the important work-product of at least two influential agencies engaged in the preparation of world-wide acceptable rules, i.e., UNIDROIT and the ICC.

C. The UNIDROIT Principles of International commercial Contracts

David A. Levy, Contract Formation Under the UNIDROIT Principles of International Contracts, UCC, Restatement, and CISG,
30 Uniform Commercial Code Law Journal 249, 253-57 (1998)

History of UNIDROIT

The International Institute for the Unification of Private Law (UNIDROIT) has a distinguished history in the field of international law unification and harmonization. It was founded in 1926 by the League of Nations in order to "examine ways of harmonizing and coordinating the private law of States and groups of States, and to prepare gradually for the adoption by the various States of uniform legislation in the field of private law."[1] Today, UNIDROIT is an autonomous intergovernmental organization headquartered in Rome. Congress, in response to private sector recognition of the importance of the development of modern laws creating predictability in international trade, authorized U.S. participation in UNIDROIT in 1964.

U.S. Participation

Participation in the unification and harmonization of private international law is accomplished through the work of the Office of the Assistant Legal Adviser for Private International Law of the Department of State (L/PIL) and its Advisory Committee on Private International Law. The Advisory Committee, made up of distinguished academics and private partitioners, includes representatives of U.S. legal groups such as the American Bar Association, the American Society of International Law, the National Commission on Uniform State Laws, and the American Law Institute. The Department draws on private sector expertise through its specialized study groups of the Advisory Committee, which work on particular projects of current interest to the global private law community. Members of the study groups and the Advisory Committee are active participants in the drafting and preparatory work that precedes the final form of a convention, model law, legal guide, or other instrument of private international law, bringing a practical knowledge to the conference table. Once a text has been drafted, the Advisory Committee and members of the specialized study

---

1. David A. Levy, *Financial Leasing Under the UNIDROIT Convention and the Uniform Commercial Code: A Comparative Analysis*, 5 INDIANA INT'L & COMP. L. REV. 267, 271 (1995) (citing Statute of the International Institute for the Unification of Private Law, done at Rome Mar. 15, 1940, art. 1, 15, UST 2494, 2501, TIAS No. 5743 (entered into force July 15, 1995; for the United States, Mar. 13, 1964). Amendments: June 15-16, 1965, 19 UST 7802, TIAS No. 6611; Dec. 18, 1967, 20 UST 2529, TIAS No. 6716; Feb. 18, 1968, 30 UST 5663, TIAS No. 9519).

groups provide sources of support and information for the project as it is circulated for approval prior to submission to the Senate where required.

Drafting the UNIDROIT Principles

UNIDROIT, in 1971, initially contemplated work on international commercial contract principles. A steering committee made of up Professors Rene David, Clive M. Schmitthoff, and Todor Popescu, reflecting civil law, common law, and socialist legal traditions was established. Subsequently, a Working Group of experts in contract and trade law was established, including jurists and academics from all major legal systems. These experts were not "philosophers," but practitioners well versed in contemporary commercial practice. As the drafts progressed, outside advice was solicited from a wide range of scholars and transactional attorneys. As Professor Bonell observes, one of the strengths of the Principles is that it is "the result of in-depth studies and extensive consultation with academics, practicing lawyers, government bodies, and business circles from all parts of the world."[2]

. . . .

The UNIDROIT Principles are divided into an Introduction; which sets forth the underlying methodology used in drafting the Principles; a Preamble, which states the purpose of the Principles; and seven chapters. More specifically, chapter One outlines basic principles that govern transactions subject to the Principles. Chapter Two addresses formation of the contract, while Chapter Three is concerned with the contract's validity. Chapter Four contains rules regarding interpretation of the terms of the contract, and Chapter Five provides gap-filler provisions and implied obligations.

Chapter Six addresses performance of the contract and is subdivided into two sections, section one setting forth basic rules of performance and section two defining "hardship" and providing for its effect on the contractual relationship of the parties. Chapter Seven, entitled "Non-Performance," deals with issues of breach of contract and remedies and is divided into four sections. Section One defines what constitutes non-performance and what effect it has on present and executory contractual obligations, while Section Two states the right to expect performance under the contract. Section Three provides rules under which the contract is deemed terminated and its effects, and Section Four is a guide to damages.

Each individual article in the Principles has a descriptive title, its basic rules set forth in "blackletter" form, along with detailed commentary, and, where appropriate, illustrations, which amplify the blackletter text, explain its underlying rationale, and provide hypothetical examples of the rule in use. Both the commentary and the illustrations, therefore, are considered by UNIDROIT to be an "integral part" of the Principles and should not be overlooked when contemplating its use.

D. The International Chamber of Commerce (ICC) and Incoterms

NOTE ON THE ICC

The International Chamber of Commerce (ICC) is a non-governmental agency representing business internationally. One of it principal functions is the development

---

2. Michael Joachim Bonell, *The UNIDROIT Principles of International Commercial Contracts: Why? What? How?*, 69 TUL. L. REV. 1121, 1147 (1995).

of standard rules and procedures to facilitate trade. To this end, the ICC began publishing in 1936 a set of international rules for the interpretation of trade terms. Its most famous work, *Incoterms*, is discussed below. The *Incoterms* were last revised by the ICC in 1990 in order to adapt terms to the increasing use of electronic data interchange (EDI).

The current version of U.C.C. Article 2 similarly contains definitions for a number of shipment and delivery terms. *See* U.C.C. Sections 2-319 through 2-324. Interestingly, the August, 1997 Tentative Draft of Article 2 repeals these definitions and leaves their meaning to trade usage, course of dealing and, in the absence of either, the *Incoterms*. *See* U.C.C. Section 2-309 (Tentative Draft August, 1997).

Jan Ramberg, Incoterms 1980, in the Transnational Law of International Commercial Transactions
Vol. 2, 137, 138

....

Trade terms constitute an early example of simplification of commercial practices. By reference to shorthand expressions, such as FOB and CIF, merchants could determine the division of important functions, costs and risks between themselves. Thus, trade terms deal with *inter alia*:

- transfer of risk;
- arranging carriage and insurance;
- export and import licences and duties;
- packing and marking of goods;
- nature and type of documents;
- checking operations and certificates of the quality of the goods;
- notifications of arrangements made.

While such trade terms to a very large extent constitute practical rules for the implementation of the international contract of sale they do *not* deal with such matters which are to be found in national laws, international conventions or general conditions relating to contracts of sale. With some simplification it could be said that trade terms are of importance in *any* international contract of sale, while other *general* rules and conditions- as distinguished from *specific* terms giving the contracts their individual characteristics- primarily deal with abnormal situations of breaches of contract and unforeseen circumstances.

It goes without saying that the need for *unification* of the interpretation of trade terms is particularly important. First, the shorthand expressions used by merchants do not specifically spell out the obligations falling upon the seller and the buyer respectively. Secondly, national laws may differ not only in various details but even in the fundamental meaning of trade terms. The International Chamber of Commerce (ICC), in the early 1920's, embarked on the task of unification by exploring the meaning of the most important trade terms and presented the first version of a set of rules for the interpretation of such trade terms as *Incoterms 1936*. The first version was later followed by *Incoterms 1953* and *Incoterms 1980*. By referring to *Incoterms*, merchants could ascertain that the chosen trade term would be interpreted as set forth in *Incoterms* and any unpleasant surprises caused by different interpretations under various applicable laws could be avoided.

QUESTIONS

1. One possible approach to the unification and harmonization of international commercial law is to unify rules of private international law (*i.e.*, choice-of-law rules). An example of such an approach is the 1955 Convention on the Law Applicable to International Sales of Goods promulgated by the Hague Conference on Private International Law. Another approach is to unify or harmonize the substantive rules. The best example of this latter effort is the CISG. What are the respective advantages and disadvantages of the two methods?

II. Does the CISG Apply to My Contract?

Documents Supplement References:

1.   *CISG Articles 1-8, 10-12, 30, 41-43, 53, 95, 96.*
2.   *U.C.C. Sections 2-105, 2-106, 2-201, 2-715.*

NOTE ON THE IMPORTANCE OF SPHERE OF APPLICATION

The first six articles of the CISG define its sphere of application. Article 1 describes when it applies. Articles 2 and 3 exclude from the CISG's coverage certain types of transactions, either because of their essential nature or because of the underlying subject matter. Articles 4 and 5 exclude certain types of issues. Finally, Article 6 is a grant of autonomy to contracting parties, permitting them to exclude, derogate from, or vary the terms of the CISG.

As noted above, the CISG is fast becoming the primary source of law governing international sales. Even if no additional countries were to ratify the convention, it would still be the presumptive sales law of the North America Free Trade Area and for most trades within the European Union. It is, therefore, critical for commercial lawyers to be familiar with its provisions and sphere of application. Without such familiarity, effective transaction planning and litigation become impossible. Consider, for example, the following case.

GPL Treatment, Ltd. v. Louisiana-Pacific Corp.,
894 P.2D 470 (Ct. App. Oregon 1994)

De Muniz, Judge.

Plaintiffs are three separate wood products corporations owned and operated by members of the Clarke family, in British Columbia, Canada. Plaintiffs sued Louisiana-Pacific Corporation (L-P) to recover lost profits on alleged agreements by plaintiffs to sell 88 truckloads of cedar shakes to L-P. The jury returned a verdict for plaintiffs for the maximum amount of each plaintiff's prayer, and L-P appeals.

Plaintiffs Scott Cedar Products (Scott Cedar) and Blackhawk Forest Products (Blackhawk), manufacture and sell raw shakes and shingles. Plaintiff GPL Treatment, Ltd. (GPL), buys raw shakes, treats them, and sells them as "Class C" shakes. Treated shakes are packaged into bundles, with five bundles constituting a "square," and are often sold by the truckload. The price for cedar shakes fluctuates widely with market demand.

In early spring of 1992, a series of hailstorms in the Midwest caused an increased demand for cedar shakes and a concomitant increase in the price of Class C shakes. Plaintiffs' principal sales person, Gerry Feaver, visited with Dan Cunnally, a shake and shingle trader for L-P. Feaver testified that telephone conversations between the two led to a May 6, 1992, deal for L-P to purchase 66 truckloads of Class C shakes. He testified that he filled out and signed six of plaintiffs' "Confirmation Form" documents and sent L-P the two top copies of each of six four-part documents.

In contrast, Cunnally testified that he made no commitment for L-P to purchase any product in any of the telephone conversations with Feaver; that he had told Feaver that the price was too high; and that L-P would not allow him to buy the volume of shakes that Feaver was offering to sell. Cunnally testified that he told Feaver that L-P would buy some shakes later and that Feaver understood that arrangement. Cunnally testified that he did not receive plaintiffs' "Confirmation Form" documents.

According to plaintiffs' evidence, plaintiffs became concerned in June 1992, when Cunnally did not ask for delivery of the shakes. Feaver testified that Cunnally had told him that L-P's customer in Dallas, Texas, was not using shakes as fast as anticipated. In the meantime, the market price for shakes had dropped. Feaver testified that plaintiffs and Cunnally had additional conversations and negotiations about adjusting the volume and price of the order. Cunnally denied any such negotiations.

On about June 30 or July 1, Feaver was on personal business in eastern Canada, and Scott Clarke was in Portland visiting the office of Scott Cedar. Clarke testified that he took it upon himself to "finalize the deal with Mr. Cunnally." According to his testimony, he wrote a new order, revising prices and quantities for materials to be sold by plaintiffs to L-P. Clarke testified that the new order was firm, to accommodate L-P's needs. Clarke testified that Cunnally was "elated" with the new arrangement because it reduced the price.

Cunnally's testimony gives a different version of the conversation. He testified that Clarke called to try to sell more shakes to L-P, at specific quantities and lower prices than had been offered by Feaver, but that otherwise the arrangement was to be the same as it had been. Cunnally testified that he did not commit L-P to the purchase of shakes.

Clarke testified that, after working out the details of the revised order with Cunnally, he immediately telephoned Rick Sherneck in Canada and told Sherneck "to phone Dan Cunnally and confirm the order, the follow up with an order confirmation." Sherneck testified that Clarke instructed him, "We have a deal with L-P. I want you to write this down and then I want you to phone Dan Cunnally and confirm it with him."

Sherneck testified that he telephoned Cunnally, and confirmed the volumes and prices for the revised order in exact detail. He testified that he filled out order confirmation forms and put the top two copies of each form into the out basket for mailing to L-P. Cunnally testified that he remembers no such telephone call from Sherneck. He testified that he did not receive any writing from plaintiffs confirming any orders.

L-P took delivery of 13 truckloads of shakes in July 1992. According to Plaintiffs, when L-P failed to give shipping instructions for an additional 75 truckloads of shakes that had allegedly been ordered by L-P, it became concerned...Plaintiffs sent a letter to L-P asserting an agreement for the delivery of 75 additional truckloads of shakes over a three-week period. L-P responded that the parties had no such agreement.

Plaintiffs brought this action to recover their respective profit losses on an alleged agreement to sell a total of 88 truckloads of cedar shakes to L-P. L-P claimed that it was responsible for only 13 truckloads, which were shipped and paid for. Plaintiffs claimed that L-P breached its agreement to accept the remaining 75 truckloads. L-P asserted as an affirmative defense that plaintiffs' claims are barred by the Statute of Frauds. The jury returned a verdict for the maximum amount of each plaintiff's prayer: $500,921 for GPL; $134,372 for Scott Cedar; and $106,984 for Blackhawk.

        . . . .

In its third assignment of error, L-P contended that the trial court erred in denying its motions *in limine* and for a directed verdict on the ground that the alleged contract for the sale of shakes fails for noncompliance with Oregon's Uniform Commercial Code Statute of Frauds. Specifically the motions sought to exclude evidence of the written order confirmations that plaintiffs allegedly sent to L-P.

ORS 72.2010 provides, in relevant part:

"(1) Except as otherwise provided in this section a contract for the sale of goods for the price of $500 or more is not enforceable by way of action of defense unless there is some writing sufficient to indicate that a contract for sale has been made between the parties and signed by the party against whom enforcement is sought or by the authorized agent or broker of the party. A writing is not insufficient because it omits or incorrectly states a term agreed upon but the contract is not enforceable under this subsection beyond the quantity of goods shown in such writing.

"(2) Between merchants, if within a reasonable time *a writing in confirmation of the contract and sufficient against the sender* is received and the party receiving it has reason to know its contents, it satisfies the requirements of subsection (1) of this section against such party unless written notice of objection to its contents is given within 10 days after it is received." (Emphasis supplied.)

Under subsection (2), the "merchant's exception" to the Uniform Commercial Code Statute of Frauds applies, when both parties to the transaction are merchants, if one merchant receives written confirmation of an oral contract from another merchant, "sufficient against the sender," the contract becomes enforceable unless the recipient objects within 10 days. L-P argued to the trial court, and argues on appeal, that the order confirmations that the plaintiffs allegedly sent to L-P are inadmissible as proof of the agreements and in satisfaction of the Statute of Frauds, because, *as a matter of law*, they are insufficient under ORS 72.2010 to constitute written confirmations of the contracts. The trial court held, as a matter of the law, that the documents were confirmations. The court submitted to the jury the factual questions of whether the confirmations were received by L-P, whether L-P knew their contents and whether L-P sent written notice of objection to plaintiffs. The assignment of error relates only to the trial court's ruling concerning the legal effect of the documents, *i.e.*, that they are, as a matter of law, sufficient to constitute "confirmations" under ORS 72.2010.

The printed order confirmation forms consist of four pages, one original page and three copies. The original and first copy are sent to the buyer. Those two pages are, for the most part, identical. At the top left of both, in large print, is the name and address of the selling company. At the top right are boxes for the date and the seller's order number. Directly underneath those boxes, in large bold print, are the words "ORDER CONFIRMATION." The form contains two address blocks of three single-spaced lines each, encaptioned "SOLD TO" and "SHIP TO." Underneath those address blocks are three slim, long boxes of one line each for shipping instructions, terms of payment and the customer number. The largest part of the form, filling approximately one half the page, is for a description of the product, with a place to note FOB mill, freight and delivery price. At the bottom right of the form is the name of the selling company, and underneath it a signature line following the word "BY." Underneath that line are the words "THANK YOU."

The original and first copy differ in one respect. At the bottom left of the original in small print, are the words:

"CONDITIONS OF SALES;

"All orders accepted subject to strikes, labor troubles, car shortages or other contingencies beyond our power to control. Any freight rate increases, sales or use taxes is for the buyer's account."

Then, beneath that block, in smaller print but highlighted, are the words: "SIGN CONFIRMATION COPY AND RETURN." At the bottom left of the first copy, the "confirmation copy," in small print, are the words "ORDER ACCEPTED BY:," followed by a line for firm name. Below that is a line for a signature and the title of the person signing, and the date.

L-P concedes that the documents contain all the elements necessary to confirm an order. However, L-P contends that, by instructing the buyer to sign the confirmation copy on the "order accepted by" line and return that copy to plaintiffs, plaintiffs have indicated an intention that the agreement is to become final only after L-P's approval of the quoted terms.

Considering the document in its entirety we conclude that it cannot reasonably be read as L-P suggests. The form is captioned "ORDER CONFIRMATION," boldly and in large print. Unlike the forms involved in the cases relied on by the dissent, *see, e.g., Great Western Sugar Co, v. Lone Star Donut Co.,* 567 F.Supp. 340 (N.D. Text *aff'd* 721 F.2d 510 (5th Cir. 1983); *Kline Iron & Steel Co., Inc. v. Gray Com. Consultants, Inc.,* 715 F.Supp. 135 (D.S.C. 1989), there is no language on this form, either on the original or the first copy, indicating that the parties are in the course of negotiations, that plaintiffs are merely proposing terms or that L-P must approve the terms. Every feature L-P of the form suggests that it is what it is labeled, a confirmation and not a mere offer. We conclude that the sign and return instruction does not alter the apparent purpose of the document, to confirm in writing a completed agreement for the sale of shakes. The trial court did not err in denying L-P's motions *in limine* and for directed verdict.

Affirmed.

[The dissenting opinion of Judge Lesson is omitted. In Judge Lesson's view, the documents were insufficient to satisfy the Statute of Frauds because of the unambiguous requirement of written acceptance. Interestingly, Judge Lesson referenced the CISG in a concluding footnote:

I would, however, address plaintiff's cross-assignment that the trial court erred in refusing to apply the United Nations Convention on Contracts for the International Sale of Goods (CISG), 15 U.S.C.A.App. (Supp.1994), instead of the U.C.C. Article 11 of the CISG does not require a contract to be "evidenced in writing" and, thus, would defeat L-P's statute of frauds defense if the trial court abused its discretion under ORCP 23 B in ruling that plaintiffs' attempt to raise the CISG was untimely and that they had waived reliance on that theory.]

QUESTIONS

1.   The defendant in the *GPL* case subsequently appealed to the Supreme Court of Oregon. That court held (with 3 justices dissenting) that the plaintiffs' forms were

sufficient confirmations notwithstanding the "sign and return" clause and "order accepted by" signature line. *See GPL Treatment, Ltd. v. Louisiana-Pacific Corp.*, 914 P.2d 682 (Or. 1996). In light of their eventual success, did it really matter that the plaintiffs neglected to timely assert the applicability of the CISG?

2.   Article 11 of the CISG provides that "[a] contract of sale need not be concluded in or evidenced by a writing." This provision would seem to have the effect of removing the Statute of Frauds from every CISG-covered case. Article 12, however, states that Article 11 is not applicable if a party to the transaction is located in a country that has ratified the Convention with the reservation permitted by Article 96. Neither the United States nor Canada has made such a reservation, but if either had, would U.C.C. Section 2-201 necessarily have determined whether the alleged contract was provable?

NOTE ON DIRECT APPLICATION OF THE CISG

The CISG applies to a contract if the requirement of internationality is met. Specifically, this requirement is satisfied if the places of business of the contracting parties are in different states that have ratified the Convention. *See* Article 1(1)(a). So, for example, if the seller has its place of business in the United States and the buyer has its place of business in Germany (both are contracting states), the CISG will govern, regardless of whether the litigation is centered in the United States or Germany. Notice that neither a party's nationality nor its civil or commercial character is a relevant consideration; all that matters is where each party's place of business is located. This determination, however, is not always easily made.

QUESTIONS

1.   Was the CISG applicable in *GPL Treatment, Ltd. v. Louisiana-Pacific Corp.*? Do you need more information before you can answer this question? If so, what additional information do you need? *See* CISG Articles 1(2) and 10.

2.   Great Britain has not ratified the CISG. In light of this fact, will a contract between the London branch of a seller with its principle place of business in the United States and a buyer with its principle place of business in Germany be subject to the CISG?

3.   Assume that a buyer with its place of business in the United States contracts to buy goods from the agent of an undisclosed foreign principal. If the agent has its place of business in the United States and the principal has its place of business in Germany, is the internationality requirement of the CISG satisfied?

NOTE ON INDIRECT APPLICATION OF THE CISG

Article 1(1)(b) expands the application of the CISG to situations where "the rules of private international law [of the forum] lead to the application of the law of a Contracting State." Thus, there are two prerequisites to the application of this provision. First, the relevant place of business of each contracting party must be in a different state; it matters not whether either state is a Contracting State. The presence of international diversity is, after all, what gives the contract its international flavor. Second, the private international law (*i.e.*, the conflict-of-laws rule) of the forum state must point to the law of a country that has ratified the Convention. To complicate matters, Article 95 allows Contracting States to declare by reservation that they will not be bound by paragraph (1)(b). So far, five Contracting States have declared that they will not be bound by Article 1(1)(b): China, Czech Republic, Singapore, Slovakia, and the United States.

Case Abstract, UNCITRAL Texts (CLOUT)
Abstract No. 104,
ICC Arbitration Case No. 7197 (1992)

The dispute concerned the failure of the Bulgarian buyer to pay the Austrian seller within the time period agreed in the sales contract.

The arbitral tribunal found that, while the parties did not specify any applicable law, the application of Austrian and Bulgarian rules of private international law led to the application of Austrian law. In view of the fact that CISG had been incorporated into the Austrian legal system, the tribunal decided to apply CISG, in accordance with Article 1(1)(b) of the Convention. The tribunal also noted that, as the applicable rules of private international law led to the application of the law of Austria, where the seller had its place of business, it was immaterial that Bulgaria, where the buyer had its place of business, was not a party to the Convention at the time the contract was concluded.

. . . .

Oberlandesgericht, Frankfurt Am Main,
September 17, 1991, 164/90
(Translation Reproduced From 12 Journal of La
and Commerce 261-270 (1993))

JOURNAL OF LAW & COMMERCE HEADNOTE:

Summary of Facts —

A seller, whose principal place of business was in Italy, contracted to manufacture shoes for a German buyer. The shoes were to be manufactured according to the buyer's instructions and marked with an "M" designation. The buyer also held a separate permit for exclusive rights to market the shoes with the designation "M." At a trade fair held in Italy from March 3 to March 6, 1989, the seller exhibited shoes marked with an "M." The buyer demanded that the shoes be removed from the exhibit, but the seller refused. The buyer then sent a telegram the day after the trade fair ended, declaring an end to the contract due to the seller's breach, and its intent to produce the shoes through another Italian manufacturer. The assignee of the seller's right sued the buyer for non-payment.

. . . .

TRANSLATED TEXT

. . . .

The lower court [the "Landgericht"], correctly based the adjudication of the legal relationships on the above-referenced CISG. The Uniform Sales Act which was declared void for the Federal Republic of Germany as of December 31, 1990 (Article 5(1), Article 7(1), Contract law of the CISG of July 5, 1989, Bundesgesetzblatt II, p.586) is not even applicable [to the instant facts], through the temporary regulations of Article 5 § 2 of the Contract law. Indeed, both Italy and the Federal Republic of Germany belong to the contracting states of the Hague Convention on the Sales of Goods of July 1, 1964; however, it was declared void by Italy already by the end of December 31, 1987. Therefore, the EKG [ULIS] is no longer applicable to German-

Italian contracts concluded after January 1, 1988 because its Article 1, Section 1 required that the place of business be located in differing Contracting States (OLG of Hamburg/IPRax 1989, 247; OLG of Koblenz RIW 1989; Asam RIW 1989 942, 943). Italy, however, was no longer a "Contracting State" at that time.

As the U.N. Convention [*i.e.*, CISG] did not take effect for the Federal Republic of Germany before January 1, 1991, it cannot become effective by the provisions of Article l(l)(a), CISG, directly as part of the German legal system (as to the time period in which it is effective, cf. Article 100, CISG). But applicability of the CISG results from the fact that the German private international law refers to the right of a contracting state which would apply the CISG to the factual circumstances to be determined (*cf.* judgment of June 13, 1991 — 3U 261/90 — RIW 1991, 501 = DB 1991, 1512: Asam RIW 1989, 942, 943).

Pursuant to Article 28, Section 1, Sentence 1, EGBGB, in the absence of a choice of law, the classification of the contract is determined by the law of the country with which it [the contract] has the closest relationships. Based on the above, the assumption is valid that this is the state in which the party, which is to execute the performance which characterizes the contract [*i.e.*, gives it its defining character], has its customary domicile or its principal place of business at the time of the concluding of the contract. In this case, a contract for labor and materials is in question, rather than a sales contract, in that the assignor assumed the obligation to manufacture the shoes, according to the [buyer's] instructions, from the raw materials which were to be procured by the assignor. With a contract for labor and materials, usually the law applied is of the country in which the entrepreneur has his usual domicile or principal place of business, because it is his performance which gives the contract its character (Reithmann/Martiny, 4th ed. 1988, marginal note No. 408; similarly for the sales contract as well as for the manufacturing contract: cf. Palandt/Heldrich, 50th ed., Article 28 EGBGB, marginal notes 8, 14). That means that Italian law is applicable because the assignor had his principal place of business in Italy and also it was from there that he was to perform.

As Italy is a Contracting State of the CISG, and the Convention has been valid in Italy since January 1, 1988 (law No. 765 1985 of December 1985, supplement to Ordinaria alla Gazetta Ufficiale No. 303 of December 27, 1985, cf. Herber/Czerwenka, International Law of Sales, 1991, before Article 1, marginal note No. 16; Schwenzer, NJW 1990, 602, Footnote 5), [the Convention] becomes effective as to the legal relations of the contracting parties through Article l(l)(b) CISG. According to this, the Convention is applicable to contracts for the sale of goods between parties which have their principal places of business in different states, if the provisions of the private international law result in the application of the law of one contracting state. A possible reservation according to Article 95 CISG which would exclude the application of Article l(l)(b) CISG (Herber/Czerwenka Article 96, marginal note No. 3), was not declared by Italy [*i.e.*, that reservation therefore will not apply] (von Caemmerer/Schlechtriem 1990, Article 2, Contract Code G, marginal note No. 2, footnote 6; Herber/ Czerwenka before Article 1, marginal note No. 16; as to the applicability of the CISG in Germano-Italian legal transactions before the enactment in the Federal Republic of Germany, further: LG Stuttgart RIW 1989, 841; Asam RIW 1989, 942, 943). The contract for labor and materials in question comes within the scope of the Convention because, pursuant to Article 3(1) CISG, sales contracts are to be considered equal to contracts for the supply of goods to be manufactured or produced. The exception of the situation in which the orderor is to provide an essential part of the raw materials necessary for the manufacturing or producing himself, does not apply here [*i.e.*, such an exception is not the case here].

. . . .

QUESTIONS

1.   Suppose that Buyer and Seller each have their relevant place of business in a different Contracting State and that suit is filed in either the Buyer's or Seller's state. If the forum's applicable rule of private international law directs application of a third non-Contracting State, will the CISG apply?

2.   Once again, assume that Buyer and Seller each have their relevant place of business in a different Contracting State. Suppose this time, however, that suit is filed in a non-Contracting State, and the rules of private international law of that state designate the law of a fourth non-Contracting State. Will the CISG apply?

3.   Assume that Buyer and Seller each have their relevant place of business in a different non- Contracting State and that the rules of private international law of the forum lead to application of the law of a Contracting State. Which law will apply: the domestic law of that state or the CISG?

4.   Suppose that the Buyer has its relevant place of business in the United States and the Seller has its relevant place of business in a non-Contracting State. If suit is brought in the United States and the rules of private international law direct application of U.S. law, is the applicable law the U.C.C. or the CISG?

5.   Suppose, once again, that the Buyer has its relevant place of business in the United States and the Seller has its relevant place of business in a non-Contracting State. Will the CISG apply if suit is brought in a third state whose rules of private international law direct application of U.S. law?

NOTE ON TRANSACTION AND SUBJECT MATTER LIMITATIONS ON THE APPLICATION OF THE CISG

Although the application of the CISG is limited to contracts for the sale of goods, the term "sale" is nowhere expressly defined in the Convention. However, a definition of this all-important term can be developed by a bit of cobbling. *Compare* U.C.C. Section 2-106(1). Article 30 and Article 53 set forth the basic obligations of the seller and of the buyer. Taken together, these provisions apparently mean that a sale is any transaction where one party is required to deliver goods, hand over any documents relating to them, and transfer the property in the goods, while the other party is required to pay the price for the goods and take delivery of them.

Yet this definition must be read in conjunction with the exclusions found in Articles 2(a)-(c), the most important of which is sales to persons who buy goods for household, family, or personal use, and Article 3. Under Article 3(1), a contract for specially manufactured goods is subject to the CISG unless the buyer supplies a "substantial" part of the materials necessary for production. Article 3(2) applies when a single contract has both a sale and service component; the CISG will not apply if the "preponderant" part of the seller's obligations is to supply services. Undefined, however, are the terms "substantial" and "preponderant."

Also missing is a definition of the term "goods." *Compare* U.C.C. Section 2-105(1). It seems clear from the exclusions in Articles 2(d)-(f) that the CISG was intended to govern only the sale of moveable tangibles. Even then, the Convention will not apply to sales of ships, vessels, hovercraft, or aircraft.

August 26 1994 (Germany)

The [seller], a Swiss market research institute, had elaborated and delivered a market analysis, which had been ordered by the [buyer], a German company. The [buyer] refused to pay the price alleging that the report did not comply with the conditions agreed upon by the parties.

The court held that the CISG was not applicable, since the underlying contract was neither a contract for the sale of goods (article 1(1) CISG) nor a contract for the production of goods (article 3(1) CISG). Noting that the sale of goods is characterized by the transfer of property in a object, the court found that, although a report is fixed on a piece of paper, the main concern of the parties is not the handing over of the paper but the transfer of the right to use the ideas written down on such paper. Therefore, the court held that the agreement to prepare a market analysis is not a sale of goods within the meaning of articles 1 or 3 CISG.

Helen Kaminski PTY. Ltd. v.
Marketing Australian Products, Inc.,
U.S. Dist. Lexis 10630 (S.D.N.Y. 1997)

Cote, District Judge

Appellant Helen Kaminski Pty. Ltd. ("Helen Kaminski") moves for leave to appeal an interlocutory order issued by the Bankruptcy Court for the Southern District of New York on March 3, 1997. Appellee Marketing Australian Products ("MAP") opposes this motion. For the reasons set forth below, the motion is denied.

BACKGROUND

Helen Kaminski is an Australian corporation with its principal place of business in Australia. It manufactures fashion accessories such as hats and bags. MAP is incorporated in Colorado, with its principal place of business in New York, and it distributes fashion accessories. Helen Kaminski and MAP negotiated an agreement in Australia in January 1996 whereby MAP had the exclusive rights to distribute Helen Kaminski goods in North America (the "Distributor Agreement"). The Distributor Agreement specified the terms on which the parties would do business, including methods of payment, warranty, delivery, etc., and anticipated that MAP would purchase a total of U.S. $ 2 million worth of products from February 1, 1996 to January 31, 1997. The parties amended the Distributor Agreement in February 1996 to address the sale of specified goods already in the United States.

MAP issued purchase orders for additional products and Helen Kaminski sent notice in October and November 1996 to MAP that the products were ready for shipment. Pursuant to the Distributor Agreement, MAP was to open a letter of credit seven days prior to shipment. When MAP failed to do so, on November 1, 1996, Helen Kaminski sent a Notice to Rectify within thirty days. On November 22, 1996, Helen Kaminski sent a notice of default requiring MAP to cure the defects under the Distributor Agreement. When MAP still did not cure, Helen Kaminski sent a notice of termination dated December 2, 1996 and commenced an action in Australia seeking a declaration that the Distributor Agreement was invalid and terminated.

MAP filed for bankruptcy in the Southern District of New York on November 29, 1996. On January 28, 1997, MAP commenced an action against Helen Kaminski seeking a declaration that Helen Kaminski was subject to the automatic stay under Section 362, Title 11, United States Code, and an order extending MAP's time to cure the defaults under the Distributor Agreement, pursuant to Section 108(b), Title 11, United States Code. Helen Kaminski then moved to dismiss this Complaint contending, among other arguments, that (1) the Convention on the International

Sale of Goods (" CISG") superseded the Bankruptcy Code and therefore MAP could not have additional time to cure under Section 108(b), and (2) the automatic stay under Section 362 should not have an extra-territorial effect.

On March 3, 1997, the Bankruptcy Court issued an Order ("March 3rd Order") which denied Helen Kaminski's motion to dismiss and determined that (1) Helen Kaminski was subject to the automatic stay and thus could not proceed with the action in Australia, and (2) extended MAP's time to cure the defaults pursuant to Section 108(b). Although the March 3rd Order does not state so explicitly, the parties agree that the bankruptcy court found that the CISG does not apply to the Distributor Agreement as it was not a contract for the sale of goods. Helen Kaminski now wishes to appeal this interlocutory order.

. . . .

Discussion

. . . .

A. The CISG and the Distributor Agreement

The CISG is an international agreement that applies to sales of goods between parties in signatory nations, unless the parties expressly contract to be bound by another source of law. There is no dispute that both the United States and Australia are signatories to the CISG.

If the CISG applies to the Distributor Agreement, as soon as MAP was in fundamental breach of the contract — and there does not appear to be a dispute that the failure to produce letters of credit was a fundamental breach — Helen Kaminski could declare the contract void and after it started an action for a breach of the contract, no court could extend MAP's time to cure the defect. CISG, Article 61(3), reprinted in 15 U.S.C. Appendix.

Thus, the dispositive issue is whether the CISG applies to the Distributor Agreement. Helen Kaminski maintains that it does, since the agreement, in addition to laying out the terms for the parties' commercial relationship, also governed the disposition of identified goods. Although it does not say so explicitly, it appears that Helen Kaminski is referring to the amendment in February 1996 which addressed specified goods already in the United States. MAP maintains that the Distributor Agreement is merely a "framework agreement" and that such agreements are not covered by the CISG. The Distributor Agreement requires MAP to purchase a minimum quantity of total goods, but does not identify the goods to be sold by type, date or price. In contrast, the CISG requires an enforceable contract to have definite terms regarding quantity and price.

While both sides cite various secondary sources, there appears to be no judicial authority determining the reach of the CISG and, in particular, whether it applies to distributor agreements. The parties do agree, however, that whether or not the CISG applies turns on whether the Distributor Agreement can be characterized as a contract for the sale of goods — that is, that it contained definite terms for specified goods. In this respect, the only contract for a specified set of goods to which Helen Kaminski points is the February 1996 amendment. As MAP correctly notes, however, these goods were not the subject of the breach. Rather, Helen Kaminski is claiming a breach for goods ordered but not shipped. Helen Kaminski makes no claim that these goods were identified in the Distributor Agreement.

For this reason, although I find that there is little to no case law on the CISG in general, and none determining whether a distributor agreement falls within the ambit of the CISG, Helen Kaminski's rationale for why the CISG applies to the debate about the breach for goods ordered but not shipped is not supported by the facts of the case. The identification in the Distributor Agreement of certain goods — about which there is no claim of breach — is insufficient to bring the Distributor Agreement within coverage of the CISG when the dispute concerns goods not specifically identified in the Distributor Agreement. Thus, while the question does present a controlling issue of law over which there may be substantial disagreement, it does not appear that a determination of the issue would materially advance the litigation as Helen Kaminski does not maintain that the general Distributor Agreement — absent the February amendment which does not concern the goods at issue — is definite enough to constitute a contract for the sale of goods.

B. Extra-territorial Effect of Section 362

Helen Kaminski cites no authority for its contention that Section 362 of the Bankruptcy Code should not have extra-territorial effect, other than an argument that such a stay is superseded by the CISG. Since I have held that, in the circumstances of this case at least, the CISG does not apply, I need not reach this second issue. I note, however, that it is a general principal that all claims against a debtor should be handled in a single proceeding to insure equitable and orderly distribution of debtor's property.

Conclusion

For the reasons given above, it is hereby *ordered* that Helen Kaminski's motion for leave to appeal the March 3rd Order of the Bankruptcy Court is denied.

. . . .

NOTE ON ISSUE LIMITATIONS ON THE APPLICATION OF THE CISG

If the CISG applies, it will not govern all issues associated with the contract. Article 4(a), for example, excludes from the Convention's coverage issues of validity. Although it does have some validity rules, like Article 11, the Convention will not apply to issues such as mistake, fraud, duress, and unconscionability. Article 4(b), moreover, provides that the Convention is not concerned with those issues concerning property claims to the goods sold. *But see* Articles 41-43. Article 5 also excludes from coverage all claims for personal injury or death. The CISG does, however, apply to claims for damage to property or to the goods themselves. *Compare* U.C.C. Section 2-715(2)(b). To fill the gaps created by the foregoing exclusions, one must necessarily resort to the rules of private international law. *See* Article 7(2).

NOTE ON OPTING OUT OF OR INTO THE CISG

The CISG is often described as an opt-out convention. What this means is that the parties, should they choose to do so, may exclude the application of the Convention or derogate from or vary the effect of any of its provisions. *See* Article 6. Such exclusion depends upon the existence of a real agreement between the parties, but the agreement may be express or implied. Further, although the CISG itself is silent on the issue, it would seem that the parties may elect to have their contract governed by the CISG in situations where it would not otherwise apply. In such cases, the opt-in provision is like any other choice of law clause.

When parties choose to opt-out of the CISG and have their contractual relations governed by a specific national law, it is not unusual for them to combine their choice of law clause with a so-called "handcuffs" clause. The object behind a handcuffs clause is to turn the contract into a partial legal system of its own by defining the remedies available to each party. So used, the handcuffs clause operates to narrow the scope of the choice of law clause by precluding application of some rules of law that, in the absence of such a clause, the proper law of the contract would put at the parties' disposal. Both the choice of law clause and the handcuffs clause are subject to mandatory provisions of the *lex contractus* and any relevant public policy.

Otto Sandrock, "Handcuffs" Clauses in International Contracts: Basic Reflections on the Autonomy of the Parties to Choose the Proper Law for Their Contracts,
31 International Lawyer 1105 (1997)

. . . .

E. Two Examples of a Valid and One Example of a Void Handcuffs Clause

. . . .

a. It is general practice in international trade that the parties to international sales contracts replace the statutory rules of the proper law governing the liability of the seller for defects in the chattels sold by special stipulations in their contract that provide for other remedies.

If the parties to an international sales contract have chosen German domestic law (and not the U.N. Sales Convention) as the proper law of their international sales contract, it is common practice for them to derogate all remedies deriving from the section of the German Civil Code dealing with the liability of the seller for such defects (section 459 *et seq.*). That section of the German Civil Code is modeled after the remedies of ancient Roman law in providing that, in general, the buyer can, in case of a defect with the good delivered, either opt for the dissolution of the contract (while demanding the repayment of the price paid to the seller) or demand a reduction of the contractual price to be paid, in proportion between the value of the chattel without the defects to its value with said defects.

These statutory remedies are completely outmoded today. It is therefore common practice to substitute for them, in domestic as well as in international contracts, other remedies that better suit the needs of the parties by providing, for example, that either the seller has the option of removing the defect within a definite period of time or that the buyer may demand such removal. There can hardly be any doubt that handcuffs clauses of that kind are fully binding, enforceable, and thus of full validity in international sales contracts.

b. Another example for the full validity of a handcuffs clause is the following:

unforeseen, unforeseeable, and unavoidable circumstances overcome the execution of an international long-term contract on the erection of an industrial plant and disturb the equivalence of the performances to be rendered by the parties. One of the parties therefore suffers a considerable hardship. The proper law of the contract, and not a special hardship clause, would assist the aggrieved party in allowing it to demand the adaption of its contractual duties to that fundamental change of circumstances. But there is a handcuffs clause in the contract providing that all remedies granted by the proper law of contract shall be unavailable to the aggrieved party.

It could hardly be doubted that, by virtue of said handcuffs clause, the remedy of the adaption of the contractual duties would not be at the disposal of the aggrieved party. For when the parties inserted the handcuffs clause into their contract, they must be deemed to have freely accepted the risk of an unbalance between their contractual performances supervening from a fundamental change in the circumstances surrounding their contract. If, in such a case, the proper law of contract would take account of the fundamental change of circumstances and, like a *clausula rebus sic stanibus* clause, would seek to alleviate the fate of the aggrieved party, that rule of the proper law could not be qualified as a public policy or mandatory provision. It would rather be considered as being of a derogatory nature permitting said handcuffs clause to display its effects by removing from the hands of the aggrieved party the remedy to claim the adaption of the mutual contractual duties.

c.   The result would be different, however, in other factual situations, for which the following might serve as a practical example: one of the parties to an international contract into which a handcuffs clause was inserted claims to have been the victim of a fraudulent misrepresentation committed by its contractual partner when entering into the contract. Such party therefore makes use of a remedy put at its disposal by the proper law of the contract, a remedy by which the aggrieved party can demand the dissolution of the contract and/or the payment of damages sustained during its execution. Its contractual partner, however, opposes the introduction of such remedy by relying on a handcuffs clause that would prohibit the exercise of that statutory tool.

The starting point for the solution of this conflict must be the following: the statutory or common law rights protecting the position of a party who, in such a manner, has become the victim of a fraudulent misrepresentation are of a mandatory nature. The parties are bound by those rules without having the option of derogating from them. The effect of the handcuffs clause would be to suppress all rights and remedies deriving from the provisions just mentioned. In such a case, a party therefore cannot be deprived by a handcuffs clause of the protection accorded to it by the proper law of the contract. In other words, the handcuffs clause would be null and void.

This result appears persuasive. A party who agrees to the insertion of a handcuffs clause into the contract cannot be supposed to have waived the exercise of remedies against a fraudulent misrepresentation of which it could neither be aware nor protect itself and to which it therefore was destined to inevitably fall victim.

The same rule has to apply when a party exerts an illegal duress or an undue influence upon his or her contractual partner: a handcuffs clause could then never deprive victims of such illegal acts of their statutory or common law rights accruing to them.

QUESTIONS

1.   Why might the parties avoid the application of the CISG?

2.   If the parties choose to be governed by New York law, is that an effective opt-out? If such a statement is not sufficient, how might an effective clause be drafted?

3.   If the CISG is applicable and the parties do not opt out, why might it still be good practice to include a choice of law provision?

Beijing Metals & Minerals Import/Export Corp. v. American Bus. Ctr., Inc.,

993 F.2D 1178 (5th Cir. 1993)

Barksdale, Circuit Judge

This appeal turns on the effect to be given two alleged oral agreements made contemporaneously with execution of a written payment agreement. American Business Center, Inc. (ABC), challenges a summary judgement granted Beijing Metals & Minerals Import/Export Corporation (MMB) on its severed claim to enforce the payment agreement, contending, inter alia, that the district courts misapplied the parol evidence rule and, on issues such as fraudulent inducement, overlooked genuine issues of material fact. We *reverse* and *remand* on the issue of fraudulent inducement and those pertaining to the quality and quantity of goods; as to all others, we *affirm*.

I.

In 1988, MMB and ABC entered into a business relationship "in order to cooperatively develop the fitness [weight lifting] equipment market in the U.S. and Canada."[1] ABC agreed to furnish MMB with "marketing information, customer names, product samples, and design prints for the research and development of products that [MMB] may be capable of manufacturing." MMB, in turn, agreed to "engage in production only" and to "not sell the products designed and ordered by [ABC] to companies other than [ABC]."

MMB also agreed that goods would be manufactured in accordance with detailed specifications, and be of the highest quality. But, according to ABC, from the very beginning, almost every shipment contained substantial amounts of defective and non-conforming goods; it notified MMB to that effect; it was assured that substitute goods would be sent; and it was instructed to retain the defective goods for later disposition.

For the shipments from MMB to ABC, the agreement originally required "documents against payment," obligating ABC to pay by letters of credit or upon presentation of bills of lading, prior to release of the goods from customs. Accordingly, ABC paid for all shipments prior to receipt. In 1988, the parties changed the payment terms to "document against acceptance," allowing ABC 90 days to pay (D/A 90). Of the shipments received on D/A 90 terms, ABC paid only approximately two invoices, and subsequently refused to pay for approximately 27 shipments totaling more than $ 1.2 million.

In July 1989, MMB notified ABC that if it did not respond with a payment plan, MMB would not ship scheduled merchandise. Accordingly, that August, Mike Lian, president of ABC, traveled to Beijing, China, to meet with MMB. After several days of negotiations, Lian signed an agreement, in which he acknowledged that ABC owed MMB $ 1,225,997.78, of which $768,529.23 was overdue as of August 15, 1989. The agreement established a payment schedule, obligating ABC to pay the amounts owed MMB in specified installments. Before he left Beijing, Lian made the first agreed payment ($ 197,503.43) by check, post-dated to August 30.

ABC maintains that the payment schedule was only part of the total agreement; that MMB orally agreed to two other items: it would ship goods to compensate for non-conforming and defective goods and shortages and would begin making new

---

1. MMB is a company formed and existing under the laws of the People's Republic of China.

shipments to ABC on D/A 90 terms, beginning September 10, 1989. Lian maintains that MMB representatives admitted that ABC had a substantial claim for defective and non-conforming goods, but that because the invoices had been entered into the accounting and banking system "the only way they could make up the problems to ABC was by shipping future goods on more favorable terms until the offsets were taken care of." According to Lian, MMB representatives stated that the signed payment agreement was necessary only to appease the bank and the controller, which would allow MMB to continue shipments to ABC on agreed-upon terms; that MMB representatives told him that the oral agreements, *i.e.* replacement of goods and future shipments on D/A 90 terms, could not be reduced to writing for "political reasons" — that "some people could go to jail over this situation;" and that he "would not have signed the Agreement had he known that MMB did not have the intention or the ability to perform their part of the bargain." Lian estimated that the total amount of defective goods and shortages was $ 500,000.

On September 1, MMB sent a letter to Lian by fax, which stated, in part, that straight D/A 90 terms would not be permitted and arguably indicated that this issue had been part of the total agreement. Lian replied twice. His first was that he could not operate on a letter of credit basis. His second, in late September, referenced the alleged oral agreement for D/A 90 terms and arguably also referenced the alleged oral agreement to provide replacement goods.

Because ABC, in early September 1989, stopped payment on the check issued in Beijing, and informed MMB that it would not honor the payment schedule, MMB filed suit against ABC (and others not parties to this appeal) to recover payment on the agreement. The substantive claim, styled as on a "sworn account," was later described by MMB as an "account stated." The defendants answered, asserting various defenses to payment, including (1) fraudulent inducement of both the payment agreement and the check issued in Beijing; (2) duress; (3) breach of agreement and breach of contract; (4) breach of express and implied warranties; and (5) offset. ABC also counterclaimed against MMB (and others not parties to this appeal) on several of the grounds asserted as defenses and for a Deceptive Trade Practices Act (DTPA) violation.

In January 1991, the district court stayed the action as to all parties except MMB and ABC until the basic account claims were adjudicated. MMB moved for summary judgment. In January 1992, after a hearing, the district court granted the motion, and subsequently ruled that "the cause of action based on the sworn account is severed from the main action" and that the "only issue remaining and not previously stayed, is the defendants' counterclaim for breach of the oral agreement for future business." A final judgment for approximately $ 1.7 million was entered for MMB.

II.

ABC contends that the summary judgment is precluded by genuine issues of material fact relating to its defenses and counterclaims.

       . . . .

A.

MMB sued to recover the amount stated in the payment agreement, asserting that it represents a binding contract in which MMB agreed to extend payment terms, and ABC agreed to pay its outstanding obligations. For summary judgment, MMB characterized the agreement as an "account stated," which is "an agreement between parties who have had previous transactions of a monetary character that all the items of the account representing such transactions, and the balance struck, are correct, together with a promise, express or implied, for the payment of such a balance." *Eastern Dev. & Invest. Corp. v. City of San Antonio*, 557 S.W.2d 823, 824-25 (Tex. Civ. App.-San Antonio 1977, writ ref'd n.r.e.). An account stated establishes a prima facie case for obligation "without other proof of price, value, quantity, or specific items." *Id*. at 826.

ABC contested the account stated characterization, contending that the written agreement reflects only one portion of their three-part agreement to resolve all disputes regarding payment and the quantity and quality of the goods: part one (written) — ABC to adhere to a payment schedule; part two (oral) — MMB to ship replacement goods to make up for non-conforming goods and shortages; and part three (oral) — MMB to resume shipment of goods on D/A 90 terms as of September 10, 1989.

The district court held that the parol evidence rule prevented the two oral agreements being a defense to ABC's obligations under the written payment agreement. It concluded that the written agreement is an unambiguous "account restatement," and that nothing in its four corners, or in the surrounding circumstances, indicates the existence of collateral contingent agreements. The court focused on the fact that the payment agreement did not refer to supply, and contained meaningful consideration (extended payment time); that, at the time of the summary judgment hearing (three years later), ABC was unable to quantify with specificity MMB's obligation to ship replacement goods; that MMB's letter denying D/A 90 terms did not refer to the payment agreement; and that Lian's subsequent letters did not characterize ABC's obligation under the payment agreement as contingent.

Under Texas law, [2] it is well settled that the parol evidence rule generally bars enforcement of prior or contemporaneous agreements introduced to vary, add to, or contradict terms of a fully integrated written instrument. *See e.g., Tripp Village v. Mbank Lincoln Centre*, 774 S.W.2d 746, 749 (Tex. App.-Dallas 1989, no writ.) "[A] written instrument presumes that all prior agreements of the parties relating to the transaction have been merged into the written instrument." *Weinacht v. Phillips Coal Co.*, 673 S.W.2d 677,679 (Tex. App.- Dallas 1984, no writ); in other words, written agreements are presumed to be completely integrated. *Jack H. Brown & Co. v. Toys "R" Us, Inc.*, 906 F.2d 169, 173 (5th Cir. 1990) (citing *Hubacek v. Ennis State Bank*, 159 Tex. 166, 317 S.W.2d 30 (Tex. 1958). [3] As discussed below, although ABC may

---

2. We apply Texas law in this diversity action. *Salve Regina College v. Russel*, 499 U.S. 225, 111 S. Ct. 1217, 113 L. Ed. 2d 190 (1991). In its complaint and thereafter, MMB relied on Texas law. ABC maintains, instead, that MMB's claim is governed by the United Nations Convention on Contracts for the International Sale of Goods (Sale of Goods Convention), codified at 15 U.S.C. Appendix (West Supp. 1993). MMB insists that Texas law controls. As noted in *Filanto S.p.A. v. Chilewich International Corp.*, 789 F. Supp. 1229, 1237 (S.D.N.Y. 1992), appeal dismissed, *984 F.2d 58 (2d Cir. 1993)* "there is as yet virtually no U.S. case law interpreting the Sale of Goods Convention." We need not resolve this choice of law issue, because our discussion is limited to application of the parol evidence rule (which applies regardless), duress, and fraudulent inducement; however, the district court may need to do so on remand.

3. ABC urges that we apply the parol evidence rule applicable to the sale of goods, which, unlike the common law, does not resume that an apparently complete writing is a total integration. *See* Tex. Bus. & Com. Code Ann. 2.202 comment 1 ("This section definitely rejects: (a) Any assumption that because a writing has been worked out which is final on some matters, it is to be taken as including all the matters agreed upon"); *Bob Robertson, Inc. v. Webster*, 679 S.W.2d 683, 688 (Tex. App.-Houston 1984, no writ). Because of the agreement, on its face, is limited to a payment schedule for overdue invoices, and more closely resembles a settlement agreement, as opposed to a sale of goods, we will apply the parol evidence rule developed by Texas common law. *Cf., Jack H. Brown & Co.*, 906 F.2d at 170-173 (applying common law rule to interpreta-

rebut this presumption, *Id.* at 174, it failed to do so. *See id.* (court determines whether written instrument is complete).

1.

In support of its contention that the payment agreement is incomplete, ABC notes evidence that it had previously complained about the quality of goods; that it traveled to Beijing to sign the payment agreement; that in discovery, MMB representatives admitted that, during the August 1989 meetings in Beijing, Lian discussed the issues of non-conforming and defective goods in past shipments (albeit for a minimal amount of time and not with specificity); and that the earlier referenced fax sent by MMB shortly thereafter referred to ABC's request for D/A 90 terms in the context of their negotiations in Beijing.

Although this evidence leads us to question why ABC signed the payment agreement, we cannot say that it is incomplete. Underneath the heading (as translated by ABC), "Agreement on installment payments of overdue merchandise amount," the parties itemized that payment schedule, listing amounts due, invoice numbers, and revised payment dates. And, the agreement in no way intimates the existence of contingent extrinsic agreements regarding future shipments of goods. Instead, it specifies that "both sides participated in the negotiation, in a friendly manner, on the *problem of the amount overdue by the American Business Center, Inc.* to the Beijing Metals and Minerals Import and Export Corporation. A *unanimous agreement has been reached*" (emphasis added). Even accepting ABC's translation of the agreement, ABC's proof is not sufficiently persuasive to convince us to ignore the clear language of the writing agreement. *Compare Jack H. Brown, Inc.*, 906 F.2d at 174 (agreement incomplete where parties admittedly made two agreements not mentioned and where agreement was facially incomplete). As this court recently stated:

> Both the parol evidence rule and the doctrine of integration exist so that parties may rely on the enforcement of agreements that have been reduced to writing. If it were not for these established principles, even the most carefully considered written documents could be destroyed by "proof" of other agreements not included in the writing.

Id. at 176

2.

In addition, the two alleged oral agreements are not "collateral" to the written agreement. Evidence of a collateral contemporaneous agreement "though it refer to the same subject matter, and may affect the rights of the parties under the written contract" may be proven if not inconsistent with the integrated contract. *Conner v. May*, 444 S.W.2d 948, 952 (Tex. Civ. App.-Austin 1969, writ. ref'd n.r.e.). To be collateral, the agreement must be made for separate consideration, or "must be such as the parties might naturally make separately and would not ordinarily be expected to embody in the writing; and it must not be so clearly connected with the principal transaction as to be part and parcel thereof." *Weinacht*, 673 S.W.2d at 680. We examine the two claimed oral agreements in turn.

First, ABC asserts that MMB conceded that ABC is entitled to an offset of roughly $ 400,000 for defective and non-conforming goods, and thus agreed to ship

---

tion of settlement agreement concerning recovery of damages for breach of contracts to purchase signs and mansards).

replacement goods. But, this extrinsic evidence contradicts the payment agreement which states that "the total amount which the American Business Center, Inc. owed to the Beijing Metals and Minerals import and Export Corporation as a result of the D/A 90 day conditions, was U.S. $1,225,997.78,"and is therefore inadmissible. *See Rinecones v. Windberg*, 705 S.W.2d 846, 849 (Tex. App.-Austin 1986, no writ) ("the parol evidence rule prohibits the admission of oral evidence which alters the payment terms of a written contract").

Second, ABC maintains that its obligation under the payment schedule was contingent upon MMB's agreement to resume shipment on D/A/ 90 day terms. We agree with ABC that this alleged oral agreement, standing alone, is not inconsistent with the payment terms stated in the written agreement, because it is silent as to future sales. However, evidence of the oral agreement is nonetheless inadmissible, because its contingent nature is inconsistent with the unconditional language of the written agreement. *Cf. Jack H. Brown & Co.*, 906 F.2d at 176 ("where a written release is unambiguous, any attempt to prove that the release was signed in return for additional consideration not mentioned in the release violates the parol evidence rule").

Moreover, we cannot conclude that a contingency of this nature would naturally be made as a separate agreement. As our court stated, when presented with a quite similar factual context in *Jack H. Brown & Co.*, 906 F.2d at 176:

It is implausible that Toys would have used explicit unconditional release language in Markham's letter, while orally agreeing to make the release contingent on some vague guarantee of future business. Nor can we believe that the alleged oral agreement is one that would be made separately...This court recognizes that even the most sophisticated businessmen often deal with each other informally and verbally, but in circumstances such as these, even an unsophisticated businessman... would either have protested the unconditional releases language or insisted on getting the alleged oral agreement in writing.

Accordingly, we conclude, as did the district court, that ABC is barred by the parol evidence rule from introducing extrinsic evidence to alter the terms of the written agreement.

B.

ABC asserts economic duress as a defense to its obligations under the payment agreement, contending that MMB used political unrest in China to convince Lian to sign it; and that MMB refused to reconcile the defective and non-conforming goods unless Lian signed, thus leaving him with no choice but to do so or lose a substantial amount of money.

Texas law is well-settled that there can be no duress unless: "(1) there is a threat to do something which a party threatening has no legal right to do; (2) there is some illegal exaction or some fraud or deception; and (3) the restraint is imminent and such as to destroy free agency without present means of protection." *Deer Creek Ltd. v. North Am. Mortgage Co.*, 792 S.W.2d 198, 203 (Tex. App.-Dallas 1990, no writ.) Additionally, the opposing party must be responsible for the financial distress. *Id.*

We conclude that ABC failed to establish material fact issue on every element of the defense. Specifically, it failed to provide probative evidence indicating it lacked a reasonable alternative to signing the agreement. According to ABC, if Lian did not sign, it would be forced to accept defective and non-conforming goods, driving it into financial ruin. In so stating, it wholly ignores the availability of pursuing its remedies under Tex. Bus. & Com. Code Ann., 2.711-2.717, or, if applicable, the Sale of Goods Convention (articles 46-52). Aside from a general reference to "cash flow problems," and a reference to the difficulty and expense of cover, there is no evidence in the summary judgment record to indicate that ABC could not pursue its legal remedies. The above conclusory statements are insufficient to establish a material fact issue.

Therefore, we conclude that ABC failed to establish economic duress. *See Palmer Barge Line, Inc. v. Southern Petroleum Trading Co.*, 776 F.2d 502, 505 (5th Cir. 1985) ("the failure or refusal to pay a contractual debt, without more, is insufficient to establish economic duress"); *Hurt v. Standard Oil Co.*, 444 S.W.2d 342, 247 (Tex. Civ. App.-El Paso 1969, no writ) (no duress where employee could have instituted suit rather than accept listed early retirement benefits).

C.

ABC asserts that the payment agreement is not enforceable because it was fraudulently induced by MMB's materially false representations that it would ship merchandise on D/A 90 terms and ship replacement goods. Of course, parol evidence is admissible to prove fraudulent inducement. *See Zoeller v. Howard Gardiner, Inc.*, 585 S.W.2d 920, 922-923 (Tex. Civ. App.-Amarillo 1979, writ ref'd n.r.e.) (Internal quotation omitted) ("When the issue of fraud is raised...all facts and circumstances leading up to and connected with the transactions are, ordinarily, admissible").

The elements for actionable fraud under Texas law are: (1) a material representation was made; (2) it was false when made; (3) the speaker knew it was false, or made it recklessly without knowledge of its truth and as a positive assertion; (4) the speaker made it with the intent that it should be acted upon; and (5) the party acted in reliance and suffered injury as a result. *Cocke v. Meridian Sav. Ass'n.*, 778 S.W.2d 516, 520 (Tex. App.-Corpus Christi 1989, no writ). Of critical importance here is that a promise to do an act in the future is not fraud, unless it is made with the intent not to perform. *M.J. Sheridan & Son Co. v. Seminole Pipeline Co.*, 731 S.W.2d 620, 624 (Tex. App.-Houston 1987, no writ).

ABC contends that Lian's affidavit and MMB's actions immediately following consummation of the agreement create material fact issues on all the elements for fraudulent inducement. We agree. Lian's affidavit, with all reasonable inferences in his favor, establishes that MMB representatives promised that it would ship replacement goods to make up for defective and non-conforming goods and would promptly begin shipping merchandise on D/A 90 terms; that these representations were false; that MMB made them with the intent that they would be acted upon; and that they induced Lian to sign the agreement to his detriment. The difficult question is whether the summary judgment record reflects material fact issues on whether MMB made representations with the intent not to perform, and whether ABC justifiably relied on MMB's representations. We examine these issues in turn.

1.

Intent not to perform a promise at the time it was made may be shown by circumstantial evidence, including the subsequent conduct of the promisor. *Pulchny v. Pulchny*, 555 S.W.2d 543, 545 (Tex. Civ. App.-Corpus Christi 1977, no writ). Needless to say, "intent is a fact question uniquely within the realm of the trier of fact because it so depends upon the credibility of the witnesses and the weight to be given to their testimony." *Spoljaric v. Percival Tours, Inc.*, 708 S.W.2d 432, 434 (Tex. 1986); thus, "summary judgment is rarely proper." *Taylor v. Bonilla*, 801 S.W.2d

553, 557 (Tex. App. 1990, writ denied). Although the failure to perform, standing alone, does not establish the issue of fraudulent intent, "slight circumstantial evidence of fraud, when considered with the breach of promise to perform, is sufficient to support a finding of fraudulent intent." *Spoljaric*, 708 S.W.2d at 435 (internal quotations omitted).

The summary judgment record contains admissible evidence, which, with all reasonable inferences in ABC's favor, establishes that ABC had objected to the goods as defective and non-conforming; that Lian traveled to Beijing to meet with MMB representatives; that MMB agreed to resume shipments on D/A 90 terms and replace defective and non-conforming goods, but stated they could not put the agreements in writing because "some people could go to jail;" that, as a result, Lian, signed the payment agreement; and that, almost immediately upon consummation of that written agreement, MMB repudiated its promise, stating that the bank refused to agree to D/A 90 terms without a letter of credit (which would require Lian to procure a commitment from his bank to pay a draft drawn by MMB). We conclude that the above evidence, particularly MMB's refusal to put the agreements in writing, followed almost immediately by its repudiation of one of them, creates a material fact issue on MMB's intent to perform.

2.

In addition, we conclude that a material fact issue exists regarding Lian's justifiable reliance. In order to establish fraud, ABC must show that its reliance on MMB's representations was justifiable as well as actual. *Haralson v. E.F. Hutton Group, Inc.*, 919 F.2d 1014, 1025 (5th Cir. 1990) (applying Texas law), modified on other grounds, 1991 U.S. App. LEXIS 1029 (Jan. 25, 1991). "Justifiable reliance' represents a lesser burden on fraud plaintiffs then what 'reasonable reliance' might imply." Id. (internal citations and quotations omitted). To determine "justifiable reliance" courts inquire whether, "given a fraud plaintiff's individual characteristics, abilities, and appreciation of facts and circumstances at or before the time of the alleged fraud - it is extremely unlikely that there is actual reliance on the plaintiff's part." *Id.* at 1026; *see General Motors Corp., Pontiac Motor Div. v. Courtesy Pontiac, Inc.*, 538 S.W.2d 3, 6 (Tex. Civ. App.- Tyler 1976, no writ) (quoted in *Haralson*, 919 F.2d at 1026) (internal quotation omitted) (plaintiff may not justifiably rely on "representations which any [person of normal intelligence, experience, and education] would recognize at once as preposterous... or which are won by facts within his observation to be so patently and obviously false that he must have closed his eyes to avoid discovery of the truth").

MMB maintains that the summary judgment record reflects that Lian's reliance was not justified because, in his disposition, he admitted that he knew that the MMB representatives had no authority to bind MMB, and, that approval from both the Chinese bank and the MMB controller was a condition precedent to future shipments. We disagree. The testimony is arguable consistent with Lian's affidavit, in which he stated that MMB representatives told him that the written payment agreement was needed "only for purposes of appeasing the bank and the controller," and that both would allow MMB to ship goods to ABC on the agreed terms. According to Lian, he "would not have signed the Agreement had he known that MMB did not have the intention or *the ability* to perform their part of the bargain" (emphasis added).

In addition, we disagree with MMB's contention that it was obvious that its representatives had authority to bind ABC as to the payment schedule, but not as to agreements on future sales. None of the prior written agreements regarding future business listed the bank or the controller as a party, or specified that the terms were subject to approval. Moreover, the actual authority of MMB representatives was peculiarly within their knowledge. *Cf. Trenholm v. Ratcliff*, 646 S.W.2d 927, 930 (Tex. 1983) (pure expressions of opinion are actionable "where the speaker purports to have special knowledge of facts that will occur or exist in the future").

In sum, because ABC established material fact issues on every element for fraudulent inducement, the district court erred in disposing of this issue by summary judgment.

D.

ABC asserted defenses and counterclaims based on defective and non-conforming goods and short shipments, including breach of express and implied warranties, breach of MMB's and ABC's underlying contract, and violation of the DTPA. The court concluded that the payment agreement constituted a novation, precluding ABC's objections to the goods. Because there are material fact issues on the enforceability of that agreement, we conclude that ABC's defenses and counterclaims that pertain to the quality and quantity of goods received were prematurely dismissed. Simply put, if the payment agreement was fraudulently induced, it is not enforceable, and the parties are restored to their prior positions on the underlying contract(s), to include defenses to the amount owed on the outstanding invoices.

III.

For the foregoing reasons, the summary judgment as to fraudulent inducement and to claims of defenses pertaining to the quality and quantity of goods received is *reversed*; the judgment in all other respects is *affirmed*; and this severed claim is *remanded* for further proceedings consistent with this opinion, to include, as to the payment agreement, extrinsic evidence not being admissible to alter its terms, but being admissible on whether it was fraudulently induced.

Affirmed in Part, *reversed* in Part, and *remanded*.

QUESTIONS

1.   Did the CISG apply to the contract between Beijing Metals and ABC? If the CISG were applicable, was the court's analysis of the parol evidence issue correct? *See* Article 8(3).

2.   If the court had recognized the applicability of the CISG, would its discussion of the fraudulent inducement and duress issues change?

MCC-Marble Ceramic Center, Inc.
v. Ceramica Nuova D'Agostino, S.P.A.,
144 F.3D 1384 (11th Cir. 1998)

Birch, Circuit Judge:

This case requires us to determine whether a court must consider parol evidence in a contract dispute governed by the United Nations Convention on Contracts for the International Sale of Goods ("CISG"). The district court granted summary judgment on behalf of the defendant-appellee, relying on certain terms and provisions that appeared on the reverse of a pre-printed form contract for the sale of ceramic tiles. The plaintiff-appellant sought to rely on a number of affidavits that tended to show both that the parties had arrived at an oral contract before memorializing their agreement in writing and that they subjectively intended not to apply the terms on the reverse of the contract to their agreements. The magistrate judge held that the affidavits did not raise an issue of material fact and recommended that the district court grant summary judgment based on the terms of the contract. The district court agreed with the magistrate judge's reasoning and entered summary judgment in the defendant-appellee's favor. We *reverse*.

BACKGROUND

The plaintiff-appellant, MCC-Marble Ceramic, Inc. ("MCC"), is a Florida corporation engaged in the retail sale of tiles, and the defendant-appellee, Ceramica Nuova d'Agostino S.p.A. ("D'Agostino") is an Italian corporation engaged in the manufacture of ceramic tiles. In October 1990, MCC's president, Juan Carlos Mozon, met representatives of D'Agostino at a trade fair in Bologna, Italy and negotiated an agreement to purchase ceramic tiles from D'Agostino based on samples he examined at the trade fair. Monzon, who spoke no Italian, communicated with Gianni Silingardi, then D'Agostino's commercial director, through a translator, Gianfranco Copelli, who was himself an agent of D'Agostino. The parties apparently arrived at an oral agreement on the crucial terms of price, quality, quantity, delivery and payment. The parties then recorded these terms on one of D'Agostino's standard, pre-printed order forms and Monzon signed the contract on MCC's behalf. According to MCC, the parties also entered into a requirements contract in February 1991, subject to which D'Agostino agreed to supply MCC with high grade ceramic tile at specific discounts as long as MCC purchased sufficient quantities of tile. MCC completed a number of additional order forms requesting tile deliveries pursuant to that agreement.

MCC brought suit against D'Agostino claiming a breach of the February1991 requirements contract when D'Agostino failed to satisfy orders in April, May, and August of 1991. In addition to other defenses, D'Agostino responded that it was under no obligation to fill MCC's orders because MCC had defaulted on payment for previous shipments. In support of its position, D'Agostino relied on the pre-printed terms of the contracts that MCC had executed. The executed forms were printed in Italian and contained terms and conditions on both the front and reverse. According to an English translation of the October 1990 contract, the front of the order form contained the following language directly beneath Monzon's signature:

The buyer hereby states that he is aware of the sales conditions stated on the reverse and that he expressly approves of them with special reference to those numbered 1-2-3-4-5-6-7-8. R2-126, Exh. 3 P 5 ("Maselli Aff."). Clause 6(b), printed on the back of the form states:

Default or delay in payment within the time agreed upon gives D'Agostino the right to...suspend or cancel the contract itself and to cancel possible other pending contracts and the buyer does not have the right to indemnification or damages. *Id.* p 6.

D'Agostino also brought a number of counterclaims against MCC, seeking damages for MCC's alleged nonpayment for deliveries of tile that D'Agostino had made between February 28, 1991 and July 4, 1991. MCC responded that the tile it had received was of a lower quality than contracted for, and that, pursuant to the CISG, MCC was entitled to reduce payment in proportion to the defects. D'Agostino, however, noted that clause 4 on the reverse of the contract states, in pertinent part:

Possible complaints for defects of the merchandise must be made in writing by means of a certified letter within and not later than 10 days after receipt of the merchandise.... Maselli Aff. P 6. Although there is evidence to support MCC's claims that it complained about the quality of the deliveries it received, MCC never submitted any written complaints.

MCC did not dispute these underlying facts before the district court, but argued that the parties never intended the terms and conditions printed on the reverse of the order form to apply to their agreements. As evidence for this assertion, MCC submitted Monzon's affidavit, which claims that MCC had no subjective intent to be bound by those terms and that D'Agostino was aware of this intent. MCC also filed affidavits from Silingardi and Copelli, D'Agostino's representatives at the trade fair, which support Monzon's claim that the parties subjectively intended not to be bound by the terms on the reverse of the order form. The magistrate judge held that the affidavits, even if true, did not raise an issue of material fact regarding the interpretation or applicability of the terms of the written contracts and the district court accepted his recommendation to award summary judgment in D'Agostino's favor. MCC then filed this timely appeal.

DISCUSSION

....

The parties to this case agree that the CISG governs their dispute because the United States, where MCC has its place of business, and Italy, where D'Agostino has its place of business, are both States Party to the Convention. *See* CISG, art. 1. Article 8 of the CISG governs the interpretation of international contracts for the sale of goods and forms the basis of MCC's appeal from the district court's grant of summary judgment in D'Agostino's favor. MCC argues that the magistrate judge and the district court improperly ignored evidence that MCC submitted regarding the parties' subjective intent when they memorialized the terms of their agreement on D'Agostino's pre-printed form contract, and that the magistrate judge erred by applying the parol evidence rule in derogation of the CISG.

I. Subjective Intent Under the CISG

Contrary to what is familiar practice in United States courts, the CISG appears to permit a substantial inquiry into the parties' subjective intent, even if the parties did not engage in any objectively ascertainable means of registering this intent. Article 8(1) of the CISG instructs courts to interpret the "statements... and other conduct of a party... according to his intent" as long as the other party "knew or could not have been unaware" of that intent. The plain language of the Convention, therefore, requires an inquiry into a party's subjective intent as long as the other party to the contract was aware of that intent.

In this case, MCC has submitted three affidavits that discuss the purported subjective intent of the parties to the initial agreement concluded between MCC and D'Agostino in October 1990. All three affidavits discuss the preliminary negotiations and report that the parties arrived at an oral agreement for D'Agostino to supply quantities of a specific grade of ceramic tile to MCC at an agreed upon price. The affidavits state that the "oral agreement established the essential terms of quality, quantity, description of goods, delivery, price and payment." ... The affidavits also note that the parties memorialized the terms of their oral agreement on a standard D'Agostino order form, but all three affiants contend that the parties subjectively intended not to be bound by the terms on the reverse of that form despite a provision directly below the signature line that expressly and specifically incorporated those terms.

The terms on the reverse of the contract give D'Agostino the right to suspend or cancel all contracts in the event of a buyer's non-payment and require a buyer to make a written report of all defects within ten days. As the magistrate judge's report and recommendation makes clear, if these terms applied to the agreements between MCC and D'Agostino, summary judgment would be appropriate because MCC failed to make any written complaints about the quality of tile it received and D'Agostino has established MCC's non-payment of a number of invoices amounting to $ 108,389.40 and 102,053,846.00 Italian lira.

Article 8(1) of the CISG requires a court to consider this evidence of the parties' subjective intent. Contrary to the magistrate judge's report, which the district court endorsed and adopted, article 8(1) does not focus on interpreting the parties' statements alone. Although we agree with the magistrate judge's conclusion that no "interpretation" of the contract's terms could support MCC's position, article 8(1) also requires a court to consider subjective intent while interpreting the conduct of the parties. The CISG's language, therefore, requires courts to consider evidence of a party's subjective intent when signing a contract if the other party to the contract was aware of that intent at the time. This is precisely the type of evidence that MCC has provided through the Silingardi, Copelli, and Monzon affidavits, which discuss not only Monzon's intent as MCC's representative but also discuss the intent of D'Agostino's representatives and their knowledge that Monzon did not intend to agree to the terms on the reverse of the form contract. This acknowledgment that D'Agostino's representatives were aware of Monzon's subjective intent puts this case squarely within article 8(1) of the CISG, and therefore requires the court to consider MCC's evidence as it interprets the parties' conduct.

II. Parol Evidence and the CISG

Given that the magistrate judge and the district court should have considered MCC's affidavits regarding the parties' subjective intentions, we must address a question of first impression in this circuit: whether the parol evidence rule, which bars evidence of an earlier oral contract that contradicts or varies the terms of a subsequent or contemporaneous written contract plays any role in cases involving the CISG. We begin by observing that the parol evidence rule, contrary to its title, is a substantive rule of law, not a rule of evidence. *See* II E. Allen Farnsworth, *Farnsworth on Contracts*, § 7.2 at 194 (1990). The rule does not purport to exclude a particular type of evidence as an "untrustworthy or undesirable" way of proving a fact, but prevents a litigant from attempting to show "the fact itself—the fact that the terms of the agreement are other than those in the writing." *Id.* As such, a federal district court cannot simply apply the parol evidence rule as a procedural matter—as it might if excluding a particular type of evidence under the Federal Rules of Evidence, which apply in federal court regardless of the source of the substantive rule of decision. *Cf. id.* § 7.2 at 196.

The CISG itself contains no express statement on the role of parol evidence. *See* Honnold, *Uniform Law* § 110 at 170. It is clear, however, that the drafters of the CISG were comfortable with the concept of permitting parties to rely on oral contracts because they eschewed any statutes of fraud provision and expressly provided for the enforcement of oral contracts. *Compare* CISG, art. 11 (a contract of sale need not be concluded or evidenced in writing) *with* U.C.C. § 2-201 (precluding the enforcement of oral contracts for the sale of goods involving more than $ 500). Moreover, article 8(3) of the CISG expressly directs courts to give "due consideration...to all relevant circumstances of the case including the negotiations..." to determine the intent of the parties. Given article 8(1)'s directive to use the intent of the parties to interpret their statements and conduct, article 8(3) is a clear instruction to admit and consider parol evidence regarding the negotiations to the extent they reveal the parties' subjective intent.

Despite the CISG's broad scope, surprisingly few cases have applied the Convention in the United States; *see Delchi Carrier SpA v. Rotorex Corp.*, 71 F.3d 1024, 1027-28 (2d Cir. 1995) (observing that "there is virtually no case law under the Convention"), and only two reported decisions touch upon the parol evidence rule, both in dicta. One court has concluded, much as we have above, that the parol evidence rule is not viable in CISG cases in light of article 8 of the Convention. In *Filanto*, a district court addressed the differences between the U.C.C. and the CISG on the issues of offer and acceptance and the battle of the forms. *See* 789 F. Supp. at 1238. After engaging in a thorough analysis of how the CISG applied to the dispute before it, the district court tangentially observed that article 8(3) "essentially rejects...the parol evidence rule." *Id.* at 1238 n.7. Another court, however, appears to have arrived at a contrary conclusion. In *Beijing Metals & Minerals Import/Export Corp. v. American Bus. Ctr., Inc.*, 993 F.2d 1178 (5th Cir. 1993), a defendant sought to avoid summary judgment on a contract claim by relying on evidence of contemporaneously negotiated oral terms that the parties had not included in their written agreement. The plaintiff, a Chinese corporation, relied on Texas law in its complaint while the defendant, apparently a Texas corporation, n15 asserted that the CISG governed the dispute. *Id.* at 1183 n.9. Without resolving the choice of law question, the Fifth Circuit cited *Filanto* for the proposition that there have been very few reported cases applying the CISG in the United States, and stated that the parol evidence rule would apply regardless of whether Texas law or the CISG governed the dispute. *Beijing Metals*, 993 F.2d at 1183 n.9. The opinion does not acknowledge *Filanto*'s more applicable dictum that the parol evidence rule does not apply to CISG cases nor does it conduct any analysis of the Convention to support its conclusion. In fact, the Fifth Circuit did not undertake to interpret the CISG in a manner that would arrive at a result consistent with the parol evidence rule but instead explained that it would apply the rule as developed at Texas common law. *See id.* at 1183 n.10. As persuasive authority for this court, the *Beijing Metals* opinion is not particularly persuasive on this point.

Our reading of article 8(3) as a rejection of the parol evidence rule, however, is in accordance with the great weight of academic commentary on the issue. As one scholar has explained:

> The language of Article 8(3) that "due consideration is to be given to all relevant circumstances of the case" seems adequate to override any domestic rule that would bar a tribunal from considering the relevance of other agreements.... Article 8(3) relieves tribunals from domestic rules that might bar them from "considering" any evidence between the parties that is relevant. This added flexibility for interpretation is consistent with a growing body of opinion that the "parol evidence rule" has been an embarrassment for the administration of modern transactions.

Honnnold, *Uniform Law* § 110 at 170-71. Indeed, only one commentator has made any serious attempt to reconcile the parol evidence rule with the CISG. *See* David H. Moore, Note, *The Parol Evidence Rule and the United Nations Convention on Contracts for the International Sale of Goods: Justifying Beijing Metals & Minerals Import/Export Corp. v. American Business Center, Inc.*, 1995 BYU L. REV. 1347. Moore argues that the parol evidence rule often permits the admission of evidence discussed in article 8(3), and that the rule could be an appropriate way to discern what consideration is "due" under article 8(3) to evidence of a parol nature. *Id.* at 1361-63. He also argues that the parol evidence rule, by limiting the incentive for perjury and pleading prior understandings in bad faith, promotes good faith and uniformity in the interpretation of contracts and therefore is in harmony with the principles of the CISG, as expressed in article 7. *Id.* at 1366-70. The answer to both these arguments, however, is the same: although jurisdictions in the United States have found the parol evidence rule helpful to promote good faith and uniformity in contract, as well as an appropriate answer to the question of how much consideration to give parol evidence, a wide number of other States Party to the CISG have rejected the rule in their domestic jurisdictions. One of the primary factors motivating the negotiation and adoption of the CISG was to provide parties to international contracts for the sale of goods with some degree of certainty as to the principles of law that would govern potential disputes and remove the previous doubt regarding which party's legal system might otherwise apply. *See Letter of Transmittal from Ronald Reagan, President of the United States,* to the United States Senate, *reprinted at* 15 U.S.C. app. 70, 71 (1997). Courts applying the CISG cannot, therefore, upset the parties' reliance on the Convention by substituting familiar principles of domestic law when the Convention requires a different result. We may only achieve the directives of good faith and uniformity in contracts under the CISG by interpreting and applying the plain language of article 8(3) as written and obeying its directive to consider this type of parol evidence.

MCC's affidavits, however, do not discuss all of the transactions and orders that MCC placed with D'Agostino. Each of the affidavits discusses the parties' subjective intent surrounding the initial order MCC placed with D'Agostino in October 1990. The Copelli affidavit also discusses a February 1991 requirements contract between the parties and reports that the parties subjectively did not intend the terms on the reverse of the D'Agostino order form to apply to that contract either. *See* Copelli Aff. P 12. D'Agostino, however, submitted the affidavit of its chairman, Vincenzo Maselli, which describes at least three other orders from MCC on form contracts dated January 15, 1991, April 27, 1991, and May 4, 1991, in addition to the October 1990 contract. *See* Maselli Aff. P 2, 25. MCC's affidavits do not discuss the subjective intent of the parties to be bound by language in those contracts, and D'Agostino, therefore, argues that we should affirm summary judgment to the extent damages can be traced to those order forms. It is unclear from the record, however, whether all of these contracts contained the terms that appeared in the October 1990 contract.

Moreover, because article 8 requires a court to consider any "practices which the parties have established between themselves, usages and any subsequent conduct of the parties" in interpreting contracts, CISG, art. 8(3), whether the parties intended to adhere to the ten day limit for complaints, as stated on the reverse of the initial contract, will have an impact on whether MCC was bound to adhere to the limit on subsequent deliveries. Since material issues of fact remain regarding the interpretation of the remaining contracts between MCC and D'Agostino, we cannot affirm any portion of the district court's summary judgment in D'Agostino's favor.

CONCLUSION

MCC asks us to reverse the district court's grant of summary judgment in favor of D'Agostino. The district court's decision rests on pre-printed contractual terms and conditions incorporated on the reverse of a standard order form that MCC's president signed on the company's behalf. Nevertheless, we conclude that the CISG, which governs international contracts for the sale of goods, precludes summary judgment in this case because MCC has raised an issue of material fact concerning the parties' subjective intent to be bound by the terms on the reverse of the pre-printed contract. The CISG also precludes the application of the parol evidence rule, which would otherwise bar the consideration of evidence concerning a prior or contemporaneously negotiated oral agreement. Accordingly, we *reverse* the district court's grant of summary judgment and *remand* this case for further proceedings consistent with this opinion.

III. Contract Formation

A. Overview

Documents Supplement References:

1. *CISG Articles 14-24, 92.*
2. *U.C.C. Sections 2-205, 2-207, 2-305.*

The Convention for the International Sale of Goods: A Handbook of Basic Materials 17-18
(Daniel Magraw& Reed Kathrein Eds., 1990)

Part II of the Convention sets out the rules governing the formation of the international sales contract. The first four articles of Part II govern the offer. These articles provide for the prerequisites of an offer (Art. 14) and the withdrawal, revocation, and termination of an offer (Arts. 15-17). The following five articles set out the corresponding rules on the acceptance. They provide for the form an acceptance may take (Art. 18), the effect of an acceptance which varies the terms of an offer (Art. 19), the time allowed for acceptance (Arts. 20-21), and withdrawal of an acceptance (Art. 22). Article 23 states that a contract is concluded when an acceptance becomes effective, *i.e.*, when it has reached the offeror. A final provision, Article 24, defines when a communication "reaches" a party.

The formation provisions embody carefully negotiated compromises between civil law and common law concepts, with several significant concessions to the common law. The Convention rejects the civil law presumption that offers are irrevocable in favor of the common law presumption of revocability with a 'firm offer' exception similar to that of the Uniform Commercial Code (U.C.C. Section 2-205). Although an acceptance will not be effective until it reaches the offeror (thus rejecting the common law 'mailbox rule'), the Convention does provide for what arguably is the most important effect of the common law rule: an offeror may not revoke an offer once an acceptance is dispatched (Arts. 16(1) & 18(2)).

The effect of the Convention will probably be to enforce somewhat fewer 'agreements' than would be the case under United States law. The Convention emphasizes the need for definiteness in an offer, which may mean, for example, that an 'open price' offer will not be effective. (Art. 14. *But see* Art. 55. *Cf.* U.C.C. Section 2-305.) Where exchanged forms do not match, application of the Convention will lead to fewer enforceable contracts because the terms of an acceptance must conform to those of the offer except where alterations are not material (Art. 19). Although United States law is more flexible on these matters (U.C.C. Section 2-207), in international trade where partes are dealing with each other at a distance, the Convention's great conceptualism is arguably desirable because it will force parties to produce more evidence of a concluded agreement.

Article 92 permits a state to declare it will not be bound by Part II. The United States did not exercise that right.

B. The Offer

Documents Supplement References:
1. *CISG Articles 6-8, 14-16, 18, 20, 24, 55, 92.*
2. *UNIDROIT Articles 1.7, 2.15, 2.2, 2.3, 2.4, 2.7, 2.8.*
3. *Restatement of Contracts Sections 24, 42, 87, 205.*
4. *U.C.C. Sections 1-203, 2-201, 2-204, 2-205, 2-305.*

NOTE ON WHAT IS AN OFFER

Article 14 (1) specifically provides that "[a] proposal for concluding a contract addressed to one or more specific persons constitutes an offer if it is sufficiently definite and indicates the intention of the offeror to be bound in case of acceptance." This criteria is not novel and should be familiar to most American lawyers. *See The Restatement (Second) of Contracts* Section 24. Unfortunately, questions concerning the purport of this section are created by its own definition of "substantially definite:" "A proposal is sufficiently definite if it indicates the goods and expressly or implicitly makes provision for determining the quantity and price." There is no fully comparable requirement in existing United States law. While there is nothing new or troublesome about the requirement that the offer "indicate the goods" and expressly or implicitly allow for the determination of the quantity term (*see* U.C.C. Sections 2-201(1) and 2- 204), difficult interpretative problems arise if the price is not explicitly set forth, and there is no applicable trade usage or prior course of dealing under Article 8(3). Although this would not cause insurmountable difficulties under the U.C.C. (*see* U.C.C. Section 2-305(1)(a)), the result under the CISG may very well be that there is no contract. The outcome will turn on how one views Article 55:

> Where a contract has been validly concluded but does not expressly or implicitly fix or make provision for determining the price, the parties are considered, in the absence of any indication to the contrary, to have impliedly made reference to the price generally charged at the time of the conclusion of the contract....

The foregoing can be read as an affirmative statement that contract formation is not dependant upon an express or implied price term. *See John Honnold, Uniform Law for International Sales Under the 1980 United Nations Convention* 163 (1982). In contrast, it can be argued that Article 55 is operative only in situations where a Contracting State made a declaration under Article 92(1) that it will not be bound by Part II of the Convention. *See* E. Allan Farnsworth, *Formation of Contract, in* INTERNATIONAL SALES: THE UNITED NATIONS CONVENTION ON CONTRACTS FOR THE INTERNATIONAL SALE OF GOODS at 3-8 (1984).

The definition of an offer under the UNIDROIT Principles is similar to Article 14 but lacks the requirement that the offer contain a description of the goods, quantity, and price terms. If there is an intent to be bound and if the "gaps" in the contract can be filled, the absence of a particular term will not preclude contract formation. *See* Article 2.2.

Case Abstract, UNCITRAL Texts (CLOUT), Abstract No. 106,

November 10 1994 (Austria)

The Austrian buyer ordered in Germany a large quantity of chincilla pelts of middle or better quality at a price between 35 and 65 German Marks per piece. The German seller delivered 249 pelts. The Austrian buyer, without opening the packaged goods, sold them further to an Italian pelt dealer at the same price. The Italian dealer returned 13 pelts arguing that they were of inferior quality to that agreed. The Austrian buyer sent to the German seller an inventory list setting out the rejected pelts and refused to pay their price arguing that it had sold the pelts further on behalf of the German seller as its agent.

The first instance court ordered the Austrian buyer to pay the price of the rejected pelts, since the pelts were as specified in the contract. Having found that pelts of middle quality were sold in the market at a price up to 60 German Marks, the court considered that a price of 50 German Marks per pelt was a reasonable one.

The Court of Appeal confirmed that decision. It found that CISG was applicable since the parties had their places of business in States parties to the Convention and the subject matter of the dispute fell within the scope of application of the Convention. The Court of Appeal further found that a valid contract had been concluded on the basis of the order, which was sufficiently definite both as to the quantity and the quality of the goods.

The Court of Appeal further found that the agreement as to the price range (35 to 65 German Marks) did not preclude the valid conclusion of a contract since under Article 55 of the Convention, if the price is not explicit or implicit in the contract, the parties are considered to have agreed on the usual market price. The Court of Appeal noted that the price of 50 German Marks per pelt, which had been established by the court of first instance based on the market price, had not been questioned by the parties. As to the currency of payment, the court found that payment was due in German Marks, since payment should be made at the place of business of the German seller (Article 57 CISG).

The Supreme Court confirmed the decision of the Court of Appeal. It found that the Convention was applicable since an international sales contract in the sense of Article 1(1)(a) CISG was involved. It also found that the order was sufficiently definite to constitute an offer under Article 14 CISG, since it could be perceived as such by a reasonable person in the same circumstances as the seller (Article 8(2) and (3) CISG). In determining that the order was sufficiently definite, the Supreme Court took into consideration the behavior of the Austrian buyer who accepted the delivered goods and sold them further without questioning their price, quality or quantity. In particular, the price was found to be sufficiently definite, so as to make the application of Article 55 CISG unnecessary. As to the place of payment, the Supreme Court found that it was the place of business of the seller since the goods were sent by post and no third party had been appointed to receive payment in Austria on behalf of the German seller.

The Supreme Court of the Republic of Hungary, Gf.I.31, 349/1992/9

(Translation Reproduced From 13 Journal of Law
and Commerce 31-47 (1993))

The Supreme Court of the Republic of Hungary has passed the following judgment against the partial judgment No.3.G.50. 289/1991/32 brought by the City Court of Budapest in the lawsuit initiated by the Plaintiff, United Technologies International Inc. Pratt & Whitney Commercial Engine Business (400 Main St., East Hartford), represented by Dr. László Szlávnits, attorney at law, of Legal Office (1053 Budapest, Károlyi M. u. 9), against the Defendant, MALÉV Hungarian Airlines (1051 Budapest, Roosevelt tér 2.), represented by Dr. Zsolt Jurasics, attorney at law, of Office of Attorneys No. 99. (1068 Budapest, Benczúr u. 3.) in respect of validity of contract due to the appeal submitted by the Defendant during the trial, held on the 25th day of September 1992.

The Supreme Court changes the partial judgment of the City Court of Budapest, the court of first instance, by revising the partial judgment as a judgment, and rejects the Plaintiff's claim.

The Supreme Court obligates the Plaintiff to pay HUF 15,150,000, *i.e.* fifteen million one hundred and fifty thousand forints, the cost of the original lawsuit and of the appeal, into the account of the Defendant's legal representative.

Plaintiff is to bear its costs itself.

Reasons adduced:

From the fall of 1990 negotiations had been conducted by the parties to the suit and the American VALSAN Co., on the one hand, about the conditions given which the Plaintiff would replace the ineffective engines on the Defendant's Soviet made Tupolyev TU-154 aircrafts with PRATT JT 8D-219 engines, manufactured by the Plaintiff (engine replacement), and on the other hand, about the Plaintiff supplying the PW 4000 series engines for the wide bodied aircrafts, to be purchased by the Defendant. On December 4, 1990 the parties signed a Letter of Intention about their negotiations on the replacement of the engines on the Defendant's already existing Soviet made aircrafts. They expressed their intention — without undertaking any obligations whatsoever — to sign a final agreement in the future in accordance with those contained in the declaration. In the above-mentioned Letter of Intention the Plaintiff stipulated a condition, among others, according to which the signing of the final agreement depended on Defendant's acceptance of Plaintiff's support offer for the purchase of PW 4000 series engines from Plaintiff by Defendant for the wide bodied aircrafts to be purchased.

Plaintiff submitted two purchase-support offers, dated December 14, 1990, to Defendant with the aim of aiding the purchase of two aircrafts, supplied with Plaintiff's engines, whose order was finalized, another one with an option to buy, furthermore, the purchase of one spare engine with a finalized order, and another one with an option to buy. These support offers replaced the one dated November 9, 1990, making that null and void. Both offers made a reference to the Appendix containing the PW 4000 series engines' Guarantee Plan. One of the offers was made in case the Defendant decided to purchase a 767-200 ER aircraft assembled with PW 4056 engines, the other in case Defendant purchased a 310-300 aircraft equipped with the new PW 4152 or 4156 jet engine systems. At this time Defendant was negotiating with two aircraft manufacturers and had not yet come to a decision about the type of the aircraft to be bought and the company to purchase from. The support offers involved financial assistance (lending), engine warranties, product maintenance and repair services in order to select the engines or jet engine systems produced by Plaintiff.

The offers were kept open by Plaintiff until December 21, 1990, on condition that the validity of Defendant's declaration of acceptance depended on the appropriate provisions to be made by the Government of Hungary and that of the United States. Point Y of both support offers contained the purchase agreements. The place where the Defendant was to sign the support offers in case of acceptance was clearly marked on the document. Defendant did not sign either support offers, but in the presence of Plaintiff's proxy, who at this time extended the offer to include the PW 4060 engine, as well, and on the basis of the discussions carried out with him/her, composed a letter together with him/ her, which was sent to the Vice-President of Plaintiff's company by telex, notifying him/her that — based on the evaluation of technical data and efficiency, furthermore taking the financial assistance also into consideration — they had selected the PW 4000 engine for the new wide bodied fleet of aircrafts. Defendant also informed Plaintiff that it is looking forward to the cooperation with PW, especially with respect to the replacement of the TU-154 aircraft engines, furthermore that the present declaration of acceptance was wholly based on the conditions included in the PW engine offer, dated December 14, 1990. In the meantime Defendant asked Plaintiff to keep this information strictly confidential until they were ready to make a joint public announcement.

Later, in the beginning of February, 1991, the Parties had a verbal discussion, with reference to which Plaintiff addressed a letter to Defendant on February 11, 1991. In this letter Plaintiff declared that an advertising budget of USD 65,000.00 "will be added" to the premium for signing, and offered assistance in selecting a partner for engine maintenance and cooperation in the creation of a spare-parts pool for the maintenance of the line. It was also said that Plaintiff would come to Budapest to continue the discussions on the replacement of the TU154 aircrafts' engines and to finalize the PW 4000 contract.

Following that Defendant notified Plaintiff in writing that Defendant would not choose PW 4000 series engines for the Boeing 767 aircraft. In response to that, still on the same day Plaintiff stated its standpoint, according to which Defendant had definitely and irrevocably committed itself to purchase the new 767 aircraft with PW 4000 engines, asked Defendant to meet its obligations without delay, notify Boeing about its selection of PW 4000 engines and make a public announcement about it. Defendant, on account of its different standpoint, refused to do so.

Plaintiff initiated a suit on July 23, 1991, asking the court to declare that the contract between the Parties legally came to force on December 21, 1990, that its provisions were violated by Defendant, that Defendant was to meet its contractual obligations, and also asked for the allowance of the legal costs. Plaintiff claimed that Defendant, with its declaration, dated on December 21, 1990, accepted Plaintiff's contractual offer, dated on December 14, 1990; thus a valid, and legally binding contract was made for the sale and purchase of PW 4056 engines and spare engines. According to Plaintiff's position, the December 14,1990 offer fully complies with the content of Paragraph 1, Section 14 of the United Nations Agreement on international sales contracts, dated in Vienna on April 11, 1980 (hereinafter the "Agreement"), and therefore with the acceptance of the offer the contract had legally come to force. For the offer clearly states the product, its quantity and contains data on the basis of which the price can be determined precisely. The circumstance that Defendant talked about PW 4000 series engines in its declaration of acceptance is insignificant, since the engines listed in the offer all belong to this series; furthermore, the offer indicated the engines' number within the series, as well. The extension of the December 14,

1990 offer to include the PW 4060 engine and the modification of the engine's maintenance and cost warranty plans by the Plaintiff's business representative was precisely in response to Defendant's request. The offer provided an opportunity for Defendant to choose the type of the aircraft from the two alternatives and, accordingly, that offer should be deemed accepted, which corresponded to the type of the selected aircraft. The quantity could also be defined on the basis of the offer, since it depended upon the Defendant purchasing two or three planes. The price was also defined, since it could be arrived at by calculating the costs. Defendant knew the technical characteristics of the engines involved in the suit, had received the engine's specifications and additional necessary documentation to which Defendant referred in its declaration of acceptance. Later in the course of the lawsuit, Plaintiff requested Defendant to be ordered to reimburse Plaintiff for costs incurred by the discovery proceedings, in relation to the present lawsuit, that had been initiated by Defendant, and indicated the amount to be USD 64,816.20.

Defendant asked for the dismissal of the suit. Defendant did not acknowledge entering into a contract with Plaintiff about the engines involved in the suit. According to Defendant's position, Plaintiff's December 14,1990, offers could not be regarded as a contractual offer, for they did not contain the data stipulated by Paragraph 1, Section 14 of the Agreement. The support offers, dated December 14, 1990, did not properly identify the goods, i.e. any one of the actual engines, that could be the subject of the contract and should be delivered by the Plaintiff. Neither did the definition of quantity comply with the provisions of Paragraph 1, Section 14 of the Agreement and the document did not indicate the price of the engines to be installed at all. For the price of the PW 4056 series spare engine is not identical with the price of the PW 4056 engine; neither is the price of the PW 4056 series engine identical with the price of the PW 4000. The so called pricing formula could only be applied if the base price of the given engines would have been defined at the time of making the contract. According to the data supplied by Plaintiff the base price would also have to be calculated; however, the data were not even sufficient for that, since Plaintiff did not indicate its own price index. Engines do not have general market prices; therefore, general market prices cannot be used for guidelines. Since the aircraft manufacturer would be paid by Defendant, while Plaintiff would be paid by the aircraft manufacturer for the engines, the precise knowledge of the price is absolutely necessary, for it is to be harmonized with the financial conditions and the terms of payment given by the aircraft manufacturer. According to Defendant's position the debated offer involved in the lawsuit does not qualify as an offer, if the cited Section of the Agreement is interpreted correctly, for it does not express Plaintiff's intention to regard itself to be under contractual obligation in case of acceptance. This is also proven by the fact that in its letter of February 11, 1991, Plaintiff still writes about the finalization of the contract and did not transfer the 1 million US dollar premium for signing either. This is the buyer's contractual premium, in case the offer is accepted within its deadline.

Defendant also referred to the fact that Plaintiff tied the validation of the contract to conditions, and the declaration of acceptance was not signed either by the United States or the Hungarian government.

According to the Defendant's position, even if Plaintiff's offer had complied with the stipulations set by the Agreement, the contract would not have been established, for Defendant's December 21, 1990 letter cannot be regarded as acceptance. This letter refers to the engine family in general terms only, and stipulated a condition that could qualify as a brand new counter-offer, when Defendant based its declaration on the replacement of the TU-154 fleet's engines.

. . . .

The court of appeals modifies and amends the bearing of the case, established by the court of the first instance, on the basis of all the accumulated data of the lawsuit, with special attention to those contained in the letter of intention, dated on December 4, 1990, the proposal, dated on December 14, 1990, and Defendant's letter, dated December 21, 1990, and also based on the Plaintiff's declaration during the appeal proceedings, as follows below.

The parties to the suit had been conducting negotiations since the fall of 1990, on the one hand, about Plaintiff replacing the engines on the Soviet built TUPOLYEV TU-154 aircrafts, on the other hand, about Defendant purchasing engines from Plaintiff for its wide bodied aircrafts, that were to be bought. On November 9, 1990 Plaintiff sent a support offer to Defendant about assembling the wide bodied aircrafts with engines manufactured by the Plaintiff. On December 4, 1990 they signed a letter of intention (memorandum) about their negotiations concerning the replacement of the engines. In this document, the Parties stated (Point 8.b) that, among other things, the contract depends on whether Defendant accepts one of the Plaintiff's two support offers, dated November 9, 1990, *i.e.* whether Defendant selects the PW 4000 series engine for the new wide bodied aircrafts. In case Defendant would not accept this offer, Plaintiff reserved the right to revise its declaration of intention in respect of the TUPOLYEV engine replacement program, which — by the way — was signed without undertaking any sort of obligations. Apart from the above, the strong connection between the replacement program and the sale of aircraft engines is also proven by Defendant's December 21, 1990 declaration and Plaintiff's letter, dated on January 11, 1991.

On December 14, 1990, Plaintiff made two different offers in case Defendant selected Boeing or in case it selected Airbus. These offers annulled the November 9, 1990 offers and replaced them. In the December 14, 1990 purchase-support offer for the Boeing scenario Plaintiff indicated two engines, taking the modification also into consideration, the PW 4056 and the PW 4060, from which, according to Point Y.1 of the offer Defendant was to choose and to notify the aircraft manufacturer about its choice. In Point Y.2 Plaintiff undertook to sell the engines to Defendant on the basis of a separate agreement with the manufacturer. In this offer Plaintiff indicated the price of the new PW 4056 engine to be USD 5,847,675, which could increase according to the stability of value calculations from December, 1989. The modified offer does not contain the base price of the PW 4060 engine and spare engine.

The other offer, dated on the same day and intended for the Airbus scenario, among the PW 4000 series engines indicated two engines, PW 4152 or PW 4156, a jet engine system and a spare engine, from which Defendant was to make its selection according to Point Y.1 and Y.2 of the offer, and upon acceptance of the offer to notify the aircraft manufacturer immediately. According to Point Y.2 Plaintiff undertook to sell the jet engine systems, the number of which was indicated, on the basis of a separate contract made with the aircraft manufacturer. In this offer Plaintiff indicated the price of the new PW 4152 spare engine base unit to be USD 5,552,675, and the price of the new PW 4156/A spare engine to be USD 5,847,675, with stabilizing their values starting from December, 1989.

According to Point Y.4 of both offers, with the acceptance of the offer Defendant was to send a finalized and unconditional order for the spare engines indicated in the offers.

In case of the offer for the Airbus scenario, the indicated jet engine system includes the engine, other parts and the gondola as well, while 'engine' means the motor only; therefore the price of the jet engine system is not identical with the price of the engine (motor). The offer contained the price of neither jet engine system.

In the appeal proceedings, based on the Defendant's appeal, a declaration was to be made also about whether, interpreting the Parties' declarations on the basis of Paragraph 1, Section 8 of the Agreement, Plaintiff's December 14, 1990 offers comply with the conditions stipulated in Paragraph 1, section 14 of the Agreement and whether Defendant's December 21, 1990 declaration qualifies as an acceptance.

According to Paragraph 1, Section 14 of the Agreement a proposal to enter into a contract, addressed to one or more persons, qualifies as a bid if it is properly defined and indicates the bidder's intention to regard itself to be under obligation in case of acceptance. A bid is properly defined if it indicates the product, expressly or in essence defines the quantity and the price, or contains directions as to how they can be defined. This means that the Agreement regards the definition of the subject of the service (product), its quantity and its price to be an essential element of a bid.

It can be determined on the basis of the given evidence and the Parties' declarations, that Plaintiff made two parallel offers for the same deal on December 14, 1990, depending on Defendant's choice of the Boeing or the Airbus aircraft. In case Boeing was selected, within the respective offer two separate engines (PW 4056 and PW 4060) were indicated. This offer did not contain the base price of the PW 4060 engine.

In case Airbus was selected, within the respective offer two different jet engine systems (PW 4152 and PW 4156), belonging to the same series, and two different spare engines (PW 4152 and PW 4156/A) were indicated. The base price of the jet engine systems is not included in the offer, only that of the spare engines, in spite of the fact that these two elements are not identical either technically or in respect of price. In case there is no base price, value stability calculations have no importance. The price cannot be determined according to Section 55 of the Agreement either, as jet engine systems have no market prices.

. . . .

It clearly follows from the above, that none of Plaintiff's offer, neither the one for the Boeing aircraft's engines, nor the one for the Airbus aircraft's jet engine systems, complied with the requirements stipulated in Paragraph 1, Section 14 of the Agreement, for it did not indicate the price of the services or it could not have been determined.

Plaintiff's parallel and alternative contractual offers should be interpreted, according to the noticeable intention of the offer's wording and following common sense, so that Plaintiff wished to provide an opportunity to Defendant to select one of the engine types defined in the offer at the time of the acceptance of the offer.

For according to the wording of Section Y of the offers:

- Defendant, following the acceptance of the proposal, immediately notifies the aircraft manufacturer about the selection of one of the numerically defined engines (jet engine systems) for use on the wide bodied aircrafts;
- Plaintiff sells the selected engine (jet engine system) to Defendant according to a separate agreement made with the aircraft manufacturer;
- Thereby (that is, with the acceptance of the proposal) Defendant sends a final and unconditional purchase order to Plaintiff for the delivery of the spare engines of the determined type.

In addition to grammatical interpretation, the assumption of Plaintiff granting "power" to Defendant, made by the court of first instance, essentially entitling Defendant to make its selection until some undetermined point of time or even during performance from the services offered alternatively, goes against economic reasoning as well. For the legal consequences of this would be that Plaintiff should manufacture the quantity, stipulated in the contract, of all four types — two engines and two jet engine systems — and prepared with its services wait for Defendant to exercise its right to make its selection with no deadline.

It follows from this all that Plaintiff provided an opportunity to choose a certain type of engine or jet engine system at the time of the acceptance of its offer.

Plaintiff's offers were alternative; therefore Defendant should have determined which engine or jet engine system, listed in the offers, it chose. There was no declaration made, on behalf of Defendant, in which Defendant would have indicated the subject of the service, the concrete type of the engine or jet engine system, listed in the offers, as an essential condition of the contract. Defendant's declaration, that it had chosen the PW 4000 series engine, expresses merely Defendant's intention to close the contract, which is insufficient for the establishment of the contract.

Therefore, the court of first instance was mistaken when it found that with Defendant's December 21, 1990 declaration the contract was established with the "power" — or, more precisely, stipulation — according to which Defendant was entitled to select from the indicated four types (PW 4056 or PW 4060 engine and spare engine, PW 4152 or PW 4156 jet engine system and spare engine) with a unilateral declaration later, after the contract had been closed. The opportunity to choose after closing the contract does not follow from the offer. If perhaps such a further condition would have been intended by Defendant, then this should have been regarded as a new offer on its behalf.

Lacking an appropriately explicit offer from Plaintiff and not having a clear indication as to the subject of the service in Defendant's declaration of acceptance, no sales contract has been established between the Parties.

It is a different issue, whether the series of discussions and Defendant's declaration of acceptance created such a special atmosphere of confidence, where Plaintiff could seriously count on closing the contract and failing that Plaintiff suffered economic and other disadvantages. With this question and with its legal grounds, no suit being initiated, the court of appeals was not entitled to deal with.

The stipulation of the contract, that the validity of the offer's acceptance dependent [sic] on the approval of the United States or of the Hungarian Government, could bear with any significance only if the acceptance of the offer would have resulted in a contract; however, since a contract was not established, the above-mentioned uncertain future circumstances bear with no significance in relation to the judgment passed in this present suit.

     ....

Plaintiff has lost the case; therefore, according to Paragraph 1, Section 78 of the Civil Procedure, in addition to bearing its own costs, it is obligated to reimburse all costs that emerged during the first and the appeal procedure to Defendant. Defendant's costs consist of legal fees, determined on the basis of Point B, Paragraph 1 of the Decree of the Minister of Justice of 12.1991 (IX.29.), and a HUF 150,000 appeal duty. Plaintiff indicated more than 2 billion forints as the subject of the suit; the court has determined the court fee, which amounts to 0.5% of the above sum for the proceedings of the first instance, while in the appeal proceeding half of that amount.

Budapest, on the 25th day of September, 1992.

Salamonné Dr. Solymosi Ibolya, the President of Council, Dr. Nemes Júlia, presenting judge, and Dr. Gyürkei Klara judge.

NOTE ON GOOD FAITH AND FAIR DEALING

In *Malév*, the Court raises, but does not discuss, the possibility that the defendant may be liable for having misled the plaintiff into believing that there would eventually be a contract for the purchase and sale of airplane engines. If so, what would be the underlying theory of recovery? Put differently, one can ask whether contract law recognizes a precontractual obligation of good faith and fair dealing. Here in the United States, the answer seems to be no. *See Restatement (Second) of Contracts* Section 205; U.C.C. Section 1-203. There may, however, be alternative doctrines under which liability may be imposed. For example, doctrines such as fraudulent nondisclosure, equitable estoppel, and promissory estoppel may operate as functional equivalents of good faith. On the other hand, civil law does recognize a good faith form of precontractual liability, commonly referred to as the doctrine of *culpa in contrahendo* ("fault in contractual negotiation"). Accordingly, courts may order the parties to continue with their negotiations and award damages, including lost profits, in the event one party refuses.

The CISG makes explicit reference to the doctrine of good faith but only as an interpretative guide. Article 7 states that "the observance of good faith in international trade" is one factor to consider in interpreting the Convention. This is a far cry, however, from the general good faith requirement found in civil law systems. By contrast, "one of the fundamental ideas underlying the [UNIDROIT] Principles" is the obligation of good faith and fair dealing. Article 1.7, cmt.1. Moreover, the Principles make clear that this obligation attaches the moment the parties begin to negotiate. *See* Article 2.15.

QUESTION

1.   What is the status of trade circulars under the CISG? What is the practical significance of whether Article 14(1) or 14(2) applies?

NOTE ON WHEN AN OFFER TAKES EFFECT AND ITS DURATION

Article 15(1) states that an offer becomes effective only when it reaches the offeree and, pursuant to Article 24, it reaches the offeree "when it is made orally to him or delivered by any other means to him personally, to his place of business or mailing address or, if he does not have a place of business or mailing address, to his habitual residence." These provisions would not drastically change present law except in the unusual case where the offer is deemed effective under the CISG before the offeree is actually aware that one has been made.

The following facts present the problem: An offer is mailed on April 5 which requires acceptance within ten days. The offeree receives the offer on April 10 and dispatches her acceptance on April 11. The acceptance reaches the offeror on April 16.

Because the time for acceptance begins to run the moment the offer was dispatched, the offer will lapse on April 15. *See* Article 20(1). Unfortunately for the offeree, the CISG rejects the common law "mailbox rule" (*See* Article 18(2)); thus, without further communication between the parties, there can be no contract. The outcome would be different, however, if the offeror were to clearly indicate in its offer that the time for acceptance begins to run from the offeree's receipt or that the acceptance would take effect when dispatched. *See* Article 6.

The UNIDROIT Principles similarly provide that "[a]n offer becomes effective when it reaches the offeree." Article 2.3. Acceptance must occur within the time fixed by the offer, or in the absence of a fixed time, within a reasonable period of time. *See* Article 2.7. If the offer provides that it must be accepted within so many days without a reference to a specific date, the time for acceptance begins to run from the date on the envelope or, if the offer were delivered by means of instantaneous communications, from the moment the offer reaches the offeree. *See* Article 2.8.

NOTE ON THE REVOCATION OF AN OFFER

The general rules under both the Convention and the Restatement (Second) of Contracts are that offers may be revoked at any time before the offeree has dispatched an acceptance, and the revocation becomes effective when it has reached the offeree. *See* Article 16(1) and Restatement (Second) of Contracts Section 42. *See also* UNIDROIT Principles Articles 2.3; 2.4. Since, under the CISG, the acceptance is not effective until it reaches the offeror, a gap is effectively created between the time of dispatch and the time of receipt during which period there is no contract, but the offer is irrevocable.

While an offer is presumed to be revocable, it may not be revoked "if it indicates, whether by stating a fixed time for acceptance or otherwise, that it is irrevocable...." Article 16(2)(a). This rule is similar to the "firm offer" rule of U.C.C. Section 2-205. *See also* UNIDROIT Principles Article 2.4. Firm offers under the Code, however, are limited in their duration to three months; there is no parallel limitation in the Convention.

An offer also becomes irrevocable in situations where there has been reasonable reliance by the offeree. *See* Article 16(2)(b). This provision is comparable to Section 87(2) of the *Restatement (Second) of Contracts*. There is, however, an important difference between the CISG and the Restatement. Section 87(2) renders the offer "binding to the extent necessary to avoid injustice," which may or may not involve full enforcement of the offered terms. No such limitation is found in Article 16(2)(b). This Article seems designed to keep the offer open so that it can be accepted and a contract formed with the same consequences that attend the formation of any other contract. *See also* UNIDROIT Principles Article 2.4.

Even if the offer is expressly made irrevocable, it can be withdrawn by the offeror "if the withdrawal reaches the offeree before or at the same time as the offer." Article 15(2). Withdrawal is permitted because the offer does not take effect until it reaches the offeree, and until that time, the offeree can have no expectations concerning the proposed transaction.

QUESTION

1.   Suppose the offer states that it will terminate on May 1. Would this language preclude the offeror from revoking prior to that date? In this regard, is there a difference between the CISG and the U.C.C.?

C. The Acceptance

Documents Supplement References:

1. CISG Articles 18-19, 21-22.

2. UNIDROIT Sections 2.11, 2.12, 2.19, 2.20, 2.21, 2.22, 2.6, 2.9

3. *Restatement Section 50.*

4. *UC.C. Sections 2-204, 2-206, 2-207.*

NOTE ON ACCEPTANCE AND WHEN IT BECOMES EFFECTIVE

The opening provision of Article 18(1) reads: "A statement made by or other conduct of the offeree indicating assent to an offer is an acceptance." The Convention's characterization of an acceptance is quite similar to that found in the Restatement (Second) of Contracts (*See* Section 50(1)) and U.C.C. Section 2-204(1)). We also find in the Convention the familiar rule that "[s]ilence or inactivity does not itself amount to acceptance." Article 18(1). This is also the rule found in the UNIDROIT Principles. *See* Article 2.6. *But see* Restatement (Second) of Contracts Section 69. Notwithstanding this similarity of approach to the issue of what constitutes an acceptance, the Convention in several respects provides rules that are different from those with which American lawyers are familiar.

The first difference relates to the question of when the acceptance takes effect. Article 18(2) provides that acceptance "becomes effective at the moment the indication of assent reaches the offeror," and it must reach the offeror within either the time set by the offer or a reasonable time if the term is left open. *See also* UNIDROIT Principles Article 2.6. Recall, however, that once the offeree has dispatched the acceptance, the offeror may no longer revoke the offer. Because no contract is formed upon dispatch of the acceptance, it may be withdrawn by the offeree if the withdrawal is received by the offeror before or at the same time as the acceptance. *See* Article 22. These provisions of the CISG suggest that after dispatching the acceptance, the offeree can speculate at the expense of the offeror. After all, should the offeree wish to escape from the deal before the acceptance reaches the offeror, she need only pick up the phone or use some other method of instantaneous communication and withdraw the acceptance.

The second difference between the Convention and domestic law concerns acceptance by conduct. The basic rule under both the U.C.C. and the Convention is that an acceptance requires communication. For example, although the U.C.C. allows the seller to accept by prompt or current shipment of conforming goods, if the buyer is not notified within a reasonable time, he may treat the offer as having lapsed before acceptance. *See* U.C.C. Section 2-206. In so far as the Convention is concerned, it seems that Article 18(3) dispenses with notice altogether where the offer expressly permits or, through trade usage or prior course of dealing, impliedly permits the offeree to "indicate assent by performing an act."

Court of Appeals (Oberlandesgericht) of Cologne, Germany February 22, 1994, Index No. 22 U 202/93

(Translation by Walter, Conston, Alexander & Green, P.C.;
Editors: William M. Barron, Esq.; Birgit Kurtz, Esq.; Coordinator:
Thomas Carlé (Referendar); Translators (Referendars): Katja Rohrbach,
Astrid Schrôtter, Carmela Schmelzer, Caroline Sierp, Sandra Wegmeyer)

EXCERPT OF GROUNDS:

Plaintiff [seller's assignee] does not have a cause of action against [buyer] for the claimed amount based on the sales contract between the [seller] and [buyer] nor for unjust enrichment.

The claim must be analyzed under German law after the parties consented to the application of German Law (EGBGB Art. 27(2)) in the hearing before the trial court (the Landgericht). As a result, the U.N. Convention on Contracts for the International Sale of Goods ("CISG") of April 11, 1980, which became effective in Germany on January 1, 1991 (BGBl.II 1989, 588), is also applicable as far as the claim is based on the law of sales. This results from CISG Art. 1(1)(b), according to which the Convention is applicable to contracts for the sale of goods between parties whose places of business are in different countries, if the Conflict of Laws rules—here EGBGB Art. 27(2)—lead to the application of the law of a Contracting State.

1. According to the provisions of the CISG, the [seller's] claim for the purchase price arose here from the contract for the delivery of the wood to [buyer], but it was voided before the assignment to plaintiff because of the cancellation of the purchase contract.

Contrary to [buyer's] argument, a sales contract was indeed formed by the [seller] and [buyer]. It may be left open whether [buyer] has already admitted this in her answer and whether such an admission is binding. In either case, [buyer's] own correspondence shows that she and the [seller] had agreed on the wood delivery in oral negotiations on January 27, 1992. Her "Purchase Order" ("Bestellschreiben") dated January 28, 1992, merely represents a written confirmation of the verbal agreement concluded earlier ("we hereby confirm our order"). According to the provisions of the CISG with respect to the conclusion of a sales contract—see CISG Art. 18(1) 2d sentence—there is no room for a reference to the German Conflict of Laws provisions regarding the conclusion of a contract by silence as an acceptance of a commercial letter of confirmation (von Caemmerer/Schlechtriem, Kommentar zum einheitlichen UN-Kaufrecht (Commentary to the Uniform U.N. Law of Sales), before CISG Arts. 14 - 24 & 6; Herber/Czerwenka, Internationales Kaufrecht (International Law of Sales), CISG Art. 14 & 18). Nevertheless, the importance of the commercial letter of confirmation as evidence for the formation of the contract remains unaffected (von Caemmerer/Schlechtriem, *supra*, citations omitted). In the present case, it can be concluded from [buyer's] letter dated January 28, 1992, and a further letter dated March 25, 1992, also referring to an "agreement" of January 27, 1992, that the [seller] and [buyer] had agreed upon a sales contract on January 27, 1992.

[Buyer's] argument that she canceled her order with the approval of the assignor was correctly rejected by the trial court as unsubstantiated. On appeal, [buyer] similarly did not set forth the content of the [seller's] verbal statement from which, by interpretation, the [seller's] approval of the cancellation of the order could possibly be inferred. The correspondence between [buyer] and the [seller] does not reveal that the [seller] agreed to the cancellation of the order. The [seller's] letter dated April 27, 1992 merely expresses regret about [buyer's] unilateral cancellation; it does not, however, contain a statement of acquiescence. As far as the [seller] asked for "reconfirmation" in the letter, it was obviously meant only as a confirmation of the order dated January 28, 1992, rather than a new contract.

Furthermore, no concrete facts have been presented to prove that [buyer] changed the purchase contract into a consignment contract through a modified agreement with the [seller]. To the contrary, [buyer's] letter dated May 5, 1992, in which she rejected a price increase by the [seller], clearly shows that even [buyer] assumed that the sales purchase agreement still existed.

Similarly, [buyer] cannot claim that she declared the contract avoided due to the delay in the [seller's] delivery. As far as [buyer] objects to the [seller's] failure to meet the desired delivery date (mid-March 1992), she could only have declared the contract avoided pursuant to CISG Art. 49(1)(b) if she had granted the [seller] an additional, reasonable period of time for the delivery (CISG Art. 47). [Buyer] failed to do so.

The parties, however, canceled the contract by mutual agreement after [buyer's] notice of the defects.

[Buyer] sufficiently set forth the claimed defects of the wood delivery and clearly expressed at the same time that she considered the defects to be material. On appeal, she further stated she had given notice of the defects to the [seller] on or before July 8, 1992, as proven by the [seller's] fax letter dated July 8, 1992, which is no longer contested by [seller's assignee]. The examination of the goods carried out by Company O in the beginning of July 1992 was still timely pursuant to CISG Art. 38; the goods had to be sent on to [buyer's] customer from H —which was known by the [seller]—with the consequence that, according to CISG Art. 38(3), the examination could be deferred until the wood delivery had arrived at Company O's facilities. The objection to the defects, which was raised on or before July 8, 1992, was made within a reasonable time after the discovery of the defects (CISG Art. 39), particularly since July 4 and July 5, 1992 were a weekend *(compare* Herber/Czerwenka, *supra*, CISG Art. 39 & 9).

It is irrelevant whether [buyer's] cancellation of the agreement based on the alleged defects was timely, *i.e.*, within a time equivalent to the reasonable time allotted for the notice of defects (von Caemmerer/Schlechtriem, *supra*, CISG Art. 49 & 44). Either way, following the notice of defects, the [seller] manifested her intention to cancel the purchase agreement, and [buyer] conclusively agreed hereto. This follows from the [seller's] written answer concerning the notice of defects, as well as from [buyer's] further conduct with respect to the agreement.

The [seller] had already announced in her letter dated July 8, 1992, that she would come to Germany in order to market the wood herself. In a further fax letter dated July 27, 1992, the [seller] confirmed [buyer's] notice of defects—with reservations—after examination of the goods ("not as bad as you claim"), and informed her that she had found a Dutch company which would market the wood for her. This was the latest indication from which [buyer] was able to infer that the [seller] did not want to be bound by the agreement any longer. Because the [seller's] intention to market the wood herself was expressed without a reservation or limitation, there was no reason, contrary to plaintiff's argument, to presume that the [seller] only wanted to assist in the marketing, while leaving the responsibility for the marketing with [buyer]. On the other hand, the [seller] could infer from [buyer's] conduct that [buyer] acquiesced in the cancellation of the agreement, since she neither objected to the letters dated July 8 and July 27, 1992, nor demanded replacement goods free of defects.

CISG Art. 29(1) expressly permits such a cancellation by agreement. The same rules apply to the formation of a contract to cancel an agreement as apply to the formation of the agreement itself (von Caemmerer/Schlechtriem, *supra*, CISG Art. 29 & 3). An offer to cancel can, therefore, pursuant to CISG Art.18(1), not be accepted by silence or inactivity of the other party; together with other circumstances, however, silence can indeed be important and may be interpreted as the acceptance of an offer of cancellation. Such circumstances exist here, because [buyer] not only remained silent but also refrained from further fulfillment of the agreement, specifically from insisting on the delivery of replacement goods or from asserting other warranty claims. Thus, the [seller] lost her claim to the purchase price.

2. A claim based on unjust enrichment (BGB § 812), which could have been assigned [by seller] to plaintiff, does not exist either. Plaintiff did not show that [buyer] had received any proceeds from reselling the delivered wood, which then had to be turned

over to the [seller] after the cancellation. Rather, [buyer] stated in the hearing that, according to available information, the wood is still stored at Company O's facilities.

NOTE ON THE EFFECT OF A LATE ACCEPTANCE

It is black-letter law that a late acceptance does not conclude a contract, and this is the same rule found in Article 18(2). Significantly, the Convention modifies this rule with several unique provisions governing late acceptances.

Article 21(1) permits the offeror to ratify a late acceptance by dispatching a notice to that effect or by orally notifying the offeree. *See also* UNIDROIT Principles Article 2.9. Notice that this is the only situation under the Convention where a particular communication takes effect upon dispatch. Subsection (2) of Article 21 provides a different rule if the acceptance indicates that it was sent in timely fashion but was received late due to transmission delays. In such cases, a contract is formed unless the offeror promptly notifies the offeree that he considers his offer as having lapsed. This rule is the basis for Article 2.9 of the UNIDROIT Principles, which requires notification "without undue delay."

NOTE ON THE EFFECT OF A VARIED ACCEPTANCE

When an acceptance varies the terms of an offer, it must be decided whether a contract has been formed and, if so, on what terms. The common-law rule was simple: the acceptance could not vary from the specific terms of the offer. This "matching acceptance" rule or "mirror image" rule was particularly troublesome in the context of the so-called "battle of the forms," where parties exchanged carefully crafted forms in an effort to secure advantageous terms. Typically, the second form (usually the seller's) would contain different or additional terms and would therefore operate as a counter offer. Later, when the goods were delivered and accepted, the buyer would discover that he had also accepted the boilerplate terms contained in the seller's form, which he presumably had never bothered to read.

The U.C.C. attempts to remedy this inequity by taking a different approach. Section 2-207 permits a response to act as an acceptance even though it contains different or additional terms than those contained in the initial offer.

Article 19(1) of the CISG, on the other hand, is a complete adoption of the pre-Code mirror image rule: "A reply to an offer which purports to be an acceptance but contains additions, limitations or other modifications is a rejection of the offer and constitutes a counter-offer." But the harshness of the rule of subsection (1) is softened somewhat by subsection (2). If the additional or different terms do not materially alter the offer, then the reply is an acceptance and the contract is concluded, *unless* the offeror promptly objects by orally informing the offeree or dispatching a notice to that effect. If the offeror does not so object, the terms of the contract are the terms of the offer as modified by the terms contained in the acceptance.

Despite this apparent movement in the direction of permitting a contract to be created on the basis of agreement on essential terms, the differences between Article 19 and U.C.C. Section 2-207 are profound. First, material alterations preclude contract formation under the CISG. This is not necessarily the case under the U.C.C. Second, if the offeror objects to an immaterial alteration under the CISG, then the varied acceptance is a rejection, and acceptance does not occur. If the offeror objects under § 2-207, in contrast, the immaterial modification does not become part of the contract, but the objection does not stop contract formation. Third, Article 19(3) lists those terms "considered to alter the terms of the offer materially." It would seem, based on the over-inclusiveness of materiality in this subsection, that nearly any alteration would be material.

What happens when the goods are tendered, accepted, and paid for after conflicting offers and acceptances are exchanged? Because the CISG does not contain a special rule analogous to U.C.C. Section 2-207(3), recourse will have to be made to general principles of the CISG and private international law to resolve such questions. Presumably, it will be necessary to discern an offer and acceptance in the conduct of the parties.

Filanto, S.p.A. v. Chilewich International Corp.,
789 F.Supp. 1229 (S.D.N.Y. 1992), Appeal Dismissed, 984 F.2D 58 (2^D Cir. 1993)

BRIEANT, CHIEF JUDGE

By motion fully submitted on December 11, 1991, defendant Chilewich International Corp. moves to stay this action pending arbitration in Moscow. Plaintiff Filanto has moved to enjoin arbitration or to order arbitration in this federal district.

This case is a striking example of how a lawsuit involving a relatively straightforward international commercial transaction can raise an array of complex questions. Accordingly, the Court will recount the factual background of the case, derived from both parties' memoranda of law and supporting affidavits, in some detail.

Plaintiff Filanto is an Italian corporation engaged in the manufacture and sale of footwear. Defendant Chilewich is an export-import firm incorporated in the state of New York with its principal place of business in White Plains. On February 28, 1989, Chilewich's agent in the United Kingdom, Byerly Johnson, Ltd., signed a contract with Raznoexport, the Soviet Foreign Economic Association, which obligated Byerly Johnson to supply footwear to Raznoexport. Section 10 of this contract—the "Russian Contract" — is an arbitration clause, which reads in pertinent part as follows:

> "All disputes or differences which may arise out of or in connection with the present Contract are to be settled, jurisdiction of ordinary courts being excluded, by the Arbitration at the USSR Chamber of Commerce and Industry, Moscow, in accordance with the Regulations of the said Arbitration." [*sic*]

> . . . .

The first exchange of correspondence between the parties to this lawsuit is a letter dated July 27, 1989 from Mr. Melvin Chilewich of Chilewich International to Mr. Antonio Filograna, chief executive officer of Filanto. This letter refers to a recent visit by Chilewich and Byerly Johnson personnel to Filanto's factories in Italy, presumably to negotiate a purchase to fulfill the Russian Contract, and then states as follows:

> "Attached please find our contract to cover our purchase from you. Same is governed by the conditions which are enumerated in the standard contract in effect with the Soviet buyers [the Russian contract], copy of which is also enclosed."

. . . The next item in the record is a letter from Filanto to Chilewich dated September 2, 1989. . . . This letter refers to a letter from Chilewich to Filanto of August 11, 1989, which "you [Chilewich] sent me with the contracts n 10001-10002-10003." These numbers do not correspond to the contract sued on here, but refer instead to other, similar contracts between the parties. None of these contracts, or their terms, are in the record, both parties having been afforded ample opportunity to submit whatever they wished.

The last paragraph of the September 2, 1989 letter from Filanto to Chilewich states as follows:

"Returning back the enclosed contracts n 10001-10002-10003 signed for acceptance, we communicate, if we do not [misunderstand], the Soviet's contract that you sent us together with your above mentioned contract, that of this contract we have to respect only the following points of it:

- n 5 Packing and marking
- n 6 Way of Shipment
- n 7 Delivery - Acceptance of Goods

We ask for your acceptance by return of post." [sic]

... The intent of this paragraph, clearly, was to exclude from incorporation by reference inter alia section 10 of the Russian contract, which provides for arbitration. Chilewich, for its part, claims never to have received this September 2 letter. In any event, it relates only to prior course of conduct.

. . . .

The next document in this case, and the focal point of the parties' dispute regarding whether an arbitration agreement exists, is a Memorandum Agreement dated March 13, 1990. This Memorandum Agreement, number 9003002, is a standard merchant's memo prepared by Chilewich for signature by both parties confirming that Filanto will deliver 100,000 pairs of boots to Chilewich at the Italian/Yugoslav border on September 15, 1990, with the balance of 150,000 pairs to be delivered on November 1, 1990. Chilewich's obligations were to open a Letter of Credit in Filanto's favor prior to the September 15 delivery, and another letter prior to the November delivery. This Memorandum includes the following provision:

"It is understood between Buyer and Seller that USSR Contract No. 32-03/93085 [the Russian Contract] is hereby incorporated in this contract as far as practicable, and specifically that any arbitration shall be in accordance with that Contract."

.... Chilewich signed this Memorandum Agreement, and sent it to Filanto. Filanto at that time did not sign or return the document. Nevertheless, on May 7, 1990, Chilewich opened a Letter of Credit in Filanto's favor in the sum of $2,595,600.00. The Letter of Credit itself mentions the Russian Contract, but only insofar as concerns packing and labeling.

. . . .

Then, on August 7, 1990, Filanto returned the Memorandum Agreement, sued on here, that Chilewich had signed and sent to it in March; though Filanto had signed the Memorandum Agreement, it once again appended a covering letter, purporting to exclude all but three sections of the Russian Contract....

. . . .

According to the Complaint, what ultimately happened was that Chilewich bought and paid for 60,000 pairs of boots in January 1991, but never purchased the 90,000 pairs of boots that comprise the balance of Chilewich's original order.... It is Chilewich's failure to do so that forms the basis of this lawsuit, commenced by Filanto on May 14, 1991.

There is in the record, however, one document that post-dates the filing of the Complaint: a letter from Filanto to Chilewich dated June 21, 1991. This letter is in response to claims by Byerly Johnson that some of the boots that had been supplied by Filanto were defective. The letter expressly relies on a section of the Russian contract which Filanto had earlier purported to exclude — Section 9 regarding claims procedures — and states that "The April Shipment and the September Shipment are governed by the Master Purchase Contract of February 28, 1989, n 32-03/93085 (the 'Master Purchase Contract')"....

This letter must be regarded as an admission in law by Filanto, the party to be charged. A litigant may not blow hot and cold in a lawsuit. The letter of June 21, 1991 clearly shows that when Filanto thought it desirable to do so, it recognized that it was bound by the incorporation by reference of portions of the Russian Contract...it had purported to exclude. This letter shows that Filanto regarded itself as the beneficiary of the claims adjustment provisions of the Russian Contract. This legal position is entirely inconsistent with the position which Filanto had professed...and is inconsistent with its present position. Consistent with the position of the defendant in this action, Filanto admits that the other relevant clauses of the Russian Contract were incorporated by agreement of the parties, and made a part of the bargain. Of necessity, this must include the agreement to arbitrate in Moscow....

Against this background based almost entirely on documents, defendant Chilewich on July 24, 1991 moved to stay this action pending arbitration, while plaintiff Filanto on August 22, 1992 moved to enjoin arbitration, or, alternatively, for an order directing that arbitration be held in the Southern District of New York rather than Moscow, because of unsettled political conditions in Russia.

....

[T]he focus of this dispute, apparent from the parties' submissions, is not on the scope of the arbitration provision included in the Russian contract; rather, the threshold question is whether these parties actually agreed to arbitrate their disputes at all....

Not surprisingly, the parties offer varying interpretations of the numerous letters and documents exchanged between them. The Court will briefly summarize their respective contentions.

Defendant Chilewich contends that the Memorandum Agreement dated March 13 which it signed and sent to Filanto was an offer. It then argues that Filanto's retention of the letter, along with its subsequent acceptance of Chilewich's performance under the Agreement — the furnishing of the May 11 letter of credit — stops it from denying its acceptance of the contract. Although phrased as an estoppel argument, this contention is better viewed as an acceptance by conduct argument, *e.g.*, that in light of the parties' course of dealing, Filanto had a duty timely to inform Chilewich that it objected to the incorporation by reference of all the terms of the Russian contract. Under this view, the return of the Memorandum Agreement, signed by Filanto, on August 7, 1990, along with the covering letter purporting to exclude parts of the Russian Contract, was ineffective as a matter of law as a rejection of the March 13 offer, because this occurred some five months after Filanto received the Memorandum Agreement and two months after Chilewich furnished the Letter of Credit. Instead, in Chilewich's view, this action was a proposal for modification of the March 13 Agreement. Chilewich rejected this proposal, by its letter of August 7 to Byerly Johnson, and the August 29 fax by Johnson to Italian Trading SRL, which communication Filanto acknowledges receiving. Accordingly, Filanto under this interpretation is bound by the written terms of the March 13 Memorandum Agreement; since that agreement incorporates by reference the Russian Contract containing the arbitration provision, Filanto is bound to arbitrate.

Plaintiff Filanto's interpretation of the evidence is rather different. While Filanto apparently agrees that the March 13 Memorandum Agreement was indeed an offer, it characterizes its August 7 return of the signed Memorandum Agreement with the covering letter as a counteroffer. While defendant contends that under Uniform Commercial Code § 2-207 this action would be viewed as an acceptance with a proposal for a material modification, the Uniform Commercial Code... does not apply to this case, because the State Department undertook to fix something that was not broken by helping to create the Sale of Goods Convention which varies from the Uniform Commercial Code in many significant ways. Instead, under this analysis, Article 19(1) of the Sale of Goods Convention would apply. That section, as the Commentary to the Sale of Goods Convention notes, reverses the rule of Uniform Commercial Code § 2-207, and reverts to the common law rule that "A reply to an offer which purports to be an acceptance but contains additions, limitations or other modifications is a rejection of the offer and constitutes a counter-offer." Sale of Goods Convention Article 19(1). Although the Convention, like the Uniform Commercial Code, does state that non-material terms do become part of the contract unless objected to, Sale of Goods Convention Article 19(2), the Convention treats inclusion (or deletion) of an arbitration provision as "material," Sale of Goods Convention Article 19(3).[1] The August 7 letter, therefore, was a counteroffer which, according to Filanto, Chilewich accepted by its letter dated September 27, 1990. Though that letter refers to and acknowledges the "contractual obligations" between the parties, it is doubtful whether it can be characterized as an acceptance.

More generally, both parties seem to have lost sight of the narrow scope of the inquiry required by the Arbitration Convention. All that this Court need do is to determine if a sufficient "agreement in writing" to arbitrate disputes exists between these parties. Although that inquiry is informed by the provisions of the Sale of Goods Convention, the Court lacks the authority on this motion to resolve all outstanding issues between the parties. Indeed, contracts and the arbitration clauses included therein are considered to be "severable," a rule that the Sale of Goods Convention itself adopts with respect to avoidance of contracts generally. Sale of Goods Convention Article 81(1)....

Since the issue of whether and how a contract between these parties was formed is obviously related to the issue of whether Chilewich breached any contractual obligations, the Court will direct its analysis to whether there was objective conduct evidencing an intent to be bound with respect to the arbitration provision *Cf. Matterhorn v. NCR Corp.*, 763 F.2d 866, 871-73 (7th Cir. 1985) (Posner, J.) (discussing cases). *See also Teledyne, Inc. v. Kone Corp.*, 892 F.2d 1404, 1410 (9th Cir. 1990) (arbitration clause enforceable despite later finding by arbitrator that contract itself invalid).

The Court is satisfied on this record that there was indeed an agreement to arbitrate between these parties.

There is simply no satisfactory explanation as to why Filanto failed to object to the incorporation by reference of the Russian Contract in a timely fashion. As noted above, Chilewich had in the meantime commenced its performance under the Agreement, and the Letter of Credit it furnished Filanto on May 11 itself mentioned the Russian Contract. An offeree who, knowing that the offeror has commenced per-

---

1. It should also be noted that, in provisions potentially relevant to this motion, the Convention essentially rejects both the Statute of Frauds and the parol evidence rule. Sale of Goods Convention Article 11; Article 8(3).

formance, fails to notify the offeror of its objection to the terms of the contract within a reasonable time will, under certain circumstances, be deemed to have assented to those terms. *Restatement (Second) of Contracts* § 69 (1981); *Graniteville v. Star Knits of California, Inc.*, 680 F. Supp. 587, 589-90 (S.D.N.Y. 1988) (compelling arbitration since party who failed timely to object to salesnote containing arbitration clause deemed to have accepted its terms); *Imptex International Corp. v. Lorprint, Inc.*, 625 F. Supp. 1572, 1572 (S.D.N.Y. 1986) (Weinfeld, J.) (party who failed to object to inclusion of arbitration clause in sales confirmation agreement bound to arbitrate). The Sale of Goods Convention itself recognizes this rule: Article 18(1) provides that "A statement made by or other conduct of the offeree indicating assent to an offer is an acceptance." Although mere "silence or inactivity" does not constitute acceptance, Sale of Goods Convention Article 18(1), the Court may consider previous relations between the parties in assessing whether a party's conduct constituted acceptance, Sale of Goods Convention Article 8(3). In this case, in light of the extensive course of prior dealing between these parties, Filanto was certainly under a duty to alert Chilewich in timely fashion to its objections to the terms of the March 13 Memorandum Agreement — particularly since Chilewich had repeatedly referred it to the Russian Contract and Filanto had had a copy of that document for some time.

There are three other convincing manifestations of Filanto's true understanding of the terms of this agreement. First, Filanto's Complaint in this action, as well as affidavits subsequently submitted to the Court by Mr. Filograna, refer to the March 13 contract: the Complaint, for example, states that "On or about March 13, 1990, Filanto entered into a contract with Chilewich..."... These statements clearly belie Filanto's post hoc assertion that the contract was actually formed at some point after that date. Indeed, Filanto finds itself in an awkward position: it has sued on a contract whose terms it must now question, in light of the defendant's assertion that the contract contains an arbitration provision. This situation is hardly unknown in the context of arbitration agreements. *See Tepper Realty Co. v. Mosaic Tile Co.*, 259 F. Supp. 688, 692 (S.D.N.Y. 1966) ("In short, the plaintiffs cannot have it both ways. They cannot rely on the contract, when it works to their advantage, and repudiate it when it works to their disadvantage").

Second, Filanto did sign the March 13 Memorandum Agreement. That Agreement, as noted above, specifically referred to the incorporation by reference of the arbitration provision in the Russian Contract; although Filanto, in its August 7 letter, did purport to "have to respect" only a small part of the Russian Contract, Filanto in that very letter noted that it was returning the March 13 Memorandum Agreement "signed for acceptance"....In light of Filanto's knowledge that Chilewich had already performed its part of the bargain by furnishing it the Letter of Credit, Filanto's characterization of this action as a rejection and a counteroffer is almost frivolous.

Third, and most important, Filanto, in a letter to Byerly Johnson dated June 21, 1991, explicitly stated that "the April Shipment and the September shipment are governed by the Master Purchase Contract of February 28, 1989 [the Russian Contract]"....Furthermore, the letter, which responds to claims by Johnson that some of the boots that were supplied were defective, expressly relies on section 9 of the Russian Contract — another section which Filanto had in its earlier correspondence purported to exclude. The Sale of Goods Convention specifically directs that "in determining the intent of a party...due consideration is to be given to...any subsequent conduct of the parties," Sale of Goods Convention Article 8(3). In this case, as the letter post-dates the partial performance of the contract, it is particularly strong evidence that Filanto recognized itself to be bound by all the terms of the Russian Contract.

In light of these factors, and heeding the presumption in favor of arbitration, Moses H. Cone, *supra*, at 24-26, which is even stronger in the context of international commercial transactions, *Mitsubishi Motors Corp. v. Soler Chrysler-Plymouth, Inc.*, 473 U.S. 614, 631, 87 L. Ed. 2d 444, 105 S. Ct. 3346 (1985), the Court holds that Filanto is bound by the terms of the March 13 Memorandum Agreement, and so must arbitrate its dispute in Moscow.

....

David A. Levy, Contract Formation Under the UNIDROIT Principles of International Contracts,
UCC, Restatement, and CISG, 30 Uniform Commercial
Code Law Journal 249, 283-296 (1998)

Article 2.11 (*Modified Acceptance*)

Article 2.11, together with Article 2.22, contains the Principles equivalent of the U.C.C. 2-207 "battle of the forms." In general, they follow closely the formation principles articulated in the current U.C.C. for "merchant" contracts, and are virtually identical to the equivalent article in the CISG. Like their domestic counterpart, neither is a model of drafting clarity.

Paragraph one states that a purported acceptance that contains "additions, limitations or other modifications" is a rejection of the offer, thereby constituting a counter-offer. Where the same communication contains "additional or different terms" that do not materially alter the terms of the offer, a contract is formed containing those modifications, unless the offeror objects to the terms. Similarly, under the U.C.C., terms that are "additional to or different from those offered" constitute acceptance under the terms of the initial offer and proposals for additional terms, which between merchants become part of the contract unless the offer expressly limits acceptance to its terms, the additional terms materially alter the offer, or the offeror objects to their inclusion either prior to or after receipt.

Draft Article 2 is somewhat simpler. Where there has been an exchange of records, a contract is formed on the basis of the terms agreed upon, whether or not contained in a record; terms supplied by applicable trade usages, course of dealing, course of performance, and U.C.C. gap-fillers; and in cases involving subsequent conformations, terms that do not materially alter the terms of the offer and were not objected to. Note that this draft provision does not contain the distinction formerly made for merchant transactions, but includes a new section that attempts to protect the reasonable expectations of consumers in records using standard terms.

While the black-letter of the Principles does not define what constitutes a "material" modification, the commentary suggests that it varies according to the circumstances, and that "[a]dditional or different terms relating to the price or mode of payment, place and time of performance of a non-monetary obligation, the extent of one party's liability to the other or to the settlement of disputes, will normally, but not necessarily constitute a material modification of the offer."

By comparison, almost any non-trivial alteration is considered a material alteration of the offer under the CISG.

The *Restatement* formulation, while embodying an elegant simplicity, does not result in contracts being formed as readily. As a basic proposition, the acceptance must be the mirror-image of the offer. While trade usages or course of dealings might permit "inconsequential variations," the offeror is entitled to insist on strict compliance with the terms of the offer, and a purported acceptance that is conditional on the offeror's acceptance of additional or different terms is considered a rejection and counter-offer.

Article 2.12 *(Writings in Confirmation)*

Article 2.12 addresses the issue of the effect of a writing received subsequent to the formation of the contract that purports to confirm the contract terms. It effectively takes an expansive view, permitting additional or different terms contained in such a writing to become part of the contract, unless they materially alter the terms of the contract, or the recipient objects without undue delay. This inclusive approach is tempered somewhat by the requirement stated in the commentary that such a writing must be sent "within a reasonable time after the conclusion of the contract," thereby limiting the ability of the parties to modify contracts with impunity. As in the previous article, whether a term "materially" alters a contract is judged contextually, with the example given that an arbitration clause contained in a writing in confirmation would not materially alter the contract in a trade where arbitration was customary.

Similarly, under traditional U.C.C. analysis, additional or different terms in a written confirmation, sent within a reasonable time after contract formation, act as an acceptance, becoming part of the contract between commercial parties unless the additional terms materially alter the contract, the offer limited acceptance to its terms, or notification of objection had been given or was forthcoming. If both parties send conflicting confirmations, the conflicting terms cancel one another out and the contract consists of terms expressly agreed to in the original contract, terms contained in the confirmations that are in agreement, and Article 2 gap-fillers. Draft Article 2 attempts to clarify 2-207's "murky prose," eliminating the reference to confirmations as acceptances, and providing that only terms contained in a confirming record that do not materially alter the prior agreement and are not seasonably objected to become part of the contract.

Analytically, the issue of confirmatory memoranda should not be troublesome under the CISG. Acceptances are effective immediately upon receipt. Subsequent communications may be seen as proposals for modification of the existing contract, which require an expression of assent to be effective. Similarly, under the Restatement, acceptances must be the "mirror-image" of the offer and are effective as soon as they are out of the possession of the offeree.

. . . .

Article 2.19 *(Contracting under Standard Terms)*

In recognition of the commercial practice of standard form contracts, the Principles state that the general rules of contract formation are to apply, subject to special rules regarding surprising terms, conflicts between standard terms and negotiated terms, and the "battle of forms" for standard term contracts.

"Standard terms" are defined under the Principles as contractual provisions "prepared in advance for general and repeated use by one party." Such standard terms may be either placed within the terms of the contract itself, expressly incorporated by reference, or impliedly incorporated by reference through an applicable trade usage of practice between the parties. Draft Article 2 deleted references to "standard form" and "standard terms" contained in earlier drafts, which drew directly from the UNIDROIT Principles.

Although the CISG does not contain a provision directly addressing the issue of standard form contracts, Professor Winship states the view that most form contracts drafted prior to the CISG will remain equally valid under the Convention. The *Restatement*, while acknowledging that standard form contracts are commonly utilized in commercial transactions and are therefore enforceable, recognizes that they are not a dickered term, are rarely read or even understood, and are subject to a variety of judge-made doctrines designed to provide a level of subjective fairness to the transaction.

Article 2.20 *(Surprising Terms)*

The Principles state the proposition that a "surprising term" that could not reasonably have been expected by a party in a standard term contract is not effective unless it has been expressly accepted by that party. Whether a term should be surprising is considered in the context of the particular transaction, including the content of the term, the language used, and the manner in which the term was presented. The commentary and illustrations are particularly informative for this article. The CISG does not contemplate the issue of surprising terms per se, and the effect of such standardized terms is a gap to be determined by applicable domestic law, or through other rules such as the Principles.

Draft Article 2 contains rather detailed rules regarding surprising standard terms in a consumer transaction. Like the Principles, any non-negotiated terms that a reasonable consumer would not reasonably expect to appear in a record for the type of transaction is excluded from the contract, subject to proof that the unexpected terms were known to the consumer prior to assenting to the record. Both the U.C.C. and *Restatement* recognize that surprising terms may be invalidated under the grounds of unconscionability.

Reasonable minds may differ about whether the focus by the Principles on surprising terms in standard form contracts is inappropriate given that, unlike its domestic counterparts, the Principles are intended only for use in international commercial, rather than consumer transactions.

Article 2.21 *(Conflict Between Standard Terms and Nonstandard Terms)*

The Principles state the familiar rule common to general contract law that negotiated terms take precedence over standard terms. While not expressed in either the CISG or the U.C.C., the Restatement provides the interpretative principles that specific terms govern general terms, and negotiated or added terms "are given greater weight than standardized terms..."

Article 2.22 *(Battle of Forms)*

The Principles contain a "knock-out" rule, providing that when both parties use standard terms, a contract is formed on the basis of agreed terms and any standard terms that are substantially common, unless one party, either in advance, or subsequently without "undue delay," states its unwillingness to be bound by a contract formed in this manner. While the formation rules of the CISG and *Restatement* prevent formation unless the acceptance essentially is the "mirror-image" of the offer, this result is similar to its domestic counterpart in U.C.C. 2-207.

Chapter 2

Performance of
the Export Contract

I. Conformity of the Goods and
Third Party Claims

A. Warranties

Documents Supplement References:
1. *CISG Articles 8-9, 33-36, 67.*
2. *U.C.C. Section 2-313.*

Richard E. Speidel, The Revision of UCC Article 2, Sales in Light of the United Nations Convention on Contracts for the International Sale of Goods

16 Northwestern Journal of International Law and Business
165, 181-83 (1995)

The starting point under the CISG and Article 2 is the same; the seller must tender goods that conform to the contract.... The problem arises when the agreement is not sufficiently clear on such things as description, basic attributes or uses to which the goods can be put. An incomplete or indefinite agreement prompts disagreement over whether the goods conformed to the contract.

Under Article 2, disputes of this sort are resolved under a warranty theory. The seller may make an express warranty, an implied warranty of merchantability, an implied warranty of fitness for a particular purpose or all three in a particular transaction. These warranties are terms of the contract to which the goods must conform.

Under CISG, the warranty rubric is not used. Rather, Article 35(1) simply provides the seller "must deliver goods which are of the quantity, quality and description required by the contract and which are contained or packaged in the manner required by the contract." Interpretation of the terms of the contract is guided by Article 8. Article 35(2), however, provides standards to which the goods must conform "except where the parties have agreed otherwise." These standards include the requirement that the goods are "fit for the purposes for which goods of the same description would ordinarily be used" and, under the proper circumstances, the goods are "fit for any particular purpose expressly or impliedly made known to the seller at the time of the conclusion of the contract."

CISG and Article 2 seemingly agree on the treatment of the so-called implied warranties. Without saying so, the standards in CISG Article 35(2) closely track the U.C.C.'s implied warranties of merchantability and fitness for a particular purpose. The track is not completely parallel, however, since under Article 2 only a merchant seller makes an implied warranty of merchantability and goods which pass without objection in the trade under the contract description may still be unfit for the "ordinary purposes for which such goods are used." Thus, when the implied warranty is made, the scope of merchantability protection is somewhat higher under Article 2 than under CISG.

These differences are trivial compared to the fact that CISG has no mechanism for dealing with affirmations of fact or commendations about the goods made by the seller to the buyer either before or after the contract is formed. Assuming that such affirmations of commendations are made, unless they are "required by the contract," the goods need not conform to them.

U.C.C. Section 2-313 of the 1990 Official Text, however, deals specifically with statements of this sort. It draws a line between affirmations of fact and statements of opinion or commendation ("puffing") and states in the comments that affirmations of fact presumptively become part of the contract unless the seller establishes that the buyer was unreasonable in concluding that they became part of the bargain.

In sum, a buyer's expectation of quality derived from the seller's express or implied representations has greater protection under Article 2 than under CISG. The standard of merchantability is somewhat higher and a presumption operates in favor of including affirmations of fact in the agreement as express warranties.... In the modern age of extensive, multi-media advertising that crosses national boundaries, this is an important difference of substance.

T.J. Stevenson & Co. v. 81,1193 Bags of Flour,
629 F.2D 338 (5th Cir. 1980), rehearing denied, 651 F.2D 77 (5th Cir. 1981)

Brown, Chief Judge

With this decision we hopefully end, in all but a minor respect, an amphibious imbroglio and commercial law practitioner's nightmare involving three shiploads of enriched wheat flour. By a coincidence in this confusing case, each shipload of flour became infested, to varying degrees, with confused (*triboleum confusam*) and red rust (*triboleum casteneum*) flour beetles (sometimes called weevils). None of the parties involved-seller, buyer, and carrier-acted faultlessly over the course of the transaction. All brought their differences to the able District Judge for resolution. The District Judge carefully considered five weeks of testimony presented by the parties, their numerous pleadings, motions, briefs and arguments, scores of interlocking mixed law-fact issues, and difficult questions of federal civil procedure, state commercial, and admiralty law. The Judge's careful and lengthy opinion, 449 F. Supp. 84 (S.D. Ala. 1976), resolved the imbroglio but failed to fully convince the parties. The District Judge convinced us, however, and we affirm in almost all respects. Without pause to reflect on the complications that simple insects-confused flour beetles or otherwise-can create in the lives of men and Courts, we proceed to explain our decision.

I. The Life-Cycle Of This Appeal: Inception, Growth, And Development

A. The Documents

In April 1974 the Republic of Bolivia entered into two contracts for the purchase of 26,618 metric tons of American enriched wheat flour from ADM Milling Co. ADM owns a number of mills throughout the Midwest. Bolivia sought the flour for distribution to her citizens. The contracts were prepared on ADM's standard form, with quantity, chemical specifications, price, mode of shipment, payment terms, and delivery details filled in. The contracts required packing the flour in 100 pound capacity cotton bags and delivering it to Mobile, Alabama. Railcar shipment was contemplated to Mobile, followed by ocean carriage to South America. This was to take place from May to September 1974. The contracts contained the following delivery terms: "F.A.S. MOBILE, ALABAMA, for export;" and "Delivery of goods by SELLER to the carrier at point of shipment shall constitute delivery to BUYER...." Upon satisfactory delivery, the price was payable by irrevocable letter of credit.

. . . .

Each contract contained an express warranty of merchantability: Except as provided on the reverse side, SELLER MAKES NO WARRANTY, EXPRESS OR IMPLIED, THAT EXTENDS BEYOND THE DESCRIPTION ON THE FACE HEREOF, except that the product sold hereunder shall be of merchantable quality....

A. The Warranty

The District Judge held that the flour in each of the three shipments failed to meet the express warranty provisions of the contracts. ADM expressly warranted that the bagged flour would be "of merchantable quality" and that it would "comply with all of the applicable provisions of the Federal Food, Drug and Cosmetic Act ('FDA')." The District Judge decided that the infested flour breached both warranties. We, however, pretermit analysis of the FDA warranty since it is difficult to interpret and unnecessary to our resolution of this case. Instead we examine only ADM's warranty of merchantability.

The Code defines the minimum standards required of "merchantable" goods:

Goods to be merchantable must be at least such as

(a) pass without objection in the trade under the contract description; and

(b) in the case of fungible goods, are of fair average quality within the description; and

(c) are fit for the ordinary purposes for which such goods are used; and

(d) run, within the variations permitted by the agreement, of even kind, quality and quantity within each unit and among all units involved; and

(e) are adequately contained, packaged, and labeled as the agreement may require; and

(f) conform to the promises or affirmations of fact made on the container or label if any.

U.C.C. § 2-314(2)... Like the District Judge we consider only the subsection (c) portion of that definition, and do not reach the arguably applicable standards of subsections (a) and (b). The question is therefore whether the flour at various critical points in time was "fit for the ordinary purposes for which such goods are used."

Official Comments 2 and 8 provide helpful clues to divining the parties' intent (emphasis supplied):

2. The question when the warranty is imposed turns basically on the meaning of the terms of the agreement as recognized in the trade. Goods delivered under an agreement made by a merchant in a given line of trade must be of a quality comparable to that generally acceptable in that line of trade under the description or other designation of the goods used in the agreement.

8. Fitness for the ordinary purposes for which goods of the type are used is a fundamental concept of the present section and is covered in paragraph (c). As stated above, merchantability is also a part of the obligation owing to the purchaser for use. Correspondingly, protection, under this aspect of the warranty, of the person buying for resale to the ultimate consumer is equally necessary, and merchantable goods must therefore be "honestly" resalable in the normal course of business because they are what they purport to be. These comments amplify what is implicit in the statute: "fit for ordinary purposes" merchantability is an ambiguous phrase which has little meaning unless trade usage and other extrinsic evidence are considered. A substantial amount of extrinsic evidence was accordingly admitted and considered by the District Judge in evaluating ADM's warranty of merchantability.

Before reviewing the facts, we observe that finding what the parties meant by "merchantability" requires some evaluation of standards in the commercial market and the state of the art in flour manufacturing. The merchantability of infested flour to be sold to consumers is a question of degree and kind. We have often recognized that no food is completely pure. The FDA has long permitted very small amounts of insect fragments and other dead infestation in food products. To declare that any contamination of flour - even by small amounts of insect fragments, renders the flour unmerchantable would no doubt be out of step with commercial reality and would wreck havoc on food manufacturers and distributors while affording little or no additional protection to the consumer. What this case involves, however, is significant amounts of live infestation, by flour beetle eggs, larvae, pupae, and adults. Here the question is: How much live infestation renders consumer-destined flour unfit for the ordinary purposes for which it is used?

The record in this case contains a number of relatively undisputed facts that shed light on the meaning of "merchantable" flour. First, flour beetle infestation in flour mills is an ever present and difficult to eliminate problem. Some flour buyers, such as the United States Government, have however been able to keep infestation problems in their flour to a bare minimum by using their own inspectors to test the flour during its manufacture and at various points thereafter. Also, the relatively stringent precautions taken in ADM-operated mills have reduced infestation problems in their flour to a very great degree. The record further shows that flour containing live infestation, though possibly not dead remains, must be completely fumigated before it can be sold to consumers. Such fumigation is, however, not a normal preparation undertaken by flour buyers. In the context the fact that the flour involved in the instant case had to be fumigated takes on great significance. Cf. U.C.C. § 1-201(1). As the District Judge stated, "Clearly, if wheat flour found to be infested with beetles would have passed the above [merchantable quality] test . . . , there would have been no need for the flour to have been fumigated, . . ." 449 F.Supp. at 126. We believe that the District Judge's observation closely tracks the Official Comments' statement that goods intended for resale to consumers, as here, are not merchantable unless " 'honestly' resalable in the normal course of business." The evidence in sum indicates that consumer-intended flour containing substantial amounts of live infestation is not merchantable under prevailing standards.

We are not aware of any precedent, in Illinois or elsewhere, which considers the issue of merchantability under circumstances similar to the instant case....

Judicial interpretation, trade usage, and course of dealing point to but one conclusion as to flour infested with significant amounts of live flour beetles: although the flour may be "fit for human consumption" in the sense that it can be eaten without causing sickness, it is nonetheless not of merchantable quality. Such flour is not what is normally expected in the trade. It is not what ADM agreed to supply to Bolivia. Our holding is a narrow one. We do not say, for example, that one live beetle egg in a batch of 10,000 bags of flour renders that flour unmerchantable. Nor do we decide the merchantability of flour containing dead infestation in large or small amounts. Furthermore, we construe only the merchantability standard for flour which will be resold to consumers, not for flour sold directly to consumers. Finally, we emphasize that merchantability is an evolving standard, so that what is unmerchantable at one time and on one record may not be so in another case. In sum, we conclude that the District Judge was not erroneous in finding that the infested flour was not in conformity with ADM's warranty of merchantability....

[Judgment affirmed.]

QUESTIONS

1.   The *T.J Stevenson* case was decided under the Code because the CISG was not yet in existence. Would the court's analysis or the outcome be different if the case were decided today under the CISG? *See* Articles 8 & 9.

2.   When must the flour be deemed merchantable: at the time it leaves the seller's mill for shipment to Alabama? When it is delivered to the ocean carrier for shipment to South America? When it arrives in Bolivia? When it is received by the buyer? *See* Articles 36 & 67.

Federal Supreme Court (Bundesgerichtshof), Civil Panel VIII, Decision Dated March 8, 1995, Index No. VIII ZR 159/94

(Translation by Walter, Conston, Alexander & Green, P.C.;
Editors: William M. Barron, Esq., Birgit Kurtz, Esq.; Coordinator:
Thomas Carlé (Referendar); Translators (Referendars): Thomas Carlé,
Nicola Heraeus, Carmela Schmelzer, Ulrich Springer)

FACTS

Defendant [buyer], who runs a fish import business in D., bought 1,750 kilograms (kg) New Zealand mussels for U.S. $3.70 per kg from Plaintiff [seller], who resides in Switzerland. [Seller] delivered the goods, as agreed, in January 1992 to a storage facility belonging to [buyer] and located at Company F. in G.G., and invoiced [buyer] on January 15, 1992 in the amount of U.S. $6,475 payable within 14 days.

At the end of January 1992, Company F. informed [buyer] that the federal veterinary agency of G.G. had taken samples of the goods for examination purposes. After the veterinary agency confirmed at the end of January/beginning of February 1992, upon [buyer's] request, that an increased cadmium content was discovered in the mussels and that further examinations by the responsible veterinary examination agency of Southern Hesse were necessary, [buyer] informed [seller] of these facts by facsimile dated February 7, 1992. According to the report by the veterinary examination agency of Southern Hesse, which was received by [buyer] on February 26, 1992 and forwarded to [seller] by [buyer], cadmium contents of between 0.5 and 1.0 milligram per kg (mg/kg) were ascertained in four of the examined bags of mussels; these contents did not yet exceed twice the amount of the 1990 standard of the federal public health agency, but further examinations by the importer were found necessary. An examination commissioned by [seller] and conducted by the federal agency for veterinary matters in Liebefeld-Bern determined a cadmium content of 0.875 mg/kg.

By facsimile dated March 3, 1992, [buyer] announced to [seller] that she was going to send the mussels back at [seller's] expense since the veterinary agency had declared them "not harmless" due to their high cadmium content; simultaneously, she complained that the goods were "no longer in their original packaging as required" and that, furthermore, the packaging was unsuitable for frozen food. Thereafter, [seller] informed [buyer] by telephone that she would not accept the goods. Consequently, [buyer] did not return the goods. According to a report of the chemical examination laboratory of Dr. B. dated March 31, 1992, which had been commissioned by [buyer] for further examination, three samples revealed 1 mg of cadmium per kg; a doubling of the federal public health agency standards could not be "tolerated," and at least 20 additional samples of the entire delivery had to be examined.

[Buyer] requested that [seller] cover, among other things, the future expenses of the examination; [seller] did not reply.

In the complaint, [seller] demands payment of the purchase price of U.S. $6,475 plus interest. She claimed that the mussels were suitable for consumption because their cadmium content did not exceed the permitted limit; furthermore, [buyer] had not given timely notice of the defects. [Buyer], on the other hand, declared the contract avoided due to a fundamental breach of contract because the mussels were defective and had been complained of by the responsible authorities. Thus, the mussels were not permitted to be delivered out of the storage facility. And by now, the "expiration date of 12/92," affixed to the merchandise by [seller], had come and gone anyway.

The trial court (here the "Landgericht") obtained an expert opinion from the federal public health agency. With respect to the question whether the mussels were suitable for consumption having the reported cadmium content, the federal public health agency elaborates that the ZEBS (central registration and evaluation office of the federal public health agency for environmental chemicals) standards are guidelines indicating an unwanted concentration of harmful substances in food for purposes of preventative consumer health protection. Occasionally exceeding the individual standard which are not toxicologically explainable, usually does not lead to harmful effects on one's health, even if the measured concentration reaches twice the amount of the standard. If twice the amount of the standard is exceeded, the responsible state control authorities usually declare that, analogous to the procedure legally required for enforcement of the meat hygiene regulations (FleischhygieneVerordnung), the relevant food can no longer be considered suitable for consumption according to the foodstuffs and consumer goods law ("Lebensmittel- und Bedarfsgegenständegesetz" or "LMBG") ' 17(1)(Nr.1).

The trial court ruled against [buyer] in accordance with [seller's] petition [see LG Darmstadt 22 December 1992]. On appeal, buyer claimed, as a precaution and with offer of proof, that the cadmium content of the mussels was even higher than 1 mg/kg. The Court of Appeals (Oberlandesgericht) dismissed [buyer's] appeal [*see* OLG Frankfurt 20 April 1994]. In the appeal to this Court, [buyer] continues to move for a dismissal, whereas [seller] pleads for a dismissal of the appeal.

Opinion

The appeal is unsuccessful.

I. The Court of Appeals has explained:

The U.N. Convention on Contracts for the International Sale of Goods dated April 11, 1980 (CISG) applies to the legal relationship between the parties. According to CISG Art. 53, [seller] is entitled to the purchase price. [Buyer] can only declare the contract avoided pursuant to CISG Art. 49(1)(a) in case of a fundamental breach of contract by seller. It is true that a delivery of goods that do[es] not conform with the contract can be a fundamental breach of contract within the meaning of CISG Art. 25; in case of a lack of express agreement, CISG Art. 35(2) governs the question whether the goods conform with the contract. The question whether only goods of average quality are suitable for ordinary use (CISG Art. 35(2)(a)) or whether it is sufficient that the goods are "marketable" may be left open. The delivered mussels are not of inferior quality even if their cadmium content exceeds the examination results known so far. The reason for this is that the standard for cadmium content in fish, in contrast to the standard for meat, does not have a legally binding character but only an administratively guiding character. Even if the standard is exceeded by more than 100%, one cannot assume that the food is no longer suitable for consumption, because mussels, contrary to basic food, are usually not consumed in large quantities within a short period of time and, therefore, even "peaks of contamination" are not harmful to one's health. That is why it is no longer relevant whether the public law provisions of those countries, to which an export was possible at the time of conclusion of the contract, have no influence on the conformity of the goods with the contract according to CISG Art. 35(2)(a).

The fact that the standard was exceeded is similarly not relevant to the elements of CISG Art. 35(2)(b) (fitness for a particular purpose). There is no evidence that the parties implicitly agreed to comply with the ZEBS-standards. Even if [seller] knew that [buyer] wanted to market the goods in Germany, one cannot make such an assumption, especially since the standards do not have legal character.

The demand to declare the contract avoided is also not legally founded based on [buyer's] allegation that the goods were not packaged properly. [Buyer's] pleadings in this respect are not substantiated and can, therefore, not be accepted. In any event, the statement to declare the contract avoided is statute-barred by CISG Art. 49(2). This is so because on March 3, 1992, Defendant (buyer) gave notice for the first time that the packaging of the goods delivered in the beginning of January did not conform with the contract; therefore, she did not give notice within a reasonably short time.

II. These elaborations hold up against a legal re-examination with respect to the result.

1. The application of the CISG provisions to the contract between the parties is expressly no longer questioned and is also correct (CISG Art. 1(1)(a)). The prerequisite to [buyer's] right to declare the contract avoided pursuant to CISG Art. 49(1)(a) due to the cadmium contamination of the delivered mussels is, therefore, a fundamental breach of contract by [seller] within the meaning of CISG Art. 25. This is the

case when the purchaser essentially does not receive what he could have expected under the contract, and can be caused by a delivery of goods that do not conform with the contract (*see, e.g.*, Schlechtriem in von Caemmerer/Schlechtriem, Kommentar zum Einheitlichen UN-Kaufrecht (Commentary on the Uniform U.N. Law of Sales) Art. 25 6 20 (2d ed.) (with further citations)). Not even non-conformity with the contract within the meaning of CISG Art. 35 can, however, be determined.

a) In this respect, an agreement between the parties is primarily relevant (CISG Art. 35(1)). The Court of Appeals did not even find an implied agreement as to the consideration of the ZEBS-standards. [Buyer] did not argue against this finding, and it is not legally objectionable. The mere fact that the mussels should be delivered to the storage facility in G.G. does not necessarily constitute an agreement regarding the resalability of the goods, especially in Germany, and it definitely does not constitute an agreement regarding the compliance with certain public law provisions on which the resalability may depend.

b) Where the parties have not agreed on anything, the goods do not conform with the contract if they are unsuitable for the ordinary use or for a specific purpose expressly or impliedly made known to the seller (CISG Art. 35(2)(a)&(b)). The cadmium contamination of the mussels, that has been reported or, above that, alleged by [buyer], does not allow us to assume that the goods, under this rule, do not conform with the contract.

aa) In the examination of whether the goods were suitable for ordinary use, the Court of Appeals rightly left open the question — controversial in the legal literature — whether this requires generic goods of average quality or whether merely "marketable" goods are sufficient (*see, e.g.*, Schwenzer in von Caemmerer/Schlechtriem, *supra*, Art. 35 6 15 (with further citations)). Even if on appeal, goods of average quality were found to be required, [buyer] has still not argued that the delivered mussels contain a higher cadmium contamination than New Zealand mussels of average quality. It is true that, according to the report from the examination laboratory of Dr. B., submitted by [buyer] to the trial court, and the contents of which is thereby alleged, "there are also other imported New Zealand mussels on the market . . . that do not show a comparable cadmium contamination." It does not follow, however, that average New Zealand mussels on the market contain a smaller amount of cadmium than the mussels delivered to [buyer].

The appeal wrongly requests that [seller] submit a statement that New Zealand mussels usually have such a high cadmium contamination. After taking delivery without giving notice of the lack of conformity, the buyer must allege and prove that the goods do not conform with the contract and the seller does not have to allege and prove that they do conform with the contract (*see, e.g.*, Herber/Czerwenka, Internationales Kaufrecht (International Law of Sales) Art. 35 6 9 (1991); Piltz, Internationales Kaufrecht (International Law of Sales) ' 5 6 21 (1993); Schwenzer, *supra*, 6 49 (with further citations)). Contrary to [buyer's] contention at trial, she accepted the mussels by physically taking delivery (CISG Art. 60(b)) at the place of destination in G.G., and she did not give notice of the lack of conformity of the goods at that time.

bb) Admittedly, from the point of view of salability and, therefore, resalability of the mussels and contrary to the Court of Appeals' opinion, even if twice the amount of the ZEBS-standard is exceeded, as [buyer] alleged, this would not change anything regarding the suitability of the mussels for consumption pursuant to LMBG '17(1)(1), and, considering the report from the federal public health agency and the documented administrative practice of the state health agencies, there would be reservations, if the public law provisions of the Federal Republic of Germany were relevant. This, however, is not the case. According to the absolutely prevailing opinion in the legal literature, which this Court follows, the compliance with specialized public law provisions of the buyer's country or the country of use cannot be expected (Schwenzer, *supra*, Art. 35 6 16 *et seq.*; Stumpf in von Caemmerer/Schlechtriem, *supra*, Art. 35 6 26 *et seq.* (1st ed.); Staudinger/Magnus, BGB (German civil code), CISG Art. 35 6 22 (13th ed.); Herber/Czerwenka, *supra*, Art. 35 66 4, 5; Piltz, *supra*, ' 5 66 35, 41; Enderlein in Enderlein/Maskow/Stargardt, Konvention der Vereinten Nationen über Verträge über den internationalen Warenkauf, Kommentar (The U.N. Convention on Contracts for the International Sale of Goods, Commentary) Art. 35 6 4 (1985); the same in Enderlein/Maskow/Strohbach, Internationales Kaufrecht (International Law of Sales) Art. 35 6 8 (1991); Bianca in Bianca/Bonell, Commentary on the international sales law Art. 35 6 2.5.1, p. 274 et seq., 6 3.2, p. 282 *et seq.* (1987); Audit, La vente internationale de marchandises (The International Sale of Goods) 6 98, p. 96 (1990); Heuzé, La vente internationale de marchandises (The International Sale of Goods) 6 290 (1993); Neumayer/Ming, Convention de Vienne sur les contrats de vente internationale de marchandises (The Vienna Convention on Contracts for the International Sale of Goods), Art. 35 6 7 (1993); probably also Hutter, Die Haftung des Verkäufers für Nichtlieferung bzw. Lieferung vertragswidriger Ware nach dem Wiener UNCITRAL-Übereinkommen über internationale Warenkaufverträge vom 11. April 1980 (The Liability of the Seller for Non-delivery or Delivery of Goods Not Conforming with the Contract pursuant to the Vienna UNCITRAL-Convention on the International Sale of Goods dated April 11, 1980) at 46 *et seq.* (doctoral thesis 1988); Otto, MDR [1] 1992, 533, 534; probably different Schlechtriem in International Sales' 6.03, 6.21 (Galston/Smit 1984); not clear Soergel/Lüderitz, BGB (German civil code), CISG Art. 35 6 11 (12th ed.); inconsistent Heilmann, Mängelgewährleistung im UN-Kaufrecht (Guaranty with Respect to Non-conformity with a Contract pursuant to the U.N. Law of Sales), *compare* p. 184 with p. 185 (1994); concerning the legal situation pursuant to the EKG, *compare, e.g.*, Dölle/Stumpf, Kommentar zum Einheitlichen Kaufrecht (Commentary on the Uniform Law of Sales) Art. 33 6 18 (1976) (with further citations) with Mertens/Rehbinder, Internationales Kaufrecht (International Law of Sales), Art. 33 6 16, 19).

Some uncertainties, noticeable in the discussions in the legal literature and probably partly caused by the not very precise distinction between subsections (a) and (b) of CISG Art. 35(2), do not require clarification in the evaluation of whether this question must be integrated into the examination of the ordinary use of the goods or the examination of the fitness for a particular purpose. There is, therefore, no need to finally decide whether, within the scope of CISG Art. 35(2)(a), as most argue, the standards of the seller's country always have to be taken into account (*see, e.g.*, Bianca, *supra*, 6 2.5.1; Piltz, *supra*, 6 41; Enderlein in Enderlein/Maskow/Strohbach, *supra*; Aue, Mängelgewährleistung im UN-Kaufrecht unter besonderer Berücksichtigung stillschweigender Zusicherungen (Guaranty with Respect to Non-conformity with a Contract pursuant to the U.N. Law of Sales under Special Consideration of Implied Promises), at 75 (doctoral thesis 1989); probably different Schlechtriem, *supra*; Hutter, *supra*, at 40), so that it is not important for the purposes of subsection (a) whether the use of the goods conflicts with public law provisions of the import country (*see, e.g.*, Herber/Czerwenka, *supra*, 6 4). In any event, certain standards in the buyer's country can only be taken into account if they exist in the seller's country as well (*see, e.g.*, Stumpf in von Caemmerer/Schlechtriem, *supra*, 6 26; Schwenzer, *supra*, 6 16; Bianca, *supra*, 6 3.2) or if, and this should possibly be examined within the scope of CISG Art. 35(2)(b), the buyer has pointed them out to the seller (*see*, *e.g.*, Schwenzer, *supra*, 66 16, 17; Enderlein, *supra*) and, thereby, relied on and was allowed to rely on the seller's expertise or, maybe, if the relevant provisions in the anticipated export country are known or should be known to the seller due to the particular circumstances of the case (*see, e.g.*, Piltz, *supra*, 6 35; Bianca, *supra*). None of these possibilities can be assumed in this case.

aaa) [Buyer], who bears the burden of proof, did not allege that there are any Swiss public law provisions concerning the contamination of mussels with toxic metals. The appeal similarly does not mention anything in this respect.

bbb) The agreement regarding the place of delivery and place of destination is in itself, even if it could be viewed as an indication by [buyer] of the anticipated marketing in Germany, neither under subsection (a) nor under subsection (b) of CISG 35(2) sufficient to judge whether the mussels conform with the contract pursuant to certain cadmium standards used in Germany (*compare, e.g.*, Stumpf, *supra*, 6 27; Schwenzer, *supra*, 6 17; Piltz, Enderlein and Bianca, each *supra*). Decisive is that a foreign seller can simply not be required to know the not easily determinable public law provisions and/or administrative practices of the country to which he exports, and that the purchaser, therefore, cannot rationally rely upon such knowledge of the seller, but rather, the buyer can be expected to have such expert knowledge of the conditions in his own country or in the place of destination, as determined by him, and, therefore, he can be expected to inform the seller accordingly. This applies even more in a case like this, where, as the reply to the appeal rightly points out, there are no statutes regulating the permissible cadmium contamination and where, instead, the public health agencies apply the provisions, that are only valid as to the meat trade (*compare* No. 3 of Exh. 6 to the regulation for meat hygiene dated Oct. 30, 1986, BGBl. I 1678, as modified by the regulation dated Nov. 7, 1991, BGBl. I 2066)), "analogously" and, seemingly, not uniformly in all the German Länder (federal states)(*compare* the announcements of the federal public health agency in Bundesgesundhbl.[4] 1990, 224 *et seq.*; 1991, 226, 227; 1993, 210, 211) to the exceeding of standards in the fish and mussels trade and where the legal bases for measures of the administrative authorities do not seem completely certain (*compare*, in a different context, *e.g.*, BVerwGE 77, 102, specifically 122).

ccc) This Court need not decide whether the situation changes if the seller knows the public law provisions in the country of destination or if the purchaser can assume that the seller knows these provisions because, for instance, he has a branch in that country (*see, e.g.*, Neumayer/Ming, *supra*), because he has already had a business connection with the buyer for some time (*see, e.g.*, Schwenzer, *supra*, 6 17), because he often exports into the buyer's country (*see, e.g.*, Hutter, *supra*, at 47) or because he has promoted his products in that country (*see, e.g.*, Otto MDR 1992, 533, 534). [Buyer] did not allege any such facts.

ddd) Finally, the appeal argues unsuccessfully that the mussels could not be sold due to the "official seizure" and were, therefore, not "tradable." There is no need to go into great detail with respect to the question whether [buyer] has even alleged a seizure of the goods and whether she could have reasonably and with a chance of success attacked such a measure. In any event, a seizure would have been based on German public law provisions which, as set forth above, cannot be applied in order to determine whether the goods conformed with the contract (*supra*, specifically II(1)(b)(bb)(bbb)).

2. The Court of Appeals also correctly denied the [buyer's] right to declare the contract avoided because of the improper packaging of the goods. The question whether [buyer's] allegations were sufficient for a conclusive statement of a funda-

mental breach of contract (CISG Art. 25) or of any lack of conformity with the contract at all (CISG Art. 35(2)(e) [sic]) may remain unanswered. In any event, Defendant (buyer) lost her rights that might have resulted from these allegations due to untimeliness. This does not, however, result from the "untimeliness" of the declaration to avoid the contract pursuant to CISG Art. 49(2)(b)(I), but from the untimeliness of the notice of the lack of conformity required by CISG Art. 39(1), which must be considered first (*compare* Huber in von Caemmerer/Schlechtriem, *supra*, Art. 49 66 45 *et seq.* (2d ed.)).

In that respect, it does not make any difference whether the mussels were delivered "in the beginning" of January 1992, as the Court of Appeals assumed, or not until January 16, 1992, as the appeal alleges pointing to the "Betreff" ("Re.") section of [buyer's] facsimile dated February 7, 1992. The first notice of the lack of conformity of the packaging in the facsimile dated March 3, 1992 was untimely even if the latter date of delivery was decisive. [Buyer] had to examine the goods or had to have them examined within as short a period after they arrived at the place of destination as practicable under the circumstances (CISG Art. 38(2) in connection with subsection (1)). At least during the working week from January 20 to 24, 1992, [buyer] could have easily done this, whether by herself at the storage facility not far from her place of business or by a person employed by company F. and designated by [buyer]. The allegedly improper packaging could have easily been ascertained in an external examination. The time limit for the notice of the lack of conformity, which starts at that moment (CISG Art. 39(1)), as well as the time limit to declare the contract avoided pursuant to CISG Art. 49(2) (*compare* judgment by this Court dated Feb. 15, 1995, VIII ZR 18/94 at II(3)(b), intended for publication) should not be calculated too long in the interest of clarifying the legal relationship of the parties as quickly as possible. Even if this Court were to apply a very generous "rough average" of about one month, taking into account different national legal traditions (*see* Schwenzer, *supra*, Art. 39 6 17 (with further citations); stricter, *e.g.*, Herber/Czerwenka, *supra*, Art. 39 6 9; Piltz, *supra*,' 5 6 59; Reinhard, UN-Kaufrecht (U.N. law of sales) Art. 39 6 5 (1991)), the time limit for the notice of the lack of conformity with the contract had expired before March 3, 1992.

The appeal's reference to an examination of the mussels already carried out by the public health agency as well as [buyer's] earlier notice of the increased cadmium content do not affect the assumption that the notice of lack of conformity was untimely. If the goods do not conform with the contract in various aspects, it is necessary to state all defects individually and describe them (*see, e.g.*, Schwenzer, *supra*, Art. 39 6 10; Herber/Czerwenka, *supra*, Art. 39 6 8). The buyer cannot claim those defects, of which he gave untimely notice.

Judgments of the lower courts: OLG Frankfurt, April 20, 1994, Index No. 13 U 51/93; LG Darmstadt, December 22, 1992, Index No. 14 O 165/92.

NOTE ON ARTICLE 5.6 OF THE UNIDROIT PRINCIPLES

Absent from the UNIDROIT Principles is the type of detailed coverage of warranty issues that one finds in the CISG and in the U.C.C. Article 5.6 alone addresses the required quality of performance, providing that in the absence of a standard of quality fixed by, or determinable from, the contract, "a party is bound to render a performance of a quality that is not less than average under the circumstances." Comment 1 to this Article and the accompanying illustration help explain its meaning:

The minimum requirement is that of providing goods of average quality. The supplier is not bound to provide goods or services of superior quality if that is not required by the contract, but neither may it deliver goods or services of inferior quality. This average quality is determined according to the circumstances, which normally means that which is available on the relevant market at the time of performance (there may for example have been a recent technological advance). Other factors may also be of relevance, such as the specific qualifications for which the performing party was chosen.

Illustration:

2. A buys 500 kgs. of oranges from B. If the contract says nothing more precise, and no other circumstances call for a different solution, those oranges may not be of less than average quality. Average quality will however suffice unless it is unreasonably defective.

Thus, in the absence of an express warranty of quality, Article 5.6 imposes its own particularized version of the warranty of merchantable quality. Although this provision is considerably less involved than, for example, U.C.C. Section 2-314, it would probably change the results of few, if any, cases.

B. Warranty Disclaimers

Documents Supplement References:

1.   *CISG Articles 4, 35, 38-40, 42-43, 49, 64, 68, 79.*

2.   *U.CC. Sections 1-103, 2-316.*

Richard E. Speidel, The Revision of UCC Article 2, Sales in Light of the United Nations International Sale of Goods

16 Northwestern Journal of International Law and Business
165, 183-84 (1995)

Since the word "warranty" is not used, CISG has no provision dealing with the "exclusion or "modification" of warranties. Rather, disputes over quality turn on what the contract "required" under Article 35(1) and whether the parties have "otherwise agreed" under Article 35(2). No special rules for interpretation are provided in these cases.

Article 2, however, offers some protection to the buyer against attempts by the seller to exclude or limit express and implied warranties by agreement. Thus, if an attempt to negate or limit cannot be construed as reasonably consistent with an express warranty, the disclaimer is "inoperative." Similarly, a disclaimer of an implied warranty of merchantability must meet certain requirements of form and disclosure. Thus, the effort to limit or exclude "must mention merchantability" and, if the disclaimer is in writing, "must be conspicuous." A disclaimer may also be vulnerable to attack on other unconscionability grounds.

Arguably, these imitations upon the enforceability of agreements limiting or excluding warranties involve the "validity of the contract or any of its provisions" with which CISG, under Article 4(a), is not concerned. If so, CISG applies to the transaction in general but does not preempt Article 2's limitations on the scope and effect of disclaimers. If not, there is a disagreement of substance between CISG and Article 2 that is subject to possible harmonization.[1]

Case Abstract, UNCITRAL texts (CLOUT), Abstract No. 168,

May 21, 1996 (Germany)

The [seller] sold a used car to the [buyer], both parties being car dealers. The documents showed that the car was first licensed in 1992 and the mileage on the odometer was low. The sales contract included the exclusion of any warranty. The [buyer] later sold the car to a customer, who discovered that the car had been first licensed in 1990 and that the actual milage on the odometer was much higher. The [buyer] paid damages to his customer and demanded the same amount as damages from the [seller].

The appellate court held that the [buyer] could claim damages under articles 35(1), 45, and 74 CISG. The [buyer's] damages caused by its liability to its customer could be claimed under article 74 CISG because such damages are foreseeable if goods are sold to a dealer who intends to resell them.

Even though the [buyer] could have detected the car's lack of conformity with the contract, the [seller] could not avail itself of article 35(3) CISG since the [seller] knew the actual age of the car and thus acted fraudulently. The appellate court held that article 35(3) CISG could not be relied on by a fraudulent seller, referring to the general principles embodied in articles 40 and 7(1) CISG. According to the appellate court, even a very negligent buyer deserves more protection than a fraudulent seller. Although, the exclusion of any warranty was possible under article 6 CISG, it was held to be invalid in this case. The appellate court found that the substantial validity of such a clause was not governed by the CISG. In this case, this question was governed by German law, according to which an exclusion of warranty is invalid if the seller acts fraudulently.

QUESTIONS

1.   Would this case be decided the same if the law governing the matter was the U.C.C.? *See* U.C.C. § 1-103 and the *Restatement (Second) of Torts* (1977) Sections 525 & 552.

2.   The CISG differentiates among (A) "knows" or is "aware" [*see* Articles 43(2), 49(2), 64 (2)(a)]; (B) "could not have been unaware" [*see* Articles 35(3), 40, 42(1),(2)]; and (C) knew or "ought to have known" [*see* Articles 38(3), 39(1), 43(1), 49(2)(b)(i), 64(2)(b)(i), 68, 79(4)]. Does the expression used in Article 35(3) impose

---

1. Professor Honnold draws a distinction between the interpretation of statements and conduct under CISG art. 8 and rules of validity under CISG art. 4(a). The former are governed by CISG and the latter are left to domestic law. He concludes, on balance, that the controls on disclaimers in U.C.C. 2-316(2) are rules of validity if they deny legal effect to a term without impairing the interpretive process under CISG art. 8 HONNOLD...at 310-312. In the process he suggests that one must first determine whether Article 2 was intended to apply to transactions subject to the Convention before one decides whether a rule of validity or a principle of interpretation is involved. HONNOLD...at 310. Professor Hartnell agrees that disclaimers or "exculpatory" clauses are rules of validity, but doubts that they should be reserved for domestic law. She prefers that the enforceability of clauses allocating risk in international sales, as opposed to doctrines of fraud or mistake, be determined by CISG. HARTNELL...at 87-93.

a duty on the buyer to investigate the condition of the goods? Does the U.C.C. impose a duty to investigate? *See* U.C.C. § 2-316(3)(b).

C. Third Party Claims

Documents Supplement References:

1. *CISG Articles 4, 41-42.*
2. *U.C.C. Section 2-312*

NOTE ON WARRANTY OF TITLE AND AGAINST INFRINGEMENT

Recall that the CISG "is not concerned with . . . (b) the effect which the contract may have on the property in the goods sold." Article 4. Thus, one would not look to the Convention to resolve a dispute between the buyer and a third-party who claims some sort of property interest in the goods. If, however, a third party does assert a claim to the goods, the Convention will indicate what rights the buyer has (if any) against the seller. CISG Article 41 requires that the seller deliver to the buyer goods that are free from any third-party right or claim. This provision is similar to U.C.C. § 2-312(1), which is also designed to protect the title expectations of the buyer.

The seller must also take into account Article 42 when dealing in goods that may infringe upon another's intellectual property rights. The seller will only be responsible to the buyer if he "knew or could not have been unaware of the claim." Moreover, the third-party claim must be based on the law of the State where the goods will be resold or used if the parties contemplated use or resale in that State or, in the absence of such contemplated resale or use, on the law of the State where the buyer has its place of business. Finally, the seller is not responsible to the buyer where (1) the buyer had actual or constructive knowledge of the third-party claim at the conclusion of the contract or (2) the claim arises because the seller followed the buyer's specifications for designs, drawings, or formulae. *Compare* U.C.C. 2-312(3).

Jeanneret v. Vichey,
693 F.2D 259 (2d Cir. 1982)

FRIENDLY

. . . .

The facts as developed at a trial before Judge Cannella and a jury were as follows:

Plaintiff Marie Louise Jeanneret, a citizen of Switzerland, is a well-known art dealer in Geneva. Defendants Anna and Luben Vichey, wife and husband, are citizens of the United States. Anna's father, Carlo Frua DeAngeli, had an extensive and internationally recognized private collection of paintings in Milan, Italy. One of these was a painting, Portrait sur Fond Jaune, by the renowned French post-impressionist, Henri Matisse, who was born in 1869 and died in 1954.

Carlo Frua DeAngeli died on July 30, 1969, and his property passed by will to his wife and three children. As a result of a settlement, evidently concluded after July 24, 1970, title to the Matisse painting ultimately vested in Anna Vichey.

The date and circumstances of the painting's exit from Italy are unclear.... It is uncontroverted that no export license or permit was obtained from the Italian government; whether any such official document was needed is in dispute. Later in 1970 the Matisse painting was brought to the Vicheys' apartment in New York City.

In January 1973 Mme. Jeanneret began negotiations for the purchase of the painting, and an agreement was reached for its sale for 700,000 Swiss francs, then equivalent to approximately $230,000. Luben Vichey delivered the painting to plaintiff in Geneva in March 1973....

In November 1974 plaintiff went to Rome. While there she encountered Signora Bucarelli, superintendent in charge of the export of paintings. Although the court excluded evidence of what Signora Bucarelli said, it allowed plaintiff to testify that as a result of the conversation Mme. Jeanneret telephoned Anna Vichey in the United States to ascertain the latter's knowledge as to how the painting had been exported from Italy. Anna referred plaintiff to her husband Luben who was in Milan. Luben in turn referred her to Dr. Magenta, the personal representative of the DeAngeli family.... According to plaintiff Dr. Magenta referred her back to Luben or the other heirs of Carlo Frua DeAngeli.

There followed a letter from Mme. Jeanneret to Anna Vichey dated November 21, 1974. This reported that Signora Bucarelli was looking for the Matisse painting because she suspected its illegal exportation, and that as a professional art dealer plaintiff could not "sell it anymore nor show it." Mme. Jeanneret proposed that the deal be annulled; she would bring the painting to New York and the Vicheys would repay the purchase price. On January 5, 1975, Luben Vichey wrote plaintiff rejecting her proposal. Other attempts to induce Mrs. Vichey to take back the painting were equally unsuccessful. This action, brought in July, 1977, was the result. The complaint was founded on breach of express and implied warranties of title, false and fraudulent misrepresentation [and breach of contract]....

II.

After Judge Cannella had denied a motion by the defendants for summary judgment, the case proceeded to trial before himself and a jury. There was much testimony on the Italian law concerning the exportation of works of art. Two different sets of provisions were involved. [The district court was presented with conflicting opinions concerning the substance and effect of the Italian statutes and regulations. It did not decide the question of what would happen if the painting were ever returned to Italy, but instructed the jury that there were three possibilities: First, the painting may be subject to confiscation. Second, the owner may be required to pay custom duties or fines. Third, nothing would happen either to the painting or the owner. The jury was also instructed that if the painting were more than 50 years old at the time of export, then the possibility that the painting would be subject to administrative proceeding would be greatly enhanced.]

III.

....

John Tancock, a vice-president of Sotheby Parke Bernet auction house and head of its Department of Impressionist and Modern Painting and Sculpture, testified that, but for the question of illegal exportation, he would appraise the painting at $750,000. On the other hand, if the painting lacked "the necessary export documents from any country where it had been located," his opinion was that it would be impossible to sell the painting since "no reputable auction house or dealer would be prepared to handle it." Hence "on the legitimate market its value is zero." He would date the painting "early 1920's, 1919, 1922, something like that." Nancy Schwartz, an art dealer associated with the Spencer Samuels & Company gallery in New York, testified that the gallery having received a number of requests for paintings by Matisse, she communicated with Mme. Jeanneret as to sending the painting to New York. Before any arrangements could be made, Ms. Schwartz wrote Mme. Jeanneret on May 1, 1975 that she would not be able to sell the painting as plaintiff had proposed to her in Geneva in February; "I had a client who was ready to buy it, but as you said that the painting left Italy clandestinely I realized that this painting cannot be sold." Graham Leader, an independent art dealer, identified letters he had written to Mme. Jeanneret from London in June and November 1974. In the former he stated that he expected a client in the next few days to whom he had indicated a price of 1,100,000 Swiss francs for the painting; in the latter he confirmed a telephone conversation announcing his refusal to consider handling the painting or advising one of his best clients to buy it "from the moment that I learned that the painting had been clandestinely exported from Italy by its former owner, Mme. Vichey-Frua DeAngeli and that it could thus be subject to suit by any authority." Finally, Dr. Bertelli, whose position we have already described, testified that Dr. Enrico Vitali, Mme. Jeanneret's lawyer, had called him to ask whether there was any record that the Matisse painting had been issued export documents after 1969 and that Dr. Bertelli had found no evidence that it had. On March 28, 1979, the Assistant Minister of Culture issued a notification... declaring the painting, "an important work by the French painter Henri Matisse, datable between 1920 and 1923," to be of "particular artistic and historical interest" within the meaning of [a 1939 law protecting items of artistic or historical interest] and "therefore subject to all the regulations regarding custody included therein." The decree was to "be notified through administrative channels to the present owner, possessor or holder of this painting," to wit, Mrs. Vichey, in care of Dr. Magenta in Milan. Dr. Bertelli also testified that on September 17, 1981, just before he had left Milan to attend the trial, the Attorney General of Italy had shown him a memorandum indicating that a penal proceeding had been instituted against Anna Frua DeAngeli, that Interpol had been requested to recover the painting, and that the Chief of the Italian Delegation for Retrieving Works of Art had been asked to present the request of the Italian Government to the United States authorities.

The defendants' evidence was sparse. Mrs. Vichey professed ignorance of the details of the exportation.... On cross-examination [Mr. Vichy] asserted that the paintings taken to Switzerland did have export documents for which Dr. Magenta had arranged.

....

IV.

The district judge charged the jury, over objection by the defendants, that "the mere casting of a substantial shadow over the title, regardless of the ultimate outcome of that dispute, is sufficient to violate a warranty of good title." [The court refused] defendants' requests to instruct the jury in detail on Italian law, partly on the ground, with which we sympathize, that he was "unable to determine what the Italian law is," and partly because in his view, the precise state of Italian law was "almost irrelevant" since plaintiff "didn't buy litigation"....

The jury returned a verdict for defendants on the first cause of action (breach of express warranty), and the third cause of action (fraudulent misrepresentation). It returned a verdict...for plaintiff on the second and fourth causes of action (breach of implied warranty of title and breach of contract)....This appeal followed.

V.

....

Both sides have assumed that defendants' liability is governed by the law of New York, where the negotiations for the sale of the painting occurred, rather than by the law of Switzerland, where it was delivered and payment received. We shall follow them in that assumption. Section 2-312 of the Uniform Commercial Code as adopted in New York, Laws, 1962, c. 553, provides:

(1) Subject to subsection (2) there is in a contract for sale a warranty by the seller that (a) the title conveyed shall be good, and its transfer rightful; and (b) the goods shall be delivered free from any security interest or other lien or encumbrance of which the buyer at the time of contracting has no knowledge.

(2) A warranty under subsection (1) will be excluded or modified only by specific language or by circumstances which give the buyer reason to know that the person selling does not claim title in himself or that he is purporting to sell only such right or title as he or a third person may have.

(3) Unless otherwise agreed a seller who is a merchant regularly dealing in goods of the kind warrants that the goods shall be delivered free of the rightful claim of any third person by way of infringement or the like but a buyer who furnishes specifications to the seller must hold the seller harmless against any such claim which arises out of compliance with the specifications.

The Official Comment on this section states in part:

1. Subsection (1) makes provision for a buyer's basic needs in respect to a title which he in good faith expects to acquire by his purchase, namely, that he receive a good, clean title transferred to him also in a rightful manner so that he will not be exposed to a lawsuit in order to protect it.

....

The warranty of quiet possession is abolished. Disturbance of quiet possession, although not mentioned specifically, is one way, among many, in which the breach of warranty of title may be established. (4) This section rejects the cases which recognize the principle that infringements violate the warranty of title but deny the buyer a remedy unless he has been expressly prevented from using the goods. Under this Article, "eviction" is not a necessary condition to the buyer's remedy since the buyer's remedy arises immediately upon receipt of notice of infringement; it is merely one way of establishing the fact of breach.

There is nothing to show that defendants breached the warranty described in § 2-312(1) (a). No one denies that Carlo Frua DeAngeli was the lawful owner of the painting and that it passed by rightful succession to Anna Vichey. While [the Italian statute protecting items of artistic and historical interest] provides that any transfers, agreements and legal acts in general carried out contrary to the law are null and void, no transfer, agreement, or comparable legal act occurred by virtue of the exportation to Switzerland; the heirs of Carlo Frua DeAngeli were exporting to themselves. The rights of the Italian Government were neither a "security interest" nor, in the normal meaning of language, an "other lien or encumbrance," especially if any weight is to be given here to the maxim *ejusdem generis*.

None of the cases from New York or other states cited by the district court deals with a situation such as is presented here. The cases holding that the buyer can recover simply by showing "the mere casting of a substantial shadow over his title, regardless of the ultimate outcome," ... deal with what would be deemed defects in title or with liens or encumbrances in the ordinary meanings of those terms. Professor Nordstrom's seemingly apposite remarks about a hypothetical sale of a painting in his *Handbook of the Law of Sales* 186 (1970) ("The buyer did not purchase a lawsuit. He purchased a painting."), lose force with respect to this case when it is realized that the author was discussing a true claim of lack of title.

The argument that there was no breach of the implied warranty created by § 2-312(1) (b) is strengthened by the terms of the Italian law and customary international law. Although [Italian] Law says that the item may be confiscated, it goes on to say that confiscation is carried out in accordance with the Customs laws and regulations pertaining to smuggled goods, which can be done only in Italy. Professor Bator, in an important article, *An Essay on the International Trade in Art*, 34 STAN. L. REV. 275, 287 (1982), has declared the "fundamental general rule" to be that "illegal export does not itself render the importer (or one who took from him) in any way actionable in a U.S. court; the possession of an art object cannot be lawfully disturbed in the United States solely because it was illegally exported from another country." He adds that "this general rule apparently obtains in all other major art-importing countries, including England, France, Germany, and Switzerland." [Italian] law makes clear that even when an item more than fifty years old has been exported from Italy, liability to pay the State the value of the exported item and any fine rests on the exporter, not on a purchaser. It is thus reasonably plain that so long as Mme. Jeanneret or any purchaser from her did not bring the painting back into Italy, it could not be confiscated and neither she nor a purchaser from her would be subject to monetary liability to Italy. There would seem no reasonable prospect that the United States or any other government would act on Italy's request for help in securing the return of the painting. This is especially true in light of the tenuous nature of the claim that a not especially notable painting by a French twentieth-century master who was testified to have left a thousand paintings constituted an important part of Italy's artistic patrimony.... Matisse's *Portrait sur Fond Jaune* bore no such relation to Italy as a Raphael or a Bellini *Madonna*.

Against all this, however, we have the testimony of Mme. Jeanneret and of the three art dealers, Tancock, Schwartz, and Leader, here uncontradicted, that the painting could not be sold to any reputable art-dealer or auction house. When we add to this evidence § 1-102(1) of the Uniform Commercial Code providing that this Act shall be liberally construed and applied to promote its underlying purposes and policies and § 1-102(2) (b) providing that one of the Code's underlying purposes and policies is "to permit the continued expansion of commercial practices through customs, usage and agreement of the parties," we find it somewhat hard to reject the commonsensical view of the district judge that an art dealer who has bought a painting which, according to the usages of her trade, she cannot sell through ordinary channels is under a heavy cloud, indeed.

We are reluctant to decide so serious a question, of particular importance to New York where so many of the country's art transactions take place, on such an unsatisfactory record and without even the slightest clue from the New York courts. Although we may ultimately be forced to decide the question without the benefit of further guidance from New York cases, defendants have at least made out a case for a new trial which may avoid the need for such a decision on our part.

We say this because in our view the court's instruction... was erroneous in several respects. One was in saying that if the painting were returned to Italy, the "owner, even if he purchased the painting in good faith, could be required to pay customs duties and/or fines." We see nothing in the Italian law that imposes any such liability on a purchaser as distinguished from the exporter. Much more important, the charge failed to focus the jury's attention adequately on the age of the painting when it was exported from Italy. The judge said only that if "the painting was more than 50 years old at the time of export, then the probability that the painting will be subject to administrative or judicial proceeding is greatly enhanced." For all we know the jury could have found that the painting was less than 50 years old when exported in the spring of 1970, yet nevertheless have rendered judgment for plaintiff because of violation of [Italian] regulations.... [V]iolation of that law alone would not constitute a sufficient cloud to breach the warranty imposed by § 2-312(1) (b) and we decline to accept the argument that plaintiff could bring herself within that section merely by showing there was enough uncertainty about the painting's age that an export violation... should be treated as colorable. Even if we should ultimately agree with plaintiff that actual violation of [Italian Law] would create an encumbrance sufficient to invoke § 2-312(1) (b), we would refuse, in the absence of instruction from the New York courts or a body of authority from courts of other states, to take the further step of holding that a claim of possible violation would suffice. If Mrs. Vichey was not in fact obliged to comply with [Italian Law] with respect to the Matisse painting, it would be altogether too drastic to hold her liable to Mme. Jeanneret simply because the Italian Government now asserts that she was. In short, plaintiff had the burden of proving that Matisse painted the *Portrait sur Fond Jaune* before the spring or early summer of 1920.

. . . .

The judgment is reversed and the case remanded for further proceedings consistent with this opinion.

QUESTION

1.   Would the transaction between the parties in *Jeanneret* be within the scope of the CISG? Assuming that the Convention were applicable, what would be the outcome?

D. Notice

Documents Supplement References:

1. CISG Articles 4, 6, 39, 40, 43, 44, 50, 74.
2. U.C.C. Sections 2-607, 2-725.

NOTE ON NOTICE

In order to understand the Convention's notice requirements, it is helpful to distinguish between cases where the goods do not conform to the contract and those cases where the breach relates to a third-party claim to the goods. Articles 39, 40, and 44 apply to the former type of breach, and Articles 43 and 44 apply to the latter type of breach.

Article 39(1) requires that notice be given "within a reasonable time after [the buyer] has discovered [a lack of conformity] or ought to have discovered it." *Com-*

pare Section U.C.C. 2-607(3)(a). Closely related to this notice requirement is Article 38, which imposes an obligation on the buyer to examine the goods as soon as practicable. Whether the goods have been examined and notice given within the time required will necessarily depend upon a number of factors, including the nature of the goods and the likelihood that the seller will attempt to cure the nonconformity. Regardless of what would constitute reasonable notice under Article 39(1), notice must be given within two years from the date the goods were handed over to the buyer, unless the two year limit "is inconsistent with a contractual period of guarantee."

If the buyer fails to notify the seller as required, the sanction is that the buyer loses all remedies. *See* Article 39(1). This rather harsh rule, however, is softened considerably by Articles 40 and 44. Article 40 excuses notice if the seller "knew or could not have been unaware" of the facts relating to the nonconformity. If notice was not given in a timely fashion and is not excused under Article 40, the buyer's only hope is try to come within the protective umbrella of Article 44. If the buyer "has a reasonable excuse for failing to give the required notice," then two remedies remain available: reduction of the price (Article 50) and recovery of damages other than lost profit (Article 74).

Under Article 43 the buyer must also notify the seller of any third-party claim under Articles 41 and 42, unless the seller "knew" of the right or claim. There is no cut-off period comparable to the one in Article 39.

Court of Appeals (Oberlandesgericht) of Düsseldorf, Decision Dated January 8, 1993, Index No. 17 U 82/93

(Translation by Walter, Conston, Alexander & Green, P.C.;
Editors: William M. Barron, Esq., Birgit Kurtz, Esq.; Coordinator:
Thomas Carlé (Referendar); Translators (Referendars): Thomas Carlé,
Nicola Heraeus, Carmela Schmelzer; Ulrich Springer)

Plaintiff [seller] is an enterprise with its place of business in Torbali, Turkey; its legal capacity and representation is in dispute between the parties. Defendant [buyer] is a commercial enterprise with its place of business in Germany.

By contract dated May 29, 1991, [buyer] purchased from [seller] approximately 1,000 tons of freshly harvested Turkish cucumbers for pickling of the sizes 3/6 and 6/9. According to the contract, the goods were to be delivered "free on refrigerated truck Turkish loading berth (Torbali)." The place of loading was also to be the place of performance. [Buyer] intended to entrust a German freight forwarder with the shipment. Subsequently, the parties agreed, by contract amendment, that [seller] hire Turkish shippers in return for reimbursement of the costs, the amount of which is in dispute.

Between June 16 and July 16, 1991, [seller] had goods loaded in Torbali for a total amount of DM 925,336.30. One Mr. T., who was hired by [buyer] to supervise the loading, was present at the loading. [Buyer] paid only an amount of DM 838,364.14 of the purchase price. The balance of DM 86,972.16 is the subject of this action. In addition, [seller] claimed DM 14,100 in freightage.

Regarding the claim for the balance, [buyer] argued that, when the goods arrived in Germany, a portion of the goods was spoiled, some of the shipments contained smaller quantities than indicated and, finally, the size of a portion of the cucumbers delivered was bigger than agreed upon. In particular, the parties disagreed as to whether the court had to look to the time of loading in Turkey or the time of arrival in Germany when determining whether the goods fit the standard set by the contract.

The record of the proceedings dated January 17, 1992, which will be referred to herein, shows that the trial court (here the Landgericht) heard evidence with respect to the contractual agreements and T.'s activities in Turkey. In its judgment [LG Krefeld 18 March 1992], which is appealed here, the trial court dismissed the claim and ordered [buyer] to pay [seller] the remainder of the purchase price in the amount of DM 86,972.16 plus interest. The court reasoned as follows: The questions whether the cucumbers were spoiled when the trucks were unloaded in Germany or whether partial quantities were missing may remain unanswered. According to the written contract and the evidence before the court, the time of loading in Turkey was determinative with respect to the question whether the goods fit the standard set by the contract. At that location, however, witness T. had examined and approved the goods. Thus, one could assume that the goods loaded by [seller] in Torbali fit the standard set by the contract. Finally, regarding the allegedly wrong sizes, [buyer's] contentions were not found to be sufficiently precise.

On appeal, [buyer] objects to the trial court's interpretation of the contract. In addition, [buyer] claims that the goods had already been defective at the time of loading in Turkey.

[Buyer] requests that the challenged decision be partially amended and that the claim be fully dismissed.

[Seller] requests a dismissal of the appeal.

GROUNDS:

[Buyer's] appeal is unsuccessful. The trial court correctly granted [seller's] claim in the amount of DM 86,972.16 plus interest.

The claim meets the formal requirements.

[Seller] is capable of being a party to a lawsuit and is legally represented by its management. According to ZPO '' 50(1) & 51(1) in connection with EGBGB Art. 7(1), the law of the country in which the legal entity has its place of business is determinative (BGH NJW [4] 1981, 522, 525; Kegel, Internationales Privatrecht (International Conflict of Laws) ' 17 II (6th ed. 1987)). Here, that is Turkey.

According to Turkish law, seller, because it is a corporation entered into the commercial register, is capable of being a party and is legally represented by its managers S.C. and B.Y. This is established by the extract from the Turkish commercial register, provided by [seller] together with a translation. [Buyer] did not oppose this in substance. She merely denied knowledge or information regarding the correctness of the translation provided. According to ZPO ' 138(2) & (4), however, that is not sufficient. Because [buyer] made a considerable deal with [seller] with a total value of almost DM 1 million and because it had witness T., who was proficient in the Turkish language, as an employee or consultant at its disposal, [buyer] could not flatly deny knowledge or information with respect to the translation of the extract from the commercial register. Rather, she should have explained any problems in detail. Furthermore, this Court does not see any reason to question [seller's] ability to be a party and its legal representation under Turkish law and to inquire *sua sponte* to this end. In particular, contrary to [buyer's] opinion, a financial collapse possibly resulting in a loss of [seller's] ability to be a party, is out of the question. [Seller] has assets, that is at least the claim granted by this judgment.

[Seller's] counsel on appeal are, contrary to [buyer's] view, duly authorized. The question whether the power of attorney provided by counsel had been signed by one of [seller's] managers may remain unanswered. [Seller's] counsel on appeal were in any case — and this is undisputed among the parties — additionally authorized by [seller's] trial counsel, and their authority has not been questioned by [buyer].

The claim is meritorious to the extent granted by the trial court.

Pursuant to Art. 53 of the U.N. Convention on the International Sale of Goods (CISG) dated April 11, 1980 in connection with the law dated July 5, 1989 (BGBl. II 586 *et seq.*), [seller] has a claim against [buyer] in the amount of DM 86,972.16 as the balance of the purchase price. Because the parties, in a statement to the trial court, agreed, pursuant to EGBGB Art. 27, that German law shall apply, the provisions of the CISG are applicable to the parties' contract, as German domestic law, pursuant to CISG Art. 1(1)(b). During the hearing, this Court pointed this out.

The amount of the purchase price balance is undisputed. [Buyer's] allegation that it had not been provided with individual invoices for each delivery is irrelevant with respect to the maturity of the purchase price claim. As far as a retention right is argued in the written pleading dated November 19, 1992, one day before the hearing, this contention is untimely as defined by ZPO " 527 & 296(1).

The purchase price claim is not reduced according to CISG Art. 50(1st sentence) in connection with Art. 35(1) & (2), Arts. 45, & 51(1). The question whether [buyer's] allegations that one part of the goods had been spoiled and that the invoiced quantities had not been delivered are correct, may remain unanswered. In any event, [buyer's] possible warranty rights are excluded under CISG Art. 39(1).

According to this provision, the buyer only has warranty rights if he gives notice of the goods' lack of conformity with the contract to the seller within a reasonable period of time. This period commences at the time the buyer should have discovered the lack of conformity with the contract. This time, in turn, is defined by CISG Art. 38(1). According to this provision, the buyer must examine the goods or have them examined within as short a period as practicable under the circumstances.

[Buyer] did not comply with this requirement. She gave notice of the alleged lack of conformity with the contract only upon the goods' arrival in Germany. That was, at the earliest, seven days after the loading of the goods in Turkey. [Buyer] should have, however, examined the goods at the time of loading in Turkey. Thus, the notice given at the earliest seven days after the loading was untimely.

The question whether the contractual relationship between the parties met the requirements of CISG Art. 38(2) and whether, therefore, an examination could have been deferred until after the goods had arrived at their point of destination, may remain unanswered. That is because CISG Art. 38(2) is not mandatory (Stumpf, in von Caemmerer/Schlechtriem, Kommentar zum Einheitlichen UN Kaufrecht (Commentary on the Uniform U.N. Law of Sales) Art. 38 6 6 (1990)), and the parties have definitely excluded this provision in their written contract dated May 29, 1991. This contract provides not only that the place of performance for the delivery was the place of loading and that the goods were to be delivered free on refrigerated trucks to the Turkish loading station. But also, the purchase price was payable "upon dispatch and approval by Mr. T." Thus, it becomes clear that the examination of the goods by witness T. as [buyer's] representative at the place of loading was not merely an internal matter of [buyer], but was to have, according to the parties' agreement, a fundamental meaning for the performance of the contract. This also accorded with the parties' respective interests. That is so because [buyer] herself intended to be responsible for the transportation of the goods. Only because of practicability reasons, [seller] later acted on behalf of [buyer], pursuant to an additional agreement, in selecting the carrier. This interpretation of the contract is substantiated by the fact that witness T., according to his own credible testimony, not only examined the quantities, but also the cucumbers' sizes and quality at the loading. The testimony of [buyer's] procurist, witness L., was comparatively unhelpful. This witness had drafted the written contract and, when doing so, assumed, according to his testimony, that only the goods' physical acceptance was to take place in Turkey, while the qualitative acceptance was to take place in Germany. That may be so. However, decisive is not what the witness assumed, but what [seller] could understand the text of the contract drafted by [buyer] to mean.

As a legal consequence of the untimely notice, [buyer] is obligated to pay the purchase price in the amount contractually agreed upon, in spite of any possible lack of conformity with the contract. In the legal literature, however, the opinion is advocated that in case of a failure to make complete delivery, the buyer, in spite of not having given timely notice, is only obligated to pay a purchase price reduced accordingly (Stumpf, *supra*, Art. 39 6 11). This Court does not agree with this opinion. It does not accord with the meaning of CISG Art. 39. With respect to the comparable provisions of HGB " 377 *et seq*., it is generally recognized that the buyer, in case of an untimely notice, is obligated to pay the full purchase price (BGH NJW 1984, 1964, 1966). The only disputed question is whether this also applies if the failure to make a complete delivery is evident from the invoice or the delivery papers, *i.e.*, in case of a so-called "open" failure to make a complete delivery (BGH, *supra*). This, however, is not the case here. Regarding the instant — not "open" — failure to make a complete delivery, the legal consequence of CISG Art. 39 cannot be different from that of HGB " 377 *et seq*. The purpose of the obligation is to quickly give the seller clarity concerning the question whether any objections can be made to his claim for the purchase price. Thus, the seller, if no notice has been given within a reasonable period of time, must be able to assume that there are no legal doubts with respect to his claim for the purchase price. Yet, that would exactly be the case where, despite the failure to give timely notice, a reduction of the purchase price due to failure to make complete delivery was permissible.

With respect to the claim for interest, the judgment of the trial court has not been challenged.

Final Judgment Rendered by the District Court (Landgericht) of München, Germany on 3 July 1989 — 17 HKO, 3726/89

(Translation by Jutta Surovic)

BACKGROUND OF CASE

Plaintiff (seller): Supplier of fashion goods with relevant place of business in Italy.

Defendant (buyer): Owner of a fashion retail company with relevant place of business in Germany.

On 4 and 12 October 1988, buyer ordered various fashion goods from the seller. Part of this order was delivered on 19 October 1988, another part on 8 November 1988. The amount due was 9,155DM. On 8 November 1988 the buyer drew a check for this amount which was postdated to 8 December 1988. On 8 November 1988, buyer also ordered other fashion goods which were delivered on 24 November 1988. The buyer drew a check for 16,385DM, the purchase price, which was postdated 25

December 1988. Neither check was honored. By writing dated 10 February 1989, the buyer canceled the sale.

Seller alleged that all contract terms have been complied with and that he received neither the requisite notice of defect of goods nor a timely demand for avoidance of the contract.

The court had issued a provisional judgment ordering the buyer to pay 25,540DM [9,155DM + 16,385DM] plus interest at the rate of 6% running from 6 December 1988 on the 9,155DM and from 23 December 1988 on the 16,385DM.

On appeal, buyer alleged that seller delivered late and defective goods; buyer reported the defects to the seller in writing on 16 November and 6 December 1988; buyer is entitled to damages of 22,173DM because of loss of profit and the credit he had to give his customers due to defective goods. Alternatively, the buyer sets these claims for damages off against the seller's claim.

The District Court (Landgericht) affirmed the provisional judgment.

Reasons For the Decision

The court reviewed the buyer's objections and held that they are not valid. This case does not require an inquiry into the evidence of alleged defects. The buyer cannot assert any claims for non-conformity because of lack of notice.

The governing law of the contract is the United Nations Convention on Contracts for the International Sale of Goods (CISG) [although the CISG was not yet effective in Germany]. German law (Article 28 EGBGB) refers to Italian law and Italy is a party to the CISG. Article 1(1)(b) of this Convention empowers application of the CISG even though one of the contracting parties does not have his residence in a Contracting State.

According to Article 39(1) of the CISG, the buyer will lose his right to rely on a lack of conformity of the goods with the contract if he does not give notice to the seller specifying the nature of the lack of conformity within a reasonable time after he has discovered it or ought to have discovered it. It may remain undecided in this case whether buyer's letters of 16 November and 6 December 1988 were actually sent to the seller. Neither letter specifies the exact nature of the defects; both letters limit themselves to notification of poor workmanship and improper fitting of the goods. The purpose of the notification of defects is to clarify the nature of the complaint. The notice sent was not adequate. Even the letter of 23 December 1988, which seller acknowledges receiving, did not contain any specification of the defects.

In consequence of the loss of rights, according to Article 39(1) of the CISG the buyer cannot claim damages.

. . . .

QUESTIONS

1.   Suppose that the buyer has a reasonable excuse for first giving notice of the nonconformity 26 months after the goods were delivered. Would Article 44 preserve the buyer's right to recover damages?

2.   May the parties by contract provide rules on timely notification of breach? *See* Article 6. What if the contract contained an unreasonably short notice period? *See* Article 4(a).

NOTE ON THE PERIOD OF LIMITATIONS

Unlike the U.C.C., the CISG contains no period or statute of limitations for instituting legal proceedings. To fill this gap, UNCITRAL has prepared a separate convention called the "United Nations Convention on the Limitation Period of the International Sale of Goods." The Convention was concluded in New York on June 14, 1974, and a Protocol to the Convention was concluded at Vienna on April 11, 1980. Both the Convention and the Protocol entered into force on August 1, 1988. On November 20, 1993, the U.S. Senate gave its advice and consent to adherence by the United States.

Article 8 of the Convention establishes a basic four-year limitation period. This four-year period begins to run or commences when a claim accrues. Article 9. If the claim is based on the non-conformity of the goods, it accrues on the date the goods are tendered or handed over. Article 10. This was intended to refer to the time when the buyer or its agent first may examine the goods to determine their conformity with the terms of the contract. *Compare* U.C.C. Section 2-725. Article 11 governs the special case of a so-called "future performance" warranty; that is, where an express undertaking has been given as to the goods which is stated to have effect for a certain period of time. In such cases, a claim for non-conformity accrues no later than the expiration of the period of the undertaking but may accrue earlier on the date the buyer notifies the seller of the fact on which the claim is based. The U.C.C. expressly adopts a similar rule under Section 2-725(2).

E. Privity

Documents Supplement References:

1. CISG Articles 4, 35.
2. U.C.C. Sections 2-313, 2-318.

Randy Knitwear, Inc. v. American Cyanamid Co.
181 N.E. 399 (N.Y. 1962)

Fuld, Judge:

"The assault upon the citadel of privity," Chief Judge Cardozo wrote in 1931, "is proceeding in these days apace." (*Ultramares Corp. v. Touche*, 255 N. Y. 170, 180.) In these days, too, for the present appeal, here by leave of the Appellate Division on a certified question, calls upon us to decide whether, under the facts disclosed, privity of contract is essential to maintenance of an action against a manufacturer for breach of express warranty.

American Cyanamid Company is the manufacturer of chemical resins, marketed under the registered trademark "Cyana," which are used by textile manufacturers and finishers to process fabrics in order to prevent them from shrinking. Apex Knitted Fabrics and Fairtex Mills are manufacturers of fabrics who were licensed or otherwise authorized by Cyanamid to treat their goods with "Cyana" and to sell such goods under the "Cyana" label and with the guaranty that they were "Cyana" finished. Randy Knitwear, a manufacturer of children's knitted sportswear and play clothes, purchased large quantities of these "Cyana" treated fabrics from Apex and Fairtex. After most of such fabrics had been made up into garments and sold by Randy to customers, it was claimed that ordinary washing caused them to shrink and to lose their shape. This action for breach of express warranty followed, each of the 3 parties being made the subject of a separate count. After serving its answer, Cyanamid, urging lack of privity of contract, moved for summary judgment dismissing the cause of action asserted against it, and it is solely with this cause of action that we are concerned.

Insofar as relevant, the complaint alleges that Cyanamid "represented" and "warranted" that the "Cyana" finished fabrics sold by Fairtex and Apex to the plaintiff would not shrink or lose their shape when washed and that the plaintiff purchased the fabrics and agreed to pay the additional charge for the cost involved in rendering them shrink-proof "in reliance upon" Cyanamid's representations. However, the complaint continues, the fabrics were not as represented since, when manufactured into garments and subjected to ordinary washing, they shrank and failed to hold their shape....

According to the complaint and the affidavits submitted in opposition to Cyanamid's motion, the representations relied upon by the plaintiff took the form of written statements expressed not only in numerous advertisements appearing in trade journals and in direct mail pieces to clothing manufacturers, but also in labels or garment tags furnished by Cyanamid.... Cyanamid delivered a large number of these labels to Fairtex and Apex and they, with Cyanamid's knowledge and approval, passed them on to garment manufacturers, including the plaintiff, so that they might attach them to the clothing which they manufactured from the fabrics purchased.

As noted, Cyanamid moved for summary judgment dismissing the complaint against it on the ground that there was no privity of contract to support the plaintiff's action. The court at Special Term denied the motion and the Appellate Division unanimously affirmed the resulting order.

Thirty-nine years ago, in *Chysky v. Drake Bros. Co.* (235 N. Y. 468), this court decided that an action for breach of implied warranty could not succeed absent privity between plaintiff and defendant and, some time later, in *Turner v. Edison Stor. Battery Co.* (248 N. Y. 73), we reached a similar conclusion with respect to express warranties, writing, "There can be no warranty where there is no privity of contract" (p. 74). This traditional privity limitation on a seller's liability for damage resulting from breach of warranty has not, however, been adhered to with perfect logical consistency and, just a year ago, in *Greenberg v. Lorenz* (9 N Y 2d 195), we noted the definite shift away from the technical privity requirement and recognized that it should be dispensed with in a proper case in the interest of justice and reason. More specifically, we held in *Greenberg* that, in cases involving foodstuffs and other household goods, the implied warranties of fitness and merchantability run from the retailer to the members of the purchaser's household, regardless of privity of contract. We are now confronted with the further but related question whether the traditional privity limitation shall also be dispensed with in an action for breach of express warranty by a remote purchaser against a manufacturer who induced the purchase by representing the quality of the goods in public advertising and on labels which accompanied the goods.

It was in this precise type of case, where express representations were made by a manufacturer to induce reliance by remote purchasers, that "the citadel of privity" was successfully breached in the State of Washington in 1932. (See *Baxter v. Ford Motor Co.*, 168 Wash. 456; same case after new trial, 179 Wash. 123.) It was the holding in the *Baxter* case that the manufacturer was liable for breach of express warranty to one who purchased an automobile from a retailer since such purchaser had a right to rely on representations made by the manufacturer in its sales literature, even though there was no privity of contract between them. And in the 30 years which have passed since that decision, not only have the courts throughout the country shown a marked, and almost uniform, tendency to discard the privity limitation and hold the manufacturer strictly accountable for the truthfulness of representations made to the public and relied upon by the plaintiff in making his purchase, but the vast majority of the authoritative commentators have applauded the trend and approved the result.

The rationale underlying the decisions rejecting the privity requirement is easily understood in the light of present-day commercial practices. It may once have been true that the warranty which really induced the sale was normally an actual term of the contract of sale. Today, however, the significant warranty, the one which effectively induces the purchase, is frequently that given by the manufacturer through mass advertising and labeling to ultimate business users or to consumers with whom he has no direct contractual relationship.

The world of merchandising is, in brief, no longer a world of direct contract; it is, rather, a world of advertising and, when representations expressed and disseminated in the mass communications media and on labels (attached to the goods themselves) prove false and the user or consumer is damaged by reason of his reliance on those representations, it is difficult to justify the manufacturer's denial of liability on the sole ground of the absence of technical privity. Manufacturers make extensive use of newspapers, periodicals and other media to call attention, in glowing terms, to the qualities and virtues of their products, and this advertising is directed at the ultimate consumer or at some manufacturer or supplier who is not in privity with them. Equally sanguine representations on packages and labels frequently accompany the article throughout its journey to the ultimate consumer and, as intended, are relied upon by remote purchasers. Under these circumstances, it is highly unrealistic to limit a purchaser's protection to warranties made directly to him by his immediate seller. The protection he really needs is against the manufacturer whose published representations caused him to make the purchase.

The policy of protecting the public from injury, physical or pecuniary, resulting from misrepresentations outweighs allegiance to an old and out-moded technical rule of law which, if observed, might be productive of great injustice. The manufacturer places his product upon the market and, by advertising and labeling it, represents its quality to the public in such a way as to induce reliance upon his representations. He unquestionably intends and expects that the product will be purchased and used in reliance upon his express assurance of its quality and, in fact, it is so purchased and used. Having invited and solicited the use, the manufacturer should not be permitted to avoid responsibility, when the expected use leads to injury and loss, by claiming that he made no contract directly with the user.

It is true that in many cases the manufacturer will ultimately be held accountable for the falsity of his representations, but only after an unduly wasteful process of litigation. Thus, if the consumer or ultimate business user sues and recovers, for breach of warranty, from his immediate seller and if the latter, in turn, sues and recovers against his supplier in recoupment of his damages and costs, eventually, after several separate actions by those in the chain of distribution, the manufacturer may finally be obliged "to shoulder the responsibility which should have been his in the first instance." ... As is manifest, and as Dean Prosser observes, this circuity of action is "an expensive, time-consuming and wasteful process, and it may be interrupted by insolvency, lack of jurisdiction, disclaimers, or the statute of limitations." (Prosser, *The Assault upon the Citadel [Strict Liability to the Consumer]*, 69 YALE L. J. 1099, 1124.)

Indeed, and it points up the injustice of the rule, insistence upon the privity requirement may well leave the aggrieved party, whether he be ultimate business user or consumer, without a remedy in a number of situations. For instance, he would be remediless either where his immediate seller's representations as to quality were less extravagant or enthusiastic than those of the manufacturer or where — as is asserted by Fairtex in this very case — there has been an effective disclaimer of any and all warranties by the plaintiff's immediate seller. Turning to the case before us, even if the representations respecting "Cyana" treated fabric were false, the plaintiff would be foreclosed of all remedy against Fairtex, if it were to succeed on its defense of disclaimer, and against Cyanamid because of a lack of privity.

Although we believe that it has already been made clear, it is to be particularly remarked that in the present case the plaintiff's reliance is not on newspaper advertisements alone. It places heavy emphasis on the fact that the defendant not only made representations (as to the nonshrinkable character of "Cyana Finish" fabrics) in newspapers and periodicals, but also repeated them on its own labels and tags which accompanied the fabrics purchased by the plaintiff from Fairtex and Apex. There is little in reason or logic to support Cyanamid's submission that it should not be held liable to the plaintiff even though the representations prove false in fact and it is ultimately found that the plaintiff relied to its harm upon such representations in making its purchases.

. . . .

The order appealed from should be affirmed, with costs, and the question certified answered in the negative.

. . . .

NOTE ON PRIVITY

Let us assume that the defendant in *Randy Knitwear* was called the Canadian Cyanamid Company with its relevant place of business in Canada, a CISG State. It seems clear enough that the CISG would govern the sale between Cyanamid and, for example, Fairtex Mills, and that the U.C.C. would govern the sale between Fairtex Mills and Randy Knitwear. The tricky question in such a case is what law governs the claim (if any) of Randy Knitwear against Cyanamid. This is by no means a purely academic question. In the modern age of marketing where manufacturers do a considerable amount of advertising across national boundaries and are responsible through a variety of dealer arrangements for much of the information that buyers receive about their goods, claims against manufacturers and other remote suppliers can be expected to grow dramatically in number and importance.

The CISG does not speak directly to the issue of privity of contract. It does, however, provide in Article 4 that the Convention "governs only the formation of the contract of sale and the obligations of the seller and the buyer arising from such a contract." Moreover, Article 35(1) limits quality disputes to what the contract requires. This language strongly suggests that the Convention applies only to the two-person sale between commercial parties. Assuming that a court would be unwilling to read the terms "seller," "buyer," and "contract" broadly so as to bring these remote sale cases within the scope of the CISG, is the buyer without a remedy against the CISG seller? Presumably, the outcome will depend on the applicable domestic sales law. Thus, under U.C.C. Article 2 the seller's liability will ultimately depend on whether the buyer is able to recover on an express warranty theory under Section 2-313 or as a third party beneficiary under the applicable alternative to Section 2-318.

II. Exemptions

Documents Supplement References:

1. *CISG Article 79.*

2. *UNIDROIT Principles Article 6.2*

Peter Winship, A Note on the Commentary of the 1980 Vienna Convention,
18 International Lawyer 37 (1984)

Although a commentary on the UNCITRAL draft sales convention had been prepared by the Secretariat and circulated to Governments, the diplomatic conference which met in Vienna did not decide to sanction the publication of an official or semi-official commentary on the final text of the international sales convention. There was no formal debate on the question of a commentary as there had been at the 1978 Hamburg Conference on Carriage of Goods by Sea, where a decision was taken not to publish a commentary. Several precedents in favor of a commentary could be cited: the official records for the 1964 conference held at the Hague included a commentary on the uniform sales laws which was written by Professor Andre Tunc Wroner; and the conference which adopted the 1974 Limitations Convention prepared under the auspices of UNCITRAL, authorized the publication of a commentary prepared by Professor Kazuaki Sono.

The United States expressed particular interest in the adoption of a commentary. In its comments on the 1978 UNCITRAL draft, the U.S. government commented as follows:

> The United States strongly urges that a commentary accompany the final text. The existing commentary has been prepared by the Secretariat and has thus far accompanied the draft as an explanation of its provisions. Such a commentary, including unofficial captions to each section, has proved most helpful to practitioners in the United States who have studied the draft CISG. It can be expected that a commentary would facilitate efforts to have the resulting convention ratified. Since the draft CISG contains a number of concepts that are unknown in common law systems, a commentary is of special importance to a common law country such as the United States.

In the absence of recorded debate on the question of a commentary one can only speculate on the reasons for not adopting the U.S. suggestion. Perhaps there was fear that the text of the convention would be ignored in favor of a more easily read, but unofficial, text of a commentary.

. . . .

Nevertheless, although the Secretariat's Commentary is not an official document and has not been updated, it remains an important source of background information about the policies behind specific provisions of the Vienna convention.

Text of Secretariat Commentary on Article 65 Of the 1978 Draft

1. Article 65 [draft counterpart of CISG article 79] governs the extent to which a party is exempted from liability for a failure to perform any of his obligations because of an impediment beyond his control.

General Rule, Paragraphs (1) and (5)

2. Paragraph (1) sets out the conditions under which a party is not liable for a failure to perform any of his obligations. Paragraph (5) provides that exemption from liability under this article prevents the other party from exercising only his right to claim damages, but does not prevent him from exercising any other right he may have.

3. Under articles 41(1)(b) and 57 (1)(b) [draft counterpart of CISG articles 45(1)(b) and 61(1)(b)] a party has a right to claim damages for any non-performance of the other party without the necessity of providing fault or a lack of good faith or the breach of an express promise on his part, as is required by some legal systems. However, under article 65 [draft counterpart of CISG article 79] the non-performing party is exempt from liability if he proves (1) that the failure to perform was due to an impediment beyond his control, (2) that he could not reasonably be expected to have taken the impediment into account at the time of the conclusion of the contract, (3) that he could not reasonably have been expected to have avoided the impediment or its consequences and (4) that he could not reasonably have been expected to have overcome the impediment or its consequences.

4. The impediment may have existed at the time of the conclusion of the contract. For example, goods which were unique and which were the subject of the contract may have already perished at the time of the conclusion of the contract. However, the seller would not be exempted from liability under this article if he reasonably could have been expected to take the destruction of the goods into account at the time of the conclusion of the contract. Therefore, in order to be exempt from liability, the seller must not have known of their prior destruction and must have been reasonable in not expecting their destruction.

5. It is this later element which is the most difficult for the non-performing party to prove. All potential impediments to the performance of a contract are foreseeable to one degree or another. Such impediments as wars, storms, fires, government embargoes and the closing of international waterways have all occurred in the past and can be expected to occur again in the future. Frequently, the parties to the contract have envisaged the possibility of the impediment which did occur. Sometimes they have explicitly stated whether the occurrence of the impending event would exonerate the non-performing party from the consequences of the non-performance. In other cases it is clear from the context of the contract that one party has obligated himself to perform an act even though certain impediments might arise. In either of these two classes of cases, article 5 [draft counterpart of CISG article 6] of this Convention assures the enforceability of such explicit or implicit contractual stipulations.

6. However, where neither the explicit nor the implicit terms of the contract show that the occurrence of the particular impediment was envisaged, it is necessary to determine whether the non-performing party could reasonably have been expected to take it into account at the time of the conclusion of the contract. In the final analysis this determination can only be made by a court or arbitral tribunal on a case-by-case basis.

7. Even if the non-performing party can prove that he could not reasonably have been expected to take the impediment into account at the time of the conclusion of the contract, he must also prove that he could neither have avoided the impediment nor overcome it nor avoided or overcome the consequences of the impediment. This rule reflects the policy that a party who is under an obligation to act must do all in his power to carry out his obligation and may not await events which might later justify his non-performance. This rule also indicates that a party may be required to perform by providing what is in all the circumstances of the transaction a commercially reasonable substitute for the performance which was required under the contract.

8. The effect of article 65 [draft counterpart of CISG article 79(1)] in conjunction with article 65(5) [draft counterpart of CISG article 79(5)] is to exempt the non-per-

forming party only from liability for damages. All of the other remedies are available to the other party, *i.e.* demand for performance, reduction of the price or avoidance of the contract. However, if the party who is required to overcome an impediment does so by furnishing a substitute performance, the other party could avoid the contract and thereby reject the substitute performance only if that substitute performance was so deficient in comparison with the performance stipulated in the contract that it constituted a fundamental breach of contract.

9. Even if the impediment is of such a nature as to render impossible any further performance, the other party retains the right to require that performance under article 42 or 58 [draft counterpart of CISG article 46 or 62]. It is a matter of domestic law not governed by this Convention as to whether the failure to perform exempts the non-performing party from paying a sum stipulated in the contract for liquidated damages or as a penalty for non performance or as to whether a court will order a party to perform in these circumstances and subject him to the sanctions provided in its procedural law for continued non-performance.

> Example 65A: The contract called for the delivery of unique goods. Prior to the time when the risk of loss would have passed pursuant to article 79 or 80 [draft counterpart of CISG article 67 or 68] the goods were destroyed by a fire which was caused by events beyond the control of Seller. In such a case Buyer would not have to pay for the goods for which the risk had not passed but Seller could be exempted from liability for any damage resulting from his failure to deliver the goods.

> Example 65B: The contract called for the delivery of 500 machine tools. Prior to the passage of the risk of loss, the tools were destroyed in similar circumstances to Example 65A. In such a case Seller would not only have to bear the loss of the 500 tools but he would also be obligated to ship to Buyer an additional 500 tools. The difference between this example and Example 65A is that in Example 65A Seller cannot provide that which was contracted for whereas under Example 65B Seller can overcome the effect of the destruction of the tools by shipping replacement goods.

> Example 65C: If the machine tools shipped in replacement of those destroyed in Example 65B could not arrive in time, Seller would be exempted from damages for late delivery.

> Example 65D: The contract called for the goods to be packed in plastic containers. At the time the packing should have been accomplished, plastic containers were not available for reasons which Seller could not have avoided. However, if other commercially reasonable packing materials were available, Seller must overcome the impediment by using those materials rather than refuse to deliver the goods. If Seller used commercially reasonable substitute packing materials, he would not be liable for damages. In addition, Buyer could not avoid the contract because there would have been no fundamental breach of the contract but Buyer could reduce the price under article 46 [draft counterpart of CISG article 50] if the value of the goods had been diminished because of the non-performing packing materials.

> Example 65E: The contract called for shipment on a particular vessel. The schedule for the vessel was revised because of events beyond the control of both Buyer and Seller and it did not call at the port indicated within the shipment period. In this circumstance the party responsible

for arranging the carriage of the goods must attempt to overcome the impediment by providing an alternative vessel.

10. Although it is probably true that the insolvency of the buyer by itself is not an impediment which exempts the buyer from liability for non-payment of the price, the unanticipated imposition of exchange controls, or other regulations of a similar nature may make it impossible for him to fulfill his obligation to pay the price at the time and in the manner agreed. The buyer would, of course, be exempted from liability for damages for the non-payment (which as a practical matter would normally mean interest on the unpaid sum) only if he could not overcome the impediment by, for example, arranging for a commercially reasonable substitute form of payment. [Note, however, that buyer does not appear to be exempt from liability for interest under the new article 78.]

Non-Performance by a Third Person, Paragraph (2)

11. It often happens that the non-performance of a party is due to the non-performance of a third person. Paragraph (2) provides that where this is the case, "that party is exempt from liability only if he is exempt under paragraph (1) of this article [under the preceding paragraph] and if the person whom he has [so] engaged would be so exempt if the provisions of that paragraph were applied to him."

12. The third person must be someone who has been engaged to perform the whole or a part of the contract. It does not include suppliers of the goods or of raw materials to the seller.

Temporary Impediment, Paragraph (3)

[Caveat: Paragraphs 13 and 14 of the Secretariat Commentary are based on a provision of the 1978 Draft that was changed, and should be evaluated accordingly. Paragraph (3) of the 1978 Draft read: "The exemption provided by this article has effect only for the period during which the impediment exists." The word "only" was deleted from paragraph (3) of the Official Text.]

13. Paragraph (3) provides that an impediment which prevents a party from performing for only a temporary period of time exempts the non-performing party from liability for damages only for the period during which the impediment existed. Therefore, the date at which the exemption from damages terminates is the contract date for performance or the date on which the impediment was removed, whichever is later in time.

> Example 65F: The goods were to be delivered on 1 February. On 1 January an impediment arose which precluded Seller from delivering the goods. The impediment was removed on 1 March. Seller delivered on 15 March. Seller is exempted from any damages which may have occurred because of the delay in delivery up to 1 March, the date on which the impediment was removed. However, since the impediment was removed after the contract date for delivery, the Seller is liable for any damages which occurred as a result of the delay in delivery between 1 March and 15 March.

14. Of course, if the delay in performance because of the temporary impediment amounted to a fundamental breach of the contract, the other party would have the right to declare the avoidance of the contract. However, if the contract was not avoided by the other party, the contract continues in existence and the removal of the impediment reinstates the obligations of both parties under the contract.

> Example 65G: Because of a fire which destroyed Seller's plant, Seller was unable to deliver the goods under the contract at the time performance

was due. He was exempted from damages under paragraph (1) until the plant was rebuilt. Seller's plant was rebuilt in two years. Although a two-year delay in delivery constituted a fundamental breach which would have justified Buyer in declaring the avoidance of the contract, he did not do so. When Seller's plant was rebuilt, Seller was obligated to deliver the goods to Buyer and, unless he decided to declare the contract avoided because of fundamental breach, Buyer was obligated to take delivery and to pay the contract price.

Duty to Notify, Paragraph (4)

15. The non-performing party who is exempted from damages by reason of the existence of an impediment to the performance of his obligation must notify the other party of the impediment and its effect on his ability to perform. If the notice is not received by the other party within a reasonable time after the party who fails to perform knew or ought to have known of the impediment, the non-performing party is liable for damages resulting from the failure of the notice to be received by the other party. It should be noted that the damages for which the non-performing party is liable are only those arising out of the failure of the other party to have received the notice and not those arising out of the non-performance.

16. The duty to notify extends not only to the situation in which a party cannot perform at all because of the unforeseen impediment, but also to the situation in which he intends to perform by furnishing a commercially reasonable substitute. Therefore, the seller in Example 65D and the party responsible for arranging the carriage of the goods in Example 65E must notify the other party of the intended substitute performance. If he does not do so, he will be liable for any damages resulting from the failure to give notice. If he does give notice but the notice fails to arrive he will be also liable for damages resulting from the failure of the notice to have been received by the other party.

Case Abstract, UNCITRAL Texts (CLOUT), Abstract No. 168, October 17, 1995

(Tribunal of International Commercial Arbitration at the Russian Federation Chamber of Commerce and Industry)

A German seller (claimant) brought a claim against a Russian buyer (respondent) in connection with the [buyer's] failure to pay for equipment supplied under a contract concluded between the two parties. The buyer acknowledged that the goods had indeed been delivered under the contract but stated that its non-payment was due to the failure on the part of the bank responsible for the buyer's foreign currency transactions to give instructions for the amount payable for the goods under the contract to be transferred to the seller. The bank did not transfer the foreign currency amounts to the seller on the grounds that there were no funds available in the buyer's account in freely convertible currency to pay for the goods. Citing these facts, the buyer requested the tribunal to discharge it from liability since, in its view, the fact that it did not have available foreign currency resources should be regarded as *force majeure* discharging it from liability for the non-performance of its contractual obligations.

The tribunal was not in agreement with the [buyer's] view that its lack of foreign currency should be regarded as *force majeure*, since the contract agreed between the two parties gave an exhaustive list of *force majeure* circumstances discharging them from liability for non-performance of their contractual obligations. The buyer's lack of foreign currency was not included in that list of *force majeure*.

In addition, the tribunal stated that, under article 54 CISG, the buyer's obligation to pay the price of the goods included taking such measures and complying with such formalities as might be required to enable payment to be made. On the basis of the case materials and the clarifications offered by the buyer during the proceedings, it was established that the only action taken by the buyer was to send instructions to the bank for the amounts payable under the contract to be transferred, but that it had not taken any measures to ensure that the payment could actually be made.

The tribunal found in favor of the [seller] and ordered the buyer to make the payment for the goods supplied.

QUESTION

1. What role, if any, should common contract clauses on exemption play in interpreting and applying Article 79?

Nuova Fucinati S.p.a. v. Fondmetall International A.B., Tribunale di Monza,

29 March 1993, 15 Journal of Law & Commerce 153 (1995)

[Synopsis by the Court:] The Vienna Convention on Contracts for the International Sale of Goods does not apply pursuant to Article 1(1)(b) when the choice of the law governing the contract is determined by the agreement of the parties instead of by the objective "criteria of connection" (for example, the place where the contract is concluded).

Article 79 of the Vienna Convention provides for release from an obligation made impossible by a supervening impediment not attributable to a party according to a rule similar to article 1463 *et seq.* of the Civil Code, but it does not seem to contemplate the remedy of dissolution for supervening excessive onerousness of a performance as provided for in article 1467 of the Civil Code for contracts involving performance over time or deferred performance.

On July 20th, 1988, upon petition of [buyer], whose place of business is in Kyrgogatan 44-S-411 15 Goteberg (Sweden), the President of the Tribunal of Monza ordered [seller], whose place of business is in Monza, to deliver to the [buyer] 1000 tons of ironchrome "Lumpy" as ordered in the contract of February 3, 1988 (at the price of Lira 545 per kilo).

[Seller] objected to this injunctive order, notice of which was given on July 25, 1988, and sued the [buyer] in this Tribunal with notice of summons given on September 29, 1988.

The [seller] pled that it was impossible to deliver the goods within the agreed delivery dates (between March 20, 1988 and April 10, 1988) because [buyer] was late in taking delivery of another load of goods (700 cubic meters of ironchrome "Fine") ordered at the same time. [Seller] demanded the repeal of the injunctive order and, as a further claim, argued for the dissolution of the February 3, 1988 contract because of supervening excessive onerousness with respect to the executory portion of the performance. In fact, [seller alleged], between the time the contract was entered into and the date for delivering the ironchrome "Lumpy," the price on the international market rose remarkably and unforeseeably to the point that it upset the balance between the corresponding performances and justified, at least, a price correction that the [buyer] refused to consider.

[Buyer] denied the factual foundation of [seller's] arguments to the injunction. [Buyer] also opposed dissolving the contract for supervening excessive onerousness by arguing that this remedy was unavailable under Article 79 of the April 11, 1980 Vienna Convention on Contracts for the International Sale of Goods, adopted in Italy by Law No. 765 of December 11, 1985. For these reasons, [buyer] demanded that [seller's] objections and claims be rejected, and urged that its opposition be ordered to pay damages for non-performance of the contract.

After the parties exchanged memoranda and submitted documents, the court held a hearing on March 1, 1990 at which counsel gave their statement of conclusions.

To investigate the possibility that the contract was governed by the April 11, 1980 Vienna Convention on Contracts for the International Sale of Goods, the Court issued an order on March 6, 1990 holding that it was necessary to ascertain if and when Sweden had ratified the Convention. It therefore reopened the judicial inquiry to acquire proper information. [The court thereafter acquired the necessary information and, after several delays, a final hearing was held on January 14, 1993.]

Reasoning: At the final hearing the [seller] relied primarily on the argument that its obligation to deliver 1000 metric tons of ironchrome "Lumpy," confirmed by order no. 002/88 of February 3, 1988, had become excessively oncrous, thus justifying [seller's] non-performance. The argument upon which it had originally relied, based on [buyer's] failure to take delivery of 700 tons of ironchrome "Fine" ordered on the same date but under a different confirmation number (003/88), was relegated to subordinate importance.

The [buyer], in turn, availed itself of the *ius variandi* provided for by Article 1453(2)[1] of the Civil Code and demanded dissolution of the contract as well as the damages already claimed in connection with its original petition for performance.

We must first determine whether Article 1467 of the Civil Code [excusing performance of a contract where one party's obligations have become "excessively onerous"] applies to the contract betwcen these parties.

The theory that the contract should be dissolved for supervening factors that upset the original economic balance between corresponding performances has been contested by the [buyer] both as a matter of law [*i.e.*, because of the preemption by Article 79 of the Sales Convention] (as recalled in the synopsis) and for factual reasons related to the requirements of Article 1467 of the Civil Code.

Since the case involves an international sale of goods between an Italian corporation (seller) and a Swedish corporation (buyer), the first question to resolve is whether the contract is subject to the Vienna Convention of April 11, 1980, adopted in Italy by Law No. 765 of December 11, 1985 and effective as of January 1, 1988. This question is anything but insignificant since that Convention, which applies only to international sales of goods, does not seem to contemplate the remedy of dissolution of contract for supervening excessive onerousness. Article 1467 of the Civil Code, in contrast, provides for this remedy with respect to contracts involving continuous or periodic or deferred performance - criteria that fit the contract under discussion (formed on February 3, 1988) because it permitted the buyer to choose a delivery date between March 20 and April 10, 1988.

The Convention, ratified by both Italy and Sweden, provides in Article 79 that a party who fails to perform any of his obligations is not liable "if he proves that the failure was due to an impediment beyond his control and that he could not reasonably be expected to have taken the impediment into account at the time of the conclusion of the contract [or to have avoided or overcome it or its consequences]."

This provision, however, governs a different case - release from a duty made impossible by a supervening impediment not ascribable to a party, according to a rule similar to Article 1463 of the Civil Code. Article 61, *et seq.*, of the Convention governs the seller's remedies for breach of contract by the buyer, providing in particular for the remedy of avoidance ("dissolution" in the terminology of our Civil Code) for breach of contract. These rules parallel those in Article 45 *et seq.* [of the Convention] governing [a buyer's remedies for] breach of contract by the seller.

Under the Convention the remedy of dissolution is associated with breach, whereas the excessive onerousness doctrine does not fit within the structure of the Convention when invoked either as a defense or as a reason to avoid (rectius: dissolve) the contract.

It is clear that, if the Convention applied to the contract in this case, one could not as a matter of law defend on the basis of the supervening excessive onerousness of the seller's obligation to deliver, whether or not the factual requirements of that doctrine were met. Article 4 of the Vienna Convention states that "[t]his Convention governs only the formation of the contract of sale and the rights and obligations of the seller and the buyer arising from such a contract," and it specifies that "except as otherwise expressly provided in this Convention, it is not concerned with (a) the validity of the contract" or "(b) the effect which the contract may have on the property in the goods sold."

Dissolution of the contract for supervening excessive onerousness affects neither the validity of the contract nor the property in the goods (except indirectly, by removing the obligation to deliver and thus affecting the transfer of title by preventing the identification of particular goods to the contract). [*i.e.*, dissolution for excessive onerousness is a matter within the scope of the Convention]. Because the Convention is "special" law [*i.e.*, one that applies to specific types of transactions], we must conclude that, if it were applicable to the case, it would preempt the general law of Article 1467 *et seq.* of the Civil Code.

The Vienna Convention came into force in Italy on January 1, 1988 - prior to the conclusion of the contract on February 3, 1988 (the date of the order confirmation that functioned as an acceptance sent by the [seller, an] Italian corporation to the [buyer, a Swedish] corporation) and prior to the March 7, 1989 [sic - March 7, 1988] telex declaring March 20 as the [first] date for delivering the goods. The Convention nevertheless cannot apply in this case because in Sweden it came into force (with a few reservations not relevant in our case) on January 1, 1989 [*i.e.*, after the confirmation and telex mentioned above], as appears from the documentation procured in the recent judicial inquiry.

Now it is true that the law applicable to the contract is Italian law, by virtue of the explicit provision inserted in the order confirmation ("law: Italian law to apply"); and it is also true that, because the Vienna Convention at this time was in force in the national system, it must be considered a law like any other law of this State.

Nevertheless, because of the conditions that this "law" [*i.e.*, the Convention] fixes for its application, we must consider the fact that the Convention came into force in Sweden after the conclusion of the contract as an obstacle to its application.

Article 1 of the Convention limits its sphere of application to contracts for the sale of goods between parties whose places of business are in different States (in this case, Italy on one side and Sweden on the other) when one of the following alternative possibilities exists: a) both States are Contracting States; or b) the rules of private international law lead to the application of the law of a Contracting State.

The second possibility does not fit the case at hand. This is not because under Article 25 of the Preliminary Provisions to the Civil Code the rules of private international law would lead to the application of the laws of Sweden (where, at the time the contract was concluded (Article 1326(1) of the Civil Code), the Convention had not yet come into force). Rather, the rules of private international law cannot apply when the parties negotiate the law applicable to an international contract, in which case only the public order principles in Article 31 of the Preliminary Provisions to the Civil Code limit private autonomy.

Thus this case is governed by the first of the two alternatives provided for by Article 1, under which the Convention applies if the sale occurs between parties whose places of business are in different Contracting States.

A Contracting State is one that has not only agreed to the Convention, but one in which the Convention has come into force (as specified in Article 100(2), under which the Convention applies to contracts concluded after the Convention has entered into force in the Contracting States referred to in Article 1(1)(a)[2]). We therefore conclude that the Vienna Convention does not apply to the contract under consideration, which was concluded before the Convention entered into force in the country where one of the contracting corporations had its place of business.

Thus, because the special law [*i.e.*, the Convention] does not apply, the parties' choice of Italian law leads to the application of the general law, Article 1467 *et seq.* of the Civil Code. As a result, the remedy of dissolution for supervening excessive onerousness is available, both as a defense and a claim. . . .

The [seller] based its claim on the ground that, between February 3, 1988 (the date on which the contract was formed) and April (the delivery date, according to [seller's] argument) the international market price of ironchrome advanced 43.71%, rising from Lire 1,496 per Kg/chrome (equal to US$ 0.545 per lb./chrome as estimated in the contract) to Lire 2,150. These facts, even though documented, do not justify the legal conclusions that the alleging party seeks to establish.

[The court rejected Plaintiff-seller's arguments based on supervening excessive onerousness and alleged breach by the Defendant-buyer.]

As a result this Tribunal renders a non-definitive decision lifting the contested injunction, declaring the contract dissolved for non-performance by the [seller], and rejecting every defense and contrary request of the latter. We submit the suit to the examining judge for further judicial inquiry into the [buyer's] request for compensatory damages.

Award of August 26, 1989, Case No. 6281, ICC Yearbook Commercial Arbitration XV 96 (1990)

(Paris, France)

Parties:

Claimant: Egyptian company (buyer)
Defendant: Yugoslav company (seller)

Facts:

On 20 August 1987, the parties concluded a contract for the sale of 80,000 metric tons of steel bars at an average price of US$ 190.00 per metric ton. The goods were delivered in accordance with the contract between 15 September 1985 and 15 January 1988 to a suitable Yugoslav port.

Claimant had the option to increase the quantity to 160,000 metric tons at the same price and conditions, provided it declared its option to purchase the additional 80,000 metric tons at the latest by 15 December 1987 and opened its letter of credit for the first delivery at the latest by 31 December 1987.

On 26 November 1987, claimant informed defendant that it would exercise the option and would open the L/C during the second half of December 1987. On 9 December 1987, defendant requested a meeting to be held that month, to discuss the prices for the additional quantity of the goods. Claimant insisted on the originally agreed price but was prepared to discuss future business transactions. At the meeting held on 28 December 1987, defendant requested US$ 215.00 per metric ton for the additional deliveries, but the claimant did not agree.

In its letter of 31 December 1987, claimant stated that defendant's behavior was a breach of contract and requested defendant to announce the beneficiaries of the future letters of credit. If defendant did not agree by 6 January 1988, claimant would hold defendant liable for any and all damage caused by breach of contract. This period was extended to 25 January 1988.

On 26 January 1988, claimant bought 80,000 metric tons of the same type of steel bars from a Romanian company at a price of US$ 216.00 per metric ton. Claimant alleged that shipping costs from Romania to Egypt were US$ 2.00 to US$ 2.50 per metric ton lower than from Yugoslavia to Egypt.

Claimant initiated arbitration under the arbitration clause in the contract which provided for arbitration at the International Chamber of Commerce, claiming compensation for the loss due to the price difference. The sole arbitrator held that the claimant was entitled to damages due to defendant's failure to deliver the additional quantity of goods at the original price.

Excerpt:

[1]   The arbitrator decided that Yugoslav law was applicable.

[2]   "It should be determined, first and foremost, in connection with the alleged unreasonableness, due to an increase in world-market prices, which legal provisions should be applied to evaluate the sales contract and, thus also, this central issue. At any rate, the Vienna United Nations Convention on Contracts for the International Sale of Goods of 11 April 1980, cannot be applied as such. The Convention is in force, both in Egypt and in Yugoslavia, as well as in France; yet, according to Art. 100(2) it applies to such sales contracts only that were concluded after the date the Convention went into force, *i.e.*, 1 January 1988. The present sales contract was concluded on 20 August 1987.

[3]   "The question, which law applies, must therefore be examined on the basis of the rules on international private law.

[4]   "According to Egyptian international private law, the law of that country applies, where the contract is signed, unless the parties agree otherwise, and, in addition, if they have their principal offices in different states (Art. 19 of the 1949 Civil Code).

[5]   "According to Yugoslav international private law, the law of that country applies, where the seller had his principal office at the time when he (or the other party) received the offer, if there is no agreement on applicable law between the par-

ties (Bill on International Private Law of 15 February 1982, Sluzbeni list No. 43/1982).

[6]   "France is a member of the Convention on the Law Applicable to the International Sales of Goods, done at the Hauge on 15 June 1955. Art. 3(2) of the above Convention states that if parties have not chosen another law, the contract is governed by the internal law of the state, where the seller has his habitual residence at the time at which he received the order....

[7]   "Since the principal office and the habitual residence of the seller at the time in question was Yugoslavia, and since the sales contract was concluded in Yugoslavia, all applicable rules on international private law refer to Yugoslav substantive law.

[8]   "Paragraphs 1 and 2 of [Art. 133 of] of the Yugoslav Law on Obligations of 1978 read as follows (in an unofficial translation):

'(1) In case of circumstances occurring after the conclusion of the contract which are of the nature to render the contractual performance of one of the parties difficult or to prevent the scope of the contract to be attained, both to such an extent that it becomes obvious that the contract ceases to correspond to the expectations of the parties and that it would be generally considered unjust to maintain it in force in the unchanged form, the party whose performance has been rendered difficult or which is prevented to attain the scope of the contact by the changed circumstances, can request that the contract be resigned.

(2) The recission of the contract cannot be claimed if the party, which invokes the changed circumstances, should have taken these circumstances into account at the time of the conclusion of the contract or could have escaped or overcome such circumstances.'

The above definition corresponds to that of a 'frustration' according to Anglo-American law or of a *Wegfall der Geschaftsgrundlage* according to German and Austrian law. Yugoslav commentaries (Blagojevic-Krulj; Vizner) speak[ing] of a *clausula rebus sic stantibus* would sustain (in a positive sense) legal relationships only for as long as there are no changes at all, giving no consideration to predictability and applicability. Such a concept cannot be found in the law of obligations, nor the commercial law, of any country (except, at the most, for unlimited obligations, such as rent and lease relationships, but mainly for support obligations). Otherwise, any business transaction would be exposed to uncertainty, or even be rendered impossible altogether, whenever the mutual covenants are not performed at the time at which the contract is concluded.

    . . . .

[10]   "In addition to Att. 133 of the Law of obligations, Usage No. 56 continues to be in force under Yugoslav law, which lists 'economic events, such as extremely sudden and high increases or decreases of prices' as one of the reasons resulting in a frustration."

[11]   The arbitrator subsequently examined whether the increase on the steel price from US$ 190.00 to US$ 215.00 per metric ton was an extreme sudden and an extremely high price increase (Art. 133(1)) and, if so, whether defendant should have taken such a development into consideration at the time when the contract was concluded (Art. 133(2)).

[12]   "The world market prices of products, such as steel, fluctuate, as is known from experience. At the time, when the contract was concluded, steel prices had begun

to go up slightly - a trend that continued between the conclusion of the contract and the exercise of the option, and became even more pronounced towards the end of 1988.

[13]   "In the opinion of Blagojevic-Krulj, *Comments on the Law of Obligations*, p. 351, the court must assess the issue, at which amount of damage contract performance is still, or no longer, reasonable, if one of the parties possibly suffers a damage when performing contractual obligations without change of contract. At any rate, such a damage must exceed a reasonable entrepreneurial risk. In the present case, the increase in world market prices, *i.e.*, from US$ 190,00 to US$ 215.00, amounts to slightly less than 13.16%. Having to sell a product at the agreed price, instead of at a price that is higher by 13.16%, is well within the customary margin.

[14]   "Furthermore, the development was also predictable. A reasonable seller had to expect that steel prices might go up further, perhaps even more dramatically than in actual fact. Whether defendant was a reasonable seller when granting the option 'at the same price' for a relatively long period, given these circumstances, is a matter beyond Arbitrator's terms of reference. In any event, even Yugoslav law precludes that a seller entices a buyer to sign a first contract, containing the option 'at the same price', while having the mental reservation that he can invoke Art. 133 of the Law of Obligations if prices should continue to go up...."

[16]   The arbitrator examined the nature of the damages:

[17]   "Defendant maintains that claimant's buying 80,000 metric tons of steel from the Romanian firm...cannot be interpreted as a purchase in replacement, since defendant was not informed in advance of claimant's specific purchasing intention, since, moreover, defendant had offered the steel at a lower price, *i.e.*, US$ 215.00 per metric ton, and since, in addition, defendant's steel was of a better quality.

[18]   "First of all, the legal interaction between Arts. 262 and 525 of the Yugoslav Law on Obligations must be defined clearly. Art. 262 grants every contracting party the right to claim compensation for the damage accruing to him, which is due to non-performance, deficient or delayed performance of the obligations by the other party. Art. 525, dealing with purchases in replacement, operates as a relief for the aggrieved party, when bringing evidence for the damage suffered. If one were to assume that damages are not due in case of non-compliance with the obligation to give notice according to Art. 525, then no sanctions could be imposed on the non-delivery of goods, for which there is no equivalent, nor on the non-deliver of goods, where it is no longer possible, in due time, to procure an equivalent by purchase in replacement.

[19]   "Neither of the parties contested that the world market price for steel (of the grade of the delivery) had gone up to a minimum of US$ 215.00 per metric ton at the time when the option was exercised. If defendant states, however, that, given these premises, claimant would have been best advised at the price to buy defendants' steel, then the only reaction to that can be that claimant would have been foolish to do so. By invoking defendant's obligation to damages, in case of non-delivery at the agreed price, claimant wanted to balance the difference in price. If claimant had bought from defendant, claimant would have been in [a] much more difficult position, since defendant would have maintained that the price had changed due to novation.

[20]   "Claimant maintains that he actually obtained a cheaper deal, in the final analysis. He paid US$ 216.50 per metric ton but saved US$ 2.00 to US$ 2.50 per metric ton in freight costs. Claimant must accept that this argument is also applied against him - with the higher amount of US$ 2.50 in case of doubt. His damage is therefore less than the difference in world market prices. It amounts only to the difference between US$ 190.00 and US$ 214.00, *i.e.*, US$ 24.00 per metric ton. Defen-

dant claims that claimant had to pay a higher import duty on the Romanian goods than he would have to pay on Yugoslav goods, which is irrelevant since claimant did not claim any additional damage, arising from the purchase in replacement. It is also of no relevance whether the steel supplied by [the Romanian firm] was of lower quality than the steel which defendant would have delivered. For the claimant, the steels were of equivalent quality.

[21] "It is also of no significance whether Art. 525 must be interpreted to mean that the infringing party must be informed in advance of an actual purchase in replacement. The claim for damages, however, arising from the purchase in replacement, is slightly less that the difference in world market prices at the time in question, when taking account of the lower freight costs. According to Art. 262 of the Law on Obligations, claimant cannot claim more than the amount of his actual damage.

[22] "It should be remarked in passing that the outcome would have been the same, if Arts. 74 to 77 of the Vienna Sales Convention had been considered, which has 19 member states so far and which one will soon be able to call universal law, on account of the large number of ratifications and accessions that are intended in the near future.

[23] "The above result is by no means surprising....

[24] "Accordingly, defendant shall reimburse claimant for a damage of 80,000 x US$24.00 = US$ 1,920,000."

[25] The arbitrator then established the amount of interest.

[26] "According to Art. 277(1) of the Yugoslav Law on Obligations, interest is due to the creditor on the amount of damages, as of the date at which the debtor begins to default. Defendant did not default by refusing to deliver at the agreed price, nor by claimant's conclusion of a purchase-in-replacement contract, nor on the date at which payment was due to the new supplier; defendant's default being so every day at which he should have delivered but did not deliver. According to the sales contract, the 80,000 metric tons of steel under the option should have been delivered in five part shipments of more or less equal quantity between January and May 1988. Defendant was therefore in default for one fifth of the amount on 1 February, 1 March, 1 April, 1 May, and 1 June 1988. For the sake of mathematics, interest can be calculated as though defendant defaulted on a total delivery, which would have been due on the date of the third shipment, i.e., on 1 April, 1988.

[27] "As mentioned before, the interest rate amounted and amounts to 6.25 to 8.25%. No prediction can be made, on how the interest rate will develop. Since there is a time delay between issuing the Arbitral Award and voluntary or enforced performance, the Arbitral Award must also fix an interest rate for the future, i.e., until the voluntary or enforced performance of the award. With a view to the mean value of the development so far, an interest rate of 7.25 % is appropriate...."

NOTE ON HARDSHIP

Traditionally, the only major exceptions to the doctrine of *pacta sunt servanda* (agreements must be kept though the heavens fall) were the doctrines of impossibility of performance or "*force majeure*" and frustration of the venture. Hardship, short of impossibility, was not a ground for the discharge of a contract. Today, in many civil and common law systems, this is no longer true; the modern case law and statutory trend is to recognize extreme hardship as a third type of excuse for nonperformance of a contract. For example, German courts will grant relief in cases where a party is unduly burdened because of changed circumstances; *see* Peter Hay,

Frustration and Its Solution in German Law, 10 AM. J. COMP. L. 345 (1961); and other countries such as Italy, Greece, and the Netherlands have reached the same result by statute. Because the UNIDROIT Principles deal with hardship and the CISG does not, one could argue that the Principles can be used in such cases to supplement the Convention.

Joseph M. Perillo, Force Majeure and Hardship Under the UNIDROIT Principles of International Commercial Contracts,

5 Tulane Journal of International and Comparative Law 5, 21-26 (1997)

. . . .

D. *Hardship*

The provisions on "hardship" contained in the chapter on performance should be compared with the provision on *force majeure* contained in the chapter on nonperformance. The rule of *force majeure* is draconian and unforgiving. Nothing short of total impossibility will excuse nonperformance or partial nonperformance. Impracticability will not suffice as an excuse. Rather, impracticability as well as hardship far short of impracticability must be tested under the hardship articles. Hardship alone never forgives nonperformance. It instead compels renegotiation and authorizes courts to "adapt" (revise) the contract to take the hardship into account. Nonetheless, the hardship provision starts with the caption: "Contract[s] to be observed." Article 6.2.1 provides that "[w]here the performance of a contract becomes more onerous for one of the parties, that party is nevertheless bound to perform its obligations subject to the following provisions on hardship."

Hardship: The Factual Predicate

The definition of hardship which appears in Article 6.2.2 is complex, because it not only defines the nature of the burden, but also other factors that must coexist with the burden to make it legally relevant. As a predicate to legally relevant hardship there must have been "the occurrence of events fundamentally alter[ing] the equilibrium of the contract either because the cost of a party's performance has increased or because the value of the performance a party receives has diminished..." When is the equilibrium of a contract fundamentally altered? "[A]n alteration amounting to 50% or more of the cost or the value of the performance is likely to involve a 'fundamental' alteration" justifying invocation of the doctrine. Thus, one illustration involves a ten-year contract for the sale of uranium at fixed prices in U.S. dollars payable in New York. The currency in the buyer's country declines to 1% of the value that it had at the time of contracting. The buyer cannot invoke *force majeure.* Similarly, if the price is increased tenfold because some Texans have almost cornered the market, *force majeure* is not present. Nonetheless, the buyer may have redress under the hardship provisions. As a factual matter, hardship exists if the "equilibrium of the contract" is "fundamentally altered" by events that occur or become known after contracting. As with the case of impossibility, hardship as a fact does not automatically trigger the juridical concept of hardship. In addition, it must be shown that the events could not reasonably have been taken into account, are not within the party's control, and the risk was not assumed. Consequently, in the two illustrations just described, a prima facie claim of hardship is made out. The following example of hardship-in-fact is given in illustration 1 of Article 6.2.2 of the Principles.

A dealer in the former German Democratic Republic contracts to buy electronic goods from a seller in another former Communist country. Prior to delivery, the German Democratic Republic is unified with the Federal Republic of Germany. There is no market for the kinds of electronic goods produced by the seller. Unless other factors dictate a contrary conclusion, the buyer may invoke the doctrine of hardship.

It has been suggested that greater hardship would be needed to trigger the hardship provisions if the obligation is an obligation to achieve a specific result than where the obligation is to exercise best efforts.

"The events could not reasonably have been taken into account by the disadvantaged party at the time of the conclusion of the contract..."

As in the case with allegations of *force majeure*, foreseeability is a central concern in hardship cases. The general notion is that if an event is foreseeable, the parties should deal with it in the contract; otherwise, the party disadvantaged by the event should bear its burden. Yet, as stated above, almost everything that even happens is in some sense foreseeable. Again, the question is whether the event was so outside the bounds of probability that reasonable parties would not provide for it. The Principles give two illustrations of the foreseeability issue. The first involves a contract for the purchase of crude oil at a fixed price for a five-year term from country X, "notwithstanding the acute political tensions in the region." Two years later, war erupts in neighboring countries, causing a world energy crisis and oil prices rise drastically. The seller cannot invoke the doctrine of hardship because "a rise in the price of crude oil was not unforeseeable." The second illustration involves a contract for sale where the price is expressed in the currency of country X. This currency was depreciating slowly prior to contracting. One month later the currency depreciated by 80% in the aftermath of a political crisis. If other circumstances do not dictate a contrary result, this constitutes legally relevant hardship.

"The events are beyond the control of the disadvantaged party..."

The Principles give no illustration of this subdivision. I will construct a hypothetical. A middleman contracts to deliver goods in the future that he does not have and has not contracted with a supplier for the acquisition of them. He could immediately contract for the goods from a manufacturer at a price that would make the resale profitable. Instead, speculating that the manufacturer will lower its price, the middleman takes no action to secure the goods. Because of changing market conditions, the manufacturer raises its prices dramatically. The middleman can only fulfill its contract at a considerable loss. Hardship cannot be invoked, because the reseller could have been avoided the loss by promptly entering into a contract with the manufacturer.

"The risk of the events was not assumed by the disadvantaged party."

The contract may expressly allocate the risk of supervening hardship, in which case the contract itself supersedes the rules of hardship in the Principles. However, it is clear from the nature of the hardship doctrine, that, unlike American law, the mere fact that the contract contains a fixed price does not allocate that risk. The allocation must be express, or be inherent in the nature of the contract. Thus, if the contract is aleatory, such as a contract of insurance, the obligor cannot complain that the risk has occurred, even thought the occurrence far exceeded what had been foreseen. Thus, if an insurer writes a policy covering the risks of war and civil insurrection, it must honor the policy even if war and civil insurrection breaks out in three countries in the same region.

The Principles allow the parties broad autonomy to determine the terms of their relationship. The grounds for invoking hardship may be broadened or reined in by the terms of the contract. Indeed, as the chairman of the working group that drafted the Principles has noted, "parties are expected to specify in more detail... the contingencies which justify invoking hardship and *force majeure*, not the least because the consequences deriving from them are fundamentally different."

E. *The Effects of Hardship*

If performance has become excessively onerous, the party so burdened is entitled to request negotiations to adapt the contract to the changed circumstances. The request should be made without "undue delay," but a delayed request is not automatically excluded. Again, the Principles stress communication; therefore, it is important that the request state the grounds for the request, unless those grounds are obvious. If the hardship claim is justified, the other party is obligated to negotiate in good faith to adapt the contract to alleviate the burden. "[A] party who negotiates or breaks off negotiations in bad faith is liable for the losses caused to the other party." In the event the parties do not reach agreement, either party may apply to the court.

An important question is whether the party who claims hardship may suspend performance until the contract is modified by agreement or by the court. The black letter test states that "[t]he request for renegotiation does not in itself entitle the disadvantaged party to withhold performance." The commentary is consistent with the text in stating that suspension of performance is permissible "only in extraordinary circumstances." However, the illustration consists of an ordinary kind of hardship in a construction case. New safety regulations require the installation of additional equipment. The illustration indicates that the contractor may "withhold the delivery of the additional apparatus, for so long as the corresponding price adaptation is not agreed." Assuming, absent the hardship defense, the contractor is obligated to install the apparatus, the circumstances do not seem very "extraordinary."

If the court finds that legally redressable hardship exists, it can terminate the contract, or revise it to restore the equilibrium of the contract. The commentary indicates that the court has great flexibility in its power to terminate or revise. The termination may be on such terms as the court deems just. It should be noted that in many cases, the reliance interest of the party not burdened by hardship ought to be redressed. Revision need not always be a price adjustment. An illustration suggests that the place of delivery could be changed. Of course, there is a strong possibility that a court will refuse to revise the contract by a declaration that the contract be performed as originally agreed.

Société Franco Tunisienne D'Armement v. Sidermar
[1961] 2 QB 278, [1960] 2 ALL E.R. 529,
[1960] 3 W.L.R. 701, [1960] 1 Lloyd's Rep. 594

. . . .

Denning, L.J. . . . .

It was suggested that this was a case of frustration. I do not regard it as a case of frustration, but it is, I think, analogous to it. It is a case where, to use LORD

SIMON'S words in the *British Movietonews* case, [1951] 2 All E.R. at p. 625; [1952] A.C. at p. 185, "a fundamentally different situation has now unexpectedly emerged." The judge agreed that a fundamentally different situation had emerged, but said that it had not "unexpectedly" emerged. He though that the parties could and should have contemplated that it might have emerged. Even so, I think it was unexpected. The plain fact is that the parties did not contemplate it. They did not expect it. They proceeded on a fundamental assumption which has turned out to be wrong.

That passage is of some interest as possibly drawing a distinction between that which is expected, that is to say, regarded by the parties as something which probably will happen, as contrasted with a mere possibility, regarded by the parties as something which perhaps might happen.

Then there is *Blane Steamships, Ltd. v. Minister of Transport*, [1951] 2 K.B. 965. It is sufficient for present purposes to say that that was a case of frustration by constructive total loss, and the possibility of constructive total loss must have been in the minds of the parties because they inserted in the contract an express provision relating to it.

Certain authorities were cited on the other side. There was *Chandler Bros., Ltd. v. Boswell*, [1936] 3 All E.R. 179. That, if I may summarise it shortly, was a case in which the defendant was the main contractor, and he contracted to divert a road for a county council, and, as incidental to that purpose, to make a tunnel. The work of excavating for the tunnel was sub-contracted to a firm called Chandler Bros. The head contract contained a provision that the engineers of the county council, if they were dissatisfied with the sub-contractor, might require the head contractors to remove him. When the sub-contract was drawn up by the parties it was drawn up with close regard to the provisions of the head contract. It was obvious that those who drew up the sub-contract had the head contract before them at the time. The sub-contract did not contain any provision to the effect that the engineers might require the removal of the sub-contractor. It was suggested that some such provision should be implied, but the court held that it could not be implied because the parties must have had fully in mind that possibility, and indeed they had drawn up the sub-contract with express relation to the head contract. It is in the light of those facts that one has to read what is said in that case by GREENE, L.J., [1936] 3 All E.R. at p. 187, and in my view what he said there was directed to the particular facts of that particular case and does not throw any light on the present question.

Secondly, there was the passage from *British Movietonews, Ltd. v. London & District Cinemas, Ltd.*, [1951] 2 All E.R. at p. 625; [1952] A.C. at p. 185, which has already appeared in an extract which I have read.

Then LORD RADCLIFFE said in *Davis Contractors, Ltd. v. Fareham U.D.C.*, [1956] 2 All E.R. at p. 161; [1956] A.C. at p. 731, (which I have already cited):

"Two things seem to me to prevent the application of the principle of frustration to this case. One is that the cause of the delay was not any new state of things which the parties could not reasonably be thought to have foreseen. On the contrary, the possibility of enough labour and materials not being available was before their eyes and could have been the subject of special contractual stipulation. It was not made so." There is that passage, and then there are a number of passages in a number of speeches in which the frustrating event is described as something "unexpected" or "not contemplated" or "not anticipated," and so on.

In my view, the explanation of those descriptions being applied to the frustrating events is partly that it happened to be an actual description in a particular case, and partly also this. The possibility, appreciated by both parties at the time of making their contract, that a certain event may occur, is one of the surrounding circumstances to be taken into account in construing the contract, and will, of course, have greater or less weight according to the degree of probability or improbability and all the facts of the case.

Now I come to the construction of the charterparty. First it has to be noticed that cl. 2 of the charterparty contains on the face of it an unqualified obligation that the vessel, having loaded at Masulipatan, is to proceed with all convenient speed to Genoa. There is no definition of the route. The parties could have said "shall proceed by way of the Suez Canal," but they did not do so. So that wording of cl. 2 is manifestly a point in favour of the charterers in this case. There is, however, the last sentence of cl. 37: "Captain also to telegraph to 'Maritsider Genoa' on passing Suez Canal." I fully accept the argument of counsel for the charterers that, for ordinary purposes, that is an unimportant provision. He compared it — I think rightly — with the provisions of cl. 19, which show that there was a similar provision for the early stage of the contract under which the vessel, on leaving the last port of discharge but before reaching Masulipatan was to wire the shippers, and, if that obligation was not performed, the penalty was that the shippers were to be allowed one extra day for loading. In my view, similarly if the captain failed to telegraph to "Maritsider Genoa" on passing the Suez Canal that would not be a fundamental breach of the contract, but would probably be an unimportant breach. The only resulting penalty on the shipowner for failure to comply with that obligation would be a liability to compensate the charterers for such damage, if any, as the breach might cause them. So it is clear enough that, for ordinary purposes, it is an unimportant provision. But, for the present purposes, it may be extremely important, because it says that the captain is "to telegraph...on passing the Suez Canal." It does not say "if the vessel passes the Suez Canal." It assumes, at any rate, that the vessel will pass the Suez Canal. That is an assumption in the contract, and, in my view, it probably goes further. There is an obligation to pass the Suez Canal. If the captain has to telegraph to "Maritsider Genoa" "on passing the Suez Canal," he must go to the Suez Canal in order to be able to do so. So, in my view, there is actually an obligation to pass the Suez Canal.

That is the main point, but there are also certain subordinate matters bearing on construction. There is the appreciated possibility, as I may now call it (because I have fully dealt with it already), and that is a point in favour of the charterers' contentions. But it is not so strong as an expectation. Then secondly — in my view, not unimportant — there is the simple geography of the matter. The route by way of the Suez Canal is a fairly direct route. It goes almost due West after passing round the southern tip of India, and then through the Red Sea and the Suez Canal, and through the Eastern and Central Mediterranean, and, I suppose, through the Straits of Messina, then up in a more or less northerly direction to Genoa. But the route via the Cape is a highly circuitous route, and, although that is obvious on a first glance at the map, it is to my mind in every sense worth emphasising. The vessel, having rounded the southern tip of India, has to pass the Equator and go far down to the South to go round the Cape of Good Hope, then into the Southern Atlantic and northwards past the Equator again into the Northern Atlantic. Then it has to take what may be called a sharp right turn through the Straits of Gibraltar into the Western Mediterranean and approach its destination from the West, having started from a point far to the East. It is a highly circuitous route. It is a route which no sensible person would take for the purpose unless either the Suez Canal were closed or the Suez Canal dues were utterly and commercially exorbitant. But otherwise it is an unnatural route if it is possible to go through the Suez Canal.

Also there are the matters with which the learned arbitrator dealt in the Special Case. There was the extra expense of going via the Cape. There was the extra journey in distance; the extra time; and the different climatic conditions, which would not affect a cargo of iron ore, but might have some effect on the vessel's cargo. There is the point about chartering arrangements, though I am not quite sure whether that has any material bearing on the matter. Perhaps it does have a bearing to this extent, that the shipowners would naturally fix a charter to begin after the conclusion of this journey as soon as possible. That they would be able to do if the journey was to go through the Suez Canal but not otherwise. If the journey was to go through the Suez Canal, or, alternatively, via the Cape of Good Hope, they would not be able to do so. On the other hand, it is pointed out, quite rightly, that what would make any such charter impossible of performance was simply the happening of the frustrating event. But, on the whole, I am not clear that this point about fixing the subsequent charter has really very much bearing. Similarly, on the facts of this case, the point about the International Load Line Convention does not have much bearing, because, by whichever route the vessel went, she would be overloaded in relation to the winter load line by the time she reached Genoa.

Then there is further point which I think is worth mentioning, but which again should not be unduly stressed. There is the figure of the freight. The freight fixed by the charterparty was 134s. per long ton. A reasonable freight for the trip via the Cape of Good Hope was 195s. per long ton. There is no express finding in the Special Case that 134s. was an appropriate rate for the trip via the Suez Canal. Also there is no finding that the rate of 134s. per long ton included any additional element to compensate the shipowners for the possibility of having to go round the Cape of Good Hope. I am rather inclined to infer that the rate of 134s. per long ton was the appropriate rate for the Suez Canal voyage, but I cannot say that it is clear from the facts as stated.

Then finally there is the point about the conduct of the parties after the frustrating event occurred. On that counsel for the charterers, quite rightly, placed some reliance as an aid to the construction of the contract if there should be ambiguity. I think that really the principle appears in *Hirji Mulji v. Cheong Yue S.S. Co., Ltd.*, [1926] All E.R. Rep. at p. 58; 17 Asp. M.L.C. at pp. 12, 13, in the passage which begins by stating that "... whatever the consequences of the frustration may be upon the conduct of the parties, its legal effect does not depend on their intention, or their opinions or even knowledge, as to the event, which has brought this about, but on its occurrence in such circumstances as show it to be inconsistent with further prosecution of the adventure."

But the last sentence of the paragraph is:

"What the parties say and do is only evidence, and not necessarily weighty evidence, of the view to be taken of the event by informed and experienced minds." [1926] All E.R. Rep. at p. 58; 17 Asp. M.L.C. at pp. 12, 13. What happened in the event here was that the parties for some days went on acting as if the charter party was still in force. Then, on Nov. 20, 1956, the shipowners informed the charterers that they considered that the contract had been frustrated, and the reply of the charterers was that they did not agree with that view. In my view, the conduct of the parties is not a consideration of any great weight, but, of course, it should be taken into account.

It is, of course, by no means an easy question whether this contract was frustrated or not, but, in my view, having regard to the express provisions of the contract and the surrounding circumstances, the proper view is that it was a term of the contract (whether express or implied) that the vessel was to go by the Suez Canal route. That was the voyage which the shipowners undertook to perform. It is true to say that the voyage is not the whole of the performance which the shipowners had to give. They had to bring the vessel by what is called the preliminary voyage to Masulipatan, and there they would have to assist in the loading of the cargo on board. Again, at the vessel's destination at Genoa they would have to assist and play their due part in unloading. But, of course, the main part, or the principal part — one might say the essential part — of their performance was the voyage itself, and that was that they were required to go via the Suez Canal. That is my view as to the meaning of the contract, and one does not have to say whether it is an express or implied term. I think it is an implied term, but a term implied directly from an express term, although also one brings in all the surrounding circumstances.

Having decided that that is the true construction of the contract, and that, on the true construction of the contract, that is the voyage which the shipowners have undertaken to make — in the language of a building contract, that is the job which the shipowners have contracted to perform — one then has to compare that with the voyage which had to be made, or the job which had to be done, after the closing of the canal. For reasons which have already been given, in effect, I think that that voyage was a fundamentally different voyage. It may help to make a simple comparison with what might happen in the case of a land journey. Supposing a lorry owner had contracted to carry goods from London to York. The natural way, I suppose, of going from London to York would be via the Great North Road, the A1. If that were temporarily closed, it might be necessary to make a journey a little further to the West, through Leicester and Nottingham, or a little further to the East, through Cambridge and Lincoln. But it may well be said that that is the same journey with a minor variation of route; there would be no frustration. But supposing some disruptive or catastrophic event had happened which caused the whole of the roads of eastern and central England to be closed, and the motor lorry's journey had to be undertaken via Oxford, Gloucester, Chester, Liverpool, Manchester and Leeds. That would be a highly circuitous route, and it may well be that it was a fundamentally different journey. The owner of the lorry might well say *"Non haec in foedera veni"*! That is a simple comparison, and, in my opinion, it is of some assistance. At any rate, my view is this, that, manifestly, the route via the Cape of Good Hope is so circuitous, and so unnatural, and so different in a number of respects, from the route via the Suez Canal that it should be regarded as fundamentally different for the present purposes. There was, therefore, in my view, frustration of the contract, that is to say, the charterparty.

Reference was made to certain cases decided with regard to c.i.f. contracts. There was *Carapanayoti & Co., Ltd. v. E. T. Green Ltd.*, [1958] 3 All E.R. 115; [1959] 1 Q.B. 131; and the cases of *Tsakiroglou & Co., Ltd. v. Noblee & Thorl G.m.b.H.*, [1959] 1 All E.R. 45; affd. C.A., [1960] 2 All ER 160, and *Albert D. Gaon & Co. v. Société Interprofessionelle des Oleagineux Fluides Alimentaires*, [1959] 2 All E.R. 693; affd. C.A., [1960] 2 All ER 160. With regard to those cases, I think that I need only read what was said by SELLERS, L.J., in the two last mentioned cases. He said:

"The effect of the blockage of the Suez Canal on shipowners was obvious, for the relatively short route through the canal was denied them and for destinations such as we are considering in these cases a different and much more prolonged journey had to be substituted. But the question is what effect that had on the contract of sale between the parties here." [1960] 2 All ER 162. Then he went on to examine the facts of the particular case and to consider what difference it made to the sale of goods contract. One may say shortly that it is obvious that the position is very different in a sale of good contract. Although it was a c.i.f. contract, the seller would sell the goods provided for and the buyer would buy the goods provided for. The seller would put the goods on board the ship at the port as contemplated by the contract and the buyer would receive the goods at the port as contemplated by the contract. The only difference would be that the seller would pay more than he expected for the freight and the buyer would have to wait longer than he expected to receive the goods. It was considered by the Court of Appeal that these were not fundamental differences and there was no frustration in the case of a c.i.f. contract.

There was also cited an American case *The Glidden Company v. Hellenic Lines, Ltd.,* unreported. That was decided by the United States Court of Appeals, second circuit. In that case there were charterparties for the transportation of ilmenite from India to "a United States Atlantic port north of Cape Hatteras." The voyage was to be "via Suez Canal or Cape of Good Hope, or Panama Canal, at owners' option declarable not later than on signing of bills of lading, to one safe U.S. Atlantic port north of Cape Hatteras, port at charterer's option." There was a typewritten insertion that the charterer's option was "to be declared not later than on vessel's passing Gibraltar." It was argued that that provision which had been inserted in typescript necessarily implied that the vessel must pass Gibraltar, and therefore must go through the Suez Canal and could not go by any other route. But, on the construction of that particular contract, if that implication had been accepted no meaning whatever would have been given to the alternatives expressly provided for, namely, a voyage via the Cape of Good Hope or Panama Canal, and it was held that it could not be accepted that, on the true construction of that contract, the voyage must necessarily be performed through the Suez Canal. It was held therefore that, when the Suez Canal was closed, that did not cause a frustration. In my view, that is merely an example of a particular charterparty being construed according to its terms, and the terms were different from those in the present case.

The next question is whether the shipowners are estopped from alleging the frustration. The charterers' contentions on this point are set out in the Special Case (para. 7 (4)) as follows:

"If the charter party was frustrated the [shipowners] were estopped and precluded from so contending. In this regard it was urged as follows: (i) When the vessel's notice of readiness to load was given on Nov. 9, 1956, the [shipowners] knew that the Suez Canal was blocked and was likely to remain blocked for a substantial period of time and that the shortest practicable route was then via the Cape of Good Hope. (ii) The [shipowners] permitted the vessel to be loaded by the agents of the [charterers] and upon completion of loading the bill of lading was issued by the [shipowners]. The bill of lading incorporated the terms, conditions, liberties, and exception of the charterparty and contained a specific stipulation that it was subject to the lien clause (cl. 21) thereof. (iii) The [shipowners] permitted the vessel, loaded as aforesaid, to sail from Masulipatan on Nov. 19, 1956. (iv) On Nov. 20, 1956 the [shipowners] by their representative intimated for the first time to the representatives of the [charterers] at Genoa the [shipowners'] contention that the charterparty had come to an end because of the blocking of the Suez Canal. (v) At all material times from Nov. 9, 1956 the [shipowners] had known that the Suez Canal was blocked and was likely to remain blocked for a substantial period of time and delay until Nov. 20, 1956 in intimating their aforesaid contention was unexplained. (vi) In these circumstances (it was contended) the [shipowners] represented: (a) that the charterparty was not frustrated and that they were ready and willing to perform it notwithstanding the blocking of the Suez Canal, (b) that they were not going to insist on their strict legal rights by desisting from further performance." ... It is clear to my mind that there was no representation of fact such as could found any estoppel at common law. The subject of equitable estoppel is obscure and insufficiently developed. Reference was made to 15 HALSBURY'S LAWS OF ENGLAND (3rd Edn.), p. 175, and to ANSON'S LAW OF CONTRACT (21st Edn.), pp. 103, 104 and 105. Reference was made also to *Birmingham & District Land Co. v. London & North Western Ry.* C3, [1888], 40 Ch.D. at p. 286, *Hughes v. Metropolitan Ry. Co.,* (1877), 2 App. Cas. 439, *Tool Metal*

Manufacturing Co., Ltd. v. Tungsten Electric Co. Ltd., [1955] 2 All E.R. 657, and *Harnam Singh v. Jamal Pirbhai*, [1951] A.C. 688. In the last-mentioned case there may have been an estoppel at common law rather than an equitable estoppel, but it is not very clear which it was. However, I have looked at those cases. They are far removed from the present case. In my view, there has been no development of this comparatively new doctrine of equitable estoppel which is wide enough to cover the present case. Moreover, it may well be that the findings of the arbitrator are in themselves sufficient to exclude the application of any equitable estoppel in the present case.

Next it is said that there is to be implied from the conduct of the parties an agreement — not a fictitious agreement, but an actual agreement — that the cargo would be carried from Masulipatan to Genoa by way of the Cape of Good Hope at the same rate of freight as that provided in the charterparty or on the charterparty terms. The main contentions of the charterers on this point are set out in the Special Case as follows:

"If the charterparty was frustrated, an agreement was in all the circumstances (including those stated in sub-para. (13) of para. 5 hereof n(55) and in sub-paras. (i) to (v) of sub-para. (4) of this paragraph [para. 7]) n(56) to be inferred between the [shipowners] and the [charterers] that the cargo would be carried from Masulipatan to Genoa via the Cape of Good Hope at the same rate of freight as that provided in the charterparty or on the charterparty terms."

The arbitrator found that there were no representations as alleged, and he held that no agreement between the shipowners and the charterers was to be inferred that the cargo would be carried from Masulipatan to Genoa via the Cape of Good Hope at the same rate of freight as that provided by the charterparty or on the charterparty terms.

It is right to consider this question broadly. There might be a different formulation of the purport of the alleged agreement, for instance, to treat the charterparty as valid whether it was or not, or to proceed according to the terms of the charterparty notwithstanding that it might be invalid. Other formulations may be suggested. One must, however, look for an actual new agreement, with each party intending to make a new agreement, or, at any rate, so conducting himself that the other party could reasonably believe that he was intending to make a new agreement. Can it be said that the shipowners, by their captain giving the notice of readiness to receive cargo, offered a new agreement to the charterers' agents, and that the charterers' agents, by tendering the cargo, accepted the offer? Or can it be said that a new agreement was made by the charterers loading the cargo and by the captain receiving the cargo and starting the voyage with the cargo on board? The necessary acts and conduct are there if the intention to make a new agreement could be inferred. There are, however, no findings of fact to establish the supposed intention or apparent intention, and the findings in para. 12 are adverse to it, and the probabilities are against it. It is probable either that the parties thought that the original charterparty was still in force and were intending to perform it, or that they did not know what the legal position was and they were trying to preserve the status quo. Moreover, the captain would not, unless expressly authorised by the shipowners, have any authority to enter into a new agreement on their behalf: SCRUTTON ON CHARTERPARTIES (16th Edn.), p. 49; CARVER's CARRIAGE OF GOODS BY SEA (10th Edn.), p. 30. Want of authority was not pleaded as such, but, in view of the normal lack of such authority, it is improbable that the captain would intend, or be supposed by the other party to intend, to enter into such an agreement, that is to say, the want of authority does come in as a factor of improbability, but only in that way.

There is the further point also that, if such an agreement were made, it would be an agreement to perform the long voyage round the Cape of Good Hope at a freight rate of 134s. per long ton; whereas, as found in the Special Case, the reasonable freight rate for such a voyage would be 195s. per long ton, and it is improbable that the shipowners would make that unreasonable agreement.

With some reluctance, I feel compelled to reject the contention that there was such a new agreement to be inferred from the conduct of the parties. I say "with some reluctance" because the shipowners did, by giving the notice of readiness and receiving the cargo and starting the voyage, restrict the field of choice which might have been open to the charterers. When the shipowners on Nov. 20, 1956, asserted frustration, the charterers could have accepted that view and had the cargo unloaded at Colombo. But they did not have the chance of finding a different ship or a different outlet for the goods at Masulipatan. However, if there was hardship on the charterers, it arose really from the frustrating event and not from any fault of the shipowners, who might well have to consider the position and take legal advice — in this case in particular on English law — before asserting frustration. It is not possible to find here any estoppel or any new agreement that the ship should make the voyage round the Cape of Good Hope at the original charterparty freight rate.

Finally, there is the agreement alleged by the shipowners for the payment of hire at a reasonable rate. The shipowners' contentions on this point are set out in the Special Case as follows:

"By Nov. 9, 1956 or, at the latest, by Nov. 13, 1956 the charterparty was frustrated and in all the circumstances (including the fact that between Nov. 13 and Nov. 18, 1956 the [charterers] by their agents tendered the cargo to the vessel for loading and loaded the same) an agreement was to be inferred between the [shipowners] and the [charterers] that the [charterers] would pay a reasonable remuneration for the carriage of the cargo from Masulipatan to Genoa and that such reasonable remuneration was not less than 200s. per long ton delivered." The charterers contended that a reasonable remuneration for the carriage of the cargo was about 178s. per long ton delivered. The arbitrator found the reasonable remuneration to be 195s., and held that if the charterparty was frustrated and the shipowners were not estopped and precluded from so alleging, an agreement was to be inferred between the shipowners and the charterers that the charterers would pay a reasonable remuneration for the carriage of the cargo from Masulipatan to Genoa and that such reasonable remuneration was at the rate of 195s. per long ton delivered. In my view, there was no actual agreement to that effect. At the material time, which was from about Nov. 9, 1956 to about Nov. 20, 1956, neither party had any actual intention, or had evinced any apparent intention, to make a new agreement. The shipowners' true claim is on a quantum meruit, which can be referred to, though perhaps not very aptly, as a fictitious agreement.

On that there is *Craven-Ellis v. Canons, Ltd.*, [1936] 2 All E.R. 1066; [1936] 2 K.B. 403. That was in the Court of Appeal. The plaintiff was appointed managing director of a company by an agreement under the company's seal which also provided for his remuneration. By the articles of association of the company each director was required to obtain his qualification shares within two months after his appointment. Neither the plaintiff nor the other directors obtained their qualification shares within two months or at all. The plaintiff having done work for the company claimed to recover the remuneration provided for in the agreement, or, alternatively, on the basis of a *quantum meruit*. It was held that the fact that the plaintiff did the work under an agreement which was in fact void did not disentitle him from recovering on a *quantum meruit*. GREER, L.J., said

"...the obligation to pay reasonable remuneration for the work done when there is no binding contract between the parties is imposed by a rule of law, and not by an inference of fact arising from the acceptance of services..." {1936] 2 All E.R. at p. 1073; [1936] 2 K.B. at p. 412.

....

Then in *Hain S.S. Co., Ltd. v. Tate & Lyle, Ltd.*, [1936] 2 All E.R. 597; 19 Asp. M.L.C. 62, there are some obiter dicta on what the position would be after a deviation had deprived the shipowner of the right to rely on, at any rate, certain provisions of the charterparty. Three of their lordshps, LORD ATKIN, LORD WRIGHT and LORD MAUGHAM, were not prepared to accept the view taken in the Court of Appeal that, in such an event, the shipowner could not recover any freight for his services. A view was indicated, certainly by LORD WRIGHT, M.R. n(62), and I think also by LORD MAUGHAM n(63), to the effect that in such a case the shipowner would have a right to recover reasonable remuneration on a *quantum meruit.*

The present case is, to some extent, *a fortiori*. There was no breach of contract or other wrongful act by the shipowners. They carried the goods from Masulipatan to Genoa for the charterers' benefit and with the consent of the charterers. In my view, the law implies or imposes an obligation for the charterers to pay reasonable freight, and the amount of the reasonable freight is found in the Special Case.

I, therefore, decide the questions of law in favour of the shipowners. Accordingly the alternative award of the arbitrator applies, which is that: (i) The charterers do pay the shipowners the sum of L 14,959 2s. 9d. together with interest thereon at L 4 per cent. per annum from Feb. 16, 1957; (ii) the charterers do bear and pay the whole of the arbitrator's costs of the reference to him and the whole of the costs of the award; (iii) if the shipowners in the first instance paid the whole or any part of the arbitrator's costs of the reference and of the award, the charterers shall forthwith refund to the shipowners the sum so paid; (iv) the charterers do pay to the shipowners the whole of the shipowners' own costs of the reference to arbitration.

Disposition:

Judgment for the shipowners, the claimants.

Tsakiroglou & Co., Ltd. V.
Noblee & Thorl G.M.B.H., [1962] AC 93,
[1961] 2 All E.R. 179, [1961] 2 W.L.R. 633,
[1961] 1 Lloyd's Rep. 329, (100 LQR 629)

INTRODUCTION:

....

VISCOUNT SIMONDS:

My Lords, on Apr. 21, 1958, the Board of Appeal of the Incorporated Oil Seed Association made an award by which they upheld the award of an umpire in an arbitration between the appellants and the respondents, awarding the latter the sum of L 5,625 against the former as damages for breach of contract. On Case Stated, DIPLOCK, J., upheld the award. His decision was affirmed by the Court of Appeal. The matter now comes before this House. Not for the first time, I venture to point out that the two first stages in proceedings which will ultimately be resolved in the highest court could conveniently be omitted.

The contract, for breach of which damages were awarded to the respondents, was made on Oct. 4, 1956. It incorporated the terms of contract form No. 38 of the Incorporated Oil Seed Association and, by it, the appellants agreed to sell to the respondents three hundred tons of Sudanese groundnuts at L 50 per one thousand kilos including bags c.i.f. Hamburg, shipment during November/December, 1956. No goods were shipped by the appellants in fulfilment of this contract in the circumstances stated in the Special Case which I summarise. All groundnuts exported from the Sudan to Europe are shipped from Port Sudan, which is the only suitable port. At the date of the contract (Oct. 4, 1956), the usual and normal route for the shipment of Sudanese groundnuts from Port Sudan to Hamburg was via the Suez Canal. Both parties then contemplated that shipment would be made by that route. It would have been unusual and rare for any substantial parcel of Sudanese groundnuts from Port Sudan to Europe to be shipped via the Cape of Good Hope. Before the closure of the Suez Canal, the appellants acquired three hundred tons of Sudanese groundnuts in shell which were held to their order in warehouses at Port Sudan as from Nov. 1, 1956. They also, before the closure, booked space for three hundred tons of nuts in one or other of four vessels scheduled to call at Port Sudan between Nov. 10 and Dec. 26, 1956. The shipping company cancelled these bookings on Nov. 4, 1956. British and French armed forces began military operations against Egypt on Oct. 29, 1956. The Suez Canal was blocked on Nov. 2, and remained closed for effective purposes until at least Apr. 9, 1957. But the appellants could have transported the goods from Port Sudan to Hamburg via the Cape of Good Hope during November and December, 1956. The distance from Port Sudan to Hamburg via the Suez Canal is about 4,386, and via the Cape about 11,137, miles. The freight ruling at the time of the contract for the shipment of groundnuts from Port Sudan to Hamburg via the Canal was about L 7 10s. per ton. After the closure of the canal, the Port Sudan United Kingdom Conference imposed the following surcharges for goods supplied on vessels proceeding via the Cape, *viz.*, as from Nov. 10, 1956, twenty-five percent, and as from Dec. 13, 1956, one hundred per cent. The market price of Sudanese nuts in shell shipped from Port Sudan c.i.f. Hamburg was L 68 15s. per ton between Jan. 1 and 15, 1957. As has been already said, the appellants did not ship any nuts. They claimed that they were entitled to consider the contract as cancelled, and to this view they adhered. The contract provided, by cl. 6, that:

"In case of prohibition of import or export, blockade or war, epidemic or strike, and in all cases of *force majeure* preventing the shipment within the time fixed, or the delivery, the period allowed for shipment of delivery shall be extended by not exceeding two months. After that, if the case of *force majeure* be still operating, the contract shall be cancelled." The award was in these terms:

"So far as it is a question of fact we find and as far as it is a question of law we hold: (i) There were hostilities but not war in Egypt at the material time. (ii) Neither war nor *force majeure* prevented shipment of the contract goods during the contract period if the word 'shipment' means placing the goods on board a vessel destined for the port of Hamburg. (iii) If the word 'shipment' includes not only the placing of the contract goods on board a vessel but also their transportation to the contract destination then shipment via the Suez Canal was prevented during the contract period of shipment by reason of *force majeure* but shipment via the Cape was not so prevented. (iv) It was not an implied term of the contract that shipment or transportation should be made via the Suez Canal. (v) The contract was not frustrated by the closure of the Suez Canal. (vi) The performance of the contract by shipping the goods on a vessel routed via the Cape of Good Hope was not commercially or fundamentally different from its being performed by shipping the goods on a vessel routed via the Suez Canal."

The first three of these findings relate to the claim of the appellants that the exceptions clause (cl. 6 of the contract) absolved them from performance of the contract. I will deal with this at once and shortly. Similar words to those in cl. 6 fell to be construed in *Re Comptoir Commercial Anversois and Power, Son & Co.*, [1920] 1 K.B. 868. BAILHACHE, J., said:

"Now, if I give to the word 'shipment' the widest meaning of which it is capable, it cannot mean more than bringing the goods to the shipping port and then loading them on board a ship prepared to carry them to their contractual destinaton."

His judgment on this point was affirmed in the Court of Appeal,   [1920] 1 K.B. at p. 89. It has never been questioned, and I see no reason for questioning it. In *Fairclough Dodd & Jones, Ltd. v. J. H. Vantol, Ltd.*, [1956] 3 All E.R. 921, the decision turned on the very particular words of the contract and is not in conflict with the earlier case.

I come, then, to the main issue and, as usual, I find two questions interlocked: (i) What does the contract mean? In other words, is there an implied term that the goods shall be carried by a particular route? (ii) Is the contract frustrated?

It is convenient to examine the first question first, though the answer may be inconclusive. For it appears to me that it does not automatically follow that, because one term of a contract, *e.g.*, that the goods shall be carried by a particular route, becomes impossible of performance, the whole contract is thereby abrogated. Nor does it follow, because, as a matter of construction, a term cannot be implied, that the contract may not be frustrated by events. In the instant case, for example, the impossibility of the route via Suez, if that were assumed to be the implied contractual obligation, would not necessarily spell the frustration of the contract. It is put in the forefront of the appellants' case that the contract was a contract for the shipment of goods via Suez. This contention can only prevail if a term is implied, for the contract does not say so. To say that that is, nevertheless, its meaning is to say in other words that the term must be implied. For this I see no ground. It has been rejected by the learned trial judge and each of the members of the Court of Appeal, and in two other cases, *Carapanyoti & Co., Ltd. v. E. T. Green, Ltd.*, [1958] 3 All E.R. 115; [1959] 1 Q. B. 131, and *Albert D. Ganon & Co. v. Société Interprofessionelle des Oleagineux Fluides Alimentaires*, [1959] 2 All E.R. 693; {1960} 2 Q.B. 318, where the same question arose, it was rejected by MCNAIR, J., and ASHWORTH, J., respectively. A variant of this contention was that there should be read into the contract by implication the words "by the usual and customary route" and that, as the only usual and customary route at the date of the contract was via Suez, the contractual obligation was to carry the goods via Suez. Though this contention has been viewed somewhat differently, I see as little ground for the implication. In this, I agree with HARMAN, L.J., for it seems to me that there are precisely the same grounds for rejecting the one as the other. Both of them assume that sellers and buyers alike intended and would have agreed that, if the route via Suez became impossible, the goods should not be shipped at all. Insamuch as the buyers presumably wanted the goods and might well have re-sold them, the assumption appears wholly unjustified. Freight charges may go up or down. If the parties do not specifically protect themselves against change, the loss must lie where it falls.

For the general proposition that, in a c.i.f. contract, the obligation, in the absence of express terms, is to follow the usual or customary route, there is a significant absence of authority. Some reliance was placed on *Re L.Sutro & Co.* and *Heilbut, Synons & Co.*, [1917] 2 K.B. 348; 14 Asp. M.L.C. 34. But the facts and the question arising on them were widely different from those in the present case. The decision was that, since the contract clearly contemplated carriage by sea from the loading port to the ultimate port of discharge, it could not be performed by carriage partly by sea and partly by rail, though the arbitrators had found that that method of transport had become a usage in the trade. It is possible that, if the decision was reviewed in this House, it might not stand; it is unnecessary now to determine that question. For, as I have said, the decisive fact there was that the actual route was different in kind from the contractual route.

Apart from this authority, the appellants relied on a passage in KENNEDY ON C.I.F. CONTRACTS (2nd Edn.), p. 39: "In the absence of express terms in the contract the customary or usual route must be followed." I cannot accept this general proposition without some qualification. In particular, since it is in any case clear that it is not the date of the contract but the time of performance that determines what is customary, the proposition must be qualified by adding to it some such words as "unless at the time of performance there is no customary or usual route." If these words are implied, the question arises: "What then?" The answer must depend on the circumstances of each case. This leads me directly to s. 32 (2) of the Sale of Goods Act, 1893, which provides that:

> "Unless otherwise authorized by the buyer, the seller must make such contract with the carrier on behalf of the buyer as may be reasonable having regard to the nature of the goods and the other circumstances of the case..."

If there is no customary route, that route must be chosen which is reasonable. If there is only one route, that must be taken if it is practicable: *see Evans, Sons & Co. v. Cunard Steamship Co., Ltd.* n(8) per WILLS, J., [1902], 18 T.L.R. at p. 375.

I turn now to what was the main argument for the appellants, that the contract was frustrated by the closure of the canal from Nov. 2, 1956, till April, 1957. Were it not for the decision of MCNAIR, J., in *Green's Case*, [1958] 3 All E.R. 115; [1959] 1 Q.B. 131, I should not have thought this contention arguable, and I must say with the greatest respect to that learned judge that I cannot think he has given full weight to the decisions old and new of this House on the doctrine of frustration. He correctly held on the authority of *Reardon Smith Lines, Ltd. v. Black Sea & Baltic General Insurance Co., Ltd., The Indian City*, [1939] 3 All E.R. 444; [1939] A.C. 562 , that

> "Where a contract expressly, or by necessary implication, provides that performance, or a particular part of the performance, is to be carried out in a customary manner, the performance must be carried out in a manner which is customary at the time when the performance is called for."

But he concluded that the continued availability of the Suez route was a fundamental assumption at the time when the contract was made, and that to impose on the sellers the obligation to ship by an emergency route via the Cape would be to impose on them a fundamentally different obligation, which neither party could, at the time when the contract was made, have dreamed that the sellers would be required to perform. Your Lordships will observe how similar this line of argument is to that which supports the implication of a term that the route should be via Suez and no other. I can see no justification for it. We are concerned with a c.i.f. contract for the sale of goods, not a contract of affreightment, though part of the sellers' obligation will be to procure a contract of affreightment. There is no evidence that the buyer attached any importance to the route. He was content that the nuts should be shipped at any date in November or December. There was no evidence and, I suppose, could not be that the nuts would deteriorate as the result of a longer voyage and a double crossing of the Equator, nor any evidence that the market was seasonable. In a word, there was no evidence that the buyer cared by what route or, within reasonable limits, when, the nuts arrived. What, then, of the seller? I recall the well-known passage in the speech of LORD ATKINSON in *Johnson v. Taylor Bros. & Co., Ltd.,* [1920] A.C. at pp. 155, 156, where he states the obligations of the vendor of goods under a c.i.f. contract, and asks which of these obligations is (to use MCNAIR, J.'s word) "fundamentally" altered by a change of route. Clearly the contract of affreightment will be different and so may be the terms of insurance. In both these respects, the seller may be put to greater cost; his profit may be reduced or even disappear. But it hardly needs reasserting that an increase of expense is not a ground of frustration: *see Larrinaga & Co. v. Societe Franco-Americaine des Phosphates de Medulla,* [1922], 28 Com. Cas. 1; affd. H.L., (1923), 29 Com. Cas. 1; 16 Asp. M.L.C. 133. "Fundamentally" altered. That is the word used by VISCOUNT SIMON in *British Movietonews, Ltd. v. London and District Cinemas, Ltd.,* [1951] 2 All E.R. at p. 625; [1952] A.C. at p. 185, and by my noble and learned friend, LORD REID, in *Davis Contractors, Ltd. v. Fareham U.D.C.,* [1956] 2 All E.R. at p. 155; [1956] A.C. at p. 723. In the latter case, my noble and learned friend, LORD RADCLIFFE, used the expression "radically different," and I think that the two expressions mean the same thing, as, perhaps, do other adverbs which have been used in this context. Whatever expression is used, I venture to say what I have said myself before and others more authoritatively have said before me, that the doctrine of frustration must be applied within very narrow limits. In my opinion, this case falls far short of satisfying the necessary conditions. Reluctant as I am to differ from a judge so experienced in commercial law as MCNAIR, J., I am glad to find that my view is shared by ASHWORTH, J., and all the members of the Court of Appeal.

On this part of the case, I have not thought it necessary to deal with the decision of PEARSON, J., in *Société Franco Tunisienne d'Armement v. Sidermar S.P.A.,* [1960] 2 All E.R. 529. There the question was whether a charterparty was frustrated by the blocking of the Suez Canal. The learned judge held that it was, but was at pains to point out that the position was very different in a contract for the sale of goods. On that point, I agree with him and need not discuss the matter further.

I come finally to a question which has given me some trouble. I refer to the sixth finding in the Special Case which I have already fully set out. It will be remembered that the vital words were "not commercially or fundamentally different." DIPLOCK, J., regarding this as a finding of fact, thought that the case was thereby concluded. I cannot regard this as a correct decision. It is a question of law whether a contract has been frustrated, and it is commonly said that frustration occurs when conditions arise which are fundamentally different from those contemplated by the parties. But it does not follow from the use by the arbitrator of the word "fundamentally" in describing the difference between the actual and the contemplated conditions that the court is precluded from forming its own judgment whether or not a contract has been frustrated. It is of great value to the court to know that lay arbitrators with special knowledge do or do not regard the new circumstances as so different from those contemplated that they think "fundamental" an appropriate word to use. But the value is evidential only. It has not the sanctity of a finding of fact. I do not say that an arbitrator should be debarred from the use of the word "fundamental" or "radical" or any other word which he thinks apt to give emphasis to his view. But, if he does so, he must not be taken indirectly to determine the question of law which the court must decide.

In my opinion, the appeal should be dismissed with costs.

LORD REID:

. . . .

The appellants' first argument was that it was an implied term of the contract that shipment should be via Suez. It is found in the Case that both parties contemplated that shipment would be by that route, but I find nothing in the contract or in the Case to indicate that they intended to make this a term of the contract, or that any such term should be implied; they left the matter to the ordinary rules of law. Admittedly, the ordinary rule is that a shipper must ship by the usual and customary route, or, if there is no such route, then by a practicable and reasonable route. But the appellants' next contention was that this means the usual and customary route at the date of the contract, while the respondents maintain that the rule refers to the time of performance. There appears to be no decided case about this and, perhaps, that is not surprising because the point cannot often arise. Apart from the opinion of MCNAIR, J., in *Carapanayoti & Co., Ltd. v. E. T. Green, Ltd.*, [1958] 3 All E.R. 115; [1959] 1 Q.B. 131, and of the Court of Appeal in this case which are against the appellants, there are a few expressions of opinion on this matter, but I shall not examine them as the precise point may not have been in the minds of their authors, and I am doing no injustice to the appellants because, on the whole, these opinions favour the respondents' contention. Regarding the question as an open one, I would ask which is the more reasonable interpretation of the rule.

If the appellants are right, the question whether the contract is ended does not depend on the extent to which the parties or their rights and obligations are affected by the substitution of the new route for the old. If the new route made necessary by the closing of the old is substantially different, the contract would be at an end, however slight the effect of the change might be on the parties. That appears to me to be quite unreasonable; in effect, it means writing the old route into the contract, although the parties have chosen not to say anything about the matter. On the other hand, if the rule is to ascertain the route at the time of performance, then the question whether the seller is still bound to ship the goods by the new route does depend on the circumstances as they affect him and the buyer; whether or not they are such as to infer frustration of the contract. That appears to me much more just and reasonable and, in my opinion, that should be held to be the proper interpretation of the rule.

I turn, then, to consider the position after the canal was closed, and to compare the rights and obligations of the parties thereafter, if the contract still bound them, with what their rights and obligations would have been if the canal had remained open. As regards the sellers, the appellants, the only difference to which I find reference in the Case — and, indeed, the only difference suggested in argument — was that they would have had to pay L 15 per ton freight instead of L 7 10s. They had no concern with the nature of the voyage. In other circumstances, they might have affected the buyers, and it is necessary to consider the position of both parties because frustration operates without being invoked by either party and, if the market price of groundnuts had fallen instead of rising, it might have been the buyers who alleged frustration. There might be cases where damage to the goods was a likely result of the longer voyage which twice crossed the Equator, or, perhaps, the buyer could be prejudiced by the fact that the normal duration of the voyage via Suez was about three weeks, whereas the normal duration via the Cape was about seven weeks. But there is no suggestion in the Case that the longer voyage could damage the groundnuts or that the delay could have caused loss to these buyers of which they could complain. Counsel for the appellants rightly did not argue that this increase in the freight payable by the appellants was sufficient to frustrate the contract, and I need not, therefore, consider what the result might be if the increase had reached an astronomical figure. The route by the Cape was certainly practicable. There could be, on the findings in the Case, no objection to it by the buyers, and the only objection to it from the point of view of the sellers was that it cost them more. And it was not excluded by the contract. Where, then, is there any basis for frustration? It appears to me that the only possible way of reaching a conclusion that this contract was frustrated would be to concentrate on the altered nature of the voyage. I have no means of judging whether, looking at the matter from the point of view of a ship whose route from Port Sudan was altered from via Suez to via the Cape, the difference would be so radical as to involve frustration, and I express no opinion about that. As I understood the argument, it was based on the assumption that the voyage was the manner of performing the sellers' obligations and that, therefore, its nature was material. I do not think so. What the sellers had to do was simply to find a ship proceeding by what was a practicable and now a reasonable route — if, perhaps, not yet a usual route — to pay the freight and obtain a proper bill of lading, and to furnish the necessary documents to the buyer. That was their manner of performing their obligations, and, for the reasons which I have given, I think that such changes in these matters as were made necessary fell far short of justifying a finding of frustration. I agree that the appellants cannot rely on the provisions of cl. 6 of the contract regarding prevention of shipment. I, therefore, agree that this appeal should be dismissed.

I should, perhaps, add a few words about the finding in the Case that performance by shipping via the Cape of Good Hope was "not commercially or fundamentally different "from performance by shipping via Suez. This cannot be intended to mean that it was neither different commercially nor different fundamentally. Plainly, there is a commercial difference between paying L 7 10s. and paying L 15 per ton freight. It must mean that performance was not fundamentally different in a commercial sense. But all commercial contracts ought to be interpreted in light of commercial considerations. I cannot imagine a commercial case where it would be proper to hold that performance is fundamentally different in a legal, though not in a commercial, sense. Whichever way one takes it, the ultimate question is whether the new method of performance is fundamentally different, and that is a question of law. The commercial importance of the various differences involved in the change of route — delay, risk to the goods, cost, etc. — is fact on which specific findings by arbitrators are entirely appropriate. But the inference to be drawn on a consideration of all the relevant factors must, in my view, be a matter of law — was there or was there not frustration?

LORD RADCLIFFE:

My Lords, I think that the outcome of this appeal depends on a short point. The real issue, as I see it, is to determine how to define the obligation of the appellants, the vendors, under the sale contract of Oct. 4, 1956, so far as it related to shipment of the goods sold and the provision of shipping documents. Once it is settled what that definition should be, there is not much difficulty in seeing what are the legal consequences that should follow, having regard to the facts found for us by the Special Case.

This is a sale of goods on c.i.f. terms. Such a sale involves a variety of obligations, both those written out in the contract itself and those supplied by implication of law for the business efficacy of the transaction. The only sector of these obligations that is relevant for the purpose of this case is the vendor's duty "to procure a contract of affreightment, under which the goods will be delivered at the destination contemplated by the contract" (see Biddell Brothers v. E. Clemens Horst Co., [1911] 1 K.B. at p. 220, per HAMILTON, J.). Even within this sector, however, there are gaps which the law has to fill in; for instance, what form of contract of affreightment will meet the needs of the transaction, and what route or routes are permissible for the carrying vessel selected? In the present case, nothing turns on the form of the bill of lading, which is not in evidence; everything turns on the question of route. The written contract makes no condition about this, its only stipulation being that shipment is to be from a West African port, by which we are asked to assume that the parties in fact meant Port Sudan. So the voyage was to begin at Port Sudan and to end at Hamburg. The primary duty under this part of the contract was to despatch the groundnuts by sea from one port to the destination of the other. At the date when the contract was entered into, the usual and normal route for the shipment of Sudanese groundnuts from Port Sudan to Hamburg was via the Suez Canal. It would be unusual and rare for any substantial parcel of Sudanese groundnuts from Port Sudan to Europe to be shipped via the Cape at any time when the Suez Canal was open. The Suez Canal was blocked on Nov. 2, 1956, and remained blocked until April, 1957. Nevertheless, during the months of November/December, 1956, the period in which the vendors had to ship under the contract, it was feasible for them to transport the goods via the Cape of Good Hope. It would have involved a voyage of some 11,137 miles as against 4,386 miles by way of Suez, and it would have meant a rise in freight rate of twenty-five per cent (and, in the last two weeks of December, one hundred per cent) above that ruling when the sale contract was made. These differences did not, however, in the opinion of the Board of Appeal of the Incorporated Oil Seed Association who state the Case, render transport by the Cape route commercially or fundamentally different from transport by way of the Suez Canal.

Now, in these circumstances, were the appellants under obligation to procure a bill of lading for the transport of the goods by the Cape route, the Suez Canal not being available? That depends on how their obligation is defined. It is said on their behalf that the duty of shipment is a duty to ship by the "customary or usual route," a route which can be ascertained as that followed by settled and established practice (see KENNEDY ON C.I.F. CONTRACTS (2d. ed.), p. 39). Failing express provision on the point by the terms of the contract, that is, in my opinion, a correct general statement of what the law would imply; but I do not accept the further proposition which the appellants' argument requires, namely that, given the existence of such a route at the date of the contract, the whole of the vendor's obligation with regard to shipment is contained in this phrase, "the customary or usual route." Putting aside exceptional cases in which there never has become established any customary route at all from one port to the other, we have to consider the case in which, while there has been a customary route at or before the date of the sale, that route is not available at the time when the vendor is ready to ship. The appellants say that, since the whole obligation consists in shipping by the customary or usual route, the contract would, in that event, become unenforceable, either because its terms had become impossible of performance or because it was avoided by frustration. In this context, the two alternatives would amount to the same thing. I think, however, that the vendor's obligation has to be determined in the light of matters as they stand at the date of shipment, and it may be proper for him to take a course in these circumstances which it would not have been proper for him to take at the date of the contract.

In my opinion, there is no magic in the introduction of the formula "customary or usual route" to describe the term implied by law. It is only appropriate because it is in ordinary circumstances the test of what it is reasonable to impose on the vendor in order to round out the imperfect form of the contract into something which, as mercantile men, the parties may be presumed to have intended. The corpus of commercial law has been built up largely by this process of supplying from the common usage of the trade what is the unexpressed intention of the parties. It is necessary first to ascertain what is the commercial nature or purpose of the adventure that is the subject of the contract; that ascertained, it has next to be asked what, within this scope, are the essential terms which, so far as not expressed, must be implied in order to make the contract efficacious as a business instrument. The natural way to answer this question is to find out what is the usual thing in the same line of business. Various adjectives or phrases are employed to describe the point of reference. I can quote the following from judicial decisions: — recognised, current, customary, accustomed, usual, ordinary, proper, common, in accordance with custom or practice or usage, a matter of commercial notoriety; and, of course, reasonable. I put "reasonable" last, because I think that the other phrases are at bottom merely instances of what it is reasonable to imply having regard to the nature and purpose of the contract. The basic proposition is, therefore, that laid down by BRETT, M.R., in *Sanders v. Maclean*, [1883], 11 Q.B.D. at p. 337; 5 Asp. M.L.C. at p. 163: "The stipulations which are inferred in mercantile contracts are always that the party will do what is mercantilely reasonable." Applying that proposition to the present case, I do not think that it is enough for the appellants to point out that the usual and customary route for the transport of groundnuts from Port Sudan to Hamburg was via the Suez Canal and that, at the date of the sale contract, both parties contemplated that shipment would be by that route. This contract was a sale of goods which involved despatching the goods from Port Sudan to Hamburg; but, of course, the transport was not the whole but only one of the incidents of the contract, in which particular incident neither vendors nor buyers were directly implicated. There was nothing to prevent the vendors from despatching the goods as contracted, unless they were impliedly bound as a term of the contract to use no other route than that of the Suez Canal. I do not see why that term should be implied; and, if it is not implied, the true question seems to me to be, since shipment was due to be made by some route during November/December, whether it was a reasonable action for a mercantile man to perform his contract by putting the goods on board a ship going round the Cape of Good Hope and obtaining a bill of lading on this basis. A man may habitually leave his house by the front door to keep his appointments; but, if the front door is stuck, he would hardly be excused for not leaving by the back. The question, therefore, is what is the reasonable mercantile method of performing the contract at a time when the Suez Canal is closed, not at a time when it is open. To such a question the test of "the usual and customary route" is *ex phypothesi* inapplicable.

On the facts found by the Special Case, I think that the answer is inevitable. The voyage would be a much longer one in terms of miles; but length reflects itself in such matters as time of arrival, condition of goods, increase of freight rates. A change of route may, moreover, augment the sheer hazard of the transport. There is nothing in the circumstances of the commercial adventure represented by the appellants' contract which suggests that these changes would have been material. Time was plainly elastic. Not only did the vendors have the option of choosing any date within a two-month period for shipment, but also there was a wide margin within which there might be variations of the speed capacity of the carrying vessel or vessels selected. There was no stipulated date for arrival at Hamburg. Nothing appears to suggest that the Cape voyage would be prejudicial to the condition of the goods or would involve special packing or stowing, nor does there seem to have been any seasonal market to be considered. With all these facts before them, as well as the measure of freight surcharge that would fall to the vendors' account, the Board of Appeal made their finding that performance by shipping on the Cape route was not "commercially or fundamentally different" from shipping via the Suez Canal. We have no material which would make it possible for us to differ from that conclusion.

It has been a matter of debate whether this finding ought to be treated as a finding of fact, by which a court would be bound, or as a holding of law, which, as such, would be open to review. It was treated as the first by the learned trial judge; it was treated more as the second by the Court of Appeal whose view of it was, I think, that, while of the utmost relevance for the determination of the final issue of he case, it did not bind the court so as to dictate what it should decide. So far as the distinction can be made between law and fact, I agree with the Court of Appeal. I regard it as a mixed question of fact and law whether transport via the Cape of Good Hope was so materially different from transport via the Suez Canal that it was not within the range of the c.i.f. contract or, alternatively, was so radically different that it left that contract frustrated. The ultimate conclusion is a conclusion of law, but, in a case of this sort, that conclusion is almost completely determined by what is ascertained as to mercantile usage and the understanding of mercantile man.

I do not believe that in this, as in many other branches of commercial law, it is possible to analyse very precisely where law begins and fact ends. That is because in this field legal obligations and legal rights are largely founded on usage and practice, which, themselves, are established as matters of fact. Many things which are now regarded as settled principles of law originated in nothing more than common mercantile practice, and the existence and terms of this practice have been vouched sometimes by questions put to and answered by special juries, sometimes by the findings and views of commercial arbitrators and sometimes by the bare statements of the judges, founded on their experience at the Bar or on the Bench. It would be difficult, for instance, to separate the judgments on commercial law delivered by three such masters as LORD ESHER, SCRUTTON, L.J., and LORD SUMNER from their personal acquaintance with mercantile usages and their translation of the one into the terms of the other. I do not think, therefore, that it is right to be very analytical in distinguishing between questions of law and questions of fact in matters of this kind. Since LORD MANSFIELD'S day, commercial law has been ascertained by a co-operative exchange between judge and jury, and, now that arbitrators have taken the place of juries, I do not think that we can start all over again with an absolute distinction between the respective spheres of judge and arbitrator. Generally speaking, I do not think that a finding in the form which we have here can ever be conclusive on the legal issue. When all necessary facts have been found, it remains a question of law for the court what, on the true construction of the contract, are the obligations imposed or whether, having regard to the terms of the contract and the surrounding circumstances, any particular term is to be implied. But, when the implication of terms depends essentially on what is customary or usual or accepted practice, it is inevitable that the findings of fact, whatever they may be, go virtually the whole way towards determining the legal result.

The finding in this case is, perhaps, unusual in that it does not speak for any usage or practice of trade — *ex hypothesi*, there was no established usage once the Suez Canal was blocked — but rather for the view of mercantile men as to the significance of adopting the alternative route. It is a summary way of stating that a voyage by that route would not involve any elements of difference that would be regarded as material by persons familiar with the trade. It would be contrary to common sense that a court, which cannot uninstructed assess the commercial significance of, say, a surcharge of L 7 10s. per ton for freight in a c.i.f. contract of this kind, should not pay careful attention to such a view from such a source; just as it would be, I think, contrary to principle that a court should regard a view so expressed as finally conclusive of the legal issue. I must add that I do not think that such a finding is altogether satisfactory for the purposes of a Special Case. It is, in essence, a summary of the commercial significance of several separate aspects of the Cape route as contrasted with the Suez Canal route, and it is embarrassing for a court which has to answer the question raised by the Case to have before it only the summary and not the arbitrators' findings on the individual aspects which make up the conclusion. I can see that, if this form came into general use, a court might feel obliged to send back the Case containing it for further and more explicit findings. It would have been better if the Special Case had identified the several aspects of difference, length, time, cost, risk, etc., which, as it is, the court is left to infer, and had made with regard to them, both separately and together, the finding that was clearly intended that they were not significant from the mercantile point of view.

I agree with the opinion already expressed by my noble and learned friends who have preceded me that the exception clause, cl. 6 of the contract, does not apply. I would dismiss the appeal.

LORD HODSON:

My Lords, the appellants have put in the forefront of their argument that it is an implied term of every c.i.f. contract, including the contract under consideration, that the goods shall be carried by the (or if more than one a) customary route. In this connection, it is contended that the relevant moment of time for determining whether a route is customary is the time when the contract is concluded. The first part of the proposition has been accepted by DIPLOCK, J., and by the majority of the Court of Appeal, while the second part was rejected, it being held in both courts that the seller's obligation, under a contract such as this, is to ship by a route usual and customary at the time of performance. If the whole of the proposition were accepted, it would be equivalent in this contract to adding by implication the words "via Suez." For the reasons already given, such implication is unnecessary and should be rejected. HARMAN, L.J., in the Court of Appeal did not accept either limb of the proposition and did not see the necessity of implying any such words as "by the usual and customary route." He pointed out that the seller's duty was to ship the goods from Port Sudan to the named port by a ship leaving within the given period. [1960] 2 All E.R. at p. 170; [1960] 2 Q.B. at p. 369.

It is true that, as the case finds: "At the date when the contract was made both parties contemplated that shipment would be made by the Suez Canal." This, however, is a contract of sale not of carriage and, unless there is some special rule applicable to c.i.f. contracts, the duty of the seller is defined by s. 32 of the Sale of Goods Act, 1893, which provides —

"(1) Where, in pursuance of a contract of sale, the seller is authorised or required to send the goods to the buyer, delivery of the goods to a carrier, whether named by the buyer or not, for the purpose of transmission to the buyer is *prima facie* deemed to be a delivery of the goods to the buyer.

"(2) Unless otherwise authorised by the buyer, the seller must make such contract with the carrier on behalf of the buyer as may be reasonable having regard to the nature of the goods and the other circumstances of the case. If the seller omit to do so, and the goods are lost or damaged in course of transit, the buyer may decline to treat the delivery to the carrier as a delivery to himself, or may hold the seller responsible in damages."

Applying the provisions of that section to this case, the seller is bound to ship by a reasonable route having regard to the nature of the goods and the other circumstances of the case. It might be...that it was essential for the buyer to receive the goods within a given time, and that this could only be done by sending them via Suez; moreover, the goods might be of a nature which would not stand a route crossing the

Equator twice. Unless persuaded by authority that this line of reasoning is wrong, I find it convincing, for the Sale of Goods Act in effect codifies the relevant law.

The appellants rely on a passage to be found in *KENNEDY ON C.I.F. CONTRACTS* (2d. ed.), p. 39: "In the absence of express terms in the contract the customary or usual route must be followed." This passage is not supported by any authority save that it was, I think, assumed to be correct by SCRUTTON L.J., in *Re L. Sutro & Co. and Heilbut, Symons & Co.*, n(22) [1917] 2 K.B. 348; 14 Asp. M.L.C. 34. The actual decision in that case is not of assistance. The majority of the Court of Appeal held that, in a contract made in 1916 for the sale of rubber to be shipped from the East to New York, a tender of goods which had been transmitted by rail from the western sea board of the United States to New York was not a good tender and the buyers were not bound to accept the same. SCRUTTON, L.J., who dissented, was of opinion that the tender was good, and the route taken by the rubber was at the time a usual route and not excluded by the terms of the contract from the means of performance open to the vendor. He did, however, use these words:

"Where there is a contract to carry from A to B if the exact route or method of carriage is not specified in the contract, the carriage must be by one of the usual routes and methods of carriage, at the option of the carrier." [1917] 2 K.B. at p. 362; 14 Asp. M.L.C. at p. 38. This language is, I think, appropriate to a contract of affreightment, but it is true that that sentence was used in a case where a c.i.f. contract was under consideration and is for that reason relied on as an authoritative dictum contained as it is in the judgment of a master of the law whose words carry great weight not least in matters appertaining to commercial transactions. Notwithstanding the fact that the procuring of a contract of affreightment is part of the obligation of the seller under a c.i.f. contract, I am not persuaded that the proposition contended for by the appellants is sound, and I [believe] that it is not necessary to imply in this contract the words "by the usual and customary route." On any view it would seem that the passage in *KENNEDY ON C.I.F. CONTRACTS* requires some qualification for, if an event happened which prevented a particular route being used so that a slightly longer journey, perhaps outside permissible deviation, was necessary, then, other routes being available, the seller could surely not say he was free from his contract.

If I have stated the obligations of the sellers correctly, one then looks to see what the position was after the closure of the Suez Canal rendered shipment impossible by what would have been the normal route but for the closure. The contract was dated Oct. 4, 1956, and provided for the sale of three hundred tons of groundnuts at a price of L 50 per one thousand kilos c.i.f. Hamburg. Shipment November/December, 1956. On Nov. 2, 1956, the canal was blocked, and transportation by that route became impossible until April, 1957. Thus, virtually the whole of the shipment period remained open to the sellers. The freight ruling at the time of the contract for shipment of groundnuts for Port Sudan to Hamburg via the Suez Canal was L 7 10s. per ton. After the closure, the freight rates were increased by surcharges for goods proceeding by the Cape of Good Hope, *viz.*, as from Nov. 10, 1956, twenty-five per cent., and as from Dec. 13, 1956, one hundred per cent. The distance from Port Sudan to Hamburg via the Suez Canal is approximately 4,386 miles, and the distance from Port Sudan to Hamburg via the Cape of Good Hope is approximately 11,137 miles. On Jan. 15, 1957, the buyers bought in a quantity of groundnuts against the sellers at a price of L 68 10s. per one thousand kilos, the market price at this time being L 68 15s. per ton. Nothing was proved or found as to the nature of the goods or other circumstances which would render the route round the Cape unreasonable or impracticable, and this route was at all times available. Unless shipment by the Cape route was so onerous to the sellers as to make the performance of the contract fundamentally different in kind from any performance they had promised, the contract of Oct. 4, 1956, remained binding between the parties.

The material date is the date of performance when the seller chooses to ship the goods by a ship of his choice which may be fast or slow and, during the shipment period, it follows from the findings in the award that the Cape route was the only reasonable and practicable route. The freight was higher than that involved in the Suez route but, even when increased by one hundred percent, still remained only a proportion of the purchase price of the groundnuts, even though a significant proportion. Freight rates go up and down, and it is exceedingly difficult in a commercial contract to escape from its terms on the ground of frustration by the increased expense involved when the time of performance is reached as compared with that contemplated when the contract is made. Indeed, the appellants did not rest their frustration argument on the increase of freight, realising the difficulty of maintaining such a submission unless the increase were astronomical, but maintained that "the long haul round the Cape" was so fundamentally different from what had earlier been the usual route that the c.i.f. contract which included the obligation to procure a contract of affreightment had been frustrated by the closure of the canal. I see no ground as a matter of law on the true construction of this contract and the facts found in the Special Case on which frustration can stand. VISCOUNT MAUGHAM pointed out in *Joseph Constantine S.S. Line, Ltd. v. Imperial Smelting Corpn., Ltd.*, [1941] 2 All E.R. at p. 174; [1942] A.C. at p. 168.

"The doctrine of frustration is only a special case of the discharge of contract by an impossibility of performance arising after the contract was made."

On the construction of the contract which appears to me to be correct having regard in particular to the dates for shipment extending over the period November/December, 1956, there is no room, in my judgment, for any application of the doctrine to this case.

I would add that I cannot agree with DIPLOCK, J., that the question in this case is answered simply by reference to the finding of mixed law and fact numbered (vi) in the Special Case where the arbitrators found, in so far as it is a question of fact, and held, in so far as it is a question of law, that "The performance of the contract by shipping the goods on a vessel routed via the Cape of Good Hope was not commercially or fundamentally different from its being performed by shipping the goods on a vessel routed via the Suez Canal." This does not purport to be a finding of fact only although it is true, I think, that a finding of fact can properly be extracted from it, namely, that nothing had been proved such as, for example, some characteristic of the goods which would have rendered the performance commercially different in kind. This finding of fact is relevant, being a conclusion by commercial men who will know what difference is permissible although, ultimately, the question whether or not there has been frustration is a question of law. The ingredients of frustration are the facts, and those facts are for the arbitrators whether they are facts found directly or by inference. For example, in *Jackson v. Union Marine Insurance Co., Ltd.*, (1874), L.R. 10 C.P. at p. 126; 2 Asp. M.L.C. at pp. 436, 444, the question left by BRETT, J., to the jury was:

"...whether the time necessary for getting the ship off and repairing her so as to be a cargo-carrying ship, was so long as...to put an end in a commercial sense to the commercial speculation entered upon by the shipowner and the charterers"?

This question was characterised in the Court of Exchequer Chamber by BRAMWELL, B., as one which could not have been left in better terms although it might be paraphrased or amplified. I only comment that the actual question there related to delay which is one of the relevant factors in reaching a conclusion as to frustration. It does not seem to me to involve that a finding of fact made by arbitrators in such general language as that contained in cl. (vi) of this award is conclusive as a matter of law in determining whether or not the contract has been frustrated. If such were the case, the same set of facts could be decided by arbitrators either way in successive cases without the court having power to intervene.

There remains only for consideration the exception clause (No. 6). Since it was at all times possible for the appellants to effect shipment of the goods at Port Sudan on a vessel which would carry them to Hamburg, this clause does not avail the appellants: see the judgment of BALLHACHE, J., in *Re Comptoir Commercial Anversois and Power, Son & Co.*, [1920] 1 K.B. 868, confirmed in the Court of Appeal.

I would dismiss the appeal.

LORD GUEST:

....

I may first dispose of a preliminary argument by the appellants. Counsel for the appellants argued that the obligation of the sellers was to procure a contract of affreightment for the buyer whereby the goods will be conveyed to the contractual destination by the usual and customary route to be ascertained when the contract was made. Authority for this proposition was said to be found in KENNEDY ON C.I.F. CONTRACTS (2d. ed.), p. 39, where it is stated: "In the absence of express terms in the contract the customary or usual route must be followed." I will assume for the purposes of this argument that this is a correct statement of the law. Counsel's argument further proceeded that, if it was a breach of the contract for the sellers to provide a contract of affreightment other than by the usual and customary route, then the closure of that route must result in frustration of the contract. "How can a route," he said, "which was in breach of the contract one day, be obligatory next day?" This is not, to my mind, a true dilemma. The fallacy of this argument, in my opinion, is to confuse a breach of contract for which damages may be due with the circumstances under which frustration of the contract occurs. It by no means follows that, assuming the sellers would have been in breach of contract to ship via the Cape of Good Hope, the sellers would be entitled to avoid the contract because the Suez Canal route was not available. This would depend on whether shipment via the Cape was a radically different thing from shipment via the Suez Canal.

The juridical basis of the doctrine of frustration was recently examined by this House in *Davis Contractors, Ltd. v. Fareham U.D.C.*, [1956] 2 All E.R. 145; [1956] A.C. 696, and it is unnecessary to deal with the earlier cases on the subject. Whether frustration is regarded as depending on the addition to the contract of an implied term or as depending on the construction of the contract as it stands does not appear to me to matter in the circumstances of the present case. LORD REID in the *Davis* case, [1956] 2 All E.R. at p. 155; [1956] A.C. at p. 723, approached the matter on the basis that frustration only occurred where a fundamentally different situation had arisen which the contract had not contemplated.

....

The contract under consideration is a c.i.f. contract. Under such a contract, the seller has to procure a contract of affreightment under which the goods will be delivered at the destination contemplated (*Johnson v. Taylor Bros. & Co., Ltd.*, [1920] A.C. at p. 156 , per LORD ATKINSON). All that is contained in the contract is "Shipment from Port Sudan as per bill or bills of lading dated or to be dated November/December, 1956." No route is given or provided for. The sellers' obligation is governed by s. 32 (2) of the Sale of Goods Act, 1893, whereby they have to make such contract with the carrier on behalf of the buyer as may be reasonable having regard to the nature of the goods and the other circumstances of the case. They must, therefore, procure a reasonable contract of affreightment. The appellants contended that the sellers' obligation was to procure a contract of affreightment which he can tender to the buyer where under the goods would be conveyed by the usual and customary route to the contractual destination, and that the usual and customary route must be ascertained at the date when the contract was made. The argument further proceeded that, when this contract was entered into, the usual and customary route was via the Suez Canal and that, as that route had been closed by the time shipment fell to be made, the contract had been frustrated. The first and critical matter to ascertain is the date when the sellers' obligation in regard to the contract of affreightment is to be judged. Under the present contract, the sellers' obligation was shipment by a bill of lading to be dated November/December, 1956. They could, therefore, fulfil their contractual obligation by shipping at any date up to Dec. 31. By the date when performance was called for, the Suez Canal was closed and the only available route was by the Cape of Good Hope. In my opinion, the sellers' obligation is to be determined by the circumstances prevailing at the date when they choose to ship the goods, and not when the contract was made. No authority was quoted by the appellants for the contention that the *tempus inspiciendum* was the date of the contract. It is also, in my view, contrary to common sense and the terms of this contract. In regard to the question whether the usual or customary role must be followed, reliance was placed on an obiter dictum of CCRUTTON, L.J., in *Re L. Sutro & Co. and Heilbut, Symons & Co.*, [1917] 2 K.B. at p. 362:

"Where there is a contract to carry from A to B if the exact route or method of carriage is not specified in the contract, the carriage must be by one of the usual routes and methods of carriage, at the option of the carrier. If the other party wishes to exclude some usual route or method of carriage, he can do so by inserting such a term into the contract, but in the absence of such a term the option of selecting a usual method of performance is with the person who has to perform." The first part of the quotation is clearly dealing with a contract of affreightment where the carrier has the option of selecting a usual route. In the second part of the quotation, I am not clear whether the learned lord justice is dealing with a c.i.f. contract or a contract of affreightment. I am not at all satisfied that this dictum, together with the quotation from KENNEDY ON C.I.F. CONTRACTS (2d. ed.), p. 39, previously referred to, is justification for implying into every c.i.f. contract an obligation on the seller to obtain a contract of affreightment by the usual and customary route.... In my opinion, all that the seller has to do is to procure a reasonable contract of affreightment. In judging whether it was a reasonable contract of affreightment, the question whether the route given is the usual or customary route may be of importance for consideration with all other relevant circumstances. Whether or not such a term is implied in the present case, at the time when performance was called for there was no usual or customary route because the Suez Canal was closed, and the only practicable route was via the Cape of Good Hope. The sellers could have fulfilled their obligation by a bill of lading via the Cape. There was, accordingly, no frustration because there was no change of circumstances to justify the application of the doctrine.

The cases dealing with contracts of affreightment are, in my view, not helpful because in such contracts very different considerations apply from those in a contract of sale. In a c.i.f. contract, the seller does not have to deliver the goods. He only has to ship them at the port indicated with a contract of affreightment to the port of destination. An example of the frustration of a contract of affreightment is *Société Franco Tunisienne d'Armement v. Sidermar S.P.A.*, [1960] 2 All E.R. 529, where PEARSON, J., held that a charterparty was frustrated by the blocking of the Suez

Canal on the ground that it was a term of the contract (express or implied) that the vessel was to go by the Suez Canal, and he was able to hold that the route via the Cape was so different that it was a fundamentally different voyage. There are no circumstances in the present case to justify the implication of a term that the route should be via the Suez Canal. The only case in which a c.i.f. contract has been held to be frustrated by closure of the Suez Canal is *Carapanayoti & Co., Ltd. v. E. T. Green, Ltd.*, [1958] 3 All E.R. 115; [1959] 1 Q.B. 131, decided by MCNAIR, J. The circumstances were almost precisely similar to the present. The learned judge held that the nature and extent of the seller's obligation in relation to the route was to be ascertained at the time of performance. He then proceeded, however, to find that the contract was frustrated, because to impose on the sellers an obligation to ship via the Cape was to impose on them a fundamentally different obligation from that which they undertook when the contract was made. The learned judge, I think, fell into the error which he had previously corrected in the seller's argument by treating the date of the contract as the date when the seller's obligation had to be ascertained. If the critical date is the time when performance is called for, there cannot be frustration.

It remains to consider the ground on which DIPLOCK, J., held that the appellants failed. He considered that what had been described as the "special finding" of the Board of Appeal — "(vi) The performance of the contract by shipping the goods on a vessel routed via the Cape of Good Hope was not commercially or fundamentally different from its being performed by shipping the goods on a vessel routed via the Suez Canal," was a conclusion of fact with which he could not interfere and that he was, accordingly, bound by that finding to hold that there was no frustration. In my opinion, the learned judge misinterpreted the finding. These findings are prefaced by the statement: "So far as it is a question of fact we find and as far as it is a question of law we hold: — "Finding (vi), in my view, is clearly a finding in law and, if I had thought that there were no facts to justify this finding, I should, for my part, not have hesitated to disregard it. But as a finding of fact it is, as SELLERS, L.J., said, [1960] 2 All E.R. at p. 166; [1960] 2 Q.B. at p. 364, of the utmost relevance in a case of frustration, although it is not, in my opinion, conclusive.

The appellants' final argument was based on cl. 6 of the contract which is in the following terms:

> "In case of prohibition of import or export, blockade or war, epidemic or strike, and in all cases of *force majeure* preventing the shipment within the time fixed, or the delivery, the period allowed for shipment or delivery shall be extended by not exceeding two months. After that, if the case of *force majeure* be still operating, the contract shall be cancelled."

It was contended that shipment was prevented by the closure of the Suez Canal and that, as the cause operated beyond two months, the contract was cancelled. In my opinion, "shipment" in the context means bringing the goods to the port of shipment and "prevention" means either physical or legal prevention (*Re Comptoir Commercial Anversois and Power, Son & Co.*, [1920] 1 K.B. 868). In no circumstances can it be said that shipment was prevented by the closure of the Suez Canal.

I would dismiss the appeal.

DISPOSITION:

Appeal dismissed.

Ocean Tramp Tankers Corporation V.
V/O Sovfracht, [1964] 2 QB 226,

[1964] 1 All E.R. 161, [1964] 2 W.L.R. 114, [1963] 2 Lloyd's Rep. 381

LORD DENNING, M.R.:

On July 26, 1956, the Government of Egypt nationalised the Suez Canal. Soon afterwards the United Kingdom and France began to build up military forces in Cyprus. It was obvious to all mercantile men that English and French forces might be sent to seize the canal, and that this might lead to it becoming impassable to traffic. It was in this atmosphere that negotiations took place for the chartering of the vessel Eugenia. She flew the Liberian flag. The proposal was to charter her to a Russian State Trading Corporation, called *V/O Sovfracht*. The Russians wanted her to carry iron and steel from the Black Sea to India. The negotiations took place in London between the agents of the parties from Aug. 29 to Sept. 9, 1956. The agents of both sides realised that there was a risk that the Suez Canal might be closed, and each agent suggested terms to meet the possibility. But they came to no agreement. And, in the end, they concluded the bargain on the terms of the Baltime Charter without any express clause to deal with the matter. That meant that, if the canal were to be closed, they would "leave it to the lawyers to sort out." The charterparty was concluded on Sept. 9, 1956, but was dated Sept, 8, 1956. The vessel was then at Genoa. By the charterparty, she was let to the charterers for a "trip out to India via Black Sea." It was a time-charter in this sense, that the charterers had to pay hire for the vessel at a fixed rate per month from the time of the vessel's delivery until her re-delivery. The charterers had, however, no wide limits at their disposal. They could not direct her anywhere they wished, but only within the following limits "Genoa via Black Sea thence to India." The charter included the printed war clause without modification. It was in these terms:

> "21 (A) The vessel unless the consent of the owners be first obtained not to be ordered nor continue to any place or on any voyage nor be used on any service which will bring her within a zone which is dangerous as the result of any actual or threatened act of war, war, hostilities, warlike operations... (B) Should the vessel approach or be brought or ordered within such zone... (i) the owners to be entitled from time to time to insure their interests in the vessel... on such terms as they shall think fit, the charterers to make a refund to the owners of the premium on demand; and (ii)... hire to be paid for all time lost...."

The Eugenia was delivered at Genoa on Sept. 20, 1956. The charterers ordered her to proceed first to Novorossik and then to Odessa (both on the Black Sea) to load. A few days later the charterers sub-chartered her to two other Russian State Trading Corporations who agreed to pay, by way of freight, whatever the charterers had to pay the owners, plus five per cent. The two sub-charterers loaded her with iron and steel goods (joists, girders, etc.). The master signed bills of lading. These made the cargo deliverable to shipper's order at Vizagapatam and Madras (both on the East Coast of India), freight pre-paid. On Oct. 25, 1956, *The Eugenia* sailed from Odessa. The customary route at this time to India was still by the Suez Canal. The charterers told the master to cable their agent in Port Said when he was within twenty-four hours' sailing of Port Said. He did so. *The Eugenia* arrived off Port Said at 11.00 a.m. on Oct. 30, 1956, and entered port at 4.30 p.m. At that time Egyptian anti-aircraft guns were in action against hostile reconnaissance planes. It was quite apparent that Port Said and the Suez Canal were zones which were "dangerous" within this war clause. Indeed, on the morning of Oct. 30, the owners' London agent called on the charterers' London agent to take action under the war clause to ensure that the ship should not enter Port Said or the Suez Canal. The charterers' agent in London, however, took no action. He let things be. But at Port Said the charterers' agent had taken action. He boarded the vessel and stated that he had made arrangements for the vessel to enter the canal the next morning. In consequence, the vessel entered the canal at 9.35 a.m. on Oct. 31 and proceeded in convoy fifty-eight kilometres south. Then the convoy tied up to allow a northbound convoy to pass. Soon afterwards English and French aircraft began to drop bombs on Egyptian targets. That evening the Egyptian Government blocked the canal by sinking ships at Port Said and Suez and in the canal and by blowing up bridges. So *The Eugenia* was trapped where she was. On Nov. 7, 1956, there was a cease-fire. Early in January, 1957, a passage was cleared northwards. But there was no hope of southward passage for a long time. So *The Eugenia* started to move north. She anchored in Port Said Roads on Jan. 8, 1957. On Jan. 11, 1957, she went to Alexandria and arrived there on Jan. 12, 1957.

Meanwhile, however, the charterers, on Jan. 4, 1957, claimed that the charterparty had been frustrated by the blocking of the canal. The owners denied that it had been frustrated and treated the charterers' conduct as a repudiation. So on either view the charter was at an end. On Jan. 15, 1957, the owners entered into a new charterparty direct with the original sub-charterers. This new charter was an ordinary Gencon voyage charter by which the owners agreed to carry the cargo already on board via the Cape of Good Hope to India. The freight was very high, for the freight market had risen rapidly; so much so, that the owners did well out of the new charter. Indeed, they might not have suffered any loss were it not for the long spell during which the ship was trapped in the canal. The owners wish to claim hire so as to cover the period in the canal, but the charterers dispute it. Hence their claim that the charter was frustrated. On Jan. 20, 1957, under this new charterparty, *The Eugenia* left Alexandria and went round the Cape. She arrived at Vizagapatam about Apr. 5, 1957, unloaded part of her cargo there, then went to Madras and unloaded the rest there, and finished discharging on May 22, 1957. The southern exit from the canal was not cleared until April, 1957. So *The Eugenia* arrived at her destination earlier by going northward out of the canal than if she had waited to get out by the southern exit.

Such being the facts, the first question is whether the charterers, by allowing *The Eugenia* to go into the canal on Oct. 31, 1956, were in breach of the war clause. Both the arbitrator and the judge held that they were in breach. Counsel for the charterers challenged this finding. He said that the war clause 21 (A) was of very limited application. It did not apply, he said, to the contract voyage itself. That was specified in the charterparty. It was "a trip out to India via Black Sea," and impliedly by the customary route. The charterers had no power to alter that trip or to give any orders to the ship to deviate from it. The war clause only applied, he said, to the places in respect of which the charterers had power to direct her, such as the orders to load at a named port in the Black Sea, or to discharge at a named port in India. If the charterers ordered her to such a port when it was dangerous, the war clause, he admitted, would apply. But it did not apply, he said, when the ship was just carrying out the contract voyage. Her route in that case was, he said, determined by the contract itself and not by any orders of the charterers. In support of this argument, counsel for the charterers urged that, although the charterparty was on a printed form applicable to a time-charter, nevertheless the "paramount feature" of it was a voyage, and it was to be construed accordingly. He cited *Glynn & Co. v. Margetson*, [1891-94] All E.R. Rep. 693; [1893] A.C. 351, and *Temple Steamship Co. v. V/O Sovfracht*, (1945), 79 Lloyd L.R. 1. He said that *The Eugenia* entered the canal by reason of the contract and not by reason of any orders of the charterers and, therefore, the war clause did not apply. I cannot accept this argument. This is a time charterparty, the essence of which is that the shipowners place the ship at the disposal of the charterers for a time — the charterers paying hire for that time. In some time-charters the time is fixed beforehand, such as six months or twelve months. In other time-charters the time is uncertain, and is to be measured by the time occupied by a particular voyage. But in either case the charterparty is a time charterparty and the ship is under the charterer's orders throughout. The charterer must, of course, give his orders within the limits permitted by the contract — if a particular voyage is contracted for he must give orders consistent with it — but still the ship is under his orders none the less. So, here, *The Eugenia* was, I think, under charterers' orders when she approached the canal, and she was under charterers' orders when she arrived off Port Said on Oct. 30, 1956, and also when she entered it. Port Said and the Suez Canal were at that time zones which were dangerous within the war clause. So they were in breach of it. But even if they did not "order" her to enter the Suez Canal, they allowed her to "continue" when it was obviously dangerous and were thus in breach of it. Counsel for the charterers argued further that, even if the charterers were in breach of cl. 21 (A), the only consequence was to bring cl. 21 (B) and (C) into operation. I do not think so. The owners can take advantage of those sub-clauses and also recover any other damages that they have suffered. I find myself in complete agreement with the arbitrator and the judge on these points.

The second question is whether the charterparty was frustrated by what took place. The arbitrator has held that it was not. The judge has held that it was. Which is right? One thing that is obvious is that the charterers cannot rely on the fact that *The Eugenia* was trapped in the canal; for that was their own fault. They were in breach of the war clause in entering it. They cannot rely on a self-induced frustration; *see Maritime National Fish, Ltd. v. Ocean Trawlers, Ltd.*, [1935] All E.R. Rep. 86; [1935] A.C. 524. But they seek to rely on the fact that the canal itself was blocked. They assert that, even if *The Eugenia* had never gone into the canal but had stayed outside (in which case she would not have been in breach of the war clause), nevertheless she would still have had to go round by the Cape; and that, they say, brings about a frustration, for it makes the venture fundamentally different from what they contracted for. The judge has accepted this view. He has held that, on Nov. 16, 1956, the charterparty was frustrated. The reason for his taking Nov. 16, 1956, was this: Prior to Nov. 16, 1956, mercantile men (even if she had stayed outside) would not have formed any conclusion whether the obstructions in the canal were other than temporary. There was insufficient information available to form a judgment. On Nov. 16, 1956, mercantile men would conclude that the blockage of the southern end would last till March or April, 1957; so that, by that time, it would be clear that the only thing to do (if the ship had never entered the canal) would be to go round the Cape. The judge said:

"I hold that the adventure, involving a voyage round the Cape, is basically or fundamentally different from the adventure involving a voyage via the Suez Canal." So he held that the contract was frustrated. He was comforted to find that, in *Société Franco Tunisience D'Armement v. Sidermar S.P.A.*, [1960] 2 All E.R. 529 at p. 544; [1961] 2 Q.B. 278 at p. 307, PEARSON, J., came to a similar conclusion. I must confess that I find it difficult to apply the doctrine of frustration to a hypothetical situation, that is, to treat this vessel as if she had never entered the canal and then ask whether the charter was frustrated. The doctrine should be applied to the facts as they really are. But I will swallow this difficulty and ask myself what would be the position if the vessel had never entered the canal but stayed at Port Said. Would the contract be frustrated? This means that, once again, we have had to consider the authorities on this vexed topic of frustration. But I think that the position is now reasonably clear. It is simply this: If it should happen, in the course of carrying out a contract, that a fundamentally different situation arises for which the parties made no provision — so much so that it would not be just in the new situation to hold them bound to its terms — then the contract is at an end.

It was originally said that the doctrine of frustration was based on an implied term. In short, that the parties, if they had foreseen the new situation, would have said to one another: "If that happens, of course, it is all over between us." But the theory of an implied term has now been discarded by everyone, or nearly everyone, for the simple reason that it does not represent the truth. The parties would not have said: "It is all over between us." They would have differed about what was to happen. Each would have sought to insert reservations or qualifications of one kind or another. Take this very case. The parties realised that the canal might become impassable. They tried to agree on a clause to provide for the contingency. But they failed to agree. So there is no room for an implied term. It has frequently been said that the doctrine of frustration only applies when the new situation is "unforeseen" or "unexpected" or "uncontemplated," as if that were an essential feature. But it is not so. It is not so much that it is "unexpected," but rather that the parties have made no provision for it in their contract. The point about it, however, is that: If the parties did not foresee anything of the kind happening, you can readily infer that they have made no provision for it. Whereas, if they did foresee it, you would expect them to make provision for it. But cases have occurred where the parties have foreseen the danger ahead, and yet made no provision for it in the contract. Such was the case in the Spanish Civil War when a ship was let on charter to the Republican Government. The purpose was to evacuate refugees. The parties foresaw that she might be seized by the Nationalists. But they made no provision for it in their contract. Yet, when she was seized, the contract was frustrated: see *W. J. Tatem, Ltd. v. Gamboa*, [1938] 3 All E.R. 135; [1939] 1 K.B. 132. So, here, the parties foresaw that the canal might become impassable. It was the very thing that they feared. But they made no provision for it. So the doctrine may still apply, if it be a proper case for it.

We are thus left with the simple test that a situation must arise which renders performance of the contract "a thing radically different from that which was undertaken by the contract;" *see Davis Contractors, Ltd. v. Fareham U.D.C.,*[1956] 2 All E.R. 145 at p. 160; [1956] A.C. 696 at p. 729, per LORD RADCLIFFE. To see if the doctrine applies, you have first to construe the contract and see whether the parties have themselves provided for the situation that has arisen. If they have provided for it, the contract must govern. There is no frustration. If they have not provided for it, then you have to compare the new situation with the old situation for which they did provide. Then you must see how different it is. The fact that it has become more onerous or more expensive for one party than he thought is not sufficient to bring about a frustration. It must be more than merely more onerous or more expensive. It must be positively unjust to hold the parties bound. It is often difficult to draw the line. But it must be done, and it is for the courts to do it as a matter of law: *see Tsakiroglou & Co., Ltd. v. Noblee & Thord G.m.b.H*, [1961] 2 All E.R. 179 at pp. 185, 187; [1962] A.C. 93 at pp. 116, 119, per VISCOUNT SIMONDS and per LORD REID.

Applying these principles to this case, I have come to the conclusion that the blockage of the canal did not bring about a "fundamentally different situation" such as to frustrate the venture. My reasons are these: (i) The venture was the whole trip from delivery at Genoa, out to the Black Sea, there load cargo, thence to India, unload cargo, and re-delivery. The time for this vessel from Odessa to Vizagapatam via the Suez Canal would be twenty-six days, and via the Cape fifty-six days. But that is not the right comparison. You have to take the whole venture from delivery at Genoa to re-delivery at Madras. We were told that the time for the whole venture via the Suez Canal would be 108 days, and via the Cape 138 days. The difference over the whole voyage is not so radical as to produce a frustration. (ii) The cargo was iron and steel goods which would not be adversely affected by the longer voyage, and there was no special reason for early arrival. The vessel and crew were at all times fit and sufficient to proceed via the Cape. (iii) The cargo was loaded on board at the time of the blockage of the canal. If the contract was frustrated, it would mean, I suppose, that the ship could throw up the charter and unload the cargo wherever she was, without any breach of contract. (iv) The voyage round the Cape made no great difference except that it took a good deal longer and was more expensive for the charterers than a voyage through the canal.

The only hesitation which I have had about this case is because of the views expressed by PEARSON, J., in *Société Franco Tunisienne D'Armement v. Sidermar S.P.A.*, [1960] 2 All E.R. 529; [1961] 2 Q.B. 278. That case can be distinguished because there was a sentence in the charter which read "Captain also to telegraph to 'Maritsider Genoa' on passing Suez Canal." PEARSON, J., held that that meant that there was actually an obligation to pass the Suez Canal, and hence that the contract was frustrated by impossibility. [1960] 2 All E.R. at p. 542; [1961] 2 Q.B. at p. 304. I think that he attached too much significance to the clause. I think that there, as here, there was no obligation to go through the Suez Canal, but only to go by the route which was customary at the time of performance; and that there is no legitimate distinction to be drawn between that case and this. That was a voyage charter and this a time charter. That makes no difference except that the burden fell on the owners and not the charterers. PEARSON, J., held that the route via the Cape was fundamentally different from the route via the Suez Canal and that the charter was frustrated on that ground also. I am afraid that I cannot take that view. It is important to notice also that, since that case, the House of Lords has held that, with goods sold c.i.f. Sudan to Hamburg, the contract of sale was not frustrated by the closure of the Suez Canal: *see Tsakiroglou & Co., Ltd. v. Noblee & Thorl, G.m.b.H....* I know that a contract of affreightment is different from a contract for the sale of goods, but I should find it strange if, in the case of a ship loaded with cargo, the contract of affreightment was frustrated by the closure of the canal and the contract of sale was not frustrated. It would lead to endless complications. I come, therefore, to the conclusion that the decision of PEARSON, J., in *Société Franco Tunisienne D'Armement v. Sidermar S.P.A.*, [1960] 2 All E.R. 529; [1961] 2 Q.B. 278, was wrong and should be overruled. It is to be noticed that, both in that case and in this, the arbitrators held there was no frustration. I think that they were right. I would allow this appeal and hold the contract was not frustrated. On this footing, I gather that there is no other point which needs to be decided.

DONOVAN, L.J.:

I also think that the charterparty is a time charterparty, the voyage being the measure of the time. I further think that the charterers were in breach of contract by sending the ship into the Suez Canal without the consent of the owners at a time when the canal was a dangerous zone as defined in cl. 21 (A) of the charterparty. This view has been contested by the charterers on the ground that cl. 21 (A) has no application to the circumstances here in question. They did not, they say, order the ship into the canal. True it is that cl. 2 (A) also provides that the ship shall not "continue" into a dangerous zone, but this word in its context means "continue in pursuance of an order," and, since the charterers gave no order, the provision leaves them still unaffected. It is admitted that cl. 21 (A) does apply to the charterers in certain circumstances, but these are confined, it is said, to the occasion when the charterers are free to give orders where the ship shall go, that is, into ports they select as ports of load-ing, of bunkering and of discharge. They selected none in the Suez Canal. The char-terparty does not, in my opinion, restrict the right of the charterers to give orders to the master as the charterers now claim. By cl. 9, the master was to be under the or-ders of the charterers as regards the employment of the ship, and by cl. 10, the char-terers were to furnish the master with all instructions and sailing directions. The ar-bitrator has found that the vessel was delivered to the charterers at Genoa, and was ordered by them to proceed first to Novorossisk, and then to Odessa to load; that at these ports the master on the instructions of the charterers signed bills of lading re-lating to the cargo; that the charterers gave the master the name and address of their agents in Port Said and instructed the master to send a cable to the agent when he was within twenty-four hours sailing of Port Said. The charterers did not order the master to follow any route other than the customary route for the voyage which, when the vessel left Odessa and up to Oct. 31, 1956, was via the Suez Canal.

On these facts, the arbitrator considered that the charterers did give implied orders that the vessel should proceed via the canal. With this conclusion I agree. It is reinforced by these further facts. On Oct. 30, 1956, the charterers' agent boarded the vessel and stated that he had made arrangements for the vessel to enter the canal next morning. On the same day, that is, Oct. 30, the owners' London agents called on the charterers' Lon-don agents to take action under cl. 21 of the charterparty to ensure that the ship should not enter Port Said or the Suez Canal. The charterers' London agents did not reply that this was not a matter for the charterers. The charterers in fact took no action on this re-quest, but it would seem that the understanding of both parties was that the charterers had a say in the matter whether the vessel should go into the canal or not. In any event, cl. 21 (A) provides that the vessel shall not be ordered "nor continue" to a danger zone, and, even if (contrary to my view) the charterers did not order the vessel into the canal, they allowed her to continue into it. I reject the argument that "continue" on this con-text means, and means only, continue in pursuance of some previous order, and that, unless the charterers gave that order, the clause does not apply. I think that this is much too narrow a construction. If the charterers were in breach of cl. 21 (A), it is common ground that they cannot rely on the delay suffered by the vessel while actually trapped in the canal as a ground for treating the contract as ended by frustration.

Whether the contract should, on other grounds, be regarded as so ended, I have little to add to what LORD DENNING, M.R., has said. There is clearly no room here for holding that the parties agreed by implication that the blocking of the Suez Canal should end the contract, or that they would have so agreed had they consid-ered this contingency. In fact, they did consider it, and, through their agents, made rival suggestions what should happen in that event. But they came to no conclusion, except to leave the terms of the contract as they were. Should the canal be blocked before the vessel passed through it, the parties were content to have their rights and duties settled on the basis of the terms of the contract which they were signing. In other words, the problem, should it arise, would be left to the lawyers. I, therefore, ask myself this question: Was there such a fundamental change in the circumstances relevant to the performance of the contract that it is just and reasonable that the par-ties should be relieved of their obligations? The contract was a contract for the hire of the vessel to carry cargo from the Black Sea to India via the customary route. Up to and including Oct. 31, 1956, the customary route was via the Suez Canal. On that day the vessel entered the Suez Canal in breach of the contract. After Oct. 31, the customary route was via the Cape. This added some thirty days to the duration of the contract. The cargo was such as not to be affected by this delay, and there was no ev-idence that the early arrival of the cargo in India was of particular importance. The ship was well found and was exposed to no additional hazard in going via the Cape except such hazard as is inherent in being longer at sea. When the charterers refused to go on with the charter, a new one was concluded with one of the sub-charterers, and he purpose of the contract, namely, the carriage of goods from the Black Sea to India was fulfilled. What resulted from the blockage of the Suez Canal, so far as the present case is concerned, is really that the voyage became more expensive. In all the circumstances, I do not think that such a fundamental change occurred in the relevant circumstances as to make it just and reasonable to relieve the parties of their obligation under the contract by reference to the doctrine of frustration.

As to the decision in *Societe Franco Tunisienne D'aimement v. Sidermar S.P.A.*, [1960] 2 All E.R. 529; [1961] 2 Q.B. 728, I agree with the observations of LORD DENNING, M.R.

DISPOSITION:
Appeal allowed. Leave to appeal to House of Lords.

III. Delivery Obligations of the Seller

Documents Supplement References:
1. *CISG Articles 9, 30-34, 52, 79.*
2. *U.C.C. Sections 2-301, 2-309.*

NOTE ON THE MANNER AND PLACE OF DELIVERY

Article 30 of the CISG sets forth the basic obligation of the seller: "The seller must deliver the goods, hand over any documents relating to them and transfer the property in the goods, as required by the contract and this Convention." *Compare* U.C.C. Section 2-301. Where, how, and when the seller must deliver goods are governed by Articles 31-33, respectively. Further, Article 34 sets out rules on the delivery of documents. Notice that the Convention does not use the concept of "tender" to describe either the seller's or the buyer's performance obligations.

Where the seller is required or authorized to send the goods to the buyer (*i.e.*, the contract involves carriage of the goods), the basic default rule is that delivery occurs when and where the seller hands the goods over to the first carrier for transmission to the buyer. *See* Article 31(a). The seller's contract with the carrier must be "appropriate in the circumstances and according to the usual terms for such transportation." *See* Article 32(2). Yet this is not all. If the goods are not clearly identified to the sales contract, by markings on the goods or by documents or otherwise, when handed over to the carrier, seller must give buyer notice of the consignment. *See* Article 32(1). Finally, the seller must hand over to the buyer any documents relating to the goods. *See* Articles 30, 34.

In most cases, however, the parties will specify the place of delivery and the seller's related duties by using one of the trade terms promulgated by the ICC, which are commonly referred to as *Incoterms*. Although there are 13 different *Incoterms*, they can be divided into four principle categories, one for each of the different first letters of the constituent terms E, F, C, and D. Each category of terms, ranging from E through D, represents a gradual increase in the responsibility of the seller.

John A. Spanogle, Incoterms and UCC Article 2—Conflicts and Confusions,
31 International Lawyer 111, 116-124 (1997)

....

II. The Terms of *Incoterms*

Under the *Incoterms* "*Ex Works*" (EXW) commercial term (including "*Ex Factory*" and "*Ex Warehouse*"), the seller needs only to "tender" the goods to the buyer by placing them at the buyer's disposal at a named place of delivery. Thus, the seller has no obligation to deliver the goods to a carrier or to load the goods on any vehicle. The seller must also notify the buyer when and where the goods will be tendered, but has no obligation to arrange for transportation or insurance. The risk of loss transfers to the buyer at the time the goods are placed at its disposal. The seller will normally provide a commercial invoice or its equivalent electronic message, but has no obligation to obtain a document of title or an export license. The *Incoterms* definition has no effect upon either payment or inspection obligations under the contract, except to require the buyer to pay for pre-shipment inspection. The *Incoterms* risk of loss provision is contrary to the default rules of both the U.C.C. and the CISG, which delay passing the risk until the buyer's receipt of the goods, both because the seller is more likely to have insurance and because the seller has a greater ability to protect the goods.

Under the *Incoterms* "*Free Carrier*" (FCA) commercial term, the seller is obligated to deliver the goods into the custody of a carrier, usually the first carrier in a multimodal transportation scheme. The *Incoterms* definition of "carrier" includes freight forwarders. The seller has no obligation to pay for transportation costs or insurance. Usually the carrier will be named by, and arranged by, the buyer. However, the seller "may" arrange transportation at the buyer's expense if requested by the buyer, or if it is "commercial practice" for the seller to do so. But, even under such circumstances, the seller may refuse to make such arrangements as long as it so notifies the buyer. Even if the seller does arrange transportation, it has no obligation to arrange for insurance coverage during transportation and need only notify the buyer "that the goods have been delivered into the custody of the carrier." The risk of loss transfers to the buyer upon delivery to the carrier, but the buyer may not receive notice until after that time. The seller must provide a commercial invoice or its equivalent electronic message, any necessary export license, and usually a transport document that will allow the buyer to take delivery — or an equivalent electronic data interchange message. The *Incoterms* definition has no provisions on either payment or post-shipment inspection terms under the contract.

This FCA term is the *Incoterms* commercial term that is most comparable to the U.C.C.'s "F.O.B. place of shipment" term. However, there are two levels of confusion. One is that *Incoterms* has an "F.O.B." term that is different, and the U.C.C. "F.O.B." term is more likely to be compared with the *Incoterms* "FOB" term. The other is that the obligations under FCA and the U.C.C. "F.O.B. place of shipment" term are, in fact, different. The norm under the U.C.C.'s "F.O.B." is for the seller to arrange transportation, while the seller need do so under FCA only in special circumstances. Further, if the seller does ship, the seller usually must also arrange insurance coverage, unless instructed otherwise by the buyer. Under *Incoterms* FCA, the seller does not seem ever to have any obligation to arrange for insurance coverage. Traditionally, under both the 1980 version of *Incoterms* and the U.C.C. "F.O.B. place of shipment" term, there is no implied special payment or inspection terms, no implied requirement of payment against documents or payment before inspection. This would also seem to be a preferable interpretation of the current *Incoterms* FCA term.

Under the *Incoterms "Free Alongside Ship"* (FAS) commercial term, the seller is obligated to deliver the goods alongside a ship arranged for and named by the buyer at a named port of shipment. Thus, it is appropriate only for waterborne transportation, and the seller must bear the costs and risks of inland transportation to the named port of shipment. The seller has no obligation to arrange transportation or insurance for the "main" (or waterborne) part of the carriage, but does have a duty to notify the buyer "that the goods have been delivered alongside the named vessel." The risk of loss will transfer to the buyer also at the time the goods are delivered alongside the ship. The seller must provide a commercial invoice and usually a transport document that will allow the buyer to take delivery, or the electronic equivalent of either. But the seller has no obligation to provide an export license, only an obligation to render assistance to the buyer to obtain one.

The *Incoterms* definition has no provisions on either payment or post-shipment inspection terms under the contract. Under the U.C.C., the term "F.A.S. vessel" requires the buyer to pay against a tender of documents, such as a negotiable bill of lading, before the goods arrive at their destination and before the buyer has any post-shipment opportunity to inspect the goods. Otherwise, the U.C.C. "F.A.S." term is similar to the *Incoterms* "FAS" term, including obligating the seller only to deliver the goods alongside a named vessel and not obligating the seller to arrange transportation to a final destination.

However, in the prior 1980 version of *Incoterms*, the definition of FAS did not provide that payment against documents was required under an FAS contract, and the 1980 *Incoterms* did contain such payment provisions in its definitions of other commercial terms. Thus, it is more likely that the current version of *Incoterms* FAS is not intended to require payment against documents, to restrict inspection before payment, or to require use of negotiable bills of lading.

Under the *Incoterms "Free on Board"* (FOB) commercial term, the seller is obligated to deliver the goods on board a ship arranged for and named by the buyer at a named port of shipment. Thus, this term is also appropriate only for waterborne transportation, and the seller must bear the costs and risks of both inland transportation to the named port of shipment and loading the goods on the ship (until "they have passed the ship's rail"). The seller has no obligation to arrange transportation or insurance, but does have a duty to notify the buyer "that the goods have been delivered on board" the ship. The risk of loss will transfer to the buyer also at the time the goods have "passed the ship's rail." The seller must provide a commercial invoice, or its equivalent electronic message, any necessary export license, and usually a transport document that will allow the buyer to take delivery — or an equivalent electronic data interchange message.

The *Incoterms* definition has no provisions on either payment or post-shipment inspection terms under the contract. The U.C.C. does define "F.O.B.," but it is not a term requiring waterborne transportation. Thus, as has been discussed above, the U.C.C. "F.O.B." is more closely linked to the *Incoterms* FCA term. But the U.C.C. also has a term "F.O.B. vessel," which does relate only to waterborne transportation and therefore is most closely linked to the *Incoterms* FOB term. Under the U.C.C., the term "F.O.B. vessel" requires the buyer to pay against a tender of documents, such as a negotiable bill of lading, before the goods arrive at their destination and before the buyer has any post-shipment opportunity to inspect the goods. Otherwise, the U.C.C. "F.O.B. vessel" term is similar to the *Incoterms* "FOB" term, including obligating the seller only to deliver the goods to a named ship's rail and not obligating the seller to arrange transportation to a final destination.

However, in the 1980 version of *Incoterms*, the definition of FOB provided that payment against documents was not required for an FOB contract, while the 1980 *Incoterms* did not contain such payment provisions in its definitions of other commercial terms. Thus, it is more likely that the current version of *Incoterms* FOB is not intended to require payment against documents or to restrict inspection before payment, unless such a term is expressly added or there is a known custom in a particular trade. In addition, it is more likely that negotiable bills of lading are not intended to be used with *Incoterms* FOB shipments, unless the parties specify "payment against documents" or use of a letter of credit in the sale contract.

Under the *Incoterms* "*Cost, Insurance, and Freight*" (CIF) commercial term, the seller is obligated to arrange for both transportation and insurance to a named destination port and then to deliver the goods on board the ship arranged for by the seller. Thus, the term is appropriate only for waterborne transportation. The seller must arrange the transportation and pay the freight costs to the destination port, but has completed its delivery obligations when the goods have "passed the ship's rail" at the port of shipment. The seller must arrange and pay for insurance during transportation to the port of destination, but the risk of loss transfers to the buyer at the time the goods pass the ship's rail at the port of shipment. The seller must notify the buyer "that the goods have been delivered on board" the ship to enable the buyer to receive the goods. The seller must provide a commercial invoice, or its equivalent electronic message, any necessary export license, and "the usual transport document" for the destination port.

The *Incoterms* definition has no provisions on either payment or post-shipment inspection terms under the contract. However, *Incoterms* does require that the transportation document "must...enable the buyer to sell the goods in transit by the transfer of the document to a subsequent buyer...or by notification to the carrier," unless otherwise agreed. The traditional method of enabling the buyer to do this, in either the "payment against documents" transaction or the letter of credit transaction, is for the seller to obtain a negotiable bill of lading from the carrier and to tender that negotiable document to the buyer through a series of banks. The banks allow the buyer to obtain possession of the document (and control of the goods) only after the buyer pays for the goods. Thus, the buyer "pays against documents," while the goods are at sea, and pays for them before any post-shipment inspection of the goods is possible. This transaction should still be regarded as the norm under *Incoterms* CIF, and the definition of the term in the 1990 version does refer to the use of a negotiable bill of lading.

The 1980 version of *Incoterms* was more precise on these payment obligations, requiring the buyer to "accept the documents when tendered by the seller...and pay the price as provided in the contract." The implication of this provision was that the buyer had no right to inspect the goods before this payment against documents. The U.C.C. also has a definition of "C.I.F." that requires the buyer to "make payment against tender of the required documents." The U.C.C. "C.I.F." term is otherwise similar to *Incoterms* CIF in that it requires the seller to deliver to the carrier at a port of shipment and bear the risk of loss only to that port, but to pay freight costs and insurance to the port of destination.

Some ambiguity is introduced in the CIF definition, because it also refers to the use of nonnegotiable documents as well. However, the ICC's Introduction to the 1990 *Incoterms* recognizes that the use of nonnegotiable documents is inappropriate in a "payment against documents" situation and thus would not "enable the buyer to sell the goods in transit by surrendering the paper document" to the sub-buyer. The introduction then explains that sometimes the parties "may specifically agree to relieve the seller from" providing a negotiable document when they "know that the buyer does not contemplate selling the goods in transit." The 1990 *Incoterms* does not have any provisions on when title to the goods passes from the seller to the buyer. Thus, when title issues arise the courts must turn to the U.C.C. for applicable provisions.

The *Incoterms* "*Cost and Freight*" (CFR) commercial term is similar to the CIF term, except that the seller has no obligations with respect to either arranging or paying for insurance coverage of the goods during transportation. Under the CFR term, the seller is obligated to arrange for transportation to a named destination point and then to deliver the goods on board the ship arranged for by the seller. Thus, the term is appropriate only for waterborne transportation. The seller must arrange the transportation and pay the freight costs to the destination port, but has completed its delivery obligations when the goods have "passed the ship's rail" at the port of shipment. The seller has no express obligation to arrange or pay for insurance on the goods during transportation, and the risk of loss transfers to the buyer at the time the goods pass the ship's rail at the port of shipment. The seller must notify the buyer "that the goods have been delivered on board" the ship to enable the buyer to receive the goods. The seller must provide a commercial invoice, or its equivalent electronic message, any necessary export license, and "the usual transport document" for the destination port. As with CIF, the *Incoterms* CFR definition has no provisions on either payment or post-shipment inspection terms under the contract. However, *Incoterms* does require that the transport document "must...enable the buyer to sell the goods in transit by the transfer of the document to a subsequent buyer," which has traditionally meant use of a negotiable bill of lading and payment against documents. Both the U.C.C. and prior versions of *Incoterms* regarded this term as requiring payment against documents while the goods were still at sea, thus restricting post-shipment inspection of the goods before payment. These provisions should still be regarded as the norm under *Incoterms* CFR.

The *Incoterms* "*Carriage and Insurance Paid To*" (CIP) and "*Carriage Paid To*" (CPT) commercial terms are similar to its CIF and CFR terms, except that they may be used for any type of transportation, including multimodal transportation, and not just for waterborne transportation. Under the CIP term, the seller is obligated to arrange and pay for both transportation and insurance to a named destination place. However, the seller completes its delivery obligations, and the risk of loss passes to the buyer, upon delivery to the first carrier at the place of shipment. Thus, the term is appropriate for multimodal transportation. The CPT commercial term is similar, except that the seller has no duty to arrange or pay for insurance coverage of the goods during transportation.

Under both CIP and CPT, the seller must notify the buyer "that the goods have been delivered" to the first carrier and also give any other notice required to enable the buyer "to take the goods." Under both, the seller must also provide a commercial invoice, or its equivalent electronic message, any necessary export license, and "the usual transport document." A list of acceptable transport documents is given, and there is no requirement that the document enable the buyer to sell the goods in transit. There are no payment or post-shipment inspection provisions in the *Incoterms* definitions, and the U.C.C. does not define these terms. Further, the Introduction to *Incoterms* contrasts CIP and CPT with CIF and CFR, indicating that there is no requirement to provide a negotiable bill of lading with CIP or CPT terms. Thus, unless the parties expressly agree to a "payment against documents" term, it is more likely that the CIP or CPT commercial terms are not intended to require payment against documents or to restrict inspection before payment.

Incoterms provides five different commercial terms for "destination" or "arrival" contracts. Two of them, *"Delivered Ex Ship"* (DES) and *"Delivered Ex Quay"* (DEQ), should only be used for waterborne transportation. The other three, *"Delivered At Frontier"* (DAF), *"Delivered Duty Unpaid"* (DDU), and *"Delivered Duty Paid"* (DDP), can all be used with any type of transportation, including multimodal transport. In all of them, the seller is required to arrange transportation, pay the freight costs, and bear the risk of loss to a named destination point. Although these definitions have no provisions on insurance during transportation, since the seller bears the risk of loss during that event, the seller must either arrange and pay for insurance or act as a self-insurer during transportation. *Incoterms* contains no provisions on payment or post-shipment inspection, but there is no requirement for use of a negotiable bill of lading, and delivery occurs only after arrival of the goods. Thus, there is no reason to imply a "payment against documents" requirement if none is expressly stated. On the other hand, the parties are free to agree expressly on both a destination commercial term and a payment against documents term.

Under the *Incoterms* DES commercial term, delivery occurs and the risk of loss passes when the goods are placed at the buyer's disposal on board ship at the named destination port. To be "at buyer's disposal," the goods must be placed (at the seller's risk and expense) so that they can be removed by "appropriate" unloading equipment. However, the goods need not be cleared for importation by customs officials; that is the buyer's obligation. Under the U.C.C., the term "ex ship" requires the seller also to unload the goods. Under the DEQ commercial term, the goods must be placed at the buyer's disposal on the quay or wharf at the named destination port. However, the parties who use a term should further specify either "Duty Paid" or "Duty Unpaid," because both DEQ (Duty Paid) and DEQ (Duty Unpaid) terms are in use. If "Duty Paid" is specified, or there is no specification, the seller must "pay the costs of customs formalities...duties, taxes...payable upon...importation of the goods, unless otherwise agreed."

In both DES and DEQ shipments, the seller must notify the buyer of the estimated time of arrival of a named vessel at a named destination port. Also, in both DES and DEQ shipments, the seller must provide the buyer with a commercial invoice or the equivalent electronic message, a "delivery order and/or the usual transport document," and an export license. For DEQ shipments, but not for DES shipments, the seller must also provide an import license, unless otherwise agreed.

Under the *Incoterms* DAF commercial term, which is most appropriately used with rail or road transportation, delivery occurs and the risk of loss passes when the goods are placed at the buyer's disposal at a named place at the frontier, but before the customs frontier of the importing country. Under the DDU commercial term, delivery occurs and the risk of loss passes when the goods are placed at the buyer's disposal at "the agreed point at the named place of destination" in the country of importation. However, the seller has no obligation to pay import duties or charges. Under the *Incoterms* DDP commercial term, delivery occurs and the risk of loss passes when the goods are placed at the buyer's disposal at the named place in the country of destination and are cleared for importation into that country. The seller must pay all import duties and charges and complete customs formalities at its own risk and expense. The only U.C.C. destination term is "F.O.B. the place of destination," which seems similar to "DDU," but without much of the detail and precision.

In each of these terms DAF, DDU, and DDP, the seller must notify the buyer of the dispatch of the goods and give any other notice necessary for the buyer "to take the goods." In each type of shipment, the seller must provide a commercial invoice or its equivalent electronic message. In a DAF shipment, the seller must provide "the usual document or other evidence of the delivery" and an export license. In a DDU shipment, the seller must also provide a "delivery order and/or the usual transport document" and an export license. In a DDP shipment, the seller must provide the delivery order or transport document and both an export license and an import license.

. . . .

Case Abstract, UNCITRAL Texts (CLOUT), Abstract No. 207,

December 2, 1997 (France)

The seller, a company with its place of business in Italy, delivered goods to a French buyer in 1992. The buyer's order form contained a jurisdiction clause in favour of the Commercial Court of Roubaix-Tourcoing in France. However, the invoices sent by the Italian [seller] to the French [buyer] referred to the jurisdiction of the Commercial Court of Prato in Italy.

Considering the goods to be defective, the French buyer sued the Italian [seller] before the Commercial Court of Roubaix-Tourcoing. The Italian seller raised an objection that the Italian, not the French, court had jurisdiction. When the Court allowed the objection to jurisdiction, the French buyer lodged an appeal.

The Court of Appeal of Douaí then determined jurisdiction according to the place of performance of the seller's obligation to deliver as the obligation on which the claim was based within the meaning of article 5(1) of the Brussels Convention. The Court considered that, the sale being governed by CISG, the place of delivery was in Italy, this being the place where the goods were handed over to the first transporter for delivery to the buyer, in conformity with article 31 CISG.

The French seller brought an appeal against this ruling. The Court of Cassation rejected the appeal on the ground that it considered that the Court of Appeal had justified its decision from the legal point of view by finding that the place of performance of the seller's obligation to deliver was in Italy, the place where the goods were handed over to the buyer, this place being further indicated by correct application of article 31 CISG.

Case Abstract, UNCITRAL Texts (CLOUT), Abstract No. 47

May 14, 1993 (Germany)

The German seller of ten electronic ear devices demanded damages for breach of contract by the Italian buyer, who had failed to take delivery despite the additional period of time set by the seller for the buyer to take delivery.

The court held that it had jurisdiction under article 5(1) of the Convention on jurisdiction and the enforcement of judgements in civil and commercial matters, which provides that a party who is domiciled in a Contracting State can be sued before the courts of the place where the obligation giving rise to the dispute had to be performed. The court applied article 31(b) CISG, which was applicable under German private international law as part of German law, and determined that Aachen, where the goods had been manufactured, was the place where the seller was obliged to deliver (art. 31(b) CISG).

The court applied articles 61(1)(b), 63 and 74-77 CISG and found that the buyer had to pay damages to the seller for failing to take delivery of the goods, even after the additional period of time set by the seller had expired.

QUESTION

1.   The language of Article 31 strongly supports the conclusion that Article 31(a) is an exception to Articles 31(b) and 31(c). In light of the dynamics of international trade, does this approach make sense?

Phillips Puerto Rico Core, Inc. v. Tradax Petroleum Ltd.,

782 F.2D 314 (2d Cir. 1985)

MANSFIELD, CIRCUIT JUDGE

Phillips Puerto Rico Core, Inc. ("Phillips"), which contracted to buy a cargo of naphtha, appeals an order and judgment of the Southern District of New York, Robert L. Carter, Judge, awarding over a million dollars in damages against it in favor of Tradax Petroleum, Ltd., for breach of its contract with Tradax. Phillips maintains that it was excused from performing because Tradax had failed to perform satisfactorily and because of the occurrence of an event of *force majeure*. We disagree and affirm.

This convoluted maritime controversy had its origins in early September 1981 when Phillips, a corporation organized under Delaware law with its principal place of business in Puerto Rico, agreed to buy 25-30,000 metric tons of naphtha from Tradax, a corporation organized under Bermuda law, with its principal place of business in Switzerland. Tradax had just purchased the naphtha from another firm, Schlubach & Co., and the naphtha was located in Skikda, Algeria. The Tradax-Phillips contract, which was made by telephone and then confirmed by telex on September 3, 1981, specified that the sale was to be "C & F" (cost and freight) Guayama, Puerto Rico and that shipment was to be made between September 20-28, 1981. No dates for delivery were specified. The agreement incorporated the International Chamber of Commerce 1980 *Incoterms*, a set of standardized terms for international commercial contracts, which define a "C & F" contract as one in which the seller arranges and pays for the transport of the goods, but the buyer assumes title and risk of loss at the time of shipment. The contract was also to include Tradax's standard contract provisions "subject to [Phillips'] review and acceptance." These standard terms, including a *force majeure* clause and an arbitration clause, were not recited in the telex but were subsequently mailed by Tradax to Phillips with a confirming letter and arrived several weeks later.

Soon after the original contract was entered into on September 8, 1981, telex from Phillips to Tradax provided documentation and delivery instructions, giving the destination in Puerto Rico and listing Phillips as consignee. The telex confirmed that "title and risk of loss to products shall pass to buyer at the time product reaches the vessel's flange at the load port." On September 16 Tradax nominated the Oxy Trader, an integrated tug barge, as the vessel for the journey, and after determining that the Trader would fit in the Puerto Rico berth and was available at the correct times, Phillips accepted the nomination.

The Trader arrived at Skikda for loading on the afternoon of September 20, 1981, and loading commenced the following day. The naphtha was completely loaded by the early morning of September 24 and at 1030 hours that morning the ship embarked for Puerto Rico. Its bill of lading listed the destination as "Rotterdam for Order," apparently a common practice in bills of lading out of Skikda, regardless of the vessel's actual destination. The cargo was consigned to Schlubach, which endorsed the bill in blank on the reverse.

Meanwhile, the admiralty press revealed that an accident had befallen another integrated tug barge — the Oxy Producer — which was the sister ship of the Oxy Trader. A September 15 report indicated that the Producer had been damaged due to foul weather. On September 17 the press reported that the damage had been caused by a problem with the bumper pads cushioning the linkage between the tug and the barge part of that integrated vessel. Five days later the newspaper stated that the Producer had sunk on September 20. On September 24 a freight manager for Tradax in London telexed Tradax in Switzerland recounting an article of that day that stated that the sinking of the Producer was "focusing attention on the safety of using combination vessels for deep-sea transport." The telex was sent at 1203 hours London time on September 24 (1303 hours Skikda time), about two and a half hours after the Trader had begun its transoceanic journey.

The Trader's voyage was cut short the following day when the ship was detained by the Coast Guard at Gibraltar for an inspection. Tradax relayed word of the delay to Phillips, which telexed back on October 1 that October 15 was the last acceptable delivery date. The next day, unbeknownst to Tradax, one Phillips office telexed another with the instruction that payment for the naphtha "should be withheld at the present time due to the delay." Three days later, Tradax telexed Phillips, objecting to Phillips' attempt to specify a delivery date. Tradax's position was that the naphtha had been sold under a shipment contract not a destination contract and that, as seller, Tradax ceased to bear responsibility for the goods when it transferred the goods to the carrier for shipment.

On October 7, Tradax received word that the Trader might have a latent defect similar to the problem encountered by the Producer, that the authorities were not letting the Trader proceed, and that the naphtha cargo would have to be transshipped. Tradax relayed this message to Phillips.

On October 9, Phillips telexed Tradax stating that it was "declaring force majeure," that it would "not make any payments under the contract until the event of force majeure abates," and that it was reserving the right to cancel the contract if delivery did not occur within 30 days. Tradax responded, reiterating its claim that its responsibility ended at the time of shipment and notifying Phillips that it would present the shipping documents for payment of the contract price the following day. Phillips again instructed its Puerto Rico office not to make payment if Tradax tendered the documents.

On October 13 a Tradax representative presented the shipping documents for payment at Phillips' Puerto Rico office. A Phillips employee examined the documents briefly — about 30 seconds according to Tradax's witness — and stated that they seemed to be in order but that he had been instructed not to pay. A telex back to Tradax that day reaffirmed Phillips' unwillingness to pay until the abatement of the claimed force majeure.

Shortly afterwards Tradax informed Phillips that the Trader would be at Lisbon for the transshipment and that Phillips should make arrangements accordingly. That same telex objected to Phillips' failure to pay for the naphtha on presentation of the documents but offered assistance with the transshipment without prejudice to Tradax's rights. Phillips then proposed to Tradax that it would pay half of the amount due when the naphtha was transshipped and the remainder on arrival. Tradax declined the offer. Phillips ultimately accepted Tradax's nomination of a vessel for the transshipment but subsequently learned that the owner of the ship had requested Tradax to indemnify the ship for the deviation between Rotterdam, the destination in the original bill of lading, and Puerto Rico. On learning of the Rotterdam destination in the original bill of lading, Phillips demanded a new bill of lading from Tradax.

Four days later, on November 9, Phillips informed Tradax that it was terminating the contract due to the "unseaworthiness" of the Trader, "discrepancies in the documents," and an "unreasonable delay" in performance. Although Phillips and Tradax representatives tried to negotiate a new contract by which Phillips would buy the naphtha on "delivery" terms as opposed to "shipment" terms, negotiations fell through when Tradax's management refused to accept that deal. The transshipment then began on November 13, with a bill of lading which left open the destination port. On November 19, Tradax informed Phillips that it would try to sell the naphtha on the open market and would hold Phillips liable for any damages. Tradax then sold the naphtha to a third party for $.88 per gallon, after first offering it to Phillips on condition that Tradax retain its right to claim in arbitration the difference between that price and the contract price. Tradax's total loss on the naphtha, compared to the contract price, was $911,710.31, plus incidental damages.

Tradax then commenced arbitration in London. Phillips protested the arbitration on the ground that the arbitration clause among Tradax's standard contract terms was not included in the contract and it also filed for a declaratory judgment in the Southern District of New York before Judge Carter. Tradax counterclaimed in the New York suit for its damages and the parties agreed to let the litigation proceed in lieu of arbitration.

On August 1, 1984, Judge Carter filed his decision in the case, finding Phillips liable to Tradax for $1,039,330.99 plus prejudgment interest from October 13, 1981. The court held that Phillips had anticipatorily breached the contract by declaring its unwillingness to pay because of *force majeure*. In his view the Coast Guard detention did not fall within the reach of the *force majeure* clause and Phillips could not in any event invoke the clause since nothing prevented its performance of the contract. The district court further rejected Phillips' claims that its performance was excused because Tradax chose an unsuitable ship and tendered defective documents. Finding that Tradax's mitigation was reasonable, the judge awarded damages with interest. From this judgment Phillips appeals.

Discussion

The 1980 *Incoterms* define a "C & F" contract as one in whiTOC3CH:

"the seller must pay the costs and freight necessary to bring the goods to the named destination but the risk of loss of or damage to the goods, as well as of any cost increases, is transferred from the seller to the buyer when the goods pass the ship's rail in the port of shipment."

. . . .

As a "C & F" seller Tradax had two duties that are relevant here: to deliver the naphtha to an appropriate carrier with which it had contracted for shipment and to tender proper documents to Phillips. Phillips in return was contractually obliged to pay for the naphtha when presented with the shipping documents by Tradax. It is undisputed that after Tradax loaded the naphtha on the Oxy Trader and presented Phillips with the shipping documents on October 13, 1981, Phillips refused to pay for the cargo. If Tradax had adequately performed its contractual duties, Phillips' refusal to pay for the naphtha constituted a breach of the contract as of October 13, unless it was somehow excused from performing.

Phillips asserts several grounds for its failure to pay Tradax on October 13: (1) the existence of a "*force majeure*," (2) unreasonable delay in Tradax's performance,

(3) discrepancies in Tradax's shipping documents, and (4) unsuitability (unseaworthiness) of the Oxy Trader. On the undisputed circumstances of this case, however, none of these theories suffice to excuse Phillips' failure to pay on Tradax's presentation of the documents.

Force Majeure

Phillips first relies on the *force majeure* clause among Tradax's standard contract terms, which were to be included in the contract "subject to [Phillips'] review and acceptance;" the contract, however, did not actually arrive at Phillips' office for review until after the Oxy Trader left port. The standard *force majeure* clause reads:

> "*FORCE MAJEURE*: In the event of any strike, fire or other event falling with[in] the term '*Force Majeure*' preventing or delaying shipment or delivery of the goods by the seller or occurring prior to shipment or delivery and preventing or delaying reception of the goods by the buyer, then the contract period of shipment or delivery shall be extended by 30 days on telex request made within seven days of its occurrence. Should shipment or delivery of the goods continue to be prevented beyond 30 days, the unaffected party may cancel the unfulfilled balance of the contract. Should the contract thus be cancelled and/or performance be prevented during any extension to the shipment or delivery period neither party shall have any claim against the other."

We assume *arguendo* that this clause became part of the contract when Phillips invoked *force majeure* on October 9, 1981.

In construing the *force majeure* clause within this "C & F" contract, we are guided by several basic principles. Although parties may agree to vary the terms of "C & F" or C.I.F. contracts,

> "the dominant outlines of the C.I.F. term are so well understood commercially that any variation should, whenever reasonably possible, be read as falling within those dominant outlines rather than as destroying the whole meaning of a term which essentially indicates a contract for proper shipment rather than one for delivery at destination. Particularly careful consideration is necessary before a printed form or clause is construed to mean agreement otherwise."

U.C.C. § 2-320, Comment 14.

We also look to the basic purpose of *force majeure* clauses, which is in general to relieve a party from its contractual duties when its performance has been prevented by a force beyond its control or when the purpose of the contract has been frustrated. The burden of demonstrating *force majeure* is on the party seeking to have its performance excused, and, as Judge Carter pointed out, the non-performing party must demonstrate its efforts to perform its contractual duties despite the occurrence of the event that it claims constituted *force majeure*.

With these principles in mind, we cannot agree that Phillips' performance was excused by its invocation of *force majeure*. Even if the detention of the ship by the Coast Guard constituted *force majeure*, and we are inclined to agree with Judge Carter that it did not, that detention did not frustrate the purpose of the contract or prevent Phillips from carrying out its obligation under the terms of the parties' contract to make payment. Indeed, to hold that the *force majeure* clause may be interpreted to excuse the buyer from that obligation, as Phillips urges, would be to wholly overturn the allocation of duties provided for in "C & F" sales. We do not find any evidence that the parties intended such a result.

Phillips' proposed interpretation is clearly inconsistent with the "C & F" terms of sale in the contract itself, which were confirmed by the pre-shipment telex from Phillips, stating that "title and risk of loss to producers shall pass to buyer at the time product reaches the vessel's flange at the load port." This conclusion is further bolstered by Tradax's cross-examination of Kurt Goehman, one of the persons who originally negotiated the contract for Phillips. Goehman gave his commercial opinion that under "C & F" terms, such as those agreed on, the risk of loss passes to the buyer upon the cargo's being loaded and that if the goods should thereafter be destroyed or if the ship should be delayed, the buyer would not be excused from paying the seller; the buyer would, however, have a claim against the carrier if the loss or delay were the fault of the ship. In sum, Tradax's only obligation regarding delivery of the goods was to deliver them to the carrier; events occurring thereafter were not its concern.

No contrary conclusion is suggested by the language of the *force majeure* clause. The clause was a standard Tradax term applicable both to delivery contracts and to shipment contracts such as this one. The language in the clause referring to a delay in delivery and to an extension in the "contract period" for delivery is simply inapplicable here where it was never the seller's duty to assure delivery and where the contract was utterly silent about any delivery date. Certainly this preprinted clause does not evince the parties' intention to revise the standard elements of a "C & F" sale. Moreover, the very manner in which the *force majeure* clause was handled belies any intention to effect radical change in the basic allocation of "C & F" duties. The clause was buried in a group of standard terms in the contract, which did not even arrive at Phillips' offices for approval until after the naphtha was shipped.

The *force majeure* clause thus did not alter the design of the "C & F" contract by requiring Tradax to assure delivery of the naphtha at the ultimate destination in Puerto Rico before it would be entitled to payment. The authorities Phillips cites in support of its contention that a "C & F" seller retains responsibility for events after the time of shipment are plainly distinguishable. The court in *Gatoil International Inc. v. Tradax Petroleum Ltd.*, 1982 G. No. 118, Slip Op. at 24 (Q.B. July 31, 1984), stated "tentative[ly]" that a "C & F" seller could be liable for having "wrongfully delayed the actual delivery of the goods," in that case by instructing a ship to wait outside the harbor at the port of discharge. Here, in contrast, the absence of any such wrongful conduct on Tradax's part makes such deviation from the standard "C & F" division of responsibility inappropriate. Phillips' other authority, *Harlow & Jones, Inc. v. Advance Steel Co.*, 424 F. Supp. 770, 776 (E.D. Mich. 1976), is also inapt. That court was presented with a different question, which is not before us, *i.e.*, whether timely delivery to a C.I.F. buyer might excuse late shipment by the seller. The court found that "delivery, not shipment...primarily concerned" the buyer. No such findings were made here nor could they be, since the contract nowhere specified a delivery date. Moreover, the *Advance Steel* court found in favor of the shipper, holding that the buyer's premature repudiation of the agreement on grounds of anticipated delay in delivery amounted to a breach of contract. Thus the result was the same as that reached by the district court in the present case.

Phillips therefore has no viable claims that *force majeure* excused it from performance under the contract.

Defects in the Documents

There is equally little merit in Phillips' claim that it was excused from payment under the contract because Tradax tendered defective shipping documents. While it is true that in a sale by documents the seller's tender of the documents is judged very strictly, Phillips' objection to the documents here, as Judge Carter noted, "is an afterthought and must fail." Without having seen the shipping documents. Phillips twice instructed its agents that because of *force majeure*, they were not to pay Tradax when the latter presented the papers for payment. When Tradax presented the papers in Puerto Rico, a Phillips employee chose to give them only a cursory examination before stating that they seemed "okay," but that he had been instructed not to pay.

To the extent that the documents might have been defective because of the incorrect destination in the bill of lading, the denomination of Schlubach as consignee and the need for an assurance that Tradax had paid the freight charges, Phillips waived its right to rely on this belatedly alleged defect as justification for its nonpayment because it did not seasonably notify Tradax and particularize any defects so that Tradax could effect a timely cure. *See* U.C.C. § 2-605(1). Under the terms of the contract, as modified by a confirming letter sent by Tradax to which Phillips never objected, *see* U.C.C. § 2-207(2)(c), payment was due in cash by telegraphic transfer on the same day as the presentation of the documents. Phillips' breach of that obligation bore no relation to its telex nearly a month later formally canceling the contract on broader grounds.

Nor is Phillips aided by U.C.C. § 2-510(1), which provides that "where a tender or delivery of goods so fails to conform to the contract as to give a right of rejection the risk of their loss remains on the seller until cure or acceptance." Assuming this section applies to a tender of defective documents (*see* Official Comment 2) the alleged defect here was immaterial. The bill of lading, although to Schlubach's order, was endorsed in blank by Schlubach, thus making Phillips the consignee. Nor is Phillips excused from performance by the bill of lading's description of the destination of the shipment as "Rotterdam for Order," wording that was commonly used with respect to shipments from Algeria in order to meet Common Market requirements. At all times the shipment was destined for Puerto Rico, not Rotterdam, and Tradax from the outset instructed the master accordingly. Finally, nothing in the parties' contract obliged Tradax to pre-pay freight. On the contrary, Part II, Clause 2 of the charter, which governed the time when freight was to be paid by Tradax, provided that payment might be made "upon the delivery of cargo at destination."

In any event, even if we were to accept Phillips' contention that its time for performance had not arrived because Tradax had failed to tender conforming documents, Phillips' earlier refusal to pay on the grounds of *force majeure* constituted an anticipatory breach of the contract. As early as October 9 Phillips declared its intention to refrain from payment until the event of *force majeure* abated, and it restated these sentiments repeatedly thereafter, even though it was beyond its rights in so insisting. Phillips anticipatorily breached the parties' contract when it "demanded...a performance to which [it had] no right under the contract and state[d] definitely that, unless [the] demand [was] complied with, [it would] not render [the] promised performance." At least by October 13 its intention to repudiate was unquestionably "positive and unequivocal." Tradax was thus excused from all performance under the contract, including any needed cure in its tender of documents.

The Suitability of the Oxy Trader

Phillips was not relieved of its contractual obligation because of Tradax's selection of the Oxy Trader. The relevant provision in the provision in the 1980 *Incoterms* requires that a "C & F" seller contract for the carriage of the goods "in a seagoing vessel...of the type normally used for the transport of goods of the contract description." Although the Oxy Trader, an integrated tug barge, was of novel design in that the tug and the barge were married together, this feature did not disqualify the Trader as a ship that might "normally" be used for transport. A new design would not carry with it such a disqualification. Indeed, the status of the Trader as a ship normally used for transport was confirmed by the United States Coast Guard's certification of it for ocean transport and for carriage of comparable cargos and by Phillips' own approval of the choice of the ship. Moreover, the Oxy Trader had safely sailed on transatlantic trips.

....

The judgment of the district court is affirmed.

CEP Interagra SA V. Select Trading GMBH, Queen's Bench Division (Commercial Court 1990)

(Lexis, UK Library, Engcas File)

PHILLIPS, JUDGE

On the morning of the 28th March of this year the tankship "JAMBUR" set sail from Constanza with a cargo of gasoil. Later that day the Plaintiffs ("the Sellers") concluded a contract whereby they sold that cargo to the Defendants ("the Buyers") under a contract which included the following terms:

Delivery: Latest by 30th April 1990, cif basis one safe berth/port Kaohsiung, Taiwan, as full cargo per mt "JAMBUR," which sailed from Constanza 10:00 am 28th March 1990

I shall refer to this provision as "the Delivery Clause."

On the 29th March 1990 the "JAMBUR" collided with another vessel in the Bosphorus. She sustained serious damage, lost some 2,500 tons of cargo and was arrested by the Turkish authorities. These misfortunes made it impossible for the "JAMBUR" to reach Kaohsiung by the 30th April.

On the 10th April the Buyers purported to treat the inability of the Sellers to procure delivery of the cargo at Kaohsiung by the 30th April 1990 as an anticipatory breach of a condition of the contract which they accepted as bringing the contract to an end.

In this Action the Sellers deny that the contract required them to procure delivery of the cargo by the 30th April and claim damages from the Buyers for their failure to perform the contract. By agreement between the parties I am invited to determine the following preliminary issue:... whether it was a condition of the contract, breach of which would entitle the Defendants to terminate the contract, that the Plaintiffs should effect physical delivery of the cargo in Taiwan by the 30th April 1990, and whether the delay caused by the collision on the 29th March 1990 put the Plaintiffs in breach, thereby entitling the Defendants to terminate the contract. That issue turns exclusively on the construction of the contract and neither party here sought to introduce any background facts as an aid to construction.

....

The merits of the rival cases as to the correct construction of this contract have been succinctly and attractively argued by Mr Simon for the Sellers and Mr Eder, QC, for the Buyers. I can summarize their submissions as follows:

The Sellers' Case

Mr Simon submitted that the delivery clause did not impose on the Sellers a positive obligation of any description in respect of the actual date of delivery of the cargo. He advanced two alternative contentions: (I) The delivery clause was incompatible with the remainder of the contract and should be disregarded. Alternatively (II) The only effect of the delivery clause was to prohibit the Sellers from doing anything which would prevent the "JAMBUR" from reaching Kaohsiung by the 30th April. It was thus a negative, not a positive covenant.

Incompatibility

Mr Simon started from what proved to be a substantial area of common ground. He submitted that, apart from the delivery clause, the contract had all the features of a classic CIF contract, subject to certain variations that are common in the oil trade. It is an important element of the CIF contract that the Seller does not have to effect physical delivery of the cargo. In circumstances where the goods do not arrive, or arrive late, the only remedies available to the CIF Buyer lie against the carriers or insurers of the cargo. Mr Simon submitted that certain specific features of the contract in the present case underlined the fact that the risk of non-delivery fell upon the Buyers, in particular:

1) The contract was described as a CIF contract in the Delivery and the Price Clauses.

2) The price fell to be paid according to the bill of lading quantity, not the delivered quantity.

3) There was no provision for inspection at the delivery port.

4) Sellers were obliged to procure a contract of insurance — a requirement which the Buyers would have no interest in imposing if the effect of the contract was that non-delivery was at Sellers' risk.

Mr Simon argued that a clause which required the Sellers to procure actual delivery before the 30th April did have the effect of putting non-delivery at Sellers' risk and was therefore at odds with the remainder of the contract and should be disregarded.

In support of this approach Mr Simon relied upon the fact that Rowlett J had adopted a similar approach in *Law and Bonar Ltd v British American Tobacco Co Ltd* [1916] 2 KB 605. In The JULIA [1949] AC 293 at p 310 Lord Porter accepted that Rowlett J's decision was proper in a case where:

"the overriding provision is the term cif under which antagonistic terms can be neglected on the ground that they are repugnant to the transaction."

These words, submitted Mr Simon, aptly applied to the present case.

In support of his submissions Mr Simon ventured a speculative suggestion as to how the inappropriate Delivery Clause might have come to be incorporated in the contract. The clause might have been agreed at an early stage of the negotiations, before a specific cargo or a specific carrying vessel had been identified. In such circumstances the delivery clause would have done no more than oblige the Sellers to load on a vessel which would, in the normal course of events, arrive at Kaohsiung prior to the 30th April.... Support for this theory could, Mr Simon suggested, be derived from the fact that the Inspection Clause was not apposite having regard to the fact that the vessel had already sailed when the contract was concluded. That also had the appearance of a clause agreed at an earlier stage and incorporated in the contract by accident. Finally, Mr Simon sought to buttress his argument by reference to commercial reality. He suggested that it was highly unlikely that the Sellers would accept the risk of the vessel being delayed beyond the 30th April when they could have no influence over factors that might delay her once she had sailed.

Negative Covenant

Mr Simon referred me to the following passage from *Benjamin on Sale of Goods*, 3rd Ed paragraph 1612:

> The point of saying that the seller performs his part of the bargain by tendering documents is that he is not obliged actually to deliver the goods at the agreed destination, he is only under a negative duty not to prevent the goods from being delivered to the buyer at that destination, by (for example) diverting them elsewhere, or by ordering the carrier not to deliver them to the buyer.

He suggested that if the Delivery Clause has to be given some effect, then it should be treated as providing a gloss on the ordinary negative duty that a CIF Seller is under. The clause made it plain that the Sellers would be in breach of duty not merely if they did anything to prevent delivery, but if they did anything to delay delivery beyond April 30th.

The Buyers' Case

Incompatibility

Mr Eder took exception to Mr Simon's speculation as to the background to the contract and the circumstances in which the Delivery Clause had come to be incorporated. He submitted that in the absence of any evidence of relevant background material it was impermissible to speculate about the genesis of the contract.

As to the contract itself, Mr Eder contended that the natural meaning of the Delivery Clause was clear. It required the Sellers to procure delivery of the cargo at Kaohsiung by the 30th April. Mr Eder contrasted the present case with "The WISE." That case involved a C & F contract in respect of an unascertained cargo to be carried on an unascertained vessel with a delivery clause which provided: Delivery: Vessel TBN. Arrival March 15-30 1986.

The Buyers argued that this clause obliged the Sellers to procure physical delivery between the 15th and 30th March. Leggatt J rejected this contention for the following reasons:

> It seems to me that since the parties have chosen to designate the contract as a c & f contract, I should approach the construction of it in the expectation that that is what it is. When I look at the delivery clause, I find that it is to be performed by a vessel to be nominated followed by the words "Arrival: March 15-30 1986." It seems to me that the natural construction of the clause is that the nominated vessel shall be such as is expected to arrive within the period mentioned. It does not wear the air of a contract designed to procure the guarantee of delivery within the period stipulated. I decline so to construe it, especially since to do so would be inconsistent with a c & f contract in classic form. I accept the plaintiffs' submission that on a true construction of the contract their obligation was to load a contractual cargo on board a nominated vessel within a time which in the ordinary course of events would enable the cargo to arrive at both discharge ports within the stipulated period.

Mr Eder pointed out that the Delivery Clause in the present case could not sensibly relate to the choice and time of loading of the vessel to perform the contract, for the "JAMBUR" had already been chosen, had loaded the cargo and had sailed. More pertinently, Mr Eder submitted that the wording of the Delivery Clause in the present case contrasted with that in "The WISE." He referred me to these comments on the meaning of "latest:"

Warde v Feedex International Inc [1985] 2 Lloyd's Rep 289, per Bingham J at p 298:

"...The reference to "the 2nd March latest" is, in my judgment, the language of deadlines. This was a mercantile contract; the term in question related to a time provision, and the parties, as I have indicated, used language indicative of an intention that the date should be complied with...."

Gill & Dufus v Societe pour l'Exportation des Sucres SA *[1986] 1 Lloyd's Rep 322, per Leggatt J:*

"...there are no words in the English language by which a deadline can be appointed more concisely, more precisely and with more finality than the words 'at latest;' and I hold they mean what they say."

The only sensible meaning that could be given to the Delivery Clause, and the obvious meaning, was that it was a condition of the contract that delivery of the cargo should be effected by April 30th.

As to the alleged incompatibility with the remainder of the contract, Mr Eder referred me to the words of Lord Porter in The "JULIA" at p 310:

"The true effect of all [the contract's] terms must be taken into account, though, of course, the description cif must not be neglected."

Mr Eder accepted that the construction of the Delivery Clause for which he contended made a significant variation to the normal CIF contract, but challenged the suggestion that there was any inconsistency between the Delivery Clause and other express provisions of the contract. In particular, he made the following points:

1)   While the contract requires payment against documents before the deadline for delivery, this is not inconsistent with the Sellers remaining under a residual obligation in respect of delivery.

2)   There were good commercial reasons why the Buyers should wish the Sellers to procure a contract of insurance. The Buyers carried the risk of contamination of the cargo, the risk of leakage between the point of discharge and the shoretank and, possibly, the risk of a degree of loss in transit. In any event the Buyers might wish to take delivery of cargo, despite loss in transit, together with an insurance policy covering such loss, whether they were obliged to or not.

Mr Eder relied upon the view of the editors of Benjamin that one can, by clear wording, vary a CIF contract to impose an obligation on the Sellers to procure physical delivery — *see* paragraph 1671.

The Negative Covenant

Mr Eder dealt with Mr Simon's alternative submission robustly. He simply submitted that the words of the Delivery Clause were quite clear and were not capable of bearing the meaning suggested.

The Correct Construction

Mr Eder was correct to object to Mr Simon's speculation as to how the Delivery Clause came to be incorporated in the final version of the contract. Such a consideration would not be admissible as an aid to construction, even if clearly established by evidence. Far less is it permissible to resort to speculation as to the nature and course of previous negotiations as an aid to construction of the contract.

Mr Simon is, however, correct to submit that the starting point when considering the Delivery Clause is that it fails to be construed in the context of a CIF contract. It is natural to seek a construction which is not antagonistic to such a contract. Such an approach does not, in my judgment, justify construing the Delivery Clause as the negative covenant suggested by Mr Simon in his alternative submission. The emphatic wording of the clause is not consistent with such a limited effect.

Mr Simon's primary submission that the clause should be disregarded as inconsistent with a CIF contract implicitly acknowledged that the natural meaning of the clause is that contended for by the Buyers. In my judgment the clear meaning of the Delivery Clause is that the Sellers have to procure physical delivery of the cargo by the 30th April.

I turn then to consider the submission that the designation of the contract as CIF should override the Delivery Clause as being antagonistic. In *Law and Bonar Ltd v British American Tobacco Co Ltd* Rowlett J adopted such an approach where the antagonistic clause was part of a printed form to which the parties had added the conflicting provisions of a CIF contract. Here the Delivery Clause is a term expressly agreed and incorporated into the contract by the parties. It can only be legitimate to disregard such a clause if it is impossible to give sensible effect to it having regard to conflicting provisions in the remainder of the contract. In the present case I find no such conflict.

It is important to bear in mind that established types of contract for the sale of goods are the servants of those who use them, not vice versa. New trades have grown up and old trades have altered with the result that the contractual requirements of buyers and sellers of goods cannot always be accommodated within the framework of the classic CIF or FOB contract. The oil trade is a case in point.

It is not uncommon for oil cargoes sold on CIF terms to reach their destination before the seller can tender the bill of lading. The ship may then give delivery to the buyer in exchange for an indemnity and the buyer may pay the seller against a letter of indemnity. Payment may precede delivery or vice versa. The contract in the present case permits of such variations to the classic CIF transaction.

I can see no reason why the Delivery Clause should not be permitted to take effect according to its natural meaning as a further variation to the classic CIF contract. It is not hard to imagine commercial justification for such a clause. It may well be that the Buyers wanted the cargo to arrive by 30th April to meet a specific delivery obligation under a delivered contract. Both Buyers and Sellers were traders. I can see no reason in principle why they should not have agreed that the risk of an untoward delay in the voyage should be born by the Sellers rather than by the Buyers.

Accordingly I hold that the Delivery Clause bears the meaning contended for by the Buyers and that due effect falls to be given to the clause in accordance with that meaning.

This conclusion raises the question of whether the obligation imposed by the Delivery Clause was a condition, an innominate term or a warranty. Mr Eder came armed with formidable authority to support the proposition that the term was a condition. In the event, while not conceding this, Mr Simon raised no positive challenge to that construction. In that he showed his customary sensible discretion. I rule that the obligation imposed on the Sellers by the Delivery Clause was a condition of the contract.

In the absence of any plea of frustration it must follow that the inability of the Sellers to comply with the Delivery Clause that was attributable to the collision and its consequences placed the Sellers in anticipatory breach of condition and entitled the Buyers to terminate the contract.

DISPOSITION:

Judgment accordingly

NOTE ON THE TIME OF DELIVERY

The primary source for determining the date for delivery is the parties' contract. *See* Article 33(a). Moreover, the date for delivery is fixed by or determinable from the contract if the date is fixed by or determinable from a usage made applicable to the contract by Article 9. If the date of delivery is fixed in terms of a period of time, the seller may choose to deliver "at any time within that period unless the circumstances indicate that the buyer is to choose a date." Article 33(b). In those cases where the parties have said nothing about the time for delivery, Article 33(c) states a default rule that the seller must perform "within a reasonable time after the conclusion of the contract." *Compare* U.C.C. Section 2-309. Should the seller deliver the goods before the date specified in the contract, Article 52(1) gives the buyer the option of either taking the goods at that time or refusing to take delivery of the goods.

QUESTION

1.   Suppose that the contract permits the buyer to choose the delivery date. Will the seller's performance be excused if the buyer fails to provide the seller with adequate notice of that date? *See* Article 79.

IV. Payment Obligation of the Buyer

Documents Supplement References:

1. *CISG Articles 53-54, 57-58.*

2. *UNIDROIT Principles Article 6.1.*

3. *U.C.C. Sections 2-301, 2-308, 2-310, 2-507, 2-513.*

4. *Restatement (Third) on Foreign Relations Law § 823.*

NOTE ON TIME AND PLACE OF PAYMENT

The principle obligations of the buyer are to pay the price for the goods and to take delivery of them "as required by the contract and [the] Convention." Article 53. *Compare* U.C.C. Section 2-301. Included within the buyer's basic obligation to pay the price is the duty to take whatever actions are necessary to enable payment to be made. *See* Article 54. Oftentimes the required steps or formalities will be dictated by the terms of the contract (*i.e.*, applying for a letter of credit or bank guarantee of payment) but not always. It will sometimes be the case that the buyer is required to comply with relevant governmental laws and regulations, such as applying for official authorization to remit the currency abroad. If the buyer fails to take the appropriate measures, the seller may then resort to remedies for anticipatory breach or damages for breach of contract.

Unless otherwise agreed, the buyer must pay the price at the seller's place of business or, if payment is to be made against the handing over of the goods or documents, the place where the handing over takes place. *See* Article 57. *Compare* U.C.C. Sections 2-308(a); 2- 310(c); and UNIDROIT Article 6.1.6. In the event that the parties have failed to contractually indicate the time for payment, the buyer is required to pay the price at the time the seller makes the goods available to the buyer by placing the goods or documents controlling their disposition at the buyer's disposal. Conversely, the seller need not hand over the goods or documents if the buyer does not pay at that time. *See* Article 58. *Compare* U.C.C. Sections 2-310(a); 2-507. Finally, the buyer is not obligated to pay for the goods until he has had an opportunity to inspect them, unless the procedures for payment or delivery are inconsistent with such an opportunity. *See* Article 58(3). *Compare* U.C.C. Sections 2-310; 2-513(1).

Magyar Kereskedelmi és Iparkamara, Mellett Szervezett, Választottbiróság,

Arbitration Court of the Chamber of Commerce and Industry of Budapest (1996)

In case of ... Claimant ... versus ... Respondent [Buyer] ... for payment of [a sum of money] with costs and interests the court of arbitration has brought today and delivers to the process parties ... the following Award

The Court of Arbitration obliges ... [Buyer] to pay ... (Claimant)

a) US $93,127 (ninety three thousand one hundred twenty seven US dollars), as well as

b) 8% interest on the amount of US $15,000 (fifteen thousand) from May 28, 1992 until payment,

c) 8% interest on the amount of US $78,127 (seventy eight thousand one hundred and twenty-seven US dollars) from November 23, 1995 until payment,

d) US $5,309 (five thousand three hundred and nine US dollars) which this Court of Arbitration established as costs of arbitration, and

e) US $3,500 (three thousand five hundred US dollars) recognized by this Court of Arbitration as attorney's fee due to Claimant.

[Buyer] is obliged to pay all these amounts (indicated under a-e) within 30 days after the receipt of the present Award.

Further demands of the Claimant pertaining to interest are denied.

Reasons for the Award

1. The Claimant has submitted in its statement of claim the ground for its claim, and annexed different correspondence of the parties to it as follows:

[Seller] a Yugoslav company exported caviar to [Buyer]. Delivery took place on May 28, 1992; Hungarian customs clearance was affected on May 29, 1992. It was not contested by [Buyer] that delivery was according to the contract in every respect. The price agreed upon between [Seller] and [Buyer] was US $93,127 — and it was never paid. ... [Seller] asked [Buyer] to pay the outstanding amount to four beneficiaries. [Buyer] agreed to it. On July 21, and on July 28, 1992 [Buyer] attempted to pay and gave orders to its bank to effect payment to the Cyprus beneficiaries, but failed. [Buyer] informed [the] beneficiaries the payments were not effected due to the UN sanctions against Yugoslavia.

During the . . . sanctions the parties made repeated endeavors to settle the outstanding debt of [Buyer]. The sanctions represented *force majeure*. In its letter of June 14, 1994 [Buyer] declared that "the purchase of caviar stock has happened, but declare that fulfillment of payment is limited by *force majeure*." On December 26, 1994, a written agreement was reached. . . . This agreement confirms that the new creditor is . . . the present Claimant in this arbitration case, since it paid to earlier creditors the amount of US $93,127. . . . [Buyer] accepted this change of creditors, it confirmed that its basic debt is US $93,127 and agreed to pay costs and interests on standard banking rates. [Buyer] answered to Claimant on May 26, 1995 that UN sanctions prevented the payment. After the UN sanction[s] were lifted, Claimant repeated its demands for payment on November 23, 1995, as well as on December 21, 1995. In its letter of January 29, 1996 [Buyer] stated that it does not contest the debt, but proposed arbitration which Claimant finally accepted.

2. The jurisdiction of the Court of Arbitration at the Hungarian Chamber of Commerce and Industry is based on a separate written agreement between the parties. Arbitration was initiated by [Buyer] in its telefax message of January, 1996. Claimant accepted all elements of [Buyer's] proposal (the jurisdiction of the Court of Arbitration of the Hungarian Chamber of Commerce and Industry, the Vienna Sales Convention as applicable law, English as language of the proceedings). Finally [Buyer] confirmed the content of the parties' mutual understanding. (Claimant enclosed the relevant telefaxes of May 1 and 2 of 1996 to its statement of claim.)

3. On ground of the statement of its claim the Claimant requested to oblige [Buyer] for the payment of US $93,127 principal sum with 8% interests from May 28 until the day of payment as well as to pay the expenses of the Arbitration proceedings.

4. [Buyer] acknowledged in its statement of defense received by the Court of Arbitration on September 18, 1996, it had concluded with [Seller] the legal predecessor of Claimant the purchase contract but emphasized the consignment was aimed for re-export. Seller delivered the product on May 28, 1992 which as a result of the international . . . sanctions, embargo coming into effect against Yugoslavia had to go outside the bonded warehouse area and [Buyer] could not take delivery of it, or clear it through the customs or return it to Sellers. [Buyer] confirmed it never contested the consignment entered into Hungary on the day prior the embargo came into effect. The goods according to the customs documents arrived for export purposes and never entered customs for local clearance. The responsibility of [Buyer] extended only to the protection of the goods which was met securing and payment of temporary cold storage. Considering [the] conservation date expired, [Buyer] was responsible to destroy the goods and bear its costs. [Buyer] emphasized the sturgeon caviar consignment could never get into its possession and ownership.

5. On basis of its reasons [Buyer] asked the Court of Arbitration to refuse the claim.

6. At the oral hearing of the Court of Arbitration of November 21, 1996, the Claimant and the [Buyer] had no objection to the composition of the panel. The Claimant and the [Buyer] confirmed their earlier statements. The Claimant submitted the original sale contract dated May 21, 1992, the relevant freight bills and invoices. The contract wrote in its Point 2 the following: "The Buyer shall pick up the fish eggs at the Seller's address and bring the goods to his facilities in Hungary." The price was agreed on FOB Kladovo basis. The freight bills contained at terms of delivery "FCO KAMION KLADOVO." The Claimant gave details of the amount of the claim. The [Buyer] disputed the deliveries were made on its behalf and that it received the relevant invoices shown at the hearing. The reasons [Buyer] confirmed its

payment obligation to Claimant several times was that [Buyer] wanted to maintain the good commercial relationship with Claimant. [Buyer] declared the mother fishes from the consignment were for local destination; therefore they were cleared by the customs. The caviar was not cleared by the customs for local destination but cleared by the customs in accordance with the rules relating to goods for re-export purposes because it was not imported for local destination. The Claimant and the [Buyer] unanimously declared there was no later amendment to their sale contract, and confirmed their common understanding relating to the 8% interests to be applied in the present proceedings.

. . . .

8. For judgment of the statement of claim as well as the rights and obligations of the parties, the Court of Arbitration had to take into account the Purchase agreement dated May 21, 1992, the protocol of the oral hearing of the Court of Arbitration, the submitted documents as well as the later statements, declarations of the parties. The parties agreed that the language of the Arbitration proceedings shall be English. The parties also agreed the United Nations Convention on Contracts for the International Sale of Goods be applied (hereinafter Vienna Convention). The Court of Arbitration — based upon § 25 of Law Decree 13 of 1979 — stated that for judgment of the present case the Yugoslav material law is applicable. The Vienna Convention was already integrated into the Yugoslav material law when the Purchase Contract was signed in 1992.

9. The Vienna Convention foresees in Art 53 that the Buyer must pay the price for the goods and take delivery of them as required by the contract and this Convention. The contract of the parties definitely provided for the basis of the delivery as follows: "The Buyer shall pick up the fish eggs at the Seller's address and bring the goods to his facilities in Hungary" (Point 2 of the Contract). The price was based FOB Kladovo (point 3 of the Contract). This was confirmed by the freight bills the Claimant enclosed. The Claimant and the [Buyer] unanimously confirmed at the oral hearing there was no later amendment to this contract. The Contract did not provide for any re-export provision. The [Buyer] could not submit to the Court of Arbitration any proof for any re-export agreement of the parties. The [Buyer] had to pay US $15,000 before the delivery and the remaining amount within two weeks after delivery of the goods in accordance with Point 6 of the Purchase Contract. Art 59 of the Vienna Convention provides the Buyer must pay the price on the date fixed by or determinable from the Contract and this Convention, without need for any request or compliance with any formality on the part of the Seller. Art 60 of the Vienna Convention confirms the Buyer's obligation to take delivery consists in taking over the goods. In the opinion of the Court of Arbitration taking over the goods means taking over the goods as foreseen in the *Incoterms* Rules, which in our case was regulated by the Contract reading to pick up the goods at Seller's address, FOB Kladovo. The Hungarian customs clearance gives a further support to this understanding. The [Buyer] itself declared during the oral hearing a part of the consignment (mother fishes) was customs cleared for local destination; the other clearance was made in accordance with the re-export provisions. Loss of or damage to the goods after the risk has passed to the Buyer does not discharge him from his obligation to pay the price, unless the loss or damage is due to an act or omission of the Seller (Art 66 of the Vienna Convention).

The Yugoslav material law has the same solution as the German, Austrian or Hungarian law when it says the title to ownership passes simultaneously when the goods are taken over by Buyer.

The Court of Arbitration came to the conclusion that the risk and the ownership has passed to Buyer...in accordance with the Contract at Kladovo. The [Buyer] could not exculpate itself proving the damage is due to an act or omission of Seller or he could not either prove Seller had known about the re-export intent of [Buyer]. In the opinion of the Court of Arbitration this means the damage caused by *force majeure* has to be borne by the party where the risk is at the moment the *force majeure* occurs.

The Court of Arbitration finds it necessary [to] point out that the risk of the freight has to be borne by the Buyer unless the Contract of the parties or the applicable law otherwise provides (Art 67 of the Vienna Convention). Therefore, the Court of Arbitration stated that the claim of the Claimant is well founded and obliged [Buyer] to pay the Claimant the US $93,127 principal sum.

10. As for the claim regarding interests the Court of Arbitration stated the following: Claimant requested the payment of 8% interest on the principal sum of US $93,127 — starting from May 1992 until payment. This position was reiterated by Claimant during the oral hearing. [Buyer] did not contest the rate of interest, but contested the principal claim, and — by implication — contested the justification for interest payment.

The Vienna Convention on the International Sale of Goods (chosen by the parties as applicable law) does not contain relevant provisions on interest for delay. Therefore, the arbitrators have to establish the applicable law by virtue of the relevant Hungarian conflict rules applicable on ground of Article 14(2) of the Rules of Proceedings of this Court of Arbitration. The relevant conflict rule is contained in § 24 of the 1979 Hungarian Act on Private International Law. According to this provision, the applicable law is the substantive law of the Seller — which is in this case Yugoslav law. In Yugoslavia, the relevant norms on interest on default are contained in the 1978 Act on Obligations (articles 277-279 in particular) as well as in the 1993 Act on the Amount of Interest on Default.

The Yugoslav rules referred to above have not made it perfectly clear whether interest on default is only due when delay in payment is attributable to the fault of the debtor, or whether such interest is a simple consequence of the objective fact that payment was not made in time. Article 277 of the Act on Obligations, and Article 1 of the Act on the Amount of Interest on Default simply state that interest on default is owed if the debtor is late with payment. In recent Yugoslav scholarly writings two justices of the Supreme Court of Serbia have taken a position that interest on default is due when the debtor is responsible for the delay. According to Justice Latinovic, "Interest on default is a consequence of breach of contract by the debtor...." (Z. LATINOVIC, ZATEZNA KAMATAZBOG DOCNJE U PLACANJU NOVCAN OBAVEZE, Pravni zivot 9-10/1992, 1426, at p. 1428). In the words of Justice Maljkovic "Interest on default regarding pecuniary claims is due from the moment the debtor is in default." (B. MALJKOVIC, ZATEZNA KAMATA NA NOVCANO POTRAZIVANJE NENOVCANE STETE, Pravni zivot 9-10/1992, 1436, at p. 1438.) Under Yugoslav law, there is no default if lack of performance is not imputable to the debtor. At the same time, according to Article 262 (4) of the 1978 Act on Obligations, the debtor will be responsible even if his performance became impossible, if it became impossible after the debtor fell into default. We shall be guided by these rules.

The UN sanctions had created a rather peculiar situation regarding the distribution of liabilities for failure to perform. We have established in this award that [Buyer] is liable to pay the purchase price notwithstanding whether he was or was not able to make proper use of the goods. Respondent/Buyer became responsible for the goods before the UN sanctions became effective in Hungary (they became effective on June 3, 1992 by virtue of Government Order No. 91/1992.) As far as payment is concerned, according to the Purchase Agreement of May 21, 1992, Buyer was supposed to pay US $15,000 before delivery, while the balance was due "within two weeks after delivery." This means that with respect to US $15,000 — Buyer was in default before the sanctions became effective, he could have and should have paid at a date when payment was possible and his status of being a defaulting party cannot be changed by a later *force majeure* under Article 262(4) of the Yugoslav Act on Obligations. This is not the case, however, with respect to the balance of US $78,127. With respect to this latter amount [Buyer] was not in default on June 3, 1992; the sanctions effectively thwarted payment. As a matter of fact, Claimant acknowledges in the statement of claim that in July 1992, [Buyer] made attempts to pay, but this was hindered by the UN sanctions. The payment of this amount became only possible when the UN sanctions were suspended. Suspension became effective on November 22, 1995 at 24:00 hours. (Resolution of the UN Security Council No. 1022/1995 — Published in Hungary in Magyar Közlöny No. 102/1995.) Therefore, from November 23, 1995, [Buyer] was in default with the payment of the amount of US $78,127 — short of convincing evidence to the contrary — and no such evidence was presented.

On ground of these considerations the arbitrators have concluded that [Buyer] owes:

a) 8% interest on the amount of US $15,000 from May 28, 1992, until payment.

b) 8% interest on the amount of US $78,127 from November 23, 1995, until payment.

. . . .

Dated this 10th December, 1996

Case Abstract, UNCITRAL Texts (CLOUT), Abstract No. 93

June 15, 1994 (Austria: Arbitral Tribunal - Vienna)

In 1990 and 1991, an Austrian seller and a German buyer concluded contracts for the sale of rolled metal sheets. The initial contracts provided that the goods were to be delivered "FOB Hamburg," by March 1991 at the latest. Later, the seller allowed the buyer to take delivery of the goods in installments. The buyer resold the goods and had to pay the price and the storage costs promptly after receiving each invoice. The buyer took delivery of some of the goods without paying, and refused to take delivery of other goods. Pursuant to an arbitration clause contained in the sales contract, the seller commenced arbitral proceedings, demanding payment of the price. In addition, the seller demanded damages, including those arising from a sale of the goods, which the buyer refused to accept, to a third party.

The sole arbitrator held that, since the parties had chosen Austrian law, the contracts were governed by CISG as the international sales law of Austria, a [C]ontracting State (Article 1(1)(b) CISG). With regard to the goods delivered but not paid for, the arbitrator found that the seller was entitled to payment of their price (Articles 53 and 61 CISG). Regarding the sale made by the seller in order to mitigate its losses, the arbitrator held that the seller had the right, and, presumably, the duty to mitigate its losses (Article 77 CISG). As a result, the seller was found to be entitled to the difference between the contract price and the substitute sale price.

The arbitrator further held that interest on the price accrued from the date payment was due (Articles 78 and 58 CISG). Since the parties' agreement required the

buyer to pay after receiving each invoice, interest accrued from the date of such receipt, which occur[r]ed within 10 days after issuance of each invoice.

Moreover, the arbitrator held that, since the interest rate was a matter governed
but not expressly settled by CISG, it should be settled in conformity with the general
principles on which CISG is based (Article 7(2) CISG). Referring to Arts. 78 and 74
CISG, the arbitrator found that full compensation was one of the general principles
underlying CISG. It was also found that in relations between merchants it was expected that the seller, due to the delayed payment, would resort to bank credit at the
interest rate commonly practiced in its own country with respect to the currency of
payment. Such currency may be either the currency of the seller's country, or any
other foreign currency agreed upon by the parties. The arbitrator observed that the
application of Article 7.4.9 of the UNIDROIT Principles of International Commercial Contracts would lead to the same result. The interest rate awarded was the average prime rate in the seller's country (Austria), with respect to the currencies of
payment (US dollars and German marks).

Franco Ferrari, Specific topics of the CISG in
the Light of Judicial Application and Scholarly Writing,
15 Journal of Law and Commerce 1, 116-25 (1995)

. . . .

1. *The Issue of Interest Rates in General*

The last issue to be discussed in this paper, the issue of interests on sums in arrears, was one of the most debated issues during the 1980 Vienna Conference. And
although this issue has been examined very often not only in legal writing, but in
many court decisions and several arbitral awards as well, it still creates difficulties,
for the reasons that will be pointed out *infra*.

This issue did not, on the contrary, cause any difficulties under the ULIS, since
Article 83 ULIS provided for "a rule for interest in arrears in the event of payment in
arrears of the price which provided for one percent above the official discount rate in
the creditor's country." This formula has not been retained by the drafters of the Vienna Sales Convention, although there were various attempts to do so. Apart from
these attempts to fix the rate of interest in the same way as the ULIS, other attempts
were made to precisely determine the rate of interests, but they were not successful
either. The German view in favour of a fixed interest rate was rejected, as was the
view of the Czechoslovakian Delegation, according to which the applicable rate of
interest should be the discount rate prevailing in the country of the debtor. The same
is true with the viewpoint held jointly by Denmark, Finland, Greece and Sweden, according to which interest should be calculated on the basis of the customary rate for
commercial credits at the creditor's place of business.

The different political, economic and religious views made it impossible to agree
upon a formula to calculate the rate of interest. Thus, the Vienna Sales Convention contains a provision —considered to work as a compromise among the different views presented during the Vienna Conference — Article 78, which limits itself to merely providing for "the general entitlement to interest" in case of payments in arrears. In other
words, Article 78 only sets forth the obligation to pay interest as a general rule, and it
does so independently from the damage caused by the payment in arrears, as pointed out
by several court decisions, which expressly stated that the entitlement to interest does
not exclude the possibility to claim damages *ex* Article 74. And since Article 78 does not

set forth a time starting from which interests may be calculated either, it has been said that "Art. 78 is more conspicuous for the questions it fails to answer than the questions it answers. In particular, it does not stipulate the rate of interest or how the rate is to be determined by a tribunal in the absence of explicit guidance in the Convention."

2. Interest Rates and Gap-Filling

The lack of a specific formula to calculate the rate of interest on sums in arrears has led some courts as well as several legal writers to consider this issue as being a gap *praeter legem*, *i.e.*, as being governed by, but not expressly settled in, the CISG, whereas other courts and legal scholars consider the issue *de quo* as falling outside the scope of application of the CISG, *i.e.*, as being a gap *intra legem*. This had necessarily to lead to diverging solutions, since under the CISG, the aforementioned kinds of gaps have to be dealt with differently. According to Article 7(2) CISG, the gaps *praeter legem* (or internal gaps) have to be filled by resorting to the general principles on which the Convention is based or, in the absence of such principles, by having recourse to the law applicable by virtue of the rules of private international law. On the contrary, if an issue is considered as falling outside the Convention's scope of application, *i.e.*, if it is an external gap, it must be solved in conformity with the law applicable by virtue of the rules of private international law *i.e.*, without any tentative recourse to the "general principles" of the CISG.

Unfortunately, the CISG does not set forth any useful criterion to determine *in concreto* when a gap is to be considered as being a *lacuna praeter legem* as opposed to a *lacuna intra legem*, although this distinction appears to be quite important for the consequences in which it results. Undoubtedly, the setting forth of a criterion to be used to decide whether a gap must be considered a *lacuna intra legem* or one *praeter legem* would have favored the uniform application of the Vienna Sales Convention.

3. The Issue of the Rate of Interest in Scholarly Writing

The absence of such a criterion raises, as already mentioned above, the question of whether the lack of a formula fixing the rate of interest must be dealt with as a *lacuna praeter legem* or as a *lacuna intra legem*.

On the one hand, it has been said that the issue of determining the rate of interest is not governed by the Vienna Sales Convention and that it is, therefore, governed by the applicable domestic law. Although many scholars hold this view, they appear not to agree on how to determine the applicable domestic law. Indeed, some scholars favor the view according to which the applicable domestic law is to be determined by virtue of the rules of private international law, thus, making applicable, "in general, the subsidiary law applicable to the sales contract [since no] special connecting points seem to have developed for the entitlement to interest." Other scholars, however, argue in favor of either the application of the law of the creditor, independently from whether this is the *lex contractus*, or the application of the law of the debtor.

On the other hand, there are a few authors holding the contrasting view according to which the issue *de quo* has to be dealt with as a *lacuna praeter legem*, on the grounds that "[t]he mandate of Article 7(1) to construe the Convention to promote 'uniformity in its application' requires us to seek a principle governing the scope of Article 78 that can be considered as a basis for uniform application of the Convention." Indeed, the "[d]eference to domestic law ... seems inconsistent with the policy underlying Article 78." Thus, it has been suggested that "the interest to be paid is defined by the function of the assessment of damages, *i.e.*, to put the seller in the same position he would have been had the sum been paid in time," a formula which, however, must be criticized for leading to a confusion of the line between damages and interest which Article 78 has expressly drawn.

4. *The Issue of the Rate of Interest in Judicial Applications*

The aforementioned dispute is not merely a doctrinal one, as evidenced by the number of different solutions adopted in the courts. These different solutions can mainly be divided into two categories: those favoring the view that the rate of interest has to be calculated on the basis of the domestic law; and those holding that the issue *de quo* must be resolved by resorting to the "need to promote uniformity in the application" of the CISG and, thus, to the general principles of the Convention.

In regard to this latter category, several cases are worth mentioning. On the one hand, there are two decisions of Argentinean courts, which invoked Article 9 CISG in order to solve the issue of the applicable rates of interest and "determined the amount of interest payable according to the relevant trading customs," thus "avoid[ing] the difficult problem of determining which domestic law applies." On the other hand, one must mention two recent arbitral awards of the *Internationales Schiedsgericht der Bundeskammer der gewerblichen Wirtschaft in Osterreich* according to which "the applicable interest rate is to be determined autonomously on the basis of the general principles underlying the Convention," on the grounds that recourse to domestic law would lead to results contrary to those promoted by the CISG, at least in those cases where the applicable domestic law would be that of a country which expressly prohibits the payment of interest. This is why in the foregoing awards the issue of the rate of interest was solved by resorting to the general principle of full compensation, which led to the application of the law of the creditor, since it is he who has to borrow money in order to be as liquid as he would be had the debtor paid the sum he owed in due time. This solution, however, contrasts with the legislative history: during the 1980 Diplomatic Conference a proposal to link the rate of interests to the law where the creditor had its place of business was rejected. Independently from this criticism, it is doubtful whether the solution suggested by the aforementioned arbitral awards really offers a new solution, as it wanted to do according to the awards themselves. As has been rightly pointed out by one commentator, the arbitral awards do not lay down a uniform substantive law rule derived from the general principles of the CISG. They merely lay down a conflict of laws rule, since this rule refers to the law of the State where the creditor has his place of business, an approach which, in the end, does not offer anything new but a uniform rule of private international law which, for the reason mentioned above, is to be rejected.

As far as the court decisions are concerned, where the issue *de quo* is solved by resorting to domestic law, a distinction must be made: there are, on the one hand, cases applying the domestic law by virtue of the rules of private international law, on the other hand, cases where the domestic law of the creditor is applied without, however, it being the law made applicable by the rules of private international law

Even though many solutions which differ greatly from each other can be found both in scholarly writing and judicial practice, there seems to be the tendency to apply the *lex contractus*, *i.e.*, the law which would be applicable to the sales contract if it were not subject to the Vienna Sales Convention. Thus, in respect of the formula to calculate the rate of interest, the interest rate of the country of the seller generally applies, at least where the rules of private international law of the forum are based upon criteria comparable to those set forth by the 1980 EEC Convention on the Law Applicable to Contractual Obligations. Absent a choice of law, this Convention makes applicable the law with which the contract has the closest connection, as already mentioned above. This is presumed to be the law where the party who is to effect the "characteristic performance" has its habitual residence, and since the characteristic performance has to be effected by the seller, it is the interest rate of the country where the seller has its place of business which generally is applicable.

Quid iuris, however, where the seller's law does prohibit the payment of interest? In this line of cases, the claim does not become unenforceable as suggested by several authors. It is here suggested, that Article 78 remains enforceable even in this line of cases, but that in order to calculate the rate of interest recourse should be had to the level of interest generally applied in international commerce in the particular trade concerned.

Case Abstract, UNCITRAL Texts (CLOUT), Abstract No. 80,

January 24, 1994 (Germany)

The plaintiff, the Italian assignee of the claim of the Italian seller for payment of the purchase price, sued the buyer, a German company, demanding payment. At issue was whether payment was due in German mark[s], as initially demanded by the seller, or in Italian lira, as agreed in the contract.

The court found that the CISG was applicable as the law of the country where the seller had its place of business. It was held that the application of the CISG could be excluded only if that was the actual and not the hypothetical intention of the parties. With regard to the validity of the assignment, the court applied other Italian law since the CISG did not address assignment.

The court held that, even if the parties had not agreed that payment should be made in Italian lira, the price would still be payable in Italian lira since the place of payment would be the place of business of the Italian seller (CISG 57(1)(a)). In addition, the court held that interest was payable from the time the purchase price became due, even if no notice was given (CISG 58).

NOTE ON THE CURRENCY IN WHICH THE PRICE IS TO BE PAID

The Convention is silent on issues dealing with the currency of the contract. This gap in coverage is particularly significant in the context of international trade where currency fluctuations and exchange control regulations are likely to have a real impact on the profitability of the contract. For the seller, the most obvious risk is that there will be a decline in value of the currency of payment relative to the currency or currencies in which he most often deals. The buyer, on the other hand, must be concerned about the possibility that his currency will depreciate relative to the currency of payment. Given these concerns and the risk that there may be a change in law by the government of the buyer's country which will prevent the payment of the purchase price in the manner agreed upon, the parties will often allocate the potential for loss or gain from these events in the contract.

For example, it is not uncommon to find a contractual stipulation that the price is to be paid in United States dollars or some other internationally respected currency (a so-called "hard" currency). In such cases, Article 6.1.9 of the UNIDROIT Principles would permit the buyer to choose between paying in the currency of account (the currency specified in the contract) or in the currency of the place for payment, provided that the latter currency is freely convertible, and the parties have not agreed otherwise. If exchange regulations or some other cause makes it impossible to pay in the currency of account, the seller may demand that the buyer pay in the currency of the place for payment even if the contract stipulated that the price was to be paid only in the currency of account. *See* UNIDROIT Principles, Article 6.1.9(2). If payment is made in the currency of the place for payment rather than in a different currency stated in the contract, the rate of exchange is that prevailing when payment is due. If, however, payment is not timely, the seller may choose between the rate of exchange prevailing when payment was due or the rate at the time of actual payment. *See* UNIDROIT Principles, Article 6.1.9(3), (4). In the infrequent case where the contract says nothing about a particular currency, payment must be made in the currency of the place where payment is to be made. *See* UNIDROIT Principles, Article 6.1.10.

QUESTIONS

1.   Assume the contract of sale quotes the price on CIF terms. Is the buyer required to pay the price before he has had an opportunity to examine the goods?

2.   Assume that the contract of sale was not on CIF terms and made no other provision for the time and place of payment. If the seller, pursuant to the authority in Article 58(2), behaves as if the contract were on CIF terms, would the buyer lose his right to examine the goods prior to paying the price?

V. Risk of Loss

Documents Supplement References:

1.   *CISG Articles 67-69.*

2.   *U.C.C. Sections 2-509, 2-510.*

3.   *Hague-Visby Rules.*

4.   *United Nations Convention on the Carriage of Goods by Sea (Hamburg Rules).*

5.   *United States Carriage of Goods by Sea Act.*

Louis F. Del Duca and Patrick Del Duca, Practice Under the Convention on International Sale of Goods (CISG): A Primer for Attorneys and International Traders (Part II)

29 Uniform Commercial Code Law Journal 99, 126-30 (1996)

Risk of Loss

Risk-of-loss rules are based on the premise that a buyer's obligation to pay arises when the seller has performed its obligations. Once the seller has performed, because the risk of loss has passed to the buyer, the buyer is required to pay, even if the goods are subsequently destroyed or damaged.

The CISG provides that once the risk has passed to the buyer, buyer must pay the full price, even if the goods have been accidentally damaged or destroyed. However, the buyer is not required to pay the price if the loss or damage was "due to an act or omission of the seller." [Article 66] In this latter situation, the loss or damage is not an accidental loss, but rather a loss for which the seller is responsible. The seller's action releases the buyer from its obligation to pay and also gives the buyer a claim for damages for breach of contract.

The CISG sets forth three sets of risk of loss rules for:

1. Contracts for sale of goods involving carriage of the goods [Article 67];

2. Contracts for sale of goods sold in transit [Article 68]; and

3. Contracts for sale of goods that are neither "carriage" of goods contracts [nor] "in transit" contracts [Article 69].

The third category involves pickup of the goods by the buyer at the seller's place of business or at some third location, as for example when the goods are in the hands of a third-party bailee.

Sale of Goods Involving Carriage

If the contract of sale involves carriage of the goods and the seller is not bound to hand them over at a particular place, the risk passes to the buyer when the goods are handed over to the first carrier for transmission to the buyer in accordance with the contract of sale [Article 67]. If the seller is bound to hand the goods over to a carrier at a particular place (*i.e.*, a destination contract), the risk does not pass to the buyer until the goods are handed over to the carrier at that place [Article 67]. These provisions do not split the risk in cases of multi modal transportation involving a combination of road, sea, or air transportation unless special provisions of the contract specify otherwise.

While the language of the CISG differs from the analogous U.C.C. provisions, these risk-of-loss rules applicable to sales of goods involving carriage appear to be essentially similar to the rules applicable to shipment and destination contracts under the U.C.C. [U.C.C. Section 2-509(1)].

Sale of Goods in Transit

Under the CISG, the risk of loss of goods sold in transit passes from the seller to the buyer at the time of the making of the contract [Article 68]. Professor John Honnold, who was intimately involved in the drafting of the CISG, has advised:

> If you are drafting a contract for the purchase of goods that are already afloat at the time of the contract, one would want a clear provision on whether the buyer bears the risk for damage (such as seeping sea-water) that occurs throughout the voyage. The Convention's rules on this awkward problem are probably no better than you find in domestic law.

Sale of Goods Not Requiring Carriage and Not in Transit

Where the sales contract does not require carriage of the goods and the buyer is to pick up the goods at the seller's place of business, the CISG provides that the risk passes to the buyer when it takes over the goods. If the buyer does not do so at the time specified by the contract, risk of loss then passes at the time when the goods are placed at buyer's disposal, and buyer commits a breach of contract by failing to take delivery [Article 69(1)]. If the goods are in the hands of a third-party bailee and the buyer is bound to take over the goods at a designated place, the risk passes when delivery is due and the buyer is aware that the goods are at his disposal at that place. This latter situation requires that the buyer have a receipt or notice that the goods are ready for delivery [Article 69(2)]. If the contract relates to goods not then identified, the goods are considered not to be placed at the disposal of the buyer until they are clearly identified to the contract [Article 69(3)].

The U.C.C. risk-of-loss rules where the goods are held by a bailee to be delivered without being moved, or where delivery is to be at the seller's place of business, are set forth in Sections 2-509(2) and 2-509(3). They are substantially similar to the CISG rules.

Effect of Seller's Breach on Risk of Loss

Both the CISG and the U.C.C. have provisions pertaining to the effect of a seller's breach on the risk of loss. The CISG provides that the normally applicable risk-of-loss rules discussed previously do not impair the buyer's remedies if the seller has committed a fundamental breach [Article 70]. The U.C.C. provides that where a tender of delivery of goods so fails to conform to the contract as to give a right of rejection, the risk of their loss remains on the seller until cure or acceptance [U.C.C. Section 2-510].

Overview

Like the U.C.C., the CISG's rules on risk of loss have abandoned the approach of making risk of loss turn on the question of whether "property" (*i.e.*, title) has passed from the seller to the buyer. Both the CISG and the U.C.C. risk-of-loss rules are applicable on the basis of the concrete commercial events such as handing over the goods to the carrier or the buyer taking over physical possession from the seller. To the extent that these physical events rather than metaphysical concepts of passage of title determine the substantive rights of the parties, a great improvement in achieving predictability and certainty of results has been made. However, the CISG risk-of-loss rules are stated in language yet to be interpreted by courts. In addition, no definitions of transportation terms are contained in the CISG. Accordingly, where negotiation postures permit, the parties may wish to insert their own specific risk of loss clauses into their contract utilizing the authorization granted by Article 6 of the CISG.

Case Abstract, UNCITRAL Texts (CLOUT), Abstract No. 191,

October 31, 1995 (Argentina)

An Argentinean buyer and a German seller concluded a contract, containing a C & F clause, for the sale of dried mushrooms to be shipped to the buyer. In the course of their transport to Buenos Aires, the goods deteriorated. The buyer sued the seller claiming lack of conformity of the goods.

In accordance with article 67 CISG, the court held that the risk passed to the buyer when the goods were handed over to the first carrier for transmission to the buyer in keeping with the contract of sale. In addition, the court held that the C & F clause obliged the seller to hand over the goods to the carrier and to pay the freight. However, a C & F clause does not affect the passing of the risk. Further, it should be noted that the buyer, pursuant to the C & F clause in the contract of sale, had taken out an insurance policy for transportation risks.

In accordance with article 66, the court held that the buyer, after passing of the risk, was not discharged from its obligation to pay the purchase price, even in the event of loss or damage to the goods, unless the loss or damage was due to an act or omission of the seller. In this case, the damage of the goods occurred after the passing of the risk to the buyer, who did not adduce that it was owing to an act or omission of the seller. Accordingly, the court dismissed the action.

QUESTIONS

1.   In lieu of the term C&F, *Incoterms* uses the term CFR. If the parties in the preceding case had used the term CIF, would the seller's obligations have been the same? If not, would the result have been the same?

2.   Consider the following *Incoterms*: FOB, FAS, CIP, CPT, DES, DDP, EXW. Under each term, when does the risk pass to the buyer?

Case Abstract, UNCITRAL Texts (CLOUT), Abstract No. 91,

November 19, 1992 (Italy)

Before the Italian Constitutional Court the argument was made that Article 1510 para. 2 of the Italian Civil Code, stating that the seller performs its obligation to deliver the goods by handing them over to the carrier and thereby implicitly placing the risk for the carriage on the buyer, was inconsistent with the principle of equality provided for by article 1228 of the Italian Civil Code [that] the carrier should be considered as the agent of the seller, who would be liable for the agent's acts.

The Constitutional Court rejected the argument, inter alia, on the ground that Article 1510 para. 2 of the Italian Civil Code reflected a rule generally accepted at international level and in this respect express reference was made to Articles 31 and 67 CISG.

NOTE ON THE LIABILITY OF OCEAN CARRIERS

Today, the liability of ocean carriers for cargo loss, damage, or delay is complicated by the unfortunate fact that carriage of goods by sea is regulated by three competing legal regimes: the Hague, Hague-Visby, and Hamburg Rules. Each, in its own way, attempts to strike an acceptable balance between freedom of contract, which would permit carriers to contractually limit their liability, and the public policy prohibiting parties from agreeing that there shall be no obligation to take precautions and hence no liability for negligence. The common law of England recognized the enforceability of such clauses, whereas the common law of the United States did not.

Attempts by international agreements to accommodate distinctions among various legal systems and to reach an acceptable compromise between carriers and shippers eventuated in a 1924 international convention usually called the Hague Rules. It was not until 1936, however, that the United States finally ratified the convention with the enactment of the Carriage of Goods by Sea Act, 46 U.S.C. Sections 1300-1315. The Hague Rules of 1924 (as embodied in the Carriage of Goods by Sea Act) is not a comprehensive set of rules regulating the liability and responsibility of ocean carriers. Rather, the Convention states certain basic responsibilities of the carrier and shipper, sets forth seventeen grounds for exempting the carrier from liability, and provides for a limitation of carrier liability.

Eventually, the decision was made to update the Hague Rules to bring them more in line with current commercial practices and needs. Thus, the Convention was amended in 1968 by the so-called Visby Amendments. The result of this amendment effort is that some states (most notably the United States) still subscribe to the original Hague Rules, while in other states, the Hague-Visby Rules are applicable.

To further complicate matters, some states (principally developing countries) believed that what was needed was a complete reexamination of the appropriate rules to regulate the carriage of goods by sea. The United Nations, through UNCITRAL, became the vehicle for this activity, and its work culminated in the International Convention on the Carriage of Goods by Sea of 1978, commonly known as the Hamburg Rules. Gone from these rules are the special exemptions for carriers found in the Hague Rules. Not surprisingly, this deletion has caused carriers to view the Hamburg Rules as being overly favorable to cargo owners, and because of such opposition, the United States and other major commercial states have so far delayed ratification. For those states that have ratified the Convention, it entered into force on November 1, 1992.

David Crystal, Inc., v. The Cunard Steam Ship Co. Ltd.
339 F.2d 295 (2d Cir. 1964)
KAUFMAN, CIRCUIT JUDGE

Our problem on this appeal, not devoid of reticulate aspects, is to determine which one of four parties shall bear the loss for the misdelivery of twenty-eight cases of shirts: the buyer and owner David Crystal, Inc., the carrier Cunard Steam-Ship Co. Ltd., the carrier's stevedore John T. Clark & Son, or the buyer's customs broker Penson & Co. After a trial in admiralty, the District Court granted Crystal recovery from Cunard and recovery over by Cunard from Clark, but denied Crystal direct recovery from Clark and dismissed Crystal's and Clark's claims against Penson for lack of admiralty jurisdiction. Crystal, Cunard, and Clark appeal from those portions of the decree adversely affecting their respective interests. We uphold the decree placing the ultimate responsibility for the loss upon Clark and find it unnecessary, because of this result, to reach the jurisdictional questions raised by the claims against Penson.

The basic facts may be stated simply enough although the resolution of liability is quite complex. Clark unloaded the shirts from Cunard's vessel to a pier in Brooklyn, N.Y., and then misdelivered them upon the presentation of a forged Penson delivery order, obtained through the complicity of one of Penson's employees.

For a full understanding of the ramifications of this case, however, a further exposition of the facts is in order. On October 31, 1957, Cunard received the shirts purchased by Crystal at Le Havre, France, for shipment aboard its vessel, the SS Trelyon. The bill of lading named Penson, Crystal's customs broker, as consignee. On November 14, after Penson received Cunard's arrival notice and obtained clearance from Customs, the file folder relating to the shipment was given to one Jose Perez, its traffic clerk. Perez prepared and signed a delivery order naming a trucker, Arrow Carriers, as agent to accept delivery at the pier. He affixed the order to the outside of the folder and placed it on his desk with other completed orders destined for the outgoing mail basket.

But shortly after Perez performed this task, the chain of events intended to effect proper delivery of the shirts to Crystal was cut at one of its most vital links. It appears that as Perez momentarily left his desk, Louis Segarra, a fellow employee who had been plotting with outsiders to steal the valued shirts, surreptitiously took the delivery order, together with a blank form. He gave the original and blank orders to Rigley, a confederate, who together with one Orlando, filled out the blank order, inserting the name of a fictitious trucker, C & L Trucking Co., in place of Arrow. They also forged Perez' signature on the new delivery order and destroyed the original.

The next morning Rigley and Orlando appeared at the pier where Clark's stevedores were unloading the Cunard vessel. They presented the forged delivery order to Keane, Clark's chief delivery clerk, and then waited until late in the afternoon while the documents were checked and the shirts loaded on their truck.

Crystal soon discovered its loss and commenced this suit by filing its libel against Cunard for breach of the contract of ocean carriage. Cunard then impleaded Clark seeking indemnity for breach of its stevedoring contract. Clark, in turn, impleaded Penson claiming negligence on its part. Both Clark and Penson answered the libel although Crystal did not assert causes of action against either until amendments to the libel were permitted by the judge upon conclusion of the trial.

The District Court held...that Cunard was fully liable to Crystal, but was entitled to be indemnified by Clark. We turn now to examine each phase of that conclusion.

I.   Crystal v. Cunard

Because Crystal's claim against Cunard was for breach of the contract of ocean carriage, we must look first to the bill of lading to determine the parties' rights and duties. The District Court was of the opinion that the bill of lading became inoperative once the cargo was discharged. We believe, however, that it is more precise to say that although the bill continued to govern the parties' relationships after discharge, its terms did not insulate Cunard from liability. It is true that the bill provided that Cunard's responsibility would cease when delivery was made from the ship's deck and that if the consignee did not immediately receive the goods, Cunard could simply abandon them on the wharf. But these clauses were clearly null and void under the Harter Act's restrictions against certain stipulations seeking to relieve carriers from liability. 46 U.S.C. § 190.

The bill of lading also provided that Cunard had the option to land or store the cargo 'at the sole expense and risk of Consignee in the Warehouse provided for that purpose.' But it is clear that Cunard did not take advantage of that option, for it discharged the goods in the custody of its stevedore on a pier and did not deposit them in a warehouse.

Since the bill of lading did not specify Cunard's obligations when it discharged the shirts to Clark, the law steps in to fill the lacuna; this it does by properly characterizing Cunard's status as a bailee. Cf. The Italia, 187 F. 113 (2d Cir. 1911); Standard Brands, Inc. v. Nippon Yusen Kaisha, 42 F.Supp. 43 (D.Mass.1941). And there is no sound reason to alter its bailee status simply because it landed the shirts on Clark's pier. Absent a valid contract to the contrary, a bailee remains liable for the safety of the goods in whatever hands he may place them; exceptions that may arise when a consignee fails to accept the goods have no relevance to this case. Cf. The Eddy, 5 Wall. 481, 72 U.S. 481, 495, 18 L.Ed. 486 (1867).

It is interesting that there is no direct precedent in the law of admiralty establishing the standard of responsibility of a bailee who misdelivers cargo. Because of this void and mindful that maritime law draws on many sources, the able District Court judge in order to shape the appropriate maritime law properly resorted to state decisional law, see 1 Harper & James, Torts 156 (1956), various uniform acts, including the Federal Bills of Lading Act, 49 U.S.C. §§ 81-124, as well as the Uniform Commercial Code, and finally fastened appropriately on the rule articulated in the Restatement, Torts § 234 (1934).

The *Restatement* rule suggests that a bailee is absolutely liable for misdelivering cargo, unless his mistake as to the person entitled to receive the goods was induced by the bailor. We agree with the District Court that considerations of uniformity and the need for certainty in commercial transactions justified application of this widely accepted rule to maritime transactions. It is not prudent to have a rule which varies a bailee's liability depending upon his proximity to the sea and susceptibility to admiralty's jurisdiction. At the same time, the rule of absolute liability represents a sound allocation of responsibility for the bailee is in a better position than the bailor to establish procedures to minimize the risk of misdeliveries and to insure against the few misdeliveries that will inevitably occur despite the most careful precautions.

Cunard was therefore absolutely liable for the misdelivery unless (a) certain bill of lading provisions not yet considered eliminated or reduced such liability or (b) the misdelivery was induced by Crystal or Penson, acting in its behalf. One of these provisions, the exception for acts of 'thieves,' seems to us inapplicable because the loss of the cargo here is more appropriately characterized as due to misdelivery rather than theft. It is true that under New York law a taking by false pretenses is larceny, Penal Law, McKinney's Consol.Laws, c. 40, § 1290, but we do not believe that the broad definition of theft in the criminal law should be extended to a commercial contract. *See Freedman v. George W. Bush & Sons Co.*, 284 Pa. 16, 130 A. 263 (1925). The law already recognizes this distinction for a warehouseman is absolutely liable for misdeliveries but is responsible in trespassory theft cases only where he has been negligent. *See North American Smelting Co. v. Moller S.S. Co.*, 204 F.2d 384 (3d Cir. 1953). These differing standards are based on sound policy considerations since it is proper that a warehouseman should bear a greater responsibility for being duped by false pretenses than for thefts that cannot be avoided despite the exercise of ordinary care.

Cunard's attempt, elsewhere in the bill of lading, to limit its liability to Pound 20 per package also must fail. This clause was clearly void while the goods were at sea, for the Carriage of Goods by Sea Act (COGSA), 46 U.S.C. § 1304(5), does not permit limitations under $ 500. It seems to us that once the law declared this clause void it should remain void forever. It would be unfair to permit the void clause to spring to life once the goods reached land, for by then Crystal had justifiably relied on the clause's inapplicability in making its decision on adequate cargo insurance. Moreover, the limitation provision in the bill of lading does not explicitly cover post-arrival damage. Furthermore, the Pound 20 limitation, when contrasted with COGSA's $ 500 figure, is such an arbitrarily small sum that it should be void as contrary to public policy. *Cf. Isbrandtsen Co. v. United States*, 201 F.2d 281 (2d Cir. 1953).

We turn, finally, to what is for us the most troublesome question on this phase of the TOC3case: whether Crystal is estopped from recovering because the misdelivery was induced by Penson's alleged negligence. The law is clear that if Penson's negligence caused the misdelivery, Crystal would be barred from recovery. *MacAndrews & Forbes Co. v. United States*, 23 F.2d 667 (3d Cir. 1928). Indeed, the chain of estoppel is firmer and shorter here than in *MacAndrews*, where an owner of furs was estopped from recovering from a carrier by imputing to the owner the negligence of a trucking firm employed by his customs broker. We are not inclined to upset the District Court's holding that Penson could not be faulted for its office procedures or for hiring and retaining Segarra. The key issue on this question is whether Segarra was acting within the scope of his authority when he took the valid delivery order and the blank form from Perez' desk.

As we read the record, Segarra's authority to prepare and sign delivery orders and hand them to truckmen did not extend to the commercial shipment involved in this case. Segarra was allowed to take delivery orders from Perez' desk but only for temporary use in answering inquiries and not for delivery to truckmen. While it is true that by trusting Segarra to this limited extent Penson may have facilitated the plot, we are unwilling to stretch the tenuous line of causation and say that Penson 'proximately caused' the misdelivery. *See Saugerties Bank v. Delaware & Hudson Co.*, 236 N.Y. 425, 141 N.E. 904 (1923). Similarly, despite Segarra's authority to take the blank form, it seems clear that this authority did not extend to completing the form; a forgery by a mere custodian of documents is not binding on the principal. *See, e.g., Ehrich v. Guaranty Trust Co.*, 194 App.Div. 658, 186 N.Y.S. 103 (1921), *aff'd*, 233 N.Y. 637, 135 N.E. 950 (1922); *Manhattan Life Ins. Co. v Forty-Second & Grand St. Ferry R. R. Co.*, 139 N.Y. 146, 34 N.E. 776 (1893).

A sound reason stands behind our holding that Segarra was not acting within the scope of his employment in the circumstances present here. If an employer were to be held liable every time an employee took advantage of a general authority to move freely about his offices, he would be placed in the role of an absolute insurer without the ability to protect himself. Instead, the law limits vicarious liability to situations where the wrongdoing can be traced to abuse of a more carefully defined authority. Here, it is clear that Segarra's actions were not sufficiently related to his delegated authority and for that reason Penson cannot be charged with responsibility for the misdelivery.

II. Cunard v. Clark

We also agree with the District Court's holding that Clark must indemnify Cunard because the misdelivery was a breach of its implied warranty of workmanlike service. The Supreme Court recently indicated, in *Italia Societa per Azioni di Navigazione v. Oregon Stevedoring Co.*, 376 U.S. 315, 84 S.Ct. 748, 11 L.Ed.2d 732 (1964), that the implied warranty may be breached even where, as here, there has been no showing of negligence on the stevedore's part. Surely, Clark was in a far better position to prevent the misdelivery than Cunard and liability should properly fall upon the party who is best situated to adopt protective measures.

It is true that Clark's contact with Cunard disclaimed responsibility for 'losses resulting from possible theft or errors in delivery.' But such disclaimers are not favored by the courts and must be strictly construed. *See* 2 Harper & James, *Torts* § 28.25 (1956); 78 Harv.L.Rev. 191 (1964); *cf. Pettus v. Grace Line, Inc.*, 305 F.2d 151, 155 (2d Cir. 1962). Somewhat similar considerations of strict construction led us to hold that a theft exception in Cunard's bill of lading, also found in the Clark-Cunard agreement, did not apply to the facts of this case. And because, as between Cunard and Clark, strong policy considerations favor placing responsibility for the misdelivery on Clark, any attempt to escape from that responsibility should be unequivocally expressed. We are not disposed to extend the agreement's exemption of 'errors in deliveries' to 'misdeliveries.' A 'misdelivery' in maritime practice is a technical term of art applied where there is a complete failure to deliver goods to the owner, consignee, or other authorized holder of a bill of lading. Although the term 'errors in delivery' is unfamiliar in this context, we are inclined to limit it to delays, incomplete deliveries, or deliveries of the wrong cargo that are ultimately rectified. Indeed, the very novelty of the expression explains our reluctance to treat it as synonymous with 'misdeliveries,' the term that naturally leaps to mind to characterize what happened here.

We believe Cunard is also entitled to reimbursement from Clark for attorneys' fees and disbursements incurred in defending against Crystal's claim. *See Paliaga v. Luckenbach S.S. Co.*, 301 F.2d 403 (2d Cir. 1962). We cannot accept the stevedore's suggestion that Cunard should be denied recovery because it could have avoided these expenses by asking Clark to defend the action on its behalf. Crystal sued Cunard only and when Cunard impleaded Clark it invoked the personal defenses already discussed against Cunard. Because those defenses were substantial and might have succeeded, Cunard's only safe course was to defend against Crystal's claims. Having forced Cunard into this position, Clark cannot now be heard to say that it should not be charged for litigation expenses unnecessarily incurred.

III. Crystal v. Clark

In light of the foregoing dispositions, which we have approved, the District Court judge saw no need to consider Crystal's direct claim against Clark, added by post-trial amendment. We recognize that because we affirm Crystal's judgment against Cunard and Cunard's against Clark, the question whether Crystal should be allowed to recover against Clark as well becomes academic. Indeed, because the issue lacks practical significance in this case, we accept without detailed analysis and discussion the authorities that impose jurisdictional obstacles to such direct recovery, *see* 1 Benedict, *Admiralty*, § 2, at 2 & n. 4 (6th ed. Knauth 1940); 3 Moore, *Federal Practice* P14.20, at 669-70, and P14.27(1), at 721 & n. 1 (2d ed. 1963), despite our observation that adherence to those precedents often needlessly fragments law suits and might deserve further consideration in the appropriate case.

IV. Crystal v. Penson; Clark v. Penson

In view of the conclusions we have reached, which are founded in part on Penson's freedom from responsibility for the misdelivery, the issues raised by the claims against Penson become wholly academic. Accordingly, we see no need to discuss the District Court's disposition of the jurisdictional problems raised by those claims.

The interlocutory decree is affirmed.

Allied Chemical International Corp., v. Companhia de Navegacao Lloyd Brasileiro,
775 F.2d 476 (2d Cir. 1985)

Meskill, Circuit Judge:

Companhia de Navegacao Lloyd Brasileiro (Lloyd), an ocean carrier, appeals from a judgment of the United States District Court for the Southern District of New York, Owen, J., finding Lloyd liable to Allied Chemical International Corporation (Allied), a shipper, for the misdelivery of goods to the consignee, Banylsa Tecelagem do Brasil S.A. (Banylsa). The carrier caused the goods to be delivered without requiring Banylsa to produce the original order bill of lading. Lloyd also challenges the district court's refusal to interpret the Carriage of Goods by Sea Act (COGSA) package limitation, 46 U.S.C. App. § 1304 (5) (Supp. I 1983), which was incorporated into the bill of lading, to reduce Allied's recovery. The court awarded damages equal to the value of the cargo in United States dollars minus an amount that Allied had already recovered from Banylsa plus interest.

We affirm the judgment of the district court.

BACKGROUND

This case was decided without a trial. The parties submitted to the district court two stipulations of fact; the deposition of Pedro Calmon Filho, an expert on Brazilian law; memoranda, one of which included an appendix; and separate proposed findings of fact and conclusions of law. Allied alleged federal jurisdiction on the basis of admiralty or, alternatively, diversity of citizenship. The pertinent, undisputed facts follow.

In September 1980, Allied, an exporter of chemical products, received from Banylsa an order for a quantity of caprolactam, a crystalline cyclic amide used in the manufacture of nylon. The sale was to be in two lots of 6,000 bags on terms of sight drafts against documents through Banco Bamerindus do Brasil S.A. of Sao Paulo, Brazil (Brazilian bank). The sight drafts were in the amount of the per lot invoice price, $266,756.92 C & F Salvador, Brazil.

In October 1980, Allied delivered to Lloyd at the Port of Norfolk, Virginia two lots of 150 double faced pallets, each lot said to contain 6,000 bags of caprolactam to be shipped to the Port of Salvador, Brazil. The cargo was loaded onto Lloyd's vessel ITAPURA. Lloyd issued clean order bills of lading that described the cargo, listed Allied as the shipper and showed that the goods were consigned to the order of Banylsa. Banylsa was also listed as the notify party. Allied, through its bank, forwarded the shipping documents — including the sight drafts, the original bills of lading and the original commercial invoices — to the Brazilian bank for handling and collection. Allied specifically instructed the Brazilian bank to deliver the documents only against payment of the sight drafts.

On or about November 12, 1980, Lloyd's vessel arrived at the Port of Salvador. In accordance with local custom and usage, the carrier unloaded the caprolactam at a warehouse under the control of the Administration of the Port of Salvador (the port authority), an agency of the Brazilian government. The caprolactam was undamaged.

Banylsa made payment on only one of the two sight drafts and therefore received from the Brazilian bank only one bill of lading. It is the bill of lading not received and the lot to which it related that are the subject of this dispute. Hereinafter, when we refer to the cargo or to the bill of lading, we refer solely to the misdelivered goods and the bill of lading that covered them.

On November 17, 1980, Banylsa through its agent delivered to Lloyd's agent in Salvador a letter explaining simply that the original bill of lading had not been received and requesting Lloyd to issue in accordance with Brazilian import regulations a "carta declaratoria," a letter declaring that the freight had been paid at the port of origin and that the Merchant Marine Renewal Tax had been paid in Salvador. That same day, Lloyd's agent issued the requested document. The parties do not dispute that to obtain the release of goods from the port authority, a party would have to produce either the original bill of lading or a carta declaratoria from the carrier. Thus, by virtue of the carta declaratoria, Banylsa was able to obtain possession of the caprolactam although it had not paid for the goods and it was not in possession of the bill of lading.

Allied first became aware that the sight draft had not been paid in January 1981. It was not until several weeks later, however, when Banylsa complained about the quality of the caprolactam, that Allied discovered that Banylsa had, notwithstanding nonpayment, obtained possession of the caprolactam. After an investigation that included an on-site inspection of the goods at Banylsa's facility, Allied rejected Banylsa's quality complaint.

In early April 1981, Banylsa filed a voluntary receivership proceeding in the Civil Court of the District of Salvador, Brazil. On May 8, 1981, Allied made a demand on

Lloyd for losses incurred as a result of the carrier's failure to request proper documentation before authorizing the release of the caprolactam. The demand letter stated that Allied had been advised by Lloyd that the goods were released on Banylsa's promise to deliver the original bill of lading within 90 days. Negotiations between the shipper and the carrier proved unavailing and Allied filed this suit in September 1981.

In May 1981, Allied filed a claim against Banylsa in the receivership proceeding. In September 1983, Banylsa deposited with the Salvador court 20,414,907 cruzeiros to pay Allied's share of the receivership distribution. The amount was equal to Allied's claim in United States dollars at the exchange rate of 76.53 cruzeiros to the dollar, the rate in effect when Banylsa filed its petition. Allied argued that it was entitled to payment at the rate in effect on the date of Banylsa's deposit, 671 cruzeiros to the dollar. On advice of counsel, Allied abandoned its appeal and accepted a sum in cruzeiros equal to less than $40,000 as of September 1983.

In its complaint against Lloyd, Allied charged that the ocean carrier had breached its contract of carriage with Allied. It also claimed that Lloyd was liable for conversion of the cargo because Lloyd authorized the delivery of the cargo to a party not entitled to possession. The district judge decided in Allied's favor and adopted Allied's proposed findings of fact and conclusions of law virtually verbatim. The findings and conclusions cited no cases and contained not a single reference to the brief but adequate record.

. . . .

On the issue of liability, Lloyd raises four challenges. First, it claims that it fully discharged its responsibility under the contract of carriage when it delivered the cargo as dictated by local custom and usage to the government controlled port authority. Second, Lloyd claims that it cannot be liable for conversion either because that would be contrary to Brazilian law or because the rights and liabilities under COGSA, 46 U.S.C. App. § 1300 *et seq.* (Supp. I 1983), are exclusive. Third and fourth, Lloyd raises related arguments, payment and waiver, based on Allied's claim and partial recovery against Banylsa in the receivership proceeding. Finally, Lloyd contends that even if it is liable, the COGSA package limitation, incorporated into the bill of lading, should reduce Allied's recovery to $500 per pallet or $75,000. For the reasons that follow, we reject Lloyd's arguments.

DISCUSSION

. . . .

B. Jurisdiction and Governing Law

This suit involves claims by a shipper against an ocean carrier arising from an alleged breach of a contract of carriage. Thus it lies within our admiralty jurisdiction. *Leather's Best, Inc. v. S.S. Mormaclynx,* 451 F.2d 800, 807 (2d Cir. 1971); *David Crystal, Inc. v. Cunard Steam-Ship Co.,* 339 F.2d 295, 298 (2d Cir. 1964), *cert. denied,* 380 U.S. 976, 14 L. Ed. 2d 271, 85 S. Ct. 1339 (1965); *see* 28 U.S.C. § 1333(1) (1982). Consequently, this action is governed by federal maritime law.

C. Liability

The liability question in this case inextricably involves the critical importance of the documentary transaction in overseas trade. *See generally* G. Gilmore & C. Black, *The Law of Admiralty* 110-12 (2d ed. 1975). The documentary sale enables the distant seller to protect himself from an insolvent or fraudulent foreign buyer by ensuring that the buyer ordinarily cannot take possession of the goods until he has paid for them. It accomplishes this rather simply. The seller tenders shipping documents, including a negotiable bill of lading, rather than goods to the buyer. By paying for the documents, the buyer gets possession of the original bill of lading. Possession of the bill entitles him to possession of the goods; it represents the goods and conveys title to them. Most likely, the bill will be an order bill of lading, made to the order of or endorsed to the buyer. *See id.* at 96-97. Absent a valid agreement to the contrary, the carrier, the issuer of the bill of lading, is responsible for releasing the cargo only to the party who presents the original bill of lading. "Delivery to the consignee named in the bill of lading does not suffice to discharge the [carrier] where the consignee does not hold the bill of lading." 2 T. G. Carver, *Carriage by Sea* para. 1593 (R. Colinvaux 13th ed. 1982). If the carrier delivers the goods to one other than the authorized holder of the bill of lading, the carrier is liable for misdelivery. *David Crystal*, 339 F.2d at 300; *Morse Electro Products Corp. v. S.S. Great Peace*, 437 F. Supp. 474, 482 (D.N.J. 1977); *The Cabo Villano*, 14 F.2d 978 (E.D.N.Y. 1926), modified as to damages, 18 F.2d 220 (2d Cir. 1927). The ocean carrier's liability arises from rights of property, 1 T. G. Carver, *supra*, at para. 120, and "delivery to a person not entitled to the goods without production of the bill of lading is prima facie a conversion of the goods and a breach of contract." 2 *id.* at para. 1593 (footnotes omitted).

The dispute herein involved precisely the consequence that the documentary transaction is intended to avert: Banylsa, which turned out to be an insolvent buyer, was given possession of goods for which it had not paid. This result would have been avoided had Lloyd, in keeping with its obligation, demanded the production of the bill of lading before permitting Banylsa to claim the caprolactam.

Before we can hold Lloyd liable for causing Allied's loss, however, we must examine the respective rights and obligations of the parties at the time of the apparent misdelivery to determine whether Lloyd was somehow relieved of its duty to take up the bill of lading. Although the cargo had been discharged from the ship and, thus, the actual carriage completed when the apparent misdelivery occurred, the relationship between Allied and Lloyd was still governed by the contract of carriage. *See Leather's Best*, 451 F.2d at 807. Our analysis begins with the bill of lading, the document evidencing the contract of carriage. *David Crystal*, 339 F.2d at 297. We bear in mind that bills of lading are contracts of adhesion and, as such, are strictly construed against the carrier. *The Caledonia*, 157 U.S. 124, 137, 39 L. Ed. 644, 15 S. Ct. 537 (1895); *West India Industries v. Tradex*, 664 F.2d 946, 951 n.9 (5th Cir. 1981); *Mitsui & Co. v. American Export Lines*, 636 F.2d 807, 822-23 (2d Cir. 1981); *E. Gerli & Co. v. Cunard S.S. Co.*, 48 F.2d 115, 116 (2d Cir. 1931) (L. Hand, J.).

Lloyd contends that clauses 1 and 12 of the bill of lading absolve it from liability. Clause 1 provides that "the Carrier shall not be liable in any capacity whatsoever for any delay, non-delivery or mis-delivery, or loss of or damage to the goods occurring while the goods are not in the actual custody of the Carrier." Clause 12 provides that "the responsibility of the Carrier, in any capacity, shall altogether cease and the goods shall be considered to be delivered and at their own risk and expense in every respect when taken into the custody of customs or other authorities."

Lloyd's reliance on these clauses is unavailing because they are null and void. In *David Crystal*, 339 F.2d at 297, we held clauses similar to 1 and 12 to be invalid under the Harter Act's proscriptions against certain limitations on carriers' liability. *See* 46 U.S.C. App. § 190 (Supp. I 1983). Although the enactment of COGSA sharply curtailed the applicability of the Harter Act, 46 U.S.C. App. § 190 *et seq.* (Supp. I 1983), to ocean bills of lading and matters of ocean carriers' liability, absent a valid agreement to the contrary, the Harter Act still governs prior to load-ing and after discharge of cargo until proper delivery is made. *Caterpillar Over-seas, S.A. v. S.S. Expeditor*, 318 F.2d 720, 722-23 (2d Cir.), *cert. denied*, 375 U.S. 942, 84 S. Ct. 347, 11 L. Ed. 2d 272 (1963); G. Gilmore & C. Black, *supra*, at 147-48. While a carrier and a shipper may specify by agreement what the respon-sibility of the carrier should be after the goods are discharged, the carrier may not simply disclaim all post-discharge responsibility. *Leather's Best*, 451 F.2d at 807.

Insofar as Lloyd relies on these clauses as agreements not to eliminate but merely to reduce its liability, which would be permissible under the Harter Act, its arguments are unavailing because the district court found that the parties did not intend the clauses to have that effect. It is undisputed that the parties agreed that COGSA, which by its terms does not apply either before loading or after discharge of cargo, 46 U.S.C. App. § 1311, was to govern before the goods were loaded and after they were dis-charged from the ship. This was a permissible agreement, *see Colgate Palmolive Co. v. S/S Dart Canada*, 724 F.2d 313, 315 (2d Cir. 1983), *cert. denied*, 466 U.S. 963, 104 S. Ct. 2181, 80 L. Ed. 2d 562, 52 U.S.L.W. 3791 (1984), and made COGSA "apply [not] of its own force as a statute, but merely as a contractual term in the bill of lading." *Id*. Because COGSA § 1303(8) provides that the parties may not, except as otherwise pro-vided by COGSA (see our discussion below), agree even to lessen the carrier's liability for loss arising from its own negligence or fault, and COGSA was incorporated into the bill of lading, the court's finding that clauses 1 and 12 of the bill of lading did not lessen Lloyd's liability for its negligent misdelivery is not clearly erroneous.

While it is clear, then, that Lloyd retained some responsibilities after discharge, the bill of lading did not specify what they might be. Therefore, "the law steps in to fill the lacuna" and provides that when Lloyd discharged the cargo, it assumed the status of a bailee. *David Crystal*, 339 F.2d at 298; *Leather's Best*, 451 F.2d at 811-12. The transfer of the cargo to the port authority, without more, did not alter this sta-tus; thus Lloyd remained presumptively responsible for the proper delivery of the goods. *Leather's Best*, 451 F.2d at 812; *David Crystal*, 339 F.2d at 298. We have pre-viously articulated the applicable standard of responsibility under admiralty law: "a bailee is absolutely liable for misdelivering cargo, unless his mistake as to the person entitled to receive the goods was induced by the bailor" or the contract of carriage otherwise reduced or eliminated his liability. *David Crystal*, 339 F.2d at 298. There is no suggestion in the record that Allied induced the misdelivery. Allied was not even aware until well after the event that Banylsa had acquired possession of the goods. We have already noted that the parties could not lawfully agree to eliminate Lloyd's liability entirely and have upheld the district court's finding that they did not intend that clauses 1 and 12 would lessen Lloyd's liability for negligent misdelivery.

The remaining question is whether the parties intended, by their incorporation of COGSA, that any provision of COGSA itself would lessen Lloyd's liability for neg-ligent misdelivery. One important consequence of the enactment of COGSA was the elimination of absolute liability of carriers. Under COGSA, carriers can be liable for loss of or damage to cargo only on the basis of fault. G. Gilmore & C. Black, *supra*, at 150. After describing a number of specific duties, the statute provides somewhat generally, in language that seems relevant to this case, that the carrier shall not be li-able for losses resulting from any...cause arising without the actual fault and priv-ity of the carrier and without the fault or neglect of the agents or servants of the car-rier, but the burden of proof shall be on the person claiming the benefit of this exception to show that neither the actual fault or privity of the carrier nor the fault or neglect of the agents or servants of the carrier contributed to the loss or damage. 46 U.S.C. App. § 1304(2)(q).

Unfortunately for Lloyd, however, this provision seems to support rather than undermine the imposition of liability for the misdelivery. COGSA specifically left unaffected the applicability of the Pomerene Bills of Lading Act, 49 U.S.C. App. § 81 *et seq.* (1982), to ocean bills of lading. Pursuant to the Pomerene Act, a carrier operating under an order bill of lading is justified in delivering the goods to one lawfully entitled to them or to one in possession of an order bill "by the terms of which the goods are deliverable to his order; or which has been indorsed to him, or in blank by the consignee." 49 U.S.C. App. § 89. When Lloyd caused the goods to be released to Banylsa, by means of the *carta declaratoria*, the bill of lading was still in the custody of the Brazilian bank because payment had not been made on the sight draft. Not having paid on the draft, Banylsa was neither lawfully entitled to the goods nor in possession of the bill. Delivery to Banylsa, therefore, was not justified. In light of its unjustified authorization of the delivery, Lloyd could not possibly show, as required by section 1304(2)(q) of COGSA, that it did not by its actual fault contribute to Allied's loss.

Having found nothing in the contract of carriage that eliminates or reduces the carrier's duty to deliver the cargo only to a party in possession of the bill of lading paid to his order or properly endorsed, we conclude that the district court correctly determined that Lloyd should be liable for the loss that resulted from its misdelivery. *See* 49 U.S.C. App. § 90; *see also Pere Marquette Ry. v. J.F. French & Co.*, 254 U.S. 538, 546, 65 L. Ed. 391, 41 S. Ct. 195 (1921); *Alderman Brothers Co. v. New York, N.H. & H.R.R.*, 102 Conn. 461, 465, 129 A. 47 (1925).

The fact that the government controlled port authority, rather than Lloyd itself, physically delivered the goods to Banylsa does not in any way relieve Lloyd from liability. As previously noted, it is undisputed that unless Banylsa presented to the port authority either the original bill of lading or a carta declaratoria issued by the carrier, the port authority would not have permitted Banylsa to take the cargo. Because Banylsa did not pay the sight draft and take possession of the bill of lading, Lloyd retained control over the goods. Thus, Lloyd acted at its peril when it authorized the release of the goods to Banylsa without demanding production of the bill. *The Cabo Villano*, 14 F.2d at 979-81.

It is surely obvious at this point that Lloyd's Brazilian law arguments are inapposite. The rights and obligations of the parties herein are rooted in United States law. Both COGSA, 46 U.S.C. App. § 1300, and the Harter Act, 46 U.S.C. App. § 190, cover transactions involving carriage from ports in the United States to foreign ports. Moreover, Lloyd's own bill of lading provided that it should "be construed and the rights of the parties thereunder determined according to the law of the United States."

Finally, Allied's claim and partial recovery against Banylsa in the receivership proceeding did not extinguish Allied's right of action against Lloyd. By misdelivering the caprolactam to Banylsa, Lloyd was responsible for Allied's loss. Allied is entitled to be compensated for the full amount of its loss in United States dollars. Of course, the amount that Allied has already recovered from Banylsa must be considered in mitigation of the damages that Lloyd must pay.

D. Damages

Citing both COGSA and clause 17 of the bill of lading, Lloyd claims that its liability is limited to $500 per pallet or $75,000 ($500 X 150 pallets). Section 1304(5) of COGSA, which Lloyd argues is applicable through the express extension of COGSA contained in the bill of lading, provides in pertinent part that the carrier shall not be liable for loss of or damage to cargo in an amount greater than $500 per package "unless the nature and value of [the] goods have been declared by the shipper before shipment and inserted in the bill of lading. This declaration, if embodied in the bill of lading, shall be prima facie evidence, but shall not be conclusive on the carrier." Clause 17 of the bill of lading provides in relevant part that the carrier's liability for damages shall be identically limited "unless the nature and value of [the] goods have been declared by the shipper before shipment and inserted in the Bill of Lading and extra freight paid." The parties apparently agree that the term "package" has the same meaning in COGSA and clause 17. We therefore need not on that ground distinguish between the COGSA and the clause 17 limitations.

Allied maintains that the district court properly refused to limit damages because Lloyd failed to plead the limitation as a special defense and never moved to amend its answer to include the defense. Our Circuit has never addressed whether a partial limitation is waived if not pleaded as a special defense. We need not decide it here because Allied also argues that the district court was correct because the pallets should not be considered to be the packages. Therefore, Allied claims, the limitation is irrelevant. We agree.

The question of what constitutes a COGSA package, a question we frequently confront, is largely and in the first instance a matter of contract interpretation. *Allied International American Eagle Trading Corp. v. S.S. "Yang Ming,"* 672 F.2d 1055, 1057, 1061 (2d Cir. 1982); *Standard Electrica, S.A. v. Hamburg Sudamerikanische Dampfschifffahrts-Gesellschaft,* 375 F.2d 943, 946 (2d Cir.), *cert. denied,* 389 U.S. 831, 19 L. Ed. 2d 89, 88 S. Ct. 97 (1967). The most obvious place for us to begin our search for the intent of the contracting parties is, of course, the bill of lading. *Binladen BSB Landscaping v. M.V. "Nedlloyd Rotterdam,"* 759 F.2d 1006, 1012 (2d Cir. 1985). The bill of lading herein contained six columns under the usual general heading, "Particulars Furnished by Shipper." Only two of those columns and only a few of the items appearing in those columns are important to our decision. The first column, headed "No. of Pkgs.," contained the entry "150." Immediately to the right of that number, squarely in the column labeled "Description of Packages and Goods," was entered "Double Faced Pallets Said to Contain: 6000 Bags Caprolactam." Just above this entry, in the same column, it stated "Rate: $110.00 LT Value: $1657.00 LT." The abbreviation LT stands for long ton, the equivalent of 2,240 pounds.

We have long accepted that a pallet may, under appropriate circumstances, be deemed to be a package. *Yang Ming,* 672 F.2d at 1062; *Standard Electrica,* 375 F.2d at 946. This may be so even where the containers on the pallet themselves constitute ordinary commercial units. Moreover, in *Yang Ming* we ruled that where, as here, the shipper gives written notice in the bill of the number of containers on the pallets, the carrier is not necessarily bound to that number if the bill elsewhere lists the number of pallets as the number of packages. *Yang Ming,* 672 F.2d at 1061. Thus the bill of lading could support either the shipper's or the carrier's position; it is not determinative. We do note, however, that in *Yang Ming,* the number of pallets was declared several times in the bill of lading to be the number of packages. *Id.* at 1063. We therefore were reasonably certain that the parties intended the pallets to constitute packages for limitations purposes. Here, however, the number of pallets was listed but once — as was the number of bags. Looking only at the numbers, we would conclude that the parties' intent is ambiguous.

But the bill contains another and potentially more significant entry — the freight charge — which we believe indicates that the parties did not intend the pallets to be packages. Lloyd contends that it would have charged a higher rate if it was potentially liable for the full value of the goods. Indeed, clause 17 explicitly and COGSA implicitly "cast upon the shipper the burden of declaring the nature and value of the goods, and paying a higher tariff, if necessary, [in order to] impose a higher liability upon the carrier." *Standard Electrica*, 375 F.2d at 945.

The excerpt cited from the bill of lading show that Allied adequately met its burden to declare the nature and value of the goods. And, despite Lloyd's attempts to introduce new evidence at this stage, we are limited to the record, and the record clearly shows that the freight rate was based on the value of the goods. Caprolactam valued at less than $2,000 per long ton was charged a rate of $110 per long ton. More valuable caprolactam was charged a rate of $131.50 per long ton. Thus, under the applicable tariff, Allied had no option to pay a higher rate. Having paid a freight charge based on the value of the goods, Allied could reasonably have expected to recover their value if they were lost. Similarly, having levied a rate keyed to value, Lloyd could reasonably have expected to be liable for that value. It would be illogical to ascribe a contrary intent to the parties.

As a final point, we reiterate that ocean bills of lading are contracts of adhesion. Ambiguities, therefore, must be resolved against the issuing carrier. *Mitsui & Co. v. American Export Lines*, 636 F.2d at 822-23. We conclude that the district court's finding that the parties did not intend the pallets to be packages was not clearly erroneous. Therefore, we affirm the district court's award of damages.

CONCLUSION

The judgment of the district court is affirmed. Appellant is liable for costs.

Brooklyn Overall Export Company Ltd. v. Amerford International Corp.,
83 A.D.2D 598; 441 N.Y.S.2D 304; 1981 N.Y. App. Div.

In an action to recover damages for breach of contract, defendant appeals, as limited by its brief, from so much of a judgment of the Supreme Court, Queens County (Calabretta, J.), entered April 7, 1980, as, after a non-jury trial, awarded plaintiffs the principal sum of $ 34,500, on two causes of action. Judgment affirmed insofar as appealed from, with costs.

The record shows that defendant breached an oral agreement with plaintiffs to structure a business transaction that involved shipping plaintiffs' goods to a buyer in Sweden and arranging for payment. Plaintiffs' employee, Jeffrey Boshnack, testified that he informed defendant's customer service agent, Ruth Witz, that he had 52 cartons of jeans to be shipped to a Stockholm buyer from his companies' Texas factory and Long Island warehouse. He said he informed her specifically that the goods were not to be handed over to this buyer except on payment. With this arrangement, he testified, he believed he had no need to investigate the credit rating of the buyer, a new customer; such was the normal procedure for his employer.

Pursuant to Witz' request, he sent her written instructions for each shipment point; the Long Island instruction was to "ship * * * against sight draft," and the Texas instruction was to "ship * * * to [buyer] * * * Ship freight collect — customer must pay on sight draft." Boshnack said he relied on defendant to prepare the paperwork necessary to carry out his intent, and assumed everything was in order and the goods were paid for on his receipt of a copy of the papers after air shipment of the goods. Boshnack admitted being unfamiliar with shipping customs. His prior experience involved shipping goods for cash in advance, cash on delivery or on letters of credit, and his understanding of those terms was limited to domestic usage. In this instance, he said, he used the term "sight draft," which he had picked up from a forwarder, even though prior shipments through defendant had been for cash on delivery terms and he was not sure what the term meant. Mrs. Witz testified that she would have insisted on using a cash on delivery term had she been told by Boshnack that he wanted assurance of payment on delivery. What Boshnack emphasized, she said, was the need for speed. After she filled in a shipper's letter of instruction form to specify drawing drafts at sight, defendant's banking department prepared certain documents. The draft for each of the two consignments specified that a Stockholm bank, acting as defendant's agent, should deliver the documents against payment. Mrs. Witz acknowledged the fact that this meant the documents would not be released to the buyer absent payment. But she admitted that the buyer could obtain the goods on arrival in Sweden without payment because the air waybills listed the buyer as consignee instead of the correspondent bank (thus obviating the buyer's need for any documents). She blamed plaintiffs' instructions that, she said, told her to consign the goods directly to the buyer without any intermediate consignee who would hold the goods pending payment. Had plaintiffs told her they wanted the drafts paid on delivery, she would have listed the correspondent bank as consignee on the waybill so that buyer would have had to obtain the documents from the bank before presenting them to the carrier for delivery of the goods.

Trial Term found that Mrs. Witz clearly understood what Boshnack had intended, and held defendant liable for delivery of the goods to the buyer without payment. We agree. Plaintiffs' intention, as expressed to defendant, was to retain control over the goods pending payment, and to rely on defendant's skill in using a sight draft rather than a cash on delivery term. Defendant could have met the obligation by arranging a documentary sale in which the air waybills were negotiable instruments of title entrusted to its banking agent in Stockholm pending buyer's honoring of the sight draft by payment, or by restricting straight (*i.e.*, nonnegotiable) waybills in such a manner that the carrier would not hand over the goods to the buyer absent instructions from defendant's agent, secured after payment. (*See Dusal Chem. Co. v. Southern Pacific Co.*, 102 Misc 222; *see also Christoffersen v. Murray Packing Co.*, 24 A.D.2d 587, *affd* 17 N.Y.2d 855; *Gubelman v. Panama R. R. Co.*, 192 App. Div. 165, 169; US Code, tit 49, §§ 82, 83, 88, 89, 112; Uniform Commercial Code, §§ 7-104, 7-303, 7-403, 7-504; Warsaw Convention, 49 Stat 3000; US Code, tit. 49, § 1502, n, arts 11, 12, 13.) Mrs. Witz' insistence at trial that Boshnack specified speed rather than security is belied by the basic incompatibility of straight waybills directly consigning goods to the buyer, with sight drafts prepared for a documentary sale. (*See Dusal Chem. Co. v. Southern Pacific Co.*, *supra*, pp 224-225.) Even if Boshnack is to be faulted...for his ignorance of the term "sight draft," nevertheless defendant should be held accountable for the negligent exercise of its relied-on expertise in carrying out the parties' understanding. Defendant also argues that its tariff filed with the Civil Aeronautics Board should apply in limiting the value of the goods delivered to the buyer and, therefore, the amount of plaintiffs' loss.

Defendant, however, acted not only as plaintiffs' agent in being an intermediate carrier of the goods from the factory and warehouse to the airports involved, but also in establishing the form for this transaction, which involved both carriage and collection. Part of its duty in this latter regard was deciding whether to make an excess valuation declaration, and there is no evidence indicating that this was not one of the several decisions necessary to the transaction that had been entrusted by plaintiffs to defendant's discretion. Defendant's further argument that the Warsaw Convention's limitation of liability is applicable to this shipment must likewise be rejected. The breach resulting in plaintiffs' injury arose in the preparation of documents prior to defendant's acceptance of the goods as a forwarder and indirect carrier (*see Orlove v Philippine Air Lines*, 257 F.2d 384, 387; *N. V. Organon [Oss] v. Coop Ver. Nederlandse Luchtvracht Groupage Centrum* [NLC], 3 *Hill & Evans Tr*

L of World 877 [Trib Haarlem, 1971]; *but see Pick v Lufthansa German Airlines*, 48 Misc. 2d 442, 454-455; *Crosby & Co. v. Compagnie Nationale Air France*, 76 Misc. 2d 990, 997-998). We therefore conclude that defendant was properly held liable for its breach of the agency agreement with plaintiffs (*see Bostwick v. Baltimore & Ohio R.R. Co.*, 45 N.Y. 712; *Dana v New York, Cent., & Hudson Riv. R. R. Co.*, 50 How. Prac. 428).

Unimac Company, Inc., v. C.F. Ocean Service, Inc.
43 F.3D 1434 (11th Cir. 1995)

KRAVITCH, Circuit Judge:

The central issue presented in this admiralty case is whether a carrier's misdelivery of goods constitutes a deviation such that the one-year statute of limitations and $ 500 per package limit on liability set forth in the Carriage of Goods by Sea Act ("COGSA"), 46 U.S.C.A.App. §§ 1300-1315 (1994), do not apply. We hold that a misdelivery is not a deviation, and *affirm* the district court's grant of summary judgment.

I.

Unimac Company, Inc. ("Unimac") is a manufacturer and seller of washing machines. C.F. Ocean Service, Inc. ("CFOS") is a non-vessel operating common carrier, engaged in the business of shipping goods from the United States to foreign destinations. At the time of the events in question, CFOS had a valid tariff on file with the Federal Maritime Commission.

On November 13, 1989, Unimac delivered a locked and sealed container to CFOS in Savannah, Georgia, for shipment to its customer, Algec Equipment ("Algec"), in Brisbane, Australia. On November 16, 1989, Unimac sent CFOS a letter of instruction directing CFOS to "handle this shipment on a 'sight draft' basis," explaining that "Algec must pay the bank [$30,650.67] for the equipment before obtaining it from the steamship line." Enclosed with the letter was the original invoice between Unimac and Algec, as well as the inland bill of lading. CFOS did not object to the terms set forth in Unimac's letter.

On January 30, 1990, Unimac again delivered cargo to CFOS for shipment to Algec in Australia. On that day, Unimac sent CFOS a letter identical to the November 16, 1989 letter, directing CFOS that the amount of the sight draft for this shipment was $ 30,411.94.

CFOS did not object to the terms set forth in this letter. CFOS issued an ocean bill of lading for each of the shipments, which bills of lading it sent to Unimac. The bills of lading were mailed after each of the ships had sailed, but prior to the ships' arrival in Australia. The reverse side of each bill of lading sets forth provisions governing the contract of carriage: Section 2(a) is a clause paramount, expressly incorporating COGSA into the contract of carriage; Section 2(e) limits the carrier's liability to $500 per package; Section 2(d) provides that "All Risk" insurance may be obtained if the shipper gives written notice to CFOS declaring the value of the cargo and pays for the insurance; Section 20(b) discharges CFOS of all liability for suits not brought within one year of the date the goods were delivered or should have been delivered; and Section 12(c) incorporates the provisions of CFOS's tariff into the contract of carriage. Unimac never objected to the terms set forth in the bills of lading, never contacted CFOS in order to obtain the extra insurance protection, and never paid the additional ad valorem rate for insurance.

On February 6, 1990, despite Algec's failure to arrange for payment of the goods, CFOS delivered the first shipment to Algec in Australia. The second shipment was delivered on March 16, 1990, and again, Algec did not arrange for payment. Algec has not paid Unimac for any merchandise it received from these shipments.

II.

After unsuccessfully demanding payment from CFOS for the delivered merchandise, Unimac brought suit against CFOS in federal district court on February 19, 1991, seeking damages for breach of contract and misdelivery of goods. The parties entered into a joint pretrial stipulation and agreed that the case could be resolved on summary judgment. CFOS filed a motion to dismiss. The district judge granted in part and denied in part each party's motion for summary judgment and denied CFOS's motion to dismiss. The court held that Unimac's claim for the first shipment was barred by COGSA's one-year statute of limitations. As to the second shipment, the court found that Unimac's letter of instruction directing CFOS to obtain a sight draft prior to delivery was part of the contract of carriage. However, the court held that pursuant to COGSA, recovery for the second shipment was limited to $ 500 for each of the seven packages delivered in the second shipment, and thus entered judgment in favor of Unimac for $ 3,500. Unimac appeals.

III.

COGSA is a comprehensive statute intended to limit the liability of carriers engaged in international shipping. It applies to "all contracts for carriage of goods by sea to or from ports of the United States in foreign trade." 46 U.S.C.A.App. § 1312. The Statute defines "foreign trade" as "the transportation of goods between the ports of the United States and ports of foreign countries." *Id.* Because the dispute between Unimac and CFOS stems from a contract for the shipment of goods from Savannah, Georgia to Australia, COGSA governs this transaction.

CFOS argues that the district court correctly concluded that COGSA bars recovery for the first shipment and limits liability for the second shipment to $ 500 per package. 46 U.S.C.A.App. § 1303(6) provides that "the carrier and the ship shall be discharged from all liability in respect of loss or damage unless suit is brought within one year after delivery of the goods or the date when the goods should have been delivered." Because the first shipment was delivered on February 6, 1990 and Unimac did not file suit until February 19, 1991, more than one year later, CFOS asserts that Unimac is barred from recovery for any damages stemming from the first shipment.

Additionally, COGSA limits the carrier's liability to $ 500 per package "unless the nature and value of such goods have been declared by the shipper before shipment and inserted in the bill of lading." 46 U.S.C.A.App. § 1304(5). CFOS asserts that the district court, pursuant to this provision, correctly limited Unimac's recovery for damages stemming from the second shipment to $ 3,500.

Unimac urges this court to hold that CFOS's failure to ensure that Algec had paid for the goods prior to releasing them, as instructed in Unimac's letters, constitutes a deviation of the contract of carriage. *See C.A. La Seguridad v. Delta Steamship Lines*, 721 F.2d 322, 324 (11th Cir.1983) (deviation from the contract of carriage strips carrier of its defenses under COGSA). Unimac also asserts that it did not have a fair opportunity to set forth a higher value for the second shipment because it did not receive the bill of lading until after the ship had sailed, and therefore could not comply with § 1304's requirement that it declare a higher value for its cargo in the bill of lading. For the reasons set forth below, we decline to hold that a misdelivery is a deviation. In addition, we hold that Unimac had notice of the requirements that it declare its goods a higher value and pay for insurance, and failed to do so.

IV.

The district court found that Unimac's letters of instructions concerning delivery on a sight draft basis constituted part of the contract of carriage and CFOS does not appeal this finding. Unimac argues that CFOS's failure to adhere to this contractual provision is a deviation, rendering the COGSA defenses unavailable to CFOS. However, even assuming that CFOS's failure to deliver the goods to Algec on a sight draft basis breached the contract of carriage, not every breach of contract is a deviation.

The doctrine of deviation developed prior to COGSA as a means of protecting shippers from contractual limits on liability. In the post-COGSA era, the doctrine provides that when a carrier deviates markedly from the contract of carriage, COGSA does not apply because the bill of lading, which acts as the contract of carriage, is nullified. Since the passage of COGSA, courts have applied the doctrine of deviation sparingly, generally only for geographical departures and unauthorized on-deck stowage. *See B.M.A. Industries, Ltd. v. Nigerian Star Line Ltd.*, 786 F.2d 90, 91 (2d Cir.1986) ("deviation" limited to geographic departures and unauthorized on-deck stowage); *SPM Corp. v. M/V Ming Moon*, 965 F.2d 1297, 1304 (3d Cir.1992) (noting that courts of appeals have declined to extend the concept of deviation and agreeing that "doctrine of quasi-deviation should be not be viewed expansively in the post-COGSA era"); *Rockwell Int'l Corp. v. M/V Incotrans Spirit*, 998 F.2d 316, 319 (5th Cir.1993) ("the notion of non-geographic deviation may be '...of questionable status under Cogsa [sic]'") (citation omitted).

Although this court has yet to decide whether a misdelivery is a deviation, we have held that a nondelivery is not a deviation. *See C.A. La Seguridad,* 721 F.2d at 325 (carrier's failure to deliver goods did not constitute a deviation); *see also C.A. Articulos Nacionales de Goma Gomaven v. M/V Aragua*, 756 F.2d 1156, 1161 (5th Cir.1985) (no deviation where cargo was loaded onto ship but inexplicably, never delivered); *Italia Di Navigazione, S.P.A. v. M.V. Hermes I,* 724 F.2d 21, 22-23 (2d Cir.1983) (refusing to extend doctrine of deviation to nondelivery of goods).

The circuits that have addressed this issue have held that a misdelivery is not a deviation. The Second Circuit, in a case factually similar to this case, held that a carrier's failure to release the shipper's cargo only upon presentation of an original, endorsed bill of lading, as agreed, was a misdelivery which did not constitute a deviation. *B.M.A. Industries, Ltd.*, 786 F.2d at 91-92. *See also Barretto Peat, Inc. v. Luis Ayala Colon Sucrs., Inc.*, 896 F.2d 656, 660 (1st Cir.1990) ("carrier's failure to collect the bill of lading in exchange for the goods is an improper delivery or misdelivery which constitutes a breach of the carriage contract subject to the COGSA one-year statute of limitations").

Consistent with our holding that a nondelivery is not a deviation and consistent with the courts' general reluctance to interpret the doctrine of deviation expansively, we join the First and Second Circuits and hold that a misdelivery is not a deviation. Accordingly, the defenses set forth in COGSA apply in this case.

V.

Unimac also argues that COGSA's $ 500 limit per package should not apply because it did not receive the bill of lading until after the ship had sailed, and thus did not have a fair opportunity to declare a higher value for the goods.

Under COGSA, a carrier has limited liability provided that the carrier gives the shipper adequate notice of the $ 500 limitation by including a clause paramount in the bill of lading and the carrier gives the shipper a fair opportunity to avoid

COGSA's limitation by declaring excess value. *Insurance Co. of North America v. M/V Ocean Lynx*, 901 F.2d 934, 939 (11th Cir.1990).

With respect to notice, CFOS's bill of lading not only contained a clause paramount, expressly incorporating COGSA, but it also contained separate provisions setting forth the liability limitation of $ 500 per package and detailing the steps that the shipper needs to take to obtain "All Risk" insurance. We recognize that Unimac did not receive the bill of lading until after the ship had sailed; nevertheless the ship had yet to reach Australia when Unimac received the document. Thus, upon receipt of the bill of lading, Unimac had notice of the limited liability.

It is also clear that Unimac had ample opportunity to declare excess value and to pay the cost of insurance. This court has held that "either a clause paramount in the bill of lading or a valid tariff filed with the Federal Maritime Commission that includes an opportunity to declare excess value...is sufficient to afford the shipper an opportunity to declare excess value." *Id.*

The bill of lading contained a clause paramount. Further, CFOS's tariff, on file with the Federal Maritime Commission, states in Rule 12(b) & (c) that if the "Shipper desires to be covered for a valuation in excess of [$ 500 per package], it must so stipulate in Carrier's Bill of Lading," and pay an additional ad valorem rate of 3.75%. Therefore, both the bill of lading and the tariff afforded Unimac notice and a fair opportunity to declare a higher value for its cargo and pay for insurance, an opportunity which Unimac did not utilize.

For the foregoing reasons, we *affirm* the district court's grant and denial of partial summary judgment in favor of Unimac and *affirm* the district court's grant and denial of partial summary judgment in favor of CFOS.

NOTE ON THE LIABILITY OF AIR CARRIERS

The liability of air carriers for cargo losses is governed by the Warsaw Convention of 1929. This Convention has been ratified by the United States and close to 100 other countries. In addition to monetary limits on damage awards, it provides carriers with a broad exemption from liability. Article 20 provides, in part, as follows:

(1) The carrier shall not be liable if he proves that he and his agents have taken all necessary measures to avoid the damage or that it was impossible for him or them to take such measures.

(2) In the transportation of goods and baggage the carrier shall not be liable if he proves that the damage was occasioned by an error in piloting, in the handling of the aircraft, or in navigation and that, in all other respects, he and his agents have taken all necessary measures to avoid the damages.

International Mining Corp. v.
Aerovias Nacionales de Columbia S.A.
45 N.Y.2d 915 (1978)

The order of the Appellate Division should be affirmed, with costs.

The issue is whether there is sufficient evidence in the record to support the jury's finding of willful misconduct within the meaning of the Warsaw Convention (49 U.S. Stat 3014). Article 25 of that Convention, which governs in this case, provides that a carrier may not avail himself of the limitations of liability fixed in the Convention "if the damage is caused by his wilful misconduct or by such default on his part as, in accordance with the law of the court to which the case is submitted, is considered to be equivalent to wilful misconduct." (49 U.S. Stat 3020.) Without undertaking a precise verbal definition of willful misconduct or its equivalent for the purposes of the Convention, we hold that the items of proof introduced, whether considered seriatim or in the aggregate, and viewed in the light most favorable to appellant shipper, while sufficient to sustain a finding of negligence, were insufficient as a matter of law to sustain the finding prescribed by the Warsaw Convention.

Against the factual background described in the opinion at the Appellate Division, it appears that following an earlier misdelivery of a shipment of platinum (later recovered) and complaint from the shipper, the carrier's vice-president of cargo sales falsely assured the shipper that appropriate disciplinary actions had been taken and that "all employees handling such matters have been reminded to carefully adhere to procedures which are designed to ensure proper delivery." It is to be noted that this assurance related to adherence to existing security procedures; no reference was made to the inauguration of any new or different procedures and none had been requested by the shipper. Appellant lists six of the procedural steps set down in the carrier's cargo traffic manual. The evidence that there had been formal compliance with each of the pertinent prescribed steps (although concededly negligently performed) was not contradicted. Indeed it was stipulated that, while constituting ordinary negligence, "the action of defendants' two employees, Robert J. Saunders and Robert Rubenstein, on June 25, 1969, in delivering two packages, numbered 862 and 863, to one Russo, an admitted impostor, was not of itself and standing alone an act of willful misconduct within the meaning of the Warsaw Convention, as applied to this case." No evidence was offered which established that the manual procedures, if carefully followed, were insufficient to provide reasonable security protection or that the carrier's security system was otherwise deficient in design or organization.

While there was other evidence, too, which would have supported a finding of negligence, we agree with the Appellate Division that there was insufficient proof as a matter of law to sustain the requisite finding of willful misconduct or its equivalent as required by the Warsaw Convention.

Manufacturers Hanover Trust Company v. Alitalia Airlines
429 F.Supp. 964 (1977)

CONNER, D.J.

On January 4, 1974, a Wells Fargo truck delivered a parcel of nondescript appearance to Cargo Building No. 86 [Building 86], the export operations facility of Alitalia Airlines at John F. Kennedy International Airport, Jamaica, New York. Within two hours of its delivery to Building 86 pending transport aboard Alitalia flight 611, the parcel — containing bank notes in the sum of $200,000 consigned to the Umma Bank of Tripoli, Libya — was to make an unscheduled landing in the hands of three gunmen. The latter, together with their prize, have to date escaped capture or recovery. What the gunmen gained, Manufacturers Hanover Trust Company lost, as shipper of the notes. Ultimate liability for that loss was the subject of a four-day, non-jury trial that began on June 8, 1976. This Opinion incorporates the Court's findings of fact and conclusions of law pursuant to Rule 52(a) F.R.Civ.P.

I.

At approximately one o'clock in the afternoon of January 4, 1974, James Brown, a security guard then employed by Beatty Protective Service, was dispatched to Building 86 on assignment, outfitted with street clothes, a .38 caliber police special, and the knowledge that he had been hired to guard high-value cargo of otherwise unidentified nature. Guided by Alitalia's assistant cargo manager and its deputy supervisor down a corridor fronted by offices, Brown was directed to a chair adjacent to an unmarked, locked door in view of a number of female typists. Thus stationed, Brown was instructed to, "Sit in this chair and watch the pretty girls." However pleasurable that initial scene according to Brown's subjective lights, the view became surely less agreeable shortly before 3:00 P.M., when Brown abruptly found himself looking into the barrel of a loaded revolver. Rather shakily holding the weapon was a man bearing the outward trappings of a Telephone Company repairman, accompanied by another similarly garbed.

Thus addressed by a gun, gripped as it was in an unsteady hand, and by the electrifying announcement, "This is a stick-up," Brown — choosing wisdom's course — eschewed the weapon in his shoulder holster and speedily retreated, with several Alitalia secretaries also in tow, through the corridor and into a men's room, obedient to directions of the gunmen.

Scant minutes earlier, the gunmen's initial contact with Nicola Amoruso, Alitalia's cargo operations manager, had been far more placid. Having proceeded into Building 86 through one of its unguarded entryways, and apparently having gained unchallenged access from the outer public area to the inner office area through a door marked "Authorized Personnel Only," the two had chanced upon Amoruso in their search for the Building 86 supervisor. After Amoruso had identified himself as the manager of operations, the pair explained that a communications problem had been traced to Building 86 and asked to be led to the building's telephone panel. The three-man procession down the corridor from Amoruso's office was suddenly halted, however, when — with revolvers freshly drawn and levelled at Amoruso — the gunmen declared their actual purpose, *i.e.*, to get "the shipment of money." Initially frozen in terror, and eventually achieving movement only by force of the gunmen's prodding, Amoruso — attempting to remain at least visibly calm — followed his assailants' order to instruct other Alitalia employees not to use their telephones pending "repairs," the gunmen meanwhile secreting their weapons beneath their jackets. That done, Amoruso and a secretary were herded into a ladies' room, soon to be involuntarily joined in the approximately 5 feet X 5 feet area by a contingent of some ten or more co-workers.

Shortly thereafter, one of the gunmen reclaimed Amoruso from the ladies'-room crush and ordered him to "open up the strong room." The sole key to the Building 86 "valuables room" was contained, Amoruso knew, in a cabinet — itself normally locked — in the assistant cargo manager's office. Impelled by the gunman's apparent determination and impatience as well as by his weapon, Amoruso made his way to his assistant's office and discovered, to his relief, that the cabinet holding the valuables-room key had fortuitously been left open. With the key in his possession and the gunman at his heels, repeatedly threatening death if he triggered an alarm, Amoruso hastily repaired to the door of the valuables room — the post from which Brown had only moments before been unceremoniously relieved. The door was thereupon unlocked, revealing on the shelves within two lone packages. One, the parcel containing the bank notes, was promptly passed from Amoruso to the gunman. The second package, thereafter reported to have contained gold dental alloy worth some $60,000, apparently was ignored. Having served his fleeting purpose, and again being pushed toward the confines of the ladies' room, Amoruso noted that his two assailants had been joined by a third, a hooded figure without the Telephone Company gear of the others, but no less potently equipped with a gun.

Redeposited in the ladies' room, Amoruso joined his dozen or so colleagues resignedly awaiting deliverance. Their release came about five minutes later, when the door to the ladies' room was opened by Anthony Baldi, then the assistant cargo manager at Alitalia. During the major portion of the robbery's course, Baldi had been occupied by business that had taken him happily beyond Building 86 and that had kept him wholly unsuspecting of the drama within. Less happily, however, Baldi was to become a momentary participant in that drama upon his return to Building 86, when, accosted by the third gunman, he was first ordered to "freeze" and then to "turn around." Apparently dissatisfied with the execution of those commands, the gunman pistol-whipped Baldi before fleeing through one of the building's exits. Bleeding and dizzy, Baldi summoned enough wit to telephone the airport police. Sounds from the lavatories nearby eventually brought Baldi to the aid of his colleagues within. By this time, all of the gunmen had quit the premises.

Their ten-to-fifteen-minute captivity ended, the Alitalia employees eagerly emerged en masse from the lavatory, only to encounter five or six strangers with guns drawn, ordering them to "freeze." Assuming this new group to be a fresh wave of robbers, the former captives turned on their heels and ran "instinctively" back to the lavatory, a proven safe retreat. The armed men, however, were subsequently identified as members of the Port Authority police, dressed in civilian clothes, summoned scarcely minutes earlier by Baldi. Beyond the battery of police questions that inevitably would follow and the administration of necessary medical aid to the wounded Baldi, normalcy had returned to Building 86.

II.

As noted at the outset, the bank notes stolen from Building 86 on January 4, 1974 have never been retrieved. The parties herein agree, as does this Court, that the extent of Alitalia's liability, if any, for that loss must be determined by reference to the Warsaw Convention [the Convention], as reproduced in its English translation at 49 Stat. 3000 (1934). *See* Article 1(1)-(2) of the Convention.

Articles 18 and 20(1) of the Convention set the measure of plaintiff's present claim, the former in relevant part providing that "[the] carrier shall be liable for * * * loss of * * * any goods * * * during [the period in] which the * * * goods are in charge of the carrier * * * ," the latter providing that "[the] carrier shall not be liable if he proves that he and his agents have taken all necessary measures to avoid the damage or that it was impossible for him or them to take such measures." Both parties herein apparently concede that Articles 18 and 20 in tandem operate to establish a presumption of carrier liability, in the event of a loss within the Convention's terms, that, in the present context, may be rebutted only by defendant's persuasive proof that it took "all necessary measures" to prevent the loss at issue. *See Wing Hang Bank, Ltd. v. Japan Air Lines Co., Ltd.*, 357 F. Supp. 94 (S.D.N.Y. 1973); *Rugani v. K.L.M. Royal Dutch Airlines*, 4 Avi. 17,257 (N.Y. Ct. of City of N.Y.), *aff'd*, 285 App.Div. 944, 139 N.Y.S.2d 899 (1st Dep't), *aff'd*, 309 N.Y. 810, 130 N.E.2d 613 (1954); *Kraus v. Koninklijke Luchtvaart Maatschappij*, N.V., 92 N.Y.S.2d 315 (Sup. Ct. N.Y. Co. 1949); *cf. Grey v. American Airlines*, 227 F.2d 282 (2d Cir. 1955); Lowenfeld & Mendelsohn, *The United States and the Warsaw Convention*, 80 HARV. L. REV. 497, 500 (1967).

Both plaintiff and defendant have devoted considerable efforts to explain and support their respective constructions of the phrase "all necessary measures." But, in the end, a common-sense reading serves best. Thus, notwithstanding plaintiff's argument to the contrary, this Court concludes that the phrase "all necessary measures" cannot be read with strict literality, but must, rather, be construed to mean "all reasonable measures." After all, there could scarcely be a loss of goods — and consequently no call for operation of Article 20 — were a carrier to have taken every precaution literally necessary to the prevention of loss. Nor, on the other hand, may a carrier escape liability under Article 20, as Alitalia suggests, by demonstrating no more than its recourse to some — as opposed to all — reasonable measures. In short, Article 20 requires of defendant proof, not of a surfeit of preventatives, but rather, of an undertaking embracing all precautions that in sum are appropriate to the risk, *i.e.*, measures reasonably available to defendant and reasonably calculated, in cumulation, to prevent the subject loss. Such construction finds implicit support in the few precedents squarely on point, *see Wing Hang Bank, Ltd. v. Japan Air Lines Co., Ltd. supra*; *Rugani v. K.L.M. Royal Dutch Airlines, supra*, and in the leading treatise on the Convention, *see* D. Goedhuis, *National Air Legislations and the Warsaw Convention* 217-38 (The Hague 1937).

With so much determined, the question of Alitalia's liability in the present case need not detain us long. Alitalia, the record makes clear, did undertake a number of measures, each intrinsically reasonable, to secure high-value cargo held in its custody. The existence and structure of the Building 86 valuables room; the armed guard hired specially to obstruct illicit access thereto; the log-book record of high-value cargo, conscientiously maintained; Alitalia's refusal to accept high-value cargo deliveries until an armed guard's arrival; certain precautions taken by Alitalia to prevent undue circulation of documents reflecting a shipment of high-value cargo — all combined to demonstrate that defendant had not been wholly unmindful of nor unmoved by considerations of security. But such precautions would be, predictably enough, likely unavailing in the circumstance of an armed robbery, as witness the scenario at Building 86 on the afternoon of January 4, 1974. To preserve against such eventuality, more could — and should — have been done. With unrestricted access into Building 86 and through it, the armed guard stationed on a chair at the valuables-room entrance was positioned no more securely than the proverbial sitting duck. As Alitalia's own witnesses agreed, restrictions on access to and through Building 86 — or, at the least, an enclosure about the valuables-room and its guard — might have discouraged or frustrated robbery, if not insured against it. Moreover, armed robbery might have been prevented — or ultimately stymied — had a silent alarm system, with a direct connection to the Port Authority police station, been installed on the premises of Building 86. The costs involved in the installation and annual maintenance of such a system, *i.e.*, $200 and $300, respectively, would have been more than reasonable in light of its robbery-prevention value.

We cannot say, of course, that such precautions would necessarily have averted the loss upon which the instant suit is based. Nor, for that matter, can we say that Alitalia's employees, under the circumstances in which they found themselves on January 4, 1974, could and should have acted otherwise for the sake of thwarting their assailants' purpose. We conclude only — but nonetheless fatally for the defense — that Alitalia did not take all reasonable measures that prudent foresight would have envisioned for the securing of high-value cargo.

Alitalia's reference to the fact that the January 4, 1974 incident at Building 86 was the first instance of armed robbery involving an airline cargo warehouse at Kennedy Airport is mentioned if only to demonstrate that it has not been overlooked. That armed robbers had so far spared such facilities could hardly have insulated the reasonably prudent airline carrier from the knowledge that an armed robbery of a cargo warehouse was a likely future contingency. Of no greater moment is defendant's observation that plaintiff had, within the space of some eighteen months preceding the robbery at Building 86, shipped without incident sixteen consignments of currency to the Umma Bank via Alitalia.

Equally unavailing to the defense is Alitalia's insistence that it necessarily be held to a standard of care no more rigorous than that observed by the majority of airlines at Kennedy Airport in 1974. In this respect, it is perhaps enough to note the following observations from Judge Learned Hand: "There are, no doubt, cases where courts seem to make the general practice of the calling the standard of proper diligence; we have indeed given some currency to the notion ourselves. *   *   * . Indeed in most cases reasonable prudence is in fact common prudence; but strictly it is never its measure; a whole calling may have unduly lagged in the adoption of new and available devices. It never may set its own tests, however persuasive be its usages. Courts must in the end say what is required *   *   *." *The T. J. Hooper*, 60 F.2d 737, 740 (2d Cir. 1932). *See also Hageman v. Signal L.P. Gas, Inc.*, 486 F.2d 479, 483 (6th Cir. 1973); *Tormo v. Yormark*, 398 F. Supp. 1159 (D.N.J. 1975); *George v. Morgan Construction, Co.*, 389 F. Supp. 253 (E.D.Pa. 1975).

Other airlines at Kennedy Airport, at least until January 1974, may well have been less security conscious than was Alitalia; few, if any, may have been more so. Nevertheless, if other airline cargo facilities might have been as, or more, awkwardly situated in the face of an armed robbery than was Building 86, that fact cannot confer added grace to Alitalia's posture herein.

III.

Under Article 22(2) of the Convention, carrier liability for the loss of freight must be limited to the sum of 250 francs per kilogram "unless the consignor has made, at the time when the package was handed over to the carrier, a special declaration of the value at delivery and has paid a supplementary sum if the case so requires." Appearing on the face of Air Waybill No. 055-3807-7830, the contract of carriage covering the bank notes now at issue, is plaintiff's special declaration of value in the amount of $200,000. Plaintiff has paid all charges imposed by the defendant carrier in connection with the air waybill, including a supplemental valuation charge of $200. In such event, the measure of plaintiff's damages is determined by the amount of value thus declared. *See Orlove v. Phillippine Air Lines, Inc.*, 257 F.2d 384, 387-88 (2d Cir.), *cert. denied*, 358 U.S. 909, 3 L. Ed. 2d 230, 79 S. Ct. 230 (1958).

In accordance with the foregoing, plaintiff shall have judgment in the amount of $200,000, with interest thereon at the rate of six per-cent per annum computed from January 4, 1974, plus costs.

Submit judgment order on notice.

Chapter 3

Remedies for Breach of the Export Contract

I. The Concept of Fundamental Breach

Documents Supplement References:
1. CISG Articles 25, 46, 49, 51, 64, 70, 72-73.
2. U.C.C. Sections 2-608, 2-610, 2-612.

NOTE ON THE SIGNIFICANCE OF THE FUNDAMENTAL BREACH CONCEPT

The Article 25 definition of "fundamental breach" is applicable to both sellers and buyers and is one of the key concepts on which the remedial structure of the CISG is built. Although Article 25 is merely a definition article, it is central to the application of other articles of the CISG. Thus, "fundamental breach" triggers the aggrieved party's right to terminate the contract under Article 49 (avoidance by buyer), Article 64 (avoidance by seller), Article 51(2) (avoidance by the buyer when the seller has delivered only a part of the goods or only a part of the goods is non-conforming), Article 72 (avoidance for anticipatory breach), and Article 73 (avoidance in the case of an installment contract). The concept is also significant in determining whether a buyer is entitled to the remedy of specific performance under Article 46 and in allocating the risk of loss following casualty to the goods. *See* Article 70.

Oberlandesgericht Frankfurt Am Main
January 18, 1994, 5 U 15/93 (Translation Reproduced From 14
Journal of Law and Commerce 201-207 (1995))

. . . .

INTRODUCTION AND SUMMARY OF FACTS

This case, decided by the Oberlandesgericht Frankfurt a.M. in January 1994, relates to a common set of facts that raises basic problems of international sales law.

In January 1991 the plaintiff [seller], whose place of business was in Italy, contracted to sell women's shoes to the defendant [buyer], located in Germany. The [seller] delivered the shoes to the [buyer] and issued invoices for the purchase price. The [buyer] paid only a portion of the price.

The [seller] sued for the balance of the purchase price and interest on that sum in German currency pursuant to the sales contract. Alternatively, the [seller] asserted the claim in Italian currency.

The [buyer] denied any further obligation for the price by asserting that the contract was avoided. The [buyer] maintained a right to avoid for (a) late delivery; and (b) non-conformity of the goods.

The court dismissed the principal claim but granted the [seller] the motion for alternative relief.

Translated Text

. . . .

Aside from a part of the interest claim, the claim is well-founded on the basis of the motion for alternative relief, because the [seller] has a right to the asserted purchase price in Italian currency pursuant to CISG, Article 53.

The sales contracts concluded by the parties to the action in 1991 are governed by the CISG pursuant to Articles 1 and 100(2) of the Convention. Both Italy and Germany are parties to the Convention. . . . The Convention came into force on January 1, 1991 in Germany and on January 1, 1988 in Italy.

The claim is based on two invoices . . . for the supply of women's shoes. The [seller] is suing the [buyer] . . . for the residual purchase money. The conclusion of the sales contract, the delivery of the shoes and the proper calculation of the purchase price are uncontested.

The [buyer] is committed to pay the purchase money only if it did not effectively declare the contract avoided (CISG, Article 49). The avoidance of the contract releases both parties from their contractual obligations subject to any damages that may be due (CISG, Article 81(1)).

Insofar as the [buyer] maintains that the shoes had not been delivered within the stipulated time period, the [buyer] does not have any right to avoid the contract, since it is not established that the [seller] failed to perform within a fixed additional period of time (CISG, Articles 49(1)(b), 47(1)).

The [buyer] also does not succeed in showing that the delivered shoes have been predominantly non-conforming.

According to the Convention, the defectiveness of goods does not qualify as non-delivery, but is a breach of contract, which has to be distinguished as to whether or not it is a fundamental one. Avoidance of contract is only available as a remedy in those cases in which non-performance of the seller's duties under the contract or under the agreement is a fundamental breach of contract (CISG, Article 49(1)(a)).

Contrary to German national sales law, which except for insignificant deviations in principle grants the right to cancellation of the contract on grounds of a defect, under the Convention, the buyer is expected to accept to a considerable extent even non-conforming goods and to invoke different remedies (reduction of price, damages) to compensate for the defect(s). For example, it is possible that there is no fundamental breach in cases in which the buyer eventually can make some use of the defective goods. . . . An examination [by the court] of this kind also is compelled in cases in which the non-conformity consists in a lack of correspondence between the goods and a sample or model presented at the conclusion of the contract (CISG, Article

35(2)(c)). Consequently, the buyer normally is required to report explicitly on the defects and the unacceptability of any further use, since otherwise the examination [by the court] would not be possible as to whether or not there had been a fundamental breach as is required for avoidance.

The allegations by the [buyer], however, overall preclude the required examination [by the court].

The [buyer] has only testified that... [the shoes] were "defective in all makings." Thus, the material had shown defects. The manufacturing had been "varying," "sometimes" the shoes had been "stitched," others had been "folded up." In all, they did not correspond to the original sample. It is not possible to draw from these submissions the precise defects alleged. As to the deviation from the sample, the evidence given by the [buyer] is not sufficient to determine whether or not she could reasonably be expected to use the shoes....

The [buyer]... also complains about the shoes being made of the material "S. Oro" instead of "Metallic Leather Gold" which caused the shoes not to be smoothly manufactured but to have heavy wrinkles. These [allegations] do not allow for any judgment as to whether or not the shoes were — apart from the different material and consequently different appearance — defective and unfit for use....

During the oral proceedings the court granted the possibility to the [buyer] to substantiate its several claims. Supplementary allegations have not been presented.

The [seller] does not have the principal claim to payment in German currency, because the purchase price had been stipulated in Italian currency. Therefore the suit had to be dismissed with respect to the principal claim.

The interest claim is well-founded only to the extent of 10%.

. . . .

Case Abstract, UNCITRAL Texts (CLOUT), Abstract No. 6
September 16, 1991 (Germany)

A German retailer ordered in September 1989 from an Italian manufacturer through a commercial agent 120 pairs of shoes "Esclusiva su B." After delivery in March 1990 and having resold 20 pairs, the buyer learned that identical shoes supplied by the Italian manufacturer were offered for sale by a competing retailer at a considerably lower price. Since attempts to enjoin the competing retailer failed, the buyer returned the unsold 100 pairs and cancelled the "order of March 1990" promising payment for the 20 pairs upon receipt of the credit.

The court, applying CISG as the relevant Italian law, held that a valid contract had been concluded at the latest at the time of delivery and that this contract had not been avoided under article 49 CISG. The cancellation of the "order of March 1990" was not an express declaration of avoidance of the order of September 1990 since it referred to another order. Even if a declaration of avoidance could be made impliedly (a point on which authors disagree), the buyer did not reject the entire contract as evidenced by the promise to pay for 20 pairs. Even assuming such rejection, the buyer was not entitled to avoid the contract for lack of a fundamental breach of the exclusive contract according to article 25 CISG. The manufacturer had no knowledge about the branches of its business partners, and any knowledge of the commercial agent could be imputed to the manufacturer only if the agent had acted as a closing agent.

The court refused reimbursement of fees incurred by the manufacturer in engaging an Italian collection agency since such engagement constitutes an appropriate measure of pursuit of right only if the collection agency can take steps superior to those that the creditor could take. No interest beyond the statutory rate was awarded and a set-off claim by the buyer based on loss of profit was rejected, both for lack of substantiation.

QUESTIONS

1.   The definition of fundamental breach in Article 25 limits the relevant detriment to what the party in breach foresaw or should have foreseen. In light of this element, would the appropriate inquiry in the preceding case be whether the seller knew or should have known of the breach or whether, if aware of the breach, the seller should have anticipated the detriment to the buyer?

2.   What, if any, is the relationship between delivery of non-conforming goods accompanied by the seller's offer of a price adjustment and fundamental breach?

Case Abstract, UNCITRAL Texts (CLOUT), Abstract No. 154
February 22, 1995 (Court of Appeal of Grenoble, France)

A French seller, a jeans manufacturer, concluded a contract for the sale of a given quantity of goods with a buyer based in the United States of America. It was specified that the jeans purchased were to be sent to South America and Africa.

Both during the negotiations preceding the contract and during the follow-up to its performance, the seller had repeatedly and insistently demanded proof of the destination of the goods sold. It became apparent during a second delivery that they had been shipped to Spain.

The seller's refusal to maintain the trade relationship and to proceed with further deliveries triggered the proceedings.

The Court of Appeal invoked article 1(1)(a) CISG in order to determine the law applicable to the case, since the buyer and seller were nationals of two different States Parties to CISG.

The court then invoked article 8(1) CISG in order to conclude that the [buyer] had not respected the wish of the [seller], namely to know the destination of the goods. That attitude constituted a fundamental breach of contract within the meaning of article 25 CISG.

Under article 64(1) the seller could declare the contract avoided. The Court of Appeal adopted this solution, invoking in addition article 73(2) with regard to the contracts for further deliveries.

Finally, it ordered the [buyer] to pay damages amounting to 10,000 French francs for abuse of process, finding that the conduct of the buyer, "contrary to the principle of good faith in international trade laid down in article 7 CISG, aggravated by the adoption of a judicial stand as plaintiff in the proceedings, constituted abuse of process."

QUESTION

1.   Suppose, in the preceding case, that at the time of contract formation the buyer was unable to foresee a serious loss to the seller if the goods were shipped to Spain, but that the buyer did have reason to know the consequences at the time of breach. Should the breach be deemed fundamental?

NOTE ON DOMESTIC LAW

Absent from the U.C.C. is a uniform material breach standard of relief that is applicable to both buyers and seller. In fact, the term "fundamental breach" appears nowhere in Article 2; what is found instead in several sections is the somewhat similar concept of "substantial impairment." *See* U.C.C. Sections 2-608 (Buyer's Revocation of Acceptance in Whole or in Part), 2- 610 (Anticipatory Repudiation), and 2-612 (Installment Contracts). Although it is difficult to imagine that many cases will be decided differently depending upon whether the materiality of the aggrieved party's loss is judged according to a standard of fundamental breach or substantial impairment of value, the additional element of foreseeability in Article 25 may indeed lead to different results. For example, the Official Comment to U.C.C. Section 2-608 explicitly rejects the notion that the impairment of value to the buyer must have been foreseeable. It provides as follows:

> [T]he test is not what the seller had reason to know at the time of contracting; the question is whether the non-conformity is such as will in fact cause a substantial impairment of value to the buyer though the seller had no advance knowledge as to the buyer's particular circumstances.

When the Code does require the impairment of value be foreseeable, it, too, fails to specify whether foreseeability should be measured at the time of contract formation or at the time of the breach. *See* Section 2-612, Official Comment 4 ("Substantial impairment... must be judged in terms of the normal or specifically known purposes of the contract.").

II. Avoidance of the Contract

Documents Supplement References:

1. *CISG Articles 34, 37, 47-49, 63-64, 75-76, 81.*

2. *UNIDROIT Principles Article 7.1*

3. *U.C.C. Sections 2-507, 2-508, 2-511, 2-601, 2-608, 2-702, 2-703, 2-709*

NOTE ON THE BUYER'S RIGHT TO AVOID
THE CONTRACT FOR NON-DELIVERY

Article 49 defines the circumstances under which the buyer may declare the contract avoided for breach. Once the seller is late in performing, the contract may be terminated if the delay in delivery constitutes a fundamental breach, *see* Article 49(1)(a), or if the seller fails to comply with the terms of a reasonable *Nachfrist* under Article 47. *See* Article 49(1)(b). The *Nachfrist* procedure is adopted with some variation from German law and can be utilized by either a buyer or a seller. The buyer's *Nachfrist* right is located in Article 47 and authorizes the buyer to fix an additional period of time of reasonable length for the seller to deliver the goods. During this additional period of time, the buyer's remedies are suspended, unless the seller notifies the buyer that it will not perform. If the seller does not perform by the stated deadline, the buyer may proceed with any of the remedial provisions available under the CISG, including avoidance.

This procedure is apparently designed to protect the buyer who is unsure whether there has been or at what point there will be a fundamental breach. In these situations, if the buyer makes a substitute purchase from a different supplier and refuses a later tender by the seller, he will be the party in breach if the delay in performance is judicially determined not to have amounted to a fundamental breach. Article 47 deals with this difficult legal and practical problem by permitting the buyer to set a deadline for performance and declare the contract avoided if the deadline is not met.

Case Abstract, UNCITRAL Texts (CLOUT), Abstract No. 136

May 24, 1995 (Germany)

The [buyer], an Egyptian businessman, and the [seller], a German company trading in used printing machines, concluded an oral contract for the sale of nine used printing machines that were to be shipped to Egypt. The parties agreed upon two shipments, the first including six machines and the second three machines. According to the contract, the [buyer] was obliged to pay a considerable part of the contract price before the first shipment, which he did. But the first shipment contained only three machines. After having demanded shipment of the missing machines several times, the [buyer] declared that it had no longer any use for three of the still missing machines. The [seller] answered: "We are sorry that we shall not deliver the machines anymore which we have kept to your disposal..." With respect to the last three machines, the [buyer] fixed a final period of two weeks for delivery. The [seller] did not deliver within that period but offered shortly afterwards shipment against advance payment. The [buyer] refused this and declared, now seven weeks after fixing the additional delivery period, the contract avoided as far as the missing machines were concerned. The [buyer] demanded compensation for its loss as well as repayment of the sum by which the advance payment exceeded the price of the three delivered machines.

The court found that the CISG was applicable as both parties had their places of business in different CISG Contracting States (article 1(1)(a) CISG), the sales contract had been concluded after the CISG had come into force for these States (article 100(2) CISG) and the application of the Convention was neither excluded (article 6 CISG) nor had the parties subsequently chosen a specific law to be applicable.

The court found the [buyer's] repayment claim to be justified according to article 81(2) CISG. As the first three missing machines were concerned, the parties had mutually terminated the contract. The [buyer] had refused to accept delivery and the [seller] had but regretted the [buyer's] refusal. A reasonable person (article 8 CISG) could have understood the [seller's] letter as an acceptance of the termination of the contract.

With regard to the last three machines the contract was avoided by the [buyer's] unilateral declaration (articles 49(1)(b), 47(1) and 51(1) CISG). The [seller] had breached the contract by not delivering the machines within the time fixed by the contract (article 33(b) CISG), thus giving the [buyer] the right to fix an additional period of time (articles 49(1)(b) and 47(1) CISG). The [buyer] was, therefore, entitled to declare the contract avoided even if the additional delivery period of two weeks was perhaps too short. According to the court, the period of seven weeks between announcement and actual declaration of avoidance was reasonable. The fact that the [seller] had offered shipment against advance payment in the meantime was found to be irrelevant since advance payment of the full contract sum was contrary to what had been agreed.

The court finally ordered the [seller] to pay interest. According to article 84(1) CISG, interest is due from the date on which the price was to be paid. The court held that the interest rate was to be determined in accordance with the applicable contract law which in the present case was German law. As the [buyer] had failed to justify a higher interest, the applicable interest rate was bound to be 4% (article 288 German Civil Code).

Case Abstract, UNCITRAL Texts (CLOUT), Abstract No. 82

February 10, 1994 (Germany)

The defendant, a German buyer, refused to pay the purchase price asserting that parts of the fabrics delivered by the plaintiff, an Italian seller of textiles, were of a colour different from that specified in the contract. The first instance court held in favour of the plaintiff.

The appellate court held that the fact that some of the textiles delivered were of a different colour did not amount to non-conformity with contract specifications, since the textiles were not unfit for the purpose for which they were bought (article 35(2)(b) CISG). The court held that such a delivery constituted partial non-performance, as a result of which the [buyer] was entitled to exercise the rights prescribed in articles 46 to 50 of the CISG (article 51 CISG). However, it was found that the [buyer] failed to fix an additional period of time of reasonable length for performance by the [seller], and consequently, it was held that the [buyer] could not exercise those rights (articles 39, 47(2) and 49(1)(b) CISG). The only right that the [buyer] had not lost as a result of its failure to fix an additional period of time for performance by the [seller] was the right to demand payment of damages for breach of contract by the [seller] (article 45 CISG). However, the court found that the [buyer] had not demanded such damages. In addition, it was held that the [buyer] had lost the right to declare the contract avoided on another ground, namely that the [buyer] had sold further the goods bought, thus having made restitution of the goods impossible (article 82(1) CISG).

QUESTION

1.   The breach in the preceding abstract apparently involved the color of the goods, not the seller's delay. Why then does the court discuss the buyer's *Nachfrist* right under Article 47? Is this right limited to situations where the seller has not timely delivered? Compare the language of Article 47(1) with that of Article 49(1)(b). Should delivery of goods of another kind be regarded as a non-conforming delivery or as no delivery at all?

Case Abstract, UNCITRAL Texts (CLOUT), Abstract No. 7

April 24, 1990 (Germany)

A German fashion retailer and an Italian clothing manufacturer concluded a contract for the sale of fashion goods, with the specification "autumn goods, to be delivered July, August, September + -". When a first delivery was attempted on 26 September, the buyer refused to accept the goods and returned the invoice on 2 October claiming expiry of the delivery period. The parties argued about the meaning of the above specification, relying on different additional factors allegedly known to both parties.

The court applied CISG as the law of the seller's country but took also into account German domestic law for filling gaps on questions of performance. The court awarded the seller the full sales price, including interest at the statutory rate in Italy plus additional interest as damages. The seller's claim was held to be justified since delivery was tendered during the agreed delivery period. Even if, as alleged by the buyer, during each of the three months one third of the goods had to be delivered, the buyer did not effectively avoid the contract by refusing acceptance of the goods without having fixed an additional period in the previous cases of non-delivery.

NOTE ON THE BUYER'S RIGHT TO AVOID THE CONTRACT FOR QUALITY DEFECTS

Once the seller has delivered the goods, the buyer has an immediate right to declare the contract avoided only if there has been a fundamental breach. Thus, the buyer's right to undo the transaction and throw the goods back on the seller will turn on the degree of injury caused by the non-conformity. *See* CISG Article 49(1). Obviously, this approach is less protective of the buyer's interests than is U.C.C. Section 2-601, which permits a buyer to reject and cancel the contract if the goods deviate from the contract "in any respect." However, this domestic "perfect tender" rule may only be employed before "acceptance;" thereafter the buyer's remedy is termed "revocation of acceptance" and is subject to different rules which tend to restrict its use. Under U.C.C. Section 2-608, the buyer may revoke his acceptance only where the non-conformity of the goods "substantially impairs its value to him." Because the CISG does not include the concept of acceptance of goods, there is no similar provision for revocation of acceptance.

NOTE ON THE SELLER'S RIGHT TO CURE

The CISG's provisions on "cure" by the seller are designed to respond to problems which arise when the seller tenders non-conforming goods or documents. Essentially, cure is one of several devices which the CISG offers to keep the contract intact, thus avoiding the economic waste that inevitably results from the needless destruction of a contractual relationship. Cure does this by giving the seller a second chance to comply with the contract. In so doing, the CISG resembles both the UNIDROIT Principles (*see* Article 7.1.4.) and the U.C.C. (*see* Section 2-508). The articles on cure may be considered separately from the viewpoint of (1) cure within the time specified for performance and (2) cure thereafter.

Article 34 (documents) and Article 37 (goods) provide that the seller may cure any non-conformity in the tender up to the delivery date in the contract. These articles aid the seller only if the exercise of this right does not cause the buyer "unreasonable inconvenience or unreasonable expense." If the non-conformity is in the goods, the seller may cure by either repair or replacement. It should be noted that there is no express requirement that the seller notify the buyer of his intention to cure. Failure to do so, however, may preclude cure if it causes the buyer "unreasonable inconvenience or unreasonable expense." Of course, even an effective cure will not deprive the buyer of its right to recover for any losses caused by the original non-conformity.

Article 48(1) allows the seller to remedy any defect in the goods or documents after the date for delivery. This opportunity for a second tender is sharply limited; the seller must cure without unreasonable delay and without causing the buyer unreasonable inconvenience or "uncertainty of reimbursement by the seller of expenses advanced by the buyer." If the seller notifies the buyer of his intention to cure and requests that the buyer inform him if the time period within which the proposed cure will be effected is acceptable, the buyer's failure to respond will preclude a later claim that cure within this period of time amounted to an "unreasonable delay" under paragraph (1). *See* Article 48(2). Moreover, even if the seller's notice says nothing about a response, it is assumed to include such a request if a time for performance is indicated. *See* Article 48(3).

QUESTIONS

1.   What is the proper relationship between the seller's right to cure and the buyer's right to avoid the contract for fundamental breach?

2.   Suppose that the contract provides for delivery in April. If the seller delivers non- conforming goods on April 15, is the right to cure governed by Article 37 or Article 48?

NOTE ON THE SELLER'S RIGHT TO AVOID THE CONTRACT

We have already seen that the buyer may avoid the contract under Article 49 if the seller's breach is fundamental, or the seller fails or refuses to deliver the goods in the additional period of time allowed by the buyer pursuant to the *Nachfrist* procedure contained in Article 47. The situations in which the seller is permitted to declare the contract avoided are substantially similar. Sellers, like buyers, may exercise this remedy if the breach is fundamental, if the seller has provided additional time for the buyer to pay or perform its other obligations under Article 63 and the buyer did not do so within that extra period, or the buyer otherwise notified the seller of his intention not to comply. *See* Article 64(1).

Roder Zelt-Und Hallenkonstruktionen GMBH v. Rosedown Park Ltd and Reginald R. Eustace

Federal Court of Australia, South Australian District, Adelaide, April 28, 1995

Van Doussa, Judge

1. In June and July 1992 the applicant ("Roder") agreed to sell goods to the first respondent ("Rosedown") to the value of Deutschmark 609,102.00 with payment to be made by a deposit and instalments after delivery. The goods were received by Rosedown in October 1992. Roder alleges that the contract contained a term for the retention of title in the goods by Roder until the purchase price had been paid in full. Rosedown fell into arrears with its payments before the end of 1992, and the payment schedule was rearranged. On 6 October 1993 the second respondent, Mr Eustace, was appointed the administrator of Rosedown under s.436A of the Corporations Law ("the Law"). Thereupon the company came under administration under Part 5.3A of the Law (ss.435-458): *see* s.435C(4). Roder immediately advised Mr Eustace that ownership of the goods remained with Roder, and Roder claimed possession. Mr Eustace disputed the existence of a retention of title term in the contract, denied both Roder's claimed interest in the goods and its right to possession, and asserted that Roder was merely an unsecured creditor for the outstanding balance of the purchase price.

2. On 8 November 1993 Roder commenced the present action against Rosedown and Mr Eustace claiming a declaration that the property in the goods remained with Roder, an order for delivering up of the goods to Roder, an order pursuant to s.440C of the Law granting leave to Roder to take possession of the goods, and various consequential orders including damages. On 9 November 1993 by specially returnable notice of motion Roder sought interlocutory injunctions restraining the respondents from removing certain of the goods from South Australia, and from selling, charging, or otherwise dealing with the goods, and for immediate delivery of the goods into the possession of Roder. The orders were opposed by the respondents. A meeting of creditors convened under s.439A of the Law was to be held on the following day to consider a resolution directing Rosedown to enter into a Deed of Com-

pany Arrangement pursuant to Part 5.3A providing for a moratorium on payment of pre-6 October 1993 debts to all creditors until March 1994 on conditions as to minimum future trading performance specified in the Deed. Mr Eustace in an affidavit sworn on 9 November 1993 deposed that: "If I am unable to use the equipment which the Applicant now claims in and about my administration of the First Respondent's business then the Deed of Company Arrangement will immediately fail and cease to operate which will be to the detriment of the creditors of the First Respondent."

3. On the hearing of the notice of motion, upon an undertaking being given by Mr Eustace to secure and maintain the goods in good working order but subject to fair wear and tear and to continue current insurance, all claims for relief were stood over pending a trial; an order was made pursuant to s.440D(1)(b) of the Law giving leave to Roder to proceed with this action notwithstanding Mr Eustace's administration of Rosedown; and directions were given to prepare the matter for trial, including directions as to pleadings and the filing of affidavit evidence.

4. The statement of claim was filed on 13 December 1993. Thereafter numerous delays occurred, times limited for procedural steps were not met, and time was lost whilst applications of security for costs and for the transfer of the proceedings to another registry were dealt with. In the meantime it seems (from statements made from the bar table during the trial) that the creditors passed a resolution under s.439C(c) requiring Rosedown to enter into the proposed Deed of Company Arrangement, and that the moratorium period was at some later stage extended from 31 March 1994 to 31 March 1995. Upon the execution of the Deed the administration of Rosedown came to an end: s.435C(2). The rights and duties of the creditors thereafter were governed by Div.10 of Part 3.5A (ss.444A to 445) and by the terms of the Deed.

5. In the preparation and presentation of their cases the parties have given little attention to the provisions of Part 5.3A, and the evidence is silent about events that have occurred in the administration after 9 November 1993, and under the Deed of Company Arrangement. It will be necessary to return to the provisions of Part 5.3A in detail later in these reasons. At this point, however, it should be noted that whilst the meeting of creditors convened under s.439A could have resolved that the administrator of the Deed be someone other than the administrator of the company: *see* s.444A(2), it appears from the conduct of these proceedings that this did not happen. It is implicit in affidavits read at trial that Mr Eustace is the administrator of the Deed.

6. In the statement of claim it was alleged that Rosedown in breach of contract failed to assign certain moneys to Roder, failed to pay interest due on the instalments and failed to pay DM 266,000 and interest of DM 9,975 due on 30 November 1993 (the latter payments falling due after the commencement of the administration and these proceedings) (para.9); that in the circumstances Rosedown had repudiated the contract and Roder had accepted the repudiation thereby determining the contract (para.10); that in the premises Roder was entitled to immediate possession of the goods (para.11); and that in October 1993 Roder requested Rosedown to deliver up the goods and further requested Mr Eustace's consent to it retaking possession which requests were refused (para.12). It was pleaded that in consequence of the breaches of contract by Rosedown, and in consequence of the respondents' refusal to give up possession of the goods, Roder suffered loss and damage. Particulars of the loss and damage were not pleaded but it was said that particulars would be given prior to trial (paras.13 and 14). The relief sought was that claimed in the application.

7. The claim for "damages" was made without further indication of the nature or legal basis for that claim or against which of the respondents it was made.

8. Defences were filed by Rosedown on 11 April 1994 and by Mr Eustace on 1 July 1994. These were amended at trial when a counter claim was also pleaded by both respondents. It was pleaded in the statement of claim and admitted by the respondents that Mr Eustace was on 6 October 1993 appointed as administrator of Rosedown. This is the only reference in the pleadings to his standing in the proceedings. He could not be a party to the counter claim in that capacity as the administration had ended before the counter claim was filed. Presumably he is a party as administrator of the Deed of Company Arrangement.

9. By the defences the allegations relating to the terms for retention of title, for payment, and for interest were either denied or not admitted.

....

11. Finally it was pleaded that if it is held that the applicant is entitled to the return of the contract goods then the respondents or either of them are entitled to the return of the moneys paid to Roder in respect of the goods (pleaded to be a deposit of DM 66,500, and an instalment of DM 72,318.75, although the evidence, such as it is, suggests the instalment was DM 66,500: *see* Ex.A1 p.42) upon a consideration that has totally failed, and that such moneys should be set off against the damages claimed. The counter claim was for the return of these moneys in the event that it is held that Roder is entitled to the return of the goods.

12. As will appear later in these reasons, the contract for the sale of the goods is one to which the United Nations Convention on Contracts for the International Sale of Goods ("the Convention") applies. The provisions of the Convention govern the rights and obligations of the parties arising from the contract. The pleadings, and the claims for relief in the statement of claim and in the counter claim, are expressed in the language and concepts of the common law, not in those of the Convention. Counsel made only passing reference to the Convention at trial. Upon consideration of the case I have concluded that the issues to be addressed, in the event that it is held that the contract of sale included a valid and effective retention of title term, are somewhat different than those stated in the pleadings. I shall return to this topic after resolving the disputed questions of fact.

13. The affidavits filed by the parties before trial concentrated solely on the events and documents that evidenced or recorded the transaction for the sale of the goods, and to aspects of German law. No attention was given in the affidavits to the claim for loss and damage alleged by Roder, or to the effect of Part 3.5A of the Law on the rights and obligations of the parties in the event that Roder established the alleged retention of title term. The affidavits dealt with the issue of liability and not the issue of damages or other consequential relief. The Court was informed that Roder had assumed that the trial was to resolve the liability issue, and that damages and consequential orders would be considered at a later date - hence no attempt had been made to give particulars of loss and damage prior to trial. The Court was informed that very shortly before trial counsel for the respondents informed Roder that the respondents wished to have all aspects of the case, including that of damages, resolved at the one trial. In his opening counsel for Roder argued that consideration of damages and other relief should be stood over for further enquiry after liability had been resolved because the assessment of Roder's loss would, in part, involve a determination of the value of the goods on their eventual return. It was said that the claim for damages included a claim for damages against Mr Eustace personally in tort for the wrongful failure to give up possession of the goods when requested in October 1993. Counsel was not precise whether the claim against Mr Eustace was one in detinue... but gave most emphasis to a claim in conversion. The assessment of damages in ei-

ther case, counsel submitted, would, in practical terms, involve assessing the difference in the value of the goods at October 1993 and when they are returned, and also a consideration of "rental value" as Rosedown, under Mr Eustace's administration, has continued to use the goods in its business. As discussion developed between counsel and the Court it became plain that neither side had worked through the implications of the provisions of Part 5.3A of the Law, and they (especially counsel for Roder) were not able at that time to present other than the case on liability.

14. In these circumstances I propose to decide the disputed questions of fact raised by the pleadings, to discuss a number of the provisions of the Convention and Part 5.3A of the Law, and then to stand the matter over for further consideration. Was there a retention of title term in the contract?

15. It is common ground that the applicant, a German company, at all material times carried on business in Germany at Budingen. It is one of the major manufacturers and suppliers in the world of large tent halls and party marquees. Rosedown is a company incorporated in Victoria. It is the trustee of the G S Tucker Family Trust which traded as Geoff Tuckers Hire and Catering from premises in Dandenong, Victoria. The business has been in operation for many years, and is one of the largest hire companies in Australia specialising in major events such as the Australian Grand Prix and the Moomba and other large festivals. The goods, the subject of these proceedings, included aluminium tent profiles and covers for five very large tents, extra gable infills and other accessories. It is admitted in the pleadings that Rosedown agreed to buy the goods from Roder. There was no dispute at trial that the purchase price was to be paid as follows: on placing the order - DM 66,500 . 30 November 1992 - DM 133,000 . 30 March 1993 - DM 66,500 and interest DM 1,496.25 . 30 November 1993 - DM 133,000 and interest DM 9,975 . 30 March 1994 - DM 66,500 and interest DM 7,481.25 . 30 November 1994 - DM 143,602 and interest DM 23,694.22.

16. Further there was no dispute that the goods were ultimately supplied "ex works" from Budingen on 27 and 28 August 1992 whence they were freighted overland to Rotterdam where they were loaded on board ship on 3 September 1992. They were delivered to Rosedown in Australia on about 3 October 1992. The tentage was urgently required in Australia to fulfil contractual commitments of Rosedown at the Adelaide Grand Prix in November 1992.

17. It was also common ground that the deposit of DM 66,500 was paid by Rosedown to Roder on 20 August 1992. Rosedown was unable to pay the next instalment of DM 133,000 due on 30 November 1992. Rosedown had hoped to do so from rental received from the Grand Prix, but money earmarked for that purpose had apparently been used to pay freight and import duty on the goods. That instalment was deferred to 30 November 1993 with the intent that following the 1993 Grand Prix Rosedown would pay two instalments totalling DM 266,000. As already noted, an administrator of the company was appointed prior to that date.

....

19. The parties were agreed that the contract for the sale of the goods was one to which the Convention applied. That Convention has become part of the law of Australia, and, relevantly for the purposes of this case, part of the law of Victoria by virtue of the Sale of Goods (Vienna Convention) Act 1987 (Vic.). The Convention applies to contracts for the sale of goods between parties whose places of business are in different contracting States (Art.1). Both Germany and Australia are contracting States....

20. However the Convention governs only the formation of the contract of sale and the rights and obligations of the seller and buyer arising from such a contract; in

particular, the Convention is not concerned with the effect which the contract may have on the property in the goods sold: Art.4. Article 7 (2) provides that: "Questions concerning matters governed by this Convention which are not expressly settled in it are to be settled in conformity with the general principles on which it is based or, in the absence of such principles, in conformity with the law applicable by virtue of the rules of private international law."

....

[The court determined initially that the property law effect of a retention of title agreement was to be determined by German private international law because Germany was where the acceptance occurred and the contract was made. According to German private international law the property law effect is to be assessed under Australian law when the goods are in Australia. Next, the court concluded that the contract for the sale of the goods was subject to a valid and effective term for the retention of title and that, therefore, the property remained with Roder and would do so until the condition as to payment was fulfilled.]

55. Whilst Roder alleges, and the respondents deny, that the contract of sale was "repudiated" by Rosedown, and that Roder has "accepted the said repudiation," these common law concepts and the common law remedies which could follow upon the acceptance of a repudiation of the contract by Rosedown are replaced by the provisions of the Convention. Relevantly the Convention provides:

"Article 25 A breach of contract committed by one of the parties is fundamental if it results in such detriment to the other party as substantially to deprive him of what he is entitled to expect under the contract...

Article 26 A declaration of avoidance of the contract is effective only if made by notice to the other party....

Article 53 The buyer must pay the price for the goods and take delivery of them as required by the contract and this Convention....

Article 61 (1) If the buyer fails to perform any of his obligations under the contract or this Convention, the seller may: (a) exercise the rights provided in articles 62 to 65; (b) claim damages as provided in articles 74 to 77. (2) The seller is not deprived of any right he may have to claim damages by exercising his right to other remedies. (3)......

Article 63 (1) The seller may fix an additional period of time of reasonable length for performance by the buyer of his obligations. (2) Unless the seller has received notice from the buyer that he will not perform within the period so fixed, the seller may not, during that period, resort to any remedy for breach of contract. However, the seller is not deprived thereby of any right he may have to claim damages for delay in performance.

Article 64 (1) The seller may declare the contract avoided: (a) if the failure by the buyer to perform any of his obligations under the contract or this Convention amounts to a fundamental breach of contract; or..."

Immediately prior to 6 October 1993 Rosedown was in continuing breach of the contract of sale in that interest payments were overdue. An amount of DM 1,496.25 had become payable on 30 March 1993. The other overdue interest payments related to interest payable under a further variation of the contract made on about 10 May 1993 when Roder agreed to extend until 30 November 1993 the time for payment of DM 133,000 originally payable on 30 November 1992. It was agreed that interest calculated at the rate of 13 % p.a. would be paid on that sum, the first payment for a six month period becoming due in late May 1993, and thereafter interest was to be paid quarterly, *i.e.* in August 1993 and the final payment with the instalment of DM 133,000 on 30 November 1993. No demand had been made for these payments, and a letter from Roder to Rosedown dated 27 September 1993 made no reference to these overdue payments. Further, Rosedown had not at 6 October 1993 assigned income expected to be received from the November 1993 Grand Prix to Roder, but that was something that could be done effectively after 6 October 1993. I am not satisfied that these breaches of contract, in the absence of notice to perform under Art. 63, constituted fundamental breaches that would justify avoidance of the contract of sale immediately prior to 6 October 1993. In any event no declaration of avoidance had been notified to Rosedown before 6 October 1993.

56. The contract of sale remained on foot when the administrator was appointed.

57. The object of Part 5.3A of the Law is stated in s.435A: "435A The object of this Part is to provide for the business, property and affairs of an insolvent company to be administered in a way that: (a) maximises the chances of the company, or as much as possible of its business, continuing in existence; or (b) if it is not possible for the company or its business to continue in existence - results in a better return for the company's creditors and members than would result from an immediate winding up of the company."

In furtherance of that object upon the appointment of an administrator under s.436A, and in the relatively short interim period whilst the company remains under administration (which in this case came to an end when the Deed of Company Arrangement was executed) the Law in Div.6 of Part 5.3A seeks to prevent creditors, secured and unsecured, from resorting to legal proceedings or self-help measures to enforce their rights against the company. Thus the company cannot be wound up during that period: s.440A. Generally, charges are unenforceable: s.440B; and owners and lessors cannot recover property used by the company: s.440C (*but see* Div.7). Proceedings in court against the company or in relation to any of its property cannot be begun or proceeded with except with the administrator's written consent or with the leave of the court: s.440D(1), and the administrator is not liable for damages if he refuses consent: s.440E. Enforcement processes in relation to the company are generally suspended: s.440F.

58. Whilst the provisions of Part 5.3A control the circumstances in which the property of the company may be recovered or taken by other parties, they do not freeze or suspend the exercise of every right held by a creditor. The provisions operate only according to their terms, and rights which are not modified or suspended may be exercised as if the administration had not occurred. Whilst s.440C curtailed Roder's right to recover the goods from Rosedown during the administration, in my opinion none of the provisions of the Law prevented Roder from notifying a declaration of avoidance of the contract. *See also* s.441J. In my opinion the appointment of an administrator by Rosedown constituted a fundamental breach of the contract within the meaning of Article 25 which would justify Roder notifying a declaration of avoidance. The resolution of the directors making that appointment amounted to an acknowledgment by them that the company was insolvent or was likely to become so. That fact, and the placement of the company under administration, in the circumstances of this case, resulted in such detriment to Roder as substantially to deprive it of what it was entitled to expect under the contract. The denial by Mr Eustace as agent for Rosedown (*see* s.437B) of the term as to retention of title also amounted to a fundamental breach of the contract.

59. The pleadings give no indication of the act which is said to constitute the "acceptance of the...repudiation." Whatever that act was, assuming there was one, it would probably constitute notification of a declaration of avoidance. I do not think

the correspondence between Roder and Rosedown, and their solicitors, in October and early November 1993 can be construed as a declaration of avoidance. The correspondence concerns Roder's claim to possession of the goods - a claim which could have been made pursuant to the contract and not only as a consequence of avoidance: *see Clough Mill Ltd v Martin* at 988. As I have earlier observed, the evidence led by the parties hardly touches on the administration, and does not deal at all with events after 9 November 1993. If there were no earlier notification of a declaration of avoidance I consider the filing of the statement of claim should be so construed as it makes it plain that Roder at that time treated the contract as at an end. The statement of claim was filed on 13 December 1993. The evidence does not disclose whether this was during or after the period when Rosedown was under administration. Whilst Rosedown was under administration Roder's rights to possession of the goods whether pursuant to the contract or on avoidance were suspended by s.440C. No action can lie against either Mr Eustace (*see* s.440E) or Rosedown in respect of the refusal to deliver up the goods during this period. That refusal was not unlawful. It was a refusal sanctioned by the Law. The only redress open to Roder was to apply to court for leave to take possession (which it did), and if it were thought necessary to apply for leave to bring proceedings for declaratory relief (which it also did).

60. Upon the administration coming to an end when the Deed of Company Arrangement was executed, the protections afforded to the property of Rosedown under Div.6 of Part 5.3A came to an end. A new legal regime then came into force, being that governed by Div.10 of Part 5.3A (ss.444A to 445). The rights and obligations of creditors and the company under a deed of company arrangement are likely to be quite different: *cf Commissioner of Taxation v. B and G Plant Hire Pty Ltd and Others* (1994) 14 ACSR 283 at 290.

. . . .

64. Subject to the question of leave, Roder is entitled to enforce the rights and obligations which arose on the avoidance of the contract under the Convention. So too is Rosedown. Relevantly the Convention provides, first as damages: "Article 74 Damages for breach of contract by one party consist of a sum equal to the loss, including loss of profit, suffered by the other party as a consequence of the breach. Such damages may not exceed the loss which the party in breach foresaw or ought to have foreseen at the time of the conclusion of the contract, in the light of the facts and matters of which he then knew or ought to have known, as a possible consequence of the breach of contract. Article 75 If the contract is avoided and if, in a reasonable manner and within a reasonable time after avoidance, the buyer has bought goods in replacement or the seller has resold the goods, the party claiming damages may recover the difference between the contract price and the price in the substitute transaction as well as any further damages recoverable under article 74. Article 76 (1) If the contract is avoided and there is a current price for the goods, the party claiming damages may, if he has not made a purchase or resale under article 75, recover the difference between the price fixed by the contract and the current price at the time of avoidance as well as any further damages recoverable under article 74. If, however, the party claiming damages has avoided the contract after taking over the goods, the current price at the time of such taking over shall be applied instead of the current price at the time of avoidance. (2) ..." and secondly as to restitution: "Article 81 (1) Avoidance of the contract releases both parties from their obligations under it subject to any damages which may be due ... (2) A party who has performed the contract either wholly or in part may claim restitution from the other party of whatever the first party has supplied or paid under the contract. If both parties are bound to make restitution, they must do so concurrently. Article 84 (1) If the seller is bound

to refund the price, he must also pay interest on it, from the date on which the price was paid. (2) The buyer must account to the seller for all benefits which he has derived from the goods or part of them: (a) if he must make restitution of the goods or part of them;..." There is no evidence before the Court which enables the application of these provisions to be further discussed. I note that immediately upon his appointment as administrator Mr Eustace obtained an "auction realisation" valuation of the plant and equipment of Roscdown, and that may be of some assistance to the parties in the application of Article 76 should that be appropriate.

65. Roder complains that its loss and damages are ongoing, and will continue until the goods are returned. As Roder cannot resell the goods for the purpose of Article 75, nor make restitution as required by Article 81, until the goods are returned, the appropriate date at which to assess the net result of applying the above Articles could be the date of return of the goods. In the unlikely event that the net result were in favour of Rosedown, there would be no practical point in Roder pursuing a claim against Mr Eustace.

66. On the other hand if the net result is in favour of Roder, Roder will obviously wish to obtain judgment against Rosedown and Mr Eustace in respect of their respective liabilities — unless the fortunes of Rosedown have now so improved that Roder is content to await payment by the company of its entitlement assessed under the Convention.

67. It is necessary therefore to consider the liability of Rosedown and of Mr Eustace for the refusal to return the goods to Roder. I have already indicated that Mr Eustace incurred no liability for the refusal to return the goods whilst Rosedown was under administration. However, when he became the administrator of the Deed he lost the protection of ss.440C and 440E.

68. By s.444A(5) the Deed is taken to include the prescribed provisions, except so far as it provides otherwise. By Regulation 5.3A.06 the prescribed provisions are those set out in Schedule 8A. Paragraph 1 of Schedule 8A provides that in exercising the powers conferred by the Deed and in carrying out the duties arising under it, the administrator (of the deed) is taken to act as agent for and on behalf of the company; and under paragraph 2(a) the administrator has the power to enter upon and take possession of the property of the company. A draft of the Deed (the only evidence of its terms before the Court) did not otherwise provide. The affidavit evidence of Mr Eustace read at trial indicates that in his capacity as administrator of the Deed, and agent of Rosedown, he has denied Roder's claim for possession and delivery up, and has defended these proceedings. In the result Roder has established that the contract of sale included a valid term for the retention of title until payment in full; that it is the owner of the goods; and that, absent an order under s.444F(4), it has been entitled to immediate possession of the goods from the time when the Deed of Company Arrangement was executed. Both Mr Eustace personally and Rosedown are liable to Roder for the tort of conversion for interfering with the possessory rights of Roder. The tort is committed by an agent even where the agent acts in good faith without any intention to commit a wrong: J G Fleming, *The Law of Torts* 8th Ed. at 56, and even though he does not act on his own account or for his personal benefit: *Salmond and Heuston on the Law of Torts*, 20th Ed. 111. *See generally Bowstead on Agency* 15th Ed. at 386 and 495 ff. The conventional measure of damages for conversion is the value of the goods at the date of the wrong: *McGregor on Damages* 15th Ed. paras. 1298 ff — in this case the value of the goods at the date when the Deed was executed. In addition Roder would be entitled to interest under the Federal Court of Australia Act 1976 (Cth), s.51A from that date. If the value of the goods at that date and interest thereafter is allowed, it is difficult to follow how Roder would have any

additional right to compensation for "rental value" from that date. If the goods are now returned, credit will have to be allowed for their present value. The judgment for damages for conversion, when assessed, will be entered jointly and severally against both Rosedown and Mr Eustace. If the loss and damage of Roder against Rosedown under the Convention provisions is assessed at the date of return of the goods there is likely to be some overlap between the judgment entered against Rosedown on that cause of action, and the judgments entered for conversion. Roder cannot recover more than its full loss. It cannot recover its loss in full under a judgment entered against one respondent, and then recover further moneys under a judgment against the other respondent. So if Rosedown is able to discharge the judgment against it that will also satisfy the judgment against Mr Eustace. If not, Mr Eustace will remain liable to discharge the judgment against him.

69. I publish these reasons and my associate will communicate with the parties to arrange a convenient time to relist the matter.

Harry M. Flechtner, Remedies Under the New International Sales Convention: The Perspective From Article 2 of the U.C.C.,
8 Journal of Law and Commerce 53, 83-86 (1988)

3. Avoidance Procedure and Time Constraints

The Convention requires that avoidance of contract be effected by notice to the other party. CISG does not specify the contents of the notice, although it presumably should contain information sufficient to inform a reasonable person in the breaching party's position that the contact has been avoided. Article 27 provides that a contract is avoided despite errors or delays in the transmission of notice of avoidance, or even failure of the notice to arrive, provided the aggrieved party attempted to communicate "by means appropriate in the circumstances." An aggrieved buyer who wishes to avoid must also take account of Article 39, which provides that a buyer "loses the right to rely on a lack of conformity of the goods" unless it gives notice specifying the non-conformity.

Article 2 of the U.C.C. contains notice requirements that parallel those under CISG. Both an Article 2 buyer that is rejecting or revoking acceptance of goods and a Convention buyer that is avoiding the contract after delivery must give notice. Both may lose their rights with respect to defects in the goods unless they notify the breaching party of the defects. Under Article 2, however, a buyer that has not received delivery and an unpaid seller need not give notice to cancel the contract, although notice is a prerequisite to one of the seller's avoidance-type remedies-resale damages. Under the Convention, in contrast, notice of avoidance is always required.

The Convention includes somewhat complex rules on the time for avoidance of the contract. Article 49(2) puts time constraints on the buyer's power to avoid. They apply, however, only where the seller has delivered the goods. Thus if the seller fails to deliver, the Convention does not specifically limit the time for avoidance by the buyer. Where the seller has delivered, the time within which the contract must be avoided depends on the type of breach. If the seller's delivery was late, the buyer will lose the right to avoid unless it does so "within a reasonable time after [the buyer] has become aware that delivery has been made." If the seller's breach is something other than late delivery-for example, delivery of goods that do not conform to the contract-the buyer must generally avoid within a reasonable time after it "knew or ought to have known of the breach." In the case of non-conforming goods, further-more, the buyer must give notice specifying the defects within a reasonable time (not to exceed two years from the date of actual delivery) after it discovered or should have discovered the non-conformities.

The avoidance rights of an unpaid seller, like those of a buyer that has not re-ceived delivery, are not limited in time. Where the buyer has paid the price, however, Article 64(2) imposes time constraints on the seller's power to avoid that are similar to those applicable to buyers who have received delivery. If the buyer's breach con-sists of late performance (e.g., delay in paying or taking delivery), the paid seller must avoid before it "has become aware that performance has been rendered." A paid seller loses the right to avoid for breaches other than late performance (e.g., wrong-ful failure to accept delivery) unless it does so within a reasonable time after it "knew or ought to have known of the breach."

Professor Honnold notes that the lack of time constraints on avoidance by sell-ers awaiting payment and buyers awaiting delivery means that an aggrieved party is not forced to estimate when delay in receiving basic performance is sufficient to con-stitute a fundamental breach. If the seller fails to deliver by the date called for in the contract, for instance, the buyer can safely put off avoid[ing] the contract. If the seller eventually delivers, the buyer still has "a reasonable time after he has become aware that delivery has been made" to determine whether the "late action" constitutes a fundamental breach and, if it does, to avoid the contract. In the case of a seller await-ing late payment, however, the Convention's execution appears flawed. The seller must avoid for late performance before it "become[s] aware that performance has been rendered," without benefit of a "reasonable time" grace period. The seller awaiting a late payment, therefore, must estimate when the buyer's delay constitutes a fundamental breach in order to preserve its avoidance rights. If the seller puts off avoiding the contract and then learns that payment has been made, it will lose the right to avoid even if the buyer's delay constituted a fundamental breach.

TEXT OF SECRETARIAT COMMENTARY
ON ARTICLE 66 OF THE 1978 DRAFT

1.   Article 66 [draft counterpart of CISG Article 81] sets forth the consequences which follow from a declaration of avoidance. Article 67 to 69 [draft counterpart of CISG Articles 82 to 84] give detailed rules for implementing certain aspects of article 66 [draft counterpart of CISG Article 81].

Effect of Avoidance, Paragraph (1)

2.   The primary effect of the avoidance of the contract by one party is that both parties are released from their obligations to carry out the contract. The seller need not deliver the goods and the buyer need not take delivery or pay for them.

3.   Partial avoidance of the contract under article 47 or 64 [draft counterpart of CISG Article 51 or 73] releases both parties from their obligations as to the part of the contract which has been avoided and gives rise to restitution under paragraph (2) as to that part.

4.   In some legal systems avoidance of the contract eliminates all rights and obligations which arose out of the contract. In such a view once a contract has been avoided, there can be no claim for damages for its breach and contract clauses relat-ing to the settlement of disputes, including provisions for arbitration, choice of law, choice of forum, and clauses excluding liability or specifying "penalties" or "liqui-dated damages" for breach, terminate with the rest of the contract.

5.   Paragraph (1) provides a mechanism to avoid this result by specifying that the avoidance of the contract is "subject to any damages which may be due" and that it "does not affect any provisions [provision] of the contract governing the respective rights [the rights] and obligations of the parties consequent upon the avoidance of the contract." It should be noted that article 66(1) [draft counterpart of CISG Article 81(1)] would not make valid an arbitration clause, a penalty clause, or other provision in respect of the settlement of disputes if such a clause was not otherwise valid under the applicable national law. Article 66(1) [draft counterpart of CISG Article 81(1)] states only that such a provision is not terminated by the avoidance of the contract.

6.   The enumeration in paragraph (1) of two particular obligations arising out of the existence of the contract which are not terminated by the avoidance of the contract is not exhaustive. Some continuing obligations are set forth in other provisions of this Convention. For example, article 75(1) [draft counterpart of CISG Article 86(1)] provides that "if the goods have been received by the buyer, and if he intends to reject them, he must take such steps as are reasonable in the circumstances to preserve them" ["If the buyer has received the goods and intends to reject them, he must take such steps to preserve them as are reasonable in the circumstances"] and article 66(2) [draft counterpart of CISG Article 81(2)] permits either party to require of the other party the return of whatever he has supplied or paid under the contract. Other continuing obligations may be found in the contract itself or may arise out of the necessities of justice.

Restitution, Paragraph (2)

7.   It will often be the case that at the time the contract is avoided, one or both of the parties will have performed all or part of his obligations. Sometimes the parties can agree on a formula for adjusting the price to the deliveries already made. However, it may also occur that one or both parties desires the return of that which he has already supplied or paid under the contract.

8.   Paragraph (2) authorizes either party to the contract who has performed in whole or in part to claim the return of whatever he has supplied or paid under the contract. Subject to article 67(2) [draft counterpart of CISG Article 82(2)], the party who makes demand for restitution must also make restitution of that which he has received from the other party. "If both parties are required to make restitution, they must do so concurrently," unless the parties agree otherwise.

9.   Paragraph (2) differs from the rule in some countries that only the party who is authorized to avoid the contract can make demand for restitution. Instead, it incorporates the idea that, as regards restitution, the avoidance of the contract undermines the basis on which either party can retain that which he has received from the other party.

10.   It should be noted that the right of either party to require restitution as recognized by article 66 [draft counterpart of CISG Article 81] may be thwarted by other rules which fall outside the scope of the international sale of goods. If either party is in bankruptcy or other insolvency procedures, it is possible that the claim of restitution will not be recognized as creating a right in the property or as giving a priority in the distribution of the assets. Exchange control laws or other restrictions on the transfer of goods or funds may prevent the transfer of the goods or money to the demanding party in a foreign country. These and other similar legal rules may reduce the value of the claim of restitution. However, they do not affect the validity of the rights between the parties.

11.   The person who has breached the contract giving rise to the avoidance of the contract is liable not only for his own expenses in carrying out the restitution of the goods or money, but also the expenses of the other party. Such expenses would constitute damages for which the party in breach is liable. However, the obligation under article 73 [draft counterpart of CISG Article 77] of the party who relies on the breach of the contract to "take such measures as are reasonable in the circumstances to mitigate the loss" may limit the expenses of restitution which can be recovered by means of damages if physical return of the goods is required rather than, for example, resale of the goods in a local market where such resale would adequately protect the seller at a lower net cost (OFFICIAL RECORDS, p. 57).

NOTE ON THE SELLER'S AVOIDANCE OPTION

If the buyer does not have possession of the goods, avoidance produces results similar to those that follow from "cancellation" under U.C.C. Article 2 when the buyer "wrongfully rejects or revokes acceptance of the goods or fails to make a payment due on or before delivery or repudiates." U.C.C. Section 2-703. However, where the seller exercises his right under the CISG to avoid after the goods have been delivered to and retained by the buyer, the remedy systems in the two bodies of law are radically different.

Under the Code, the seller will typically lose all right of recourse against the goods once they have been delivered to the buyer unless he has retained a security interest in them under U.C.C. Article 9; instead of a claim to the goods, the seller's remedy will be an action for the price under section 2-709. Article 2 does provide the seller with a limited right to take the goods back in two situations. A credit seller who complies with the requirements of Section 2-702(2) may reclaim the goods where the buyer has received them on credit while insolvent. If successful, however, the seller is denied all other remedies including the right to resale or market-price damages. *See* Section 2-702(2). The second situation in which recovery of the goods may be possible is the so-called cash sale where payment is by a check that is subsequently dishonored upon presentment at buyer's bank. *See* U.C.C. Sections 2-507(2) & 2-511.

An avoiding CISG seller will always have a right to restitution of the goods under Article 81(2). Moreover, the fact that the seller retakes possession of the goods will not preclude a claim for resale or market-price differential damages under Articles 75 and 76. In short, the seller's right of avoidance under the Convention produces a right of reclamation which is substantially broader and more potent than its U.C.C. counterpart.

III. Specific Performance

Documents Supplement References:

1.   *CISG Articles 28, 45-46, 62, 64.*
2.   *U.C.C. Sections 2-709, 2-716*

NOTE ON THE BUYER'S RIGHT TO COMPEL PERFORMANCE

Consistent with the Civil Law notion that specific performance is the aggrieved party's entitlement, Article 46 of the CISG grants the disappointed buyer a broad right to compel the seller's performance as originally agreed. If the seller has not delivered the goods, the buyer may exercise this right provided he has not resorted to a remedy which is inconsistent with an action to compel performance. *See* Article

46(1). It seems clear that a declaration by the buyer that the contract is avoided under Article 46 is inconsistent with compelling delivery of the goods as contracted, whereas a claim for damages is not. *See* Article 45 (2).

If the seller has delivered non-conforming goods, efficiency concerns justify a somewhat less liberal application of the specific performance remedy. Additional limitations, therefore, on the remedy are found in paragraphs (2) and (3). Under paragraph (2), the buyer can demand substitute goods only if the non-conformity constitutes a fundamental breach, and he may not demand that the seller repair the defect under paragraph (3) if it would be "unreasonable in the circumstances." In the event the buyer elects to require the seller to deliver substitute goods, he is, of course, obligated to make restitution of the unsatisfactory goods "substantially in the condition in which he received them." Article 82(1).

Notwithstanding the broad scope of the remedy of specific performance under the Convention, the common law-civil law compromise in Article 28 may have the effect of negating its availability in a wide variety of cases. This Article allows the court to refrain from ordering specific performance if it would not do so under its own domestic law. The outcome may, therefore, ultimately depend on the choice of forum. In the United States, for example, a court might withhold the remedy in any case in which the buyer could readily purchase replacement goods elsewhere. *See* U.C.C. Section 2-716. But it is important to note that while Article 28 would not mandate specific performance in such a situation, neither would it necessarily preclude it. A U.S. court could presumably rely on Article 7 and conclude that the domestic restrictions on specific performance should be loosened in the context of CISG cases. One point of contention among commentators is whether Article 28 is limited to specific performance requests under Article 46(1) or whether it also limits the availability of the remedy under paragraphs (2) and (3). *Compare* Jacob Ziegel, *Report to the Uniform Law Conference of Canada on Convention on Contracts for the International Sale of Goods* 105 (1981) (Article 28 also impacts upon Articles 46(2) & 46(3)) *with* Amy Kastely, *Rhetorical Analysis of the Convention*, 8 N.W. J. INT'L L. 615, 635-37 (1988) (Article 28 does not impact upon Article 46(2) & 46(3)).

Court of Appeals (Oberlandesgericht) of Hamm, Germany

June 9, 1995, Index No. 11 U 191/94 (Translation by Walter, Conston, Alexander & Green, P.C.; Editors: William M. Barron, Esq., Birgit Kurtz, Esq.; Coordinator: Thomas Carlé (Referendar); Translators (Referendars): Katja Rohrbach, Astrid Schrütter, Carmela Schmelzer, Caroline Sierp, Sandra Wegmeyer)

[Seller], a manufacturer of windows and doors located in South Tyrol/Italy, asserts a balance of purchase price claim against [buyer] (located in Germany).

[Buyer] ordered 19 window elements altogether from [seller] for the building project of his customer F. The window elements were delivered by [seller] between July 9 and July 19, 1991, and, after that, were installed by [buyer]. On July 5, 1991, [seller] billed [buyer] in the amount of DM 15,363.80 for the window elements.

After the installation of the window elements by [buyer], it was discovered that a part of the ISO window-panes had defects. Because of [buyer's] complaint, [seller] delivered new window-panes which were installed by [buyer] himself.

[Buyer] paid DM 2,131.20 of the invoice. For the balance of DM 13,232.60, [seller] obtained a court order to pay the debt, which was delivered on February 8,

1993 and to which [buyer] objected in due time. [Seller] then abandoned the action for the amount of DM 724.50 because she acknowledged that the costs for the removal of the defects were justified. After [buyer] paid DM 6,313.94 by check dated February 1, 1993, the parties agreed that the main issue was settled. This claim is for the balance of DM 6,194.16.

[Buyer] set off his claim for the costs of the installation of the replacement window-panes against [seller]'s claim.

Excerpt of the Court's Opinion

The admissible appeal of [buyer] is, in its essential part, legally justified.

I.

The U.N. Convention on Contracts for the International Sale of Goods ("CISG"), which took effect in Italy on January 1, 1988 and in Germany on January 1, 1991, applies to the legal relationship of the parties.

The fact that the parties chose German law, as indicated by their behavior in the litigation proceedings is without consequence. Such an implicit choice of law is deemed to have taken place where the parties assumed, throughout their lawsuit, that a certain legal system applies, especially where they referred to its statutory provisions. This happened here; the parties have referred to the provisions of the BGB in the proceedings before the two lower courts. This choice of German law, in turn, leads to the application of the CISG which is part of German law and which has, within its scope of application, priority over the German Civil Code. Indications that the parties have excluded the CISG by their implicit choice of law are neither submitted nor apparent in any other way.

II.

[Seller's] purchase price claim under CISG Art. 53 (the basis and amount of which is not in dispute between the parties) was voided by way of set-off by [buyer] with a counterclaim of at least an equal amount.

1. The set-off itself is not regulated in the CISG. The requirements and consequences of the set-off can be found in the legal system that is applicable, under the principles of Conflict of Laws, to the principal claim that has been set off. As a result of the choice of law due to the trial conduct of the parties, German law applies.

2. The counterclaim, which, pursuant to BGB § 387, is necessary for a set-off, is legally justified. [Buyer] is, contrary to the trial court's (the Landgericht) view, entitled to demand the costs and expenses for the exchange of the ISO windows.

a) An explicit basis for a claim for reimbursement of the costs is, however, not contained in the CISG.

b) But CISG Art. 46(2) provides that if the goods do not conform to the contract, the buyer may require delivery of substitute goods if the lack of conformity constitutes a fundamental breach of contract and a request for substitute goods is made either in conjunction with notice given under CISG Art. 39 or within a reasonable time thereafter. Pursuant to CISG Art. 46(3), the buyer may require the seller to remedy the lack of conformity by repair if the goods do not conform to the contract. In the case at bar, it is not disputed that the ISO window-panes delivered by [seller] do not conform to the contract; [seller] has agreed to deliver goods that conform to the contract, and there is no need to decide whether this is considered a delivery of substituted goods or a repair.

One can conclude from CISG 48(1) that the seller bears the costs for the delivery of substitute goods or for the repair. Moreover, according to subparagraphs 1(b) and

2 of CISG Art. 45, the seller must reimburse the buyer for all other damages caused by nonconformity of the first delivery in so far as they cannot be remedied by a delivery of substituted goods or a repair. Those damages include the costs for the exchange of the ISO window-panes by [buyer]. This applies at least where, as in this dispute, the buyer's own performance does not injure the [seller's] interests. [Seller] did not allege such a scenario....

c) As a result, [buyer's] set-off has voided the claim in full (BGB § 389)....

d) Further, [buyer's] counterclaim, which he set off against [seller's] claim, is not barred by the statute of limitations. The CISG does not contain any provisions concerning the limitation of actions. Rather, the applicable provisions are found in the law that applies to the contract as determined by... German law. Therefore,... even after the expiration of the limitations period, the buyer may refuse to pay the purchase price as far as he may have declared the contract avoided or reduced the purchase price and has given notice of the defective goods within a reasonable time. Here, these requirements are undoubtedly met; the replaced ISO windows did not conform to the contract, and [buyer] immediately gave notice of the fact that the goods did not conform to the contract.

QUESTIONS

1.   What are some of the factors that a rational buyer might consider when deciding whether to pursue specific performance rather than restitution or damages for non-performance?

2.   Article 46(3) provides that the buyer may not require repair by the seller when "this is unreasonable having regard to all the circumstances." What are some of the circumstances that ought to be considered?

3.   Suppose that the U.S. is the forum and that if the CISG were not applicable, Italian law would govern the transaction under private international law principles. Which state's law would be the relevant law for purposes of Article 28?

NOTE ON THE SELLER'S RIGHT TO COMPEL PERFORMANCE

CISG Article 62 is the seller's version of the specific performance remedy. Although one imagines that this Article will be used most often as a vehicle to enforce the buyer's obligation to pay the price, its use is not so limited. The seller may also require the buyer to "take delivery or perform his other obligations." The availability of this remedy is, not surprisingly, subject to two now familiar limitations. The first is that the seller must not have acted in a way inconsistent with the continued viability of the contract, such as by avoiding the contract under Article 64. The other limitation derives from Article 28. In the United States, for example, the seller in a CISG case might be denied recovery of the price unless the goods were accepted or were destroyed after risk of loss passed to the buyer, or the seller is unable to resell the goods on reasonable terms. See U.C.C. Section 2-709.

Morales Y/O Son Export, S.A. Dec. v. Nez Marketing

Dictamen de la Comisión Para la Protección del Comercio
Exterior de México (Translation Reproduced
From 16 Journal of Law and Commerce 363-367 (1997))

Advisory opinion concerning the claim stemming from a transaction of foreign commerce between the private parties Jose Luis Morales and/or Son Export, S.A. de

C.V., from Hermosillo Sonora, Mexico and Nez Marketing from Los Angeles, California, U.S.A.

....

In Mexico City, Federal District, on April 7, 1993, the Mexican Commission for the Protection of Foreign Commerce (Compromex), based on Article 2, section IV and Article 14 of its Organic Law, analyzed the file M/66192. This file was comprised as a consequence of the complaint presented by Mr. Jose Luis Morales and/or Son Export, S.A. de C.V., from Hermosillo Sonora, Mexico (hereinafter the [seller]) against the Nez Marketing from Los Angeles, California, U.S.A. (hereinafter the [buyer]) in order to deliver the following opinion.

Conclusions

I.—In a writing of August 12, 1992, the State Directors of Bancomext in Hermosillo Sonora, sent to this commission an initial written claim signed by [seller], who pleaded the intervention of this organization in order to aid in the recovery of US $15,700.00, which was originally US $20,000.00, from the sale of purple garlic made to [buyer].

II.— The claimant based its claim on the following facts:

a) On May 8, 1992, the [buyer], through the mediation of Mr. Francisco Enriquez, agreed to the purchase of twenty-four tons of purple garlic harvested in 1992. The garlic was tendered in the city of Nogales, Arizona on May 6, 1992.

b) It was agreed that the payment would be in four checks for US $5,000.00 each, which would be cashed by the claimant on May 8, 14, 21, and 28, 1992. However, none of these checks could be cashed, the first because of insufficient funds and the rest because of cancellation of the account. For this reason the [seller] traveled to Los Angeles, California, U.S.A. to interview the [buyer] and demand payment. At that time the [buyer] gave him a partial payment of US $4,300.00.

c) The [buyer] also informed the [seller] that a partial payment of US $3,700 had already been made in the respondent's name through Mr. Francisco Enriquez. However, the [seller] never received said sum nor authorized said person to receive the money in his name.

III.— On August 17, 1992, the Executive Secretary of the Mexican Commission for the Protection of Foreign Commerce (Compromex), after the receipt of the claim in question, proceeded to notify the North American [buyer] about the claim through the Commercial Council of Mexico in Los Angeles, California, U.S.A., and gave him a fifteen working day period to argue his rights. The period, however, passed without any response to the Commission.

IV.— At this stage of the proceeding, and in accordance with Article 12 of the Organic Law of Compromex, the parties were summoned to appear on October 6, 1992 to reconcile their differences. Only [seller] appeared by sending a written notice; the [buyer] did not appear through an agent or by sending a written notice. In the notice, the [seller] confirmed his initial written claim and requested the payment of the debt plus the expenses incurred due to lack of payment.

V.— In relation to the statements made by the [seller] in the aforementioned meeting, this Commission decided to notify the respondent company that it had a seventeen day period beginning on October 6 to argue its right and interest. This period expired on October 30, 1992, without a response from the [buyer].

VI.— When the [mediation] procedure to reconcile the interests of the parties was completed without achieving the objective, and in accordance with Article 14 of the Organic Law of Compromex and the [seller's] petition, the commission must continue with the analysis of the file as follows:

Legal Reasons

1.— In conformity with Articles 2, Section IV and 14 of the Organic Law of Compromex, this organization is competent to submit a recommendation in this case, given the impossibility of reconciling the interests of the parties; the fact that the respondent did not submit to this Commission's arbitration; and the [seller's] plea as described above, as it states in the proceedings on page 51 of the record pertaining to this case filed at the Mexican Commission for the Protection of Foreign Commerce (Compromex).

2.— The substance of the controversy is the lack of payment of US $15,700.00 owed by the [buyer] that bought twenty-four tons of purple garlic harvested in 1992 from the Mexican [seller]. This situation has been proven by the invoice 007 dated on April 22, 1992 in the proceedings on page 57 of the record pertaining to this case filed at Compromex.

3.— Although there is not a specific written contract for this sales transaction, this situation should be understood in reference to Article 11 of the United Nations Convention on Contracts for International Sale of Goods (hereinafter United Nations Convention), adopted in Vienna, Austria, on April 11, 1980, and published in the Official Publication of the Federation on March 17, 1988, ratified by the United States of America on December 11, 1986. Said article of the Convention states: "A contract of sale need not be concluded in or evidenced by writing and is not subject to any other requirement as to form...." Therefore, it can be assumed that the contractual relation between the claimant and the respondent in accordance with the terms stated in subparts II b and c of the conclusion section of this opinion as proven by the following documents: invoice 007 dated April 22, 1992 where the price of U.S. $1,030.00 per ton is indicated for a total of U.S. $24,915.70; goods that were received by the driver in charge of its transfer; the bill of lading indicating that the final destination of the goods would be [buyer]; photocopied documentary evidence shown on pages, 57, 58 and 59 of the record pertinent to this case filed at the Mexican Commission for the Protection of Foreign Commerce (Compromex).

4.— Likewise, Article 62 of the United Nations Convention, states: "The seller may require the buyer to pay the price, take delivery or perform his other obligations, unless the seller has resorted to a remedy which is inconsistent with this requirement." Based on this provision, the Mexican [seller] has the right to demand that the [buyer] firm pay the price of the merchandise, a situation that has been proven with the checks issued by Bank of America. The check numbered 3645 was not paid because of insufficient funds, and the checks 1149, 1150, and 1151 were canceled by order of the [buyer]. [See the] photocopied documentary evidence found on pages 5, 6, and 7 of the record filed at the Mexican Commission for the Protection of Foreign Commerce (Compromex).

5.— Article 81(2) of the United Nations Convention states: "A party who has performed the contract either wholly or in part may claim restitution from the other party of whatever the first party has supplied or paid under the contract...." Based on this provision, the Mexican [seller] also has the right to claim payment from the North American [buyer] for the sale of purple garlic, which is the object of the controversy, as has been demonstrated through the invoice 007 dated April 22, 1992 and through the photocopy of the bill of lading which is within the proceedings on pages 58 and 59 of the record pertinent to this case filed at the Mexican Commission for the Protection of Foreign Commerce(Compromex).

For the legal reasons expressed above and in conformity with Article 2, Section IV and Article 14 of the Organic Law of the Mexican Commission for the Protection of Foreign Commerce, the Commission finds as follows:

Recommendation:

First. The present claim stems from a foreign commercial transaction between private parties involving the sale of twenty-four tons of purple garlic concluded between [a seller], from Hemmosillo Sonora, Mexico, and [a buyer] from Los Angeles, California, U.S.A.

Second. Based on the findings and legal reasons in this recommendation, we conclude that the instant case could not be resolved through conciliation, nor through arbitration, because the [buyer] did not submit to these proceedings. For this reason this Commission, because of the petition of the Mexican [seller] and the terms of its own Organic Law, is entitled to make a recommendation in this controversy.

Third. In conformity with the provisions of law discussed in paragraphs 3, 4, and 5 of the legal reason portion of this opinion and based on the documentary evidence cited in those sections, we conclude that the [seller] proved his allegations, but the [buyer] did not prove its defenses.

Fourth. This Commission recommends to [buyer] that in order to preserve its commercial ties it considers the importance of completing its obligation to pay the sum of U.S. $15,700.00 to [seller].

Fifth. The rights of the [seller] and [buyer] will be left intact to allow their exercise before an authority in the form most convenient to the parties' interests.

Sixth. Notice to the parties—

In the city of Mexico, Federal District, on the 4th day of the month of May 1993, this recommendation was approved by the members of the Honorable [acting in plenary session] Mexican Commission for the Protection of Foreign Commerce.

The Secretary hereby certifies that the foregoing is entitled to its proper legal effect. Mexican Commission for the Protection of Foreign Commerce.- Executive Secretary.-

[officially signed by] Arturo Guajardo Estrada, Executive Secretary.

QUESTION

1.   Assume that the buyer in the preceding case had resold the purple garlic at a higher price. What are the remedial consequences to the seller? *See* CISG Article 84(2).

IV. Damages

Documents Supplement References:

1. *CISG Articles 6, 46, 50, 62, 72, 74-77.*
2. *U.C.C. Sections 2-706, 2-708, 2-712, 2-713, 2-714, 2-715.*

NOTE ON NON-AVOIDANCE DAMAGES

In assessing the Convention's rules for measuring damages, it is helpful to distinguish between those situations where the contract has been avoided and those situations where it has not. Whenever the contract has not been declared avoided by the injured party, Article 74 provides the means of calculating damages. This right to be compensated in damages is not, however, inconsistent with any other remedy that may be available. Thus, in an appropriate case, Article 74 damages may be available to a party who elects to seek specific performance and to a buyer who chooses to reduce the price under Article 50, requests substitute goods under Article 46(2), or demands that the seller repair defective goods under Article 46(3).

The basic premise underlying Article 74 is that the injured party is entitled to be placed in the same economic position he would have been in if the contract had been performed. To this end, the injured party may recover as damages "a sum equal to the loss, including loss of profit, suffered...as a consequence of the breach." Article 74. In the very next sentence, however, this principle of full recovery is limited by the familiar requirement of foreseeability derived from *Hadley v. Baxendale,* 156 Eng. Rep. 145 (1854).

It should be pointed out that although Article 74 functions in a manner similar to U.C.C. Sections 2-714(2) and 2-715, there is a distinct difference in drafting style. This difference may or may not have substantive consequences. Article 74, for example, has no specific rules for determining "the loss...suffered...as a consequence of the breach." U.C.C. Section 2-714(2), in contrast, states that damages for breach of warranty are measured by the difference between the value of the goods delivered and "the value they would have had if they had been as warranted." Presumably, a court will apply the same measure under Article 74, but one cannot be certain. Moreover, unlike U.C.C. Section 2-714(2), Article 74 is silent on the time and place for calculating the loss. The 1978 Commentary on Article 70 (the counterpart of Article 74) offers some guidance: "[T]he place for measurement should be where the seller delivered the goods" and the point in time should be an appropriate one "such as the moment the goods were delivered, the moment the buyer learned of the non-conformity of the goods" or the moment that the non-conformity "would not be remedied by the seller under article [37, 46, 47 or 48], as the case may be."

Delchi Carrier SpA v. Rotorex Corp.
71 F.3d 1024 (2nd Cir. 1995)

WINTER, CIRCUIT JUDGE

Rotorex Corporation, a New York corporation, appeals from a judgment of $1,785,772.44 in damages for lost profits and other consequential damages awarded to Delchi Carrier SpA following a bench trial before Judge Munson. The basis for the award was Rotorex's delivery of nonconforming compressors to Delchi, an Italian manufacturer of air conditioners. Delchi cross-appeals from the denial of certain incidental and consequential damages. We affirm the award of damages; we reverse in part on Delchi's cross-appeal and remand for further proceedings.

BACKGROUND

In January 1988, Rotorex agreed to sell 10,800 compressors to Delchi for use in Delchi's "Ariele" line of portable room air conditioners. The air conditioners were scheduled to go on sale in the spring and summer of 1988. Prior to executing the contract, Rotorex sent Delchi a sample compressor and accompanying written performance specifications. The compressors were scheduled to be delivered in three shipments before May 15, 1988.

Rotorex sent the first shipment by sea on March 26. Delchi paid for this shipment, which arrived at its Italian factory on April 20, by letter of credit. Rotorex sent a second shipment of compressors on or about May 9. Delchi also remitted payment for this shipment by letter of credit. While the second shipment was en route, Delchi discovered that the first lot of compressors did not conform to the sample model and accompanying specifications. On May 13, after a Rotorex representative visited the Delchi factory in Italy, Delchi informed Rotorex that 93 percent of the compressors were rejected in quality control checks because they had lower cooling capacity and consumed more power than the sample model and specifications. After several unsuccessful attempts to cure the defects in the compressors, Delchi asked Rotorex to supply new compressors conforming to the original sample and specifications. Rotorex refused, claiming that the performance specifications were "inadvertently communicated" to Delchi.

In a faxed letter dated May 23, 1988, Delchi cancelled the contract. Although it was able to expedite a previously planned order of suitable compressors from Sanyo, another supplier, Delchi was unable to obtain in a timely fashion substitute compressors from other sources and thus suffered a loss in its sales volume of Arieles during the 1988 selling season. Delchi filed the instant action under the United Nations Convention on Contracts for the International Sale of Goods ("CISG" or "the Convention") for breach of contract and failure to deliver conforming goods. On January 10, 1991, Judge Cholakis granted Delchi's motion for partial summary judgment, holding Rotorex liable for breach of contract.

After three years of discovery and a bench trial on the issue of damages, Judge Munson, to whom the case had been transferred, held Rotorex liable to Delchi for $ 1,248,331.87. This amount included consequential damages for: (i) lost profits resulting from a diminished sales level of Ariele units, (ii) expenses that Delchi incurred in attempting to remedy the nonconformity of the compressors, (iii) the cost of expediting shipment of previously ordered Sanyo compressors after Delchi rejected the Rotorex compressors, and (iv) costs of handling and storing the rejected compressors. The district court also awarded prejudgment interest under CISG art. 78. The court denied Delchi's claim for damages based on other expenses, including: (i) shipping, customs, and incidentals relating to the two shipments of Rotorex compressors; (ii) the cost of obsolete insulation and tubing that Delchi purchased only for use with Rotorex compressors; (iii) the cost of obsolete tooling purchased only for production of units with Rotorex compressors; and (iv) labor costs for four days when Delchi's production line was idle because it had no compressors to install in the air conditioning units. The court denied an award for these items on the ground that it would lead to a double recovery because "those costs are accounted for in Delchi's recovery on its lost profits claim." It also denied an award for the cost of modification of electrical panels for use with substitute Sanyo compressors on the ground that the cost was not attributable to the breach. Finally, the court denied recovery on Delchi's claim of 4000 additional lost sales in Italy.

On appeal, Rotorex argues that it did not breach the agreement, that Delchi is not entitled to lost profits because it maintained inventory levels in excess of the maximum number of possible lost sales, that the calculation of the number of lost sales was improper, and that the district court improperly excluded fixed costs and depreciation from the manufacturing cost in calculating lost profits. Delchi cross-appeals, claiming that it is entitled to the additional out-of-pocket expenses and the lost profits on additional sales denied by Judge Munson.

DISCUSSION

The district court held, and the parties agree, that the instant matter is governed by the CISG, reprinted at 15 U.S.C.A. Appendix (West Supp. 1995), a self-executing agreement between the United States and other signatories, including Italy.[1] Because there is virtually no caselaw under the Convention, we look to its language and to "the general principles" upon which it is based. *See* CISG art. 7(2). The Convention directs that its interpretation be informed by its "international character and...the need to promote uniformity in its application and the observance of good faith in international trade." *See* CISG art. 7(1); *see generally* John Honnold, *Uniform Law for International Sales Under the 1980 United Nations Convention* 60-62 (2d ed. 1991) (addressing principles for interpretation of CISG). Caselaw interpreting analogous provisions of Article 2 of the Uniform Commercial Code ("U.C.C."), may also inform a court where the language of the relevant CISG provisions tracks that of the U.C.C. However, U.C.C. caselaw "is not *per se* applicable." *Orbisphere Corp. v. United States*, 13 C.I.T. 866, 726 F. Supp. 1344, 1355 (Ct. Int'l Trade 1989).

We first address the liability issue. We review a grant of summary judgment de novo. *Burgos v. Hopkins*, 14 F.3d 787, 789 (2d Cir. 1994). Summary judgment is appropriate if "there is no genuine issue as to any material fact" regarding Rotorex's liability for breach of contract. *See* Fed. R. Civ. P. 56(c).

Under the CISG, "the seller must deliver goods which are of the quantity, quality and description required by the contract," and "the goods do not conform with the contract unless they...possess the qualities of goods which the seller has held out to the buyer as a sample or model." CISG art. 35. The CISG further states that "the seller is liable in accordance with the contract and this Convention for any lack of conformity." CISG art. 36.

Judge Cholakis held that "there is no question that [Rotorex's] compressors did not conform to the terms of the contract between the parties" and noted that "there are ample admissions [by Rotorex] to that effect." We agree. The agreement between Delchi and Rotorex was based upon a sample compressor supplied by Rotorex and upon written specifications regarding cooling capacity and power consumption. After the problems were discovered, Rotorex's engineering representative, Ernest Gamache, admitted in a May 13, 1988 letter that the specification sheet was "in error" and that the compressors would actually generate less cooling power and consume more energy than the specifications indicated. Gamache also testified in a deposition that at least some of the compressors were nonconforming. The president of Rotorex, John McFee, conceded in a May 17, 1988 letter to Delchi that the compressors supplied were less efficient than the sample and did not meet the specifications provided by Rotorex. Finally, in its answer to Delchi's complaint, Rotorex admitted "that some of the compressors...did not conform to the nominal performance information." There was thus no genuine issue of material fact regarding liability, and summary judgment was proper. *See Perma Research & Dev. Co. v. Singer Co.*, 410 F.2d 572, 577-78 (2d Cir. 1969) (affirming grant of summary judgment based upon admissions and deposition testimony by nonmoving party).

---

1. Generally, the CISG governs sales contracts between parties from different signatory countries. However, the Convention makes clear that the parties may by contract choose to be bound by a source of law other than the CISG, such as the Uniform Commercial Code. *See* CISG art. 6 ("The parties may exclude the application of this Convention or...derogate from or vary the effect of any of its provisions."). If, as here, the agreement is silent as to choice of law, the Convention applies if both parties are located in signatory nations. *See* CISG art. 1.

Under the CISG, if the breach is "fundamental" the buyer may either require delivery of substitute goods, CISG art. 46, or declare the contract void, CISG art. 49, and seek damages. With regard to what kind of breach is fundamental, Article 25 provides:

> A breach of contract committed by one of the parties is fundamental if it results in such detriment to the other party as substantially to deprive him of what he is entitled to expect under the contract, unless the party in breach did not foresee and a reasonable person of the same kind in the same circumstances would not have foreseen such a result. CISG art. 25.

In granting summary judgment, the district court held that "there appears to be no question that [Delchi] did not substantially receive that which [it] was entitled to expect" and that "any reasonable person could foresee that shipping non-conforming goods to a buyer would result in the buyer not receiving that which he expected and was entitled to receive." Because the cooling power and energy consumption of an air conditioner compressor are important determinants of the product's value, the district court's conclusion that Rotorex was liable for a fundamental breach of contract under the Convention was proper.

We turn now to the district court's award of damages following the bench trial. A reviewing court must defer to the trial judge's findings of fact unless they are clearly erroneous. *Anderson v. City of Bessemer*, 470 U.S. 564, 575, 84 L. Ed. 2d 518, 105 S. Ct. 1504 (1985); *Allied Chem. Int'l Corp. v. Companhia de Navegacao Lloyd Brasileiro*, 775 F.2d 476, 481 (2d Cir. 1985), *cert. denied*, 475 U.S. 1099, 89 L. Ed. 2d 903, 106 S. Ct. 1502 (1986). However, we review questions of law, including "the measure of damages upon which the factual computation is based," *de novo*. *Wolff & Munier, Inc. v. Whiting-Turner Contracting Co.*, 946 F.2d 1003, 1009 (2d Cir. 1991) (internal quotation marks and citation omitted); *see also Travellers Int'l, A.G. v. Trans World Airlines*, 41 F.3d 1570, 1574-75 (2d Cir. 1994).

The CISG provides:

> Damages for breach of contract by one party consist of a sum equal to the loss, including loss of profit, suffered by the other party as a consequence of the breach. Such damages may not exceed the loss which the party in breach foresaw or ought to have foreseen at the time of the conclusion of the contract, in the light of the facts and matters of which he then knew or ought to have known, as a possible consequence of the breach of contract. CISG art. 74.

This provision is "designed to place the aggrieved party in as good a position as if the other party had properly performed the contract." Honnold, *supra*, at 503.

Rotorex argues that Delchi is not entitled to lost profits because it was able to maintain inventory levels of Ariele air conditioning units in excess of the maximum number of possible lost sales. In Rotorex's view, therefore, there was no actual shortfall of Ariele units available for sale because of Rotorex's delivery of nonconforming compressors. Rotorex's argument goes as follows. The end of the air conditioner selling season is August 1. If one totals the number of units available to Delchi from March to August 1, the sum is enough to fill all sales. We may assume that the evidence in the record supports the factual premise. Nevertheless, the argument is fallacious. Because of Rotorex's breach, Delchi had to shut down its manufacturing operation for a few days in May, and the date on which particular units were available for sale was substantially delayed. For example, units available in late July could not be used to meet orders in the spring. As a result, Delchi lost sales in the spring and early summer. We therefore conclude that the district court's findings regarding lost sales are not clearly erroneous. A detailed discussion of the precise number of lost sales is unnecessary because the district court's findings were, if anything, conservative.

Rotorex contends, in the alternative, that the district court improperly awarded lost profits for unfilled orders from Delchi affiliates in Europe and from sales agents within Italy. We disagree. The CISG requires that damages be limited by the familiar principle of foreseeability established in *Hadley v. Baxendale*, 156 Eng. Rep. 145 (1854). CISG art. 74. However, it was objectively foreseeable that Delchi would take orders for Ariele sales based on the number of compressors it had ordered and expected to have ready for the season. The district court was entitled to rely upon the documents and testimony regarding these lost sales and was well within its authority in deciding which orders were proven with sufficient certainty.

Rotorex also challenges the district court's exclusion of fixed costs and depreciation from the manufacturing cost used to calculate lost profits. The trial judge calculated lost profits by subtracting the 478,783 lire "manufacturing cost" — the total variable cost — of an Ariele unit from the 654,644 lire average sale price. The CISG does not explicitly state whether only variable expenses, or both fixed and variable expenses, should be subtracted from sales revenue in calculating lost profits. However, courts generally do not include fixed costs in the calculation of lost profits. *See Indu Craft, Inc. v. Bank of Baroda*, 47 F.3d 490, 495 (2d Cir. 1995) (only when the breach ends an ongoing business should fixed costs be subtracted along with variable costs); *Adams v. Lindblad Travel, Inc.*, 730 F.2d 89, 92-93 (2d Cir. 1984) (fixed costs should not be included in lost profits equation when the plaintiff is an ongoing business whose fixed costs are not affected by the breach). This is, of course, because the fixed costs would have been encountered whether or not the breach occurred. In the absence of a specific provision in the CISG for calculating lost profits, the district court was correct to use the standard formula employed by most American courts and to deduct only variable costs from sales revenue to arrive at a figure for lost profits.

In its cross-appeal, Delchi challenges the district court's denial of various consequential and incidental damages, including reimbursement for: (i) shipping, customs, and incidentals relating to the first and second shipments — rejected and returned — of Rotorex compressors; (ii) obsolete insulation materials and tubing purchased for use only with Rotorex compressors; (iii) obsolete tooling purchased exclusively for production of units with Rotorex compressors; and (iv) labor costs for the period of May 16-19, 1988, when the Delchi production line was idle due to a lack of compressors to install in Ariele air conditioning units. The district court denied damages for these items on the ground that they "are accounted for in Delchi's recovery on its lost profits claim," and, therefore, an award would constitute a double recovery for Delchi. We disagree.

The Convention provides that a contract plaintiff may collect damages to compensate for the full loss. This includes, but is not limited to, lost profits, subject only to the familiar limitation that the breaching party must have foreseen, or should have foreseen, the loss as a probable consequence. CISG art. 74; *see Hadley v. Baxendale, supra*.

An award for lost profits will not compensate Delchi for the expenses in question. Delchi's lost profits are determined by calculating the hypothetical revenues to be derived from unmade sales less the hypothetical variable costs that would have been, but were not, incurred. This figure, however, does not compensate for costs actually incurred that led to no sales. Thus, to award damages for costs actually incurred in no way creates a double recovery and instead furthers the purpose of giving the injured party damages "equal to the loss." CISG art. 74.

The only remaining inquiries, therefore, are whether the expenses were reasonably foreseeable and legitimate incidental or consequential damages.[2] The expenses incurred by Delchi for shipping, customs, and related matters for the two returned shipments of Rotorex compressors, including storage expenses for the second shipment at Genoa, were clearly foreseeable and recoverable incidental expenses. These are up-front expenses that had to be paid to get the goods to the manufacturing plant for inspection and were thus incurred largely before the nonconformities were detected. To deny reimbursement to Delchi for these incidental damages would effectively cut into the lost profits award. The same is true of unreimbursed tooling expenses and the cost of the useless insulation and tubing materials. These are legitimate consequential damages that in no way duplicate lost profits damages.

The labor expense incurred as a result of the production line shutdown of May 16-19, 1988 is also a reasonably foreseeable result of delivering nonconforming compressors for installation in air conditioners. However, Rotorex argues that the labor costs in question were fixed costs that would have been incurred whether or not there was a breach. The district court labeled the labor costs "fixed costs," but did not explore whether Delchi would have paid these wages regardless of how much it produced. Variable costs are generally those costs that "fluctuate with a firm's output," and typically include labor (but not management) costs. *Northeastern Tel. Co. v. AT&T*, 651 F.2d 76, 86 (2d Cir. 1981). Whether Delchi's labor costs during this four-day period are variable or fixed costs is in large measure a fact question that we cannot answer because we lack factual findings by the district court. We therefore remand to the district court on this issue.

The district court also denied an award for the modification of electrical panels for use with substitute Sanyo compressors. It denied damages on the ground that Delchi failed to show that the modifications were not part of the regular cost of production of units with Sanyo compressors and were therefore attributable to Rotorex's breach. This appears to have been a credibility determination that was within the court's authority to make. We therefore affirm on the ground that this finding is not clearly erroneous.

Finally, Delchi cross-appeals from the denial of its claimed 4000 additional lost sales in Italy. The district court held that Delchi did not prove these orders with sufficient certainty. The trial court was in the best position to evaluate the testimony of the Italian sales agents who stated that they would have ordered more Arieles if they had been available. It found the agents' claims to be too speculative, and this conclusion is not clearly erroneous.

---

2. The U.C.C. defines incidental damages resulting from a seller's breach as "expenses reasonably incurred in inspection, receipt, transportation and care and custody of goods rightfully rejected, any commercially reasonable charges, expenses or commissions in connection with effecting cover and any other reasonable expense incident to the delay or other breach." U.C.C. § 2-715(1) (1990). It defines consequential damages resulting from a seller's breach to include "any loss resulting from general or particular requirements and needs of which the seller at the time of contracting had reason to know and which could not reasonably be prevented by cover or otherwise." U.C.C. § 2-715(2)(a).

CONCLUSION

We affirm the award of damages. We reverse in part the denial of incidental and consequential damages. We remand for further proceedings in accord with this opinion.

QUESTIONS

1.   In granting the right to recover consequential damages, Article 74 does not limit recovery to the buyer. *Compare* U.C.C. Section 2-715(2). Of what might consequential damages for the seller consist?

2.   To what extent are the texts of U.C.C. Section 2-715(2) and Article 74 regarding the foreseeability of consequential damages substantively different?

Case Abstract, UNCITRAL Texts (CLOUT), Abstract No. 166

Arbitration March 21, 1996 (Germany)

[CLOUT Abstract 166 summarizes awards handed down in two related proceedings: proceedings of 21 March 1996 (award on substantive issues); and proceedings of 21 June 1996 (award on costs of proceedings)]

The [seller], a Hong Kong company, and the [buyer], a German company, had concluded a general agreement for the exclusive delivery and distribution of Chinese goods. Under this agreement, the [seller] was responsible for the business relations with Chinese manufacturers while the [buyer] was responsible for the distribution of the goods in Europe. On this basis, the parties concluded regularly separate sale of goods contracts. Owing to financial difficulties, a Chinese manufacturer could not deliver the ordered goods to the [seller], who consequently could not fulfill its contractual obligation to the [buyer].

The [seller] demanded payment of the sum due resulting from previously delivered goods. The [buyer] set off against this claim a damage claim for lost profit owing to the termination of the business relation with the [seller] and refused to pay.

The arbitral tribunal applied the CISG as the relevant German law under article 1(1)(b) CISG. The arbitral tribunal upheld the [seller's] demand for payment. It further held that the [buyer] could set off against the [seller] a claim resulting from the breach of the relevant sales contract but not from the general distribution agreement.

With respect to the damages claim for the non-performance of the sales contract, the arbitral tribunal held that the contract could be declared void and damages could be claimed under article 45(2). It further held that a [seller] could be deemed to have unlawfully refused performance if it made delivery dependent on payment of arrears from previous sales contracts, even if the parties had agreed on cash payment in advance. The arbitral tribunal also held that the [buyer's] damage claim was not precluded under article 79 CISG since the financial difficulties of the [seller's] Chinese manufacturer were within the sphere of the [seller's] responsibility.

With respect to the general distribution agreement, the arbitral tribunal held that the damages claim was without sufficient merit since it was not a consequence of the breach of a sales contract by the [seller] in the sense of article 74 CISG.

The arbitral tribunal, in rendering its award on the costs of the proceedings, held that the [seller] could claim its attorney's fees for the arbitration proceedings as damages according to articles 61 and 74 CISG. It also held that, if the [buyer] refused to pay because it set off an alleged claim for damages, the [seller] did not have to fix an additional period of time for payment according to article 63 CISG.

NOTE ON AVOIDANCE DAMAGES

In the event that a contract is avoided for fundamental breach, the injured party may recover damages under either CISG Article 75 or Article 76. In addition, the injured party may recover incidental and consequential damages under Article 74.

The underlying assumption of Article 75 is that sometime after the breach, the injured party entered into a reasonable substitute transaction. If the buyer purchased replacement goods elsewhere or if the seller resold the goods to a third party, then the injured party recovers the difference between the original contract price and the price received or paid in the substitute transaction. *Compare* U.C.C. Sections 2-706 and 2-712. All, however, may not be quite so simple. First, recovery under this Article requires that the substitute sale or purchase be made in a reasonable manner and within a reasonable time after avoidance. Failure to satisfy this test of reasonableness means that recovery must be had, if at all, under Article 76 and, if applicable, Article 74. A second complicating factor is the need to adjust the substitute contract price to reflect any increased costs or expenses saved. Presumably, the extra costs associated with the transaction are recoverable under Article 74 and any savings can be accounted for by a proper adjustment to the substitute transaction price.

Article 76 provides an alternative measure of damages for those cases where no substitute transaction can be linked to the contract which was breached or, if there was a substitute transaction, it was not reasonable under Article 75. Because there is no actual substitute price, damages are measured by "the difference between the price fixed by the contract and the current price." The current market price is determined "at the time of avoidance," and the price prevailing is determined "at the place where delivery of the goods should have been made." *Compare* U.C.C. Sections 2-708(1) and 2-713.

Final Award in Case No. 7585 OF 1992,

Extracts from ICC Awards, the ICC International Court of Arbitration Bulletin 1995, pp. 60-64

[In March 1991, Claimant (Seller, an Italian Company) and Defendant (Buyer, a Finnish Company) entered into an agreement for the sale of a production line of foamed boards. According to the agreement, Buyer made down payments, and Sseller issued an on demand guarantee. An amendment to the agreement provided that after the inspection of the machine, buyer would make a third down payment and issue letters of credit. As Buyer did not make the third down payment nor did he notify the letters of credit, Seller declared that the contract was terminated, withheld the production line, and filed a request for arbitration claiming damages and interest.

The contract provided that: "this agreement shall be governed by and construed in accordance with the United Nations Convention on Contracts for the International Sale of Goods of April, 11, 1980."]

. . . .

Breach of Contract

The legal consequences of the described facts are the following:

Article 25 of the Vienna Sales Convention gives the following definintion of fundamental breach: *"A breach of contract committed by one of the parties is fundamental if it results in such detriment to the other party as substantially to deprive him of what he is entitled to expect under the contract."*

This general provision has to be read in connection with the provisions relating to the obligations of the buyer, which are stated in Part III, Chapter III of the Convention:

-Article 53 clearly obliges the buyer to pay the price. Buyer didn't pay the third down payment.

-Article 54 includes in this obligation to pay the price *"taking such steps and complying with such formalities as may be required under the contract."*

The fact that Defendant did not notify the letters of credit which were foreseen in the contract at the date of the inspection test falls into this broad definition of price payment according to the Convention.

However, the mere fact that a buyer has some delay in payment is not always in itself a fundamental breach. According to the circumstances, delay on payment for the buyer or delay of delivery for the Seller cannot be the cause of immediate avoidance of the contract.

Acting wisely, Claimant did not terminate the contract immediately after the date of inspection test.

Claimant waited several months before declaring the contractual relations terminated.

In spite of the fact that it was absolutely clear that Defendant did not have financial resources, Claimant still waited.

The time period between November 28th, 1991 (date of equipment inspection) and March 10th, 1992 (date of termination) has to be analyzed as the "additional period" fixed by Seller as set out in Articles 63.1 and 64.1 (b) of the Convention.

Consequently, Claimant may *"declare the contract avoided"* as allowed by Article 64.1 (b).

The sole arbitrator approves the avoidance.

It could be helpful to emphasize that in the Vienna Sales Convention the power to avoid a contract belongs to the parties. It has not to asked to a judge or an arbitrator. Nevertheless, it is the duty of the arbitrator to appreciate if the termination was rightly decided. In the present case, it was rightly decided and Buyer is justified to ask for compensation.

(. . .)

Examination of the Damages Claimed Interest:

This claim raises three connected problems:

- the right of the creditor to interest,
- the starting point of interest,
- the rate of interest.

The Right to Interest

Article 78 of Vienna Sales Convention provides that the creditor is entitled to interest *"without prejudice to any claim for damages."* The purpose of this provision is to make a distinction between interest and damages and to give compensation for the financial loss due to the men; fact that delay in payment has a financial cost. The same general idea is at the origin of Article 84 which obliges the seller who is bound to refund the price, to pay interest on it from the date on which he received money.

The practical consequence for the present case is that Seller is entitled to claim interest on any sum that was in arrears.

The Starting Point of Interest

Article 78 which declares: *"If a party fails to pay the price or any other sum that is in arrears, the other party is entitled to interest on it"* means that any delay in payment entitles the creditor to interest.

Contrary to what is sometimes provided in several legal systems, the right to interest doesn't need a formal notice (*cf. la mora del articolo 1224 del Codice Civile Italiano; la mise en demeure* of Article 1153 of the French Civil Code).

For the above reasons, Seller is entitled to interest from the date on which Buyer had to pay (the date of acceptance test and the expected date of installation).

Rate of Interest

The question of the rate of interest is not solved in the Convention. The Diplomatic conference did not agree on this issue (*See* Official Records I p. 138; II p. 223-226, p. 388-392, 415-419, 429-430).

Several solutions are conceivable:

- the rate in force in the state whose law is applicable;
- the rate in force in the place of business of the creditor;
- the rate in force in the place of procedure.

The arbitrator shares another view. In his opinion, the rate of interest is linked to a precise currency. It would be rather illogical to base interest for the delayed payment of a price agreed in strong currency on the legal rate in force at a place of business located in a country which has a high inflation figure and, consequently, a high rate of interest.

The same reasoning would lead to the exclusion of the law applicable to the contract the *lex fori,* or that of the place of payment.

In the present case, the parties agreed that the price had to be paid in German marks. The first and the second down payments had been paid in DM. The same currency was used for the payment of the bank guarantee issued by the Seller.

Clearly, the financial aspects of the sale are linked with the German Mark. The applicable rate of interest is therefore the German one.

. . . .

Other Claims

The other claims are

- on the one hand, damages for storage, care and maintenance of the non delivered machinery and costs and expenses (legal costs, arbitration),
- on the other hand, damages for loss of profit.

Referring to these claims, Article 74 of the Vienna Sales Convention provides that *"damages for breach of contract by one party consist of a sum equal to the loss, including loss of profit, suffered by the other party as a consequence of the breach.*"

This article limits the amount of damages to the foreseeable loss.

The claims under the present case are usual in situations of avoidance of a contract for breach of one party. They should therefore by considered as foreseeable and do not fall into the scope of the exclusion provided in the second sentence of Article 74 (which excludes non-foreseeable loss).

—The first part of the claim (charges for storage..., costs and expenses) belongs to the category of the well known Roman law *damnum emergens.*

The Convention, at Article 77 states that the *"party who relies on a breach of contract" has a duty "to mitigate the loss, including loss of profit, resulting from breach."*

In the present case, the size of the machinery and its specification obliged Buyer to expenses of carriage and storage in a warehouse, to care and maintenance.

Claimant sent to the sole arbitrator invoices for these costs. The invoices referred also to modification of electrical equipment for the needs of the new buyer. Claimant has based the conversion from Italian Lira to German marks of these costs on the rate of 1 DM for 784, 760 Italian Lira.

The sole arbitrator therefore awards the total amount of DM [...].

The other part of the claims consists of loss of profit. These claims belong to the category of *lucrum cessans* of Roman law. As above said, this sort of claim is expressly stated in Article 74 of the Convention.

A specific provision in Article 75 gives the seller who resells the goods the right to *"recover the difference between the contract price and the price in the substitute transaction."* This provision is applicable to the present case.

Claimant sent to the arbitrator an invoice...evidencing that it had resold the machinery to another firm of Turn. The agreed price was ITL 1 800 000 000 (the resale is a domestic sale, the price of which is payable in Italian Lira). The difference between the price of sale to Defendant and the price of resale, is the loss of profit, ITL 900,000,000;

ITL 900,000,000: 784,760 (rate of exchange) = DM 1,146,847. These figures are supported by the evidence submitted and are not disputed by Defendant.

Compensation Fee

At the hearing, Claimant gave to the arbitrator a written statement asking for the payment of the compensation fee provided by the contract, equivalent to 30% of the price of equipment.

There is a construction difficulty referring to the meaning of the wording "compensation fee."

Article XX of the contract is drafted as follows: *"If the agreement is terminated by fault of the supplier before the goods have been delivered, the purchaser will be returned any sum he has previously transferred to the supplier as down payment, without interest.*

If the agreement is terminated by fault or request of the purchaser - including force majeure- the supplier is entitled to a compensation fee of 30% of the price."

The wording "compensation fee" is not usual in legal vocabulary. From the point of view of the claimant it is "a price, a consideration other than and in addition to damages suffered."

This particular contract clause has to be interpreted in accordance with the Vienna Sales Convention rules and *"in conformity with the general principles on which it is based"* as it is provided in Article 7 of the Convention.

The arbitrator notices that Article XX draws a distinction between Seller's and Buyer's situation in cases where the contract is terminated by an act originated by one or other party.

If the cause of the termination is the fault of Seller, buyer will be returned the money he has previously transferred to Seller. Is this a lump sum compensating for all the damages he could have suffered?

In the opinion of the arbitrator, Article 19.3 is not precise enough to be construed in such a way that it means a renunciation of the right to be compensated as stated in Article 73 of the Vienna Sales Convention.

On the contrary, Article XX of the contract clearly states that Buyer has no right to the interest based on the money momentarily transferred to Buyer. This is an express exception to the Convention Article 84.1 provision.

In the sole arbitrator's opinion, a similar reasoning from the Seller's side, leads to the following solutions;

In the absence of an express wording meaning that the right to interest as provided by Article 78 of the Vienna Sales Convention is excluded, interest has to be recovered.

Referring to damages, the wording "compensation fee" has not the meaning of a lump sum for compensation. Again, as the sole arbitrator stated for the benefit of Buyer, Article XX of the contract has not a language precise enough to be construed in such a way as meaning a renunciation to the right to damages expressly given by Article 74 of the Convention.

. . . .

The wording "compensation fee" has to be interpreted as an amount of money payable in consideration of the termination of the contract independently of any damages suffered by Seller.

It has to be paid independently for any contractual liability on behalf of Buyer. It is expressly stated in Article 19.3 of the contract that compensation fee is due even in a "force majeure" situation.

According to Article 79 of the Convention, a party has not to pay damages *"if he proves that the failure was due to an impediment beyond his control."*

The mere fact that the compensation fee has to be paid in such a situation evidences that it has a nature different from damages in compensation of a loss.

The conclusion is that Defendant has to pay the provided "compensation fee" (30% of the price) added to the damages.

QUESTION

1.   The subject of liquidated damages is not explicitly covered in the Convention. However, a clause agreed upon by the parties should be given effect under the Article 6 principle of freedom of contract. Even though this principle suggests that the "compensation fee" provision in the preceding case should be respected, what countervailing principles would have justified a decision by the arbitrator that the provision was invalid?

Joseph M. Perillo, UNIDROIT Principles of International Commercial Contracts: The Black Letter Text and a Review,

63 Fordham Law Review 281, 313-14 (1994)

XIV. PENALTYCLAUSES

Nowhere in the law of contracts has the clash of common law and civil law notions seemed as irreconcilable as in the treatment of penalty clauses. They have been void in the common law world for two centuries, three, if we count back to the time the enforcement of penal bonds was enjoined. Whatever merit this rule continues to have in consumer transactions, it is a rule that deserves overturning in commercial transactions between businesses. Although some economic analysts have supported the rule on the ground that the enforcement of penalty clauses would deter efficient breaches, the contrary has been cogently demonstrated. It represents paternalistic interference with contractual freedom. The civil law perhaps went too far in the other direction. Under the Code Napoleon, penalty clauses were binding and could not be modified by the court except in cases of part performance of the principal obligation of the contract. In 1975, however, Article 1152 of the French Civil Code was amended to provide: "Nevertheless, the Judge may reduce or increase the agreed upon penalty if it is manifestly excessive or ridiculously small. Any contrary stipulation will be considered not written." This revision removes any possible rational opposition to the validity of penalty clauses. *Principles* adopts a rule consistent with the modern civil law. So should we. Under *Principles*, penalty clauses are valid but agreed penalty sums may be reduced if they are "grossly excessive." [Article 7.4.13]

Final Award in Case No. 7531 OF 1994,

Extracts From ICC Awards, The ICC International Court of Arbitration Bulletin 1995, pp. 67-68

[This arbitration arises out of a dispute over the quality of goods supplied to the Claimant (an Austrian company) by Defendant (Chinese corporation).

In 1990, Claimant entered into a contract with Defendant for the purchase of 80,000 scaffold fittings. Delivery was made to Claimant's customer in England. The goods were subsequently rejected by Claimant as non-conforming. Claimant declared the contract avoided and allegedly sold the goods. Claimant claims damages and interest for losses suffered because he has been able to resell only part of the goods at a lower price.]

Applicable Legal Framework

The parties have not expressly agreed on the law applicable to the substance of the contract. Neither party has expressly argued what national law should be held applicable; claimant bases its argument directly on the United Nations Convention on Contracts for the International Sale of Goods. The Convention entered into force for the People's Republic of China on 1 January 1988 (with reservations in respect of Articles 1.1 (b) and Article 11 and provisions relating to Article 11, none of which is relevant here) and in respect of Austria on 1 January 1989. The respective place of business of each party, as stated in the contract was in a State which is a Contracting state at the time when the contract was concluded (cf. Article 1(1)(a) of the Convention):

In the light hereof - and notwithstanding that Claimant's liaison office in Beijing may have been involved in the negotiation process - the Convention therefore applies to the contract and governs the rights and obligations for the parties arising from the contract, and I intend so to apply it without going further into determining any national law which might be applicable in a dispute.

....

Conformity of the Goods. Breach of the Agreement?

As allowed under the contract, an independent inspection company was engaged on the buyer's side to carry out examination and testing of the goods supplied.

....

Defendant has complained in its letter of (...) that Claimant did not allow a Defendant representative to inspect the goods after delivery or to have the technical inspection repeated by a "reference notary organization," but there is no obligation on claimant to do so (unless the inspection arranged by the buyer's side was flawed, which has not been proven) (...) Claimant has estimated the cost of sorting out bad fittings at USD 17,000, which may be compared with the involved price of the supplies, USD 46,397. [T]he estimate has been communicated to Defendant and has not been disputed.

Under Article 35.1 of the Convention the seller must deliver goods which are of the quality required by the contract. According to Article 35.2 the goods do not conform with the contract unless they are fit for the purposes for which goods of the same description would ordinarily be used and possess the qualities of goods which the seller has held out to the buyer as a sample. The lack of conformity of an important part of the goods supplied amounts to a breach of the contract which, under Article 25, is fundamental since the buyer is deprived of substantially what he was entitled to expect under the contract. Defendant is not entitled to supply substitute items after the delivery date specified in the contract without the consent of the Claimant.

Compensation

The breach of contract committed by Defendant entitles Claimant to remedies under the Convention (article 45(1)). According to Articles 49(1)(a), [the] contract [is] avoided, and under Article 75 Claimant becomes entitled to damages equal to the loss, including loss of profit, to the extent the loss was, or ought to have been, foreseen by the seller. Under Article 86 the buyer is entitled to have his reasonable expenses for preservation of the goods reimbursed by the Seller; he may deposit the goods in a warehouse at the expense of the seller if the expense is not unreasonable (article 87); and he may sell the goods by appropriate means if there has been an unreasonable delay by the seller in taking possession of the goods. (Article 88.1)

Claimant has declared the contract avoided and, as appears from its claim, has sold the goods. The individual items claimed in damages are set out above and have not been disputed by Defendant. However, I cannot find that the amount claimed for the travel costs of Mr. X -an employee of Claimant's consumer- are such as could reasonably have been foreseen and accordingly Defendant should not be liable therefor. The remaining items of damages claimed, which have been justified by invoices, should be granted.

The damage suffered by Claimant includes the cost of credit which has been stated by Claimant undisputedly, at 11% per annum and which should be compensated at the rate as an element of the damages due according to Article 74. Claimant claims interest from the date when it communicated the amount of its claim to Defendant by telex. The Convention is silent on the question of the maturity date of damage claims. [S]ince this particular aspect of the claim is also undisputed, interest should be granted from the date claimed by the Claimant.

Case Abstract, UNCITRAL Texts (CLOUT), Abstract No. 130

January 14, 1994 (Germany)

The [buyer], a German company, ordered 140 pairs of winter shoes from the [seller], an Italian shoe manufacturer. After having manufactured the ordered shoes, the [seller] demanded security for the sales price as the [buyer] still had other bills to settle with the [seller]. The [buyer], however, did neither pay nor furnish security. Therefore the [seller] declared the contract avoided and resold the shoes to other retailers: only 21 pairs for the same price as agreed upon with the [buyer], 109 pairs for a much lower price, 10 pairs remaining unsold.

The [seller] demanded compensation for various damages caused by the breach of the contract: (1) compensation for the difference between the contract price and the price in the substitute transactions, (2) the attorney's fees, (3) interest loss of 16,5%, (4) exchange rate loss of 15%, (5) and current interest of 16,5%. The [buyer] accepted responsibility in general but disputed the extent of damages which it attributed to the [seller's] failure to resell the shoes in a reasonable manner.

The appellate court held that the [seller] was entitled to avoid the contract according to article 72 CISG and consequently granted the [seller] the rights listed in articles 74 and 75 CISG. Accordingly, the [seller] was allowed to recover the difference between the contract price and the price in the substitute transactions (art. 75 CISG). In addition, the court found that the [seller] had performed the resale in a reasonable time noting that the [seller] was not obliged to resell the shoes before the date of avoidance. In the court's view, a resale nearly 2 months after avoidance (avoidance on 7 August, resale on 6 and 15 October) still succeeded within reasonable time and was no breach of the [seller's] obligation under art. 77 CISG to mitigate the loss. In that regard, the court accepted the [seller's] argument, who had offered the shoes on the Italian market, that in August most retailers have already filled their stock for the coming season and have no reason to buy more goods for the winter season.

The court also granted the interest loss according to article 74 CISG. The [seller] argued that it had made use of a bank loan with an interest rate of 16,5%. The court accepted this allegation according to article 287 of the German Civil Procedure Code. However, the [seller's] claim for attorney's fees was rejected. Although such fees in general could be recovered under article 74 CISG, in the present case this would lead to double compensation as the attorney had demanded his costs already in the special procedure for fixing costs.

The court also rejected the [seller's] claim for damages to cover the exchange rate loss between the Italian Lira and the German Mark. The court found that there existed no general custom to exchange money paid in the local currency to a foreign one unless this was the claimant's usual practice. As this could not be established, it was held that the [seller] had not suffered a damage.

Neri v. Retail Marine Corp.

30 N.Y.2d 393, 334 N.Y.S.2d 165, 285 N.E.2d 311 (N.Y. Ct. App. 1972)

GIBSON, JUDGE

The appeal concerns the right of a retail dealer to recover loss of profits and incidental damages upon the buyer's repudiation of a contract governed by the Uniform Commercial Code. This is, indeed, the correct measure of damage in an appropriate case and to this extent the code (§ 2-708, subsection [2]) effected a substantial change from prior law, whereby damages were ordinarily limited to "the difference between the contract price and the market or current price." Upon the record before us, the courts below erred in declining to give effect to the new statute and so the order appealed from must be reversed.

The plaintiffs contracted to purchase from defendant a new boat of a specified model for the price of $ 12,587.40, against which they made a deposit of $ 40. They shortly increased the deposit to $ 4,250 in consideration of the defendant dealer's agreement to arrange with the manufacturer for immediate delivery on the basis of "a firm sale," instead of the delivery within approximately four to six weeks originally specified. Some six days after the date of the contract plaintiffs' lawyer sent to defendant a letter rescinding the sales contract for the reason that plaintiff Neri was about to undergo hospitalization and surgery, in consequence of which, according to the letter, it would be "impossible for Mr. Neri to make any payments." The boat had already been ordered from the manufacturer and was delivered to defendant at or before the time the attorney's letter was received. Defendant declined to refund plaintiffs' deposit and this action to recover it was commenced. Defendant counterclaimed, alleging plaintiffs' breach of the contract and defendant's resultant damage in the amount of $ 4,250, for which sum defendant demanded judgment. Upon motion, defendant had summary judgment on the issue of liability tendered by its counterclaim; and Special Term directed an assessment of damages, upon which it would be determined whether plaintiffs were entitled to the return of any portion of their down payment.

Upon the trial so directed, it was shown that the boat ordered and received by defendant in accordance with plaintiffs' contract of purchase was sold some four months later to another buyer for the same price as that negotiated with plaintiffs. From this proof the plaintiffs argue that defendant's loss on its contract was recouped, while defendant argues that but for plaintiffs' default, it would have sold two boats and have earned two profits instead of one. Defendant proved, without contradiction, that its profit on the sale under the contract in suit would have been $ 2,579 and that during the period the boat remained unsold incidental expenses aggregating $ 674 for storage, upkeep, finance charges and insurance were incurred. Additionally, defendant proved and sought to recover attorneys' fees of $ 1,250.

The trial court found "untenable" defendant's claim for loss of profit, inasmuch as the boat was later sold for the same price that plaintiffs had contracted to pay; found, too, that defendant had failed to prove any incidental damages; further found "that the terms of Section 2-718, subsection 2(b), of the Uniform Commercial Code are applicable and same make adequate and fair provision to place the sellers in as good a position as performance would have done" and, in accordance with paragraph (b) of subsection (2) thus relied upon, awarded defendant $ 500 upon its counterclaim and directed that plaintiffs recover the balance of their deposit, amounting to $ 3,750. The ensuing judgment was affirmed, without opinion, at the Appellate Division and defendant's appeal to this court was taken by our leave.

The issue is governed in the first instance by Section 2-718 of the Uniform Commercial Code which provides, among other things, that the buyer, despite his breach, may have restitution of the amount by which his payment exceeds: (a) reasonable liquidated damages stipulated by the contract or (b) absent such stipulation, 20% of the value of the buyer's total performance or $ 500, whichever is smaller (§ 2-718, subsection [2], pars. [a], [b]). As above noted, the trial court awarded defendant an offset in the amount of $ 500 under paragraph (b) and directed restitution to plaintiffs of the balance. Section 2-718, however, establishes, in paragraph (a) of subsection (3), an alternative right of offset in favor of the seller, as follows: "(3) The buyer's right to restitution under subsection (2) is subject to offset to the extent that the seller establishes (a) a right to recover damages under the provisions of this Article other than subsection (1)."

Among "the provisions of this Article other than subsection (1)" are those to be found in Section 2-708, which the courts below did not apply. Subsection (1) of that section provides that "the measure of damages for non-acceptance or repudiation by the buyer is the difference between the market price at the time and place for tender and the unpaid contract price together with any incidental damages provided in this Article (Section 2-710), but less expenses saved in consequence of the buyer's breach." However, this provision is made expressly subject to subsection (2), providing: "(2) If the measure of damages provided in subsection (1) is inadequate to put the seller in as good a position as performance would have done then the measure of damages is the profit (including reasonable overhead) which the seller would have made from full performance by the buyer, together with any incidental damages provided in this Article (Section 2-710), due allowance for costs reasonably incurred and due credit for payments or proceeds of resale."

The provision of the code upon which the decision at Trial Term rested (§ 2-718, subsection [2], par. [b]) does not differ greatly from the corresponding provisions of the prior statute (Personal Property Law, § 145-a, subd. 1, par. [b]) except as the new act includes the alternative remedy of a lump sum award of $ 500. Neither does the present reference (in § 2-718, subsection [3], par. [a]) to the recovery of damages pursuant to other provisions of the article differ from a like reference in the prior statute (Personal Property Law, § 145-a, subd. 2, par. [a]) to an alternative measure of damages under section 145 of that act; but section 145 made no provision for recovery of lost profits as does Section 2-708 (subsection [2]) of the code. The new statute is thus innovative and significant and its analysis is necessary to the determination of the issues here presented.

Prior to the code, the New York cases "applied the 'profit' test, contract price less cost of manufacture, only in cases where the seller [was] a manufacturer or an agent for a manufacturer" (1955 Report of N. Y. Law Rev. Comm., vol. 1, p. 693). Its extension to retail sales was "designed to eliminate the unfair and economically wasteful results arising under the older law when fixed price articles were involved. This section permits the recovery of lost profits in all appropriate cases, which would include all standard priced goods." (Official Comment 2, McKinney's Cons. Laws of N. Y., Book 62 1/2, Part 1, p. 605, under Uniform Commercial Code, § 2-708.) Additionally, and "[in] all cases the seller may recover incidental damages" (id., Comment 3). The buyer's right to restitution was established at Special Term upon the motion for summary judgment, as was the seller's right to proper offsets, in each case pursuant to Section 2-718; and, as the parties concede, the only question before us, following the assessment of damages at Special Term, is that as to the proper measure of damage to be applied. The conclusion is clear from the record — indeed with mathematical certainty — that "the measure of damages provided in subsection (1) is inadequate to put the seller in as good a position as performance would have done" (Uniform Commercial Code, §2-708, subsection [2]) and hence — again under subsection (2) — that the seller is entitled to its "profit (including reasonable overhead) * * * together with any incidental damages ***, due allowance for costs reasonably incurred and due credit for payments or proceeds of resale."

It is evident, first, that this retail seller is entitled to its profit and, second, that the last sentence of subsection (2), as hereinbefore quoted, referring to "due credit for payments or proceeds of resale" is inapplicable to this retail sales contract.[1] Closely parallel to the factual situation now before us is that hypothesized by Dean Hawkland as illustrative of the operation of the rules: "Thus, if a private party agrees to sell his automobile to a buyer for $ 2,000, a breach by the buyer would cause the seller no loss (except incidental damages, *i.e.*, expense of a new sale) if the seller was able to sell the automobile to another buyer for $ 2000. But the situation is different with dealers having an unlimited supply of standard-priced goods. Thus, if an automobile dealer agrees to sell a car to a buyer at the standard price of $2000, a breach by the buyer injures the dealer, even though he is able to sell the automobile to another for $ 2000. If the dealer has an inexhaustible supply of cars, the resale to replace the breaching buyer costs the dealer a sale, because, had the breaching buyer performed, the dealer would have made two sales instead of one. The buyer's breach, in such a case, depletes the dealer's sales to the extent of one, and the measure of damages should be the dealer's profit on one sale. Section 2-708 recognizes this, and it rejects the rule developed under the Uniform Sales Act by many courts that the profit cannot be recovered in this case." (Hawkland, *Sales and Bulk Sales* [1958 ed.], pp. 153-154; and *see* Comment, 31 FORDHAM L. REV. 749, 755-756.)

The record which in this case establishes defendant's entitlement to damages in the amount of its prospective profit, at the same time confirms defendant's cognate right to "any incidental damages provided in this Article (Section 2-710)" [2] (Uniform Commercial Code, §2-708, subsection [2]). From the language employed it is too clear to require discussion that the seller's right to recover loss of profits is not exclusive and that he may recoup his "incidental" expenses as well (*Procter & Gamble Distr. Co. v. Lawrence Amer. Field Warehousing Corp.*, 16 N Y 2d 344, 354). Although the trial court's denial of incidental damages in the uncontroverted amount of $ 674 was made in the context of its erroneous conclusion that paragraph (b) of subsection (2) of section 2-718 was applicable and was "adequate * * * to place the sellers in as good a position as performance would have done," the denial seems not to have rested entirely on the court's mistaken application of the law, as there was an explicit finding "that defendant completely failed to show that it suffered any incidental damages." We find no basis for the court's conclusion with respect to a deficiency of proof inasmuch as the proper items of the $ 674 expenses (being for storage, upkeep, finance charges and insurance for the period between the date

---

1. The concluding clause, "due credit for payments or proceeds of resale," is intended to refer to "the privilege of the seller to realize junk value when it is manifestly useless to complete the operation of manufacture" (Supp. No. 1 to the 1952 Official Draft of Text and Comments of the Uniform Commercial Code, as Amended by the Action of the American Law Institute of the National Conference of Commissioners on Uniform Laws [1954], p.14). The commentators who have considered the language have uniformly concluded that "the reference is to a resale as scrap under * * * Section 2-704."

2. "Incidental damages to an aggrieved seller include any commercially reasonable charges, expenses or commissions incurred in stopping delivery, in the transportation, care and custody of goods after the buyer's breach, in connection with return or resale of the goods or otherwise resulting from the breach." (Uniform Commercial Code § 2-710).

performance was due and the time of the resale) were proven without objection and were in no way controverted, impeached or otherwise challenged, at the trial or on appeal. Thus the court's finding of a failure of proof cannot be supported upon the record and, therefore, and contrary to plaintiffs' contention, the affirmance at the Appellate Division was ineffective to save it.

The trial court correctly denied defendant's claim for recovery of attorney's fees incurred by it in this action. Attorney's fees incurred in an action such as this are not in the nature of the protective expenses contemplated by the statute (Uniform Commercial Code, § 1-106, subd. [1]; § 2-710; § 2-708, subsection [2]) and by our reference to "legal expense" in *Procter & Gamble Distr. Co. v. Lawrence Amer. Field Warehousing Corp.* (16 N Y 2d 344, 354-355, *supra*), upon which defendant's reliance is in this respect misplaced.

It follows that plaintiffs are entitled to restitution of the sum of $ 4,250 paid by them on account of the contract price less an offset to defendant in the amount of $ 3,253 on account of its lost profit of $ 2,579 and its incidental damages of $ 674.

The order of the Appellate Division should be modified, with costs in all courts, in accordance with this opinion, and, as so modified, affirmed.

QUESTIONS

1.   *Neri* involved what is commonly called a "lost volume" seller. Do the damages provisions of the CISG allow for lost volume damages? How does a seller prove lost profits?

2.   Are there circumstances in which the seller might choose to forego damages under Article 76 and instead seek to recover lost profits under Article 74?

3.   Are there circumstances in which the defaulting buyer might argue that the seller should not be permitted to recover under Article 76 but rather should be restricted to the recovery of lost profits under Article 74?

NOTE ON MITIGATION

Located in CISG Article 77 is the familiar mitigation principle that the injured party must take reasonable steps to limit the harm he will suffer from breach. Although this obligation to mitigate damages is frequently characterized as a duty, this is not quite accurate. After all, the party in breach has no affirmative remedy in the event the injured party fails to take measures to prevent further loss; he may only "claim a reduction in the damages in the amount which should have been mitigated." Mitigation, therefore, plays no part in a case where the injured elects a remedy other than damages. Thus, for example, a seller who seeks the price pursuant to Article 62 or a buyer who exercises his right to reduce the price under Article 50 may ignore Article 77 with impunity. It should be noted, however, that the application of Article 77 is not limited to situations where a current obligation has been breached. It applies with equal force to an anticipatory breach under Article 72. *See infra.*

Case Abstract, UNCITRAL Texts (CLOUT), Abstract No. 133

February 8, 1995 (Germany)

The plaintiff [buyer], an Italian trading company, and the defendant [seller], a German automobile marketing company, concluded a sales contract concerning eleven cars for the price of about DM 400.000, —. The contract provided that the [buyer] was to furnish a bank guarantee for the sales price. A bank guarantee in the amount of DM 55.000 was granted in favour of the [seller]. After the conclusion of the contract, the parties had some communications on the time of delivery and special features of the ordered cars. Five cars were finally ready for delivery in August, the remaining six in October. In October, the [buyer] informed the [seller] that, due to extreme exchange rate fluctuations between the Lira and the Mark, acceptance of delivery of the cars was impossible. The [buyer] asked the [seller] to try to defer delivery from the supplier. In the beginning of November, the [seller] cancelled all orders it had made with its suppliers and demanded payment of the bank guarantee which was paid out. The [buyer] claimed repayment of the guaranty sum and damages.

The appellate court found the [buyer] to have a repayment claim against the [seller]. It was held that, although the CISG will normally apply to German-Italian sales, it does not regulate the seller's rights concerning bank guaranties. The court, applying its rules of private international law, determined that German law was applicable.

The court found the [seller] to have been unjustifiedly enriched according to 812 (1) 1 German Civil Code since the [seller] obtained the payment of the bank guarantee without legal grounds. The court held that the bank guarantee was agreed upon to cover an obligation to pay and dismissed the [seller's] argument that the bank guaranty should serve as a penalty for not taking delivery by the [buyer].

Furthermore the court found that the [seller] had not taken the appropriate legal measures to mitigate its loss (article 77 CISG). By giving notice that the cars were ready to be picked up, the [seller] had in fact fulfilled its contractual obligations (article 31 CISG) and the [buyer] committed a breach of contract by not taking delivery of the cars (article 53 CISG). The [seller], therefore, was entitled to the remedies provided by articles 61 (1) (b) and 74 CISG. But, as the [seller] never avoided the contract, it had disregarded its duty to mitigate its loss and could not claim damages. Therefore, the [seller] was not entitled to the guaranty sum.

However, the court dismissed the [buyer's] claim for damages against the [seller] according to articles 45 (1)(b), 45 (2), 49 (1)(a) and 25 CISG. Since the parties had not agreed on the precise date of delivery, the [seller's] readiness to deliver in August and October was no breach of contract, let alone a fundamental one. Thus, the right to declare the contract avoided because of the non-delivery of the cars was lost by the [buyer]. To allow the [buyer] now, i.e., 2 1/2 years later, to declare the contract avoided would violate the principle of good faith (article 7 (1) CISG).

The court held that the [buyer] was entitled to interest according to article 84 CISG. Even though the claim for repayment was based on article 812 German Civil Code, the claim for interest derived from the CISG, because the repayment was a refund of the price. As the CISG does not regulate the interest rate, German Law was applicable. In view of the fact that both parties were merchants, the interest rate of 5% applied (article 352 German Civil Code).

QUESTION

1.   Suppose the buyer repudiates the contract before the seller has completed manufacturing the goods. Should the seller ever be required to complete the manufacture? If the seller is not required to complete the manufacture, should he be permitted to do so? What damages may the seller recover from the buyer if he completes the goods? What damages may the seller recover from the buyer if he ceases manufacturing at once?

V. The Price Reduction Remedy

Documents Supplement References:

1. *CISG Articles 50, 74, 79.*
2. *U.C.C. Section 2-717.*

Eric E. Bergsten and Anthony J. Miller, The Remedy of Reduction of Price

27 American Journal of Comparative Law 255, 256-58 (1979)

Civil law origins

The remedy of reduction of price for the purchaser of defective goods derives from the *actio quanti minoris* in Roman Law. At the risk of considerable over-simplification, this action originated from an Edict of the Aediles which sought to "repress the sharp practices of sellers of slaves and cattle in the City markets." If a buyer became aware, after delivery, of certain specified defects which the vendor did not declare and which, had the buyer been aware of them at the time of sale would have led him to pay a lesser price, he could bring an action for reduction of price or for recission of contract. Defects which were evident at the time of conclusion of the contract were excluded from this remedy since the buyer should have taken them into account when calculating the price he was willing to pay.

The Roman law origins of the remedy are reflected in contemporary provisions in Civil law countries. For example, if the goods contain hidden defects, art. 1644 of the French Civil Code enables a buyer to recover part of the purchase price, the amount to be determined by experts, or to rescind the contract and recover the total purchase price. In the Federal Republic of Germany, § 459 BGB provides that if the goods lack promised qualities or contain defects which diminish the ordinary use of the goods or the use provided for in the contract, the buyer has the option of rescinding the contract or of reducing the price according to a formula set out in § 472.

It has been pointed out that in the Civil law, rescission and reduction of price are the normal remedies for a buyer who has been delivered non-conforming goods, and damages are, in principle, the exception. In large measure this is because damages can be recovered in the Civil law only if the non-performing party was at fault. Contractual fault can, of course, be understood in ways that lead to a blurring of the distinction between fault and no-fault liability. However, to the extent that contractual fault requires more than the mere showing that the goods delivered were non-conforming, reduction of price provides a remedy by way of monetary relief even though damages are not available for that non-conformity. The Civil law also offers a remedy similar in effect, though not in theory, to reduction of price for delivery of an insufficient quantity of goods. The theory is that there has been a partial non-execution of the contractual obligation to deliver. Therefore, if the price has not been paid and the buyer is faced with a partial non-delivery, he can rely upon the *exceptio non adimpleti contractus* to withhold that part of the purchase price related to the non-performance. This remedy also finds a place in art. 46 [draft counterpart of Article 50].

NOTE ON THE REMEDY OF REDUCTION OF PRICE

CISG Article 50 gives the injured party the right to reduce the price in proportion to the loss in value if the goods do not conform to the contract. This remedy should not be confused with a set-off or counterclaim to an action for the price. *Compare* U.C.C. Section 2-717. Although set-off and counterclaim may lead to the same result as Article 50 in some situations, the remedies are distinctly different. The price reduction formula of Article 50 is not measured by the buyer's damages under Article 50 and may actually yield a result which is entirely inconsistent with traditional remedial principles. In fact, to fully appreciate Article 50 one must understand that it is distinct from a claim for damages. It is for this reason that the buyer may reduce the price even if the seller is excused from paying damages by virtue of Article 79, and it also explains why the remedy is not subject to the requirement of foreseeability under Article 74.

Harry M. Flechtner, More U.S. Decisions on the U.N. Sales Convention: Scope, Parol Evidence, "Validity" and Reduction of Price Under Article 50

14 Journal of Law and Commerce 153, 171-76 (1995)

To date, English-language commentaries on Article 50 have focused on the provision's Civil Law origins; methods for calculating the amount of the price reduction; the distinction between damages governed by CISG Articles 74-77 and proportional price reduction under Article 50; and the tendency of common law lawyers to misperceive the price reduction remedy as a mere setoff provision. One of the more striking observations on Article 50, made by several commentators, is that in some circumstances the provision yields results inconsistent with a fundamental principle of common law remedies: protection of the expectation interest.

Indeed, the price reduction remedy of CISG operates in a fashion that cannot be justified by any of the remedial principles recognized in U.S. contract law. In other words, Article 50 is not designed to protect the expectation interest, the reliance interest, or the restitution interest. An example will illustrate. On April 1 Seller contracts to sell 100,000 barrels of oil with a sulphur content not to exceed 1% for $25/barrel, delivery on May 1. On May 1 Seller delivers 100,000 barrels with a 2% sulphur content, and Buyer elects to accept the shipment. By May 1 the market value of 1% sulphur oil is only $20/barrel, and the 2 % sulphur oil actually delivered is worth even less— $15/barrel. If Buyer chooses to pursue damages, which it can do under Article 74 of the Convention, its recovery will be measured by the difference between the $20/barrel value that 1% sulphur oil would have had and the $15/barrel value of the 2% sulphur oil that was actually delivered. Thus Buyer is entitled to damages of $5/barrel, with the result that Buyer would end up paying $20/barrel ($25/barrel contract price less $5/barrel damages) for the 2% sulphur oil worth$15/barrel. Article 74 damages calculated in this fashion will (as the common law has long viewed the matter) put Buyer in the position it would have been if Seller properly performed the contract.

If Buyer chooses to reduce the price under Article 50, on the other hand, it would pay only $18.75/barrel — $6.25/barrel less than the contract price. The reduction is calculated by multiplying the contract price by a fraction—the ratio of the value, as of the delivery date, of the goods actually delivered to the value of conforming goods on that date. Since the 2% sulphur oil was worth $15/barrel on the delivery date, and conforming (1% sulphur) oil would have been worth $20/ barrel, the ratio is 15/20, or 3/4. Multiplying the $25/barrel contract price by 3 /4 yields $18.75/barrel. Obviously that result departs from expectation damages as calculated under Article 74. Nor does it correspond to a reliance-based or restitutionary recovery. If the market value of oil was higher than the contract price on the delivery date, the result under Article 50 would again differ from expectation damages under Article 74 — although in that case the Article 74 damages would exceed the reduction in price under Article 50.

In other words, the amount of the price reduction under Article 50 seems to be based on a principle unknown to the common law. To phrase the matter in a fashion that echoes the traditional description of common law remedy principles, one could say that Article 50 puts an aggrieved buyer in the position she would have been in had she purchased the goods actually delivered rather than the ones promised — assuming she would have made the same relative bargain for the delivered goods. For example, if at the time non-conforming goods were delivered the contract price was 80% of the market price of conforming goods, the buyer can buy the non-conforming goods for 80% of their market value. Put another way, expectation damages are designed to preserve for an aggrieved party the benefit of her bargain; reduction in price under Article 50 attempts to preserve the proportion of her bargain.

Alternatively one could view the Article 50 remedy as a modification of the sales contract. From this perspective a seller could be seen as offering such a modification by shipping non-conforming goods. The buyer accepts the offer by keeping the goods at an implied price proportional to the original contract price. The "modification" view, however, should be handled with care. There are important differences between the fictitious modification permitted by Article 50 and an actual modification. For one thing, a buyer who accepts non-conforming goods and reduces the price under Article 50 is entitled to recover damages beyond the amount of the price reduction — although this could be rationalized as part of the implied price term of the modification. Additionally, the seller might be bound to a price reduction under Article 50 even if she made it clear that she did not intend to be so bound. Thus suppose a seller shipped non-conforming goods accompanied by notice that, if the buyer was unwilling to pay full price despite the nonconformity, the goods should be returned to the seller. It is not clear whether this expedient would prevent the buyer from keeping the goods and reducing the price under Article 50.

There are many other issues surrounding Article 50. For example, although the provision specifies the time as of which the value of goods is to be determined ("the time of the delivery"), it is unclear where (*i.e.*, in what geographical market) value should be measured. It is also unclear whether the Article 50 remedy is available against sellers who violate their obligations under Articles 41 or 42 to deliver goods free of rights and claims of third parties and whether a buyer is bound by an election of remedies if it avails itself of Article 50. For U.S. lawyers, however, the most pressing job is to apprehend the nature of the price reduction remedy — how it departs from the remedial concepts with which we are familiar, and how it establishes a new remedy principle of substantial potential significance in certain scenarios.

Case Abstract, UNCITRAL Texts (CLOUT), Abstract No. 56

April 27, 1992 (Switzerland)

The [seller], an Italian wholesaler of furniture, claimed the purchase price, which the [buyer], a Swiss retailer, refused to pay alleging lack of conformity of the goods.

The court, applying Swiss private international law, found that CISG was applicable as the law of Italy. It was held that as the [buyer] had resold some of the defective furniture without notifying the [seller] in time about the resale, the [buyer] had lost its right to rely on non-conformity of the goods (art. 38 and 39 CISG). With regard to other goods, the [buyer] was granted a reduction of price, since it had promptly notified the [seller] about the defects and the [seller] had refused to remedy the defects (art. 50 CISG). The court rejected an offer made by the [seller] during the proceedings to pay the repair cost, holding that article 50 CISG was not intended to provide for restitution of the repair cost but a reduction of the purchase price in the same proportion as the value that the goods actually delivered had at the time of delivery bore to the value that conforming goods would have had at that time.

QUESTIONS

1.   Does a claim of price reduction under Article 50 bar a claim of incidental and consequential losses under Article 74? *See* Article 45(a), (b).

2.   Is Article 50 an available remedy if the seller's performance is deficient in some respect other than the quality of the goods? *See* Article 35(1).

VI. Anticipatory Breach and Installment Contracts

Documents Supplement References:

1.   *CISG Articles 51, 71-73, 77.*

2.   *U.C.C. Sections 2-609, 2-610, 2-612, 2-705.*

NOTE ON INSTALLMENT CONTRACTS

CISG Article 73 deals with some of the problems that arise when a sales contract calls for deliveries of goods in separate installments, and there is a breach by a party with respect to one or more of the installments. Three distinct problems arise: (1) May the injured party avoid the contract with respect to that installment; (2) May the injured party avoid the contract with respect to future installments; and (3) May the injured party avoid the contract with respect to past installments? The Convention's handling of these questions is similar to the U.C.C. *See* U.C.C. Section 2-612.

Paragraph (1) of Article 73 deals with the first of the three problems outlined above. This provision permits either party to declare the contract avoided with respect to a particular installment if the other party has committed a "fundamental breach of contract with respect to that installment." In those cases where the seller is in breach, this rule is similar to that found in Article 51(1).

Paragraph (2) is concerned with the question whether failure to comply with the contract with respect to one or more installments empowers the injured party to avoid the contract with respect to future deliveries. The basic test is whether the default(s) which have occurred give the injured party "good grounds" to anticipate a fundamental breach as to future deliveries. In effect, a special rule of anticipatory repudiation exists which requires far less certainty about the future than that which would otherwise be required by Article 72. This provision allows the injured party to avoid as to future installments regardless of the seriousness of the current breach. Moreover, there is no reason why the injured party is to rely on a series of minor breaches to establish the necessary "good grounds." A final point worth noting is that although Article 73(2) requires avoidance "within a reasonable time," there is not the slightest hint as to when such period is to begin running.

Finally, Article 73(3) provides that if the buyer avoids an installment under Paragraph (1), he may also avoid past and future installments "if, by reason of their interdependence, those deliveries could not be used for the purposes contemplated by the parties at the time of the conclusion of the contract." This would be the case, for example, where the contract calls for the seller to separately deliver parts of a single machine or any other collection of items intended as part of an integrated whole.

NOTE ON ANTICIPATORY BREACH

CISG Articles 71 and 72 provide for the special case where prior to the scheduled date for performance, one party is seriously concerned about the other party's willingness or ability to perform. *Compare* U.C.C. Sections 2-609 and 2-610. Article 71(1) deals with one aspect of this problem by providing that a party may suspend its performance if "it becomes apparent that the other party will not perform a substantial part of his obligations" for one of the reasons specified in Article 71(1)(a) or (b). A party suspending performance must immediately give notice of suspension to the other party. Once notified, the other party can then reinstate the suspending party's duty to perform if he provides adequate assurance of performance. *See* Article 71(3). The *Draft Commentary* on Article 62 (draft counterpart of Article 71) prepared by the Secretariat gives several examples of what might in the circumstances constitute adequate assurance of performance:

Example 62E: The contract of sale provided that Buyer would pay for the goods 30 days after their arrival at Buyer's place of business. After the conclusion of the contract Seller received information.... [on the Buyer's creditworthiness which permitted Seller to suspend his performance pursuant to paragraph (1)]. After he suspended performance and so notified Buyer, Buyer offered either (1) a new payment term so that he would pay against documents, or (2) a letter of credit issued by a reputable bank, or (3) a guarantee by a reputable bank or other such party that it would pay if Buyer did not, or (4) a security interest in sufficient goods owned by Buyer to assure Seller of reimbursement. Since any one of these four alternatives would probably give Seller adequate assurances of being paid... Seller would be required to continue performance.

Example 62F: The contract of sale called for the delivery of precision parts for Buyer to use in assembling a high technology machine. Seller's failure to deliver goods of the requisite quality on the delivery date would cause great financial loss to Buyer. Although Buyer could have the parts manufactured by other firms, it would take a minimum of six months from the time a contract was signed for any other firm to be able to deliver substitute parts. The contract provided that Buyer was to make periodic advance payments of the purchase price during the period of time Seller was manufacturing the goods. When Buyer received information... [which made it apparent that] Seller would not be able to deliver on time, Buyer notified Seller that he was suspending any performance due the Seller. Seller gave Buyer written assurances that he would deliver goods of the contract quality on time and offered a bank guarantee for financial reimbursement of all payments made under the contract if he failed to meet his obligations. In this case Seller has not given adequate assurance of performance. Seller's statements that he would perform, unless accompanied by sufficient explanations of the information which...[made it apparent] that Seller would not deliver on time, were only a reiteration of his contractual obligation. The offer of a bank guarantee of reimbursement of payments under the contract was not an adequate assurance to a Buyer who needs the goods at the contract date in order to meet his own needs.

Paragraph (2) of Article 71 gives the seller the right to stop delivery to the buyer of goods in the possession of a carrier in circumstances where the seller becomes aware of grounds for suspending performance after the goods have been dispatched. *Compare* U.C.C. Section 2-705. The seller may intercept the goods in transit even though he has parted with title and even though he has not preserved control through possession of a negotiable document of title.

It will be observed, however, that this Paragraph grants rights against the buyer only. Whether the carrier must obey the seller's instructions is another matter entirely. Moreover, the seller will surely lose the right to recapture the goods in most cases where a negotiable document of title has been transferred to a third party.

Article 72(1) grants the injured party the right to avoid the contract, if prior to the date of performance, it is clear that the other party will commit a fundamental breach. The only procedural prerequisite to avoidance is that, if time permits, the injured party must give reasonable notice of his intention to avoid in order to permit the other party to provide adequate assurance of his performance. *See* Article 72(2). There is no requirement of notice, however, if "the other party has declared that he will not perform his obligations." Article 72(3).

As mentioned previously, the duty to mitigate damages under Article 77 applies with equal force in the context of anticipatory breach. Once again, consider a couple of examples drawn from the Secretariat's *Draft Commentary,* this time on Article 73 (draft counterpart of Article 77).

Example 73A: The contract provided that Seller was to deliver 100 machine tools by 1 December at a total price of $50,000. On 1 July he wrote Buyer and said that because of the rise in prices which would certainly continue for the rest of the year, he would not deliver the tools unless Buyer agreed to pay $60,000. Buyer replied that he would insist that Seller deliver the tools at the contract price of $50,000. On 1 July and for a reasonable time thereafter, the price at which Buyer could have contracted with a different seller for delivery on 1 December was $56,000. On 1 December Buyer made a cover purchase for $61,000 for delivery on 1 March. Because of the delay in receiving the tools, Buyer suffered additional losses of $3,000.

In this example Buyer is limited to recovering $6,000 in damages, the extent of the losses he would have suffered if he had made the cover purchase on 1 July or a reasonable time thereafter, rather than $14,000, the total amount of losses which he suffered by awaiting 1 December to make the cover purchase.

Example 73B: Promptly after receiving Seller's letter of 1 July, in Example 73A, pursuant to article 62 [draft counterpart of CISG Article 71] Buyer made demand on Seller for adequate assurances that he would perform the contract as specified on 1 December. Seller failed to furnish the assurance within the reasonable period of time specified by Buyer.

Buyer promptly made a cover purchase at the currently prevailing price of $57,000. In this case Buyer can recover $7,000 in damages rather than $6,000 as in Example 73A

(OFFICIAL RECORDS, p. 61).

Case Abstract, UNCITRAL Texts (CLOUT), Abstract No. 51

January 31, 1991 (Germany)

The plaintiff, an Italian manufacturer of shoes, demanded payment of the balance due under the contract with defendant, a German company. The contract provided for payment of 40% of the purchase price upon delivery and the balance within sixty days after delivery. The seller sent an invoice in September 1989 and shipped the goods in January 1989 [1990] but suspended delivery without notifying the buyer, who was forced to pay more tha[n] 40% of the purchase price upon delivery in order to obtain the goods.

The court held that the seller committed a breach of contract by suspending delivery without giving notice of the suspension to the buyer and set off the claim of the seller for the balance of the purchase price against the claim of the buyer for damages (art. 45(1)(b), 73(1) and 74 CISG).

Case Abstract, UNCITRAL Texts (CLOUT), Abstract No. 124

February 15, 1995 (Germany)

The German plaintiff sold to the Swiss [buyer] a key stamping machine, which was manufactured by a German third party. The price had to be paid in three installments. The parties agreed that the seller would retain title to the machine until payment of the last installment. The manufacturer of the key stamping machine imposed a delivery stop upon the [seller]. In October 1991, the manufacturer delivered the machine directly to the [buyer]. The [buyer] refused to pay the remaining two installments to the [seller] asserting that the [seller] would not be able to transfer the property of the key stamping machine, since the [seller] could not obtain the property directly from the manufacturer because of the delivery stop.

The court of first instance ordered the [buyer] to pay the purchase price whereas the Court of Appeal decided in favor of the [buyer]. The [seller] appealed to the Supreme Court.

The Supreme Court held that the [buyer] was not entitled to declare the contract avoided under article 72 CISG. The period of time within which the buyer could declare the contract avoided under article 72 CISG was the time prior to the date of performance. After the contract had been performed by the parties, neither party could declare the contract avoided under article 72 CISG. The [buyer] accepted the machine in October 1991 and had to pay the last installment in November 1991. Therefore, both parties fixed the date of performance for November 1991. As a result, the [buyer] could no longer invoke article 72 CISG in March 1992.

Leaving the question undecided whether the behavior of the [seller] constituted a fundamental breach of contract, the court held that, in any event, the [buyer] had lost the right to avoid the contract under article 49 CISG, since the [buyer] had claimed avoidance of the contract five months after being informed of the delivery stop. This delay could not be considered as a reasonable time under article 49(1)(b) CISG.

Thus, the Supreme Court reversed the decision of the Court of Appeals, restored the decision of the court of first instance and ordered the [buyer] to pay the purchase price.

QUESTIONS

1.   A party may not declare a contract avoided under Article 71 if the other side fails to provide adequate assurances. If, however, adequate assurances are not forthcoming, might that be a basis for avoidance under Article 72?

2.   Suppose that one party has suspended performance under circumstances where he could not avoid the contract under Article 72 because there was no clear threat of a fundamental breach. If adequate assurances are not forthcoming, should there be a time limit on how long the obligation to perform can remain suspended?

3.   The *Draft Commentary* on Article 63 (draft counterpart of Article 72) advises that "[a] party who intends to declare the contract avoided...should do so with caution." Explain.

VII. What if the Buyer Importer Goes Bankrupt?

NOTE ON CROSS-BORDER INSOLVENCY PROCEEDINGS

The tremendous increase in international trade and the growing number of multinational corporations have inevitably led to a proliferation of transnational insolvency cases. Some of the best-known recent cases include *Axona International Credit & Commerce Limited, Bank of Credit & Commerce International, Maxwell Communication Corporation plc, Olympia & York Developments Limited,* and *LJ Hooker Corporation Inc.* The basic problem in these so-called "international bankruptcies" stems from the fact that some type of insolvency proceedings will often be commenced in every nation in which the insolvent enterprise does business. When the legal systems of two or more nations are implicated, difficulties are likely to arise because the local laws of various nations differ with regard to many elements of an insolvency. For example, the United States Bankruptcy Code will recognize a valid claim of any creditor, regardless of identity. English law, in contrast, will not recognize foreign revenue service claims. *See* Insolvency Act, 1986 (c45) (Eng.). Assume that an enterprise has assets in the United States and England and is indebted to the Internal Revenue Service. Now assume that an insolvency proceeding is commenced in both nations. What is the resolution if the I.R.S. seeks to have its claim allowed in each proceeding? Complicating matters further is the fact that the U.S. Bankruptcy Code accords priority to tax claims. *See* 11 U.S.C. § 507(a)(8) (1994).

Historically, two divergent philosophies have been employed in addressing transnational insolvencies. The most common one is the principle of "territoriality." Each nation takes control of the assets within its borders and administers those assets according to local law, which typically favors local creditors over foreign creditors. In most cases, little or no regard is given to the legal positions of other nations or what they may be doing.

The other philosophy is variously called "unity" and "universality." In its various forms, the emphasis is on cooperation. Unity is often used to mean the international equivalent to a domestic bankruptcy. That is, the goal is to have one proceeding, where all assets would be administered and all claims and interests would be resolved. The term "universality" carries a slightly different meaning. Although this approach assumes that there will be a "primary" forum, it recognizes that it also may be necessary to have one or more "ancillary" proceedings in other courts. These other courts will, however, defer to the law and the rulings of the primary forum.

Traditionally, courts in the United States have vacillated among universality, territoriality, and points in between. The situation changed dramatically in 1978 with the enactment of Section 304 of the Bankruptcy Code. This section permits a foreign representative to file a case in a United States bankruptcy court in order to protect local assets. This is not a full-blown bankruptcy proceeding in the conventional sense; rather, it is an ancillary case in aid of the principle insolvency proceeding abroad. Because this approach stresses cooperation with and deference to the primary foreign proceeding, it is clearly a form of universality, albeit a somewhat watered-down form. The guidelines enumerated in Section 304 give courts broad discretion when deciding whether to grant the relief requested by the foreign representative. Courts are directed to consider such factors as comity and the extent to which United States creditors would be prejudiced and inconvenienced in the foreign proceeding.

A search for international cooperation and harmony in the bankruptcy area has led to a number of recent initiatives to improve the international insolvency process. For example, in May, 1997, the United Nations Commission on International Trade Law ("UNICTRAL") adopted the final text of a Model Law on Cross-Border Insolvency. Although the model law leaves many issues unresolved, its adoption by the United States and by other nations should dramatically increase the potential for coordination and cooperation in transnational bankruptcies. Another example is the "Convention on Insolvency Proceedings," issued by the European Union. The convention provides for uniform conflicts of law rules as well as for recognition and enforcement of proceedings and judgments. A final example is the on-going effort by the American Law Institute ("ALI") to harmonize insolvency administrations and promote enhanced levels of cooperation in cross-border cases involving members of the North American Free Trade Agreement (NAFTA).

Chapter 4

Cross-Border Payments

I. Importing/Exporting and Commercial Letters of Credit

A. Transactional Aspects of Commercial L/Cs

Boris Kozolchyk, The Immunization of Fraudulently Procured Letter of Credit Acceptances: All Services Exportacao, Importacao Comercio, S.A. v. Banco Bamerindus Do Brazil, S.A. and First Commercial v. Gotham Originals

58 Brooklyn Law Review 369, 380-85 (1992)

. . . .

Unlike checks, letter of credit drafts [referred to in England as "bills of exchange"] even after they have been accepted, do not become part of settlements and clearing mechanisms. As a rule the collecting bank in the letter of credit collection process sends the draft and documents directly to the issuing or confirming bank or presents them to a nominated paying bank. None of the banks that act as intermediaries in the process of collecting the letter of credit draft or demand for payment credit or debit their predecessors' or successors' accounts until the issuing or confirming banks decide to pay.... [S]uch payment can be made by the issuing or confirming banks themselves or by their correspondents authorized to debit or credit the appropriate accounts. Hence, the specification of a time within which the issuing or confirming bank must honor a beneficiary's draft or demand for payment in letter of credit law practice is neither the transactional nor the legal equivalent of [Uniform Commercial Code, or "U.C.C."] Article 4's "midnight deadline."

Both the *Uniform Customs and Practices for Documentary Credits ("UCP")* requirement that the issuing bank examine the beneficiary's documents within a "reasonable time" [not to exceed seven banking days following the day of receipt of the documents, according to U.C.P. Article 13(b)] and the U.C.C.'s deferral "until the close of the third banking day following receipt of the documents" reflect a desire to give banks enough time to examine carefully the draft and documents. The examination period also allows a beneficiary the opportunity to cure discrepancies and either re-sell or re-ship the goods if the documents are rejected by a bank.....

245

The issuing or confirming bank's commitment to pay varies with the kind of draft required by the letter of credit. If the letter of credit requires payment upon presentation of a draft drawn on the issuing or confirming bank, the draft is termed a "sight" draft and will be paid as soon as the bank determines that the draft and accompanying documents comply with the terms and conditions of the credit. The meaning of the sight payment in letter of credit customary law, then, is actually to pay the credit or to assure that payment will be made by the designated party. This meaning coincides with the layman's understanding of final payment as "cash in his pocket." The UCP [Article 9(a)(iv)] also makes clear that when the payment is made by a negotiating bank, the bank pays "without recourse to drawers and/or bona fide holders of drafts drawn by the beneficiary...."

If the letter of credit requires payment at a certain time after the presentation of the draft and documents, it is known as an "acceptance" credit and the draft is known as a "time," "tenor" or "usance" draft. If the draft and documents comply with the terms and conditions of the credit, the bank will accept the beneficiary's draft, thereby promising to pay at a future time. The act of acceptance is affected by the bank's writing or stamping the word "accepted" across the draft's face or on the acceptor's column, and then signing and dating it. [At this point, the instrument is known as a "bankers acceptance," or "BA."] It should be noted, however, that the accepting bank's obligation to honor an acceptance is not discharged by merely accepting the draft. As stated in [Article 9(a)(iii)]... of the UCP, to honor an acceptance credit the honoring bank must not only accept the draft but, must also pay it at maturity.

Once the issuing or confirming bank accepts a letter of credit draft, its liability on that credit is no longer contingent. It becomes an unconditional liability: the accepting bank has determined that the documents comply with the terms and conditions of the credit and that payment is due on the date specified in the accepted draft. The bank's unconditional acceptance does not mean that the issuing or confirming bank cannot raise defenses against the beneficiary holder of the draft. By accepting the item, the issuing or confirming bank is not limited to post-payment actions such as unjust enrichment or mistaken payment, against the beneficiary. The same rules on availability of defenses... in connection with checks apply to accepted drafts in the hands of the payee-beneficiary. As a party who has dealt with a beneficiary who is not a holder in due course, the drawee bank can raise defenses such as setoff, accord and satisfaction and beneficiary's consent to post-acceptance amendments, which require additional or modified documents. In addition, U.C.C. Section 5-114 expressly leaves it to the bank's discretion to raise the defense of fraud by allowing banks to refuse to honor the allegedly fraudulent draft or demand for payment.

If the mere writing or stamping of an acceptance on a time draft were to entail not only unconditionality, but also finality of payment, letter of credit practice would be significantly changed. As of the moment the issuing bank signified its acceptance, the confirming bank would be able to wipe out its confirmation liability from its books. Conversely, if the confirming bank were the one signifying the acceptance, the issuing bank would have to provide prepayment immediately preceding or reimbursement immediately following the writing or stamping of the acceptance. Since such changes would inevitably lead to unjust enrichment by requiring payment or reimbursement for moneys not paid and not likely to be paid in the immediate future, banks could not adopt them.

....

Letter of credit acceptances,... are often bought or "discounted" by the accepting bank itself or bought in the open market by other banks, investors or speculators.

[Indeed, BAs are widely traded international money market instruments, *i.e.*, there is a very liquid BA market. In addition, BAs meeting Federal Reserve eligibility criteria are used in overnight or other short-term repurchase (or "repo") transactions with a Federal Reserve Bank.] Where the acceptance is bought by a bank or other holder under circumstances that would qualify such a buyer as a holder in due course, payment will be much more certain than if it were to the beneficiary or his agent. As a holder in due course, the negotiating bank is not subject to the issuing or confirming bank's personal defenses against the beneficiary and is also immune to the defense of fraud and to the fraud injunction alluded to in U.C.C. Section 5-114.

Sight and acceptance credits are by far the most common types of letters of credit payable against the presentation of drafts. Nevertheless, in the last fifty years of international banking practice, variations have emerged as a result of demands by customers and beneficiaries for more advantageous credit terms and stamp tax avoidance. One of these variations, the "deferred payment" credit, was first used in Japanese Far Eastern trade in the early 1950s and is now widely used in Europe. On its face, a deferred payment credit looks like an irrevocable sight credit, except for a stipulation that payment will be made at a specified period after the beneficiary's presentation of the documents. The documents, meanwhile, are released by the issuing bank to its customer.

The bank that issues or confirms a deferred payment credit occasionally issues a statement to the beneficiary acknowledging that the documents received from the beneficiary complied with the terms and conditions of the credit. This statement is usually issued as a letter or memorandum and not as a negotiable instrument such as a draft or promissory note. Frequently, however, the only acknowledgment issued by the issuing or confirming bank is simply a receipt for the tendered documents. The removal of the conditionality of a deferred payment credit by the issuance of an express statement of compliance or of a receipt of documents is not unlike the issuance of an acceptance.... Yet, as with the payment of sight drafts and of time drafts in the hands of the beneficiary or his collection agent, payment of a deferred payment credit is "not over until it is over." In fact, many European issuing banks warn the beneficiaries of their deferred payment credits that even if their advising banks issue commitments to pay at maturity, such commitments will not be recognized as binding by the issuing bank.

....

Urquhart Lindsay and Company, Limited v. Eastern Bank, Limited

[1922] 1 K.B. 318 (King's Bench Division)

....

ROWLATT J. read the following judgment: In this case the essential facts are few and simple. The plaintiffs in this country arranged with the Benjamin Jute Mills, Calcutta, to manufacture and ship to them over a series of months a quantity of machinery, at prices mentioned in a pro forma invoice; subject however to a stipulation not infrequently insisted upon by manufacturers at the date when the arrangement was made, that should the cost of labour or wages advance there would be a corresponding advance in the prices to be paid by the buyers. The goods were to be paid for by means of a confirmed irrevocable credit to be opened by the buyers in favour of the plaintiffs with a bank in this country, who were to pay the plaintiffs for each shipment as it took place. In pursuance of this arrangement the defendant bank at the instance of the buyers issued to the plaintiffs a document the terms of which I need not rehearse in detail, it being sufficient to state that the defendants undertook up to a certain amount and within a certain limit of time to pay the plaintiffs, against bills drawn upon the buyers accompanied by corresponding invoices and shipping documents, the amount of such invoices. This credit was by its terms to be irrevocable and the invoices were to be for machinery. There can be no doubt that upon the plaintiffs acting upon the undertaking contained in this letter of credit consideration moved from the plaintiffs, which bound the defendants to the irrevocable character of the arrangement between the defendants and the plaintiffs; nor was it contended before me that this had not become the position when the circumstances giving rise to this action took place.

Having received the letter of credit, the plaintiffs proceeded to manufacture the machinery and actually shipped two instalments of it, receiving payment from the defendants under the letter of credit against bills accompanied by invoices and other documents called for by that instrument. Before the third shipment was made the buyers, finding that the plaintiffs were including in their invoices an addition to the prices originally quoted, in respect of an alleged rise in the cost of wages or materials, instructed the defendants only to pay so much of the next invoices as represented the original prices. These instructions (very unfortunately, as I think, from many points of view) the defendants obeyed. The plaintiffs however refused to part with the documents representing their goods unless they received the full amount of the invoices; and upon the defendants maintaining their position canceled the contract as to further shipments, as upon a repudiation by the buyers, and have brought this action against the defendants, claiming as damages the loss on material thrown on their hands, and loss of profit; in other words, the same damages as they would claim against the buyers on their repudiation of the contract. After the action had been commenced the defendants paid to the plaintiffs the amount of the invoices, the original refusal of which had caused the dispute.

In my view the defendants committed a breach of their contract with the plaintiffs when they refused to pay the amount of the invoices as presented. Mr. Stuart Bevan contended that the letter of credit must be taken to incorporate the contract between the plaintiffs and their buyers; and that according to the true meaning of that contract the amount of any increase claimed in respect of an alleged advance in manufacturing costs was not to be included in any invoice to be presented under the letter of credit, but was to be the subject of subsequent independent adjustment. The answer to this is that the defendants undertook to pay the amount of invoices for machinery without qualification, the basis of this form of banking facility being that the buyer is taken for the purposes of all questions between himself and his banker or between his banker and the seller to be content to accept the invoices of the seller as correct. It seems to me that so far from the letter of credit being qualified by the contract of sale, the latter must accommodate itself to the letter of credit. The buyer having authorized his banker to undertake to pay the amount of the invoice as presented, it follows that any adjustment must be made by way of refund by the seller, and not by way of retention by the buyer.

There being thus in my view a breach of contract, the question arises what damages the plaintiffs can recover. . . . In the present case, . . . the credit was irrevocable; and the effect of that was that the bank really agreed to buy the contemplated series of bills and documents representing the contemplated shipments just as the buyer agreed to take and pay for by this means the goods themselves. Now, if a buyer under a contract of this sort declines to pay for an instalment of the goods, the seller can cancel and claim damages upon the footing of an anticipatory breach of the contract of sale as a whole. These damages are not for non-payment of money. It is true that non-payment of money was what the buyer was guilty of; but such non-payment is evidence of a repudiation of the contract to accept and pay for the remainder of the goods; and the damages are in respect of such repudiation. I confess I cannot see why the refusal of the bank to take and pay for the bills with the documents representing the goods is not in the same way a repudiation of their contract to take the bills to be presented in future under the letter of credit; nor, if that is so, why the damages are not the same.... What is the difference ... between the obligation to take the goods and pay the invoice, and the obligation to take bills and documents representing the goods and pay the invoice? The whole purpose of the arrangement is that the seller shall have a responsible paymaster in this country to protect him against the very contingency which has occurred and the very damages which he claims.

....

The damages to which the plaintiffs are entitled are the difference between on the one hand the value of the materials left on their hands and the cost of such as they would have further provided, and, on the other hand, what they would have been entitled to receive for the manufactured machinery from the buyers, the whole being limited to the amount they could in fact have tendered before the expiry of the letter of credit.

B. The Proper Law

Documents Supplement References:

1. Uniform Customs and Practices for Documentary Credits (UCP 500, 1993)
2. New York Uniform Commercial Code Article 5 (1998)

Power Curber International Ltd. v. National Bank of Kuwait
[1981] 1 W.L.R. 1233 (Court of Appeal)

LORD DENNING M.R. This case raises an important point in international trade. It has nothing to do with England except that an action has been brought here. It is brought by plaintiffs, American sellers, who exported goods from the United States to buyers in Kuwait. They were to be paid by a letter of credit issued by the National Bank of Kuwait S.A.K., the defendants. The bank wishes to honour their obligations. They wish to pay the sums due under the letter of credit. But the courts in Kuwait have forbidden the bank to pay. What is the bank to do?

The plaintiff company's name is Power Curber International Ltd. You might think that it was an English company seeing that its name ends with "Ltd." But it is in fact an American corporation which carries on business at Salisbury in North Carolina. I will call it "Power Curber." It exports machinery to countries in the Middle East. It operates through a firm of distributors in Kuwait called Hammoudeh & Al Fulaij General Trading & Contracting Co. W.L.L. I will call the firm "Hammoudeh." The directors have close contacts with America and spend their time between that country and the Middle East. They are the "distributors" for Power Curber in the Middle East. By which I take it they buy goods on their own account from Power Curber and re-sell them on a commission or other basis in the Middle East.

About July 1979 Power Curber agreed to supply machinery to Hammoudeh to be shipped from the U.S.A. not later than March 1, 1980, on c.i.f. terms and paid as to 25 per cent. on presentation of documents and the remaining 75 per cent. one year after date of shipment. The buyers (Hammoudeh) were to give usance drafts (that is, bills of exchange payable at a later date) for this remaining 75 per cent.

In order to be sure of payment, Power Curber required Hammoudeh to open a letter of credit in their favour. Hammoudeh went to their bank, the National Bank of Kuwait S.A.K., and asked them to issue a letter of credit. No doubt Hammoudeh put the bank in funds or otherwise secured the bank so that the bank would be indemnified against their liability under the letter of credit.

The letter of credit

The letter of credit is dated "Kuwait September 6, 1979." It was issued by the National Bank of Kuwait S.A.K. (the issuing bank) to the Bank of America, Florida, Miami, U.S.A. (the advising bank) through the North Carolina National Bank in Charlotte, North Carolina. It was an irrevocable credit but not a confirmed credit. It is so important that I will set out most of it.

"To Bank of America,   Kuwait

Florida, Miami, U.S.A.   September 6, 1979

Our Irrevocable Credit No. A02/164018/7

"Dear Sirs,

"At the request of Hammoudeh & Al Fulaij General Trading & Contracting Co WLL (A/c 59554-9), please advise our irrevocable credit through North Carolina National Bank in Charlotte, North Carolina in favour of Power Curber International Ltd., P.O. Box 1639, Salisbury, North Carolina, 28144, U.S.A. (A/c No. 411003742), to the extent of U.S. $300,000...irrevocably valid in U.S.A. until March 1, 1980, and available by drafts without recourse as shown below drawn on the opener for 100 per cent. of the invoice value and accompanied by the documents marked (X) below..." Here were set out invoices, bills of lading, insurance policy, etc.

"The value of the usance drafts will be remitted by us at relative maturity dates provided all credit terms should have been fully complied with evidencing current shipment not later than March 1, 1980...from U.S.A. to Kuwait of: — 'Equipments and spare parts'...Payment terms: 25 per cent. of the Ex-works value...to be paid against presentation of documents called for in order as per credit terms. Remaining 75 per cent. of the Ex-works value after one year of the date of shipment...

"All drafts drawn under this credit must contain the clause:-

"'Drawn Under L/C No. (as above) of them National Bank of Kuwait, S.A.K. Dated (dated of this advice).'

"In reimbursement of your negotiations under this credit, please draw on our account with Bank of America (International), New York, in respect of sight payment provided you certify to us that all terms of the credit have been complied with, and forward the original documents direct to us by first registered airmail, duplicates by following airmail.

"This credit is irrevocable on our part and we hereby undertake that all drafts drawn in compliance with the terms hereof will be duly honoured....

"Except as otherwise stated herein, this credit is subject to the *Uniform Customs and Practice for Documentary Credits* (1974 Revision) International Chamber of Commerce Publication No. 290.

Yours faithfully,

For the National Bank of Kuwait, S.A.K. . . ."

The goods are shipped

On December 26, 1979, the goods were duly shipped from the U.S.A. The shipment value was U.S. $101,059. 28. Twenty-five per cent. of it was paid against presentation of documents. Hammoudeh drew a usance draft on the National Bank of Kuwait for the remaining 75 per cent. which a was $75,794.46, maturing on December 26, 1980. It was accepted by the National Bank of Kuwait who wrote on March 4, 1980, to the North Carolina National Bank:

"Our Letter of Credit No. A02/164018/7.

". . . please note that the relative usance draft for U.S. $75,794 . 46 maturing on December 26, 1980, has been accepted by our principals. We shall not fail to remit to you the above mentioned amount through Morgan Guaranty Trust Co. New York at maturity on December 26, 1980."

The effect of the letter of credit

The law on the point is clear. I take it first from *Edward Owen Engineering Ltd. v. Barclays Bank International Ltd.* [1978] Q.B. 159, 169:

"It has been long established that when a letter of credit is issued and confirmed by a bank, the bank must pay it if the documents are in order and the terms of the credit are satisfied. Any dispute between buyer and seller must be settled between themselves. The bank must honour the credit. That was clearly stated in *Hamzeh Malas & Sons v. British Imex Industries Ltd.* [1958] 2 Q.B 127. Jenkins L.J. giving the judgment of this court, said, at p. 129: '. . . it seems to be plain enough that the opening of a confirmed letter of credit constitutes a bargain between the banker and the vendor of the goods, which imposes upon the banker an absolute obligation to pay, irrespective of any dispute there may be between the parties as to whether the goods are up to contract or not. An elaborate commercial system has been built up on the footing that bankers' confirmed credits are of that character, and, in my judgment, it would be wrong for this court in the present case to interfere with the established practice.'

"To this general principle there is an exception in the case of what is called established or obvious fraud to the knowledge of the bank."

Those words apply not only to confirmed credits but also to irrevocable credits. To which I would add these provisions of the *Uniform Customs and Practice for Documentary Credits* (1974 revision) which I take from *Gutteridge and Megrah, The Law of Bankers' Commercial Credits*, 6th ed. (1979), pp. 221-222:

"(c) Credits, by their nature, are separate transactions from the sales or other contracts on which they may be based and banks are in no way concerned with or bound by such contracts. . . .

"A.   Form and notification of credits. . . .

"ARTICLE 3

"(a) An irrevocable credit constitutes a definite undertaking of the issuing bank, provided that the terms and conditions of the credit are complied with: (i) to pay, or that payment will be made, if the credit provides for payment, whether against a draft or not; (ii) to accept drafts if the credit provides for acceptance by the issuing bank or to be responsible for their acceptance and payment at maturity..."

The order made in Kuwait

It appears that early in November 1980 Hammoudeh filed a claim in the courts of Kuwait against Power Curber for 50,000 Kuwaiti dinars. That is about $180,000. We do not know the nature of the claim but it is thought that it may be a claim for commission. Following on that claim, Hammoudeh applied to the court in Kuwait for an order for "provisional attachment" of the sums payable by the National Bank of Kuwait under the letter of credit to Power Curber. On November 5, 1980, the court in Kuwait ordered the "provisional attachment." This order prevented the bank from making any further payment under the letter of credit in Kuwait or outside Kuwait: and made the bank accountable to the court for the amount involved. The bank lodged a protest against the attachment: and applied to the court in Kuwait to set aside the order for provisional attachment. But the court refused to set it aside. And its refusal has been upheld by the Court of Appeal in Kuwait.

The steps taken by Power Curber

As Power Curber did not receive payment, they sent a telex to the bank in January 1981, saying:

"We have not received the payment in the amount of U.S. $75,794.46 which matured for payment on December 26, 1980. You had agreed to honour the draft upon maturity under the rules and regulations of the *Uniform Customs and Practices for Documentary Credits* (1974 revision) International Chamber of Commerce publication No. 290.

"Unless we receive this payment immediately, we will begin legal proceedings against you for failure to pay the balance legally due us..."

Power Curber started proceedings in North Carolina, but afterwards discontinued them and started proceedings in England.

On January 27, 1981, Power Curber issued a writ in the High Court in England against the National Bank of Kuwait (which was trading here and had a registered address in London). They claimed $75,794.46 and applied for judgment under Order 14.

On March 27, 1981, Parker J. gave judgment in favour of Power Curber against the National Bank of Kuwait for that amount but stayed execution on it until further order. There is now an appeal Power Curber against the stay and by the bank against the judgment.

The questions debated before us were these: I. Should Power Curber be granted summary judgment? II. Even if granted summary judgment, should execution be stayed?

By our English law a plaintiff is entitled to have summary judgment given for him if the defendant has no arguable defence to the claim. Parker J. gave summary judgment for the plaintiffs. But he stayed execution on it until further order. Each side appeals. I will deal first with summary judgment.

I. Summary judgment

On the face of it, the National Bank of Kuwait [is] in default. They promised to pay the sums due under the letter of credit at maturity. They have not paid those sums.

Mr. Longmore submits, however, that the "provisional attachment" gives the bank an arguable defence. He says that the proper law of the contract was Kuwaiti law and that, by that law, the payment of the sums was unlawful. Alternatively, he says that the lex situs of the debt was Kuwait: and it is that law which governs the effect of the attachment. If the attachment was lawful by Kuwaiti law, he says that all other countries should give effect to it.

I cannot accept Mr. Longmore's submissions. The proper law of the contract is to be found by asking: With what law has the contract its closest and most real connection? In my opinion it was the law of North Carolina where payment was to be made (on behalf of the issuing bank) against presentation of documents. Mr. Longmore sought to say that *Offshore International S.A. v. Banco Central S.A.* [1977] 1 W.L.R. 399 decided by Ackner J. was either wrongly decided or was distinguishable on grounds parallel to those canvassed in *Gutteridge and Megrah, The Law of Bankers' Commercial Credits*, 6th ed., pp. 213-214. But I think the case was rightly decided and cannot be distinguished on any valid grounds. The letter of credit, and the payments under it, were certainly valid by its proper law.

Nor can I agree that the lex situs of the debt was Kuwait. It was in North Carolina. A debt under a letter of credit is different from ordinary debts. They may be situate where the debtor is resident. But a debt under a letter of credit is situate in the place where it is in fact payable against documents. I would hold therefore that Parker J. was right in giving summary judgment against the National Bank of Kuwait for the sums due.

If it were a case where leave to defend should be given, I would hold that the action should be tried in England. By bringing the action in England, Power Curber has legitimate juridical advantage of which it would not be right to deprive them: see *MacShannon v.- Rockware Ltd.* [1978] A.C. 795, 812, *per* Lord Diplock.

II. *Stay of execution*

In considering the "provisional attachment" order, it must be remembered that the orders of a foreign court fall into three categories. First, those which are enforceable in England by our English courts. Second those which are recognised in England by virtue of the comity of nations: so that we will do nothing contrary to them. Third, those which will not be recognised here in England because they do not accord with the public policy of our law.

On this question of recognition, I must draw attention to the importance of letters of credit in international trade. They are the means by which goods are supplied all the world over. It is vital that every bank which issues a letter of credit should honour its obligations. The bank is in no way concerned with any dispute that the buyer may have with the seller. The buyer may say that the goods are not up to contract. Nevertheless the bank must honour its obligations. The buyer may say that he has a cross claim in a large amount. Still the bank must honour its obligations. A letter of credit is like a bill of exchange given for the price of goods. It ranks as cash and must be honoured. No set off or counterclaim is allowed to detract from it: see *Nova (Jersey) Knit Ltd. v. Kammgarn Spinnerei G.m.b.H.* [1977] 1 W.L.R. 713. All the more so with a letter credit. Whereas a bill of exchange is given by buyer to seller, a letter credit is given by a bank to the seller with the very intention of avoiding anything in the nature of a set off or counterclaim. This is borne out by the *Uniform Customs and Practice for Documentary Credits* which has been adopted by the banks in all, or practically all, the countries of the world — from China to Andorra — from Cuba to Nauru. All subscribe to the *Uniform Customs and Practice* which declare[s]:

"Credits, by their nature, are separate transactions from the sales or other contracts on which they may be based and banks are in no way concerned with or bound by such contracts."

If the court of any of the countries should interfere with the obligations of one of its banks (by ordering it not to pay under a letter of credit) it would strike at the very heart of that country's international trade. No foreign seller would supply goods to that country on letters of credit—because he could no longer be confident of being paid. No trader would accept a letter of credit issued by a bank of that country if it might be ordered by its courts not to pay. So it is part of the law of international trade that letters of credit should be honoured—and not nullified by an attachment order at the suit of the buyer.

Added to this, it seems to me that the buyer himself by his conduct has precluded himself from asking for an attachment order. By opening the letter of credit in favour of the seller, he has implicitly agreed that he will not raise any set off or counterclaim — such as to delay or resist payment. He has contracted under the terms of the *Uniform Customs and Practice* by which he promises that the bank will pay without regard to any set off or counterclaim: and implicitly that he will not seek an attachment order. I gather that, if the court in Kuwait had looked at the case in this way, they would not have granted the "provisional attachment." To my mind, it is implicit in the *Uniform Customs and Practice* that such an attachment is precluded.

Yet another consideration occurs to me. Many banks now have branches in many foreign countries. Each branch has to be licensed by the country in which it operates. Each branch is treated in that country as independent of its parent body. The branch is subject to the orders of the courts of the country in which it operates; but not to the orders of the courts where its head office is situate. We so decided in the recent case about bankers' books in the Isle of Man: *Reg. v. Grossman*, The Times, March 6, 1981. In this case I think that the order for "provisional attachment " operates against the head office in Kuwait, but not against the branch office in London. That branch is subject to the orders of the English courts. Only the other day this court held that a Mareva injunction should not be granted to stop payment of a bank guarantee outside the jurisdiction: see *Intraco Ltd. v. Notis Shipping Corporation of Liberia*, The Times, July 7, 1981.

It is my opinion that the courts of England are not bound by the comity of nations to recognise the "provisional attachment" issued by the courts in Kuwait. We should not grant a stay of execution. The judgment here should operate against the branch in London so as to require it to pay the sums due under the letter of credit.

Conclusion

The striking fact is that the courts here in London are asked to enforce a letter of credit opened by buyers in Kuwait in favour of sellers in the United States for payment in the United States. But this is because London is an important centre of international trade. Merchants from all the world come here to settle their disputes. Banks from all the world over have branches here to receive and make payments. So far as we can be of service to international trade, we will accept the task and fulfil it to the best of our ability.

I would approve the judgment of Parker J. in favour of the sellers. I would not grant a stay of execution.

Griffiths L.J. I will deal first with the cross-appeal. The bank submits that the judge should give leave to defend because payment of the sums due under the letter of credit is unlawful according to the proper law of the contract. This submission depends upon the proper law of the letter of credit being Kuwaiti law. In my view the proper law of the letter of credit was the law of the state of North Carolina. Under the letter of credit the bank accepted the obligation of paying or arranging the payment of the sums due in American dollars against presentation of documents at the sellers' bank in North Carolina. The bank could not have discharged its obligation by offering payment in Kuwait. Furthermore the bank undertook to reimburse the advising bank if they paid on their behalf in dollars in America. In *Offshore International S.A. v. Banco Central S.A.* [1977] 1 W.L.R. 399 Ackner J. held that the place at which the bank must perform its obligation under a letter of credit determines the proper law to be applied to the letter or credit. In my view that case was correctly decided.

Secondly, it was submitted that payment was unlawful according to the lex situs of the debt which it is said is Kuwait. But this is a debt that is owed in American dollars in North Carolina; I do not regard the fact that the bank that owes the debt has a residence in Kuwait as any reason for regarding Kuwait as the lex situs of the debt. The lex situs of the debt is North Carolina, and this ground for giving leave to defend cannot be supported.

No other grounds were advanced for resisting judgment under R.S.C., Ord. 14 and I agree that the cross-appeal should be dismissed.

Now as to the appeal: should the judge have granted a stay of the judgment? At the time the case was before Parker J. the order of the Kuwait court was under appeal to the Kuwait Court of Appeal. In those circumstances, I think I should have been very tempted to grant a short stay to await the outcome of the decision of the Court of Appeal because I fear that I should have thought it highly unlikely that the Court of Appeal would uphold an order that interfered so seriously with the well recognised international obligation of a bank under an irrevocable letter of credit. By granting the stay I should have been relieved of the disagreeable obligation to refuse to recognise the order of a court of a friendly state.

But now we know the result of the Court of Appeal hearing in Kuwait and must face the choice between enforcing the obligation upon the bank to pay under its irrevocable letter of credit or recognising the order of the Kuwait court.

I have no doubt that we should uphold the obligation to pay under the irrevocable letter of credit and remove the stay. Letters of credit have become established as a universally acceptable means of payment in international transactions. They are regarded by merchants the world over as equivalent to cash; they have been rightly described by that most distinguished commercial lawyer Kerr J. as "the life-blood of international commerce": see *R. D. Harbottle (Mercantile) Ltd. v. National Westminster Bank Ltd.* [1978] Q.B. 146, 155. The bankers' promise to pay the seller is wholly independent of the underlying contract of sale between the seller and the buyer, or of any contractual dispute that may arise between them. The whole purpose of this form of payment is that a seller should not be kept out of his money by litigation against him at the suit of the buyer. In the absence of fraud the seller is entitled to be paid on presentation of genuine documents.

In the present case we do not even know with certainty the nature of the buyer's claim in Kuwait because he obtained his provisional attachment order at an ex parte hearing and has never served the American seller with any documents specifying the claim. It may be in respect of commission, or it may arise in respect of the goods in respect of which the letter or credit was issued. There is no suggestion of fraud and in the absence of fraud an English court would not have interfered with the banker's obligation to pay under the letter of credit: see *Discount Records Ltd. v. Barclays Bank Ltd.* [1975] 1 W.L.R. 315; *R. D. Harbottle (Mercantile) Ltd. v. National Westminster Bank* [1978] Q.B. 146 and *Edward Owen Engineering Ltd. v. Barclays Bank International Ltd.* [1978] Q.B. 159.

We should do the Bank of Kuwait a grave disservice if we were not to remove this stay for it would undoubtedly seriously damage their credibility as an international bank if it was thought that their paper was not worth holding because an ex parte application to their domestic courts could prevent payment under an expressedly irrevocable obligation.

There is no recognised rule of international law that compels this court to recognise this ex parte order of the Kuwaiti court. It is of course entitled to be treated with respect and wherever possible this court will in the interests of comity seek to recognise and uphold the order of the court of a friendly state. But unhappily in this case the approach of the Kuwaiti court appears to be so out of step with that of our own courts and the courts of other trading nations that I fear we cannot recognise it. The choice lies between upholding the world-wide practices of international commerce or the order of the Kuwaiti court. I choose the first option and would remove the stay.

Waterhouse J. (read by **Griffiths L.J.**). I agree that this appeal should be allowed and that the cross-appeal should be dismissed. Despite the forceful argument of counsel for the bank, I am unable to accept that leave to defend the action should have been granted. On the issue as to the proper law of the letter of credit, I respectfully agree with what has been said by Lord Denning M.R. and Griffiths L.J. about the correctness and the application to the instant case of the reasoning of Ackner J. in *Offshore International S.A. v. Banco Central S.A.* [1977] 1 W.L.R. 399. The more difficult issue for me has been that relating to the lex situs of the debt.

A debt is generally to be looked upon as situate in the country where it is properly recoverable or can be enforced and it is noteworthy that the sellers here submitted voluntarily to the dismissal of their earlier proceedings against the bank in North Carolina. We have been told that they did so because of doubts about the jurisdiction of the North Carolina court, which was alleged in the pleadings to be based on the transaction of business by the bank there, acting by itself or through another named bank as its agent. As for the question of residence, the bank has been silent about any residence that it may have within the United States of America. In the absence of any previous binding authority, I have not been persuaded that this debt due under an unconfirmed letter of credit can be regarded as situate in North Carolina merely because there was provision for payment at a branch of a bank used by the sellers in Charlotte: and I do not regard the analogy of a bill of exchange or a security transferable by delivery as helpful.

Nevertheless, Parker J. was right, in my judgment, to refuse the bank leave to defend because the Kuwaiti provisional order of attachment did not affect the existence of the debt. Counsel for the bank has submitted that the effect of that order was to alter the debt from one due to the sellers to a debt due to the court or held to the order of the court awaiting a decision as to whom it should be paid. I agree with Parker J. that this submission is based upon a single sentence in an affidavit and that it does not bear that weight. There is no acceptable evidence that, according to the law of Kuwait, the debt has ceased to be due to the sellers. There is no ground, therefore, for granting leave to defend and counsel for the bank has not sought to argue that a stay of proceedings is justified if leave to defend was properly refused. If there had been arguable defence, I would have held that the action should be tried in England because there is a legitimate juridical advantage to the sellers in proceeding here, which outweighs any disadvantage to the bank.

The sellers' appeal against the stay of execution granted by Parker J. has to be considered in the changed circumstance that the bank's appeal to the Court of Appeal in Kuwait against the provisional order of attachment has failed. Although a further appeal to the *Cour de Cassation* there is proceeding, we have been told that it will not be heard until the end of the year. I agree, therefore, that the overwhelming balance of the argument now is in favour of removal of the stay of execution. Part of the argument for the bank on this issue has been that it is inexpedient for the court to permit execution to proceed pending resolution of the dispute between Hammoudeh and the sellers: it is suggested that the bank may be exposed to the risk of proceedings for contempt in Kuwait or of double payment. One has sympathy with bank in its dilemma, and its good faith is not in doubt, not least because it has already paid to the plaintiffs $82,546.80 due earlier on November 7, 1980, in respect of the same letter of credit, despite the provisional attachment order. However, the action of the opener, Hammoudeh, and the reasoning of the Kuwait Court of Appeal appear to me to strike at the essential foundations of the international acceptability of letters of credit so that the stay ought not to continue.

> *Appeal allowed with costs.*
> *Cross-appeal dismissed with costs.*
> *Leave to appeal refused.*

C. Defects in Documents and Strict Compliance

Equitable Trust Company of New York
v. Davson Partners, Ltd.

[1927] 27 Lloyds' List L.R. 49 (House of Lords)

. . . .

JUDGMENT

The **LORD CHANCELLOR (VISCOUNT CAVE)**, in moving that the appeal should be dismissed, said: The respondents, Messrs. Dawson Partners, Ltd., are importers and merchants, and in the month of February, 1925, they were minded to take from a man called Rogge, trading at Batavia under the name of Messrs. J. H. Rogge & Co., a consignment of vanilla beans for sale on commission. Rogge required that before he shipped the beans a credit should be opened in a bank in Batavia in his favour to the extent of 25s. per lb. [25 shillings per pound weight] of the goods to be consigned; and accordingly, on Feb. 9, 1925, the respondents wrote to the appellants, the Equitable Trust Company of New York (who are bankers) requesting them to open by cable, confirmed credit with a certain bank at Batavia (which has been referred to as the Escompto Bank), authorising that bank to pay a draft to the extent of £ 8,300 drawn by Messrs. J. H. Rogge & Co. on the appellants. The draft was to be drawn at 90 days' sight and was to be accompanied by a complete set of shipping documents made out to the order of the appellants (consisting of an "on board" bill of lading, an invoice and a policy of insurance) and also by a Dutch Government certificate certifying the goods to be sound and sweet and of prime quality. The documents were to be surrendered to the respondents against payment, and the respondents undertook to reimburse the appellants and presentation of the documents to the respondents, plus interest and a commission. This proposal was afterwards modified at the request of the respondents by substituting for the Escompto Bank, as the correspondents through whom the credit was to be opened, the Hongkong & Shanghai Banking Corporation. With these modifications the proposal was accepted by the appellants, and at their request the Hongkong & Shanghai Bank in London communicated the arrangement by cable to their branch in Batavia.

Subsequently a further change was made which has given rise to all the trouble. The respondents were informed by Rogge by cable that it was not the practice of the Dutch East Indian Government to give certificates of quality, and the respondents on Feb. 18 wrote, to the appellants as to the above and other proposed credits as follows:—

> In these credits we stipulated for a Government certificate of quality. We have just heard by cable from our friends in Batavia to the effect that the Government does not issue a certificate of quality for these goods, but that they have arranged for a certificate of quality to be issued by experts who are sworn brokers, signed by the Chamber of Commerce. We agree to this, and shall be obliged if you will amend the credits accordingly by cable. All charges for our account.

The appellants consented to this change, and by letter to the Hongkong & Shanghai Bank in London dated Feb. 19 requested that bank to cable the modification, which they described in the identical terms which were contained in the above letter of Feb. 18 to their branch Batavia. The Hongkong & Shanghai Bank thereupon dispatched in their secret cypher code to their office in Batavia a telegraphic message which, before being coded, read as follows:—

> L/C wired 12th J. II. Rogge & Co. £ 8,3OO. In place of Dutch Government certifying goods to be sound, &c., you may accept certificate of quality issued by experts who are sworn brokers, signed by Chamber of Commerce.

Unfortunately they made use of a code in which the code words for "experts who are sworn brokers" denoted either the plural or the singular, and so were capable of being read as meaning either "experts who are sworn brokers" or "expert who is sworn broker"; and when the message reached their Batavian branch the code words were decoded by the branch in the singular. On the faith of this error (if error it can be called) the branch wrote to Messrs. Rogge & Co. in these terms:—

> We beg to advise having received a telegram from our London Office dated 20th inst., and translating as follows:

> "L/C wired Feb. 12 J. H. Rogge & Co., £ 8,300. In place of Dutch Government certificate goods being sound, &c., you may accept certificate of quality issued by expert who is sworn broker signed by Chamber of Commerce."

> Our London L/C of Feb. 12 was advised to you in our letter of the 13th inst. to which please attach this advice.

Rogge accordingly drew on the appellants for £ 8,270 10s. 6d. and procured the draft to be discount[ed] by the Escompto Bank, to whom he delivered, together with the shipping documents which had been stipulated for, a certificate of quality issued by a single sworn broker named Droop, whose signature was countersigned by the Handelsvereeniging te Batavia; and the Escompto Bank sent the documents to the Westminster Bank in London for presentation to the appellants.

By the time when the documents arrived in London, it was known that Rogge had committed a fraud by substituting for the goods to be shipped, presumably after he had obtained a certificate of quality, a quantity of wood and iron with a small sprinkling of beans; and it is said that Rogge is now in prison for this or some other fraud. The appellants, before accepting the draft, showed the documents to the respondents, who (in addition to other objections which have since disappeared) objected to the certificate of quality on the ground that it was signed by one broker only and that his signature was countersigned, not by the Chamber of Commerce as agreed, but by the above named Handelsvereeniging (or Commercial Association) of Batavia. The appellants at first took the same view of the meaning of the contract and expressed their intention of not accepting the draft; but after taking advice they took up and paid the draft and claimed to be reimbursed by the respondents the amount so paid, with interest and commission, less a trifling sum realised by the sale of the substituted goods, or in all £8288. The claim was resisted, and this action was brought by the appellants against the respondents to enforce it.

Bateson, J., by whom the action was tried, gave judgment for the plaintiffs (the present appellants), but the Court of Appeal by a majority (Bankes and Atkin, L.JJ., Scrutton, L.J., dissenting) reversed that decision and directed judgment to be entered for the defendants. Hence the present appeal.

My Lords, one of the objections insisted upon by the respondents may be disposed of at once. It was held by Bateson, J., on the evidence called before him, that the *Handelsvereeniging te Batavia*, a semi-official institution performing the functions commonly performed by chambers of commerce, corresponded to the expression "Chamber of Commerce" in the agreement; and in the Court of Appeal Bankes and Scrutton, L.JJ., took the same view, Atkin, L.J., expressing no decided opinion on this point. The evidence upon this point has been read to your Lordships, and having heard it, I agree with the opinion of the learned trial Judge and the majority of the Court of Appeal. I therefore put this objection aside.

The second objection is of a more serious character, and its validity turns on the answer to be given to two arguments which have been put forward on behalf of the appellants. First, it is said that upon the true construction of the letter of Feb. 18, 1925, which embodies the agreement of the parties on this point, the stipulation for a "certificate of quality to be issued by experts who are sworn brokers" was complied with by the presentation of a certificate issued by a single expert who was a sworn broker. In support of this contention it was argued that the expressions "experts" and "brokers" may in a business document of this kind be used to connote the singular as well as the plural, and such expressions as "my solicitors" or "my accountants" were referred to as having an elastic meaning. At all events, it was argued the expression was ambiguous and might reasonably be understood by the appellants in either sense.

I am unable to accept this argument. The plural number is deliberately used, and it must be inferred that the respondents, failing to obtain the guarantee of the Dutch Government for which they had at first stipulated, desired to be protected by the opinions of not less than two experts, who might or might not be partners but who would at least be severally responsible for the exercise of care and reasonable skill in giving the certificate of quality. The correspondence makes it clear that the expression was understood in this sense by the appellants' letter of Feb. 19 already mentioned, used the plural number, and in a later letter of Mar. 19, written to the Escompto Bank before the present dispute arose, wrote that it was "a condition of the credit that the quality and value [of the goods] were to be substantiated by two experts approved by the Batavia Chamber of Commerce." I will add that it is at least possible that, if a second expert had been employed, he would have exercised more care than Mr. Droop (who appears to have contented himself with inspecting certain beans shown to him in Rogge's go down) and would have satisfied himself that the goods which he had inspected and certified were actually shipped.

It was suggested that the request contained in the respondents' letter of Feb. 18, to amend the credit "by cable" makes a difference, for that it must be inferred that the respondents, who knew that the codes in common use did not distinguish between the plural and the singular, contemplated that an ambiguous instruction would be given; but this argument seems to me quite untenable. The respondents were entitled to assume that the communication to Batavia to be made on behalf of the appellants would accurately represent the agreement, and that either figures or code words free from ambiguity would be used, or that the expressions would be telegraphed en clair. I think, therefore, that the argument on construction fails.

But, secondly, it is said that the ambiguity in the instructions was introduced in the coded telegram dispatched by the Hongkong & Shanghai Bank in London to their branch in Batavia—a telegram which contained code words capable of being decoded either in the singular or in the plural number—and that as the respondents had requested the appellants to make the communication to Batavia through that bank and by cable, the respondents must be bound by the message as sent and decoded in Batavia. If (as Scrutton, L.J., suggested) the Hongkong & Shanghai Bank could be said to have been the agents of the respondents in the matter, then this contention would have force, and the principle of cases like Ireland v. Livingston, 5 H.L. 395, might be found to apply: but it does not appear to me that they were such agents, or were otherwise in such relation to the respondents as to bring the doctrine of Ireland v. Livingston into operation. The effect of the correspondence is that at the request of the Hongkong & Shanghai Bank in Batavia [it] was substituted as the bank through which the credit should be communicated to Rogge, and so became the correspondents for that purpose of the appellants: and I think that the effect was to make them the agents for this purpose, not of the respondents, but of the appellants.

Upon the whole I have come to the conclusion that one of the conditions on which the respondents undertook to reimburse the appellants—namely, that there should be presented to the respondents (with the other documents) a certificate of quality to be issued by experts who were sworn brokers—has not been complied with, and accordingly that this appeal fails. I move your Lordships that it be dismissed with costs.

Viscount Sumner: The appellants sued, according to their statement of claim, for damages for breach of the respondents' obligation to accept documents tendered by the plaintiffs and to reimburse to them the amount of a bill of exchange which they had accepted under a confirmed credit opened at the defendants' request. Alternatively, the amount is claimed as an indemnity against all losses and liabilities incurred in consequence of having accepted the bill under the credit. The substance of the claim is really the indemnity for which in terms the letter of credit provides.

The contract sued on—a confirmed credit of an ordinary kind—was made in writing in London between the parties to the action themselves. By its terms reimbursement is to be made on presentation of "the documents," and "the documents," in terms of the credit as ultimately agreed, include "a certificate of quality to be issued by experts who are sworn brokers." What the plaintiffs tendered, as one of the documents and as the only certificate of quality, was one issued by only one expert who was a sworn broker, and by nobody else. There is really no question here of waiver or of estoppel or of diligence or of negligence or of breach of a contract of employment to use reasonable care and skill. The case rests entirely on performance of the conditions precedent to the right of indemnity, which is provided for in the letter of credit.

It is both common ground and common sense that in such a transaction the accepting bank can only claim indemnity if the conditions on which it is authorised to accept are in the matter of the accompanying documents strictly observed. There is no room for documents which are almost the same, or which will do just as well. Business could not proceed securely on any other lines. The bank's branch abroad, which knows nothing officially of the details of the transaction thus financed, cannot take upon itself to decide what will do well enough and what will not. If it does as it is told, it is safe; if it declines to do anything else, it is safe; if it departs from the conditions laid down, it acts at its own risk. The documents tendered were not exactly the documents which the defendants had promised to take up, and *prima facie* they were right in refusing to take them.

The plaintiffs sought to bring the certificate tendered within the documents stipulated for by saying that on a business construction of a business document the certificate of one expert really is or may be what is meant by the "certificate of experts." This list expression, it is accordingly suggested, means in a business sense the certificate either of one or of more than one. In plain English, of course, it does not. A certificate of experts may, I suppose, be that of any number from two to infinity, but it cannot be satisfied by the certificate of one expert only. People may, and I dare say do talk loosely of consulting "solicitors" and of calling in "surveyors" without troubling about the distinction between the case of a single professional man, practising by himself, and that of two or more practising in partnership. So, too, in talking of a ship one speaks of the owners or of the charterers doing this or that, without much troubling whether they actually are of the singular or of the plural number. In a written and highly formal contract this laxity is inadmissible. In the absence of any evidence to prove a special meaning acquired by the word as a term of art or as a commercial slang word, "experts" must be taken to mean what it says, and it does not say "an expert." If support for this is needed, I think it is found in the words "who are sworn brokers." I do not known why brokers are sworn or what exactly swearing them adds to their integrity or to their status, but, at any rate, the taking of oaths is a personal matter. No one can swear "for self and partners" and "experts who are sworn brokers" are neither a firm of expert brokers, one of whom is sworn, nor one sworn and expert broker carrying on business by himself. The latter was the position of Mr. Droop, of Batavia, who alone issued this certificate of quality, and I think his certificate would not do.

The argument being, as have said, that on this occasion commercial colloquialism would treat "more than one" and "not more than one" as the same thing, the contention is next raised that the contract contained an ambiguity proceeding from the respondents, who must therefore accept as a sufficient performance the action taken on the message as coded. This alleged ambiguity can only be latent, for the words are as plain as can be. The respondents requested that the credit should be opened by cable. They no doubt knew that the message would be sent in the main, if not entirely, in code. Their own code, the ABC, used the same group or letters— "ECIZX" — for "expert" and for "experts," and in otherwise determined whether the singular or the plural was the real meaning. They knew that the Hongkong & Shanghai Bank would use a code of their own, and, if they considered the point, they would see that this code might—as in fact it did—adopt the same loose system of letters. That is all. The clerk in London who coded the written message knew that "experts" was the word in the contract. He knew that the sign he used in the code message was common to both numbers. The decoding clerk in Batavia did not know which it was to be, and the result was that, when Mr. Rogge presented among his documents the certificate in question, somehow or other it was accepted as a correct compliance with the coded instructions. But for Rogge's frauds, no doubt it would not have mattered, nor did the respondents suppose that it would matter, until detection overtook him. In fact, the certificate was exactly what had been arranged for by Rogge according to his cable of Feb. 19, 1925, though again owing to the old confusion the respondents did not know it. When Rogge's fraud was found out and the documents came forward, its importance became apparent, for it might enable them to escape from taking up the documents and paying for them. Why should they not take the point? In any case, where is the ambiguity in the language and the letter of credit? I fail to find any.

. . . .

...I think the judgment in the respondents' favour was right.

Lord Atkinson: The action out of which this appeal has arisen was brought by the appellants to recover from the respondents the sum of £ 8,298 12s. 8d. with interest, to which it was alleged they were entitled under the provision of a certain agreement in writing dated Feb. 9, 1925, whereby the appellants, at the request of the respondents, undertook to open by cable a confirmed credit with their correspondents in Batavia, authorising them to pay a draft or drafts to the amount of £ 8,300 drawn by Messrs. J. H. Rogge & Co., of Batavia, on the appellants. By this agreement, as it originally stood, it was provided that the draft or drafts of Messrs. Rogge & Co should be accompanied by a complete set of shipping documents, made out to the order of the appellants, consisting of, among others, a certificate of the Dutch Government certifying that certain Java vanilla beans sold by Messrs. Rogge & Co. to the defendants were sound, sweet and of good quality. By the said agreement the respondents undertook, on the presentation to them of the above-mentioned documents, to reimburse the appellants the amount their advances plus commission for their service.

It was subsequently ascertained by Messrs. Rogge & Co. that the Dutch Government would not give any certificate of the kind specified, and, accordingly, it was arranged that some other mode of procuring a reliable certificate as to the soundness, sweetness and prime quality of these beans should be adopted. The mode selected is set out in a letter dated Feb. 18, 1925, sent by the respondents to the appellants, which runs thus:—

Dear Sir,

Re Confirmed Credit No. 2791 and No. 2792; *re* Unconfirmed Credit No. 2793.

In these credits we stipulated for a Government certificate of quality. We have just heard by cable from our friends in Batavia to the effect that the Government does not issue a certificate of quality for these goods, but that they have arranged for a certificate of quality to be issued by experts who are sworn brokers, signed by the Chamber of Commerce.

We agree to this, and shall be obliged if you will amend the credits accordingly by cable. All charges for our account.

Please confirm.

Yours faithfully,
Dawson Partners, Ltd.

To this letter the appellants sent the following reply:—

Gentlemen,

Re Credits Nos. 2791/3 in favour of J. H. Rogge & Co., Batavia, Java.

We beg to acknowledge receipt of your favour of the 18th inst., advising us of a modification in the documents required under the above credits, and we have accordingly requested the Hongkong & Shanghai Banking Corporation to cable their Batavia Branch, Java, to notify Messrs. J. H. Rogge & Co., or Batavia, of this modification.

We will advise you in due course as to cost of cable.

Yours faithfully,
C. Avery,
Cashier.

On the same day the appellants sent to the Hongkong & Shanghai Banking Corporation the following letter:—

Gentlemen,

Re Confirmed Credit No. 2791 in favour of J. H. Rogge & Co., Batavia, Java, a/c Dawson Partners, Ltd., London, for £ 8,300 0s. 0d.

Referring to our letter of the 11th inst., relative to the issuance of the above credit, we shall be obliged if you will cable to your Batavia branch, Java, to notify Messrs. J. H. Rogge & Co., of Batavia, that in place of the certificate required under this credit of the Dutch Government, certifying goods to be sound and sweet and prime quality, it will be in order to deliver a certificate of quality, to be issued by experts who are sworn brokers, signed by the Chamber of Commerce.

We shall be glad, also, if you will state in your cable that this modification applies to Irrevocable Letter of Credit No. 2792 and Unconfirmed Credit No. 2793 dated 10th inst. which we handed to you with our letter of the same date, to be mailed out to your Batavia branch for delivery to the beneficiaries.

Awaiting a note of cable expenses.

Yours faithfully,
Manager.

On Feb. 20, 1925, the Hongkong & Shanghai Bank sent to the appellants the following letter:—

Dear Sir,

In accordance with your request, have dispatched a telegraphic message (using our cypher code as required) to our office at Batavia, translating as follows:

"L/C wired 12th J. H. Rogge & Co. £ 8,300. In place of Dutch Government certifying goods to be found sound, &c., you may 'accept certificate of quality issued by experts who are sworn brokers, signed by Chamber of Commerce.' This modification also applies to Equitable Trust Co. of New York L/C's 2792/3 on the way our Nos. 61/10215/6."

This message has been sent on the understanding that it is at your risk in every respect and that we are not liable for the consequences of any delay, mistake or omission in transmission or payment.

Please hand us £ 3 12s. 10d. for cost of our telegram.

Yours faithfully,
Sub-Manager.

It will be observed that in all these documents the all-important words "experts who are sworn brokers" are used. It is difficult to believe that this was not a correct translation of the telegram they purported to repeat. From this correspondence it appears to me to be perfectly clear what, according to the intention of the parties concerned, including the appellants, the respondents and the Hongkong & Shanghai Bank, was to be the nature and meaning of the certificate which, under the new arrangement, the respondents were to be entitled to receive with the shipping documents before they became liable to reimburse the appellants for the sums to be advanced by the latter, as provided by letter of Feb. 9, 1925. It was to be a document certifying that the vanilla beans mentioned in this last-named letter were sound, sweet and of prime quality. It was to be issued "by experts who are sworn brokers," and was to be signed by the Chamber of Commerce. Until a certificate answering completely that description had been presented to the respondents, together with the shipping documents, the latter did not, they, contend, become liable to reimburse the appellants the sums mentioned in the letter of Feb. 9, 1925. This was apparently the respondents' rights. They never waived, released or consented to modify them in any way, or to accept any substitute for them. It is because of this that they take their stand upon these rights and defend themselves against the claim of the appellants.

In my opinion they are clearly justified in so doing. It was suggested in argument, as I understood, that this conduct of the respondents was rather grasping, inconsiderate and ungenerous. I express no opinion on that point; it may be so, but I do venturer to express a confident opinion that their action was legally justifiable, and that it is the business of Courts of law, from the lowest to the highest, to enforce legal rights rather than the obligations which generosity or benevolence may impose. I am not quite certain as to the grounds urged to support the appeal of the appellants on this point. I do not know whether it was intended to be contended that the respondents consented to accept a certificate signed by one sworn expert instead of by two or more, or that, as a certificate signed by one expert was quite as good as one signed by two or more, they ought to have so consented. In my view it is clear that the respondents never consented to accept a certificate signed by one expert as a substitute for one signed by two or more. As I have already said, they were not under any obligation to do so. *Prima facie* in a case of this character a better security will be afforded, that the thing the quality of which is to be certified will be honestly, carefully and efficiently examined and judged of, if there are a number of experts engaged in the work than if only one was engaged in it. If there are two or more engaged in it they can observe each other. No "collective responsibility," to use Atkin, L.J.'s word, is secured under the latter method as it is likely to be under the former.

In my view, the respondents, as competent men of business, with a prudent regard for their own interests, would be entirely justified in refusing to accept the certificate of a single expert as to the quality of these vanilla beans as the thing, or as a substitute for the thing, which under the contract contained in the letter of Feb. 9, 1925, as modified by the letters of Feb. 18 and 19, 1925, they were entitled to receive. If the translations of the messages sent by the code of the bank given in the above-mentioned letters be correct — and it is difficult to imagine why they should not be — it shows conclusively that it is possible by adding the words experts "*en clair*" or by attaching some numerals to it or by some other means to express the word "experts" in the plural.

....

Lord Carson, who *dissented* said: I agree with the conclusions arrived at by Bateson, J., the trial Judge, and by Scrutton, L.J., in the Court of Appeal, and I am therefore of opinion that this appeal should be allowed.

Before dealing with the letter of instructions from the respondents to the appellants dated Feb. 18, 1925, upon which the claim of the respondents is mainly based, it is necessary to trace the alterations of the original proposals of Feb. 9, 1925, whereby the complete set of shipping documents to be presented were to include "Dutch Government certificate certifying, goods to be sound and sweet and prime quality." On Feb. 18, Messrs. Rogge & Co., by cable, informed the respondents that the Government did not issue certificates of sweetness and quality, whereupon on the same day the respondents cabled Messrs. Rogge & Co. using the ordinary and customary code words that they "must have Chamber of Commerce certificate of quality and/or issued by trade experts." It is to be noted that the code word used, "ECIZX," could be decoded either in the singular or the plural as meaning either "expert" or "experts," and it will be observed that Messrs. Rogge & Co., in replying by cable on Feb. 19, 1925, used the same code word which was decoded by the respondents as "experts," while there is no evidence whether Messrs. Rogge & Co. meant to use it in the singular or the plural. It was in consequence of this cable that the letter of Feb 18, 1925, relied upon by the respondents, was sent. In the letter they state:—

> We have just heard by cable from our friends in Batavia to the effect that the Government does not issue a certificate quality for these goods, but that they have arranged for a certificate of quality to be issued by experts who are sworn brokers, signed by the Chambers of Commerce. We agree to this, and shall be obliged if you will amend the credits accordingly by cable.

On the next day the appellants accordingly requested the Hongkong & Shanghai Bank to cable this alteration to their branch in Batavia. It was proved in evidence, which was not contradicted, that not only in the code used by the respondents in their communications with Messrs. Rogge & Co., but also in the private code used by the Hongkong & Shanghai Bank, the same three groups of five letters signify "expert" or " experts," "who is" or "who are," "broker" or "brokers," and there was further evidence that such a system of alternative singular or plural meanings is universal or at least usual in all codes. Accordingly, the Java branch of the Hongkong & Shanghai Bank seem to have decoded the message from the same bank in London as "expert who is sworn broker," and to have notified this alteration in similar terms to Messrs. Rogge & Co.

Now, my Lords, it is to be observed that from beginning to end no one had suggested that the arrangement was that two experts were necessary, and, although the respondents and Messrs. Rogge & Co. had each of them by cable arranged the alteration consequent upon the information "that the Government does not issue a certificate of quality," neither of them ever thought it necessary by ambiguous code word to qualify that ambiguous code word which meant either the singular or the plural.

Bearing these facts in mind, it is necessary to consider the terms of the letter of Feb. 18, 1925, upon which the whole case of the respondents depends. Do the words therein necessarily imply that two or more experts were to sign the certificate which took the place of the certificate originally provided for?

My Lords, in my opinion they do not. In the first place it only refers to "a certificate to be issued," and in the second place it puts no limitation on or makes any suggestion as to what will satisfy the word "experts." I agree Scrutton, L.J., that in common commercial experience to use the plural when what is meant is one of a class of more than one—"I will require the opinion of sanitary engineers as to the drains of the house before I buy it," or "the opinion of accountants" or the "certificate of brokers," are, I think, common expressions when it is not in contemplation that more than one person should be employed.

Further, I am of opinion that the request by the respondents to amend the credits by cable after they themselves had arranged the matter by an ambiguous code with Messrs. Rogge & Co. and without making any request as to the necessity of having two or more experts specifically introduced into the cable gives further colour to the view that the respondents had not in their minds any necessity for having the certificate signed by more than one expert.

. . . .

I am therefore of opinion that as the respondents themselves made the arrangement with Rogge in a cable that was ambiguous, and by the terms of the letter of Feb. 18, 1995, asked in ambiguous terms to have the communication made by the Hongkong & Shanghai Bank in London to their branch in Batavia, they cannot rely as a defence to their liability on the fact that the communication reached the third party in a sense other than that in which it is now said was intended. In other words, I agree with the ninth reason stated in the appellants' case that this appeal should succeed "because the respondents' instructions as to the terms of the credit were ambiguous and the certificate tendered complied with such instructions upon an interpretation which they were unreasonably capable of bearing."

Voest-Alpine International Corporation v. Chase Manhattan Bank
707 F.2D 680 (2D. Cir. 1983)

. . . .

CARDAMONE, Circuit Judge:

This appeal involves an interpretation of the law applied to commercial letters of credit. When analyzing that law the unique characteristics of a letter of credit must be kept firmly in mind. Otherwise, a court may unknowingly paint broadly over the letter of credit's salient features and compromise its reliability and fluidity.

Background

Originally devised to function in international trade, a letter of credit reduced the risk of nonpayment in cases where credit was extended to strangers in distant places. Interposing a known and solvent institution's (usually a bank's) credit for that of a foreign buyer in a sale of goods transaction accomplished this objective. A typical letter of credit transaction, as the case before us illustrates, involves three separate and independent relationships—an underlying sale of goods contract between buyer and seller, an agreement between a bank and its customer (buyer) in which the bank undertakes to issue a letter of credit, and the bank's resulting engagement to pay the beneficiary (seller) providing that certain documents presented to the bank conform with the terms and conditions of the credit issued on its customer's behalf. Significantly, the bank's payment obligation to the beneficiary is primary, direct and completely independent of any claims which may arise in the underlying sale of goods transaction.

Several distinct features characterize letters of credit. By conditioning payment solely upon the terms set forth in the letter of credit, the justifications for an issuing bank's refusal to honor the credit are severely restricted, thereby assuring the reliability of letters of credit as a payment mechanism. Banks readily issue these instruments because they are simple in form. Hence, they are convenient and economical for a customer (buyer) to obtain. Further, employing concepts which underlie letters of credit in non-sale of goods transactions enables these devices to serve a financing function. And it is this flexibility that makes letters of credit adaptable to a broad range of commercial uses.

Letters of credit evolved as a mercantile specialty entirely separate from common law contract concepts and they must still be viewed as entities unto themselves. Completely absorbed into the English common law by the 1700s along with the Law Merchant — of which it had become an integral part by the year 1200 — 2 W. Holdsworth, *A History of English Law* 570-72 (1922), letter of credit law found its way into American jurisprudence where it flourishes today. Its origins may be traced even more deeply into history. There is evidence letters of credit were used by bankers in Renaissance Europe, Imperial Rome, ancient Greece, Phoenicia and even early Egypt. *See* Trimble, *The Law Merchant and The Letter of Credit*, 61 HARV. L. REV. 981, 982-85 (1948). These simple instruments survived despite their nearly 3000-year-old lineage because of their inherent reliability, convenience, economy and flexibility.

Since the great utility of letters of credit arises from the independent obligation of the issuing bank, attempts to avoid payment premised on extrinsic considerations — contrary to the instruments' formal documentary nature — tend to compromise their chief virtue of predictable reliability as a payment mechanism. Viewed in this light it becomes clear that the doctrine of strict compliance with the terms of the letter of credit functions to protect the bank which carries the absolute obligation to pay the beneficiary. Adherence to this rule ensures that banks, dealing only in documents, will be able to act quickly, enhancing the letter of credit's fluidity. Literal compliance with the credit therefore is also essential so as not to impose an obligation upon the bank that it did not undertake and so as not to jeopardize the bank's right to indemnity from its customer. Documents nearly the same as those required are not good enough.

We note that there is a distinction between rights obtained and obligations assumed under letter of credit concepts. While a party may not unilaterally alter its obligations, nothing in the purpose or function of letters of credit forecloses the party from giving up its rights.

Facts

Metal Scrap Trading Corporation (MSTC) is an agency of the Indian government that had contracted to buy 7000 tons of scrap steel from Voest-Alpine International Corporation (Voest), a trading subsidiary of an Austrian company. In late 1980 MSTC asked the Bank of Baroda to issue two letters of credit in the total amount of $1,415,550 — one for $810,600 and the other $604,950 — to Voest to assure payment for the sale. The credits were expressly made subject to the *Uniform Customs and Practice for Documentary Credits*.

The parties originally contemplated that Chase Manhattan Bank, N.A. (Chase or Bank) would serve as an advising bank in the transaction. As such, Chase was to review documents submitted by Voest in connection with its drafts for payment. Amendments to the letters of credit increased Chase's responsibilities and changed its status to that of a confirming bank, independently obligate on the credit to the extent of its confirmation.

The contract between MSTC and Voest provided that Voest, as seller, would ship the scrap metal no later than January 31, 1981. The terms and conditions of the credits required proof of shipment, evidenced by clean-on-board bills of lading; certificates of inspection indicating date of shipment; and weight certificates issued by an independent inspector. Sometime between February 2 and February 6 (beyond the January 31 deadline), the cargo was partially loaded aboard the M.V.

ATRA at New Haven. Unfortunately, the ATRA never set sail for India. A mutiny by the ship's crew disabled the ship and rendered it unseaworthy. The scrap steel was later sold to another buyer for slightly over a half million dollars, nearly a million dollars less than the original contract price.

On February 13, two days before the expiration date of the credits, Voest presented three drafts with the required documentation to Chase. The documents contained what the district court termed "irreconcilable" inconsistencies. The bills of lading indicating receipt on board of the scrap metal were signed and dated January 31 by the captain of the ATRA. The weight and inspection certificates accompanying the drafts revealed, however, that the cargo was loaded aboard the ATRA sometime between February 2 and February 6.

Despite this glaring discrepancy Chase advised the Bank of Baroda on February 25 that the drafts and documents presented to it by Voest conformed to the terms and conditions set forth in the letters of credit. At Voest's request (Chase having provided Voest with an advance copy of the advice it planned to forward to the Bank of Baroda), Chase added the following language: "PAYMENT OF ABOVE-MENTIONED DRAFT...WILL BE MADE AT MATURITY ON JULY 30, 1981, TO VOEST...." The Bank of Baroda apparently looked at the documents with more care than Chase. It promptly advised Chase that the documents did not comply with the requirements of the letters of credit, that it would therefore not honor the drafts, and that it would hold the documents at Chase's disposal. When Voest presented the drafts for payment on July 30 Chase refused to honor them.

Voest thereupon instituted the present suit. It asserted that Chase waived the right to demand strict compliance with the terms of the credits and therefore wrongfully dishonored the drafts. Voest further alleged that regardless of whether the documents conformed to the letters of credit Chase was liable on the drafts because it accepted them. Chase, in turn, served a third-party complaint on the Bank of Baroda, alleging that were Chase to be held liable for wrongfully dishonoring the drafts, the Bank of Baroda should be liable to Chase in the same amount. In granting summary judgment against Voest the United States District Court for the Southern District of New York (Duffy, J.), found that Chase had not waived compliance with the terms and conditions of the letters of credit and that the drafts had not been wrongfully dishonored. The district court also rejected Chase's affirmative defense that Voest committed fraud in presenting documents which contained such obvious discrepancies. Voest has appealed from the order insofar as it granted summary judgment against it and Chase has cross-appealed from that part of the order which dismissed its third-party complaint against the Bank of Baroda.

DISCUSSION

I. Waiver

Voest urges that summary judgment was inappropriate because there were disputed factual issues as to whether Chase accepted the documents submitted and, if so, thereby waived any deficiencies in them. Chase contends that a waiver analysis is inappropriate because the defects in Voest's documentation were "incurable." In urging that such defects preclude any waiver on its part, Chase relies upon *Flagship Cruises Ltd. v. New England Merchants National Bank of Boston*, 569 F.2d 699 (1st Cir. 1978) and *American Employers Insurance Co. v. Pioneer Bank and Trust Co.*, 538 F. Supp. 1354 (N.D. Ill. 1981). These cases afford the Bank little comfort. In neither case was there any indication that the issuing or confirming bank accepted defective or untimely documents.

Two other cases including a decision of this Court have indicated that the terms and conditions of a letter of credit may be waived. In *Marino Industries Corp. v. Chase Manhattan Bank, N.A.*, 686 F.2d at 117, one of the questions raised was whether an official of Chase, with apparent authority to act, had waived the expiration date of a letter of credit. Since that issue had not been resolved by the trial court the case was remanded for further consideration. By remanding on the waiver issue, the *Marino* court impliedly approved a waiver analysis even though it reaffirmed its adherence to the rule of strict compliance. Moreover, the Court apparently recognized that a confirming bank may waive the requirements contained in the credit without approval of either the issuing bank or its customer who originally established the credit. In the instant case Chase could have waived the right to demand strict compliance without approval from either the Bank of Baroda or MSTC.

In *Chase Manhattan Bank v. Equibank*, 550 F.2d 882 (3d Cir. 1977), Chase, as beneficiary of a letter of credit, contended that its untimely presentation of documents resulted from an agreement with the issuing bank (Equibank) to extend the time beyond that specified in the credit. The Third Circuit held that the possibility of a waiver of the time requirement by Equibank existed. The court stated that in such instances the "beneficiary bases his claim on the letter of credit as modified by the bank and acceptable to him." The court noted that such a waiver merely jeopardizes a bank's right to reimbursement from its customer, in the case of an issuing bank, or from the issuing bank, in the case of a confirming bank.

Chase argues that *Equibank* is distinguishable because in that case the defects were arguably curable while in the present case they are not. Chase contends that incurability of defect defeats any possibility of waiver. We reject this argument because it is totally at odds with the concept of waiver, which is defined as the intentional relinquishment of a known right. Whether or not a defect can be cured is irrelevant, for it is the right to demand an absence of defects that the party is deemed to have relinquished.

Since a waiver by Chase of the inconsistencies in the documents is possible, we must determine whether Voest presented sufficient evidence which, if believed, could establish a waiver. As proof of waiver Voest relies most heavily on deposition testimony by the Chase official who inspected the documents that he "must have noticed" the discrepancy between the dates in the documents. Other evidence of waiver included: an initialed approval of the documents by a Chase official on the Voest letter which accompanied the presentation of the documents; a letter from Voest to Bank of Baroda, allegedly co-authored by a Chase official, stating that the documents had been accepted; the statement which appeared at the bottom of Chase's advice to Bank of Baroda that payment of the draft would occur on July 30; and a deposition by a Voest official in which he quotes an unknown Chase employee as stating that Chase had accepted the drafts and that payment would definitely be forthcoming.

All parties seem to agree that New York law governs. To establish waiver under New York law one must show that the party charged with waiver relinquished a right with both knowledge of the existence of the right and an intention to relinquish it. There is little doubt that Voest sufficiently established Chase's knowledge of an existing right. Chase clearly had the right to demand strict compliance with the specifications required by the letters of credit, and since it is an established commercial bank we may assume that it had constructive, if not actual, knowledge of that right. The remaining question is whether that right had been intentionally relinquished.

The intention to relinquish a right may be established either as a matter of law or fact. Examples of the former include instances of express declarations by a party or situations where the party's undisputed acts or language are "so inconsistent with his purpose to stand upon his rights as to leave no opportunity for a reasonable inference to the contrary." More commonly, intention is proved through declarations, acts and nonfeasance which permit different inferences to be drawn and "do not directly, unmistakably or unequivocally establish it." In these instances intent is properly left to the trier of fact.

Claims by a beneficiary of a letter of credit that a bank has waived strict compliance with the terms of the credit should generally be viewed with a somewhat wary eye. As noted earlier, if equitable waiver claims are treated too hospitably by courts, letters of credit may become less useful payment devices because of the increased risk of forfeiting the right to reimbursement from their customers which banks would soon face. Nonetheless, because Voest offered evidence which, if believed by the trier of fact, could establish the requisite intentional relinquishment of Chase's right to insist on strict compliance, summary judgment was inappropriately granted to Chase in this case.

. . . .

III. Fraud

Presentation of fraudulent documents to a bank by a beneficiary subverts not only the purposes which letters of credit are designed to serve in general, but also the entire transaction at hand in particular. Falsified documents are the same as no documents at all. We are not persuaded upon the present record, as was the trial court, that Voest did not intend to deceive Chase when it submitted deliberately backdated documents falsely indicating compliance with the terms of the credits in order to have the documents accepted. Since Chase has raised a sufficient question of fact regarding fraud, a trial of this issue is mandated. If it is found that fraud on the part of Voest caused Chase to act, then Voest would be estopped from claiming any benefit accruing to it from its misconduct.

IV. Chase's Cross-Appeal

Finally, we affirm the judgment in favor of the Bank of Baroda. All parties have acknowledged that the documents tendered to Chase did not conform to the established terms and conditions of the letters of credit. The Bank of Baroda, as the issuing bank, was entitled to strict compliance and there is no claim that it waived that right. Further, Chase itself has acknowledged that its cross-appeal has been rendered academic in light of Voest's admission regarding the nonconformity of the documents.

CONCLUSION

This case must be remanded to determine the factual issues raised by the claims of waiver, . . . and fraud. The order appealed from is thus affirmed in part, reversed in part and remanded for further proceedings in accordance with this opinion.

Beyene v. Irving Trust Company
762 F.2D 4 (2d Cir. 1985)

. . . .

KEARSE, CIRCUIT JUDGE:

Plaintiffs Dessaleng Beyene and Jean M. Hanson appeal from a final judgment of the United States District Court for the Southern District of New York, Morris E.

Lasker, *Judge*, dismissing their complaint seeking damages for the alleged wrongful refusal of defendant Irving Trust Company ("Irving") to honor a letter of credit. The district court granted Irving's motion for summary judgment dismissing the complaint on the ground that, since the bill of lading presented to Irving misspelled the name of the person to whom notice was to be given of the arrival of the goods and thereby failed to comply with the terms of the letter of credit, Irving was under no duty to honor the letter of credit. On appeal, plaintiffs contend, *inter alia*, that the mere misspelling of a name should not relieve a bank of its duty to honor a letter of credit. We agree with the district court that the misspelling in this case was a material discrepancy that relieved Irving of its duty to pay the letter of credit, and we affirm the judgment.

FACTS

The material undisputed facts may be stated briefly. In March 1978, Beyene agreed to sell to Mohammed Sofan, a resident of the Yemen Arab Republic ("YAR"), two prefabricated houses. [On 22 May 1990, the Yemen Arab Republic and the People's Democratic Republic of Yemen united to become a single sovereign state, the Republic of Yemen.] Sofan attempted to finance the purchase through the use of a letter of credit issued by the Yemen Bank for Reconstruction and Development ("YBRD") in favor of Beyene. YBRD designated Irving as the confirming bank for the letter of credit, and Irving subsequently notified Beyene of the letter's terms and conditions. Beyene designated the National Bank of Washington ("NBW") as his collecting bank.

In May 1979, NBW sent Irving all of the documents required under the terms of the letter of credit. Thereafter, Irving telephoned NBW to inform it of several discrepancies in the submitted documents, including the fact that the bill of lading listed the party to be notified by the shipping company as Mohammed Soran instead of Mohammed Sofan. The NBW official contacted testified at deposition that Irving never waived the misspelling discrepancy and continued to assert that it was a discrepancy, though it undertook to request authorization from YBRD to pay the letter of credit despite the discrepancy. Such authorization was not forthcoming, and Irving refused to pay.

Plaintiffs instituted the present suit seeking damages for Irving's failure to pay the letter of credit. Irving moved for summary judgment dismissing the complaint on a variety of grounds. The district court granted the motion on the sole ground that the misspelling of Sofan's name in the bill of lading constituted a material discrepancy that gave Irving the right to dishonor the letter of credit. This appeal followed.

DISCUSSION

On appeal, plaintiffs contend principally that (1) the district court's ruling is unsound as a matter of precedent and of policy, and (2) Irving should be required to pay the letter of credit on grounds of waiver and estoppel. We find merit in none of plaintiffs' contentions. We need discuss only the first.

The nature and functions of commercial letters of credit have recently been explored by this Court, *see Voest-Alpine International Corp. v. Chase Manhattan Bank, N.A.*, 707 F.2d 680, 682-83 (2d Cir. 1983), and will not be repeated in detail here. The terms of a letter of credit generally require the beneficiary of the letter to submit to the issuing bank documents such as an invoice and a bill of lading to provide "the accredited buyer [with] some assurance that he will receive the goods for which he bargained and arranged payment." The issuing bank, or a bank that acts as confirming bank for the issuer, takes on an absolute duty to pay the amount of the credit to the beneficiary, so long as the beneficiary complies with the terms of the letter. In order to protect the issuing or confirming bank, this absolute duty does not arise unless the terms of the letter have been complied with strictly. Literal compliance is generally "essential so as not to impose an obligation upon the bank that it did not undertake and so as not to jeopardize the bank's right to indemnity from its customer." *Voest-Alpine International Corp. v. Chase Manhattan Bank*, 707 F.2d at 683....

While some variations in a bill of lading might be so insignificant as not to relieve the issuing or confirming bank of its obligation to pay, we agree with the district court that the misspelling in the bill of lading of Sofan's name as "Soran" was a material discrepancy that entitled Irving to refuse to honor the letter of credit. First, this is not a case where the name intended is unmistakably clear despite what is obviously a typographical error, as might be the case if, for example, "Smith" were misspelled "Smithh." Nor have appellants claimed that in the Middle East "Soran" would obviously be recognized as an inadvertent misspelling of the surname "Sofan." Second, "Sofan" was not a name that was inconsequential to the document, for Sofan was the person to whom the shipper was to give notice of the arrival of the goods, and the misspelling of his name could well have resulted in his nonreceipt of the goods and his justifiable refusal to reimburse Irving for the credit. (Indeed the record includes a telex from Beyene, stating that Sofan had not been notified when the goods arrived in YAR and that as a result demurrage and other costs had been incurred.) In the circumstances, the district court was entirely correct in viewing the failure of Beyene and NBW to provide documents that strictly complied with the terms of the letter of credit as a failure that entitled Irving to refuse payment.

Plaintiffs do not contend that there was any issue to be tried as to the fact of the misspelling of Sofan's name. Their assertions that Irving waived the admitted discrepancy or was estopped from relying on it were not supported sufficiently to withstand a motion for summary judgment and were properly rejected by the district court for the reasons stated in its opinion.

Conclusion

The judgment of the district court is affirmed.

D. The Independence Principle and Its Exceptions

Maurice O'Meara Company v.
National Park Bank of New York

239 N.Y. 386 (N.Y. Ct. App. 1925)

MCLAUGHLIN, J. This action was brought to recover damages alleged to have been sustained by the plaintiff's assignor, Ronconi & Millar, by defendant's refusal to pay three sight drafts against a confirmed irrevocable letter of credit. The letter of credit was in the following form:

"The National Park Bank
"of New York.

"Our Credit No. 14956   *October* 28, 1920
"MESSRS. RONCONI & MILLAR,
"49 Chambers Street,
"New York City, N.Y.:

"DEAR SIRS. —In accordance with instructions received from the Sun-Herald Corporation of this City, we open a confirmed or irrevocable credit in your favor for account of themselves, in amount of $224,853.30, covering the shipment of 1322 2/3 tons of newsprint paper in 72 1/2" and 36 1/2" rolls to test 11-12, 32 lbs. at 8 1/2¢ per pound net weight — delivery to be made in December 1920 and January 1921.

"Drafts under this credit are to be drawn at sight on this Bank, and are to be accompanied by the following documents of a character which must meet with our approval:

"Commercial Invoice in triplicate

"Weight Returns

"Negotiable Dock Delivery Order actually carrying with it control of the goods.

"This is a confirmed or irrevocable credit, and will remain in force to and including February 15th, 1921, subject to the conditions mentioned herein.

"When drawing drafts under this credit, or referring to it please quote our number as above.

"Very truly yours,
"R. STUART
"*Assistant Cashier*
"(R.C.)"

The complaint alleged the issuance of the letter of credit; the tender of three drafts, the first on the 17th of December, 1920, for $46,301.71, the second on January 7, 1921, for $41,446.34, and the third on January 13, 1921, for $32,968.35. Accompanying the first draft were the following documents:

"1. Commercial invoice of the said firm of Ronconi and Millar in triplicate, covering three hundred (300) thirty-six and one-half (36 1/2) inch rolls of newsprint paper and three hundred (300) seventy-two and one-half (72 1/2) inch rolls of newsprint paper, aggregating a net weight of Five Hundred and forty-four thousand seven hundred and twenty-six pounds (544,726), to test eleven (11), twelve (12), thirty-two (32) pounds.

"2. Affidavit of Elwin Walker, verified December 16, 1920, to which were annexed samples of newsprint paper, which the said affidavit stated to be representative of the shipment, covered by the accompanying invoices and to test twelve (12) points, thirty-two (32) pounds.

"3. Full weight returns in triplicate.

"4. Negotiable dock delivery order on the Swedish American Line, directing delivery to the order of the National Park Bank of three hundred (300) rolls of newsprint paper seventy-two and one-half (72 1/2) inches long and three hundred (300) half rolls of newsprint."

The documents accompanying the second draft were similar to those accompanying the first, except as to the number of rolls, weight of paper, omission of the affidavit of Walker, but with a statement: "Paper equal to original sample in test 11/12-32 pounds;" and a negotiable dock delivery order on the Seager Steamship Co., Inc.

The complaint also alleged defendant's refusal to pay; a statement of the amount of loss upon the resale of the paper due to a fall in the market price; expenses for lighterage, cartage, storage and insurance amounting to $3,045.02; an assignment of the cause of action by Ronconi & Millar to the plaintiff; and a demand for judgment.

The answer denied, upon information and belief, many of the allegations of the complaint, and set up (a) as an affirmative defense, that plaintiff's assignor was required by the letter of credit to furnish to the defendant "evidence reasonably satisfactory" to it that the paper shipped to the Sun-Herald Corporation was of a bursting or tensile strength of eleven to twelve points at a weight of paper of thirty-two pounds; that neither the plaintiff nor its assignor, at the time the drafts were presented, or at any time thereafter, furnished such evidence; (b) as a partial defense, that when the draft for $46,301.71 was presented, the defendant notified the plaintiff there had not been presented "evidence reasonably satisfactory" to it, showing that the newsprint paper referred to in the documents accompanying said drafts was of the tensile or bursting strength specified in the letter of credit; that thereupon an agreement was entered into between plaintiff and defendant that the latter should cause a test to be made of the paper represented by the documents then presented and if such test showed that the paper was up to the specifications of the letter of credit, defendant would make payment of the draft; [and] (c) for a third separate and distinct defense that the paper tendered was not, in fact, of the tensile or bursting strength specified in the letter of credit....

The claim for damages for the non-payment of the third draft was apparently abandoned at or prior to the time the motion was made. It is unnecessary, therefore, to further consider that and it will not be again referred to in the discussion as to the first two drafts.

The motion for summary judgment was denied and the defendant appealed to the Appellate Division, where the order denying the same was unanimously affirmed, leave to appeal to this court granted, and the following question certified: "Should the motion of the plaintiff for summary judgment herein have been granted?"

....

I am of the opinion that the order of the Appellate Division and the Special Term should be reversed and the motion granted. The facts set out in defendant's answer and in the affidavits used by it in opposition to the motion are not a defense to the action.

The bank issued to plaintiff's assignor an irrevocable letter of credit, a contract solely between the bank and plaintiff's assignor, in and by which the bank agreed to pay sight drafts to a certain amount on presentation to it of the documents specified in the letter of credit. This contract was in no way involved in or connected with, other than the presentation of the documents, the contract for the purchase and sale of the paper mentioned. That was a contract between buyer and seller, which in no way concerned the bank. The bank's obligation was to pay sight drafts when presented if accompanied by genuine documents specified in the letter of credit.

If the paper when delivered did not correspond to what had been purchased, either in weight, kind or quality, then the purchaser had his remedy against the seller for damages. Whether the paper were what the purchaser contracted to purchase did not concern the bank and in no way affected its liability. It was under no obligation to ascertain, either by a personal examination or otherwise, whether the paper conformed to the contract between the buyer and seller. The bank was concerned only in the drafts and the documents accompanying them. This was the extent of its interest. If the drafts, when presented, were accompanied by the proper documents, then it was absolutely bound to make the payment under the letter of credit, irrespective of whether it knew, or had reason to believe, that the paper was not of the tensile strength contracted for. This view, I think, is the one generally entertained with reference to a bank's liability under an irrevocable letter of credit of the character of the one here under consideration.

The defendant had no right to insist that a test of the tensile strength of the paper be made before paying the drafts. Nor did it even have a right to inspect the paper before payment, to determine whether it in fact corresponded to the description contained in the documents. The letter of credit did not so provide. All that the letter of credit provided was that documents be presented which described the paper shipped as of a certain size, weight and tensile strength. To hold otherwise is to read into the letter of credit something which is not there, and this the court ought not to do, since it would impose upon a bank a duty which in many cases would defeat the primary purpose of such letters of credit. This primary purpose is an assurance to the seller of merchandise of prompt payment against documents.

It has never been held, so far as I am able to discover, that a bank has the right or is under an obligation to see that the description of the merchandise contained in the documents presented is correct. A provision giving it such right, or imposing such obligation, might, of course, be provided for in the letter of credit. The letter under consideration contains no such provision. If the bank had the right to determine whether the paper were of the tensile strength stated, then it might be pertinent to inquire how much of the paper must it subject to the test? If it had to make a test as to tensile strength, then it was equally obligated to measure and weigh the paper. No such thing was intended by the parties and there was no such obligation upon the bank. The documents presented were sufficient. The only reason stated by defendant in its letter of December 18, 1920, for refusing to pay the draft, was that "there has arisen a reasonable doubt regarding the quality of the newsprint paper. *   *   *. Until such time as we can have a test made by an impartial and unprejudiced expert we shall be obliged to defer payment." This being the sole objection, the only inference to be drawn therefrom is that otherwise the documents presented conformed to the requirements of the letter of credit. All other objections were thereby waived.

. . . .

Defendant largely relies upon *Bank of Montreal v. Recknagel* (109 N. Y. 482, 492) and *Portuguese American Bank v. Atlantic National Bank* (200 App. Div. 575). Each of these cases is distinguishable from the present case. In *Bank of Montreal v. Recknagel* the letter of credit expressly required that the description of the goods should be contained in the bills of lading and this court said: "It was an integral part of the agreement of the parties that the bills of lading should contain a statement that manila hemp was shipped." As the bill of lading did not contain this statement, the court held that the bank was not justified in paying the drafts.

In *Portuguese American Bank v. Atlantic National Bank* the letter of credit did not call for any documents whatever. The defendant guaranteed payment of a draft drawn to cover the purchase price of certain specified merchandise to be shipped by the drawers to the drawees and it was held that the bank was not liable on the guaranty where it appeared that neither the draft nor the express company's receipt described the merchandise specified in the guaranty.

Finally, it is claimed that the plaintiff was not entitled to a summary judgment since there was an issue raised as to the amount of damages. It appears from the affidavits in support of the motion that after the defendant had refused to pay the drafts, due notice was given to it by the plaintiff of its intention to sell the paper for the best price possible, although no notice of such resale was necessary. No attention was paid to the notice and the paper was sold as soon as practicable thereafter and for the best price obtainable, which represented the fair market value at the time of the sale. The plaintiff's damages were, primarily, the face amount of the drafts. Plaintiff, of course, was bound to minimize such damage so far as it reasonably could. This, it undertook to do by reselling the paper, and for the amount received, less expenses connected with the sale, it was bound to give the defendant credit. There was absolutely no statement in defendant's affidavits to the effect that the plaintiff did not act in the utmost good faith or with reasonable care and diligence in making the resale. The only reference thereto is that defendant did not get the best price possible. The defendant gave no evidence, however, of a market value at the time and the plaintiff submitted the affidavits of three dealers in paper that the paper was sold at the fair market value at the time of the sale. Plaintiff's damages were, therefore, liquidated by a resale on notice. This is the rule which has long prevailed between seller and buyer. The only requirement is that the resale must be a fair one.

. . . .

There was a loss on the resale of the paper called for under the first draft of $5,447.26, and under the second draft of $14,617.53, making a total loss of $20,064.79, for which amount judgment should be directed in favor of the plaintiff.

The orders appealed from should, therefore, be reversed and the motion granted with costs in all courts. The question certified is answered in the affirmative.

Cardozo, J., *dissenting.* I am unable to concur in the opinion of the court.

I assume that no duty is owing from the bank to its depositor which *requires* it to investigate the quality of the merchandise. I dissent from the view that if it chooses to investigate and discovers thereby that the merchandise tendered is not in truth the merchandise which the documents describe, it may be forced by the delinquent seller to make payment of the price irrespective of its knowledge. We are to bear in mind that this controversy is not one between the bank on the one side and on the other a holder of the drafts who has taken them without notice and for value. The controversy arises between the bank and a seller who has misrepresented the security upon which advances are demanded. Between parties so situated, payment may be resisted if the documents are false.

I think we lose sight of the true nature of the transaction when we view the bank as acting upon the credit of its customer to the exclusion of all else. It acts not merely upon the credit of its customer, but upon the credit also of the merchandise which is to be tendered as security. The letter of credit is explicit in its provision that documents sufficient to give control of the goods shall be lodged with the bank when drafts are presented. I cannot accept the statement of the majority opinion that the bank was not concerned with any question as to the character of the paper. If that is so, the bales tendered might have been rags instead of paper, and still the bank would have been helpless, though it had knowledge of the truth, if the documents tendered by the seller were sufficient on their face. A different question would be here if the defects had no relation to the description in the documents. In such circumstances, it would be proper to say that a departure from the terms of the contract between the vendor and the vendee was of no moment to the bank. That is not the case before us. If the paper was of the quality stated in the defendant's answer, the documents were false.

I think the conclusion is inevitable that a bank which pays a draft upon a bill of lading misrepresenting the character of the merchandise may recover the payment when the misrepresentation is discovered, or at the very least the difference between the value of the thing described and the value of the thing received. If payment might have been recovered the moment after it was made, the seller cannot coerce payment if the truth is earlier revealed.

We may find persuasive analogies in connection with the law of sales. One who promises to make payment in advance of delivery and inspection may be technically in default if he refuses the promised payment before inspection has been made. None the less, if the result of the inspection is to prove that the merchandise is defective, the seller must fail in an action for the recovery of the price. The reason is that "the buyer would have been entitled to recover back the price if he had paid it without inspection of the goods."

I think the defendant's answer and the affidavits submitted in support of it are sufficient to permit a finding that the plaintiff's assignors misrepresented the nature of the shipment. The misrepresentation does not cease to be a defense, partial if not complete, though it innocently made.

The order should be affirmed and the question answered "no."

Sztejn v. J. Henry Schroder Banking Corporation
31 N.Y.S.2d 631 (N.Y. Sup. Ct. 1941)

. . . .

SHIENTAG, Justice.

This is a motion by the defendant, the Chartered Bank of India, Australia and China, (hereafter referred to as the Chartered Bank),...to dismiss the supplemental complaint on the ground that it fails to state facts sufficient to constitute a cause of action against the moving defendant. The plaintiff brings this action to restrain the payment or presentment for payment of drafts under a letter of credit issued to secure the purchase price of certain merchandise, bought by the plaintiff and his co-adventurer, one Schwarz, who is a party defendant in this action. The plaintiff also seeks a judgment declaring the letter of credit and drafts thereunder null and void. The complaint alleges that the documents accompanying the drafts are fraudulent in that they do not represent actual merchandise but instead cover boxes fraudulently filled with worthless material by the seller of the goods. The moving defendant urges that the complaint fails to state a cause of action against it because the Chartered Bank is only concerned with the documents and on their face these conform to the requirements of the letter of credit.

On January 7, 1941, the plaintiff and his co-adventurer contracted to purchase a quantity of bristles from the defendant Transea Traders, Ltd. (hereafter referred to as Transea) a corporation having its place of business in Lucknow, India. In order to pay for the bristles, the plaintiff and Schwarz contracted with the defendant J. Henry Schroder Banking Corporation (hereafter referred to as Schroder), a domestic corporation, for the issuance of an irrevocable letter of credit to Transea which provided that drafts by the latter for a specified portion of the purchase price of the bristles would be paid by Schroder upon shipment of the described merchandise and presentation of an invoice and a bill of lading covering the shipment, made out to the order of Schroder.

The letter of credit was delivered to Transea by Schroder's correspondent bank in India, Transea placed fifty cases of material on board a steamship, procured a bill of lading from the steamship company and obtained the customary invoices. These documents describe the bristles called for by the letter of credit. However, the complaint alleges that in fact Transea filled the fifty crates with cow hair, other worthless material and rubbish with intent to simulate genuine merchandise and defraud the plaintiff and Schwarz. The complaint then alleges that Transea drew a draft under the letter of credit to the order of the Chartered Bank and delivered the draft and the fraudulent documents to the "Chartered Bank at Cawnpore, India, for collection for the account of said defendant Transea." The Chartered Bank has presented the draft along with the documents to Schroder for payment. The plaintiff prays for a judgment declaring the letter of credit and draft thereunder void and for injunctive relief to prevent the payment of the draft.

For the purposes of this motion, the allegations of the complaint must be deemed established and "every intendment and fair inference is in favor of the pleading." Therefore, it must be assumed that Transea was engaged in a scheme to defraud the plaintiff and Schwarz, that the merchandise shipped by Transea is worthless rubbish and that the Chartered Bank is not an innocent holder of the draft for value but is merely attempting to procure payment of the draft for Transea's account.

It is well established that a letter of credit is independent of the primary contract of sale between the buyer and the seller. The issuing bank agrees to pay upon presentation of documents, not goods. This rule is necessary to preserve the efficiency of the letter of credit as an instrument for the financing of trade. One of the chief purposes of the letter of credit is to furnish the seller with a ready means of obtaining prompt payment for his merchandise. It would be a most unfortunate interference with business transactions if a bank before honoring drafts drawn upon it was obliged or even allowed to go behind the documents at the request of the buyer and enter into controversies between the buyer and the seller regarding the quality of the merchandise shipped. If the buyer and the seller intended the bank to do this they could have so provided in the letter of credit itself, and in the absence of such a provision, the court will not demand or even permit the bank to delay paying drafts which are proper in form. *O'Meara Co. v. National Park Bank of New York*, 239 N.Y. 386.... Of course, the application of this doctrine presupposes that the documents accompanying the draft are genuine and conform in terms to the requirements of the letter of credit.

However, I believe that a different situation is presented in the instant action. This is not a controversy between the buyer and seller concerning a mere breach of warranty regarding the quality of the merchandise; on the present motion, it must be assumed that the seller has intentionally failed to ship any goods ordered by the buyer. In such a situation, where the seller's fraud has been called to the bank's attention before the drafts and documents have been presented for payment, the principle of the independence of the bank's obligation under the letter of credit should not be extended to protect the unscrupulous seller. It is true that even though the documents are forged or fraudulent, if the issuing bank has already paid the draft before receiving notice of the seller's fraud, it will be protected if it exercised reasonable diligence before making such payment. However, in the instant action Schroder has received notice of Transea's active fraud before it accepted or paid the draft. The Chartered Bank, which under the allegations of the complaint stands in no better position than Transea, should not be heard to complain because Schroder is not forced to pay the draft accompanied by documents covering a transaction which it has reason to believe is fraudulent.

Although our courts have used broad language to the effect that a letter of credit is independent of the primary contract between the buyer and seller, that language was used in cases concerning alleged breaches of warranty; no case has been brought to my attention on this point involving an intentional fraud on the part of the seller which was brought to the bank's notice with the request that it withhold payment of the draft on this account. The distinction between a breach of warranty and active fraud on the part of the seller is supported by authority and reason. As one court has stated: "Obviously, when the issuer of a letter of credit knows that a document, although correct in form, is, in point of fact, false or illegal, he cannot be called upon to recognize such a document as complying with the terms of a letter of credit." *Old Colony Trust Co. v. Lawyers' Title & Trust Co.,* 2 Cir., 297 F. 152 at page 158, *certiorari denied* 268 U.S. 585,....

No hardship will be caused by permitting the bank to refuse payment where fraud is claimed, where the merchandise is not merely inferior in quality but consists of worthless rubbish, where the draft and the accompanying documents are in the hands of one who stands in the same position as the fraudulent seller, where the bank has been given notice of the fraud before being presented with the drafts and documents for payment, and where the bank itself does not wish to pay pending an adjudication of the rights and obligations of the other parties. While the primary factor in the issuance of the letter of credit is the credit standing of the buyer, the security afforded by the merchandise is also taken into account. In fact, the letter of credit requires a bill of lading made out to the order of the bank and not the buyer. Although the bank is not interested in the exact detailed performance of the sales contract, it is vitally interested in assuring itself that there are some goods represented by the documents.

On this motion only the complaint is before me and I am bound by its allegation that the Chartered Bank is not a holder in due course but is a mere agent for collection for the account of the seller charged with fraud. Therefore, the Chartered Bank's motion to dismiss the complaint must be denied. If it had appeared from the face of the complaint that the bank presenting the draft for payment was a holder in due course, its claim against the bank issuing the letter of credit would not be defeated even though the primary transaction was tainted with fraud. This I believe to be the better rule despite some authority to the contrary.

The plaintiff's further claim that the terms of the documents presented with the draft are at substantial variance with the requirements of the letter of credit does not seem to be supported by the documents themselves.

Accordingly, the defendant's motion to dismiss the supplemental complaint is denied.

United Bank Limited v. Cambridge Sporting Goods Corp.
41 N.Y.2d 254 (N.Y. Ct. App. 1976)

. . . .

GABRIELLI, Justice.

On this appeal, we must decide whether fraud on the part of a seller-beneficiary of an irrevocable letter of credit may be successfully asserted as a defense against holders of drafts drawn by the seller pursuant to the credit. If we conclude that this defense may be interposed by the buyer who procured the letter of credit, we must also determine whether the courts below improperly imposed upon appellant buyer the burden of proving that respondent banks to whom the drafts were made payable by the seller-beneficiary of the letter of credit, were not holders in due course. The issues presented raise important questions concerning the application of the law of letters of credit and the rules governing proof of holder in due course status set forth in Article 3 of the Uniform Commercial Code....

In April, 1971 appellant Cambridge Sporting Goods Corporation (Cambridge) entered into a contract for the manufacture and sale of boxing gloves with Duke Sports (Duke), a Pakistani corporation. Duke committed itself to the manufacture of 27,936 pairs of boxing gloves at a sale price of $42,576.80; and arranged with its Pakistani bankers, United Bank Limited (United) and The Muslim Commercial Bank (Muslim), for the financing of the sale. Cambridge was requested by these banks to cover payment of the purchase price by opening an irrevocable letter of credit with its bank in New York, Manufacturers Hanover Trust Company (Manufacturers). Manufacturers issued an irrevocable letter of credit obligating it, upon the receipt of certain documents indicating shipment of merchandise pursuant to the contract, to accept and pay, 90 days after acceptance, drafts drawn upon Manufacturers for the purchase price of the gloves.

Following confirmation of the opening of the letter of credit, Duke informed Cambridge that it would be impossible to manufacture and deliver the merchandise within the time period required by the contract, and sought an extension of time for performance until September 15, 1971 and a continuation of the letter of credit, which was due to expire on August 11. Cambridge replied on June 18 that it would not agree to a postponement of the manufacture and delivery of the gloves because of its resale commitments and, hence, it promptly advised Duke that the contract was canceled and the letter of credit should be returned. Cambridge simultaneously notified United of the contract cancellation

Despite the cancellation of the contract, Cambridge was informed on July 17, 1971 that documents had been received at Manufacturers from United purporting to evidence a shipment of the boxing gloves under the terms of the canceled contract. The documents were accompanied by a draft, dated July 16, 1971, drawn by Duke upon Manufacturers and made payable to United, for the amount of $21,288.40, one half of the contract price of the boxing gloves. A second set of documents was received by Manufacturers from Muslim, also accompanied by a draft, dated August 20, and drawn upon Manufacturers by Duke for the remaining amount of the contract price.

An inspection of the shipments upon their arrival revealed that Duke had shipped old, unpadded, ripped and mildewed gloves rather than the new gloves to be manufactured as agreed upon. Cambridge then commenced an action against Duke in Supreme Court, New York County, joining Manufacturers as a party, and obtained a preliminary injunction prohibiting the latter from paying drafts drawn under the letter of credit; subsequently, in November, 1971 Cambridge levied on the funds subject to the letter of credit and the draft, which were delivered by Manufacturers to the Sheriff in compliance therewith. Duke ultimately defaulted in the action and judgment against it was entered in the amount of the drafts, in March, 1972.

The present proceeding was instituted by the Pakistani banks to vacate the levy made by Cambridge and to obtain payment of the drafts on the letter of credit. The banks asserted that they were holders in due course of the drafts which had been made payable to them by Duke and, thus, were entitled to the proceeds thereof irrespective of any defenses which Cambridge had established against their transferor, Duke, in the prior action which had terminated in a default judgment. The banks' motion for summary judgment on this claim was denied and the request by Cambridge for a jury trial was granted. Cambridge sought to depose the petitioning banks, but its request was denied and, as an alternative, written interrogatories were served on the Pakistani banks to learn the circumstances surrounding the transfer of the drafts to them. At trial, the banks introduced no evidence other than answers to several of the written interrogatories which were received over objection by Cambridge to the effect that the answers were conclusory, self-serving and otherwise inadmissible. Cambridge presented evidence of its dealings with Duke including the cancellation of the contract and uncontested proof of the subsequent shipment of essentially worthless merchandise.

The trial court concluded that the burden of proving that the banks were not holders in due course lay with Cambridge, and directed a verdict in favor of the banks on the ground that Cambridge had not met that burden; the court stated that Cambridge failed to demonstrate that the banks themselves had participated in the seller's acts of fraud, proof of which was concededly present in the records. The Appellate Division affirmed, agreeing that while there was proof tending to establish the defenses against the seller, Cambridge had not shown that the seller's acts were "connected to the petitioners [banks] in any manner."

We reverse and hold that it was improper to direct a verdict in favor of the petitioning Pakistani banks. We conclude that the defense of fraud in the transaction was established and in that circumstance the burden shifted to petitioners to prove that they were holders in due course and took the drafts for value, in good faith and without notice of any fraud on the part of Duke (Uniform Commercial Code, § 3-302)....

This case does not come before us in the typical posture of a lawsuit between the bank issuing the letter of credit and presenters of drafts drawn under the credit seeking payment. Because Cambridge obtained an injunction against payment of the drafts and has levied against the proceeds of the drafts, it stands in the same position as the issuer, and, thus, the law of letters of credit governs the liability of Cambridge to the Pakistani banks. Article 5 of the Uniform Commercial Code, dealing with letters of credit, and the *Uniform Customs and Practice for Documentary Credits* promulgated by the International Chamber of Commerce set forth the duties and obligations of the issuer of a letter of credit. A letter of credit is a commitment on the part of the issuing bank that it will pay a draft presented to it under the terms of the credit, and if it is a documentary draft, upon presentation of the required documents of title (*see* Uniform Commercial Code, § 5-103). Banks issuing letters of credit deal in documents and not in goods and are not responsible for any breach of warranty or nonconformity of the goods involved in the underlying sales contract (*see* Uniform Commercial Code, § 5-114, subd. [1]; *Uniform Customs and Practice*, [Articles 2, 9, and 13-14]; *O'Meara Co. v. National Park Bank of N.Y.*, 239 N.Y. 386. Subdivision (2) of Section 5-114, however indicates certain limited circumstances in which an issuer *may* properly refuse to honor a draft drawn under a letter of credit or a customer may enjoin an issuer from honoring such a draft. Thus, where "fraud in the transaction" has been shown and the holder has not taken the draft in circumstances that would make it a holder in due course, the customer may apply to enjoin the issuer from paying drafts drawn under the letter of credit. This rule represents a codification of precode case law most eminently articulated in the landmark case of *Sztejn v. Schroder Banking Corp.*, 31 N.Y.S.2d 631, Shientag, J., where it was held that the shipment of cow hair in place of bristles amounted to more than mere breach of warranty but fraud sufficient to constitute grounds for enjoining payment of drafts to one not a holder in due course. Even prior to the Sztejn case, forged or fraudulently procured documents were proper grounds for avoidance of payment of drafts drawn under a letter of credit and cases decided after the enactment of the code have cited *Sztejn* with approval.

The history of the dispute between the various parties involved in this case reveals that Cambridge had in a prior, separate proceeding successfully enjoined Manufacturers from paying the drafts and has attached the proceeds of the drafts. It should be noted that the question of the availability and the propriety of this relief is not before us on this appeal. The petitioning banks do not dispute the validity of the prior injunction nor do they dispute the delivery of worthless merchandise. Rather, on this appeal they contend that as holders in due course they are entitled to the proceeds of the drafts irrespective of any fraud on the part of Duke (*see* Uniform Commercial Code, § 5-114, subd. [2], par. [b]). Although precisely speaking there was no specific finding of fraud in the transaction by either of the courts below, their determinations were based on that assumption. The evidentiary facts are not disputed and we hold upon the facts as established, that the shipment of old, unpadded, ripped and mildewed gloves rather than the new boxing gloves as ordered by Cambridge, constituted fraud in the transaction within the meaning of subdivision (2) of Section 5-114. It should be noted that the drafters of Section 5-114, in their attempt to codify the *Sztejn* case and in utilizing the term "fraud in the transaction," have eschewed a dogmatic approach and adopted a flexible standard to be applied as the circumstances of a particular situation mandate. It can be difficult to draw a precise line between cases involving breach of warranty (or a difference of opinion as to the quality of goods) and outright fraudulent practice on the part of the seller. To the extent, however, that Cambridge established that Duke was guilty of *fraud* in shipping, not merely nonconforming merchandise, but worthless fragments of boxing gloves, this case is similar to *Sztejn*.

If the petitioning banks are holders in due course they are entitled to recover the proceeds of the drafts but if such status cannot be demonstrated their petition must fail. The parties are in agreement that Section 3-307 of the Code governs the pleading and proof of holder in due course status and that Section provides:

"(1)   Unless specifically denied in the pleadings each signature on an instrument is admitted. When the effectiveness of a signature is put in issue

"(a)   the burden of establishing it is on the party claiming under the signature; but

"(b)   the signature is presumed to be genuine or authorized except where the action is to enforce the obligation of a purported signer who has died or become incompetent before proof is required.

"(2)   When signatures are admitted or established, production of the instrument entitles a holder to recover on it unless the defendant establishes a defense.

"(3)   After it is shown that a defense exists a person claiming the rights of a holder in due course has the burden of establishing that he or some person under whom he claims is in all respects a holder in due course."

Even though Section 3-307 is contained in Article 3 of the code dealing with negotiable instruments rather than letters of credit, we agree that its provisions should control in the instant case. Section 5-114 (subd. [2], par. [a]) utilizes the holder in due course criteria of Section 3-302 of the Code to determine whether a presenter may recover on drafts despite fraud in the sale of goods transaction. It is logical, therefore, to apply the pleading and practice rules of Section 3-307 in the situation where a presenter of drafts under letter of credit claims to be a holder in due course. In the context of Section 5-114 and the law of letters of credit, however, the "defense" referred to in Section 3-307 should be deemed to include only those defenses available under subdivision (2) of Section 5-114, *i.e.*, noncompliance of required documents, forged or fraudulent documents or fraud in the transaction. In the context of a letter of credit transaction and, specifically subdivision (2) of Section 5-114, it is these defenses which operate to shift the burden of proof of holder in due course status upon one asserting such status. Thus, a presenter of drafts drawn under a letter of credit must prove that it took the drafts for value, in good faith and without notice of the underlying fraud in the transaction (Uniform Commercial Code, § 3-302).

Turning to the rules of Section 3-307 as they apply to this case, Cambridge failed to deny the effectiveness of the signatures on the draft in its answer and, thus, these are deemed admitted and their effectiveness is not an issue in the case. However, this does not entitle the banks as holders to payment of the drafts since Cambridge has established "fraud in the transaction." The courts below erroneously concluded that Cambridge was required to show that the banks had participated in or were themselves guilty of the seller's fraud in order to establish a defense to payment. But, it was not necessary that Cambridge prove that United and Muslim actually participated in the fraud, since merely notice of the fraud would have deprived the Pakistani banks of holder in due course status.

In order to qualify as a holder in due course, a holder must have taken the instrument "without notice *   *   * of any defense against *   *   * it on the part of any person" (Uniform Commercial Code, § 3-302, subd. [1], par. [c]). Pursuant to subdivision (2) of Section 5-114 fraud in the transaction is a valid defense to payment of drafts drawn under a letter of credit. Since the defense of fraud in the transaction was shown, the burden shifted to the banks by operation of subdivision (3) of Section 3-307 to prove that they were holders in due course and took the drafts without notice of Duke's alleged fraud. As indicated in the Official Comment to that subdivision, when it is shown that a defense exists, one seeking to cut off the defense by claiming the rights of a holder in due course "has the full burden of proof by a preponderance of the total evidence" on this issue. This burden must be sustained by "affirmative proof" of the requisites of holder in due course status (see Official Comment, MCKINNEY'S CONS. LAWS OF N.Y., Book 62 1/2, Uniform Commercial Code, § 3-307, p. 212). It was error for the trial court to direct a verdict in favor of the Pakistani banks because this determination rested upon a misallocation of the burden of proof; and we conclude that the banks have not satisfied the burden of proving that they qualified in all respects as holders in due course, by any affirmative proof. The only evidence introduced by the banks consisted of conclusory answers to the interrogatories which were improperly admitted by the Trial Judge. The failure of the banks to meet their burden is fatal to their claim for recovery of the proceeds of the drafts and their petition must therefore be dismissed.

Accordingly, the order of the Appellate Division should be reversed, with costs, and the petition dismissed.

II. Securing Performance and Standby Letters of Credit

Documents Supplement References:

1. *Uniform Customs and Practices for Documentary Credits (UCP 500, 1993)*

2. *New York Uniform Commercial Code Article 5, with Official Comments (1998)*

3. *United Nations Convention on Independent Guarantees and Stand-by Letters of Credit, with Explanatory Note (1995)*

A. Transactional Aspects of Standby L/Cs

Boris Kozolchyk, The Emerging Law of Standby Letters of Credit and Bank Guarantees

24 Arizona Law Review 319, 320-30 (1982)

A. *The Commercial Letter of Credit, the Standby Letter of Credit and the Guarantee of the Performance*

A commercial or "documentary" letter of credit may be defined as a formal promise by a bank or another party of known solvency to accept and pay, or only to pay, the draft or demand of payment of the beneficiary upon the latter's compliance with the terms of the credit. As a financial intermediary, the bank issuing or confirming a commercial letter of credit performs the service of payment for the seller or supplier of services and of verification of documentary compliance for the buyer, who is the recipient of such goods or services. By contrast, the purposes of the bank's mediation in the standby letter of credit are as varied as the beneficiaries' needs for assurances of payment or reimbursement.

As an assurance of payment against the presentation of specified documents accompanied by a draft or demand for payment, the standby credit can encompass virtually every obligation known to man.... [W]hat characterizes the usage of the standby letter of credit is the likely occurrence of a default because of a failure to perform, as well as poor performance by the bank's customer of the underlying obligation to the beneficiary. This negative antecedent in the standby letter of credit contrasts with the positive antecedent in the commercial letter of credit. The issuance of a commercial letter of credit is meant to trigger the seller's bargained-for delivery of required or customary documents to the buyer through the banking intermediaries. In fact, one of the first reported instances of use of standby credits revealed the negative antecedent of a buyer's failure to pay directly to his seller. A bank was asked to issue a commercial letter of credit payable upon the presentation of duplicate documents (invoice, bill of lading and insurance policy) accompanied by the seller's demand for payment. Upon inquiry into the reason for payment against duplicate documents, the bank found out that its letter of credit was to be used only if the buyer had not paid the seller directly once the latter had tendered the original set of documents to the buyer. The bank's credit therefore was standing by, awaiting, as it were, the buyer's non-payment to take effect.

Given its negative antecedent, the documents required by a standby credit differ from those required by a commercial letter of credit. As a documentary letter of credit, the assertions in the documents are adaptable to assure payment on any underlying transaction by the mere expedient of requiring assertions of lack of performance or default. These could range from elaborate third party certifications to terse statements by the beneficiary in the form of "simple demands" of payment. Thus, the standby letter of credit must be regarded as a genus which includes all types of documentary assurances of payment or reimbursement, including notably the "tender bond" as well as "performance" and "repayment" guarantees commonly required of large national and international building and services contractors by their clients or financiers. [[A] "tender bond" [provides] an assurance of the party submitting the tender (principal) to sign the contract if the tender is accepted; a "performance guarantee" [safeguards] against the party to whom the contract is awarded (principal) failing to meet his obligations under the awarded contract; and a "repayment guarantee" [assures] the party awarding the contract that advances made by him will be repaid in the event of the principal not fulfilling the contract terms.]

A standby letter of credit can be drafted so as to incorporate any negative antecedent into its documentary specifications. It can stipulate, for example, payment against a certification of failure to execute the final contract after the award of the bid, or of a failure to perform or to effect repayment of advances or the total amount of the contract. Such variations of the commercial letter of credit do not alter the basis upon which it became one of the most relied-upon trade instruments of our time.

The standby letter of credit, as an offspring of the commercial letter of credit, will continue to be relied upon as long as the financial intermediary continues to provide two distinct assurances. The first is an "abstract" assurance of payment to the beneficiary (seller or provider of services). An abstract promise of payment is one which is independent of the equities in underlying transactions, such as those between the seller or provider and his buyer or client; the bank's customer or account party and the issuing or confirming bank; and between the requesting, issuing, notifying, confirming, negotiating and paying banks. Thus, the beneficiary of an established commercial letter of credit can demand the enforceability of the bank's promise strictly on the terms and conditions specified in the letter of credit, regardless of the inadequacy of consideration in an underlying sale. He can also claim payment regardless of a reimbursement agreement or of insufficiency of collateral between the account party and the issuing or confirming bank, or of mistaken or inconclusive communications between the issuing, notifying, confirming, negotiating and paying banks.

The second essential assurance is that the banks involved in the commercial letter of credit transaction will use their professional skill and integrity in verifying that the beneficiary complied with the terms and conditions of the credit instrument. The party interested in this assurance is the bank's customer or account party. Clearly these assurances can be made available to both the beneficiary and customer of a standby letter of credit. For this reason, no objections can be raised to the 1977 opinion of the International Chamber of Commerce Commission on Banking Technique and Practice that standby credits fall within the definition of documentary credits provided in paragraph (b) of the general provisions and definitions of the *Uniform Customs and Practice for Documentary Credits (U.C.P.)*. [Article 2 of UCP 500, *i.e.*, the 1993 revision of the *UCP*, on the meaning of credit, specifically mentions standby letters of credit. Thus, the *UCP* clearly governs both commercial (or documentary) and standby letters of credit.]

The issuing or confirming bank ceases to act in its professional banking capacity, however, when it undertakes in a standby credit to ascertain the occurrence of acts or events of default by its customer or by third parties. The distinction between acting as a commercial banker and as a "dealer" in goods, whatever their nature and volume, was taught vividly to two generations of letter of credit bankers by First National City Bank's Frank Sauter with the following illustration: a customer wants the bank to issue a letter of credit predicated upon the bank's ascertaining that the olive oil shipped by the beneficiary is as found in a sample bottle provided to the bank. Sauter suggested that:

> Of course we could have accommodated him if we wanted to, but experience has taught us to mind our own business, and that is the banking business.... No bank that knows the commercial credit business would enter into a transaction of this kind just to accommodate even its best customer. It would be impractical for a bank to do so anyhow when you stop to think about it.

The U.C.P. reflects the international banking community's endorsement of separation between the bank's and the customer's business when they declare, proverbially, that banks deal in documents and not in goods.

In verifying the beneficiary's compliance with the terms and conditions of the commercial letter of credit, the bank is protected by standards of diligence that take into account that which is known in the banking trade about documents emanating from other trades. This knowledge is restricted only to some effects of those documents. Thus a bank is supposed to know what is a marine "on board" as opposed to a "received for shipment" bill of lading. But an issuing banker is not expected to know whether the bill of lading in question is in full conformity with the laws of the country in which it was issued. What the commercial letter of credit banker is supposed to know is objectively ascertainable by referring to the written banking customs such as found in the U.C.P. and the unwritten rules as to what experienced bankers would have done under the circumstances. In addition, a standby letter of credit banker should be held responsible for distinguishing between a document clearly labelled "bid" and one labelled "contract" or between one labelled "release of contractual liability" and one labelled "lien waiver." He cannot, however, be held responsible for the knowledge and skills peculiar to each of the numerous underlying trades or professions. Accordingly, a bank departs from sound commercial letter of credit practice when it issues a performance guarantee in the manner described in the International Chamber of Commerce Uniform Rules for Contract Guarantees (I.C.C. Rules). Upon proof of nonperformance, the beneficiary will be entitled to demand either a stipulated sum of money or a completed performance of the contract. Even if the bank is willing to act on the basis of the expert advice of consulting contractors, engineers, architects, or nuclear scientists, it must be prepared to face the consequences of their negligence or the validity of contrary opinions. Therefore, the bank guaranteeing performance as such (as contrasted with a guarantee of payment) is exposed to significant liability both at time of determination of performance and when deciding to undertake the completion of performance. If it chooses to complete performance instead of paying the beneficiary, it cannot ignore the likelihood of additional liabilities to injured workmen, tenants or passers by, unpaid tax authorities and so on.

B. *Types of Standbys*

1. *According to Type of Bank*

A recent [September 1979] study and a survey by P. Lloyd-Davies of the Research Staff Board of Governors of the Federal Reserve Board shed light on the types of banks that issue standby credits and on their most common uses. Predictably large banks are the most extensive issuers. Banks with assets of over 1 billion dollars account for more than 90% of the total standby letters of credit outstanding in terms of amount of money issued. Of these banks, the First National City Bank of New York (Citibank) accounts for about twenty-five percent of the total of approximately-thirty-five billion dollars issued in the first three months of 1980. But while large banks account for the largest percentage of standbys in terms of the amount of money issued, over one-half of all the banks issuing these credits have less than fifty million dollars in total assets. This fact prompts Lloyd-Davies' conclusion that standbys "have the potential to cause problems for small banks as well as large ones."

The Lloyd-Davies study lists three reasons for the dominant presence of large multinational banks in the standby issuing business. The first is that beneficiaries are most apt to rely on a standby issued by a large bank than by a smaller one. The second is the expertise developed by large banks with regard to commercial letters of credit, an expertise not generally available in smaller banks. Finally, since the issuance of standbys frequently involves very large amounts, especially in connection with construction projects, only large banks have the sufficient resources to issue such credits without violating their lending limits to the specific customer-borrower.

An unmentioned, but in this writer's opinion equally significant, cause of the dominance of large multinational banks is their wider network of correspondent relations, including foreign and domestic branches and subsidiaries. Unlike sureties of different nationalities and places of business, correspondent banks communicate with each other rapidly, easily, inexpensively and in a binding manner. They also have a much wider pool of information on customers, beneficiaries and corresponding banks than do smaller banks. Chances are that a given customer requesting a large issuance will be better known to them than he will be to smaller banks and surety companies. Communications between correspondent banks use uniform terminology, and their legal instruments are frequently accorded similar legal effects in different jurisdictions. Further, correspondent banks often enjoy lines of credit with different "facilities" which include discounts of commercial paper and overdrafts. Transactions are routinely assigned to the appropriate facility and the accounts are credited or debited with consensually binding effects upon both parties. Thus, correspondent banks are able to transact business and to assume, pay, charge and collect liabilities worth billions of dollars with a minimum of formality and legal expense. When the ease, rapidity, binding effect and economy of their communications are added to the ability to rely on their combined financial resources and to charge lower fees than sureties or bonding companies, it becomes apparent why large banks have taken over, internationally and nationally, a substantial segment of the suretyship and bonding business.

2. *According to Type of Use*

The most significant use of standbys issued to foreign beneficiaries is in connection with construction projects. Of the eleven billion standbys supporting transactions abroad at the time of a survey in the spring of 1979, approximately one-half were issued in connection with construction projects. In this type of standby, the foreign correspondent is sometimes asked to issue its own standby and to seek reimbursement from the balances of the U.S. bank in its account with the foreign correspondent. On other occasions the U.S. bank is required to issue a "counterguarantee," which consists of the U.S. bank's own standby credit payable upon presentation of documents indicating payment of its standby by the foreign correspondent.

By contrast, approximately seventy-five percent of standby credits supporting U.S. domestic transactions were used in connection with what the Lloyd-Davies study describes as "financial" transactions, particularly among the largest banks. The study refers to a financial transaction as meaning one in which the issuing bank assures the beneficiary that he will receive payment for his financing of the bank's customer's borrowing. For example, one such assurance is that of payment of the commercial paper such as promissory notes or accepted drafts issued by the customer, an assurance without which the customer could not have borrowed in the commercial paper market. The beneficiary of the financial standby is the holder of the customer's commercial paper or a trustee representing all holders of such paper. The issuing bank's payment is due upon presentation of the commercial paper with a statement or document indicating its non-payment at maturity. A significant reason for the popularity of financial standbys with customers and issuing banks alike is that they have often served as means to circumvent costly regulations such as [the Federal Reserve's former] Regulation Q on interest ceilings. If, for example, the rise of interest rates made it harder to attract deposits and grant loans, banks were able to meet their customers' credit needs by the issuance of standbys that would allow prior customers' borrowing in the open market or from other lenders unaffected by the interest rate ceilings. Similarly, reserve requirements were circumvented throughout the 1960's by "documented notes" or notes accompanied by a standby commitment of the banks' holding companies that promised payment of their member banks' unpaid notes at maturity. Until 1970, the proceeds procured by the banks through these notes were deemed nonreservable funds by regulatory authorities. And while in 1970 they were deemed reservable deposits, shortly thereafter the member banks began issuing standby credits on behalf of their customers to allow them to borrow in the commercial paper market. The standby issuance prevented the need to put up the required reserves, as the loan funds were not channeled through the banks as deposits.

There is no doubt that the difference between non-financial and financial issuances is significant. A bank that assumes the liability to pay upon the presentation of, say, a certificate of inspection stating that the bridge built or merchandise shipped by its account party is defective does not assume the same debt as when it promises to pay upon the presentation of a draft drawn against its branch as a result of the latter's borrowing in the commercial paper market. In the case of payment against the certificate of inspection, the unreimbursed issuing bank has, in effect, lent its money to its customer (shipper or builder), whereas in the case of payment against presentation of the draft, it paid for what was the bank's own borrowing. This situation is fraught with peril, particularly when it disguises the true borrower behind "dummy" corporations. The differences between these, then, must be taken into account by bank and governmental officers concerned with the safety and soundness of banking practices, and is reflected in rules governing lending limits and collateralization. Yet from the standpoint of the risk of unreimbursed payments, the non-financial standby can be as risky as its financial counterpart. Take, for example, the same landmark decision, *American Bell International v. Islamic Republic of Iran*. [This case is excerpted below.] A large American company, American Bell International, requested large seaboard bank in the United States to issue a standby credit guaranteeing its performance of a construction contract in the Shah's Iran. The Iranian government required a local bank, also the United States bank correspondent, to issue the operative letter of credit. As a condition for its issuance, the Iranian bank requested from the United States bank a standby credit "counter-guaranteeing" its own credit to the Iranian government. The standby credit issued by the United States bank was payable upon "simple demand."

When the American Bell International standby credit was issued, the issuing bank's and its customer's assumption was that the then Iranian ruler (or his kind of rule) was to remain in power for a long time. Yet, with changes in ruling groups come changes in contractual relations with the outside world and, not infrequently, demands for payment of standby on bases justifiably deemed fraudulent by the foreign contractor. In *American Bell International*, the U.S. contractor's resort to the equitable remedy of an injunction in the United States against the U.S. bank's payment to its correspondent caused the bank hardships vividly described by the United States District Court of New York as follows:

> To be sure, Bell faces substantial hardships upon denial of its motion [seeking to enjoin the issuing bank's payment of the credit to the revolutionary government of Iran or to its correspondent bank in Iran]....
>
> But Manufacturers [the U.S. issuing bank] would face at least as great a loss, and perhaps a greater one, were we to grant relief. Upon Manufacturers' failure to pay, Bank Iranshahr could initiate a suit on the Letter of Credit and attach $30.2 million of Manufacturers' assets in Iran. In addition, it could

seek to hold Manufacturers liable for consequential damages beyond that sum resulting from the failure to make timely payment. Finally, there is no guarantee that Bank Iranshahr or the government, in retaliation for Manufacturers recalcitrance, will not nationalize additional Manufacturers' assets in Iran in amounts which counsel at oral argument represented to be far in excess of the amount in controversy here.

Thus, the availability of correspondent relations with Iran on the one hand allowed Manufacturers to become involved in what appeared at first sight as a safe and lucrative transaction, but on the other hand, limited its options by increasing its exposure. The ever-present risk of unreimbursed payments, in non-financial and financial standbys alike, makes proper collateralization a central regulatory concern. . . .

The Lloyd-Davies survey reports a utilization of collateral by large banks amounting, on average, to eighteen percent of the value of the standby, whereas the percentage for smaller banks was thirty-eight percent. Mr. Lloyd-Davies attributes the disparity in these averages to the greater likelihood of payments or "takedowns" in the standbys issued by the smaller banks. A sharp disparity, however, was left unexplained in the Lloyd-Davies survey and study. This disparity arises in the collateralization of non-financial standbys issued to foreign and U.S. beneficiaries. The ratio of large bank collateralization in connection with insuring contract performance associated with construction projects to U.S. beneficiaries was approximately $1 of collateral to $30 issued, whereas when issued to foreign beneficiaries the ratio was approximately $1 to $4.50. Since the definition of collateral used by the survey included only "marketable securities, readily marketable commodities and guarantees or standby letters of credit issued by the government, insurance companies or other banks," and did not include balances in the customer's or correspondent's accounts, it may be hypothesized that these balances are being relied upon by large banks as "de facto" collateral when issuing or confirming standbys. The issuance of a standby by a large bank to a U.S. beneficiary can be requested by a bank's local customer, usually a substantial enough depositor to prompt a thinly-collateralized issuance. It is also frequently requested by a foreign correspondent bank with sufficient balances in its account so as to allow the placement of a "hold" ticket or notation on the appropriate amount of the balance once the standby liability ceases to be contingent. In both instances account balances can be used as "de facto" or non-identified collateral until the moment of effective, as distinguished from contingent, liability. Smaller banks generally do not have access to such healthy balances, which could explain the much higher rates of collateralization for the same issuances. Yet, as shown by the *American Bell International* proof of hardship analysis, when the balances are those of a foreign correspondent bank, the collateralization value could well be minimal. Any debiting in the United States would be more than matched by the foreign debiting, attachment, expropriation or confiscation of the U.S. bank's assets.

3. *According to Method and Documentation of Payment*

Banks can issue, notify or confirm another bank's issuance of a standby credit much as they do commercial letters of credit. Standby letters of credit, however, are invariably issued as irrevocable promises of payment, since revocable standbys could not be regarded as reliable assurances of payment. Nevertheless, given the unpredictability of commercial ingenuity, revocable standbys could appear in practice. By the same token, while standbys are most effective assurances when payable at sight, time or acceptance standbys are conceivable and nothing in theory prevents their use.

Standbys are usually payable not against the customary documents in a sale of goods transaction, but against documents that evidence either the beneficiary's performance or the customer's default in the underlying transaction. Significantly, even when the bank's payment is against a document indicating the beneficiary's performance, the standby presupposes a negative antecedent, that is, the customer's lack of payment in the underlying transaction. The operative document that triggers payment varies significantly from credit to credit and can be classified only in accordance with the nature of the issuer and whether or not it purports to prove or certify anything.

The document may be issued by the beneficiary himself, by a third party, or by both the beneficiary and a third party or parties. Documents issued by the beneficiary or by third parties can function as purported evidence of the occurrence or non-occurrence of an act or event, or as formal certifications that the terms and conditions specified in the operative instrument have been met. The less assertive the document is in terms of the occurrence of an act or event, the less is the need for the bank's scrutiny. A failure to supply, say, building materials according to underlying contract specifications in a certificate of inspection is bound to contain more troublesome terms and assertions than is a mere statement by the beneficiary that "the failure described in the letter of credit has taken place." And when the required document is the "simple demand" type of guarantee, or is one in which the beneficiary only expresses his demand for payment without need of proof of the occurrence of any act or event or certification of the existence of the conditions for payment, the bank's scrutiny is limited to establishing the authenticity of the beneficiary's signature or his identity. By contrast with other types of documentation, the beneficiary in a simple demand type of credit makes no representations to the bank and is therefore immune from the issuing, confirming, or paying bank's actions for misrepresentation or for unjust enrichment as a result of a mistaken payment, except for the warranties of genuineness of his signature and accuracy of his identification. Undoubtedly, all these reasons must have weighed heavily in the decision not to include simple demand guarantees in the I.C.C. Rules.

Simple demand standby credits are as objectionable as simple demand guarantees. A simple demand beneficiary implicitly rejects the bank's role as the issuer of the basic assurances to both parties and transforms the bank into a pliant custodian of funds which can become the beneficiary's at his discretion. Here, then, lies a key distinction from the so-called "clean" or non-documentary commercial letter of credit, or a letter of credit payable simply against the beneficiary's draft. When a customer agrees to a clean commercial letter of credit, it is not as a result of the beneficiary's imposition but of the customer's own convenience. Since their inception these credits have been issued, as Karl Llewellyn reported, in anticipation of consignment shipments or where the beneficiary was the customer's trusted agent for the purchase of merchandise. By contrast, for example, the Libyan Government bank's status as a beneficiary of the simple demand credit objected to by the German Banker's Association entitled it to payment even in the face of a court of appropriate jurisdiction's injunction against payment. The Libyan bank's disregard for the issuing bank's role as a trusted intermediary and for the function of courts in pluralistic legal systems is characteristic of a contemporary Persian Gulf version of the Golden Rule: "He who has the black gold, rules." Predictably, however, as more and more account parties become the victims of beneficiary arbitrariness, the simple demand standby will be rejected by all but the neediest, silliest or greediest of account parties.

. . . .

B. Standby L/Cs Versus Guarantees

Banque Paribas v. Hamilton Industries International, Inc.
767 F.2D 380 (7th Cir. 1985)

POSNER, Circuit Judge.

This appeal presents a dispute over an international letter of credit. Hamilton Industries International, a Wisconsin corporation, bid for a subcontract with Saudi Medcenter, Ltd. (SMC), a Saudi Arabian corporation that had bid on a contract to do construction work for a Saudi Arabian university. SMC required that Hamilton's bid be guaranteed. Bid guarantees are common in construction work. If the contractor has to guarantee his bid (as in fact Saudi Arabian law requires...), he will want guarantees of his subcontractors' bids. If Hamilton backed out of its deal with SMC, the latter might not be able to make good on its bid guarantee at all, and at least would have to make a new subcontract with someone else, maybe on much worse terms.

Hamilton obtained a letter of credit from American National Bank in Chicago for $290,700, the amount of security demanded by SMC (equal to one percent of the amount of Hamilton's bid). This is what is called a "standby" letter of credit, as its purpose was to provide security for the beneficiary, SMC, against a default by its supplier, Hamilton. The letter of credit names the Bahrain branch of the Banque de Paris et des Pays-Bas (Paribas) as "advising" bank, and states that American National Bank will pay Paribas the amount of the letter of credit upon Paribas' demand if accompanied by "your [Paribas'] signed statement certifying that you have been called upon to make payment under your guaranty issued in favor of" SMC. As the letter of credit thus contemplates that Paribas will pay the beneficiary of the letter of credit (SMC), pursuant to Paribas' guarantee, and then be reimbursed by American National Bank, the issuing bank, Paribas' actual status was probably that of a "confirming" rather than "advising" bank. An alternative characterization is that the guarantee was actually a letter of credit issued by Paribas, with American National Bank the beneficiary. We shall see that for purposes of deciding this appeal nothing turns on whether Paribas is deemed the confirming bank or the issuer of a second letter of credit of which the American National Bank was the beneficiary.

The letter of credit issued by American National Bank states, "we have issued the above letter of credit in your favor in consideration of your [Paribas'] issuance of a letter of guarantee in favor of" SMC, the letter "to expire on February 28, 1983" and to be "in accordance with Exhibit A attached." Exhibit A is a "Form of Tender Letter of Guarantee," addressed to SMC, and intended to be signed by Paribas. The critical undertakings in the guarantee are the following: "we the Guarantor hereby unconditionally agrees [sic] to pay to you forthwith following demand made by you in writing (which writing shall refer to the number and date of this letter of guarantee) to our agent" the amount guaranteed, i.e., $290,700; and "the Guarantor's Agent must receive your written demand hereunder within the period of the effectiveness of this letter of guarantee"—i.e., no later than February 28. The letter of credit itself was to expire on March 15. The guarantee recites that it shall be construed in accordance with Saudi Arabian law.

Paribas retyped the guarantee on its own letterhead, signed it, and sent it to SMC. On February 24, 1983, SMC telephoned Paribas, demanding payment under the guarantee. Paribas cabled American National Bank the same day advising it that Paribas had been called upon to pay SMC under the terms of the guarantee, and requesting American National Bank to treat the cable as Paribas' formal demand for payment to it under the letter of credit. Before the letter of credit expired on March 15 Paribas followed up the cabled demand to American National Bank with a signed written statement certifying that Paribas had been called on to make payment to SMC in accordance with the guarantee.

According to Paribas, on February 28, the last day on which the guarantee was in force, Paribas received the following telex from SMC: "Subject: King Saud Project. . . . This confirms the telephone conversation the undersigned had with you this afternoon, wherein it was requested that the letter of credit established by Hamilton Industries in favor of SMC in connection with a bank guarantee on the above subject be called off." Paribas' deputy manager in Bahrain testified by affidavit that this telex was intended (despite the wording, which suggests the opposite, and the discrepancy in dates) to confirm the telephone demand of February 24 for payment of the guarantee. But it was not until March that SMC sent Paribas a written demand that actually recited the number and date of the guarantee. Although the guarantee had expired, Paribas paid SMC anyway, and then repeated its demand for reimbursement by American National Bank, which refused and brought this suit.

The suit bases jurisdiction on diversity; interpleads Hamilton, SMC, and Paribas under Rule 22 of the Federal Rules of Civil Procedure; and asks the court to decide who is entitled to the $290,700 that American National Bank has refused to pay Paribas. Since Hamilton has agreed to hold American National Bank harmless should American be ordered to pay Paribas, the real fight is between Hamilton and Paribas. A separate fight between Hamilton and SMC over the subcontract is not involved in this appeal.

On Hamilton's motion for summary judgment against Paribas, the district court held that Paribas had paid SMC under the guarantee in violation of the terms of the letter of credit. It reasoned as follows: the guarantee was a part of the letter of credit, so that American National Bank was not obligated to make good on the letter of credit unless Paribas complied with the terms of the guarantee; Paribas had failed to comply with those terms, by paying SMC even though the only written demand that SMC had made before the guarantee expired — the telex of February 28 — contained no reference to the number and date of the guarantee. Having concluded that Paribas was not entitled to payment from American National Bank under the letter of credit, the district court dismissed as moot Hamilton's cross-claim against Paribas (a claim we take up at the end of this opinion). The court certified both of its orders — the order granting Hamilton's motion for summary judgment against Paribas and the order dismissing Hamilton's cross-claim as moot — under Rule 54(b) of the Federal Rules of Civil Procedure for immediate appeal. This was proper, since the two orders, between them, disposed of the entire dispute between Paribas and Hamilton.

The parties have treated us to a learned debate on many fine points of commercial law, but it seems to us that the decision of this appeal must turn on the simple principle that a contract dispute cannot be resolved on summary judgment when the meaning of the contract depends on the interpretation of ambiguous documents and can be illuminated by oral testimony. The critical issue on which Paribas' right to reimbursement for the money it paid out to SMC turns is whether it was a condition precedent to that right that Paribas receive a written demand from SMC specifying the date and number of the guarantee that Paribas had issued to SMC. This issue can be decomposed into two questions: Did the guarantee make such specification a condition precedent? If so was the guarantee meant to be incorporated in American National Bank's letter of credit, which defines Paribas' right of reimbursement? Only if both questions can be answered "yes" on the record of the summary judgment proceeding was Hamilton entitled to summary judgment.

1. Conceivably, although improbably, the requirement in the guarantee of a written demand that "shall refer to the number and date of this letter of guarantee" is solely for the protection of the guarantor, Paribas, and waivable by it, rather than even partly for the protection of American National Bank. (The expiration date on the letter of credit is an example of a provision clearly intended for the protection of the issuing bank, American National Bank, and its customer, Hamilton.) If Paribas in response to an incomplete written demand paid the wrong person or paid too much, it would be stuck; it could not get reimbursement from American National Bank. *See Voest-Alpine Int'l Corp. v. Chase Manhattan Bank, N.A.*, 707 F.2d 680, 686 (2d Cir. 1983). But as a matter of fact it paid the right amount to the right person, and it is not obvious why American National Bank (or Hamilton) should benefit from Paribas' risk-taking. It was not, to repeat, a risk taken with American National Bank's money or Hamilton's money, since if Paribas made a mistake it would be its mistake, and it would bear the cost. True, there is another problem with the demand. The telex of February 28 is mysterious; on its face, it isn't a demand at all. But its sufficiency is not an issue that can be resolved on summary judgment. Maybe in light of earlier phone conversations, in particular the one on February 24, the telex was perfectly clear.

All this, however, may take too narrow a view of the situation. It ignores the long tradition of requiring strict compliance with the terms of a letter of credit, a tradition which, though challenged, as so many of the strict requirements of the law are challenged nowadays, has managed to retain its vitality. *See, e.g., Beyene v. Irving Trust Co.*, 762 F.2d 4, 6 (2d Cir.1985). We may assume, without affecting our decision, that it continues in full force. In defense of the traditional approach it can be pointed out that since the customer of the issuing bank may have no practical recourse against the beneficiary of the letter of credit who makes a fraudulent demand for payment under it — Hamilton might have trouble obtaining relief from a Saudi Arabian corporation, though in fact it is litigating with SMC in the district court — the customer depends on the issuing bank to scrutinizing the demand for payment with great care and to insist upon literal compliance with all the conditions on payment. This case may seem different in that the customer has the additional protection represented by the confirming bank, but the additional protection may be quite illusory. That bank may be a local firm in cahoots with the beneficiary, yet once it pays the beneficiary the issuing bank has to reimburse it. This makes it all the more important that the confirming bank be required to comply with the literal terms of the letter of credit, to minimize the likelihood that a fraudulent demand for payment will be made and accepted.

This insight may lie behind the rule that the confirming bank has the same obligations to the issuing bank, viewed as its customer, as the issuing bank has to the original customer. *See, e.g., Voest-Alpine Int'l Corp. v. Chase Manhattan Bank, N.A., supra*, 707 F.2d at 686....It thus would make no difference whether Paribas was a confirming bank, as we have suggested was probably the case, or the issuer of a second letter of credit (the guarantee) of which American National Bank was the beneficiary, which would make this a case of "back to back" letters of credit. Paribas' obligations, and the argument for insisting on strict compliance, would be the same.

But the argument for strict compliance comes up against an insuperable obstacle in the present TOC3case: the stipulation in the guarantee that it is to be interpreted in accordance with Saudi Arabian law. Hamilton does not argue that such a stipulation is unenforceable. And according to the affidavit by Paribas' deputy manager in Bahrain, under Saudi law the guarantee, despite its apparently clear wording, would have required Paribas to pay SMC in response to an oral demand (provided that the documents specified in the letter were furnished later, as they were), because the mails are very uncertain in Saudi Arabia. The affidavit, which was competent and uncontradicted though not conclusive evidence of foreign law, suggests — not implausibly in light of what little we have been able to learn about the commercial law of Saudi Arabia on our own, that Saudi Arabia does not insist on strict compliance even with guarantees incorporated in letters of credit; substantial compliance, generously construed, is quite enough. Supposing this is so — a hypothesis that the district judge was not entitled to reject when no contrary evidence had been introduced, or independent research into Saudi law conducted by him — Paribas could not be refused reimbursement by American National Bank. It would put Paribas in an intolerable position for the courts to say, your obligations to SMC are governed by the guarantee as interpreted under Saudi law but your rights against American National Bank are governed by the guarantee as inconsistently interpreted under American law. The effect would be to make Paribas rather than Hamilton the ultimate guarantor of Hamilton's subcontract with SMC; and that was no one's intention.

Of course Paribas would deserve no judicial sympathy if it were in cahoots with SMC to obtain money from Hamilton though no default had occurred. Fraud is a defense to payment of a letter of credit, *see, e.g., Harris Corp. v. National Iranian Radio & Television*, 691 F.2d 1344, 1354-55 (11th Cir.1982); . . . and has been a hot issue in connection with another Middle Eastern country recently. Maybe at trial American National Bank and Hamilton can prove that Paribas schemed with SMC to defraud Hamilton, but this question cannot be decided on a summary judgment record that contains, in fact, no evidence of fraud. It would be premature for us to attempt to determine the outer bounds of the defense of fraud in this setting. . . .

Even if, contrary to what we have said, Paribas violated the guarantee as a matter of law when it paid SMC, it would not follow that Paribas violated the terms of the letter of credit. The issue would then be, did the parties intend the guarantee to be incorporated in the letter of credit, so that compliance with the guarantee was required for compliance with the letter of credit? Unresolved factual questions make it impossible to resolve this issue on summary judgment.

The letter of credit — explicitly anyway — attaches only one condition to paying Paribas: that before the date of expiration of the letter on March 15 Paribas submit a "signed statement certifying that you have been called upon to make payment under your guaranty issued in favor of" SMC. Paribas mailed such a statement to American National Bank on February 28, which was well before the expiration date of March 15; American National Bank acknowledged the receipt of the statement by telex sent on March 15. There thus was literal compliance with the terms of the letter of credit; whether more was required cannot be resolved on the record of the summary judgment proceeding.

The district court thought that the cable Paribas sent American National Bank on February 24 advising that it had been called on to make payment to SMC "under the terms of your letter of credit" was a false representation that dis-entitled Paribas to payment under the letter of credit. However, there was no falsity if the letter of credit did not incorporate the guarantee (or if, as discussed above, Paribas did not violate the guarantee). The letter of credit does not in words make payment conditional on compliance with every detail of the guarantee; the guarantee is described merely as consideration for American National Bank's promise to pay Paribas upon demand. It is possible that the purpose of all this is to incorporate the guarantee in the letter of credit, but no more than possible. After all, the guarantee was intended for SMC's protection rather than Hamilton's. Maybe therefore the parties did not intend to condition Paribas' right to payment under the letter of credit on strict compliance with the conditions in the guarantee.

To summarize, we are clear neither that Paribas paid SMC in violation of the guarantee nor that a violation of the guarantee would automatically violate the letter of credit. Interpreted as it must be in accordance with Saudi Arabian law, the guarantee is ambiguous; and the letter of credit is ambiguous as to whether it incorporates the guarantee. Ambiguities in a letter of credit, as in other contracts, are resolved against the drafter, in this case American National Bank, which therefore was not entitled to summary judgment. On remand, the district court should first determine, in accordance with Rule 44.1 of the Federal Rules of Civil Procedure, whether there was any violation of the guarantee, when that guarantee is interpreted in accordance with Saudi Arabian law. If not, then unless some fraud between Paribas and SMC is shown, Hamilton's claim against Paribas must be rejected. If there was a violation of the guarantee, the issue whether the guarantee was incorporated in the letter of credit will then become material and will be an issue for trial since the letter is ambiguous.

The district judge dismissed Hamilton's cross-claim against Paribas as moot, an action Hamilton challenges on the ground that Paribas' payment of the guarantee to SMC imposed certain costs on Hamilton, so that even if it does not have to make good the $290,700 to Paribas (via American National Bank) it still has a dispute with Paribas. Since the finding of mootness is based on an order (holding that Paribas is not entitled to reimbursement of the $290,700 from Hamilton) that we are reversing, the order dismissing the cross-claim must also be reversed. Costs in this court are awarded to Paribas.

Reversed and Remanded.

C. Expiration of Standby L/Cs

Exxon Company, U.S.A. v. Banque de Paris et des Pays Bas
828 F.2D 1121 (5th Cir. 1987)

ALVIN B. RUBIN, CIRCUIT JUDGE:

Standby letters of credit are issued by banks to assure the prompt payment of money to a party to another contract in the event that the other contract is not performed in accordance with its terms. The issuing bank is required to make payment only if it is presented with specified documents. The function of letters of credit requires that they be succinct and clear, for their utility lies in the assurance they provide that payment will be made on the specified terms without delay or litigation.

In this action for the wrongful dishonor of a letter of credit on which payment was demanded after the stated expiry date of the credit, we find that the obligation of the issuing bank had terminated even though it might not have been possible to present to the bank the documents required for payment before the expiry date. We therefore reverse the district court judgment holding the bank liable.

I.

In July 1981, Houston Oil & Refining, Inc. entered into a contract with Exxon Company, U.S.A., under which Exxon would deliver 558,000 barrels of crude oil to Houston in July and Houston would deliver an equal quantity of crude oil to Exxon "during September through December 1981." Exxon made this trade because it had closed part of one of its refineries for maintenance and therefore had a surplus of crude oil. The contract required Houston to provide an irrevocable standby letter of credit to cover the value of the oil delivered by Exxon. It stated that the letter of credit was to be payable to Exxon "on presentation of invoices or [a] statement of an officer of Exxon certifying that invoices are unpaid and past due ten (10) days or more."

Houston then applied to Banque de Paris et des Pays-Bas, also known as Paribas, for a letter of credit in the amount of $19,530,000. In its application, Houston stated that the letter of credit was to be payable upon presentation of specified invoices; pipeline tickets or transfer statements; and a

> [s]tatement signed by an authorized representative certifying that Houston Oil & Refining, Inc. has *failed to deliver to* Exxon Company, U.S.A. 558,000 barrels of one of the following: South Louisiana to St. James, La., West Texas Sour to Shell, McCamey or Exxon, Crane, Arab Light to U.S. Gulf Coast or Alaskan North Slope to U.S. Gulf Coast *between September and December, 1981.*

The application also expressly requested that the letter of credit expire on October 31, 1981.

Because the transaction was in effect an extension of credit to Houston, Paribas required Houston to provide security sufficient to cover the amount of the credit, and, as part of the security arrangement, the bank blocked certain funds coming into Houston's account. In addition, Paribas charged Houston a fee of $53,000 for establishing the credit.

On July 16, 1981, Paribas "opened" the credit by telex and delivered a copy of it to Exxon as requested by Houston. The credit stated that it was to be paid against the documents specified in the application, and that these documents "must be presented not later than October 31, 1981." Because October 31 would be a Saturday, the documents could also be presented on the next business day, Monday, November 2. The credit also stated that it was subject to the 1974 revision of the *Uniform Customs & Practice for Documentary Credits*, a set of rules promulgated by the International Chamber of Commerce.

Because the letter *expired on October 31*, yet covered deliveries *between September and December*, Paribas checked with Houston twice — both before and after issuing the letter — to make sure that the terms specified by Houston in its application were indeed what it had intended. Before the letter was issued, Flozella Telfair, the Paribas employee who dealt with the application, noted the apparent inconsistency and communicated with Houston. Upon receiving Houston's affirmation that the terms were correct, Telfair drew circles on the application around both the October 31 expiration date and the September-December period specified for delivery, and next to these terms made the notation "OK as per HOR and R.P." (HOR was Houston, and R.P. was Rene Perdreaux, a Paribas lending officer responsible for the Houston account.) Subsequently, after the letter had been issued, Hal Peist, a letter of credit professional at Paribas, discussed its terms with Robert Wheelock at Houston and asked whether a change in the expiration date was desired. Wheelock responded negatively.

When the credit was opened, Paribas sent a copy of the letter to the attention of Don Meiers, the Exxon employee responsible for receiving and transmitting letters of credit and monitoring their expiration dates. Meiers received the letter of credit and transmitted it to the appropriate executives at Exxon with a letter stating that it "is due to expire October 31, 1981." Meiers' transmittal letter also noted that the credit covered the delivery of crude oil by Exxon during July and "the return" of the crude by Houston "between September and December 1981." No one at Exxon complained or even suggested that these terms were not fully satisfactory.

Exxon was an experienced trader of crude oil. It commonly balanced its crude oil supply by entering into exchanges and, unless it was dealing with a major oil company, secured those exchanges by receiving letters of credit issued in its favor. Exxon knew from its experience that it could insist on the amendment of unsatisfactory letters of credit, and it followed the practice of delaying the delivery of crude oil to its trading partners until it had actually received a satisfactory letter.

Houston made no delivery of crude oil to Exxon during September or October of 1981. Before October 31, Meiers brought the problem of Exxon's exposure to loss under the exchange contract to the attention of higher management at Exxon. Exxon asked Houston to obtain an extension of the letter of credit, but did not communicate with Paribas. On October 30, Joe Imparato, the president of Houston and a former Exxon employee, said that he would extend the letter of credit on Monday, November 2; however, he did not do so. When Imparato visited Exxon during the week of November 2, he stated that Houston would not be able to return the crude oil under the contract, and asked whether Exxon would be willing to convert Houston's obligation into a long term debt. Exxon's representatives told Imparato that such an arrangement would be unsatisfactory, and that they would insist on performance as required by the contract.

During November, Paribas released both the security that it had held for its extension of credit to Houston and the funds that it had blocked in Houston's account. Subsequently, on November 30 and on December 1, Exxon attempted to obtain payment by presenting documents to Paribas. Paribas rejected both presentations as untimely.

II.

The district court found a "clash" between the expiry date in the letter and the dates specified for performance of the underlying contract. It held, however, that the letter of credit was not ambiguous because its meaning could be made certain "by application of the rules of [contract] construction." The court resolved the "inconsistency" in part by interpreting the letter of credit against its author, the bank — a rule of construction that generally applies only to clarify ambiguity — and by reading the letter in such fashion as to make performance possible. The court thus construed the contract "in favor of Exxon" and, extending but not defining the expiry date, entered summary judgment in Exxon's favor.

III.

A letter of credit "means an engagement by a bank...made at the request of a customer...that the issuer will honor drafts or other demands for payment upon compliance with the conditions specified in the credit." The purpose of a standby letter is to insure that one or more parties to a contract will perform their duties under it. The credit substitutes a known, accessible, and demonstrably impeccable source of funds in the event of default by the party whose performance it guarantees. Letters of credit facilitate commercial transactions, particularly in international commerce, by assuring certainty in application, consistency in interpretation across jurisdictional boundaries, and swiftness in execution. By eliminating credit risks, they reduce the cost of commercial transactions.

The transaction involves three separate contracts: The first one is the underlying commercial contract between two parties, one of whom will later apply to a bank for the letter, and the other of whom will be the beneficiary of the letter. The terms of this contract may not become known to the bank. The second contract is between the issuer of the letter of credit — typically a commercial bank — and its customer, who in applying for the letter asks the bank to draft the letter in conformance with specified terms. The third contract, the letter of credit itself, is between the issuer and the beneficiary. The issuer unconditionally and irrevocably binds itself to pay a specified sum upon presentation of documents complying with the terms of the credit. The issuer's obligation to pay the beneficiary is generally independent of any obligation of the issuer's customer to the beneficiary, and the issuer has no obligation to pay unless the beneficiary strictly complies with the conditions contained in the credit. An issuer who makes payment upon a presentation that does not conform to the requirements of the credit loses its right to repayment from its customers.

A letter of credit is therefore strictly construed. The issuer is required to act in good faith and to observe any general banking usage, but is not charged with the responsibility for knowledge or lack of knowledge of any usage of the trade in which the customer and beneficiary are involved. It must determine whether to make payment to the beneficiary "on the basis of the documents [presented to it] alone." A half century ago, when a particular letter of credit did not specify an expiration date, courts required that necessary documents be presented to the issuing bank "within a reasonable time." Eventually, that formulation proved to be commercially unsatisfactory because it left a bank's obligation uncertain and open-ended. To solve this problem, the International Chamber of Commerce adopted the *Uniform Customs & Practice for Documentary Credits*. Article 37 of the *Uniform Customs* requires all letters of credit made subject to it to stipulate an expiry date. [This provision is contained in Article 43 of the 1993 revision of the UCP, UCP500.] Paribas' letter of credit expressly incorporated by reference the *Uniform Customs*, and therefore by necessity stated a specific termination date.

The need for a precise expiration date is particularly acute when a standby letter of credit is issued. Although such a credit is different from a surety bond or a guaranty, it does assure payment in the event the account party fails to perform an underlying contract with the beneficiary, the terms of which may be unknown to the issuer. The standby credit is therefore an extension of a bank's credit to its customer and, for this reason, it is subject to the statutory and regulatory loan limits imposed upon lending institutions. Because the issuer of a standby credit does not hold documents representing goods in a commercial transaction, it cannot look to those documents as security for repayment by its customer. Therefore, the issuer must look solely to the financial strength of its customer and to whatever security it has required for issuance of the credit. The length of time that an issuer remains liable for a failure to perform by its customer is obviously a matter of critical importance to the issuing bank, to the customer who must pay for the credit, and to the regulatory authorities that monitor the bank's activities. Good banking practice and common sense require that the bank's liability terminate at a date certain.

IV.

The issue before us is not the clarification of a contract susceptible to more than one interpretation. The expiry date in the letter of credit is as certain as words permit. The requirement in the letter that Exxon certify, no later than October 31, 1981, that Houston "has failed to deliver...between September and December, 1981" created no uncertainty on the face of the letter as to its expiration date.

Counsel for both sides have stated that the phrasing of the required certification, that Houston *"has failed to deliver"* the crude oil, excludes the possibility of presentation before the end of the stated delivery period. If that were indeed Exxon's understanding, then it should have refused the letter when tendered. The terms of the credit departed in more than one respect from the Exxon-Houston contract. As we have noted, that contract provided that the credit was to be payable "on presentation of invoices or [a] statement of an officer of Exxon certifying that invoices are unpaid and past due ten (10) days or more," and also provided that deliveries were to be made during September through December. Houston instead applied to Paribas for a letter of credit requiring a statement "by an authorized representative certifying that Houston has failed to deliver... between September and December." If either these discrepancies or the expiry date did not satisfy Exxon, it simply should have declined to accept the credit and refused to deliver oil to Houston. Exxon's decision to deliver suggests the possibility that, as contended by counsel for Paribas, Exxon was relying at least in part on its business dealings with Houston and its relationship with Imparato, a former crude oil trader at Exxon.

Exxon does not suggest that Paribas acted fraudulently. Nor does Exxon allege that Houston specified the expiration date of October 31 as the result of inadvertence or mistake, or that Exxon was mistaken as to that date when it accepted the letter. Indeed, the evidence shows that Exxon employees noted the expiry date upon their receipt of the letter of credit and that in late October Exxon asked Houston to obtain an extension of the expiry date.

Exxon does assert that Paribas did not act in "good faith" toward Exxon when it issued a letter of credit that its employees had questioned as "not mak[ing] sense" when Paribas knew that the letter was designed to secure Houston's contractual obligations to Exxon. No authority has been cited to us, and we have found none, that imposes on an issuer a duty to the beneficiary to "make sense" of the customer's application. As provided by Tex.Bus. & Com.Code Ann. § 5.109(a), Paribas did owe a duty of good faith to Houston, its customer. Tex.Bus. & Com.Code Ann. § 1.201(19) defines the standard of "good faith" as "honesty in fact in the conduct or transaction concerned." As mentioned earlier, Paribas checked with Houston both before and after issuing the letter to make sure that the terms specified in the application were what Houston intended. Thus, Paribas acted honestly toward Houston. Paribas' acceptance of Houston's assurances could not indicate dishonesty toward Exxon, for the expiration date was apparent on the letter when Paribas delivered it to Exxon. Paribas could tell Exxon no more than what was on the face of the letter, and Paribas knew that Exxon could insist on amendments to the letter if it was not satisfied. Moreover, as already noted, Exxon has not alleged fraud against the bank or Houston. Paribas therefore complied entirely with the terms of the letter when it interpreted the credit as having expired on November 2 and released its security to Houston.

As a lawyer experienced in letter of credit transactions has written, cautioning issuers, "the legality of a letter-of-credit transaction should not be equated with its prudence or commercial sense." In like measure, the issuer is not charged with determining the utility to, or prudence of, a beneficiary who acts in reliance on its letter of credit. In letter-of-credit transactions, as in many other legal areas, certainty of result and practicality of performance by laymen are of paramount importance. As Exxon asserts, it was required to comply with "whatever requirements that Paribas established" "to the last comma, the last semicolon, ... and, if they [did] that, they [were] entitled to be paid." It follows that, if Exxon did not do that, it was not entitled to be paid.

We therefore hold that the letter of credit issued by Paribas required no construction and that it terminated on its express expiry date. The summary judgment is *reversed* and judgment is entered for Paribas.

D. Enjoining Payment on a Standby L/C

Stromberg-Carlson Corporation v. Bank Melli Iran
467 F.Supp. 530 (S.D.N.Y. 1979)

EDWARD WEINFELD, DISTRICT JUDGE.

This is a diversity action by Stromberg-Carlson Corporation ("Stromberg-Carlson"), a Delaware corporation engaging in the manufacture and sale of telecommunications equipment, against Bank Melli Iran ("Melli"); an Iranian banking corporation with an agency office in New York registered with the State Superintendent of Banks. Stromberg-Carlson seeks to enjoin Melli from making payment on two bank guarantees in favor of the "Imperial Government of Iran" without first notifying plaintiff in writing of receipt of a demand for payment and giving plaintiff ten days in which to (1) provide evidence as to lack of authenticity or fraudulent nature of the demand, or (2) take such other action as plaintiff deems appropriate.....

On or about October 6, 1976, plaintiff entered into an agreement ("the contract") with the Imperial Government of Iran, which at that time was headed by His Imperial Majesty Mohammed Reza Shah Pahlavi Aryamehr ("Shah of Iran"), pursuant to which plaintiff agreed to engineer, manufacture, ship, install and maintain in Iran certain telecommunications equipment for which it would receive in excess of $5,500,000 from the Imperial Government. Of this amount $1,390,230 was paid by the Imperial Government to plaintiff as an advance payment.

As a condition of the contract and to secure the advance payment, Stromberg-Carlson was required to obtain two bank guarantees in favor of the Imperial Government. These guarantees, which were issued by defendant Melli, are in the respective amounts of $556,091, guaranteeing performance of the contract, and $1,390,230, guaranteeing repayment of the advance payment in the event of a failure to perform the contract. The two guarantees are now outstanding and are payable by Melli on demand by the Imperial Government without notice to plaintiff.

To obtain the bank guarantees, plaintiff caused irrevocable letters of credit to be issued by Continental Illinois Bank & Trust Co. of Chicago for the benefit of Melli in amounts corresponding to the guarantees. The letters of credit are payable upon Melli's declaration that it has been called upon to effect payment to the Imperial Government, again without notice to plaintiff.

By early February 1979, Stromberg-Carlson had engineered, manufactured and shipped all of the equipment required under the contract and had installed and maintained a substantial portion thereof. Recent events in Iran, however, both before and after the return of the Ayatollah Ruhollah Khomeini, have interrupted transportation and communication systems and disrupted governmental, business and banking functions in Iran. The "present period is one of crisis and uncertainty." According to plaintiff, this state of affairs poses a substantial threat that individuals within Iran, neither duly authorized by the Imperial Government nor in accord with its policies at the time the contract, guarantees and letters of credit were entered into, may issue an unauthorized demand for payment under the bank guarantees for reasons entirely unrelated to performance by Stromberg-Carlson of its duties under the contract.

Plaintiff has no practical means of determining the authenticity of, or absence of fraud in, any demand for payment which might be made under the Melli guarantees, nor can any reliable information be obtained as to whether such demands have been or are about to be made.

In light of the foregoing, plaintiff has established its entitlement to a preliminary injunction under the standard prevailing in this Circuit. Under the present circumstances in Iran, there is a serious risk that a fraudulent or nonauthentic demand could be issued on the Melli guarantees. [Under the Uniform Commercial Code § 5-114(a)(2), a court may enjoin a bank from honoring the demand for payment when the bank has been notified by its customer that a required document is forged or fraudulent or that there is fraud in the transaction. The "fraud" exception to the traditional reluctance of courts to interfere with commercial letters of credit and guarantees has been liberally construed in the decisional law both prior and subsequent to the adoption of the Code. *See, e.g.,... United Bank Ltd. v. Cambridge Sporting Goods Corp.*, 41 N.Y.2d 254,..., (1976); *Sztejn v. J. Henry Schroder Banking Corp.*, 31 N.Y.S.2d 631 (Sup. Ct. 1941)....The provisions of the *Uniform Customs and Practice for Documentary Credits* promulgated by the International Chamber of Commerce are not to the contrary. *United Banking Ltd. v. Cambridge Sporting Goods Corp.*, 41 N.Y.2d at 258 n.2....] It is clear that the "Imperial Government" with which plaintiff negotiated its contract and in favor of which the bank guarantees were issued has ceased to function. Moreover, the views of the current government with respect to the contract are completely unknown and may well differ, in fact conflict with those of the former government.

Plaintiff does not seek to alter the terms of the underlying contract nor does it now request an injunction against eventual payment. Although the modest relief requested would require reading a notice requirement into the provisions of the bank guarantee, "the fluid and precarious circumstances now prevailing in Iran justify deviation from what would otherwise be a strong reluctance" to do so.

In the absence of an injunction, plaintiff, in the event of a fraudulent demand, would be called upon to pay close to $2 million under the guarantees without notice and an opportunity to call the fraud to the attention of the bank. Plaintiff's sole remedy would be to institute an action in the courts of Iran, which in light of the present situation would make any relief questionable. Finally, defendant has not alleged that it would be prejudiced in any way if a ten-day notice requirement is imposed.

In sum, plaintiff has raised serious questions going to the merits of the litigation and the balance of hardships tips decidedly in its favor. The requested injunction is therefore granted.

American Bell International, Inc. v. Islamic Republic of Iran
474 F.Supp. 420 (S.D.N.Y. 1979)
MACMAHON, DISTRICT JUDGE.

Plaintiff American Bell International Inc ("Bell") moves for a preliminary injunction pursuant to Rule 65(a), Fed. R. Civ. P, enjoining defendant Manufacturers Hanover Trust Company ("Manufacturers") from making any payment under its Letter of Credit No. SC 170027 to defendants the Islamic Republic of Iran or Bank Iranshahr or their agents, instrumentalities, successors, employees and assigns. We held an evidentiary hearing and heard oral argument o August 3, 1979. The following facts appear from the evidence presented.

The action arises from the recent revolution in Iran and its impact upon contracts made with the ousted Imperial Government of Iran and upon banking arrangements incident to such contracts. Bell, a wholly-owned subsidiary of American Telephone & Telegraph Co. ("AT & T"), made a contract on July 23, 1978 (the "Contract") with the Imperial Government of Iran—Ministry of War ("Imperial Government") to provide consulting services and equipment to the Imperial Government as part of a program to improve Iran's international communications system.

The Contract provides a complex mechanism for payment to Bell totaling approximately $280,000,000, including a down payment of $38,800,000. The Imperial Government had the right to demand return of the down payment at any time. The amount so "callable, however, was to be reduced by 20% of the amounts invoiced by Bell to which the Imperial Government did not object. Bell's liability for return of the down payment was reduced by application of this mechanism as the Contract was performed, with the result that approximately $30,200,000 of the down payment now remains callable.

In order to secure the return of the down payment on demand, Bell was required to establish an unconditional and irrevocable Letter of Guaranty, to be issued by Bank Iranshahr in the amount of $38,800,000 in favor of the Imperial Government. The Contract provides that it is to be governed by the laws of Iran and that all disputes arising under it are to be resolved by the Iranian courts.

Bell obtained a Letter of Guaranty from Bank Iranshahr. In turn, as required by Bank Iranshahr, Bell obtained a standby Letter of Credit, No. SC 170027, issued by Manufacturers in favor of Bank Iranshahr in the amount of $38,800,000 to secure reimbursement to Bank Iranshahr should it be required to pay the Imperial Government under its Letter of Guaranty.

The standby Letter of Credit provided for payment by Manufacturers to Bank Iranshahr upon receipt of:

"Your [Bank Iranshahr's] dated statement purportedly signed by an officer indicating name and title or your Tested Telex Reading: (A) 'Referring Manufacturers Hanover Trust Co. Credit No. SC170027, the amount of our claim $ represents funds due us as we have received a written request the Imperial Government of Iran Ministry of War to pay them the sum of under our Guarantee No. issued for the account of American Bell International Inc. covering advance payment under Contract No. 138 dated July 23, 1978 and such payment -has been made by us'...."

In the application for the Letter of Credit, Bell agreed — guaranteed by AT & T — immediately to reimburse Manufacturers for all amounts paid by Manufacturers to Bank Iranshahr pursuant to the Letter of Credit.

Bell commenced performance of its Contract with the Imperial Government. It provided certain services and equipment to update Iran's communications system and submitted a number of invoices, some of which were paid.

In late 1978 and early 1979, Iran was wreaked with revolutionary turmoil culminating in the overthrow of the Iranian government and its replacement by the Islamic Republic. In the wake of this upheaval, Bell was left with substantial unpaid invoices and claims under the Contract and ceased its performance in January 1979. Bell claims that the Contract was breached by the Imperial Government, as well as repudiated by the Islamic Republic, in that it is owed substantial sums for services rendered under the Contract and its termination provisions.

On February 16, 1979, before a demand had been made by Bank Iranshahr for payment under the Letter of Credit, Bell and AT & T brought an action against Manufacturers in the Supreme Court, New York, County, seeking a preliminary injunction prohibiting Manufacturers from honoring any demand for payment under the Letter of Credit. The motion for a preliminary injunction was denied in a thorough opinion by Justice Dontzin on March 26, 1979, and the denial was unanimously affirmed on appeal by the Appellate Division, First Department.

On July 25 and 29, 1979, Manufacturers received demands by Tested Telex from Bank Iranshahr for Payment of $30,220,724 under the Letter of Credit, the remaining balance of the down payment. Asserting that the demand did conform with the Letter of Credit, Manufacturers declined payment and so informed Bank Iranshahr. Informed of this, Bell responded by filing this action and an application by way of order to show cause for a temporary restraining order bringing on this motion for a preliminary injunction. Following argument, we granted a temporary restraining order on July 29 enjoining Manufacturers from making any payment to Bank Iranshahr until forty-eight hours after Manufacturers notified Bell of the receipt of a conforming demand, and this order has been extended pending decision of this motion.

On August 1, 1979, Manufacturers notified Bell that it had received a conforming demand from Bank Iranshahr. At the request of the parties, the court held an evidentiary hearing on August 3 on this motion for a preliminary injunction.

Criteria for Preliminary Injunctions

The current criteria in this circuit for determining whether to grant the extraordinary remedy of a preliminary injunction are set forth in *Caulfield v. Board of Education*, 583 F.2d 605, 610 (2d Cir. 1978):

> "[T]here must be showing of possible irreparable injury *and* either (1) probable success on the merits *or* (2) sufficiently serious questions going to the merits to make them a fair ground for litigation *and* a balance of hardships tipping decidedly toward the party requesting the preliminary relief."

We are not persuaded that the plaintiff has met the criteria and therefore deny the motion.

A. *Irreparable Injury*

Plaintiff has failed to show that irreparable injury may possibly ensue if a preliminary injunction is denied. Bell does not even claim, much less show, that it lacks an adequate remedy at law if Manufacturers makes a payment to Bank Iranshahr in violation of the Letter of Credit. It is too clear for argument that a suit for money damages could be based on any such violation, and surely Manufacturers would be able to pay any money judgment against it.

Bell falls back on a contention that it is without any effective remedy unless it can restrain payment. This contention is based on the fact that it agreed to be bound by the laws of Iran and to submit resolution of any disputes under the Contract to the courts of Iran. Bell claims that it now has no meaningful access to those courts.

There is credible evidence that the Islamic Republic is xenophobic and anti-American and that it has no regard for consulting service contracts such as the one here. Although Bell has made no effort to invoke the aid of the Iranian courts, we think the current situation in Iran, as shown by the evidence, warrants the conclusion that an attempt by Bell to resort to those courts would be futile. *Cf. Stromberg-Carlson Corp. v. Bank Melli*, 467 F. Supp. 530 (Weinfeld, J.) (S.D.N.Y. 1979). However, Bell has not demonstrated that it is without adequate remedy in this court against the Iranian defendants under the Sovereign Immunity Act which it invokes in this very case. 28 U.S.C. §§ 1605(a)(2), 1610(b)(2)....

Accordingly, we conclude that Bell failed to demonstrate irreparable injury.

B. *Probable Success on the Merits*

Even assuming that plaintiff has shown possible irreparably injury, it has failed to show probable success on the merits.

In order to succeed on the merits, Bell must prove, by a preponderance of the evidence that either (1) a demand for payment of the Manufacturers Letter of Credit conforming to the terms of that Letter has not yet been made, or (2) a demand, even though in conformity, should not be honored because of fraud in the transaction, *see, e.g.*, N.Y. UCC § 5-114(2); *United Bank Ltd. v. Cambridge Sporting Goods Corp.*, 41 N.Y.2d 254,.... It is not probable, in the sense of a greater than 50% likelihood, that Bell will be able to prove either nonconformity or fraud.

As to nonconformity, the August 1 demand by Bank Iranshahr is identical to the terms of the Manufacturers Letter of Credit in every respect except one: it names as payee the "Government of Iran Ministry of Defense, Successor to the Imperial Government of Iran Ministry of War" rather than the "Imperial Government of Iran Ministry of War."' It is, of course, a bedrock principle of letter of credit law that a demand must strictly comply with the letter in order to justify payment. Nevertheless, we deem it less than probable that a court, upon a full trial would find nonconformity in the instant case.

At the outset, we notice, and the parties agree, that the United States now recognizes the present Government of Iran as the legal successor to the Imperial Government of Iran. That recognition is binding on American Courts. Though we may decide for ourselves the consequences of such recognition upon the litigants in this case, we point out that American courts have traditionally viewed contract rights as vesting not in any particular government but in the state of which that government is an agent.

Accordingly, the Government of Iran is the successor to the Imperial Government under the Letter of Guaranty. As legal successor, the Government of Iran may properly demand payment even though the terms of the Letter of Guaranty only provide for payment to the Government of Iran's predecessor and a demand for payment under the Letter of Credit reciting that payment has been made by Bank Iranshahr to the new government is sufficient. We are fortified in this conclusion and made confident that a court, upon full trial, would reach the same result... that the Government of Iran was the legal successor to the Imperial Government Iran.

Finally, an opposite answer to the narrow question of conformity would not only elevate form over substance, but would render financial arrangements and undertakings worldwide wholly subject to the vicissitudes of political power. A nonviolent, unanimous transformation of the form of government, or, as this case shows, the mere change of the name of a government agency, would be enough to warrant an issuer's refusal to honor a demand. We cannot suppose such uncertainty and opportunity for chicanery to be the purpose of the requirement of strict conformity.

If conformity is established, as here, the issuer of an irrevocable, unconditional letter of credit, such as Manufacturers normally has an absolute duty to transfer the requisite funds. This duty is wholly independent of the underlying contractual relationship that gives rise to the letter of credit. Nevertheless, both the Uniform Commercial Code of New York, which the parties concede governs here, and the courts state that payment is enjoinable where a germane document is forged or fraudulent or there is "fraud in the transaction." N.Y.U.C.C. § 5-114(2); *United Bank Ltd. v. Cambridge Sporting Goods Corp., supra.* Bell does not contend that any documents are fraudulent by virtue of misstatements or omissions. Instead, it argues there is "fraud in the transaction."

The parties disagree over the scope to be given as a matter of law to the term "transaction." Manufacturers, citing voluminous authorities, argues that the term refers only to the Letter of Credit transaction, not to the underlying commercial transaction or to the totality of dealings among the banks, the Iranian government and Bell. On this view of the law, Bell must fail to establish a probability of success, for it does not claim that the Imperial Government or Bank Iranshahr induced Manufacturers to extend the Letter by lies or half-truths, that the Letter contained any false representations by the Imperial Government or Bank Iranshahr, or that they intended misdeeds with it. Nor does Bell claim that the demand contains any misstatements.

Bell argues, citing equally voluminous authorities, that the term "transaction" refers to the totality of circumstances. On this view, Bell has some chance of success on the merits, for a court can consider Bell's allegations that the Government of Iran's behavior in connection with the consulting contract suffices to make its demand on the Letter of Guaranty fraudulent and that the ensuing demand on the Letter of Credit by Bank Iranshahr is tainted with the fraud.

There is some question whether these divergent understandings of the law are wholly incompatible since it would seem impossible to keep the Letter of Credit transaction conceptually distinct. A demand which facially conforms to the Letter of Credit and which contains no misstatement may, nevertheless, be considered fraudulent if made with the goal of mulcting the party who caused the Letter of Credit to be issued. Be that as it may, we need not decide this thorny issue of law. For, even on the construction most favorable to Bell, we find that success on the merits is not probable. Many of the facts alleged, even if proven, would not constitute fraud. As to others, the proof is insufficient to indicate a probability of success on the merits.

Bell, while never delineating with precision the contours of the purported fraud, sets forth five contentions which, in its view, support the issuance of an injunction. Bell asserts that (1) both the old and new Governments failed to approve invoices for services fully performed; (2) both failed to fund contracted-for independent Letters of Credit in Bell's favor; (3) the new Government has taken steps to renounce altogether its obligations under the Contract; (4) the new Government has made it impossible to assert contract rights in Iranian courts; and (5) the new Government has caused Bank Iranshahr to demand payment on the Manufacturers Letter of Credit, thus asserting rights in a transaction it has otherwise repudiated.

As to contention (4), it is not immediately apparent how denial of Bell's opportunity to assert rights under the Contract makes a demand on an independent letter of credit fraudulent.

Contentions (1), (2), (3) and the latter part of (5) all state essentially the same proposition — that the Government of Iran is currently repudiating all its contractual obligations, with American companies, including those with Bell. Again, the evidence on this point is uncompelling.

Bell points to (1) an intra-governmental order of July 2, 1979 ordering the termination of Iran's contract with Bell, and (2) hearsay discussions between Bell's president and Iranian officials to the effect that Iran would not pay on the Contract until it had determined whether the services under it had benefitted the country. Manufacturers, for its part, points to a public statement in the Wall Street Journal of July 16, 1979, under the name of the present Iranian Government, to the effect that Iran intends to honor all legitimate contracts. Taken together, this evidence does not suggest that Iran has finally and irrevocably decided to repudiate the Bell contract. It suggests equally that Iran is still considering the question whether to perform that contract.

Even if we accept the proposition that the evidence does show repudiation, plaintiff is still far from demonstrating the kind of evil intent necessary to support a claim of fraud. Surely, plaintiff contends that every party who breaches or repudiates his contact is for that reason culpable of fraud. The law of contract damages is adequate to repay the economic harm caused by repudiation, and the law presumes that one who repudiates has done so because of a calculation that such damages are cheaper than performance. Absent any showing that Iran would refuse to pay damages upon a contract action here or in Iran, much less a showing that Bell has even attempted to obtain such a remedy, the evidence is ambivalent as to whether the purported repudiation results from non-fraudulent economic calculation or from fraudulent intent to mulct Bell.

Plaintiff contends that the alleged repudiation, viewed in connection with its demand for payment on the Letter of Credit, supplies the basis from which only one inference — fraud — can be drawn. Again, we remain unpersuaded

Plaintiff's argument require us to presume bad faith on the part of the Iranian government. It requires us further to hold that government may not rely on the plain terms of the consulting contract and the Letter of Credit arrangements with Bank Iranshahr and Manufacturers providing for immediate repayment of the down payment upon demand, without regard to cause. On the evidence before us, fraud is no more inferable than an economically rational decision by the government to recoup its down payment, as it is entitled to do under the consulting contract and still dispute its liabilities under that Contract.

While fraud in the transaction is doubtless a possibility, plaintiff has not shown it to be a probability and thus fails to satisfy this branch of the *Caulfield* test.

C. *Serious Questions and Balance of Hardships*

If plaintiff fails to demonstrate probable success, he may still obtain relief by showing, in addition to the possibility of irreparable injury, both (1) sufficiently serious questions going to the merits to make them a fair ground for litigation, and (2) a balance of hardship tipping decidedly toward plaintiff. Both Bell and Manufacturers appear to concede the existence of serious questions, and the complexity and novelty of this matter lead us to find they exist. Nevertheless, we hold that plaintiff is not entitled to relief under this branch of the *Caulfield* test because the balance of hardships does not tip *decidedly* toward Bell, if indeed it tips that way at all.

To be sure, Bell faces substantial hardships upon denial of its motion. Should Manufacturers pay the demand, Bell will immediately become liable to Manufacturers for $30.2 million, with no assurance of recouping those funds from Iran for the services performed. While counsel represented in graphic detail the other losses Bell faces at the hands of the current Iranian government, these would flow regardless of whether we ordered the relief sought. The hardship imposed from a denial of relief is limited to the admittedly substantial sum of $30.2 million.

But Manufacturers would face at least as great a loss, and perhaps a greater one, were we to grant relief. Upon Manufacturers' failure to pay, Bank Iranshahr could initiate a suit on the Letter of Credit and attach $30.2 million of Manufacturers' assets in Iran. In addition, it could seek to hold Manufacturers liable for consequential damages beyond that sum resulting from the failure to make timely payment. Finally, there is not guarantee that Bank Iranshahr or the government, in retaliation for Manufacturers recalcitrance, will not nationalize additional Manufacturers' assets in Iran in amounts which counsel, at oral argument, represented to be far in excess of the amount in controversy here.

Apart from a greater monetary exposure flowing from an adverse decision, Manufacturers face a loss of credibility in the international banking community that could result from its failure to make good on a letter of credit.

Conclusion

Finally, apart from questions of relative hardship and the specific criteria of the *Caulfield* test, general considerations of equity counsel us to deny the motion for injunctive relief. Bell, a sophisticated multinational enterprise well advised by competent counsel, entered into these arrangements with its corporate eyes open. It knowingly and voluntarily signed a contract allowing the Iranian government to recoup its down payment on demand, without regard to cause. It caused Manufacturers to enter into an arrangement whereby Manufacturers became obligated to pay Bank Iranshahr the unamortized down payment balance upon receipt of conforming documents, again without regard to cause.

Both of these arrangements redounded tangibly to the benefit of Bell. The Contract with Iran, with its prospect of designing and installing from scratch a nationwide and international communications system, was certain to bring to Bell both monetary profit and prestige and good will in the global communications industry. The agreement to indemnify Manufacturers on its Letter of Credit provided the means by which these benefits could be achieved.

One who reaps the rewards of commercial arrangements must also accept their burdens. One such burden in this case, voluntarily accepted by Bell, was the risk that demand might be made without cause on the funds constituting the down payment. To be sure, the sequence of events that led up to that demand may well have been unforeseeable when the contracts were signed. To this extent, both Bell and Manufacturers have been made the unwitting and innocent victims of tumultuous events beyond their control. But, as between two innocents, the party who undertakes by contract the risk of political uncertainty and governmental caprice must bear the consequences when the risk comes home to roost.

. . . .

Accordingly, plaintiff's motion for a preliminary injunction, pursuant to Rule 65(a), Fed. R. Civ. P., is denied. . . .

Harris Corporation v. National Iranian Radio and Television

691 F.2D 1344 (11th Cir. 1982)

James C. Hill, Circuit Judge:

National Iranian Radio and Television ("NIRT") and Bank Melli Iran appeal from a district court order granting plaintiff-appellee Harris Corporation preliminary injunctive relief. The court enjoined: (1) NIRT from making a demand on Bank Melli under a certain bank guaranty letter of credit; (2) Bank Melli from making payment to NIRT under that letter of credit; and (3) Bank Melli from receiving payment from Continental Illinois National Bank and Trust Company ("Continental Bank") under a standby letter of credit issued by Continental Bank in favor of Bank Melli. The appellants challenge the jurisdiction of the district court,... and argue that the court abused its discretion by ordering preliminary relief. After careful consideration of the issues presented, we affirm.

I. The Facts

On February 22, 1978, the Broadcast Products Division of Harris Corporation entered into a contract with NIRT ("the contract") to manufacture and deliver 144 FM broadcast transmitters to Teheran, Iran, and to provide related training and technical services for a total price of $6,740,352. Harris received an advance payment of $1,331,470.40, which was to be amortized over the life of the contract by deducting a percentage of the payment due upon shipment of the equipment or receipt of the services and training from the balance of the advance.

Pursuant to the contract, Harris obtained a performance guarantee in favor of NIRT from Bank Melli, an agency of the State of Iran. The guarantee provides that Melli is to pay NIRT any amount up to $674,035.20 upon Melli's receipt of NIRT's written declaration that Harris has failed to comply with the terms and conditions of the contract. The contract between Harris and NIRT makes the guarantee an integral part of the contract and provides that NIRT must release the guarantee upon termination of the contract due to *force majeure*. Before Melli issued the guarantee it required that Harris obtain a letter of credit in Melli's favor. Continental Bank issued this standby, which provides that Continental is to reimburse Melli to the extent that Melli pays on the guarantee it issued. Harris, in turn, must indemnify Continental Bank to the extent that Continental Bank pays Melli.

From August 1978 through February 1979, Harris shipped to Iran 138 of the 144 transmitters (together with related equipment for 144 transmitters) and also conducted a 24-week training program in the United States for NIRT personnel. In February 1979, the Islamic Republic of Iran overthrew the Imperial Government of Iran. After the overthrow, one shipment of goods which Harris sent could not be delivered safely in Iran. Harris notified NIRT, by telex dated February 27, that those goods were taken to Antwerp, Belgium, and Sharjah, United Arab Emirates.

Frank R. Blaha, the Director of Customer Products and Systems Operations of the Broadcast Products Division of Harris Corporation, met either NIRT officials in Teheran in early May, 1979, to help them obtain the goods in Antwerp, to discuss amendments to the contract, and to discuss a revised delivery schedule made necessary to Iranian events. Harris, offering Blaha's affidavit, contends that all parties at those meetings acknowledged the existence of *force majeure* as defined in the contract....

Blaha worked in May to obtain the Antwerp goods for NIRT, then returned to Teheran to continue discussions with NIRT officials. At these discussions, NIRT agreed to delay shipment of the final six transmitters until the fall of 1979 due to the conditions in Iran.

Negotiations on contract modifications continued during the summer and fall of 1979. On August 18, 1979, Harris formally advised NIRT of the additional costs it had incurred with respect to the goods that had been re-shipped from Antwerp, and Harris requested payment for the additional amount in accordance with the contract's *force majeure* clause and with a letter from NIRT authorizing Harris to re-ship the goods.

On November 4, 1979, Iranian militants took 52 hostages at the United States Embassy in Teheran. Harris received no further communications from NIRT after the seizure of the hostages.

Harris completed the remaining six transmitters in November 1979 and inventoried them for future delivery. Harris, supported by Blaha's affidavits, has argued that disruptive conditions created by the Iranian revolution initially prevented shipment of the final six transmitters. Subsequently, Harris contends, it was unable to ship the materials as a result of the Iranian Assets Control Regulations effective November 14, 1979. In particular, Harris points out, the Treasury voided all general licenses to ship to Iran and required sellers to obtain special licenses on a case-by-case basis before exporting goods. *See* 31 C.F.R., § 535.533 (1979). An affidavit submitted by Blaha states that Harris's counsel was advised by the Office of Foreign Assets Control that special licenses would be issued only in emergency situations or for humanitarian reasons and would not be issued for the transmitters. This request is not documented, and Harris did not inform NIRT of its inability to ship. On April 7, 1980, Treasury Regulation 535.207 became effective and prohibited the shipment of nonessential items to Iran. 45 Reg. 24,434 (1980).

On June 3, 1980, Continental Bank received a telex from Melli reporting that NIRT had presented Melli with a written declaration that Harris had failed to comply with the terms of the contract and stating that NIRT had demanded that Melli extend or pay the guarantee. Melli demanded that it be authorized to extend the guarantee and that Continental Bank extend its corresponding letter of credit to Melli, or else Melli would pay the guarantee and demand immediate payment from Continental.

In response to the demand by Melli, Harris sought and obtained the preliminary injunction at issue in this case. On July 11, 1980, Harris filed a verified complaint against NIRT and Melli in the United States District Court for the Middle District of Florida, seeking to enjoin payment and receipt of payment on the guarantee and receipt of payment on the letter of credit. The complaint also sought a declaratory judgment that the contract underlying the guarantee and the letter of credit had been terminated by *force majeure*. The court granted a temporary restraining order on June 13, 1980, pending a hearing on Harris's motion for a preliminary injunction.

On June 16, 1980, a copy of the TRO was mailed to Melli's counsel and on the following day was hand-delivered to Melli's branch office in Manhattan. On June 20, 1980, three days after receipt of the June 13th TRO at its Manhattan branch office, and despite the restraint against payment contained in the TRO, Melli telexed Continental Bank that it had paid the full amount of the guarantee "after receipt of a demand for payment from the National Iranian Radio and Television stating that there has been a default by Harris Corporation, Broadcast Products Division[,] to comply with the terms and conditions of contract F-601-1...." The telex also demanded that

Continental pay Melli by crediting Melli's London office with the amount of the letter of credit. After a hearing on August 15, 1980, the district court issued the preliminary injunction at issue here.

....

III. Jurisdiction

...Melli claims that it has sovereign immunity, which would deprive the court of...subject matter jurisdiction.....

A. Subject Matter Jurisdiction

1. The Statutory Requirement:

An Exception to Sovereign Immunity

The asserted basis for jurisdiction here is [the Foreign Sovereign Immunities Act of 1976] § 1330(a) [of title 28 of the United States Code], which permits a district court to exercise:

> original jurisdiction without regard to amount in controversy of any non-jury civil action against a foreign state as defined in § 1603(a) of this title as to any claim for relief in personam with respect to which the foreign state is not entitled to immunity either under §§ 1605-1607 of this title or under any applicable international agreement.

If Melli is entitled to sovereign immunity, then § 1330(a) does not confer subject matter jurisdiction. Harris contends, however, that exceptions to judicial immunity are invoked by statute.....

....

...Harris contends, the FSIA itself provides an exception to sovereign immunity here. Section 1605(a)(2) provides that a foreign state shall not be immune in any case in which the action is based "upon an act outside the territory of the United States in connection with a commercial activity of the foreign state elsewhere and that act caused a direct effect in the United States." This case falls within those parameters.

The appellants have clearly been involved in commercial activity in Iran; the issue that Melli contests is whether there has been an act having a "direct effect" in this country. Harris asserts that the appellants' demands for payment on the letters of credit have involved the requisite effect because they "trigger the entry of a blocked account on Harris's books in Melbourne [, Florida,] and discharged the letter of credit." Melli responds by arguing that such an effect is insufficient since the "direct effect" contemplated by the FSIA "is one which has no intervening element, but, rather, flows in a straight line without deviation or interruption." *Upton v. Empire of Iran*, 459 F. Supp. 264, 266 (D.D.C. 1978), *aff'd mem.* 607 F.2d 494 (D.C.Cir. 1979) (no "direct effect" in United States caused by injuries suffered by United States citizens in Teheran airport although injury was "endured here"). Moreover, Melli contends, the direct effect standard requires a substantial impact in the United States that occurs as a directly foreseeable result of conduct outside the country. *See Harris v. VAO Intourist*, 481 F.Supp. 1056, 1062 (E.D.N.Y.1979) (death of American citizen in fire in Moscow hotel did not cause direct effect in United States).

Essentially, the question presented is, "was the effect sufficiently 'direct' and sufficiently 'in the United States' that Congress would have wanted an American court to hear the case?" The answer is yes. The letter of credit arrangement — which was structured according to the wishes of the appellants — extends into this country, and the appellants' demands thus have significant, foreseeable financial consequences here. This sufficiently establishes a "direct effect" within the meaning of § 1605(a)(2).... Sovereign immunity is thus waived by the applicable statutory provision.....

....

IV. The Preliminary Injunction

A. The Framework for Review

The appellants contend that the district court erred in entering the preliminary injunction against payment or receipt of payment on the NIRT-Melli guarantee letter of credit and against receipt of payment on the Melli-Continental letter of credit. The four prerequisites for the injunction are: (1) a substantial likelihood that the plaintiff will prevail on the merits; (2) a substantial threat that the plaintiff will suffer irreparable injury if the injunction is not granted; (3) threatened injury to the plaintiff must outweigh the threatened harm that the injunction may cause to the defendant; and (4) granting the preliminary injunction must not dis-serve the public interest. In reviewing these factors, a court must keep in mind that the granting of the preliminary injunction rests in the sound discretion of the district court and will not be disturbed on appeal unless there is a clear abuse of discretion.

B. Substantial Likelihood of Success on the Merits

The merits of this case involve letter of credit law. Harris asserts that the existence of *force majeure* terminated its obligations under the contract with NIRT, making illegitimate NIRT's subsequent attempt to draw upon the performance guarantee issued by Melli. The appellants respond by relying upon a fundamental principle of letter of credit law: the letter of credit is independent of the underlying contract. Harris advanced two ways to overcome this barrier to enjoining a letter of credit transaction.

First, Harris asserts that the independence principle was modified by the parties here. It points to those paragraphs of its contract with NIRT which make "the bank guarantees" an "integral part" of the contract and which state that NIRT shall release all guarantees upon termination of the contract due to *force majeure*. Harris contends that it has demonstrated a substantial likelihood that *force majeure* occurred and terminated both the contract and the guarantee.....

We choose not to rely upon Harris's first line of argument, for we hesitate to hold that the letters of credit were automatically terminated by the operation of the contractual provisions. Accepting Harris's first argument would create problems; a bank could honor a letter of credit only to find that it had terminated earlier. While parties may modify the independence principle by drafting letters of credit specifically to achieve that result, there is no assertion by Harris that the performance guarantee or the letter of credit contain provisions (conditions) which would modify the independence of the banks' obligations. Since the banks were not parties to the underlying contact, it would appear that the contractual provisions relied upon by Harris would have the same effect as a warranty by NIRT that it would not draw upon the letter of credit issued by Melli if the contract were to terminate due to *force majeure*.

The second avenue pursued by Harris is the doctrine of "fraud in the transaction." Under this doctrine, a court may enjoin payment on a letter of credit, despite the independence principle, where there is shown to be fraud by the beneficiary of the letter of credit. Unfortunately, one unsettled point in the law is what constitutes fraud in the transaction, *i.e.*, what degree of defective performance by the beneficiary justifies enjoining a letter of credit transaction in violation of the independence principle?

Contending that a narrow definition of fraud is appropriate, the appellants assert that an injunction should issue only upon a showing of facts indicating egregious misconduct. They argue that fraud in the transaction should be restricted to the type of chicanery present in the landmark case of *Sztejn v. Henry Schroeder Banking Corp.*, 31 N.Y.S.2d 631 (Sup. Ct. 1941), where a seller sent fifty crates of "cow hair, other worthless material, and rubbish with intent to simulate genuine merchandise and defraud [the buyer]."

The appellants further contend that Harris does not and cannot allege conduct on the part of NIRT or Melli that would justify a finding of fraud under *Sztejn*. The egregious conduct, they assert, was by Harris. They state that it was Harris which failed to ship the remaining goods, unreasonably refused to extend the letter of credit obtained from Continental, and deliberately abandoned and destroyed the underlying contract. In contrast, they point out that they informed Continental that they would have been satisfied if the letter of credit had been extended long enough for Harris to complete performance. According to the view of NIRT and Melli, all that Harris has — taking its assertions as true — is an impossibility defense to an action on the underlying contract.

Appellants' arguments are not persuasive in the context of this case. *Sztejn* does not offer much direct guidance because it involved fraud by the beneficiary seller in the letter of credit transaction in the form of false documentation covering up egregiously fraudulent performance of the underlying transaction. That does not mean that the fraud exception should be restricted to allegations involving fraud in the underlying transaction, nor does it mean that the exception should be restricted to protecting the buyer in the framework of the traditional letter of credit. The fraud exception is flexible, *e.g.*, *United Bank v. Cambridge Sporting Goods Corp.*, 41 N.Y.2d 254, 260 (1976), and it may be invoked on behalf of a customer seeking to prevent a beneficiary from fraudulently utilizing a standby (guarantee) letter of credit.

Thus, the independent contracts rule does not make a fraudulent demand completely irrelevant to a bank's obligation to honor a standby. The differences between the allegations in this case and those in *Sztejn* merely require us to focus on the conduct of the buyer rather than the seller as we evaluate the beneficiary's conduct in light of the terms of the particular documents involved in the demand.

In order to collect upon the guarantee letter of credit, NIRT was required to declare that Harris had failed to comply with the terms and conditions of the contract. Harris contends that NIRT intentionally misrepresented the quality of Harris's performance; Harris thus asserts fraud as it has been defined traditionally.

We find that the evidence adduced by Harris is sufficient to support a conclusion that it has a substantial likelihood of prevailing on the merits. The facts suggest that the contract in this case broke down through no fault of Harris's but rather as a result of problems stemming from the Iranian revolution. NIRT apparently admitted as much during its negotiations with Harris over how to carry out the remainder of the contract. Nonetheless, NIRT sought to call the performance guarantee. Its attempt to do so necessarily involved its representation that Harris had defaulted under the contract. Yet the contract explicitly provides that it can be terminated due to *force majeure*. Moreover, NIRT's demand was made in a situation that was subtly suggestive of fraud. Since NIRT and Bank Melli had both become government enterprises, the demand was in some sense by Iran upon itself and may have been an effort by Iran to harvest undeserved bounty from Continental Bank. Under these circumstances, it was within the district court's discretion to find that, at a full hearing, Harris might well be able to prove that NIRT's demand was a fraudulent attempt to obtain the benefit of payment on the letter of credit in addition to the benefit of Harris's substantial performance.

C. Irreparable Injury

The district court did not abuse its discretion in finding a substantial likelihood of irreparable injury to Harris absent an injunction. Harris has sufficiently demonstrated that its ability to pursue a legal remedy against NIRT and Melli (*i.e.*, to recover the proceeds of the standby) has been precluded. It is clear that the Islamic regime now governing Iran has shown a deep hostility toward the United States and its citizens, thus making effective access to the Iranian courts unlikely. *See American Bell International v. Islamic Republic of Iran*, 474 F.Supp. 420, 423 (S.D.N.Y.1979). Similarly, the cooperative response of agencies of Iran to orders of a United States court would be unlikely where the court's order would impose a financial obligation on the agencies. Harris's possible resort to the Iran-United States Claims Tribunal does not, in our eyes, ameliorate the likelihood of irreparable injury for purposes of this requirement for preliminary relief.

D. The Balance of Harms

Neither appellant argues that the preliminary injunction has caused or will cause it any harm. Since there would otherwise be a likelihood that Harris would suffer irreparable injury, the balance of harms weighs heavily in Harris's favor.

E. The Public Interest

In a Statement of Interest filed with the district court on July 16, 1982, the United States indicated that new amendments to the Iranian Assets Control Regulations governing letter of credit claims still permit American litigants to proceed in United States Courts and to obtain preliminary injunctive relief. The supplementary information explaining the changes provides a good indication that preliminary injunctions such as the one entered here are in the public interest:

> Iran filed more than 200 claims with the Iran-U.S. Claims Tribunal (the "Tribunal") based on standby letters of credit issued for the account of United States parties. United States nationals have filed with the Tribunal a large number of claims related to, or based on, many of the same standby letters of credit at issue in Iran's claims. Other United States nationals have litigation pending in United States courts concerning some of these same letters of credit.

> The purpose of the amendment is to preserve the *status quo* by continuing to allow U.S. account parties to obtain preliminary injunctions or other temporary relief to prevent payment on standby letters of credit, while prohibiting, for the time being, final judicial action permanently enjoining, nullifying or otherwise permanently disposing of such letters of credit.

> Preservation of the *status quo* will provide an opportunity for negotiations with Iran regarding the status and disposition of these various letter of credit claims. Preservation of the status quo for a period of time also permits possible resolution in the context of the Tribunal of the matters pending before it. The amendment will expire by its terms on December 31, 1982.

Melli has charged, however, that the entry of a preliminary injunction here would threaten the function of letters of credit in commercial transactions. Admittedly, that has given us pause, for it would be improper to impose relief contrary to the intentions of parties that have contracted to carry out their business in a certain manner. Some might contend that the use of the fraud exception in a case such as this damages commercial law and that Harris could have chosen to shift the risks represented in this case. Under the circumstances, however, we disagree. First, the risk of a fraudulent demand of the type which Harris has demonstrated a likelihood of showing is not one which it should be expected to bear in light of the manner in which the documents in this transaction were structured. Second, to argue that Harris could have protected itself further by inserting special conditions in the letters of credit and should be confined to that protection is to ignore the realities of the drafting of commercial documents. Third, unlike the first line of argument presented by Harris, the issuance of a preliminary injunction based on a showing of fraud does not create unfortunate consequences for a bank that honors letters of credit in good faith; it is up to the customer to seek and obtain an injunction before a bank would be prohibited from paying on a letter of credit. Finally, foreign situations like the one before us are exceptional. For these reasons, the district court's holding is not contrary to the public interest in maintaining the market integrity and commercial utility of guarantee letters of credit.

V. Conclusion

The requisite jurisdictional elements...have been waived, and the requirements for preliminary injunctive relief have been met. Accordingly, the decision of the district court is

Affirmed.

III. Export Credits

NOTE ON EXPORT CREDIT SUBSIDIES AND
THE UNITED STATES EXPORT-IMPORT BANK*

Introduction

Governments grant official export credits to support the export sector of their economies. The government-established institutions that carry out this task are referred to generically as "export credit institutions." There are many different ways an export credit institution supports exports. It can provide political or commercial risk insurance to domestic exporters, it may make loans to exporters to allow them to establish their exports abroad, and it may also provide buyers in foreign countries with loans and/or letters of credit through which they may buy exports. These topics are addressed below.

Origins of Export Credit Schemes

Export credit programs began to develop in Europe following the First World War, as countries sought to give their industries an edge against international com-

---

* This Note was prepared by Gregory D. Logerfo, Esq.

petition. Europe's industrialized nations created institutions to support the export sectors of their economies.[1] Some countries, such as Great Britain and France, created insurance-oriented credit agencies to facilitate exports.[2] For example, Britain's Export Credit and Guarantee Department (ECGD), under the Secretary of State for Trade, was created in 1919. The ECGD provides political and commercial risk insurance to exporters, but also issues loans directly to exporters or overseas buyers of British goods. It makes available subsidized loans, working closely with commercial banks. COFACE, the French counterpart to the ECGD, also issues commercial and political risk insurance policies. It receives financial backing from the state-owned Banque Française du Commerce Extérieur, as well as from commercial banks, depending on the type of loan or letter of credit being issued.[3]

Countries such as the United States, Japan and Canada have established banks, as opposed to insurance agencies, to operate as their export credit institutions. As such, these institutions obviously do not need to rely on commercial banks for loans — a contrast with insurance-type credit granting institutions. The government-established export credit banks employ their own loan officers and other experts to assess the creditworthiness of prospective borrowers, and to make loans directly to borrowers. However, because these institutions are in fact banks, they may be quite susceptible to economic downturns. In particular, their ability to provide export credits in times of recession may be hampered.

The Creation and Mission of the United State Export-Import Bank

The Ex-Im Bank is first and foremost a bank, according to its authorizing statute (12 U.S.C. Section 635). The Ex-Im Bank was created in 1934 by the Roosevelt Administration and established under its present law in 1945 to aid in the financing and to facilitate American exports. The Bank is a corporation whose sole shareholder is the United States Department of the Treasury. The Ex-Im Bank is authorized to operate as any normal bank does, keeping in mind its sole purpose: to aid in the financing and facilitation of exports from the United States.[4] Because the Ex-Im Bank's mission is to "create jobs through exports,"[5] its modern-day programs include providing guarantees of working capital loans for American exporters, establishing letters of credit and/or loans for foreign buyers, and providing commercial and political risk insurance. The loans to foreign buyers are subject to OECD guidelines established to limit government sponsored loans to promote exports.[6]

The Ex-Im Bank is, therefore, a bank in the sense that it makes loans like any ordinary commercial bank. But, it also functions like an insurance company, in that it backs commercial and political risk insurance policies to domestic exporters, an operation not normally performed by commercial banks. The mission of Ex-Im thus is described in its statute, 12 U.S.C. Section 635(a)(1)(A), as follows:

> It is the policy of the of United States to foster expansion of exports of manufactured goods, agricultural products, and other goods and services, thereby

1. See John M. Duff Jr., *The Outlook for Official Export Credits*, 13 L.& POL'Y INT'L. BUS. 891-959 (1981).
2. Duff, *supra*, at 927-28
3. *Id.* at 932.
4. 12 U.S.C. § 635(a)(1).
5. See Export-Import Bank of the United States, General Information 1 (October 1997).
6. Duff, *supra*, at 929.

contributing to the increased development of the productive resources of the United States.

While the Ex-Im Bank is authorized to implement insurance and loan programs to meet this goal, it must do so in a manner that does not compete with or take normal business from commercial lending and insurance institutions. Section 635 (B) of title 12 of the United States Code clearly indicates the Ex-Im Bank shall not compete with private capital, but rather shall supplement and encourage private capital to support exports of the United States. The Ex-Im Bank, therefore, is not designed to give American exporters an advantage, but merely to "level the playing field."[7] As regards export credit banks, the Ex-Im Bank is unique in this regard. All other export credit banks compete with the private capital markets for customers to some extent.[8] The Ex-Im Bank must endeavor to operate in the black and earn profits through its programs. It must, however, be careful not to wander into the domain of private capital.

In addition, the Ex-Im Bank is directed to work with government-supported export financing institutions of other countries to minimize competition in government supported export financing, and is further obligated to seek international agreements to reduce such financing.[9] After all, without some restraints, countries could compete with one another to, in effect, subsidize their exporters, and the international playing field would become very uneven indeed. The international agreement to which Ex-Im adheres regarding government sponsored export loan programs is the Organization of Economic Cooperation and Development's (OECD) *Arrangement on Guidelines for Officially Supported Export Credit*. The *OECD Arrangement* urges countries with export credit institutions to work to limit their activity, and seek solutions to their export dilemmas through private capital markets.[10] This *Arrangement* merely provides guidelines. It offers no steadfast remedy to a country that is beset by the unfavorable export credit programs of another.[11] As one scholar notes, "[c]ompliance (with the OECD) is voluntary, without any specific legal obligation. At best, under paragraph 9 of the *Arrangement*, a country faced with a competitive nation's nonconforming interest rates can provide matching finance of its own."[12] Hence, the term "arrangement" as opposed to "agreement" is used.

Cooperating with the Insurance Industry: Commercial and Political Risk Insurance

The Ex-Im Bank is authorized to cooperate with private insurance companies, and to issue commercial and/or political risk insurance policies in conjunction with them to insure exporters against loss. Ex-Im also can employ private insurance companies on an agency basis in order to issue and service its guarantees and insurance

---

7. *See* General Information, *supra*, at 1.

8. *See* Statement of Benjamin F. Nelson, Before the Subcommittee On Domestic and International Monetary Policy, Committee on Banking and Financial Service, House of Representatives (April 29, 1997).

9. *See* 12 U.S.C. § 635a(1)(A).

10. *See* Nelson Testimony, *supra*.

11. For an interesting case of an export credit agency essentially disregarding the *OECD Arrangement* in order to stimulate exports to the United States, see Mark S. Sullivan, *Export Subsidies: Predatory Financing and the MTA-Bombardier Contract*, 9 BROOKLYN J. INT'L L. LAW 385-409 (1983). The Canadian aerospace company, Bombardier, was able to secure a $570 million contract to provide subway cars to New City's Mass Transit Authority through a loan that clearly exceeded the lowest allowable interest rate under the *Arrangement*.

12. Sullivan, *supra*, at 390.

policies, and to adjust claims arising from these commitments. Pursuant to the Ex-Im statute, and at the encouragement of Ex-Im, the Federal Credit Insurance Association was established in 1961.[14] The FCIA is an unincorporated association of insurance companies, and as such originally bore ultimate responsibility for the risk associated with commercial risk insurance policies issued to exporters. The FCIA served as agent for the private insurance companies when commercial risk insurance was involved, and as agent for Ex-Im when political risk insurance was involved. FCIA and its member insurance companies, with the support of Ex-Im financing, were able to offer commercial risk insurance policies that were unavailable in the private insurance market.

After the establishment of FCIA, fewer and fewer private insurance companies were willing to take on commercial risk policies without Ex-Im bearing ultimate responsibility for such policies. Private insurance companies were unwilling to participate in FCIA programs due to the considerable political and commercial uncertainties in the world economy during the 1970s and 1980s. In *Hamilton Bank v. Export-Import Bank of the United States and Foreign Credit Insurance Association*,[15] an American commercial bank, Hamilton, sought to recover losses resulting from default on payments by a number of Mexican companies on a loan issued by Hamilton. The defaults occurred after the Mexican government forbade Mexican nationals from repayment of such debts in United States dollars.

Hamilton sued Ex-Im and FCIA, alleging breach of contract and intentional misrepresentation. Hamilton also alleged Ex-Im and FCIA made "bad faith denials" towards Hamilton's insurance claim. In a motion for summary judgment, the defendants argued that Hamilton did not suffer an insured loss, and more importantly, that they were immune from suit under the doctrine of sovereign immunity and/or official immunity for any misrepresentation or bad faith denials.[16] The court held that the plaintiff's exclusive tort remedy (relevant to the claim of a bad faith denial, and also to the claim of intentional misrepresentation) against Ex-Im was through the Federal Tort Claims Act (FTCA).[17] The FTCA provides government agencies with immunity against tort action, and specifies exceptions thereto.

The trickier question for the court was whether the FCIA, an organization of several dozen private insurance companies organized at the behest of Ex-Im, was able to use the FTCA. The FCIA argued that it was acting within the scope of its official authority as an agent for Ex-Im and, therefore, was immune under the FTCA. The court held that Hamilton deserved the opportunity to determine whether FCIA was truly acting within the scope of its relationship with Ex-Im, and allowed for discovery on this issue. Thus, the court left open the door for possible claims against FCIA as a private entity.

Only a short time thereafter, the FCIA and Ex-Im were in court again. NF Industries, an American company insured by an FCIA political and commercial risk insurance policy, followed FCIA risk analysis to its detriment during the 1982 crisis in the Falkland (Malvinas) Islands. Ex-Im denied a claim for coverage issued by FCIA, after NF had followed the FCIA's advice as to how to deal with wartime currency transactions in Argentina after the outbreak of the Falklands War. In *NF Industries v. Export Import Bank of the United States*,[18] the FCIA asserted official immunity (as a government entity) as a

---

14. 7 F.3d 158 (9th Cir. 1993)
15. 634 F. Supp. 195 (E.D. Pa.1986)
16. *Id.* at 199.
17. 28 U.S.C. § 2671-80
18. 846 F.2d 998 (5th Cir. 1988) (*per curiam*)

defense to various claims asserted by the plaintiff, NF Industries, including breach of contract. The Fifth Circuit held that the insured party, NF Industries, was not in direct privity with Ex-Im, but rather with FCIA. Although FCIA had a re-insurance policy with Ex-Im, FCIA was not acting as a government entity when it granted the insurance policy to NF Industries. Therefore, it was not allowed an official claim of immunity.[19]

In *Seattle Fur Exchange, Inc. v. FCIA et al*,[20] the question of whether Ex-Im was the ultimate insurer of a commercial risk policy arose again. By this time, Ex-Im had re-drafted their agreements in the wake of the *NF Industries* decision. In *Seattle Fur*, the plaintiff, Seattle Fur Exchange, brought suit against FCIA and its member private insurance companies after the buyers of their exported goods defaulted on payments. The plaintiff argued on appeal that "the District Court erred in applying to private insurance companies an insurance law rule applicable only to federally issued insurance."[21] Further, the plaintiff argued, the FCIA actually was acting as a group of private insurance carriers, and hence not acting as a government agent. The United States Court of Appeals for the Ninth Circuit Court held that Ex-Im was, in fact, responsible for issuing the commercial risk insurance to the plaintiff, because the insurance policy specifically identified Ex-Im as the re-insurer of the policy. This result illustrates the departure from the policy issued in *NF Industries,* where FCIA was not directly backed by Ex-Im. In *Seattle Fur*, the policy made clear that Ex-Im was the insurer and, therefore, there could be no argument as to whether the FCIA actually was acting as a government agent.[22]

Finally, as a result of the political and commercial risks associated with FCIA loans, private insurance companies discontinued insuring FCIA policies. Ex-Im took up the slack, and began to guarantee 100 percent of the FCIA's potential liability.[23] A limited number of private insurance companies were participants, acting as "fronting" companies for FCIA policies, or acting in an advisory capacity regarding the insurance programs. These companies were not liable for the FCIA insurance policies. In 1989, FCIA again was allowed to re-insure private insurers, but Ex-Im made clear that a "fronting" private insurance company was indemnified against non-payment by Ex-Im. Ultimately, Ex-Im was behind these policies, and presumably FCIA was acting as a "government agent," so that the FCIA was eligible for the immunity privileges it had sought unsuccessfully in *NF Industries.*

Ex-Im's contract with FCIA allowing FCIA to sell insurance was terminated in 1992, and today Ex-Im assumes complete responsibility for operation of the Ex-Im Bank program.[24] Commercial and political risk insurance policies are both ultimately backed by Ex-Im. This results from pressure from the FCIA member companies. It also is designed to provide the legal benefits Ex-Im gains from being in privity with the insured party, *i.e.*, a greater likelihood of utilizing the government immunity from breach of contract.

The Programs of the Export-Import Bank Today

Today, Ex-Im touts itself as a "lean" government bank responsive to the needs of American exporters. Ex-Im is particularly concerned with supporting small busi-

---

19. *See* NF Industries, Inc. v. Export Import Bank of the United States, 846 F.2d 998 (5th Cir. 1988). *See also* Nu-Air Mfg. Co. v. Frank B. Hall Co. of New York, 822 F. 2d 987 (11th Cir.1987), *cert. denied,* 485 U.S. 976 (1988).
20. 7 F.3d 158 (9th Cir. 1993)
21. 7 F.3d at 161.
22. 7 F.3d at 163.
23. *See* General Information, *supra*, at 31.
24. *See* General Information, *supra*, at 31.

nesses, but also has created programs to facilitate exports of aircraft.[25] Recently, Ex-Im has focused its efforts on supporting exports to less developed countries (LDCs), and also on increasing exports of environmental goods and services. Ex-Im works with agencies that foster development overseas, such as the United States Agency for International Development and the World Bank. Ex-Im is potentially interested in any American export, be it a good or a service, with the only exception being on military-related goods or services.[26]

1. The Working Capital Guarantee Program

The Working Capital Program is designed to assist small business by supplying them with the capital necessary for exporting activities. [27] Clearly, it is time consuming, expensive and risky for a small business to set up the framework through which it can export its goods and services. These loans may be used to purchase raw materials and/or finished products for export, to pay for materials or labor to produce goods and/or services for export, or to provide financially backing for standby letters of credit.[28] The Ex-Im working capital guarantee covers 90 percent of the loan's principal and accrued interest. An exporter applies directly to Ex-Im for a preliminary commitment to a working capital guarantee. Once approved, the exporter may solicit loan packages from commercial lenders, and then apply to Ex-Im for a final commitment. Ex-Im will guarantee 90 percent of the loan made by the commercial lender, and this backing allows commercial banks to offer attractive loan packages. The loans must be for amounts greater than U.S. $ 833,333. Loans below that amount may be financed through programs offered by the Small Business Administration (SBA).

2. The Export Credit Insurance Program

The purpose of Ex-Im's export credit insurance program is to provide credit risk protection, in the form of commercial and/or political risks, but not to provide insurance policies covering transport, liability or performance insurance.[29] Ex-Im considers "commercial risk" to be the risk of default or of the inability of a foreign purchaser to meet payment obligations. It defines "political risk" to include events beyond the control of a foreign purchaser, such as political violence (*i.e.*, war), government intervention, cancellation of an export or import license, transfer or inconvertibility risk (*i.e.*, the inability to buy United States dollars in a legal market).

Commercial and political risk cover may be purchased together, or political risk cover may be purchased alone, but commercial risk cover alone is not available. Coverage is offered for short term credits (up to 180 days) and medium term credits (up to five years). The percentage of cover applicable to the insured amount, the principal and interest amounts covered are all variable (within certain guidelines), to be determined by the insured party and Ex-Im.[30] Ex-Im determines the availability of risk insurance on a country-by country and a buyer-by-buyer basis. Ex-Im publishes a

---

25. Ex-Im allows for financing of large-passenger aircraft, (those having 70 seats or more) with repayment terms as long as twelve years. It should be noted that aircraft export subsidies are governed by the *Understanding on Export Credits for Civil Aircraft*. *See* United States Export-Import Bank, *Aircraft Finance Program* (1997).

26. *See* General Information, *supra*, at 1.

27. *See* General Information, *supra*, at 7.

28. *See* General Information, *supra*, at 26.

29. *See* General Information, *supra*, at 32.

30. *See* General Information, *supra*, at 32.

"Country Limitation Schedule" (CLS) that lists the countries that have been approved by Ex-Im to insure against. Cuba, for example, is not on the CLS, nor is Rwanda or Pakistan. On the other hand, Turkey is on the CLS, approved for both the public and private sector.[31] To be sure, because Ex-Im competes with export-credit granting agencies from other countries, it revises the CLS monthly. More generally, it is not afraid to launch programs that target specific countries and/or products for export to serve American interests.

It is critical to understand that Ex-Im rules prevent a company exporting goods from the United States with Ex-Im support if those goods are not really "made in the U.S.A." The rules specify minimum domestic content standards for goods if those goods are to be eligible for Ex-Im insurance policies. Specifically, there is a 50 percent United States content for short-term policies, and an 85 percent for medium-term policies.[32]

There are two categories of Ex-Im Bank policy types, "single buyer" and "multi buyer." Single buyer policies cover a sale or a number of sales to a single importer in a foreign country. They are available for short or medium term credits, or a combination of the two. In addition, there are many types of specific policies, including those that deal with leasing and services.

In contrast, multi buyer policies cover a number of importers in several countries, and require the insured exporter to cover all or a reasonable spread of its export credit sales to enable Ex-Im to mitigate risks involved in the policy. For example, an exporter of shoes may have several buyers in several South American countries, and it may be laborious and impractical for the exporter to have a policy with the Ex-Im Bank for each individual buyer. There are aggregate credit limits (ACLs) in multi buyer insurance policies that delineate the amount of goods that may be covered through the policy and to whom they may be sold. Multi buyer policies are available only to cover short-term credits, and covers shipments made over the period of one year.

How does an exporter apply for an insurance policy with Ex-Im? Applications for insurance may be obtained from Ex-Im, and may be submitted to any of Ex-Im's regional offices. These offices are in Chicago, Houston, Long Beach, Miami and New York City. In addition, applications may be submitted through an insurance broker or an umbrella or trade association policy member.[33]

The application review is a two step process. First, Ex-Im reviews the operating history, financial condition, and nature of the business applicant. Second, the foreign purchasers must provide credit reports to show their creditworthiness. Financial statements of the foreign buyers may be required, depending on the type and amount of the policy. Significantly, Ex-Im does *not* require an applicant to show evidence of foreign competition in order to qualify for an Ex-Im insurance policy.

In fiscal year 1996 (the year ending 30 September 1996), the Ex-Im Bank authorized $ 3.9 billion in insurance cover. It insured shipments of $ 2.3 billion, 86 percent of which was insured through short-term transactions. A total of 1,900 insurance policies were issued, the vast majority of these (84 percent) were made to small businesses.[34] Mexico and Brazil were the top two countries, respectively, to which insured

---

31. *See* Export-Import Bank of the United States, *Country Limitation Schedule*, (Oct. 21, 1997).

32. *See* General Information *supra*, at 34.

33. *See* General Information *supra*, at 37.

34. *See* General Information *supra*, at 39.

shipments were made. The top ten countries to which insured shipments were made in 1996 were, in order of importance: Mexico, Brazil, Canada, Argentina, Japan, the United Kingdom, Chile, Hong Kong, Germany, and India.

3. Direct Loans and Guarantees, and Attendant Legal Issues

The Ex-Im Bank provides loans directly to buyers of American capital goods and services.[35] The Bank also guarantees commercial financing that is loaned for the same purpose. In both cases, the Ex-Im Bank covers up to 85 percent of the total value of the exported goods and/or services. The Bank is bound by OECD agreements when determining the market and term for each loan.[36] The loans must be repaid over a term of two or more years. The Ex-Im Bank also has various programs involving medium-term financing to make it easier for American exporters to buy capital equipment associated with the export of their products (*e.g.*, to purchase a machine tool used to make a product for export).[37]

Ex-Im, as a bank, is in the business of making loans. It makes loans to domestic producers, of exports as well as to foreign purchasers of American exports.[38] In the case of foreign importers, Ex-Im makes loans either to private entities or to public, or governmental, institutions. The Bank determines the risk level for such loans on a country-by-country basis, and also appraises private entities and public institutions of a given country separately.

In *Atwood Turnkey Drilling Inc., et al. v. Petroleo Brasileiro, S.A.*,[39] the government of Brazil sought protection under the United States Foreign Sovereign Immunities Act (FSIA) (28 U.S.C. Section 1602) after its state-owned oil company, Petroleo Brasileiro (Petrobras), breached a contract with an American company, Atwood. Ex-Im had issued Petrobras with a letter of credit. After determining it had appellate jurisdiction, the United States Court of Appeals for the Fifth Circuit turned to the issue of whether Petrobas could have FSIA immunity. The Court held that under Section 1603 of the Act, Petrobras was entitled to protection as an instrumentality of a foreign state. But, when Petrobras was granted the letter of credit from Ex-Im, it waived its immunity under FSIA through the following language:

> The Borrower [Petrobras] acknowledges and agrees that the activities contemplated by the provisions of this agreement and the notes are commercial in nature rather than government or public and therefore acknowledges and agrees that it is not entitled to any right of immunity in the grounds of sovereignty or otherwise.[40]

Thus, the court allowed the Ex-Im Bank to contract around the FSIA with an entity (Petrobras) controlled by a foreign government (Brazil).

In addition to upholding Ex-Im's efforts at contracting around the FSIA, courts have allowed Ex-Im to circumvent the Freedom of Information Act (FOIA). In *Comstock International (U.S.A.) Inc. v. Export-Import Bank of the United States*,[41] the plaintiff, Comstock, brought an action under the FOIA to compel disclosure of loan

---

35. *See* General Information *supra*, at 3.
36. *See* Alfred C. Holden, *The Reposition of Ex-Im Bank*, 31 COLUM. J. WORLD BUS.82-93 (1996)
37. *See* Export-Import Bank of the United States, *A Map of Programs* (September 1997).
38. *See* *A Map of Programs*, *supra*, at 31.
39. *See* 875 F. 2d 1174 (5th Cir. 1989).
40. 875 F. 2d at 1177.
41. *See* 464 F. Supp. 804 (D.C. Cir. 1979).

agreements and related materials made by Chase Manhattan Bank (Chase) and Ex-Im to an Algerian corporation, Sonatrach. Ex-Im had guaranteed a letter of credit equal to the amount of the loan made by Chase, and therefore was directly involved in both loans to Sonatrach. Sonatrach and Comstock were involved with a pipeline project in Algeria, but Comstock had withdrawn from the project and now sought information regarding the Sonatrach loan to be used in arbitration proceedings against Sonatrach. Ex-Im informed Sonatrach that the information was protected under the commercial and financial information exemption to the FOIA (codified at 5 U.S.C. § 552(b)(4)). Ex-Im argued that the release of the information would cause considerable harm to the competitive position of the two commercial parties involved in the transaction, Chase and Sonatrach. The United States District Court for the District of Columbia held that the information could be withheld from Sonatrach. The Court recognized the need for Ex-Im to withhold the information requested by Sonatrach in order to remain competitive as an export credit-granting agency:

> Because Ex-Im competes in the world market with other government-supported export credit unions that are not required to disclose financing agreements to outside parties, potential loan applicants might seek financing outside the United States because of their unwillingness to subject themselves to the possible risk of disclosure. [42]

Thus, Ex-Im avoided a ruling that had the potential to crimp its ability to compete with overseas export credit institutions for loan customers.

4. Project Finance

Ex-Im also is involved in large-scale infrastructure project finance transactions in developing countries.

The Political Debate About the Ex-Im Bank.

Ex-Im is under constant pressure from Congress and the Executive branch to remain efficient and to pursue effectively its goals as set forth in Section 635 of title 12 of the United States Code. It is also scrutinized to see whether it promotes contemporary American economic interests and thus, for example, has endeavored to promote environmental and aircraft exports. In 1993, President Clinton authorized an initiative to "reinvent" the Ex-Im Bank.[43] This initiative was made largely in response to an OECD arrangement that effectively barred OECD member states from giving certain export credits to "wealthier" developing countries, i.e., countries with per capita incomes of over $2,500. Ex-Im was re-positioned as part of a national strategy to act as a "significant" export credit agency.[44] The budget for the Ex-Im Bank increased, and fiscal year 1994 was the Bank's second busiest year in supporting American exports.[45] However, in 1995 the debate over the need for the Ex-Im Bank resurfaced after Congress attempted to cut the Bank's budget.

The Ex-Im Bank has its share of detractors, including many members of Congress who vote regularly to curtail, or even shut down completely, the Bank. According to Ian Vasquez of the Cato Institute in Washington, D.C., the Ex-Im Bank

---

42. 464 F. Supp. at 808.
43. *See* Holden *supra*, at 90.
44. *See* Holden *supra*, at 84.
45. *See* Nelson Testimony, *supra*.

backs only about two percent of all American exports.[46] Vasquez and others correctly point out that neo-classical economic theory predicts a country cannot improve its overall welfare by subsidizing exports. Allow the market to determine the appropriate rate of return and risk involved in each international transaction, and those countries that lower the commercial and political risk in their countries and/or companies will be rewarded. Put bluntly, these critics dub Ex-Im's programs "corporate welfare."

> It [Ex-Im] has long been known as "Boeing's Bank," for its support of Boeing Co.'s aircraft sales. The deal is simple: taxpayers provide the cash; exporters collect the profit. There is perhaps no better example of corporate welfare than the Ex-Im Bank.[47]

Those who are for shutting down the Bank see it as a New Deal agency with no place in a liberal global economy.[48] From the vantage of an economist, the reasons for closing Ex-Im are clear. Neo-classical economic theory holds that subsidies are inefficient.[49] International trade is a means through which nations can specialize, increase the productivity of their resources, and thereby realize a larger total output. The concept of *comparative advantage* underlies the reasoning that specialization is the key to increased economic growth for the world as a whole. The total output of the world economy will be greatest when each good or service is produced by the nation (or region) with the lowest overall cost in producing, *i.e.*, the greatest comparative advantage, in producing that good or service. Thus, although the United States may be able to produce coffee, it would be inefficient for it to do so when Brazil can grow and export coffee to the United States more efficiently. Conversely, Brazilian coffee farmers would be acting inefficiently if they chose to produce wheat, as Brazil can import wheat produced in the United States at a lower cost. The United States, then, has a comparative advantage in wheat while Brazil has a comparative advantage in coffee.

Critics point out that the Export-Import Bank does not make its decisions to loan and/or insure goods and services based on comparative advantage. In fact, they claim it does just the opposite by supporting the export of goods that can be produced more efficiently elsewhere. American exporters, indeed exporters wherever located, should make choices about what to produce based on efficiency criteria, not handouts from government-established export credit agencies.

But, the perspective of neo-classical economists from developed countries is not the only one to weigh. Consider the position of developing countries.[50] They tend to have comparative advantages in the agricultural sector of the world economy. Yet, for a developing country like Brazil to progress economically, it needs to establish its own manufacturing and service sectors. Brazil does not want to rely on coffee ex-

---

46. *See* Ian Vasquez, *No Need for Export-Import Bank*, BALTIMORE SUN, Aug. 15, 1997, at 27a.

47. Doug Bandow, *Get Business Off Welfare, Shut the ExIm Bank*, INVESTOR'S BUS. DAILY, Aug. 11, 1997.

48. *See* Testimony of Ian Vasquez, U.S. Senate Committee on Banking, Housing and Urban Affairs, Subcommittee on International Finance. July 17, 1997.

49. *See generally* Campbell R. McConnell & Stanley L. Brue, *International Economics and the World Economy*, in ECONOMIC PRINCIPLES, PROBLEMS AND POLICIES 773-96 (11th ed. 1990) (discussing the distortive effects of subsidies).

50. *See generally* Roger Cohen, *A Region At Risk*, N.Y. TIMES, February 5-6, 1998 (considering the impact of globalization, and in effect the impact of comparative advantage, on Brazil and Argentina, and the different responses of the governments of those countries).

ports, and have to import computers, automobiles, and aircraft forever. It thus is easy for a neo-classical economist to extol the virtues of comparative advantage doctrine, when the United States has a comparative advantage in nearly all high-technology sectors of the world economy. How can a country such as Brazil possibly develop these sorts of comparative advantages without its own export credit institutions? If the United States and other developed countries maintain their own export credit agencies, and developing countries do not establish them, then will not the pattern of trade and investment remain skewed against developing countries? So goes the anti-neo-classical logic — or fear — anyway.

To be sure, supporting export credit institutions in a developing country is a conceptually different problem from supporting the Ex-Im Bank in the United States. Support for Ex-Im comes from policy makers that want to ensure the United States maintains important sectors of its economy. Arguably, an aircraft industry is necessary for the last remaining superpower. It is no surprise then, that Ex-Im supports aircraft exports. Ex-Im also is necessary for the United States to maintain leverage against nations who use their export credit agencies in an excessive manner. In addition, Ex-Im supporters argue, in the absence of government support, it is unlikely that American small businesses could obtain export financing.

Supporters contend that the Ex-Im Bank is necessary in a global market that does not offer American exporters a "level playing field."[51] They note that the authorizing statute for the Ex-Im Bank (12 U.S.C. Section 635) makes clear that Ex-Im's ultimate objective is to work with international forums such as the OECD to reduce and eventually eliminate subsidized export finance programs.[52] However, it is unlikely the United States government will achieve this end without the negotiating leverage that Ex-Im provides the United States.[53] How could the United States negotiate a favorable OECD agreement on export credits without the ability to affect the export credit arena?

Supporters of the Ex-Im Bank further argue that it is not clear the free market allocates resources most efficiently in all circumstances. The free market relies on the price system to communicate information about the value of goods and services. In the international arena, information about prices, supply, and demand in other countries is often murky at best, and therefore it may be less likely that the free market will allocate resources efficiently. Private financial institutions may be unwilling to support exports to emerging markets, even when the risk is *correctly* priced. For example, it is entirely plausible that pre-conceived biases against certain developing countries within the "free market" lending community may preclude a truly efficient allocation of loans and insurance programs.

Finally, defenders of the Ex-Im Bank observe that most other countries in the Group of Seven (G-7) have export credit agencies. These countries are France, the United Kingdom, Japan, Canada, Germany and Italy. Indeed, a total of 73 export credit agencies now exist worldwide.[54] However, in 1995, U.S. $ 258 billion of the $533 billion in total export financing came from the G-7 nations. The export credit

---

51. Nelson Testimony, *supra.*

52. 12 U.S.C. § 635 (a)(1)(B)

53. *See* Nelson Testimony, *supra.* Nelson notes that "given the importance of exports to national economic performance, achieving the objective of eliminating all financial subsidies may prove difficult."

54. *See* Nelson Testimony, *supra.*

agencies of other G-7 countries all appear, on some level, to compete with private commercial capital, yet Ex-Im is not allowed to because of its authorizing statute.[55]

As debate rages, Ex-Im has tried to position itself to promote exports of leading market sectors, such as environmental and aircraft exports. For example, in the first half of fiscal year 1997, Ex-Im authorized $1.65 billion in asset-based financing for 10 separate commercial export transactions. Ex-Im, in this time frame, helped to finance sales or leases of Boeing and McDonnell-Douglas aircraft to the Czech Republic, Egypt, India, Kenya, Korea, Morocco, Turkey, and Uzbekistan. Ex-Im also guaranteed a long-term lease valued at $105 million to China for American-built aircraft.[56]

Ex-Im also has large programs designed to boost the export of American environmental technology. At the 1992 "Earth Summit" in Rio de Janeiro, the most ambitious environmental monitoring system ever was proposed in an effort to monitor the Amazon rain forest and protect it from continued destruction. Raytheon, a Massachusetts based corporation, was awarded the contract to build the "System for Vigilance of the Amazon" (SIVAM). Ex-Im provided over $1 billion in financing to support the project.[57]

Conclusion

Although it may be unclear whether the Ex-Im Bank can increase the total number of American exports through its programs, it is unlikely the Bank will be "shut down" any time in the near future. The fact that other countries have export credit agencies necessitates — politically if not economically — the Ex-Im Bank's existence, if for no other reason than to provide leverage for American negotiators trying to eliminate export credits altogether. Further, the Ex-Im Bank can be used by American policy makers indirectly as an instrument of foreign policy.[58] For example, the United States has clear interests in maintaining a long-standing, strong strategic interest in Turkey, hence Ex-Im offers all of its programs for exports to Turkey. On the other hand, Cuba receives (and presumably expects) no Ex-Im Bank export credit support, given long-standing American policy to isolate its Communist regime. Even countries that have economic and political track records similar to Turkey, such as Brazil, are not eligible for all Ex-Im programs.[59] It is clear that the Ex-Im Bank's determinations of political and commercial risk are influenced by larger American policy concerns.

In addition, special interest lobbies, such as environmental groups and companies, and well-organized, powerful industries, such as the aircraft industry, are likely to be successful in their efforts to keep the Ex-Im Bank alive. The Bank, as mentioned, has programs that cater specifically to these groups.

In short, it seems inconceivable that the United States can afford to give up on the Ex-Im Bank, based on the perceived advantages it affords the United States in the international business and political arenas. In an imperfect international political

---

55. *See* 12 U.S.C. § 635.

56. *Eximbank Authorizes $1.65 Billion in Aircraft Exports in First Half*, AVIATION DAILY, April 22, 1997.

57. Scott Allen, *"Eye" on the Rain Forest Relies on Space, Ground, Air Sensors*, BOSTON GLOBE, Mar. 31, 1997.

58. *See* Duff *supra*. The most notable example occurred in the late 1960s. Inserted into Ex-Im's Charter was a provision prohibiting lending to communist nations without a prior presidential determination that the proposed loan is in the national interest. This provision essentially excluded loans to the former Soviet Union and Cuba, but has not kept Ex-Im loans and programs from reaching China.

59. *See* Country Limitation Schedule, *supra*.

economy replete with interventionist public- sector organizations and institutions, the Ex-Im Bank seems to have a purpose. Not surprisingly, in November 1997, Ex-Im was re-authorized by Congress for an additional four years. It will be up again for re-authorization in 2001.[60]

QUESTIONS

1.   What is the primary difference between the Ex-Im Bank's mission and those of export credit institutions for other developed nations?

2.   What program from Ex-Im Bank is available to a small American company seeking to obtain capital to support exports?

3.   Explain the concept of *comparative advantage* and how it relates to export credit programs. Does the concept lend support for Ex-Im Bank or not? What other considerations must be made in appraising the utility of the Bank?

IV. Wire Transfers

Documents Supplement References:

1. *United Nations Model Law on International Credit Transfers (1992)*
2. *Uniform Commercial Code Article 4A (1989 official text), with Official Comments*

A. Transactional and Legal Overview

NOTE ON WIRE TRANSFER LAW*

Introduction

This Note explains the interactions among the main pillars of law which should govern large-value credit transfer systems, also known as "funds" or "wire" transfer systems. The Note highlights the importance of certainty, efficiency, and fairness in funds transfer law. It does so by focusing on the essence of the American legal regime governing large-value credit transfer systems. The same

---

60. *Ex-Im Charter Renewed by Congress*, 14 INT'L TRADE REP. (BNA) 1947 (Nov. 12, 1997).
 * This Note was presented as a paper at the World Bank-CEMLA Seminar on Payments Systems in Mexico City on 22 July 1997. An earlier version of the Note was published as a World Bank Discussion Paper entitled *Towards A Payments System Law for Developing and Transition Economies*. All footnotes from the paper have been omitted. For more detailed treatments of wire transfer law, see ERNEST T. PATRIKIS, THOMAS C. BAXTER, JR. & RAJ BHALA, WIRE TRANSFERS (1993); Raj Bhala, *Paying for the Deal: An Analysis of Wire Transfer Law and International Financial Market Interest Groups*, 42 KAN. L. REV. 667 (spring 1994); Raj Bhala, *The Inverted Pyramid of Wire Transfer Law*, 82 KY. L. J. 347 (winter 1993-94).

essential principles discussed herein are found in the new international legal regime governing these systems. Accordingly, the Note will be useful to international business lawyers concerned with the development of funds transfer laws in other countries.

The Note consists of five parts. In Part 1, the relationship between the legal framework for a large-value credit transfer system and the development of an ideal system is discussed. Part 2 briefly surveys the five foundations of a legal framework for large-value credit transfer systems. These foundations are: (1) a rule defining the scope of the law; (2) a rule establishing when the rights and obligations of parties to a funds transfer are triggered; (3) a receiver finality rule; (4) a rule assigning liability for interloper fraud; and (5) a money-back guarantee rule, coupled with provisions on discharge. Part 3 introduces a case study of a funds transfer and employs essential legal terminology. In Part 4, the five foundations of a legal regime governing funds transfer law are discussed in detail using the essential legal terminology. Part 5 considers general principles of drafting a funds transfer law in the special context of developing and transition economies. The countries of the former Soviet Union and Baltic region are considered as examples. Finally, concluding observations are set forth.

1. The Importance of the Governing Legal Regime

A necessary (but not sufficient) condition for a thorough discussion of large-value credit transfers is a treatment of U.C.C. Article 4A. Whether these transfers are popular means of payment from the view of individual transactors, and whether they are conducted in a safe and sound manner from the view of bank supervisors, are issues that necessarily involve the law. Funds transfer law should serve the interests of the commercial parties who look to large-value credit transfer systems to settle their payment obligations and in particular should facilitate growth in domestic and international transactions. As discussed below, ill-conceived funds transfer rules, or a legal void, can retard the growth and development of large-value credit transfer systems. In turn, the underlying transactions which generate payments obligations may be hampered.

Large-value credit transfers are of enormous importance. For example, over 80 percent of the dollars transferred in the United States are sent over large-dollar electronic funds transfer networks. Every day in the United States, roughly two trillion U.S. dollars are transferred by means of Fedwire and the Clearing House Interbank Payments System (CHIPS). Every two to four days, the total gross national product of the G-10 countries turns over on the wires. Depending on the structure of the laws governing funds transfers, potential users and providers of funds transfer services may find these services either more or less attractive.

With so much money transferred "by wire" each day, and with the average value of each transfer so high, the potential for large losses is great. Thus, commercial parties making and receiving such payments require a clear, comprehensible, and sensible legal regime to answer two basic questions. First, how should a funds transfer normally work? Second, what happens if a mishap occurs? There is a third public policy issue of particular concern to central bankers, namely, systemic risk — how can this risk be minimized and contained?

One way to approach these issues is to consider the theoretical underpinnings of an ideal payments system. Arguably, an ideal payments system must have three salient features: it must be certain (*i.e.*, reliable), efficient (*i.e.*, high speed, low cost, and high security), and fair (*i.e.*, equitable in its apportionment of liability). That is, large amounts of funds must be transmitted at low cost and with high security, and the rights and obligations of parties to the funds transfer must be allocated in a fair manner. A legal framework for a large-value credit transfer system is essential to ensuring that all three features are present in the system.

First, burdensome or unclear legal rules raise the costs of a funds transfer, thereby reducing efficiency. In turn, the system becomes less attractive to potential providers of system services, users of those services, or both. For example, suppose an automobile company instructs its bank to make a $5 million payment to a steel supplier. The payment is made through the Bank of Credit and Commerce International (BCCI), but before the payment transaction is complete BCCI fails. Does the automobile company, the steel company, the creditors of BCCI, or some other party bear the $5 million loss? If the legal framework fails to provide an unequivocal answer, then uncertainty is generated. In reaction to uncertainty, system providers and users must take precautions — that is, insure against risks — hence, the cost of providing and using the system inevitably will increase.

Second, the lack of rules on authenticity and security reduces reliability. Consequently, the system creates uncertainties and risk for both its providers and users. For example, suppose an American bank that receives a $500,000 payment instruction from one of its customers discovers — after the payment is made to an offshore bank — that the instruction is unauthorized. What are the rights and obligations of the American bank, its customer, and the offshore bank? If the legal framework does not provide a clear answer, then the system will be viewed as unreliable by prospective users and providers of system services.

Third, an over-allocation of duties to system providers or to system users can be unfair. In addition, it may lead to a non-level playing field. For example, where liabilities are skewed toward non-bank users of a large-value funds transfer system, banks may enjoy a monopoly position. When potential users or providers perceive a system to be unfair, they simply will not use or provide, respectively, system services.

In sum, there is an integral link between the (1) legal foundations of a large-value credit transfer system and (2) extent to which that system is an ideal one. The essence of the American and United Nations legal regimes governing large-value credit transfer systems can be grasped by understanding five legal rules. These rules — the five legal foundations — are designed to make the systems to which the rules apply more efficient, reliable, and safe. To be sure, these are not the only rules in United States or international funds transfer laws. Reasonable people may contend that there are other equally or even more essential statutory provisions. For example, there are important rules on liability and damages, including a rule against consequential damages in all cases except where a beneficiary's bank wrongfully withholds payment from a beneficiary. Nevertheless, distilling this complex legal field to five foundational rules assuredly yields much of the essence of the law.

2. A Brief Mention of the Five Legal Foundations

To appreciate the rules, it is first necessary to master the terminology of funds transfer law and to use applicable terms in the context of a typical funds transfer. (The terms "funds transfers" and "credit transfers" are used interchangeably, as are the terms "funds transfer systems" and "large-value credit transfer systems.") Accordingly, the five critical elements in the American and international funds transfer laws are set forth in the appropriate legal terminology and context.

All of the economic and policy justifications for the five legal rules are beyond the scope of this Note. Similarly, there is no attempt to argue or prove that the rules discussed herein are the exclusive legal pillars of funds transfer law. By setting forth the important provisions in American funds transfer law, the presentation will serve as a point of departure for the future work and study of the lawyer, banker, or scholar.

The five rules are set forth in Article 4A of the Uniform Commercial Code (U.C.C.), the principal law in the United States governing funds transfers, and the United Nations Model Law on International Credit Transfers (U.N. Model Law), the main international legal agreement on funds transfer rules. They are:

(1) a *scope rule* to differentiate the parties and payment instructions that are included in the law from those that are not included;

(2) a *trigger event* to indicate the moment when the rights and obligations of a party to a funds transfer are manifest;

(3) a *receiver finality rule* to establish when credit to an account is irrevocable;

(4) a *money-back guarantee* to cover situations where a funds transfer is not completed, coupled with a discharge rule for cases where the transfer is completed; and,

(5) an *anti-fraud rule* to allocate liability for fraudulent payments instructions.

3. A Case Study

A discussion of the five key rules of U.C.C. Article 4A is aided by reference to a case study of a funds transfer. Consider the following hypothetical:

(1)   An automobile manufacturer buys steel worth $100,000 from a steel company to make vehicles. The steel company delivers the steel to the automobile manufacturer, and the manufacturer now seeks to pay the company for the steel by funds transfer.

(2)   The manufacturer and steel company hold their accounts at different banks.

(3)   The manufacturer instructs its bank to pay $100,000 to the steel company. The instruction contains the name and account number of the steel company and the name and identifying number of the steel company's bank.

(4)   The automobile manufacturer's bank complies with the instruction of its customer by further instructing a second bank to pay $100,000 to the steel company. This second instruction again contains the relevant information about the steel company and its bank.

(5)   The second bank also complies with the instruction it received. It further instructs the bank at which the steel company has an account to pay $100,000 to the steel company.

(6)   The steel company's bank complies with the third instruction and pays the company.

This hypothetical transaction is represented in the following diagram. The chronological steps in the transaction are indicated by numbers in parentheses. The defined terms of U.C.C. Article 4A are used, highlighted, and explained in detail below.

Each of these parties, and the actions each undertakes, has a specific legal label in U.C.C. Article 4A. Applying the correct labels is the first step in the process of distilling Article 4A to its essential ingredients. Each payment instruction is a *"payment order"* if it meets the requirements of the definition of that term. This term is critical in defining the scope of the law.

The automobile manufacturer is the *"originator"* of the funds transfer, that is, "the sender of the first payment order in a funds transfer." The bank at which the au-

Diagram 4.1. Hypothetical Example of a Funds Transfer

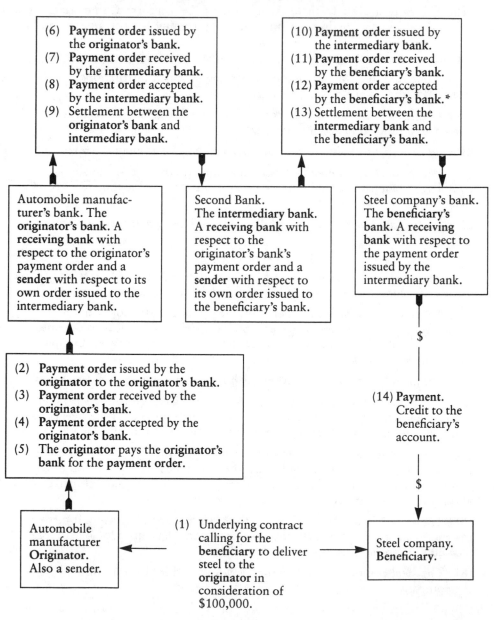

(6) **Payment order** issued by
    the **originator's bank.**
(7) **Payment order** received
    by the **intermediary bank.**
(8) **Payment order** accepted
    by the **intermediary bank.**
(9) Settlement between the
    originator's bank and
    intermediary bank.

(10) **Payment order** issued by
     the **intermediary bank.**
(11) **Payment order** received
     by the **beneficiary's bank.**
(12) **Payment order** accepted
     by the **beneficiary's bank.** *
(13) Settlement between the
     intermediary bank and
     the **beneficiary's bank.**

Automobile manufac-
turer's bank. The
originator's bank. A
receiving bank with
respect to the originator's
payment order and a
sender with respect to its
own order issued to the
intermediary bank.

Second Bank.
The **intermediary bank.**
A **receiving bank** with
respect to the
originator's bank's
payment order and a
sender with respect to
its own order issued to
the beneficiary's bank.

Steel company's bank.
The **beneficiary's
bank.** A receiving
bank with respect to
the payment order
issued by the
intermediary bank.

(2) **Payment order** issued by the
    originator to the **originator's bank.**
(3) **Payment order** received by the
    originator's bank.
(4) **Payment order** accepted by the
    originator's bank.
(5) The **originator** pays the **originator's
    bank** for the **payment order.**

(14) **Payment.**
     Credit to the
     beneficiary's
     account.

$

Automobile
manufacturer
Originator.
Also a sender.

(1) Underlying contract
    calling for the
    beneficiary to deliver
    steel to the
    originator in
    consideration of
    $100,000.

Steel company.
Beneficiary.

$

* Adjunct to (12). Obligation of
the **originator** to pay $100,000 to
the **beneficiary** is **discharged** when
the **beneficiary's bank** accepts the
payment order.

tomobile manufacturer maintains an account and to which the first payment order is addressed is the "*originator's bank*." The steel company is the "*beneficiary*" of the originator's payment order. Also, it is the beneficiary of each payment order issued in the funds transfer chain that implements the originator's order, *i.e.*, the payment order issued by the originator's bank and the second bank. The "beneficiary" is simply "the person to be paid by the beneficiary's bank." The bank at which the steel company maintains its account and to which funds are credited is the "*beneficiary's bank*." This term is reserved for "the bank identified in a payment order in which an account of the beneficiary is to be credited pursuant to the order or which otherwise is to make payment to the beneficiary if the order does not provide for payment to an account." The second bank is the "*intermediary bank*" in that it is "a receiving bank other than the originator's bank or the beneficiary's bank."

The terms "*sender*" and "*receiving bank*" are generic: a sender is "the person giving the instruction to the receiving bank" and the receiving bank is "the bank to which the sender's instruction is addressed." The automobile manufacturer (the originator), the bank of the automobile manufacturer (the originator's bank), and the second bank (the intermediary bank) are all senders. The originator's bank, intermediary bank, and beneficiary's bank (the steel company's bank) are receiving banks.

The "*funds transfer*" is the entire "series of transactions, beginning with the originator's payment order, made for the purpose of making payment to the beneficiary of the order." It includes the payment orders issued by the originator's bank and the intermediary bank, because these are "intended to carry out the originator's payment order." The funds transfer "is *completed* by acceptance by the beneficiary's bank of a payment order for the benefit of the beneficiary of the originator's payment order."

The sale of steel by the steel company to the automobile manufacturer is the underlying contract between the beneficiary and originator of the funds transfer. Under the terms of the contract, the originator has a $100,000 payment obligation, and the originator begins the funds transfer for the purpose of *discharging* this obligation.

The concept of discharge is tricky in two senses. First, its legal importance is not always clearly understood. The crucial point is that until the funds transfer is completed, which occurs when the beneficiary's bank accepts a payment order for the beneficiary, the originator is legally liable on this obligation — it is not discharged. The originator's obligation to pay the beneficiary based on the contract for steel is not discharged until the beneficiary's bank accepts a payment order for the benefit of the beneficiary. Thereafter, the originator cannot be sued by the beneficiary for breach of contract on the grounds of non-payment.

Second, seemingly synonymous uses of the terms "payment obligation" (or "payment"), "settlement obligation" (or "settlement") and "discharge" sometimes generate confusion. In the funds transfer context, the underlying payment obligation refers to the obligation of the originator to pay the beneficiary. This obligation arises from the underlying contractual obligation between those two parties. When the obligation is satisfied, it is said to be legally discharged. Each sender whose payment order is accepted by a receiving bank has a payment obligation to that bank, namely, to pay for the accepted order. The terms "settlement" and "settlement obligation" refer to an interbank payment obligation that arises from the acceptance of a payment order. That is, they refer to the payment obligation as between a sending and receiving bank. However, these interpretations are based more on customary and trade usage than specific sections of U.C.C. Article 4A.

Each receiving bank has a decision to make when it receives a payment order: should it *accept* or *reject* the order? The receiving bank is not obligated to accept an order. A receiving bank may reject an order because the sender does not have sufficient funds in its account to pay for the order. Or, a receiving bank may reject a payment instruction because it states conditions with which the bank is unwilling or unable to comply. A receiving bank other than the beneficiary's bank (*i.e.*, the originator's bank and intermediary bank) accepts a payment order by executing the order. "Execution" of a payment order means that the bank "issues a payment order intended to carry out the payment order received by the bank." Thus, the originator's bank accepts the payment order of the originator by issuing an order that conforms with the instructions set forth in the order of the originator. Similarly, the intermediary bank accepts the payment order of the originator's bank by issuing a conforming order designed to implement the originator's bank's order.

A beneficiary's bank, however, does not accept a payment order by execution. Rather, the beneficiary's bank, if it accepts the order, is required to pay the beneficiary the amount of the order. Typically, it does so by crediting the account of the beneficiary maintained at the beneficiary's bank.

A receiving bank's decision to accept or reject a payment order is partly a credit judgment: if the order is accepted, then the sender must *pay* for the order (*e.g.*, the originator must pay $100,000 to the originator's bank if the bank accepts the originator's order, the originator's bank must pay $100,000 to the intermediary bank if the intermediary bank accepts the originator's bank's order, and so forth.) The credit issue arises where a sender does not currently have funds in its account with the receiving bank sufficient to pay for the payment order. The receiving bank may, in its discretion, grant the sender an overdraft. But, any receiving bank, including a central bank, may charge interest to the sender for the amount and duration of the overdraft.

If the bank entitled to payment is a receiving bank other than the beneficiary's bank (*i.e.*, the originator's bank or an intermediary bank), then the obligation to pay arises upon acceptance but does not mature until the *execution date*. That is, payment is not due until the day on which it is proper for the receiving bank to execute the order. Generally, the execution date is the day the order is received. This is referred to as "same-day execution," which means that the receiving bank executes the order on the day it is received from the sender. On or before that day, the sender must pay for the order. Payment by a sender to a receiving bank for a payment order issued by the former and accepted by the latter may be made by a number of means. These include receipt of final settlement on the books of a central bank or through a funds transfer system (which may involve bilateral or multilateral netting), a credit to an account of the receiving bank with the sender, or a debit to an account of the sender with the receiving bank.

If the bank entitled to payment is the beneficiary's bank, then again the obligation to pay arises upon acceptance by that bank. Here, however, the sender (in the hypothetical, the intermediary bank) need not pay the beneficiary's bank until the *payment date*. That is the date on which the amount of the payment order accepted by the beneficiary's bank is payable to the beneficiary. Typically, it is the date of receipt. The beneficiary's bank can pay the beneficiary by crediting its account. The beneficiary is paid as a matter of law when it "is notified of the right to withdraw the credit" or funds "are otherwise made available to the beneficiary," or the bank lawfully applies the credit to a debt of the beneficiary."

The above discussion has not expressly highlighted the role of a central bank in a funds transfer. The conventional but incomplete view is that a central bank is the intermediary bank. To be sure, a central bank often is the intermediary between two commercial banks (the originator's and beneficiary's bank), the upstream originator, and the downstream beneficiary. However, a central bank can play any role in a funds transfer: originator, originator's bank, intermediary bank, beneficiary's bank, or beneficiary. Thus, the critical point is that a central bank can be a sender or receiving bank at any point in a funds transfer chain.

Insertion of the central bank at any point in the funds transfer would not alter the case study as a legal matter unless funds transfer rules set forth in U.C.C. Article 4A (or the U.N. Model Law) are modified by the rules of the central bank. However, there is an important practical difference. A central bank cannot go bankrupt, thus there is no credit risk associated with sending a payment order to, or receiving a payment order from, a central bank. If the funds transfer is not completed, then the reason for the non-completion will lie with a party other than the central bank.

4. In-depth Treatment of the Five Legal Foundations

Foundation I: Scope Rule — Promotes Certainty and Efficiency (Low Litigation Costs)

What is the scope of application of the law? How does a party seeking to send funds electronically know whether the transmission is a funds transfer governed by applicable funds transfer law? Who is included and who is excluded? Appropriate answers to these questions foster certainty and efficiency, in part by reducing the likelihood of litigation about the coverage of the law and thus reducing potential legal costs.

These questions are answered in U.C.C. Article 4A by referring to the definition of "payment order." *If an instruction is not a "payment order," then Article 4A is not applicable.* The term "payment order" means:

an instruction of a sender to a *receiving bank*, transmitted orally, electronically, or in writing, to pay, or to cause another bank to pay, a *fixed or determinable* amount of money to a beneficiary, if:

(i)   the instruction *does not state a condition* to payment to the beneficiary other than time of payment,

(ii)   the receiving bank is to be *reimbursed* by debiting an account of, or otherwise receiving payment from, the sender, and

(iii) the instruction is transmitted by the sender directly to the receiving bank or to an agent, funds-transfer system, or communication for transmittal to the receiving bank.

There are five salient features of this definition. First, the instruction must be issued to a "bank." While any person can be a "sender," only a "bank" can be a "receiving bank." A "bank" is "a person engaged in the business of banking and includes a savings bank, savings and loan association, credit union, and trust company." This definition is flexible, applying to a variety of financial institutions that offer account services — regular commercial banks and certain other types of financial institutions that take deposits and make loans. Thus, the scope of application is potentially wide.

Second, the amount of the instruction must be "fixed or determinable." In most cases, the application of this requirement is straightforward. In the hypothetical, the $100,000 amount is "fixed."

Third, the definition of "payment order" requires that the instruction contain no condition other than time of payment. If the automobile manufacturer's instruction to its bank said "pay $100,000 on day 10 if you receive delivery of shipping documents pertaining to the purchased steel," then the requirement would not be satisfied. Only the statement regarding day 10 is permissible; the statement regarding presentation of documents to the bank is a condition other than time of payment. If both statements are included in the instruction, then it is not a "payment order" and U.C.C. Article 4A is inapplicable.

The fourth requirement concerns payment for the payment instruction. A receiving bank that receives a payment instruction from its sender must be reimbursed by debiting an account of, or otherwise receiving payment from, the sender. This means that credit transfers are included, but all electronic funds transfers that are debit transfers are excluded. In the hypothetical, if the originator's bank is reimbursed for the automobile company's payment order by debiting an account of the company, then this requirement is met.

The way in which this result is obtained raises the important distinction between a credit and debit transfer. "In a credit transfer the instruction to pay is given by the person making payment. In a debit transfer the instruction to pay is given by the person receiving payment." The classic example of a debit transfer involves a check or other negotiable instrument. In a check transaction, a debtor (the drawer of the check) gives authority to the creditor (the payee of the check) to draw on the debtor's account which is maintained at the payer bank (also called the drawee). The authority is given by drawing the check and transferring the check to the payee. In turn, the payee issues the instruction to pay to the payer bank when it deposits the check. That is, the payee (not the drawer) issues the instruction by depositing the check in the depositary bank (at which the payee maintains an account), and the check is presented to the payer bank through the check collection process. Assuming the payer bank honors the check, it is reimbursed by the debtor, not the person giving the instruction (the payee). "Article 4A is limited to transactions in which the account to be debited by the receiving bank is that of the person in whose name the instruction is given." In sum, in a funds transfer the payer (originator) issues the instruction (payment order) to the paying bank (originator's bank) and reimburses that bank. In a check transaction the payee issues the instruction (the check) and the paying bank (payor bank) is reimbursed by the drawer of the check.

Finally, to qualify as a payment order, an instruction must be transmitted directly by the sender to the receiving bank (or its agent, funds transfer system, or communication system for subsequent transmission to the receiving bank). In the hypothetical, each instruction is directly transmitted from sender to receiving bank. This requirement serves to exclude from U.C.C. Article 4A payments made by means of a check or credit card, for example.

Assume that the parties know that U.C.C. Article 4A applies to their transfer. Does it apply to the entire transfer, from the originator to the beneficiary? This is the issue of "end-to-end" coverage. Generally speaking, U.C.C. Article 4A is intended to apply end-to-end. The rules of a funds transfer system like Fedwire — namely, Regulation J of the Board of Governors of the Federal Reserve System — ensure such coverage. For example, if the funds transfer is through Fedwire, then whether remote parties (*i.e.*, those that are not in privity with a Federal Reserve Bank) are bound by Regulation J depends on whether they had prior notice that (1) Fedwire might be used and (2) the applicable law governing Fedwire is Regulation J. Privity means that the parties send payment orders directly to or receive orders directly from a Reserve Bank. These requirements presumably avoid the unwarranted extension of Regulation J or the extraterritorial application thereof in inappropriate situations. Regulation J, however, essentially states that U.C.C. Article 4A is the law governing Fedwire. Similarly, the rules of the CHIPS system make clear that Article 4A governs that system.

Foundation II: Trigger Event — Promotes
Certainty and Efficiency (High Speed)

At what point are the rights and obligations of a party to a funds transfer triggered? In other words, when does the party gain certain legal entitlements, and when is it legally "on the hook" to perform certain duties? Appropriate answers to these questions can promote certainty. The answers also can ensure that funds transfers are conducted efficiently, specifically, in a high speed manner.

The answers are provided in U.C.C. Article 4A by the concept of acceptance. *"Rights and obligations under Article 4A arise as the result of 'acceptance' of a payment order by the bank to which the order is addressed."* Only when a receiving bank accepts a payment order issued by its sender are the rights and obligations of the receiving bank and sender triggered.

As the hypothetical suggests, acceptance is divided according to the class of receiving bank. A receiving bank other than the beneficiary's bank, in the example, the originator's bank and the intermediary bank (the automobile manufacturer's bank and the second bank, respectively), can accept a payment order only by executing the order. "Execution" means the issuance of a payment order that conforms with the terms of the order received from the sender.

In contrast, a beneficiary's bank is responsible for crediting the account of the beneficiary (or otherwise lawfully applying funds received on behalf of the beneficiary). There are essentially three acts that constitute "acceptance" by a beneficiary's bank: (1) payment by the beneficiary's bank to the beneficiary; (2) notification from the beneficiary's bank to the beneficiary that a payment order has been received; or (3) receipt of payment by the beneficiary's bank from the sender that issued the payment order to the beneficiary's bank. Acceptance occurs at the earliest of these times. The first two acts involve the "downstream" relationship between the beneficiary's bank and its customer, the beneficiary. The third act involves the "upstream" relationship between the beneficiary's bank and its sender.

What rights and obligations are triggered upon acceptance of a payment order? Again, there is bifurcation. The basic duty of a sender whose payment order is accepted by a receiving bank is to pay the receiving bank for the order. Conversely, the basic right of the receiving bank is to be paid for the accepted order. While this right-duty set is triggered upon acceptance, it does not mature until the execution date. In addition, the sender has a right to have its payment order, upon acceptance, executed at the right time, in the right amount, and to the right place. This is a trinity of rights which, from the receiving bank's perspective, constitute a trinity of duties.

The right-duty set pertaining to the beneficiary's bank and the beneficiary is straightforward. Upon acceptance of a payment order, the beneficiary's bank has an obligation to pay the order, and the beneficiary has a right to be paid. These mature on the payment date, which typically is the day the order is received by the beneficiary's bank.

Foundation III: Receiver Finality — Promotes
Certainty, Efficiency (High Speed), and Fairness

When does a beneficiary know that it has received "good funds"? If the steel company receives a $100,000 credit to its account, is the credit provisional (revocable), on the one hand, or final on the other hand? If the credit is revocable, then the steel company cannot irrevocably commit the $100,000 to other uses (*e.g.*, paying its bills, paying dividends, investing in new projects, and the like). This is because the steel company's bank (the beneficiary's bank) might demand that the $100,000 be returned if the bank does not finally receive payment from the intermediary bank. An answer to this dilemma is crucial if a funds transfer is to be a certain, efficient (especially high speed), and fair mode of payment.

Once a beneficiary's bank has paid the beneficiary, it has thereby satisfied the obligation to pay the beneficiary that arises from its acceptance of a payment order on behalf of the beneficiary. The payment is final. The payment for the funds transfer cannot be recovered by the beneficiary's bank. This is the receiver finality rule. Even the beneficiary's right to withdraw a credit (*i.e.*, even if the beneficiary's account has been credited but the beneficiary has not withdrawn the credit) cannot be revoked. One of the greatest contrasts, however, between Article 4A and the U.N. Model Law is that the latter does *not* contain a receiver finality rule. Why? Because the Model Law does not purport to govern the relationship between the beneficiary's bank and the beneficiary. That relationship is governed by local law.

The Article 4A receiver finality rule is subject to one important exception. Consider a major settlement failure in a funds-transfer system that nets payment obligations on a multilateral (or net-net) basis and has a loss-sharing arrangement among participants in the system to handle a settlement failure by one or more participants. If a beneficiary's bank accepts a payment order but the multilateral netting system fails to complete settlement in spite of the operation of the loss-sharing scheme, then the acceptance is nullified and the beneficiary's bank can recover funds from the beneficiary. In this unwind scenario, the funds transfer is not completed, the originator is not discharged on its underlying obligation to the beneficiary, and each sender is excused from its obligation to pay for its payment order. This exception to the receiver finality rule supports the development of loss-sharing agreements and other methods to achieve finality on privately operated funds transfer systems that rely on netting. The unwind exception is a "last resort escape" from potentially expensive settlement guarantees that remaining (and presumably solvent) participants in the funds transfer system might be unable to meet. Only by accounting for the potential trade-off between settlement guarantees and finality can the law promote netting systems designed to offer their users finality on a routine basis.

Because of this exception to the receiver finality rule, some observers (*e.g.*, officials at the Bundesbank and Bank for International Settlements) contend that a real-time, gross-settlement (RTGS) funds transfer system is preferable to a netting system. In a RTGS system, there is no worrisome overhang of a possible settlement unwind, yet this possibility plagues a multilateral netting system. Of course, netting serves the purpose of lowering systemic risk by reducing the number and volume of funds transfers. Ultimately, the choice between the systems may depend on country, market, and technological conditions.

The receiver finality rule is constrained when the beneficiary's bank (having accepted a payment order) has a "reasonable doubt concerning the right of the beneficiary to payment." But, the beneficiary's bank risks incurring liability for consequential damages as a result of its nonpayment if the beneficiary demands payment, the bank has notice of "particular circumstances that will give rise to consequential damages as a result of nonpayment," and it is shown that the bank lacked reasonable doubt. This is the only instance in U.C.C. Article 4A where consequential damages are a remedy provided by the statute, absent a written agreement between parties that calls for consequential damages.

Foundation IV: Interloper Fraud Rule — Promotes
Certainty, Efficiency (High Speed), and Fairness

Modern day electronic pirates abound. An example of such modern day electronic pirates arises in the fascinating Australian case involving Swiss Bank and the Bank of New South Wales. A frauds-person (also called an interloper) claiming to be an official of the automobile manufacturer could send a payment order to the automobile manufacturer's bank instructing that $100,000 be paid to an account #10017 at the Bank of Credit and Commerce International (BCCI) in the Grand Cayman Islands. How is the automobile manufacturer's bank to determine whether the payment order is really that of its customer, the automobile manufacturer? If the bank executes the order and debits the automobile manufacturer's account for $100,000, is the bank obliged to re-credit the account when it is discovered that the payment order was not authentic? What if the payment order is issued by an employee or agent of the automobile manufacturer that has access to its bank account information? Appropriate answers to these questions promote certainty, efficiency in the sense of high security, and fairness.

U.C.C. Article 4A addresses the interloper fraud problem through the concept of a "*security procedure*" and rules based on the existence or non-existence of such a security procedure.

A security procedure is the generic term for a device or method (whether an electronic message authentication or other computer algorithm, code words, telephone call-back, or the like) for "verifying that a payment order is that of the customer...." The U.C.C. Article 4A rules are summarized as follows:

> In a large percentage of cases, the payment order of the originator of the funds transfer is transmitted electronically to the originator's bank. In these cases it may not be possible for the bank to know whether the electronic message has been authorized by its customer. To ensure that no unauthorized person is transmitting messages to the bank, the normal practice is to establish security procedures that usually involve the use of codes or identifying words. If the bank accepts a payment order that purports to be that of its customer after verifying its authenticity by complying with a *security procedure agreed to by the customer and the bank*, the customer is bound to pay the order even if it was not authorized. But there is an important limitation on this rule. The bank is entitled to payment in the case of an unauthorized order only if the court finds that the security procedure was a *commercially reasonable* method of providing security against unauthorized payment orders. The customer can also avoid liability if it can prove that the unauthorized order was *not initiated by an employee or other agent* of the customer having access to confidential security information or by a person who obtained that information from a source controlled by the customer.... If the bank accepts an unauthorized payment order without verifying it in compliance with a security procedure, the loss falls on the bank.

Three analytical steps are apparent from the summary: the agreement; commercial reasonability; and the "not an insider" defense.

First, has a security procedure been established pursuant to an agreement between the sender and receiving bank? If no procedure exists, then interloper fraud issues are resolved under non-U.C.C. Article 4A principles, specifically, the law of agency, that is, the law that establishes when one person is considered to be acting on behalf of another. The resolution that might be achieved under this law will turn on whether the frauds-person sent the payment order with the authority (whether actual or apparent) of the

purported sender. Thus, if no security procedure exists between the automobile manufacturer and its bank, then whether the payment order issued by the frauds-person was
authorized by the automobile manufacturer will be determined under applicable agency
law principles.

A security procedure, in theory, is not unilaterally imposed by one party or
the other, but rather results from negotiations culminating in a written account
agreement. To be sure, many customers are likely to have a standard-form contract specifying a particular procedure presented to them by their banks. Assuming that a security procedure has been agreed to between the bank and its customer, the next step is to consider whether that procedure is "commercially
reasonable."

"Commercial reasonability" is a question of law, not fact. The judge's discretion is limited by U.C.C. Article 4A, which sets out criteria for evaluating whether
a security procedure is commercially reasonable in a case at bar: "the wishes of the
customer expressed to the bank, the circumstances of the customer known to the
bank, including the size, type and frequency of payment orders normally issued by
the customer to the bank, alternative security procedures offered to the customer,
and security procedures in general use by customers and receiving banks similarly
situated."

To avoid liability, the originator's bank in the hypothetical must prove that the
security procedure it agreed to with its customer is commercially reasonable. In
addition, the bank must show that it accepted the payment order in "good faith"
and in compliance with the procedure. Acting in good faith and following the security procedure are issues of fact and, therefore, matters for a trier of fact such as
a jury.

In the hypothetical funds transfer, suppose the originator argues that the
$100,000 issued in its name and accepted by the originator's bank was unauthorized,
and the ensuing $100,000 debit to its account should be reversed. Suppose also that
the automobile manufacturer's bank proves to a judge that the security procedure in
operation between it and the automobile manufacturer by which the payment order
was verified was commercially reasonable. Suppose further that the bank also proves
to the trier of fact that it acted in good faith in accepting the order and in compliance
with the procedure. Has the purported originator, the innocent customer of the bank,
lost the case?

Not necessarily, because of the "not an insider" defense. The suspect payment
order may have been issued by a person who was not an employee or agent of the automobile manufacturer, and who did not gain access to the manufacturer's bank account information through someone controlled by the manufacturer. In other words,
the frauds-person may not have been an "insider" of the automobile manufacturer
or someone close to an insider. If the "innocent" automobile manufacturer proves
these facts, then the automobile manufacturer's bank cannot retain payment for the
payment order. Note that the burden of proof has shifted: the automobile manufacturer's bank has the burden on the matters of a security procedure agreement, commercial reasonability, and good faith and compliance; but the customer purporting
to be a victim of fraud has the burden of the "not an insider" defense. Note also that
the "not an insider" defense is difficult to maintain successfully. A large number of
fraud, and even attempted fraud, cases appear to involve insiders.

There is no comparative negligence analysis or sharing of liability in this legal
scheme. The purported sender/innocent customer (the automobile manufacturer) bears
the full $100,000 loss (in that its account is not re-credited) if (1) the bank proves that

it acted in good faith and complied with a commercially reasonable security procedure and (2) the customer cannot meet the innocent customer defense requirements.

Foundation V: Money-back Guarantee and Discharge — Promotes Certainty, Efficiency (Low Litigation Costs), and Fairness

In the hypothetical funds transfer, what rights does each sender (the originator, originator's bank, and intermediary bank) have if the funds transfer is not completed? For example, is the automobile manufacturer entitled to a refund of $100,000, or must it commence litigation against some downstream party to recover the funds? What rights do the automobile manufacturer's bank and the second bank have in the event of non-completion? Does completion have an effect on the underlying contractual obligation of the automobile manufacturer to pay $100,000 to the steel company? Appropriate answers to these questions promote certainty, efficiency in the form of low litigation costs, and fairness.

A money-back guarantee rule ensures that the originator of a funds transfer, and each subsequent sender of a payment order in the funds transfer chain, obtains its money back in the event the transfer is not completed. A funds transfer is said to be completed when the *beneficiary's bank accepts* a payment order on behalf of the beneficiary. If the transfer is not completed, then each sender of a payment order in the funds transfer chain is *entitled to a refund* of the principal amount of the payment order, plus any accrued interest. If the transfer is completed, then the originator's underlying contractual obligation to the beneficiary is *discharged*.

In the hypothetical funds transfer, as soon as the steel company's bank accepts the payment order issued by the second bank, the funds transfer is complete and the automobile manufacturer is discharged on its underlying obligation to pay $100,000 to the steel company. In the event of non-completion, each sender — the automobile manufacturer, the automobile manufacturer's bank, and the second bank — is entitled to a refund of any amount it paid for its payment order, plus interest.

The money-back guarantee may not be varied by an agreement between the sender and receiving bank. However, the rule is subject to the exception that a sender that selects a particular intermediary bank through which to route a funds transfer bears the risk of loss associated with the failure of that bank.

Suppose the automobile manufacturer instructed its bank to route the $100,000 transfer through BCCI instead of the second bank, and the automobile manufacturer's bank complies with this instruction and debits its customer's account. Assume that BCCI is closed by banking supervisors. The closure occurs after BCCI accepts the payment order issued by the automobile manufacturer's bank and is paid for the order by that bank, but before the funds transfer is completed (*i.e.*, before the steel company's bank accepts BCCI's order). The effective result of these facts is that the funds are "stuck" at BCCI. Then, the originator is not entitled to a re-credit of $100,000. The automobile manufacturer's bank can keep the $100,000, and the automobile manufacturer is subrogated to the right of its bank to claim against the receiver or trustee of BCCI's assets. (That is, the automobile manufacturer's ability to retrieve the $100,000 depends on the right of its bank to claim against the receiver.) In sum, the party (here, the originator) who designates the failed intermediary bank should and does bear the risk of adverse consequences of that choice.

A Note on Bank Failure

The consequences of bank failure on account holders depend in part on the time the failure occurs and on which bank in the funds transfer chain fails.

Failure of an Intermediary Bank Before Completion: In the above example, BCCI fails before the funds transfer is complete, therefore, the risk of loss is assumed by the party that designated the use of the intermediary bank.

Failure of an Intermediary Bank After Completion: If BCCI fails after the transfer is complete, then the beneficiary's bank must have accepted a payment order from BCCI, and the originator must have been discharged, before the failure. This is because of the definition of "completion" and the discharge rule. Payment by the beneficiary's bank to the beneficiary is final because of the receiver finality rule. Whether the beneficiary's bank was paid by BCCI for the order it received and accepted from BCCI before the beneficiary's bank paid the beneficiary depends on the facts of the case. If the beneficiary's bank accepts BCCI's order by paying the beneficiary before receiving settlement from BCCI, then the beneficiary's bank assumes the risk of loss from a BCCI failure.

Failure of the Originator's Bank Before Acceptance: The above discussion prompts the question of what happens if BCCI remains solvent, but the originator's bank or the beneficiary's bank fails. Consider first the case where the originator's bank fails before accepting the originator's payment order. Plainly, the funds transfer is not complete and the originator's obligation to pay $100,000 to the beneficiary is not discharged. Under U.C.C. Article 4A, because the originator's bank failed before acceptance, the duty of the originator to pay the originator's bank for its order never matured, hence the originator is not liable for the order it issued. It is entitled to a refund of any money it might have paid to the originator's bank for its payment order.

Failure of the Originator's Bank After Acceptance: If the originator's bank fails after accepting the order, then the originator is obligated to pay for its order. Assuming a same-day execution scenario, the originator's bank will have accepted the originator's payment order by issuing a conforming order, *i.e.*, by executing the originator's order, on the day it received the originator's order. Under U.C.C. Article 4A, if BCCI accepts the order of the originator's bank, then the originator's bank is liable to pay for its order. Whether this liability is affected by applicable Federal bank regulatory provisions is beyond the scope of this presentation, but the issue raises potentially intriguing legal and policy issues.

For example, the originator is not discharged until the beneficiary's bank accepts an order from BCCI, but suppose BCCI is unwilling to accept the order issued by the originator's bank until the originator's bank provides settlement for its order. In this instance, BCCI presumably is unwilling to assume the risk that the originator's bank fails after BCCI accepts the order but before BCCI has been paid for the order. The originator will then bear that risk, because it may have paid the originator's bank for its payment order but not have been discharged on its underlying payment obligation to the beneficiary. If the originator's bank fails before discharge occurs, then the originator is liable to the beneficiary for $100,000 on the underlying contract and must claim against the originator's bank (or its receiver or liquidator) under the money-back guarantee (or perhaps other applicable law). This might be justified on the ground that the originator is the party that selected the use of the originator's bank by maintaining an account at, and issuing a payment order to, that bank.

Failure of the Beneficiary's Bank: Consider the scenario in which the beneficiary's bank fails. If this occurs after acceptance, then the originator is discharged on its obligation. The beneficiary bears the risk of loss and must make a claim against the failed bank (or its receiver or liquidator). Again, this might be justifiable because the beneficiary is the party that designated to the originator in its underlying contract with the originator that payment should be made at the beneficiary's bank. If failure occurs before acceptance, then the funds transfer is not complete. The originator (and each subsequent sender) are entitled to the money-back guarantee. Presumably, the originator will pay the beneficiary through a funds transfer directed to a different beneficiary's bank (or through an alternative payments mechanism).

5. Drafting Principles for Developing Countries

Point 1: Interest Groups

Law, including payments system law, is not handed down from God. Rather, law results from a long and complicated interaction of interest groups that advance their economic, political, and social agendas. U.C.C. Article 4A and the U.N. Model Law are examples of this interaction. Accordingly, neither Article 4A nor the Model Law appeared in the law books quickly. The drafters negotiated for years, working and re-working concepts and specific legal language. It would be foolish to suggest that the work of every drafter reflected the same or even similar theories as those held by every other drafter. To the contrary, different drafters had different theories and they negotiated, argued, and ultimately compromised with one another.

However, it is possible to group the drafters of U.C.C. Article 4A into three broad interest groups: system users, system providers, and system supervisors. The delegates to the United Nations Commission on International Trade Law (UNCI-TRAL) that drafted the U.N. Model Law also tended to reflect these constituencies. The users of large-value credit transfer systems — typically corporate customers and some (usually smaller) financial institutions — had consumer interests in mind. Their aim was to ensure that stringent liabilities were imposed on system providers. Hence, they sought clear rules on misdirected payment orders, and to hold banks liable for consequential as well as actual damages under certain circumstances. Often, the arguments of users were cast in terms of fairness.

Conversely, system providers — generally, large banks and owners of particular systems — sought to minimize their liabilities. They struggled to avoid the imposition of consequential damages, and ensure that stringent rules governing authenticity and security procedures were drafted. Typically, their arguments were cast in terms of efficiency and reliability.

Finally, system supervisors — central banks and finance ministries — sought to minimize systemic risks. Accordingly, they strongly advocated the receiver finality and discharge rules. They did not consistently side with users or providers. Indeed, often they played the role of mediator between users and providers, while at the same time keeping a watchful eye on their own interests. They would employ the language of fairness, efficiency, or reliability depending on the needs of the problem at hand.

When drafting a funds transfer law, it may be useful to think in terms of users, providers, and supervisors as three distinct interest groups whose concerns must be addressed. However, it is not necessarily desirable to encourage this tripartite division of interest groups during the drafting process. The countries of the former Soviet Union, and the Baltic countries, must draft legal frameworks for large-value funds transfer system in different environments from the one in which U.C.C. Article 4A and the U.N. Model Law were created. Thinking in terms of consumer, bank, and supervisory interests may not necessarily reflect these different environments.

Instead, it may be particularly fruitful to consider what questions are most pressing. For example, to what extent is the general commercial law framework well articulated and well developed? In some instances, the answer is that only a skeletal framework exists. Are bankruptcy rules in place to handle bank and customer insolvencies? In some cases, only nascent rules exist, and in other instances no such rules have been implemented. To what extent is fraud present in commercial transactions? Sadly, in some cases fraud is relatively commonplace.

Point 2: The Rule of Law

The special environment in developing and transition economies — present, for example, in the countries of the former Soviet Union, and the Baltic countries — suggests five fundamental drafting principles. First, as a threshold matter the importance of the rule of law must be established firmly. The payments system law should be manifest at the highest level of the hierarchy of rules in a particular country. If in a country's legal system a statute has greater force and effect than a regulation, and in turn a regulation has greater force and effect than an administrative order, then the law governing funds transfers should take the form of a statute. This form should afford greater protection against political or bureaucratic meddling in the payments system. Of course, in certain countries — for instance, Vietnam — passing a statute is a more cumbersome process than issuing a regulation. Nonetheless, the rule of law is fundamental to the certain, efficient, and fair operation of a funds transfer system, thus procedural hurdles in passing laws must be overcome.

Point 3: Accountability

Institutions involved in funds transfers should be held accountable for their own behavior. Such parties should not expect assistance from the government in the event of mishaps or financial difficulties. The utmost importance must be accorded rules of law, not relationships among parties or between a party and the government. In general, a funds transfer law must be part of a larger legal environment that is founded on individual financial accountability, not central planning and control. In this regard, the participation of the central bank in the funds transfer system should not be overemphasized. There is no necessary reason why it must own and operate a system. Indeed, private party action and responsibility ought to be encouraged, not only in transition and developing economies, but also in developed market economies.

Point 4: Integration with Other Bodies of Law

Funds transfer law ought not to develop in a vacuum. This law must be seen as part of the broad commercial and bankruptcy framework and not developed in a piecemeal fashion. Accordingly, the rules governing large-value credit transfers must be consistent with those established for contracts, negotiable instruments, letters of credit, secured transactions, and insolvencies. Thus, for example, the concepts of "commercial reasonability" or "good faith" must be used consistently throughout the framework. The economic incentives created by the different parts of the framework must also be consistent. Commercial law is a seamless web, and thus there must be a holistic integrity to the law.

Point 5: Fraud Prevention

Especially in developing and transition economies, particular emphasis must be given to fraud prevention. Accordingly, appropriate safeguards must be implemented that create incentives for all parties to a large-value credit transfer to exercise at least reasonable care. More generally, the legal framework must be seen as a primary guarantor of the integrity of the payments system. Nothing undermines that integrity faster than fraud. However, in drafting rules on fraud prevention, an inevitable tension between security and efficiency must be managed. On the one hand, requiring receiving banks and their sender customers to exercise great diligence in preventing fraud raises the level of security. On the other hand, the greater the burden on receiving banks and senders to act as policemen against fraud, the higher the monetary cost of a funds transfer, and the longer it may take to process a transfer. There is no simple recipe for managing this tension; rather, the appropriate solution will depend on the country in question.

Point 6: Supporting Emerging Financial Markets

The legal framework for large-value funds transfers should accommodate the anticipated growth and development of the economy and its constituent sectors. In the United States and other post-industrial societies, the primary motivation for engaging in such transfers is not to settle payments obligations arising from the sale of goods. In this sense, the case study discussed above concerning the automobile manufacturer and steel company is antiquated. In truth, the bulk of credit transfer activity is generated by financial transactions — the buying and selling of foreign exchange, short-term money market instruments, and various types of investment securities. Accordingly, in developing a legal framework for large-value credit transfers systems, the future needs of the financial community must be anticipated and addressed.

Summary

The legal foundations of the large-value credit transfer systems in the United States, Fedwire and CHIPS are set forth in U.C.C. Article 4A. The same legal foundations are found in the U.N. Model Law. Among the many provisions in these legal texts, at least five are particularly noteworthy: (1) a rule defining the scope of the law; (2) a rule establishing when the rights and obligations of parties to a funds transfer are triggered; (3) a receiver finality rule; (4) a rule assigning liability for interloper fraud; and (5) a money-back guarantee rule, coupled with provisions on discharge. The rules are articulated through precise terminology identifying each party to a funds transfer and the actions that each party undertakes.

Must the five rules exist in any funds transfer statute? To what extent can one generalize from the Article 4A or U.N. Model Law experience? These questions deserve two levels of analysis. First, comparative legal research on the laws governing large-value credit transfer systems in other jurisdictions is needed to identify the foundations of those laws. In other words, those laws need to be distilled. Second, theoretical debate, involving economic rationales and public policy goals, is required to determine the justifications for alternative statutory foundations.

While these analyses have yet to be performed, one point of caution is appropriate: commercial law, including funds transfer law, is not immutable. It serves commercial parties and their transactions, but because both of these change over time, individual needs and systemic concerns vary as well. Accordingly, the legal foundations of a regime for large-value credit transfer systems, should be viewed as dynamic, not static.

B. The Relationship Between Wire Transfer Law and Other Law

Sheerbonnet, Ltd. v. American Express Bank, Ltd.
951 F.Supp. 403 (S.D.N.Y. 1995)

PRESKA, DISTRICT JUDGE:

Instructed by the Court of Appeals not to abstain from further determinations, *Sheerbonnet v. American Express Bank, Ltd.*, 17 F.3d 46 (2d Cir.), *cert. denied*, 513 U.S. 813 (1994), I return to this case to address the remaining arguments in defendant's renewed motion to dismiss. The facts...will...be summarized here. They should be considered retrospectively, in light of the seizure by the Superintendent of Banks of the State of New York ("Superintendent"), as part of a worldwide seizure in July of 1991, of the New York assets of the Bank of Credit and Commerce, S.A.("BCCI"). The collapse of BCCI and the subsequent seizure of its assets has spawned a legion of lawsuits, of which this is but one.

FACTS

Plaintiff Sheerbonnet, Ltd. ("Sheerbonnet") is a British trading company which contracted in 1990 to sell troop carriers to the Hady Establishment ("Hady"), a Saudi Arabian company. The carriers were to be used by Allied forces during the Persian Gulf War. For payment, Hady obtained an irrevocable $14,080,000 letter of credit from Banque Scandanave, in Geneva, Switzerland. Ten percent of this price was down payment, the remainder due after delivery. After receiving the down payment and fulfilling its obligations under the contract, Sheerbonnet awaited the balance, approximately $12.4 million, due on July 5, 1991.

Sheerbonnet requested that the payment be made through a funds transfer to its account at BCCI in London. Because Sheerbonnet was to be paid in U.S. dollars, Banque Scandanave initiated payment on July 3rd by instructing its correspondent bank in New York, Northern Trust International ("Northern Trust"), to transfer $12.4 million to American Express Bank ("AEB") for credit to BCCI's account at AEB in New York on July 5th.

On the morning of July 5th, regulators in England and Luxembourg suspended the operations of the faltering BCCI. On the same day in the United States, the Federal Reserve Bank advised AEB and other banks of the suspension of BCCI accounts worldwide, including the seizure of BCCI's New York operations. At 9:00 a.m., the Superintendent closed BCCI's New York Agency and announced the seizure of all "business and property" of BCCI in New York.

Shortly thereafter, AEB received by wire from Northern Trust the payment order for the transfer of $12.4 million to the BCCI account at AEB in New York. Knowing the account was frozen, AEB nevertheless credited to it the $12.4 million. Because of the freeze, these assets remained in New York.

After crediting the funds to the BCCI account, AEB asserted its rights over virtually the entire account as an off-set against debts owed to it by the insolvent BCCI. The $12.4 million transferred by wire from Northern Trust on July 5, 1991 remains in AEB's control, none of this money having ever reached Sheerbonnet.

The Superintendent, pursuant to New York Banking Law § 606(4)(a), thereafter began liquidation proceedings to dispose of BCCI's assets in New York. In March of 1992, the Superintendent petitioned the Supreme Court of the State of New York

("Liquidation Court") for an order compelling AEB and several New York banks to turn over any BCCI funds held in their accounts. A settlement agreement was reached, and the Liquidation Court entered a Turnover Order on April 27, 1992 instructing the banks to cede BCCI funds to the Superintendent, less set-offs claimed by the banks. Upon remittance, the Turnover Order provided that the banks would be "discharged from liability with respect to claims for funds of BCCI, S.A. located in New York." Having already claimed the BCCI London account as a set-off, AEB did not turn over any funds to the Superintendent.

In September of 1992, Sheerbonnet commenced suit against AEB in this Court. After motion by the defendant, I abstained from the case under the federal abstention doctrine enunciated by the Supreme Court in *Burford v. Sun Oil Co.*, 319 U.S. 315, (1943). That order was reversed by the Court of Appeals, and defendant now renews its motion to dismiss.

DISCUSSION

AEB has moved to dismiss the complaint on three grounds: (1) that Sheerbonnet has failed to state a claim upon which relief can be granted, under Fed.R.Civ.P. 12(b)(6); (2) that the claim is barred by a previous order of the Liquidation Court; and (3) that Sheerbonnet has failed to join an indispensable party, under Fed.R.Civ.P. 19. I will address these arguments in order. For the reasons set forth, I find each argument to be unpersuasive. [The Court's discussion of the second and third points is omitted.]

I. Failure to State a Claim

AEB has offered two reasons why Sheerbonnet's claim fails to state a legally cognizable claim. The first is that Article 4A of the New York Uniform Commercial Code provides the exclusive remedy for the type of injury alleged, and the complaint not only ignores Article 4A but is inconsistent with several of its provisions. The question of the exclusivity of Article 4A as a whole, or the preclusive effect of any of its parts, has yet to be directly addressed in this Circuit. The second reason offered by AEB is that Sheerbonnet's common law claims, even if not excluded by Article 4A, are inadequate as a matter of law. Neither position is supportable.

A. N.Y.—U.C.C. Art. 4A Does Not Bar Sheerbonnet's Claim

Effective as of January 1, 1991, Article 4A is the latest addition to New York's Uniform Commercial Code. Its exact contours, its reach, and the implications of its various provisions have not yet been tested in state or federal courts. The provisions of Article 4A are dense, and a preliminary discussion of their subject matter is helpful before addressing AEB's first argument for dismissal, grounded as it is on the purpose and scope of the provisions. Article 4A governs "funds transfers" or "wire transfers." N.Y. U.C.C. § 4A-102 (McKinney 1991). A by-product of new communications technology, funds transfers are a specialized "method of payment in which the person making the payment ('the originator') directly transmits an instruction to a bank either to make payment to the person receiving payment ('the beneficiary') or to instruct some other bank to make payment to the beneficiary." N.Y. U.C.C. § 4A-104, Official Comment, at p. 561. A funds transfer is initiated by a "payment order," which is an instruction from the person making the payment to a "receiving" or "intermediary" bank to transfer the funds to the bank account of the beneficiary, normally in the "beneficiary's bank." N.Y. U.C.C. § 4A-103. A payment order may pass through several banks on its route from the sender, or originator, to the beneficiary. A payment order must be for a fixed or determinable sum, must not state a condition for payment to the beneficiary other than time, must require the receiving bank to be reimbursed by debiting or otherwise receiving payment from the originator, and must be communicated directly to the receiving bank (as opposed to the originator's bank). *See id.* Furthermore,

> payment by the originator to the beneficiary is accomplished by providing to the beneficiary the obligation of the beneficiary's bank to pay. Since this obligation arises when the beneficiary's bank accepts a payment order, the originator pays the beneficiary at the time of acceptance and in the amount of the payment order accepted.

N.Y. U.C.C. § 4A-406, Official Comments, at p. 623.

Most often, funds transfers are made to discharge an underlying payment obligation which arose through earlier commercial dealings between the originator (*e.g.*, a purchaser of goods or services) and the beneficiary (*e.g.*, a provider of goods or services). Insofar as they facilitate the efficient, high-speed, low-cost, national and international transfer of huge sums of money, usually between sophisticated institutional parties, funds transfers have become an integral component of large business transactions.

1. Article 4A is not Exclusive

Article 4A responded to the growing use of funds transactions and the absence of a "comprehensive body of law—statutory or judicial—that defined the juridical nature of a funds transfer or the rights and obligations flowing from payment orders." N.Y. U.C.C. § 4A-102, Official Comment, at p. 559. The pastiche of laws—statutory, administrative and judicial—applied to funds transfers prior to Art. 4A was found to be unsatisfactory. *See id.*

The drafting committee made "a deliberate decision...to use precise and detailed rules to assign responsibility, define behavioral norms, allocate risks and establish limits on liability, rather than rely on broadly stated, flexible principles." *Id.* AEB relies heavily on passages selected from the official commentary to support its argument that Article 4A is the exclusive remedy for claims like Sheerbonnet's arising out of funds transfers:

> In the drafting of Article 4A, a deliberate decision was made to write on a clean slate and to treat a funds transfer as a unique method of payment to be governed by unique rules that address the particular issues raised by this method of payment....
>
> ...The[se] rules...represent a careful and delicate balancing of [competing] interests and are intended to be the exclusive means of determining the rights, duties and liabilities of the affected parties in any situation covered by particular provisions of the Article. Consequently, resort to principles of law or equity outside of Article 4A is not appropriate to create rights, duties and liabilities inconsistent with those stated in this Article.

N.Y. U.C.C. § 4A-102, Official Comments, p. 559.

These passages are the foundation for AEB's conclusion that "[be]cause Sheerbonnet has not alleged that AEB violated any provision of Article 4A, the Complaint has failed to state a cognizable cause of action and should be dismissed." AEB's conclusion is unjustified for several reasons.

On their face, the above passages fail to establish a legislative intent to preclude any and all funds transfer actions not based on Article 4A. A desire to start on a "clean slate" implies only that in drafting the Article, the legislature was neither borrowing from related U.C.C. regulations, such as Article 4 (Bank Deposits and Collections) or Article 3 (Commercial Paper), nor from principles of common law or equity. Clearly, parties whose conflict arises out of a funds transfer should look first and foremost to Article 4A for guidance in bringing and resolving their claims, but the Article has not completely eclipsed the applicability of common law in the area. The exclusivity of Article 4A is deliberately restricted to "any situation covered by particular provisions of the Article." Conversely, situations not covered are not the exclusive province of the Article. The legislative intent reflected here is that carefully drafted provisions, designed to bring uniformity, predictability, and finality to an increasingly important area of commercial law, are not be side-stepped when convenient by reference to other sources of law. But where the provisions do not venture, the claimant need not turn back; he or she may seek other guides, statutory or judicial. The only restraint on the plaintiff seeking such relief is that "resort to principles of law or equity outside of Article 4A" must not be inconsistent with provisions within the Article.

Commentators uniformly recognize that Article 4A is not a hermetic legal seal over funds transfers. *See* J.J. White & R.S. Summers, *Uniform Commercial Code*, § 1-2, at p. 132 (1993 pocket part) ("With the adoption of Article 4A, electronic funds transactions are governed not only by Article 4A, but also common law, contract, Federal Reserve rules, Federal Reserve operating letters, rules of automated clearing houses, CHIPS and Title IX of the Federal Consumer Credit Protection Act."). ["CHIPS" is the New York Clearing House Interbank Payment System, a system of rules for funds transfers.] Professor White goes on to discuss how Article 4A's

> scope questions come in two basic forms. First—as to transactions partly covered by 4A, but also partly covered by contract, by CHIPS' rules or by Fedwire rules, or other law—which part is covered by 4A and which part by other rules? Second—as to transactions completely beyond Article 4A—which are these and what are their characteristics?

White & Summers, § 1-2, at p. 133 (1993 pocket part). As explained elsewhere, "the Drafting Committee intended that Article 4A would be supplemented, enhanced, and in some places, superseded by other bodies of law.... the Article is intended to synergize with other legal doctrines." T.C. Baxter & R. Bhala, *The Interrelationship of Article 4A with Other Law*, 45 BUSINESS LAWYER 1485, 1485. (1990) (describing eleven "points of contact" between the Article and other law, including tort law.) [The Court stated in footnote 4 that "Baxter and Bhala, however, argue somewhat ambiguously that these "points of contact" are selective, and that where not made explicit by the drafters, no contact with other law is intended. "Silence is the immune system the draftpersons gave to the body of Article 4A. To protect against the unlicensed importation of undesirable legal doctrines, the draftpersons omitted any mention of that which was not wanted." Baxter & Bhala at 1486. The Court said it understood this passage "to argue that when a provision is on point, and does not invite recourse to common law, then common law is not to be relied on; this is not to say that recourse to common law is foreclosed when there is no provision on point."]

The Article itself is replete with references to common law remedies. Many sections borrow freely from the tort concepts of "ordinary care," "reasonableness," and "the law governing mistake and restitution." *See, e.g.,* § 4A-205(2) (the sender of an erroneous payment order who is notified by the receiving bank that the order was executed or the sender's account was debited has "a duty to exercise ordinary care ... to discover the error"); § 4A-404(2) (if payment order does not instruct notice from the beneficiary's bank to the beneficiary, notice may be by "any means reasonable in the circumstances"); § 4A-205 (if a payment order erroneously instructs payment in an amount greater than intended, the sender is not obliged to pay to the beneficiary the excess amount but the receiving bank is entitled to recover from the beneficiary "to the extent allowed by the law of mistake and restitution").

Based on the foregoing, I conclude that Article 4A of the New York Uniform Commercial Code is not the exclusive means by which a plaintiff can seek to redress an alleged harm arising from a funds transfer.

2. Plaintiff's Allegations are not Inconsistent with Article 4A

Having determined that Article 4A is not an automatic bar to electronic funds transfers claims grounded elsewhere, the remaining question is whether Sheerbonnet's common law causes of action are nonetheless inconsistent with any of the Article's provisions and therefore must be dismissed. Neither the case law nor the specific provisions argued by AEB demonstrate such inconsistency.

Typical of AEB's myopic argumentation on this point is its reliance on the New York Court of Appeals decision in *Banque Worms v. BankAmerica Int'l*, 77 N.Y.2d 362 (Ct. of App. 1991). To support its assertion that "case law also rejects Sheerbonnet's limited vision of the reach of Article 4A," AEB cites the pronouncement in *Banque Worms* that the National Conference of Commissioners on Uniform State Laws and the American Law Institute "undertook to develop a body of unique principles of law that would address every aspect of the electronic funds transfer process and define the rights and liabilities of all parties involved in such transfers." AEB fails to recognize, however, that the issue in *Banque Worms*, taken by the Court of Appeals as a certified question from the Second Circuit, was which of two common law doctrines, "discharge for value" or detrimental reliance, would be imported into Article 4A to remedy an erroneous electronic transfer of funds. The Court ultimately decided that the "discharge for value" rule, the product of "a myriad of cases," was the most appropriate supplement to Article 4A because it was the most consistent with its policy goals. It reached this finding despite expressly noting that the Article did not invite an application of this judicially constructed rule:

> We believe such an application accords with the legislative intent and further the policy considerations underlying Article 4A of the New York Uniform Commercial Code. Although no provision of Article 4A calls, in express terms, for the application of the "discharge for value" rule, the statutory scheme and the language of various pertinent sections, as amplified by the Official Comments to the UCC, support our conclusion that the "discharge for value" rule should be applied in the circumstances here presented.

As the reasoning of our Court of Appeals and the New York Court of Appeals make clear, despite its exhaustive aspirations, Article 4A has not completely filled in the area of law surrounding funds transfers. Common law and equitable principles, where they compliment the important policy considerations of the Article and are not inconsistent with any of its specific provisions, can and should be used to resolve conflicts between parties to this type of transaction.

In *Aleo Int'l, Ltd. v. Citibank N.A.*, 160 612 N.Y.S.2d 540 (Sup.Ct. N.Y.Co.1994), also relied on by AEB, plaintiff brought an action to recover funds which Citibank had transferred to a third party pursuant to instructions that the plaintiff unsuccessfully retracted. Citibank claimed not to have received the cancellation until payment had been accepted. The court dismissed the complaint, which alleged negligence, holding that "unless Citibank's failure to cancel [plaintiff's] transfer order was not in conformity with Article 4A, plaintiff...has failed to state a cause of action, and this action must be dismissed." In its one-page opinion, however, the court was able to refer to two provisions of Article 4A directly applicable to the facts alleged. Reference to § 4A-211(2) (governing cancellation and amendment of payment orders) and § 4A-209(2) (governing acceptance of payment orders), quickly demonstrated that, because the stop transfer order was received after the payment and acceptance had occurred, cancellation was ineffective, and Citibank bore no liability. Were the allegations in this action so clearly circumscribed by applicable sections of Article 4A, Sheerbonnet could not be heard to protest if its common law claims were dismissed on the pleadings. *Aleo* is an excellent example of how the underlying policies of Article 4A—predictability, consistency, finality—are well-served by its clear and careful drafting. We are not so fortunate here.

As in *Aleo*, another recent State Supreme Court case resolved a dispute arising out of an allegedly erroneous funds transfer by reference to Article 4A provisions directly on point. *See Southtrust Bank of Ala., N.A v. Turkiye ve Ihracat Bankasi, A.S., et al.*, no. 116581/94 (Sup.Ct.N.Y.Co. Jan. 19, 1995). In *Southtrust*, plaintiff's bank relayed a payment order to American Express for the transfer of $500,000 to the account of a creditor of the plaintiff. The order included correct verbal instructions, but an erroneous written account number. It was into this wrong account that American Express transferred the $500,000. Neither American Express nor the holder of the account into which the funds were sent agreed to return the funds to plaintiff, who in turn sought unsuccessfully to have the funds garnished. As in our facts, American Express in *Southtrust* used the funds which it credited as a set-off against debts owed to it by the account holder.

The court dismissed plaintiff's complaint, based in negligence, and denied leave to amend to substitute other common law tort claims which it said were inconsistent with Article 4A. Again the court was able to point to specific provisions with which the plaintiff's tort theories conflicted. The section on point, which eclipsed plaintiff's claims no matter how they were styled, was § 4A-207 ("Misdescription of a Beneficiary"). Clearly from the language of the Section, American Express was entitled to rely on the representation of the account number as it appeared on the payment order it received, even if that number conflicted with the accompanying description of the account. Only because it ignored this plainly applicable and inconsistent provision was plaintiff's complaint dismissed.

Further distinguishing *Southtrust* from this case was American Express's ability to argue lack of knowledge. Plaintiff in *Southtrust* could not prove that American Express was aware of the discrepancy between the account number and its description. In the instant case, however, AEB's knowledge of the insolvency and seizure of BCCI's accounts—before accepting the Northern Trust payment order and crediting the BCCI London account—is undisputed. Nor was the sender in our case responsible for conveying an erroneous order or tardy cancellation. AEB's knowledge that the $12.4 million it was asked to receive and transfer was destined for a seized account seems relevant to its decision to accept the order and credit the frozen account, but there is no provision in Article 4A dealing with such circumstances.

AEB fares no better in direct reliance on specific provisions of Article 4A, three of which it argues are inconsistent with, and thus preclude, Sheerbonnet's theory of tort liability.

First, AEB argues that § 4A-209 is both applicable and inconsistent insofar as it gives the receiving bank full discretion to accept or reject a payment order. Since it is granted full discretion, AEB argues that it would be inconsistent to impose tort liability for the acceptance of the payment order. The intent of granting this discretion is explained in the commentary, however, which stresses the receiver's ability to *reject* the order: "Section 4A-209 is based on a general principle that a receiving bank is not obliged to accept a payment order unless it has agreed or is bound by a funds transfer rule to do so. Thus, provision is made to allow the receiving bank to prevent acceptance of the order." N.Y. U.C.C. § 4A-209, Official Comments, at p. 593. Section 4A-209 is primarily devoted to describing how and when acceptance, and the liability attendant to it, occurs—not to how and when a receiving bank's discretion should be exercised. There is no indication that such discretion is meant to serve as a veil against liability for the manner in which the discretion to accept is exercised. A payment order is merely a request by the sender that the receiving bank pay or execute the order. With acceptance of an order comes certain obligations. A receiving bank may refuse requests which would expose it to unreasonable high risk of loss—as when there does not seem to be adequate funds to cover the order. It can hardly promote the purposes of Article 4A to equate a general discretion to accept or reject payment orders with a ban on judicial inquiry into the circumstances under which that discretion was exercised and what followed its exercise.

AEB also looks to § 4A-212 as a shield from Sheerbonnet's claims. This Section governs the "Liability and Duty of Receiving Bank Regarding Unaccepted Payment Order." Specifically, AEB relies on a part of the provision which reads that, "[a] receiving bank ... owes no duty to any party to the funds transfer except as provided in this Article or by express agreement." N.Y. U.C.C. § 4A-212. First, in full context this Section indicates that (1) no liability attaches to a receiving bank before it accepts a payment order, (2) absent an express agreement to the contrary, the receiving bank is not obliged to accept the order, and (3) the receiving bank is not an agent of any party to the funds transfer and hence, outside its acceptance of the order, owes no intrinsic duty stemming from an agency relationship. *See id.*; N.Y. U.C.C. § 4A-212, Official Comments, at p. 602; White & Summers, at § 3-5 (1993 pocket part). Second, it is not clear whether this Section applies to banks that are acting as *both* a receiving bank and the beneficiary's bank, as AEB argues it was. Third, and perhaps most telling, § 4A-212, governing liability for unaccepted payment orders, should be read in tandem with § 4A-212, governing rejection of payment orders. Section 4A-210 indicates that, if not constrained by agency principles, receiving banks cannot conduct their business with blinders on to extenuating circumstances. Comment 1 to § 4A-210 reads in part:

> In some cases, the receiving bank may not be able to carry out the instruction because of equipment failure, credit limitation on the receiving bank, *or some other factor that makes proper execution of the order infeasible.* In those cases notice of rejection is a means of informing the sender of the facts so that a corrected payment order can be transmitted or the sender can seek alternate means of completing the fund transfer.

N.Y. U.C.C. § 4A-210, Official Comment, at pp. 595-96.

The final section relied on by AEB to bar Sheerbonnet's claim as inconsistent is § 4A-502, governing set-offs. This Section is inapplicable in light of the pleadings. AEB argues that it is expressly entitled to set off any funds credited to BCCI's account against debt owed to AEB by BCCI. It is correct in this assertion. *See* N.Y. U.C.C. § 4A-502(3)(a) ("If a beneficiary's bank has received a payment order for payment to the beneficiary's account ... (a) The bank may credit the beneficiary's account. The amount credited may be set off against an obligation owed by the beneficiary to the bank. ..."). Sheerbonnet does not challenge AEB's right to a set-off, however. Instead, it challenges AEB's preliminary decision to *credit* the BCCI account. As stated in Sheerbonnet's Brief on Appeal to the Court of Appeals on the issue of abstention:

2. *The Conversion Here Was the Wrongful Credit, Not American Express's Attempted Setoff.*

...The conversion alleged by Sheerbonnet in this action is the purported crediting of funds to the BCCI London account; American Express's attempted setoff was at most the motive for the wrongful "credit," and is not even mentioned in Sheerbonnet's complaint.

Reply Brief of Plaintiff-Appellant, at 12.

Whether AEB's set-off was in bad faith, as Sheerbonnet later alleged, is immaterial at this juncture. For purposes of this motion, Sheerbonnet's claim that AEB's crediting of the BCCI account was an intentionally tortious and unjustly enriching act is not inconsistent with the provisions of § 4A-502 regarding set-offs and therefore is not barred by it.

Unlike *Aleo* or *Southtrust*, the allegations here and the circumstances giving rise to them do not fit neatly into any of Article 4A's "precise and detailed rules." The rules of the Article are transactional, aimed essentially at resolving conflicts created by erroneous instruction or execution of payment orders, whether by the originator, by an intermediary or receiving bank, or by the beneficiary's bank. A major objective is to reduce and control risks that arise in payment systems by defining when and how rights and obligations are incurred and discharged. As organized by the Article, funds transfer errors fall into three main categories. Errors may occur during the issuance and acceptance of the payment order—as when a payment order is made for the wrong amount, or identifies the wrong beneficiary, or, as in *Aleo*, is untimely canceled. Errors may also occur during the execution of the payment order by the receiving bank—as when the originator's instructions are not followed, or the order is executed late, or is issued in an improper amount, or is not executed at all. Errors may also stem from payment issues—as in the obligation of the originator to pay the receiving bank, of the beneficiary's bank to pay the beneficiary, and notification of payment and discharge of duties requirements. None of these three areas, nor any of Article 4A's miscellaneous provisions, directly addresses the allegations here.

Sheerbonnet does not complain of an erroneous instruction or execution in the processing of Northern Trust's payment order, causing it to be credited to the wrong party, or in the wrong amounts or at the wrong time. Ironically, we are here now because AEB apparently followed its instructions to the letter. Sheerbonnet argues that in light of the unprecedented and superseding seizure of BCCI, AEB's decision to credit the BCCI London account, knowing that it was frozen and knowing that AEB would use these very funds as a $12.4 million set-off against BCCI's debt to AEB, was an exercise in self-serving, tortious tunnel vision. AEB did not ask either the originator or the beneficiary how they would like to proceed in light of the seizure, nor did it confer with the Superintendent of Banks.

There is no doubt, as Sheerbonnet contends, that the global seizure of BCCI was an unprecedented event that tests the limits of Article 4A in a novel way. More at issue is whether AEB, seizing on the seizure, unfairly capitalized on this event. As plead, it appears that AEB was at least in a position to do so, functioning as it was as both the receiving bank and the benefit's bank. As the receiving bank, AEB had full discretion to accept or deny the payment order; as the beneficiary's bank AEB had full discretion to off-set against debts owed to it by the beneficiary. In isolation, these two provisions of Article 4A are clear, harmonious, and equitable. But when linked in a transaction through a single entity, and placed in the crucible of the BCCI insolvency and seizure, the clarity, harmony, and equity fracture. The separate links of the funds transfer at issue here are whole, yet the chain was broken. Sheerbonnet agreed to sell troop carriers to Hady, on the basis of an irrevocable letter of credit issued by Banque Scandanave. The carriers were delivered. Sheerbonnet had an account with BCCI in London, which it wished credited in fulfillment of the letter of credit. Banque Scandanave directed its correspondent bank in New York, Northern Trust, to credit BCCI's London account through AEB in New York. Northern Trust so instructed AEB. AEB so credited the (frozen) BCCI London account. AEB then set-off the credit against BCCI debts.

When the electronic transfer was "completed," step-by-step according to Article 4A, only one element was missing: the seller was never paid for its goods. The irony of this was not lost on the Court of Appeals. Thus, the money originally destined for Sheerbonnet ended up not in the hands of the buyer or seller, but of a bank whose only role was to transfer the funds." *Sheerbonnet*, 17 F.3d at 48.

A further peculiarity manifest in these facts is that under the terms of the payment order BCCI is itself the beneficiary, not Sheerbonnet. What agreement existed between BCCI and Sheerbonnet for final payment is beyond the pleadings. Thus, although in the real world Sheerbonnet was to be the "beneficiary" of the $12.4 million, in the electronic world of funds transfers it was BCCI—and that has made all the difference. When the intended beneficiary became insolvent, the normal payment process was disrupted. When AEB off-set against BCCI debts, the credit to that account initiated by Hady and destined for Sheerbonnet was effectively pulled back, as if on an electronic string, before it was within Sheerbonnet's grasp. Professor White, in a discussion of issues that could interfere with the completion of a funds transfer, calls the insolvency of one of the banks within the system during a funds transfer the "least likely of all" scenarios and "the bank equivalent of nuclear holocaust." White & Summers, § 2-1, at p. 146 (1993 pocket part). He, like Article 4A, does not even raise the specter of the insolvency of the beneficiary itself.

As in *Banque Worms*, these circumstances, not specifically provided for in an otherwise thorough statutory scheme, demand resort to other legal principles in order to reach a fair resolution. Article 4A is an attempt to balance competing interests, namely "those of the banks that provide the funds transfer services and the commercial and financial organizations that use the services, as well as the public interest." N.Y. U.C.C. § 4A-102, Official Comment, at p. 559. A necessary risk taken by the drafting committee in eschewing "broadly stated, flexible principles" in favor of "precise and detailed rules" is that maneuvering among these competitors will eventually land them somewhere in between precise rules, and dependent on broader principles to resolve their conflict. This is such a case.

Article 4A is a thorough but not exhaustive legislative treatment of funds transfers. Nevertheless, resort to judicial or other legal principles is prohibited if those principles conflict with any discrete components of the statutory scheme. Sheerbonnet's common law claims, based in tort and equity, do not conflict with any of Article 4A's provisions. In fact, in the context of the circumstances giving rise to them, these claims compliment primary policy goals of the Article, including consistency, predictability, finality, and the fair allocation of risk. For the foregoing reasons, defendant's motion to dismiss for failure to bring this claim under Article 4A is denied.

B. Plaintiffs Common Law Claims Are Legally Cognizable

AEB argues in the alternative that "[e]ven if not preempted, Sheerbonnet's tort and equity causes of action should be dismissed for failure to state a cognizable claim." AEB claims that it only did what it was instructed and entitled to do and therefore cannot have any liability as a matter of law. This approach misses the forest for the trees.

Freed from the confines of Article 4A, Sheerbonnet's claims—conversion, tortious interference with contract, unjust enrichment—all turn in varying degrees around one narrow question: what is the standard of care that is to be exercised by a receiving bank, also serving as the beneficiary's bank, in the handling of a payment order to be credited to the seized account of an insolvent bank that is also the beneficiary of the payment order—particularly when the crediting of the frozen account will have the effect of increasing the receiving/beneficiary's bank offset against debts owed to it by the beneficiary, thus ensuring that the transferred funds will not in fact reach the beneficiary?

The absence of language in Article 4A expressly restraining AEB from completing the transfer, and the allegedly porous restrictions attending the Supervisor's seizure of BCCI accounts no more vitiates Sheerbonnet's claims than does AEB's protestation that it was simply following orders. Plaintiff has made out a *prima facie* claim on each cause of action.

. . . .

V. Political Risk and Cross Border Payments

Libyan Arab Foreign Bank v. Bankers Trust Co.

[1988] 1 Lloyd's L. Rep. 259 (Queen's Bench Division (Commercial Court))

MR. JUSTICE STAUGHTON: The plaintiffs are a Libyan corporation, wholly owned by the Central Bank of Libya. They carry on what is described as an offshore banking business, in the sense that they do not engage in domestic banking within Libya. I shall call them "the Libyan bank." The defendants are a New York corporation with their head office there. They no doubt have a number of branches in various parts of the world; but I am concerned with one in particular, their branch in London. I shall refer to them as "Bankers Trust," and when it is necessary to refer to particular offices as "Bankers Trust London" or "Bankers Trust New York."

In January, 1986, the Libyan bank had an account with Bankers Trust London, denominated in U.S. dollars. That was a call account, which meant that no cheque book was provided, interest was payable on the balance standing to the credit of the account at rates which varied from time to time, and some minimal period of notice might be required before instructions relating to the account had to be complied with. The suggestion in this case is that instructions would have to be given before noon if they were to be carried out that day. In English practice it would, I think be described as a species of deposit account. The amount standing to the credit of that account at the close of business on Jan. 8, 1986, was $131,506,389.93. There may be a small element of subsequent adjustment in that figure. But the point is not material.

The Libyan bank also had an account with Bankers Trust New York, again denominated in United States dollars. This was a demand account. No interest was paid on the balance, and no significant period of notice was required before instructions had to be complied with. But there was not, so far as I am aware, a cheque book. In England it would have been a current account. The amount standing to the credit of that account at the close of business on Jan. 8, 1986, was $251,129,084.53.

Relations between Libya and the United States in January, 1986 were not good. At 8:06 p.m. New York time on Jan. 7 the President of the United States of America issued an executive order, which had the force of law with immediate effect. It provided, so far as material, as follows:

Section 1. The following are prohibited, except to the extent provided in regulations which may hereafter be issued pursuant to this Order:...

(f)   The grant or extension of credits or loans by any United States person to the Government of Libya, its instrumentalities and controlled entities.

That order did not in itself have any great effect on the events with which this case is concerned. But there followed it at 4:10 p.m. New York time on Jan. 8 a second order, reading as follows:

I, RONALD REAGAN, President of the United States, hereby order blocked all property and interests in property of the Government of Libya, its agencies, instrumentalities and controlled entities and the Central Bank of Libya that are in the United States that hereafter come within the United States or that are or hereafter come within the possession or control of U.S. persons including overseas branches of U.S. persons.

The Secretary of the Treasury, in consultation with the Secretary of State, is authorized to employ all powers granted to me by the International Emergency Economic Powers Act 50 U.S.C. 1701 et. seq. to carry out the provisions of this Order.

This Order is effective immediately and shall be transmitted to the Congress and published in the Federal Register.

RONALD REAGAN
THE WHITE HOUSE
January 8, 1986.

It is not in dispute that Bankers Trust are a U.S. person; or that Bankers Trust London are an overseas branch of a U.S. person; or that the Libyan bank are an agency, instrumentality or controlled entity of the government of Libya. Consequently by the law of and prevailing in the State of New York (which I shall refer to as New York law for the sake of brevity) it was illegal at and after 4:10 p.m. on Jan. 8, 1986, for Bankers Trust to make any payment or transfer of funds to or to the order of the Libyan bank in New York, either by way of debit to the Libyan bank's account or as the grant of credit or a loan. Similarly it was illegal, by the law of New York or of any other American state, for Bankers Trust to make any such payment or transfer of funds in London or anywhere else.

The United Kingdom Parliament did not enact any similar legislation. No doubt there were reasons of high policy for that forbearance; but with them I am not concerned. It is sufficient to say that nothing in English domestic law prohibited such a transaction. So the main issues in this case are concerned with the rules of conflict of laws, which determine when and to what extent the law of New York is given effect in our Courts, and with the contractual obligations of banks. In a word, Bankers Trust say that they cannot, or at any rate are not obliged to, transfer a sum as large as $100m. or more without using the payment machinery that is available in New York; consequently they have a defence to the Libyan bank's claim, because performance of this contract would have required them to commit an illegal act in New York. Alternatively they say that their contract with the Libyan bank is governed by the law of New York, so that performance is the time being illegal by the proper law of contract.

The Libyan bank's claims

These are as follows...

(1) The first claim is for the balance $131,506,389.93 standing to the credit of London account at the close of business on Jan. 8, 1986. It is said that this sum is due to Libyan bank, and can be claimed on a cause of action in debt. Alternatively it is said that Bankers Trust ought to have responded demands for $131m. that were made by Libyan bank in various different ways after Jan. 8, and are liable in damages.

(2) If they are right on the first claim, Libyan bank further say that one or other three sums ought to have been transferred from the New York account to the London account on Jan. 7 or 8, thus increasing the amount which they are entitled to recover. These are: (i) $165,200,000 on Jan. 7, *or* (ii) $6,700,000 Jan. 8, *or* (iii) $161,400,000 on Jan. 8. Indeed it is said that the sum of $6,700,000 was in fact transferred to London on Jan. 8, with the consequence that the Libyan bank are in any event entitled to recover that additional amount. [The remaining claims of the Libyan Bank, concerning damages for failure to execute a payment instruction, breach of duty of confidence, frustration, and deprivation of interest owed, are omitted, as is Judge Staughton's discussion of these claims.]

....

The issues thus raised, or at any rate those that arise under par. (1) above, are of great interest and some difficulty. Similar problems occurred a few years ago in connection with the freeze on Iranian assets by executive order of Nov. 14. 1979, and litigation was commenced. But before any of those actions could come to trial the freeze was lifted. This time the problems have to be resolved.

History of the banking relationship

This can be considered in three stages. The *first stage* was from 1972 to Dec. 15, 1980.

The Libyan bank came into existence in June, 1972. A correspondent relationship was established between the Libyan bank and Bankers Trust. Initially an account was opened for that purpose with the Paris branch of Bankers Trust. But in April, 1973 that account was closed, and an account opened with the London branch. It was described as a 7-day notice account. However, any requirement that notice of that length should be given before debits were allowed on the London account was not enforced. In this period the Libyan bank did not wish to have any account with Bankers Trust New York. Transfers for the credit of the Libyan bank used regularly to arrive at Bankers Trust New York, in accordance with the system most often used for transferring large dollar amounts, which I shall describe later. But they were dealt with by an instruction from Bankers Trust New York to Bankers Trust London to credit the account of the Libyan bank there. Indeed the Libyan bank insisted on that from time to time. Thus on July 14, 1973, they said in a telex to New York:

> We also request immediate transfer of any funds you may receive in future for our favour to your London office.

And on July 17, 1973, to London:

> When we have agreed to have the account of Libyan Arab Foreign Bank with Bankers Trust I have made it very clear that no balance at all should be kept in New York and should be transferred immediately to our call account which started in Paris and now with you in London.

Certainly one motive for that attitude, and in 1973 possibly the only motive, was that dollar credit balances outside the United States earned a higher rate of interest than was obtainable in the United States. That is all that Euro-dollars are-a credit in dollars outside the United States, whether in Europe or elsewhere. (It may be that one should add to this definition "at a bank" or "at an institution.") The interest rate is higher owing to the terms of the requirement imposed by the Federal Reserve Board that banks should maintain an amount equal to a proportion of the deposits they receive on deposit interest-free with the Federal Reserve system. That requirement is less demanding in connection with deposits received by overseas branches.

In fact Bankers Trust New York had operated an account in New York, for the handling of transactions by the Libyan bank. But that account was closed on Dec. 17, 1973 in consequence of the above and other protests by the Libyan bank.

There followed a long period of discussion and negotiation. Bankers Trust were dissatisfied because the London, so-called 7-days notice, account was used as a current account. Large numbers of transactions occurred on it, but interest was paid on the balance. This was not thought to be profitable for Bankers Trust. Furthermore, transfers to or from the account would commonly be made through New York, with a risk of delay and the possibility of error. On Nov. 23, 1977, Mr. Ronai of Bankers Trust New York wrote to the Libyan bank as follows:

> ...I am writing to outline our proposal for clearing up the operational difficulties encountered in your dollar-clearing activity through Bankers Trust in New York.
>
> I feel that the problems stem from the number of intermediate steps required to effect a large number of transfers to and from your London Call account via New York. In order to simplify this situation, my proposal is to set up a fully-managed account relationship with Libyan Arab Foreign Bank. This should provide you with several major benefits, among which are:
> - more timely information for yourselves
> - simplification of transactions
> - greater ease in researching possible errors
> - the ability to tailor the system to your requirements
>
> The basic elements of a managed account consist of a Current account in New York and a Call account in London with Bankers Trust Company. The Current account will be used for your daily dollar-clearing activity; the Call account should be considered as an investment of liquid funds. An explanation of the operation of your managed account follows.
>
> On a daily basis, all transactions concerning the demand account are reviewed, and the balance is "managed" so that it does not exceed or fall below a predetermined target or "peg" balance. Excess funds will be credited to your Call account, or your Current account will be funded from your Call account, as the case may be.

In 1980 that proposal was more actively pursued. At first it was suggested by Bankers Trust that the current account should be in London. But by the time of a meeting in New York on July 7 it was again proposed that there should be a demand account there. Following that meeting Bankers Trust wrote from London to Libyan bank with details of the proposed managed account system:

> We will establish a "peg" (or target) balance for the demand account of $750,000. That amount is intended to compensate Bankers Trust Company for the services which we expect to provide, and is subject to periodic renegotiation as appropriate, for example when our costs increase, when interest

rates decline significantly or when our level of servicing is materially changed. Each morning our Account Management Team will review the demand account's closing book balance from the previous business day. If that balance is in excess of the "peg," they will transfer in multiples of $100,000 the excess amount to your call account in London with value the previous business day.

Similarly, if the demand account balance is below the $750,000 peg, they will transfer funds back from your call account with value the previous business day.... As you can appreciate, our Account Management Team must closely follow the balance in your call account. Given time zone differences with London, all entries to your call account must be passed by that Team in New York, and all your instructions to effect payments or foreign exchange settlements must be directed to our Money Transfer Department in New York.

The figure of $750,000 as the peg balance was later agreed at $500,000.

There was some discussion of political risk at the New York meeting. I am confident that political risk was at any rate in the minds of both parties, seeing that the freeze on Iranian assets had occurred only eight months previously. Mr. Abduljawad, then deputy chairman, is recorded as saying:

Placing at call is not an effort to avoid political risk, which he believes to be unavoidable.

Whilst I accept that record as accurate, I also accept Mr. Abduljawad's oral evidence that "political risk is always being taken into consideration." Mr. Van Voorhees, who was among those attending the meeting on behalf of Bankers Trust, accepted that the Iranian crisis was at the back of everyone's mind in 1980.

A further meeting took place in Paris on Oct. 28, 1980 between Mr. Abduljawad and Mr. Van Voorhees. At that meeting too no complete agreement was reached, so there was no new agreement or variation of the existing agreement. But important progress was made. Mr. Van Voorhees explained in plain terms that all the Libyan Bank's transactions would have to pass through New York. According to Mr. Van Voorhees, Mr. Abduljawad at first objected to that requirement, but later agreed to it. Mr. Abduljawad's evidence was that he did not reject it and equally did not agree to it. I do not need to resolve that conflict. It is plain to me that one of the terms which Bankers Trust were putting forward for the new arrangement was that all transactions should pass through New York; whether or not it was accepted at that stage is immaterial.

There followed a meeting in Tripoli and correspondence between the parties, and agreement was finally reached by Dec. 11, 1980. Thus the managed account system was agreed on. Bankers Trust New York would open a demand account for the Libyan bank, with a peg balance of $500,000. Transfers between that account and the call account in London would be made, as the need arose, in multiples of $100,000. The need for a transfer would be determined each morning by examining the closing balance of the New York account for the previous business day; if appropriate a transfer to or from London would be made with value the previous business day — in other words, it would take "effect from that date for interest purposes."

It was, as I find, a term of that arrangement that all the Libyan bank's transactions should pass through New York. Although not mentioned in the correspondence by which agreement was ultimately reached, this had plainly been a requirement of Bankers Trust throughout the later stages of the negotiations, and I conclude that it was tacitly accepted by the Libyan bank. It was virtually an essential feature of the system: Bankers Trust New York would know about and rely on the credit balance in London in deciding what payments could be made from New York; they might be exposed to risk if the balance in London could be reduced without their knowledge. It was argued that such a term is not to be found in the pleadings of Bankers Trust; but in my judgment it is, in par. 3(4)(v) of the re-reamended points of defence. There remains an important question whether the managed account arrangement was irrevocable, or whether it could be determined. I shall consider that later.

The *second stage* ran from December, 1980, to November, 1985. Before very long Bankers Trust took the view that the remuneration which they received from the relationship, in the form of an interest-free balance of between $500,000 and $599,999 in New York, was insufficient reward for their services. On Mar. 15, 1983, they proposed an increase in the peg balance to $1.5m. Negotiations continued for a time but without success. By Mar. 15, 1984, Bankers Trust had formed the view that the Libyan bank would not agree to an increase in the peg balance; so, on Apr. 3, 1984, they decided unilaterally on a different method of increasing the profitability of the relationship for Bankers Trust; and it was put into effect on Apr. 17.

The new method required a consideration of the balance on the New York account at 2:00 p.m. each day. If it exceeded the peg balance of $500,000 the excess was transferred in multiples of $100,000 to the London account with value that day. Consideration was also given on the following morning to the balance at the close of the previous day. If it was less than the peg balance, a transfer of the appropriate amount was made from London to New York on the next day, with value the previous business day; if it was more than the peg balance there was, it seems, a transfer to London with value the same day. The effect of the change was that the Libyan bank lost one day's interest whenever (i) credits received after 2:00 p.m. exceeded payments made after 2:00 p.m., and (ii) the closing balance for the day would under the existing arrangement have required a transfer (or a further transfer if one had been made at 2:00 p.m.) to be made with value that day. If a weekend intervened, three days interest might be lost. I am not altogether sure that I have stated the effect of the change correctly; but precision as to the details is not essential.

Bankers Trust did not tell the Libyan bank about this change. Indeed an internal memorandum of Bankers Trust dated Aug. 14, 1984, wondered whether Libya (possibly referring to the Libyan bank) would notice the drop in interest earnings. Although the effect was on any view substantial, I am satisfied that the Libyan bank did not in fact appreciate what was happening until mid-1985; and they complained about it to Bankers Trust in October, 1985. I am also satisfied that the Libyan bank could have detected, if they had looked at their statements from Bankers Trust with a fair degree of diligence, that they were not receiving the full benefit by way of interest to which they were entitled. Indeed, they did, as I have said, eventually detect that. But I am not convinced—if it matters—that they could have divined precisely what system Bankers Trust were now operating.

The *third stage* began on Nov. 27, 1985, with a telex from Bankers Trust which recorded the agreement of the Libyan bank to a new arrangement. This telex is important, and I must set out part of it:

> As discussed with you during our last meeting in our office in Tripoli, we have changed the method of investment from same day by means of next day back valuation, to actual same day with investment cut off time of 2:00 p.m. New York time.... In this regard, those credits which are received after our 2:00 p.m. New York time cut off which result in excess balances are in-

vested with next day value. This you will see from observing your account. For your information, the way our same day investment system works, is as follows:

Each day, at 2:00 p.m., the balance position of your account is determined and any credits received up to that time, less payments and less the peg balance, are immediately invested. An example of this investment system can be seen for instance by comparing both statements of your demand and call accounts for September 26 and 30, 1985 which indicate same day investment on September 26th for US D 33.7 million which is reflected on your London call account statement on September 27th and value September 26th and on September 30th for US D 181.3 million which is reflected on your London call account statement on October lst value September 30th.

That was not in substance any different from the system which Bankers Trust had been operating since April 1984 without informing the Libyan bank. It was now accepted by them.

January 7 and 8, 1986

At 2:00 p.m. on Jan. 7 the balance to the credit of the New York account was $165,728,000 (For present purposes I use figures rounded down to the nearest $1000, save where greater accuracy is desirable.) Subject to two points which I shall consider later, a transfer of $165.2m. should then have been made to London. Mr. Fabien Arnell, an account manager of Bankers Trust New York, says somewhat laconically in his statement:

On 7th January 1986 I instructed the Managed Account Clerk not to make a 2 p.m. investment. I cannot now recall the precise reason why I gave that instruction.

During the rest of that day there were substantial transfers out of the New York account, with the result that it would have been overdrawn to the extent of $157,925,000 if the 2:00 p.m. transfer had been made. There would then have had to be a recall of $158,500,000 from London on Jan. 8, with value the previous business day, to restore the peg balance. As no 2:00 p.m. transfer had been made, the closing balance was in fact $7,275,000 in credit.

On the morning of Jan. 8 there was an amount of $6,700,000 available to transfer to London. The same amount would have been left as a net credit to the London account if $165.2m. had been transferred at 2:00 p.m. on Jan. 7 and $158.5m. recalled on Jan. 8 with value the previous day. An instruction for the transfer $6,700,000 was prepared. But in the event the computer which kept the accounts in New York was not ordered to effect this transfer, nor was the London branch informed of it.

At 2:00 p.m. on Jan. 8 the balance to the credit of the New York account was $161,997,000. After deducting the peg balance of $500,000 there was a sum of $161,400,000 available to transfer to London. No transfer was made. Those figures I assume, as was the fact, that $6,700,000 had not been transferred to London in respect of the excess opening balance on that day.

Bankers Trust New York had received payment instructions totaling $347,147,213.03 for execution on Jan. 8. All of them had been received by 8:44 a.m. New York time. None of them were executed, for reasons which I shall later explain. (In case it is thought that not even the combined London and New York accounts could have sustained such payments, I should mention that substantial credits were received in New York during Jan. 8 for the account of the Libyan bank. If all the payment instructions had been implemented, there would still at the end of the day have been a net balance due to the Libyan bank on the total of the two accounts).

In the hope of rendering those figures somewhat more intelligible, I set out a summary of the actual state of the New York account on Jan. 7 and 8, 1986, with notes:

Balance at 2:00 pm Jan. 7

Post 2:00 pm operations		
	$165,728,000	(1)
Opening balance Jan. 8	(158,453,000)	
Receipts before 2:00 pm		
	7,275,000	(2)
Balance at 2:00 pm Jan. 8	154,722,000	
Receipts after 2:00 pm		
	161,997,000	(3)
Closing balance Jan. 8	89,132,000	(4)
	251,129,000	

Notes:

(1) $165.2m. available for transfer to London

(2) $ 6.7m. available for transfer

(3) $161.4m. available for transfer

(4) This figure contains some minor adjustments of no consequence.

Next I turn to the Civil Evidence Act statement of Mr. Brittain, the chairman of Bankers Trust. Late in the afternoon of Jan. 7 he received a telephone call from Mr. Corrigan, the President of the Federal Reserve Bank of New York. Mr. Corrigan asked that Bankers Trust should pay particular attention on the next day to movement of funds on the various Libyan accounts held by Bankers Trust, and report anything unusual to him.

Late in the morning of the next day Mr. Brittain informed the New York Fed (as it is sometimes called) that-

...it looked like the Libyans were taking their money out of the various accounts.

(So far as the Libyan bank were concerned, it will be remembered that they had already given instructions for payments totaling over $347m. on that day.) Later Mr. Brittain learnt that sufficient funds were coming in to cover the payment instructions; he telephoned Mr. Corrigan and told him that the earlier report had been a false alarm. Mr. Corrigan asked Mr. Brittain not to make any payments out of the accounts for the time being, and said that he would revert later.

That assurance was repeated several times during the early afternoon. Mr. Brittain's statement continues:

Finally I telephoned Mr. Corrigan at about 3.30 p.m. and told him that we now had sufficient funds to cover the payments out of the various Libyan accounts and were going to make them. Mr. Corrigan's response to this was, "You'd better call Baker" (by which he meant the Secretary of the United States Treasury, Mr. James A. Baker III). I said that I would release the payments and then speak to Mr. Baker. Mr. Corrigan's reply to this was. "You'd better call Baker first."

Mr. Brittain was delayed for some 20 minutes talking to Mr. Baker and to an assistant secretary of the Treasury on the telephone. Then at approximately 4:10 to 4:15 p.m. Mr. Baker said:

The President has signed the order, You can't make the transfers.

Mr. Brittain adds in his statement that this was the first occasion on which he became aware that an order freezing the assets was contemplated. In a note made a few weeks after Jan. 8 he adds: "That is how naive I was." I am afraid that I can but agree with Mr. Brittain's description of himself. It seems to me that a reasonable banker, on the afternoon of Jan. 8 would have realized, in the light of the first executive order made on the previous day, the requests of Mr. Corrigan, and particularly his saying "You'd better call Baker first," that a ban on payments was a distinct possibility.

There is other evidence as to Mr. Brittain's telephone conversations. First, Mr. Blenk was in Mr. Brittain's office and heard what was said by him. There was not, it seems, any reference name to Libyan Arab Foreign Bank, but merely to "the Libyans," which meant some six Libyan entities (including the Libyan bank) which had accounts with Bankers Trust. Secondly, Mr. Sandberg, a senior Vice-President of the Federal Reserve Bank of New York, heard Mr. Corrigan's end of the conversations. He accepted in evidence that the New York Fed probably knew which Libyan banks held accounts with Bankers Trust.

. . . .

The demands made

On Apr. 28, 1986, the Libyan bank sent a telex to Bankers Trust London in these terms:

We hereby instruct you to pay to us at 10.30 a.m. U.K. time on Thursday 1st, May 1986 out of our U.S. dollar account number 025-13828 at Bankers Trust London the sum of US dollars one hundred and thirty one million. We make demand accordingly.

This sum is to be paid to us in London at the said time and date either by a negotiable banker's draft in such amount (U.S. dollars 131,000,000.00) drawn on Bankers Trust London payable in London to ourselves (Libyan Arab Foreign Bank) or to our order.

Alternatively we will accept payment in cash although we would prefer to be provided with a banker's draft as aforesaid.

On the same day a demand in similar terms was made for $161m., on the basis that this amount should have been transferred from the New York account to the London account at 2:00 p.m. on Jan. 8, 1986.

Neither demand was complied with. Bankers Trust replied that it would be unlawful (sc. by New York or any other United States law) for them to pay in London. That was factually correct. The question is whether it was relevant. Bankers Trust also denied that the $161m. transfer should have been made on Jan. 8.

The action 1986 L. No. 1567 was than started by the Libyan bank against Bankers Trust. In correspondence between the parties' solicitors various other methods of payment were discussed. In addition the Libyan bank's solicitors by letter dated July 30, 1986, said that, in so far as notice was required to terminate the managed account arrangement-

(1) notice had been given by the Libyan bank's telex of Apr. 28, 1986, or

(2) notice was then given by the solicitors in their letter.

Finally, there was a further demand made in a telex from the Libyan bank to Bankers Trust on Dec. 23, 1986:

> ... We now hereby further demand that you pay to us within seven days from receipt of this telex in London, England, the said sums of US dollars 131,000,000 — and US dollars 161,000,000 — respectively, either by the means set out in our April demands or by any other commercially recognised method of transferring funds, which will result in our receiving unconditional payment in London within the said seven-day period. In particular (but without prejudice to the foregoing) the said sums of US dollars 131,000,000 — and U.S. dollars — 161,000,000 — (or either of them) may be transferred in compliance with these demands by any such commercially recognised method to the U.B.A.F. Bank Limited London for the credit of our dollar account number 0000104-416. We reiterate, however, that our demands are for us to receive unconditional payment in London, within the said seven-day period. If therefore, a transfer or clearing procedure is employed by you to comply with our demands, such procedure must be such that funds or credits said to represent any part of the debt which you owe to us in London are not, in the result, frozen or otherwise impeded in the United States. We would not object to your exercising your right to pay us in sterling, and, if so, our sterling account number at the above bank is 0000103-919.

A second action was commenced eight days later on the basis of that demand (1986 L. No. 4048), and the two actions have been consolidated.

....

(1) The $131 million claim

(a) Conflict of laws — the connecting factor

There is no dispute as to the general principles involved. Performance of a contract is excused if (i) it has become illegal by the proper law of the contract, or (ii) it necessarily involves doing an act which is unlawful by the law of the place where the act has to be done. I need cite no authority for that proposition (least of all my own decision in *Euro-Diam Ltd. v. Bathurst*, [1987] 1 Lloyd's Rep. 178 at p. 190; [1987] 2 W.L.R. 1368 at p. 1385) since it is well established and was not challenged. Equally it was not suggested that New York law is relevant because it is the national law of Bankers Trust, or because payment in London would expose Bankers Trust to sanctions under the United States legislation, save that Mr. Sumption Bankers Trust desires to keep the point open in case this dispute reaches the House of Lords.

There may, however, be a difficulty in ascertaining when performance of the contract necessarily involves doing an illegal act in another country. In *Toprak Mahsulleri Ofisi Finagrain Compagnie Commerciale Agricole et Financiere S.A.*, [1979] 2 Lloyd's Rep. 98, Turkish buyers of wheat undertook to open a letter of credit "with and confirmed by a first class U.S. or West European bank." The buyers were unable to obtain exchange control permission from the Turkish Ministry of Finance to open a letter of credit, and maintained that it was impossible for them to open a letter of credit without exporting money from Turkey. It was held that this was no answer to a claim for damages for non-performance of the contract. Lord Denning M.R. said (at p. 114):

> In this particular case the place of performance was not Turkey. Illegality by the law of Turkey is no answer whatever to this claim. The letter of credit had to be a confirmed letter of credit, confirmed by a first-class West European or U.S. bank. The sellers were not concerned with the machinery by which the Turkish state enterprise provided that letter of credit at all. The place of performance was not Turkey.

> This case is really governed by the later case of *Kleinwort, Sons & Co. v. Ungarisch Baumwolle Industrie Aktiengesellschaft an Another*, [1939] 2 K.B. 678 where bills of exchange were to be given and cover was to be provided in London, but at the same time there was a letter saying, "We have to get permission from Hungary." It was said that because of the illegality by Hungarian law in obtaining it, that would be an answer to the case. But Mr. Justice Branson and the Court of Appeal held that the proper law of the contract was English law; and, since the contract was to be performed in England, it was enforceable in the English Courts even though its performance might involve a breach by the defendants of the law of Hungary.

> That case has been quoted in all the authorities as now settling the law. . . .

> The only way that Mr. Johnson (for the Turkish state enterprise) could seek to escape from that principle was by saying -

>> . . . Although there was no term, express or implied, in the contract that anything had to be done in Turkey as a term of the contract, nevertheless it was contemplated by both parties. It was contemplated by both parties that the Turkish buyers would have to go through the whole sequence in Turkey of getting exchange control permission, and all other like things: and, if the contemplated method of performance became illegal, that would be an answer. Equally, if it became impossible, that would be a frustration.

> I am afraid that those arguments do not carry the day. It seems to me in this contract, where the letter of credit had to be a confirmed letter of credit —confirmed by a West European or U.S. bank—the sellers are not in the least concerned as to the method by which the Turkish buyers are to provide that letter of credit. Any troubles or difficulties in Turkey are extraneous to the matter and do not afford any defence to an English contract.

From that case I conclude that it is immaterial whether one party has to equip himself for performance by an illegal act in another country. What matters is whether performance itself necessarily involves such an act. The Turkish buyers might have had money anywhere in the world which they could use to open a letter of credit with a U.S. or West European bank. In fact it would seem that they only had money in Turkey, or at any rate needed to comply with Turkish exchange control regulations if they were to use any money they may have had outside Turkey. But that was no defence, as money or a permit was only needed to equip themselves for performance, and not for performance itself.

Mr. Sumption [Queen's Counsel, for the defendants Bankers Trust] took the same route as Mr. Johnson did in the *Toprak* case. He argued that the Court could look at the method of performance which the parties had contemplated, and relied on *Regazzoni v. K. C. Sethia (1944) Ltd.,* [1957] 2 Lloyd's Rep. 289; [1958] A.C.

301. (Mercifully he refrained from citing *Foster v. Driscoll*, [1921] 1 K.B. 470). In *Regazzoni's* case the plaintiff had agreed to buy 500,000 jute bags from the defendants c.i.f. Genoa. It was, of course, open to the defendants as a matter of law to ship the goods to Genoa from anywhere in the world. But in practice the goods had to be obtained from India, both parties knew that this was intended, and they also knew that the plaintiff intended to re-export the goods to South Africa. It was illegal by Indian law, again as both parties knew, to export goods from India destined to South Africa directly or indirectly. The plaintiff's claim failed.

I am relieved from the task of distinguishing between the *Toprak* principle and *Regazzoni's* case by a most helpful analysis of Mr. Justice Robert Goff in the *Toprak* case itself at first instance, which I gratefully adopt. He there held (at p. 107) that there were two related but distinct principles. The principle of *Regazzoni's* case was derived from the judgment of Lord Justice Sankey in *Foster v. Driscoll* (at p. 521):

> An English contract should and will be held invalid on account of illegality if the real object and intention of the parties necessitates them joining in an endeavour to perform in a foreign and friendly country some act which is illegal by the law of such country notwithstanding that there may be, in a certain event, alternative modes or places of performing which permit the contract to be performed legally.

Even if that principle can be applied to supervening illegality as opposed to illegality *ab initio* (a point which I would regard as open to question), it does not apply in this case. At no stage was it the real object and intention of the Ubyan bank that any illegal act should be performed in New York. That was not suggested in argument or in the course of the evidence. This case accordingly raises only the other principle, that performance is excused if it necessarily involves doing an act which is unlawful by the law of the place where the act has to be done.

Some difficulty may still be encountered in the application of that principle. For example, if payment in dollar bills in London was required by the contract, it would very probably have been necessary for Bankers Trust to obtain such a large quantity from the Federal Reserve Bank of New York, and ship it to England. That, Mr. Sumption accepts, would not have been an act which performance necessarily involved; it would merely have been an act by Bankers Trust to equip themselves for performance, as in the *Toprak* case. By contrast, if the contract required Bankers Trust to hand over a banker's draft to the Libyan bank in London, Mr. Sumption argues that an illegal act in New York would necessarily be involved, since it is very likely that the obligation represented by the draft would ultimately be honoured in New York. I must return to this problem later.

(b) The proper law of the contract

As a general rule the contract between a bank and its customer is governed by the law of the place where the account is kept, in the absence of agreement to the contrary. Again there was no challenge to that as a general rule, the fact that no appellate decision was cited to support it may mean that it is generally accepted. However, since the point is of some importance, I list those authorities that were cited. They are *X AG v A. Bank*, [1983] 2 Lloyd's Rep. 535; [1983] 2 Lloyd's Rep. 535; 1983 2 All E.R. 464,... *Dicey & Morris, The Conflict of Laws* (11th ed.) p. 1292 n. 51,... *Restatement (2d) Conflict of Laws*, p. 622....

That rule accords with the principle, to be found in the judgment of Lord Justice Atkin in *N. Joachimson v. Swiss Bank Corporation*. [1921] 3 K.B. 110 at p. 127, and other authorities, that a bank's promise to repay is to repay at the branch of the bank where the account is kept.

In the age of the computer it may not be strictly accurate to speak of the branch where the account is kept. Banks no longer have books in which they write entries; they have terminals by which they give instructions; and the computer itself with its magnetic tape, floppy disc or some other device may be physically located elsewhere. Nevertheless it should not be difficult to decide where an account is kept for this purpose, and is not in the present case. The actual entries on the London account were, as I understand it, made in London, albeit on instructions from New York after December, 1980. At all events I have no doubt that the London account was at all material times "kept" in London.

Mr. Sumption was prepared to accept that the proper law governing the London account was English law from 1973 to December 1980. But he submitted that a fundamental change then took place, when the managed account arrangement was made. I agree that this was an important change, and demands reconsideration of the proper law from that date. That the proper law of a contract may be altered appears from *James Miller & Partners Ltd. Whitworth Street Estates Ltd.*, [1970] 1 Lloyd's Rep. 269; [1970] A.C. 583, per Lord Reid at pp. 271 and 603, Lord Wilberforce at pp. 279 and 615.

Mr. Cresswell [Queen's Counsel] for the Libyan bank submits that there then arose two separate contracts, of which one related to the London account and remained governed by English law; alternatively he says that there was one contract, again governed by English law; or that it had two proper laws, one English law and the other the law of New York. Mr. Sumption submits that there was from December 1980 one contract I only, governed by New York law.

Each side has relied on a number of points in support of its contentions. I do not set them out, for they are fairly evenly balanced, and in my view do little or nothing to diminish the importance of the general rule, that the proper the law of the place where the account is kept. Political risk must commonly be an important factor to those who deposit large sums of money with banks; the popularity of Swiss bank accounts with some people is due to the banking laws of the Cantons of Switzerland. And I have already found, on the evidence of Bankers Trust, that the Iranian crisis was at the back of everyone's mind in 1980. Whatever considerations did or did not influence the parties to this case, I believe that banks generally and their customers normally intend the local law to apply. So I would require solid grounds for holding that the general rule does not apply, and there do not appear to me to be such grounds in this case.

I have, then, to choose between the first and third of Mr. Cresswell's arguments —two separate contracts or one contract with two proper laws. It would be unfortunate if the result of this case depended on the seemingly unimportant point whether there was one contract or two. But if it matters, I find the notion of two separate contracts artificial and unattractive. The device of a collateral contract has from time to time been adopted in the law, generally to overcome some formal requirement such as the ci-devant parole evidence rule, or perhaps to avoid the payment of purchase tax, and at times for other purposes. No doubt it has achieved justice, but at some cost to logic and consistency. In my judgment, the true view is that after December, 1980, there was one contract, governed in part by the law of England and in part by the law of New York. It is possible, although unusual, for a contract to have a split proper law, as Mr. Sumption accepted—see *Dicey & Morris* p. 1163, *Chitty on Contracts* (25th ed.) par. 2081. Article 4 of the E.E.C..Convention on the Law Applicable to Contractual Obligations (as I write not yet in force) provides:

1. To the extent that the law applicable to the contract has not been chosen in accordance with Article 3, the contract shall be governed by the law

of the country with which it is most closely connected. Nevertheless, a severable part of the contract which has a closer connection with another country may by way of exception by governed by the law of that other country.

That such a solution is not necessarily unacceptable to businessmen is shown by one of the Australian printed forms of charter-party, which adopts it.

Mr. Sumption argues that difficulty and uncertainty would arise if one part of the contract was governed by English law and another by New York law. I do not see that this would be so, or that any difficulty which arose would be insuperable.

There is high authority that branches of banks should be treated as separate from the head office. See for example *R. v. Grossman,* [1981] 73 Cr. App. Rep. 302, where Lord Denning, M.R. said (at p. 307):

> The branch of Barclays Bank in Douglas, Isle of Man, should be considered as a different entity separate from the head office in London.

That notion, of course, has its limits. A judgment lawfully obtained in respect of the obligation of a branch would be enforceable in England against the assets of the head office. (That may not always be the case in America). As with the theory that the premises of a diplomatic mission do not form part of the territory of the receiving state, I would say that it is true *for some purposes* that a branch office of a bank is treated as a separate entity from the head office.

This reasoning would support Mr. Cresswell's argument that there were two separate contracts, in respect of the London account and the New York account. It also lends some support to the conclusion that if, as is my preferred solution, there was only one contract, it was governed in part by English law and in part by New York law. I hold that the rights and obligations of the parties in respect of the London account were governed by English law.

If I had not reached that conclusion, and if the managed account arrangement was brought to an end as suggested by the Libyan Bank's solicitors in their letter of July 30, 1986, I would have had to consider whether the London account then ceased to be governed by New York law and became governed by English law once more.

(c) The nature of a bank's obligations

It is elementary, or hornbook law to use an American expression, that the customer does not own any money in a bank. He has a personal and not a real right. Students are taught at an early stage of their studies in the law that it is incorrect to speak of "all my money in the bank." See *Foley v. Hill,* (1848) 2 H.L.C. 28 at p. 36, where Lord Cottenham said:

> ...Money, when paid into a bank, ceases altogether to be the money of the principal.... It is then the money of the banker, who is bound to return an equivalent by paying a similar sum to that deposited with him when he is asked for it.... The money placed in the custody of a banker is, to all intents and purposes, the money of the banker, to do with as he pleases.

Naturally the bank does not retain all the money it receives as cash in its vaults; it if did, there would be no point or profit in being a banker. What the bank does is to have available a sufficient sum in cash to meet all demands that are expected to be made on any particular day.

I mention these simple points in order to clarify the real problem, which is what the obligation of a bank is. There are passages in the experts' reports which appear inconsistent with what I have said. Thus Dr. Marcia Stigum, who gave evidence for Bankers Trust, wrote:

> Dollars deposited and dollars lent in wholesale Eurodollar transactions never leave the United States.

That statement no doubt makes sense to an economist. For a lawyer it is meaningless.

The obligation of a bank is not, I think, a debt pure and simple, such that the customer can sue for it without warning. Thus in *Richardson v. Richardson*, [1927] P. 228 at p. 232 Mr. Justice Hill said:

> Certain contractual obligations of a bank and its customer, in the absence of special agreement, are well ascertained. They include these implied terms, as stated by Lord Justice Atkin in *Joachimson v. Swiss Bank Corporation: (a)* the promise of the bank to repay is to repay at the branch of the bank where the account is kept, and (b) the bank is not to be called upon to pay until payment is demanded at the branch at which the account is kept. (p. 233) If a demand is made at the branch where the account is kept and payment is refused, the position is altered. Undoubtedly the bank is then liable to be sued wherever it can be served.

That in itself is, in my judgment, an answer to one of the ways in which the Libyan bank put their claim. They cannot sue on a cause of action in debt without more. They must allege a demand made which Bankers Trust were obliged to comply with. Or, to put the point in another way, English law currently recognizes that an obligation to pay money can be frustrated.

What is the customer entitled to demand? In answering that question one must, I think, distinguish between services which a bank is obliged to provide if asked, and services which many bankers habitually do, but are not bound to, provide. For a private customer with a current account I would include in the first category the delivery of cash in legal tender over the bank's counter and the honouring of cheques drawn by the customer. Other services, such as standing orders, direct debits, banker's drafts, letters of credit, automatic cash tills and foreign currency for travel abroad, may be in the second category of services which the bank is not bound to but usually will supply on demand. I need not decide that point. The answer may depend on the circumstances of a particular case.

The problem in this case does not arise from the current account of a private customer. There was a correspondent relationship between the two banks, and a call account in London credited with very large sums denominated in United States dollars. The class of demands to which Bankers Trust were obliged to respond may be very different, and must be considered afresh.

. . . .

(d) Means of transfer

The credit balance of the Libyan bank with Bankers Trust constituted a personal right, a chose in action. At bottom there are only two means by which the fruits of that right could have been made available to the Libyan bank. The first is by delivery of cash, whether dollar bills or any other currency, to or to the order of the Libyan bank. The second is the procuring of an account transfer. (I leave out of account the delivery of chattels, such as gold, silver or works of art, since nobody has suggested that Bankers Trust were obliged to adopt that method. The same applies to other kinds of property, such as land.)

An account transfer means the process by which some other person or institution comes to owe money to the Libyan bank or their nominee, and the obligation of Bankers Trust is extinguished or reduced *pro tanto*. "Transfer" may be a somewhat misleading word, since the original obligation is not assigned (notwithstanding dicta in one American case which speak of assignment); a new obligation by a new debtor is created.

Any account transfer must ultimately be achieved by means of two accounts held by different beneficiaries with the same institution. In a simple case the beneficiaries can be the immediate parties to the transfer. If Bankers Trust held an account with the A bank which was in credit to the extent of at least $131 m., and the Libyan bank also held an account at the A bank, it would require only book entries to achieve an account transfer. But still no property is actually *transferred*. The obligation of Bankers Trust is extinguished, and the obligation of A bank to Bankers Trust extinguished, or reduced; the obligation of A bank to the Libyan bank is increased by the like amount.

On occasion a method of account transfer which is even simpler may be used. If X Ltd. also hold an account with Bankers Trust London, and the Libyan bank desires to benefit X Ltd., they instruct Bankers Trust to transfer $131 m. to the account of X Ltd. The obligation of Bankers Trust to the Libyan bank is extinguished once they decide to comply with the instruction, and their obligation to X Ltd. is increased by the like amount. That method of account transfer featured in the case of *Momm v. Barclays Bank International Ltd.*, [1977] Q.B. 790.

In a complex transaction at the other end of the scale there may be more than one tier of intermediaries, ending with a Federal Reserve Bank in the United States. Thus the payer may have an account with B bank in London, which has an account with C bank in New York; the payee has an account with E bank in London, which has an account with D bank in New York. Both C bank and D bank have accounts with the Federal Reserve Bank in New York. When an account transfer is effected the obligations of the New York Fed. to C bank, of C bank to B bank, and of B bank to the payer are reduced; the obligations of the New York Fed. to D bank, of D bank to E bank, and of E bank to the payee are increased. That is, in essence, how the CHIPS system works, by which a large proportion of transfers of substantial dollar amounts are made.

I shall call the three methods which I have described a correspondent bank transfer, an in-house transfer and a complex account transfer. There are variations which do not precisely fit any of the three, but the principle is the same in all cases. Sooner or later, if cash is not used, there must be an in-house transfer at an institution which holds accounts for two beneficiaries, so that the credit balance of one can be increased and that of the other reduced. In the example of a complex account transfer which I have given that institution is the New York Fed, which holds accounts for C bank and D bank.

Evidence was given by Professor Scott of a method which, at first sight, did not involve an in-house transfer at any institution. That was where different Federal Reserve Banks were used. However, the Professor assured me that an in-house transfer was involved, although it was too complicated to explain. That invitation to abstain from further enquiry was gratefully accepted.

Thus far I have been assuming that only one transaction affecting any of the parties takes place on a given day. But manifestly that is unlikely to be the case; there may be thousands, or tens of thousands. One purpose of a clearing system between banks must be to set off transfers against others, not only between the same parties but also between all other parties to the clearing system. Thus C bank and D bank, in my example of a complex account transfer, may have made many transactions between themselves on the same day. Only the net balance of them all will be credited to one by the New York Fed. and debited to the other at the end. So the identity of the sum which the payer wished to pay to the payee may be entirely lost in one sense. The net balance may be the other way, and a sum be credited to C bank and debited to D bank instead of vice versa. Or, by a somewhat improbable coincidence, the net balance may be nil.

There are two further complications. The first is that set-off occurs not only between C bank and D bank, but between all other participants to the clearing system. An amount which would otherwise fall to be debited to C bank and credited to D bank may be reduced (i) because F bank has made transfers on that day to C bank, or (ii) because D bank has made transfers on that day to G bank.

Secondly, an intermediate clearing system maybe used, such as London dollar clearing. If the chain of transmission on each side reaches a bank that is a member of the London dollar clearing, and if the item in question is eligible for that clearing system, it may be put through it. Then it will go to make up the net credit or debit balances that are due between all the members at the end of the day—and they in turn are settled in New York.

(e) Particular forms of transfer

I set out below those which have been canvassed in this case, and discuss the extent to which they involve activity in the United States.

(i) In-house transfer at Bankers Trust London

This is quite simple. It involves no action in the United States. But it cannot take place unless the Libyan bank are able to nominate some beneficiary who also has an account with Bankers Trust London.

(ii) Correspondent bank transfer

Again, this is relatively simple and involves no action in the United States. But for it to be effective in this case a bank must be found outside the United States where two conditions are satisfied: the first is that Bankers Trust have a credit balance there of $131 m. or more; the second, that an account is also held there for the Libyan bank or for some beneficiary whom they nominate.

(iii) CHIPS or Fedwire

These are two methods of complex account transfer which are used for a high proportion of large dollar transactions. They can only be completed in the United States.

(iv) Banker's draft on London

A banker's draft is, in effect, a promissory note, by which the banker promises to pay to or to the order of the named beneficiary. When the beneficiary receives the draft he can negotiate it, or hand it to another bank for collection. If he negotiates the draft the beneficiary's part in the transaction ends. He has received all that he bargained for, and so far as he is concerned no action in New York is required. Hence the view which emerges in the shipping cases that a banker's draft is as goods as cash. But there still remains for the bank the task of honouring the draft when it is presented. The issuing bank, by debiting the customer's account and issuing a draft, has substituted one personal obligation for another. It still has to discharge the obligation represented by the draft. That it may do, in theory at any rate, by another of the means of transfer that are under discussion—in-house transfer, correspondent bank transfer, CHIPS, Fedwire, London dollar clearing, cash. So in one sense a banker's draft does not solve the problem; it merely postpones it. One cannot tell whether action is required in the United States until one knows how the draft is to be honoured.

There would be a further problem for the Libyan bank if they received a draft from Bankers Trust. While the freeze was still operative the draft would in practice be difficult or impossible to negotiate, since nobody would want an instrument made by an American bank which on its face contained a promise to pay to or to the order of the Libyan bank. That, as it seems to me, would be the case whether the draft was drawn on London or New York. If instead of negotiating the draft the Libyan bank presented it to another bank for collection, the problem would have been postponed rather than solved for both parties. The Libyan bank would receive no credit until the draft had been honoured; and Bankers Trust would have to use another means of transfer in order to honour it.

(v) *Banker's payment*

This is an instrument issued by one bank in favour of another bank. As the shipping cases show, it too is treated as the equivalent of cash in the ordinary way, so that the receiving bank might well allow the customer who presented it to draw against it forthwith. I am not sure whether that would happen in present circumstances, if the receiving bank knew that the banker's payment was issued for the account of the Libyan bank.

Apart from the possibility of negotiation, which does not arise with a banker's payment, the same problem remains as with a banker's draft. It has to be cleared or honoured (whichever is the right word) by one of the other means of transfer under discussion. Normally the document will specify a clearing system which is to be used.

(vi) *London dollar clearing*

It may not be right to describe this as a means of transfer in itself, but rather as a method of settling liabilities which arise when other means of transfer are used, such as a banker's draft or banker's payment, or indeed a cheque. Bankers Trust are not themselves members of London dollar clearing, but use it through Lloyds Bank p.l.c.

Suppose H bank, also a member of the clearing presented a banker's draft issued by Bankers Trust to or to the order of the Libyan bank for $131 m. At the end of the day net debits and credits of all the members of the clearing would be calculated— and settled by transfers in New York. As already explained, there would not necessarily be a transfer there of $131 m. or any sum by Lloyds Bank of their New York correspondent to the New York correspondent of H bank. But somewhere in the calculation of the sum that would be transferred by some bank in New York to some other bank in New York the $131 m. would be found.

That is the first aspect of the transaction which requires action in New York. But thus far only the liabilities of the clearing members between themselves have been settled. What of the liabilities of the banks that have used the clearing but are not members? Bankers Trust owe Lloyds Bank $131 m. That sum will go into a calculation of all the credits and debits between Bankers Trust and Lloyds Bank on that day; the net balance will be settled by a transfer in New York between Bankers Trust New York and Lloyds Bank or their New York correspondent.

Since I have assumed that H bank are a member of the London dollar clearing, no similar transfer is required in their case. They have already received credit for

$131 m. in the clearing process and the transfers which settled the balances which emerged from it.

There is another aspect of the London dollar clearing which featured a great deal in the evidence. This is that a rule, at the time unwritten, excluded from the clearing -

...cheques drawn for principal amounts of interbank Eurocurrency transactions.

The system is described in the Child report, where it is said that -

...by mutual consent "wholesale" interbank foreign exchange deals and Eurodollar settlements are excluded.

That in turn raises a question as to the meaning of "wholesale." Bankers Trust argue that it includes transactions on interest-bearing call accounts between banks, at any rate if they are for large amounts. The Libyan bank say that it refers only to transactions for time deposits traded between the dealing rooms of banks.

I prefer the evidence of Bankers Trust on this point. The reason for the exclusion appears to be that the introduction of a very large sum by one participant into the clearing system would impose an excessive credit risk. The average value of transactions passing through the system is $50,000, and the vast majority of items are of the order of $10,000. It is not normally used for transactions over $30 m.; indeed, there were not many transactions in millions. I find that a transfer of $131 m. by Bankers Trust to or to the order of the Libyan bank would not, in the circumstances of this case, be eligible for London dollar clearing.

(vii) *Other clearing systems outside the United States*

Apart from the last point about eligibility, it seems to me that much the same considerations must apply to the other three systems discussed—Euroclear, Cedel and Tokyo dollar clearing. Although the identity of a particular transaction will be difficult or impossible to trace in the net credits or debits which emerge at the end of the clearing, these debits and credits must "ultimately" be settled in the United States. (The word "ultimately" constantly recurs and is of importance in this case, as was stressed in the course of the evidence.)

But whether that be so or not, there are other points relevant to the use of these systems. Euroclear in Brussels is a system run through Morgan Guaranty Trust Company for clearing securities transactions and payments in respect of such transactions. If it so happened that Bankers Trust had a credit of $131 m. in the system, it could arrange for that sum to be transferred to the Libyan bank or any nominee of the Libyan bank which had an account with Euroclear. That would be a species of correspondent transfer. Alternatively, it could order the transfer to be made anywhere else—but that would involve action in New York.

Cedel, in Luxembourg, is similar to Euroclear in all respects that are material.

The Tokyo dollar clearing system is run by Chase Manhattan Bank at its Tokyo branch. Bankers Trust did not have an account with the system. If they had done, and had used it to pay $131 m. to the Libyan bank, they would have had to reimburse Chase Manhattan via New York.

(viii) *Certificates of deposit*

These are issued by banks for large dollar sums, and may be negotiable. Once again they raise the problem that one personal obligation of Bankers Trust would be substituted for another and the substituted obligation still has to be honoured by some means at maturity. Furthermore, the terms of the certificate be subject to agreement. . . as to its maturity date and interest rate.

(ix) *Cash—dollar bills*

I am told that the largest notes in circulation are now for $100, those for $500 having been withdrawn. Hence there would be formidable counting and security operations involved in paying $131 m. by dollar bills. Bankers Trust would not have anything like that amount in their vault in London. Nor, on balance, do I consider that they would be likely to be able to obtain such an amount in Europe. It could obtained from a Federal Reserve Bank and sent to London by aeroplane, although several different shipments would be made to reduce the risk. The operation would take some time—up to seven days.

Banks would seek to charge for this service, as insurance and other costs would be involved, and they would suffer a loss of interest from the time when cash was withdrawn from the Federal Reserve Bank to the time when it was handed over the counter and the customer's account debited—assuming that the customer had an interest-bearing account. I cannot myself see any basis on which a bank would be entitled to charge, although there might be a right to suspend payment of interest. If a bank chooses, as all banks do for their own purposes, not to maintain a sum equal to all its liabilities in the form of cash in its vaults, it must bear the expense involved in obtaining cash when a demand is made which it is obliged to meet. If a customer demanded $1,000 or $10,000 in cash, I do not see how a charge could be made. When the sum is very much larger it is an important question—which I shall consider later—whether the bank is obliged to meet a demand for cash at all. If it is so obliged, there is not, in my opinion, any right to charge for fulfilling its my opinion, any right to charge for fulfilling its obligation.

As I have already mentioned, it is accepted that there would be no breach of New York law of cash in New York and despatching it to their London office.

(x) *Cash—sterling*

There would be no difficulty for Bankers Trust in obtaining sterling notes from the Bank of England equivalent in value to $131 million, although once again, there would be counting and security problems. Bankers Trust would have to reimburse the Bank of England, or the correspondent through whom it obtained the notes, and this would probably be done by a transfer of dollars in New York. But, again, was not argued that such a transfer would infringe New York law.

(f) *Termination of the managed account arrangement*

Those means of transfer are all irrelevant so long as the managed account arrangement subsists; for I have found it to be a term of that arrangement that all the Libyan bank's transactions should pass through New York. Apart from some minor teething problems at the start in 1980, that term was observed. The only entries on the London call account were credits from, or debits to, the New York demand account. It was the New York account that was used to make payments to, or receive credits from, others with whom the Libyan bank had business relations. If the arrangement still exists, the London account can only be used to transfer a credit to New York, which would be of no benefit whatever to the Libyan bank.

In my judgment, the Libyan bank was entitled unilaterally to determine the managed account arrangement on reasonable notice, which did not need to be more than 24 hours (Saturdays, Sundays and non-banking days excepted). The important feature of the arrangement from the point of view of Bankers Trust was that their operators could make payments in New York, on occasion giving rise to an overdraft in New York, safe in the knowledge that there was a credit balance in London which they could call upon and which would not disappear. If it were determined, Bankers Trust New York would be entitled to refuse to make payments which would put the account there into overdraft. For the Libyan bank an important feature was that they obtained both the speed and efficiency with which current account payments could be made in New York, and the advantage of an account in London bearing interest at Eurodollar rates. If the arrangement were determined and the Libyan bank began once again to use the London account as if it were a current account, Bankers Trust would be entitled (again on notice) to reduce the rate of interest payable on that account, or to decline to pay interest altogether.

I find nothing surprising in the notion that one party to a banking contract should be able to alter some existing arrangement unilaterally. Some terms, such as those relating to a time deposit, cannot be altered. But the ordinary customer can alter the bank's mandate, for example by revoking the authority of signatories and substituting others, or by canceling standing orders or direct debits; he can transfer sums between current and deposit account; and he can determine his relationship with the bank entirely. So too the bank can ask the customer to take his affairs elsewhere. In this case it does not seem to me at all plausible that each party was locked into the managed account arrangement for all time unless the other agreed to its determination, or the entire banking relationship were ended. I accept Mr. Cresswell's submission that the arrangement was in the nature of instructions or a mandate which the Libyan bank could determine by notice. For that matter, I consider that Bankers Trust would also have been entitled to determine it on reasonable notice—which would have been somewhat longer than 24 hours in their case. I hold that the arrangement was determined, implicitly by the Libyan bank's telex of Apr. 28, 1986, and if that were wrong, then expressly by their solicitors' letter of July 30, 1986.

What, then, was the position after determination? The New York account remained, as it always had been, a demand account. Subject to New York law, Bankers Trust were obliged to make transfers in accordance with the Libyan bank's instructions to the extent of the credit balance, but they were not obliged to allow an overdraft—even a daylight overdraft, as it is called when payments in the course of a day exceed the credit balance but the situation is restored by further credits before the day ends. The London account remained an interest bearing account from which Bankers Trust were obliged to make transfers on the instructions of the Libyan bank, provided that no infringement of United States law in the United States was involved. If Bankers Trust became dissatisfied with the frequency of such transfers, they were, as I have said, entitled on notice to reduce the rate of interest or bring the account to an end. And if I had not held that the rights and obligations of the parties in respect of the London account were governed by English law at all times, I would have been inclined to hold that they were once more governed by English law when the managed account arrangement was determined, although there is clearly some difficulty in recognizing a unilateral right to change the system of law governing part of the relations between the parties.

....

(h) Obligations in respect of the London account

Having considered and rejected [a] method [ ] by which Bankers Trust seek to limit their obligations in respect of the London account—that is, an express term from the managed account arrangement still subsisting, . . . - I have to determine what those obligations were. What sort of demands were the Libyan bank entitled to make and Bankers Trust bound to comply with? [I]t is necessary to distinguish between services which a bank is obliged to provide if asked, and services which many bankers do provide but are not obliged to.

Dr. Mann in his book The Legal Aspects of Money (4th ed.) pp. 193-195, discusses this question in the context of the Eurodollar market. I have given careful attention to the whole passage. His conclusion is this:

> The banks, institutions or multinational companies which hold such deposits, frequently of enormous size, and which deal in them are said to buy and sell money such as dollars. In law it is likely, however, that they deal in credits, so that a bank which has a large amount of dollars standing to the credit of its account with another (European) bank probably does not and cannot except it to be "paid" or discharged otherwise than through the medium of a credit to an account with another bank. In the case of dollars it seems to be the rule (and therefore possibly a term of the contract) that such credit should be effected through the Clearing House Interbank Payments System (CHIPS) in New York... In short, as economists have said, the Eurodollar market is a mere account market rather than a money market.

Dr. Mann cites Dr. Stigum's book, and finds some support for his view — which he describes as tentative — in an English case which has not been relied on before me. The passage in question appeared for the first time in the 1982 edition of Dr. Mann's book after the litigation about the Iranian bank freeze.

I am reluctant to disagree with such great authority on money in English law, but feel bound to do so. There is one passage which appears to me to be an indication of economic rather than legal reasoning:

> It could often be a national disaster if the creditor bank were entitled to payment, for in the last resort this might mean the sale of a vast amount of dollars and the purchase of an equally large sum of sterling so as to upset the exchange rates.

But if a person owes a large sum of money, it does not seem to me to be a sound defence in law for him to say that it will be a national disaster if he has to pay. Countries which feel that their exchange rates are at risk can resort to exchange control if they wish.

Furthermore, the term suggested by Dr. Mann — that all payments should be made through CHIPS — is negatived by the evidence in this case. It may for all I know be the rule for time deposits traded between the dealing rooms of banks, but I am not concerned with such a case here.

Professor Goode, in *Payment Obligations in Commercial and Financial Transactions*, p. 120 writes:

> Would an English court have declared the Executive Order effective to prevent the Iranian Government from claiming repayment in London of a dollar deposit maintained with a London bank? At first blush no, as it is unlikely that an English court would accord extra-territorial effect to the United States Executive Order. However, the argument on the United States side (which initially appeared to have claimed extraterritorial effect for the Order) was that in the Eurocurrency market it is well understood that deposits cannot be withdrawn in cash but are settled by an inter-bank transfer through the clearing system and Central Bank of the country whose currency is involved. So in the case of Eurodollar deposits payment was due in, or at any rate through, New York, and the Executive Order thereby validly prevented payment abroad of blocked Iranian deposits, not because the Order was extra-territorial in operation but because it prohibited the taking of steps within the United States (i.e.

through CHIPS in New York) to implement instructions for the transfer of a dollar deposit located outside the United States.

That was published in 1983. 1 have not accepted the argument which Professor Goode refers to, that it is well understood that deposits cannot be withdrawn in cash. I find that there was no implied term to that effect.

I now turn again to the forms of transfer discussed in sub-section (e) of this judgment, in order to consider in relation to each whether it was a form of transfer which the Libyan bank were entitled to demand, whether it has in fact been demanded, and whether it would necessarily involve any action in New York.

(i) *In-house transfer at Bankers Trust London.*

[and]

(ii) *Correspondent bank transfer.*

I consider that each of these was a form of transfer which the Libyan bank were entitled to demand as of right. But I find that no demand has in terms been made for a transfer by either method. This may well be because, in the case of an in-house transfer, there is no other institution with an account at Bankers Trust London which the Libyan bank wish to benefit; and in the case of a correspondent bank transfer, the Libyan bank have been unable to nominate a bank outside the United States which holds accounts both for Bankers Trust and also for the Libyan bank or some beneficiary whom they wish to nominate. It is not shown that U.B.A.F. Bank Ltd. (referred to in the telex of Dec. 23, 1986) fulfilled this requirement.

As to action in New York, none would have been required in respect of an in-house transfer at Bankers Trust London. Whether any would have been required in the case of a correspondent bank transfer depends on whether the correspondent bank in question did or did not already owe Bankers Trust $131 m. or more. On the evidence, it is at the least unlikely that any bank outside New York could be found owing Bankers Trust $131 m.

(iii) *CHIPS or Fedwire*

There is no doubt that the Libyan bank were entitled to demand such a transfer. But they did not demand it. Such a transfer would have required action in the United States which was illegal there. The only doubt which I have felt on that point is as to whether the ultimate entries on the books of a Federal Reserve bank would have been so remote from the underlying transaction—being perhaps between different parties, for a different sum, and even in the opposite direction to the underlying transaction —that they would not be unlawful. Professor Felsenfeld, who gave evidence on behalf of the Libyan bank, was inclined to think that such a transaction would be unlawful, and so was Mr. Knake. Professor Scott took a different view. Whichever be correct, I am convinced that *some* illegal action in the United States would be required by a CHIPS or Fedwire transfer.

(iv) *Banker's draft on London*

[and]

(v) *Banker's payment*

Bankers Trust did not in practice issue banker's drafts on their London office. Instead they would provide a cheque drawn on Lloyds Bank p.l.c. That does not seem to me a point of much importance. I consider that Bankers Trust were obliged to provide such instruments to the Libyan bank if asked to do so, subject to one important proviso—that the instruments were eligible for London dollar clearing. If they were not, then there was no such obligation, since in normal times and in the absence of legislation it would be simpler to use CHIPS or Fedwire in the first place.

A banker's draft was demanded in the telex of Apr. 28, 1986; and a banker's payment was within the description "any other commercially recognized method of transferring funds" demanded by the telex of Dec. 23, 1986. But since, as I have found, an instrument for $131 m. would not have been eligible for London dollar clearing in the circumstances of this case, Bankers Trust were not obliged to comply with that aspect of the demands.

It was argued that Bankers Trust might still have made interest payments through the London dollar clearing, since the exclusion is only of the *principal* amount of inter-bank Eurocurrency transactions. There are, in my judgment, three answers to that point. First, it is not relied on in the points of claim; secondly, there was no demand for interest payments as such; thirdly, the interest due had been capitalized once credited to the account. Indeed, if that were not so it would be impossible, or very difficult, to say how much of the $131 m. was interest.

That makes it unnecessary to answer the question, which I regard as particularly difficult, whether the issue of a banker's draft or banker's payment by Bankers Trust to the Libyan bank would necessarily involve illegal action in New York. Even if the instrument were cleared through London dollar clearing, action in New York would, as I have already mentioned, ultimately be required. (The same is true, in all likelihood, if one of the other clearing systems outside the United States had been used.) Although the identification of a particular payment would be even more difficult than in the case of a straight CHIPS transfer, I am inclined to believe that Bankers Trust would have a second defence to a claim based on failure to issue such an instrument, on the ground that performance of their obligation would necessarily involve illegal action in New York. However, Mr. Sumption appeared at one stage to accept that the issue of a draft drawn on London would not, or might not, involve illegal action in New York.

I need not consider problems as to the worth of a banker's draft or banker's payment to the Libyan bank in present circumstances or the damages they would have suffered by not obtaining one.

(vi) *London dollar clearing*

[and]

(vii) *Other clearing systems outside the United States*

In effect these have already been considered. Bankers Trust were not obliged to issue an instrument with a view to its being passed through London dollar clearing if it was not eligible; and an instrument for $131m. in this case would have been disqualified.

The other clearing systems give rise to similar problems. There is no evidence that Bankers Trust had an existing credit of $131m. with Euroclear or Cedel arising from a transaction in securities, and they were under no obligation to acquire one. Nor were they obliged to become participants in the Tokyo dollar clearing. If they had done so, the issue of an instrument to be cleared in Tokyo would, as with London dollar clearing, have necessarily involved action that was illegal in the United States.

(viii) *Certificates of deposit*

The issue of these comes in my judgment into the class of service which banks habitually do provide but are not obliged to. If for no other reason, that is because agreement is involved, as to the maturity of the instrument and the interest rate. It cannot be that a customer is entitled to demand any maturity and any interest rate that he chooses. Nor would a reasonable maturity and a reasonable interest rate provide a practicable solution.

In addition there would again be the problem whether a certificate of deposit could be honoured at maturity without infringing the law of the United States; and whether the Libyan bank had suffered any damage by not obtaining one.

(ix) *Cash — dollar bills*

Of course it is highly unlikely that anyone would want to receive a sum as large as $131m. in dollar bills, at all events unless they were engaged in laundering the proceeds of crime. Mr. Osbourne said in his report:

> As to the demand for payment in cash, I regard this simply as the assertion of a customer's inalienable right. In practice, of course, where such a large sum is demanded in this manner, fulfilment of the theoretical right is unlikely, in my experience, to be achieved. A sensible banker will seek to persuade his customer to accept payment in some more convenient form, and I have yet to encounter an incident of this nature where an acceptable compromise was not reached, even where the sum was demanded in sterling.

I would substitute "fundamental" for "inalienable;" but in all other respects that passage accords with what, in my judgment, is the law. One can compare operations in futures in the commodity markets: everybody knows that contracts will be settled by the payment of differences, and not by the delivery of copper, wheat or sugar as the case may be; but an obligation to deliver and accept the appropriate commodity, in the absence of settlement by some other means, remains the legal basis of these transactions. So in my view every obligation in monetary terms is to be fulfilled, either by the delivery of cash, or by some other operation which the creditor demands and which the debtor is either obliged to, or is content to, perform. There may be a term agreed that the customer is not entitled to demand cash; but I have rejected the argument that there was any subsisting express term, or any implied term, to that effect. Mr. Sumption argued that an obligation to pay on demand leaves very little time for performance, and that $131m. could not be expected to be obtainable in that interval. The answer is that either a somewhat longer period must be allowed to obtain so large a sum, or that Bankers Trust would be in breach because, like any other banker they choose, for their own purposes, not to have it readily available in London.

Demand was in fact made for cash in this case, and it was not complied with. It has not been argued that the delivery of such a sum in cash in London would involve an illegal action in New York. Accordingly I would hold Bankers Trust liable on that ground.

(x) *Cash — sterling*

Dicey & Morris (11th ed.) state in par. 210 at p. 1453:

> If a sum of money expressed in a foreign currency is payable in England, it may be paid either in units of the money of account or in sterling at the rate of exchange at which units of the foreign legal tender can, on the day when the money is paid, be bought in London...

See also Chitty on Contracts (25th ed.) par. 2105:

> Where a debtor owes a creditor a debt expressed in foreign currency...the general rule is that the debtor may choose whether to pay in the foreign currency in question or in sterling.

Mr. Sumption argues that there is no such rule, at any rate since the decision in *Miliangos v. George Frank (Textiles) Ltd.*, [1976] 1 Lloyd's Rep. 201; [1976] A.C. 443, that the judgment of an English Court does not have to be given in sterling.

Since the *Miliangos* decision the rule in *Dicey & Morris*, or rather an earlier version of it, has been approved obiter by Mr. Justice Mocatta in *Barclays Bank International Ltd. v. Levin Brothers (Bradford) Ltd.*, [1977] Q.B. 270, at p. 278. It must be admitted that the foundations of the rule appear to be somewhat shaky, and the reasoning upon which it has been supported open to criticism. Furthermore, in *George Veflings Rederi A/S v. President of India*, [1979] 1 Lloyd's Rep. 123 at p. 125; [1979] 1 W.L.R. 59, at pp. 63, Lord Denning, M. R. said:

> I see no reason to think that demurrage was payable in sterling. So far as demurrage was concerned, the money of account was U.S. dollars and the money of payment was also U.S. dollars...When you find, as here, that the demurrage is to be calculated in U.S. dollars and that there is no provision for it to be paid in sterling, then it is a reasonable inference that the money is payable in U.S. dollars.

The rule in *Dicey & Morris* had been cited in the Court below in that case; and it would appear at first sight that the Master of the Rolls disagreed with it. However, his conclusion evidently was that by implication the contract provided that demurrage should be paid only in U.S. dollars. In other words, the parties had contracted out of the rule. Furthermore, in that case a payment in sterling had in fact been made. The issue was not whether the charterer was entitled to pay in sterling, but how much credit should be given for the payment which he had made.

The pendulum swung the other way in *Re Lines Brothers Ltd.*, [1983] Ch. 1. Both the *Barclays Bank* case and the *George Veflings* case were cited in argument. Lord Justice Oliver, speaking of the argument of counsel for the creditors, said this (at p. 25):

> Now his argument has an engaging—indeed an almost unanswerable—logic about it once one accepts his major premise, but it is here that I find myself unable to follow him, for what, as it seems to me, he is seeking to do is to attribute to the *Miliangos* case a greater force than it has in fact. In effect what he seeks to do is to suggest that because *Miliangos* establishes that a creditor in foreign currency is owed foreign currency, it follows that the debtor is a debtor in foreign currency alone and cannot obtain his discharge by anything but a foreign currency payment. But this is to stand *Miliangos* on its head. What *Miliangos* is concerned with is not how the debtor is to be compelled to pay in the currency of the debt but the measure of his liability in sterling when, ex hypothesi, he has not paid and is unwilling to pay in the currency of the debt.

That, as it seems to me, is authority of the Court of Appeal that the *Miliangos* case does not affect the question whether a foreign currency debtor has a choice between payment in sterling and payment in foreign currency. I should follow the dicta of Lord Justice Oliver and Mr. Justice Mocatta, and the passages cited from *Dicey & Morris* and *Chitty*. That is also Dr. Mann's preferred solution and has the support of the Law Commission.

Still it may be agreed, expressly or by implication, that the debtor shall not be entitled to pay in sterling. There is no subsisting express term to that effect in the present case. Nor do I consider that such a term should be implied, in the present context of a banking contract where the obligation of Bankers Trust is to respond to demands of the Libyan bank.

It remains to be considered whether there is a true or business option such that payment in dollars is the primary or basic obligation but the debtor may choose to pay in sterling if it suits him to do so. Or are there alternative methods of performance, with the consequence described by Lord Devlin in *Reardon Smith Line Ltd. v. Ministry of Agriculture, Fisheries and Food*, [1963] A.C. 691, at p. 730:

> Where there is no option in the business sense, the consequence of damming one channel is simply that the flow of duty is diverted into the others and the freedom of choice thus restricted.

No other authority was cited on the point, and I feel that the material on which to decide it is somewhat meagre. Given that a foreign currency debtor is entitled to choose between discharging his obligations in foreign currency or sterling, I consider that he should not be entitled to choose the route which is blocked and then claim that his obligation is discharged or suspended. I prefer the view that he must perform in one way or the other; so long as both routes are available he may choose; but if one is blocked, his obligation is to perform in the other.

A further complication arises from the fact that a bank's obligation is to respond to a demand, and there are or may be various different kinds of demand which a customer is entitled to make. When the general doctrine of *Dicey & Morris* is considered in the context of a bank account such as that of the Libyan bank, and there is (as I have held) no express or implied term that the obligation must be discharged only in dollars, I hold that the customer is entitled to demand payment in sterling if payment cannot be made in dollars. (I need not decide whether payment in sterling could be demanded if it was still possible to pay in dollars.) In this case there was an alternative demand for sterling in the telex of Dec. 23, 1986; and it is not suggested that this would have involved any illegal activity in New York. I am not sure that it was a demand specifically for sterling notes, rather than an account transfer in sterling. But if the Libyan bank were entitled to demand sterling, no separate point arises as to the manner in which it should be provided. So if I had not held that payment should have been made in cash in United States dollars, I would have held that it should have been made in sterling.

(2) *The claim that a further sum should have been transferred from New York*

This arises in three different ways on the facts. First it is said that $165.2m. should have been transferred to London at 2:00 p.m. on Jan. 7, 1986.

Bankers Trust have two answers to this claim. First they say that instructions had been received and were pending for further payments to be made on Jan. 7 after 2:00 p.m., which exceeded the amount then standing to the credit of the New York account (and, for that matter, the London account as well). It was only because further receipts also occurred after 2:00 p.m. that the New York account ended the day with a credit balance of $7.275 m., and the London account remained untouched.

Secondly, Bankers Trust say that, if they were obliged to make a transfer to London on Jan. 7, they could lawfully have postponed it until after 8:06 p.m. New York time, when the first Presidential order came into force. Thereafter, they say, the transfer would have been illegal because it would have left the New York account over-drawn, and would have constituted the grant of credit or a loan to the Libyan bank.

In my judgment both those arguments fail. The telex of Nov. 27, 1986, from which I have already quoted, contained this passage:

> Each day, at 2:00 p.m., the balance position of your account is determined and any credits received up to that time, less payments and less the peg balance, are immediately invested.

It is said that "payments" there are not confined to payments actually made, and include payments for which instructions were pending. In view of the precision with which the time of 2:00 p.m. is stated, and the word "immediately," I do not consider that to be right. Mr. Sumption argued that "immediately" is coloured (one might say contradicted) by the illustration given in the telex; but I do not agree. The argument that Bankers Trust were entitled to delay the transfer until after 8:06 p.m. also fails, for the same reason, and it is unnecessary to decide whether it would have been a breach of the first Presidential order to allow an overdraft in New York which was less than the credit balance in London. They would certainly have been entitled in any event not to make payments which exceeded the net credit balance of the two accounts. But after credits which were received during the afternoon there was no need to do that.

Mr. Sumption also argued that the passage in the telex set out above was merely an illustration of how the arrangement would work, and not part of the revised terms of the managed account arrangement. That argument I also reject.

Some attention was paid to the course of dealing on these points. Mr. Blackburn's evidence showed that there was no consistency in the treatment of unprocessed payments; sometimes they were taken into account in deciding whether a 2:00 p.m. transfer should be made, and at other times they were ignored. As to the actual of the transfer, it was always booked in New York on the same day, and in London on the following day with one day's back value. The important feature to my mind is that, so long as there was no legislative interference, it did not make any difference to the parties whether the actual transfer was made at 2:00 p.m. or at any time up to midnight. Banking hours in London had already ended. Nor did it necessarily make a difference whether unprocessed payments were taken into account; if they were not, and a debit balance in New York resulted at the end of the day, Bankers Trust would recall an appropriate amount next morning from London, with one day's back value. It was only when the Presidential orders came to be made that timing became important. Bankers Trust were, as I hold, in breach of contract in failing to transfer $165.2m. to London at 2:00 p.m. on Jan. 7.

If they had done so, they would have been entitled to recall $158.5m. from London next morning, so that the net loss to the London account was only $6.7m. Mr. Cresswell argues that, in practice, Bankers Trust only recalled sums from the London account late in the day, and therefore after 4:10 p.m. when the second Presidential order came into effect; a transfer from London would thereafter have been illegal. In point of fact that may well be correct. But I have no doubt at all that, if there had been a large overdraft on the New York account on the morning of Jan. 8, 1986, Bankers Trust would on that particular day have recalled the appropriate sum from London with the utmost despatch.

No transfer to London having in fact been made on Jan.7, and no recall the next morning, $6.7m. should then have been transferred, as the amount by which the New York balance exceeded the peg of $500,000. The only issue of potential importance here is whether the transfer was actually made. Although preparations were made for effecting the transfer, I am satisfied that it was countermanded and did not take effect. There is no need for me to decide precisely when the transfer ought to have been made, since that is subsumed in the next point.

The Libyan bank's third complaint under this head is that, no transfers between New York and London having in fact been made at 2:00 p.m. on Jan. 7 or in the morning of Jan. 8, the balance in New York at 2:00 p.m. on Jan. 8 was $161,997,000. It is said that a sum of $161.4 should then have been transferred to London. In answer to that Bankers Trust rely on points that are the same as, or similar to those raised in respect of 2:00 p.m. on Jan. 7: they say they were entitled to delay payment until after 4:10 p.m. when the second Presidential order had been made, which certainly prohibited such a transfer. I reject both arguments for the reasons already given, based on the telex of Nov. 27, 985. It is true that if the pending payment instructions were to be executed in the afternoon, there were grounds for apprehension that the New York account would become overdrawn, which might be a breach of the first Presidential order; and even that the total of both accounts would be overdrawn, which would plainly be a breach of that order. The solution for Bankers Trust was not to execute those pending instructions unless and until further credits were received—in New York. Some were in fact received—the New York account ended the day in credit to the extent of $251,129,000. Payment instructions for that day totalled $347,147,213.03, and none of them were in fact executed. So on any view the New York account would have been overdrawn if all had been executed, and that much more overdrawn if all had been transferred to London at 2:00 p.m. But the net total of the two accounts would still have been a credit balance. If Bankers Trust took the view that an overdraft on the New York account would itself be a breach of the Presidential order, and if they were right, the solution as I have said was to execute the pending instructions only as and when credits received permitted them to do so.

Accordingly I hold that -

(i)   Bankers Trust were in breach of contract in failing to transfer $165.2m. to London at 2:00 p.m. on Jan. 7;

(ii)   if they had done that, they could and would have recalled $158.5m. from London in the morning of Jan. 8; but,

(iii)   on the assumption that both those steps had been taken, there would have been a further breach in failing to transfer $154.7m. to London at 2:00 p.m. on Jan. 8. (I trust that the calculation of this last figure is not too obscure. The 2:00 p.m. transfer on Jan. 8 should have been $161.4m. if *neither* of the previous transfers had been made—as in fact they were not. If they had both been made, the figure would have been reduced to $154.7m.)

The balance resulting from those three figures is a net loss to the London account of $161.4m. I hold that this must be added Libyan bank's first claim, as an additional sum for which that claim would have succeeded but for breaches of contract by Bankers Trust. It is said that this loss is not recoverable, because it arose from a new intervening act and is too remote. In the circumstances as they were Jan. 7 and 8 I have no hesitation in rejecting that argument.

. . . .

Conclusion

The Libyan bank are entitled to recover $131 m. on claim (1) and $161 m. (the amount of their demand) on claim (2)....

QUESTIONS

1.   What do you think of the proposition that all United States dollars ultimately are sourced (*i.e.*, must clear and settle through) New York City? *See* Hal S. Scott, *Where Are the Dollars? — Off-Shore Funds Transfers*, 3 BANKING & FIN. L. REV. 243 (June 1989).

2.   Even if the United States government can freeze dollar deposits held abroad through its control of the United States payments system, are such freezes good policy?

Part II

Foreign Direct Investment

Chapter 5

Negotiating and Structuring the Deal

I. Trends in FDI

A. Basic Concepts and Patterns

NOTE ON THE DEFINITION AND IMPORTANCE OF FDI[*]

Defining "FDI"

Before discussing the motivations for and recent trends in foreign direct investment (FDI), it is essential to understand what "FDI" is. Generally speaking, FDI is a type of overseas investment that involves the "transfer of tangible or intangible assets from one country into another for the purpose of use in that country to generate wealth under the total or partial control of the owner of the assets."[1] Alternatively, "it may be characterized as the transfer of funds or materials from one country (called the capital exporting country) to another country (called the host country) to be used in the conduct of an enterprise in that country in return for a direct or indirect participation in the earnings of the enterprise."[2] Further, "[f]oreign direct investment (FDI) occurs when an investor based in one country (the home country) acquires an asset in another country (the host country) *with the intent to manage the asset.*"[3]

FDI, as a subset of overseas investment, should be distinguished from its sibling, portfolio investment. Where portfolio investment involves the investor acquiring debt instruments, bonds, or equities through capital markets, FDI involves "new ventures, or acquisition of existing enterprises"[4] in the host country, generally providing the investor with a higher level of managerial control. "The management dimension is what distinguishes FDI from portfolio investment in foreign stocks, bonds, or other

---

[*] This Note was prepared by Christopher C. Matteson, Esq.

1. M. Sornarajah, The International Law on Foreign Investment 4 (1994) (citations omitted).

2. Stefan A. Reisenfeld, *Foreign Investments, in* II Encyclopedia of Public International Law 435, (R. Bernhardt ed.) (1995).

3. *Special Topic: Trade and Foreign Direct Investment, in* I World Trade Organization Annual Report 1996 46 (August 31, 1996) (emphasis original).

4. Reisenfeld, *supra*, at 435.

financial instruments."[5] Further, FDI generally involves a greater degree of potential liability on the part of the investor than does portfolio investment. For example, a direct investment may take the shape of a corporation organized under the laws of the host country and therefore does not operate under the protection or environment of United States laws and regulations. Investment through a direct ownership of material assets is not as liquid as an ownership of securities, for example, for which there is more likely to be an active market and an accordingly greater degree of asset fungibility.

Why Invest Overseas?

The world certainly has been "getting smaller." The increase in global intercourse, whether through travel, commerce, communication, or other means, illustrates the growing interdependence of economies and markets throughout the world. Recently, the entities that thrive in the international environment have increased their capabilities through means such as the Internet, satellite communications, intermodal shipping, and aviation. Commercial success no longer relies purely on a successful local or regional approach, and it is indisputable that the global marketplace is a source of tremendous potential for investors and businesses.

The prevalence of FDI has grown very rapidly in recent years. For example, the growth of FDI has outpaced world trade, and the expanding role of multinational corporations ("MNCs") in the global economy has influenced this trend significantly. Consider the following facts:

1st: During 1986-89, and again in 1995, outflows of FDI grew much more rapidly than world trade. Over the period 1973-95, the estimated value of annual FDI outflows multiplied 12 times (from $25 billion to $315 billion), while the value of merchandise exports multiplied eight-and-a-half times (from $575 billion to $4,900 billion).

2nd: Sales of foreign affiliates of [MNCs] are estimated to exceed the value of world trade in goods and services (the latter was $6,100 billion in 1995).

3rd: Intra-firm trading among MNCs is estimated to account for about one third of world trade, and MNC exports to all other firms for another third, with the remaining one third accounted for by trade among national (non-MNC) firms.[6]

The largest commercial entities in the world thus endeavor to reap the benefits of the global economy.

The role of the industrialized nations in this unprecedented rise in FDI flows over time is key. Consider the year 1995: "Developed countries were the key force behind the record 1995 flows. Inflows rose by 53 per cent in 1995, to $203 billion; outflows rose by 42 per cent in 1995 to $271 billion.... The United States was the star performer, with $60 billion of inflows and $96 billion of outflows."[7] The largest outflows have come from the United States, Germany, the United Kingdom, Japan, and France, together accounting for approximately two thirds of the world FDI outflow.

---

5. WTO ANNUAL REPORT 1996, *supra*, at 46.

6. WTO ANNUAL REPORT 1996, *supra*, at 73. These reports are an excellent source for researching the trends in world trade and investment. They are available for ordering online through the World Trade Organization's excellent website, <www.wto.org>.

7. *Investment, Trade, and International Policy Arrangements, in* UNITED NATIONS CONFERENCE ON TRADE AND DEVELOPMENT — WORLD INVESTMENT REPORT 1996 3 (1996).

The large role played by the developed world, however, did not detract from the increase in FDI flows into the developing world.

> At $100 billion, (an increase of 15 per cent over 1994), they, too, set a record in 1995, although their *share* in global inflows declined to 32 per cent, after having increased consecutively for the previous six years. While continuing to be small, FDI inflows to the group of 48 least developed countries increased as well, by 29 per cent in 1995 to $1.1 billion.[8]

Developing nations certainly participate in the global economy to varying degrees and at different levels over time.

The main thrust of these recent trends seems to indicate that business entities in both developed and developing nations are turning to overseas investment to respond to competition and take advantage of economic opportunities. FDI, as one component of overseas investment, certainly has become a field of opportunity for many.

Counsel to investors hoping to harness this tremendous potential should endeavor to assist their clients in effective use of FDI as a means of achieving a successful growth strategy. FDI presents unique challenges and rewards in this regard. Accordingly, the lawyer who can successfully operate in the 21st century global economy will be one who appreciates the risks, requirements, advantages, and long-term implications of overseas investment. Although written over twenty years ago, consider the following:

> While the world community of today is very interdependent, upon a closer scrutiny, it presents a kaleidoscopic picture of about 150 different countries, each with its own cherished history, economic development, socio-political and legal framework, its identifications and expectations. The accelerated tempo of scientific and technological advances has not only dramatically increased our interdependence resulting in a fast shrinking world in terms of physical distances has also been instrumental in contributing to the ever-growing transnational contacts, including investment and trade.... The vast area with which the lawyer in international business may be concerned includes the laws, the economic, social and political conditions and prospects in the foreign country. *The lawyer in a given case may have to familiarize himself with the different forms of foreign business organization, the advantages and disadvantages of selecting a particular type of business enterprise.*[9]

Clearly, the above statement is even more valid in the world of today, where the rewards of and demand for foreign direct investment is greater than ever before.

Current Trends: Less Restrictions, More Flexibility

The current shift toward globalization of the world economy has caused a change in the somewhat distrustful attitudes regarding FDI in the past.[10] Nations are seeking to encourage inflows of capital and technology, creating a competitive global marketplace in which many countries are attempting to stimulate, encourage, and attract FDI. "The overall policy trend is toward less control and more promotion and [cooperation]."[11] Indeed, consider the following facts:

---

8. UNCTAD World Investment Report, *supra*, at 4.

9. Stephen Gorove, *Advising Clients in International Business and Investment: The Lawyer's Role, in* Legal Aspects of International Investment 1 (Stephen Gorove ed., 1977) (emphasis added).

10. *See* Jose Luis Siqueros, *Bilateral Treaties on the Reciprocal Protection of Foreign Investment*, 24 Cal. W. Int'l L.J. 255 (1994).

11. Siqueros, *supra*, at 255-56 (citations omitted).

1st: Since the early 1980s, there has been a widespread trend towards lib-
       eralization of national laws and regulations relating to foreign invest-
       ment, especially in developing and transition countries. However, uni-
       lateral action has not been found sufficient as regards either the
       locking-in of reforms and their credibility in the eyes of investors or the
       compatibility with other FDI regimes. In the absence of a multilateral
       regime, the liberalization of national FDI regimes has been accompa-
       nied by a rapid proliferation of intergovernmental arrangements deal-
       ing with foreign investment issues at the bilateral, regional (for exam-
       ple, NAFTA and MERCOSUR), and plurilateral levels. Some two
       thirds of the nearly 1,160 bilateral investment treaties concluded up to
       June 1996 were signed during the 1990s.

2nd: In addition, OECD members—which currently account for about 85
       per cent of world outflows of FDI—have been negotiating since May
       1995, with the aim of concluding a Multilateral Agreement on Invest-
       ment (MAI)....The objective is for an independent international
       treaty, open to OECD members and the European Community and to
       accession by non-OECD countries.[12]

Many of the host nations of the world seem to recognize that less regulation is better and that attracting investors through incentives can be beneficial to their
economies.

Another excellent example of this reduction in control and liberalization of the
laws governing FDI is found in the energy sector.[13] In the 1970s, the international energy investment sector was characterized by a "strong assertion of state sovereignty
over economic and political emancipation of developing countries, resulting in large-
scale nationalization, renegotiation, and emergence of strong state resource companies
supported by foreign loans. Capital investment was seen as an important lever to gain
economic power, and private investment generally was excluded,de-packaged, and restricted."[14]

The climate has changed from being restrictive to one where privatization, deregulation, liberalization, and encouragement of FDI are emphasized. Nations are
"rushing into foreign investment as a panacea for their woes."[15] Examples of host
nation policy changes include relaxation or elimination of traditional host government majority ownership requirements and reductions in the number of approvals
required by the relevant host government agencies. Governments have attempted to
develop and implement multilateral guidelines for international energy investment.
For example, the Energy Charter Treaty (ECT)[16] attempts to create legal and policy
foundations for the modernization of the energy sector in Eastern Europe.[17] "The
ECT is likely to create a new type of regional and industry-focused international investment law."[18] Governments are including innovative features that reflect this fundamental shift in policy in international energy investment contracts. For example,

---

12. WTO ANNUAL REPORT 1996, *supra*, at 74.
13. Comments about the role of FDI in the energy sector are drawn significantly from
Thomas W. Waelde, *International Energy Investment,* 17 ENERGY L.J. 191 (1996).
14. Waelde, *supra*, at 191.
15. *Id.*
16. Fifty OECD, Eastern European, and CIS nations have signed the ECT. The United States
and Canada, however, have not yet done so.
17. *See* Waelde, *supra*, at 212-213 and accompanying footnotes.
18. Waelde, *supra*, at 213.

entering into flexible taxation regimes and royalty agreements, emphasizing environmental quality issues in contracts, and evaluating the socio-economic impact of energy operations at local and regional levels.

Further, there has been a greater deference to the corporate decision-makers in recent international energy legislation and agreements. Presumably, petroleum rich host nations have realized that companies investing their money know how to do so properly. It also has been suggested that government participation will be far less present in the future, and there will be a continuing reevaluation of the impact of host government regulation and taxation on corporate energy operations.[19]

Generally speaking, there are frequent incentives offered by host countries to attract inward FDI. In industrialized countries, often there are tax and other incentives offered to investors, such as reduced property taxes or offers to fund certain portions of local road improvements. These types of incentives can encourage investors to initiate an investment relationship in such a host country, as the investors' bottom line is inevitably helped in some way. "The United States Commerce Department (1994) found in a survey of United States-owned affiliates abroad that 26 per cent of affiliates had been offered tax concessions, 16 per cent tariff protection, and 9 per cent subsidies."[20]

However, there is a negative side to these FDI incentives. "Such incentives not only bias FDI towards countries with "deep pockets", but the reality of their operation—they are no different from any other kind of subsidy programme—is a source of considerable concern."[21] The reason for concern stems from the fact that there is a "hidden cost" of such subsidies, that host countries begin to compete by offering incentives, thereby driving up the cost of attracting FDI. Also, they are subject to manipulation by political interest groups in host nations. Clearly, the globalist position as advocated by the WTO would imply that, although inward investment is a desirable factor in local labor markets, and increases the transfer of technology, excessive competition in the attraction of FDI can reduce its benefits to all. "Too often, policies are designed to attract firms through incentives or protected markets, which erode or even negate the potential gains from that investment."[22] Adherence to bilateral and regional investment agreements, supplemented by a multilateral legal and regulatory regime would enhance stability in the FDI sector.

Opportunities in Developing Nations[23]

Investment in developing and newly liberalized nations (DVANLN) has increased in the past fifteen years. The outlay of capital to these nations has increased steadily, from $12.5 billion worldwide in 1985 to $48.9 billion in 1993.[24] Asia has seen the largest increase in its share of worldwide FDI, rising from 39.3 percent in

---

19. *See* Waelde, *supra*, at 194.

20. Stephen Thompson, *Attracting Investment in an Integrating World Economy*, *in* THE NEW GLOBALISM AND DEVELOPING COUNTRIES 214, 223 (John H. Dunning & Khalil A. Hamdani eds., 1997) (citation omitted).

21. WTO ANNUAL REPORT 1996, *supra*, at 74.

22. Thompson, *supra*, at 223.

23. For a thorough and economically-oriented treatment of the topic of FDI and developing nations, *see* THE NEW GLOBALISM AND DEVELOPING COUNTRIES (John H. Dunning and Khalil A. Hamdani eds., 1997).

24. *See* George Thomas Ellinidis, *Foreign Direct Investment in Developing and Newly Liberalized Nations*, 4 DET. C.L. AT MICH. ST. U. J. INT'L L. & PRAC. 299, 300-01 (1995), *citing* MULTILATERAL INVESTMENT GUARANTEE AGENCY (MIGA), ANNUAL REPORT 1994.

1985 to 60.5 percent in 1993.[25] One reason for this increase is that there are great advantages to investing in these relatively high-risk markets. Growth rates are often relatively high in these nations, natural resources may be present in the host country, labor costs are often lower, and many host countries are potential consumer markets for the investor, as their home market share may have peaked.

Also, many developing nation governments have instituted policy frameworks[26] that encourage FDI due to the many possible benefits, including, an increase in net private capital inflows, a decrease in unemployment, a transfer of technology and management skills, and overall modernization.[27] From a developing host country perspective, FDI thus can be an extremely beneficial component of a development plan. It may enhance the successful use of other forms of development finance, as both foreign direct investment and debt tend to flow into developing economies. The accompanying economic growth tends to further attract multinationals and other entities to invest in the host country, raising return for investors and reducing risk for lending entities in a circular process.

> Foreign direct investment is not only complementary with other forms of international capital flows, but it has been suggested that it may also serve to complement local capital in the host country. Even in-house technology transfer and external mechanisms of technology transfer can be complementary in the sense that both affect the capability of the host country to utilize and to absorb technologies. Because of this complementarity, all policies that attempt both to hire capital, technology, etc., or to increase exports will probably affect both inward investment and arm's length transactions.[28]

Thus, the benefits of FDI extend beyond participation in the global economy, it can enhance things on the local and regional levels as well.

However, "developing country [pro-FDI] policies need to be judged not only by the number of firms that they attract, but also by the technological and other spillovers from that investment."[29] In other words, there are many components to a mutually beneficial FDI arrangement. The presence of FDI ventures in a host country alone does not automatically result in a benefit to the host economy.

Certainly, investing in the developing world involves risks. Political instability can result in unfavorable events, such as insurrection, and a consequent change in climate for the investor. Expropriation[30] is another possibility, as there is no universally accepted definition of "fair compensation."[31] Further, currency inconvertibility may result in the investor failing to meet external financial commitments. Consequently, there has been a demand for insurance against these types of risks.

---

25. *See* Ellinidis, *supra*, at 301 (citing the MIGA ANNUAL REPORT 1994).

26. Examples include tax reductions or exemptions, decreased regulation, or product promotion.

27. *See* IBRAHIM F. I. SHIHATA, LEGAL TREATMENT OF FOREIGN INVESTMENT 9-12 (1993) (discussing FDI's benefits to the host country).

28. Thompson, *supra*, at 223.

29. *Id*. at 223.

30. Expropriation is defined as "the taking of an investor's property without compensation or with inadequate compensation." Ellinidis, *supra*, at 314 (citation omitted).

31. *See* Ellinidis, *supra*, at 315 (discussing the right of a nation under international law to nationalize foreign owned property if (1) there is no discrimination, (2) there is a public purpose, and (3) there is fair compensation) (citations omitted).

Private companies, such as Lloyd's of London, Citicorp International Trade Indemnity, and American International Underwriters have responded to this need by offering appropriate policies for sale.[32] Developed nations and the World Bank also have developed insurance programs that can provde coverage against these risks. For example, the Overseas Private Investment Corporation (OPIC) in the U.S. and the Multilateral Investment Guarantee Agency (MIGA) both offer insurance coverage to foreign direct investors. A detailed discussion of the factors involved with regard to political risk follows, in the note entitled *Political Risk: Implications and Mitigation Techniques*.

Although risks are involved, investment in developing nations can be lucrative. Both host countries and source countries have instituted policies to encourage FDI and alleviate the potential risks. It is likely that the upward trend in FDI flows to developing nations will continue, with positive consequences for source nations and host nations, and for the overall development of the world economy.

Conclusion

The basic incentives for the use of FDI as a vehicle by which to harness the power of the global economy remain intact, despite varying levels of risk and cyclical economic downturns in the developing world. As long as the globalization of world commerce continues, the flow of capital and resources across borders will likely continue to rise in amount and importance. Many host nations will seek to capitalize on this trend by reducing regulation and, indeed, welcoming FDI. Thus, lawyers should be aware of the motivations behind the use of FDI, the issues involved, and the special risks and opportunities provided in developing countries.

QUESTIONS

1. What is the difference between FDI and portfolio investment?

2. What policy changes have affected the landscape of international energy investment?

3. How have multinational corporations (MNCs) fared in the new global economy?

4. Should multinationals play such an instrumental role in the global economy? Are corporations replacing nations as the foci of power and leverage over the population of the world?

B. The Historical Development of Multinational Corporate Networks

Raymond Vernon, Where Are the Multinationals Headed?

In Foreign Direct Investment 57-77 (Kenneth A. Froot Ed. 1993)

Four decades ago, the multinational enterprise was widely regarded as a peculiarly American form of business organization, a manifestation of the existence of a *pax Americana*. Today, every industrialized country provides a base for a considerable number of multinationals, which collectively are becoming the dominant form of organization responsible for the international exchange of goods and services. In-

---

32. *See* Ellinidis, *supra*, at 320.

deed, by the end of the 1980s, even the larger firms in some of the rapidly industrializing countries of Asia and Latin America had joined the trend.

For scholars who want to understand the factors affecting international trade in
goods and services, these changes are of consummate importance. In the past, whenever the international behavior of multinationals appeared at odds with a world regulated by comparative advantage and capital market theory, the deviation could be
treated as idiosyncratic, the basis for a footnote in passing. But today, with multinationals dominating the international traffic in goods and services, the question of
what determines their behavior takes on considerable significance.

I cannot pretend to provide a definitive answer to this central question... but I
have two goals in mind which contribute to that central task. The first is to persuade
the reader that explanations of the behavior of multinational enterprise which draw
on the national origins of the enterprise as a major explanatory variable are rapidly
losing their value, to be replaced by an increased emphasis on the characteristics of
the product markets in which the enterprises participate. The second is to plant a few
ideas regarding the motivations and responses of the multinational enterprise that I
believe must figure in any rounded explanation of the behavior of these enterprises in
the various product markets they face.

3.1 U.S. Firms Ascendant

The sudden growth of U.S.-based multinational networks after World War II
was in fact some time in the making. Many decades earlier, the first signs that
large enterprises might find themselves pushed to develop a multinational structure were already beginning to appear. Setting the stage for the development of
these multinational networks were the dramatic improvements in tho technologies
of transportation and communication, coupled with the vastly increased opportunities for scale economies in industrial production. Operating with high fixed costs
and low variable costs, a new crop of industrial giants felt especially vulnerable to
the risks of price competition. And by the beginning of the twentieth century, these
risks were beginning to be realized; the country's industrial leaders, including
firms in machinery, metalworking, and chemicals, were coming into bruising contact not only with rivals from the United States but also with some from Europe.

Facing what they perceived to be dangerous and destructive competition, the
leaders in many U.S. industries went on the defensive. By the beginning of the century, many of the new industries of the country had organized themselves in restrictive market-sharing arrangements and were reaching out to their European competitors to join agreements that were global in scope.

From the first, however, it was apparent that these restrictive arrangements were
fragile responses to the threat of competition, especially for firms based in the United
States. The diversity and scope of the U.S. economy, coupled with a hostile legal environment, made it difficult for U.S. leaders to stifle the appearance of new firms inside the country; those same factors put a brake on the leaders' engaging in overt collusion with European rivals. Nevertheless, global market-sharing agreements
persisted at times, especially when patents and trademarks provided a fig leaf for the
participants. By and large, though, the role of U.S. firms in these restrictive arrangements was cautious and restrained.

While participating in the international division of markets in a number of products before World War II, many large firms also established the first of their subsidiaries in foreign locations during that period. Commonly, however, large firms
used these subsidiaries to implement their restrictive agreements with other firms, as

in the case of the Du Pont-ICI subsidiaries located in Latin America. Often, too, firms established such subsidiaries as cautionary moves against the possibility that competitors might be in a position to cut them off from raw materials in times of shortage or from markets in times of glut. U.S. firms that were engaged in extracting and processing raw materials, for instance, typically developed vertically integrated structures that covered the chain from wellhead or mine shaft to the final distribution of processed products; and because other leading firms shared the same fear, partnerships among rivals commonly appeared at various points in these vertical chains, in the form of jointly owned oil fields, mines, and processing facilities. Meanwhile, other U.S. firms, such as General Motors, Ford, and General Electric, established subsidiaries in Europe, to serve as bridgeheads in the event of warfare among industry leaders. Such bridgeheads, consistent with their function, were usually allowed to operate with considerable independence and autonomy.

For a decade or two after World War II, the defensive responses of U.S.-based firms to their perceived risks in world markets were a little less in evidence. The reasons were too obvious to require much comment. The proverbial "animal spirits" of U.S. business were already at an elevated level as a result of the technological lead and financial advantages that U.S. firms enjoyed over their European rivals. Dramatic advances in communication and transportation were enlarging the stage on which those spirits could be released. The real cost of those services was rapidly declining; and with the introduction of containerized freight, airborne deliveries, and the telex, the range of those services was widening. These improvements expanded the business horizons of U.S.-based firms, allowing them to incorporate more distant locations in the marketing of their products and the sourcing of their needed inputs.

The first reaction of most U.S. firms to their expanding product markets was to meet demands by increasing exports from the home base. But, as numerous case studies attest, the establishment of local producing subsidiaries soon followed. Almost all of the first wave of manufacturing subsidiaries established in foreign countries after World War II were dedicated principally to serving the local markets in which they were placed. As a consequence, about four-fifths of the sales of such subsidiaries during the 1960s were directed to local markets.

The motives of the firms in serving local markets through producing subsidiaries rather than through exports were usually complex. In some cases, for instance, the establishment of a producing subsidiary was simply perceived as a more efficient means for serving the foreign market, a consequence of the fact that sales in the market had achieved a level sufficient to exploit the existing economies of scale in production. But other factors contributed to the scope and timing of these decisions as well. There were indications, for instance, that the decisions taken to establish subsidiaries abroad, whether for the marketing of products or for the production of required materials and components, were often reactive measures, stimulated by and intended as a hedge against some perceived threat. Once a U.S. firm lost its unique technological or marketing lead, as seemed inevitable in most products over the course of time, governments might be tempted to restrict imports in order to encourage domestic production. In that case, the foreign subsidiary served to protect existing market access.

But even without the threat of action by governments, U.S.-based firms frequently faced threats posed by rivals in the product markets in which they operated. And some rich anecdotal evidence strongly suggests that foreign subsidiaries were often created as a hedge against such threats.

That hypothesis may help to explain why, in the first few decades after World War II, U.S.-based firms were engaged in follow-the-leader behavior in the establish-

ment of new producing subsidiaries abroad. Once a U.S.-based firm in an oligopolis-
tically structured industry set up a producing subsidiary in a given country, the
propensity of other U.S.-based firms in the oligopoly to establish a subsidiary in the
same country was visibly heightened. Such a pattern, of course, does not conclusively
demonstrate that the follower is responding defensively to the behavior of the leader.
Alternative hypotheses also need to be entertained, such as the possibility that both
follower and leader were responding to a common outside stimulus or that the follower was responding in the belief that the leader had done a rational analysis
equally applicable to both their situations.

However, stimulated by my reading of various individual cases, I am strongly inclined to attribute such follow-the-leader behavior in many cases to the follower's desire to hedge a threat posed by the leader. Although the follower may be unsure
whether the leader has properly analyzed the costs and benefits of its move in establishing a foreign subsidiary, the follower is understandably fearful of allowing a rival
to enjoy the benefits of undisturbed exploitation of its foreign opportunities. As long
as the number of rival producers in the market is small, therefore, following the leader
often seems to entail smaller downside risks than failing to follow. Failing to follow a
leader that was right in making its move would give that leader an unrivaled opportunity to increase its competitive strength, whether by increasing its marketing opportunities or by reducing its production costs; if the leader was wrong, the follower's risks
from committing the same error would be limited by the leader's having shared in it.

If the hedging of a threat was sometimes necessary for the growth of U.S.-based
multinational enterprises, however, it was certainly not sufficient for such growth. Still
to be explained was why in so many cases U.S.-based firms chose to establish producing subsidiaries rather than to exploit their strengths through licensing or other
contractual arrangements with a local firm. In some cases, the high transaction costs
associated with searching out and dealing with local firms may provide an adequate
explanation. But here too, I am inclined to put heavy weight on explanations that see
the establishment of a subsidiary in part as a hedge against various risks. Whenever licensing agreements are negotiated, both parties face the uncertainties generated by
asymmetrical information; the licensee is uncertain of the value of the information it
is to receive, while the licenser is uncertain of the use to which the licensee proposes
to put the information. Moreover, enforcing the provisions of any licensing agreement
carries both parties into areas of major uncertainty, based partly on the difficulties of
monitoring the agreement and partly on the difficulties of enforcing its provisions.

In any event, the late 1960s registered a high watermark in the spread of the
multinational networks of U.S.-based industrial enterprises, as the number of foreign
affiliates added annually to such networks reached an all-time high. For at least a
decade thereafter, the number of foreign affiliates added annually was much reduced.
Without firm-by-firm data of the kind compiled by the Harvard Multinational Enterprise Project for the period up to 1975, it is hard to know more precisely what was
going on at the firm level during the succeeding years. But the rate of growth of these
networks appeared to pick up again in the late 1980s.

The high rate of growth in recent years, however, appears to be based on somewhat different factors from those that prevailed in earlier decades. Anecdotal evidence indicates that U.S.-based firms continue to use their multinational networks to
transfer newly generated products and processes from the United States to other
countries. But with the U.S. lead greatly diminished in the generation of new products and processes, it is doubtful that the transmission of new products and processes
from U.S. parents to foreign subsidiaries plays as important a role in the business of

U.S.-based enterprises as it did some decades ago. Indeed, by the 1990s, the ostensible purpose of some U.S.-based firms in establishing foreign subsidiaries in Japan was not to diffuse existing skills but to acquire new skills for their multinational network in the hope that their Japanese experience would strengthen their competitive capabilities in markets all over the world. With Japanese and European firms acquiring subsidiaries in the United States at the same time for the same purpose, it was apparent that the distinctive characteristics of U.S.-based multinational networks were beginning to fade.

Another factor that began to change the behavior of U.S.-based enterprises was the increasing familiarity of their managers with the problems of operating in foreign environments. At least until the 1970s, in their decisions when and where to establish subsidiaries in foreign countries, U.S.-based firms had been giving a heavy preference to the familiar. Careful analyses of the geographical sequence by which these firms established manufacturing facilities abroad demonstrated a historically heavy preference for setting up the first foreign production unit in Canada, with the United Kingdom taking second place and Mexico third. By the 1960s, U.S.-based firms were bypassing Canada for Europe and Latin America as the first point of foreign manufacture; by the 1970s, although Europe and Latin America continued to provide the principal first-production sites, Asian sites were beginning to turn up with increasing frequency.

The role played by experience during these early postwar decades could be seen even more directly by trends in the reaction times of U.S.-based firms in setting up foreign production facilities. Where new products were involved, U.S.-based firms characteristically set up their first production sites within the United States. Eventually, however, they set up production sites abroad as well; as these firms gained experience with producing in a given country, the time interval involved in setting up production facilities in the country for new products showed a marked decline. Moreover, as the number of foreign production sites in any product increased, the time interval in setting up another facility in a foreign country also declined. By the 1970s, therefore, U.S.-based firms were beginning to show less hesitation in setting up production subsidiaries abroad for their new products and were scanning a rapidly widening circle of countries for their production sites.

The pattern toward which U.S.-owned multinational networks seem to be moving, ... is one in which the parent firm in the United States is prepared to survey different geographic locations on their respective merits, with a much reduced presumption in favor of a U.S. location. Instead, when assigning tasks to the various units of their multinational networks, U.S. business managers are increasingly likely to discount the distinction between home-based and foreign facilities, except as governmental restraints compel them to recognize that factor. This does not mean that the role played by geography is altogether obliterated. U.S.-based firms, for instance, continue to rely on Latin America more than on Asia to provide their low-cost labor needs, while the reverse is true for Japanese firms. But the sense of uncertainty associated with producing outside the home economy has substantially declined, and the preference for nearby production locations such as those in Latin America over more remote locations such as those in Asia has declined as well.

For enterprises operating in oligopolistic markets, however, a major source of uncertainty remains. Even when such enterprises are fully familiar with the foreign environments in which they are obliged to operate, they are still exposed to the predatory and preemptive tactics of their rivals in the oligopoly. The reasoning that led the international oil and minerals firms to develop vertically integrated structures before World War II, therefore, can be glimpsed in more recent decades in the behavior of U.S.-based firms operating in oligopolistic markets. For instance, U.S.-based oil companies, having been separated from some of their captive crude oil supplies by the nationalizations in the 1970s, remain unwilling to rely upon the open market for the bulk of such supplies despite the existence of a large public market for the product. Facing the latent threat posed by the vertical integration of the Saudi and Venezuelan state-owned oil companies, U.S.-based firms are repairing and strengthening their upstream links.

Such cautionary behavior is not confined to the raw materials industries. Similar behavior is apparent among U.S. firms in the electronics industry: under pressure to reduce the costs of-labor-intensive components, firms such as IBM and Texas Instruments have chosen to manufacture a considerable part of their needs within their own multinational networks rather than to rely upon independent suppliers. A major factor in that decision, according to many observers, has been the fear that predatory rivals might withhold the most advanced versions of those components from competitors while incorporating them in their own products.

For some U.S.-based enterprises, it was only a small step from using their foreign subsidiaries as feeders for manufacturing facilities in the United States to using those facilities to fill requirements arising anywhere in the network; by the 1980s, it had become apparent that this process was well advanced. Of course, in practically every multinational network, the parent unit in the United States typically continued to occupy a unique position: characteristically, the parent's U.S. sales still accounted for the bulk of network sales, its U.S. facilities were responsible for the most important research and development work in the network, and its U.S. offices still coordinated some of the network's functions that might benefit from a centralized approach, such as the finance function. But the direction was clear. Although the centralized functions of the network would presumably remain in the United States indefinitely, the historical and institutional forces that resisted the geographical diffusion of other functions to locations outside the United States were growing weaker.

A more novel trend, however, has been the growing propensity of U.S.-based firms to enter into alliances of one kind or another with multinational networks based in other countries—typically, in other highly industrialized countries. Such alliances, for instance, sometimes take the form of a joint subsidiary established to perform a specified function or of an exchange of licenses in a specified field. At times, the arrangements link suppliers to their customers; at other times, the parties involved in such limited linkages appear to be direct rivals.....Although the definitions are muddy and the data far from complete, such alliances seem to be concentrated in industries in which barriers to entry are high and technological change is rapid and costly.

Part of the motivation for these alliances is apparent: an effort of each of the participating firms to reduce the risks associated with lumpy commitments to new research and development projects and to ensure that they are abreast of their competitors in their research resources. The alliances, therefore, are not much different in function from the jointly owned mines and oil fields that rival refiners and marketers shared in decades gone by, such as ARAMCO in Saudi Arabia, Southern Peru Copper in Peru, and HALCO in Guinea. Moreover, with common interests linking rivals to their suppliers and to one another in these new alliances, the likelihood that any one of the rivals might steal a technological lead on the others is obviously reduced. As with the partners in the raw material subsidiaries, therefore, there may well be a sense among some of the partners in the new alliances that their ties with rivals and suppliers could be used to reduce the harshness of future competition among them.

In one respect, however, many of the new alliances differ from those in the raw material industries. In industries with rapidly changing technologies and swiftly changing markets, the interests of the participants in any given alliance are likely to be relatively unstable; such firms will be constantly withdrawing and regrouping in order to satisfy their rapidly shifting strategic needs. Nevertheless, the possibility remains very real that these arrangements will serve at times to take the edge off the competition in some product markets.

For all the evidence that defensive motivations have been dominating the behavior of U.S.-based enterprises, there are various signs that the animal spirits of some U.S. managers can still be roused. One sign of such spirits is the global spread of U.S.-based firms in various service industries, including fast foods, advertising services, and management consulting. Some of these service-oriented firms developed multinational networks simply by following their multinational clients abroad in an effort to maintain an existing relationship; others, relying on a technological or managerial capability that their foreign rivals had not yet matched, bravely set out to master new environments without any apparent defensive motivation. Such initiatives, it appears, depend on the extent to which enterprises feel protected by some unique firm capability, such as a technological or managerial lead, or a patent or trademark. But whether such situations are common or not in the future, defensive responses can be counted on to compel many large firms in the United States to maintain and extend their multinational networks.

3.2 Emergence of the Europeans

European industry often enjoys a reputation among Americans for sophistication and urbanity that equips them especially for the role of global entrepreneurs. But their performance as a group after World War II presents a very mixed picture.

In the decades just prior to World War II, the principal strategy of the leading European firms was to protect their home markets from competition, not to seek out new foreign markets. When they established subsidiaries in foreign countries, they tended to concentrate on countries to which their home governments had close political ties. And their typical reaction to the threat of international competition in those decades was to develop market-sharing arrangements along national lines.

In the immediate postwar period, European firms continued to cling to their home markets. Absorbed in the rebuilding of their home economies and saddled with the need to catch up technologically, they had little slack to devote to the establishment of new foreign facilities. True, enterprises headquartered in some of the smaller countries that possessed a technological edge, such as the pharmaceutical companies of Switzerland and the Netherlands and the machinery firms of Sweden, often felt compelled to set up subsidiaries outside their home countries in order to exploit their technological lead and to finance their ongoing innovational efforts; and the subsidiaries they set up in foreign countries typically operated with greater autonomy in foreign locations than did subsidiaries of some of their U.S. rivals. Moreover, manufacturing firms headquartered in the larger European countries were not altogether averse to establishing producing subsidiaries in areas over which their home governments still exercised strong political or economic influence. Between 1945 and 1965, for instance, British parents established about four hundred manufacturing subsidiaries in Australia, Canada, and New Zealand.

The disposition of European firms to identify closely with their home governments has some of its roots in history. Until recently, many were family-owned enterprises, with a long history of dominance in some given city or region. Some were so-called national champions, accustomed to especially favorable treatment by their governments in the provision of capital and the purchase of output. The idea of maintaining close ties to their home government when operating abroad therefore represented an easy extension of their relationship at home.

After 1960, the emergence of a common market on the European continent began to affect the strategies of European firms. At first, however, these developments did little to encourage European firms to set up subsidiaries in other countries within the area. For one thing, the promise of a duty-free market among members of the European Community actually served to eliminate one of the motivations for creating such subsidiaries, namely the threat that frontiers might be closed to foreign goods. And with land distances relatively small and national markets relatively limited in size, the economic reasons for establishing such subsidiaries often did not appear compelling.

On the other hand, by the 1960s, U.S.-based companies were beginning to set up their subsidiaries in Europe in large numbers. Data from the Harvard Multinational Enterprise Project show that whereas, in the fifteen years between 1945 and 1959, U.S. parents had established some three hundred manufacturing subsidiaries in Europe, between 1960 and 1975 these parents established nearly two thousand manufacturing subsidiaries in Europe. Typically, the first landing of the U.S. invaders was in the United Kingdom, despite that country's delay in entering the European Community; but the U.S.-based firms were not long in establishing subsidiaries on the continent as well.

One might have expected the appearance of these subsidiaries to stimulate moves to renew the restrictive market-sharing agreements of the prewar period, but the environment following the end of World War II was much less conducive to such agreements. For one thing, rapidly expanding markets and swiftly changing technologies generated an environment that made agreements difficult. In addition, although enforcement of U.S. antitrust laws had grown lax in the postwar period, the European Community itself had adopted and was occasionally enforcing some exemplary measures aimed at preventing enterprises from dividing up the European market.

Eventually, however, most large European firms were led through the same defensive cycle that some U.S.-based firms had already experienced. Having reestablished export markets for their manufactured goods in many areas, including the Middle East and Latin America, they faced the same kind of threat that had moved their U.S. counterparts to set up producing subsidiaries abroad, namely the fear of losing a market through import restrictions. By 1970, manufacturing firms based in Europe were adding affiliates to their multinational networks in numbers over twice as high as those recorded by their U.S. counterparts.

Moved largely by defensive considerations, European firms were adding rapidly to their holdings in the United States. There they showed a strong preference for investing in existing firms rather than in wholly new undertakings, and a strong disposition to team up with a U.S. firm in the process. Such entries, some European managers supposed, would give them exposure to the latest industrial technologies and marketing strategies, thus strengthening their ability to resist the U.S. onslaught in their home markets and in third countries.

By the end of the 1960s, however, the Europeans had begun to have less reason to fear the dominance of U.S.-based firms. The differences in technological achievement between U.S. firms and European firms had obviously shrunk, and access to capital no longer favored the Americans. Not surprisingly, then, some of the motivations that lay behind the expansion of the European networks grew more nearly akin to that of the Americans—that is, largely defensive moves aimed at protecting a foreign market from import restrictions or copycat responses to the initiatives of rivals in setting up a subsidiary abroad. In an apparent response to such stimuli, the number of European-owned subsidiaries appearing in various parts of the world increased rapidly.

These new transborder relations have not wholly obliterated the distinctive national traits that have characterized European firms. German enterprises, for instance, continue to huddle in the shelter of their big banks, French companies in the protective cover of their national ministries. Moreover, despite the existence of the European Community, European firms continue to owe their existence to their respective national enabling statutes, which reflect wide differences in philosophical values and political balance. The United Kingdom, for instance, cannot agree with its continental partners on such fundamental issues as the responsibilities of the corporation to its labor force; whereas the British tend to see corporate managers primarily as the agents of their stockholders, continental governments generally take the view that labor has a quasi-proprietary stake in the enterprise that employs it, which stake managers are obliged to recognize. Differences such as these have served to block projects for the creation of a European company under the European Community's aegis.

Nevertheless, cross-border mergers are growing in number in Europe. In 1987, among the large industrial enterprises based in the community, only 75 cases were recorded in which a firm based in one EC country gained control of a firm based in another, but by 1990 the number had risen to 257. Indeed, in this universe of large industrial firms, the number of such transborder acquisitions in 1990 for the first time exceeded the number of like acquisitions involving firms in a single member country.

In part, the trend toward cross-border mergers is a consequence of the many liberalizing measures that the member countries of the European Community have taken with regard to capital flows. In addition, however, there appears to be a visible weakening of the family conglomerate, a distinctly national form of big business. In Italy, for instance, where that kind of structure has been particularly prominent in the private sector, the country's leading family conglomerates have fallen on especially hard times.

. . . .

In explaining the growth of the networks of firms based in Europe, then, I return to some of the same themes that were stressed in the case of U.S.-based firms. The summary of the factors that have pushed U.S.-based enterprises to develop and expand their multinational networks in the past decades stressed the continuous improvements in the technology of communication and transportation as the powerful exogenous factor; the decisions of the U.S.-based firms to expand their enterprises were seen in large part as a response aimed at reducing the uncertainties and countering the threats that accompanied such developments. I feel sure that these generalizations will carry the observer considerable distance in understanding the behavior of Europe-based firms as well. Over time, the differences that heretofore have distinguished U.S.-based from Europe-based multinational networks are likely to diminish as the conditions of their founding and early growth begin to lose their original importance.

3.3 Latecomer Japan

Studying the factors behind the growth of multinational enterprises based in Japan, a phenomenon of the past two or three decades, will bring us back to the same defensive motivations, including the need of Japanese enterprises to protect their interests against the hostile acts of foreign governments and business competitors, and their desire to build up competitive strengths by exposing themselves to the most challenging technological and marketing environments.

Indeed, the defensive motivations that commonly lie behind the creation and spread of multinational enterprises are likely to act even more powerfully on the Japanese than on their U.S.-based and Europe-based competitors. To see why, it helps to review briefly the evolution of Japan's industrial structure.

From the earliest years of the Meiji restoration in the last decades of the nineteenth century, the industrial structure of Japan exhibited some distinctive national characteristics. Dominating the core of Japan's modern economy were half a dozen conglomerate organizations, each with its own captive bank, trading company, and portfolio of manufacturing and service enterprises. The conglomerate structure, well developed before World War II, was modified only a little by Japan's loss of its foreign territories and by the ensuing occupation. Japanese firms lost their investments in the territories its armies had occupied, but these investments had largely been controlled by the so-called new zaibatsu, companies that depended for their existence on Japan's foreign conquests and that had very little stake in the home economy itself.

In Japan proper, the holding companies that sat at the apex of each conglomerate were liquidated during the occupation. But the member firms of the conglomerates maintained their old ties by cross-holdings of stock and by shared memories of past loyalties. And in the 1960s and 1970s, as foreign enterprises began to show some interest in acquiring control over Japanese firms, member firms within each conglomerate systematically built up their cross-holdings even further as a means of repelling foreign boarders.

From the early emergence of these conglomerate organizations, a fierce rivalry existed among them—but a rivalry based much more on comparative rates of growth and market shares than on nominal profits. Within each conglomerate, the financing of the contest was left to the conglomerate's captive bank rather than to public capital markets. But the general scope and direction of the lending by these banks to their affiliates were largely determined by continuous consultation with key government agencies, especially the Ministry of Finance, the Bank of Japan, and the Ministry for International Trade and Industry.

By the 1980s, however, it was becoming apparent that major changes were taking place in the conglomerate structures. Perhaps the most obvious change was the dramatic shift in the financing practices of the industrial firms. As the rate of growth of the Japanese economy slowed up a little in the 1980s and as the need to finance capacity expansion grew less urgent, Japanese firms found that internally generated cash was going a much longer way toward meeting their capital needs.

At the same time, under pressure from foreign sources and from Japan's own financial intermediaries, the Ministry of Finance was gradually relaxing its tight controls over the development of internal capital markets, thereby providing Japanese companies for the first time with a real option for raising their capital needs through the sale of securities in public markets. Concurrently, Japanese firms were being granted permission to raise capital in foreign currencies by selling their securities abroad or borrowing from foreign banks. Japanese banks, trading houses, and other service facilities, therefore, were strongly represented in the outflow of direct investment from Japan to major foreign markets." And because Japanese manufacturing firms were always a little uncomfortable when dealing with foreigners as service suppliers, the existence of those service facilities in foreign markets eased the way for the manufacturers to establish their foreign subsidiaries outside of Japan.

In accounting for the changes in the character of the multinational networks based in Japan, however, one must place particularly heavy emphasis on the increasing technological capabilities of these enterprises. In the very first stages of the development of multinational networks by Japan-based firms, in the 1960s and 1970s, some scholars entertained the hypothesis that these firms would develop a pattern of foreign direct investment quite different from that pioneered by U.S.-based and Europe-based firms. At that stage, Japan's penetration of foreign markets for manufactured goods was most in evidence in South and Southeast Asia and was heavily concentrated in relatively simple items such as batteries, noodles, radios, and other consumer goods—items in which Japan's comparative advantage was already fading. Given the unsophisticated nature of the products and the lack of a need for after-sales services, Japanese producers usually used their affiliated trading companies as their agents in these foreign markets; indeed, in many cases, the Japanese producers were not large enough even to consider marketing their own products abroad and so had no choice but to rely on trading companies.

In these cases, when the risk that the government might impose restrictions became palpable, the trading company typically took the lead in establishing a local production facility, often through a three-way partnership that combined the trading company with a local distributor and with the erstwhile Japanese exporter. From this early pattern, it appeared that the Japan-based multinational enterprise might root itself much more deeply in its foreign markets than did the U.S.-based and Europe-based companies, with results that might prove more benign from the viewpoint of the host country.

By the 1980s, however, the patterns of foreign direct investment by Japanese firms were converging toward the norms recorded by their U.S. and European rivals. As with U.S.- and Europe-based firms, the object of Japanese firms in establishing a producing subsidiary in a foreign country was commonly to protect a market in a relatively differentiated product that originally had been developed through exports from Japan.

Compared with U.S.-based or Europe-based firms, however, the stake of Japanese firms in the export markets of other industrialized countries soon grew very large. The spectacular growth of Japanese exports to the markets of such countries exposed Japanese firms once more to threats of restrictive action on a major scale. At this advanced stage, however, the markets to be protected were considerably different in character from those that the first generation of Japan-based multinationals had developed. One difference was in the identity of the markets under siege, now located mainly in the United States and Europe. Another was the nature of the products involved; these were relatively sophisticated products, such as automobiles, camcorders, and computer-controlled machine tools. And a third was the channels of distribution involved; such sophisticated products were usually marketed through channels under the direct control of the manufacturers rather than through trading companies.

The networks that Japan-based firms created in response to the new threats came closer to emulating those of the U.S.-based and Europe-based firms with multinational networks. Moreover, as with their European rivals, many of the foreign acquisitions by Japan-based firms were explained by a desire to acquire advanced technological skills; this motive was especially apparent in the acquisition of various medium-sized high-tech firms in the United States.

Although the multinational networks that Japan-based firms produced in this second generation bore a much greater resemblance to the networks of their counterparts from other advanced industrialized countries, some characteristic differences remained. One such characteristic was the high propensity of Japan-based multinationals to control their producing subsidiaries tightly from Japan. Symptomatic of that fact was the near-universal use of Japanese personnel to head their foreign subsidiaries. A striking illustration of the same desire for control was the limited leeway allowed subsidiaries in the acquisition of capital equipment. Australian subsidiaries of Japanese firms, for instance, possessed far less leeway in the selection of new machinery than did the subsidiaries of U.S.-based or Europe-based firms. Some signs existed in the 1990s that a few Japanese firms were breaking away from their traditional controls and giving their foreign subsidiaries greater leeway, but the illustrations were still exceptional.

The early reluctance of Japan-based firms to develop a multinational network and the tendency of the foreign subsidiaries of such firms to rely upon their established sources in Japan have been attributed to a number of different factors. They have been variously explained as a consequence of the relative inexperience of Japanese firms with the novel problems of producing abroad, as a result of the heavy reliance on the consensual process in decision making, or as a consequence of the extensive use of just-in-time producing processes, which demand the closest coordination between the firms and their suppliers. Introducing strangers into the system, according to the argument, entails major modifications in firm practices that cannot be achieved overnight.

Nevertheless, by the end of the 1980s, Japan-based firms were expanding their multinational networks at an unprecedented rate. What is more, their manufacturing affiliates in the United States and Europe were drawing a considerable fraction of their inputs from sources located in the host country. Moreover, it appeared that some of the very factors that had slowed the growth of Japan-based multinational networks in the past could be expected to reinforce the expansion rather than to slow it down. For example, the desire of Japanese firms to rely on Japanese sources means that the foreign subsidiaries of major Japanese firms are pulling large numbers of satellite suppliers with them into foreign locations. While this has not been an unknown phenomenon in the establishment of the multinational networks of firms based in the United States, it appears to be an especially powerful force in the case of Japan-based firms. Moreover, if one pair of authoritative observers is to be believed, Japanese firms already are being drawn into Europe by the conviction that they must assimilate some distinctive regional emphases if they are to be successful in major industries, such as automobiles and electronic equipment. Finally, given the intense rivalry of Japanese firms, with their stress on market share, it is not unreasonable to expect a pattern of copycat behavior even stronger than that observed with respect to firms based in other countries.....

3.4 Patterns of the Future

....

I anticipate that multinational networks and transborder alliances, already a major factor in international economic flows, will grow in importance.

3.4.1 The Response of Governments

How governments will respond to that situation is a little uncertain. Although globalization and convergence may prove to be major trends defining the behavior of multinational enterprises in the future, it is implausible to assume that national governments will stand aside and allow such behavior to develop as it may. With jobs, taxes, payment balances, and technological achievement seemingly at stake, governments are bound to act in an effort to defend national interests and respond to national pressures. Their efforts, involving carrots in some cases and sticks in others, will continue to pose threats and offer opportunities to the multinationals.

Some governmental responses will take the form of restrictions, unilaterally, adopted, aimed at holding inbound and outbound foreign investment in check. But from all the signs, political leaders in the major industrialized countries seem aware that national autarky is not an available option unless a country is prepared to absorb some overwhelming costs. That recognition explains so many countries now eye the possibility of developing regional blocs—areas large enough to satisfy the modern requirements of scale and scope, and small enough to promise member countries that they will exert some influence in shaping their joint economic policies.

    ....

In any case, when seen through the eyes of the managers of multinational enterprises based in the industrialized areas, the managers' principal stake by far lies in other industrialized areas, not in the hinterlands of their respective "regions." That has been the case for decades, and it has shown no signs of changing in recent years. To be sure, such enterprises will not hesitate to use the influence of their respective governments to promote their interests in these regions. But from the viewpoint of the firms, such efforts will be a sideshow compared to their respective stakes in other industrialized economies.

At the same time, the influence that individual governments are in a positions to exert over their respective multinational enterprises appears rapidly on the decline. Although governments have been known to remain blind to the obvious for remarkably prolonged periods of time, that ineluctable fact should eventually lead them to limit their unilateral efforts at control. Where control of some sort still seems necessary or desirable, the option remaining will be to pursue mutually agreed-upon measures with other countries. In the decades ahead, the United States, Europe, and Japan are sure to find themselves addressing the feasibility and desirability of international agreements that define more fully the rights and obligations of multinational enterprises. Although most other countries may be slower to address the issue, a few such as Singapore and Mexico along with the non-European members of the Organization for Economic Cooperation and Development (OECD) are likely to be involved as well. Already some of the elements of an international system are in place with respect to a few functional fields, such as the levying of corporate income taxes. It does not stretch the imagination very much to picture international agreements on such subjects as the competition of governments for foreign direct investment, the threats to market competition posed by restrictive business practices and mergers, the rights and obligations of multinational enterprises in national political processes, and other issues relating to the multi-national enterprise.

3.4.2 The Development of Theory

In the past, as multinational networks appeared and grew, some researchers concerned with understanding the causes of their behavior found it useful, even indispensable, to distinguish such enterprises according to their national base. If I am right in seeing strong tendencies toward national convergence, distinctions based on the national origin of the network are likely to lose their analytic and descriptive value, and distinctions on other dimensions are likely to grow in importance. Even more than in the past, distinctions based on the characteristics of the product market and the production process are likely to prove particularly fruitful.

As I observed earlier, many multinational enterprises created global networks in response to perceived threats and operated under circumstances in which ignorance and uncertainty were endemic. For the most part, the enterprises operated in product markets with significant barriers to entry, including static and dynamic scale economies, patents, and trademarks. With the passage of time, however, a considerable proportion of these multinational enterprises overcame their sense of acute uncertainty in foreign markets, especially as the products and their related technologies grew more stable and standardized.

These tendencies often reduced barriers to entry, increased the number of participants, and elevated the role of price competition. In the production and sale of metals and petroleum, for instance, the number of sellers on world markets inexorably increased, and the role of competitive pricing grew. In big-ticket consumer electronics, an intensification of competitive pricing among multinational enterprises also has become commonplace, despite the persistent efforts of sellers to differentiate their products. In such cases, there is considerable utility in models that cast the participants as fully informed actors operating in a market in which their choices are known, under conditions in which some scale economies exist. I see no reason why models based on these assumptions should not generate useful first approximations to the behavior of multinational enterprises in a considerable number of industries.

Other models may also have something to contribute, such as those that view multinational networks as the consequence of decisions by firms to internalize certain types of transactions. The international market for the sale of technology and management skills, for instance, is a grossly inefficient market from the viewpoint of both buyer and seller. Internalization can be viewed as a response to those inefficiencies, in a setting in which the enterprises are otherwise fully aware of the set of choices they confront and of the facts bearing on those choices.

Models based on the internalization hypothesis therefore fit comfortably into the structure of the models described earlier, which are based essentially on a neoclassical framework driven by costs and prices. But they have tended to crowd out the analysis of other motivations that seem at least as important in explaining the behavior of the managers of such enterprises. For instance, various measures taken by the firm to create a multinational network may be driven by another motive, namely a desire to avoid being exposed to the predatory behavior of rivals, including the risk that such rivals might cut off needed supplies or deny access to a distribution system during some future contingency.

That possibility pushes the modeler in a very different direction in attempting to explain the behavior of multinational enterprises. Such enterprises continue to figure prominently in many product markets that have not yet attained a stable middle age. In such markets, the number of producers is often sharply limited, products and related services are often highly differentiated, technologies are in flux, and price differences are not the critical factor in competition. Moreover, externalities of various kinds commonly play a dominant role in locational decisions, as when enterprises try to draw on various national environments to produce the stimuli they think will improve their competitive strengths. Firms engaged in producing microprocessors, aircraft engines, and wonder drugs, for instance, are strongly influenced by one or another of these factors.

Needless to say, where the number of rivals in a market is low, that fact fundamentally conditions the strategies of the participants. Some of them may long for the security of a market-sharing arrangement and may even take some tentative steps in that direction, such as entering into partnerships with some of their rivals. But developing an effective market-sharing arrangement is usually difficult and dangerous.

In any event, when a limited number of participants are involved in a product market, theorists must entertain the possibility that the firms that are engaged in such markets see any given transaction as only one move in a campaign stretching across time. In each transaction, the principal objective of the firm is to strengthen its position in relation to its rivals or to neutralize the efforts of its rivals to steal a march; with that objective paramount, share of market becomes a critical measure of success. In such circumstances, invading a rival's principal market may prove a useful defensive strategy, aimed at reducing the rival's propensity for warfare elsewhere. And, given the imperfect knowledge under which each firm is assumed to operate, a policy of following a rival into new areas of supply and new markets may be seen as a prudent response to the rival's initiatives.

Of course, by shedding many of the assumptions underlying the neoclassical model, models built on such behavioral assumptions relinquish the support provided by a comprehensive body of well-explored theory. Instead, the analyst is thrown into a world of uncertain outcomes, explored so far largely by game theorists, specialists in signaling theory, and others outside the neoclassical mainstream. It is hardly surprising, therefore, that most of the scholars who have sought to model the behavior of the multinational enterprise have avoided the implications of high uncertainty and limited numbers, preferring instead to concentrate on hypotheses that require less radical departures from neoclassical assumptions.

Nevertheless, any serious effort to project the behavior of multinational enterprises in the future will have to recognize that the players in many major product and service markets will see themselves as engaged in a campaign against specific adversaries in a global market, with individual decisions being shaped in light of that perception. At different times and places, there will be efforts to call a truce, efforts to weaken specific adversaries, and efforts to counter the aggressive behavior of others. The behavior that emerges will not be easily explained in terms of models that satisfy neoclassical conditions. Therein lies a major challenge for those who are attempting to cast light on the behavior of multinational enterprises through systematic modeling.

C. The Link Between FDI and International Trade

Obie G. Whichard and Jeffrey H. Lowe, An Ownership Based Disaggregation of the U.S. Current Account
1982-93, 75 Survey of Current Business 52, 53 (October 1995)

With the growing integration of the world economy, foreign direct investment has flourished, and the multinational company (MNC) has become a major force in the delivery of goods and services to overseas markets. Interest in analyzing foreign trade from the perspective of MNC's has grown accordingly. In response, BEA [the Bureau of Economic Analysis of the United States Department of Commerce] has prepared a supplemental disaggregation of the U.S. current account along ownership lines by combining information from its direct investment surveys with information from the standard current account. The new disaggregation builds on a proposal introduced in an earlier BEA study of alternative balance-of-payments frameworks. It presents information on the sales by MNC's through their affiliates as well as through crossborder trade. By viewing the activities of MNC's and their affiliates in the context of a formal economic accounting framework, these activities can be analyzed in a more consistent fashion than previously was possible.

This new disaggregation, presented for 1982-93, breaks down cross-border trade according to whether it is between affiliated parties—that is, within MNC's—or between unaffiliated parties. Trade within MNC's ("intrafirm trade") is further disaggregated according to whether it is between U.S. parent companies and their foreign affiliates or between U.S. affiliates of foreign companies and their foreign parent groups. In addition, details on receipts and payments of direct investment income are provided to show how the income is derived from the production and sales of affiliates.

The disaggregation of the current account presented here provides information not available in the standard disaggregation. The standard disaggregation breaks down cross-border trade in goods and services on the basis of the commodity classifications of the goods and services traded and the geographic location of the parties involved, but it generally does not indicate relationships between the exporters and importers. Nor does it show how production and sales by foreign affiliates give rise to income on direct investments.

. . . .

The following are among the patterns that emerge when the current account is viewed along ownership lines. Many of these patterns confirm or reinforce the conclusions of earlier BEA analyses of affiliate operations.

- Transactions within MNC's accounted for a significant share—about one-third—of both U.S. exports and U.S. imports of goods and services throughout 1982-93. Intrafirm trade accounted for a growing share of U.S. imports of goods and services—37 percent in 1993, compared with 32 percent in 1982—reflecting the rapid rise in foreign direct investment in the United States during the late 1980's. However, much of this trade simply represented goods imported by U.S. wholesale trade affiliates established by foreign companies to facilitate the distribution of their goods, largely to unaffiliated customers, in the United States. The share of intrafirm trade in U.S. exports fluctuated somewhat, but it ended the 1982-93 period at the same level—30 percent—as it began.

- Trade in goods—rather than in services—accounted for the predominant share of both unaffiliated trade and intrafirm trade, but the share was higher for intrafirm trade. For exports, goods tended to account for about 85 percent of intrafirm trade, compared with about 70 percent of unaffiliated trade. For imports, the difference was even more marked, with goods tending to account for about 95 percent of intrafirm trade, compared with about 75 percent of unaffiliated trade. The higher share of goods in intrafirm trade partly reflects the absence of some types of services—such as travel and other services sold to individuals—from trade within firms.

- Both intrafirm exports and intrafirm imports of goods and services were largely accounted for by transactions in which affiliates were used as distribution channels for their parents' output (sometimes with further processing), rather than as sources of supply. Exports by U.S. parent companies to their foreign affiliates accounted for roughly two-thirds to three-quarters of total intrafirm exports, while imports by U.S. affiliates from their foreign parents accounted for 55-64 percent of total intrafirm imports.

- Direct investment income—that is, net returns to direct investors resulting from sales by their affiliates—was a small component of both total exports and total imports of goods, services, and income: 7-9 percent of exports and less than 2 percent of imports. The particularly low import share largely reflects the low returns foreigners have realized on their direct investments in the United States.

- All account balances—that on the overall current account and those on various groupings of its components—were more negative at the end of 1982-93 than at the beginning. However, the balance on goods, services, and net receipts resulting from sales by affiliates was more favorable than the others in every year since 1985. This balance, which shows the net result of all active participation of companies in international markets (that is, through both cross-border trade and sales by affiliates), went from a $2.2 billion deficit in 1982 to an $18.5 billion deficit in 1993. By comparison, the deficit on cross-border trade alone increased from $24.2 billion to $74.8 billion during the same period. The difference between the two balances is attributable to the sizable surplus throughout the period on net receipts and payments resulting from sales by affiliates.

- Notwithstanding the importance of affiliates as distribution channels for their parents' output, most of the content of affiliates' sales is of local (or, for foreign affiliates, non-U.S.) origin: 88-92 percent of the content of the output of foreign affiliates originated abroad, and 80-84 percent of the output of U.S. affiliates originated in the United States. Most of the local content represented payments for locally procured inputs.

....

II. Negotiating FDI Deals

William F. Fox, Jr., International Commercial Agreements
154, 159-64, 177-82 (2nd ed. 1992)

ESTABLISHING A BASIC FRAMEWORK FOR NEGOTIATION: A SHORT EXCURSUS IN NEGOTIATION THEORY

....

Notwithstanding the lack of a unifying theory, virtually all of the literature [on negotiation] recognizes essentially three points: (1) negotiation is a function of leverage (leverage is the allocation of power or control between the two sides), (2) negotiation can often turn as much on the personalities and behavior of the negotiators as on the relative merits of the parties' positions; and (3) in a commercial setting, as well as many other settings, legal principles frequently shape the outcome, irrespective of the desires of the individual parties. Consider these propositions in a little more depth. First, all bargaining is a function of leverage. People come together to bargain because they want something (in either the affirmative or negative sense of the term). Merchants want to buy and sell telescopes, not for the mere doing of the transaction, but to make either short-run or long term profits. Divorcing spouses frequently want not only a monetary benefit from the dissolution of the marriage, but also possibly some kind of psychological vindication, or even some type of retribution. Leverage is simply the ingredient that forces people to bargain. Anyone who is completely lacking in leverage is totally at the mercy of the other side. Such parties have no reason to negotiate.

Leverage is almost always present in commercial dealings because commercial relationships are normally characterized by (1) parties who wish to do business together; (2) a range of possible outcomes that will be generally satisfactory to both parties...and (3) a fairly dispassionate approach to the deal making itself. While high emotion occasionally intrudes into commercial decision making and while vindication and retribution are not totally foreign to the behavior of business people, these ingredients are not commonplace. Leverage in business dealings is derived mainly from information and knowledge, whether openly held or secretly acquired, on the type and quality of the goods or services offered for sale, on the status of foreign markets, the trends in national currencies, anticipated consumer interests and behavior, and the like.

To establish a non-quantitative analytical framework for negotiation, many dispute resolution professionals now use Roger Fisher's and William Ury's *Getting to Yes* as a starting point. *Getting to Yes* is probably the single most popular book ever written on negotiation and has attracted both praise and criticism from an entire spectrum of readers.....Fisher and Ury believe that there is virtually no conflict that cannot be negotiated if parties engage in what they refer to as *principled negotiation*. Principled negotiation begins when both parties appreciate and began to accommodate the fact that each has both conflicting and compatible interests. By building on the identification of compatible interests it becomes far easier for the parties to reach some kind of reconciliation on the conflicting issues. Indeed, even when interests directly collide and seem totally irreconcilable, there may be—at the very least—a shared interest in preserving the negotiation as a dispute resolution device rather than resorting to more costly and cumbersome forms of conflict resolution.

From these basic premises, *Getting to Yes* moves to a series of what look suspiciously like anecdotal rules of thumb for negotiators but which are, arguably, general principles applicable to virtually any negotiation. Since these guidelines have a great deal of applicability to the relatively harmonious, non-belligerent discussions of people in business, they bear close analysis by persons interested in succeeding in international commercial negotiations. The guidelines are:

a.   Separate the people from the problem

b.   Focus on interests, not positions

c.   Invent options for mutual gain

d.   Insist on objective criteria

e.   Know your "best alternative to a negotiated agreement" (BATNA)

SEPARATING THE PEOPLE FROM THE PROBLEM.

When initially set out, these guidelines sound intriguing, but they are not easily understood without putting them into a more practical setting. Assume that two people in business, a seller in the United States and a buyer in Japan, wish to negotiate a contract for the sale of telecommunications equipment. While thinking through the negotiation beforehand, a negotiator (or the parties themselves as is often the case) may wish to begin by understanding that there is a great difference between the problem (executing an equipment contract) and the people who are going to be negotiating that contract (the lawyers, for example) or the people (buyer and seller themselves) who are standing behind that contract. A negotiator can over generalize by simply deciding that profit is the single motivating force in the transaction and may try to hammer through a deal on that basis. However, a more careful, more sophisticated negotiator will recognize that business executives, like all other human beings, are an amalgam of personal needs and professional goals.

For example, a U.S. negotiator may be put off by the personal desire of the Japanese to begin the project with some social amenities or by the inclination of Japanese to bow rather than shake hands. The U.S. party may, conceivably, harbor some residual dislike of Japanese for that country's role in World War Two. But those things are not the *problem*; they are the *people*. The problem is mainly to consummate a purchase and sale agreement within the instructions given the negotiator by the client, not to refight World War Two or muse over the relative wisdom of shaking hands or bowing as a greeting.

....

FOCUS ON INTERESTS, NOT POSITIONS.

This is another concept that frequently gets lost in the negotiation process. Inexperienced negotiators may hear a statement from the other side to the effect that "I will not agree to a letter of credit" and automatically turn on the heat, deciding that this is obviously a time to get tough. The positions then become hardened and a shouting match ensues that frequently leads to a total breakdown in the negotiation. There is another way to view such a statement, however.

In an international commercial setting, a buyer may enter a negotiation with the announced *position* that he will simply not execute a letter of credit. It could be that he was hurt in an earlier unrelated transaction in which a seller shipped non-conforming goods—a defect that may have taken years to resolve—yet the seller received instant payment in full under the letter of credit. Even if the seller ultimately has to reimburse the buyer for the non-conforming goods, it frequently happens in international transactions that the reimbursement is made with inflated funds, so the buyer is never made fully whole. A seller may take the position that she absolutely demands a letter of credit because she shipped goods to another buyer and was years collecting on the invoice. However the buyer may hear the demand for a letter of credit as an accusation that his credit is no good.

Note that the *position* of the buyer is flatly: "No letter of credit." Yet his *interest* is much different: he really wants protection against the risk of having to receive and contend with non-conforming goods while the seller walks away with all the money due under the contract. Simply recognizing this difference may make all the difference between a successful and unsuccessful negotiation because recognition will permit the parties to work with the third Fisher/Ury guideline.

CREATE OPTIONS FOR MUTUAL GAIN.

This factor is nearly self-explanatory. But as Fisher and Ury explain, it is not so easily factored into an on-going negotiation. They recognize that there is more than a little tension and pressure associated with even the smoothest and friendliest negotiations: "Trying to decide in the presence of an adversary narrows your vision. Having a lot at stake inhibits creativity. So does searching for the one right solution." This is, nonetheless, a factor that marks a good negotiation. Take the letter of credit imbroglio. Buyer and seller could simply butt heads forever on this and eventually walk away from what could be a very lucrative deal simply because of mutual stubbornness. A wise negotiator will take a step back and ask: "Is there any reasonable alternative to the letter of credit?" It could be that some other payment device would sufficiently protect the seller's interest. Not every international commercial agreement is accompanied by a letter of credit. If seller suspects the buyer's creditworthiness, some kind of credit check such as a Dun & Bradstreet report might provide the assurances she needs to let the deal go forward on an open account basis. She might be willing to accept a partial payment on the goods before shipment in lieu of a letter of credit. Granting that none of these forms of payment provide the absolute security of a letter of credit, the seller might be persuaded to accept a less-secure form of payment in order to consummate the transaction. On the buyer's part, his *interest* in obtaining conforming goods (the underlying reason for his reluctance to execute the letter of credit) may be satisfied by having some right to inspect the goods prior to payment; for example, the letter of credit might be made payable only after he has had an opportunity to inspect. In the alternative, the buyer could appoint a third party inspector who inspects the goods at the seller's factory immediately prior to shipment, releasing for shipment only those goods which are truly conforming. In commercial transactions, there are usually a myriad of options available for any situation. Creativity, rather than intransigence, ought to be the hallmark of commercial negotiators.

INSIST ON OBJECTIVE CRITERIA.

This factor ties in with the previous factor. It recommends that crucial evaluations be measured by devices that are outside the control of either party. The public international law prototype is the use of United Nations military peacekeeping forces composed of personnel from wholly uninvolved nations to monitor and keep separate belligerent forces. Consider again the problem with the letter of credit. Assume that the seller will agree to on-site inspection of goods prior to shipment. Seller may say something such as: "We'll inspect the goods before we crate them up and make sure they're okay." Buyer may like the idea of inspection before shipment as one part of a quality control protocol, but will likely object to the seller's employees performing that crucial inspection. At the same time, buyer may not have the financial wherewithal to station an employee at the seller's factory; and even if she could afford it, seller may worry that an employee of the buyer's would object to the tiniest discrepancy, however insignificant. One way to incorporate objective criteria into this agreement is to have that final pre-shipment inspection performed by a third party who is trusted by both seller and buyer. The presence and reputation of this third person will frequently provide all the objectivity required by the contracting parties.

KNOW YOUR "BEST ALTERNATIVE TO A NEGOTIATED AGREEMENT (BATNA)"

This guideline urges negotiators to understand what may take place if the negotiations prove unsuccessful. For lawyers negotiating settlement agreements in ongoing litigation, the alternative is usually a return to litigation. Thus, the parties give over their dispute to a judge or jury for resolution. A parallel alternative in international commercial dispute resolution is to hand the matter over to an arbitrator. As a result, parties engaged in renegotiation or mediation following some breach of contract should always consider how an arbitrator might dispose of the issues as part of their evaluation of BATNA. However, in pre-contractual international negotiation BATNA has only limited applicability. A breakdown in negotiations in a commercial setting means simply that the parties do no business with each other. As a result, pre-contractual BATNA means either that a party does no deal or that a party does the deal with someone else. An Indonesian entrepreneur whose negotiation to purchase and operate a McDonald's hamburger franchise in Jakarta falls through may have to consider a deal with Burger King or may look for some other business opportunity.

In initial contract negotiations a BATNA is sometimes useful as leverage ("If you don't sign, I'll take my business to IBM") but is rarely as important a factor as it is in negotiations prior to litigation.

To some readers, the Fisher/Ury guidelines may seem not much more than simplistic rules of thumb that may or may not work in any particular setting. They are really much more than that. For example, they can serve as an analytical framework that may be applied either before the fact or after the fact to virtually any negotiation. This permits observers and participants to evaluate a number of different negotiations from the same perspective. To that extent, the criteria constitute an attempt to develop a unified theory of negotiation. They represent a quantum leap beyond the merely anecdotal approach to negotiation.....

....

THE ETHICS OF NEGOTIATION

Ethics Generally

There are three ethical dimensions in negotiation. [These dimensions are ethics generally, professional responsibility rules, and relevant statutes.] The first is simply the normal duty one human being owes to another human being. In this context, the term *ethics* is used in its dictionary sense of morality: as the Oxford English Dictionary puts it—a set of principles that "direct men's actions to the production of the greatest possible quantity of happiness." All negotiators are subject to certain constraints on their behavior as human beings wholly apart from the subject matter of the negotiation. While cultures differ greatly in their approach to and definition of morality, some minimal ethical conditions apply to virtually all negotiations. Consider, for example, the issue of lying in negotiation. While defining "lie" is never easy, most people will probably concede that telling an outright misrepresentation on which the other side is expected to rely is a lie....[A] seller-negotiator who describes his fittings as being able to bear a stress of 100 pounds per square inch when he knows for a fact that they will bear only 50 pounds is clearly lying. The lie is compounded if the negotiator knows for certain that stress-bearing capacity is an important factor in the buyer's purchasing decision and further knows that the buyer is not likely to have instrumentation capable of measuring stress-bearing capacity. Virtually no culture or legal system excuses this kind of affirmative misrepresentation.

The harder question is whether simply remaining silent in negotiation is also a lie. For example, if the buyer acts as if he believes that the fittings can bear a stress of 100 foot pounds and the seller says nothing to disabuse him of that notion, is the seller's inaction a lie? Would the definition turn on the specific context of the non-disclosure; as, for example, when the seller knows that the buyer's processes will never expose the fitting to a stress greater than 10 pounds. Would non-disclosure constitute a lie if the seller knows that the fittings are to be a part of, say, an aircraft wing exposed to varying stresses?

Ethicists may debate these questions at length. A number of legal systems have attempted to deal with such issues. The Anglo-American legal system centuries ago established the doctrine of *caveat emptor* (let the *buyer* beware). This doctrine places virtually all risks on the buyer and imposes virtually no duties of disclosure on the seller. But it is an exceptionally harsh doctrine, particularly when it is imposed in a setting where most of the knowledge and information is in the hands of the seller. In the United States, the harsher aspects of *caveat emptor*—particularly in consumer transactions—have been modified by legislation. Most countries now have legal principles that place some burden of disclosure on the party who is in the best position to know of defects or limitations in a product.

At the same time, there is a thin line between the sort of misrepresentation or non-disclosure discussed above and the more innocuous statements that takes place in most negotiations. Is it ethically impermissible for the seller to tell buyer: "our fittings are the best in the world"? Probably not. This type of behavior, commonly referred to as *puffing*, is age-old business conduct and has almost never led to either official or unofficial sanctions. Most people, whether they are consumers or business executives automatically discount such comments as soon as they are offered.

A purely philosophical discussion of these issues may make many business executives uncomfortable. In the United States it is a commonplace that morality bears very little relation to business practices. For readers who find the philosophical dimension unproductive, it is entirely possible to address these questions from a pragmatic standpoint. Setting philosophy aside, a negotiator should simply ask the question: "what may happen if the other side finds out I'm lying?" This analysis forces a negotiator to consider the risks of lying (whether affirmative misrepresentation or non-disclosure) in a practical context. There could be legal ramifications involved in a negotiator's misleading the other side on the stress-bearing capacity of fittings used in an airplane wing. If the aircraft crashes, a product liability lawsuit may implicate the seller as well as the buyer. But even in a non-life-threatening context, truth-telling has a lot of advantages. For example, assume a negotiator who comes into the room with instructions from her client to do two things: make the best deal possible on the transaction at hand *and* do everything you can to build toward a long-term business relationship. A negotiator armed with these instructions would normally not only not commit an affirmative misrepresentation, but would probably go out of her way to make full disclosure even where she might not be faced with a specific request for information. Buyers who are lied to are unlikely to want to continue the business enterprise. Can there be any doubt, for example, that a stainless steel fitting negotiator armed with these instructions would have an obligation to disclose stress capacity even if the buyer forgot to ask the question? When the risk of lying is the possible destruction of the long-term business relationship, the negotiator has very little alternative but to tell the truth.

There are other issues that a good negotiator should consider. In the examples discussed above, the misrepresentation or non-disclosure involved the capability of the good to be sold—what the lawyers would call the heart of the bargain. Now assume a situation in which a fitting negotiator needs some time to think during the actual negotiation and obtains this thinking time by implying that he cannot set the price when in fact his price-setting authority runs from $0 to $45 per unit (i.e., encompasses virtually the entire range of possible price outcomes). Is it a lie for the negotiator to leave the room pretending to make a telephone call to the client when he already has all possible authority to agree? While there may be a misrepresentation here, the misrepresentation does not relate to the quality of the goods. A price for the fittings is eventually going to be established if the parties are to have a contract at all. The actions of the negotiator here are more in the nature of a delaying ploy, rather than a lie that goes to the heart of the bargain. Second, the risk of some adverse reaction by the other side if the buyer finds out that the negotiator did have price-setting authority is likely to be minimal. Many negotiators use such techniques, and it is virtually certain that the other negotiator is engaged in similar activities. The end product of lying on one's price setting authority may make the other side a little more skeptical in later negotiations but is not likely to drive them away from the bargaining table. It is doubtful that such a ploy would damage long-term relationships or in any way affect the health or safety of the ultimate users of the product.

The issue might be resolved differently, however, if the negotiator gets a direct question from the other side: "Do you have independent authority to set the price of this contract?" A negative response to such a direct question would be, by definition, an affirmative misrepresentation and might lead to future hostility between the parties. In this instance, a negotiator might permissibly choose either not to answer the question or to give an evasive response if she believes that concealing her price-setting authority is important to the negotiation. It is highly unlikely that concealment in this setting will poison the business relationship.

Many commentators on negotiation go even further. If negotiation is viewed as a game, then it is axiomatic that good gamesmanship will pay results. It is something of a conundrum, at least as seen by Professor James White, who has written:

> On the one hand the negotiator must be fair and truthful; on the other he must mislead his opponent. Like the poker player, a negotiator hopes that his opponent will overestimate the value of his hand. Like the poker player, in a variety of ways he must facilitate his opponent's inaccurate assessment. The critical difference between those who are successful negotiators, and those who are not, lies in this capacity both to mislead and not to be misled.

Readers should not be misled. Professor White is mainly concerned with win/lose bargaining where winner takes all, while most business negotiation is a matter of win/win bargaining, permitting both sides to gain advantages from the deal.

There are no easy answers here. Cynical readers...can point to large numbers of ethical abuses on the part of negotiators who seem to be highly successful. But at least in win/win negotiation, ethical issues can best be handled by application of the famous golden rule: "Do unto others as you would have them do unto you."

Ethical Constraints on U.S. Lawyer-Negotiators

Lawyers in the United States and in many other countries are subject not only to general constraints on their behavior but also to express principles governing their professional behavior. Violations of the lawyers' code of ethics can lead to disciplinary action against the lawyer irrespective of whatever effect the ethical abuses have on the client. One U.S. code of ethics, the *Model Code of Professional Responsibility*, addresses dishonesty (including the matter of lying to others) mainly in generalities. The Code admonishes a lawyer to "represent his client zealously within the bounds of the law." In so doing, however, a lawyer is not to "engage in conduct involving dishonesty, fraud, deceit, or misrepresentation." The Code contains some other restrictions on lying, but those restrictions essentially prohibit lying to a court—as contrasted to lying to another lawyer or to a third person. A new statement of ethical behavior, the *Model Rules of Professional Conduct*, has been adopted by a majority of the states in the U.S. and, for the first time, contains some specific admonitions on lying in a negotiation context. Rule 4.1 requires that a lawyer "shall not knowingly: (a) make a false statement of material fact or law to a third person; or (b) fail to disclose a material fact to a third person when disclosure is necessary to avoid assisting a criminal or fraudulent act by a client [unless, however, the matter is covered by attorney-client privilege]." This principle is limited by a comment to the rule that states: "whether a particular statement should be regarded as one of fact can depend on the circumstances. Under generally accepted conventions in negotiation, certain types of statements ordinarily are not taken as statements of material fact. Estimates of price or value placed on the subject of a transaction and a party's intentions as to an acceptable settlement of a claim are in this category."

These express constraints may not be terribly helpful in raising the level of the typical lawyer/negotiator's conduct. There are virtually no reported instances involving sanctions imposed on a U.S. lawyer for violating Rule 4.1, for example. Nonetheless, Rule 4.1 is one of the first instances of a lawyer-drafted code of conduct that specifically refer to conduct in a negotiation and that attempt to establish at least some principle of minimally acceptable behavior. . . . .

Statutory Controls on Negotiator Conduct

There are other restrictions on the negotiating behavior of both lawyers and non-lawyer negotiators imposed by U.S. law. Article One of the U.S. Uniform Commercial Code provides expressly that: "Every contract or duty within this Act imposes an obligation of good faith in its performance or enforcement." But it remains unclear whether this provision governs pre-contract negotiations. In the United States the controversial Foreign Corrupt Practices Act (FCPA), places severe constraints on the giving of certain gratuities to foreign agents in order to obtain business. [The FCPA is discussed later in this Casebook.] While there are no constraints in the act specifically devoted to the negotiation process, the FCPA may constrain negotiating behavior that in the past has been regarded as normal and permissible. Even so, the FCPA, . . . is mainly a constraint on the paying of bribes to foreign government officials, rather than a specific constraint on international business negotiations.

Jeswald W. Salacuse, Making Global Deals
1-3, 28-33, 58-71, 73-82 (1991)

. . . .

Globalization has placed many new demands on business executives, one of the most important of which is the ability to negotiate deals around the world to get what their companies need. Whether they are from Boise or Beijing, managers have to master what is quickly becoming a basic element of modern business life—the global deal.

For many executives, the move from the domestic to the global deal is not easy. They have had little experience outside their own countries. They speak no foreign language. They have paid scant attention to the constantly shifting relations among nations. Conditioned to see business basically as a domestic activity, managers are often unprepared to conduct international business negotiations with skill and confidence. They frequently approach the task with one of two contradictory, but equally fallacious, attitudes.

For some, international business negotiation is an uncharted sea that is dangerous and mysterious, a place where exotic cultures, foreign languages, unfathomable business practices, and arbitrary bureaucratic traditions make negotiating risky and uncertain. Every deal is different. Experience in China is useless in Saudi Arabia.

Other managers see global deal making merely as an extension of domestic business, an arena in which the skills, attitudes, and knowledge so useful in Akron and Kansas City will work just as well in Accra and Kuala Lumpur. After all, business is business, products are products, and when you come right down to it, international business is really nothing more than making deals in strange places.

Both attitudes are wrong. International deal making is shaped by many common forces, whether negotiations concern a joint venture with a rural commune in China, a Eurodollar loan with a group of London banks, a technology transfer agreement with a Japanese multinational, or a barter arrangement with a Russian trading organization. At the same time, negotiating international business transactions is fundamentally different from making domestic deals.

. . . .

Effective negotiation is not just a matter of following fixed rules and formulas. Every negotiation is special. Each negotiation is affected by a host of different factors in many different ways. The effective deal maker must identify those factors, evaluate them, and then determine a course of action. In many situations, the answer to the question "How should I proceed?" is, quite frankly, "It depends." It depends on the culture; it depends on the political system; it depends on the negotiating environment. In order to develop an appropriate strategy for a particular situation, a negotiator must know the right questions to ask. . . . .

Your Words or Mine?

"The language of international business," one purist has said, "is broken English." Fortunately for American executives, who usually have few linguistic gifts, much of the world's business is conducted in English—an English with a profusion of different accents, cadences, and syntaxes, but a mutually understandable English nonetheless. Language, of course, is crucial to deal making, and it is an important element of the negotiating environment. Because of the widespread use of English in business, the American global deal maker in many instances, but certainly not all, will be negotiating with persons who speak the American's language. Often the American enters this linguistic exchange with the advantage that English is his or her native tongue, while for the other side it is a second or third language.

The degree of fluency in and command of English by the two sides affects the pace and progress of the talks. Therefore, negotiations between an American educated at Harvard Business School and a Nigerian trained at the London School of Economics will ordinarily proceed smoothly from a linguistic point of view. On the other hand, the experienced negotiator knows that English is by no means uniform throughout the globe, and that differences in usage and meaning occur even among the highly educated. As George Bernard Shaw pointed out, England and America are two countries separated by the same language.

Often the other side in a negotiation does not have a strong command of English, a fact that can have a direct effect on the talks. For one thing, it slows the pace of discussions, as each side seeks through repetition and rephrasing to clarify its own and the other side's meaning. In addition, language difficulties can lead to misunderstanding about the nature of the transaction, and they can ultimately create conflict between the two parties. An example of this type occurred in a negotiation between an English construction company and the Sudanese government to build villages for Nubians forced from their traditional homes by the rising Nile waters caused by the construction of the Aswan Dam. When the Sudanese side stated that "time was of the essence in the contract," the English negotiator replied that his company "expected" to meet the deadline. The Sudanese negotiator claimed to have heard him say that the English company "accepted" to meet the deadline. The difference between "expected" (which would merely require the English company to make a good faith effort to finish the work on time) and "accepted" (which legally bound them to do so) may not have sounded like much to the untrained ear, but of course it affected the very nature of the deal. When the company failed to finish the job on the date specified in the contract, a serious conflict arose as to its obligation to pay damages. It was eventually settled only by international arbitration.

The use of linguistic superiority to overwhelm an adversary for whom English is a second or third language rarely works. The wise global deal maker, knowing that future conflict between business partners is *always* costly for *both* sides, seeks be sure that the other party understands the nature of the deal.

Despite the widespread use of English in international business, American managers occasionally encounter foreign executives who either cannot or will not use English in negotiations. Even if they know the language, they may refuse to negotiate in it because to do so would give the other side a tactical advantage. In this case, an American has only two choices: negotiate in the other side's language, if he or she knows it, or employ an interpreter.

Speaking the other side's language can be extremely useful in building a good relationship with them. But as a generate rule you should not negotiate in a foreign language unless you know it extremely well. Otherwise, you will be focusing your attention on the language, rather than on the substance of the deal you are trying to make. Having a translator, even if you know the language, gives you additional time to consider your response to the other side's statements.

Most of the time, parties with different languages employ an interpreter. Linguistic differences and the presence of interpreters change the negotiating environment significantly from that which exists when the two sides speak the same language and can communicate directly. For one thing, the need for an interpreter increases the time required to conduct the negotiation. For another, it raises the risk of misunderstanding between the parties. The linguistic ability of persons calling themselves "professional interpreters" often varies considerably in many countries. Hiring a mediocre professional interpreter can create conflict between the parties that neither may understand. For example, one American company in China was astounded to find that its simple request to bring three typewriters into the country was angrily rejected by government officials on the other side of the table, until it became clear, after an hour of wrangling, that the interpreter had mistranslated the English word "typewriter" as the Chinese word "stenographer."

Even if the interpreter is an expert in the language of the two sides, he or she is rarely also an expert in their own businesses. The context of words is important in giving them meaning, and interpreters are seldom knowledgeable about the relevant business context. The presence of an interpreter increases the number of persons involved in a negotiation and increases its costs. Moreover, instead of coming to know one another directly, the parties have to rely on the interpreter for that knowledge. Depending on his or her degree of skill and integrity, the interpreter can be a clear lens or a murky filter through which information passes easily or is obstructed. But in all cases, the needs for an interpreter, at least to some extent, impedes the development of a close working relationship between the two sides. According to one experienced executive, involving an interpreter in a deal is a lot like trying to kiss your girlfriend through a screen door.

There are two types of foreign language interpretation: simultaneous and consecutive. Simultaneous interpretation, frequently found at the United Nations and in diplomatic conferences, is rarely used in international business negotiations because of its great expense and the need for special equipment. Consecutive interpretation, in which a negotiator makes a statement in one language and the interpreter then translates it into another, is by far the more common method. Although the process may seem simple, it complicates deal making and must be managed carefully.

Seven Rules for Using Interpreters

By following a few simple rules, the international business negotiator can make effective use of an interpreter.

1. A negotiation team should hire its own interpreter. Except in cases where special reasons for trust exist, do not rely on the other side's interpreter, unless someone on your team understands the language and can check the translation. Before hiring an interpreter, try to determine his or her skill and experience from independent, reliable sources.

2. Before negotiations actually begin, hold a briefing meeting with the interpreter to explain the nature of the deal, what you want in the way of translation, and why you want it. For example, if you want a word-for-word translation rather than a summary, make your requirements clear.

3. Guard against interpreters who, because of personal interest or ego, try to take control of the negotiations or slant them in a particular way. This risk may be present if the interpreter also works as a middleman, agent, or business consultant.

4. When negotiating, speak in short, bite-size statements, and pause after each one to give the interpreter a chance to translate your words.

5. Plan each statement carefully so that it is clear, devoid of abbreviations, slang, and business jargon, and delivered slowly. Constantly ask yourself: How can my statements be misunderstood? One inexperienced American executive forgot this rule when he proudly told his Saudi counterparts that he represented a "blue chip company." This drew quizzical looks from both the interpreter and the Saudi executives. The American then launched into a long discussion of the expression "blue chip," only to be told that Saudi Arabia did not allow gambling.

6. Interpretation is difficult and extremely tiring work, so give your interpreter ample opportunity to take periodic breaks.

7. Treat the interpreters, both yours and the other side's, with the respect due professionals. Because the other side's interpreter speaks your language and presumably has insights into your psyche and culture that his employers do not, they may seek his advice about you—whether you are trustworthy, telling the truth, seem honest. If you have slighted or offended their interpreter in some way during the negotiations, he or she may not give the other side the kind of advice that you would like them to hear. Conversely, if you develop a friendly relationship with the interpreter, he or she may provide you with much useful information about the other side, as one Japanese interpreter did when he let it slip that the head of his delegation believed he would lose face if he returned to Tokyo without a contract.

A final linguistic decision is to determine the language of the contract. An American company normally wants English alone to be the language of its agreement, but the other side may push just as hard to have the contract written in its own language. A compromise is to have both an English- and foreign-language version of the contract and to provide that both versions are equally authoritative. Unless the translations are done extremely skillfully, the parties may later find differences in the two versions that require further negotiations to settle.

. . . .

Ten Ways Culture Affects Negotiations

While warning against cultural stereotypes and oversimplifications, all experienced negotiators acknowledge that cultural differences between negotiators are an important and special factor in global deal making. A knowledge of the other side's culture allows a negotiator to communicate, to understand, to plan, and to anticipate more effectively. The enormous number and great diversity of the world's cultures make it impossible for any negotiator, no matter how skilled and experienced, to understand fully the culture that he or she encounters. How, then, should an executive entering international negotiations prepare to cope with cultures in making global deals? One approach is to try to identify the specific ways in which cultural traits affect the negotiating process.

While culture can influence a business deal in many ways,...it generally has a direct impact on the dealmaking process itself in only ten substantial ways. A knowledge of these ten factors allows you to analyze the negotiator you are facing and enables you to develop an effective way of communicating with your counterpart. It is also useful to measure your own negotiating style against these ten factors to see how you appear as a negotiator to executives from other countries. Each factor represents a continuum along which negotiating behavior may be placed between two identified poles.

   ....

1. Negotiating Goal: Contract or Relationship?

An initial question is whether the two sides in a negotiation have the same goal and see the deal-making process in the same light. It is possible for business persons from different cultures to interpret the very purpose of their negotiation differently. For many Americans, the purpose of a business negotiation, first and foremost, is to arrive at a signed contract between the parties. Americans view a signed contract as a definitive set of rights and duties that strictly binds the two sides, an attitude succinctly summed up in the declaration that "a deal is a deal."

Japanese and certain other cultural groups consider that the goal of negotiation is not a signed contract but a relationship between the two sides. Although the written contract expresses the relationship, the essence of their deal is the relationship itself. For the American, signing a contract is closing a deal; for the Japanese, signing a contract might more appropriately be called opening a relationship. As will be seen, these differing goals can affect certain other aspects of the negotiating process.

If a "relationship" negotiator sits on the other side of the table, you need to be aware that merely convincing him of your ability to deliver on a low-cost contract will not get you the deal. You have to convince him instead, from the very first meeting, that your two organizations have the potential to build a rewarding relationship over the long term. On other hand, if the other side is basically a "contract" deal maker, trying to build a relationship may be a waste of time and energy.

2. Negotiating Attitude: Win/Lose or Win/Win?

Because of culture or personality, or both, business persons appear to approach deal making with one of two basic attitudes: that a negotiation is either a process through which both can gain (win/win) or a process through which, of necessity, one side wins and the other loses (win/lose). As you enter negotiations, it is important to know which type of negotiator is sitting across the table from you. If one side has much greater bargaining power than the other, the weaker side has a tendency to see the negotiation as a win/lose situation: every gain for the powerful side is automatically a loss for the weaker party. As one Indian executive put it, "Negotiations between the weak and the strong are like negotiations between the lamb and the lion. Invariably, the lamb gets eaten." Win/win negotiators see deal making as a collaborative and problem-solving process; win/lose negotiators view it as confrontational.

Developing-country officials often view their negotiations with large multinational corporations as win/lose competitions. For example, in negotiating investment contracts, they sometimes take the view that any profits earned by the investor are automatically losses to the host country. As a result, they may focus rather fixedly in negotiations on limiting investor profit in contrast to discovering how to maximize the benefits from the project to both the investor and the host country.

The presence of a win/lose deal maker on the other side may block any deal. Searching constantly for the negative implications of every proposal while failing to evaluate the positive side, this type of negotiator may simply take a position and refuse to budge. How should you negotiate with a win/lose deal maker?

First, without appearing to condescend, explain fully the nature of the proposed transaction. Do not assume that the other side has the same degree of business sophistication as you. Part of their intransigence may stem from lack of understanding of the deal and an unwillingness to show ignorance.

Second, try to find out the other side's real interests—what do they really want out of the deal? Negotiators who encourage the other side to provide information about themselves, their interests, and their preferences generally achieve better results than those who do not. To do this you have to look behind the positions they take at the table. Here, the question is your most powerful tool. But questioning at the negotiating table requires a high degree of sophistication. On the one hand, you do not want to appear ignorant and therefore reduce your credibility with the other side. On the other, you do not want to seem indiscreet by appearing to ask for business secrets. Many foreign companies attach a much greater importance to secrecy than do American corporations, which have to contend daily with the disclosure requirements of U.S. law and business practice. For example, although the salary of the chairman of a U.S. publicly traded corporation is a matter of public record, the salary of the president of a French corporation is a tightly kept secret. The cultural differences on what is and what is not considered secret can complicate information exchange, which is so vital to determining interests. But one principle that all cultures seem to respect is reciprocity. If you are open and provide information easily, the other side will be led to provide you with information. Your own openness may be the best way to get persons across the table to open up.

Third, to understand the other side's interests, you need to know something about its history and culture. For instance, Mexico's history of domination by the United States invariably leads Mexican corporations to pursue both profits and prestige in their negotiations with American companies. A lucrative deal that places a Mexican corporation in a visible second-class position will probably fail.

And finally, once you have been able to identify the other side's interests, you have to develop proposals directed at satisfying those interests. Here, creativity and innovation are essential. In one negotiation between an American contractor and a foreign manufacturing corporation for the construction and sale of an electrical cogeneration plant, the foreign negotiators insisted that if the plant did not work up to a specified standard, the American corporation would have to dismantle the entire plant and take it all away. The American company was unwilling to make that kind of guarantee. As the negotiations appeared to disintegrate, the American negotiators realized that the real interest of the foreign corporation was not in having a cogeneration plant but in having a reliable supply of electricity. The Americans therefore proposed that, if the plant was defective and could not be fixed, they would take over and run it, provided the foreign corporation agreed to purchase all the electricity it produced. Ultimately, the two sides struck a deal on this basis. An understanding of interests led to the creation of innovative proposals, which in turn led to a deal.

3. Personal Style: Informal or Formal?

An executive's "style" at the negotiating table is usually characterized as formal or informal. References to style focus on the way a negotiator talks to others, uses titles, dresses, speaks, and interacts with other persons. A negotiator with a formal style insists on addressing the other team by their titles, avoids personal anecdotes, and refrains from questions touching on the private or family life of members of the other side. An informal style of negotiator tries to start the discussion on a first-name basis, quickly seeks to develop a personal, friendly relationship with the other team, and may take off his jacket and roll up his sleeves when deal making begins in earnest. Each culture has its own formalities, which have special meaning. They are another means of communication among the persons sharing that culture. For an American or an Australian, calling someone by his first name is an act of friendship and therefore a good thing. In other cultures, such as the French, Japanese, or Egyptian, the use of a first name at a first meeting is an act of disrespect and therefore a bad thing.

Negotiators in a foreign culture must take care to respect appropriate formalities. As a general rule, it is always safer to adopt a formal posture and gradually move to an informal stance, if the situation warrants it, than to assume an informal style too quickly. Degrees of appropriate formality vary from culture to culture. As an illustration, in the Sudan, an Arab country, informality is more readily and quickly tolerated than in Egypt, its Arab neighbor down the Nile.

4. Communication: Direct or Indirect?

Methods of communication vary among cultures. Some place emphasis on direct and simple methods of communication; others rely heavily on indirect and complex methods. The latter may use circumlocutions, figurative forms of speech, facial expressions, gestures, and other kinds of body language. In a culture that values directness, such as the German, you can expect to receive a clear and definite response to questions and proposals. In cultures that rely on indirect communication, reaction to your proposal may be gained only by interpreting a series of signs, gestures, and seemingly indefinite comments. What you will not receive at a first meeting is a definite commitment or rejection.

The presence of conflict in a negotiation may lead to the use of extreme forms of indirect communication. In one case, a small U.S. manufacturing concern located in New York was having difficulty paying its Japanese suppliers, who had been asking for their money without success for some time. The American company was allied with a Canadian partner for certain business in Canada. One day the Japanese called the Canadian and asked to meet with him at his office in Toronto, to which the Canadian agreed. When the Japanese arrived for the meeting, they asked where John, the owner of the American company, was. Surprised, the Canadian replied that he had had no idea that they wanted to see John. They said they did and asked the Canadian if he would mind calling John to invite him to Toronto for a meeting with them. After receiving the call, John flew to Toronto for discussions about his financial problems. The Japanese indirectly brought about the meeting that they were reluctant to arrange directly.

5. Sensitivity to Time: High or Low?

Discussions of national negotiating styles invariably treat a particular culture's attitudes toward time. So it is said that Germans are always punctual, Mexicans are habitually late, Japanese negotiate slowly, and Americans are quick to make a deal.

Commentators claim that some cultures "value" time more than others, but this may not be an accurate characterization of the situation. Rather, they value differently the amount of time devoted to and measured against the goal pursued. For Americans, the deal is a "signed contract" and "time is money," so they want to make a deal quickly. Americans therefore try to reduce formalities to a minimum and get down to business. For members of other cultures, who view the purpose of the negotiation as creating a relationship rather than simply signing a contract, there is a need to invest time in the negotiating process so that the parties can get to know one another well and determine whether they wish to embark on a long-term relationship. Aggressive attempts to shorten the negotiating time may be viewed by the other side as efforts to hide something and therefore may be a cause of distrust. These elements should be taken into account in planning and scheduling negotiation sessions and in dealing with other factors affecting the pace of negotiations.

6. Emotionalism: High or Low?

Accounts of negotiating behavior of persons from other cultures almost always point to a particular group's tendency or lack thereof to act emotionally. According to the stereotype, Latin Americans show their emotions at the negotiating table, but Japanese hide their feelings. Obviously, individual personality plays a role here. There are passive Latins and hotheaded Japanese. But various cultures have different rules as to the appropriateness of displaying emotions, and these rules are usually brought to the negotiating table as well.

7. Form of Agreement: General or Specific?

Cultural factors also influence the form of agreement that parties try to make. Generally, Americans prefer very detailed contracts that attempt to anticipate all possible circumstances, no matter how unlikely. Why? Because the "deal" is the contract itself, and one must refer to the contract to determine how to handle a new situation that may arise. Other cultures, such as that of China, prefer a contract in the form of general principles rather than detailed rules. Why? Because, it is claimed, the essence of the deal is the relationship of trust that exists between the parties. If unexpected circumstances arise, the parties should look to their relationship, not the contract, to solve the problem. So in some cases, the American drive at the negotiating table to foresee all contingencies may be viewed by persons from another culture as evidence of lack of confidence in the stability of the underlying relationship.

Some persons argue that differences over the form of an agreement are caused more by unequal bargaining power between the parties than by culture. In a situation of unequal bargaining power, the stronger party always seeks a detailed agreement to "lock up the deal" in all its possible dimensions, while the weaker party prefers a general agreement to give it room to "wiggle out" of adverse circumstances that are almost bound to occur in the future. So a Chinese commune as the weaker party in negotiations with a multinational corporation will seek a general agreement as a way of protecting itself against the future. According to this view, it is not culture context that determines this negotiating trait.

. . . .

8. Building an Agreement: Bottom Up or Top Down?

Related to the form of an agreement is the question of whether negotiating a business deal is an *inductive or deductive* process. Does it start from agreement on general principles and proceed to specific items, or does it begin with agreement on specifics, such as price, delivery date, and product quality, the sum total of which becomes the contract? Different cultures tend to emphasize one approach over the other.

Some observers believe that the French prefer to begin with agreement on general principles, while Americans tend to seek agreement first on specifics. For Americans, negotiating a deal is basically making a whole series of compromises and trade-offs on a long list of particulars. For the French, the essence is to agree on basic general principles that will guide and indeed determine the negotiation process afterward. The agreed-upon general principles become the framework, the skeleton, upon which the contract is built.

A further difference in negotiating style is seen in the dichotomy between the "building down" approach and the "building up" approach. In the building-down approach, the negotiator begins by presenting a maximum deal if the other side accepts all the stated conditions. In the building-up approach, one side starts by proposing a minimal deal that can be broadened and increased as the other party accepts additional conditions. According to many observers, Americans tend to favor the building-down approach, while the Japanese prefer the building-up style of negotiating a contract.

9. Team Organization: One Leader or Group Consensus?

In any international business negotiation, it is important know how the other side is organized, who has the authority to make commitments, and how decisions are made. Culture is one important factor that affects the way executives organize themselves to negotiate a deal. One extreme is the negotiating team with a supreme leader who has complete authority to decide all matters. Americans tend to follow this approach, described as the "John Wayne style of negotiations": one person has all the authority and plunges ahead to do a job, and to do it as quickly as possible. Other cultures, notably the Japanese and the former Soviets, stress team negotiation and consensus decision making. When you negotiate with such a team, it may not be apparent who is the leader and who has the authority to commit the side. In the first type, the negotiating team is usually small; in the second, it is often large. For example, in negotiations in China on a major deal, it would not be uncommon for the Americans to arrive at the table with three persons and for the Chinese to show up with ten. Similarly, the one-leader team is usually prepared to make commitments and decisions more quickly than a negotiating team organized on the basis of consensus. As a result, the consensus type of organization usually takes more time to negotiate a deal.

10. Risk Taking: High or Low?

Studies seem to support the idea that certain cultures try to avoid risk more than others. In any given deal, the willingness of one side to take "risks" in the negotiation process—to divulge information, to be open to new approaches, to tolerate uncertainties in a proposed course of action—can be affected by the personality of the negotiator and the context of the negotiation. Nonetheless, there are certain cultural traits to this effect. The Japanese, with their emphasis on requiring enormous amounts of information and on their intricate group decision-making process, tend to be risk adverse. Americans, by comparison, are risk takers.

If you determine that the team on the other side of the table is risk adverse, focus your attention on proposing rules, mechanisms, and relationships that will reduce the apparent risks in the deal for them.

TYPE A AND TYPE B NEGOTIATORS

Negotiating styles, like personalities, have a wide range of variation. The ten negotiator traits listed above and the range of variation within each trait easily show the complexity of the problem. For purposes of simplification one might divide negotiators into two types, A and B, just as a famous cardiology study grouped the human race into type A and type B personalities. The following table may be helpful in identifying the two types.

TRAIT	TYPE A NEGOTIATOR		TYPE B NEGOTIATOR
Goal	Contract	↔	Relationship
Attitudes	Win/Lose	↔	Win/Win
Personal Styles	Informal	↔	Formal
Communications	Direc	↔	Indirect
Time Sensitivity	High	↔	Low
Emotionalism	High	↔	Low
Agreement Form	Specific	↔	General
Agreement Building	Bottom-up	↔	Top-down
Team Organization	One leader	↔	Consensus
Risk-taking	High	↔	Low

Unlike the purpose of the cardiology study, the purpose this categorization is not to argue that one type is better than another or to persuade a type A negotiator to become more like a type B negotiator. Individual negotiators may not fit neatly into either of these two categories. While Americans may tend to be type A and Japanese type B, Russians, Germans, and Poles may have negotiating traits that draw from both types. The purpose of the checklist is to identify the specific cultural and personality characteristics that affect deal making, and to show the possible variation that a particular trait may take. With this knowledge, a global deal maker is better prepared to cope with the complexities of culture in an international business negotiation.

. . . .

THE ELEMENTS OF IDEOLOGY

Ideology is deadly serious business. Whether it is socialism or capitalism, nationalism or Islamic fundamentalism, ideology gives authoritative answers to some basic questions. What should be the relationship between the individual and the community? How should that relationship be guaranteed and enforced? How should the means of producing goods and services be organized and governed? What should be the role of the state in the lives of its citizens? How should the state and its citizens treat the citizens of other states?

. . . .

Some American managers tend to think of ideologies in sweeping, general categories: capitalism, socialism, nationalism. But these categories are much too broad to guide deal makers in foreign countries. Existing ideologies in a particular country have usually been adapted to suit that country's particular needs. The socialism of China is different from that of North Korea, and the capitalism of the United States is different from that of Canada.

Numerous factors shape and influence a particular ideology. Internal factors, such as a country's geography, demography, culture, and resources are powerful forces in shaping an ideology. Thus Japan's dense population, island structure, poor resource base, and homogeneous ethnic background have given it a communitarian ideology that emphasizes the importance of cooperating for the common good. Similarly, external forces such as colonialism and invasion also play a role. Latin America's history of outside domination has surely prompted the strong nationalist ideology that prevails throughout the continent.

....

IDEOLOGY AND THE DEAL-MAKING PROCESS

Ideology has a dual impact on global deals: it affects the negotiation process and it influences the nature of the transaction ultimately agreed upon. Ideological differences between two sides can complicate the deal-making process in numerous ways.

First, ideologies have an adversarial quality. They have their good guys and bad guys, friends and foes, right and wrong ways. Thus ideological differences at the negotiating table can increase mistrust between the parties and raise suspicions about the other side's intentions, honesty, and reliability. As a result, the parties may come to see themselves not as jointly engaged in solving a business problem, but as ideological adversaries to be watched very carefully.

Second, ideological differences can complicate communication between deal makers. The use of ideological jargon may seem natural and value-free to a person holding that ideology, but it often appears provocative to the other side. An American executive may consider "free enterprise," "profit," and "private property" to be unquestionably good things; however, an Argentinean government official or Chinese manager may consider them more ambivalently.

Third, ideology may lead negotiators to take hard-and-fast positions. As a result, they may obstruct the process of shaping an agreement by exploring areas of mutual interests and developing creative options to advance them. In the negotiation of a joint venture in a developing country, the local government may insist on 51 percent ownership for reasons of nationalism requiring that enterprises be under local control. Although the purpose behind its position on ownership is to assure local control, ideology may prevent the government from exploring ways for controlling the enterprise without owning 51 percent of its shares. For instance, it might hold a class of shares with more power than that owned by its foreign partner.

....

DEALING WITH IDEOLOGIES

How should you deal with the barrier of ideology at the negotiating table? The basic strategy to follow is avoidance. You will not change the other side's ideology, and they will certainly not change yours. Therefore, if you really want to make a global deal, you must duck ideology.

That piece of advice is not as easy to put into practice as it sounds. The following are eight simple rules you should observe for ducking ideology.

1. *Know your own ideology.* American executives tend to think of themselves as pragmatists. They have viewpoints, even philosophies. But few self-respecting corporate executives believe they have an ideology. The ideologies are on the other side of the table. They, not we, are the zealots and the fanatics.

That reaction is self-delusion. We all have ideologies. We all have answers to the basic questions raised earlier... questions that every ideology tries to answer. And even if our political beliefs seem to us to be obvious and eternal truths, acknowledged by mankind as laws of nature, those beliefs will inevitably appear to be an ideology to somebody on the other side of the negotiation table. Thus you should also try to understand how the other side views the ideology that you hold.

2. *Once you have learned your own ideology, don't preach it.* You are at the table to make deals, not converts. Trumpeting your own ideology may antagonize the other side. At the very least, your gratuitous praise of "free enterprise" in a socialist country will be interpreted to be criticism of the country's prevailing ideology. Do not transform a business negotiation into an ideological struggle. Even in these days, when capitalism seems to have won over communism as an economic system, becoming a missionary for capitalism, rather than focusing on your job as a business negotiator, may lose you a deal in the end.

3. *Know the other side's ideology and take it seriously.* Ideology, like culture, gives you important insights into the other side. You should therefore seek to understand that ideology and how it came about.

One way you can begin to gain that knowledge is by reading a modern political history of the country in which you want to do business. Local newspapers and magazines and discussions with embassy officials and your consultants can also be extremely helpful in this respect. Of course, members of the other negotiating team, often in social conversation, can give important information on the prevailing ideology in the country, as well as on their own political beliefs.

Understanding the other side's ideology helps you to understand its interests. Once you understand interests, you can begin to shape an acceptable deal. In one socialist country a major U.S. soft-drink producer wanted to set up a bottling plant and distribution network. The prevailing ideology in the country stressed the importance of the group over the individual, and the need to develop industrial capacity at the expense of consumer goods. Soft drinks hardly seemed to fit the country's ideological priorities. Indeed, one government official dismissed the product as a "useless drink." Eventually a deal was struck, but not on the basis that the drink would satisfy the local population's thirst. Instead, the U.S. negotiators justified the project on the ground that it would contribute to the country's industrial development. The project was restructured to include a heavy training component for local workers and managers, as well as a farm where certain ingredients would be grown. In addition, the U.S. manufacturer promised to make efforts to persuade other American companies to consider investments in the country.

Americans not only feel that they themselves have no ideology, but they also tend to believe that the proclaimed ideologies of other persons are not genuine. For many U.S. executives, ideological statements merely justify interests. They assume that foreign business executives and officials just parrot the ideological line to get along with their governments: nobody really believes that stuff.

It is dangerous to arrive at the negotiating table with that attitude. It is far better to assume that negotiators on the other side believe the ideological line they are giving you—at least until you have direct evidence that they don't.

4. *Look for ideological divisions on the other side.* In negotiating any deal you have to be concerned about the other side's ideology at three different levels: personal, organizational, and national. Specifically, you need to determine: (1) the ideology of the persons you are negotiating with; (2) the ideology of the organization you hope to make a deal with; and (3) the ideology prevailing in the country where you want to do business.

In many but not all instances, the ideologies at the three levels are the same. It sometimes happens that the personal, organizational, and national ideologies of the other side are all different, even inconsistent. These differences in ideology may either facilitate or complicate deal making. For example, if a foreign executive with whom you are negotiating is clearly not sympathetic to his country's prevailing socialist ideology, the opportunity to make a deal may be greater than if he were a genuine socialist. However, if a country has a declared open-door policy toward foreign investment, but the official with whom you are negotiating holds strong nationalist and socialist views, making a deal on a foreign investment project may prove to be difficult.

U.S. companies discovered the problem created by ideological diversity in the 1970s, when Egypt, under President Anwar Sadat, actively tried to promote foreign investment. Despite favorable policies and laws, prospective investors in Egypt encountered significant barriers in the offices of government agencies and state corporations. Officials in those offices had formed a set of beliefs, known as Arab Socialism, during the previous twenty years under the rule of President Gamal Nasser. As a result, they came to view foreign investors as a threat to Egypt's sovereignty and to existing public-sector companies. The arrival of a new president, with new laws and policies, did not cause them to put aside those beliefs suddenly. So regardless of Sadat's speeches inviting foreign capital to Egypt, many Egyptian officials continued to bring their old ideology to the table and therefore obstructed deal making. To counter this situation, American companies sought to shift negotiations to a higher level in the bureaucracy, where they felt they would find an ideology more in tune with what they were hearing from President Sadat.

5. *Avoid discussion of ideological positions and focus instead on interests.* If a country has taken a strong ideological position on an issue, say, the predominance of public-sector enterprise over that of the private sector, it does little good to try to persuade officials of that country that its position is wrong. Rather, try to determine the goals that the other side is pursuing through that ideological position, then seek to propose options that will enable that side to achieve those goals. In the case of the soft-drink plant in the socialist country, it would have been confrontational and counterproductive for the U.S. company to have tried to persuade the government to provide more goods for consumers. Instead, it identified the country's interests in developing its industrial capacity and convinced the government that the soft-drink plant, distribution system, and farm would help the country to advance its interests.

6. *Look for the gaps between ideology and reality.* As we have seen in Eastern Europe, reality changes faster than ideology. With that change, a gap develops between the two as ideology's explanation of society and its proposed solutions seem more and more inadequate. Eventually, when the gap becomes too great, the prevailing ideology is abandoned or reformed. Thus, when communism became less and less relevant to the problems of East Germany, it was discarded as that country's prevailing ideology.

Similarly, as deal makers come to know a country, they should seek to identify gaps between ideology and the realities of the local business and economic environment. The existence of large gaps between ideology and reality may provide business opportunities and suggest areas in which official ideology is less of an obstacle to deal making. For example, if the ideology of a state stresses the importance of the group over the individual, but the role of the individual is increasing in the society, opportunities for business deals in consumer goods may arise. Then, too, the existence of big gaps between official ideology and the social realities may mean that major political changes will soon take place.

7. *Try to structure deals around ideological obstacles.* Often ideological principles crystalize into laws, rules, and institutions that threaten to block deals. Nation-

alism requires that all natural resources belong to the state, and that no one else can own them. Islamic fundamentalism prohibits interest payments on loans. Egyptian socialism demands that workers participate both in the management and in the profits of an enterprise. Each of these principles can be an obstacle to deal making in particular cases. Yet, with some creativity, it is possible to structure a deal in such a way that the ideological principle is respected, but business goes forward. A loan to a project might be secured by its assets and paid for by an annual administrative fee and a percentage of the profits in lieu of interest. A petroleum development contract could be written in such a way that ownership of the oil is transferred not when the oil is in the ground, but at the point where it leaves the flange of the well. And worker participation in management need not mean a seat on the board of directors but merely an advisory committee that meets regularly with an officer of the company.

Some countries, such as the former Soviet Union, appear to have an ideological aversion to paying for services, especially at the going international rates. Influenced by their own egalitarian wage structure, they often resisted paying high fees for engineering, technical, and managerial services. One way of dealing with this kind of ideological barrier is to repackage a deal as a sale of a product rather than of services alone: the provision of management services to a new factory could be included as part of the contract of sale for the factory instead of being spelled out in a separate contract.

8.   *Maintain confidentiality.* The more public the negotiations, the more likely that ideological differences will surface. In the glare of publicity, local executives and officials feel strong need to show to the government, the public, and their colleagues that they are adhering to appropriate ideological positions. For example, in a mineral negotiation that receives a great deal of publicity, the officials representing the host country may feel obliged to show that they are not selling out to foreigners. As a result, their positions may harden, and they may prove to be inflexible at the table.

Executives should therefore seek to establish and maintain confidentiality in negotiations as one way of softening the influence of ideology. To create a confidential atmosphere, the U.S. team should be careful in what they say to others outside the negotiating room. They should naturally avoid comments to the press and indeed should specifically agree that the host country side will be the principal source of public commentary on the negotiations. Another way to foster confidentiality . . . is to hold discussions in another country or some out-of-the-way site.

David A. Victor, Cross-Cultural Awareness, in the ABA Guide to International Business Negotiations
15, 19-21 (James R. Silkenat & Jeffrey M. Aresty Eds. 1994)

Few areas of international negotiations are as important as cross-cultural awareness to understanding and developing appropriate responses. Yet, for the most part, American lawyers have received very little in the way of formal training in those areas of behavior most likely to be affected by cultural difference. How each culture differs is highly variable. That they differ in specific ways is a constant.

. . . .

. . . While experience in an international setting is unquestionably the best means for acquiring cross-cultural skills, even those well-versed in international transactions often find it difficult to pass on what they know in any organized way to those new to the culture in question. In short, some of the best international negotiators know when something feels right or wrong but would not be able to specifically explain why. . . .

FIGURE 2.1
Cultures Ranked by Level of Contexting

High Contexting Cultures		Japanese	*Information*
		Arabic	*implicitly*
		Latin American	*contained*
		Italian	
		English	
SENDER		French	RECEIVER
		North American	
Low		Scandinavian*	*Information*
Contexting		German	*explicitly*
Cultures		Swiss-German	*conveyed*

* Scandinavian category excludes Finland.

Moreover, a lawyer's experience in one culture is rarely valid when dealing with another. Negotiation in Tokyo, Frankfurt, and Mexico City are as conceptually different as they are geographically so. Yet in an increasingly integrated world economy, the lawyer expert in only one other culture is often called on to interact with those from cultures far removed from his or her area of experience. Still no international lawyer is able to know every negotiation approach common in every nation. The sheer number of possible cultures the international lawyer may face at a given time thus presents a dilemma; to practice international law effectively, the lawyer must know the specifics about a vast array of cultures....

. . . .

CONTEXTING AND FACE-SAVING

Directness in legal negotiations shifts drastically across cultures. Arguably, no two cultures negotiate exactly in the same manner. International negotiations in legal matters are particularly tied up with two key issues: contexting and face-saving.

Contexting is a term...to describe the way people read into what is communicated in words based on the surrounding circumstances. Contexting deals with the amount one pays attention to how something is said over what is actually put into words. No two cultures share the same level of contexting. All cultures can be seen as either higher contexted or lower contexted than another.

High contexting refers to the practice of relying heavily on how something is said or written and on the circumstances surrounding that communication. In a high-context culture, negotiations are based more on what is understood than on what is explicitly stated. *Low contexting* refers to the practice of relying heavily on what is said. In a low-context culture, negotiations are based on hammering out specifics and on establishing the exact wording of an agreement. Relatively little importance is given to implied arrangements.

All cultures can be placed on a contexting scale from low to high. Figure 2.1 shows the relative level of contexting of several major groups. Note that the United States is generally considered a very low context culture.

High- and low-context cultures have predictable reactions relative to one another. Figure 2.2 contrasts high- and low-context negotiation style.

FIGURE 2.2
Variation in the Reliance on Verbal Communication
Between Extreme High- and Low-Context Cultures

	High context	Low context
Reliance on words to communicate	Low	High
Reliance on nonverbal communication	High	Low
View of silence	Respected; communicative	Anxiety-producing; non-communicative
Attention to detail	Low	High
Attention to intention	High	Low
Communication approach	Indirect; inferential	Direct; explicit
Literalness	Low literalness; interpretive	High literalness; non-interpretive

Face-saving may be defined as the act of preserving one's prestige or outward dignity. Face-saving — like contexting — varies drastically from culture to culture. In cultures with a strong face-saving element, negotiations may end if one party or the other is caused to lose face.

In such cultures, face is more important than most business dealings. In cultures with a weak face-saving element, negotiations may continue if one or the other party is caused to lose face. In such cultures (including the United States), business dealings are generally considered more important than face.

High and low face-saving cultures have predictable characteristics affecting negotiation. Figure 2.3 illustrates these.

The most significant of these differences is how the law is viewed. In high face-saving cultures, shame and fear of losing face keep people in line. The courts serve as a resolution method of last resort. In low face-saving cultures such as the United States, the law is often the option of first recourse. The law — not face — keeps people in line.

. . . .

Robert C. Ciricillo et al., International Negotiations: A Cultural Perspective, in the ABA Guide to International Business Negotiations

5, 7-14 (James R. Silkenat & Jeffrey M. Aresty Eds. 1994)

To negotiate an international transaction successfully, it is necessary to understand and develop appropriate responses, where necessary, to cultural attitudes and expectations. For example, the often indirect communication and consensus-building style of the Japanese may make it necessary to pay more attention to implicit messages conveyed by their conduct and to set aside more time for the negotiation phase

FIGURE 2.3
Characteristics of High- and Low-Face Saving Cultures

	High Face-Saving	Low Face-Saving
Contexting	High	Low
Favored business communication approach	Politeness strategy; indirect plan	Confrontation strategy; direct plan
View of directness	Uncivil; inconsiderate; offensive	Honest, inoffensive
View of indirectness	Civil; considerate; honest	Dishonest; offensive
Amount of verbal self-disclosure	Low	High
Vagueness	Tolerated	Untolerated

of a transaction than would be necessary for negotiations with an American party. Likewise, it is important for an American negotiator to appreciate that some cultures, such as the Chinese and Japanese, do not place the same emphasis upon the written document that Americans do. Therefore, it may be necessary to place more stress on the binding nature of the written contract when doing business in these cultural environments. It may also be wise to keep in mind that Russian and Arab negotiators are more likely to assume a win/lose negotiating posture, and to expect these foreign parties to use competing offers to their advantage — sometimes even negotiating with the American party's competitors at the same time that negotiations are under way with the American.

Insight into cultural attitudes and expectations such as these are vital to the negotiation, documentation, and performance of almost every type of international business transaction, whether the sale of merchandise, the setting up of a joint venture, or the licensing of technology. The potential for cultural misunderstandings abounds, and the American company that has best understood the cultural attitudes of its overseas counterpart will be able to develop its business abroad in a more efficient and cost-effective manner.

. . . .

THE LAWYER'S ROLE IN INTERNATIONAL NEGOTIATIONS

The lawyer's role in the United States is more prominent than it is abroad. While it is common in the United States for lawyers to be actively involved in a negotiation, even at the earliest stages, it may be unusual for lawyers to be similarly involved in business transactions outside of the United States. The mere presence of a lawyer during a negotiation may, in some cases, actually present the threat of litigation to a foreign negotiator. Thus, in negotiating an international transaction, it may be appropriate for the American lawyer to assume a lower profile, perhaps by being available only on an as-needed basis to deal with specific issues or questions, rather than attending each negotiation session, particularly in the early stages of a transaction. Much may depend on whether the foreign party with whom one is negotiating includes a lawyer on its team.

Closely connected to the prominence of the lawyer's role in the United States is the American inclination to engage in litigation as a means of dispute resolution. In some countries, litigation is the exception rather than the rule, and negotiations are regarded as the best mechanism to resolve disputes. For example, the Japanese view their relationship with a business partner as a dispute-settling mechanism in itself, and trust and honor are important. The relationship is expected to weather disputes. In this context, the presence of a lawyer threatening suit at the first sign of disagreement is likely to provoke and offend, rather than expedite settlement. It may, however, be somewhat more acceptable for a lawyer to function as a mediator or intermediary once a dispute arises.

A method of settlement or dispute resolution is often specified in an agreement, but in an international transaction the negotiation of such a clause must be handled delicately. Creativity can help. For example, in one transaction with an Egyptian party, a clause calling for arbitration in the event of a dispute was successfully negotiated after the parties agreed that before the arbitration clause could be invoked, the chief executive officer of the American entity and his counterpart at the Egyptian firm would have to meet to try to resolve the dispute within a specified time period. An aggressive approach, on the other hand, may offend: presenting a highly detailed arbitration clause without having established a rationale for its necessity may fail to produce agreement on a dispute-resolution mechanism.

CULTURAL CHARACTERISTICS

Stereotypes about a particular nationality or region can be misleading, and observations about different cultures should not be obscured by the particular personalities with whom an American negotiator is dealing and the context in which the negotiations take place. Nonetheless, certain generalizations and patterns that emerge from exposure to a foreign culture can help improve communication during the negotiation process. These insights can help us understand not only the foreign culture, but also how our words and conduct will be received by a foreign party, thereby guiding and, hopefully, contributing to the success of the negotiations. One noted commentator has suggested that there are 10 specific cultural characteristics that affect negotiations: the negotiating goal (contract or relationship); the negotiating attitude (win/lose or win/win); personal style (formal or informal); communication (direct or indirect); sensitivity to time (high or low); emotionalism (high or low); form of agreement (general or specific); building an agreement (inductive or deductive); team organization (one leader or group consensus); and risk-taking (high or low)....
The following summary of cultural characteristics that may affect negotiations with members of the Russian, Japanese, Brazilian, Chinese, and Arab cultures is organized around many of the foregoing characteristics, and is intended to aid the commercial negotiator in recognizing the affect of cultural differences when transacting business with members of these cultures.

Russia

Because the rule of law, so common in western market-oriented societies, is not yet as structured in Russia, commercial transactions are not law- or rule-based, but are based primarily on relationships. The Russian focus on relationships in part explains why many Russians place much more emphasis on the quality of a relationship with a potential western partner than on the detailed negotiation and documentation of the transaction. Consequently, it is too often the case that the secret to successful business dealings in Russia unfortunately is "getting to" the right political connection rather than having the right project in an important industrial or business sector of the Russian economy.

. . . .

Russia's recent emergence from a culture dominated by a totalitarian political system has influenced negotiating behavior in that country. Under that system, the predominant motivation for behavior was fear arising from the avoidance of retribution by the Communist party, KGB, and other instruments of the Soviet regime. While much progress has been made in removing fear as a primary incentive for behavior, the cautious and formalistic approaches often followed by Russian entities, particularly entities with strong governmental ties, have their roots in this psychological orientation. This mind-set helps explain why Russians often submit unquestioningly to authority and are reluctant to challenge or appeal to governmental authorities. Accordingly, an American may need to encourage his Russian joint-venture partner to be a more aggressive advocate in negotiations with the Russian authorities for necessary governmental approvals.

Another vestige of the Soviet totalitarian system is the Russians' reluctance to resolve disputes by consensus. Russian organizations have exemplified to an extreme degree the principle of one-man rule. The general director of a Russian enterprise is the supreme authority. The delegation of authority is uneven and tends to occur only when the general director is absent. Moreover, Russians generally fall into two categories: those who give orders and those who receive and implement them. One of the key reasons for the difficulties in resolving the fundamental political disputes that exist today over questions of authority in Russia is that those people who customarily gave orders in the Soviet society have been deprived of much of that authority (or at least the means to enforce their authority) and those who customarily received and implemented orders have been given more authority to make decisions. Neither group is accustomed to the roles in which they find themselves, and it is likely to be some time before Russian business people develop skills in resolving disputes by consensus and in handling obligations that require both submission to authority and the exercise of responsibility.

In part because of the historical decision that cut off the Russian people from access to foreign influences, Russians have been suspicious and often resentful of foreigners operating in their country. The latest manifestation of this tendency toward xenophobia is the allegation raised by certain "hard-line" politicians and media that foreigners are seeking to "steal" Russian assets by paying low prices. There has also been criticism of efforts by western natural resource companies to acquire control over key Russian natural resources, such as oil and gas reserves, timber, and precious metals. Moreover, some unscrupulous western businesspeople have invaded Russia in the hopes of earning a fast buck, a particularly unfortunate development since it feeds the already existing antiforeign sentiment among Russian hard-liners.

It is important to note that in many cases the values and practices of today's new Russian business class are rooted in the "business culture" of the former Soviet system. The business experience of a number of Russians was shaped in the black market in the old Soviet Union where private business transactions were largely outlawed. In many cases, these individuals learned to survive and succeed by avoiding the law at all costs. Others were former Communist Party officials whose status allowed them to operate above the law and in disregard of the rights of others. However, in addition to these individuals, there is also a group of new Russian entrepreneurs who appear to be promising business partners, but limited in commercial experience.

Finally, several other observations about Russians' negotiating style are worth mentioning. Russians appear to be tough negotiators, viewing negotiation as a win/lose situation and compromise as a sign of weakness. Profit-maximization consequently assumes much less prominence than in the American negotiation process, as the Russian negotiator seeks to win a point, rather than enlarge the total gain of each party. In addition, because the goal of a Russian negotiation is not to consummate an isolated transaction, but to foster a long-term relationship, a Russian negotiator may seek to prolong and make difficult a negotiation to "test" his counterpart, believing that if the American can survive the negotiation process, a long-term relationship will be strong enough to withstand setbacks. Indeed, it is because of the Russian's emphasis on relationship building that the success of initial contracts with Russians is critical, paving the way for long-term mutually beneficial relationships.

. . . .

Japan

In conducting negotiations with Japanese parties, it is critical to appreciate the significance of the relationship between the parties. The relationship, not the contract, is viewed by the Japanese as the end goal of any negotiation. Consequently, negotiations can be expected to take longer than they would in dealing with an American entity and to proceed at a slower pace while the parties come to know and trust each other. Moreover, from the Japanese perspective, the specific terms of a contract are subordinated to the need to create a long-term relationship that will consistently benefit the Japanese party and not always its foreign counterpart. Rather than building upon specific terms, contract negotiations in Japan tend to begin with a general approach. Preparing an opening statement that purports to evince an intent to foster a mutually beneficial long-term relationship is a critical part of preparing for negotiations, but the American negotiator must always realize that the Japanese party will be acting primarily in its own self-interest.

Also characteristic of the negotiation process in Japan is the emphasis on consensus building. It is because of the importance of consensus building that Japanese negotiating teams may often be comprised of as many as fifteen or more members. If the negotiation is to succeed, agreement usually must be reached with all of them. Naturally, this takes time. In addition, because this consensus-building approach is mirrored in the corporation from which the representatives are sent to negotiate, any counter-proposals made in response to suggestions by the Japanese team may require the Japanese to return to their company and gain consensus there for the new proposal. Once consensus on a proposal has been reached within a Japanese organization, it is difficult and time-consuming to alter the proposal. A successful result requires not only patience, for the new proposal will have to be routed through the organization again, but also an awareness of the Japanese organization's needs and desires. Only a proposal that furthers the Japanese interests will succeed; important in assessing these interests is an awareness of the significance to the Japanese firm of reputation and standing within the business community.

It is often noted that Japanese are indirect in their means of communication. This has been linked to the Japanese desire to avoid confrontation and preserve respect. By not committing to one position, the Japanese businessperson can reverse his or her position if a superior demands a reversal, without sacrificing what appears to be the American party's respect. American negotiators are therefore wise to permit their Japanese counterparts leeway to reverse themselves without losing face. Also, it is often the Japanese practice not to have the individuals with ultimate authority participate in a negotiation, and Japanese negotiators' indirectness may well be a result of their lack of authority to make final decisions. Finally, indirectness is another product of the consensus-building style noted above. By offering what seem to be vague responses to proposals, Japanese negotiators permit their colleagues, as well as the other party, an opportunity to fully participate in the decision-making process. American directness of approach can be out of place in this environment and attention to conduct, as well as words, is critical; for example, long periods of silence are common, indicating contemplation rather than evasiveness, and should not be interrupted with a barrage of explanations or suggestions. When nuances of language are important, an interpreter is essential.

Related to the Japanese tendency to be indirect is an aversion to say "no" directly, probably animated by a desire to promote harmony and a long-term relationship. However, inactivity, a suggestion for alternatives or of weaknesses in the proposal offered, as well as a simple failure to draw up a suggested proposal, all probably mean "no."

Also important to the Japanese is an emphasis on long-term, rather than short-term, gain. Their cooperative style of negotiating means that in realizing this gain, they will attempt to maximize profit for all parties: a win/win approach. Renegotiation of contracts is not unusual if circumstances change, and some recommend a contract review every two to three years.

In Japan (as in China) small courtesies and gifts are appropriate and in many cases expected among negotiating parties. Formality is also important to the Japanese. Nonetheless, the parties will frequently get to know each other during social activities, paving the way for a relationship of trust and understanding between them.

American firms beginning a relationship with the Japanese are advised to be cautious. Information assumed by an American party to be proprietary, or even characterized as such, may be freely disclosed by a Japanese party with whom the American has entered a joint-venture agreement. Likewise, selective enforcement of regulations has been observed to occur to the detriment of American firms doing business in Japan. Forging long-term and ongoing relationships with both private entities and governmental authorities in Japan can be important in avoiding or mitigating these types of problems.

Brazil

In their communication style, Brazilians are more subtle than Americans, though not so indirect as the Japanese. One attorney tells of assisting with the negotiation of a joint venture between a Brazilian company and a Japanese company. The Brazilian company made a simple request of the Japanese company. The Japanese company sent a voluminous telex in response. The Brazilian company could not decipher it and, referring it to a Japanese employee of the Brazilian company, asked if he understood what it meant. After spending several minutes perusing the lengthy document, the Japanese employee responded, "It says no." Thus, while the Brazilian should be expected to be less direct than the American during negotiations, he will likely be less difficult for the American to understand than a Japanese party. Indeed, one business study reports that relative to both Japanese and Americans, a Brazilian more often says "no" in disagreeing with a point made by his negotiating counterpart.

In keeping with their tendency to express disagreement outright, Brazilians are regarded as tough negotiators. For example, Brazilians have been observed to make fewer promises and commitments and more demands than their American counterparts; they may often make more overreaching first offers, demanding more profits at the outset. They are also known, however, to make higher initial concessions. One study suggests that a party who is more difficult to size up may be more successful in negotiating with a Brazilian.

The Brazilian negotiating style is also less linear, and may create an impression of disorder to the American. A Brazilian may jump from point to point during a negotiation, and return to points that his or her American counterpart might have thought had previously been resolved. This can be particularly disconcerting when it occurs just prior to the scheduled closing of a transaction.

In many cases, Brazilians appear to devote less effort to preparation for a negotiation than Americans. They do not seem to be as sensitive to time constraints and may be less inclined to read successive drafts of a document. Rather, they focus on the final draft and may not propose changes until after reading it. Contributing to this tendency of many last-minute changes is the fact that principals will often be involved only in the decision to make a deal and at the closing of the deal, rather than in the negotiation process. For example, one lawyer recalls a representative from a U.S. company flying to New York to sign a closing document for a transaction with a Brazilian company. Successive drafts of the document had been negotiated, and the final draft sent to the Brazilian company in advance of the meeting. Nonetheless, the principal from the Brazilian entity began reading the final document on the day it was to be signed, and consequently, the closing had to be put off, and the other party's stay extended, until the Brazilian principal's comments had been discussed.

The Brazilians, more than their Japanese counterparts, place emphasis on the written contract but are less likely to be as focused on detail as Americans. This less detail-oriented style is reflected by the Brazilian concept of *jeito*, which, roughly translated, means an improvised solution. Rather than anticipate every contingency, the Brazilians prefer to resolve problems as they arise (an attitude that may be rooted in the unpredictability of the Brazilian political and economic systems). Since noncompliance with the law is likely to have less draconian consequences in Brazil than in America, there is more of a "fix-it-later" attitude among Brazilian negotiators than among their counterparts in the United States, where legal repercussions are usually considered in advance.

This improvisational attitude, however, should not be interpreted to mean that Brazilians do not intend to be bound by the written document. Brazilians are less familiar with the letter of intent as a nonbinding document, and, therefore, may be reluctant to sign it for fear of its binding effect. One solution to this problem may be to take minutes of initial meetings that can then later be referred to or to prepare a list of terms that does not require the parties' signatures.

Also not to be overlooked is the backlogged bureaucracy in Brazil. Discretionary government approval is often necessary, and time should be allowed for it to be obtained. Because local politics may often be involved in obtaining the best incentives for a particular transaction, it may be prudent to establish relationships with local consultants who can expedite government processing and who have political access to assist in obtaining such incentives. Brazilian negotiators are less formal than their counterparts in many other countries, but probably not as informal as Americans. Social activities and entertainment are critical to the parties' getting to know each other, and in cementing business relationships. It is not uncommon for an American executive and spouse, at the conclusion of a transaction, to visit the Brazilian counterpart's home.

China

As with the Japanese, the goal of negotiations for the Chinese is to build a long-term relationship. The American "time is money and let's get down to business" approach does not sit well with the Chinese, and ample time should be allowed to form a relationship with the Chinese party. Americans should also be aware that in entering a relationship with a Chinese party, they will be expected to grant favors and confer material benefits over the long term. Chinese view the relation as one of interdependency, rather than (as Americans are wont to do) of complementary interests.

Many people are involved in decision making within a Chinese organization. Moreover, most business transactions with foreign parties require approval from a Chinese governmental body, so the number of people involved in the decision-making process extends beyond the personnel within the Chinese organization negotiating the transaction. Time must be permitted for everyone involved (many of whom will not be present at the negotiating table) to consider an American party's proposal before acceptance or rejection will be indicated. Pressure for closure may destroy a deal, particularly where the Chinese party perceives that he or she will lose face with the American by failing to respond, or lose face with superiors for making promises that cannot be kept if they reject the deal.

Also important to the Chinese is the emphasis on societal or collective gain. Indeed, whereas American parties focus on profit maximization (a private goal), the Chinese negotiator is frequently required to seek to benefit the state in negotiating transactions. They often begin negotiations with a statement of broad principles that may appear to an American as a litany of platitudes and euphemisms. In fact, such broad principles are imposed on the Chinese negotiator by the Chinese government's approval authority and reflect national goals. These principles will influence the substantive terms of the negotiation. The Chinese will rigidly adhere to these principles, once they are accepted by the American party, who frequently has no statement of goals to offer the Chinese party, and, by his or her silence, indicates assent to the Chinese principles. The American negotiator will find the Chinese party reluctant to compromise and trade for fear of deviating from these principles.

In keeping with their focus both on relationship building and on the statement of principles, Chinese normally prefer to proceed from general principles in performing their obligations to another party, rather than from the terms of a detailed written contract. As a result, they are not accustomed to the American focus on detail, and patience will be important in working out the details of the transaction.

In addition to patience during the negotiation process, American negotiators should at all times maintain a consistent position with their Chinese counterparts. Too frequently American negotiators modify their proposals during the negotiating process in order to encourage the Chinese side to respond favorably. Since the cause of the Chinese failure to respond is most often that a decision maker has been unavailable to approve the original proposal, the revised proposal (by appearing more attractive) causes the Chinese side to become even more cautious, since it is now obvious that the first proposal was not the best proposal. To avoid this unfavorable result, American negotiators should generally maintain the original proposal offered until such time as the Chinese side provides specific comments on the proposal.

Unless restrained by the terms of a written agreement, the Chinese may appropriate and disseminate what is viewed by an American party as confidential information; in China, trade secrets enjoy no special protection and Chinese are so used to sharing information that technical know-how or expertise simply is not regarded as proprietary. Consequently, caution—and the clear communication that certain information shared with a Chinese party is expected not to go farther—are important, especially in the context of a joint venture, or any transaction involving the transfer of technology.

When an American desires to communicate scientific or technological information, China's relative inexperience with technical matters is a handicap; careful explanations and translation are important to communicate technical know-how. This inexperience is exacerbated by the fact that often members of a negotiating team, or even the person with ultimate authority over the terms of a transaction, attain their positions not because of technical knowledge or competence, but because of social and political prominence. Consequently, it is important to communicate fully and provide explanations where needed of technical information. It is also important to be aware that while the "boss" of an American party may have the technical competence to make decisions, his or her Chinese counterpart, before making a decision, will frequently need to consult with more junior advisors who have such expertise.

China's past, which spans over four thousand years, is a source of considerable pride and great importance to the Chinese, and an American negotiator should be familiar with Chinese history before beginning a negotiation. This familiarity will denote respect to the Chinese party and confer status upon the American.

Arab Countries

The Muslim religion has a major impact on negotiations conducted in the Arab world. For example, in the more religious countries, such as Saudi Arabia, the work week begins on Saturday and ends on Thursday morning, so that there is time for observance of the Sabbath on Friday. Many businesses close, and negotiations are interrupted, so that the official prayer times, which occur five times a day, may be observed. During the month of Ramadan, many businesses are closed during the day and open only after sunset. Finally, women's ability to engage in business is severely restricted by both religious and social proscriptions in the more conservative Arab nations.

A large part of the law in some Arab countries is grounded in religion, and some aspects of this law will naturally affect the terms of negotiations. For example, the primary law of Saudi Arabia is the Shari'a, which is derived from the Muslim scripture, the Koran. While regulations are increasingly being adopted to supplement the Shari'a, there is no comprehensive civil and commercial code system in Saudi Arabia. Because the Koran prohibits the charging of interest, investments in Saudi Arabia are often structured to provide for a payout of a share of the profits. Likewise, the absence of any statute of limitations in the Shari'a requires that claim cutoff periods be dealt with as a matter of contract.

The Arabs have a well-deserved reputation as tough and able negotiators. As many Americans who have worked in the region are aware, Gulf countries like Kuwait and the United Arab Emirates, located at the crossroads of historic East-West trade routes, are well experienced in international trade and negotiations. During skillfully orchestrated negotiations, many Arabs adopt win/lose strategies, and may effectively use time delays and competing offers to their advantage. An Arab buyer may invite several competitors to be available for negotiations at the same time, and conduct a series of separate negotiations with each until the best deal has been reached.

As important, and perhaps even more important, to the Arabs as to the Chinese and Japanese is the nature of the personal relationships that are formed during negotiations. It is considered an affront to proceed immediately to negotiations in the Arab world. The parties first socialize. During negotiations, the Arab's sense of connectedness with all those in the community may mean negotiations are frequently interrupted by visits and phone calls. Arabs expect Americans to understand that these interruptions are not rude, but, rather, that to refuse those who call upon them be.

The Arab's emphasis upon personal relationships may also be due to a relative lack of technical expertise. Though they may frequently rely on lawyers and technical experts, Arabs are adept at using an intuitive grasp of their negotiating partners' personalities to their advantage. Time is needed for Arabs to come to know the individuals with whom they negotiate so that their honesty may be gauged.

Because many Arab countries have strong ties to the United States — and because of their familiarity with oil industry practice — Arabs are often comfortable with long-form transactional documents common in the American and English legal worlds. At least one government owned entity in Saudi Arabia has used resident lawyers seconded from a prominent U.S. law firm to aid it in negotiating transactions.

Like the Japanese, the Arabs are indirect and may be difficult to read. They do not enjoy confrontation and it may be hard to decipher when they are saying "no." They are demanding and cautious, perhaps because of bad experience with foreign suppliers, and may insist on onerous penalties and guarantees to ensure performance. Americans negotiating in the Arab world should expect to assume greater contractual risks, unless they have developed a relationship with or demonstrated a history of reliable performance to their Arab counterpart.

Finally, the boycott regulations of the League of Arab States, which restrict trade activities with Israel and with firms doing business with Israel, illustrate how deeply cultural, political, and legal issues are interconnected within the Arab world. In preparing for negotiations with an Arab party, American negotiators should be prepared to deal with these boycott regulations, both from the Arab perspective and the perspective of U.S. anti-boycott legislation. [The Arab boycott and United States anti-boycott legislation are discussed later in this Casebook.]

. . . .

QUESTIONS

1.   As discussed in the excerpt above from Professor Fox's book, *International Commercial Agreements*, in their celebrated 1981 work, *Getting to Yes*, Roger Fisher and William Ury develop a theory of principled negotiation that calls for (1) separating the people from the problem, (2) focusing on interests, not positions, (3) inventing options for mutual gain, (4) using objective criteria, and (5) understanding the best alternative to a negotiated agreement, or BATNA. However, what happens if the other side in a negotiation will not engage in a principled negotiation?

2.   In an international business negotiation, what considerations are relevant in deciding whether the American investor's counsel or counsel to the foreign counterparty should produce the first (and possibly subsequent) drafts of the agreement? In other words, should the American investor's counsel walk into the first negotiating session and present a draft to her counterparty?

3.   You are counsel to a party in an FDI deal, and the other side presents you with a draft agreement at the start of negotiations. How might you respond to this opening gambit?

III. Types of FDI

NOTE ON THE TYPES OF FDI*

Introduction

Although investors may accomplish FDI in various ways, this note concentrates on the major forms of choice in today's global marketplace. There are five principle

---

* This Note was prepared by Christopher C. Matteson, Esq.

ways in which an international business lawyer and her client in one country, the "home" (or "source") country, can structure an investment in another country, the "host" (or "target") country. The forms are: (1) *"greenfield" or de novo* investments, where an investor seeds with capital a new and distinct corporate entity in the host country; (2) *franchising*, where the investor opens an operation similar to another in the source or other country, with standardized commercial marks, procedures, and goals; (3) *mergers and acquisitions*, where a company in the host country is purchased directly or joins with that of the investor; (4) *joint ventures*, where a company in the host country and the investor embark upon a combined commercial operation; and (5) *distributorships*, where the investor institutes a network, or harnesses an existing one, to market, distribute, and sell its product or service. Each of these forms is discussed in turn below.

There exists, of course, a myriad of possible hybrids of these five forms. In addition, some observers classify an overseas branch of a corporation as a form of FDI, although as a general corporate law matter a branch is not a separate entity from its parent. In effect, a branch is a "corporate face" manifest through a desk or office, with little or no distributional or other operational network, and very little commitment by the parent. It should be noted that Section 403 of the *Restatement (Third) of the Foreign Relations Law of the United States* indicates that it is easier for the United States government to exert extraterritorial jurisdiction over an overseas branch of an American corporation, in part because a branch is part and parcel of the home company.

1. Form #1: "Greenfield" or *De Novo* Investment

"Greenfield" or *de novo* foreign investment, as the name implies, involves the creation of a legal entity in the host country under host country corporation or company law. For purposes of this Note, discussion focuses on incorporation of a new entity—a subsidiary, for example—under the local laws of the host country. The procedures and implications of incorporating under United States law will serve as a measure by which to compare the incorporation laws and procedures of a sample host country, in this case, Japan. Although the incorporated entity in the host nation may be a completely separate and free-standing business operation, it also may be a subsidiary of the investor, or any of a variety of business forms.

a. United States Corporation Law

First, it is necessary to define a corporation. "A corporation is an entity that consists of an intangible structure for the conduct of the entity's affairs and operations, the essence of which is created by the state, and that possesses the rights and obligations more or less parallel those of natural persons."[1] The Model Business Corporation Act (MBCA) sets forth the incorporation laws adopted in many American states. It serves as an ample representative of the various corporation statutes, and is a good benchmark for comparison of the incorporation environments in other nations.

(1) Advantages of the Corporate Form

The corporation usually is chosen over other business forms, and essentially, there are five reasons for this fact: (1) limited liability of shareholders; (2) structure of management; (3) structure of capital, (4) status as a separate entity; and (5) commonality and magnitude of use as a business form.

---

1. MODEL BUS. CORP. ACT.

1st — Limited Liability

Limited liability of shareholders, under United States corporation law, is often the most important advantage of incorporation. Limited liability provides the investor, who may or may not have any control over the operations of the corporation, with protection from potential liability for the acts or omissions by the company. This creates, therefore, an incentive to invest in operations that may require large amounts of capital, therefore providing "fuel" for growth, innovation, and risk-taking. One practitioner's even states that "[t]he nineteenth century industrial revolution could not have advanced significantly without the availability of massive amounts of capital, which investors would not have provided without the guarantee of limited liability."[2] Incorporation as a business form allows the investor to have a greater ability to raise capital.

2nd — Management Structure

The second advantage, management structure, is useful and has evolved over time. Further, the corporation statutes generally provide that a business may alter the management structure to meet unusual needs. Traditional corporate structure is made up as follows: Shareholders elect the directors and approve certain corporate activities out of the normal course. The directors elect officers and manage the corporation, and the officers are able to manage the corporation as they see fit, within the bounds of the powers defined for them by the directors. This structure is helpful in that it allows the directors to vary the amount of power delegated to the officers. Further, it allows the shareholders to have some input as well. Section 35 of the MBCA (pre-1984 version) contains a provision allowing for variations in the degree of control held by each level of management. In practice, however, few actually deviate from the traditional structure other than some closely held corporations.

3rd — Capital Structure

The third advantage, capital structure, is present in that it is variable according to the corporation's needs. For instance, a simple capital structure might be to have the sole ownership interest in the corporation be all common stock. The variations on this simple structure can be almost infinite. One possibility is having both common and preferred stock with the ownership interest split between the two. Another possibility is to have a similar structure, but with various promissory notes, bonds, and debentures issued, all with a different degree of convertibility. "In the usual situation...a full range of permutations in capital structure is already in existence and well known to corporate lawyers, so that the need for the creation of a unique structure is available 'off the shelf.'"[3]

4th — Separate Entity

The fourth advantage, the corporation's status as a separate entity, creates advantages in two ways. First, the death of an equity owner has no effect on the existence of the corporation. Secondly, a shareholder may pass on the ownership interest to an heir as personal property, without the complexities of probating the interests in each state where the deceased owns property. This allows for the corporation to exist in a desired status after the owner dies, allowing for the formation of long-term obligations, contracts, and debt.

---

2. LARRY D. SODERQUIST & A.A. SOMMER, JR., UNDERSTANDING CORPORATION LAW 51 (1990).
3. SODERQUIST & SOMMER, *supra*, at 54.

5th — Use

The final advantage, the frequent usage of the corporation as a business form, is important. Complex business forms may require unique procedures for simple tasks, including leasing real property or equipment, borrowing funds from a bank, or entering into contracts. Corporations are very common, and are frequently encountered in these types of situations, making transactions somewhat routine. "Those on the other side of the transaction are used to dealing with corporations and are familiar with how documents are signed on behalf of corporations. With other forms of business, save perhaps the partnership, that is usually not the case."[4]

(2) Disadvantages of the Corporate Form

There are a few disadvantages, however, of the corporation as a business mode, particularly the expense and complexity of incorporation, required formalities for maintaining the corporation, and potential taxation problems.

1st — Costs

Formation can be costly, in terms of time and money. It entails various complexities and formalities. The drafter of the articles of incorporation needs to construct the articles in accordance with the laws of the state and file them with the proper authorities. Corporate bylaws are required, and must be drafted as well. Requirements for annual reports, legal and accounting fees, and other costs are incurred, making the formation and maintenance of a corporation a potentially costly process.

Continuing formalities are required for the operation of a corporation. For example, meetings must be conducted, or written consent for action must be received. Further, the accounting records and meeting minutes must be maintained, and the funds of the owner/shareholders may not be mixed with those of the corporation. Failure to satisfy the formalities may result in a court disregarding the corporate form and allowing creditors to collect from the owner/shareholders, or "piercing the corporate veil."[5]

2nd — Double Taxation

A second disadvantage is double taxation. The earnings of the corporation are taxed once at the corporate level, and then once again as earnings are distributed to the shareholders. Although, at times, this can be avoided, "the fact that [double taxation] exists as a possibility and that corporate managers must devote efforts to avoiding it makes double taxation a clear disadvantage of operating in the corporate form.

(3) Incorporation in the United States Under Model Business Corporation Act

The process of incorporation in the United States has been improved upon and simplified from its earlier condition in the era prior to the inception of the MBCA.[6] The incorporation process is covered in Sections 2.01 through Section 2.07 of the

---

4. SODERQUIST & SOMMER, *supra*, at 57.

5. SODERQUIST & SOMMER, *supra*, at 59.

6. *See* SODERQUIST & SOMMER, *supra*, at 74 (comparing incorporation laws in force prior to the MBCA, noting their complexity and the occasional confusion as to when the corporation actually came into existence).

MBCA. Section 2.01 states that "[o]ne or more persons may act as the incorporator or incorporators of a corporation by delivering articles of incorporation to the secretary of state for filing."[7] The official commentary states that the only functions of incorporators are to sign the articles of incorporation, deliver them to the appropriate office, and complete the formation of the corporation as stipulated in § 2.05 of the Act. The Model Act simplified the requirements for execution and filing by eliminating the previous requirement that the articles be acknowledged and verified, and in duplicate originals. The current form requires only that the incorporator(s) submit a signed original and an "exact or confirmed copy".[8]

The articles of incorporation, set forth in Section 2.02 of the MBCA, must enumerate three requirements. First, a corporate name must be selected.[9] Second, the number of shares that the corporation is authorized to issue;[10] and lastly, the street address of the corporation's office and the name of the corporation's registered agent must be listed. The MBCA only requires that the drafter furnish this information in the articles.

Subsection (b), however, sets forth optional categories of information that may be included in the articles.[11] Under the optional information that the drafter may include in the articles are a number of specifics, including naming the initial directors, stating a purpose for and duration of the corporation, par value for the shares, shareholder and director liability, corporate powers, and indemnification.[12] These provisions are relevant to the authority, directors and officers, and management of the internal affairs of the corporation.

The mandatory requirements are quite brief, while there is still room for the drafter to be specific as to purpose and other information. This distinction is important because a corporation formed in compliance with the mandatory requirements only will generally possess the "broadest powers and least restrictions on activities permitted by the [MBCA]. The [MBCA] thus permits the creation of a 'standard' corporation by a simple and easily prepared one-page document."[13] This is a simplification that has made much of American corporation law somewhat more "user friendly" than in the past.[14]

The process of incorporation in the United States can be relatively simple, as in the case of a close corporation that includes only the required information in its articles of incorporation. On the other hand, it can be complex, allowing the drafter of the articles to specifically enumerate, for example, the duration of the corporation's existence, the capitalization, purpose, and powers and liability of the directors and shareholders. Corporate practice requires know-how, a detail-oriented approach, and a prospective viewpoint on the part of counsel. When considering the corporation as a form of FDI, counsel will need to be capable of dealing with the technicalities, formalities, and have an understanding of the implications of choosing such a form of investment

---

7. MODEL BUS. CORP. ACT. § 2.01.

8. *See* MODEL BUS. CORP. ACT. official cmt. to § 2.01.

9. MODEL BUS. CORP. ACT. § 2.02(a)(1).

10. MODEL BUS. CORP. ACT. § 2.02(a)(2).

11. *See* MODEL BUS. CORP. ACT. official cmt. to § 2.02, at ¶ 1.

12. *See* MODEL BUS. CORP. ACT. § 2.02(b).

13. *See* MODEL BUS. CORP. ACT. § 2.02(b).

14. *See* Historical Background at ¶ 1, MODEL BUS. CORP. ACT. ANNOTATED § 2.02.

b. Greenfield or *De Novo* Investment in Japan[15]

Foreign direct investment in Japan serves as a good example for many reasons, among them are the following. First, it holds great potential for foreign investors, despite cyclic economic changes. "Japan is an important market because it provides a solid manufacturing base and a workforce capable of efficient production in high technology industries."[16] Secondly, foreign direct investment in Japan gives the foreign operation a presence in the economy there, allowing it to gauge consumer trends, better serve its market, and hopefully, achieve higher market share than if the investor had remained overseas.[17] Despite this potential, the idea of investing in Japan can be intimidating, likely because of cultural differences and the historically and presently low levels of foreign investment by foreign entities in Japan.[18] The Japanese government, however, likely would counter this assertion by indicating its efforts to encourage greater levels of FDI in Japan:

> Direct investment... not only contributes to the improvement of the Japanese economy and the internationalization of domestic business, but also serves as an effective stimulant to the economies of the counterpart nations.... [T]he Japan External Trade Organization (JETRO) established the Investment Promotion Division... the specific aim of which is to further promote direct investment between Japan and other nations.[19]

(1) Issues Involved

The Japanese government has taken special steps to encourage FDI in certain sectors. For example, Japan's Ministry of International Trade and Industry (MITI) will certify an investor as a "designated inward investor" if three conditions are met. First, the investment must be in the form of a branch or subsidiary, with a foreign capitalization rate of at least 33 percent. Secondly, the company must have been operating for less than five years since its initial establishment, and lastly, it must be engaged in the manufacturing, wholesale, retail, or services sector in Japan, and the parent company must be engaged in the software or manufacturing industry.

Establishing a *de novo* investment in Japan may be accomplished in many ways, but for purposes of example, this section will focus on the *Kabushiki Kaisha* ("KK"), or joint-stock company. This form is the most common, and is close to the American style of incorporation discussed above. The advantages of the KK are similar to those of the corporation in the U.S. (*i.e.* limited liability of shareholders, structure of management, status as a separate entity, and commonality and magnitude of use as a business form). Most significantly, the fact that the investors face only limited liability makes this form the most preferred for many foreign investors. "The most typical and widely used form by foreign investors in establishing a... company is a joint-stock company which has the merits of giving limited liability to investors and of allowing the participation of many to acquire stocks."[20]

---

15. This section draws significantly upon materials obtained through the kind assistance of the Japan External Trade Organization (JETRO) office in Richmond, Virginia.

16. Charles O. Roehrdanz, *Reducing the U.S. Trade Deficit by Eliminating Japanese Barriers to Foreign Direct Investment*, 4 MINN. J. GLOBAL TRADE 305, 308 (1995).

17. *See id.* at 308.

18. *See id.* at 305 (comparing the low levels FDI in Japan ($2.975 billion in 1993) versus the high levels of Japanese direct investment in the rest of the world ($32.604 billion in 1993).

19. SETTING UP A BUSINESS IN JAPAN: A GUIDE TO FOREIGN BUSINESSMEN 2 (JETRO, 1992).

20. SETTING UP A BUSINESS IN JAPAN, *supra*, at 16.

As is the case in the United States, this form of direct investment also has its disadvantages. Formalities, for example, must be completed. The incorporation must be done in accordance with the Commercial Code of Japan, including accounting procedures and auditing requirements. Further, the minimum capitalization requirement present in Japanese law makes it necessary for investors to place at least ¥ 10,000,000 as paid-in capital, with at least 25 percent paid in upon incorporation.[21] It has been suggested that this capitalization requirement and other formalities may encourage foreign investors to evaluate and use other forms to achieve entry into the Japanese economy.[22]

(2) Incorporation under Japanese Law

The process of establishing a KK through incorporating under the Commercial Code of Japan is relatively elaborate, when compared to the process set forth under the MBCA. In addition to searching for a similar corporate name, checking the necessity to obtain governmental permits, and confirming whether prior notification is required under the Japan's Foreign Exchange Law, the investor must consider other issues. These include: (1) corporate objectives, (2) capital, (3) preparation of a register of shareholders, (4) officers, (5) financial year, and (6) bank selection.[23]

The Commercial Code of Japan requires a greater degree of mandatory information in the articles of incorporation than does the MBCA. The "Compulsory Provisions" are items, "omission of which invalidates the articles of incorporation."[24] There are also "Principal Voluntary Provisions", which "will have effect against the corporation only when included in the articles of incorporation."[25] Finally, there are provisions which are deemed "Optional Provisions" under the Commercial Code, such as the number of directors and statutory auditors, date of the shareholders meeting, financial year, and procedures for registration of transfers of shares.

The articles of incorporation must list the objectives of the corporation, which must be stated as specifically as possible. This requirement may force the investor's hand into emphasizing one area of business, rather than allowing for a flexible approach, such as under the MBCA, which does not require that the purpose be stated expressly. As with United States law, the corporate name must be listed in the articles of incorporation, however it must be "expressed only in Japanese and Chinese characters and contain the word "*kabushiki kaisha*."[26] The drafter of the articles must list the total number of shares to be issued by the corporation, and if par-value shares are to be issued, the value of each must be at least ¥ 50,000.[27] Further, the total number of shares to be issued must be listed in the articles of incorporation, and at least one quarter of the total number of shares to be issued must be issued upon incorporation.

---

21. SETTING UP A BUSINESS IN JAPAN, *supra*, at 16.

22. For example, the *Yugen Kaisha*, or limited liability company, which operates under the Commercial Code with a paid-up capital requirement of only ¥ 3,000,000. The requirements for the number of directors, auditors, and procedures for establishment of the YK are "not so strict that it is unsuitable for small and medium size business operation." *See* SETTING UP A BUSINESS IN JAPAN, *supra*, at 14.

23. *See* JETRO, SETTING UP A BUSINESS IN JAPAN 206-14 (TMI Associates, Shimazaki International Law Office, Chuo Coopers & Lybrand International Tax Office eds., 1992).

24. *See* SETTING UP ENTERPRISES, *supra*, at 220.

25. *See id.*

26. *See id.*

27. *See id.* The concept of par value is also present in United States corporation law, although capitalization is not a required piece of information under the post 1984 version of the MBCA.

Finally, the drafter must include the location of the head office, the method of public notice, and the names and addresses of the promoters.

Under the "Principal Voluntary Provisions," more general guidance is provided. Among the information that may be included under this category are provisions relating to anomalous or nonstandard incorporation, such as special benefits to be enjoyed by the promoters, assets to be transferred to the corporation upon formation, amount of remuneration to accrue to the promoters, alteration of the voting rights of the shareholders, restrictions on share transfers, and expenses of incorporation. It should be noted, however, that if this type of information is provided, then special procedures are required:

> The above provisions are called "anomalous provisions", and will have effect against the incorporated corporation only when included in the articles.... When such anomalous provisions are included in the articles...inspection by examiners appointed by the court is required, except in certain cases relating to contribution in kind and undertakings of assets transfers. Because such inspection is a time-consuming procedure, it may be preferable to avoid anomalous incorporation in cases where rapid incorporation is desired.[28]

Thus, adherence to the basic "boilerplate" type of incorporation process is advised for reasons of time and expense.

(3) Legal Barriers to Entry

Incorporation by foreign entities also invokes reporting requirements. Under Japan's Foreign Exchange Law, foreign investors must file a report after, and sometimes prior to, the incorporation if: (1) the foreign investor establishes a legal entity in Japan, and (2) the investor intends to acquire stocks or equity in the corporation. If the acquisition requires a prior notification, then the investor must file a report of the acquisition through the Bank of Japan, and the reports must be filed by an attorney-in-fact who is a resident of Japan.[29] One of the directors must be a resident of Japan, and the incorporation must be registered by a representative director with the Bureau of Legal Affairs before the commencement of business in Japan. Naturally, the resident of Japan might serve as this representative.

It is often argued and widely perceived that there are substantial barriers to foreign direct investment in Japan.[30] These barriers are both formal barriers created by the government of Japan, and informal ones that may be social, cultural, or systemic in nature.

An example of a formal barrier that exists in Japan is the required consultation with the Ministry of Finance and the Bank of Japan. This consultation may often give Japanese industry sectors that may be threatened by the investment a "tip-off" and a subsequent chance to oppose the merger, acquisition, or other investment because of a high degree of cross-shareholding.[31] The foreign investment laws in Japan also allow the government to restrict investment, importation of technology, and operations in some industries, which may threaten national security, public order, or the "smooth functioning of the Japanese economy."[32]

---

28. *See* Setting Up Enterprises, *supra*, at 220.
29. *See* Setting Up a Business, *supra*, at 16.
30. *See, e.g.*, Roehrdanz, *supra*.
31. *See, e.g.*, Roehrdanz, *supra*, at 311 (describing the phenomenon of cross-shareholding among Japanese companies, which can allow shareholders to prevent acquisition of Japanese enterprises by foreign entities).
32. Roehrdanz, *supra*, at 311.

A good example of an informal barrier is the culture of Japan and its homogeneity:

> Whereas takeovers of businesses and corporations by foreigners are commonplace in the United States, they are rare in Japan. In Japan, the corporation is a kind of family, and the employees are a part of that family. When a foreigner (*gaijin*) purchases the corporation, it is seen as a sign of weakness, and the "family" is disgraced. The loyalty of Japanese employees to their companies even interferes with friendly mergers. These cultural phenomena demonstrate xenophobia with respect to foreign direct investment in Japan.[33]

Despite the difficulties, Japan can be an excellent prospect as a host country for FDI, if the investor is willing to adhere to the legal and regulatory scheme created for FDI, and to take note of cultural factors when making the investment.

2. Form #2: International Franchising[34]

Franchising involves "a license from [the] owner of a trademark or trade name permitting another to sell a product or service under that name or mark."[35] In a more general sense, franchising "has evolved into an elaborate agreement under which the franchisee undertakes to conduct business or sell a product or service in accordance with methods and procedures prescribed by the franchisor, and the franchisor undertakes to assist the franchisee through advertising, promotion and other advisory services."[36]

The prevalence of franchises as a commercial presence in global commerce is evident to many who have traveled abroad. From fast food restaurant chains and soft drink bottling operations, to well known retail stores, successful franchise relationships have been created around the world.

> If we look at the world in 1964 and compare it with the world we have now so far as franchising is concerned, there has been an amazing transformation. Perhaps because of the nature of franchising, and the growth which can be achieved, its impact on the market place has been significant.

Franchising is present in more countries around the world than we realize. Certainly, the figure of 120 countries would not understate the situation.[37]

a. Risks and Benefits

International franchising is subject to all of the risks and benefits associated with any form of FDI. Risks, such as currency and market fluctuations, expropriation and political instability, and lack of appeal to the product itself are balanced against the benefits, namely increases in sales, revenue, and diversification into the global marketplace. Expanding a business specifically through franchising overseas has numerous advantages, including expansion of the trademark, product name, or identity,

---

33. Roehrdanz, *supra*, at 314 (citations omitted) (emphasis original).

34. This section draws upon RALPH H. FOLSOM & MICHAEL W. GORDON, INTERNATIONAL BUSINESS TRANSACTIONS ch. 18 (1995). For an excellent introduction to the many issues encountered in an international franchise relationship, consult the collection of articles regarding international franchising published in 25 INT'L BUS. LAW. 193 (May 1997).

35. BLACK'S LAW DICTIONARY 658 (6th ed. 1990).

36. BLACK'S LAW DICTIONARY at 658 (6th ed. 1990) (*citing H & R Block v. Lovelace*, 208 Kan. 538 (1972)).

37. Martin Mendelsohn, *International Franchising Over 30 Years*, 25 INT'L BUS. LAW. 197 (May 1997).

greater coverage in overseas consumer markets, and increased income through franchise fees, supply agreements, or operating revenues. Franchising in the developing world—and, indeed, other host countries—allows the franchisor to capitalize on the popularity of American products abroad.

The latter of these advantages is described well in the following observation.

[T]he attraction is even bigger than money, says James Watson, anthropology professor at Harvard University, who has been visiting China since the end of the Cultural Revolution. "The Chinese want the American lifestyle, a modern lifestyle, the way they think Americans live."

. . . .

And why not? After half a century of isolation under the Communist Party, the Chinese are desperate to catch up. "Chinese, young and old, are tired of political movements," says a Western correspondent in Beijing. The American Dream may be frayed at the edges, he adds, but Chinese still want all the amenities associated with it: a car, a house filled with appliances, in short, the good life. "America represents an ideal in China," says King Lai, CEO of Saatchi & Saatchi Advertising China. "For the Chinese, it's the lifestyle that they aspire to, the spirit of America."[38]

The appeal of American products and the element of lifestyle identification they carry is an obvious benefit to international business lawyers and their clients who seek to expand into many markets, such as China and Eastern Europe. For better or worse, it seems to be a fact of 21st century life, that much of the world aspires to consume such notable American name- brand products as Levi's jeans, Timberland shoes, Dallas Cowboy t-shirts, Timex ironman watches, John Grisham novels, Sylvester Stallone movies, National Basketball Association games, Janet Jackson's compact discs — and, of course, McDonald's hamburgers and Pepsi.

However, American culture does not sell well to everyone in all markets. There are many people who prefer *haute culture* to Americana, and thus choose Albert Camus over John Grisham, soccer over pro basketball, Edith Piaf over Janet Jackson, and Perrier over Pepsi. Examples provided by high-profile, but somewhat less-than-successful, ventures like Euro Disneyland should be a poignant reminder to international business lawyers and their clients who perceive that franchising to sell "all things American" overseas is a "sure bet" success. Consider these cautionary words:

Not all American companies agree with the ["America is best"] thesis. In fact, many shy away from highlighting any U.S. association. Both Nike and Coca-Cola present themselves as global, rather than U.S., brands. "Overt American advertising is a recipe for disaster," warns Soames Hines, managing director of advertising agency J. Walter Thompson in Shanghai. "Being American carries baggage...It's much better to position yourself as an *international* brand."[39]

Consequently, counsel to an investor seeking to franchise abroad should consider the cultural and language aspects of the host country. "For example, the appearance of a franchise building or trademark symbol may conflict in a foreign setting with tradi-

---

38. Ron Gluckman, *THE AMERICANIZATION OF CHINA: Forget Politics: U.S. Culture has Invaded the Mainland and the Chinese will Never Be the Same,* Asia Week, July 4, 1997, *available in* Westlaw, ASIAWK database, doc. no. 1997 WL 10819924.

39. Gluckman, *supra* (emphasis added).

tional architectural forms (such as in European cities) or nationalist feelings hostile to the appearance of foreign trademarks on franchised products (such as in India or Mexico)."[40] With respect to language issues, recall the oft-mentioned example of the Chevrolet Nova in Spanish-speaking nations: "*no va*" carries the meaning, "doesn't go." One experienced practitioner states that "...not every society, and not every business, is a candidate for cultural transplant. Lawyers are not equally essential everywhere. What one experiences in other businesses can be applied to franchising. America is not the fount of all wisdom. And appearances can be deceiving."[41] Clearly, counsel should consider these issues, as cultural and language conflicts can severely hamper the franchisor in his or her attempt to succeed in the global marketplace.

One other important issue involved in international franchising worth mentioning is the applicability of U.S. franchising laws, such as the FTC Franchise Rule—requiring, *inter alia*, that the franchisor supply an offering circular to prospective franchisees. The offering circular must contain the terms of the agreements to be used and other specific information. State laws also may come into play, as some states require that the circular be registered with the state government as well. The applicability of U.S. franchising law in the global marketplace is a difficult issue, one which is beyond the scope of treatment in this context. Suffice it to say that the determination of applicability of the U.S. laws and compliance therewith is an important issue to counsel assisting U.S. overseas investors in the franchising sphere.[42]

b. Specific Concerns

Any international franchising agreement needs to address a number of issues. Provisions relating to fees and royalties, training, the term of the relationship, and termination should be included in the agreement. Also, it may require provisions that relate to tax, antitrust, intellectual property, and licensing issues. While international franchising agreements require a special approach, it is emphasized that the agreement, and indeed the relationship that it formalizes, should not alter the franchisor's "successful business formula."[43]

Of the major concerns associated with international franchising agreements, there are three that deserve special mention in this context. Counsel to an investor should not overlook the range of issues that stem from intellectual property protections, quality controls, and host country regulations in the franchising context.

(1) Intellectual Property

There are two basic concerns with respect to intellectual property issues. First, will the host country have regulations to protect trademarks, copyrights, and trade secrets of the franchisor; and secondly, how should intellectual property protections be incorporated into the franchise agreement?

Most countries provide some protection to trademarks, whether through common law or a statutory scheme. This generally will involve trademark registration in each host country where the investor seeks to establish a franchise. "Roughly 40,000 trademarks applications are filed each year by United States citizens with the appro-

---

40. FOLSOM & GORDON, *supra*, at 687.

41. Philip F. Zeidman, *An International Encounter*, 25 INT'L BUS. LAW. 229 (1997).

42. For an in-depth discussion of this issue, *see* Andrew P. Loewinger, *International Franchising: Suggestions for Compliance*, 15 FRANCHISE L.J. 60 (Fall 1995).

43. Loewinger, *supra*, at 691.

priate authorities in other countries."[44] Trademark laws vary in different countries with respect to duration of the trademark and prohibitions on speculative trademarks (those that have not actually been used on a product), or prohibitions on "offensive trademarks" such as those forbidden by the People's Republic of China. There are also multilateral and bilateral trademark treaties in effect that will assist investors in the trademark registration process.

Copyrights may be involved in a franchising scheme. Often they may be associated with emblems, logos, or instruction manuals sold to the franchisee. The Universal Copyright Convention (UCC) of 1952 and the Berne Convention of 1886 apply to international copyrights. The UCC gives national treatment to copyright holders, and essentially waives any registration requirement so long as the franchisor provides adequate notice of a copyright claim.

Trade secrets must also be protected when a franchisor enters a new host country. A trade secret in a franchising context may be a drink formula or ingredient proportion, a food recipe, a preparation technique, or even market and customer information.

It is extremely difficult to protect such trade secrets under United States law. The first problem arises from the concept of what is a trade secret. Generally speaking, abstract ideas or business practices which do not involve an element of novelty are not considered trade secrets. Even if franchise trade secrets are involved, maintaining such secrets can be difficult given the wide number of persons who may have access to the confidential information. Even though the franchisees may warrant to maintain such secrets, once released into the business public there may not be an effective way to recapture the secret or remedy the harm.[45]

Given the difficulty of the franchisor's position with regard to trade secrets, it is prudent for counsel to expressly incorporate prohibitions against disclosure into the franchise agreement, and to extend this to all employees and agents of the franchise. For example, consider the famous salad dressing available on sandwiches at The Cheese Shop in Williamsburg, Virginia. If the owner of The Cheese Shop were to have a franchisee in London, it would be nearly impossible for the franchisor to prevent the franchisee, manager, and kitchen staff of the London Cheese Shop restaurant from knowing the formula for the dressing, as it is a critical component of The Cheese Shop's success. The most cautious approach would be to disseminate the recipe to only the personnel who require it, and to incorporate prohibitions into the relevant portions of the franchise agreement.

(2) Quality Controls

Quality controls are a crucial element of a successful franchise, as product and business process standardization may be the hallmark of the enterprise. In the above example of The Cheese Shop franchise, if the dressing for the sandwiches is produced in London using a lower grade of olive oil, the taste of a sandwich made by the London franchisee will be different. Aside from incorporating quality control standards into the agreement, the franchisor must maintain a relationship with the franchisee in order that the integrity and quality of the overall operation will be maintained. In short, the franchisor must keep a close watch on the operations of the franchisee to the extent practicable. This view should be tempered, however, by the following commentators' point:

---

44. Loewinger, *supra*, at 688.
45. FOLSOM & GORDON, *supra*, at 690 (citations omitted).

On the other hand, excessive control or the public appearance of such control may give rise to an agency relationship between the franchisor and the franchisee. Such a relationship could be used to establish franchisor liability for franchisee conduct, including international product and other tort liabilities. It may be possible to minimize these risks through disclaimer or indemnification clauses in the franchise agreement.[46]

Clearly, the success of many global franchising operations such as McDonald's restaurants support the proposition that maintaining a similar level of quality in the products and services of a franchisee is important.

(3) Regulation

Regulation of franchise relationships by a host nation is a third noteworthy issue when establishing a franchise operation. Various nations have instituted regulation of franchise agreements with respect to monetary, economic, social, and antitrust issues. One example of such a regulation is a requirement that the franchise use local products. Counsel generally can expect host country regulations to be more beneficial to the franchisee, as would many foreign investment laws governing cross-border contractual relationships, such as those regulations affecting distributorships.

c. Examples of International Franchising Operations

As mentioned above, franchising has been an enormously successful means of expansion for many enterprises. Consider, for example, the case of New Zealand, where franchising has become very successful in the past five years.

According to Simon Lord, founder and publisher of Franchise New Zealand magazine, it is not only the availability of franchised services, but also the public perception of franchising which has changed dramatically in [the last five years].

"Back in 1992, franchising was a dirty word," Mr. Lord says. "There had been a couple of high profile failures, and the only time you ever saw franchising mentioned in the newspapers was when the Commerce Commission took action against yet another shady operator."

"The effect was to make people suspicious of this franchising stuff. If you included the word 'franchise' in a business opportunities advert, it actually reduced response by about 50 [percent]."

However, he says, that attitude ignored the successes of not only the big brands such as McDonald's, but also the small companies like Stirling Sports who had proved that a franchise could be a realistic and profitable way of going into business for yourself."

. . . .

"We now have a significant number of successful, home-grown franchises in New Zealand which have achieved maturity. We've had more franchises imported from Australia and, increasingly, ideas are coming direct from the United States and Europe."[47]

---

46. FOLSOM & GORDON, *supra*, at 689 (citations omitted).

47. *Franchising Enjoys Massive Growth*, THE DOMINION, June 24, 1997 at 9, *available in* LEXIS, ASIAPC database, CURNEWS file.

An example of a successful international franchising operation can be found in virtually any sector of the market. The automobile industry in Malaysia and the personal computer retail market in Thailand provide interesting examples of successful franchising operations. On a somewhat different plane exist the various fast food franchising operations in many countries, including New Zealand and Vietnam.

In the automobile industry, General Motors' (GM) successful European venture Opel has been further expanded into the Asia-Pacific region through franchising. Europel Sdn. Bhd. is the sole seller of Opel automobiles in Malaysia, where Opel has achieved tremendous success and popularity in the market:

> Many car critics have attributed Opel's success in capturing a large following in Malaysia to its "striking difference." With a reputation of being the best-selling car in Europe as well as the most popular car in Germany—the home of automotive precision, quality and technology—the local market for Opel's range of completely built-up units (CBU) has indeed grown by leaps and bounds.
>
> Europel Sdn Bhd is the sole distributor of Opel vehicles in Malaysia. It commenced operations in 1992 after securing the franchise from renowned American car manufacturer, General Motors Corporation.[48]

Opel is yet another example of a franchising operation that has been able to capitalize on its overseas reputation and popularity by commencing operations in another market. To illustrate the earlier point regarding trademark selection, consider whether the GM nameplate would have been as successful, in light of Asian perceptions of quality in the American automobile industry.

The retailing sector is also one where franchising is an excellent expansion vehicle. In Thailand, personal computer (PC) superstores are predicted to capture up to fifty percent of the PC market, and franchising has been used by players in the information technology (IT) retail market to facilitate the planned expansion.

> IT superstores have been forecast to capture 10 per cent of the total IT market this year. They will capture 50 per cent next year, according to Ekachai Sirijirapatana, president and CEO of IT City Co Ltd., an IT superstore in Thailand.
>
> These figures have attracted many computer vendors to jump into this market as IT superstore operators. There are now three IT superstores in Thailand; Computec's Datamation, M Information Technology's Imart and SVOA Group's IT City.[49]

One Thai IT superstore executive posits that franchising will help increase distribution channels and generate a greater percentage of total profits as the sector develops. This executive's IT superstore, Imart, plans to open up four new franchise operations per year. This sector might be a ripe opportunity for an American computer superstore operator such as CompUSA, if it is willing to accept the level of risks associated with such an investment. After all, American businesses pioneered the superstore concept, and many are experienced franchisors.

The example provided by the fast food industry is ubiquitous to any American who has traveled overseas. In almost every corner of the globe, it is almost impossi-

---

48. *Europel's Stable of Opel Cars Captures the Malaysian Motorist's Imagination and His Wallet,* NEW STRAITS TIMES, Scpt. 1, 1997.

49. *Battlelines are Drawn in Great IT Store War,* NATION, Emerging Markets Datafile, Apr. 7, 1997, *available in* LEXIS, ASIAPC database, CURNEWS file.

ble not to be able to get the same fast food that is a staple of the American diet, and indeed to many travelers the homogenization of global taste buds and restaurants is to be lamented. Nonetheless, from a business perspective, the success of American fast-food franchises has to be admired. Like it or not, much of the world wants to eat American hamburgers, fries, pizza, and ice cream and drink American sodas. In Vietnam, once a well-known bastion of violent anti-capitalism, fast food franchises are flourishing. Along with Connecticut-based Carvel ice cream, "Baskin-Robbins is here and expanding. TGI Friday's and Kentucky Fried Chicken are scheduled to open their first outlets in Ho Chi Minh City next year."[50] New Zealand, as mentioned above, also has seen a dramatic increase in franchising, in which the fast food industry has participated.

> Pizza Hut and KFC stores are hardly a gourmet's paradise [, but] the chains are considered ideal by a large sector of the population which likes its food hot and now.
>
> KFC and Pizza Hut are the key assets of Restaurant Brands, the company being set up to own and manage the two food chains in New Zealand....
>
> ...Restaurant Brands will be a franchisee, paying 6% of sales as royalties and another 5% for advertising. It also has to meet strict standards of outlet design, service, and quality of products.[51]

In sum, franchising is a rapidly growing mode of expansion and investment, both domestic and overseas. The examples provided above illustrate the success of franchising in the automotive, PC retail, and fast food markets. Clearly, there is great potential for U.S. investors seeking to "go international" to use franchising as a successful expansion vehicle in many different industries and market sectors.

3. Form #3: Mergers and Acquisitions (M&A)[52]

a. Definition and Implications

Exactly what is meant by "mergers and acquisitions," or M&A? A merger involves "an amalgamation of two corporations [or other entities] pursuant to statutory provision in which one of the corporations survives and the other disappears."[53] It is also defined as an "absorption of one company by another, the former losing its legal identity, and the latter retaining its own name and identity and acquiring assets, liabilities, franchises, and powers of [the] former, and absorbed company ceasing to

---

50. Mai Hoang, *In New Fight for Vietnam, Franchise Count Rises; Returnees Help to Spread U.S. Influence*, INT'L HERALD TRIBUNE, May 12, 1997 *available in* LEXIS ASIAPC database, CURNEWS file.

51. David McEwen, *New Zealand: Investors Desperate to Queue for Fast Food*, NAT'L BUS. REV., May 16, 1997, *available in* LEXIS ASIAPC database, CURNEWS file.

52. This discussion draws heavily on THE HANDBOOK OF INTERNATIONAL MERGERS & ACQUISITIONS (BenDaniel & Rosenbloom eds., 1990), as well as on H. LEIGH FRENCH, INTERNATIONAL LAW OF TAKE-OVERS AND MERGERS: ASIA, AUSTRALIA, AND OCEANA (Quorum 1986).

   Mergers and acquisitions is a very broad and deep topic, about which entire law school courses exist. It is difficult to treat the topic in a simple, consolidated fashion; hence the discussion is only a general one designed to present some of the most salient issues involved in international M&A deals.

53. BLACK'S LAW DICTIONARY (6th ed. 1990) at 988.

exist as a separate business entity."[54] An acquisition is "[t]he act of becoming the owner of certain property."[55] For the purposes of this work, however, perhaps the best conceptual definition is stated by one observer as:

> ...The route by which some firms choose to grow involves getting together with another enterprise....Analytically, it is possible to distinguish between two main ways that firms can get together....(1) *Takeover*: technically known as an "acquisition," and where there is a dominant firm and where the owners of the subordinate enterprise give up their interest for a consideration given by the other enterprise....(2) *Merger*: technically known as a "uniting of interest" or an "amalgamation," where two or more companies...agree to transfer their capital to another company newly formed for the purpose and the old company is dissolved. For example, firm A merges with firm B to form firm C.
>
> ....
>
> Whatever the motivation, or route taken, the objective of companies engaging in such transactions is to improve growth, profits, and the quality of earnings.[56]

This definition suggests it is important for the international business lawyer to consider her client's potential motivations. No doubt the general reasons supporting an investor's desire to "go international" are relevant to the M&A form. But, there are a few implications particular to the M&A form, however, which deserve mention.

First, the size of the investment desired is important. That is, does the magnitude of the investor's financial interest in the particular market warrant an M&A approach? In other words, would the client be better served by other, perhaps less ambitious and resource-intensive means of accomplishing FDI?

Second, does the investor have a specific length of time in mind for the duration of the project? Does the investor realize the long-term nature of the M&A approach to foreign investment?

Third, what structure is preferred? Is the investor looking for a 100 percent equity ownership, or a controlling ownership? The percentage of foreign ownership may be restricted by the governing law in the host country.

Finally, with respect to the M&A transaction itself, will it be a friendly or a hostile one? This dimension of the issue has important cultural implications. For example, while hostile bids are commonplace in the United States, they are indeed seen as unfriendly in Europe, and downright irresponsible in Japan.[57] This choice has implications that reach beyond the immediate sphere of the transaction itself, possibly into the future operations of the firm after the transaction is completed. It cannot be disputed that the investor's goals, resources, and intentions as to the duration of the investment should be guiding factors in planning a direct foreign investment, especially a merger or an acquisition.

---

54. BLACK'S LAW DICTIONARY (6th ed. 1990) at 988 (*citing* Morris v. Investment Life Ins. Co., 27 Ohio St. 2d 26 (1971)).

55. BLACK'S LAW DICTIONARY (6th ed. 1990) at 24.

56. PETER MOLES & NICHOLAS TERRY, THE HANDBOOK OF INTERNATIONAL FINANCIAL TERMS 350-51 (1997) (emphasis original).

57. Laurance R. Newman, *Strategic Choices, in* THE HANDBOOK OF INTERNATIONAL MERGERS & ACQUISITIONS 1, 20 (BenDaniel & Rosenbloom eds., 1990).

b. Advantages[58]

A merger or acquisition can provide a number of advantages to the foreign investor desiring to enter a new overseas market. These advantages include supply and distribution, contacts, personnel and facilities, and name recognition/reputation.

Establishing new supply and distribution networks for an operation in a foreign country may prove difficult and resource-intensive for a new investor in an overseas environment. Specifically, entering a new market means that the investor will have to expend a significant amount of time and resources in comprehending the complexities of, and subsequently harnessing, a foreign supply and distribution system. Unfamiliarity can hinder the venture's ability to recoup initial capital expenditures, enter the wholesale or retail markets in the host country, or export its product from the host country.

Initiating a merger with or acquiring an existing firm in the host country can ameliorate these problems. Consider the following hypothetical. Tom's Toys, a Richmond, Virginia-based retailer of toys. This company seeks to enter the Malaysian market. Merging with, or acquiring, a leading national toy retailer in Malaysia would allow Tom's Toys to receive its supplies and distribute its product through the existing networks of the Malaysian toy company.

The principle applied in the above example also applies with respect to contacts. For instance, without the existing contacts between the Malaysian toy company and Malaysian government consumer product safety regulators, Tom's Toys might face difficulty in creating an amicable relationship with the authorities. In turn, the process for obtaining necessary government product approvals could be inhibited. Obviously, the fact that a target of an overseas M&A transaction has contacts that are already established with regulators, as well as local counsel, distribution agents, and others, is an advantage of entering an overseas market through an M&A deal.

Regarding personnel and facilities, the investor often must face the difficult task of hiring workers in the host country with no expertise in hiring practices and labor laws. In the case of a merger, the firm in the host country already has employees in place. The toy company, for example, has a workforce that has sustained it in its operations thus far, and so Tom's Toys can harness this capability. The same concept applies to facilities, in that the target of the merger likely already has facilities in place in which it conducts its business. In contrast, a *de novo* or greenfield investor faces the challenge of constructing a facility or facilities in the host country, which may prove to be time consuming, resource-intensive, and otherwise problematic.

Finally, the reputation of the merger target in the host country can be an additional vehicle for success for an American investor. The name recognition of a local, regional, or national toy retailer in Malaysia would allow the American firm to harness an already existing market share, whereas the *de novo* or greenfield investor would be required to again "carve out" a place for itself in the domestic market.

---

58. For an interesting discussion of the risks and benefits associated with an American business merging with or acquiring a foreign firm (in particular, a Japanese firm), *see* Bernard Wysocki Jr., *The Outlook, Buying a Japanese Firm is Still a Tricky Matter*, WALL ST. J., November 17, 1997 at A1. The author states that

> buying into Japan hasn't been this cheap in many years. For some American companies, it might be the right time to consider buying control of a Japanese company. Or is it?...Even takeovers could have a place in the Japanese economy, some hopeful officials say. As... Kiyoshi Goto of the Japan Development Bank put it recently, "[p]eople in Japan think the real boom for M&A is coming, in pharmaceuticals, hospitals, finance, retailing."...Maybe.

Id.

Tom's Toys, for example, may face an uphill battle in acquiring market share in Kuala Lumpur. With a locally recognized name, this task becomes easier.

c. Disadvantages

There are a few common disadvantages to M&A as a form of FDI. Due to the risk, an exceedingly thorough knowledge of the culture, geography, local business climate, regulatory structure, and industry is required for a merger or acquisition to be successful. Further, to a greater degree than in other forms of FDI, a long-term approach is required. Finally, a merger may involve an additional layer of complexity in terms of the clearances required from the government of the host nation than other forms of FDI.

Knowledge of the culture, geography, business climate, and industry in the host nation is crucial in any foreign investment situation, but especially so in the case of a merger or acquisition. As one practitioner rightly cautions, "[b]e sure to understand the culture, the people, the country, and the business environment of the potential acquisition. The Japanese and Chinese are very different, as are the Koreans and the Taiwanese."[59]

An acquisition of an existing firm in another country entails the formation of relationships that are more complicated and more difficult to terminate than, for example, an arm's-length sale of goods or licensing transaction. The investor in an M&A transaction likely will have expended significant effort, capital, and time in the acquisition process. Accordingly, the time needed to recoup this initial investment, whether the investor decides to maintain the presence in the host country or not, will be longer than in other transactions.

With respect to government permissions that may be required, the host country may have foreign investment laws that restrict inbound investment, or there may be special benefits or incentives available. The issue is crucial:

> Like Hart-Scott-Rodino [Act] in the United States, many countries require government permission for a transaction to be made, especially if that transaction requires foreign currency being brought into the country. (Sometimes a foreign government can require a local company to bid against a multinational purchase.) This process of government approval can be time consuming and difficult. Many countries, especially [developing nations], have erected legal and procedural barriers to protect local industry. In addition to restricting the level and type of foreign ownership, many countries have erected significant procedural approval processes.[60]

A specific example of a host-country legal and regulatory approach — Indonesia — is discussed later. The point for now is that any international M&A deal must comply with all applicable laws and regulations imposed by relevant foreign jurisdictions.

> These... obstacles may take the form of [I]nvestment approvals, [e]xchange control approvals or consents, [t]ax clearances, [c]learances under local or international competition laws, [u]nusual problems arising in the due diligence investigation of a foreign target, [t]he necessity of agreeing on an allocation of the purchase price among assets located in various jurisdictions, and [b]urdensome mechanics required to comply with local law or practice relating to the documentation necessary to effect the acquisition for local purposes.[61]

---

59. Newman, *in* HANDBOOK, *supra*, at 12.
60. Newman, *in* HANDBOOK, *supra*, at 23.
61. McCarthy, *in* HANDBOOK, *supra*, at 62-63.

To be sure many of these factors, such as tax and anti-competition clearances, apply in the case of a domestic merger. Yet, typically, an international M&A deal is more complex with regard to each factor, and the greater the number of jurisdictions are involved, the greater the complexity.

d. Legal Documentation[62]

Documenting an international M&A deal occurs in two basic stages: the letter of intent, and the acquisition agreement. The letter of intent is likely to be drafted following the initial negotiation phase between the parties, when the parties have come to a general consensus that they are seriously considering some sort of merger or acquisition. Signed before the contract between the parties, this document will reflect the main points or tenets of their pending agreement. As such, the letter of intent will help the parties in structuring the transaction, identifying the various issues that they have deemed to be significant, those that need further clarification and negotiation, and those to which they have agreed thus far.

Although the letter of intent is not legally binding, parties from outside the United States often regard the letter of intent as more flexible than do their American counterparts.

> Parties outside the United States feel free to propose departures from the letter of intent than would an American party. Nonetheless, all matters of importance to the parties, especially the structure of the transaction, should be considered and reviewed with counsel and other consultants before a letter of intent is signed.[63]

As in a domestic M&A transaction, the key document in an international M&A deal is the acquisition agreement. Generally speaking, the agreements that are drafted for international deals are less complex than agreements for domestic mergers or acquisitions. International M&A agreements often lack any representation or warranty provisions. When an American investor participates in an overseas acquisition, however, the agreement will be closer in terms of complexity to that of a domestic transaction. In fact, there may be areas that will be more detailed than in the purely domestic transaction, because the international transaction will frequently entail a greater degree of risk in certain areas, particularly labor, regulation, or taxation.

The contract associated with an international M&A deal may have two separate sub-categories, a master agreement and local agreements. The master agreement will govern the overall transaction. The local agreements are important in the event that the American investor is acquiring an entity with assets and operations in multiple countries. Consider again the Malaysian toy company, and suppose it also has a manufacturing operation in Singapore and an assembly plant in Taiwan. Tom's Toys should be advised to create a separate local agreement for each country. Why? First, a local agreement can be short, which simplifies translation and may make it easier to register the agreement with local authorities, if that is necessary. Second, a local agreement may obviate the need for each local tax authority to re-calculate and re-allocate the purchase price of the deal with a view to increasing local income taxes or local transfer taxes. Third, a dual-agreement structure allows for more flexibility to tailor each component of the transaction to the peculiarities of the jurisdiction in which it takes place.

---

62. This section of this Note is derived significantly from Paul McCarthy, *Legal Aspects of Acquiring Non-U.S. Enterprises*, in HANDBOOK, *supra*, at 61.

63. McCarthy, *in* HANDBOOK, *supra*, at 69.

What issues typically are dealt with in an international merger or acquisition agreement? They include the following: (1) consideration, (2) assumption of liabilities, (3) warranties, (4) covenants, (5) conditions, (6) closing, and (7) indemnification.

(1) Consideration

Undoubtedly, the issue of consideration is important to both parties. The price may be represented by a set figure, or it may fluctuate in accordance with an index or the value of the target's assets at a specific point in time. In the event there is a master agreement and multiple local agreements, the price will be set forth in the master agreement, along with the specific amount designated for each sub-component of the deal. Each local agreement will, of course, contain the price representing the local portion of the transaction. Payment will generally be accomplished via wire transfer, which requires substantial coordination in the event there are multiple jurisdictions requiring payment at the same time.

(2) Assumption of Liabilities

Generally, the acquirer becomes subject to all liabilities of the target firm, which may include leases, loans, payables, and other agreements. The target firm may, of course, enumerate and indemnify the buyer against specific liabilities, such as contingent liabilities. Significantly, certain liabilities will transfer automatically to an acquiror, depending on the laws of the host country. For example, liabilities for employees will transfer automatically in some jurisdictions.

(3) Warranties

Warranties and representations will (or at least ought to) be given regarding any areas of concern to the acquirer or investor. Of course, a thorough due diligence investigation should uncover these areas of concern. However, some situations may remain unknown that may cause the acquirer to want the target to make a warranty or representation. After all, the practice in some countries is to be less inclusive than in the United States with respect to disclosure. As a result, it may not be easy to persuade the target to make the desired warranty or representation. For instance, "in Europe, the sellers may flatly refuse to provide the extensive representations common in the United States. In that case, the buyer will have to choose with care the particular matters that it wishes covered and independently investigate any other important matters."[64] Any warranties and representations the target does agree to make are likely to be incorporated into the master agreement, rather than in local agreements.

(4) Covenants

Covenants apply to matters taking place between the signing of a merger or acquisition agreement and the culmination, or closing, of the transaction. One example of a covenant frequently incorporated into the agreement is that the target firm continue its operations in the normal course of business, and that it refrain from participating in any substantial transaction without the acquirer's consent. Although the local agreements may contain covenants regarding issues specific to that portion of the transaction, "most pre- and post-closing covenants will appear only in the master agreement,"[65] as is the case with representations and warranties.

---

64. McCarthy, *in* HANDBOOK, *supra*, at 71.
65. McCarthy, *in* HANDBOOK, *supra*, at 71.

(5) Conditions

Examples of conditions in an acquisition agreement are the obtaining of any required permissions or approvals from government or other bodies, the execution of any required secondary agreements, and the absence of any serious adverse changes in the condition of the industry. Conditions such as these will be included in the master agreement, fulfillment of which is required for the deal to close.

(6) Closing

With regard to the closing, a master agreement also will contain a description of the mechanics of the closing. There are many details to a closing, and the pressure on an international business lawyer to "get it right" is especially acute during the period just prior to closing, when each detail is addressed. Of course, the exact nature of the details are likely to differ from one M&A deal to the next.

(7) Indemnification

Finally, indemnification provisions may be contained in the master agreement. These serve the same purpose as in any contract; namely, they attempt to distribute the risks between the acquirer and the target. Negotiating an indemnification provision into a contract with a non-United States party may be difficult, unless the target is a sophisticated party familiar with such provisions from previous contracts or agreements with American firms.

e. M&A in Indonesia[66]

Indonesia, the world's largest Muslim country, is a fascinating case study. It is a civil law country surrounded by common law nations such as Australia, Malaysia, Singapore, Brunei, and the Philippines. For most of the post-World War II era, Indonesia has experienced rapid economic progress. Between roughly 1970 and 1995, Indonesia's average annual growth rate was approximately seven percent, and its yearly *per capita* income exceeded $1,000. While Indonesia's early growth was mostly due to petroleum exports, it has now moved away from this approach, and its reliance on oil and gas revenue has decreased to about twenty-five percent of total exports. While the 1997 currency crisis and subsequent economic slump have hurt Indonesia, nevertheless it remains an attractive developing market for FDI in the long run. (Indeed, many western businesses are finding bargain-priced investments in Indonesia and other Far Eastern economies.)

"Indonesia's rapid economic progress has spurred calls from both local businessmen and foreign investors for a new company law more suited to Indonesia's modern commercial sector."[67] The new company law in Indonesia attempts to respond to this concern. The new Indonesian Company Law, entitled the Undang-Undang Tentang Perseroan Terbatas, or "UUPT" was promulgated in 1995 and adopted on March 7, 1996. It supersedes articles thirty-six through fifty-six of the old Indonesian Commercial Code. The Indonesian Commercial Code, entitled *Wetboek van Koophandel*, was instituted in 1847 by the Dutch (who colonized Indonesia during the nineteenth and early twentieth centuries), and revised only once after Indonesia became independent in 1945. The old code was silent on the topic of merg-

---

66. This discussion is drawn from Darrel R. Johnson, *Indonesia*, in COMMERCIAL LAWS OF EAST ASIA (Alan S. Gutterman & Robert Brown eds., 1997) and Benny S. Tabalujan, *The New Indonesian Company Law*, 17 U. PA. J. INT'L ECON. L. 883 (1996).

67. Tabalujan, *supra*, at 883.

ers and acquisitions, whereas the new expressly recognizes them — one improvement among many. A very significant attribute stated in the UUPT pertaining to M&A transactions is that "any merger, consolidation, or acquisition must also be in the interest of the target company, its employees and minority shareholders and must not be against the public interest. Any merger, consolidation or acquisition must be done with due consideration for fair competition." The UUPT, along with the Foreign Investment Law of 1967 ("FIL"), as amended, thus affect foreign investors in Indonesia. However, a few certain significant sectors are not covered by the FIL, such as petroleum and finance.

With respect to the FIL, there are a number of requirements placed on foreign investors that warrant discussion. First, the investor must obtain a foreign investment license by applying to the Indonesian Capital Investment Coordinating Board, or BKPM. The license issued to the investor will be valid for thirty years. There are a number of specific permits that are required, for example, a limited import license, a personnel utilization plan approval, and a permanent operating license. These will be approved and issued as necessary during the approval process for the investment as a whole. The second major requirement is that the investor must check the Negative Investment List, known as the DNI list. This list enumerates certain sectors of the Indonesian economy that are areas where foreign investment is prohibited. Significantly, however, investments are permitted unless expressly prohibited, subject to specific government regulations pertinent to a particular sector.

A foreign investment in Indonesia must take the form of a limited liability company, or "PT." The foreign investment operation in Indonesia also may be called a PMA, which means "foreign capital investment." A PMA may acquire another company in Indonesia, with some exceptions, as may a foreign individual or corporation. The acquisition may be effected via a direct investment or a purchase in the Indonesian capital markets. In the case of a direct investment, the acquisition

> must meet at least one of the following four criteria: (a) the acquired company's project must be in the construction stage; (b) the new shareholder is a lender which is converting its debt to equity; (c) the acquisition is made to improve the acquired company's product marketing; or (d) the acquisition is made to improve the acquired company's exports or to obtain the benefits of new technology.[68]

The Indonesian government has allowed an additional criterion to remain in effect, which is that a target company may be acquired if it is in financial distress.

If the target is a publicly traded, native Indonesian company and is to be acquired by way of a portfolio equity investment (*i.e.*, buying shares on the Jakarta Stock Exchange or other securities market on which the target's shares are traded), then there are requirements as to foreign equity holdings. "The general rule is that the foreign investor may own a maximum of 80 percent of the equity, which must be reduced to 49 percent or less within 20 years after the [company's] commencement of commercial production."[69] However, the forty-nine percent shareholder may actually posses the largest portion of outstanding shares of a firm, and this still may constitute *de facto* control of the firm.

---

68. Johnson, *in* COMMERCIAL LAWS, *supra*, at 219.
69. Darrel R. Johnson, *Going International in Indonesia, in* COUNSELING EMERGING COMPANIES IN GOING INTERNATIONAL 567 (Alan S. Gutterman, ed., 1994).

4. Form #4: International Joint Ventures

A joint venture, or JV, is a "legal entity in the nature of a partnership engaged in the joint undertaking of a particular transaction for mutual profit,"[70] or "a one-time grouping of two or more [companies] in a business undertaking."[71] In a more fundamental sense, an international JV is "essentially a collaboration among parties among more than one nationality."[72]

JVs entail many of the risks and problems associated with other forms of FDI, but "the joint venture is often properly viewed as a way of reducing some of the problems and risks a stranger assumes in operating in a new market."[73] Thus, it is often an appropriate form of investment for an excursion into a new market in a country which one of the partners has had no previous presence or experience. One overriding point should be emphasized: the investors and their counsel should define clearly and precisely a set of realistic expectations, and devise a practical approach to realize those expectations.[74]

a. Major Issues in Establishing an International JV

Establishing an international JV requires careful attention to at least seven major issues: (1) what structure will the JV take?; (2) what will the tax position of the JV be?; (3) what liability will the JV partners bear?; (4) how will the JV be capitalized?; (5) how will the JV be managed?; (6) how will disputes between (or among) the JV partners be resolved?; and (7) will interests in the JV be transferable, and relatedly, how will the JV be terminated? These issues are considered in turn below.

(1) Structure

There is no one model of a JV. Rather, a JV can be structured in a number of ways. At one end of the continuum, a JV can be as loose as a strategic alliance. At the other end, it can be as specific and integrated as a new corporation, formed with equity from both partners, under local law in the host country.[75] There are many choices between these two extremes. The choice is important for many reasons, particularly with respect to taxes and limitation of liability.[76]

(2) Tax

It is a fact of the life of an international business lawyer that every decision her client makes may have tax implications. In the JV context (as well as other contexts), possibly the most important situation to avoid is double taxation, which occurs when

---

70. BLACK'S LAW DICTIONARY at 839 (6th ed. 1990) (citing Tex- Co Grain Co. v. Happy Wheat Growers, Inc., 542 S.W.2d 934 (1976)).

71. BLACK'S LAW DICTIONARY at 839 (6th ed. 1990) (citing Tex- Co Grain Co. v. Happy Wheat Growers, Inc., 542 S.W.2d 934 (1976)).

72. International Joint Ventures, in YOUNG LAWYERS DESKTOP REFERENCE GUIDE 1 (American Bar Association, Young Lawyers Division ed., 1994).

73. Peter D. Ehrenhaft, International Joint Venture Basics, 41 PRAC. LAW. 57 (1995).

74. For a discussion of planning and strategy in international Jvs, see Michael B. Nelson, Critical Analysis and Strategies for U.S. Overseas Businesses Participating as a Foreign Joint Venture Partner, 9 Transnat'l Law. 1 (1996).

75. A detailed discussion of international JVs, including the structuring options, is set forth in RONALD CHARLES WOLF, A GUIDE TO INTERNATIONAL JOINT VENTURES WITH SAMPLE CLAUSES (1995). A description of the types of clauses employed in each form also is provided therein.

76. See DESKTOP REFERENCE, supra, at 6.

the United States and host country tax the venture at the same time. The American side of the JV should obtain a tax credit from the Internal Revenue Service (IRS) for taxes paid to a foreign government at the site of the venture. "Under the Internal Revenue Code...a U.S. corporate venturer owning at least 10 percent of the voting stock of the foreign joint venture may claim a credit upon repatriation of the venture's earnings, as if the venturer had paid a share of the foreign taxes paid by the venture."[77] Tax analysis is very fact-specific and detailed, however, and "advice from local tax counsel is crucial to structuring a joint venture successfully."[78] In addition, there are many published articles about the tax implications of an international JV,[79] and these discussions should be consulted. When in doubt, before proceeding with the structuring of a JV, an international business lawyer may save herself and a client considerable grief in the future by obtaining a private letter ruling from the IRS in which the IRS explains the position it would take in response to a set of facts presented by the lawyer and her client.

(3) Liability

There is a close connection between liability and the needs of the JV partners. Obviously, the structure of the JV ought to meet those needs. For example, if a limited partnership or shareholder status meets the partner's needs, then either of those two forms should be selected. In turn, the choice of structure will determine the degree of liability, expense, and time needed to initiate the joint venture. The preferences of the JV partners on these matters is likely to depend on their overall corporate structure in their respective organizations,[80] as well as their risk tolerances and corporate culture. Naturally, the limitation on liability is an advantage in JVs for the same reasons set forth above regarding the advantages of incorporation.

(4) Capitalization

In addition to tax and liability concerns, JV partners need to consider capitalization. They must, first, agree on the timing and type of the initial capital contributions from the respective partners. What intellectual property, real property, cash, services, and machinery will be contributed and by whom? The law regarding transfer of non-cash capital — e.g., intellectual property — is particularly relevant. It is very common for a local JV partner to seek a JV with an American business largely to benefit from technology transfer. The American partner may be chary of transferring too much technology too quickly, lest it be exploited by competitors. Yet, "[i]n some countries, particularly underdeveloped countries [which obviously are hungry for technology inflows to assist their businesses and thereby accelerate their economic development process], the licensor of intellectual property [i.e., the American JV partner] will be deemed to have essentially made a sale to the licensee [i.e., the local JV partner]. No license agreement can prevent it."[81] In addition, technology transfer laws may come into play at any time during the capitalization process. For instance, the United States Department of Commerce's Export Administration Regulations ("EAR") may affect the American partner seeking to license computer technology to its JV partner in Malaysia.

---

77. *See* DESKTOP REFERENCE, *supra*, at 6-7.
78. *See* DESKTOP REFERENCE, *supra*, at 7.
79. *See, e.g.*, D. Kevin Dolan, Esq., *Special issues in Structuring International Joint Ventures-Part One*, 22 TAX MGMT. INT'L J. 51 (1993).
80. *See* DESKTOP REFERENCE, *supra*, at 7.
81. *See* DESKTOP REFERENCE, *supra*, at 7.

Second, what happens if more capital is needed in the future? Inevitably, some JVs will require more financial support to be profitable than initially anticipated, or to tide them over through unforeseen market slumps. The partners ought to agree initially in their JV agreement upon "a mechanism for providing additional capital over the life of the joint venture, and a response to the failure to make a contribution."[82] This point may be a delicate in the event a local law limits certain remedies.

Third, further refinements in the capitalization plan may be needed. It may be prudent to earmark capital for certain purposes, and to direct the flow of capital upon achieving specific milestones, so that the JV partners do not quarrel about mis-allocation of funds. Here again, a resolution to these issues ought to be negotiated and contained in the final JV agreement. *Chipman v. Steinberg* is a case in point of what can go wrong.[83] Here, one partner violates its fiduciary duty by wrongfully diverting profits from the venture. "It is an accepted principle of longstanding that profits which are wrongfully diverted from a joint adventure are subject to the imposition of a constructive trust, and a faithless fiduciary must account to his associates in the enterprise."[84] The law in Delaware, for example, requires "good faith, honesty, and integrity . . . in dealings with each other and with the venture."[85]

(5) Management

Plainly, tax, liability, and capitalization issues require careful negotiation and resolution among the JV partners. However, almost invariably the most highly negotiated issue is control and governance, *i.e.*, management. Many questions need to be addressed. "Who controls what decisions? Who appoints which officers? What decisions are so important to all partners that they should be subject to super-majority or unanimous consent provisions?"[86] Who will approve budgets? Expenditures? Hiring? Compensation? Stock issuance? Matters not in the ordinary course of business? How will all of the decisions that need to be made actually get made? For example, "ventures based in the U.S. tend to have more committee decision-making and detailed governance provisions than ventures based outside of the U.S."[87] Local law also may affect the decision making process. For instance, certain host countries require the most senior management position, or a certain percentage of senior management positions or the board of directors, to be held by a national of that country. Even if practical solutions are found to all of these questions, they may not be executed as planned for cultural reasons. An American JV partner may find its local partner less forthcoming with information needed to make decisions than expected. The local partner may find the American side pushy and impatient. Either situation can breed a non-cooperative atmosphere. The international business lawyer must appraise her client of these possibilities, try and prevent them, and negotiate amicable solutions in the event they arise. It is an example of the fact that an encyclopedic knowledge of the law is a necessary but not sufficient condition to be a great lawyer; what is needed is also outstanding "people skills."

---

82. *See* DESKTOP REFERENCE, *supra*, at 8.

83. *See* 483 N.Y.S.2d 256 (1984).

84. JOHN P. KARALIS, INTERNATIONAL JOINT VENTURES, A PRACTICAL GUIDE § 3.13 at 120, fn. 10, *citing* Chipman v. Steinberg, 43 N.Y.S.2d 256, 257 (1984).

85. KARALIS, *supra*, at fn. 8.

86. *See* DESKTOP REFERENCE, *supra*, at 8.

87. *See* DESKTOP REFERENCE, *supra*, at 9.

(6) Dispute Resolution

The above discussion suggests yet another key issue in structuring a JV is dispute resolution. When (not if) a dispute among the partners arises, by what procedure will it be resolved? The best course for the international business lawyer drafting a JV agreement is to

> ...craft the management and control provisions so well that there are few, if any disputes which cannot be resolved. For example, if most decisions are subject to majority or supermajority decision, then the only risk of deadlock is if there are an equal number of, *e.g.*, members of the board, or the venture cannot continue without an affirmative act, *e.g.*, approving a loan or a capital contribution when the venture is out of funds.[88]

In other words, deadlock can be avoided by careful planning for foreseeable conflicts, and by minimizing disputes.

To be sure, regardless of skillful drafting of a JV agreement, proper planning, and conflict avoidance, disputes certainly are ineluctable — if for no other reasons than cultural misunderstandings or market downturns. When they occur, the JV parties have various options. "The standard approach is that, since the parties have provided the rules, they must live by them. Therefore, an infraction is a breach of contract to be decided by the appropriate court in light of the circumstances at the time of breach."[89] This principle is based on deterrence, and litigation between the partners will ensue if the dispute is not solved informally. Another option is arbitration. It may be less costly than litigation. But, the host country's legal regime may not accept it as a legitimate mechanism, hence an award would not necessarily be binding under local law. A third option is a sort of "sunset" provision in the JV agreement. It mandates formal negotiations for a specific time period. If unsuccessful, the JV is dissolved. This option might minimize losses to the respective JV partners by avoiding protracted litigation, but it may prematurely end what might have been a profitable venture if only the partners could have resolved their dispute. In sum, no one dispute resolution option can be prescribed for all international JVs. The parties must decide the mechanism that best serves their particular needs.

(7) Transferability and Termination

Some final issues that warrant consideration by investors and their counsel in international JVs concern the transferability of interests and termination or dissolution of the venture. Transferability revolves around each partner's commitment to the JV, *i.e.*, whether each partner is a long or short-term player. How one partner can transfer its interest in the event it "wants out" to a third party should be spelled out in the JV agreement. Regarding termination or dissolution, it is necessary to determine whether the parties want the venture to be "iron clad" or more fluid, allowing for termination if certain conditions occur, such as insolvency. As in most JV issues, local law is important, and the final disposition of assets will depend on the laws of the situs of the JV.[90]

b. Steps in Forming an International JV

Conceptually, there are six steps to the formation of an international JV: (1) preparation, (2) strategic planning, (3) hiring local counsel, (4) partnering, (5) for-

---

88. *See* DESKTOP REFERENCE, *supra*, at 9.
89. *See* DESKTOP REFERENCE, *supra*, at 10.
90. *See* DESKTOP REFERENCE, *supra*, at 13.

malizing the relationship, and (6) negotiating and drafting the JV agreement.[91] These steps are discussed in turn below.

(1) Preparation

Preparation is a key ingredient for success. The client should prepare for the venture by gathering information about the host country. A thorough country profile describing the risks and opportunities for the prospective JV should be generated, and the client should become familiar with the economy, politics, culture, and legal framework in the host country. It is not possible to make informed business judgments without a solid understanding of these and other relevant factors. For example, if the economy lacks sufficient basic infrastructure (roads, power plants, and telecommunication facilities), then the investor may have to provide that infrastructure for the JV, or choose another host country. If there is an insufficient supply of well-trained, English speaking workers, then the investor may have to provide educational facilities or choose a different host country. If the political situation in the host country is unstable, then an American investor might consider purchasing political risk insurance from the Overseas Private Investment Corporation (OPIC), or from a private underwriter.

(2) Strategic Planning

The second step, strategic planning for the venture, includes defining its goals, limits, and alternatives. To some extent, strategy evolves as the JV proceeds, in response to new developments and as the investor gains more information and experience in dealing with important third-party players like government officials, business competitors, and customers. The point is that

> [a]t the outset, your client should: set limits *before* expending significant time, funds, and other resources on the venture; form clear business goals and fallback positions *before* approaching potential joint venture partners; develop a clear notion of the amount of equity and degree of operating control desired; and formulate a time frame for investment and return on investment.[92]

In brief, proceeding with a JV without a strategic plan is like cooking without a recipe, and is likely to have analogous disastrous results.

(3) Hiring Local Counsel

Hiring trustworthy, competent local counsel adept at operating in the host country is important for any American investor, regardless of whether the form of FDI is a JV. "If you are involved in a foreign joint venture, or your client is entering into any relationship under foreign law, then it is imperative that you engage a smart, reliable, responsive, experienced, English-speaking local counsel."[93] Further, local counsel ought to know how to establish the type of JV the American investor and its partner seek.

(4) Selecting a Partner

Perhaps the fourth step, choice of a partner is the most important one of all. Many JVs have failed when all other steps have been taken with care, and when the business climate has been robust, simply because of a bad local partner. The

---

91. *See* DESKTOP REFERENCE, *supra*, at 5.
92. *See* DESKTOP REFERENCE, *supra*, at 3 (emphasis original).
93. *See* DESKTOP REFERENCE, *supra*, at 3.

partner must bring to the venture capital at least one critical ingredient that the American partner lacks, for example, particular business skills, experience, or connections, political acumen, or technological expertise. Above all else, the local partner must be trustworthy. An American investor rushing into an international JV without a thorough investigation of a potential partner is foolish. The investor must dig deep and uncover information the potential partner might not want to disclose, for example, (1) adverse data on its financial condition, (2) the true identity and percentage ownership of its shareholders, (3) its role (or the role of one of its shareholders) in corruption or scandals in the host or a third country, and (4) its ability to provide what it claims to offer the venture. In brief, a thorough investigation may yield information that will assist the investor in making decisions concerning the venture and the nature of the relationship, if any, with a potential partner.

(5) Formalizing the Relationship

The fifth step, formalizing the relationship between the JV partners, may be accomplished by way of a teaming agreement or letter of intent (LOI). Either document can provide a "quick temporary framework in which the parties can proceed while working through the substantive issues."[94] Further, these documents allow for the partners to share costs, and they provide exclusivity and confidentiality during the negotiations. An LOI may take one of two forms, with or without annexed legal documents. This difference affects the degree to which portions of the LOI are binding.

> The usual letter of intent without legal documents should never be relied upon by any parties who may be incurring substantial financial commitments or who are proceeding with corporate plans prematurely.... Annexing [warranted] legal documents... normally arises because of hurried circumstances compelling a "final deal," when a letter of intent, after ratification, becomes transformed from a declaration of purpose into an abbreviated joint venture agreement.[95]

It is possible for an LOI to evolve into an abbreviated JV agreement, but this arrangement is not advisable. A JV agreement, properly constituted, ought to be a more comprehensive, forward-looking document that better protects the partners in the event of future problems than an LOI.

(6) Devising a JV Agreement

As with any contract, producing a JV agreement — the final step in forming an international JV — requires foresight, sensitivity, and attention to detail. An international business lawyer and her client should "aim for negotiating a clear, concise, and complete agreement, with the stated purpose being that the parties fully understand what they are doing and the consequences of their actions."[96] Investors should have an idea whether the agreement ought to follow a form common in the host country, or a typical American form. Local laws that may affect the enforceability of the agreement also should be considered and verified with local counsel. For example, "equitable relief, which may be the only effective remedy, may not be available or only in limited circumstances."[97]

---

94. *See* DESKTOP REFERENCE, *supra*, at 5.
95. WOLF, *supra*, at 21-22.
96. WOLF, *supra*, at 5.
97. WOLF, *supra*, at 6.

Standard Clauses

At a basic level, a JV agreement will contain provisions similar to most FDI agreements, such as a choice of law clause, a choice of forum clause, a *force majeur* clause, and a detailed description of the JV's scope and purpose.

> It would be legally reckless to enter into an international joint venture without a detailed agreement. The agreement should speak of the present and future and as a consequence be a living constitution to be consulted when problems arise between partners in the future. It should be a document that treats specific and general topics so that third parties will later be able to understand the economic reasons which gave origin to the joint venture. The appropriate clauses for a joint venture agreement are many and there is no defined limit to them.[98]

Two of these very important categories of clauses that warrant special discussion are safety and management clauses.

Safety Clause

A safety clause protects the parties from general problems and from the "unknowns" that may arise, even after a detailed "due diligence" investigation is conducted. Through due diligence, the parties examine thoroughly the companies involved in the transaction in order to learn as much as possible about each company. In other words,

> [i]t provides, so to speak, an X-ray of the legal and financial condition of the company and it may bring to the surface problems which even the company being examined did not suspect. Depending on the investment involved, due diligence ranges from a simple review of accounting information and the basic legal documents to a far-reaching, probing investigation into all aspects of the target company.... [99]

There are many types of safety clauses in a JV agreement.

For instance, they may pertain to disclosure, representations and warranties, non-competition, and equal opportunity. Disclosure clauses are important because they compel the JV partners to disclose material information, knowledge of which may affect the negotiations or agreement. Examples include undisclosed liabilities, accounting information, and net worth. There may be various representations and warranties made by the parties. "The intention is to ensure that there is legal responsibility for what the parties have said, or represented by documents, which the other party has relied upon."[100] One of the partners may warrant, for example, it is legally organized under the applicable corporation laws of its jurisdiction. A non-competition clause purports to limit the ability of one JV partner to open, for example, a competing business in a neighboring geographical area, and thereby profit itself at the expense of the JV. The final example of a safety clause, an equal opportunity clause, deals with future opportunities similar to the JV. An equal opportunity clause will spell out the intention of the partners as to whether they will pursue them together.

---

98. Wolf, *supra*, at 57.

99. Wolf, *supra*, at 127. New associates in large firms acting as counsel to a transaction party often are "foot soldiers" in the due diligence process, poring over documents in search of issues of possible importance to the agreement.

100. Wolf, *supra*, at 98.

Management Clause

A management clause pertains to the control and governance of the many aspects of the JV's administration and operation. As mentioned earlier, almost certainly the most highly negotiated issue in a JV negotiation is control and governance. Moreover, this issue may be of particular concern to the minority partner in the venture, who may fear being effectively "frozen out" of key decisions.

Management clauses are not so complex in a legal sense, but they can be crucial for the successful and conflict-free operation of a JV. Examples include qualified majority clauses, clauses relating to the board of directors, capital expenditure limits, accounting rules, salaries, and dividend distributions. Qualified majority clauses seek to give a level of management power to the minority partner that may be greater than that party's level of equity ownership. JV's board of directors needs to have express provisions describing its role and powers of governance. Clauses relating to financial matters cover essential matters such as capital expenditure limitations, accounting standards to be used (*e.g.*, United States Generally Accepted Accounting Principles (GAAP) or some other system), salaries for management and other employees of the venture, and the distribution of dividends.

In sum, although the joint venture agreement is a multi-faceted document, its purpose is clear. It must protect the partners and the venture itself from mismanagement, conflict, or unseen problems. Counsel to investors seeking to initiate a JV must draft and use a thorough and well-prepared agreement which serves well the intentions of the partners.[101]

c. Joint Ventures in China[102]

It is obvious that the Peoples Republic of China ("China," or "PRC") is a dominant economic power in the global economy. As Hamish McRae points out in his fascinating 1994 book, *The World in 2020*, the size of China's economy will be larger than that of the United States early in the 21st century. Indicia of China's dramatic economic success include the gains in the personal wealth of many urban-dwelling, educated Chinese, as well as of entrepreneurial farmers, and the surge in trade between China and many other countries. The PRC, therefore, presents unique opportunities for overseas investors looking to produce or market their goods in a nation of about 1.2 billion people.[103] Indeed, China is an interesting case study of international JVs because of the special circumstances involved with investing in a nation making a transition to a market economy from a planned, centralized economy.

The first major issue encountered when establishing a JV in China concerns a feasibility study. Completing this study is important for two reasons. First, the Chinese government requires it. Second, as discussed earlier, planning is an important

---

101. For guidance in preparing a JV agreement, Stephen P.H. Johnson, *Negotiating and Drafting International Contract Joint Ventures, in* NEGOTIATING AND STRUCTURING INTERNATIONAL COMMERCIAL TRANSACTIONS: LEGAL ANALYSIS WITH SAMPLE AGREEMENTS, (Shelly P. Battram & David N. Goldsweig eds., 1991) provides a thorough discussion of the various clauses and issues involved.

102. This section is drawn from DONG SHIZHONG ET AL., TRADE AND INVESTMENT OPPORTUNITIES IN CHINE (1992), and Wang Weiguo, *The Legal Characteristics of Chinese-Foreign Cooperative Ventures,* 26 U. BRIT. COLUM. L. REV. 375 (1992).

103. *See, e.g.*, ABA SECTION OF INTERNATIONAL LAW AND PRACTICE, CHINA'S LEGAL SYSTEM IN TRANSITION, A REPORT OF THE ABA DELEGATION TO CHINA (Malcolm S. McNeil ed. 1995) (discussing investment opportunities, and success stories, in China).

step in the establishment of any JV. A feasibility study serves as a strategic planning tool.

A feasibility study has two components, the preliminary report and the formal report. First, the prospective Chinese partner must conduct a preliminary feasibility study before any commitment is made to a foreign entity. "A Chinese enterprise does not have the legal capacity to enter into a joint venture contract with foreign parties until such proposal and preliminary feasibility study report are approved."[104] The preliminary study must establish a necessity for cooperation with a foreign partner, and the explanation must satisfy relevant Chinese government authorities before they will grant approval to proceed. These authorities consider macroeconomic, social, political, and viability factors in the approval process. Consequently, an overseas investor ought to assure itself that it can clear these hurdles before entering into a formal contractual relationship with a Chinese JV partner. The second component of a feasibility study, the formal feasibility study report, must be completed and signed jointly by both partners. Formation of the venture is contingent upon approval from the relevant authorities of this document.

It should be apparent that completing a feasibility study is time-consuming and expensive. To do it right, the parties need to allocate proper resources and time to the completion of the study, as the studies are seminal in nature. Because the documents will be reviewed by various ministries and agencies in the Chinese government — possibly not only in Beijing, but also at the regional and local levels — the overseas partner in particular needs healthy doses of patience and stamina. (For example, if the JV concerns utilities, then investors must submit the project for review to the authorities responsible for each utility needed.) The overseas partner also needs a well-connected, trustworthy Chinese partner on which it can rely to deal effectively with government officials. Finally, given the time and expense associated with a feasibility study, the overseas and Chinese partner had better estimate the costs of the study before embarking upon it, and decide up front how to allocate these costs if a government authority does not grant approval, as well as if approval is granted.

To do it right, however, obtaining Chinese government approvals should be regarded only as a minimum threshold. The partners ought to include in their study more than what is simply compelled under Chinese law. For example, they should analyze market conditions, production programs, the capabilities and needs of the prospective venture, and appraise realistically the chances for success. Again, a more expansive feasibility study can serve as a strategic plan.

Assuming a feasibility study is completed and approved by Chinese authorities, the next major issue involved is material (*i.e.*, productive input) supply. As a planned economy in transition, the Chinese government still controls many important materials, raw or finished, needed in the production of goods. Potential supply problems can devastate a JV. Suppose the venture seeks to make leather wallets and purses for export to the United States and Europe. Where will the leather come from? If the right type of leather does not come to the Chinese JV factory in the right amount, and at the right time, then American and European wholesalers will not receive the wallets promised them in the right amount at the right time — for example, 10,000 mens' brown wallets with credit card pouches in time for the Christmas shopping season. The wholesalers will cancel their contract with the JV if the JV fails to deliver. Accordingly, the feasibility study should include the JV's material supply needs, so as to alert the Chinese authorities to the necessity for the

---

104. SHIZHONG *et al.*, *supra*, at 181.

products. In turn, the JV agreement should include provisions that address material supply issues if difficulties arise. As another example, building materials for construction of the JV's premises may be scarce, so investors may have to consider importing them from abroad. In that event, the agreement should provide that sufficient foreign exchange (namely, hard currencies like United States dollars, Japanese yen, German marks, British pound sterling, and French francs to pay for the imported construction materials) be available to accomplish the necessary importation. This availability may hinge on permission from China's central bank, the People's Bank of China.

Still more problems may arise concerning interaction with the Chinese government over government-controlled materials. For instance, the government may reject requests for materials if they are on a controlled list, especially if the request is for a quantity of materials exceeding the amount specified in the feasibility study report and JV agreement. Hence, the partners should consider alternative supply sources for both the short and the long term. As yet another example, transportation may be in short supply. "[I]t is not unusual for a large number of users to be placed upon waiting lists. It can be difficult to gauge exactly how long an enterprise must wait for transportation services in these circumstances because relative efficiency is dependent on the conscientiousness of the domestic transportation enterprise."[105] Thus, the JV partners should endeavor to speed the transportation process as best they can, or to attempt to arrange for their own transportation services.

If the products made by a JV are to be exported from China, then they can be sold through any one (or more) of four channels: (1) a sales agent of the foreign JV partner (*e.g.* the American partner's network), (2) a Chinese foreign trade agency, (3) an export fair in China, or (4) a separately established and approved marketing institution created by the JV partners. However, depending on the product it produces, a JV may have a sizeable market within China. Partners planning to sell products for domestic Chinese consumption must verify whether the products are on a government distribution plan. If so, then the partners must adhere to the requirements of the distribution plan's requirements. The key point here is that the partners do not have complete freedom as to the selection of customers or clients — a position that might be very unusual for the overseas partner in particular, which may be used to selling its product to anyone it likes. For example, consider consumer goods. The vehicle by which such goods are likely to be distributed is a Chinese commercial institution. The Chinese government will choose a suitable wholesaler to distribute the products to retail operations in China. Overseas partners need not be put off by this situation, but rather simply need to realize it is endemic to planned economies, even those engaged in market reforms. Even though the government-approved wholesaler is likely to take a "cut" of the JV's sales revenues, and that wholesaler may be entirely unnecessary, the venture may be very profitable.

How should a JV price a product sold domestically? Chinese investment law provides that prices for goods sold domestically must be consistent with state-controlled prices for similar goods available on the domestic market. Clearly, the Chinese government does not want international JVs undermining its state pricing system (*e.g.*, as a result of local consumers buying a significantly cheaper JV product, and thus diminishing demand for goods made by wholly Chinese companies or state-owned enterprises). In contrast, the products of a JV intended for export do not have to be priced in accordance with government-mandated price controls. These prices can be

---

105. SHIZHONG *et al.*, *supra*, at 185.

established by the partners, though they must file their price lists with the appropriate regulatory body and with the Price Control Administration.

These factors indicate an overseas investor must plan for and accommodate potential Chinese government constraints on the marketing, sales, distribution, and pricing scheme of the JV enterprise. Failure to do so may result, for example, in the JV being held to price controls that cause it to be less profitable than expected. In other words, here again planning is the foundation on which the success of an international JV rests.

Labor is another issue for JVs in China. A JV may hire from the Chinese partner's employee pool, it may take the suggestions of the Chinese partner in hiring from another pool, or it may enter into a contract with a Chinese labor service company. In addition, the Chinese government may allow the JV to recruit locally, or even outside the area if specifically requested. As to compensation, the wages of the Chinese employees of a JV "typically must exceed 120% of the wages that the employee would receive if employed in a similar capacity by a domestic state-owned enterprise."[106] The JV also must pay for employee benefits, such as unemployment insurance, health insurance, accident insurance, retirement pension, housing assistance, subsidies for food, fuel, and other consumables depending on locale, and trade union expenses. These expenses— for example, for housing, food, fuel, consumer items, and trade union dues—typically are not what an American company would pay to its workers. Another interesting requirement placed on JV enterprises in China is that the JV must allocate a fixed portion of its net profits to a "bonus fund" administered jointly by the relevant trade union and the JV itself. Most importantly, an American partner needs to establish and preserve a positive working relationship between its Chinese partner. This necessarily involves appropriate treatment of its partner and Chinese employees. "Foreign managers know that a positive working atmosphere between the Chinese and foreign workers is vital to the success of the entity and that a deterioration of that atmosphere will almost certainly be detrimental to the enterprise.... [E]ffective and open communication is a key to success in the inherently suspicious business environment of the PRC."[107]

Nascent and evolving Chinese environmental protection requirements are a final important consideration for JVs. Although the concept of environmental protection is relatively new in China, and environmental legislation is recent and developing, a JV must be informed of, and adhere to, applicable environmental standards. Specifically, China's National Environmental Protection Bureau is authorized to review construction contracts to ensure compliance. Local government bodies also may have supplemental regulations in place to account for possible changes in conditions that would result from the JV.

In sum, planning, maintaining good relations, and knowing what to expect in terms of the intricacies of working with government bureaucracies are crucial to the success of a JV in China. Although there are complexities associated with dealing with a communist economy in transition, a JV in China may present unparalleled opportunities to overseas investors.

5. Form #5: International Distributorships[108]

A distributorship is "[a]ny individual, partnership, corporation, association, or other legal relationship which stands between the manufacturer and the retail

---

106. SHIZHONG et al., supra, at 187.

107. SHIZHONG et al., supra, at 189.

108. This discussion is drawn from COMMERCIAL LAWS OF EAST ASIA (Alan Gutterman & Robert Brown eds. 1997), and Sales Agent and Distributorship Agreements, in 1 RALPH H. FOLSOM & MICHAEL W. GORDON, INTERNATIONAL BUSINESS TRANSACTIONS 1 (1995).

seller in purchases, consignments, or contracts for sale of consumer goods. [Thus, examples of distributors include a] wholesaler, jobber, or other merchant middleman authorized by a manufacturer or seller to sell chiefly to retailers and commercial users."[109] Simply put, this arrangement involves a sale of a product by a manufacturer in one country (the home country) to an agent — the distributor — in another or other countries (the host country or countries). In turn, the distributor re-sells the product to retailers (*e.g.*, stores), or directly to purchasers in the consumer market.[110]

A distributor is not simply a reseller, however. It is linked closely to its supplier. In particular:

1. in its capacity as reseller, the distributor deals with the promotion and or organization of distribution in the assigned territory;

2. the supplier confers a privileged position in the territory on the distributor: generally the exclusive right to purchase the products from the supplier;

3. the relationship must be for a certain duration and sets conditions for collaboration that, by definition, cannot be episodic;

4. the relationship creates a fairly close tie of loyalty between the parties, which usually implies that the distributor refrains from distributing competing products;

5. the distributor is virtually always distributing brand-name products.[111] As this list of characteristics involved in a distribution arrangement suggests, there is a higher degree of connectivity and mutual dependence between a manufacturer and its distributor than between independent players in a sale-resale arrangement.

A distributorship provides an American investor, which typically wants to export its product, with an agent in the overseas destinations to which the investor seeks to sell its wares (again, the host country or countries). A distributor offers an existing sales network through which the exporter can sell its product. The distributor benefits from the differential between the price at which it sells the product in the host country, and the price at which it purchases the product from the exporter. The distributor also benefits from a standpoint of comparative advantage. For example, the distributor of American auto parts in Mexico is able to introduce new parts and products without incurring a development or manufacturing cost.

To be sure, distributorships are subject to host country regulation. Yet, as distinct from other forms of FDI, the foreign investment law of a host nation is not likely to embrace distributorships. It is not an unintentional omission from a foreign investment law that distributorships are excluded, but merely a recognition that distributorships are the least intrusive and direct form of FDI. The overseas investor is not establishing a subsidiary or JV, but rather simply hiring an agent. Most foreign investment laws are aimed at overseas investments that result in a more involved physical presence and the attendant ownership arrangements. Accordingly, in most instances the most important areas of host country law regulating the activities of a distributor are simply standard

---

109. BLACK'S LAW DICTIONARY (6th ed. 1990) at 476.

110. There may be a number of variations on those forms. For instance, the distributor might not take title to the goods before sale. For purposes of the above discussion, the sale-resale arrangement is assumed.

111. International Chamber of Commerce, *The ICC Model Distributorship Contract* VI-VII (ICC International Contracts Series, Pub. No. 518 1993).

contract law and sale of goods law. In addition to standard commercial law, agency, competition, or antitrust law may be relevant to distributorships:

> In addition, many countries have special laws regulating the activities of sales agents and distributors, as well as the terms of sales agency and distribution arrangements. Also, a number of developing countries regulate distribution arrangements under the antitrust/competition laws in much the same way as they regulate licensing arrangements. Regulators in [developing] countries are particularly concerned about the competitive effects of exclusive distribution arrangements.[112]

Thus, an international business lawyer needs to consider the legal system of the host country and ascertain exactly which areas of this system apply to a proposed distributorship arrangement.

a. Establishing an International Distributorship

A distributorship arrangement should be memorialized in a written agreement. As in many international transactions where a relationship between parties from different countries is less trusting at the outset due to lack of familiarity, cultural or language differences, or lack of an established track record, the parties to a distributorship deal need a writing to allocate the risks of the deal.[113] Hence, a distribution agreement is the central document in a distributorship relationship. Of course, the agreement is only a second best substitute to careful selection of a distributor. As with setting up a JV, where selecting a suitable partner is crucial, the success of a distributorship rests ultimately on proper selection of a distributor.

Once a host country, market sector, choice of distributor, and desired scope of a relationship have been determined, and the parties have initiated negotiations, the agreement will begin to take shape. The International Chamber of Commerce *Guide to Drafting International Distributorship Agreements*, ICC Publication No. 441(E) (1988) explains how to draft an international distributorship agreement, and provides detailed recommendations on each provision of the agreement.[114] In general, a careful international business lawyer will devise an agreement that protects the exporter/manufacturer and the distributor from as many contingencies as possible, and that allows the distributorship to work in reality in the manner envisioned by the parties. In particular, a well-planned agreement will cover at least eight key areas: (1) the product covered by the distributorship arrangement, (2) the scope and duration of the distributorship arrangement, (3) pricing of the product, and payment for the product, that is provided to the distributor by the manufacturer, (4) shipping and supply of the product by the manufacturer to the distributor, (5) retail pricing of the product, (6) warranties associated with the product, (7) the obligations of the distributor, and (8) termination of the distributorship arrangement. These areas are discussed in turn below.

(1) The Product

The terms of a distributorship agreement relating to the product are noteworthy, because the product is the medium by which the agreement becomes mutually bene-

---

112. Gutterman & Brown, *supra*, at 61.

113. *See Sales Agent and Distributorship Agreements, in* FOLSOM & GORDON, *supra*, at 2.

114. For another excellent source, see Steven C. Nelson, *Negotiating and Drafting Agency, Distribution, and Franchise Agreements, in* NEGOTIATING AND STRUCTURING INTERNATIONAL COMMERICAL TRANSACTIONS, *supra*.

ficial. The description, quantity, spare parts, and replacement information should be set forth in the agreement. The agreement also should set forth the rights of and limitations on the distributor to enhance, improve, or modify the product. After all, the distributor may want to tailor the product to local market conditions, whereas the exporter may be concerned about standardization, particularly with respect to quality.

(2) Scope and Duration

A distributorship agreement should define the scope and duration of the distributorship arrangement. In what geographic region and market, and to which customers, is the distributor permitted to sell the product? Is this permission exclusive, or may other distributors of the product sell in the same area or to the same customers? The answer is important for an exporter seeking to avoid distributors with overlapping territories and clientele, and for a distributor seeking to minimize competition. Indeed, the distributor may want a territorial monopoly, though local antitrust laws may address this matter. Likewise, a distributorship agreement should address exclusivity: Does the distributor have exclusive rights to distribute the product, or can the exporter sell the product through another—and potentially competing—distributor? The distributor is quite likely to want a monopoly, but again anticompetition laws may limit or foreclose this option. Still another matter for the agreement to address is whether the distributor is permitted to use a sub-distributor or other dealer. Such use may give the distributor needed flexibility and the ability to take advantage of effective marketing networks. Finally, the agreement should define the length of time of the distributorship relationship.

(3) Pricing and Payment

Pricing and payment terms (as between the exporter and distributor) are another crucial component of the agreement. Over what time period, and by what means, will the distributor pay for the product it ships to the distributor for subsequent re-sale? One common possibility is a credit arrangement whereby the distributor can pay for the product, for example, in ninety days. This arrangement allows the distributor to pay the exporter with the proceeds from the re-sale of the product. Of course, the agreement also should explain what happens in case of nonpayment by the distributor.

(4) Shipping and Supply

Because the point of a distributorship arrangement is to establish a new overseas market for a product, provisions in a distributorship agreement on shipping and supply are important to both exporter and distributor. On one hand, the exporter may need time to increase the flow of the product to the distributor gradually, as the exporter's manufacturing capacity, the demand for its product, and its level of comfort with the distributor all increase. On the other hand, the distributor may need time to build new plants in which to make its product, and time to develop a successful advertising campaign that creates greater demand for the product. Accordingly, the provisions in the agreement on shipping and supply should balance these concerns. They ought not, for example, to call for the exporter to provide an unrealistically large product volume in an artificially compressed period of time. Rather, these provisions should be flexible, and also allow for occasional shortages or delays.

(5) Retail Price Levels

With respect to retail price levels, as noted earlier, a distributor profits from the differential between the re-sale and purchase prices. There is, as a result, a possible divergence of interests between the distributor and exporter. For instance, the exporter may want a relatively low re-sale price level for its product in order to maintain an image as a "discount product," whereas the distributor may want a relatively higher re-sale price level in order to make a greater profit. "In some cases, distributors may demand some form of protection against the adverse effects of price decreases and in almost all cases the manufacturer must provide the distributor with prior notice of any price changes."[115]

(6) Guarantees and Warranties

Depending on the sophistication of the product, a distributor may want to obtain guarantees or warranties with respect to the design and operation of the product. Indeed, the purchasers of the product may demand such guarantees and warranties. Generally, an exporter will limit potential warranty claims to a specified period, and also limit the extent of any claimant's remedy. Recall that most imported consumer electronics products sold in the United States have a 60- or 90-day manufacturer's warranty, valid for repair done at one of a few specified service facilities. Additionally, an exporter may be asked by its distributor to provide a warranty regarding the legal status of the product, stating that in manufacturing the product, the exporter did not violate any intellectual property (*e.g.*, patent or trademark) rights of others.

(7) Obligations of the Distributor

Enumerating the obligations of a distributor in a distributorship agreement ensures the expectations of the exporter are understood by the distributor. Possibly the most important such expectation concerns are the minimum market share or sales revenue needed to maintain operations in the host country. Hence, an exporter may be well advised to insist on a "best efforts" provision in the agreement, so as to obligate the distributor to market, sell, and service properly the product. Likewise, the exporter may seek a non-competition provision, which prevents its distributor from selling a competing product during the pendency of the distributorship relationship.

(8) Termination

Termination is an area of the distributorship that is often troublesome for the overseas investor:

> [I]n the sphere of distribution agreements, the most difficult issues arise upon termination, especially when the agent or distributor is terminated against its will.... There is often a sense that the foreign distributor, usually an individual rather than a large corporation, was treated unfairly by the assumed foreign seller, particularly when the local distributor has worked to develop clients and goodwill for the foreign company. The consequence of complaints by local agents and distributors in foreign nations that they have been mistreated, especially terminated unfairly, has been the enactment of foreign, host nation regulation of many forms of distribution agreements.[116]

A farsighted distribution agreement will define with reasonable particularity, but not necessarily exclusively, the events of termination, *i.e.*, the grounds for ending the distribution arrangement. It also will set forth a means of resolving disputes, such as an arbitration clause, because invocation of the termination provision by one party may

---

115. Gutterman & Brown, *supra*, at 63.
116. INTERNATIONAL BUSINESS TRANSACTIONS, *supra*, at 3.

be contested by the other party. For example, there may be a dispute about unsold inventory, goods unpaid for, or whether damages are owed, and if so the amount thereof. As suggested in the above excerpt, many host nations have laws protecting distributors or sales agents in the event of a termination. These laws may, for example, provide a remedy for the distributor to be compensated for loss of future profits, goodwill established during the term of the agreement, employee severance costs, or capital investments.

b. The Amway Example

One of the most well-known international distributorships headquartered in the United States is Amway. Reduced to its essentials, Amway operates through a multi-tiered distribution arrangement whereby the corporation sells products, which it or any number of other companies may have manufactured, to supplier/distributors. In turn, the supplier/distributors sell products to other downstream supplier/distributors, and so forth, until the products reach the consumer.

Amway has enjoyed tremendous success in overseas markets. "There are more than 2.5 million independent Amway distributors in more than 75 countries worldwide. Amway and its affiliates employ more than 13,000 worldwide."[117] Consider Amway's activities in Japan, where Amway Japan has agreements with American exporter/manufacturers to sell their products through Amway's distribution network in Japan:

> Amway Japan Ltd. today announced its million-plus distributors will start selling Rubbermaid Inc. products this spring in Japan.
>
> . . . .
>
> Amway Japan and Rubbermaid will jointly develop and sell a line of food storage containers, according to the announcement fromboth [sic] companies today.
>
> Amway Japan's alliance with Rubbermaid is the second distribution pact the company has signed with a U.S.-based consumer products company in the past quarter.
>
> Amway Japan recently announced an agreement to distribute lingerie made by the Playtex Apparel Division of Chicago-based Sara Lee Corp.[118]

Amway's success also may be evidenced by its recent expansion into the Philippines. Amway initially invested six million dollars in the Philippines and set up three distribution centers, anticipating sales figures in the range of ten to twenty million dollars, selling personal care, household, and home electronics. They joined Avon, Sara Lee, and Mondragon Industries in the Philippine direct marketing/distributorship sector.[119]

Using Amway's distribution network in a foreign country has significant advantages, particularly for a small American manufacturer seeking to export its product, or a large one with little or no international business experience. Such a manufacturer will lack a network of overseas contacts. In contrast, Amway is a sophisticated

---

117. Leda A. Esguerra, *Amway Plans on Becoming Major Direct Seller,* Bus. World (Manila), Apr. 18, 1997, at 8, *available in* WESTLAW, ALLNEWS database, file no. 1997 WL 10162587.

118. *Amway Japan Signs Deal with Rubbermaid,* GRAND RAPIDS PRESS, Jan. 17, 1997, *available in* WESTLAW, ALLNEWS database, file no. 1997 WL 7861727.

119. *See* Esguerra, *supra.*

player with considerable experience in international distributorships. In sum, an international distributorship, as evidenced by the example of Amway, is a significant opportunity for an investor seeking to "go international."

Conclusion

Although there are many means by which an investor may participate in the global economy through FDI, the five major forms of greenfield, franchise, joint venture, M & A, and distributorship investments serve as excellent examples. In order to become aware of the benefits, risks, and complexities of global commerce and investment, a detailed study of the goals and means of the client, the business form of choice, and the local cultural and business climate of the host nation is crucial.

QUESTIONS

1. What are the five major modes of foreign direct investment?

2.   What is the most commonly preferred form of incorporation for an American investor operating in Japan?

3.   What are some of the potential areas of difficulty that an investor might encounter in a joint venture investment in China?

4.   Why does pricing of the product become such a significant issue in creating and maintaining an international distributorship?

5.   What are three reasons why countries seek to attract FDI?

Chapter 6

International Project Finance

I. Syndicated Loans and Registration-Exempt Securities

NOTE ON INTERNATIONAL PROJECT FINANCE*

Introduction[1]

How is FDI financed? For example, consider a German company specializing in infrastructure projects that seeks to build a power generation project in China. Or, consider an American corporation specializing in oil drilling that seeks to develop a large petroleum extraction facility for the Vietnamese government. The price tag may run into the billions of dollars, hence these investors are highly unlikely to be in the position of financing the project out of their own retained earnings. Rather, to finance their proposed projects, these investors will need legal counsel, as well as commercial and investment banking expertise. As discussed below, while there are many financing vehicles, two of the most common are (1) a syndicated loan and (2) the issuance of securities exempt from formal securities laws and regulations pertaining to registration.

1. Defining "Project Finance"

The term "project finance" is used to describe an arrangement whereby "the claims of the debt holders are against an asset or project [*i.e.*, a "stand-alone activ-

---

* This Note was prepared by Christopher C. Matteson, Esq. and Professor Raj Bhala. For a thorough explanation of project finance transactions from a practitioner's perspective, see David H. Spencer, *Project Financing, in* International Banking and Capital Markets: Innovation, Regulation, and Transactions (1994).

1. This portion of the Note draws upon William M. Stelwagon, *Financing Private Energy Projects in the Third World,* 37 Cath. Law. 45 (1996). Patrick D. Harder, *Infrastructure Privatization in South Asia,* 15 Construction Law. 34 (April 1995), also provides significant support.

For a thorough explanation of project finance transactions from a practitioner's perspective, see David H. Spencer, *Project Financing, in* International Banking and Capital Markets: Innovation, Regulation, and Transactions (ABA Section of Int'l L. & Prac, 1994). For a draft of proposed model legislation regarding international project finance, see United Nations, General Assembly, Commission on International Trade Law, Privately Financed Infrastructure Projects, Draft Chapters of a Legislative Guide on Privately-Funded Infrastructures Projects, Report of the Secretary-General, Addendum 1, U.N. Doc. A/CN.9/438/Add.1 (December, 1996).

ity" involving a "medium- to long-term commitment of resources", and in most cases, involving infrastructure] rather than against the sponsor [or host country] as a whole."[2]

Infrastructure projects in developing nations may be financed in many ways. For example, the government of the host country may itself issue bonds in its own domestic market to finance a project, it may use government agencies and labor to build the project out of its own budget, or it may borrow from a multilateral aid or development agency such as The World Bank. Further, the host country may receive United States loan guarantees to assure creditors that finance the project, or it may borrow the finds from a commercial bank or lending syndicate. All of the above, however, are avenues of financing that involve the host country financing the project itself, through whatever means, in its role as sovereign. In other words, these are *public* methods of finance.

The discussion below presents two of the most common *private* funding methods, a syndicated loan from commercial banks, and an issuance of registration-exempt securities. An investor and its counsel must consider these options in relation to the level of risk involved in the project. One writer explains the relationship between risk and financing choices:

> When determining project feasibility, developers most often appeal first to commercial lenders to obtain financing. If the lender cannot obtain adequate security and mitigate its exposure to project risks, financing will be refused. When commercial lending is unavailable, the developer may seek to obtain financing through securities markets, which divide project risks among a larger number of investors. Access to these markets, however, requires the developer to consider the relative cost of different types of offerings, as well as the risk tolerance of different classes of investors. In the United States, private placements of debt or equity followed by resale under Rule 144A [of the Securities and Exchange Commission (SEC)] may offer the best alternative for developers. Such transactions avoid the registration costs associated with Section Five of the Securities Act of 1933 and require placement of securities with sophisticated institutional investors that are better able to bear risk. Public offerings, in contrast, are less appealing to developers because they generate high registration costs and because investors are less willing to assume risks at rates of return acceptable to the developer.[3]

2. The Nature of and Demand for Infrastructure Projects

In general, as suggested above, international project finance is undertaken in relation to a major infrastructure project in another nation. Such a project is defined as follows:

> Privately-financed infrastructure projects are transactions pursuant to which the national, provincial, or local Government engages a private entity to develop, maintain, and operate an infrastructure facility in exchange for the right to charge a price, either to the public or to the government, for the use of the facility or the services or goods it generates.[4]

---

2. Peter Moles & Nicholas Terry, The Handbook of International Financial Terms 437 (1997).

3. Stelwagon, *supra*, at 67-68 (citations omitted).

4. United Nations, General Assembly, Commission on International Trade Law, Privately Financed Infrastructure Projects, Draft Chapters of a Legislative Guide on Privately-Funded Infrastructures Projects, Report of the Secretary-General, Addendum 1, U.N. Doc. A/CN.9/438/Add.1 (December, 1996). This document provides clear and

Note, then, that investing in an infrastructure project is one type of FDI, and is to be distinguished from the establishment of a manufacturing facility (*e.g.*, a textile or personal computer factory). (Both types of FDI are, of course, to be distinguished from portfolio investment, *e.g.*, investing in the equity or debt of an overseas company.)

What drives the need for international project finance? At bottom, it is the tremendous demand for infrastructure development, particularly in the developing world, and the inability or unwillingness of sovereign governments to undertake the project themselves and finance it through tax revenues or the issuance of sovereign debt. Put bluntly, international project finance is needed because roads, schools, power plants, seaports and airports, telecommunications facilities, irrigation systems, and the like need to be built, and these projects are very expensive. Private companies step into to meet the demand for the projects, and private financial institutions step into finance the project. Thus, international project finance allows a host country to modernize and expand its infrastructure without having to fund the project directly. It also allows the host country to benefit from the foreign expertise and technology in the specific area it wishes to develop. Naturally, the arrangement also provides the investors and developers with the ability to realize profits and to expand their global market share.

At the same time, the reality of the extremely high costs involved in infrastructure construction and improvement must be dealt with by those organizing a project:

> Given the significant capital cost involved in undertaking major infrastructure projects, private sector parties typically seek to finance such projects off-balance; that is, on a limited recourse or non-recourse basis. Such form of financing (which as you know is generally referred to as "project finance" and is typically based on 80:20 debt/equity ratio) requires lenders to look wholly or substantially to the cash flows and earnings of the project as the source of funds for repayment of the debt by the project and to the assets of the project as security for the project loan.[5]

Thus, an investor may well have sufficient funds to build a manufacturing facility overseas, or may be able to pool these funds with other investors (*e.g.*, joint venture partners), or with a commercial bank loan. In contrast, because of the much higher cost of an infrastructure project, project finance almost certainly will be needed.

Costs aside, it is difficult to overstate the tremendous demand overseas for infrastructure projects, particularly in the developing world. The Third World seeks economic expansion that requires a supporting infrastructure. That is, less developed countries (LDCs) need to create new infrastructure and modernize that which already exists. Reasons supporting this high level of demand include an increased migration of rural population into the cities, the antiquated state of existing facilities, higher electricity demands due to greater industry needs, and a greater availability and use of consumer appliances in the cities of developing nations. The connection between population growth and infrastructure demand is especially noteworthy. The bulk of the world's population lives in LDCs, and LDCs have the fastest growing population rates in the world. The present and inevitable future

---

well explained definitions of much of the terminology associated with the topic of privately financed infrastructure projects. It also provides a good step-by-step explanation of the roles of the various parties, and the phases of execution involved in a project finance deal.

5. Nicholas Grambas, *Role of Government in Project Finance: Host Government Support*, 23 INT'L BUS. LAW. 196 (May 1995)

population pressures in LDCs add to the strain on their already over-taxed infrastructures, exacerbating the need for infrastructure projects and, therefore, project
finance.

How do infrastructure projects in LDCs catalyze economic growth in those
countries? There seem to be three links. First, they increase the commercial capabilities of the host country. Second, the projects attract overseas investors to do
business in the host country. Third, they improve economic conditions in the host
country. In short, enhanced infrastructure allows developing nations to modernize further and harness the power of the global economy. Roads, bridges, seaports, and airports exist for the traffic of goods, electricity and water are provided
for factories, schools help train workers, and telecommunication networks allow
for the rapid transfer of information. Finally, the process of strengthening infrastructure may lead to valuable technology transfer, and the end result of a
stronger infrastructure may reduce dependence on aid agencies. As one practitioner puts it,

> such schemes reduce the need for governments to use existing public finds
> or to borrow funds from traditional infrastructure lenders such as the
> World Bank, the Asian Development Bank (ADB), and the Overseas Eco-
> nomic Cooperation Fund (OECF) by transferring the funding obligations to
> private companies. This is especially important where governments have
> reached borrowing limits, whether such limits are self-imposed, or are im-
> posed by lenders, international agencies or credit-rating bodies. In addition,
> governments normally require investors to transfer important technology to
> local companies and train local people in the operation and maintenance of
> such technology. By bringing valuable technology into local hands, coun-
> tries can potentially boost their own technological competitiveness in world
> markets.[6]

As suggested earlier, the demand for infrastructure projects far outstrips the capacity of most developing countries to fund such projects. The gap is being filled by
American, European, Japanese, and Korean companies, as many developing country
governments have allowed (sometimes reluctantly) foreign investors to invest in their
local infrastructure. For example:

> According to recent news accounts, [Asia's] need for new power genera-
> tion capacity is staggering — as much as 460,000 megawatts in the next ten
> years according to estimates by General Electric Co. That is equal to about 75
> percent of the current capacity in Asia — or 60 percent of U.S. capacity — at a
> cost, according to Chase Manhattan Bank, of between (U.S.) $50 billion to
> (U.S.) $60 billion a year. In fact, GE estimates that at least 50 percent of its
> power equipment unit's future business will come from Asia.[7]

> Two Asian countries in particular are drawing a great deal of attention be-
> cause of the sheer size of their power needs: 170,000 megawatts for China
> and 60,000 megawatts for India in the next ten years, according to GE's esti-
> mates. China and India will between them order half of Asia's total equipment
> purchases.

Clearly, the demand for such infrastructure project construction, improvement, and
financing is and will be substantial for some time into the future.

---

6. Harder, *supra*, at 34 (citations omitted).
7. *Id.*

3. Risks

One fundamental difference between an overseas infrastructure project and other overseas investments (*e.g.*, FDI not involving infrastructure, or portfolio investments), is that the financing of an infrastructure project is limited, or often non-recourse. That is, investors and creditors may not secure their interests against assets of the host country. Their return on their investment must come from future project income or cash flow. "A project financing at bottom is setting up a new company, with the lenders' recourse limited to the bundle of physical assets that — one hopes — will work as predicted and generate revenues exceeding costs, all as provided in a complex series of construction, off-take, management, operational, financing, and security contracts."[8] Due to the non-recourse nature of the financing, investors often require credit enhancements to mitigate risks. These enhancements may include guarantees against political risks associated with the host country, or insurance from a multilateral or regional development financing institution such as the World Bank's Multilateral Investment Guarantee Agency (MIGA), the Overseas Private Investment Corporation (OPIC), or the United States Export Import Bank (Eximbank).[9] (A detailed treatment of political risk and these sorts of risk-mitigating strategies, as well as commercial risks mentioned below, is provided in a later chapter of this Casebook.)

Consider, for example, an arrangement whereby a syndicate of banks led by National Westminster Bank (Nat West) lends the capital necessary for Halliburton, an American conglomerate, whose Brown & Root Construction division is to develop a toll road in the Philippines.[10] Assume the creditors cannot use Philippine government assets as collateral. Therefore, future income from the operation of the project — the tolls — must constitute the return on investment for the lending syndicate. A separate agreement among the developer, syndicate, and host country is drafted. This agreement creates the stream of revenue from the tolls against which financing is arranged, and from which the investors get their return.[11] The arrangement makes sense be-

---

8. John C. Ale *et al.*, *Capital Markets Provide Finds for Projects Abroad*, NAT'L L.J., December 22, 1997, at B11.

9. *See* Stelwagon, *supra*, at 50-51.

10. To emphasize the applicability of this particular example, consider this passage, written in 1995 regarding project finance in the Philippines.

> Legislation authorising the financing, construction, operation, and maintenance of infrastructure projects by the private sector passed in 1990. Government agencies have been authorised to enter build-operate-transfer, and build and transfer [turnkey] arrangements for infrastructure projects.
>
> For BOT projects where the operation requires a public utility franchise, at least 60 per cent of the capital of the project company must be owned by Filipino citizens. Examples of such projects are railways, distribution of electricity and gas, water distribution, sewerage, and telephone systems serving the general public.
>
> ...
>
> Outside the power sector, the first privately financed toll road will be built by the Indonesian Citra Group under a concession arrangement with the Philippine National Construction Company; and the ubiquitous Renong Group has recently entered into a joint venture agreement with the Philippine Estates Authority under which United Engineers will construct and finance a number of toll roads for the PEA; PEA has an existing franchise to collect tolls from these roads. An expressway running parallel to the railway from Manila to [the former] Clark Air Base, which then will be extended to Subic Bay, is also to be built under a BOT contract.

Kevin Julian, *Infrastructure Privatisation in Asia*, 23 INT'L BUS. LAW. 219 (1995).

11. In the context of a power project, the agreement is called a power purchase agreement, or "PPA." Although the example provided in this Note involves a toll road, which would not in-

cause the syndicate is directly financing the project, rather than lending the funds directly to the Philippine government or its agencies.

The developer, Brown & Root, and the Nat West-led lending syndicate in the Philippine toll road example are likely to purchase political risk insurance, and insurance against the risk of currency inconvertibility, from a private insurance provider such as AIG, or from organizations such as the Asian Development Bank (ADB) or OPIC. After all, the special risks involved a project-based financing arrangement warrant special credit-enhancement arrangements. These risks fall into two basic categories: commercial risks and political risks.

Generally speaking, commercial risks stem from the contracts between the parties involved in the project, including the developer, sponsoring entity in the host country, investors, creditors, and lenders. Examples of these types of risks associated with the hypothetical Philippine toll road include (1) whether the developer can repatriate profits from the Philippines, (2) whether the service life and effectiveness of the toll road are sufficient to meet investor and host country needs, (3) whether the toll road will be well-traveled (sufficient to create an adequate revenue stream), and (4) whether construction is completed in a timely and cost-effective manner. It is important for international business lawyers to be aware of the existence of commercial risks, allocate them satisfactorily in the appropriate agreements, and that properly insure against these risks.

Political risks, obviously, are greatest in developing countries lacking stable political and economic climates and the rule of law—the very countries with the greatest demand for infrastructure projects. International business lawyers will need to identify and allocate these risks, as well as the commercial risks mentioned above. Political risks include (1) currency risks (inconvertibility or devaluation of the Philippine Peso), (2) risk of non-payment by the project operator (likely a Philippine government agency or department, but possibly a private operator), (3) risk of civil disturbance or unrest (such as that posed by guerillas), and (4) expropriation risk. As intimated earlier, obtaining political risk insurance may be necessary. For example, the risk of civil unrest can be mitigated by purchasing political risk insurance from the Asian Development Bank (ADB).

4. Project Structure

There is no one formula for structuring a major overseas infrastructure project. Every deal is in some way—large or small—unique. However, there are two "textbook" structures, which are well described as follows:

> Generally, private [infrastructure] projects take one of two forms. First, the project might be conducted in a Build-Own-Operate basis ("BOO"). In such transactions, the developer builds the [infrastructure project] inside the host country, owns the plant, and sells the [project output to the relevant party in] the host nation. Second, the project might be conducted Build-Own-Operate-Transfer basis ("BOOT"). In a BOOT project, the developer also builds, owns, and operates the [project] inside the host nation. A BOOT project ultimately requires the developer to transfer ownership of the [project] to the [relevant party in the host nation].[12]

---

volve a PPA, the agreement might be similar, as it would provide "a revenue stream against which financing is obtained and from which investment returns are realized." Stelwagon, *supra*, at 50.

12. Stelwagon, *supra*, at 49 (citations omitted). The term BOOT is used by Harder, *supra* note 1. It should be noted that the term "Build-Operate Transfer," ("BOT") also is used to describe the BOOT project. BOT is well described in this example involving Vietnam. The Vietnamese government approves BOT projects, allowing project consortia to enter into ancillary contracts in order to "construct, supply, finance, advise, insure, or invest in BOT project." The

In sum, the BOO scheme usually involves the developer or developer's consortium operating the project post-completion, whereas the BOOT scheme would involve a post-completion transfer of ownership (a so-called "turnkey" operation).[13] One might correctly surmise that a BOOT arrangement is appropriate "where a customer base exists for the end product."[14] The Philippine toll road is an excellent example of such a project.

Certainly, these textbook formulas may be varied in a myriad of ways. Consider again the Philippine toll road project. The developer might build the toll road in the Philippines directly for the Philippine authority, without ever actually owning or operating the project. The purchase agreement, or variant of the power purchase agreement (PPA), would guarantee the stream of revenue to the developer, investors, and lending syndicate after completion and transfer.

Option "1: Commercial Lending—The Syndicated Loan[15]

Commercial lending is the traditional, and often the least expensive, form of financing an overseas infrastructure project. But, as the funding requirements are large in the case of an infrastructure project such as a toll road, easily running into the billions of dollars, the credit risk is considerable. It is unlikely that any one commercial bank will be willing or able to lend the amount needed by the developer to complete the project—hence a lending syndicate will be needed. Why?

First, no commercial bank wants to be left "holding the bag" if a toll road construction project fails. The bank could lose billions of dollars depending on its loan exposure to the failed debtor, the assets of the debtor available to pay out claims, the priority of the bank's claim, and the extent to which the bank has credit enhancements on which it can draw. (Regarding priority, a commercial lender, like most other creditors, ought always to seek to be the "most senior in terms of repayment priority."[16]) Second, prudential bank regulations limiting loans to one borrower (*e.g.*, a rule against loaning an amount in excess of 10 percent of the bank's assets to one borrower) may prohibit any single bank from extending such a large loan to one debtor. Likewise, regulatory bank capital adequacy requirements—such as those set forth in the 1988 Basle agreement on risk-based capital—may preclude one bank from financing the entire project. Finally, aside from banking law proscriptions, any one commercial bank simply is unlikely to have sufficient liquidity to lend such a large amount.

Vietnamese government requires investors in BOT projects to "have responsibility to organize and manage project within time period of sufficient length to recover their invested capital and reasonable profit; after which they have obligation to transfer project, without compensation, to Vietnamese Government." Martindale-Hubbell International Law Digest, Vietnam Law Digest, *available in* LEXIS-NEXIS, MARHUB database, INTDIG file.

13. For an interesting case study of such a turnkey project and some sample documentation, see John I. Huhs, *Actual Case Study of a Soviet Turnkey Project, in* NEGOTIATING AND STRUCTURING INTERNATIONAL COMMERICAL TRANSACTIONS: LEGAL ANALYSIS WITH SAMPLE AGREEMENTS 323 (Shelly P. Battram & David N. Goldsweig eds., 1991). Although it describes an arrangement of the Cold War era, the principles mentioned therein are helpful in gaining an understanding of a ?rather typical? (in the author's words) turnkey project.

14. Harder, *supra*, at 36 (citation omitted).

15. This portion draws significantly upon the chapters on syndicated lending in NICHOLAS L. DEAK & JOANNE CELUSAK, INTERNATIONAL BANKING (1984) and RAVI C. TENNEKOON, THE LAW & REGULATION OF INTERNATIONAL FINANCE (1991), and on Richard Slater, *Syndicated Bank Loans*, J. BUS. L. 173-99 (May 1982).

16. Stelwagon, *supra*, at 63-64.

Given the reasons for the inability or unwillingness of a commercial bank to be the sole lender, a developer will have to consider a syndicated loan arrangement to finance the project at sufficient levels. A syndicate of banks, with risks distributed with relative equality among them, will be more willing and able to extend the huge sums required to finance a large infrastructure project.

Loan requirements for international finance are often so substantial that no institution could or would want to undertake the entire credit commitment. This economic reality has lead to the development of the syndicated loan, whereby several banks join together to share the rights and responsibilities connected with the extension of a substantial loan. Therefore, syndication involves a number of lending banks, which when acting in concert are effectively able to extend the size limit of loans that could be made individually on the Eurodollar market. ["Eurodollars" are United States dollars deposited or on loan from a bank located outside of the United States.] The banks are also able to spread their risks amongst themselves. Each lender's obligation is generally separate.[17]

Thus, the syndicated loan is an appropriate vehicle and suits both lenders and creditors in an infrastructure project financing scheme.

1. Issues Involved

As suggested above, a principal reason why a developer chooses a syndicated commercial loan as an infrastructure project finance vehicle is the accessibility of a large "pool" of funds raised and lent in concert by the syndicate members. There are additional advantages to syndicated loan arrangements, such as the accessibility of the global lending market to less sophisticated commercial banks, the increased availability of large Eurodollar loans to groups such as governments, multinationals, and other market institutions, and the spreading of risk among members of the syndicate. Finally, syndicated loans provide the debtor with access to financing options for ventures that may involve a higher than average degree of risk, for which routine financing options might not be available.

Commercial banks lacking the resources, experience, or capitalization to extend a large loan directly can participate, and reap the rewards of such loans through membership in a lending syndicate. The "managing bank" or "lead bank" (the head of the syndicate) provides the expertise necessary to arrange such a transaction, while the resources and capital are provided by the banks as a group. To be sure, there are risks associated with membership in a lending syndicate, but the rewards can be great. With the global lending market open to a wider range of banks, these risks are spread among a larger segment of the lending industry, and the opportunities to participate in large transactions in the developing world, for example, allow American banks to expand their profit and customer base.

The genesis of syndicated lending stemmed from the needs for governments, multinational corporations, and other entities to access large credits. Financing large acquisitions such as airline and merchant shipping fleets, as well as petroleum and gas product extraction, transport and processing facilities, and even government budgets (as in sovereign syndicated lending) requires vast sums. Naturally, the financial market rose to meet this need in the form of syndicated lending. This form of financing has, for instance, met a need for large Eurodollar credits which continues today. "Institutional participation in bank loans jumped 139.4% in 1996, according

---

17. DEAK & CELUSAK, *supra*, at 176.

to a study.... [Also, syndicated B]ank loans were the most sought-after types of trans-actions in the private market last year[.]"[18]

With respect to the allocation of risk, consider again the example of the Philip-pine toll road project. If one bank—say Nat West—were to lend (directly) eighty percent of the funds necessary in a large Eurodollar loan to Brown & Root and the project consortium, then Nat West would bear almost the entire commercial and po-litical risk of the project. Suppose this project turns sour, and in addition Nat West experiences a default on another large Eurodollar loan, or on a series of loans in other countries. Nat West could well go bust, and in turn a chain reaction of liquid-ity problems could arise for creditors of Nat West, leading to serious "systemic" risk, *i.e.*, the risk that problems suffered by one bank spread throughout the banking sys-tem because of exposures of banks to one another. Even if the commercial creditor, Nat West, is at the head of the line when it comes to repayment, it will not want to be in the position of a creditor trying to collect from a "deadbeat" debtor, especially one in a developing nation subject to local insolvency law. Doubtless that Nat West will prefer to be a partial creditor to a failed toll road construction project in the Philippines than the sole creditor. Importantly, "...lenders prefer [syndicated] bank loans because, in short, they offer an alternative to investors unwilling to move down the credit scale. Although the yields are often not as attractive as those that could be obtained through participation in below-investment grade private debt offerings, the security is better."[19]

2. Responsibilities of the Lead Bank

The principal commercial bank in charge of the syndicate is called the "lead bank," "manager," or sometimes, the "lead manager." In order to gain a thorough understanding of the structure of a syndicated loan deal, it is necessary to understand the role and responsibilities of the lead bank.

The lead bank essentially initiates the process by negotiating with the borrower. Enveloped in this negotiation process is a very thorough review of the risks and ben-efits of the project itself, and of the loan transaction in particular. Intuitively, the de-gree of risk involved necessarily influences the lead bank's negotiation position, as a high risk project might cause the lead bank to be able to request a higher yield or even to refuse to finance certain portions of the project. During this phase, the lead bank will determine the most profitable way of marketing the loan to potential syn-dicate members.

The lead bank solicits participation in the syndicate from other commercial banks with which it has dealt in the past, or from those banks interested in extend-ing credit in the global syndicated lending market. For example, as lead bank, Nat West may contact commercial departments of banks such as Credit Lyonnais, the Hong Kong Shanghai Banking Corporation, Banque Indosuez, Bank of Tokyo-Mit-subishi, and Citibank, and solicit their participation in a syndicated loan to the Philippine toll road consortium. The manner of solicitation is important. Some legal authorities suggest there is a possibility that a solicitation to the general commercial bank market will be considered an offering of securities, thus becoming subject to registration and disclosure requirements under applicable securities regulation. A lead bank does not offer a "prospectus" to the participating banks; it is instead called

---

18. *Institutions Devour Syndicated Bank Loan Deals*, 12 BANK LOAN REP. no. 37 (Sept. 15, 1997), *available in* LEXIS, MARKET library, PROMT file.
    19. *Id.*

a placement memorandum. Normally, the placement memorandum would be subject to the strict registration and disclosure requirements of the United States Securities Act of 1933. Indeed, during the Third World debt crisis of the late 1970s and early and mid 1980s, one scholar suggested that, as a general proposition, loan syndications should be considered securities:

> As the current debt crisis continues, banks in creditor countries will have to respond to the likely inability of debtor countries to repay their loans in full. These banks may react by trying to collect from one another. One possible approach would be for participant banks in international loan syndications (most likely U.S. regionals) to sue their lead banks (typically U.S. money center banks) for breach of the securities laws.[20]

However, if done "right," the transaction will not be considered subject to the Act because syndicated loan participations will not be considered "securities" within the meaning of the Act.[21] Still, lead banks should be cautious as to disclosures and the accuracy of the statements contained in the placement memorandum, because some authorities suggest lead banks are subject to American and British securities regulations concerning fraudulent and misleading statements.

Full and accurate disclosure hardly is the end of the lead bank's responsibility (indeed, liability). It must conduct an independent credit investigation of the project. Prudence dictates that the other commercial banks in the syndicate investigate as well. Of course, the information supplied by the project consortium and the developer—in our example, Brown & Root—will be cast in a positive light because it is promotional in nature. Nat West certainly will hire counsel to perform a "due diligence" inspection and review of the project, as should the syndicate members.

> Nevertheless, the effectiveness of such safeguards against liability varies and depends to a large degree upon the extent of diligence and culpability found on the part of the lead [bank]. For this reason, it is prudent practice to secure independent outside legal counsel, as well as aiming for accurate and complete disclosure in the placement memorandum.[22]

There are three basic ways by which the lead bank may market the syndicated loan to prospective commercial bank members. Although there may be variations on each or hybridization among these three methods, they are "best efforts," "firm com-

---

20. David Z. Nirenberg, *International Loan Syndications: The Next Security,* 23 Colum. J. Transnat'l L. 155 (1984).

21. *See, e.g.,* UBAF Ltd. v. European American Banking Corp., 1 Lloyd's Rep 258 (C.A. 1984). Participants sued the lead bank in a syndicated loan to Colocotronis for vessel finance purposes. After default, the members sued under United Kingdom law, alleging misrepresentation.

"Colocotronis loan participations were sold to plaintiffs—American participating banks—who alleged that this constituted a sale of securities within the meaning of United States (and state) securities laws." Deak & Celusak, *supra,* at 181. "As a result of a number of suits brought in the United States against European-American Banking Corporation in 1976, there was much discussion in United States legal circles at the end of that year and in 1977 about whether the anti-fraud provisions of the [1933 and 34 Acts] apply to certain aspects of syndicated loans.... The question has in fact never been properly resolved and United States bank lawyers remain nervous about the applicability of the Acts to certain activities by banks in syndicated loans. No such worries afflict their English brethren. It is quite clear that none of the rules regulating securities and dealing in securities in England applies to syndicated loans." Slater, *supra,* at 185-86. In sum, it appears that under United States securities regulation, syndicated loan participations are not "securities" within the meaning of the term.

22. Deak & Celusak, *supra,* at 181.

mitment," and "pre-advanced." A "best efforts" syndication involves a pre-determined set of terms and conditions offered by the lead bank to potential participants.
If the potential lenders do not accept the pre-determined terms and conditions, then
the marketing effort is terminated with no obligation to the borrower. "Firm commitment" syndication, as the name implies, involves a commitment by the lead bank
to arrange financing and provide the loan. If the marketing effort is not successful,
then the lead bank will lend the un-marketed portions. Finally, a "pre-advanced"
syndication entails a firm commitment arrangement, with the added caveat that the
lead bank "may participate the loan out at a later date."[23] In other words, at some
point in the future, the lead bank can sell the un-marketed portions rather than continue to bear the obligations and risks associated with these portions.

What is the relationship between the lead bank and the other commercial banks in
the syndicate? There are two basic arrangements, "direct" and "indirect." With "direct" loans, the participants actually hold notes that represent the indebtedness of the
owner, developer, or consortium, providing for direct recourse against the borrower in
the event of default. In essence, the participants can bypass the lead bank. In the case
of "indirect" loans, the lead bank funds the loan directly, and the participants receive
certificates representing the indebtedness of the lead bank. The obvious difference between these two arrangements is a significant one. In a direct arrangement, the borrower remains liable to each syndicate participant, whereas in an indirect arrangement,
the lead bank has sole right of recourse against the borrower. One implication of this
difference is that the direct loan might be more appropriate in the case of a well-established and creditworthy borrower, so that the participating banks are comfortable with
having the right of recourse directly against the project consortium or developer.

After the participants have been recruited, the syndicate has been formed, and
the terms and conditions agreed upon, the lead bank's role diminishes and becomes
largely administrative. It is responsible for calculating interest, overseeing funds
transfers, and monitoring and ensuring compliance on the part of the borrower.

3. Syndicated Loan Documentation

What does a syndicated loan "look like" in terms of legal documentation? There are
three main parts: a mandate letter or a letter of intent, a placement memorandum, and
a loan agreement. Each part represents a distinct phase in the syndicated lending process.

Mandate Letter/Letter of Intent

The mandate letter is a pre-contractual document representing the culmination
of the negotiation process between the lead bank and the borrower. To illustrate
using the above example, the mandate letter represents negotiations and contains the
principal terms of the initial arrangement between NatWest and Brown & Root for
the Philippine toll road project. Terms of credit, price, fees, and type of syndication
(*i.e.*, firm commitment, best efforts, or pre- advanced) will be in the letter. Often, this
negotiation is a difficult part of the process, as the parties may have differing expectations with respect to items such as interest rate and repayment. Once this document
is signed by the borrower, it acts as a "go-ahead" for the lead bank to pursue the organization of the syndicate and arrange for credit on the borrower's behalf.

The letter of intent, often used in a sovereign lending context, is "...an agreement to agree.... Before a business or financial transaction is formally set up, preliminary negotiations should come about and some written or oral understanding

---

23. *Id.* at 178.

will establish the frame for concluding an agreement between the parties."[24] As with a mandate letter, a letter of intent is a pre-contractual document. But, it may be enforceable in varying degrees depending on the cultural context and legal regime in which it was prepared and signed. Both a mandate letter and letter of intent represent the culmination of the negotiation process between the lead bank and the borrower.

Placement Memorandum

As suggested above, the placement memorandum is largely a solicitation tool. It is a source of information source for potential syndicate participants, and thus catalyzes the formation of the syndicate. In the Philippine toll road example, Nat West would issue the placement memorandum. Its contents would include the basic terms of the loan, an analysis of the financial and credit background of the borrower, and relevant information concerning the risks involved in the toll road project. The document also can and should be an exercise in "preventative law." Counsel for Nat West should seek to avoid future litigation among members of the syndicate by ensuring they have exercised all requisite due diligence, and have been thorough and accurate in drafting the placement memoranda.

Loan Agreement

Without doubt, the document most central to the syndicated loan transaction is the loan agreement. It contains the "essential agreements to lend and repay, with interest, funds of a certain variety and amount...[and] descriptions of certain contingencies representing risk to one or all parties and of provisions included to reduce those risks."[25] The basic provisions of a syndicated loan agreement are described below in terms of the Philippine toll road hypothetical. These include (1) *conditions precedent*, (2) *representations and warranties*, (3) *financial arrangements*, (4) *covenants*, (5) *default*, and (6) *choice of law*.

Conditions precedent are those which must be satisfied by Brown & Root and the project consortium before the Nat West syndicate extend any credit. These conditions generally include the requirement that the borrower provide

> various documents relating to its [the borrower's] constitution, its powers, its status and capacity, internal authorizations and exchange control permissions (where necessary) as well as legal opinions from specified lawyers with regard to these and other matters. These conditions precedent seek to ensure that the loan agreement is a valid and legal agreement and that the borrower has the power and all necessary authorizations to enter into the agreement.[26]

Nat West and the syndicate may include further conditions precedent, such as one regarding default; specifically, that Brown & Root and the consortium has not defaulted between the signing of the loan agreement and the first extension of credit.

Representations and warranties in the syndicated loan agreement are factual in nature and form the basis of the loan syndicate's extension of credit. As opposed to covenants, which are points with which the Brown & Root consortium must comply prior to disbursement, representations and warranties give Nat West the ability to

---

24. Alfred G. Romero, *The Letter of Intent in Syndicated Financing: An Analysis of the English and American Law from a Sovereign Borrowers' Perspective*, 3 NAFTA: L. & Bus. Rev. Americas 74 (1997). This excellent article analyzes in depth the legal nature of the letter of intent in the context of sovereign syndicated lending.

25. *Id.* at 182.

26. Tennekoon, *supra*, at 68.

take action if the representations are untrue or inaccurate. Appropriate action may be to (a) terminate the agreement, (b) accelerate the loan (demand faster repayment), or (c) nullify the agreement. Essentially, this portion of the loan agreement provides the Nat West syndicate with a contractual remedy against the project consortium. One example of a warranty in this context might be that the Brown & Root consortium represent and warrant the accuracy of all accounting reports and forecasts of the Philippine toll road project.

The *financial arrangements* in the loan agreement are central to the operation of the syndicated loan transaction. They concern the "nuts and bolts" aspects of the relationship between lender and borrower. These logistics include the mechanics and procedures for funds transfers and interest payment. They also include the currency in which credit is to be extended, the period of the loan, the amount of the loan and amount of disbursements and repayments to be made, and when, procedures for disbursement and repayment, and provisions relating to prepayment.[27]

The *covenants* in a syndicated loan transaction exist to protect the lenders. There are six types of covenants in a typical international syndicated loan agreement. First, financial performance covenants exist to compel the borrower to maintain a specific minimum level of performance, at which repayment of the loan is not problematic. There also may be financial information covenants, which compel the borrower to disclose information sufficient to allow the syndicate to determine compliance with the financial performance covenants mentioned above. Asset disposal covenants may be embodied in the agreement in order to preserve the borrower's asset base. One interesting covenant is the negative pledge, which seeks to prevent other lenders (outside the syndicate) from obtaining a secured or higher position in the repayment "food chain." An events of default covenant grants the syndicate the right to accelerate the loan in the event that the borrower fails to meet the financial performance covenant. Lastly, a cross-default clause allows the syndicate to accelerate the borrower's repayment obligation in the event that other syndicates who may have lent to the borrower accelerate their loans. Of great importance to the lending syndicate, these covenants are very complex and may retain potency for as long as forty years.

Some of the covenants may pose difficulties from a systemic perspective. Consider the cross-default clause. Suppose other lenders, outside the Nat West syndicate, accelerate the obligations of the borrower. These lenders act largely on rumors about the financial condition of the borrower, the borrower's industry, or the borrower's country, but not necessarily on a thorough review of the true state of the individual borrower. In fact, however, the borrower is in fairly good shape. Hearing that other creditors have accelerated their obligations, the Nat West syndicate follows suit. Now, there is a "run" on the borrower. It cannot repay all of its obligations at once, and thus faces a liquidity problem. In turn, the financial position of some of its large creditors may be jeopardized because of any delay in repayment, or non-payment. In other words, a cross-default clause can turn a healthy borrower into a shaky debtor, or exacerbate the problems of an already-shaky debtor. Each creditor may be acting rationally based on its existing information set about the borrower, but when every creditor accelerates the obligation owed to it, the creditors as a whole are made worse off because they are injuring the borrower. The creditor "grab race" — the race to grab the borrower's assets before some other creditor gets them — depletes the value of the borrower as a going concern, making full repayment of the creditors less

27. For a detailed discussion of each of the different provisions contained in the financial arrangements section of a syndicated loan agreement, see TENNEKOON, *supra*, at 73.

likely, and possibly sending the borrower into bankruptcy. This is precisely the problem Professor Jackson described in his 1986 book, *The Logic and Limits of Bankruptcy Law*. The end result is that the creditors hurt themselves insofar as they are not repaid in full. No doubt banking regulators worry about this sort of "systemic" risk: the individual action of commercial bank creditors leads to difficulties for a debtor, which reverberates back to the commercial banks.

The last two types of provisions in a syndicated loan agreement are easily described and common to many commercial agreements. *Default* provisions in the agreement would define acts (*i.e.*, events) of default, and convey the legal right to accelerate the loan and terminate the agreement if default occurs. These events should be drafted very carefully, and the possible clash of interests between the syndicate and borrower ought to be realized in advance. For instance, the syndicate may want a large number of events listed, including several broadly worded events, so that it can call the loan virtually whenever it feels insecure. The borrower, in contrast, is likely to want to protect itself from "trigger-happy" creditors by, *inter alia*, a short list of tightly-worded events.

A *choice of law* provision designates the law to be applied in the event of any dispute. A choice of jurisdiction, or forum-selection clause, is a concomitant provision specifying the situs of any litigation. Generally speaking, as in most international business contracts, in a syndicated loan agreement, New York and United Kingdom law are chosen. This selection reflects the widespread understanding about these laws, and thus the certainty and predictability they provide. It also reflects the generally pro-creditor leaning of the those laws. Following the selection of New York or United Kingdom law, the loan agreement might well specify a court in New York (such as the United States District Court for the Southern District of New York), or a court in England (such as a commercial court in London), as the forum in which to adjudicate any disputes.

In sum, it is important for international business lawyers to understand the legal and business elements of a syndicated loan transaction. It is, after all, the traditional, and an extremely common, form of project finance.

Option "2: Sales of Registration-Exempt Securities[28]

While commercial loans are the traditional source of infrastructure project finance,[29] a sale of securities[30] also is a common way of raising the necessary funding or a portion thereof. Indeed, the increasingly frequent resort to the international cap-

---

28. Securities regulation is a complex topic and, of course, the subject of one or more law school courses. This discussion is hardly an exhaustive treatment of exempt offerings under United States or other securities laws. Rather, it is intended to introduce the reader to the existence and utility of securities offerings in the project finance context and highlight some of the important attendant securities regulation issues. For a thorough treatment of relevant United States securities regulations, see LOUIS LOSS & JOEL SELIGMAN, FUNDAMENTALS OF SECURITIES REGULATION (3rd ed. 1995).

29. Especially in the Asian project finance market, there is a general preference for syndicated bank loans rather than sales of securities. Accordingly, the volume of this type of private financing has increased: "European banks reporting to the BIS [Bank for International Settlements in Basle, Switzerland] had claims of $26.05 billion in China by the end of [1996], a 28 per cent increase over the previous year." Sheel Kohli, *Europe Banks Aim to Win Top Spot for Loans*, SOUTH CHINA MORNING POST, July 3, 1997, *available in* WESTLAW, ALLNEWS database, file No. 1997 WL 2268586.

30. The term "securities" in this context includes debt instruments, such as bonds, as well as equity instruments, such as stocks. For an authoritative treatment of the definition of a "security," see LOSS & SELIGMAN *supra*, at 169-239.

ital markets reflects at least two developments: the inability or unwillingness of commercial banks to meet all of the demand for international project finance, and the ability of more and more project sponsors to tap the markets directly on favorable financing terms.

The global turn to the private sector [*i.e.*, privatization of state-owned enterprises] during the past 10 years has generated new demands for private capital to fund new infrastructure projects.

. . . .

Yet the sheer numbers of these projects—in Europe and throughout the world—has taxed the capacity of...conventional sources for infrastructure financing. Moreover, in the case of economies [of developing nations], risks inherent in any emerging country deal—political and currency risks, restrictions on repatriation of profits, less creditworthy revenue sources, immature legal and commercial regimes—make these projects all the more difficult to finance. Traditional financing sources have not been able to fill all the demand, even when risks have been managed. The pressures for broader financing sources recently have lead many companies to seek funds from a new source for limited-recourse project debt: the capital markets.[31]

Naturally, issuing securities raises important legal problems under the securities regulations of the jurisdiction(s) in which the securities are being issued. What regulations apply? How onerous are they? Do they require a large amount of disclosure? What sorts of liabilities do they impose on the issuer? Do they raise the cost of capital materially? What exemptions exist from the otherwise regulations? What are the requirements for qualifying for these exemptions, and can they be met?

As might be imagined, the process of registering an initial public offering (IPO) of securities with the United States Securities and Exchange Commission (SEC) is expensive and time consuming, and an extremely high level of disclosure required. In other words, the expense, time, regulatory burden, and complexity of an IPO raises the cost of capital. Hence, those involved in international project finance are likely to find an "exempt offering," *i.e.*, a sale of securities exempt from registration requirements under United States securities laws, to be an attractive choice.

Developers who are unable to obtain commercial loans may utilize several other potential sources of capital. First, the developer can issue a private placement of securities. Second, the developer can offer securities outside the United States and enjoy the exemption to United States registration embodied in SEC Regulation S. With both private placements and offshore offerings, the developer can issue either debt or equity instruments. In addition, the buyer in each of these situations may resell these securities within the United States without registration if the security complies with SEC Rule 144A. Rule 144A provides a safe harbor from registration in the United States for resales to "qualified institutional buyers" of securities that are not of the same class of securities publicly traded in United States markets. Finally, the developer can offer both debt and equity securities to the public in the United States. Public offerings, however, generate onerous and expensive registration requirements under section five of the Securities Act of 1933.[32]

---

31. Ale *et al.*, *supra*, at 5.
32. Stelwagon, *supra*, at 64-65.

As suggested in the above-quoted passage, two of the most appropriate types of exempt offerings in the project finance context are private placements and offshore offerings. These are discussed in turn below.

1. Private Placements and Section 4(2)[33]

Overview

The statutory basis for the registration requirement for securities offerings in United States law is found in the Securities Act of 1933, which is intended to regulate the distribution of securities when first offered. The operative provision of the Act is Section 5, which, simply stated, prohibits sale of, or offers to sell, securities unless a registration statement is filed and in effect. Violations of Section 5 may subject the issuer to SEC actions such as injunctions and investigations, criminal sanctions, or civil liability to the purchasers of the unregistered security.

Clearly, the avoidance of such consequences is a top priority. Section 4(2) of the 1933 Act provides an opportunity to avoid both the registration requirements of Section 5 and the consequences of violating the provision — it is the "private placements exemption." A "private placement" is

> [a] type of placement where new securities are sold by the lead manager (often called an *arranger*) to a limited number of investors, usually their own clients, rather than being offered to a wider public. It is private in the sense that little need be disclosed to third parties and usually the securities are not listed.[34]

Section 4(2) provides that the registration requirements of Section 5 "shall not apply to 'transactions by an issuer not involving any public offering.'"[35] An excellent practitioners' summary of the Section 4(2) exemption states:

> The seminal case is *SEC v. Ralston Purina*, 346 U.S. 119 (1953).
>
> * The focus of the exemption is on offerees and whether they need the protection of the 33 Act or whether they can "fend for themselves."
>
> * The primary question that must be asked in determining whether investors can fend for themselves is whether an offeree has the ability to realize and comprehend the risks involved with the particular offering through access to the kind of information contained in a registration statement or due to the offeree's sophistication.
>
> * It is thought to be critical that no offers be made to even one unsuitable investor. There is an ill-defined limit on the number of permissible offerees in a Section 4(2) private placement (perhaps 35).[36] To be sure, it is advisable for the issuer to hire counsel with expertise in private placement transactions, because there are many difficult areas in which problems may arise.

---

33. This treatment of private placements draws significantly from Leigh Walton & Lori B. Morgan, *Exempt Transactions: Practical Ways to Sell Securities, in* NUTS & BOLTS OF SECURITIES LAW 1997 283 (PLI Corporate Law and Practice Course Handbook Series, No. B-992, Larry D. Soderquist, Chair, 1997), and MARC I. STEINBERG, UNDERSTANDING SECURITIES LAW (2nd ed. 1996).

34. FINANCIAL TERMS, *supra*, at 435.

35. TENNEKOON, *supra*, at 422.

36. Walton & Morgan, *supra*, at 285-86.

Key Requirements

The need for competent securities counsel is evident from the following requirements associated with a private placement. First, *all* offers must be within the limitations of the exemption—one offeree without access to the requisite information may invalidate the offering. Second, with respect to sophistication, generally speaking, the term means the offerees "must be financially sophisticated or be advised by someone who has the requisite acumen (called an "offeree representative"). Under case law, individual wealth does not make one sophisticated for Section 4(2) private placement purposes."[37] Third, there may be no advertising or general solicitation. The term "general solicitation" has not yet been well-defined, but the number of offerees solicited and their levels of sophistication should be considered. Fourth, the resale of privately placed securities is restricted. One can hardly expect there not to be limits on the development of an active secondary market for privately placed securities. Accordingly, the issuer should place legends on the certificates as a precaution against resale. If purchasers of privately placed securities subsequently try to resell their securities prematurely, then the legend on the certificate serves as a "forewarning." The legend may preserve the Section 4(2) exemption for the issuer in case subsequent resale occurs.

The Private Placement Memorandum

What disclosure is required by the issuer in a private placement? Consider again the Philippine toll road project consortium example used earlier to help explain syndicated lending. The issuer of securities—the Philippine toll road project consortium—will prepare a document called the Private Placement Memorandum, or "PPM," to solicit prospective buyers for the securities. This document serves two purposes and has two (somewhat contradictory) goals: to attract potential buyers, and to disclose relevant information, particularly the material risks of the project. One helpful practice tip regarding drafting the PPM is that "[h]aving a clear discussion with the client early in the process regarding these conflicting goals, including an explanation of how the PPM can serve as a potential shield from litigation, will enhance the lawyer's ability to draft an appropriately conservative disclosure document."[38]

Any oral or written sales presentations used to solicit buyers ought to be within guidelines set in the PPM. In other words, they should not contradict each other, and the PPM should be the blue print for all marketing efforts. Also, the contents of the PPM should be updated as needed during the offering period, when there are any material changes in the information "with respect to the issuer's business, management, financial condition or other matter..."[39]

2. Offshore Sales and Regulation S[40]

Overview

Regulation S provides a "safe harbor" for offshore offerings of securities—sales in the "Euromarkets." That is, if a project consortium wishes to offer securities outside of the United States capital markets—on the Hong Kong and Singapore Stock

---

37. *See* STEINBERG, *supra*, at 47.

38. Walton & Morgan, *supra*, at 298.

39. *Id.* at 299.

40. The section on Regulation S draws upon Marc I. Steinberg & Daryl L. Landsdale, Jr., *Regulation S and Rule 144A: Creating a Workable Fiction in an Expanding Global Securities Market*, 29 INT'L LAW. 43 (Spring 1995).

Exchanges, for example—it may do so under the Regulation S safe harbor without triggering SEC registration requirements. This point may seem intuitive: why should there be any registration in the United States if the securities are not offered for sale there? However, the law prior to Regulation S essentially stated that registration requirements applied to United States persons regardless of where they lived or the situs of the offering.

The promulgation of Regulation S in 1990 reflected a fundamental policy shift to a new territorial approach. Simply stated, only offers and sales of securities inside the United States are subject to the registration requirements of Section 5. The SEC's new approach as embodied in Regulation S reflects a more global philosophy. "The [Securities and Exchange] Commission stated: 'The territorial approach recognizes the primacy of the laws in which a market is located. As investors choose their markets, they choose the laws and regulations applicable in such markets.'"[41] This approach is consistent with the promotion of freer, cross-border markets: let issuers and investors operate in the markets, and under the concomitant legal regimes, which they decide are best for them. In turn, the level of regulation on issuers (and resellers) in the markets is reduced, if for no other reason than they will not be saddled with both American and foreign securities law requirements.

Are the Offering and Sale "Outside the United States"?

The main issue as to the availability of Regulation S is "whether the offer and sale occurs 'outside the United States.' If the offer and sale are outside the United States within the meaning of [SEC] Rule 901, the registration provisions of section 5 are not applicable; if the offer or sale occurs within the United States, the registration provisions (absent the perfection of an exemption) are applicable."[42] How does an issuer determine whether an offer or sale actually is made outside the United States? SEC Rule 903 and Rule 904, both part of Regulation S, are the actual safe harbor provisions. If either Rule is satisfied, then the transaction is deemed to have taken place outside the United States and is exempt from registration requirements. Rule 903 provides an "issuer safe harbor." It would be available, for example, for the Philippine toll road project consortium in the above example. Rule 904 is known as the "resale safe harbor" provision. It is for the investors in the exempt securities who want to resell the securities without having to register.

Prerequisites for the Safe Harbors

Two prerequisites must be satisfied regardless of the safe harbor on which the transaction is based. The structure of these prerequisites is well presented by one scholar:

> The general conditions applicable to all offers and sales, whether based on the issuer or resale safe harbor, are that (1) the offer or sale is made in an "offshore transaction"; and (2) there are no "directed selling efforts" in the United States in connection with the distribution or resale of securities. To engage in an offshore transaction there can be no offer or sale to a person in the United States and either of two additional requirements must be satisfied. The first of the alternative requirements is that the buyer is outside the United

---

41. Steinberg & Lansdale, *supra*, at 48, *quoting* Offshore Offers and Sales, Securities Act Release No. 6863, [1989-1990 Transfer Binder] Fed. Sec. L. Rep. (CCH) ¶ 80,665 (Apr. 24, 1990).

42. *Id.* at 48 (citations omitted).

States, or the seller reasonably believes that the buyer is outside the United States, at the time the buy order is originated.... The second alternative means of satisfying the offshore transaction requirement is to execute the transaction on a designated offshore securities market.[43]

There is, further, a prohibition against pre-arranging the transaction with a buyer in the United States. If this were to occur, then the offshore securities market alternative would not be satisfied. So, for instance, if the Philippine toll road consortium decides to offer the securities on the Hong Kong capital markets, the transaction will be considered an offshore one.

With respect to the second basic prerequisite, the prohibition against direct selling efforts in the United States, the issuer (or its distributors and their affiliates) may not undertake any action that "could reasonably be expected to have the effect of conditioning the market in the United States for any of the securities being offered in reliance on Regulation S."[44] Conditioning the market, which includes methods whereby media such as radio, television, mail, newspapers or seminars are used, will result in a loss of the exemption from registration requirements for the issuer. An obvious example would be that the Philippine toll road consortium must be careful not to solicit investors via an interview publicizing the project as an investment opportunity on CNN-FN or CNBC, as these cable channels are broadcast to viewers in the United States.

SEC Rule 903: Issuer Safe Harbor

The first safe harbor, Rule 903, would be applicable to the Philippine toll road consortium directly, as it is an issuer attempting to raise capital through an offshore offering of securities. For purposes of Regulation S, the SEC divides securities into three separate categories, depending on the probability of the securities flowing back into the United States. As can be imagined, the greater the chance that the securities will re-enter the United States, the more stringent the requirements for the issuer to maintain the availability of the safe harbor.

Category I securities are least likely to re-enter the United States. They include "securities of foreign issuers for which there is no 'substantial U.S. market interest,' securities offered and sold in 'overseas directed offerings,' [and] securities backed by the full faith and credit of a 'foreign government.'"[45] Examples of a Category I security might be a local Malaysian corporation's stock, or a Myanmar government security. Because these securities are quite unlikely to re-enter the United States, they encounter less regulatory scrutiny. An issuer of a Category I security need only satisfy the two basic prerequisites mentioned above, namely, that the offering is an offshore transaction, and that there are no directed selling efforts in the United States.

Category II securities, deemed by the SEC as more likely to re-enter the United States, "are those by foreign and U.S. companies that are subject to the [1934 Securities] Exchange Act's reporting requirements as well as offerings of debt securities by non-reporting foreign issuers."[46] In order for an issuer to qualify for the Category II

---

43. *See* STEINBERG, *supra*, at 68 (citations omitted).

44. *Id.* at 69.

45. *Id.* at 70 (citations omitted).

46. *Id.* at 71. To clarify the terminology, a company subject to reporting requirements under the Securities Exchange Act of 1934 essentially means a company that has had a public offering, has securities traded on a national stock exchange, and has at least $ 5 million in assets and 500 equity shareholders.

safe harbor, the offering must comply not only with the two basic prerequisites stated above, but also with two additional restrictions. These restrictions are: (1) transactional restrictions and (2) offering restrictions.

The transactional restriction is that offers to United States persons or in the United States are prohibited within a 40-day period. When the securities are sold by distributors to dealers before the end of the period, the distributor must send a notice to the dealer notifying them of this restriction (so that the dealer does not re-sell the securities to retail investors during the 40-day period). The offering restrictions are that all of the distributors agree in writing that "all offers and sales during the applicable restricted period be made only in accordance with a Regulation S safe harbor or pursuant to registration under the [1933 Act] or an exemption therefrom."[47] The securities also must be designated in the offering materials as "unregistered."

Category III securities are those that do not fall within either Category I or II. They include "offerings of non-reporting United States issuers and equity offerings of non-reporting foreign issuers when there is a substantial United States market interest in such securities."[48] Category III securities must meet the basic prerequisites for a Regulation S transaction. Further, the offering restrictions of Category II are applicable, and the transactional restrictions are even greater than those applicable to Category II securities. For example, the restriction period is one year, not merely 40 days, for equity offerings in Category III.

SEC Rule 904: Resale Safe Harbor

As mentioned above, Rule 904, promulgated pursuant to Regulation S, contains a resale safe harbor. Generally speaking, the resale safe harbor is not available to issuers and their affiliates or distributors and their affiliates (with one exception in the case of officers and directors of affiliates and securities professionals). It is fairly simple in its approach. The exemption from registration is available to resellers if they adhere to the two basic prerequisites of the Regulation S transaction: (1) it is an offshore transaction and (2) there are no directed selling efforts in the United States. Thus, for example, the resale safe harbor would be used by the purchasers of the Philippine toll road securities if they subsequently wanted to resell the securities in offshore transactions.

3. Rule 144A[49]

Overview

SEC Rule 144A, promulgated in 1990, is a powerful tool in international project finance. It allows securities privately placed (pursuant to Section 4(2)) or sold in an overseas offering (pursuant to Regulation S) to be resold in the United States to *certain* buyers. That is, Rule 144A authorizes the development of a secondary market in the United States for securities initially offered in a private placement or to a foreign primary market. Rule 144A provides a non-exclusive safe harbor (meaning it can be used along with other exemptions from Section 5 of the 1933 Act, such as a Section 4(2) private placement or Regulation S) from the registration requirements

---

47. *Id.* at 72.

48. *Id.* at 72.

49. A thorough treatment of the complex requirements of Rule 144A is beyond the scope of this Note. This introduction and summary of its requirements presents a snapshot of this important Rule and its advantages.

for resales of restricted securities already to *"qualified institutional buyers,"* or "QIBs."

Obviously, because Rule 144A may be used in conjunction with United States private placements or Regulation S offerings, it is a versatile tool for international project finance. It is an important attraction for institutional investors in the global securities markets, and it thereby enhances the ability of issuers to raise capital for overseas investments. The nub of the attraction is resale. Resale is an important issue in project finance, as in any prospective investment. The ability to resell securities adds to their value simply because the market for the securities is considered "liquid." That is, there is an assured broad and deep market of participants ready, willing, and able to buy the securities. Because the issuer of liquid securities is more attractive to buyers, the issuer is likely to fetch a higher price for the securities, thus raising more capital for the issuer's project. Indeed, Rule 144A was introduced to

> increase the liquidity and efficiency of the U.S. private placement market, thereby making it easier for companies, including start-up and small companies, to raise capital. By eliminating the costs and delays inherent in the registration process with respect to purchases by large institutional investors—which may not need the protection of the [1933] Act—it was believed that the discount commonly associated with private placements would be lowered and more issuers, foreign and domestic, would be attracted to the U.S. private placement market.[50]

Thus,

> [i]f [securities] sold privately are marketed under the exemption provided by Rule 144A of the Securities and Exchange Commission, the [securities] become essentially freely tradeable among "qualified institutional buyers," such as insurance companies, pension plans, banks, mutual funds, and credit companies—still a vast market indeed. The same issue also can be sold and listed on European and Asian exchanges through the safe-harbor provisions of SEC Regulation S, reaching even more potential purchasers.[51]

The policy behind adopting Rule 144A is in line with that behind Regulation S, namely, to enhance the efficiency of the international capital markets. Rule 144A, in particular, rightly is hailed as "help[ing] [to] increase the demand and marketability in the United States of securities issued by foreign entities."[52]

Key Requirements

There are five key requirements for satisfying the Rule 144A safe harbor. First, the resale must be to a QIB, such as an insurance company, mutual fund, pension plan, or venture capital firm. A QIB must have at least $100 million invested in securities at the end of its most recent fiscal year, and commercial banks and saving and loan associations also must have a net worth of at least $25 million. Second, the seller of the securities must reasonably believe the prospective purchaser to be a QIB. Third, the securities for sale must not be of the same class as a security offered on public markets (such as one quoted on the New York Stock Exchange or NASDAQ).

---

50. Marvin E. Pollock, *Rule 144A, in* RESALES OF RESTRICTED SECURITIES UNDER SEC RULES 144 AND 144A AT A-24 (BNA Corp. Prac. Series Portfolio no. 46-2nd, 1991).

51. Ale *et al., supra,* at 5.

52. Steinberg & Lansdale, *supra,* at 44 (citations omitted).

That is, fungible securities must be excluded. Fourth, the issuer of the securities (in our example, the Philippine toll road project consortium) must provide information on its business and financial status to the QIB/prospective purchaser upon request. Lastly, the seller must take reasonable steps to notify the prospective QIB/prospective purchaser that the sale is made in reliance on Rule 144A.

Conclusion

Using syndicated loans and sales of securities — both offshore and through private placements, possibly resold to QIBs — to finance large infrastructure projects is a complex but fascinating process. At bottom, though, the process is nothing more than channeling billions of dollars worth of private capital from savers to investors. Because, however, the savers tend to be in developed countries, and the need for the capital tends to be concentrated in developing countries, where the bulk of the demand for infrastructure exists, this process is very much part of the story of Third World economic development. The financing options yield opportunities for American, Western European, Japanese, and other developed-country companies that seek to expand their business and market share, and purvey their expertise abroad. But, syndicated lending and registration-exempt offerings are not just about helping companies from wealthy countries realize their strategic business aims, any more than they are about just making money for Wall Street commercial and investment bankers. They also are about helping disadvantaged countries move up the development ladder by making infrastructure projects happen. In turn, this much-needed infrastructure supports the development of agricultural and manufacturing industries. In sum, international project finance assists in the creation and better distribution of wealth, and thereby contributes to human betterment.

QUESTIONS

1.   What are some of the differences between a project finance transaction and an infrastructure project undertaken directly by a host government?

2.   Why would an American construction firm, for example, seek to underwrite a project in a country such as Chile? What might be some of the risks and advantages?

3.   Why does international project finance require a creative approach?

4.   What advantages do firms from the United States and other members of the Organization for Economic Co-operation and Development (OECD) have in the bidding process for overseas infrastructure project contracts?

5.   Do project finance transactions tend to create a new colonization of the developing world, or are developing nations benefitting from the inflow of capital and expertise from their wealthier brethren?

6.   How would you assess World Bank or International Monetary Fund (IMF) lending to developing countries in relation to international project finance?

II. A Latin American Case Study

Peter V. Darrow, et al., Financing Infrastructure Projects in the International Capital Markets: The Tribasa Toll Road Trust
1 The Financier 9-19 (August 1994)

INTRODUCTION

....

The U.S. institutional market, which is approximately $14 trillion in size, is the deepest investment market in the world. Approximately $4 trillion of this market consists of pension assets, which usually seek long-term investments. The U.S. institutional market is therefore naturally attractive to infrastructure projects which require long-term financing.

The attraction of the U.S. capital market for infrastructure financing has been enhanced considerably by the adoption in 1990, by the Securities and Exchange Commission (the "SEC"), of Rule 144A ("Rule 144A") under the Securities Act of 1933 (the "Securities Act"). As discussed in detail below, Rule 144A established a non-exclusive exemption from the registration requirements of the Securities Act for resales by investors to eligible institutions of privately- placed securities, subject to certain limitations. By facilitating resales of securities issued in private placements, the Rule has created liquidity in the secondary market for privately-placed securities, causing the U.S. private placement market to become more attractive to foreign issuers, including those offering debt securities to finance infrastructure development.

The recent successful implementation of several financings for infrastructure projects in less developed countries through the international capital markets has reinforced the attractiveness of this financing alternative. In particular, the successful syndication by Salomon Brothers, in November 1993, of an offering of $110 million of debt securities issued by a special purpose Mexican trust to finance two existing Mexican toll roads, collateralized by the collection rights under two toll road concessions and toll revenues therefrom, has been instrumental in persuading the international financial community that financings of this type for projects in Latin America and elsewhere in the developing world are feasible and economically attractive....

II. Infrastructure Financing Alternatives

Financing for infrastructure development is available from several traditional sources: government funding (consisting of grants, loans and credit enhancement), government direct investment, suppliers (with respect to construction financing), multi- and bilateral agency funding, credit facilities provided by banks or other financial institutions (provided in reliance upon the credit of the corporate sponsor of the particular infrastructure project (contractor, owner or operator) or sovereign sponsor of the infrastructure project), capital markets financing based on such credit (in the form of domestic public offerings, domestic municipal bond offerings, Eurobond offerings, medium term note programs and private placements), project financing (dependent solely or principally on the assets and cash flow of the project in question) and some form of securitization (consisting of the transfer of the right to receive the revenue from the project, often under a government-granted concession, to a special purpose vehicle, and the contemporaneous issuance of securities that are payable from revenues generated by the project).

Financing which is based upon the credit of a corporate or sovereign sponsor is limited in availability, and is also subject to changes in the perception of the credit-worthiness of the sponsor, local market considerations and developments unrelated to any particular project that may adversely influence the financial condition or business of the sponsor. In addition, sponsors of infrastructure projects generally seek to avoid incurrence of indebtedness that permits creditors to have recourse to the sponsor: limitation of on-balance sheet indebtedness is one of the principal objectives of most project sponsors.

By contrast, project financing and securitization are forms of financing which are structured so as to be reliant only (or principally) upon a specific project, and the revenues anticipated from an identified source (such as toll revenues, take-or-pay contracts or power purchase agreements) under contractual arrangements negotiated as part of the financing. Thus, the risks arising in this type of financing are limited primarily to those associated with the particular project, and the industry (or segment of the economy) served by the project. Provided the relevant industry (or segment of the economy) performs as anticipated, repayment of the financing should be isolated from most factors (other than currency devaluation) which might otherwise adversely affect a more traditional cross-border credit-based financing. The typical project financing or securitization is structured to provide lenders with only limited recourse to the sponsor which relieves the sponsor of a general contractual obligation to repay the infrastructure financing. Under this approach, individual projects or select groups of projects can be financed separately, to minimize the effect of the financial condition and profitability of the sponsor, on the availability of its financial resources, and to limit the risk to the sponsor from the financial problems of a particular project. Accordingly, through reliance upon project finance or securitization techniques, infrastructure can be financed through high-yield limited recourse securities which, if structured correctly, carry manageable (and therefore marketable) risks.

III. FORCES MAKING PROJECT FINANCE AND SECURITIZATION OF INFRASTRUCTURE ATTRACTIVE

A. Unavailability of Traditional Financing Sources

The need for infrastructure development, and for corresponding infrastructure financing, is enormous worldwide, especially in Latin America, Asia and the Eastern Bloc nations. In most developing nations, the governments do not have the financial resources to finance even essential infrastructure projects, resulting in an effort to shift to the private sector (typically through the granting of concessions, and the right to finance those concessions) the responsibility for undertaking basic infrastructure projects. This effort to shift infrastructure development to the private sector, which has characterized many of the largest privatizations in Latin America and elsewhere in the developing world, also reflects the growing consensus that the private sector is often better suited to correctly identifying, building and operating large-scale infrastructure projects.

B. The Adoption of Rule 144A, and the Development of a Rule 144A Securities Market

With the adoption of Rule 144A, a broader market for private financing in the U.S. capital markets has become available, especially for foreign issuers, characterized by greater liquidity than existed prior to adoption of the Rule, and ease-of-entry for foreign issuers. Prior to adoption of Rule 144A, privately-placed securities were subject to significant restrictions upon resale under applicable U.S. securities rules, rendering such securities illiquid, and resulting in an illiquidity premium on resale.

Rule 144A, adopted by the SEC in April 1990, provides a non-exclusive safe harbor from the registration requirements of the Securities Act for resales of certain securities to "qualified institutional buyers" ("QIBs"). The expressed intention of the SEC in adopting Rule 144A was to increase the liquidity of privately-placed securities, by allowing unrestricted resales of such securities among QIBS, and to increase access to the U.S. capital markets by foreign issuers.

In a Rule 144A placement, an issuer will sell, in a traditional private placement (in reliance upon an exemption from the registration requirements), its securities to one or more investment banking firms which will then resell, in reliance upon Rule 144A, the securities to a larger number of QIBs. [The traditional private placement relies on the exemption from registration requirements that is contained in Section 4(2) of the Securities Act and Regulation D promulgated by the SEC pursuant thereto.] From an issuer's standpoint, the way in which Rule 144A placements are conducted is very similar to traditional underwritten public offerings.

A sale in compliance with Rule 144A must meet four basic criteria, . . . (a) the securities must be offered and sold only to QIBs; (b) the securities must not, when issued, be of the same class as securities listed on a U.S. securities exchange or quoted in a U.S. automated interdealer quotation system (such as the NASDAQ System); (c) the seller and the prospective purchaser must have the right to obtain certain information about the issuer if such information is not publicly available; and (d) the seller must ensure that the prospective purchaser knows that the seller may rely on Rule 144A.

Since 1990, in response to adoption of Rule 144A, a large number of foreign and domestic companies have issued securities in the U.S. private placement market in reliance upon the resale exemption afforded by Rule 144A and, as expected, there has developed a moderately liquid secondary market for these securities among QIBs. The creation of this market, and the growing appetite among U.S. institutional investors for high-yield securities (which, by definition, includes those issued by private or public sector issuers in the emerging markets), have made it possible to structure a capital markets financing for infrastructure projects targeted to the U.S. private placement market.

C. Sponsors' View

From the perspective of the sponsors, project finance and securitization involve high levels of leverage (typically between 80% and 100%), reducing the need for sponsor-provided funding. In some cases the use of project financing or securitization is more tax efficient, and financing costs can be reduced accordingly. In addition, the limited recourse nature of such financing allows a sponsor to "encapsulate" its exposure in the event of a troubled project and, in most cases, enables sponsors to remove the project liabilities from their balance sheets.

IV. Risk Considerations

Structuring an international financing—especially a capital markets financing—of an infrastructure project requires the mitigation of a number of risks to ensure marketability of the financing.

A. Cross-border Considerations

Arranging cross-border infrastructure financing requires that the participants assume certain risks, in addition to those customary to infrastructure projects.

1. Currency Risk

Currency risk with respect to an international financing has three components: the risk related to the currency in which project revenues are generated, the risk arising from incurring liabilities to fund a project denominated in a currency (typically U.S. dollars) different from the currency of project revenues and the risk of inconvertibility of the currency arising from exchange controls or other currency restrictions. Investors in financings for foreign borrowers must consider and evaluate the risks associated with foreign currencies, including the possibilities of devaluations, exchange requirements and repatriation restrictions.

Any devaluation of the local currency in which project revenue is denominated will require a corresponding increase in the project's cash flow to assure that economic returns are sustained, and to service the project's debt(especially if denominated in another currency). Any significant devaluation of a local currency, without offsetting factors, will directly impair the project's likelihood of repaying its lenders and other investors.

Additionally, exchange controls could result in international investors not being able to receive payments in specified currencies on a timely basis. If only a limited supply of a specified currency is available, or if new approvals or extra fees are required to effect conversion to the currency of payment, the adequacy of project cash flow could be impaired, or investors could have to settle for payment in another currency. Repatriation restrictions could prohibit or limit the ability of lenders to move payments received out of the country in which the project is located.

2. Political Risks

Loans and investments based on revenue streams from foreign projects are subject to risks specific to the country involved, causing investors to examine differences in law and politics from their own nation. Country-specific risk must be taken into account, including (i) the political stability of the government (central and local), (ii) the attitude (historical and current) of the government towards foreign investment regarding currency exchange, repatriation of earnings, taxation, privatization and the need for infrastructure development, (iii) the degree of involvement of the government in the economy, and (iv) the current and projected state of the economy.

Furthermore, investors must also take into consideration the risk of unanticipated developments that might adversely affect the project, or the sector of the economy which the project serves. These risks include the risk that underlying contracts will be changed or impaired, the risk of expropriation or confiscation of project assets (both outright and creeping), and risks of war and civil unrest. Investors must also consider the likelihood, and probable effect, of any change in regime, and whether policies and attitudes toward the particular project, towards international financing in general or towards the sponsors in particular will change.

. . . .

B. Project Considerations

1. Economic Sensitivity

Insulation from the general credit risk of the sponsor is one of the benefits of project or securitization infrastructure financing. In addition, infrastructure tends to involve basic products and services needed by the public. However, such financing is also insulated from (and deprived of the benefit of) any diversity in activities of the sponsor which may cushion an economic downturn. Consequently, a financing which is wholly dependent on the demand for a particular product or service from a particular facility (such as a single power plant with a single power purchaser, or a toll road with only a limited distance and destination) is directly subject to the economy of the country in general, and to the specific industry or segment of the economy served by the project. Historical use, projected trends and economic expectations are therefore very important considerations.

2. Limited Remedies

Project finance and securitization, as financing tools, involve limited recourse to sponsors and other nonproject assets. Institutional investors also need to recognize that financing of infrastructure is subject to additional restrictions in the exercise of traditional remedies. For example, foreclosure on a power plant with a sole power purchaser (such as a state-owned power company) is of little use if the problem is an inability of the power purchaser to make required payments. If there are no other significant purchasers of power available in the relevant market, the plant, to the extent physically and legally removable, may have only salvage value to lenders.

Similarly, where the financing is structured as a securitization of concession rights (which, unlike the related cash flows, are generally non-transferrable) upon the occurrence of an event of default there may be no asset on which to foreclose (since, as a practical matter, toll roads and bridges cannot be moved).

3. Construction and Technology Risk

Infrastructure projects tend to be large, complex transactions with long lead times, occasionally involving new technology or novel applications of old technology, and requiring extensive governmental approvals and sophisticated financing. Infrastructure assets generally have long useful lives, and only by financing these projects with indebtedness that has a correspondingly long maturity is it possible to minimize the cost of the service provided by the project.

Since there is often incomplete data or in some cases no reliable data concerning project revenues prior to completion, lending for construction of a project is likely to be perceived as a relatively high-risk proposition. The ability to finance any project, particularly in the capital markets, is therefore directly tied to its stage of development and the availability of operational data. A project that is in place and operating is considerably easier to finance than a project subject to construction risk, completion risk, technology risk or performance risk. A project with an operating history is easier to finance than a project subject to unquantified operating risk. Historical and pro forma operating data, and a careful analysis thereof by an independent expert, are essential.

C. Transferability

Project financing and securitizations are usually secured financings, secured by the cash flows (including, in the case of financing a concessioned project, the right to receive revenues under the concession), the underlying contracts and, in the case of project finance, the project assets themselves. In evaluating any limited recourse financing, secured creditors always want to know the likelihood and cost of being able to foreclose upon, and realize the benefit from, the assets which secure repayment of their financing. The ability to perfect a security interest and, more importantly, to be able to transfer the asset at the time of foreclosure to reduce or repay in full the out-standing indebtedness are highly important considerations to institutional lenders, particularly in the context of project finance and securitization. In considering the transferability of financed assets, institutional lenders focus on the following issues:

- Are the licenses, permits and concessions transferable to someone who can finish the project and operate it?

- Are hard assets transferable or removable?

- Is there a fully effective legally enforceable assignment of all rights to future cash flow?

- Are the underlying operational contracts transferable for performance by someone else?

V. TRIBASA TOLL ROAD TRUST 1: A CASE STUDY

In view of the foregoing discussion regarding the factors making project finance and securitization of infrastructure projects attractive, and the obstacles which need to be overcome in order to make such financing viable and marketable, it is educational to look at the Tribasi Toll Road Trust I financing, and to examine the structure for the financing devised by Salomon Brothers, which enabled both the investors and the sponsors to participate in this innovative financing.

1. The Mexican Government's Toll Road Program

In Mexico, infrastructure has been built primarily with public sector funds or pursuant to public programs which serve to stimulate private-sector investment. These programs (at the federal or state government level) include the grant, through a competitive bidding process, of concessions for the construction or improvement of highways to private sector entities (concessionholders). Under the highway concession program, the government grants a concession to a concessionholder to finance, build or improve, operate and maintain a highway (subject to government regulation) for a specified period of time, in exchange for the right of the concessionholder to receive toll revenues generated by the highway during such period.

Concessioned highways are typically financed in stages through short-term borrowing and equity contributions during construction and, thereafter, through longer-term financing secured by an assignment of the toll revenues from the concession once the highway is in use. Concessionholders may assign their rights and duties under concessions only with the approval of the governments.

The government provides the design for the highways and monitors construction and operation. Each concession sets forth its term, the construction or improvements to be done, a schedule of tolls by category of vehicle (and generally the conditions for toll adjustments upward or downward), standards for operations, standards for maintenance reserve requirements and specified fees payable to the government. The term of concessions may be lengthened if actual highways use falls short of levels specified in the concession. Recent concessions generally provide that, if actual traffic exceeds the specified volumes, the term of the concession may be reduced or the concessionholder may be required to pay a portion of the toll revenues to the government. The concessionholder is required to operate the highway and to correct any defects in the highway that arise during the concession.

Upon termination of the concession, the right to operate the highway and to collect toll revenues reverts to the government. The highway itself remains the property of the government throughout the term of the concession.

Concessions may be terminated by the governments without compensation before specified expiration dates upon the occurrence of certain events, including nonpayment of any amounts due to the government, failure to comply with the conditions specified in the concession, negligence in the operation of the highway, failure to maintain the highway and establishment of tolls in excess of those approved. The government may also seize all assets related to a concession in the event of war, significant public disturbance or threats to internal peace and for other reasons of economic or public older or pursuant to rights of the nature of eminent domain.

2. Background

Grupo Tribasa, S.A. de C.V. ("Tribasa"), acting through two subsidiaries, obtained concessions to construct, operate and maintain two toll roads. The Ecatepec-Pirámides toll road, which is a 13.9 mile highway located north of Mexico City, in the State of Mexico, was opened in 1965, and has been operated by a subdivision of Tribasa since 1991. The Armaría-Manzanillo toll road is a 29 mile highway located on the west coast of Mexico, in the State of Colima, and is one of the principal routes leading to the resort and port city of Manzanillo. A subsidiary of Tribasa has operated a significant portion of the Manzanillo toll road under concession since 1991, and has operated the entire toll since 1992.

Construction and initial operations of both toll roads were funded in part by contractor financing, private local commercial financing and financing obtained through local Mexican capital markets. The Pyramids concession was originally 1991 for a period of three years and 11 months, which was later extended to a term ending in December 2011. The Manzanillo concession was granted initially for a term of nine years and three months, and was later extended to November 2004. Further extensions are permitted if traffic volumes do not meet specified levels.

Once reliable historical data was available, Tribasa decided to seek financing in the international capitals markets, and selected Salomon Brothers to be the underwriter and financial adviser for the offering. The offering was oversubscribed, and was widely considered to be highly successful.

3. Overview

The Tribasa Toll Road Trust 1 offering (the "Tribasa Toll Road financing") in November of 1993, which combined a simultaneous Eurobond offering and a U.S. private placement (eligible for resale under Rule 144A) U.S. $110,000,000 of 10_% Notes due 2011 (the "Notes"), was the first successfully syndicated securitization in the international capital markets of U.S. dollar-denominated securities supported by Mexican Pesodenominated cash flow.

4. The Trust and Its Assets

A single special purpose Mexican trust (a Fideicomisoadministration and guaranty trust- organized under the laws of the United Mexican States) sponsored by the two toll road concessionholders was formed (the "Trust"). The two concessionholders (both of which are wholly-owned subsidiaries of Tribasa), as sponsors of the Trust (the "Sponsors"), contributed the following assets to the Trust:

(i) rights to collect tolls pursuant to the concessions ("Toll Collection Rights");

(ii) toll revenues actually collected (net of Value Added Tax (VAT));

(iii) investment income earned on Trust assets;

(iv) accounts maintained by or on behalf of the Trust (e.g., a general operating account and major maintenance account);

(v) insurance proceeds; and

(vi) certain operator and sponsor payments.

The Trust was established pursuant to a Trust Agreement among the Sponsors and a Mexican bank, as trustee (the "Trustee"). The Trust Agreement appoints the Trustee and specifies:

(i) the obligations and rights of the Trustee as administrator of the Trust and the Sponsors, including performance covenants;

(ii) the mode of governance of the Trust;

(iii) the Accounts (defined below);

(iv) the Debt Service Reserve Fund (defined below); and

(v) the collection and disposition of toll revenues.

The Trustee is a Mexican bank, which performs more extensive duties than a U.S. trustee normally performs. The Trust is managed by a technical committee, consisting of the independent engineer, the Sponsors, the Operator and an independent representative of the Noteholders (in this case a member of a Mexican investment bank).

The Trustee established several accounts (the "Accounts") and a reserve fund (the "Debt Service Reserve Fund") on behalf of the Trust, to hold the Trust's assets.

The Accounts consisted of the followings:

(i) the General Account, established to hold revenues until expended for operating expenses or debt service or other applications;

(ii) the SCT Account, established to hold amounts collected over time to make annual fee payments to the federal government in respect of the concessions; and

(iii) the Major Maintenance Account, established to ensure that funds are available in Pesos to make necessary repairs and major maintenance.

The Noteholders are the beneficiaries of the Trust, with the Sponsors having the residual interest after payment of the Notes.

5. The Debt Service Reserve Fund

The Debt Service Reserve Fund was established with a U.S. bank serving as Fiscal Agent, to ensure that funds are available in U.S. dollars to pay debt service on the Notes on a timely basis, where otherwise available funds from the General Account are insufficient. Initially, the Debt Service Reserve Fund was substantially funded from proceeds of the offering. The balance is then to be funded out of cash flow prior to the commencement of amortization. Thereafter, the Debt Service Reserve Fund is to be maintained at specified levels, and replenished from cash flow from time to time as may become necessary.

6. Structure

The Trustee, on behalf of the Trust, issued the Notes in a private placement eligible for resale pursuant to Rule 144A, and contemporaneously in a Eurobond offering pursuant to Regulation S under the Securities Act. The Trustee entered into a fiscal and paying agency agreement with a U.S. bank serving as fiscal and paying agent, providing fiscal agent and paying agent services and preparing certain reports, as well as holding the Debt Service Reserve Fund in a fiduciary account in the U.S.

The Trustee, on behalf of the Trust, entered into an operating agreement with a subsidiary of Tribasa (the "Operator"), at closing. The Operator has responsibility for running the toll roads, collecting the tolls, paying VAT, maintaining the roads, paying employees, paying the deductible on any insurance, making weekly deposits of funds into the Trust's General Account, and preparing operation and performance reports for the Trust, the Noteholders, the technical committee and the independent engineer. The Operator is paid a monthly fee based on revenues less SCT reserves (government concession fees). The performance obligations of the Operator are guaranteed by Tribasa.

7. Debt Service and Cash Flow

All toll revenues are collected by the Operator and held in a segregated account, and applied in the following fashion:

- VAT is deducted and held by the Operator in a segregated account for payment to the government of the United Mexican States;

- weekly, the collected toll revenues (net of VAT) are deposited by the Operator with the Trustee into the General Account;

- upon receipt of insurance proceeds, the Trustee will deposit such funds into the General Account;

- monthly, funds are withdrawn from the General Account for the following purposes, with the following priority:

    (i) funds are deposited into the SCT Account, established to collect funds for payment of the annual fee to the government in respect of the concessions;

    (ii) funds are applied to pay administrative and operating fees and expenses of the Trust, such as the Trustee, the Fiscal Agent, the Operator, legal counsel, accountants, the independent engineer, the independent Noteholder representative and other providers of service to the Trust;

    (iii) funds are set aside, in Pesos, within the General Account for the later payment (semi-annually) of withholding taxes (so that payments received by Noteholders are free of withholding taxes);

    (iv) if required, funds are converted to U.S. dollars and transferred to the Fiscal Agent to maintain the Debt Service Reserve Fund at the specified level; and

    (v) if required, funds are transferred to the Major Maintenance Account, maintained in Pesos by the Trustee, to bring the balance tip to levels specified by the independent engineer.

- Semi-annually, funds are withdrawn from the General Account for the following purposes, with the following priorities:

    (i) funds are transferred to the taxing authorities to pay withholding taxes in respect of payments on the Notes that are to be made on the semi-annual payment date;

    (ii) funds are transferred to the Fiscal Agent for payments to Noteholders in U.S. dollars of interest and principal;

(iii) funds are transferred to the Fiscal Agent in U.S. dollars for deposit into the Debt Service Reserve Fund, to bring the balance to the required levels;

(iv) funds are set aside in the General Account for payment of withholding taxes due with respect to payments to Noteholders scheduled to be made on the next payment date;

(v) if required, funds are transferred to the Major Maintenance Account to bring its balance up to specified levels;

(vi) if available, and required, funds are transferred to the Fiscal Agent for payment in U.S. dollars to the Noteholders of a late payment premium; and

(vii) if no default or blockage event exists, and if there is excess cash flow on a quarterly payment date, after payment of all of the above and cash is available to cover projected operating expenses and certain financial ratios are satisfied, any remaining funds are transferred as distributions to the Sponsors.

8. Advantages of the Structure

a) The Sponsors' View

The Tribasa Toll Road financing provided a means for Tribasa to remove infrastructure indebtedness from its balance sheet while retaining control of the assets. In addition, Tribasa, through its subsidiary, the Operator, receives income for the services provided. Furthermore, Tribasa's continuing involvement in the operation of the toll roads ensures its satisfaction with the maintenance and operation of the projects. Moreover, through the Sponsors, Tribasa will receive current income, in the form of distributions, if all prior uses for cash flow are satisfied.

The transfer of the cash flow to the Trust also gave Tribasa the reversionary right to receive cash flow from the toll roads after the infrastructure debt is fully repaid. Payment of the transaction costs, the initial funding of the Debt Service Reserve Fund and the withholding tax reserve were the only proceeds of the offering not paid to the Sponsors to retire existing debt. However, Tribasa did remain liable as a guarantor of the performance of the Operator and for certain insurance liabilities.

b) The Investors' View

The Notes offered were high-yield securities based on infrastructure which carried no construction risk, and had a long and well-documented operating history. The toll roads are located in Mexico, which is democratic, stable and near investment grade. In addition, certain features were incorporated into the structure to minimize certain risks to the investors, including a dual amortization structure, as more fully described below, a Debt Service Reserve Fund and tax gross-up requirements.

9. Risk Minimization

a) Dual Amortization Schedules

The debt repayment requirement—the amortization schedule—used in the Tribasa Toll Road financing was separated into two schedules. This separation served the purpose to (i) take into account variable revenue streams, (ii) restrict and capture otherwise permitted distributions to prevent shortfalls in cash flow, (iii) compensate investors for a slower return of capital and (iv) lessen the need for drastic Noteholder remedies, such as acceleration and foreclosure.

The Notes are due in 2011, which is the outside maturity date, assuming the "contractual" amortization schedule is adhered to. Failure to make payments consistent with the contractual amortization results in a default, permits acceleration of the Notes and removal of the Operator and prohibits distributions to the Sponsors. However, the Notes require the Trust to try to make repayments based on the more aggressive "scheduled" amortization schedule, which would result in an earlier payout (if strictly adhered to) in 2005. Failure to make payments consistent with the scheduled amortization results in a prohibition of distributions to the Sponsors, as discussed below, and the imposition of a late payment premium in the amount of 1% per annum on all unpaid scheduled amortization amounts. Failure to satisfy scheduled amortization does not result in a default, but merely "traps" funds payments so long as contractual amortization is being satisfied.

The dual amortization schedules provide the Trust with flexibility. It is theoretically possible for the financing to move back and forth between the two amortization schedules over the life of the transaction. The late payment premium is only payable to the extent of any shortfall from scheduled amortization, thereby providing the Sponsors value in being part-way between the two amortization schedules. Thus, investors are compensated for holding longer term securities-securities which could have a final maturity occurring anytime between 2005 and 2011—while the Sponsors are provided with some of the pricing benefits of the more aggressive amortization schedule, without being as heavily penalized (foreclosure, acceleration, etc.) for having misjudged future cash flows and only meeting the contractual amortization (or partially meeting the scheduled amortization).

b) Currency Risk

Devaluations were a major concern in structuring the Tribasa Toll Road financing. The Debt Service Reserve Fund is maintained in the United States in dollars and, to the extent additional funds are required to be added thereto, Pesos are required to be converted monthly and promptly remitted to the U.S. Accordingly, the Debt Service Reserve Fund is not subject to Peso devaluation risk, and provides a source of repayment if devaluation or other unrelated problems cause a cash flow shortfall.

Payments to the Operator are made in Mexican Pesos, not U.S. dollars, thus eliminating the need for dollars or devaluation risk to the Trust for these payments. Moreover, pursuant to the terms of the toll road concessions, toll increases are permitted for various reasons (including to reflect inflation), thereby enabling some further protection from revenue stress. As noted above, the dual amortization structure provides added cushion for stresses in cash flow, whatever the source.

These techniques help lessen the likelihood that fluctuations in the exchange rate will jeopardize the ability of a project which is performing up to, or near, expectations to make required U.S. dollar payments.

c) Restricted Payments and Blockage Events

The availability of adequate cash flow for operations, maintenance and debt service was further protected through restrictions placed on distributions to the Sponsors. Distributions are only permitted semi-annually (i) after all other applications of cash flow on such semi-annual payment date (as described above) have been made, (ii) after provision for one month's operating and administrative expenses and for withholding taxes to be paid on the next semi-annual payment date has been made,

(iii) so long as no blockage event (referred to below), default or event of default has occurred and is continuing, (iv) so long as the ratio of net cash flow to scheduled debt service for the immediately preceding four semi-annual periods meets certain specified levels and (v) so long as the amount in certain Accounts and the Debt Service Reserve Fund (taken together) are in excess of a specified amount and, then, only to the extent of any such excess. Accordingly, distributions to the Sponsors are only permitted when performance achieves certain standards and there has been retained in the Trust a specified level of funds.

To provide remedial protections which are less drastic than acceleration, certain blockage events are specified. Upon the occurrence and during the duration of any blockage event, distributions to Sponsors, the incurrence of subordinated indebtedness and the payment on any existing subordinated indebtedness are all prohibited, and the frequency of certain deposits for the benefit of Noteholders is accelerated. Upon the occurrence of an event of default, in addition to the measures described above, acceleration of the Notes is permitted. The right to accelerate is of limited benefit, however, since the toll roads belong to the government, the concessions cannot be foreclosed upon and sold, and the Notes are nonrecourse to the Sponsors. The inclusion of blockage events serves the useful purpose of permitting the exercise of remedies short of acceleration, and providing additional means to retain cash flow in the Trust.

d) Political Risks

The toll roads are located in Mexico, a stable democracy with a regard for the enforceability of private contracts. In addition, Mexico has a publicly announced policy (including the adoption of NAFTA) of encouraging international infrastructure financing. The Mexican government has approved revisions to certain concessions to make them more readily financeable, and has revised its concession program accordingly. The Tribasa concessions were amended and supplemented to increase their term, permit toll increases and permit transferability of revenues. Mexican sovereign debt is at or near investment grade, and the expectations for the future are generally positive. Moreover, Tribasa is a large and prominent Mexican construction company with broad experience in concessions granted by the Mexican government.

. . . .

f) Economic Sensitivity

Toll roads in Mexico, while superior to other roadway alternatives, are not exclusive routes and are used largely by commercial and tourist traffic, making toll roads particularly market and economy sensitize (unlike power or water use). The granting of toll road concessions in Mexico is conditioned on the existence of a non-toll road alternative.

To enable investors to quantity this economic sensitivity, Tribasa commissioned and included in the offering circular a detailed traffic report from an independent consultant. The traffic report provided a detailed historical analysis of the operations of the toll roads, and analyzed the prospective use of the toll roads (taking use, location and the Mexican economy and governmental policies into account). The completeness and independence of this report was an important consideration to prospective investors.

Structuring elements were also included to deal with economic sensitivity. The dual amortization structure was employed allowing for variability of revenue stream. The Debt Service Reserve Fund was established (which provided a six-month cushion for debt service short falls). Distributions to the Sponsors are permitted only after all other uses for cash flow had been currently satisfied and funds were available to cover projected operating expenses and certain financial ratios are satisfied. In addition, the concessions permit toll increases which can offset reductions in income. The Operator's fee is based on a percentage of revenue.

g) Limited Remedies

As neither the toll roads nor the concessions (as distinguished from the related cash-flow) could be transferred or mortgaged, distributions to the Sponsors are prohibited during times of stress on the cash flows. In addition, a dual amortization schedule was being employed, giving rise to late payment premiums during periods when the contractual amortization or any less than scheduled amortization was being followed.

Additionally, the Trust could remove the Operator when appropriate or insist on toll increases or operating changes during the pending specified events of default. The Trust also has the Accounts, the Debt Service Reserve Fund and the maintenance reserve fund to call upon, as well as required insurance protection. Each of these features serves as a less drastic measure exercisable in addition to the right to accelerate the debt (a non-recourse obligation to the Sponsors).

h) Construction and Technology Risk

The Tribasa transaction involved no construction risk. In addition, the technology risk was minimal as the two roads had established operating histories as described in the traffic report. In addition, business interruption insurance and property and liability insurance were required. The payment for insurance was expressly provided for in the cash flow and specified deductibles were guaranteed by the Operator. The independent engineer examined each toll road, as reflected in the traffic report, and is one of the four members of the Technical Committee governing the Trust.

i) Transferability

The Tribasa offering involved the effective transfer of cashflows evidenced by filed documents and confirmed by opinions of counsel. A sole purpose entity — the Trust — was employed to provide insulation from bankruptcy risk relating to the Sponsor and the Operator.

III. Internationalization of Capital Markets and the Problem of Integrated Disclosure

Edward F. Greene et al., Hegemony or Deference: U.S. Disclosure Requirements in the International Capital Markets

50 The Business Lawyer 413-21, 423-43 (February 1995)

INTRODUCTION

The past decade has witnessed a significant increase in the internationalization of the world's capital markets. Companies have become increasingly more willing to raise money outside their domestic markets, and investors have become increasingly more willing to purchase shares of issuers that are "foreign" to their home markets. At the same time, the level of secondary market trading in all markets and across markets has substantially increased, dwarfing the amounts raised in primary offerings. As an illustration of these developments, consider that U.S. investors owned $190 billion of non-U.S. equity securities compared to $19 billion in 1992.

The United States Securities and Exchange Commission (SEC) has responded to this trend by adapting the U.S. regulatory system, to some extent, to accommodate the desires of non-U.S. companies to raise capital in the United States and of U.S. investors to purchase shares of non-U.S. companies in both primary distributions and secondary trading. The accommodations made to date, however, have not yet been considered in light of the theories surrounding the revolutionary changes to the U.S. regulatory system brought about by the adoption of the integrated disclosure system in the early 1980s. In adopting this system, the SEC recognized that the size of the secondary trading market warranted at least as much regulatory concern as primary distributions. Furthermore, the SEC acknowledged that decisions to buy securities in the secondary trading markets, whether over-the-counter or on a securities exchange, required just as much information as decisions to purchase securities in an offering registered under the Securities Act of 1933 (Securities Act).

In connection with implementing the integrated disclosure system, the SEC revised the disclosure requirements of the Securities Exchange Act of 1934 (Exchange Act) to parallel those of the Securities Act. Once the disclosure requirements under the two statutes were made equivalent, the integrated disclosure system assumed that, for a certain class of companies and for certain securities, information contained in a company's periodic reports, together with all other relevant information made public about the company, would immediately be reflected in the price at which the securities traded in the secondary markets. The integrated disclosure system also recognized that this *old* information would not have to be repeated subsequently in a prospectus required by the Securities Act (but instead could be incorporated by reference); only material developments since the company's last periodic or current report, together with information about the intended financing, would have to be set forth in the prospectus and delivered to investors. Thus, the burden of increased periodic reporting was offset by the benefit of short-form prospectuses and, later, the efficiencies of shelf registration.

Under the integrated disclosure system, a particular company would be entitled to the benefits of short-form prospectuses and shelf registration if information with respect to all material developments about the company could reasonably be expected to be made publicly available and if all publicly available information about the company could reasonably be expected to be reflected in the price of its securities. The SEC chose two criteria to implement this policy: (i) compliance with the periodic reporting requirements of the Exchange Act for a specified period, and (ii) a specified minimum value of voting stock eligible to trade freely (the *float*). The theory was that market professionals, including analysts who would publish their research, would follow a company with a large, publicly traded capitalization and a history of reporting. Thus, it would be reasonable to expect that all new public information from whatever source—periodic or current reports filed by the company with the SEC, press releases by the company, analysts' research reported, or stories in the press—would be reflected promptly in the price of the company's securities. Although predicating the system on mandated disclosure, the SEC recognized that this disclosure alone was not sufficient. Rather, a professional market following was necessary to ensure that the information would be analyzed and disseminated to the marketplace. The SEC noted that "investors are protected by the market's analysis of information about certain companies which is widely-available, both from the Commission's files and other sources, and . . . such analysis is reflected in the price of the securities offered."

Form 20-F and the F-series of forms apply the integrated disclosure system to non-U.S. companies, but make some accommodations to disclosure standards of non-U.S. markets. These accommodations, however, are quite insignificant; in particular, non-U.S. companies are still required either to prepare their financial statements on the basis of U.S. Generally Accepted Accounting Principles (U.S. GAAP), or to show numerical reconciliations of the key line-items to what they would have been had U.S. GAAP been applied. It appears that little consideration was given to whether the pricing of shares of certain classes of non-U.S. companies in the secondary trading markets could be deemed efficient [i.e., the prices of shares reflect all material development] in ways that might allow those companies to offer their shares to the U.S. public, or to list their shares on a U.S. securities exchange, or to arrange for them to be quoted on NASDAQ, without complying with the full range of U.S. disclosure requirements, including in particular the requirement to prepare or reconcile financial statements pursuant to U.S. GAAP.

The time is now right to consider this question. Developing criteria for determining when the pricing of non-U.S. securities in the secondary market could be deemed efficient would not only allow the shares of certain non-U.S. companies to be offered to the public and listed on the U.S. securities exchanges or quoted on NASDAQ more easily, thereby enhancing the ability of U.S. investors to buy and trade non-U.S. shares, but also could influence in a positive way the direction in which regulators of non-U.S. markets might seek to move their systems. Although it is unlikely that many non-U.S. regulators or *world class* companies will eventually adopt U.S. accounting principles as their own, it may be possible to move the regulatory systems of the major non-U.S. markets towards increased disclosure and more comprehensive trade reporting requirements that would be sufficient for U.S. regulators to conclude that the quoted price of a company's shares fully reflects material developments and is comparable to the pricing of shares in the U.S. markets. The incentive for non-U.S. regulators to move in this direction would be easier access to the U.S. capital markets for the major companies operating in their jurisdictions.

In addition to the benefits to be gained from easing the access of certain non-U.S. companies to the U.S. public markets, there are harms to be avoided—harms that may soon arise out of the current arrangements. The process of internationalization, in combination with a number of recent SEC initiatives such as Regulation D, Rule 144A, and Regulation S, is undermining the rationale for the accommodation reached with non-U.S. companies in the mid-1960s over the circumstances that would require a non-U.S. company to register and be subject to the periodic reporting requirements of the Exchange Act. This accommodation, embodied in Rule 12g3-2(b) under the Exchange Act, essentially exempts non-U.S. companies from the periodic reporting requirements of the Exchange Act so long as they do not offer their securities to the public in the United States, or arrange for them to be listed on a U.S. securities exchange or, since 1983, quoted on NASDAQ. The accommodation made sense in 1967, when Rule 12g3-2(b) was adopted, but the assumptions underlying it are now questionable in light of the increased purchasing by U.S. investors of shares in non-U.S. companies.

It now appears that Rule 12g3-2(b) permits, or will soon permit, a degree of U.S. secondary market trading that is well beyond what those who adopted the rule could reasonably have expected. Moreover, the scope of disclosure now considered appropriate to support secondary market trading has increased significantly beyond what was thought necessary in 1967 because of the changes made to the periodic reporting requirements of the Exchange Act. The current scope is virtually coextensive with what is required for primary offerings. As a result, significant secondary market trading in shares of non-U.S. companies may be taking place in the United States on the basis of information considered inadequate to support investment decisions in either the primary or the secondary markets.

The current regulatory regime thus gives rise to two significant problems. First, in circumstances where the non-U.S. trading market for the company's shares may be considered efficient, U.S. investors are needlessly denied the benefits that result from the following: (i) secondary market trading on a U.S. securities exchange or NASDAQ, (ii) easy participation in attractively priced primary distributions, and (iii) the full protections afforded by the securities acts for misleading disclosure. Second, if information about a company is genuinely insufficient to support U.S. secondary market trading because of the inadequacies of home country requirements, Rule 12g3-2(b) does not require that U.S. investors be given information that would permit them to make informed investment decisions.

. . . .

EVOLUTION OF THE INTEGRATED DISCLOSURE SYSTEM

... Over time, ... the SEC increased the reporting requirements under the Exchange Act in order to ensure that investors in the primary and secondary markets would have access to the same information when purchasing securities. . . .

The process of linking disclosure under the Securities Act and the Exchange Act was not completed, however, until 1982, when the SEC adopted the integrated disclosure system. The releases proposing adoption of this system focused on the importance of providing the same information to investors in the primary and secondary markets:

> Integration, as a concept, involves a conclusion as to equivalency between transactional (Securities Act) and periodic (Exchange Act) reporting. If a subject matter is material information (other than a description of the transaction itself), then it will be material both in the distribution of securities and to the trading markets. Moreover, requirements governing the description of such subject matters should be the same for both purposes.

The SEC also considered circumstances in which information would not have to be provided to investors in primary offerings. The SEC explained that "the concept of integration also proceeds from the observation that information is regularly being furnished to the market through periodic reports under the Exchange Act. Therefore, an assumption underlying the SEC's concept of integration in general, and the development of simplified prospectus forms in particular, was that periodic reports under the Exchange Act were a primary source of the information that would be digested by market professionals, disseminated to investors, and reflected in the price of a company's securities in the secondary trading market.

. . . .

When periodic reports and other information from an issuer's earlier offering are expected to be fully digested by the secondary trading market, and hence reflected in the market price of the securities being distributed, there is no need to repeat the earlier disclosures in prospectuses for later primary offerings of such securities.

. . . .

The SEC extended the integrated disclosure system to non-U.S. issuers through the adoption of the F-series of forms and through a revision of Form 20-F designed to reflect the increased disclosure requirements of the Exchange Act. Although the SEC made some accommodations to the disclosure requirements of foreign markets in adopting these forms, it did not consider whether, for certain classes of companies, non-U.S. disclosure or accounting requirements might afford adequate protection to U.S. investors if combined with U.S. liability rules. The model followed was *national treatment*, at least insofar as complying with core accounting and business disclosures was concerned. Although *foreign private issuers* were recognized as a class, deference to their home country disclosure requirements was minimal once they decided to offer their securities to the U.S. public or arrange for their securities to be listed on a U.S exchange or, after 1983, quoted on NASDAQ. Thus, an extremely efficient system for the distribution of securities was available, but only to those companies willing to comply with U.S. standards of disclosure, in particular U.S. accounting rules. Many non-U.S. companies have chosen not to comply with these requirements; 2000 non-U.S. companies were estimated to be eligible at the end of 1993 to list their shares on the NYSE, compared to the nearly 600 non-U.S. companies that were traded in all U.S. public markets at that time.

NON-U.S. COMPANIES AND RULE 12g3-2(b): THE DEPARTURE FROM THE INTEGRATED DISCLOSURE IDEAL

The theory that led to gradual erosion of the distinction between the disclosure requirements of the Securities Act and the Exchange Act (i.e., an investment decision in the secondary market ought to be as informed as one in the primary market) has not been fully applied to securities of non-U.S. issuers. When section 12(g) was added to the Exchange Act in 1964 in order to subject more equity securities traded in the over-the-counter markets to the reporting requirements of the Exchange Act, the SEC temporarily exempted non-U.S. securities in order to consider the appropriateness of treating them in the same manner as domestic securities. The SEC noted that it was trying to achieve "the greatest practicable benefits for American investors, while at the same time not disrupting existing trading markets or penalizing foreign issuers." Based on its study, including an evaluation of the reporting by non-U.S issuers abroad, the SEC adopted Rule 12g3-2(b).

Under section 12(g), and Rules 12g-1 and 12g3-2(a) thereunder, any foreign issuer meeting the minimum asset requirement must register any class of equity securities held of record by 500 or more persons worldwide if 300 or more of such persons are resident in the United States. Rule 12g3-2(b) exempts such securities from registration if the issuer is eligible for and claims exemption pursuant to the rule. To obtain the exemption, a non-U.S. company must furnish to the SEC, in its initial submission and from time to time thereafter, certain information that it makes public pursuant to the laws of its home country, files with any stock exchange, or distributes to its security holders.

In adopting section 12(g)3-2(b), the SEC recognized that strictly applying section 12(g) and Rule 12g-1 to non-U.S. issuers in order to protect U.S. investors would probably lead to U.S. persons being excluded from holding their shares. Also, bearing in mind that no other jurisdiction compels U.S. companies to register under their laws as a consequence of foreign shareholdings, the SEC developed a compromise approach based on the notion of *voluntary* entry into the U.S. market. If a company raised capital through a public offering in the United States or arranged for its securities to be listed on a U.S. exchange or, after 1983, quoted on NASDAQ, it would be required to comply with the U.S. disclosure requirements; if, in contrast, its securities ended up in the hands of U.S. investors only as a result of secondary trading, the company would not be required to register under the Exchange Act....

For unexplained reasons, private placements and the creation of sponsored Level I American Depositary Receipt (ADR) programs were not considered to be voluntary entries into the U.S. market for this purpose. [There are three types of sponsored ADR programs. A Level I ADR program that trades in over-the-counter markets through so-called "pink sheets." A Level II ADR program established in connection with a listing, but there is no public offering. A Level III program is established in connection with a public offering.] Developments after 1967, suggest that considering these entries not to be *voluntary* and allowing non-U.S. companies to take such steps while still relying on Rule 12g3-2(b) may no longer be appropriate in certain circumstances.

There were a number of other factors supporting the adoption of Rule 12g3-2(b). First, the SEC was relatively satisfied with the level of information being disclosed by non-U.S. companies in their home markets at the time. In this regard, it is important to bear in mind that in 1967 the reporting requirements of the Exchange Act were less comprehensive than they are today....

Second, there was no reason to think that a very significant U.S. shareholder base would develop for issuers relying on Rule 12g3-2(b), which was adopted before Regulation D, Rule 144A, and Regulation S. Public offering-style private placements such as those possible under Rule 144A or Regulation D today were barely conceivable in 1967. Limitations on the number of offerees and concerns about general solicitation and general advertising, including U.S. roadshows, would have restricted the number of U.S. investors likely to purchase shares in a private placement by a non-U.S. company, and concerns about the legality of resales by private placers while the securities remained restricted would have limited the number of U.S. holders that could result from such a placement. SEC Release No. 4708, *Registration of Foreign Offerings by Domestic Issuers*, released by the SEC only three years before the adoption of Rule 12g3-2, was silent as to when non-U.S. securities offered in non-U.S. markets could be resold into the United States, and this uncertainty probably operated to limit *flow-back* into the United States through secondary market trading. Perhaps more important, it gave no guidance as to when or under what circumstances privately placed shares of non-U.S. companies in the United States could be resold in the principal market offshore. Not until after the SEC issued the College Retirement Equities fund (CREF) no-action letters, in the context of the French privatizations in the late 1980s, was it generally accepted that privately placed securities could be immediately resold in certain markets outside the United States. Uncertainty about the ability to resell privately placed securities into their principal markets reduced the likelihood that U.S. investors, other than those willing to hold for the long term, would be interested in privately placed securities of non-U.S. companies.

Third, in 1967, integration of the world's capital markets had not nearly reached current levels, and it is very unlikely that the SEC believed that Rule 12g3-2(b) would affect as many holders of non-U.S. securities as it does today. The absolute value of holdings by U.S. investors of non-U.S. securities has grown dramatically over the years. Furthermore, the volume of trading of non-U.S. securities in the secondary market substantially outweighs the volume of primary offerings. Based on the number of ADR programs that are not listed on a U.S. exchange or quoted on NASDAQ, the trading figure for unregistered American depositary shares is likely to be substantial....

The arguments supporting the adoption of Rule 12g3-2(b) are no longer valid. The reporting requirements under the Exchange Act have increased significantly, and since 1967 there has been no reassessment of whether reports prepared by non-U.S. issuers in their home countries are still comparable, as the SEC believed was the case in 1967. Moreover, the opportunities are much greater to obtain a significant U.S. shareholder base through actions deemed by the SEC to be involuntary. Level I ADR programs can be established through which pink sheet or electronic bulletin board trading, even for retail investors, takes place. Rule 144A offerings involving large numbers of institutional investors also are common and are not infrequently followed by the creation of Level I ADR programs. Following a Rule 144A offering, trading among large numbers of institutional investors can also take place in the restricted securities, and when the restrictions are lifted, retail investors can begin to trade the securities.

Furthermore, Regulation S permits increased holdings of non-U.S. securities by U.S. investors. It clarifies when *seasoning* of securities occurs, thereby opening the way for securities placed in primary offerings outside the United States, based entirely on home country disclosure standards, to flow into the United States after the seasoning period. It also allows U.S. institutional investors to establish offices outside the United States in order to participate in primary distributions by certain non-U.S. issuers; securities so purchased offshore can then be resold into the United States after the seasoning period. Finally, Regulations S makes privately placed securities of certain non-U.S. companies more attractive by permitting immediate resale into the principal market outside the United States, whether on a securities exchange or in the over-the-counter market.

THE STATUS QUO: ARGUMENTS FOR AND AGAINST

Because internationalization and the SEC initiatives discussed previously have undermined the rationale for Rule 12g3-2(b), it is time to reconsider in a comprehensive way the treatment of non-U.S. companies under the U.S. securities laws. Under the current regulatory regime, all non-U.S. companies raising capital in the U.S. public market, listing their securities on a U.S. exchange, or arranging for them to be quoted on NASDAQ are required to comply fully with U.S. disclosure and accounting standards, and are allowed to reap the benefits afforded by the integrated disclosure system; in all other cases Rule 12g3-2(b) provides for complete deference non-U.S. standards. There is no middle ground. Although there are a number of arguments supporting the balance that has been struck between national treatment on the one hand and deference to non-U.S. standards on the other, some adjustments are in order.

Several arguments are made in favor of the status quo. One argument is that the United States, as a result of U.S. GAAP and the disclosure requirements embodied in SEC rules and regulations, has the most "transparent financial reporting and full and complete disclosure" system in the world, and this system should be followed whenever the U.S. public is given the opportunity to buy securities in a primary offering or in organized secondary trading market. A second argument is that because making an informed choice between competing investments requires comparable information, financial statements of non-U.S. companies and U.S. companies that trade in the public markets must be prepared on the basis of the same accounting principles; these principles should be U.S. GAAP because U.S. GAAP are the best. Finally, proponents of the status quo argue that equally applying U.S. standards to all issuers ensures that U.S. issuers are not placed at a disadvantage in their own capital markets.

Many supporters of the status quo also believe that the U.S. capital markets are so important that most world-class issuers will eventually give in and comply with U.S. requirements. The recent decision by Daimler-Benz to comply with U.S. disclosure requirements, notwithstanding a history of opposition by German companies, is seen as supporting this view. If the United States is winning, why change the order of battle before U.S. hegemony is complete? Daimler-Benz was only one of thirty-seven non-U.S. companies that listed shares on the NYSE in 1993 out of a total of 306 U.S. and non-U.S. companies that listed common or preferred shares on the NYSE that year.... The more such companies come to the United States, the greater the likelihood that the superiority of the U.S. system will be acknowledged by other regulators, and the greater the likelihood that they will adopt such requirements. The biggest market in the world should be expected to set world standards.

Although the arguments for preserving the status quo are strong, the arguments for changing it are stronger. First, U.S. investors are needlessly disadvantaged under the current system in circumstances when the information about non-U.S. companies would be adequate for informed investment decision-making without requiring those companies to comply with U.S. GAAP and the other U.S. disclosure requirements. For such companies, U.S. investors, both retail and institutional, are merely driven to the less efficient and less transparent over-the-counter markets and non-U.S. markets. At the same time, U.S. retail investors who are not substantial or sophisticated enough to make arrangements to buy securities offshore are denied the benefits of attractively priced foreign privatizations and other primary offerings.

Moreover, if the status quo remains unchanged, the problems arising out of Rule 12g3-2(b) can only be expected to grow. Because Rule 12g3-2(b) does not distinguish between non-U.S. companies on the basis of the quality of the information they make public, and because it places no limit on the extent of a non-U.S. company's U.S. shareholder base, significant secondary market trading can take place in the United States under Rule 12g3-2(b) without adequate information. Also, Rule 12g3-2(b), unlike the rules of the principal U.S. stock exchanges and NASDAQ, does not require that material developments with respect to the company be disclosed. Thus, unless required by non-U.S. law, information about non-U.S. companies whose securities trade in the United States on the basis of Rule 12g3-2(b) may not be kept current. Finally, information furnished to the SEC pursuant to Rule 12g3-2(b) is not subject to the same U.S. liability rules as information provided by non-U.S. companies that list their securities on U.S. exchanges or arrange to have their securities quoted on NASDAQ.

Those who advocate preserving the status quo generally ignore Rule 12g3-2(b), and thus the arguments they make are subject to question. In particular, the emphasis on U.S. GAAP appears to be misplaced. The accounting systems of a number of other countries, as well as International Accounting Standards, may be as good as U.S. GAAP—and in certain respects may even be better—as systems of rules for fairly presenting the financial position of a company. Moreover, for purposes of complete disclosure, other types of disclosure, such as the supplemental disclosure required under Industry Guide 3 in the case of public offerings by banks and management's discussion and analysis of financial condition and results of operations, are as important, and perhaps even more important, than the particular system of accounting rules that a company chooses for its financial statements.

Finally, and perhaps the most important, there is no evidence that presenting information on the basis of U.S. GAAP has a significant effect on the market price of shares of a non-U.S. company.

. . . . It is not surprising that reconciliation to U.S. GAAP does not have a significant impact on price. Accounting principles, after all, are merely sets of rules for fairly presenting the historical financial condition of a company and its results of operations. Valuation starts from, but is not determined by, these rules. Assuming that the rules meet a certain minimum standard and that they are understood, one set of rules should be just as good as another as a starting point for valuation.

If it is correct that, (i) U.S. GAAP is merely one of a number of systems of accounting rules that can fairly present a company's financial position, (ii) narrative discussions are as important elements of fair disclosure as the accounting rules chosen, and (iii) presentation of the financial results of a non-U.S. company according to U.S. GAAP has little impact on the price of that company's shares, then the only substantive argument in favor of the status quo must be that informed choice between two companies' shares requires that both companies prepare their financial statements on the same basis. Although this proposition has a superficial appeal, it is wrong. The extent of trading by U.S. investors in shares of non-U.S. companies that have not reconciled their accounts to U.S. GAAP suggests that comparisons are in fact being made, although the basis on which this is being done is not clear and would be a good topic for empirical research. It is interesting to note that when the largest and most powerful U.S. institutional investors and investment banks have had the ability to influence the disclosure of non-U.S. companies, they have not insisted on reconciliations to U.S. GAAP. The best prospectuses prepared for U.S. placements of non-U.S. securities under Rule 144A, for example, contain much of the information that would be required in a prospectus for a U.S. public offering, with the notable exception of reconciliation to U.S. GAAP. Moreover, market professionals who prepare research about non-U.S. companies do not appear to require U.S. GAAP-reconciled financial information in order to make comparisons in their research.

Even if all the substantive arguments of those who wish to preserve the status quo are answered, two other points remain: fairness to U.S. issuers and influencing non-U.S. regulators and companies to improve their disclosure by adopting U.S. requirements. Affording greater deference to home country disclosure would not be unfair to U.S. companies. First, U.S. companies would not be subject to any new requirements. Second, they would be at no greater disadvantage than at present, bearing in mind the existing size of secondary market trading in non-U.S. securities and the ability of U.S. investors to participate in primary offerings by non-U.S. issuers under Regulation S, Regulation D, and Rule 144A. Third, greater deference to home country rules would only be permitted for those countries that similarly deferred to U.S. rules when U.S. companies raised capital or listed shares there. Fourth, at some point the level of U.S. ownership of the shares of a non-U.S. company could justify treating that company as equivalent to a U.S. company. For example, if a *foreign private issuer* were to cease satisfying the U.S. shareholder percentage and other requirements for treatment as such, it would no longer be entitled to follow the different registration and other requirements applicable to non-U.S. issuers. Finally, an approach based on the premise that no change need be made because non-U.S. regulators and non-U.S. companies ultimately will accept U.S. accounting standards is confrontational and unlikely to succeed. Surely an approach based on greater deference, where appropriate, would be more acceptable to other jurisdictions than insistence on the U.S. system, and particularly U.S. GAAP, as a whole. Greater deference might be more likely to produce acceptance of U.S. disclosure standards if the quid pro quo is easier access to the U.S. capital markets and it might in turn make it easier to reach agreement on common international standards. After all, greater deference does not mean that standards will be frozen in time. They will continue to evolve, and in all likelihood in the direction of more, not less, disclosure.

REGULATORY ALTERNATIVES

There are a number of regulatory alternatives to the status quo. U.S. regulators could (i) attempt to turn back the clock by repealing Rule 12g3-2(b), (ii) establish different systems for retail and institutional investors, or (iii) devote their energies to harmonizing the disclosure and accounting requirements of the principal capital markets. In the end, none of these alternatives is as attractive or realistic as an approach based upon greater deference to non-U.S. requirements in circumstances where deference is appropriate.

TURNING BACK THE CLOCK

Turning back the clock to 1967 and repealing Rule 12g3-2(b) would be too disruptive. The rule's survival over the years, despite the significant increase in U.S. holdings of non-U.S. securities, indicates implicit satisfaction with the pragmatic judgments that led to its adoption. Further, full application of the Exchange Act to non-U.S. issuers would lead to a hue and cry about regulatory imperialism. But it must be recognized that the gap between the information available about those issuers that *come to the United States* and those that do not is great, and that the level of trading in shares of the latter is increasing. Moreover, confining such issuers to the pink sheet market also may put U.S. investors at a disadvantage because most such issuers raise capital by way of rights offerings, and the SEC has not yet permitted such offerings without full registration.

THE SOPHISTICATED INVESTOR MODEL

Many regulatory initiatives are premised on the notion that if investors are sophisticated, they can fend for themselves and therefore do not need the protection of mandated disclosure and accounting rules when making primary or secondary market investments. If this approach were followed, non-U.S. issuers would be able, without complying with U.S. disclosure requirements, to offer their securities to sophisticated investors in the United States and to list their securities on a special section of a U.S. exchange (or have them quoted on a special section of NASDAQ) for trading limited to sophisticated investors. The exchanges and NASDAQ would be expected to adopt listing or quotation criteria likely to result in eligibility for seasoned world-class issuers.

This approach, however, is flawed. It would prevent retail investors from trading securities of many world-class companies on U.S. exchanges or NASDAQ, instead driving them into the less efficient and less transparent over-the-counter markets and non-U.S. markets. Moreover, retail investors not substantial or sophisticated enough to buy securities in non-U.S. markets would be denied the opportunity to participate in attractively priced primary offerings, including privatizations. Although this approach would be an improvement over the status quo, it would not be as desirable as one based on greater deference, which would allow retail investors to buy shares of certain of the companies in question in U.S. public offerings and in organized trading markets in the United States.

HARMONIZATION

Under the *harmonization* proposals, each regulatory system would share a basic set of disclosure and accounting standards. The European Community's common disclosure and accounting standards illustrate such an approach.

Some of those who support the status quo also advocate harmonization, perhaps because they suspect that any widely accepted international standards would involve significant deference to existing U.S. requirements, which are the oldest and most extensive. Unfortunately, few anticipate that the disclosure requirements of the world's major capital markets will be harmonized at any point in the near future.

GREATER DEFERENCE, WHERE APPROPRIATE

The most reasonable alternative is to acknowledge that markets outside the United States can efficiently price certain securities in those markets, evaluate the circumstances in which greater deference to the disclosure requirements of those markets is appropriate, and extend the current benefits of the integrated disclosure system of reporting and distribution to certain companies in those markets. The premise of such an approach is that in certain markets outside the United States all material developments about a company could reasonably be expected to be made publicly available, and all publicly available information about the company could reasonably be expected to be reflected in the price at which its shares trade in its home market. The role of market professionals is significant in achieving this result, as the SEC recognized when it adopted the integrated disclosure system. It is clear not only that this role is being played by such professionals in many other jurisdictions, but also that the importance of research analysis in markets outside the United States is increasing.

It would be an extremely narrow interpretation of the efficient market theory to contend that it works only within U.S. borders because of the U.S. mandated disclosure system. If it can operate outside U.S. borders, then for certain companies all investors should be permitted to trade those shares on the basis of pricing in that market without the delivery of any disclosure document other than what may be required locally. Distributions, as new events, would require that additional information be disseminated to investors, the content of which should be the subject of discussion.

The goal of the greater deference approach would be to agree upon criteria for deciding when non-U.S. markets could be acknowledged as functioning in a manner comparable to the U.S. markets. A key component would be the frequency of periodic reporting as well as the minimum disclosure requirements that would be sufficient for raising capital in the United States by non-U.S. issuers and for secondary market trading in their shares without adherence to U.S. standards. This approach would need to be consistent with the principles articulated by the SEC regarding its dealings with non-U.S. issuers:

> The legislative history of the Securities Act indicates an intent to treat foreign private issuers (as distinct from foreign governments) the same as domestic issuers. Therefore, the Commission has generally perceived its function as neither discriminating against nor encouraging foreign investment in the United States or investments in foreign securities.

This position of neutrality, however, would not be subverted by the acceptance of different disclosure about non-U.S. issuers because the SEC settled on an integrated disclosure system that "parallels the system for domestic issuers but also takes into account the different circumstances of foreign registrants."...

There would be many benefits from such a new approach. First, it would increase the access of U.S. investors to the companies whose disclosure satisfies certain minimum standards. This access would not be limited to investors who are able to participate in the private placement market or are otherwise able to purchase shares offshore. Instead, access would be through the U.S. exchanges and NASDAQ, the most liquid and transparent markets, and not through the over-the-counter markets or non-U.S. markets. Second, the condition that the non-U.S. disclosure requirements meet certain minimum standards could improve the quality of information about certain non-U.S. companies that is made available both in the United States and abroad. Third, it would subject these non-U.S. companies to the full panoply of U.S. liability rules. Finally, as more non-U.S. companies enter the U.S. public market, competition between the world's securities exchanges and over-the-counter markets in the areas of trading efficiency and simplicity of clearance and settlement might increase....[S]uch an approach could also be coupled with tightening Rule 12g3-2(b) to address some of the anomalies created by the rule.

IMPLEMENTING THE APPROACH

Deference to Home Country Disclosure

Permission to rely upon home country disclosure would be limited to circumstances when the market for the securities in question is considered efficient. Efficiency would be a reflection of certain characteristics of both the company and its home market. The main criteria could be the following: (i) minimum disclosure standards, (ii) minimum periodic reporting requirements, (iii) satisfactory rules aimed at preventing market manipulation and ensuring market transparency, and (iv) minimum market capitalization and trading volume requirements. It is thought that a company meeting minimum capitalization and trading volume requirements implies a significant following of the company's stock by analysts. If there were some concern about this correlation, perhaps minimum research requirements would also be developed.

Minimum Disclosure Standards

The most important step to implementing an approach of greater deference would be to determine minimum disclosure standards. Although U.S. disclosure standards are the most comprehensive, other alternatives may provide adequate protection for investors. The SEC has accepted limited departures from U.S. disclosure requirements in the past for non-U.S. issuers, and these departures have not been found detrimental to U.S. investors or disadvantageous to U.S. issuers. Indeed, by setting certain minimum disclosure standards, the SEC will in fact be improving the quality of information about certain non-U.S. companies that is made available in the United States and abroad.

It is often argued that greater deference would result in a *race to the bottom*. There are two main responses. First, it is unlikely that regulators in the United States would accept standards that do not at least satisfy the fundamental features of existing U.S. standards. Indeed, the current requirements of Form 20-F, without U.S. GAAP reconciliation, could be a starting point that is likely to be acceptable to many non-U.S. issuers and regulators. Minimum financial statement criteria could also apply. Financial statements should be prepared on a consolidated basis. The treatment of hidden reserves should also be considered, with a view to determining whether full numerical disclosure would be required or whether narrative disclosure about the policies involved in establishing the reserves and their order of magnitude would be sufficient.

Second, the market professionals upon whom the SEC relied in adopting the integrated disclosure system would not permit such a race to the bottom. Both financial intermediaries who publish research about non-U.S. companies and the institutions who purchase their securities surely would cease to recommend and purchase such securities if they felt that the information available about the issuers was inadequate.

Greater deference might be thought to constitute an improper departure from the basic principle of the U.S. securities laws that certain specified information is required to be disclosed. This assumes, however, that U.S. GAAP and all the other U.S. disclosure requirements are essential elements of investor protection. The new approach would be based on the premises that disclosure meeting certain minimum standards will be prepared in the relevant non-U.S. markets, and that for certain companies in efficient markets, this information and all other public information about that company will be reflected in the pricing. Absent satisfaction of such minimum standards, deference would not be granted....

The high U.S. liability standards should also provide comfort that a disclosure document would be prepared with much care, even in circumstances where the formal requirements as to content were dictated by non-U.S. rules. This would be the case particularly where the disclosure document is being used for a U.S. public offering, in which the most rigorous U.S. liability standards apply.

Minimum Periodic Reporting Requirements

Consistent with the basic premise of the U.S. system, periodic updating of available disclosure on a timely basis could be another criterion for deciding which companies are entitled to rely upon home country disclosure. This could be a significant improvement over the current system under Rule 12g3-2(b), which does not have an updating requirement.

Satisfactory Rules Aimed at Preventing Market Manipulation and Ensuring Market Transparency

Regulators would need to be confident that the home markets are protected from market manipulation through appropriate rules prohibiting market manipulation and similar practices. They might conclude that only issuers from jurisdictions with which the SEC has information-sharing or similar agreements would be entitled to rely on home country disclosure.

Regulators also would need to be confident that home market rules ensure market transparency with respect to price and trading information. Information about securities trades need not be made available to the public in the same manner as in the United States, although the procedures in the home market for disseminating such information, and the timing of such dissemination, would need to satisfy certain minimum standards.

Minimum Market Capitalization and Trading Volume Requirements

The SEC has often granted exemptions from certain U.S. rules when the issuers met specified market capitalization levels. The logic of granting these exemptions is that, given the size of such issuers, the market for their shares is presumably efficient, and pricing in the U.S. market is likely to be closely tied to pricing in the home country market. The exemptions were also based in part on the likelihood of a significant following by research analysts and trading in several markets, and the knowledge that such a following would contribute to market efficiency. A minimum market capitalization also is one of the primary eligibility criteria for the use of the short-form prospectuses under the Securities Act and the ability to incorporate previously filed documents by reference into such prospectuses.

The greater deference approach could therefore be limited to companies that satisfy certain market capitalization and trading volume tests. To be eligible to use Form F-3, a company must have a float of at least $75 million, but no trading volume test need be satisfied. In this context, however, it may be desirable to apply a higher float requirement and to add a trading volume requirement.

Minimum Research Coverage Requirements

If the essential role of intermediaries is given full recognition, regulators might even choose to buttress a system that involves greater deference to home country requirements by institutionalizing the role of the intermediaries in disseminating to investors available information about issuers. For example, home country deference might only be continued so long as a specific number of independent financial intermediaries disseminate customary research about the issuer in the U.S. markets. The requirement could be that a certain number of financial intermediaries agree at the outset of an offering to disseminate research about the issuer for a specified period of time. Perhaps only financial intermediaries who meet specified size and qualification standards, such as those used in the National Association of Securities Dealers (NASD) rules that define *qualified independent underwriters*, might be allowed to satisfy this requirement. Also eligibility probably would depend on an intermediary's history of disseminating research in the United States.

NARROWING THE AVAILABILITY OF RULE 12g3-2(b)

The approach of Rule 12g3-2(b) is outmoded and its effect is to allow significant departures from the basic premises of securities regulation. An alternative approach would be to limit the use of the exemption to truly involuntary entry. As is the case today, the exemption provided by Rule 12g3-2(b) would not be available to companies that have their shares listed on a U.S. exchange or quoted on NASDAQ. The rule would be amended to provide that it would not be available to companies that sponsor Level I ADR programs or conduct private placements, under Rule 144A or otherwise, if in either case their U.S. shareholders exceed a certain number, which could be higher than the current threshold of 300. To avoid disruption from changes to the availability of the Rule 12g3-2(b) exemption, companies that currently rely upon the exemption would be grandfathered.

Chapter 7

Political Risk

I. The Concept of "Political Risk"

Documents Supplement References:

1. *1962 United Nations Resolution on Permanent Sovereignty Over Natural Resources.*
2. *1974 United Nations Declaration on the Establishment of a New International Economic Order.*
3. *1974 United Nations Charter of Economic Rights and Duties of States.*
4. *Restatement Sections 712-713.*

NOTE ON FDI AND POLITICAL RISK[*]

Introduction

An international business lawyer must appreciate the role of political risk and its effect on FDI decisions. This Note defines, explains, and treats the relationship between FDI and political risk. Initially, "political risk" is defined and explored as a term. A taxonomy of the various types and manifestations of political risk follows, along with examples of each. Next, the legal doctrines relevant to political risk, including the conflicting viewpoints and philosophies, and theories behind the doctrines, are explained. Thereafter, the various means available to investors to mitigate political risk is explored. Finally, dispute resolution regimes and methods for managing disputes between investors and host nations are discussed. Some of these regimes and methods also are treated in a later chapter in this Casebook dealing with the regulation of FDI.

Conceptual Definitions and Species of "Political Risk"

Simply defined, "political risk" represents the threat that a host country will interfere with the property rights of a foreign investor in connection with their invest-

---

* The assistance of Christopher C. Matteson, Esq. in preparing this Note is gratefully acknowledged. Much of this Note draws on PAUL E. COMEAUX & N. STEPHAN KINSELLA, PROTECTING FOREIGN INVESTMENT UNDER INTERNATIONAL LAW: LEGAL ASPECTS OF POLITICAL RISK (1997) for support. The authors of this excellent work provide a useful structure for the study of political risk, and thus deserve special mention. Their work also is recommended for further research, as the authors provide an exhaustive treatment of the many aspects of political risk.

ment in the host country. In other words, it is the risk that the host country's government will take some action that adversely affects the investment.

Political risk tends to accompany investment in developing countries, where typically there is less certainty and predictability in the existing legal, political, business,
and economic frameworks. For example, a petroleum corporation based in Dallas,
Texas would be accustomed to a certain level of comfort as regards its investments in
its extraction operations in the Gulf of Mexico near the coast of Louisiana. United
States law would apply to many aspects of its operations. No doubt, Texas and
Louisiana state laws would apply to other aspects of the company's activities. Furthermore, the corporation likely would have little fear that its assets would be seized
by either the federal or a state government without due regard to their property
rights, other than in connection with a proceeding in bankruptcy or the like, as such
action would be patently unconstitutional.

The concept most closely resembling political risk in a domestic context is called
"regulatory risk." This term describes the possibility that Congress or the Environmental Protection Agency (EPA), for instance, might change rules pertaining to offshore petroleum extraction in the Gulf of Mexico, possibly resulting in a loss to the
Texas petroleum firm. After all, Congress is in the business of enacting legislation,
and administrative agencies are in the business of promulgating regulations. So, the
possibility of rules changing—it is hoped not from day to day—always exists. As
pointed out by the late Italian legal theorist Bruno Leoni in his 1961 book *Freedom
and the Law*, even if a given statute is written clearly, "we are *never certain* that tomorrow we shall still have the rules we have today."[1]

Naturally, the Texas-based petroleum corporation might not have the same level
of comfort as regards its extraction operations in, say, Algeria. The level of stability
and certainty present in the legal, political, business, and economic frameworks in
that and many other host countries is considerably lower than in the United States.
The difference between these two scenarios provides a simple conceptual illustration
of "political risk."

However, the basic definition of "political risk" offered above must be expanded. The notion that an investor's property rights may face confiscation or interference in a host country requires that the property right itself be defined. Property
rights may vary in nature based on culture, geography, and the applicable political
and legal frameworks. As Professor Herz wrote in 1941, a few rudimentary points
seem clear, though even they give rise to uncertainties.

> The meaning of "property" is not so easily to be determined. Since the law
> of property is a matter regulated by the municipal laws of the different coun-
> tries in various ways, it might be expected that international law, when deal-
> ing with property, would have its own definition or, at least, refer to some de-
> finition of municipal law. Some sort of an international definition of property
> can indeed be derived from the practice of states and the jurisdiction of inter-
> national tribunals. International law concerning the protection of foreign
> property is a product of the evolution of [the] world economy in the nine-
> teenth century. It has taken over from internal legal conceptions the largest
> and, as it were, most advanced definition of property. First of all, it comprises
> the usual form of what, in most civil codes, is called property, *i.e.*, "tangible"

---

1. BRUNO LEONI, FREEDOM AND THE LAW 1 n. 1 (Liberty Fund 3d ed. 1991) (1961) (emphasis original, citations omitted).

property in the sense of the highest right of dealing with a thing, "the highest degree of possession."....

Property...however, means more. According to a great array of diplomatic and judicial cases and the great majority of authors, it comprises rights as well as tangible property, above all contractual rights, such as rights arising from contracts of concession, purchases, loans, etc. A difficult problem, however, arises here with respect to what constitutes interference with these rights. The breach of a contract, the modification of contractual obligations said to amount to expropriation, and similar interferences are for the most part open at first to local lawsuits and internal procedure, to be dealt with by municipal courts or other state authorities.....

A still more difficult problem is that of the demarcation between rights, or vested rights, as they are often called, and mere interests, expectancies, favorable situations, etc. The civil law of a country in almost every one of its specific rules, and often also in its constitutional and administrative law, creates situations in the continuation of which an individual may be interested. By acts of legislation, or even of administrative practice, this situation may be changed. To give foreigners vested rights against each of these changes would mean to insure them against every change which may concern their interests. It is clear that somewhere a line of demarcation has to be drawn between *droits acquis* [acquired rights] and that which is beyond their sphere. But international law by no means gives a clear-cut solution. The destruction of the good will of an enterprise or the annihilation of a business by the erection of a state monopoly is one of those contested cases where, on the basis of precedents and expressed opinion, as much can be said pro as con.[2]

From a developed country standpoint, "property rights" probably ought to be defined in an inclusive manner to cover (1) intellectual property (such as a patent, copyright, trademark, or semiconductor mask work), (2) real property (such as a plot of land on which a factory sits), (3) a property right in one's labor, (4) personal property (such as an automobile), and (5) contract rights. But, not every legal culture is likely to agree with this expansive approach. Conceptions of "property rights" are sure to be different across common, civil, and Islamic legal systems, legal systems governing economies in transition from communism or socialism to capitalism, and inchoate legal systems in underdeveloped countries. The variations in the concept surely heightens the degree of political risk a foreign direct investor faces. For example, in certain African nations, land is considered ultimately to be vested in the head of state, or alternatively in the chief of the local tribe. Even though a factory may be built upon a plot of land, the investor may be forced to contend with the head of state and/or the chief to realize certain use rights of what (under a western conception) is the investor's property.

In sum, "political risk" is a broad term indeed. At one level, it is the threat an investor faces that the host country's government interferes with some aspect of the investor's property rights in the investment. At another level, however, it can arise from a variety of government action or inaction, on a local, regional, or national basis, or from quasi- or non-governmental sources, like revolution or terrorism. Indeed, Professor Kennedy suggests the following classification, dividing political risk into legal and extra-legal categories, and macro- and micro-level categories.

---

2. John Herz, *Expropriation of Foreign Property*, 35 Am. J. Int'l L. 243, 244-26 (1941).

Diagram: Types of Political Risk[3]

	EXTRA-LEGAL	LEGAL-GOVERNMENT
MACRO	Revolution	Investment Laws
MICRO	Terrorism	Trade Regulations

Not surprisingly—and quite rightly—Professor Kennedy suggests that perhaps it is best to consider political risk as "one that threatens a firm with financial, strategic, or personnel loss due to *non-market* forces."[4]

Taking a broad conception of "political risk," and given the broad conception of "property" as a bundle of rights to use, take the fruits of, and dispose of many different types of "property," it follows that *all* of the following are manifestations or species of political risk:

I.		Expropriation or confiscation of the investor's real and personal property by the host country's government.

II.		Refusal by the host country's government to allow the investor to remove its machinery and other equipment from the host country.

III.	Imposition of regulation and taxes by the host country's government to such a degree that the investment becomes practically worthless or economically unfeasible.

IV.		Legislation implemented by the host country's government compelling transfer of technology or permitting violations of the investor's intellectual property rights.

V.		Repudiation or forced renegotiation by the host country's government of a contract between it and the investor.

VI.		Nonpayment of debt owed by the host country's government to the investor, including the possibility of nonpayment of compensation owed for an expropriation.

VII.	Currency inconvertibility, or the inability of the investor to transfer currency out of the host country.

VIII.	Unfair calling of performance on a bond or letter of credit by the host country's government.

IX.		Loss of assets or contract rights of the investor due to war, civil war, insurrection, revolution, terrorism, or related conditions arising from political instability in or near the host country.[5]

No doubt this long list is yet incomplete. For example, what about "corruption risk"? This is the risk that a government official, or intermediary, in the host country seeks "extra compensation" (*i.e.*, a bribe) from a foreign direct investor in order to provide necessary authorizations, goods, or services for the investment to go forward. Problems of corruption are so pervasive that they, the nascent international anti-bribery regime, and the highly significant United States Foreign Corrupt Practices Act, are treated in a separate Chapter of this Casebook.

Implicit in the concept of "political risk" is the idea that the occurrences itemized above are unanticipated, or not fully anticipated, at the time the investment is made.

---

3. CHARLES R. KENNEDY, JR., POLITICAL RISK MANAGEMENT 7, fig. 1 (1987).

4. KENNEDY, *supra*, at 5 (emphasis added).

5. *See* COMEAUX & KINSELLA, *supra*, at 2-3.

Thus, still another way of defining "political risk" is to say it is the risk faced by any foreign direct investor that the host country's government will interfere with the investment in a way not expected by the investor at the time the investor makes its investment decision. This way of defining the concept highlights the need for investors and their counsel to try to anticipate as many problems as possible, devise ways to reduce the chances the problems actually arise, minimize the adverse effects of problems that do occur, and agree upon a means of settling any disputes with the host country's government.

Expropriation, Exchange Controls, and Political Violence

Special mention should be made of items I and VII, as these species of political risk are particularly common. Regarding item I, expropriation is the classic form of political risk typically emphasized in international business law books. Indeed, several of the cases below in this portion of the Chapter arise from expropriation, and expropriation is discussed in greater detail in a subsequent Note.

Regarding item VII, by the early 1990s it seemed that currency controls were part of the history, not present or future, of some developing countries (particularly in Latin America) and, therefore, were not a serious threat to FDI. But, in response to the Asian and Russian economic crises of the mid and late 1990s, several countries seriously debated implementing currency controls, and some—including Malaysia—implemented such controls. Accordingly, "exchange control risk" is discussed in the Chapter of this Casebook dealing with currency risk.

Special mention also should be made of item X in the above-quoted list. Political violence includes "war, revolution, insurrection, or politically motivated civil strife, terrorism and sabotage."[6] It is a threat to an investor's property in an immediate sense, as it can result in damage, loss of use, or complete destruction. To "add insult to injury," in the longer term, a confiscation or expropriation may result from such an activity.

However, there is a grey area with respect to political violence. So long as the activity is in the control of the government of the host country, it generally is compensable under international law.[7] How, then, does one know whether political violence occurs in the context of government control? In the case of *Sea-Land*,[8] the Iran-United States Claims Tribunal noted that for the act to be determined an expropriation, "the tribunal [must] be satisfied that there was deliberate governmental interference with the conduct of Sea-Land's operation, the effect of which was to deprive Sea-Land of the use and benefit of the Investment."[9]

To be sure, there is a risk that some act of political violence will cause a loss to a foreign investor without the knowledge of the host country's government, and without the requisite deliberate governmental action. Consider, for example, the following hypothetical of an American petroleum extraction facility in Algeria, operating with the permission of and under contract with the government in Algiers. During the night, armed insurgents, affiliated with the group known as the Islamic Salvation Front, or "F.I.S.," enter the perimeter of the American operation and destroy U.S.

---

6. OVERSEAS PRIVATE INVESTMENT CORPORATION, PROGRAM HANDBOOK 13 (October 1995).

7. *See* COMEAUX & KINSELLA, *supra*, at 16.

8. *See* Sea-Land Service, Inc. v. Government of the Islamic Republic of Iran, Awd. No. 135-33-1, 6 IRAN-U.S. C.T.R. 149 (1984).

9. COMEAUX & KINSELLA, *supra*, at 16, *citing* Sea-Land, 6 IRAN-U.S. C.T.R. 149 at 166.

$500,000 worth of vehicles and computer equipment. They also set fire to a building, causing an additional U.S. $1 million in damage to the investment. Should the government in Algiers be held responsible for the destruction? Certainly not, if the destruction was not a result of a deliberate governmental interference with the property of the investor, and there was no government complicity in the FIS violence.

What can a foreign direct investor such as the American company in Algeria due to mitigate the risk of political violence? Fortunately, it is possible to insure against this risk,[10] though there may be certain host countries where insurance against acts of political violence is either unavailable or prohibitively expensive. Political risk insurance is discussed later in this Chapter.

Distinguishing Political Risk from Other Risks

Armed with some perspectives on what "political risk" is, it is important to understand how the term relates to the oft-heard terms "country risk" and "sovereign risk." "Country risk" refers to risks or threats to property interests in an investment stemming solely from an action of the host country government. "Sovereign risk" refers to a risk or threat to property interests in an investment by the host country government (or a sovereign unit under that government, such as a province or state). Thus, the terms "political risk," "country risk, and "sovereign risk" are somewhat interchangeable, though "political risk" seems to have a broader connotation.

It is even more important to distinguish "political risk" from other types of risk that exist in any FDI transaction. These risks include "market risk," "credit risk," and "legal risk." "Market risk" describes the category of threats to an investment that may occur in relation to changes in the values of foreign exchange, capital market instruments, products, and raw materials and intermediate goods, and changes in the competitive landscape. In other words, it is a risk that the value of a financial market instrument, finished good, or input into the production process will move in an adverse direction.

For example, a Japanese manufacturer of cars operating in Indonesia faces market risk that may result from a change in currency values. Suppose this manufacturer imports auto parts from Japan, pays for these parts in Japanese yen, and thereafter assembles the parts in its Indonesian plant. Suppose further that the manufacturer sells the cars it makes in Indonesia to Indonesians, thus earning revenue denominated in Indonesian rupiah. Finally, suppose the rupiah depreciates relative to the yen. Clearly, the manufacturer is worse off: it will need more rupiah than before the depreciation to convert to the same amount of yen and buy the needed auto parts. This is the sort of currency risk that occurred during the Asian economic crisis of the late 1990s. Indeed, currency risk is so important to consider in any FDI deal that it is treated separately in this Casebook.

At the same time, currency risk is hardly the only form of market risk to worry a foreign direct investor. The Japanese company in the above example also faces market risk in the form of a decline in the value of the securities (equity and debt) that it has issued. This risk is exacerbated if the securities are traded on a local exchange that is highly volatile. As another instance, the Japanese company will be hurt by any increase in the price of raw materials or intermediate goods it uses in the production process, such as a hike in the price of auto parts notwithstanding any currency fluctuations. Market risk could arise from changes in consumer preferences. Perhaps In-

---

10. *See* OVERSEAS PRIVATE INVESTMENT CORPORATION ANNUAL REPORT 14 (1996) (listing eligibility and coverage of investment insurance).

donesians no longer like the kind of car the Japanese company makes, and the company experiences a drop in sales. Finally, market risk can arise from a change in the competitive landscape. A German car manufacturer might open a new factory in Indonesia, and its output might take market share away from the cars made by the Japanese company. Plainly, "market risk" and "political risk" are the same in one respect: they are both very broad concepts.

"Credit risk" describes the threats to an investment from problems in payment, lending, or borrowing. Consider, for example, the risks that might be present in a financing arrangement with a local or regional bank in a host country. The bank might accelerate the loan, raise interest rates beyond the expected level, or fail to disburse funds. Surely, obtaining funds can be a crucial element of a successful venture, such as in a situation where a manufacturing operation needs to access a credit line in order to procure raw materials or components. The logical but unfortunate extreme of credit risk is "insolvency risk," that is, the risk that a party in a transaction goes bankrupt and, therefore, cannot repay all of its obligations in full.

"Legal risk" ought to be most familiar to international business lawyers. Indeed, the concept resonates throughout this Casebook. The term is generic. It encompasses any legal development adverse to a foreign direct investor. The development can result from private party behavior, such as where a supplier breaches a contract that, in turn, threatens the well-being of the investment operation. It could result from official legislative or regulatory action, in which case it overlaps with political risk. It could also result from judicial action, such as where a judge rules a contract invalid — as, for example, did an English judge in the celebrated *Hammersmith* case, finding that a local government entity did not have the authority to enter into swap contracts.

De-constructing the Distinctions

It may seem strange to attack the distinctions among types of risk in FDI transactions after expending considerable effort to draw these distinctions. But, de-construction is exactly what is called for. In everyday international legal practice, these are blurred, or even disappear. For example, as intimated earlier, legal risk can arise from official action, which means that the legal risk also involves a political risk. Likewise, the currency of a host country may depreciate through heavy market selling pressure, as distinct from official de-valuation. But, the reason foreign exchange traders are dumping the currency could be bad monetary policy in the host country. Then, currency risk is really both a market and political risk phenomenon. As still another example, suppose the Korean distributor of products made by a multinational corporation defaults in its contractual obligations. Ostensibly, this is simply a legal risk problem. But, it becomes a hybrid between legal and political risk if the distributor is a wholly-owned government corporation, and the default results from cancellation of a government procurement deal.

In sum, conceptual lines between the various types of risk involved in FDI are useful insofar as they frame the thinking of an international business lawyer and help the lawyer anticipate and take precautions against potential future problems. But, in practice, when disaster strikes, the different risks tend to meld together. As two astute practitioners, who developed a five-part method for classifying political risk, admit:

> For analytical purposes, five types of political risk may be identified: expropriation (including confiscation and nationalization), *de facto* expropriation (including creeping and indirect expropriation), currency risk, the risk of po-

litical violence, and the risk of breach of contract by the host state. While these distinctions are useful in understanding the nature of political risk and the various ways [in which] it can manifest itself, the lines among these types of political risk are often blurred in actual situations, which usually involve elements from more than one of these five categories.[11]

Is it, then, fair to conclude that at bottom all risk is one form or another of political risk? This proposition may, at first blush, seem overly broad. Perhaps, however, it is defensible, if it is agreed that the behavior of private parties is directly or indirectly impacted by official action. Then, many instances of market, credit, or legal risk can be seen as prompted by political acts.

II. Expropriation

A. Overview

NOTE ON EXPROPRIATION[*]

The Risk of Expropriation

"Expropriation risk" — a species of "political risk" as defined in the Note above — is the threat that a host country government where a foreign direct investment is situated will take the property of the investor. That is, "'[e]xpropriation is the taking by a host state of property owned by an investor and located in the host state, ostensibly for a 'public purpose.' The state accomplishes the 'taking' by declaring that the investor is no longer the owner of the property being expropriated. The taking will, if necessary, be enforced through the use of force against the investor."[1]

Are "expropriation" and "nationalization" synonymous? Both terms are, indeed, used interchangeably. "Nationalization" describes a scenario where the host country's government takes property in pursuance of a centralized plan to take over an entire sector or industry, generally with the objective of effecting broader economic or social change. An example is provided by Chile's nationalization of the copper mining sector in 1971.[2] Interestingly, the idea that the Russian government ought to nationalize businesses run by criminal elements and robber barons gained considerable cache in the fall 1998, when Russia faced a severe economic crisis.

A host country's government can accomplish expropriation of an investor's property through various means. It may take over an operating investment enterprise through direct action, including the use of military force to seize the premises and eject the occupants. This occurred in *Amco Asia*, where the Indonesian military took control of an American investment group's hotel.[3]

---

11. KENNEDY, *supra*, at 3.

* This Note was prepared by Christopher C. Matteson, Esq. and Professor Raj Bhala.

1. PAUL E. COMEAUX & N. STEPHAN KINSELLA, PROTECTING FOREIGN INVESTMENT UNDER INTERNATIONAL LAW: LEGAL ASPECTS OF POLITICAL RISK 3 (1997)

2. *See* Orrego Vicuna, *Some International Law Problems Posed by the Nationalization of the Copper Industry by Chile*, AM. J. INT'L L. 711 (1973).

3. Amco Asia Corp., Pan American Development Ltd., and P.T. Amco Indonesia v. Republic of Indonesia, 24 INT'L LEGAL MATERIALS 1022 (1984), *annulled on other grounds*, 25 INT'L LEGAL MATERIALS 1439 (1986). This case was handled by an arbitration panel of the Interna-

In the *AMCO* case, the dispute arose between foreign investors, AMCO Asia, its affiliates and assignees and Indonesia about the construction and subsequent management of the Kartika Plaza Hotel in Jakarta.

The hotel construction was completed substantially as planned but a dispute arose over AMCO's performance of the management portion of the Agreement. Finally, the owner, an Indonesian organisation linked with the Indonesian Army, sought to discontinue AMCO's involvement in the Agreement, and the Tribunal found that it enlisted armed forces of the Indonesian Government to take over control and ownership of the hotel. It also found that the Indonesian organisation persuaded the Indonesian Government to revoke the investment license. Accordingly, the Tribunal held that the Republic of Indonesia should pay to the investors the amount of US $3,200,000 with interest at the rate of 6% per annum on the ground that the acts of the owner were illegal self-help and that the assistance or lack of protection afforded to the foreign investor by the Army/Police was an international wrong attributable to the Republic [of Indonesia].[4]

Another means of expropriation is for the host country's government to "confiscate a controlling share of equity in the entity owning or holding the enterprise."[5] This tactic was used by the Iranian government after the Islamic revolution in 1979. "Examples of expropriation by taking shares of foreign investors can be seen in *American International Group* and *INA Corp. v. Iran*. In both cases, the Iranian government expropriated claimants' shares of Iranian insurance companies pursuant to the law of nationalization of insurance and credit enterprises on June 25th, 1979."[6]

Expropriation stories are not always as dramatic as the above Indonesian and Iranian instances. Expropriation can take place through a slow, cumulative process —with the same end result as a rapid, tumultuous taking. The government of the host country may initiate changes in the regulatory framework, tax structure, or legal rules that gradually interfere with the use rights of the investor. In turn, this leads "to the sale or abandonment of the project to the government or local private investors. It is the cumulative effect of the measures which has a *de facto* confiscatory effect, and...their combined effect results in depriving the investor of ownership, control, or substantial benefits over his enterprise, even when each such measure taken separately does not have this effect."[7] This type of expropriation is called "creeping expropriation."[8] The rubric is apt, as suggested by the following description:

> [A]n enterprise established by a foreign investor may sometimes be subjected to measures which do not in themselves constitute nationalization [or expropriation] but whose effect is such that the investor becomes unable to operate his venture effectively. Such measures may, for example, include wage and labour controls, price control and import and export restrictions, which cripple the investment and make it no longer economically viable.[9]

---

tional Center for Settlement of Investment Disputes (ICSID), a World Bank Group entity. ICSID is discussed below.

4. Amco Asia, 25 INT'L LEGAL MATERIALS, *supra*, at 1439-40.

5. COMEAUX & KINSELLA, *supra*, at 4.

6. *Id.* at 5, *citing* American International Group, Inc., *et al.* (AIG) v. Islamic Republic of Iran, Awd. No. 93-2-3, 4 IRAN-U.S. C.T.R. 96 (1983).

7. *Id.* at 8-9 (citation omitted).

8. *See* Burns H. Weston, *Constructive Takings Under International Law: A Modest Foray Into the Problem of Creeping Expropriation*, 16 VA. J. INT'L L. 103 (1975).

9. INGRID DELUPIS, FINANCE AND PROTECTION OF INVESTMENTS IN DEVELOPING COUNTRIES 104-105 (Halsted Press, 1973). Although this particular work was written during a

There exists a conflict, however, between the incremental confiscatory effect of such regulations and policies, and the sovereign right of a nation to regulate its affairs. "Investors and their enterprises in foreign states are subject to the laws of that country and have to abide by such rules as the state may promulgate. Only rarely would there be any provisions in investment agreements to protect an investor against such measures: and, even if there were, a state would still be entitled to enact such rules if they are indispensable for the public welfare."[10]

Issue #1: Lawfulness

Expropriation raises three basic questions: *lawfulness, compensation,* and *defenses*. These are discussed in turn below.

First, was the taking of the foreign investor's property by the host country government lawful? Professor Herz addressed this question in 1941 by making a threshold distinction between expropriation as a result of the exercise of the power of eminent domain, and expropriation as a result of the exercise of police power, neither of which would result in the state incurring legal obligations (most notably, compensation).

We now come to the motives and purposes which underlie the [expropriation] measures in question. Are they material or immaterial in giving to, or taking from, a measure its character of expropriation? We here meet with the first great exception to the rule that *any* interference, by action of the state, with foreign property constitutes expropriation. According to the theory and practice of the early nineteenth century, the function of the state in a *laissez-faire* society was merely to protect private property. Actual interference with this private sphere was to occur only in exceptional cases, for reasons of public utility and with full compensation; thus, *e.g.*, when internal improvements such as the construction of railways made the transfer of property from one owner to another necessary. The state's right to expropriate for such purposes became known as its right of eminent domain. However, even in the era of most radical non-intervention policy there were always certain cases in which state interference with private property was not considered expropriation entailing an obligation to pay compensation but a necessary act to safeguard public welfare: *e.g.*, measures taken for reasons of police, that is, for the protection of public health or security against internal or external danger.

The right of the state to interfere with private property in the exercise of its police power has been recognized by general international law as referring to foreign property also: interference with foreign property in the exercise of police power is not considered expropriation. The state is deemed to be free to take all necessary steps in this respect without incurring any of the obligations which accompany ordinary expropriation. Again it is very difficult to draw a sharp line of demarcation between the exercise of the right of eminent domain and that of police power, especially since states have more and more abandoned the *laissez-faire* conception of their functions and become "welfare" states interfering daily in all imaginable realms of private activities by all imaginable measures and procedures. It may be often difficult to ascertain whether such interference is one which is necessary to protect the public

---

markedly different era in terms of global commerce, it states eloquently the basic incentives and risks that have been and remain present in the area of FDI in developing nations.

10. *Id.* at 105.

against a direct danger threatening its safety or one which refers to public utility only. There is the great controversy as to whether general legislative reform
measures interfering with rights in order to establish what is deemed to be a
better social order in certain branches or the whole of national economy
(measures of "socialization" or "nationalization" or "social reform") constitute measures of an extended police power, whether they fall under the traditional conception of expropriation for public utility, or whether they form a
new kind of motivation which leads to new legal consequences. . . . Suffice it to
say here that, in spite of difficulties of demarcation, the distinction between
measures of police and expropriation for public utility is one of positive international law. . . .

Apart from this distinction, however, the different purposes and motivations are entirely irrelevant as far as legal consequences are concerned. In particular, there is no relevant distinction between cases of real public utility and
arbitrary acts: international law does not contain its own definition of "public use" but leaves it to the expropriating state to judge what it considers useful for the welfare of its people. Even in the extreme case where a state expressly takes foreign property without giving any reason or motivation for its
action, international law does not contain any special rule dealing with such
a case in a way different from ordinary expropriation for public use.[11]

However, as Professor Herz suggests at the end of this passage, it is troubling that a
state contemplating the expropriation of foreign property decides, in its sole discretion, whether such an act is in the public interest.

In other words, the question of the lawfulness of an expropriation seems to boil
down to whether the expropriation was in pursuit of an appropriate public policy
purpose, and that question is answered by the host country's government that is responsible for the expropriation—hardly an objective party. Nonetheless, various
United Nations pronouncements confirm the right of countries to exercise complete
sovereignty over their economic resources, and their right to expropriate foreign
business assets if necessary to exercise this sovereignty. These pronouncements—
such as those calling for a "New International Economic Order"—reflect the interests of developing countries, many of which suffered from colonial exploitation and
imperial domination. Most of them date from the 1960s and 1970s, a very different,
and in some ways more politically divisive, era in the world economy.

Still, to satisfy international law, the expropriating state must give at least some
minimum justification for its act. After all, there ought to be a difference between expropriation and official acts of piracy. It does not seem to require the state to explain
to the world why its behavior does not fall into the latter category. Perhaps it is a
formality, because any government worthy of holding office ought to be able to provide a plausible, or at least face-saving, explanation. The formality, then, is a bit of a
restraint, however weak.

As can be imagined, there arises a problem of relative perceptions when analyzing what constitutes an expropriation, an incremental portion of "creeping expropriation," or a legitimate regulatory action by a host country's government. This
legal issue is complex. There is a line drawing problem as to which actions are legitimate and which are confiscatory. Central to the analysis is the intent of the host nation. Consider the following hypothetical. On the one hand, a new tax levied by the
Indonesian government upon garments produced in a joint venture factory may not

---

11. John Herz, *Expropriation of Foreign Property*, 35 Am. J. Int'l L. 243, 251-53 (1941).

be a confiscatory action if it was not intended to drive out the American partner. On the other hand, it may be a part of a creeping expropriation scheme if it were levied to cause fiscal pain, in order to encourage the American partner to cease operations there.

Issue #2: Compensation

In many if not most cases, it is not difficult for a host country government to come up with a plausible public policy justification for expropriating foreign assets. Consequently, much of the controversy focuses on the second key issue. Was the foreign investor provided with acceptable compensation for the taking? This question is devilishly complex in that there is no single universal standard of compensation. Must it be "prompt, adequate and effective"—the formula proposed by President Franklin Roosevelt's Secretary of State, Cordell Hull?

> Apart from the use of force, no subject of international law seems to have aroused as much debate—and often strong feelings—as the question of the standard for payment of compensation when foreign property is expropriated. In the United States especially, the issue—as every student of international law knows—has centered largely on the requirement of "prompt, adequate and effective compensation," the phrase used by Secretary of State Hull in 1938 in his notes to the Mexican Government claiming compensation for expropriated agrarian lands owned by U.S. nationals. Since that time the U.S. Government has maintained in numerous statements that "prompt, adequate and effective compensation" is required by international law. While the United States Supreme Court in the *Sabbatino* case of 1964 referred to the "disagreement" among states as to the relevant international law standards and applied the act of state doctrine, the Congress in the two Hickenlooper Amendments asserted that international law requires "speedy compensation in convertible foreign exchange equivalent to the full value" of the property taken. Other congressional enactments have also affirmed the "prompt, adequate and effective" formula as a requirement of international law.[12]

Alternatively, must the compensation be "just"—the standard in Section 712 of the *Restatement (Third) on the Foreign Relations Law of the United States* (as well as the Fifth Amendment to the United States Constitution)? Must it cove the "fair actual value," as some international arbitrators and judges have said, or possibly the "fair market value" as is stated in Article 1110 of Chapter 11 of the North American Free Trade Agreement (NAFTA)?

> Arguably, the formula that seems to come closest to reflecting what international law requires is that an investor must receive "appropriate" compensation for an expropriation. If this formula does reflect the consensus, then perhaps it is because "appropriate" is so vague that it can be interpreted to be consistent with most if not all of the above suggested formulas. In other words, perhaps the law on compensation for expropriation really is not that much clearer than in 1941, when Professor Herz queried:

> What does compensation or indemnification imply?... [I]t does not mean restitution of the property taken, but payment for its value. The ever repeated statement that this compensation must be just or fair does not seem to be very helpful, as it is rather vague. More concrete is the rule that only full and im-

---

12. Oscar Schachter, Comment, *Compensation for Expropriation*, AM. J. INT'L L. 121 (1984) (citations omitted).

mediate compensation in cash fulfills the conditions of international law. Though in practice deferred payments have frequently been accepted or agreed upon, the fact that interest has usually been paid for the delay seems to corroborate this rule. On the other hand, there is less unanimity as to what constitutes full indemnification. . . . .

In practice it seems to be difficult to ascertain the value of an object which has no usual market price without having recourse to average profits or returns; investment may exceed or fall below the actual value. But it is difficult to ascertain any definite positive rule, since practice "is always affected by what is practicable under the particular circumstances of the case."[13]

Issue #3: Defenses

The third key issue arises when a foreign direct investor sues the host country government that has expropriated its property interests. What defenses under international law are available to the host country government that expropriated an investor's property? The answer involves the Act of State, Sovereign Immunity, and Calvo doctrines.

1. The Act of State Doctrine

The Act of State doctrine is a construct of American jurisprudence. Essentially, the doctrine says a United State court will not adjudge an act of a foreign state. The doctrine was laid down in initially the 1897 *Underhill* case,[14] and it has been applied ever since, most notably in the famous *Sabbatino* case,[15] excerpted below. In *Sabbatino*, the United States Supreme Court reiterated the holding of *Underhill* regarding the Act of State doctrine:

The classic American statement of the act of state doctrine, which appears to have taken root in England as early as 1674, and began to emerge in the jurisprudence of this country in the late eighteenth and early nineteenth centuries, is found in *Underhill v. Hernandez*, where Chief Justice Fuller said for a unanimous Court:

Every sovereign state is bound to respect the independence of every other sovereign state, and the courts of one country will not sit in judgment on the acts of the government of another, done within its own territory. Redress of grievances by reason of such acts must be obtained through the means open to be availed of by sovereign powers as between themselves."[16]

Although "originally based on principles of comity and sovereign immunity,"[17] the *Sabbatino* Court held that the Act of State doctrine precluded the Court from "interfering in matters that were primarily the responsibility of the executive or legislative branches of the government."[18] In this case, the Act of State doctrine (based on separation of powers theory) precluded the Court from invalidating the Cuban government's title to a quantity of sugar that was, prior to being nationalized, the property of respondent Sabbatino.

---

13. Herz, *supra*, at 255-56.
14. Underhill v. Hernandez, 168 U.S. 250 (1897).
15. Banco Nacional de Cuba v. Sabbatino, 376 U.S. 398 (1964).(citations omitted).
16. Sabbatino at 416, *quoting* Underhill, 168 U.S. 250, 252 (1964) (citations omitted).
17. COMEAUX & KINSELLA, *supra*, at 52.
18. COMEAUX & KINSELLA, *supra*, at 52.

It should be of comfort to foreign direct investors, however, that there are a number of exceptions to the Act of State doctrine. "The first is the '*Bernstein* Exception,' which states that a court need not apply the [Act of State] doctrine where the executive branch has advised that it is unnecessary to do so."[19]

Secondly, there is an exception to the Act of State doctrine that applies to nations that are involved in commerce with the United States. The rationale behind the so-called "commercial activity exception" is that a state should not be able to benefit from commerce with the United States and, at the same time, shield itself from the jurisdiction of United States courts with the Act of State doctrine and the doctrine of Sovereign Immunity.[20]

Third, if an expropriation were in violation of a treaty between the United States and the host country whose government expropriated American property, then an American court may adjudicate the case. After all, it is only right that an American court be able to interpret a treaty to which the United States is a party.

Fourth, the "Second Hickenlooper Amendment,"[21] a Congressional reaction to the Supreme Court's decision in *Sabbatino*, creates an exception. The Amendment requires a United States court to adjudicate claims that arise as a result of illegal expropriation, namely those whereby the investor did not receive compensation for the expropriated property.[22] It is often said, therefore, that the Second Hickenlooper Amendment effectively overrules the *Sabbatino* decision.

2. The Concept of Sovereignty and the Doctrine of Sovereign Immunity

Sovereign immunity is a second defense a host country government might make in a suit brought against it by a foreign direct investor arising out of an expropriation. Understanding this defense, however, pre-supposes an understanding of sovereignty. What does "sovereignty" mean?

Fundamentally, "sovereignty" dictates that a nation has the right to act as it wishes within its own boundaries. Of course, this right is qualified by the existence of treaties, customs, and international legal norms to which the sovereign nation subscribes or is a party.

> [A]ll states are sovereign within their own territory, and... "*pari parim non habet imperium*" ... means that no state could be expected to submit to the laws of another. This finds expression, for example, in the claims of certain developing states that they have the absolute right to expropriate property of foreign investors located within their territory, and are not bound by any law external to their own with regard to compensation to be paid to the investor.[23]

---

19. COMEAUX & KINSELLA, *supra*, at 53, *citing* Bernstein v. N. V. Nederlandsche-Amerikaansche Stoomvart-Maatschappij, 210 F.2d 375 (2d Cir. 1954). The *Bernstein* case is an interesting one, involving stock in a German corporation taken from a Jewish investor by the Nazi government. The United States Department of State notified the court in writing of its desire that the court exercise its jurisdiction and sit in judgment of the acts of Nazi Germany in confiscating the property. The court held the Act of State doctrine was inapplicable.

20. COMEAUX & KINSELLA, *supra*, at 53, *citing* Alfred Dunhill v. Cuba, 425 U.S. 682 (1976), from which the commercial activity exception has been derived.

21. Codified at 22 U.S.C. § 2370(e)(2).

22. *See* 22 U.S.C. § 2370(e)(2). *See also*, COMEAUX & KINSELLA, *supra*, at 54, explaining the Amendment and its application only to expropriated property that has entered the United States.

23. COMEAUX & KINSELLA, *supra*, at 24 (citation omitted).

To what extent, if any, should an absolute approach to sovereignty be circumscribed by a requirement that if an expropriation takes place, then the aggrieved investor must be compensated in order for it to be legal? As discussed earlier, "[u]nder international law, expropriation is considered 'legal' only if [it] meets certain requirements. Thus, it is said that expropriation is legal if the expropriation is : (1) 'nondiscriminatory'; (2) 'for a public purpose'; and (3) accompanied by full compensation."[24]

What, then, is the doctrine of Sovereign Immunity? It "prohibits one state from exercising jurisdiction over another state, its agents or instrumentalities."[25] Although this doctrine was once considered absolute, there developed a restrictive theory. Under this theory, the immunity still applies to acts of a sovereign foreign government that were considered to be public acts, but the immunity does not extend to a sovereign's acts that are commercial in nature.[26] For example, suppose the United States is sued in a court in the United Kingdom in connection with a breach of contract, such as for nonpayment of the agreed- upon price for a defense procurement from British Aerospace. Sovereign immunity will not apply, as the basis for the suit is a commercial act of the United States government. But, suppose a British subject sues the United States in a British court in the United Kingdom, claiming to have been damaged by President Clinton's August 1998 decision to launch missiles against alleged terrorist targets in Sudan and Afghanistan. Perhaps, for instance, this plaintiff owned property damaged in the American missile attack. Here, sovereign immunity will apply, as the policy decisions of the Executive branch are acts of public authority.

The United States recognizes the restrictive theory of Sovereign Immunity, and it has codified this theory in the Foreign Sovereign Immunities Act (FSIA) of 1976, as amended.[27] The FSIA sets forth the requirements for a United States court to have jurisdiction over a foreign state. Generally speaking, the FSIA provides for immunity of foreign states against the jurisdiction of the United States courts, but articulates three main exceptions.[28] First, there is obviously no immunity if a host country government has waived immunity in an agreement between it and the foreign direct investor. Second, as just suggested, there is no immunity if the foreign sovereign's behavior is a commercial activity. Third, there is no immunity in cases of an illegal (non compensated) expropriation.

3. The Calvo Doctrine

The Calvo Doctrine is derived from the work of Carlos Calvo, a nineteenth century Argentinian legal scholar. A response to intervention by the United States and European powers in the affairs of Latin American countries at the time, the Doctrine remains integrally related to the concept of Latin American sovereignty. "The doctrine's two basic principles are: (1) the 'national treatment standard,' which provides that foreigners should not be granted more rights and privileges than those accorded nationals; and (2) the 'diplomatic intervention' provision that foreign states may not

---

24. *Id.* at 5, *citing* RESTATEMENT (THIRD) OF THE FOREIGN RELATIONS LAW OF THE UNITED STATES § 712. The *Restatement* provides a description of customary international law with respect to expropriation.
25. COMEAUX & KINSELLA, *supra*, at 45 (citation omitted).
26. *See id.*
27. *See* 28 U.S.C. §§ 1602-1611.
28. *See* 28 U.S.C. §§ 1605 (a) (1)-(3).

enforce their citizen's private claims by violating the territorial sovereignty of host states either through diplomatic or forceful intervention."[29]

Has the Calvo Doctrine been superseded by widespread acceptance of the principle of multilateralism, frequent use of arbitral tribunals, and the inescapable trend toward global economic interdependence? One observer points out that the first principle of the Calvo Doctrine—national treatment—has become more prevalent in trade and commercial intercourse among countries. While "the Calvo Clause has become ineffective and will eventually become obsolete in a new [framework for global business] based on supranational organizations and individuals, ... paradoxically, one of the primary principles of the Calvo Doctrine will be vindicated: equality of foreign and national investors."[30] To be sure, this vindication hardly is good news for a foreign direct investor. After all, the national treatment provision of the Calvo Doctrine strips foreign direct investors of the right to call upon their home country governments to intervene on their behalf in the event of expropriation. If they do, then the host country may forfeit any rights to compensation they might otherwise have. The logic is that local host country businesses do not have an analogous right; *i.e.*, national treatment, in the Calvo Clause context, means that both foreign and local investors must be accorded the same rights in the event of expropriation. Local investors are limited to local courts, and so too should be foreign investors.

Nor can the Calvo Doctrine—particularly the diplomatic intervention provision—be considered a boon to home country governments. Why, for example, should the United States, as the home country of a business whose assets have been expropriated in Paraguay, comply with Argentina's Calvo Doctrine calling for the United States government to eschew assisting its businesses? The United States government surely views itself has having a duty to its corporate citizens to provide assistance whenever and wherever necessary.

Whatever the merits of the conflicting arguments, the Calvo Doctrine probably has not deterred recent FDI flows into Latin America. "In 1995, inflows of FDI into the non-OECD area totaled an estimated $112 billion. Of this, approximately $65 billion went to Asia, and another *$27 billion to Latin America (including Mexico)*. The remaining $20 billion was divided almost equally between transition economies in Europe on the one hand, and the Middle East on the other."[31] These numbers indicate that, after Asia, Latin America drew the largest amount of FDI in the non-OECD world. In part, they may signal the lack of enthusiasm for the Doctrine among contemporary Latin governments.

QUESTIONS

1.   What are the three major types of political risk?

2.   What are the two basic tenets of the Calvo Doctrine?

---

29. Christopher K. Dalrymple, Note, *Politics and Foreign Direct Investment: the Multilateral Investment Guarantee Agency and the Calvo Clause*, Cornell Int'l L.J. 161 at 163 (1996) (citations omitted).

30. Denise Manning-Cabrol, Note, *The Imminent Death of the Calvo Clause and the Rebirth of the Calvo Principle: Equality of Foreign and National Investors*, 26 LAW & POL'Y INT'L BUS. 1169 (1995).

31. WORLD TRADE ORGANIZATION, ANNUAL REPORT 1996, SPECIAL TOPIC: TRADE AND FOREIGN DIRECT INVESTMENT, vol.1 (1996) (emphasis added).

B. The Act of State Defense

Documents Supplement References:

1. *Restatement Sections 443-444.*
2. *The Second Hickenlooper Amendment, 22 U.S.C. § 2370(e)(2).*

Banco Nacional de Cuba v. Sabbatino
376 U.S. 398 (1964)

MR. JUSTICE HARLAN delivered the opinion of the Court.

The question which brought this case here, and is now found to be the dispositive issue, is whether the so-called act of state doctrine serves to sustain petitioner's [Banco Nacional de Cuba] claims in this litigation. Such claims are ultimately founded on a decree of the Government of Cuba expropriating certain property, the right to the proceeds of which is here in controversy. The act of state doctrine in its traditional formulation precludes the courts of this country from inquiring into the validity of the public acts a recognized foreign sovereign power committed within its own territory.

I.

In February and July of 1909, respondent Farr, Whitlock & Co., [the respondent] an American commodity broker, contracted to purchase Cuban sugar, free alongside the steamer, from a wholly owned subsidiary of Compania Azucarera Vertietes-Camaguey de Cuba (C.A.V.), a corporation organized under Cuban law whose capital stock was owned principally by United States residents. [C.A.V. appears in an amicus position in the litigation. Farr, Whitlock adopts C.A.V.'s contentions, and vice versa, though each presents its arguments separately. Thus, while Farr, Whitlock is the only formal respondent, the Court explains in Footnote 9 of the opinion that it refers to both Farr, Whitlock and C.A.V. as respondents.] Farr, Whitlock agreed to pay for the sugar in New York upon presentation of the shipping documents and a sight draft.

On July 6, 1960, the Congress of the United States amended the Sugar Act of 1948 to permit a presidentially directed reduction of the sugar quota for Cuba. On the same day President Eisenhower exercised the granted power. The day of the congressional enactment, the Cuban Council of Ministers adopted "Law No. 851," which characterized this reduction in the Cuban sugar quota as an act of "aggression, for political purposes" on the part of the United States, justifying the taking of countermeasures by Cuba. The law gave the Cuban President and Prime Minister discretionary power to nationalize by forced expropriation property or enterprises in which American nationals had interest. Although a system of compensation was formally provided, the possibility of payment under it may well be deemed illusory. Our State Department has described the Cuban law as "manifestly in violation of those principles of international law which have long been accepted by the free countries of the West. It is in its essence discriminatory, arbitrary and confiscatory."

Between August 6 and August 9, 1960, the sugar covered by the contract between Farr, Whitlock and C.A.V. was loaded, destined for Morocco, onto the *S.S. Hornfels*, which was standing offshore at the Cuban port of Jucaro (Santa Maria). On the day loading commenced, the Cuban President and Prime Minister, acting pursuant to Law No. 851, issued Executive Power Resolution No. 1. It provided for the compulsory expropriation of all property and enterprises, and of rights and interests arising therefrom, of certain listed companies, including C. A. V., wholly or principally owned by American nationals. The preamble reiterated the alleged injustice of the American reduction of the Cuban sugar quota and emphasized the importance of Cuba's serving as an example for other countries to follow "in their struggle to free themselves from the brutal claws of Imperialism." In consequence of the resolution, the consent of the Cuban Government was necessary before a ship carrying sugar of a named company could leave Cuban waters. In order to obtain this consent, Farr, Whitlock, on August 11, entered into contracts, identical to those it had made with C.A.V., with the Banco Para el Comercio Exterior de Cuba, an instrumentality of the Cuban Government. The *S.S. Hornfels* sailed for Morocco on August, 12.

Banco Exterior assigned the bills of lading to petitioner, also an instrumentality of the Cuban Government, which instructed its agent in New York, Societe Generale, to deliver the bills and a sight draft in the sum of $175,250.69 to Farr, Whitlock in return for payment. Societe Generale's initial tender of the documents was refused by Farr, Whitlock, which on the same day was notified of C.A.V.'s claim that as rightful owner of the sugar it was entitled to the proceeds. In return for a promise not to turn the funds over to petitioner or its agent, C.A.V. agreed to indemnify Farr, Whitlock for any loss. Farr, Whitlock subsequently accepted the shipping documents, negotiated the bills of lading to its customer, and received payment for the sugar. It refused, however, to hand over the proceeds to Societe Generale. Shortly thereafter, Farr, Whitlock was served with an order of the New York Supreme Court, which had appointed Sabbatino as Temporary Receiver of C.A.V.'s New York assets, enjoining it from taking any action in regard to the money claimed by C.A.V. that might result in its removal from the State. Following this, Farr, Whitlock, pursuant to court order, transferred the funds to Sabbatino, to abide the event of a judicial determination as to their ownership.

Petitioner then instituted this action in the Federal District Court for the Southern District of New York. Alleging conversion of the bills of lading, it sought to recover the proceeds thereof from Farr, Whitlock and to enjoin the receiver from exercising any dominion over such proceeds. Upon motions to dismiss and for summary judgment, the District Court, sustained federal *in personam* jurisdiction despite state control of the funds. It found that the sugar was located within Cuban territory at the time of expropriation and determined that under merchant law common to civilized countries Farr, Whitlock could not have asserted ownership of the sugar against C.A.V. before making payment. It concluded that C.A.V. had a property interest in the sugar subject to the territorial jurisdiction of Cuba. The court then dealt with the question of Cuba's title to the sugar, on which rested petitioner's claim of conversion. While acknowledging the continuing vitality of the act of state doctrine, the court believed it inapplicable when the-questioned foreign act is in violation of international law. Proceeding on the basis that a taking invalid under international law does not convey good title, the District Court found the Cuban expropriation decree to violate such law in three separate respects: it was motivated by a retaliatory and not a public purpose; it discriminated against American nationals; and it failed to provide adequate compensation. Summary judgment against petitioner was accordingly granted.

The Court of Appeals, affirming the decision on similar grounds, relied on two letters (not before the District Court) written by State Department officers which it took as evidence that the Executive Branch had no objection to a judicial testing of the

Cuban decree's validity. The court was unwilling to declare that any one of the infirmities found by the District Court rendered the taking invalid under international law, but was satisfied that in combination they had that effect. We granted certiorari because the issues involved bear importantly on the conduct of the country's foreign relations and more particularly on the proper role of the Judicial Branch in this sensitive area....

....

II.

It is first contended that this petitioner, an instrumentality of the Cuban Government, should be denied access to American courts because Cuba is an unfriendly power and does not permit nationals of this country to obtain relief in its courts. Even though the respondents did not raise this point in the lower courts we think it should be considered here. If the courts of this country should be closed to the government of a foreign state, the underlying reason is one of national policy transcending the interests of the parties to the action, and this Court should give effect to that policy *sua sponte* even at this stage of the litigation.

Under principles of comity governing this country's relations with other nations, sovereign states are allowed to sue in the courts of the United States. This Court has called "comity" in the legal sense "neither a matter of absolute obligation, on the one hand, nor of mere courtesy and good will, upon the other." *Hilton v. Guyot*, 159 U.S. 113, 163-164. Although comity is often associated with the existence of friendly relations between states, prior to some recent lower court cases which have questioned the right of instrumentalities of the Cuban Government to sue in our courts, the privilege of suit has been denied only to governments at war with the United States, or to those not recognized by this country.

Respondents, pointing to the severance of diplomatic, relations, commercial embargo, and freezing of Cuban assets in this country, contend that relations between the United States and Cuba manifest such animosity that unfriendliness is clear, and that the courts should be closed to the Cuban Government. We do not agree. This Court would hardly be competent to undertake assessments of varying degrees of friendliness or its absence, and, lacking some definite touchstone for determination, we are constrained to consider any relationship, short of war, with a recognized sovereign power as embracing the privilege of resorting to United States courts. Although the severance of diplomatic relations is an overt act with objective significance in the dealings of sovereign states, we are unwilling to say that it should inevitably result in the withdrawal of the privilege of bringing suit. Severance may take place for any number of political reasons, its duration is unpredictable, and whatever expression of animosity it may imply does not approach that implicit in a declaration of war.

It is perhaps true that non-recognition of a government in certain circumstances may reflect no greater unfriendliness than the severance of diplomatic relations with a recognized government, but the refusal to recognize has a unique legal aspect. It signifies this country's unwillingness to acknowledge that the government in question speaks as the sovereign authority for the territory it purports to control. Political recognition is exclusively a function of the Executive. The possible incongruity of judicial "recognition," by permitting suit, of a government not recognized by the Executive is completely absent when merely diplomatic relations are broken.

The view that the existing situation between the United States and Cuba should not lead to a denial of status to sue is buttressed by the circumstance that none of the acts of our Government have been aimed at closing the courts of this country to

Cuba, and more particularly by the fact that the Government has come to the support of Cuba's "act of state" claim in this very litigation.

Respondents further urge that reciprocity of treatment is an essential ingredient of comity generally and, therefore, of the privilege of foreign states to bring suit here. Although *Hilton v. Guyot*, 159 U.S. 113, contains some broad language about the relationship of reciprocity to comity, the case in fact imposed a requirement of reciprocity only in regard to conclusiveness of judgments, and even then only in limited circumstances. In *Direction der Disconto- Gesellschaft v. United States Steel Corp.*, 300 F. 741, 747 (S.D.N.Y.), Judge Learned Hand pointed out that the doctrine of reciprocity has apparently been confined to foreign judgments.

There are good reasons for declining to extend the principle to the question of standing of sovereign states to sue. Whether a foreign sovereign will be permitted to sue involves a problem more sensitive politically than whether the judgments of its courts may be re-examined, and the possibility of embarrassment to the Executive Branch in handling foreign relations is substantially more acute. Re-examination of judgments, in principle, reduces rather than enhances the possibility of injustice being done in a particular case; refusal to allow suit makes it impossible for a court to see that a particular dispute is fairly resolved. The freezing of Cuban assets exemplifies the capacity of the political branches to assure, through a variety of techniques, that the national interest is protected against a country which is thought to be improperly denying the rights of United States citizens.

Furthermore, the question whether a country gives *res judicata* effect to United States judgments presents a relatively simple inquiry. The precise status of the United States Government and its nationals before foreign courts is much more difficult to determine. To make such an investigation significant, a court would have to discover not only what is provided by the formal structure of the foreign judicial system, but also what the practical possibilities of fair treatment are. The courts, whose powers to further the national interest in foreign affairs are necessarily circumscribed as compared with those of the political branches, can best serve the rule of law by not excluding otherwise proper suitors because of deficiencies in their legal systems.

We hold that this petitioner is not barred from access to the federal courts.

. . . .

IV.

The classic American statement of the act of state doctrine, which appears to have taken root in England as early as 1674, *Blad v. Bamfield*, 3 Swans. 604, 36 Eng. Rep. 992, and began to emerge in the jurisprudence of this country in the late eighteenth and early nineteenth centuries, is found in *Underhill v. Hernandez*, 168 U.S. 250, where Chief Justice Fuller said for a unanimous Court (p. 252):

> "Every sovereign State is bound to respect the independence of every other sovereign State, and the courts of one country will not sit in judgment on the acts of the government of another done within its own territory. Redress of grievances by reason of such acts must be obtained through the means open to be availed by sovereign powers as between themselves."

Following this precept the Court in that case refused to inquire into acts of Hernandez, a revolutionary Venezuelan military commander whose government had been later recognized by the United States, which were made the basis of a damage action in this country by Underhill, an American citizen, who claimed that he had been un-lawfully assaulted, coerced, and detained in Venezuela by Hernandez.

None of this Court's subsequent cases in which the act of state doctrine was di-rectly or peripherally involved manifest any retreat from *Underhill. See American Ba-nana Co. v. United Fruit Co.*, 213 U.S. 347; *Oetjen v. Central Leather Co.*, 246 U.S. 297; *Ricaud v. American Metal Co.*, 246 U.S. 304; *Shapleigh v. Mier*, 299 U.S. 468; *United States v. Belmont*, 301 U.S. 324; *United States v. Pink*, 315 U.S. 203. On the contrary in two of these cases, *Oetjen* and *Ricaud*, the doctrine as announced in *Un-derhill* was reaffirmed in unequivocal terms.

Oetjen involved a seizure of hides from a Mexican citizen as a military levy by General Villa, acting for the forces of General Carranza, whose government was rec-ognized by this country subsequent to the trial but prior to decision by this Court. The hides were sold to a Texas corporation which shipped them to the United States and assigned them to defendant. As assignee of the original owner, plaintiff replevied the hides, claiming that they had been seized in violation of the Hague Conventions. In affirming a judgment for defendant, the Court suggested that the rules of the Con-ventions did not apply to civil war and that, even if they did, the relevant seizure was not in violation of them. 246 U.S. at 301-302. Nevertheless, it chose to rest its deci-sion on other grounds. It described the designation of the sovereign as a political question to be determined by the legislative and executive departments rather than the judicial department, invoked the established rule that such recognition operates retroactively to validate past acts, and found the basic tenet of *Underhill* to be ap-plicable to the case before it.

> "The principle that the conduct of one independent government cannot be successfully questioned in the courts of another is as applicable to a case in-volving the title to property brought within the custody of a court, such as we have here, as it was held to be to the cases cited, in which claims for damages were based upon acts done in a foreign country, for it rests at last upon the highest considerations of international comity and expediency. To permit the validity of the acts of one sovereign State to be re-examined and perhaps con-demned by the courts of another would very certainly 'imperil the amicable relations between governments and vex the peace of nations.'" *Id.* at 303-304.

In *Ricaud* the facts were similar — another general of the Carranza forces seized lead bullion as a military levy — except that the property taken belonged to an Amer-ican citizen. The Court found *Underhill, American Banana*, and *Oetjen* controlling. Commenting on the nature of the principle established by those cases, the opinion stated that the rule

> "does not deprive the court of jurisdiction once acquired over a case. It requires only that, when it is made to appear that the foreign government has acted in a given way on the subject-matter of the litigation, the details of such sanction or the merit of the result cannot be questioned but must be accepted 'by our courts as a rule for their decision. To accept a ruling authority and to decide accord-ingly is not a surrender or abandonment of jurisdiction but is an exercise of it. It results that the title to the property in this case must be determined by the result of the action taken by the military authorities of Mexico...." 246 U.S. at 309.

To the same effect is the language of Mr. Justice Cardozo in the *Shapleigh* case, *supra*, where, in commenting on the validity of a Mexican land expropriation, he said (299 U.S. at 471): "The question is not here whether the proceeding was so conducted as to be a wrong to our nationals under the doctrines of international law, though valid under the law of the situs of the land. For wrongs of that order the remedy to be followed is along the channels of diplomacy."

In deciding the present case the Court of Appeals relied in part upon an exception to the unqualified teachings of *Underhill, Oetjen*, and *Ricaud* which that court had earlier indicated. In *Bernstein v. Van Heyghen Freres Societe Anonyme*, 163 F.2d 246, suit was brought to recover from an assignee property allegedly taken, in effect, by the Nazi Government because plaintiff was Jewish. Recognizing the odious nature of this act of state, the court, through Judge Learned Hand, nonetheless refused to consider it invalid on that ground. Rather, it looked to see if the Executive had acted in any manner that would indicate that United States Courts should refuse to give effect to such a foreign decree. Finding no such evidence, the court sustained dismissal of the complaint. In a later case involving similar facts the same court again assumed examination of the German acts improper, *Bernstein v. N.V. Nederlandsche-Amerikaansche Stoomvaart-Maatschappij*, 173 F.2d 71, but, quite evidently following the implications of Judge Hand's opinion in the earlier case, amended its mandate to permit evidence of alleged invalidity, 210 F.2d 375, subsequent to receipt by plaintiff's attorney of a letter from the Acting Legal Adviser to the State Department written for the purpose of relieving the court from any constraint upon the exercise of its jurisdiction to pass on that question.

This Court has never had occasion to pass upon the so-called *Bernstein* exception, nor need it do so now. For whatever ambiguity may be thought to exist in the two letters from State Department officials on which the Court of Appeals relied, 307 F.2d at 858, is now removed by the position which the Executive has taken in this Court on the act of state claim; respondents do not indeed contest the view that these letters were intended to reflect no more than the Department's then wish not to make any statement bearing on this litigation.

The outcome of this case, therefore, turns upon whether any of the contentions urged by respondents against the application of the act of state doctrine in the premises is acceptable: (1) that the doctrine does not apply to acts of state which violate international law, as is claimed to be the case here; (2) that the doctrine is inapplicable unless the Executive specifically interposes it in a particular case; and (3) that, in any event, the doctrine may not be invoked by a foreign government plaintiff in our courts.

V.

Preliminarily, we discuss the foundations on which we deem the act of state doctrine to rest, and more particularly the question of whether state or federal law governs its application in a federal diversity case.

We do not believe that this doctrine is compelled either by the inherent nature of sovereign authority, as some of the earlier decisions seem to imply, or by some principle of international law. If a transaction takes place in one jurisdiction and the forum is in another, the forum does not by dismissing an action or by applying its own law purport to divest the first jurisdiction of its territorial sovereignty; it merely declines to adjudicate or makes applicable its own law to parties or property before it. The refusal of one country to enforce the penal laws of another is a typical example of an instance when a court will not entertain a cause of action arising in another jurisdiction. While historic notions of sovereign authority do bear upon the wisdom of employing the act of state doctrine, they do not dictate its existence.

That international law does not require application of the doctrine is evidenced by the practice of nations. Most of the countries rendering decisions on the subject fail to follow the rule rigidly. No international arbitral or judicial decision discovered suggests that international law prescribes recognition of sovereign acts of foreign governments, and apparently no claim has ever been raised before an international tribunal that failure to apply the act of state doctrine constitutes a breach of international obligation. If international law does not prescribe use of the doctrine, neither does it forbid application of the rule even if it is claimed that the act of state in question violated international law. The traditional view of international law is that it establishes substantive principles for determining whether one country has wronged another. Because of its peculiar nation-to-nation character the usual method for an individual to seek relief is to exhaust local remedies and then repair to the executive authorities of his own state to persuade them to champion his claim in diplomacy or before an international tribunal. Although it is, of course, true that United States courts apply international law as a part of our own in appropriate circumstances, the public law of nations can hardly dictate to a country which is in theory wronged how to treat that wrong within its domestic borders.

Despite the broad statement in *Oetjen* that "The conduct of the foreign relations of our Government is committed by the Constitution to the Executive and Legislative...Departments," 246 U.S., at 302, it cannot of course be thought that "every case or controversy which touches foreign relations lies beyond judicial cognizance." *Baker v. Carr*, 369 U.S. 186, 211. The text of the Constitution does not require the act of state doctrine; it does not irrevocably remove from the judiciary the capacity to review the validity of foreign acts of state.

The act of state doctrine does, however, have "constitutional" underpinnings. It arises out of the basic relationships between branches of government in a system of separation of powers. It concerns the competency of dissimilar institutions to make and implement particular kinds of decisions in the area of international relations. The doctrine as formulated in past decisions expresses the strong sense of the Judicial Branch that its engagement in the task of passing on the validity of foreign acts of state may hinder rather than further this country's pursuit of goals both for itself and for the community of nations as a whole in the international sphere. Many commentators disagree with this view; they have striven by means of distinguishing and limiting past decisions and by advancing various considerations of policy to stimulate a narrowing of the apparent scope of the rule. Whatever considerations are thought to predominate, it is plain that the problems involved are uniquely federal in nature. If federal authority, in this instance this Court, orders the field of judicial competence in this area for the federal courts, and the state courts are left free to formulate their own rules, the purposes behind the doctrine could be as effectively undermined as if there had been no federal pronouncement on the subject.

....

VI.

If the act of state doctrine is a principle of decision binding on federal and state courts alike but compelled by neither international law nor the Constitution, its continuing vitality depends on its capacity to reflect the proper distribution of functions between the judicial and political branches of the Government on matters bearing upon foreign affairs. It should be apparent that the greater the degree of codification or consensus concerning a particular area of international law, the more appropriate it is for the judiciary to render decisions regarding it, since the courts can then focus on the application of an agreed principle to circumstances of fact rather than on the sensitive task of establishing a principle not inconsistent with the national interest or with international justice. It is also evident that some aspects of international law touch much more sharply on national nerves than do others; the less important the implications of an issue are for our foreign relations, the weaker the justification for exclusivity in the political branches. The balance of relevant considerations may also be shifted if the government which perpetrated the challenged act of state is no longer in existence, as in the *Bernstein* case, for the political interest of this country may, as a result, be measurably altered. Therefore, rather than laying down or reaffirming an inflexible and all-encompassing rule in this case, we decide only that the (Judicial Branch) will not examine the validity of a taking of property within its own territory by a foreign sovereign government, extant and recognized by this country at the time of suit, in the absence of a treaty or other unambiguous agreement regarding controlling legal principles, even if the complaint alleges that the taking violates customary international law.

There are few if any issues in international law today on which opinion seems to be so divided as the limitations on a state's power to expropriate the property of aliens. There is, of course, authority, in international judicial and arbitral decisions, in the expressions of national governments, and among commentators for the view that a taking is improper under international law if it is not for a public purpose, is discriminatory, or is without provision for prompt, adequate, and effective compensation. However, Communist countries, although they have in fact provided a degree of compensation after diplomatic efforts, commonly recognize no obligation on the part of the taking country. Certain representatives of the newly independent and underdeveloped countries have questioned whether rules of state responsibility toward aliens can bind nations that have not consented to them and it is argued that the traditionally articulated standards governing expropriation of property reflect "imperialist" interests and are inappropriate to the circumstances of emergent states.

The disagreement as to relevant international law standards reflects an even more basic divergence between the national interests of capital importing and capital exporting nations and between the social ideologies of those countries that favor state control of a considerable portion of the means of production and those that adhere to a free enterprise system. It is difficult to imagine the courts of this country embarking on adjudication in an area which touches more sensitively the practical and ideological goals of the various members of the community of nations.

When we consider the prospect of the courts characterizing foreign expropriations, however justifiably, as invalid under international law and ineffective to pass title, the wisdom of the precedents is confirmed. While each of the leading cases in this Court may be argued to be distinguishable on its facts from this one — *Underhill* because sovereign immunity provided an independent ground and *Oetjen, Ricaud*, and *Shapleigh* because there was actually no violation of international law — the plain implication of all these opinions, and the import of express statements in *Oetjen*, 246 U.S., at 304, and *Shapleigh*, 299 U.S. at 471, is that the act of state doctrine is applicable even if international law has been violated. In *Ricaud*, the one case of the three most plausibly involving an international law violation, the possibility of an exception to the act of state doctrine was not discussed. Some commentators have concluded that it was not brought to the Court's attention, but Justice Clarke delivered both the *Oetjen* and *Ricaud* opinions, on the same day, so we can assume that principles stated in the former were applicable to the latter case.

The possible adverse consequences of a conclusion to the contrary of that implicit in these cases is highlighted by contrasting the practices of the political branch with the limitations of the judicial process in matters of this kind. Following an expropriation of any significance, the Executive engages in diplomacy aimed to assure that United States citizens who are harmed are compensated fairly. Representing all claimants of this country, it will often be able, either by bilateral or multilateral talks, by submission to the United Nations, or by the employment of economic and political sanctions, to achieve some degree of general redress. Judicial determinations of invalidity of title can, on the other hand, have only an occasional impact, since they depend on the fortuitous circumstance of the property in question being brought into this country. Such decisions would, if the acts involved were declared invalid, often be likely to give offense to the expropriating country; since the concept of territorial sovereignty is so deep seated, any state may resent the refusal of the courts of another sovereign to accord validity to acts within its territorial borders. Piecemeal dispositions of this sort involving the probability of affront to another state could seriously interfere with negotiations being carried on by the Executive Branch and might prevent or render less favorable the terms of an agreement that could otherwise be reached. Relations with third countries which have engaged in similar expropriations would not be immune from effect.

The dangers of such adjudication are present regardless of whether the State Department has, as it did in this case, asserted that the relevant act violated international law. If the Executive Branch has undertaken negotiations with an expropriating country, but has refrained from claims of violation of the law of nations, a determination to that effect by a court might be regarded as a serious insult, while a finding of compliance with international law, would greatly strengthen the bargaining hand of the other state with consequent detriment to American interests.

Even if the State Department has proclaimed the impropriety of the expropriation, the stamp of approval of its view by a judicial tribunal, however impartial, might increase any affront and the judicial decision might occur at a time, almost always well after the taking, when such an impact would be contrary to our national interest. Considerably more serious and far-reaching consequences would flow from a judicial finding that international law standards had been met if that determination flew in the face of a State Department proclamation to the contrary. When articulating principles of international law in its relations with other states, the Executive Branch speaks not only as an interpreter of generally accepted and traditional rules, as would the courts, but also as an advocate of standards it believes desirable for the community of nations and protective of national concerns. In short, whatever way the matter is cut, the possibility of conflict between the Judicial and Executive Branches could hardly be avoided.

Respondents contend that, even if there is not agreement regarding general standards for determining the validity of expropriations, the alleged combination of retaliation, discrimination, and inadequate compensation makes it patently clear that this particular expropriation was in violation of international law. If this view is accurate, it would still be unwise for the courts so to determine. Such a decision now would require the drawing of more difficult lines in subsequent cases and these would involve the possibility of conflict with the Executive view. Even if the courts avoided this course, either by presuming the validity of an act of state whenever the international law standard was though unclear or by following the State Department declaration in such a situation, the very expression of judicial uncertainty might provide embarrassment to the Executive Branch.

Another serious consequence of the exception pressed by respondents would be to render uncertain titles in foreign commerce, with the possible consequence of altering the flow of international trade. If the attitude of the United States courts were unclear, one buying expropriated goods would not know if he could safely import them into this country. Even were takings known to be invalid, one would have difficulty determining after goods had changed hands several times whether the particular articles in question were the product of an ineffective state act.

Against the force of such considerations, we find respondent's countervailing arguments quite unpersuasive. Their basic contention is that United States courts could make a significant contribution to the growth of international law, a contribution whose importance, it is said, would be magnified by the relative paucity of decisional law by international bodies. But given the fluidity of present world conditions, the effectiveness of such a patchwork approach toward the formulation of an acceptable body of law concerning state responsibility for expropriations is, to say the least, highly conjectural. Moreover, it rests upon the sanguine presupposition that the decisions of the courts of the world's major capital exporting country and principal exponent of the free enterprise system would be accepted as disinterested expressions of sound legal principle by those adhering to widely different ideologies.

It is contended that regardless of the fortuitous circumstances necessary for Untied States jurisdiction over a case involving a foreign act of state and the resultant isolated application to any expropriation program taken as a whole, it is the function of the courts to justly decide individual disputes before them. Perhaps the most typical act of state case involves the original owner or his assignee suing one not in association with the expropriating state who has had "title" transferred to him. But it is difficult to regard the claim of the original owner, who otherwise may be recompensed through diplomatic channels, as more demanding of judicial cognizance than the claim of title by the innocent third party purchaser, who if the property is taken from him, is without any remedy.

Respondents claim that the economic pressure resulting from the proposed exception to the act of state doctrine will materially add to the protection of United States investors. We are not convinced, even assuming the relevance of this contention. Expropriations take place for a variety of reasons, political and ideological as well as economic. When one considers the variety of means possessed by this country to make secure foreign investment, the persuasive or coercive effect of judicial invalidation of acts of expropriation dwindles in comparison. The newly independent states are in need of continuing foreign investment; the creation of a climate unfavorable to such investment. Foreign aid given to many of these countries provides a powerful lever in the hands of the political branches to ensure fair treatment of Untied States nationals. Ultimately the sanctions of economic embargo and the freezing of assets in this country may be employed. Any country willing to brave any or all of these consequences is unlikely to be deterred by sporadic judicial decisions directly affecting only property brought to our shores. If the political branches are unwilling to exercise their ample powers to effect compensation, this reflects a judgment of the national interest which the judiciary would be ill-advised to undermine indirectly.

It is suggested that if the act of state doctrine is applicable to violations of international law, it should only be so when the Executive Branch expressly stipulates that it does not wish the courts to pass on the question of validity. We should be slow to reject the representations of the Government that such a reversal of the *Bernstein* principle would work serious inroads on the maximum effectiveness of United States diplomacy. Often the State Department will wish to refrain from taking an official position, particularly at a moment that would be dictated by the development of private litigation but might be inopportune diplomatically. Adverse domestic consequences might flow from an official stand which could be assuaged, if at all, only by revealing matters best kept secret. Of course, a relevant consideration for the State Department would be the position contemplated in the court to hear the case. It is highly questionable whether the examination of validity by the judiciary should depend on an educated guess by the Executive as to probable result and, at any rate, should a prediction be wrong, the Executive might be embarrassed in its dealings with other countries. We do not now pass on the *Bernstein* exception, but even if it were deemed valid, its suggested extension is unwarranted.

However offensive to the public policy of this country and its constituent States an expropriation of this kind may be, we conclude that both the national interest and progress toward the goal of establishing the rule of law among nations are best served by maintaining intact the act of state doctrine in this realm of its application.

. . . .

The judgment of the Court of Appeals is reversed and the case is remanded to the District Court for proceedings consistent with this opinion.

It is so ordered.

MR. JUSTICE WHITE, *dissenting.*

I am dismayed that the Court has, with one broad stroke, declared the ascertainment and application of international law beyond the competence of the courts of the United States in a large and important category of cases. I am also disappointed in the Court's declaration that the acts of a sovereign state with regard to the property of aliens within its borders are beyond the reach of international law in the courts of this country. However clearly established that law may be, a sovereign may violate it with impunity, except insofar as the political branches of the government may provide a remedy. This backward-looking doctrine, never before declared in this Court, is carried a disconcerting step further: not only are the courts powerless to question acts of state proscribed by international law but they are likewise powerless to refuse to adjudicate the claim founded upon a foreign law; they must render judgment and thereby validate the lawless act. Since the Court expressly extends its ruling to all acts of state expropriating property, however clearly inconsistent with the international community, all discriminatory expropriations of the property of aliens, as for example the taking of properties of persons belonging to certain races, religions or nationalities, are entitled to automatic validation in the courts of the United States. No other civilized country has found such a rigid rule necessary for the survival of the executive branch of its government; the executive of no other government seems to require such insulation from international law adjucations in its courts; and no other judiciary is apparently so incompetent to ascertain and apply international law.

I do not believe that the act of state doctrine, as judicially fashioned in this Court, and the reasons underlying it, require American courts to decide cases in disregard of international law and of the rights of litigants to a full determination on the merits.

I.

Prior decisions of this Court in which the act of state doctrine was deemed controlling do not support the assertion that foreign acts of state must be enforced or recognized or applied in American courts when they violate the law of nations. These cases do hold that a foreign act of state applied to persons or property within its borders may not be denied effect in our courts on the ground that it violates the public policy of the forum. Also the broad language in some of these cases docs cvince an attitude of caution and self-imposed restraint in dealing with the laws of a foreign nation. But violations of international law were either not presented in these cases, because the parties or predecessors in title were nationals of the acting state, or the claimed violation was insubstantial in light of the facts presented to the Court and the principles of international law applicable at the time. These cases do not strongly imply or even suggest that the Court would woodenly apply the act of state doctrine and grant enforcement to a foreign act where the act was a clear and flagrant violation of international law, as the District Court and the Court of Appeals have found in respect to the Cuban law challenged herein.

II.

Though not a principle of international law, the doctrine of restraint, as formulated by this Court, has its roots in sound policy reasons, and it is to these we must turn to decide whether the act of state doctrine should be extended to cover wrongs cognizable under international law.

Whatever may be said to constitute an act of state, our decisions make clear that the doctrine of nonreview ordinarily applies to foreign laws affecting tangible property located within the territory of a government which is recognized by the United States. This judicially fashioned doctrine of nonreview is a corollary of the principle that ordinarily a state has jurisdiction to prescribe the rules governing the title to property within its territorial sovereignty, a principle reflected in the conflict of laws rule, adopted in virtually all nations, that the *lex loci* is the law governing title to property. This conflict rule would have been enough in itself to have controlled the outcome of most of the act of state cases decided by this Court. Both of these rules rest on the deeply imbedded postulate in international law of the territorial supremacy of the sovereign, a postulate that has been characterized as the touchstone of private and public international law. That the act of state doctrine is rooted in a well-established concept of international law is evidenced by the practice of other countries. These countries, without employing any act of state doctrine, afford substantial respect to acts of foreign states occurring within their territorial confines. Our act of state doctrine, as formulated in past decisions of the Court, carries the territorial concept one step further. It precludes a challenge to the validity of foreign law on the ordinary conflict of laws ground of repugnancy to the public policy of the forum. Against the objection that the foreign act violates domestic public policy, it has been said that the foreign law provides the rule of decision, where the *lex loci* rule would so indicate, in American courts.

The reasons that underlie the deference afforded to foreign acts affecting property in the acting country are several; such deference reflects an effort to maintain a certain stability and predictability in transnational transactions, to avoid friction between nations, to encourage settlement of these disputes through diplomatic means and to avoid interference with the executive control of foreign relations. To adduce sound reasons for a policy of nonreview is not to resolve the problem at hand, but to delineate some of the considerations that are pertinent to its resolution.

Contrary to the assumption underlying the Court's opinion, these considerations are relative, their strength varies from case to case, and they are by no means controlling in all litigation involving the public acts of a foreign government. This is made abundantly clear by numerous cases in which the validity of a foreign act of state is drawn in question and in which these identical considerations are present in the same or a greater degree. American courts have denied recognition or effect to foreign law, otherwise applicable under the conflict of laws rules of the forum, to many foreign laws where these laws are deeply inconsistent with the policy of the forum, notwithstanding that these laws were of obvious political and social importance to the acting country. For example, foreign confiscatory decrees purporting to divest nationals and corporations of the foreign sovereign of property located in the United States uniformly have been denied effect in our courts, including this Court; courts continued to recognize private property rights of Russian corporations owning property within the United States long after the Russian Government, recognized by the United States, confiscated all such property and had rescinded the laws on which corporate identity depended. Furthermore, our courts customarily refuse to enforce the revenue and penal laws of a foreign state, since no country has an obligation to further the governmental interests of a foreign sovereign. And the judgments of foreign courts are denied conclusive or prima facie effect where the judgment is based on a statute unenforceable in the forum, where the procedures of the rendering court markedly depart from our notions of fair procedure, and generally where enforcement would be contrary to the public policy of the forum. These rules demonstrate that our courts have never been bound to pay unlimited deference to foreign acts of state, defined as an act or law in which the sovereign's governmental interest is involved; they simultaneously cast doubt on the proposition that the additional element in the case at bar, that the property may have been within the territorial confines of Cuba when the expropriation decree was promulgated, requires automatic deference to the decree, regardless of whether the foreign act violates international law.

III.

I start with what I thought to be unassailable propositions: that our courts are obliged to determine controversies on their merits, in accordance with the applicable law; and that part of the law American courts are bound to administer is international law.

.... The doctrine that the law of nations is a part of the law of the land, originally formulated in England and brought to America as part of our legal heritage, is reflected in the debates during the Constitutional Convention and in the Constitution itself. This Court has time and again effectuated the clear understanding of the Framers, as embodied in the Constitution, by applying the law of nations to resolve cases and controversies. As stated in *The Paquete Habana*, 175 U.S. 677, 700, "[i]nternational law is part of our law, and must be ascertained and administered by the courts of justice of appropriate jurisdiction, as often as questions of right depending upon it are duly presented for their determination." Principles of international law have been applied in our courts to resolve controversies not merely because they provide a convenient rule for decision but because they represent a consensus among civilized nations on the proper ordering of relations between nations and the citizens thereof. Fundamental fairness to litigants as well as the interest in stability of relationships and preservation of reasonable expectations call for their application whenever international law is controlling in a case or controversy.

....

The Court accepts the application of rules of international law to other aspects of this litigation, accepts the relevance of international law in other cases and announces that when there is an appropriate degree of "consensus concerning a particular area of international law, the more appropriate it is for the judiciary to render decisions regarding it, since the courts can then focus on the application of an agreed principal to circumstances of fact rather than on the sensitive task of establishing a principle not inconsistent with the national interest or with international justice." The Court then, rather lightly in my view, dispenses with its obligation to resolve controversies in accordance with "international justice" and the "national interest" by assuming and declaring that there are no areas of agreement between nations in respect to expropriations. There may not be. But without critical examination, which the Court fails to provide, I would not conclude that a confiscatory taking which discriminates against nationals of another country to retaliate against the government of that country falls within that area of issues in international law "on which opinion seems to be so divided." Nor would I assume, as the ironclad rule of the Court necessarily implies, that there is not likely to be a consensus among nations in this area, as for example upon the illegality of discriminatory takings of alien property based upon race, religion or nationality. But most of all I would not declare that even if there were a clear consensus in the international community, the courts must close their eyes to a lawless act and validate the transgression by rendering judgment for the foreign state at its own request. This is an unfortunate declaration for this Court to make. It is, of course, wholly inconsistent with the premise from which the Court starts, and, under it, banishment of international law from the courts is complete and final in cases like this. I cannot so cavalierly ignore the obligations of a court to dispense justice to the litigants before it.

IV.

The reasons for non-review, based as they are on traditional concepts of territorial sovereignty, lose much of their force when the foreign act of state is shown to be a violation of international law, including those rules which mark the bounds of lawful state action against their property located within the territorial confines of the foreign states. Although a state may reasonably expect that the validity of its laws operating on property within its jurisdiction will not be defined by local notions of public policy of numerous other states (although a different situation may well be presented when courts of another state are asked to lend their enforcement machinery to effectuate the foreign act), it cannot with impunity ignore the rules governing the conduct of all nations and expect that other nations and tribunals will view its acts as within the permissible scope of territorial sovereignty. Contrariwise, to refuse inquiry into the question of whether norms of the international community have been contravened by the act of state under review would seem to deny the existence or purport of such norms, a view that seems inconsistent with the role of international law in ordering the relations between nations. Finally, the impartial application of international law would not only be an affirmation of the existence and binding effect of international rules of order, but also a refutation of the notion that this body of law consists of no more than the divergent and parochial views of the capital importing and exporting nations, the socialist and free-enterprise nations.

The Court puts these considerations to rest with the assumption that the decisions of the courts "of the world's major capital exporting country and principal exponent of the free enterprise system" would hardly be accepted as impartial expressions of sound legal principle. The assumption, if sound, would apply to any other problem arising from transactions that cross state lines and is tantamount to a declaration excusing this Court from any future consequential role in the clarification and application of international law. This declaration ignores the historic role which this Court and other American courts have played in applying and maintaining principles of international law.

Of course, there are many unsettled areas of international law, as there are of domestic law, and these areas present sensitive problems of accommodating the interests of nations that subscribe to divergent economic and political systems. It may be that certain nationalizations of property for a public purpose fall within this area. Also, it may be that domestic courts, as compared to international tribunals, or arbitral commissions, have a different and less active role to play in formulating new rules of international law or in choosing between rules not yet adhered to by any substantial group of nations. Where a clear violation of international law is not demonstrated, I would agree that principles of comity underlying the act of state doctrine warrant recognition and enforcement of the foreign act. But none of these considerations relieve a court of the obligation to make an inquiry into the validity of the foreign act, none of them warrant a flat rule of no inquiry into the validity of the foreign act, none of them warrant a flat rule of no inquiry at all. The vice of the act of state doctrine as formulated by the Court and applied in this case, where the decree is alleged not only to be confiscatory but also retaliatory and discriminatory and had been found by two courts to be a flagrant violation of international law, is that it precludes any such examination and proscribes any decision on whether Cuban Law No. 851 contravenes an accepted principle of international law.

The other objections to reviewing the act challenged herein, save for the alleged interference with the executive's conduct of foreign affairs, seem without substance, both in theory and as applied to the facts of the instant case. The achievement of a minimum amount of stability and predictability in international commercial transactions is not assured by a rule of non-reviewability which permits any act of a foreign state, regardless of its validity under international law, to pass muster in the courts of other states. The very act of a foreign state against aliens which contravenes rules of international law, the purpose of which is to support and foster an order upon which people can rely, is at odds with the achievement of stability and predictability in international transactions. And the infrequency of cases in American courts involving foreign acts of state challenged as invalid under international law furnishes no basis at all for treating the matter as unimportant and for erecting the rule the Court announces today.

There is also the contention that the act of state doctrine serves to channel these disputes through the processes designed to rectify wrongs of an international magnitude, see *Oetjen v. Central Leather Co., supra; Shapleigh v. Mier, supra.* The result of the doctrine, it is said, requires an alien to seek relief in the courts or through the executive of the expropriating country, to seek relief through diplomatic channels of his own country and to seek review in an international tribunal. These are factors an American court should consider when asked to examine a foreign act of state, although the availability and effectiveness of these modes of accommodation may more often be illusory than real. Where alternative modes are available and are likely to be effective, our courts might well stay their hand and direct a litigant to exhaust or attempt to utilize them before adjudicating the validity of the foreign act of state. But the possibility of alternative remedies, without more, is frail support for a rule of automatic deference to the foreign act in all cases. The Court's rule is peculiarly inappropriate in the instant case, where no one has argued that C.A.V. can obtain relief in the courts of Cuba, where the United States has broken off diplomatic relations with Cuba, and where the United States, although protesting the illegality of the Cuban decrees, has not sought to institute any action against Cuba in an international tribunal.

V.

There remains for consideration the relationship between the act of state doctrine and the power of the executive over matters touching upon the foreign affairs of the Nation. It is urged that the act of state doctrine is a necessary corollary of the executive's authority to direct the foreign relations of the United States and accordingly any exception in the doctrine, even if limited to clear violations of international law, would impede or embarrass the executive in discharging his constitutional responsibilities. Thus, according to the Court, even if principles of comity do not preclude inquiry into the validity of a foreign act under international law, due regard for the executive function forbids such examination in the courts.

Without doubt political matters in the realm of foreign affairs are within the exclusive domain of the Executive Branch, as, for example, issues for which there are no available standards or which are textually committed by the Constitution to the executive. But this is far from saying that the Constitution vests in the executive exclusive absolute control of foreign affairs or that the validity of a foreign act of state is necessarily a political question. International law, as well as a treaty or executive agreement, see *United States v. Pink*, 315 U.S. 203, provides an ascertainable standard for adjudicating the validity of some foreign acts, and courts are competent to apply this body of law, notwithstanding that there may be some cases where comity dictates giving effect to the foreign act because it is not clearly condemned under generally accepted principles of international law. And it cannot be contended that the Constitution allocates this area to the exclusive jurisdiction of the executive, for the judicial power is expressly extended by that document to controversies between aliens and citizens or States, aliens and aliens, and foreign states and American citizens or States.

A valid statute, treaty or executive agreement could, I assume, confine the power of federal courts to review or award relief in respect of foreign acts or otherwise displace international law as the rule of decision. I would not disregard a declaration by the Secretary of State or the President that an adjudication in the courts of the validity of a foreign expropriation would impede relations between the United States and the foreign government or the settlement of the controversy through diplomatic channels. But I reject the presumption that these undesirable consequences would follow from adjudication in every case, regardless of the circumstances. Certainly the presumption is inappropriate here.

Soon after the promulgation of Cuban Law No. 851, the State Department of the United States delivered a note of protest to the Cuban Government declaring this nationalization law to be in violation of international law. Since the nationalization of the property in question, the United States has broken off diplomatic relations with the present Government of Cuba. And in response to inquiries by counsel for the respondent in the instant case, officials of the State Department nowhere alleged that adjudication of the validity of the Cuban decree nationalizing C.A.V. would embarrass our relations with Cuba or impede settlement on an international level. In 1963, the United States Government issued a freeze order on all Cuban assets located in the United States. On these facts — although there may be others of which we are not aware — it is wholly unwarranted to assume that an examination of the validity of Cuban Law No. 851 and a finding of invalidity would intrude upon the relations between the United States and Cuba.

But the Court is moved by the specter of another possibility; it is said that an examination of the validity of the Cuban law in this case might lead to a finding that the Act is not in violation of widely accepted international norms or that an adjudication here would require a similar examination in other more difficult cases, in one of which it would be found that the foreign law is not in breach of international law. The finding, either in this case or subsequent ones, that a foreign act does not violate widely accepted international principles, might differ from the executive's view of the act and international law, might thereby seriously impede the executive's functions in negotiating a settlement of the controversy and would therefore be inconsistent with the national interest. "[T]he very expression of judicial uncertainty might provide embarrassment to the Executive Branch." These speculations, founded on the supposed impact of a judicial decision on diplomatic relations, seem contrary to the Court's view of the arsenal of weapons possessed by this country to make secure foreign investment and the "ample powers [of the political branches] to effect compensation," and wholly inconsistent with its view of the limited competence and knowledge of the judiciary in the area of foreign affairs and diplomacy. Moreover, the expression of uncertainty feared by the Court is inevitable under the Court's approach, as is well exemplified by the *ex-cathedra* pronouncements in the instant case. While premising that a judicial expression of uncertainty on whether a particular act clearly violates international law would be embarrassing to the executive, this Court, in this very case, announces as an underpinning of its decision that "[t]here are few if any issues in international law today on which opinion seems to be so divided as the limitations on a State's power to expropriate the property of aliens," and proceeds to demonstrate the absence of international standards by cataloguing the divergent views of the "capital exporting," "free enterprise" nations, of the "newly independent and underdeveloped countries," and of the "Communist countries" toward both the issue of expropriation and international law generally. The act of state doctrine formulated by the Court bars review in this case and will do so in all others involving expropriation of alien property precisely because of the lack of a consensus in the international community on rules of law governing foreign expropriations. Contrariwise, it would seem that the act of state doctrine will not apply to a foreign act if it concerns an area in which there is unusual agreement among nations, which is not the case with the broad area of expropriations. I fail to see how greater embarrassment flows from saying that the foreign act does not violate clear and widely accepted principles of international law than from saying, as the Court does, that non-examination and validation are required because there are no widely accepted principles to which to subject the foreign act. As to potential embarrassment, the difference is semantic, but as to determining the issue of its merits and as to upholding a regime of law, the difference is vast.

There is a further possibility of embarrassment to the executive from the blanket presumption of validity applicable to all foreign expropriations, which the Court chooses to ignore, and which, in my view, is far more self-evident than those adduced by the Court. That embarrassment stems from the requirement that all courts, including this Court, approve, validate, and enforce any foreign act expropriating property, at the behest of the foreign state or a private suitor, regardless of whether the act arbitrarily discriminates against aliens on the basis of race, religion, or nationality, and regardless of the position the executive has taken in respect to the act. I would think that an adjudication by this Court that the foreign act, as to which the executive is protesting and attempting to secure relief for American citizens, is valid and beyond question enforceable in the courts of the United States would indeed prove embarrassing to the Executive Branch of our Government in many situations, much more so than a declaration of invalidity or a refusal to adjudicate the controversy at all. For the likelihood that validation and enforcement of a foreign act which is condemned by the executive will be inconsistent with national policy as well as the goals of the international community is great. This result is precisely because the Court, notwithstanding its protestations to the contrary, has laid down "an inflexible and all-encompassing rule in this case."

VI.

Obviously there are cases where an examination of the foreign act and declaration of invalidity or validity might undermine the foreign policy of the Executive Branch and its attempts at negotiating a settlement for a nationalization of the property of Americans. The respect ordinarily due to a foreign state, as reflected in the decisions of this Court, rests upon a desire not to disturb the relations between countries and on a view that other means, more effective than piecemeal adjudications of claims arising out of a large-scale nationalization program of settling the dispute, may be available. Precisely because these considerations are more or less present, or absent, in any given situation and because the Department of our Government primarily responsible for the formulation of foreign policy and settling these matters on a state-to-state basis is more competent than courts to determine the extent to which they are involved, a blanket presumption of non-review in each case is inappropriate and a requirement that the State Department render a determination after reasonable notice, in each case, is necessary. Such an examination would permit the Department to evaluate whether adjudication would "vex the peace of nations," whether a friendly foreign sovereign is involved, and whether settlement through diplomacy or through an international tribunal or arbitration is impending. Based upon such an evaluation, the Department may recommend to the court that adjudication should not proceed at the present time. Such a request I would accord considerable deference and I would not require a full statement of reasons underlying it. But I reject the contention that the recommendation itself would somehow impede the foreign relations of the United States or unduly burden the Department. The Court notes that "[a]dverse domestic consequences might flow from an official stand," by which I take it to mean that it might be politically embarrassing on the domestic front for the Department of State to interpose an objection in a particular case which has attracted public attention. But an official stand is what the Department must take under the so-called *Bernstein* exception, which the Court declines to disapprove. Assuming that there is a difference between an express official objection to examination and the executive's refusal to relieve "the court from any constraint upon the exercise of its jurisdiction," it is not fair to allow the fate of a litigant to turn on the possible political embarrassment of the Department of State and it is not this Court's role to encourage or require non-examination by bottoming a rule of law on the domestic public relations of the Department of State. The Court also rejects this procedure because it makes the examination of validity turn on an educated guess by the executive as to the probable result and such a guess might turn out to be erroneous. The United States in its brief has disclaimed any such interest in the result in these cases, either in the ultimate outcome or the determination of validity, and I would take the Government at its word in this matter, without second-guessing the wisdom of its view.

This is precisely the procedure that the Department of State adopted voluntarily in the situation where a foreign government seeks to invoke the defense of immunity in our courts. If it is not unduly disruptive for the Department to determine whether to issue a certificate of immunity to a foreign government itself when it seeks one, a recommendation by the Department in cases where generally the sovereign is not a party can hardly be deemed embarrassing to our foreign relations. Moreover, such a procedure would be consonant with the obligation of courts to adjudicate cases on the merits except for reasons wholly sufficient in the particular case. As I understand it, the executive has not yet said that adjudication in this case would impede his functions in the premises; rather he has asked us to adopt a rule of law foreclosing inquiry into the subject unless the executive affirmatively allows the courts to adjudicate on the merits.

Where the courts are requested to apply the act of state doctrine at the behest of the State Department, it does not follow that the courts are to proceed to adjudicate the action without examining the validity of the foreign act under international law. The foreign relations considerations and potential of embarrassment to the executive inhere in examination of the foreign act and in the result following from such an examination, not in the matter of who wins. Thus, all the Department of State can legitimately request is non-examination of the foreign act. It has no proper interest or authority in having courts decide a controversy upon anything less than all of the applicable law or to decide it in accordance with the executive's view of the outcome that best comports with the foreign or domestic affairs of the day.... But where a court refuses to examine foreign law under principles of international law, which it is required to do, solely because the Executive Branch requests the court, for its own reasons, to abstain from deciding the controlling issue in the controversy, then in my view, the executive has removed the case from the realm of the law to the realm of politics, and a court must decline to proceed with the case. The proper disposition is to stay the proceedings until circumstances permit an adjudication or to dismiss the action where an adjudication within a reasonable time does not seem feasible. To do otherwise would not be in accordance with the obligation of courts to decide controversies justly and in accordance with the law applicable to the case.

It is argued that abstention in the case at bar would allow C.A.V. to retain possession of the proceeds from the sugar and would encourage wrongfully deprived owners to engage in devious conduct or "self-help" in order to compel the sovereign or one deriving title from it into the position of plaintiff. The short answer to this is that it begs the question; negotiation of the documents by Farr, Whitlock and retention of the proceeds by C.A.V. is unlawful if, but only if, Cuba acquired title to the shipment by virtue of the nationalization decree. This is the issue that cannot be decided in the case if deference to the State Department's recommendation is paid (assuming for the moment that such a recommendation has been made). Nor is it apparent that "self-help," if such it be deemed, in the form of refusing to recognize title derived from unlawful paramount force is disruptive of or contrary to a peaceful international order. Furthermore, a court has ample means at its disposal to prevent a party who has engaged in wrongful conduct from setting up defenses which would allow him to profit from the wrongdoing. Where the act of state doctrine becomes a rule of judicial abstention rather than a rule of decision for the courts, the proper disposition is dismissal of the complaint or staying the litigation until the bar is lifted, regardless of who has possession of the property title to which is in dispute.

VII.

The position of the Executive Branch of the Government charged with foreign affairs with respect to this case is not entirely clear. As I see it no specific objection by the Secretary of State to examination of the validity of Cuba's law has been interposed at any stage in these proceedings, which would ordinarily lead to an adjudication on the merits. Disclaiming, rightfully, I think, any interest in the outcome of the case the United States has simply argued for a rule of non-examination in every case, which literally, I suppose, includes this one. If my view had prevailed I would have stayed further resolution of this issues in this Court to afford the Department of State reasonable time to clarify its views in light of the opinion. In the absence of a specific objection to an examination of the validity of Cuba's law under international law, I would have proceeded to determine the issue and resolve this litigation on the merits.

C. The Sovereign Immunity Defense

Documents Supplement References:

1. *Foreign Sovereign Immunities Act, 28 U.S.C. §§ 1602-11.*

2. *Restatement Sections 451-460.*

Verlinden B.V. v. Central Bank of Nigeria
461 U.S. 480 (1982)

CHIEF JUSTICE BURGER delivered the opinion of the Court.

We granted *certiorari* to consider whether the Foreign Sovereign Immunities Act of 1976, by authorizing a foreign plaintiff to sue a foreign state in a United States district court on a nonfederal cause of action, violates Article III of the Constitution.

I

On April 21, 1975, the Federal Republic of Nigeria and petitioner Verlinden B.V., a Dutch corporation with its principal offices in Amsterdam, the Netherlands, entered into a contract providing for the purchase of 240,000 metric tons of cement by Nigeria. The parties agreed that the contract would be governed by the laws of the Netherlands and that disputes would be resolved by arbitration before the International Chamber of Commerce, Paris, France.

The contract provided that the Nigerian Government was to establish an irrevocable, confirmed letter of credit for the total purchase price through Slavenburg's Bank in Amsterdam. According to petitioner's amended complaint, however, respondent Central Bank of Nigeria, an instrumentality of Nigeria, improperly established an unconfirmed letter of credit payable through Morgan Guaranty Trust Co. in New York. [Morgan Guaranty acted solely as an advising bank; it undertook no independent responsibility for guaranteeing the letter of credit.]

In August 1975, Verlinden subcontracted with a Liechtenstein corporation, Interbuco, to purchase the cement needed to fulfill the contract. Meanwhile, the ports of Nigeria had become clogged with hundreds of ships carrying cement, sent by numerous other cement suppliers with whom Nigeria also had entered into contracts. In mid-September, Central Bank unilaterally directed its correspondent banks, including Morgan Guaranty, to adopt a series of amendments to all letters of credit issued in connection with the cement contracts. Central Bank also directly notified the suppliers that payment would be made only for those shipments approved by Central Bank two months before their arrival in Nigerian waters.

Verlinden then sued Central Bank in the United States District Court for the Southern District of New York, alleging that Central Bank's actions constituted an anticipatory breach of the letter of credit. Verlinden alleged jurisdiction under the Foreign Sovereign Immunities Act, [and] 28 U.S.C. § 1330. [Section 1330(a) provides that "[t]he district courts shall have original jurisdiction without regard to amount in controversy of any non-injury civil action against a foreign state as defined amount in controversy of any non-injury civil action against a foreign state as defined in section 1603(a) of this title as to any claim for relief in personam with respect to which the foreign state is not entitled to immunity either under sections 1605-1607 of this title or under any applicable international agreement." In actual fact, the Foreign Sovereign Immunities Act is codified at 28 U.S.C. Sections 1602-1611. Its provisions are discussed in this case, the following case, and the excerpt from the *Restatement (Third) on the Foreign Relations Law of the United States* that appears in the *Documents Supplement*.]

The District Court first held that a federal court may exercise subject-matter jurisdiction over a suit brought by a foreign corporation against a foreign sovereign. Although the legislative history of the Foreign Sovereign Immunities Act does not clearly reveal whether Congress intended the Act to extend to actions brought by foreign plaintiffs, Judge Weinfeld reasoned that the language of the Act is "broad and embracing. It confers jurisdiction over 'any non-jury civil action' against a foreign state." Moreover, in the District Court's view, allowing *all* actions against foreign sovereigns, including those initiated by foreign plaintiffs, to be brought in federal court was necessary to effectuate "the Congressional purpose of concentrating litigation against sovereign states in the federal courts in order to aid the development of a uniform body of federal law governing assertions of sovereign immunity." The District Court also held that Art. III subject- matter jurisdiction extends to suits by foreign corporations against foreign sovereigns, stating:

> "[The Act] imposes a single, federal standard to be applied uniformly by both state and federal courts hearing claims brought against foreign states. In consequence, even though the plaintiff's claim is one grounded upon common law, the case is one that 'arises under' a federal law because the complaint compels the application of the uniform federal standard governing assertions of sovereign immunity. In short, the Immunities Act injects an essential federal element into all suits brought against foreign states."

The District Court nevertheless dismissed the complaint, holding that a foreign instrumentality is entitled to sovereign immunity unless one of the exceptions specified in the Act applies. After carefully considering each of the exceptions upon which petitioner relied, the District Court concluded that none applied, and accordingly dismissed the action.

The Court of Appeals for the Second Circuit affirmed, but on different grounds. The court agreed with the District Court that the Act was properly construed to permit actions brought by foreign plaintiffs. The court held, however, that the Act exceeded the scope of Art. III of the Constitution. In the view of the Court of Appeals, neither the Diversity Clause nor the "Arising Under" Clause of Art. III is broad enough to support jurisdiction over actions by foreign plaintiffs against foreign sovereigns; accordingly it concluded that Congress was without power to grant federal courts jurisdiction in this case, and affirmed the District Court's dismissal of the action. [The Foreign Diversity Clause provides that the judicial power extends "to Controversies...between a State, or the Citizens thereof, and foreign States, Citizens or Subjects." U.S. Const., Art. III, § 2, cl. 1. The so-called "Arising Under" Clause provides: "The judicial power [of the United States] shall extend to all Cases...arising under this Constitution, the Laws of the United States, and Treaties made, or which shall be made, under their Authority." *Ibid*].

We granted *certiorari*, and we reverse and remand.

II

For more than a century and a half, the United States generally granted foreign sovereigns complete immunity from suit in the courts of this country. In *The Schooner Exchange v. M'Faddon*, 7 Cranch 116 (1812), Chief Justice Marshall concluded that, while the jurisdiction of a nation within its own territory "is susceptible of no limitation, not imposed by itself," the United States had impliedly waived jurisdiction over certain activities of foreign sovereigns. Although the narrow holding of *The Schooner Exchange* was only that the courts of the United States lack jurisdiction over an armed ship of a foreign state found in our port, that opinion came to be regarded as extending virtually absolute immunity to foreign sovereigns.

As *The Schooner Exchange* made clear, however, foreign sovereign immunity is a matter of grace and comity on the part of the United States, and not a restriction imposed by the Constitution. Accordingly, this Court consistently has deferred to the decisions of the political branches—in particular, those of the Executive Branch—

on whether to take jurisdiction over actions against foreign sovereigns and their instrumentalities.

Until 1952, the State Department ordinarily requested immunity in all actions
against friendly foreign sovereigns. But in the so-called Tate Letter, the State Department announced its adoption of the "restrictive" theory of foreign sovereign immunity. Under this theory, immunity is confined to suits involving the foreign sovereign's
public acts, and does not extend to cases arising out of a foreign state's strictly commercial acts.

The restrictive theory was not initially enacted into law, however, and its application proved troublesome. As in the past, initial responsibility for deciding questions of sovereign immunity fell primarily upon the Executive acting through the
State Department, and the courts abided by "suggestions of immunity" from the
State Department. As a consequence, foreign nations often placed diplomatic pressure on the State Department in seeking immunity. On occasion, political considerations led to suggestions of immunity in cases where immunity would not have been
available under the restrictive theory.

An additional complication was posed by the fact that foreign nations did not always make requests to the State Department. In such cases, the responsibility fell to
the courts to determine whether sovereign immunity existed, generally by reference
to prior State Department decisions. Thus, sovereign immunity determinations were
made in two different branches, subject to a variety of factors, sometimes including
diplomatic considerations. Not surprisingly, the governing standards were neither
clear nor uniformly applied.

In 1976, Congress passed the Foreign Sovereign Immunities Act in order to free
the Government from the case-by-case diplomatic pressures, to clarify the governing
standards, and to "assur[e] litigants that... decisions are made on purely legal
grounds and under procedures that insure due process," H.R. REP. NO. 94-1487, p.
7 (1976). To accomplish these objectives, the Act contains a comprehensive set of
legal standards governing claims of immunity in every civil action against a foreign
state or its political subdivisions, agencies, or instrumentalities.

For the most part, the Act codifies, as a matter of federal law, the restrictive theory of sovereign immunity. A foreign state is normally immune from the jurisdiction of federal and state courts, 28 U.S.C. § 1604, subject to a set of exceptions
specified in §§ 1605 and 1607. Those exceptions include actions in which the foreign state has explicitly or impliedly waived its immunity, § 1605(a)(1), and actions
based upon commercial activities of the foreign sovereign carried on in the United
States or causing a direct effect in the United States, § 1605(a)(2). When one of
these or the other specified exceptions applies, "the foreign state shall be liable in
the same manner and to the same extent as a private individual under like circumstances," § 1606.

The Act expressly provides that its standards control in "the courts of the United
States and of the States," § 1604, and thus clearly contemplates that such suits may
be brought in either federal or state courts. However, "[i]n view of the potential sensitivity of actions against foreign states and the importance of developing a uniform
body of law in this area," H.R. REP. NO. 94-1487, *supra*, at 32, the Act guarantees
foreign states the right to remove any civil action from a state court to a federal
court, § 1441(d). The Act also provides that any claim permitted under the Act may
be brought from the outset in federal court, § 1330(a). If one of the specified exceptions to sovereign immunity applies, a federal district court may exercise subject-matter jurisdiction under § 1330(a); but if the claim does not fall within one of the ex-

ceptions, federal courts lack subject-matter jurisdiction. In such a case, the foreign state is also ensured immunity from the jurisdiction of state courts by § 1604.

III

The District Court and the Court of Appeals both held that the Foreign Sovereign Immunities Act purports to allow a foreign plaintiff to sue a foreign sovereign in the courts of the United States, provided the substantive requirements of the Act are satisfied. We agree.

On its face, the language of the statute is unambiguous. The statute grants jurisdiction over "any non-jury civil action against a foreign state... with respect to which the foreign state is not entitled to immunity," 28 U.S.C. § 1330(a). The Act contains no indication of any limitation based on the citizen of the plaintiff.

The legislative history is less clear in this regard. The *House Report* recites that the Act would provide jurisdiction for "*any* claim with respect to which the foreign state is not entitled to immunity under sections 1605-1607," H.R. REP. NO. 94-1487, *supra*, at 13 (emphasis added), and also states that its purpose was "to provide when and how *parties* can maintain a lawsuit against a foreign state or its entities," *id.*, at 6 (emphasis added). At another point, however, the Report refers to the growing number of disputes between "American citizens" and foreign states, *id.*, at 6-7, and expresses the desire to ensure "*our citizens*... access to the courts," *id.*, at 6 (emphasis added).

Notwithstanding this reference to "our citizens," we conclude that, when considered as a whole, the legislative history reveals an intent not to limit jurisdiction under the Act to actions brought by American citizens. Congress was aware of concern that "our courts [might be] turned into small 'international courts of claims[,]'... open... to all comers to litigate any dispute which any private party may have with a foreign state anywhere in the world." *Testimony of Bruno A. Ristau*, HEARINGS ON H.R. 11315, at 31. As the language of the statute reveals, Congress protected against this danger not by restricting the class of potential plaintiffs, but rather by enacting substantive provisions requiring some form of substantial contact with the United States. *See* 28 U.S.C. § 1605. If an action satisfies the substantive standards of the Act, it may be brought in federal court regardless of the citizens of the plaintiff.

IV

We now turn to the core question presented by this TOC3case: whether Congress exceeded the scope of Art. III of the Constitution by granting federal courts subject-matter jurisdiction over certain civil actions by foreign plaintiffs against foreign sovereigns where the rule of decision may be provided by state law.

This Court's cases firmly establish that Congress may not expand the jurisdiction of the federal courts beyond the bounds established by the Constitution. Within Art. III of the Constitution, we find two sources authorizing the grant of jurisdiction in the Foreign Sovereign Immunities Act: the Diversity Clause and the "Arising Under" Clause. The Diversity Clause, which provides that the judicial power extends to controversies between "a State, or the Citizens thereof, and foreign States," covers actions by citizens of States. Yet diversity jurisdiction is not sufficiently broad to support a grant of jurisdiction over actions by foreign plaintiffs, since a foreign plaintiff is not "a State, or [a] Citize[n] thereof." We conclude, however, that the "Arising Under" Clause of Art. III provides an appropriate basis for the statutory grant of subject-matter jurisdiction to actions by foreign plaintiffs under the Act.

The controlling decision on the scope of Art. III "arising under" jurisdiction is Chief Justice Marshall's opinion for the Court in *Osborn v. Bank of United States*, 9 Wheat. 738 (1824). In *Osborn*, the Court upheld the constitutionality of a statute that granted the Bank of the United States the right to sue in federal court on causes of action based upon state law. There, the Court concluded that the "judicial department may receive...the power of construing every...law" that "the Legislature may constitutionally make," *id.*, at 818. The rule was laid down that

> "it [is] a sufficient foundation for jurisdiction, that the title or right set up by the party, may be defeated by one construction of the constitution or law[s] of the United States, and sustained by the opposite construction." *Id.*, at 822.

Osborn thus reflects a broad conception of "arising under" jurisdiction, according to which Congress may confer on the federal courts jurisdiction over any case or controversy that might call for the application of federal law. The breadth of that conclusion has been questioned. It has been observed that, taken at its broadest, *Osborn* might be read as permitting "assertion of original federal jurisdiction on the remote possibility of presentation of a federal question." *Textile Workers v. Lincoln Mills*, 353 U.S. 448, 482 (1957) (Frankfurter, J., dissenting). We need not now resolve that issue or decide the precise boundaries of Art. III jurisdiction, however, since the present case does not involve a mere speculative possibility that a federal question may arise at some point in the proceeding. Rather, a suit against a foreign state under this Act necessarily raises questions of substantive federal law at the very outset, and hence clearly "arises under" federal law, as that term is used in Art. III.

By reason of its authority over foreign commerce and foreign relations, Congress has the undisputed power to decide, as a matter of federal law, whether and under what circumstances foreign nations should be amenable to suit in the United States. Actions against foreign sovereigns in our courts raise sensitive issues concerning the foreign relations of the United States, and the primacy of federal concerns is evident. *See, e.g., Banco Nacional de Cuba v. Sabbatino*, 376 U.S. 398, 423-425 (1964).

To promote these federal interests, Congress exercised its Art. I powers by enacting a statute comprehensively regulating the amenability of foreign nations to suit in the United States. The statute must be applied by the district courts in every action against a foreign sovereign, since subject matter jurisdiction in any such action depends on the existence of one of the specified exceptions to foreign sovereign immunity, 28 U. S. C. § 1330(a). At the threshold of every action in district court against a foreign state, therefore, the court must satisfy itself that one of the exceptions applies —and in so doing so it must apply the detailed federal law standards set forth in the act. Accordingly, an action against a foreign sovereign arises under federal law, for purposes of Art. III jurisdiction.

V

A conclusion that the grant of jurisdiction in the Foreign Sovereign Immunities Act is consistent with the Constitution does not end the case. An action must not only satisfy Art. III but must also be supported by a statutory grant of subject-matter jurisdiction. As we have made clear, deciding whether statutory subject-matter jurisdiction exists under the Foreign Sovereign Immunities Act entails an application of the substantive terms of the Act to determine whether one of the specified exceptions to immunity applies.

In the present case, the District Court, after satisfying itself as to the constitutionality of the Act held that the present action does not fall within any specified exception. The Court of Appeals, reaching a contrary conclusion as to jurisdiction under the Constitution, did not find it necessary to address this statutory question. Accordingly, on remand the Court of Appeals must consider whether jurisdiction exists under the Act itself. If the Court of Appeals agrees with the District Court on that issue, the case will be at an end. If, on the other hand, the Court of Appeals concludes that jurisdiction does exist under the statute, the action may then be remanded to the District Court for further proceedings.

It is so ordered.

Letelier v. Republic of Chile
748 F.2D 790 (2d Cir. 1984)

CARDAMONE, Circuit Judge:

The critical question posed on this appeal is whether the assets of a foreign state's wholly owned airline are subject to execution to satisfy a default judgment obtained against the foreign state. The district court, believing that Congress under the Foreign Sovereign Immunities Act of 1976, 28 U.S.C. §§ 1602-11 (1982) (FSIA or the Act), would not have established a right to jurisdiction over the foreign state without also providing a remedy, ordered execution. We reverse although we recognize that our decision may preclude the plaintiffs from collecting on their judgment. How one wishes to decide a case comes lightly to mind, on a wing; but often how one must decide it comes arduously, weighed down by somber thought. To rule otherwise here would only illustrate once again that hard cases make bad law.

Facts

Orlando Letelier, the former Chilean Ambassador to the United States, his aide, Michael Moffitt, and Moffitt's wife, Ronni, were riding to work in Washington, D.C. in September, 1976 when an explosive device planted under the driver's seat in their car was detonated killing both Letelier and Ronni Moffitt and seriously injuring Michael Moffitt. That assassination gives rise to the present appeal.

Investigation by agencies of the United States government into these murders revealed the identity of nine assassins and their alleged connection to the government of Chile. Of the nine only Michael Vernon Townley, an American citizen working for Chilean intelligence, was convicted of a criminal offense. Three of those indicted were members of the Cuban Nationalist Movement who, although found guilty in the trial court, had their convictions reversed on appeal. Of the other five individuals indicted, none were brought to trial: three were Chilean nationals that Chile refused to extradite, and two remain at large.

In August 1978 the personal representatives of Letelier and Moffitt instituted a civil tort action in the United States District Court for the District of Columbia against the indicted individuals and the Republic of Chile. The complaint asserted five causes of action: (1) a conspiracy to deprive Letelier and Moffitt of their civil rights under 42 U.S.C. § 1985; (2) assault and battery; (3) reckless transportation and detonation of explosives; (4) violation of the "law of nations" (international law); and (5) murder of an internationally protected person under 18 U.S.C. § 1116. The complaint alleged that the noncommercial tort exception of § 1605(a)(5) of the FSIA applied and that Chile was not entitled to sovereign immunity in the tort action.

All defendants defaulted, although Chile sent two Diplomatic Notes to the United States Department of State asserting its sovereign immunity and that the allegations against it were false. The State Department forwarded these Notes to the clerk of the district court. In August 1978 the trial court granted default judgment against the individual defendants. During 1979 and 1980 the district court heard plaintiffs' motion for a default judgment against Chile, *see Letelier v. Republic of Chile*, 488 F.Supp. 665 (D.D.C.1980), and finally resolved that motion. *See Letelier v. Republic of Chile*, 502 F.Supp. 259 (D.D.C.1980). In the former case, the court ruled that it had subject matter jurisdiction pursuant to the exception to immunity found in § 1605(a)(5) of the Act. In the latter case the trial court relying on Townley's testimony at the criminal trial, where he had pled guilty and testified for the prosecution, granted a default judgment against the Republic of Chile and awarded plaintiffs over five million dollars including interest, compensatory and punitive damages, counsel fees and out-of-pocket expenses. The Republic of Chile did not take an appeal from either of these judgments.

The resulting judgment against the Republic of Chile was entered in the United States District Court for the District of Columbia. Plaintiffs subsequently filed the judgment in the United States District Court for the Southern District of New York, for the purpose of executing on the property interests that The Republic of Chile has in the Chilean national airline, Linea Aerea Nacional-Chile or LAN, which is located in New York, and for the appointment of Michael Moffitt as a receiver of those interests to satisfy the judgment against Chile. The application for execution against LAN's assets came before District Court Judge Morris E. Lasker. LAN moved to dismiss claiming that it should not be held to answer for Chilean debts and that its assets were immune from execution. Relying upon a recent decision of the United States Supreme Court, *First National City Bank v. Banco Para El Comercio Exterior de Cuba (Bancec)*, 462 U.S. 611, (1983), which based a decision to disregard separate corporation identities on "international equitable principles," Judge Lasker first held in an opinion and order dated July 28, 1983 that, were the facts as asserted, LAN's role in the assassination was commercial activity under the Act. He further held that to adhere to LAN's separate corporate identity would, as in *Bancec*, violate equitable principles. *Letelier v. Republic of Chile*, 567 F. Supp. 1490, 1496 (S.D.N.Y. 1983).

Having concluded that LAN's assets were subject to execution to satisfy a judgment against Chile, the district court concluded that the language of § 1610(a)(2) did not limit execution only to commercial assets used for commercial purposes, as LAN claimed, but also permitted execution to satisfy tort judgments "so long as the assets on which the judgment creditor seeks to execute were also used commercially in the activity giving rise to the claim." The rationale for this reading of the statute was that a statute should not be interpreted to create a right without a remedy. The court reasoned that if jurisdictional immunity is lifted, the presumption is that there will be a right to execute.

Plaintiffs later sought discovery against The Republic of Chile by serving it with interrogatories and requests to produce documents and admit facts. Chile refused to comply and again filed Diplomatic Notes asserting its refusal to recognize either the validity of the default judgment or the district court's jurisdiction in the supplementary proceedings for enforcement. Judge Lasker in an order dated December 20, 1983 granted plaintiff's motions for [F.R.Civ.P.] Rule 37 sanctions against LAN consisting of adverse findings of fact that provided a basis to disregard LAN's juridical separateness, and appointed Moffitt as a receiver of LAN's assets in the United States. 575 F. Supp. 1217 (S.D.N.Y.1983). From the rulings of July 28 and December 20, 1983 LAN has appealed and raised a number of issues.

Discussion

The principal issue is whether LAN's assets may be executed upon to satisfy the judgment obtained in the District of Columbia against Chile. This discussion necessarily focuses on the Foreign Sovereign Immunities Act of 1976, which is the exclusive source of subject matter jurisdiction over all suits involving foreign states or their instrumentalities. According to § 1604, foreign states are immune from suit in our courts unless the conduct complained of comes within the exceptions set forth in §§ 1605 to 1607 of the Act. Similarly, under § 1609 foreign states are immune from execution upon judgments obtained against them, unless an exception set forth in §§ 1610 or 1611 of the FSIA applies.

The judgment creditors claim that § 1610(a)(2) allows them to execute upon LAN's assets in this case. Section 1610(a)(2) provides:

> The property in the United States of a foreign state...used for a commercial activity in the United States, shall not be immune from attachment in aid of execution, or from execution...if...the property is or was used for the commercial activity upon which the claim is based....

We consider first whether LAN's separate juridical existence may be ignored, thereby making its assets "[t]he property in the United States of a foreign state."

I. *Separate Juridical Existence*

In *Bancec* the Supreme Court determined whether a claim of a foreign agency plaintiff was subject to a set-off for the debts of its parent government. *Bancec* deserves close scrutiny because it provides a conceptual framework for resolving plaintiffs' assertion that LAN's assets should be treated as assets of Chile and because the district court relied on it to reach that conclusion.

In *Bancec*, the Cuban bank of the same name brought suit against Citibank to collect on a letter of credit issued in its favor in 1960. Citibank counterclaimed arguing that it was entitled to set-off amounts as compensation due it for the Cuban government's expropriation of Citibank's assets in Cuba. We ruled that as Bancec was not the alter ego of the Cuban Government, it could not be held to account for Cuban debts. The Supreme Court reversed, relying on the Act's legislative history, the Court noted that it was not intended to affect the substantive law of liability of a foreign state or the attribution of liability among its entities and proceeded to resolve the appeal on "equitable principles." The *Bancec* Court recognized that "government instrumentalities established as juridical entities distinct and independent from their sovereign should normally be treated as such." 103 S.Ct. at 2600. FSIA's legislative history provided support for that conclusion:

> Section 1610(b) will not permit execution against the property of one agency or instrumentality to satisfy a judgment against another, unrelated agency or instrumentality. There are compelling reasons for this. If U.S. law did not respect the separate juridical identities of different agencies or instrumentalities, it might encourage foreign jurisdictions to disregard the juridical divisions between different U.S. corporations or between a U.S. corporation and its independent subsidiary. However, a court might find that property held by one agency is really the property of another. H.R. REP. No. 94-1487, pp. 29-30, U.S. CODE CONG. & ADMIN. NEWS 1976, 6604, pp. 6628, 6629 (citation omitted).

The Supreme Court concluded in *Bancec* that the presumption of separateness had been overcome. It reasoned that the real beneficiary of any recovery would be the

Cuban government, and that Cuba should not be permitted to obtain relief in American courts without answering for its seizure of Citibank's assets. The Court commented that "Cuba cannot escape liability for acts in violation of international law simply by re-transferring the assets to separate juridical entities." 103 S.Ct. at 2603.

Thus, *Bancec* rests primarily on two propositions. First, Courts may use set-off as a unique, equitable remedy to prevent a foreign government from eluding liability for its own acts when it affirmatively seeks recovery in an American judicial proceeding. The broader message is that foreign states cannot avoid their obligations by engaging in abuses of corporate form. The *Bancec* Court held that a foreign state instrumentality is answerable just as its sovereign parent would be if the foreign state has abused the corporate form, or where recognizing the instrumentality's separate status works a fraud or an injustice.

The district court analyzed the present case in light of *Bancec* and ruled that Chile's alleged use of LAN to transport Townley and explosives to the United States were "significant steps in the conspiracy" that if proven "would constitute a gross abuse of the corporate form." Accordingly, it held, "If Chile ignored LAN's separate existence in accomplishing the wrong, it may not invoke that separate existence in order to deny the injured a remedy."

The district judge "found" the following facts based "on the record" and "established" by evidentiary sanctions imposed pursuant to Rule 37(b)(2)(A): From January 1975 through January 1979 LAN's assets and facilities were under the direct control of Chile, which had the power to use them; Chile could have decreed LAN's dissolution and taken over property interests held in LAN's name; Chile, through its agencies, officers, and employees, intentionally used facilities and personnel of LAN to plan and carry out its conspiracy to assassinate Orlando Letelier by (a) transporting Michael Vernon Townley between Chile and the United States, (b) transporting explosives on several occasions, (c) assisting with currency transactions involved in paying off the co-conspirators in the assassination, (d) providing a meeting place for the co-conspirators, (e) arranging for Townley to exit the United States under an alias after the assassination. By using LAN in these endeavors, the district court found, Chile ignored LAN's separate existence and abused the corporate form.

In our view this is not the sort of "abuse" that overcomes the presumption of separateness established by *Bancec*. Joint participation in a tort is not the "classic" abuse of corporate form to which the Supreme Court referred. In *Bancec* the Court relied by analogy on the domestic law of private corporations that ignores separate juridical status "where a corporate entity is so extensively controlled by its owner that a relationship of principal and agent is created," where "the corporate form . . . is interposed to defeat legislative policies," or where recognition of corporate form "'would work fraud or injustice.'" The facts that the district court "found" here do not add up to anything that resembles the abuses in the decisions cited in *Bancec*. None of these facts shows that Chile ignored LAN's separate status. Instead, they simply demonstrate that Michael Townley was able to enlist the cooperation of certain LAN pilots and officials with whom he had a pre-existing social relationship in pursuing his sinister goal. There was no finding that LAN's separate status was established to shield its owners from liability for their torts or that Chile ignored ordinary corporate formalities.

Plaintiffs had the burden of proving that LAN was not entitled to separate recognition. A creditor seeking execution against an apparently separate entity must prove "the property to be attached is subject to execution." *Palmiter v. Action, Inc.*, 548 F. Supp. 1166, 1172 (N.D. Ind. 1982). The evidence submitted by the judgment creditors does not reveal abuse of corporate form of the nature or degree that *Bancec* found sufficient to overcome the presumption of separate existence. As both *Bancec* and the FSIA legislative history caution against too easily overcoming the presumption of separateness, we decline to extend the *Bancec* holding to do so in this case.

II. *Commercial Activity*

Even assuming the district court was correct in disregarding LAN's corporate form and finding that LAN's assets were Chile's property in the United States, § 1610(a)(2) also requires that the property, be "used for the commercial activity upon which the claim is based." In permitting execution against LAN's assets the court below essentially concluded that LAN's activities aided Townley in the assassination and constituted the "commercial activities" that § 1610(a)(2) requires. We cannot agree because a consistent application of the Act, analysis of the background of its enactment, its language and legislative history, and the case law construing it compel the opposite conclusion.

We first note that the district court for the District of Columbia found that Chile lost its immunity from jurisdiction pursuant to § 1605(a)(5), the "tortious activity" exception to jurisdictional immunity. Section 1605(a)(5) specifically states that it applies to situations "not otherwise encompassed in paragraph (2)." Section 1605(a)(2) is the commercial activity exception. This language suggests that the commercial activity exception to jurisdictional immunity under (2) and the tort exception under (5) are mutually exclusive. If the district court in the District of Columbia lifted jurisdictional immunity based on its finding that the activities complained of were tortious, not commercial, it is inconsistent for this court to lift execution immunity based on a finding that the activities were commercial.

Our disagreement with the finding that LAN's activities were commercial rests on more than the resulting lack of symmetry in application of the FSIA. If LAN, as the trial court found, acted in complicity with the Chilean secret police in the assassination, its activities had nothing to do with its place in commerce. The nature of its course of conduct could not have been as a merchant in the marketplace. Its activities would have been those of the foreign state: governmental, not private or commercial.

Chief Justice Marshall with his decision in *The Schooner Exchange v. McFaddon*, 11 U.S. (7 Cranch) 116, 3 L.Ed. 287 (1812) upheld France's plea of sovereign immunity. In that case American citizens claimed ownership of a French vessel of war berthed in Philadelphia. The executive department recommended to the Supreme Court that it dismiss the claim and the Supreme Court complied with that suggestion. After *The Schooner Exchange* it became the rule that American courts would exercise jurisdiction over foreign states unless the matter was intimately connected with foreign policy and the executive department charged with the conduct of foreign policy asked for judicial abstention. In 1976 Congress, acting pursuant to its Article I powers, changed that practice by enacting the Foreign Sovereign Immunities Act. The Act assigns the task of deciding whether a foreign sovereign is immune solely to federal and state courts sitting without juries.

The FSIA adopts a restrictive view of sovereign immunity. The absolutist view, which found foreign sovereigns immune from suit for any activity, fell into disfavor in other countries and a more restrictive rule succeeded it. In 1952 the United States Department of State signaled with its Tate Letter, 26 DEP'T OF STATE BULL. 984, that it embraced the new rule. This restrictive view grants immunity for "governmental" acts of a foreign state and denies it for acts of a "private" nature. This translates into the "commercial activity" exceptions in the FSIA.

FSIA § 1602 contains the findings and declaration of purpose for the Act. That section states:

> Under international law, states are not immune from the jurisdiction of foreign courts insofar as their *commercial activities* are concerned, and their commercial property *may be levied upon for the satisfaction of judgments rendered against them in connection with their commercial activities.* (emphasis furnished).

Under § 1603(d) commercial activity is defined as "either a regular course of commercial conduct or a particular commercial transaction or act." S. REP. NO. 94-1310, 94th Cong., 2d Sess. (1976) (*Senate Report*) recognizes that activities fall along a "spectrum" bounded by "commercial" behavior on one end of the spectrum and "governmental" activity on the other:

> Certainly, if an activity is customarily carried on for profit, its commercial nature could readily be assumed. At the other end of the spectrum, a single contract, if of the same character as a contract which might be made by a private person, could constitute a "particular transaction or act."

Id. at 15. The *Senate Report* contains examples of commercial activities:

> Activities such as a foreign government's sale of a service or product, its leasing of property, its borrowing of money, its employment or engagement of laborers, clerical staff or public relations or marketing agents or its investment in a security of an American corporation, would be among those included within the definition.

Id. at 16. Congress specifically designed the execution immunity rules to "conform" to the jurisdictional immunity provisions of § 1605. H.R. REP. NO. 94-1487, 94th Cong. 2d Sess. (1976), *reprinted in* 1976 U.S. CODE CONG. & AD. NEWS 6604, 6626 (*House Report*).

Congress intended the "essential nature" of given behavior to determine its status for purposes of the commercial activities exception, and gave the courts a "great deal of latitude" to decide this issue. *Id.* at 6615. The legislative history makes clear that courts should not deem activity, "commercial" as a whole simply because certain aspects of it are commercial. The example given is that the AID programs remain governmental even though they involve behavior traditionally performed by private persons.

The district court correctly noted that under § 1603(d) the court must inquire into the nature of conduct, not its purpose, to determine if it is "commercial." *See Texas Trading & Milling Corp. v. Federal Republic of Nigeria*, 647 F.2d 300, 310 (2d Cir.1981), *cert. denied*, 454 U.S. 1148, (1982) (Nigerian government's purchase of cement was a commercial activity irrespective of its purposes for so doing). The commercial activity exception of § 1605(a)(2) has been interpreted broadly, *In re Rio Grande Transport*, 516 F.Supp. 1155, 1162 (S.D.N.Y. 1981). "The determination of whether particular behavior is 'commercial' is perhaps the most important decision a court faces in an FSIA suit." *Texas Trading, supra*, 647 F.2d at 308. As with any statutory term, the "commercial activity" requirement must be given a logical and reasonable interpretation. Inquiry therefore ordinarily focuses on whether the specific acts are those that private persons normally perform. *See Texas Trading, supra*, 647 F.2d at 309; *Rios* 309; *Rios v. Marshall*, 530 F.Supp. 351, 371-72 (S.D.N.Y. 1982) (joint venture agreement with private corporation is "commercial activity"). Yet, not every act of a foreign state that could be done by a private citizen in the United States is "commercial activity," *see In re Sedco, Inc.*, 543 F.Supp. 561, 565 (S.D.Tex. 1982) (holding that the Mexican national oil company's drilling of the infamous IXTOC I well in the Gulf of Mexico was not "commercial activity"). The court must inquire whether the activity is of the type an individual would customarily carry on for profit. One of the few decisions that has construed § 1610(a)(2) also searched for evidence of a profit motive on the foreign sovereign's part. *United States v. County of Arlington, Va.*, 702 F.2d 485, 488 (4th Cir.1983). *See also Frolova v. U.S.S.R.*, 558 F. Supp. 358 (N.D.Ill.1983) (refusal to allow immigration is public, not commercial, activity).

A case that involved facts analogous to those before us is *Arango v. Guzman Travel Advisors Corp.*, 621 F.2d 1371 (5th Cir. 1980), which was decided under § 1605, not § 1610. In *Arango*, the plaintiffs sued the wholly owned, national airline of the Dominican Republic after being expelled from a flight because that country's officials would not permit them entry. Although the Court dismissed the appeal because it was taken from a non-appealable order, it discussed (in *dicta*) whether the "commercial activity" exception of § 1605(a)(2) would allow plaintiffs to bring their tort action against the airline. The *Arango* court considered the airline's actions in rerouting plaintiffs noncommercial because it concluded that the airline acted merely as the agent of the Dominican government.

We agree with the *Arango* analysis. The *Arango* court found that alleged "kidnapping" by a foreign state is not "commercial activity" under the FSIA because a private person cannot lawfully engage in that activity. A private person cannot lawfully engage in murder any more than he can in kidnapping or criminal assault. Carriage of passengers and packages is an activity in which a private person could engage. But it is not for those activities that LAN's assets are being executed against. Rather, plaintiffs assert that LAN itself participated in the assassination and essentially accuse LAN of being a co-conspirator or joint tort-feasor. In other words, LAN is accused of engaging in state-sponsored terrorism the purpose of which, irrelevant under the FSIA, was to assassinate an opponent of the Chilean government. Politically motivated assassinations are not traditionally the function of private individuals. They can scarcely be considered commercial activity. Viewed in this light, LAN's participation, if any, in the assassination is not commercial activity that falls within the § 1610(a)(2) exception and its assets therefore are not stripped of immunity.

III. *Right Without a Remedy*

The district court's principal concern with finding LAN immune from execution on its assets was that "[h]aving determined to grant jurisdiction in both commercial and tort claims, it appears out of joint to conclude that Congress intended the surprising result of allowing only commercial creditors to execute on their judgments." Hence, it concluded that Congress would not create a right without a remedy. Few would take issue with the district judge's comment as an abstract principle of statutory interpretation. Nevertheless, when drafting the FSIA Congress took into account the international community's view of sovereign immunity. That makes a world of difference in the Act's interpretation. The Act's history and the contemporaneous passage of similar European legislation strongly support the conclusion that under the circumstances at issue in this case Congress did in fact create a right without a remedy. Congress wanted the execution provisions of the FSIA to "remedy, *in part*, the [pre-FSIA] predicament of a plaintiff who has obtained a judgment against a foreign state." *House Report, supra*, at 6605-06 (emphasis added). It is to that pre-FSIA plaintiff's predicament that we now turn.

To put the execution immunity provisions of the 1976 Act in proper perspective it is helpful to examine them in light of the European Convention on State Immunity and Additional Protocol adopted in 1972 and the United Kingdom's enactment of The State Immunity Act of 1978. Although these two codifications contain vastly different approaches to execution of judgments, they are relevant to this discussion in that neither Act ensures that a party may execute on a judgment against a foreign state by attaching property, even if it may validly assert jurisdiction over that foreign state. The European Convention, because of its members' conflicting views, decided not to provide machinery for the enforcement of judgments by execution. The Convention relied instead on the obligation of an individual State to honor judgments taken against it. A judgment creditor must ordinarily obtain satisfaction through executive or administrative channels, though when both States involved have made certain declarations the European Court of Human Rights provides a judicial remedy. In effect, the European Convention leaves execution by judgment creditors at the mercy of the defendant State's policies. This is scarcely surprising as Article 2, paragraph 7 of the Charter of the United Nations declared the same rule 37 years earlier. Paragraph 7 prohibits the United Nations from intervening "in matters which are essentially within the domestic jurisdiction of any state."

The State Immunity Act, like the FSIA, grants general immunity from execution over a foreign state's property except that, unlike the FSIA, which permits execution only on property upon which the claim is based, courts in England may execute on property in use or intended to be used for commercial purposes. Hence, The State Immunity Act restricts immunity from execution more than the FSIA and subjects *any* property of the foreign state used for commercial purposes to execution.

The FSIA distinguishes between execution against property of an agency or instrumentality of a foreign state, which may be executed against regardless of whether the property was used for the activity on which the claim is based under § 1610(b)(2), and the property of the foreign state itself, which may be executed against only when the property was used for the commercial activity on which the claim is based under § 1610(a)(2). In so distinguishing, Congress sharply restricted immunity from execution against agencies and instrumentalities, but was more cautious when lifting immunity from execution against property owned by the State itself. Congress passed the FSIA on the background of the views of sovereignty expressed in the 1945 charter of the United Nations and the 1972 enactment of the European Convention, which left the availability of execution totally up to the debtor state, and its own understanding as the legislative history demonstrates, that prior to 1976 property of foreign states was absolutely immune from execution. *House Report, supra,* at 6606. It is plain then that Congress planned to and did lift execution immunity "in part." Yet, since it was not Congress' purpose to lift execution immunity wholly and completely, a right without a remedy does exist in the circumstances here. Our task must be to read the Act as it is expressed, and apply it according to its expressions.

CONCLUSION

We hold, therefore, that the Foreign Sovereign Immunities Act does not allow execution against the assets of LAN, the Chilean National Airlines. The court below improperly ignored defendant LAN's separate juridical status from the Republic of Chile. Ordinarily, we would remand for further evidentiary hearings on the separateness issue, but we are further persuaded, even were LAN and Chile found to be alter egos, that Congress did not provide for execution against a foreign state's property under the circumstances of this case. Congress provided for execution against property used in commercial activity upon which the claim is based. An act of political terrorism is not the kind of commercial activity that Congress contemplated.

Accordingly, we reverse the orders appealed from and dismiss the supplementary proceedings.

III. Political Risk Management

Documents Supplement References:

1. *North American Free Trade Agreement, Chapter 11:B—Settlement of Disputes between a Party and an Investor of Another Party.*

2. *United States Model Bilateral Investment Treaty (BIT) (1998) (especially Article IX).*

A. Overview

NOTE ON MITIGATING POLITICAL RISK*

Introduction

There are a few basic ways in which political risk can be mitigated in the context of planning an FDI venture. Naturally, these mitigation techniques are pre-transactional insurance schemes, namely, the purchase of political risk insurance from public or private insurers. Before discussing them, however, it is important to appreciate that the degree of exposure and time frames involved vary depending on the nature of the venture. This factor should be taken into account when evaluating the needs of an investor. For instance, manufacturing ventures may face a wider variety of risks, including nationalization, political violence, natural resource availability, loss of intellectual property or technology, and others. Banks, however, are exposed to political risks through the loans that they extend, and generally are exposed to political risk in a shorter term than are manufacturers.[1]

There does exist common ground, though, in that

[b]anks and manufacturing companies also face many common concerns about political risk. Most fundamentally, of course, the macroeconomic and political environment of the [host] country in which the business relationship exists is vitally important to both kinds of firms. It is when analysis moves on to questions of the environment's impact on specific companies that crucial differences between banks and manufacturing firms emerge.[2]

The "bottom line" is that the needs of investors differ, and the type of insurance and the requisite coverage will vary accordingly.

Political risk insurance is purchased by a foreign direct investor in order to cover losses from the various types of political risk mentioned in the section above. For example, a joint American-Peruvian agribusiness venture likely should obtain political risk insurance to cover the venture's potential losses from political violence caused by the *Sendero Luminoso* or Shining Path guerilla groups. The providers of this type of insurance include (1) the United States Overseas Private Investment Corporation (OPIC), (2) the Multilateral Investment Guarantee Agency (MIGA), a member of

---

*. This Note was prepared by Christopher C. Matteson, Esq.

1. *See* CHARLES R. KENNEDY, JR., POLITICAL RISK MANAGEMENT 77-78 (1987).

2. KENNEDY, *supra*, at 78.

The World Bank Group, and (3) private insurers, such as the American International Group's American International Underwriters.[3]

OPIC

The Overseas Private Investment Corporation (OPIC) was founded by the Foreign Assistance Act of 1969,[4] and began operations in 1971. It is a self-sustaining government corporation, and returned its start-up appropriation to the United States Treasury in 1983. As a provider of political risk insurance, it has been active in this market since its inception. In 1996, it supported a record 169 projects, and sold U.S. $16.5 billion worth of insurance.

OPIC's affiliation with the United States government makes it an instrument of foreign policy, and as such, there are stipulations placed on its issuance of insurance. For example, the Corporation's literature states:

OPIC-Backed Investment Supports U.S. Foreign Policy Goals.

OPIC support helps stabilize key regions. Leveraging capital from the private sector, OPIC helps support economic stability in countries that are a focus of U.S. foreign policy. Since 1971, OPIC has supported more than $107 billion in investment in developing countries and emerging economies through its support to small and large U.S. companies. In 1996 alone, OPIC-backed projects accounted for more than $23 billion in new investment in 44 countries, an increase of 115% over the total investment in 1995, and the highest level achieved in the agency's history.[5]

OPIC policies dictate that their programs be available only for projects on their list of eligible countries, and "[a]t times, statutory and policy constraints may limit the availability of OPIC programs in certain countries."[6] One example of the ways in which eligibility for OPIC programs interface with foreign policy goals is the fact that the People's Republic of China is not on the list of eligible countries, whereas Taiwan is on the list.

Further foreign-policy based restraints exist on OPIC's operations, such as performance, environmental impact, worker rights, and development contribution requirements. For instance,

OPIC is required by statute to conduct an environmental assessment of every project proposed for financing or insurance that would significantly affect the environment of the host country, and to decline support for projects that, in OPIC's judgment, would have an unreasonable or major adverse impact on the environment of the host country.... Of particular concern are adverse effects on tropical forests, national parks, protected areas, and endangered species, as well as on the health and safety of employees and the public.[7]

---

3. This example was possible by the ready availability of information on AIG's website, <http://www.aiu.aig.com/>. Of course, there are numerous other private insurers offering political risk coverage. "Private insurance companies offering political risk insurance include the Chubb Group (New Jersey), Lloyd's of London, Citicorp International Trade Indemnity (CITI), Professional Indemnity Association (PIA, New York), Pan Financial (London and New York),... and Poole d'Assurance des Risques Internationaux et Speciaux (P.A.R.I.S.). KENNEDY, *supra*, at 182 (citation omitted).

4. The pertinent section is codified at 22 U.S.C. § 2191.

5. OVERSEAS PRIVATE INVESTMENT CORPORATION ANNUAL REPORT 19 (1996)(emphasis in original).

6. OPIC ANNUAL REPORT, *supra*, at 3.

7. OPIC ANNUAL REPORT, *supra*, at 5.

Clearly, then, the availability of OPIC programs to investors is subject to a number of political constraints.

OPIC political risk insurance can cover (1) currency inconvertibility, (2) expropriation, and (3) political violence. It is available for purchase by "U.S. investors, contractors, exporters, and financial institutions involved in international transactions."[8]

The currency inconvertibility coverage is an excellent way to mitigate currency risks (discussed later in this Chapter). It can compensate a foreign direct investor who cannot convert or transfer profits or remittances from its investments. It should be noted, though, that the distinction between currency devaluation (an official act to reduce the value of one currency relative to another currency) and depreciation (a market phenomenon resulting from selling of a currency relative to another currency) is relevant in this situation. The OPIC coverage "insures investors against the consequences of conversion restrictions that occur after an insurance contract is issued."[9] Notably, depreciation in the currency due to market forces is a contingency under which OPIC compensates an investor.

Expropriation coverage offered by OPIC is available to mitigate the risk that a host government will expropriate the investor's property in the situs country.[10] Specifically, the coverage protects against the "nationalization, confiscation, or expropriation of an enterprise, including 'creeping expropriation' — government actions that for a period of at least six months deprive the investor of fundamental rights in a project."[11] However, the coverage excludes any losses to the investor incurred as a result of a host country government's legitimate regulation or taxation of the project. In order to receive compensation from OPIC, the investor must assign all rights to the investment. Presumably, to the extent possible, OPIC then would pursue an action against the host government for the unlawful expropriation, hoping to recover its payout on the claim.[12]

As regards political violence, OPIC's program insures foreign direct investors against losses to property and loss of revenue due to "violence undertaken for political purposes. Declared or undeclared war, hostile actions by national or international forces, civil war, revolution, insurrection, and civil strife (including politically-motivated terrorism and sabotage) are all examples of political violence covered by OPIC."[13] Interestingly, the policies issued by OPIC expressly exclude coverage of actions by groups aimed at changing labor or student conditions. For example, on the one hand, damages incurred as a result of an action by Kashmiri separatists in India might be covered. On the other hand, those incurred as a result of a labor union or university student demonstration in Seoul might not be covered.

In an era of government down-sizing, there is a vigorous debate about the utility of OPIC's programs, and indeed, its existence. In 1996, its re-authorization legisla-

---

8. OPIC Annual Report, *supra*, at 13.

9. OPIC Annual Report, *supra*, at 14.

10. For an interesting case involving the interpretation of a political risk insurance contract with regard to confiscated property, *see* Enterprise Tools v. Export-Import Bank of the United States, 799 F.2d 437 (8th Cir. 1986).

11. OPIC Annual Report, *supra*, at 14.

12. *See, e.g.,* Foremost-McKesson v. Islamic Republic of Iran, 905 F.2d 438 (D.C. Cir. 1990), to which OPIC was a party suing the Iranian government for compensation for a policy payout. It was alleged that the Iranian government used its majority position in the enterprise to deny the American investor its profits.

13. OPIC Annual Report, *supra*, at 14.

tion was in jeopardy. Critics in Congress claimed OPIC was a form of "corporate welfare," and that it encouraged the export of American jobs to developing nations overseas. Although Congress ultimately re-authorized OPIC, the arguments lingered, even in light of the fact that OPIC is a government corporation that actually makes a profit from its operations and is self-sustaining.[14] (Indeed, in 1994 it earned $167 million in net income.[15])

Since 1993, OPIC, which marked its 25th anniversary last year, has been headed by Ruth Harkin, a dynamic woman who seems to be always on the go promoting her agency. Her efforts have been rewarded: Over the last four years, Harkin has shepherded the agency through a growth spurt. In fiscal 1996, OPIC committed $2.2 billion to finance projects and new private-investment funds, compared to $1.8 billion in 1995, and earned revenue by selling $16.5 billion in political risk insurance, compared to $8.6 billion the prior year.[16]

In addition to its political risk coverage, OPIC offers project financing on a limited recourse basis through direct loans and loan guarantees. The Corporation also offers investment promotion, as it offers "[p]re-investment services. Finally, OPIC offers pre-investment services to potential American investors. For example, OPIC investment missions to various countries and regions in which OPIC does business are designed to introduce American business executives to key business leaders, potential joint venture partners and government officials of a host country."[17]

MIGA

The Multilateral Investment Guarantee Agency (MIGA), established in 1988, is a financially independent arm of The World Bank Group. MIGA's mission is defined as follows: "to enhance the flow to developing countries of capital and technology for productive purposes under conditions consistent with their developmental needs, policies, and objectives, on the basis of fair and stable standards for the treatment of foreign investment."[18] MIGA was founded to provide support for FDI through investment insurance. The protection offered by MIGA investment insurance is issued to cover investors for losses incurred as a result of noncommercial risks, namely, political risks.

Do MIGA's programs overlap with those of OPIC? Not necessarily. A key feature of MIGA's insurance is that it is issued to *"fill gaps* left by national insurance programs, which, due to their respective national objectives, often contain strict eligibility requirements that exclude many investors and investments."[19] Its policies are issued as co-insurance, and can be issued "through parallel or joint underwriting."[20]

---

14. *See* Maura B. Perry, *A Model for Efficient Foreign Aid: the Case for the Political Risk Insurance Activities of the Overseas Private Investment Corporation*, 36 VA. J. INT'L L. 511 (1996). This article sets forth an in-depth analysis of OPIC's activities, the roles played by private and public sources of political risk insurance, and OPIC's role as an efficient provider of political risk insurance.

15. Frederick E. Jenney, *Mitigating the Political Risk of Infrastructure Projects with OPIC Political Risk Insurance*, 734 PLI/COMM. L. & PRAC. COURSE HANDBOOK SERIES 199 at 203 (1996).

16. *See Risky Business (interview with Overseas Private Investment Corp. CEO Ruth Harkin)*, ACROSS THE BOARD, May 1, 1997, 1997 WESTLAW 10026415. This interview with the OPIC CEO contains interesting, succinct observations of OPIC's role and activities.

17. Jenney, *supra*, at 202.

18. *Multilateral Investment Guarantee Agency: the Mission and the Mandate*, (visited Mar. 12, 1998) <http://www.miga.org/>.

19. PAUL E. COMEAUX & N. STEPHAN KINSELLA, PROTECTING FOREIGN INVESTMENT UNDER INTERNATIONAL LAW: LEGAL ASPECTS OF POLITICAL RISK 168 (1997) (emphasis added).

20. COMEAUX & KINSELLA, *supra*.

MIGA offers political risk insurance in four separate categories. Policies cover losses to investors due to (1) currency inconvertibility, (2) expropriation, (3) breach of contract, and (4) war and civil disturbance.

The euphemistic term found in MIGA promotional materials in lieu of "currency inconvertibility" is "transfer restriction."

> Transfer Restriction. Protects against losses arising from an investor's ability to convert the local currency (capital, interest, principal, profits, royalties, and other remittances) into foreign exchange for transfer outside the host country. The coverage insures against excessive delays in acquiring foreign exchange caused by host government action or failure to cat, by adverse changes in exchange control laws or regulations, and by deterioration in conditions governing the conversion and transfer of local currency.[21]

Notably, as with OPIC's currency inconvertibility insurance, currency depreciation is not covered. Only explicit action by the host country government to lower the value of its currency will trigger a pay out by MIGA. The currency in which compensation is paid is determined by what is specified in the Contract of Guarantee, which presumably is a hard currency.

MIGA's expropriation coverage is issued in largely the same form as is issued by OPIC. The insurance covers acts of expropriation by host governments where there is no compensation paid, it covers "creeping expropriation," and the insured must assign the interest in the FDI venture to the Agency if a claim is paid. For example, if a MIGA-insured investor lost her investment in Burma due to illegal expropriation, the investor must assign its equity interest in the expropriated facility to MIGA.

The breach of contract coverage is interesting, as it is intended to cover a foreign direct investor's losses resulting from a quasi-political risk, namely legal or contract risk. The coverage applies to situations where the government of a host country breaches or repudiates a contract with the investor. MIGA policy, with regard to the breach of contract coverage, endeavors to invoke standard international dispute resolution mechanisms before paying out a claim. Accordingly, one important qualification to this coverage is that

> [i]n the event of an alleged breach or repudiation, the investor must be able to invoke a dispute resolution mechanism (*e.g.*, an arbitration) in the underlying contract and obtain an award for damages. If, after a specified period of time, the investor has not received payment or if the dispute resolution mechanism fails to function because of actions taken by the host government, MIGA will pay compensation.[22]

Therefore, MIGA's breach of contract coverage compensates an investor who exhausts its remedies through an international dispute resolution mechanism, such as an arbitration tribunal of the International Center for Settlement of Investment Disputes (discussed below).

The magnitude of MIGA's investment guarantee program is not that of OPIC, at least according to information from 1994 and 1995. "In fiscal year 1995, ending June 30, 1995, MIGA issued 54 guaranty contracts totaling $672 million in net coverage, compared to 38 contracts for $372.6 million in fiscal year 1994."[23]

---

21. *Multilateral Investment Guarantee Agency, Investment Guarantee Guide* (visited Mar. 14, 1998) <http://www.miga.org/>.

22. *Id.* at "Guarantee Program" section.

23. COMEAUX & KINSELLA, *supra*, at 169, *citing* MIGA Press Release dated Aug. 10, 1995. (The figure for political risk insurance issued for OPIC for 1995 was $8.6 billion.)

To be sure, MIGA programs do not come without politically-motivated qualifications. For example, MIGA approval is contingent on, among other things, economic and environmental soundness. Still, "[p]olitical considerations are not as important under MIGA as under OPIC. For example, there is no 'human rights' standard that must be met by the host country, as is required by OPIC."[24]

It should be clear that the advantage of MIGA's coverage is in its flexibility and gap filling potential. For example, if an investor wishes to obtain political risk insurance for a venture in Thailand and North Korea, the North Korean portion of the venture will not be eligible for OPIC insurance. MIGA, however, might issue investment guarantee coverage for that portion.

Private Insurers

Private insurers may provide an avenue to manage political risk in an FDI transaction. For example, consider the political risk insurance coverage offered by the American International Group (AIG) through its American International Underwriters (AIU) division. AIU insures investors against specifically enumerated perils in international trade and FDI.

Insurance issued by AIU covers basic political risks in a similar fashion as do the insurance and guarantee programs of OPIC and MIGA. For example, AIG's expropriation coverage includes "Confiscation, Expropriation, Nationalization (CEN) of an investor's permanent or mobile assets. This includes discriminatory government action that causes the permanent cessation of the operations."[25] Currency inconvertibility insurance includes perils such as "the inability to convert and transfer dividends or proceeds from a forced sale of the shareholding.... [and] currency inconvertibility and exchange transfer due to political or economic difficulties which prevent the conversion and transfer of foreign exchange."[26] Further, AIU political risk coverage insures against "[w]ar and [p]olitical violence [and] [p]hysical damage to the investor's assets caused by any military action, civil war, revolution, rebellion, insurrection, *coup d'etat*, strike, riot, sabotage, terrorism, or other civil disturbance which takes the form of organized violence."[27]

AIU insurance plan is flexible. In addition to the basic political risks covered, the group will insure investors against perils such as

> deprivation or the inability to export finished product from the foreign investment or to repatriate mobile assets, forced abandonment of the investment or mobile assets due to the foreign country's deteriorating security situation and where such abandonment is at the direction of the investor's government.... Abrogation of a production, concession or other government guaranteed agreement which such an act is expropriatory and discriminatory in nature, forced divestiture of the shareholding by either the government of the investor's country or the foreign government, and law, order, decree, or import/export restriction by the foreign government which selectively discriminates against the foreign investment so as to cause the permanent cessation of activities, failure to repossess where the foreign government interferes with the investor's rights to repossess under a mortgage, lease agreement or

---

24. COMEAUX & KINSELLA, *supra*, at 173 (citation omitted).

25. *American International Underwriters, Political Risk Insurance for Projects, Description of Product* (visited Mar. 31, 1998) <http://www.aiu.aig.com/pr000001.htm>.

26. *Id.*

27. *Id.*

sales contract subsequent to a default in payment. Arbitration award default or the failure of a government joint venture partner to honor an arbitration award for payment as set out in the joint venture agreement.[28]

AIU's political risk coverage potentially is somewhat broader than that offered by OPIC and MIGA. There are no express political criteria for the availability of the insurance, and additional risks can be insured against by modifying the coverage agreement.

To summarize, the decision to purchase political risk insurance from OPIC, MIGA, or a private insurer requires a comparison and contrast of the different programs, specifically, what each covers, and what each costs. "[G]overnment subsidized insurance is generally less expensive, and can also be issued for longer terms. Also, OPIC and MIGA ... have better facilities for covering currency inconvertibility risks than do private insurers."[29] Political factors also enter the calculation. OPIC and MIGA, but not private insurers, are subject to some political constraints. AIU, for example, has greater freedom than OPIC or MIGA in deciding what perils against which it will insure, and what countries in which it will operate. Political factors may, however, way in favor of OPIC or MIGA. Because OPIC is an agency of the United States Government, perhaps there is some "deterrent value" in the fact that OPIC insures a certain FDI venture. Similarly, developing country host governments will wish to "stay on the good side" of MIGA, because it is a member of The World Bank Group.[30]

Dispute Resolution

Even if a foreign direct investor has accounted for, and attempted to insure against, as many political risks as possible, there will be times when it is not enough. That is, careful planning of an FDI transaction and the purchase of political risk insurance do note preclude the possibility that an investor and the host country government will end up on opposite sides of a dispute. These unhappy situations call for formal dispute resolution.

Fortunately, there is no shortage of available forums. Among the more commonly used mechanisms are (1) arbitration under the auspices of an International Center for Settlement of Investment Disputes (ICSID) tribunal, (2) a dispute resolution panel established pursuant to a regional trade arrangement like the North American Free Trade Agreement (NAFTA), and (3) invocation of the provisions of a bilateral investment treaty (BIT). These mechanisms are discussed briefly in turn below.

1. ICSID Arbitration

In general, arbitration is an outstanding method for resolving FDI disputes for at least three reasons.[31] First, if the parties to an international agreement specify arbitration as a means of solving a dispute, the opportunities for one of the parties to complain about the use of the other party's laws for adjudication are reduced. It seems to "equalize" the parties. Second, the laws of the host country may not have

---

28. *Id.* (The above-quoted passage is modified slightly from its Internet format to make it more readable.)

29. COMEAUX & KINSELLA, *supra*, at 184 (citations omitted).

30. *See id.*

31. *See* W. MICHAEL REISMAN ET AL., INTERNATIONAL COMMERCIAL ARBITRATION, CASES, MATERIALS AND NOTES ON THE RESOLUTION OF INTERNATIONAL BUSINESS DISPUTES lxxvii (1997).

developed to the point where they are appropriate for problem solving in a particular area. Finally, arbitration is often said to be less expensive, and solves disputes quicker than does litigation.

ICSID was created under the auspices of The World Bank Group in 1966. It was intended to relieve the President and staff of the World Bank from frequently becoming involved in international commercial dispute resolution proceedings. Thus,

> ICSID provides facilities for the conciliation and arbitration of disputes between member countries and investors who qualify as nationals of other member countries. Recourse to ICSID conciliation and arbitration is entirely voluntary. However, once the parties have consented to arbitration under the ICSID Convention, neither can unilaterally withdraw its consent. Moreover, all ICSID members, whether or not parties to the dispute, are required by the Convention to recognize and enforce ICSID arbitral awards.....Provisions on ICSID arbitration are commonly found in investment contracts between governments of member countries and investors from other member countries. Advance consents by governments to submit investment disputes to ICSID arbitration can also be found in about twenty investment laws and in over 700 bilateral investment treaties. Arbitration under the auspices of ICSID is similarly one of the main mechanisms for the settlement of investment disputes under four recent multilateral trade and investment treaties (the North American Free Trade Agreement, the Energy Charter Treaty, the Cartagena Free Trade Agreement and the Colonia Investment Protocol of MERCOSUR)....
> .To date, 41 cases have been registered by the Centre, 3 involving conciliation and the remaining 38 arbitration. Ten of the arbitrations are currently pending before the Centre. The majority of the other cases have concluded with settlements by the parties on agreed terms, before the rendition of an award.[32]

ICSID is thus an experienced and capable provider of arbitration services, and as evidenced by the above quoted passage, many of the cases have been settled by the parties prior to an award. One example of an ICSID arbitration that resulted in a decision is the case of *AMCO Asia*,[33] discussed earlier in this Chapter.

An important issue for foreign direct investors and their counsel to understand is that "[t]here are three conditions that must be satisfied before the ICSID Centre may assume jurisdiction over a dispute. First, the dispute must involve a Contracting State and a national of another Contracting State. That is, both the host country and the investor's home country must have signed and ratified the ICSID Convention. Second, both the host country and the investor must agree to submit the particular dispute for arbitration to the ICSID Centre. These first two requirements are known as the "double consent" requirement of the ICSID Convention. Finally, the dispute must "arise directly out of the investment."[34] Once the jurisdictional requirements are met, the investor and host government may elect to settle the dispute through this mechanism.

What approach to American courts take to the enforcement of international arbitral awards? In brief, the courts grant a high degree of deference to the results

---

32. *The International Center for Settlement of Investment Disputes, An Overview of ICSID* (visited Mar. 25, 1998) <http://www.worldbank.org/html/extdr/icsid.html>.

33. Amco Asia Corp., Pan American Development Ltd., and P.T. Amco Indonesia v. Republic of Indonesia, 24 INT'L LEGAL MATERIALS 1022 (1984), *annulled on other grounds*, 25 INT'L LEGAL MATERIALS 1439 (1986).

34. COMEAUX & KINSELLA, *supra*, at 201 (citations omitted).

of binding arbitration.[35] The policy supporting this notion is that courts are eager to encourage parties to use alternative remedies to disputes, in order to ease the pressure on overcrowded courts. Moreover, many provisions of United States international trade and investment law encourage other countries to enforce international arbitral awards. For example, receipt of preferential trading benefits under the Generalized System of Preferences (GSP) is contingent on respect for these awards.

2. NAFTA Chapter 11

An excellent example of a dispute resolution mechanism in a regional trade arrangement is Chapter 11 of NAFTA.[36] Of particular interest is Sub-chapter B, which prescribes the use of ICSID arbitration panels or arbitration under the rules established by the United Nations Commission on International Trade Law (UNCITRAL), or litigation in the judicial system of a NAFTA Party. Sub-chapter B of Chapter 11 does not establish a preference for any one of the above measures. Rather, "[i]t seeks to preserve the maximum scope for amicable settlement of disputes."[37] Thus, by allowing a foreign direct investor to choose the appropriate dispute resolution mechanism for its case, NAFTA provides flexibility.

The political significance of NAFTA Chapter 11:B ought not to be under-emphasized. It signifies consent by the NAFTA Parties to be sued by private investors —in effect, a waiver of the sovereign immunity to which the Parties might otherwise be entitled. Viewed in historical terms, this is particularly remarkable with respect to Mexico—a country that during much of the 1950s, 1960s, and 1970s not only made FDI difficult, and nationalized many foreign assets, but also embraced the Calvo Doctrine. "The encouraging note is that Mexico's acceptance of the Chapter 11:B procedures represents an abandonment of the ill-starred Calvo Doctrine."[38]

NAFTA Chapter 11:B is politically significant in a second respect. It may well serve as a catalyst for other regional trading blocks to establish a framework for investment dispute resolution procedures. This, in turn, will encourage FDI by providing certain, predictable, and standardized procedures for the resolution of disputes.[39]

3. Bilateral Investment Treaties

Bilateral Investment Treaties (BITs) typically contain a set of dispute resolution provisions. This set plays a similar role to that of Chapter 11:B of NAFTA in providing a variety of options to the parties with regard to dispute resolution. For example, Article IX of the United States Model BIT contains provisions, similar to NAFTA, that prescribe the use of an ICSID arbitration panel, the courts of the par-

---

35. *See, e.g.,* Revere Copper and Brass v. Overseas Private Investment Corporation, 628 F.2d 81 (D.C. Cir. 1980), *cert. denied* 100 S.Ct. 2964, excerpted below.

36. *See* Hope H. Camp & Andrius R. Kontrimas, *Direct Investment Issues 3.2.4, in* NAFTA AND BEYOND (Joseph J. Norton & Thomas L. Bloodworth, eds.) (Kluwer, 1995).

37. Gloria L. Sandrino, *The NAFTA Investment Chapter and Foreign Direct Investment in Mexico: A Third World Perspective*, 27 VAND. J. TRANSNAT'L L. 259 at 320 (1994).

38. Malcolm Richard Wilkey, *Introduction to Dispute Settlement in International Trade and Foreign Direct Investment*, 26 LAW & POL'Y INT'L BUS. 613 at 618 (1995). *See also,* discussion of the Calvo Doctrine, *supra.*

39. *See generally,* THE NORTH AMERICAN FREE TRADE AGREEMENT: IT'S SCOPE AND IMPLICATIONS FOR NORTH AMERICA'S LAWYERS, BUSINESSES, AND POLICYMAKERS, (ABA Sec'n Int'l L. & Prac. 1993).

ties, or in accordance with the arbitration rules established by UNCITRAL. The Model BIT is discussed in another Chapter of this Casebook.

B. OPIC

Revere Copper and Brass, Inc. v. Overseas Private Investment Corporation
628 F.2D 81 (D.C. Cir. 1980), cert. denied 100 S.Ct. 2964

Per Curiam:

Appellant, Revere Copper and Brass Incorporated (Revere), seeks reversal of the district court's denial of Revere's motion to correct or vacate in part an arbitration award. The origin of the arbitration award in question is an insurance contract under which the appellee, Overseas Private Investment Corporation (OPIC), an agency of the United States, insured Revere against losses incurred by expropriation of Revere's investment in its wholly-owned subsidiary's aluminum mining and refinery complex in Jamaica. Section 10.01 of the contract provides that any disputes thereon "shall be settled by arbitration... [and]... [t]he award rendered by the arbitrator shall be final and binding upon the parties...."

Following a change in administration of the Jamaican government, Revere made claim upon OPIC for compensation, alleging that actions by the new government constituted an expropriation of Revere's property. When OPIC denied the claim, Revere submitted the dispute to arbitration. The arbitrators determined that there was expropriatory action but awarded Revere $1,131,144, instead of the $64,131,000 that Revere had claimed.

Revere then filed its motion in the district court, seeking to correct or vacate the portions of the arbitrators' award in which the amount of the award was determined. Judge Charles R. Richey concluded that "Revere's claims amount to no more than the contention that the arbitrators misconstrued the contract.... [which] is not open to judicial review." Judge Richey rejected Revere's claim that the award must be set aside for public policy reasons because it violates the rule of *contra proferentem*. *Contra proferentem* is "the rule of construction that ambiguities in insurance contracts are resolved favorably to the insured." The rule developed in recognition that insurance policies are usually written by the insurer, and the insurer ought not be allowed to benefit from any ambiguities in the language which it chose. After questioning whether any ambiguity in the Revere-OPIC insurance contract had been shown, Judge Richey declared that "[p]ublic policy is involved in this case, but not in the manner the petitioner [Revere] contends. There is a strong public policy behind judicial enforcement of binding arbitration clauses." From this ruling Revere appeals. We affirm.

Revere's motion in the district court was made pursuant to sections 10 and 11 of the Federal Arbitration Act, 9 U.S.C. §§ 10-11 (1976). The Act was originally passed in 1925. Pub. L. No.-68-401, 43 Stat. 883. As stated in the Act's preamble, Congress intended it to be "An Act to make valid and enforceable written provisions or agreements for arbitration of disputes arising out of contracts, maritime transactions, or commerce among the States or Territories or with foreign nations." In the ensuing years, "[t]he federal courts have recognized a strong federal policy in favor of voluntary commercial arbitration, as embodied in the [Act]...." The goal of Congress in passing the Act was to establish an alternative to the complications of litigation. As a result, judicial review of an arbitration award has been narrowly limited. This court has acknowledged its restricted function in that capacity.

Seeking to avoid the restrictions upon our review of the award in question, Revere points to the rule that enforcement of arbitration awards is subject to public policy considerations. Revere mis-perceives the nature of the public policy exception to the enforcement of arbitration awards. It is not available for every party who manages to find some generally accepted principle which is transgressed by the award. Rather, the award must be so misconceived that it "compels the violation of law or conduct contrary to accepted public policy." *Union Employers Division of Printing Industry, Inc. v. Columbia Typographical Union No. 101*, 353 F. Supp. 1348, 1349 (D.D.C. 1973), *affd mem.*, 160 U.S. App. D.C. 403, 492 F.2d 669 (1974). A proper description of the limits of the public policy exception is provided in *Interinsurance Exchange of Automobile Club v. Bailes*, 219 Cal. App.2d 830, 33 Cal. Rptr. 533, 538 (1963):

> While, in one sense, all rules of adjective and substantive law set forth the "public policy" of the state, there is a vast difference between the enforcement of a void contract and the mere misunderstanding or misapplication of rules of law involved in the application to a particular dispute of a [valid] contract....

There being no question as to the validity of the insurance contract between Revere and OPIC, or the legitimacy of the parties' bargained-for performances, the public policy exception is inapplicable here.

Revere argues that arbitration clauses are entitled to varying degrees of enforcement depending upon the subject matter of the contract in question. The Federal Arbitration Act provides no basis for this view. Section 9 of the Act expressly provides for the confirmation of arbitration awards which arise out of the kind of binding arbitration clause which is present in Revere's contract with OPIC. *See* U.S.C. § 9 (1976). If indeed there are particular considerations that lead parties to different types of contracts to favor or disfavor arbitration, that is for the parties to determine when they decide whether to include an arbitration clause in their contract. It has nothing to do with the judicial enforcement of arbitration clauses pursuant to the Federal Arbitration Act. The strong federal policy in favor of voluntary commercial arbitration would be undermined if the courts had the final say on the merits of the award.

If Congress wanted to exempt insurance contracts from the purview of the Federal Arbitration Act in the manner suggested by Revere, Congress could do so. In fact, the cases cited by Revere to demonstrate that arbitration of disputes between customer and broker is disfavored, stand for the proposition that Congress can abrogate an arbitration procedure previously contracted for. Congress has done no such thing in the insurance area. On the contrary, in the Foreign Assistance Act of 1969, Congress expressly sanctioned the use of arbitration in OPIC's insurance and guaranty programs. *See* 22 U.S.C. § 2197(i) (1976). As Judge Fuchsberg cogently stated in a case relied upon by Revere, "The notion that courts may freely assume the role of arbiters of public policy is a very much exaggerated one. Most especially, they should avoid doing so in the face of a statutory scheme which bespeaks its own policy considerations...." *Susquehanna Valley Central School Dist. v. Susquehanna Valley Teachers' Ass'n*, 37 N.Y.2d 614, 376 N.Y.S.2d 427, 430, 339 N.E.2d 132, 134 (1975) (concurring opinion).

We see no reason for holding that the failure of arbitrators to apply the rule of *contra proferentem* is sufficient cause for upsetting the award. In *Amicizia Societa*

Navegazione v. Chilean Nitrate & Iodine Sales Corp., 274 F.2d 805 (2d Cir. 1960), the court was faced with a challenge to "arbitrators" reliance upon the principle that ambiguous language is to be construed against the author." *Id*. at 808. The court, resolved the issue in declaring that "the misapplication.... of such rules of contract interpretation does not rise to the stature of a 'manifest disregard' of law." *Id*.

Our disposition makes it clear that we do not find credence in Revere's claim that it was compelled to accept the arbitration provision in its contract with OPIC. This allegation appears to have surfaced after the arbitration award was announced. Revere is willing, on the other hand, to let stand the arbitrators' majority decision in Revere's favor that the Jamaican government expropriated Revere's property. Such an after-the-fact, pick-and-choose approach to an arbitration award is hardly consonant with the underlying concept of arbitration or with Revere's claim that it was forced to agree to arbitration in the first place.

As for Revere's argument that the arbitrators "rewrote" the contract in excess of their authority, a cursory reading of the arbitration award indicates that it "draws its essence" from the Revere-OPIC contract.

We are satisfied that the arbitration award should be sustained. The judgment of the district court, therefore, is

Affirmed.

QUESTIONS

1.   Are OPIC's political constraints legitimate? Should it be free of such constraints?

2.   Name two advantages and two disadvantages of purchasing private political risk insurance.

3.   Why would investor choose to submit her dispute with a host country to arbitration rather than litigate in the host country?

C. Enron and India

NOTE ON POLITICAL RISK MANAGEMENT IN INTERNATIONAL PROJECT FINANCE: THE ENRON CASE*

Introduction

In August 1995, multinational developers and foreign investors received a tremendous shock when the new Hindu nationalist government of the State of Maharashtra canceled the Dabhol Power Company project, originally a U.S. $2.8 billion, 2,015 megawatt power plant under construction on India's west coast. Although the Maharashtra government decided eventually to reinstate the Dabhol project in January 1996, it did so only after numerous lawsuits and seven months of renegotiations. To date, the project and its main sponsor, America's Enron Development Corporation, have been the subject of thirteen lawsuits in India alone. The costs

---

* This Note was prepared by Stephen P. Diamond, Jr., Esq., New York, N.Y.

of delay from the cancellation, furthermore, are expected to exceed U.S. $175 million.

The events that led up to the cancellation of the project, namely increasing public opposition to the project and a general election that replaced a government supportive of the project with a hostile one opposed to the project, fall under the category of "political risk." Dabhol is a classic example of the danger that may occur when political risk is mismanaged.

A full understanding of the failure to manage the political risk in the Dabhol project, as well as the steps Enron took to prevent a full disaster, is essential, because similar issues and circumstances lurk beneath the surface of every international project financing. This Note demonstrates the importance of evaluating and addressing political risk in international project finance, and to provide an organized structure for doing so.

The first part of this Note provides a review of international project finance and political risk. The first section defines "project finance" and explains its basic structure and importance of project finance. The second section furnishes a broad picture of the risk inherent in project financing, and then argues that the events falling under political risk are the manifestation of two distinct forces: political pressure and project-regime dynamics. This part concludes by reviewing the unique problems that political risk presents to project participants.

The second part of the Note gives a history of the Dabhol Power Project and identifies the various participants and the chain of events that led up to the cancellation of the project.

The final part of the Note offers an organized procedure for managing political risk and examines whether such measures were employed in Dabhol, and if so, to what effect. The first section identifies and examines the different factors that influence political pressure and project-regime dynamics. The second section offers four general methods for addressing political risk: (1) minimizing political opposition through negotiation, structure and management of the project; (2) limiting political risk through contract; (3) spreading political risk; and (4) hedging against political risk through insurance and financial instruments. The third section examines damage control and how to stave off disaster in an adverse political climate. Damage control measures are divided under two broad headings. The first broad heading is "dispute resolution." Under it, the effectiveness of using operating committees to handle disputes internally among project participants prior to renegotiation and international commercial arbitration is analyzed. The second broad heading is "the role of multinational organizations (MNOs)." The focus here is on the London Courts of International Arbitration (LCIA), the World Trade League (WTL) and the International Chamber of Commerce (ICC), and on how sponsors can turn to them to help resuscitate an imperilled project. This section also reviews similar provisions in NAFTA that may be applicable for projects undertaken in Mexico.

This Note concludes by arguing that the lesson to be drawn from Dabhol is that effective political risk management in any project financing must occur on three distinct levels. First, steps should be taken to rein in the forces that trigger political risk events and disperse the impact that a project will have on these forces. Second, devices should be employed to minimize the effect that political risk events will have on the project should they occur. Finally, dispute resolution contingencies should be negotiated up front to revive a project in the event its existence is threatened by the occurrence of a political risk event.

I. PROJECT FINANCE AND POLITICAL RISK

A. What is Project Finance?

Put simply, "project finance" is the financing of the construction, development or exploitation of a "right, natural resource or other asset," where repayment of the financing does not rest primarily on the credit support of the sponsors or the physical assets of the project company. Instead, lenders in project financing rely primarily on the income stream, or revenues, that is expected to be generated by the operation of the project for repayment of the project loans. The lenders also rely on the income stream as a measure of the value of the project's assets. Depending on the structure of the transaction, a project financing may be considered "non-recourse" or "limited recourse" in nature. "Non-recourse" finance means that in the event of default or non-payment, lenders can have recourse (or access) only to the underlying physical assets of the project, but never to the borrower. This type of project financing arrangement is extremely rare. "Limited recourse" finance, although preserving some of the borrower's immunity against suit by the lender, nevertheless, provides a lender with some remedies against the borrower in the event he does not comply with his obligations.

Project financing is arranged for large infrastructure development projects that demand a tremendous amount of capital, but present equally substantial risks. The projects involved in this type of financing most often involve the energy, resource recovery, mining, transportation, resort and hotel industries. Recent well-publicized project financings have included the English Channel tunnel (cited as "the largest project financing of this century"), the development of oil pipelines in Colombia, toll roads in Asia, copper mines in Indonesia and Chile, the exploitation of goldfields in Kazakhstan, and the construction of numerous power plant projects around the world. The financing for any of a number of these types of projects easily can exceed one billion dollars.

1. Project Finance as a Capital-Raising Method

A form of limited-recourse lending that earned its current sobriquet during the energy crisis of the late-1970s, project finance now has become an important means of providing capital for much-needed infrastructure improvement in lesser developed countries (LDCs). In 1993, approximately 150 infrastructure projects financings were undertaken worldwide, at a total cost of U.S. $60 billion, half of which were in developing countries. Infrastructure development needs in Asia alone are estimated at U.S. $2 trillion dollars for the period between 1995 and 2004. Yet Third World governments, on their own, are unable to raise the vast sums of money needed to develop their infrastructure. Project finance, on the one hand, addresses the capitalization needs of the Third World, while, on the other hand, providing sponsors and lenders with a greater return than other forms of investment.

Before undertaking an infrastructure development project, however, sponsors must overcome two considerable obstacles. First, as suggested above, an inordinate amount of capital is needed to realize such a project; second, infrastructure projects in LDCs often carry a high risk of default. If not managed properly, the latter can become an obstacle to the financing of a particular project, as lenders (banks and other financial institutions) may be reluctant to make loans available to a project with a high level of risk, or will seek term so strict as to make financing practically unavailable. The parties in a project financing, however, assume or are assigned, through negotiation, those project risks which they are in the best position to bear. This type of risk allocation scheme reduces the overall project risk for all participants. In short, project finance is a legal means for removing a major obstacle to economic progress in LDCs.

2. Structure of Project Finance

a. Phases of Development

Typically, a project financing has four phases of completion, each of which presents different risk-bearing consequences for project participants.

(1) Pre-Development/Design Engineering Phase

This is the preliminary stage of project development. At this stage, sponsors commission plans for the construction of the project and arrange for experts to conduct a study on its feasibility (the "feasibility study"). After the feasibility study is completed, the next step is for the sponsors to negotiate the various project agreements, such as the supply and revenue contracts. The final step in this phase is for the sponsors to obtain the necessary financing for the project.

(2) Construction Phase

Once construction of the project is underway, the project moves to its second stage, during which the majority of the risk is borne by the lenders and to a limited extent, by the contractor. Lenders do so because they are best positioned to analyze a commercial risk, such as currency risk, and hedge against it. Because they are in the best position to do so, contractors will assume the construction risk often by providing performance guarantees, which lowers the costs of financing. The general concern of participants at the construction phase is whether the project will be constructed on time and for the projected contract price. Cost and pace of construction are susceptible to material shortages, construction delays, design changes, political interruption and strikes. The exposure of the lenders to loss is highest during the construction period.

(3) Start-up Phase

In this phase, the participants learn whether the project has been constructed properly to certain pre-set standards agreed upon earlier by all of the parties in the project agreements. Successful completion of the start-up phase often occasions the transfer of the project risk to both the project company and operator, from the contractors. The concern during start-up is whether the project will be able to operate at the contracted for-level of performance that is necessary to maintain debt payments and pay its operating costs. Upon verification by independent experts that the project meets the pre-set standards, the project is considered operational.

(4) Operating Phase

The operating phase is the period after acceptance of start-up results or preliminary operation of the project. During this period, the project company begins servicing the project debt with cash flows from its operation.

3. Participants

Hundreds of different parties may become involved in a project financing. However, the main participants in a project financing are: (1) the sponsors; (2) the lenders; (3) the contractors; (4) the project company; (5) the financial advisor; (6) the suppliers; (7) the host country's government; and (8) the purchaser (also called the product "off-taker").

a. Sponsors

A company or consortium of companies that undertakes the development of the project and shepherds the project from its initial development to operation. The goal of the sponsors is to earn a profit, either through management fees, by selling equipment or raw materials to the project company, by buying and then reselling the project's product, or simply as a return on investment. Contractors, suppliers, or output purchasers, therefore, often will be sponsors.

b. Lenders

Because of the enormous size of most projects, financing usually is spread among a syndicate of banks. One view among experts is that a syndicate of banks representing a broad spectrum of countries is desirable to discourage the host government from interfering with the project. Local financing also may be obtained from host country banks and their inclusion in the syndicate is advisable, especially if the laws of the host country impose restrictions on the ability of foreign banks to take security over *in situ* assets. For lenders, however, the most important form of security are the product purchase agreements, as they guarantee a stream of income for repayment of the project loans.

c. Contractors

The contractors are the companies responsible for constructing the project. The primary goal of the contractor is to deliver a project at a fixed price, by a specified date, which is warranted to perform at certain agreed-upon levels.

d. Project Company

Usually a special purpose vehicle (SPV), which is a company created specifically to construct and operate the project. The project company is usually established as a company in the host country of the project. A SPV is used primarily to insulate the sponsors from any potential liabilities arising out of the ownership of the project. The shareholders of the project company generally will include the sponsors and, in some instances, may include the contractors, operators and output purchasers as well as local investors.

e. Financial Advisor

A commercial or merchant bank with expertise and contacts in the host country, hired by the sponsors to provide advice on project financing feasibility, security alternatives for financing and local conditions. The financial advisor is also the party responsible for contacting lenders to finance the project.

f. Suppliers

Entities which supply the project with construction materials, fuel, power and other supplies or services necessary for the construction and operation of the project. Contracts are executed between the project company and its main suppliers to ensure a steady stream of supplies at a specified price and on guaranteed terms, to avoid shortfalls, which can lead to costly delays or shut-downs.

g. Host Country's Government

The host country's government often is involved either directly, or through one of its agencies, as either (i) a project sponsor; (ii) partial guarantor of loans, licenses, or tax benefits; or (iii) as an output purchaser. Additionally, in some projects, called B-O-T (build-operate-transfer) projects, the host government may take over eventually the operation and ownership of the project.

h. Purchaser ("Off-Taker")

For projects which produce or transfer a given commodity (*i.e.*, a mineral, electricity, petroleum) or service, the purchaser is a private company or governmental organization that enters into a long-term contract to purchase all, or in some cases part, of the output of the project, and has executed a contract or agreement, usually called an off-take agreement, take-or-pay contract or output purchase agreement, to that effect.

B. Political Risk

1. Risk Generally

A risk may be defined generally as an exposure to the chance of an injury or loss. Many common forms of risk exist in international project finance, although the degree of uncertainty growing out of these risks will vary with each project. Project risk is allocated through an intricate series of contractual agreements between the project participants. Risk allocation is predicated on two theories. The first is the "fundamental theory of exchange," which argues that "a risk should be shifted to the person or entity that is best able to control or manage the risk." The second is the "general theory of competitive equilibrium," which explains that "a risk should be shifted until the marginal cost to the risk bearer of bearing the risk is equal to the marginal benefit to the risk shifter of shifting the risk."

The risks in a project financing are identified as (i) Credit Risk; (ii) Construction and Development Risks; (iii) Market and Operating Risk; (iv) Financial Risk; (v) Legal Risk; and (vi) Political Risk. Although the focus of this Note is political risk, a brief overview of the other inherent risks is helpful in obtaining a broad understanding of the contractual dynamics that occur in a project financing.

a. Credit Risk

Credit risk is the risk that the project company will default on its loans. The primary concern of the lenders here is to protect their interest in the project's revenues, and their ability to operate the project in the event of default, or sell it to a party who will do so.

If the project generates hard currency revenues, lenders may protect their interest in project revenues by establishing an offshore collateral account, usually in a New York or London bank, into which such hard currency project revenues must be deposited. An offshore collateral account, also called a "lockbox" account, gives lenders considerable control over the disbursement of project revenues in excess of debt service requirements.

The need to protect the lenders' security interest is two-fold. First, lenders must have security in the relevant project contracts; second, the contracts must remain in place after the lenders enforce security rights. The first concern is accomplished by ensuring that each relevant contract can be charged or assigned to the lenders as security, and that all consents from the counterparties necessary to accomplish this are obtained. The second concern is accomplished by ensuring that the termination clauses in the project contracts do not include insolvency of the project company or assertion of security as terminating events.

b. Construction and Development Risks

Several risks fall under this heading. First, the risk that a shortfall of expected mineral reserves, capacity, output or efficiency of the project itself will occur. Other construction and development risks ("C&D risk") include the risk that the project will incur cost overruns and delays in completion, or that the project may suffer a shortage in building materials, energy and work force. Generally, lenders arrange fixed-price construction contracts, called "turnkey" contracts, to minimize the risk of cost overruns. Essentially, the contractor in a turnkey contract agrees to construct the project for a predetermined price, subject to changes approved by the lenders.

C&D risk also includes non-political *force majeure* risk. *Force majeure* risk covers the risk that a party to a contract will be unable to perform his obligations under the contract because of the occurrence of certain events beyond the control of the parties. Generally speaking, *force majeure* risk includes natural disasters (referred to as "Acts of God"), war, revolution and strikes. *Force majeure* risk, as defined within a specific project, also may be affected by the host government's participation in the project, particularly with respect to risk of expropriation (*i.e.*, the risk that the host government will expropriate the project). If a project is comprised of private sector participants only, then risk of expropriation is not within the control of the parties and it falls under *force majeure* risk. If the host government is a project participant, however, then expropriation risk would not constitute a *force majeure* risk (because it is an event that is most likely within the control of one of the participants, namely, the host government), but rather a political risk. *Force majeure* risk in construction and development is addressed through the insertion of a *force majeure* clause into both the construction and the output purchase agreements. A *force majeure* clause excuses performance or suspends penalty provisions against a party for the consequences of a failure to perform his obligations, for reasons arising from the occurrence of a *force majeure* event. Lenders, however, often are reluctant to excuse repayment of loans despite the occurrence of a *force majeure* event. Additionally, certain events may constitute *force majeure* for one party but not the others. Consequently, participants in a project financing will negotiate very carefully which risks are included in the definition of *force majeure*, as well as the effects upon their contractual obligations of a *force majeure* event. One way to manage non-*force majeure* C&D risk is to obtain construction insurance. Non-*force majeure* C&D risk may be limited also through contract, by arranging long-term fixed price contracts for the supplies, fuel, power and transportation required in the construction of the project. Some risk also may be transferred from the lenders to the contractors contractually through the insertion of penalty provisions for delays and performance shortfalls up to and including the start-up phase of a project.

c. Market and Operating Risk.

Market and operating risk are the risks connected with the operating phase of a project and include the risk that a market for the product will be unavailable; price changes; obsolescence of product or production facilities; and failure of the product or facility. One method of minimizing market risk is for the sponsors or the project company to execute a product purchase agreement with a product purchaser, which ensures a market for the project's product. The product purchase agreement essentially is the guts of project finance. By controlling the revenues that a project receives for selling its product and ensuring a constant market for the product for a specified length of time, the purchase agreement reduces the market risk assumed by the sponsors.

d. Financial Risk

Risk of fluctuation in exchange and interest rates, world commodity prices, and international trade and tariffs. Also includes risk of inflation and of price drops for the project's output product on world markets. Financial risk can be allocated from the power supplier to the power purchaser. Additionally, financial risk is manageable through use of conventional financial hedging instruments, such as interest rate swaps and currency forward contracts.

e. Legal Risk

Legal risk encompasses all manner of legal risks that can be encountered in the host country. Legal risk includes the risk that in the case of limited recourse financing, an inadequate legal regime or facilities exist for the taking and enforcing of security against the project.

f. Political Risk

Although political risk enjoys (or suffers from) a somewhat amorphous definition, some commentators define it as "the occurrence of events in the political sphere which impede the normal operations of a business venture and detrimentally impact the commercial viability of the venture." For a variety of reasons, political risk, among all of the risks present in project financing, has the greatest potential to imperil the success of a project. In project financing, furthermore, political risks are more serious because a host government's decision to undertake a project often may be the product of a highly politicized public debate.

At least four types of events fall under the heading of political risk: (1) a change in government; (2) governmental actions; (3) politically motivated insecurity in the country; and (4) international conflict.

(1) Change in Government

Simply put, the installation of a political leader or administration that is different from the one which negotiated and executed project agreements with the other project participants. A change in government may be effected either through general election, or a revolution or coup.

To be sure, a newly-elected government is not necessarily harmful to a project. The new government may decide that it and the country will benefit by supporting the development of the project. In LDCs, however, political parties often will have diametrically opposing views on foreign investment. A new government that wishes to distinguish itself from the previous government may be tempted to use a foreign project to illustrate this point, or it may decide that what its predecessor thought was essential, is not. The sheer size of infrastructure projects also guarantees that a cancellation will stir up local passions and generate a good amount of visibility for the new government and its policies.

A final note on change in government is that such change differs from the other three events in that, often, it may precede the occurrence of the other three events (although it is not a necessary predicate for the other three to take place).

(2) Governmental Actions

Governmental actions that pose significant risk to a project include breach of agreement by the government, governmental expropriation or requisition of the project, and risk of currency inconvertibility or non-transferability. Very little can be done to protect against governmental expropriation, other than for the sponsors' and lenders' respective governments to pressure the host government not to undertake such action, when it is foreseeable.

Risk of currency inconvertibility is the risk that the host country will experience a pronounced foreign exchange shortfall, currency devaluation or economic inflation, and either render the host country's central bank incapable of converting local currency into hard foreign currency or cause the host country's central bank to impose strict exchange controls on its currency.

Risk of currency non-transferability is the risk that the host country's central bank will not permit the free conversion of convert soft currency into hard currency (*i.e.*, Eurodollars) and will prohibit the transfer of its hard currency out of the host country.

Currency inconvertibility or non-transferability can make service of debt problematic for sponsors because financing for a project is primarily denominated in hard currency (*i.e.*, the United States dollar). Whether a project's income stream is denominated in hard or soft currency will be determined to a large extent by who the consumer of the project's output will be. Because electricity, for example, is produced largely for domestic consumption, power project revenues will be denominated in local currency. Likewise, toll roads and water projects. Alternatively, hotels, oil and gas exploitation, and mineral extraction projects, which create goods or services consumed primarily by overseas buyers, will generate hard currency income streams.

Take for example a power project in Thailand, and assume that the project loans were made in United States dollars. Because the loans are hard currency denominated, they must be repaid in hard currency (*i.e.*, the United States dollar). The power produced by the project is destined for domestic consumption, and so, will be paid for in local currency, here, the baht. The project company, therefore, must convert the baht-denominated income stream into dollars to meet its obligations to the lenders. If the baht, depreciates relative to the dollar, however, service of debt payments will become more expensive. As the Thai currency devaluates, the project company will be forced to spend increasing amounts of baht to buy the same amount of dollars for its loan payments. Currency devaluation is particularly pernicious for projects with soft currency income streams because a devaluation quickly can turn an otherwise profitable project into a loser. The best way for sponsors to hedge against fluctuations in the currency markets is through the use of derivatives and currency forward or futures contracts.

Sponsors also can encounter serious difficulties in servicing their debt if the host government decides to prohibit the transfer of hard currency out of the host country. Sponsors in such a scenario may be squeezed into obtaining short-term financing overseas to meet their project loan obligations. The interest rate on such short-term loans, of course, is an additional cost of currency non-convertibility.

One way to limit the above form of currency risk is to obtain a guarantee from the host government, usually from its central bank, that the local currency the project company receives for selling its product may be converted freely into hard currency and remitted abroad to service loans denominated in hard currency.

Another way to protect partially against currency risk in projects with hard currency income streams, is for the sponsors or the project company to set up an account in an offshore bank into which the output purchaser deposits the payments it makes for the project's product in hard currency. This type of payment structure, a form of "pass-through" structure (so-called because the risk is "passed through" the project company) transfers the currency risk from the project company to the purchaser. By making payment offshore, the project company's funds are immune to subsequent "meddling" by the host country's central bank. The project company is free then to service its debt directly from the offshore account.

(3) Politically Motivated Insecurity in the Host Country

Civil unrest, revolution, political crisis, protests against a project or foreign investment are all examples of politically motivated insecurity in a host country that can increase the political risk of a project.

(4) International Conflict

International conflict may include trade war, economic sanctions and, ultimately, war itself. For obvious reasons, an international conflict between the host country and the home government(s) of the sponsors, lenders or other project participants presents a significant threat to the completion of a project.

2. Forces that Influence Occurrence of Political Risk Events

Political risk events, simply put, are events that occur as responses to two forces: political pressure, and what this Note terms project-connected relation dynamics.

a. Political Pressure

All project financing, at one stage or another, require some form of cooperation or favorable concession from one or more governments (including the host government), the duration of which is subject to political pressure. Political pressure exists on both the micro- and macro-levels.

Micro-level political pressure is pressure exerted by the public in the host country upon the host government to modify (or in some instances, eliminate) a "benefit" that it has granted to the project company. This benefit usually concerns a matter of the host country government's domestic policy (*i.e.*, a loan guarantee, special regulatory approval, an individualized tax regime, land right, or foreign exchange repatriation scheme). The host country government's motivation in granting the project a benefit is to encourage FDI in the host country. In granting the benefit, the host country's government, in turn, may also receive a benefit from the project company. For example, the host government may demand one or more licensing fees for certain activities conducted in connection with a project, or certain taxes, or a lower-priced product.

The general public, however, may perceive the host government's concession as overly-favorable pandering to a foreign company or companies, or discrimination against domestic companies. Such mis-perceptions often lead to political criticism against the host government and its negotiators. A host government facing mounting political pressure and criticism for what its citizenry perceives as capitulation to foreign demands or the making of a bad deal, will either revoke its concessions and seek to renegotiate, or be replaced by an opposition government that will do it for them (in the latter instance, the opposition is likely to capitalize on such misguided but prevailing public sentiment by running for office on a "foreigner-bashing" platform).

Macro-level political pressure is exerted upon project participants by persons or actors outside the host country, usually in response to the domestic policies of a host government, or certain conditions occurring within the host country, such as human or civil rights violations. Such external public pressure may prompt a project sponsor's own government to respond by imposing debilitating economic and diplomatic policies against the host country. In the past, such policies have included the revocation of governmental loan guarantees and project subsidies and reactive import-export controls on certain types of technology.

In 1995, for example, the United States Government prohibited the Export-Import Bank from conducting business in Colombia because it thought Colombia was not making a sincere effort to curb drug trafficking. At the time, Colombia was considered by institutional investors to be a "hot" country for privatization projects, but the absence of Ex-Im Bank support sidelined many projects underway in Colombia at the time.

Another example of macro-level political pressure, in the form of reactive import-export controls, is the United States Treasury Department's Office of Foreign Assets Control (OFAC). OFAC regulations restrict, *inter alia*, the exportation of U.S. goods and services to countries such as Iran, Iraq, Libya, North Korea, and other countries suspected of sponsoring terrorism (as well as the importation or use of goods and services from those countries by U.S. persons), or viewed as "hostile" to the foreign policy or national security of the United States.

Macro-level political pressure also may be applied directly against project participants in the form of consumer boycotts and unfavorable publicity, which may cause potential sponsors to view participation in a project as economically disadvantageous.

During the 1980s, anti-apartheid human rights groups in the United States instituted boycotts of companies such as Coca-Cola, I.B.M. and Eastman Kodak in an effort to force these companies to divest their holdings in South Africa. More recently, British Petroleum's project financing activities in Colombia have faced public opposition in the wake of accusations concerning BP's complicity in human rights abuses by the Colombian military, as well as its environmental record in Colombia.

b. Project-Connected Relation Dynamics

The term "project-connected relation dynamics" describes the shift of advantage and bargaining power from the sponsors to the host government. This shift is explained best by the theory of the "obsolescing bargain," which illustrates the "hostage effect" of sunk investment.

The obsolescing bargain theory posits that sponsors and lenders often have the upper hand in the initial stages of negotiations because the host country's need to obtain a certain project probably exceeds the sponsors' or lenders' need to undertake a high-risk investment in that particular country. After the sponsors have begun the project and the lenders have "sunk" considerable investment into the project, however, their ability to walk away from the project decreases dramatically, making them vulnerable to a host government willing to exploit this shift in bargaining power by requesting renegotiation of the project terms. The occurrence of certain events, such as the discovery of a possible adverse environmental impact from the project, or a sudden change in world demand for the output product, may also exacerbate the sponsors' vulnerability.

II. HISTORY OF THE DABHOL POWER PROJECT

> *"[We will] bundle Enron into the sea."*[2]
> *"My God, what happened there?"*[3]

A stunning example of the "deal-breaking potential" of political risk occurred in August 1995 with the cancellation of the Dabhol power project in India. The event

---

2. Gopinath Munde, Maharashtra's former Energy Minister, *quoted in* RICHARD DONKIN, SURVEY OF MAHARASHTRA.

3. Hazel O'Leary, U.S. Secretary of Energy, *Decision Time. But see, So What Happened At Dabhol?*, COAL & SYNFUELS TECH., Oct. 4, 1996, *available in* 1996 WL 8375174.

sent shockwaves through the international investment community. Because the Dabhol project was resuscitated eventually, an examination of the project and the circumstances behind the cancellation provide an excellent method of analyzing the effectiveness of political risk management techniques and post-breach defensive contingencies.

A. Historical Background to the Project

When India's central government introduced sweeping economic reforms in 1991, it also embarked on a plan to address India's dire shortfall in electricity, which the national government recognized would only worsen with the economic growth it had planned. In 1993, the Congress Party-led central government placed eight power projects on a "fast-track" program and opened the projects, worth a total of almost U.S. $8 billion and representing over 4,000 megawatts of installed capacity, to foreign investors. Rather than putting the fast-track projects to tender through an open competitive bidding process, however, the central government, anxious to avoid delay and maintain the smooth flow of foreign investment into India, negotiated the projects privately with select international power groups. The Dabhol project, originally a U.S. $2.8 billion, 2,015 megawatt liquid natural gas (LNG)-fired powerplant, to be built 180 kilometers south of Mumbai (ex-Bombay), in the state of Maharashtra, on India's west coast, is one of these "fast-track" projects.

As originally negotiated, the Dabhol project was a joint venture of three U.S. Sponsors, the Enron Development Corporation ("Enron"), which owned 80 percent of the project, General Electric Capital Services ("GECS") and Bechtel Enterprises, Inc. ("Bechtel"), each of whom owns 10 percent (collectively, the "Dabhol Sponsors"). Bechtel Power Corporation was to construct the Dabhol Powerplant, and affiliates of General Electric were to supply the equipment. Enron was to operate the plant upon completion. The electricity that the plant produces was to be sold to the Maharashtra State Electricity Board ("MSEB") under a 20-year power purchase agreement. Dabhol was funded by a commercial bank syndicate led by Bank of America and ABN Amro, which provided U.S. $150 million; OPIC provided U.S. $100 million; the United States Export-Import Bank provided U.S. $298 million, based on a guarantee from a group of Indian financial institutions led by the Industrial Development Bank of India ("IDBI"); additionally, IDBI was the lead arranger for a rupee loan equaling U.S. $96 million. The remaining costs would be funded by the Dabhol Sponsors through owners' equity, in amounts correlating to their respective ownership interests. Enron, however, encountered problems with the deal in the spring of 1995, after it had received its financing, and initial construction of the project had begun.

In India, electricity is managed mostly on a state level by the State Electricity Boards (SEBs), which for the most part, are inefficient political animals. SEBs, for instance, subsidize the cost of producing electricity. In India, the SEBs maintain low electricity prices to keep local voters, particularly, the farmers, happy. SEBs also are a big source of political patronage. A conflict exists, thus, between the central government, which is charged with setting India's national power policy, and the various state governments, which must implement that policy through the SEBs.

The Dabhol project became a hotly contested issue in the Maharashtra state elections in March 1995. During the state election campaign, two Hindu-nationalist parties, Shiv Sena and the Bharatiya Janata Party (BJP), ran against the incumbent Congress on an anti-foreign platform that targeted the Dabhol project, specifically. The Shiv Sena-BJP Alliance, alleging that the project was "too costly, 'corruptly' negotiated and environmentally unfriendly," went on to win the state elections. Upon taking office, the new Maharashtra government "scrapped" the project.

Enron entered into negotiations with the new government immediately and seemed on the verge of reaching an agreement with the MSEB in June 1995, when the U.S. Energy Department, at Enron's prompting, threatened India with economic sanctions if the Maharashtra government did not live up to its bargain. Outraged by what it perceived as foreign economic imperialism, the MSEB immediately canceled all further negotiations with Enron. In October 1995, however, after suffering several public setbacks, and recognizing that public opinion had shifted in favor of increasing the amount of available electricity, the Alliance reversed its policy on Dabhol and resumed negotiations with Enron. In June 1996, a renegotiated agreement was signed by the MSEB and the Dabhol Sponsors, which provided for a reduction in the project's cost to U.S. $2.5 billion, and an increase in its total power output to 2,184 megawatts. Changes also were made to the project structure. Under the renegotiated agreement, the MSEB was given a 30% interest in the Dabhol Power Company, reducing Enron's share accordingly, to 50%.

On December 2, 1996, the Bombay High Court dismissed the final lawsuit against the Dabhol Power Company. Construction has since resumed on Phase I of the Dabhol Power Project.

B. A Recipe for Disaster

The Dabhol crisis was unique in the sense that an unusual set of circumstances (some of which should have been apparent to the Dabhol Sponsors during negotiations), combined with Enron's own actions, created a recipe for disaster.

1. Conflicts Over Power Authority Between India's Central and State Governments

In Dabhol, the federalism conflict that existed (and still does) between India's central government and the SEBs presented jurisdictional tension, which is a big political risk factor. This risk might have been magnified when the central government issued counter-guarantees for the project loans. The guarantees would become effective in the event the MSEB failed to pay its obligations under the power purchase agreement. This arrangement was problematic because the central government made it easier for the SEB to walk away from the deal. By delegating the authority to implement a power project to a state entity without retaining any control over the MSEB's ability to do so, and then issuing a guarantee on behalf of that entity, the central government eliminated a major economic incentive for the MSEB to see the project through to completion. Because the SEB was not required to cover the costs of its breach, it had nothing to lose by breaching, and everything to gain (in the form of obtaining more favorable terms from the sponsors). This power-sharing relationship was also dangerous because it placed implementation of the project into the hands of an entity that was more likely to fall under the influence of radical or extremist forces and, thus, buckle to local political pressure.

Looking back, one can understand easily why India's central government was desperate to avert disaster at Dabhol. Permanent cancellation of the project not only would have jeopardized future foreign investment in India, but because of the loan guarantees, the central government also would have had to repay whatever portion of the U.S. $644 million in financing had been expended — up to the point of cancellation — on construction of the first phase of Dabhol. Maharashtra's xenophobic state government, however, had no such constraints to hamper its actions.

2. Indian Distrust of Foreign Companies

Indians have a well-documented and deep-seated suspicion, and in some instances, an outright hostility, to foreign multinational companies, and what Indians view as economic imperialism. This attitude is, of course, a legacy of the British colonial period and the activities of companies such as the famous British East India Company. Such deeply entrenched views and suspicions meant that Dabhol faced an uphill battle from its start. In order to win over the Indian public successfully (or at least, the people of Maharashtra), Enron would have had to have behaved in a manner that dispelled any suspicions of aggressive economic expansion on its part. Unfortunately, Enron did the exact opposite.

3. Secret Negotiations Between Enron and the SEB

Although the Congress-led central government did not want to delay its fast-track projects with an open bid tendering process, conducting negotiations with Enron behind closed doors served to feed another ravenous Indian belief: the prevalence of systemic governmental corruption.

4. Rate Structure Analysis

The original agreement called for the Maharashtra SEB to pay the Dabhol Power Company a power tariff of Rs. 2.40 (rupees) per kilowatt hour (kW/h) of power. Renegotiation subsequent to the SEB's breach brought the tariff down to Rs. 1.86 per kilowatt hour. Nevertheless, this still is more than the Rs. 1.74 that the MSEB pays presently for its power, which it then turns around and supplies to Maharashtrans at drastically reduced prices. The SEBs, therefore, incur heavy losses in order to provide power to the public at reduced rates. These losses, in turn, are subsidized by the central government.

Private power projects such as Dabhol charge higher rates for the electricity they produce, because sponsors obviously are seeking to make a profit from their investment. Sponsors, however, will run into problems if they overcharge for power, because the SEBs will be able to subsidize only so much of the cost of power before they are forced to pass some of the added cost onto their customers (an action, which naturally, they are reluctant to undertake).

In the case of Dabhol, Enron became greedy and negotiated unreasonably high tariff rates in a blatant attempt to maximize Dabhol profit margins. The subsequent reduction in tariff rates that the more virulent BJP-Shiv Sena-dominated MSEB obtained from Enron in renegotiation tends to validate the view that Enron got greedy. The higher tariff rate Enron initially negotiated became a fundamental problem in Dabhol for two reasons. First, rather than serving as evidence of Enron's good faith, an exploitative tariff rate had the opposite effect. Second, the unreasonably high tariff rate gave opponents of the project a sound economic basis for opposing it.

5. Political Forces at Play

India's internal politics also were a driving force behind Dabhol's cancellation. The BJP decided that an anti-foreign campaign platform, capitalizing on Indian fears of foreign investment, would help it win the election in Maharashtra. To be sure, electoral showdowns between the Congress party and the Shiv Sena and BJP were neither new nor unforeseeable at the time. Historically, however, the BJP, had always been oriented towards a free market. Thus, a fair argument may be made that at the time Enron negotiated the Dabhol project, it could not have foreseen the BJP would seek to gain political advantage by opposing Dabhol (and foreign investment in India in general), in apposition to their traditional policy.

III. HOW DABHOL'S POLITICAL RISK COULD HAVE BEEN MINIMIZED FURTHER

"The terrain is to be assessed in terms of distance, difficulty or ease of travel, dimension, and safety."[4]

To manage political risk effectively, the essential first step is identifying where the risk lies, and what will exacerbate or ameliorate the occurrence of a political risk event. Once identified, the second step is to address the political risk, either by minimizing it, limiting it, or hedging against it. After addressing political risk, the final step is to control any adverse effects which may occur if the political risk is addressed insufficiently or incompletely in the second stage.

A. Identification of Political Risk.

Identification of political risk is accomplished by examining four independent factors that affect political pressure: the history of the host country, the internal political and economic climate of the host country, the role of the host country in the global political economy, and the effect of the host country's legal regime upon the sponsor-host government relationship. By analyzing these four areas, project participants can gauge more accurately the amount of political pressure they can expect their project to encounter in the host country.

1. History of the Host Country

A thorough analysis of a host country's history is vital in planning a project financing, simply because it reveals much about how project participants should behave in the host country. Ignoring a host country's history can lead to missteps that may anger the public and help give birth to political pressure.

Studying the host country's history also provides sponsors with a valuable perspective on the host country, and how its citizens view them. The salient point being that old beliefs and suspicions, especially those ingrained in a nation's character, die hard. Ethnic atrocities in the former Yugoslavia, tribal strife in Central and Eastern Africa and continuing tensions in the Middle East all demonstrate that historical rivalries based on nationalistic or ethnic lines persist. One would be extraordinarily naive to think that such beliefs and suspicions do not carry over into the realm of international commerce.

Enron's actions in Dabhol, betrayed a general ignorance of India's history and prevailing mores. For instance, the "legacy of the [British] East India Company, coupled with Gandhian distaste for foreign corporate control, has left Indians with a deep suspicion of [foreign] investment." Had Enron minded the prevailing prejudice in India against foreign investment and undertaken measures to diminish or even contain it, then most likely Dabhol would have encountered far less political pressure than it did. Instead, as one of Enron's critics pointed out, the Company "behaved in what appeared to many Indians to be an arrogant colonialist manner."

Indians came to view Enron as a malicious aggressor for two reasons. First, Enron elected not to involve a local Indian partner in the project, a step which would have built local support and helped allay fears of foreign expansion. Second, the closed nature of the project negotiations, although initiated by the Indian government, gave birth to suspicions of improper dealing. Finally, and perhaps most dam-

---

4. SUN TZU, THE ART OF WAR 44 (Shambhala Dragon ed., transl. by Thomas Cleary, 1988).

aging, the threat of the United States Department of Energy of economic retaliation angered many Indians who previously had supported the project, and put a swift end to the negotiation sessions.

These missteps allowed the BJP/Shiv Sena Alliance to portray Enron as a "rapacious predator," mobilize the public against the Dabhol project, and eventually cancel the contract outright.

2. Internal Political and Economic Climate of the Host Country

An understanding of the current political climate is important because sponsors need to know what the host country's sentiments are towards a project and foreign investment. Expropriation is an obvious risk, however, the negative effects of indirect governmental actions, such as tax increases or demands for equity participation, are more difficult to predict without a careful analysis of the local political climate. If, for example, a robust opposition party adopts a strong policy opposing a particular project, then the sponsors may want to consider withdrawing from the project, if that opposition party is capable of making a change in the host country's political environment (either through common political discourse or a change in government). Similarly, even a strong governing party firmly in control of the government can present a similar danger if it is composed of different internal factions, each pursuing conflicting agendas. A recent example of this occurred in Colombia, with the Termobarranquilla power project, which was also sponsored by Enron. In that situation, internal bidding over power tariff rates led the Colombian government to "meddle" with the price of power in that project. The Colombian government also revoked the project's tax exemptions. Enron, frustrated ultimately by the level of government interference, pulled out of the project.

A less drastic alternative to withdrawal is for sponsors to negotiate an agreement with the host government that, in the words of Rebecca Mark, Chairman and Chief Executive Officer of Enron Development Corporation, "makes it as painful as possible for any party to walk out of [the] deal." Of course, the more unstable the political situation, the more "painful" the penalties of cancellation shall need to be.

Sponsors and lenders, however, must be aware that this option is an imperfect solution because it also can increase the political risk. As participants attempt to decrease political risk by negotiating stiffer penalties for a breach by the government, the externalities of the project will increase, thus, raising the cost of the project. Higher project costs increase the likelihood of public opposition to the project, which in turn, increases the political risk. Additionally, the host government, though obligated by contract to pay penalties for breach, in fact may not be able to pay these penalties.

Participants, therefore, need to be keenly aware of the political climate in order to plan their negotiation strategy and project structure effectively, and be able to strike the proper balance between the cost of the project, and the penalties for breach.

Knowledge of the domestic economic climate of the country also is important. Sponsors need to know whether the price or tariff, the public is willing and capable of paying for the product (or service) that the project produces will be enough to service the project's debt. For the most part, the analysis of the host country's economic situation is conducted in the formal project feasibility study undertaken in the first stage of project development.

As discussed above, sponsors enter into product purchase agreements to limit market and operating risk as much as possible. Proper economic analysis will provide insight on the prices the public is willing or expects to pay for the project's product, and whether the sponsors' or the lenders' anticipated tariff structure is too high.

3. Role of the Host Country in the Global Political Economy

Political risk management of a project must not be restricted only to the political risk presented within the host country ("internal political risk"), because a project also can be jeopardized by certain events occurring outside the host country ("external political risk"). External political risk is manifested, for example, by war, trade embargoes, international treaties, and generally, by the state of relations between the home country (or countries) of the various participants and the host country.

In 1995, for instance, the United States government prohibited the Export-Import Bank from conducting business in Colombia, (whose investment grading made it then, and still makes it, an attractive country for private financing) because the Clinton Administration decided that Colombia was not making an earnest effort to reduce drug trafficking. Because American sponsors (such as Enron, General Electric, and Westinghouse) are dependent upon Ex-Im Bank financing to complete a project financing, several American-sponsored projects in Colombia had to be abandoned.

4. Effect of the Host Country's Legal Regime upon the Sponsor-Host Government Relationship

Any international project financing, by its nature, will touch upon many different areas of law. As discussed earlier, because a project financing is structured on a series of interrelated contracts, obviously, it must involve contract law. A host country's contract law, however, rarely will govern the major project agreements, because participants usually designate the law of another jurisdiction, usually New York or England because of their well-developed commercial laws, through a choice-of-law provision as the governing law. Environmental, labor, social and tax laws, however, are all examples of the laws of a host country that can have a substantial impact on the success or failure of a project.

Environmental law, in particular, often presents a major legal concern for sponsors and lenders. Infrastructure projects involving such endeavors as resource extraction, highway or airport construction, and energy development, all have significant (though not necessarily adverse) environmental impacts. Environmental regulation is a particularly tricky problem because, by its very nature, it is a dynamic regime. Environmental law develops constantly, evolving as a result of technological innovations, new understanding of what causes environmental damage, and new methods of dealing with those causes.

In modern industrialized countries, unforeseen environmental opposition to a project is considered a major political risk facing sponsors and lenders. Similarly, though environmental law in most LDCs is non-existent, or nascent at best, nevertheless, this is changing. As more LDCs begin creating their own environmental regimes, participants no longer are able to assume that projects undertaken in the developing world will be free from the burdens of complying with environmental regulation. The dynamic nature of environmental law and the adverse financial impact it can have on a project require sponsors to "lock-in" or stabilize environmental regulations prior to construction, to protect the project from revisions and developments in the environmental regime of the host country.

At the negotiation stage of a project financing, sponsors enjoy a superior bargaining position because the host government is anxious to attract foreign investment. Sponsors, therefore, need to be familiar with the laws of the host country, to devise a coordinated and effective negotiation strategy that will enable them to stabilize the various laws and regulations that can affect their project.

B. Addressing Political Risk

Political risk in international project finance ought to be addressed in four ways. First, political opposition to a project should be minimized through the negotiation, structure and management of the project. Second, political risk should be limited contractually through the insertion of certain clauses in the project agreements. Third, several structural methods exist for spreading a project's political risk to additional parties, thus, lowering the overall exposure of lenders and sponsors. Finally, political risk should be hedged against by obtaining political risk insurance.

1. Minimizing Political Opposition in the Negotiation, Structure and Management of the Project

Political opposition to a project, the genesis of most political risk, should be minimized in the negotiation, structure and management of the project in three ways. The first method is by introducing more transparency into project negotiations and bidding. A second method relates to limiting the size of the project itself. Third, entering into local private partnerships with companies in the host country is an effective method of minimizing political opposition in the host country. Fourth, local public partnerships also help minimize political opposition to a project. Finally, project participants may limit some political opposition through effective management of public relations in the host country.

a. Transparency of Negotiations

In the past, many infrastructure projects were awarded through bids that lacked competition, and negotiations were conducted in processes that lacked transparency. Project participants are well-advised to steer clear of such bidding structures, simply for the reason that secret negotiations will produce a void of information on a project. Such a void serves only to plant doubts in the minds of the public about the project. These doubts, in turn, can easily be exploited by opponents of a project to stir up public opinion against the project. Two concerns most frequently associated with negotiations that lack competition or transparency are corruption and unfairness.

Throughout the world, many countries suffer governmental corruption. Closed bidding and negotiations between a host government and foreign developers can feed a public's distrust of government and give rise easily to public suspicion that a project has been negotiated corruptly.

Even if the negotiation process is not perceived to be corrupt, the closed nature of such negotiations can give rise to allegations of unfairness and charges that the host country's government is favoring foreign multinational corporations over domestic industry. Such allegations and public sentiment are dangerous, because they create an environment ripe for opposition parties to challenge the ruling government and raise questions about the necessity and legitimacy of a project (whether such is the case or not).

A major criticism of the Dabhol Project (also shared by the other "fast-track" power projects in India), has been the lack of transparency in the negotiation process. Observers have noted that the secret nature of the Dabhol project negotiations perpetuated popular Indian fears of government corruption and foreign imperialism. When Indians learned how much they would have to pay for Dabhol power, without any further information on the negotiations, they naturally viewed the deal as unfair.

Project negotiations must be open to public scrutiny, especially with respect to the expenditure of initial monies and the costs of the project. In other words, "[d]eals must be fair and be seen to be fair."

Admittedly, competitive bidding and more transparency may cause greater delays up front during the negotiation stage than a "fast-track" process will. Such steps, however, will help disarm some public fears concerning a project, thereby reducing the political risk, and in the long run, allowing the project to be completed more quickly.

b. Local Private Partnerships

Engaging local partners in the host country is a useful means of reducing political risk, and is also good business sense. For example, turning to local manufacturers for project components, often referred to as "outsourcing," can improve a sponsor's chances of winning the project contract. Adding a reputable local partner also gives sponsors a better understanding of local markets and regulations. Finally, by involving local companies sponsors spread the local economic benefits of a project and help build local support by dispelling the possible public perceptions of foreign economic imperialism that often accompany a project.

In structuring the Dabhol project, Enron did not make any attempt to involve a local partner, a fact which critics allege jeopardized the success of the project. Whether engaging a local partner in Dabhol would have avoided some of the problems that the project encountered is impossible to say for certain, nevertheless, a comparison with a contemporaneous, American-sponsored power plant project in the South Indian state of Andhra Pradesh, which did involve a local partner, is illuminating.

The other project, built near the city of Rajahmundry, was sponsored jointly by CMS Energy of Dearborn, Michigan and GVK Industries Ltd., which is based in Hyderabad, Andhra Pradesh's capital. Construction on the Rajahmundry project began in early 1995, roughly at the same time as Dabhol, however, the Rajahmundry project's success stands in stark contrast to Dabhol's problems. The Rajahmundry project was generating electricity by July 1996, and became fully operational in June 1997. A large part of the credit for that project's success has been attributed to GVK's chairman, G.V. Krishna Reddy, whose contacts in Andhra Pradesh and experience with India's mammoth bureaucracies, as well as his Indian citizenship, kept the project away from many of the political risks that sidelined Dabhol.

c. Local Public Partnerships

Engaging the host government as a partner in the project reduces the political risk and the chances of interference, because it gives the host government a vested interest in the success of the project. Government support for a project not only leads to more effective risk sharing, but also can expedite the completion of a project.

One public partnership option is to structure a project on the Build-Operate-Transfer (B-O-T) model. A B-O-T structure usually is based on a concession agreement (essentially, a licensing agreement) between the host government, or a host government agency, and the project company to develop and construct the project, and then to operate the project for a certain period of time. At the conclusion of the initial operation period, the project company transfers the project back to the state authority that granted it the concession.

Under the original project structure, the MSEB was not a partner in the Dabhol project, nor was the project structured on the B-O-T model. Aside from the unfounded allegations of corrupt negotiation, another charge brought against Enron and Dabhol was that the power tariff structure (*i.e.*, the negotiated rate at which the MSEB is required to purchase power from the DPC under a power purchase agreement) was too high and exploited the MSEB unfairly. Such a charge would have been difficult to make, however, had the MSEB been an equity partner in the Dabhol Power Company at the beginning of the project. In the spring of 1997, subsequent to renegotiations, the MSEB obtained a 30 percent equity stake in the DPC, reducing Enron's stake to 50 percent, and a 25 percent drop in the price of power.

d. Size of the Project

The size of a project can determine whether a project will encounter political opposition and, if so, to what degree. Generally speaking, "smaller projects... are simpler to negotiate, easier to build and less risky—as opposed to mega-projects such as Paiton and Dabhol... which world financiers find tricky to digest." The reason for this is that a small project has lower visibility, making it less likely to be noticed and, ultimately, made a target of public opposition.

As discussed above, Dabhol is a massive project, and as such quickly became a lightning rod for anti-foreign sentiment. Whether the Dabhol project would have escaped controversy had it been planned as a U.S. $300 million, 235 megawatt power plant is hard to say. Enron's behavior also bears a large portion of the blame for Dabhol's problems. Dabhol's mammoth size gave it a high profile, which, doubtless, would have engendered fierce opposition in any event.

Often, the size of a particular project will be dictated by the needs of the host country and the policies of the host government. Lenders, however, are warier of larger projects because of the increased political risk they present, and the externality of managing the increased risk of larger project will raise the cost of financing that project.

e. Effective Management of Public Relations

Effective management of public relations takes two forms. The first form is more strategic, involving the adoption of an inconspicuous management structure, unobtrusive operations, and the creation of domestic equity. The goal of this strategy is to create a perception of "fairness" and "domestic benefit" embodied by the project.

The second form entails the creation of an organized public relations campaign to promote a project. The value of a carefully designed public relations campaign has long been recognized in other types of financial transactions, such as domestic mergers and acquisitions. Yet, international project financings, for the most part, have not involved extensive public relations programs. In light of the potential pejorative effects of political opposition to a project in a host country, especially a large high-visibility project such as Dabhol, sponsors ought to engage a highly competent, possibly local, public relations consultant. In many instances, a project may have to be "sold" to a host country's public. Sponsors need to market and present their projects effectively. A public relations consultant located in the host country is sure to be familiar with the public attitude toward foreign investment, and will be best-placed to organize an effective information campaign aimed at dispelling local fears and uncertainties about a project. Finally, as discussed earlier, it is sometimes best that a project maintain a low profile in the host country. Again, a local public relations consultant is best-placed, with respect to local media contacts and expertise, to accomplish that goal.

Subsequent events demonstrated that Enron's efforts to educate Maharashtrans about the benefits of the Dabhol project were woefully inadequate. Even Enron officials have admitted "with hindsight, that perhaps more information should have been provided to win over the hearts and minds of Maharashtrans." One of the lessons to be gleaned from the Dabhol transaction is that, at least for large high-visibility projects, sponsors must manage their relations with the host country's public constructively. Sponsors are well-advised to craft an information campaign, in consultation with local experts, that effectively conveys the benefits of the project to the host country's citizens.

2. Limiting Political Risk Through Contract

Political risk in a project finance ought to be limited through the use of two contractual mechanisms. The first is to obtain guarantees from the host government for some of the project loans. A second method, for high-risk LDCs with evanescent legal or regulatory regimes, is to include stabilization clauses in the project agreements.

a. Government Loan Guarantees

Government, or sovereign, guarantees can be an effective method of limiting the effects of political risk. A government guarantee is a way of assuring sponsors and lenders that "certain events within the government's control will or will not occur." Essentially, a government loan guarantee will cover debt service defaults resulting from the host government's failure to comply with its contractual obligations.

In a host country where both the national and state governments share authority over a project and where action by either of them can occasion a debt service default, sponsors and lenders are advised either to obtain loan guarantees from both entities, or persuade the national government to incorporate actions by the state government into its guarantee. With the latter alternative, sponsors and lenders should ascertain whether the national government is capable of ensuring that the state government will live up to its obligations, otherwise, the state government will be insulated from liability for its actions—to the detriment of both the national government and project participants.

Finally, because service of debt in project finance relies upon the income stream generated by sales of a project's product or service, a government guarantee may require the government to stimulate investment in an area where market demand for that good or service is uncertain.

In high-risk projects, lenders generally require some manner of government guarantee in order to make the project "bankable." In some instances, where a project is "well-structured," involves a "creditworthy" off-take purchaser with a "good track record of meeting debt-service commitments," and the host country's political and economic environment is "favorable," lenders may not require a government guarantee.

The Dabhol crisis demonstrates the importance of obtaining government loan guarantees in high-risk project financing. In the Dabhol project, Enron obtained performance guarantees from the State of Maharashtra to guarantee payment by the MSEB, of power tariffs in the event the MSEB was unable to meet its obligations under the power purchase agreement. The Government of India also guaranteed the State of Maharashtra's payment. By guaranteeing an income stream for the project, these guarantees effectively ensured payment of the project loans. In the long run, the Government guarantees made scrapping the Dabhol project extremely painful for the MSEB, because it committed the MSEB, willy-nilly, to make tariff payments to the DPC until the financing expended on the initial construction of the first phase of the project was paid off. The government loan guarantees may have provided one economic incentive for the state government to keep the window of renegotiation open.

b. Stabilization Clauses

A modern stabilization clause simply is "a risk-allocation provision" whereby a state company (that is to say, a company that is wholly- or partially-owned by the host government, such as PEMEX, Mexico's national petroleum company, or CODELCO, Chile's national copper company) indemnifies a foreign contractor for any increased project expenses resulting from government legislation passed subsequent to the execution of the project agreements (for example, tougher environmental regulations). A stabilization clause may include an assurance against government expropriation of the project, though such assurances are not standard. The specific method of compensation can take several forms, including: (1) discounting payments that a contractor may owe to the state company by the amount of additional expenses that arise from the subsequent legislation; (2) counter-payments from the state company to the contractor that correspond to the increased expenses; or (3) reduction of tax liability.

Stabilization clauses, however, do present significant problems for sponsors, and are by no means foolproof. If the host country's government changes a particular regime, for instance, the range of a sponsor's claims for remuneration of expenses caused by that change are limited to the specific terms articulated in the stabilization clause. Furthermore, the range of claims available to a sponsor may be even narrower if the state company is one of limited liability.

If the host country's government makes a change in a law that is covered by a stabilization clause, the sponsor can exercise its right of recompensation under the project agreements against the state company. Although the sponsor may have a valid claim, nevertheless, a host government can still find ways of avoiding payment. One way the host government can accomplish this is by means of a "creeping expropriation." A creeping expropriation occurs when the host government taxes the state company so heavily that it eliminates that company's capital and, thus, its ability to recompense the foreign contractor under the stabilization clause. Because the state company (and not the host government specifically) owes the sponsor the duty to pay for any change in law, the host government, by syphoning funds out of the state company, effectively avoids its obligation under the stabilization clause.

Alternatively, selecting a reduction in the sponsor's tax liability as the method of compensation may not necessarily cover fully the added costs to the sponsor of the change in legislation. Also, the host government can elect to annul the contract between the state company and the sponsor. In such a situation, a sponsor's options for recovery of added costs are limited to arbitration, diplomatic remedies, and other forms of international law remedies.

3. Spreading Political Risk

Two fundamental principles underlie the strategy of spreading political risk. The first principle, and the most obvious, is that spreading risk reduces a participant's individual exposure to political risk. The second principle of political risk spreading is that political risk is deterred by the existence of greater bargaining power. An effective risk-spreading strategy spreads political risk across a wide spectrum of participants, presenting a "united front" against an "interventionist host country", and giving participants greater bargaining power than an individual actor or smaller group of participants.

As suggested above, one effective method of spreading political risk is by creating a wide breadth of international involvement. By bringing in suppliers and contractors from as many countries that trade with the host country as possible, the sponsors increase their leverage with the host government, because the host government will be disinclined to allow problems with the project to damage its trade relations with its trading countries.

A related method of risk spreading involves the syndication of project loans. Drawing together a broad syndicate of lenders accomplishes both principles of risk spreading. First, it takes a large, quantified amount of risk (*i.e.*, the total loan amount), breaks it down into smaller amounts, which are then taken on by each lender in the syndicate. Breaking down the loan, thus, reduces each lender's overall risk exposure to its portion of the loan only. Second, by syndicating a loan, the sponsors and primary lenders are increasing the representation and involvement of host country trading partners (in the form of lenders) that can be affected adversely by a default, which may help reduce the chance of default or breach by the host government.

A third method of spreading risk is to obtain multilateral development bank guarantees with partners. A multilateral development bank is an international, nongovernmental organization whose purpose is to support investment in developing countries. Examples of multilateral development banks include The World Bank Group (the International Bank for Reconstruction and Development (IBRD), the International Development Agency (IDA), the International Finance Corporation (IFC), and MIGA), the Asian Development Bank (ADB), and the European Bank for Reconstruction and Development (EBRD).

The World Bank provides partial risk guarantees for risks that the international insurance markets either will not bear, or will make prohibitively expensive. A World Bank partial risk guarantee covers the lenders from the "risks arising from nonperformance of sovereign contractual obligations...in a project." In exchange for its coverage, the World Bank will obtain an indemnity (or a counter-guarantee) from the host country for any payments it makes under its guarantee. The World Bank will also charge a fee for its guarantees, which is payable by either the project company or the lenders. The World Bank's participation through the International Finance Corporation (IFC) ensures that necessary export credit financing can be obtained, lowers the costs of financing, and decreases the risk to investors and lenders. The risk guarantees and involvement of the EBRD are essentially similar to those of the World Bank.

Spreading risk to multilateral development banks is effective particularly because multilateral investment agencies carry a great deal of clout with LDCs, as they are often the only lenders willing to extend credit to such countries. A host government is less likely to breach its obligations in a project if, by doing so, it may jeopardize its ability to borrow from a multilateral development bank in the future.

A related method to involving multilateral development agencies is to spread risk also to export credit agencies. An export credit agency is a government agency that provides export credit loans or guarantees and absorbs export credit risks that will not be covered by the private insurance market. Examples of export credit agencies include the United States Ex-Im Bank and OPIC, the Export-Import Bank of Japan (JEXIM), and Britain's Export Credit Guarantee Department (ECGD). An export credit agency is a governmental organization in the home country of one or more of the sponsors or a country of export, which involves that government, at least indirectly, in the project.

A fourth method for sponsors and lenders to spread political risk, as well as an increasingly popular means of raising project financing, is through a private placement of debt, in the name of the project company, in the United States, under Rule 144A. Rule 144A, promulgated by the SEC in 1990, exempts certain types of securities offerings from the registration requirements of the 1933 Securities Act. The "catch" is that the securities can neither be sold nor offered to the general public in the United States. They may be offered and sold, however, to large financial institutions, classified as "qualified institutional buyers" (QIBs).

One of the first Rule 144A debt offerings for a project financing occurred in 1993. A U.S. $105 million offering of secured notes to help finance the Enron-sponsored Subic Power Corporation, a 113.4 megawatt power project in the Philippines. By the end of 1996, more than U.S. $1.3 billion of project financing had been raised from the Rule 144A market. A Rule 144A debt offering operates as a political risk spreading measure in much the same way as the syndication of a project loan. Essentially, the sponsors and lenders merely are apportioning a share of the risk to another group of lenders: institutional investors.

A U.S. $150 million Rule 144A offering was contemplated as a means of raising financing for Dabhol. A decrease in international interest associated with the Mexican peso crisis of the early 1990s, however, scuttled Enron's efforts to float a Rule 144A offering. Enron arranged alternative means of financing through its lead lenders, Bank of America and ABN AMRO.

4. Hedging Against Political Risk through Political Risk Insurance

Project participants should consider arranging to hedge against the impact of political risk by obtaining political risk insurance through export credit agencies, such as OPIC, or possibly a multilateral development agency. OPIC is a self-sustaining government corporation, which provides trade and foreign investment insurance and investment for American companies that is unavailable from the private markets. OPIC's total insurance portfolio limit is U.S. $13.5 billion, and it is authorized to lend up to U.S. $9.5 billion.

The mainstay of OPIC's insurance program is political risk insurance. OPIC provides political risk insurance for project financing, but subject to several conditions. First, although OPIC does not require that a foreign project be entirely owned or controlled by American investors in order to be insured, it only provides political risk insurance for the American portion of that project. Additionally, it only provides loan insurance for projects in which the majority of the project is owned by American investors. A second requirement is that the United States government and the host country must have a favorable relationship, and the host country must have executed a bilateral agreement with OPIC. At present OPIC programs are available in over 140 countries. OPIC also examines various factors relating to a project's impact on the host country, including, contribution to development, environmental impact, worker's rights, host government participation in the project, and the specific industrial sector relating to the project.

Political risk insurance also may be obtained from other export credit agencies, such as Ex-Im Bank and ECGD, among others; private insurers, such as American International Group, Inc. (AIG); and from some multilateral development agencies.

C. Damage Control: Staving Off Disaster in an Adverse Political Climate

Despite an effective political risk management strategy, some projects cannot avoid political risk. When a political risk event occurs, sponsors and lenders naturally will attempt to surmount the obstacle to a project's success. There are at least three methods to resolve disputes in an international project financing. The first is the creation of operating committees, comprised of project participants, to resolve disputes internally. A second method is to renegotiate the project to attempt to eliminate the source of the dispute. The final method is to submit to international commercial arbitration.

1. Operating Committees to Handle Disputes Among Participants Internally

The establishment of an operating committee within a project structure, as a means of resolving disputes, has several benefits. First, operating committees are comprised of representatives from both the host government and the investors, thus, all of the members of an operating committee are intimately familiar with the structure of a project and its surrounding issues. Second, having worked on the project itself, they are already accustomed to working together as a formal group. Finally, having worked on the project, the members of an operating committee ultimately want to see the success of a project, and have an incentive to resolve project disputes. A final benefit is that operating committees can reduce the costs of a delay, because they avoid expensive litigation.

2. Renegotiation

Ultimately, this may be what the host government is seeking when it breaches a project agreement or passes a new law that impacts a project negatively. As mentioned above, renegotiation is a cost of the "obsolescing bargain." As the Dabhol transaction demonstrates, sponsors and lenders are well-advised to attempt to learn whether a host government finds certain previously agreed-upon project terms objectionable, and attempt to renegotiate the project agreements. This tactic, along with the strong support that Enron received from its lenders, is what saved the Dabhol project from disaster.

3. International Commercial Arbitration

A final option for sponsors and lenders prior to litigating claims against a host government, is to seek a resolution of the project dispute in an international commercial arbitration hearing. Various arbitration tribunals exist in which sponsors and lenders can proceed to obtain a judgement. Among the tribunals are the American Arbitration Association (AAA), the International Chamber of Commerce (ICC), the London Courts of International Arbitration (LCIA), the Stockholm Chamber of Commerce, the United Nations Commission on International Trade Law (UNCITRAL), the Inter-American Commercial Arbitration Commission (IACAC), and the International Center for Specialized Investment Disputes (ICSID).

Conclusion

The lesson to be learned from the Dabhol project is that to be effective, political risk management must occur on three distinct levels. First, steps should be taken to rein in the forces that trigger political risk events and disperse the adverse impact that a project will have on these forces. Second, devices should be employed to minimize the effect that political risk events will have on the project, should they occur. Finally, dispute resolution contingencies should be negotiated up front to revive a project in the event its existence is threatened by a political risk event.

Chapter 8

Currency Risk

I. Foreign Exchange Markets and Rates

Francesco Caramazza and Jahangir Aziz, Fixed or Flexible?
1-11, 13 (International Monetary Fund 1998)

Analysts agree that "getting the exchange rate right" is essential for economic stability and growth in developing countries. Over the past two decades, many developing countries have shifted away from *fixed* exchange rates (that is, those that peg the domestic currency to one or more foreign currencies) and moved toward more *flexible* exchange rates (those that determine the external value of a currency more or less by the market supply and demand for it). During a period of rapid economic growth, driven by the twin forces of globalization and liberalization of markets and trade, this shift seems to have served a number of countries well. But as the currency market turmoil in Southeast Asia has dramatically demonstrated, globalization can amplify the costs of inappropriate policies. Moreover, the challenges facing countries may change over time, suggesting a need to adapt exchange rate policy to changing circumstances.

. . . .

From Fixed to Flexible

A Brief History

The shift from fixed to more flexible exchange rates has been gradual, dating from the breakdown of the Bretton Woods system of fixed exchange rates in the early 1970s, when the world's major currencies began to float. At first, most developing countries continued to peg their exchange rates-either to a single key currency, usually the U.S. dollar or French franc, or to a basket of currencies. By the later 1970s, they began to shift from single currency pegs to basket pegs, such as to the IMF's special drawing right (SDR). Since the early 1980s, however, developing countries have shifted away from currency pegs toward explicitly more flexible exchange rate arrangements.... This shift has occurred in most of the world's major geographic regions.

Back in 1975, for example, 87 percent of developing countries had some type of pegged exchange rate. By 1996, this proportion had fallen to well below 50 percent. When the relative size of economies is taken into account, the shift is even more pronounced. In 1975, countries with pegged rates accounted for 70 percent of the developing world's total trade; by 1996, this figure had dropped to about 20 percent. The overall trend is clear, though it is probably less pronounced than these figures indicate because many countries that officially describe their exchange rate regimes as "managed floating" or even "independently floating" in practice often continue to set their rate unofficially or use it as a policy instrument.

Several important exceptions must be mentioned. A prime example is the CFA franc zone in sub-Saharan Africa, where some 14 countries have pegged their rate to the French franc since 1948—with one substantial devaluation in 1994. In addition, some countries have reverted, against the trend, from flexible to fixed rate regimes. These include Argentina, which adopted a type of currency-board arrangement in 1991, and Hong Kong SAR (Special Administrative Region), which has had a similar arrangement since 1983.

Nevertheless, the general shift from fixed to flexible has been broadly based worldwide. In 1976, pegged rate regimes were the norm in Africa, Asia, the Middle east, nonindustrial Europe, and the Western Hemisphere. By 1996, flexible exchange rate regimes predominated in all these regions.

Why the Shift?

The considerations that have led countries to shift toward more flexible exchange rate arrangements vary widely; also, the shift did not happen all at once. When the Bretton Woods fixed rate system broke down in 1973, many countries continued to peg to the same currency they had pegged to before, often on simple historical grounds. It was only later, when major currencies moved sharply in value, that countries started to abandon these single-currency pegs. Many countries that traditionally pegged to the U.S. dollar, for instance, adopted a basket approach during the first half of the 1980s, in large part because the dollar was appreciating rapidly.

Another key element was the rapid acceleration of inflation in many developing countries during the 1980s. Countries with inflation rates higher than their main trading partners often depreciated their currencies to prevent a severe loss of competitiveness. This led many countries in the Western Hemisphere, in particular, to adopt "crawling pegs," whereby exchange rates could be adjusted according to such pre-set criteria as relative changes in the rate of inflation. Later, some countries that suffered very high rates of inflation shifted back to a pegged exchange rate as a central element of their stabilization efforts. (These exchange-rate-based stabilization programs have typically been short-lived, with the median duration of a peg about 10 months.)

Many developing countries have also experienced a series of external shocks. In the 1980s, these included a steep rise in international interest rates, a slowdown of growth in the industrial world, and the debt crisis. Often, adjustment to these disturbances required not only discrete currency depreciations but also the adoption of more flexible exchange rate arrangements. In recent years, increased capital mobility and, in particular, waves of capital inflows and outflows have heightened the potential for shocks and increased pressures for flexibility.

The trend toward greater exchange rate flexibility has been associated with more open, outward-looking policies on trade and investment generally and increased emphasis on market-determined exchange rates and interest rates. As a practical matter, however, most developing countries are still not well-placed to allow their exchange rates to float totally freely. Many have small and relatively thin financial markets, where a few large transactions can cause extreme volatility. Thus, active management is still widely needed to help guide the market. In these circumstances, a key issue for the authorities is where and when to make policy adjustments—including the use of official intervention to help avoid substantial volatility and serious misalignments.

Macroeconomic Performance Under Different Regimes

Neither of the two main exchange regimes—fixed or flexible—ranks above the other in terms of its implications for macroeconomic performance. Although in previous years inflation appeared consistently lower and less volatile in countries with pegged exchange rates, in the 1990s the difference has narrowed substantially. Output growth also does not seem to differ across exchange rate regimes. While the median growth rate in countries with flexible exchange rates has recently appeared higher than in those with pegged rates, that result reflects the inclusion of the rapidly growing Asian countries in the "flexible" category; yet many of these countries in practice have operated a tightly managed policy. When these countries are excluded, growth performance does not differ significantly between the two sets of countries.

Evidence also suggests that, contrary to conventional wisdom, misalignments and currency "crashes" are equally likely under pegged and flexible exchange rate regimes. Indeed, in 116 separate cases between 1975 and 1996-where an exchange rate fell at least 25 percent within a year—nearly half were under flexible regimes. For both types, there was a large cluster of such crashes during the period immediately following the debt crisis of 1982. In part, this may reflect the fact that relatively few developing countries have truly floating exchange rates—and that, even if they had an officially declared flexible rate policy, they were often in practice pursuing an unofficial "target" rate that was then abandoned.

Choosing a Regime

The early literature on the choice of exchange rate regime took the view that the smaller and more "open" an economy (that is, the more dependent on exports and imports), the better it is served by a fixed exchange rate. A later approach to the choice of exchange rate regime looks at the effects of various random disturbances on the domestic economy. In this framework the best regime is the one that stabilizes macroeconomic performance, that is, minimizes fluctuations in output, consumption, the domestic price level, or some other macroeconomic variable. The ranking of fixed and flexible exchange rate regimes depends on the nature and source of the shocks to the economy, policymakers' preferences (that is, the type of costs they wish to minimize), and the structural characteristics of the economy.

In an extension of this approach, economists have viewed the policymaker's decision not simply as a choice between a purely fixed and a purely floating exchange rate but as a range of choices with varying degrees of flexibility. In general, a fixed exchange rate (or a greater degree of fixity) is preferable if the disturbances impinging on the economy are predominantly monetary—such as changes in the demand for money—and thus affect the general level of prices. A flexible rate (or a greater degree of flexibility) is preferable if disturbances are predominantly real—such as changes in tastes or technology that affect the relative prices of domestic goods—or originate abroad.

Credibility Versus Flexibility

In the 1990s another strand of analysis has focused on the credibility that authorities can gain under a fixed regime. Some argue that adopting a pegged exchange rate—by providing an unambiguous objective "anchor" for economic policy—can help establish the credibility of a program to bring down inflation. The reasons for this seem intuitively obvious. In fixed regimes, monetary policy must be subordinated to the requirements of maintaining the peg. This in turn means that other key aspects of policy, including fiscal policy, mut be kept consistent with the peg, effectively "tying the hands" of the authorities. A country trying to maintain a peg may not, for example, be able to increase its borrowing through the bond market because this may affect interest rates and, hence, put pressure on the exchange rate peg.

So long as the fixed rate is credible (that is, the market believes it can and will be maintained), *expectations* of inflation will be restrained—a major cause of chronic inflation. The risk is, of course, that the peg becomes unsustainable if confidence in the authorities' willingness or ability to maintain it is lost.

A flexible exchange rate provides greater room for maneuver in a variety of ways. Not least, it leaves the authorities free to allow inflation to rise—which is also a way, indirectly, to increase tax revenue. The danger here is that it will probably be harder to establish that there is a credible policy to control inflation—and expectations of higher inflation often become self-fulfilling.

But the discipline of a pegged exchange rate need not necessarily be greater. Even with a peg, the authorities still retain some flexibility, such as an ability to shift the inflationary cost of running fiscal deficits into the future. Ways to do this include allowing international reserves to diminish, or allowing external debt to accumulate until the peg can no longer be sustained. In a more flexible regime, the costs of an unsustainable policy may be revealed more quickly—through widely observed movements in exchange rates and prices. If this is the case, then a flexible regime may exert an even stronger discipline policy. In any event, a policymaker's commitment to a peg may not be credible for long if the economy is not functioning successfully. For example, maintaining interest rates at very high levels to defend the exchange rate may over time undermine the credibility of the peg—especially if it has damaging effects on real activity or the health of the banking system.

In many cases, the apparent trade-off between credibility and flexibility may depend not only on the economy but also on political considerations. For instance, it may be more costly in political terms to adjust a pegged exchange rate than to allow a flexible rate to move gradually by a corresponding amount. Authorities must shoulder the responsibility for adjusting a peg, whereas movements in an exchange rate that is allowed, to some degree at least, to fluctuate in response to changes in the demand and supply for the currency can be attributed to market forces. When the political costs of exchange rate adjustments are high, a more flexible regime will likely be adopted.

Pegging: A Single Currency or Basket?

For those that do adopt an exchange rate anchor, a further choice is whether to peg to a single currency or to a basket of currencies. The choice hinges on both the degree of concentration of a country's trade with particular trading partners and the currencies in which its external debt is denominated. When the peg is to a single currency, fluctuations in the anchor currency against other currencies imply fluctuations in the exchange rate of the economy in question against those currencies. By pegging to a currency basket instead, a country can reduce the vulnerability of its economy to fluctuations in the values of the individual currencies in the basket. Thus, in a world of floating exchange rates among the major currencies, the case for a single currency peg is stronger if the peg is to the currency of the dominant trading partner. However, in come cases, a significant portion of the country's debt service may be denominated in other currencies. This may complicate the choice of a currency to which to peg.

Challenges Posed by Fast Growth and Capital Inflows

The successful development of an emerging market economy should, economists often conjecture, tend to result in an appreciation of the domestic currency in real (inflation-adjusted) terms. Such an appreciation over the long term has been evident in Korea, Taiwan Province of China, Singapore, Hong Kong SAR, and—to a lesser extent—Chile.

This relationship between economic growth and real appreciation is assumed to stem from a tendency for productivity growth in the manufacture of traded goods to outpace that of goods and services that are not traded internationally. In practice, that tendency has been apparent, so far at least, only in Korea and Taiwan province of China. In other emerging market economies, the phenomenon appears muted or absent. This may be because those economies are at a (relatively) early stage of their development or perhaps because other influences—such as shifts in the international distribution of production of traded goods and changes in trade restrictions and transportation and other costs of market penetration—have obscured it.

In these circumstances, the choice between fixed and flexible exchange rate arrangements hinges largely on the preference of policymakers between nominal exchange rate appreciation and relatively more rapid inflation. The results in terms of real exchange rate changes may be nearly the same with either approach. For example, between 1980 and 1996, while Hong Kong SAR, which has had a type of currency board arrangement since 1983, experienced relatively higher inflation than Singapore, which had a managed floating regime, their real exchange rates appreciated at roughly similar rates.

Adjusting to Capital Inflows

In many fast-growing emerging market economies, upward pressure on the exchange rate in recent years has stemmed largely from vastly increased private capital inflows. When capital inflows accelerate, if the exchange rate is prevented from rising, inflationary pressures build up and the real exchange rate will appreciate through higher domestic inflation. To avoid such consequences, central banks have usually attempted to "sterilize" the inflows—by using offsetting open market operations to try and "mop up" the inflowing liquidity.

Such operations tend to work at best only in the short term for several reasons. First, sterilization prevents domestic interest rates from falling in response to the inflows and, hence, typically results in the attraction of even greater capital inflows. Second, given the relatively small size of the domestic financial market compared with international capital flows, sterilization tends to become less effective over time. Finally, fiscal losses from intervention, arising from the differential between the interest earned on foreign reserves and that paid on debt denominated in domestic currency, will mount, so sterilization has a cost.

As capital inflows increase, tension will likely develop between the authorities' desire, on the one hand, to contain inflation and, on the other, to maintain a stable (and competitive) exchange rate. As signs of overheating appear, and investors become increasingly aware of the tension between the two policy goals, a turnaround in market sentiment may occur, triggering a sudden reversal in capital flows.

Since open market operations have only a limited impact in off-setting the monetary consequences of large capital inflows, many countries have adopted a variety of supplementary measures. In some countries the authorities have raised the amount of reserves that banks are required to maintain against deposits. In others, public sector deposits have been shifted from commercial banks into the central bank—to reduce banks' reserves. A number of countries have used prudential regulations, such as placing limits on the banking sector's foreign exchange currency exposure. Some central banks have used forward exchange swaps to create offsetting capital outflows— although there appear to be limits on how long such a policy can be used, given the likelihood, as with open market operations, that it can cause fiscal losses. In other cases the authorities have responded by widening the exchange rate bands for their currencies, thus allowing some appreciation. And a few have introduced selective capital controls.

While such instruments and policies can for a time relieve some upward pressure on a currency and ease inflationary pressure, none appears to have been able to prevent an appreciation of the real exchange rate completely.

Can exchange rate flexibility help manage the impact of volatile capital flows? As mentioned earlier, if interest rates and monetary policy are "locked in" by an exchange rate anchor, the burden of adjustment falls largely on fiscal policy—that is, government spending and tax policies. But often taxes cannot be raised or spending reduced in short order, nor can needed infrastructure investments be postponed indefinitely. (Clearly, policymakers who cannot adjust fiscal policy in the short run should not adopt a rigidly fixed exchange rate regime.) Allowing the exchange rate to appreciate gradually to accommodate upward pressures would appear to be a safer way of maintaining long-run economic stability. Furthermore, by allowing the exchange rate to adjust in response to capital inflows, policymakers can influence market expectations. In particular, policymakers can make market participants more aware that they face a "two-way" bet—exchange rate appreciations can be followed by depreciations. This heightened awareness of exchange rate risks should discourage some of the more speculative short-term capital flows, thereby reducing the need for sharp corrections.

. . . .

Capital Account Convertibility

In recent years, many emerging economies have gradually relaxed or removed capital controls and are now proceeding toward full capital account convertibility. Remaining restrictions are nevertheless significant, and are mostly asymmetric— placing more restrictions on capital flowing out than on capital flowing in. More liberal rules in both directions would have the advantage of increasing economic efficiency (allowing more capital to flow to where it gets the best returns). Liberalization would also provide domestic investors with more opportunities to diversify their portfolios and reduce the concentration of exposure to domestic market risks.

A movement toward full capital account convertibility, however, can succeed only in the context of sound economic fundamentals, a sound banking sector, and an exchange rate policy that allows adequate flexibility. The increasing number of developing countries adopting more flexible exchange rate regimes probably reflects, at least in part, a recognition that increased flexibility may be helpful in making the transition to full convertibility.

As developing countries become ever more integrated with global financial markets, they will likely experience more volatility in cross-border capital flows. How to manage such volatility has thus become an important issue for policymakers. One obvious way to contain volatility is to try to reduce reliance on short-term capital flows. It would be unrealistic, however, to try to distinguish between those flows that are destabilizing and those that perform important stabilizing functions in the foreign exchange and other markets. It would also be undesirable to eliminate short-term flows entirely — given that, among other things, they help provide liquidity to the currency market.

II. Foreign Exchange Instruments and Hedging

Raj Bhala, Risk Trade-Offs in the Foreign Exchange Spot, Forward and Derivative Markets
1 The Financier 34-49 (August 1994)

I. DIMENSIONS OF THE GLOBAL CURRENCY BAZAAR

The foreign exchange market is the world's largest financial market. Average daily turnover exceeds one trillion dollars. The most prominent participants in the market are roughly 200,000 active foreign exchange traders employed by commercial and investment banks, treasury officials in corporations, and institutional investors like mutual pension funds. Among the two most significant types of transactions are spots and forwards, which are conducted over-the-counter (OTC). These are made for leading "hard" (*i.e.*, freely convertible and widely accepted) foreign currencies like yen, marks, pounds, and dollars, as well as less liquid, softer currencies like the Kuwaiti dinar and the Portuguese escudo. Trading in spots and forwards never ceases. It occurs not only in leading centers such as London, New York, and Tokyo, but also through telephone and computer linkages among markets participants in peripheral locations.

The markets for foreign exchange derivative products are where the world's largest financial market intersects with the world's most advanced financial technology. When this technology is applied to spot and forward transactions, the results are large, electronic, liquid, twenty-four hour global markets for derivatives. These products are financial instruments whose value is derived from an underlying financial asset such as stocks, bonds, or commodities. With respect to foreign exchange derivatives, the underlying real asset is a currency, and the value of these derivatives is derived from exchange rates in the spot market. In the fast-paced and sometimes volatile OTC foreign exchange derivatives market, trading occurs in currency futures, foreign exchange options, and currency swaps.

As in the spot and forward markets, the participants in the derivatives market include bank traders, corporate traders, and portfolio managers. They buy and sell foreign exchange derivatives around the clock. Their hope is to make huge profits by correctly speculating on movements in the underlying currency markets or avoid huge losses by hedging currency risk incurred as a result of underlying currency positions. In other words, they have one of two purposes in mind: hedging or speculating.

. . . .

. . . [T]rading foreign exchange instruments, particularly derivative products, entails risk trade-offs. That is, buying and selling derivatives creates as well as mitigates serious risks. These risk trade-offs are rarely appreciated. On the one hand, some market participants and commentators approach foreign exchange derivative products from an excessively favorable perspective: they see only the risk-reducing aspects of the products. On the other hand, some legislators and regulators approach the products from an unjustifiably alarmist standpoint: they dwell on the risk-enhancing features of the products. The truth lies somewhere in between these two extreme perspectives. The risk trade-offs imply that foreign exchange derivative products have a dualistic nature insofar as they simultaneously reduce certain risks and exacerbate others.

Two critical risk trade-offs are analyzed here. First, derivatives can minimize currency risk, the risk of financial loss from an adverse exchange rate movement. But, hedging against currency risk can result in large losses. Thus, there is a trade-off between minimizing currency risk and increasing risk of loss. Second, there is a risk trade-off between currency risk and *Herstatt* risk. *Herstatt* risk refers to the risk that one of the payment obligations associated with the purchase and sale of the instrument will not be fulfilled. Each of these risk trade-offs must be carefully weighed by market participants before entering into a transaction.

> ....

II. THE FUNDAMENTAL PRODUCT—SPOTS

The most basic foreign exchange transaction is a spot. The value of every derivative foreign exchange action is derived in part from prices in the spot market, *i.e.*, the spot exchange rate. Hence, understanding the spot deal is essential to grasping the derivative deals.

A. Direct Dealing

A spot foreign exchange contract is a commitment by one party to deliver a specific quantity of one currency against the other party's delivery of a specific quantity of a second currency. Generally, the deliveries occur within two business days of the contract. The ratio of the quantities delivered reflects the price of one currency in terms of the other, which is the spot rate. Suppose an investment bank, the London office of Merrill Lynch ("Merrill") and a commercial bank, the Hong Kong office of Sumitomo Bank ("Sumitomo") enter into a dollar-yen spot foreign-exchange transaction on November 1. Sumitomo wants to sell yen and buy dollars, and Merrill wants to do the opposite. Merrill agrees to buy 120 million yen from Sumitomo in exchange for U.S. dollars at a spot rate of 105 yen per dollar. This means that Merrill will pay Sumitomo $1,142,857.10 for the yen. Payment of the dollars, and the reciprocal yen payment, must occur on the value date, which is two days after the trade date, *i.e.*, November 3. The trade date is the day on which the terms of the deal are established, *i.e.*, November 1.

The dollar-yen spot agreement could be entered into by traders at Merrill and Sumitomo in one of three ways. First, the traders may communicate directly with each other by telephone. Second, Merrill and Sumitomo may be members of the same electronic direct-dealing system sponsored by a third-party vendor such as Reuters. The traders at each bank communicate with each other through their respective computer terminals. Third, the traders may deal with each other indirectly through one or more foreign-exchange brokers. The brokers would act as agents for their respective principals. The telephone conversations between the banks and between banks and brokers are taped. Moreover, written confirmations of the terms of the spot transaction are exchanged between the banks and between the brokers.

> ....

D. *Herstatt* Risk

The settlement of payments obligations on the value date creates a risk known as "*Herstatt* risk," after a 1974 case in which a German bank (Bankhaus I.D. Herstatt

K.G.a.A.) that had entered into foreign exchange contracts was closed by German bank regulators. In the case, Herstatt had received settlement of foreign currency to which it was entitled under the contracts, but was closed by the authorities before it could fulfill its settlement obligations to its counterparty (Delbrueck & Company). *Herstatt* risk arises whenever the settlement of the two portions or "legs" of a spot foreign exchange transaction do not occur simultaneously. The settlements rarely occur simultaneously when they involve currencies whose home countries are in different time zones. Clearly, Sumitomo will be open for business before Merrill because of the time difference between Hong Kong and London—but, that is not the difficulty. The problem is that dollar payments must be made through the U.S. electronic fund transfer system, namely, Fedwire (owned and operated by the Federal Reserve Banks) or the Clearing House Interbank Payments System (CHIPS) (owned and operated by the New York Clearing House). Yen payments must be made through the Japanese electronic funds transfer system, principally BOJNET sponsored by the Bank of Japan. Fedwire and CHIPS may not be open for business at the same time as BOJNET because of the time differences between New York and Tokyo. Assume, for example, that dollar payments can be made between 8 a.m. and 6 p.m. Eastern Time (ET), while yen payments can be made between 8 a.m. and 6 p.m. Japan Time (JT). Assume further that JT is twelve hours ahead of ET. When the Japanese electronic funds transfer system opens for business at 8 a.m. JT, the U.S. system is closed, and vice versa.

Accordingly, Sumitomo will deliver 120 million yen to the designated account of Merrill before Merrill delivers $1,142,857 to Sumitomo's designated account. During the time gap between the yen and the dollar deliveries, Sumitomo is exposed to *Herstatt* risk. If Merrill becomes insolvent or is closed by regulatory authorities before it is able to pay $1,142,857.10 to Sumitomo, then Sumitomo will become a general unsecured creditor of Merrill. It is likely to receive the proverbial "ten cents on the dollar" (or just $114,285.71). (The failure of Merrill is not the only source of *Herstatt* risk. An asset freeze imposed by the U.S. government on dollar payments to Japan would place Sumitomo in a similar unsatisfactory position.)

Herstatt risk would be eliminated if settlements occurred in the same time zone. This would be possible if a multi-currency payments system existed—yet, thus far, none does. In the spot deal, the yen will be delivered by Sumitomo to a yen-denominated account of Merrill in Japan through BOJNET. Conversely, dollars will be delivered by Merrill to a dollar-denominated account of Sumitomo through Fedwire or CHIPS. The principal barriers to the development of multi-currency systems appear to be political and economic, not technological. The U.S. is not prepared for dollar transfers to be handled through a network that does not own, operate, or at least regulate in some fashion. Such an arrangement would imply a diminution of sovereignty insofar as control over one's own currency is an important manifestation of independence and authority. Moreover, it might have untoward monetary policy effects. If overdrafts could be created in dollar-denominated accounts held at, for example, the Bank of Japan as part of a Tokyo-based multi-currency system, then a foreign central bank effectively would have the power to grant credit in the U.S. currency. Heretofore, that power remains with the Federal Reserve and U.S.-related commercial banks.

Theoretically, *Herstatt* risk could be eliminated even if the dollar and yen settlements did not occur in the same time zone. All that is needed is some overlap between the hours of operation of the relevant payments system and coordination of payments. Suppose the hours of operation of Fedwire or CHIPS, or of BOJNET, were expanded in order to ensure an overlap between the U.S. and Japanese electronic funds transfer systems. For example, assume that Fedwire accepted dollar transfer instructions at 6:30 a.m. and BOJNET remained open to accept yen transfer instructions until 7 p.m. Then, a one half-hour overlap between the two systems—from 6:30 a.m.-7 a.m. (ET) (6:30 p.m.-7 p.m. (JT)—would exist. If the dollar and yen settlements are made simultaneously during this half-hour, then *Herstatt* risk will not materialize. However, in practice parties to foreign exchange transactions tend not to synchronize their payments in such a manner. One explanation may be that it is operationally infeasible to do so given that active participants in the foreign exchange markets make thousands of payments every day. A second explanation may be that participants do not yet fully appreciate *Herstatt* risk or, if they do, they simply discount this risk. [Central banks such as the Federal Reserve are taking steps to minimize *Herstatt* risk by, for example, lengthening the operating hours of their payments systems, and supporting the development of centralized foreign exchange clearing and settlement systems in which currency delivery obligations are netted against one another on a bilateral or multilateral basis. Indeed, recently the Federal Reserve expanded the operating hours of Fedwire to provide for a brief overlap with other funds transfer systems, most notably, BOJNET.]

. . . .

III. FORWARDS AND FUTURES

A. Currency Risk and Risk of Loss

Suppose Sumitomo and Merrill enter into a dollar-yen transaction with a value date that is further than two days from the trade (*e.g.*, the trade date is November 1 and the value date is November 30). Their transaction is not a dollar-yen spot but rather a forward. A forward contract is almost identical to a spot contract, except that the date set for delivery of the underlying currencies is more than two days, (and is generally between one week and two years) from the date of the contract. Therefore, the above discussion of spots is equally applicable to forwards, except for the postponed delivery of currencies. . . . *Herstatt* risk pervades both the forward and spot markets.

The classic example of the purpose of a forward involves an importer of foreign products that must pay for the products in the exporter's currency—for example, an electronics store in the U.S. like Circuit City buying compact disc (CD) players from a Japanese manufacturer such as Panasonic. Because Panasonic seeks payment in yen, Circuit City must purchase yen in exchange for dollars. One alternative is to purchase the yen on the spot market just before payment is due. However, this strategy means Circuit City assumes currency risk, *i.e.*, the risk that the yen will appreciate before the date of the spot purchase. To hedge against this risk, Circuit City can purchase yen forward against dollars.

Forward contracts are ideal for this situation because of their flexibility. Their critical terms, including the amount of the currencies involved, delivery date, and exchange rate (known as the forward rate), are individually negotiated by the principals involved. If Circuit City knows it will need to pay for the CD players in ninety days, then it can enter into a ninety-day forward contract to buy yen. Forward contracts are made for periods as short as a week and as long as one year (though forwards that mature in one or more are very rare). Generally, most forward contracts last thirty, sixty, or ninety days.

Businesses engaged in international commerce are not the only users of forwards. Commercial and investment banks actively participate in the forward market for hedging purposes. Assume Merrill has a long position in dollars (*i.e.*, it has bought dollars. Merrill perceives a weakness in the dollar against the German mark and expects the dollar will depreciate against the mark in both the spot and forward markets. Yet, Merrill is unwilling to liquidate its dollar holdings for fear that dumping a large quantity of dollars in exchange for marks might accelerate the depreciation of one dollar.

Merrill decides to buy 10 million 30-day marks forward against the dollar. The purchase occurs on November 1 at 1.75 marks per dollar and the contracts are for thirty days. Suppose that by November 30 the dollar has sank to a spot rate of 1.65 marks per dollar. The value in terms of marks of Merrill's long position in dollars has fallen. However, some of this lost value can be recouped through the forward hedge whereby Merrill has bought a currency (marks) that has strengthened. Merrill is entitled to receive 10 million marks at the forward rate of 1.75 marks per dollar, a total cost of $5,714,235.70, on November 30. Merrill will re-sell the marks immediately in the spot market at 1.65 marks for dollar, garnering $6,060,606.06, and earn a profit of $346,320.36.

The same transaction illustrates the use of forwards for speculative purposes. If there were no underlying dollar position, then there would be no reason to buy forwards to guard against currency risk. Any such purchases would be purely for speculative purposes, *i.e.*, to profit from the expectation that the spot price of marks would appreciate relative to the dollar and that marks purchased in a forward contract could be re-sold at the higher spot rate.

Finally, the above transaction highlights the pitfalls of using forwards to hedge currency risk. Suppose that on November 30 the dollar has strengthened against the mark to a spot rate of 1.85 marks per dollar. Because Merrill has locked in the forward rate of 1.75 marks per dollar, it must pay $5,714,285.70 for the marks. If it sells them at the spot rate, it will receive only, $5,405,405.40, incurring a loss of $308,880.30. Merrill's attempt to hedge currency risk resulted in a risk of loss that materialized.

B. Forwards Versus Futures

At first blush, foreign currency forward and futures contracts seem quite similar. Like a forward contract, a futures contract calls for the later purchase and sale of a designated amount of foreign currency. Moreover, the same market participants — commercial and investment banks, corporations, and institutional investors — transact in both types of contracts.

A futures contract is defined as "[a]n agreement to purchase or sell a commodity for delivery in the future: (1) at a price that is determined at initiation of the contract; (2) which obligates each party to the contract to fulfill the contract at the specified price; (3) which is used to assume or shift price risk; and (4) which may be satisfied by delivery or offset." This definition suggests three differences between a forward and futures contract.

First, unlike a forward contract, the material terms of a futures contract are standardized. The terms of a futures contract — namely, the quantity of currency and delivery date — are not tailored to the individual needs of the principals in the transaction. In particular, the quantity of the currency underlying a futures contract cannot be negotiated by the parties. Similarly, the delivery date pre-set. However, like forward contracts, most futures contracts expire within six months.

Second, very few futures contracts result in the actual delivery of foreign exchange. Unlike forwards, futures are not a means to transfer ownership in an underlying currency. Instead, a party discharges its obligation to make or take delivery of foreign currency pursuant to a futures contract by "closing out" its "open" position. Close out is effected by entering into equal and opposite offsetting transaction. Thus, if Merrill bought one futures contract that calls for it to deliver 1 million Venezuelan bolivars on December 1, it would close out its open position by selling a futures contract for delivery of the same amount of bolivars on the same date.....Whether a party profits from futures transactions depends on whether it closes out its positions for a net gain. Suppose Merrill bought the contract for 115.30 bolivars per dollar, paying $8,673.03, and sells an offsetting contract for 116.60 per dollar, receiving $8,576.33. Then, Merrill incurs a loss of $96.70.

A third critical difference between forward and futures contracts is where they are traded. Currency futures are not traded OTC but on one of the eleven organized U.S. futures exchanges, such as the International Money Market (IMM) division of the Chicago Mercantile Exchange (CME) or the New York Mercantile Exchange (NYMEX). In addition, they are traded on many overseas exchanges such as the London International Financial Futures Exchange (LIFFE) and the Singapore Monetary Exchange (SIMEX).

As a result of this difference, the credit risk appraisal process associated with forward transactions is different from that which occurs for currency futures trading. Only members of the exchange can trade on an exchange. Non-members must execute trades through a member. Membership is regulated by the exchange, which attempts to ensure that members are well capitalized and operate in a safe and sound manner. In contrast, there is no watchdog to ensure that participants in the forward market are creditworthy. It is left to each participant to appraise the creditworthiness of other participants. More generally, a federal regulatory agency, the Commodity Futures Trading Commission (CFTC), and a self-regulatory organization, the National Futures Association oversee futures trading.

Futures exchanges like the CME impose security deposit requirements on members. These requirements include original margin deposits when a member first buy or sells a currency future, and maintenance margin deposits resulting from daily revaluations or "marking-to-market" of the member's positions. There is no organized system mandating security deposits in the forward market. Again, this is a matter for participants to negotiate as they see fit. Finally, the counterparty in a forward deal is the other commercial or investment bank, corporation, or institutional investor involved. In a futures deal, the exchange clearinghouse is interposed between the two parties. The clearinghouse is better organized than most prospective individual counterparties and thus is more likely to fulfill its obligations on the futures contract.

. . . .

IV. SPOT PLUS FORWARD EQUALS CURRENCY SWAP

A. The Basic Transaction

A currency swap is a "pair of foreign exchange deals in the same two currencies but for different delivery dates and in opposite directions.... The amount involved will be identical for one of the currencies and similar for the other, the difference here being the result of the difference in exchange rates for different dates. In terms of its constituent elements, a currency swap is a spot plus a forward transaction. It effectively gives the parties the use of a different currency for a fixed period of time and cost.

Suppose that Sumitomo and Merrill decide to enter into a dollar-pound currency swap transaction on November 2. Sumitomo swaps 100,000 pounds against U.S. dollars. The transaction occurs through two steps. The first step is the spot transaction where Sumitomo sells Merrill 100,000 pounds. Because the trade date is November 2, the value date in the spot deal is November 4.

Assume that the exchange rate for the spot transaction is $1.50/pound. On November 4, Merrill receives 100,000 pounds from Sumitomo. Merrill's pound-denominated account in London is credited and Sumitomo's pound-denominated account in London is debited. Conversely, Merrill delivers $150,000 to Sumitomo. Merrill's dollar-denominated account in New York is debited and Sumitomo's dollar-denominated account in New York is credited. The deliveries are effected by means of wire transfers that are governed by the law of the jurisdiction in which the transfers occur.

The second step of the currency swap is a thirty-day forward transaction. The principals enter into the forward deal at the same time as they enter into the swap, *i.e.*, on November 2. The forward effectively unwinds the spot, *i.e.*, the currency flows are reversed. Sumitomo buys 100,000 pounds from Merrill for delivery on December 4 at an exchange rate of $1.49/pound. On December 4, Merrill delivers 100,000 pounds to Sumitomo and receives $149,000 from Sumitomo. Again, reciprocal debit and credit entries are made to the appropriate bank accounts and the funds are transferred electronically.

B. Results

The results of the currency swap are readily apparent. First, the quantity of pounds exchanged is the same—100,000 pounds. Merrill receives this amount in the forward transaction on November 4 and delivers this amount in the forward transaction on December 4. As the definition of a currency swap states, the quantity of one currency involved in the transaction always remains the same.

Second, as the definition of a currency swap suggests, the quantity of the second currency exchanged—here dollars—is similar but not exactly the same. Merrill pays $150,000 on November 4, but receives only $149,000 on December 4. The difference in the dollar amounts arises because the dollar is at a premium for forward delivery.

Third, each principal in the transaction has the use of the currency it "swapped in" for thirty days. Sumitomo has the benefit of 100,000 dollars from November 4 to December 4. Merrill has the use of 100,000 pounds for one month. Each of the banks can profitably invest the currency swapped in for the duration of the swap. For example, Sumitomo might extend a short-term dollar loan to a corporate borrower, thereby earning interest income on the loan. Merrill might purchase a short-term interest-bearing note.

Fourth, the cost to each principal is certain. Merrill pays a fixed price, $1,000. This cost reflects the difference between the number of dollars delivered on November 4 and received on December 4. Thus, even if the dollar-pound spot and forward exchange rates move dramatically away from $1.50 per pound and $1.49 per pound respectively, it does not matter—Merrill has locked in its cost at the rates prevailing on November 4. Sumitomo also pays a fee for the pounds. This might take the form of a commission paid to a swaps broker for finding counterparty.

C. *Herstatt* Risk Again

The deliveries of currencies entails *Herstatt* risk. As in any spot or forward transaction, the deliveries in a currency swap are made to accounts designated in payments instructions exchanged by the principals. These accounts will be maintained at banks located in different time, namely, in the home country of each currency involved. Sumitomo and Merrill will maintain pound accounts in London and dollar accounts in New York, and one currency will be delivered before the second currency. Pounds will be delivered several hours before dollars because the business day begins in London while banks and the payments system for transferring dollars in New York is closed.

How would *Herstatt* risk materialize? Suppose Sumitomo delivers 100,000 pounds to Merrill's pound account in London at 10 a.m. on November 4. It is 5 a.m. in New York, so Merrill is unable to effect a transfer of $150,000 dollars to Sumitomo's dollar account in New York for at least a few hours. At 9 a.m. New York time Merrill is closed by regulatory authorities or declares bankruptcy—before the dollar delivery is made to Sumitomo's account. Sumitomo thereby becomes a creditor of its failed counterparty.

Herstatt risk also could materialize on December 4, when the deliveries pursuant to the forward part of the currency swap are made. Assume Merrill re-delivers 100,000 pounds to the London-based pound account of Sumitomo at 9 a.m. on December 4. For the aforementioned reason, this delivery is made before Sumitomo transfers $149,000 to Merrill. If Sumitomo is closed or becomes insolvent before the dollar settlement occurs, then Merrill becomes a creditor of its failed counterparty.

To be sure, *Herstatt* risk would be eliminated if the settlement of dollars took place in London along with the pound settlement, or if the pound and dollar settlements occurred simultaneously in New York. However, as explained above, neither the U.S. nor any other country operates a multi-currency payments system whereby electronic funds transfers can be made in currencies other than that of the home country.

D. Variations and Hedging Currency Risk

To hedge against currency risk where a payment date is uncertain, a variant of the above currency swap transaction could be used. The principals might be a U.S. oil company building a petroleum refinery in Britain and a British engineering consultant performing services in the U.S. The U.S. company will be paid in pounds in five years when the project is finished. Conversely, the British company will be paid in dollars in five years when the consultancy project is completed. The payments to be made in five years entail currency risk—the U.S. company must convert pounds to dollars, and the British company must do the reverse—and the spot rate in five years is likely to vary dramatically from the current rate. A five-year currency swap will minimize the currency risk: the U.S. company will swap its pound revenues for dollars, and the British company will do the reverse. Each company thereby locks in the amount of its home currency that its foreign currency revenues represent. In effect, the currency swap resembles a long-term forward contract.

A currency swap may consist of two forward transactions instead of a spot plus a forward. Consider a U.S. importer that buys goods from an exporter in Chile on January 1. Assume the exporter wants to be paid in Chilean pesos. Payment will be required in two or six months. The precise date is not known because the dates on which the goods will be shipped and arrive are not yet certain. The U.S. importer wants to hedge against currency risk, namely, that the Chilean peso will appreciate relative to the U.S. dollar during the February 1-July 1 period.

Exhibit 1. Timeline of Currency Swap Transaction

Jan. 1	Feb. 1	Apr. 1	July 1
U.S. importer buys Chilean goods but exact payment date is not set. Importer buys 90-day peso forward based on a presumed payment date of April 1.	Importer learns that payment for imports is due July 1. Importer adjusts its peso position to hedge against currency risk from April 1 to July 1 by selling a 60-day peso forward and buying a six-month peso forward.	90-day peso forward purchase contract matures. 60-day peso forward sale contract matures.	Payment for imports due. Six-month peso forward purchase contract matures, thereby funding the payment for the imports.

Accordingly, the importer purchases a 90-day Chilean peso forward on January 1. Assume that on February 1, the importer learns that payment will be due on July 1. The 90-day forward will not protect the importer against currency risk because it matures on April 1, thus leaving an exposure from April 1-July 1. The importer can hedge against this exposure by entering into a currency swap on February 1 that consists of two forward dollar-peso transactions. February 1 is the "adjustment date" in that the importer alters its foreign exchange position to account for the finalization of the payment date of July 1.

The first part of the swap is the sale of a 60-day Chilean peso forward contract. The maturity date of the forward sale matches the maturity date of the original Chilean peso purchase—April 1. The pesos obtained from the forward purchase will fund the forward sale.

In the second part of the swap, the importer buys Chilean pesos in the forward market with a value date of July 1. Therefore, it must purchase a six-month peso forward. (The forward is purchased on February 1, matures on July 1, and thereby covers the April 1-July 1 exposure.) On July 1, the importer will obtain the Chilean pesos it needs to pay for the imports by virtue of this forward contract.

The effect of this currency swap is that the importer has "rolled out" the delivery date of Chilean pesos from a presumptive initial date of April 1 until the actual date of July 1. This arrangement can be used to hedge currency risk whenever the date on which currency will be needed is not certain. A time line depicting the swap transaction is set forth in Exhibit 1.

However, the strategy is not without risk of loss. Suppose that the original forward contract entered into on January 1 is for 5 million Chilean pesos purchased at an exchange rate of 411 Chilean pesos per dollar. Suppose further that from January 1-February 1 the Chilean peso is the subject of intense speculation. As a result, on February 1 the 60-day forward rate is 451 Chilean pesos per dollar, *i.e.*, the Chilean peso has depreciated relative to the dollar during January. The U.S. importer will lose money from these transactions. It has purchased 5 million Chilean pesos at the more expensive rate of 411 per dollar for a total cost of $12,165.45. It must sell this amount pursuant to the 60-day forward at 451 per dollar, earning $11,086.47. The net result is a loss of $1,078.98. It is incurred because the importer hedged against an appreciation in the Chilean peso, when in fact that currency depreciated.

V. OPTIONS

A. Distinguishing Features

A critical distinguishing feature of foreign exchange spots, forwards, futures, and swaps is that they entail binding legal obligations on the principals engaged in the deal. One party must buy a currency, while the other party must sell a currency. This feature does not exist with respect to currency options. Only one party in an option transaction, the seller, is legally obligated to render performance to the buyer. An option involves the payment of an up-front premium by the buyer and imposes a binding delivery obligation on the seller. The buyer, on the other hand, has a legal right, but not an obligation, to exercise the option according to its terms.

There are two types of options. A call option gives the buyer the right, but not the obligation, to buy a specific quantity of an underlying currency at a fixed exchange rate at any time up to, or in some instances on, a stated expiration date. The seller of a call option is obligated to deliver (*i.e.*, sell) that currency in the event the buyer exercises the option.

A put option gives the buyer the right, but not the obligation, to sell a specific quantity of an underlying currency at a fixed exchange rate at any time up to, or in some instances on, a stated expiration date. The seller of a put option is obligated to accept delivery (*i.e.*, buy) of the currency if the buyer exercises the option. Both types of options specify the exercise or strike price, which is the exchange rate at which the buyer has the right to buy (in the case of a call option) or sell (in the case of a put option) the underlying currency.

The risk of loss incurred by a buyer of a call or put is limited and pre-determined. It is the amount of the premium paid to the seller, *i.e.*, the non-refundable price paid to the seller, *i.e.*, the non-refundable price paid to the seller. In contrast, as explained below the risk of loss assumed by the seller is potentially dramatic. The intuitive reason for this disparity is that a seller is obligated to sell (in the case of a call option) or buy (in the case of a put option) and will be called upon to do so (by virtue of the buyer's exercise of the option) precisely when exchange rates are more favorable in the spot market.

Calls and puts come in two styles. An option that can be exercised on any business day up to and including the expiration date of the option is an "American-style option." An option that can be exercised only on the expiration date of the option is a "European-style option."' Most options expire within five months. The important practical question is whether the buyer of a call or put will exercise the option or allow it to expire unexercised. The buyer will exercise only if the option has value, which is only when the option is "in the money." As discussed below, a call is in the money if its exercise price is below the spot price of the underlying currency. Conversely, a put is in the money if its exercise price is above the spot above the spot price of the underlying currency.

A second key feature that distinguishes options from the instruments previously described is the forum in which they are traded. Spots, forwards, and swaps are exclusively OTC instruments, while futures are traded on an organized exchange. In contrast, options are traded both OTC and on exchanges such as the IMM and the Philadelphia Stock Exchange. Market participants have the choice of dealing in OTC options that are individually negotiated and tailored or in exchange-sponsored options that are standardized contracts. Moreover, the same differences in the credit appraisal process regarding forwards versus currency futures exist with respect to OTC options versus exchange-traded options.

B. Call Options

Suppose that on December 1 Merrill buys a call option on Mexican pesos from Sumitomo. The purchase is arranged directly over the telephone. The option expires in 30 days and is American-style. Merrill pays Sumitomo a premium for the option, which is the purchase price of the option. As the buyer, Merrill has the right but not the obligation to buy 70 million Mexican pesos at an exercise price of 3.50 pesos per dollar. As the seller, Sumitomo is obligated to sell 70 million Mexican pesos at an exercise price. Consequently, Merrill has locked in the price for the pesos—$20 million—regardless of dollar-peso spot market fluctuations.

When is this call option in-the-money? The answer depends entirely on the dollar-peso spot exchange rate. Assume that during the life of the option (December 1-30) the dollar appreciates and the rate becomes 3.75 pesos per dollar. If Merrill were to purchase 70 million pesos on the spot market, then it would have to pay $18,666,666.66. Because this is a lower cost than would be incurred if the option were exercised, the option is not in-the-money. Of course, Merrill cannot re-coup the fixed cost represented by the premium, but it saves $1,333,333.33 (the difference between $20,000,000 and $18,666,666.66) by buying the pesos on the spot market instead of exercising the option.

Conversely, suppose the dollar weakened to 3.25 pesos per dollar during the life of the option. Purchasing 70 million Mexican pesos at that rate will cost $21,533,462.00, plainly more than the cost incurred by exercising the option. Hence, the option is in-the-money and should be exercised. The intuitive reason it is profitable to exercise is that the underlying currency, that is the subject of the call option has appreciated, *i.e.*, Merrill has an option to buy a currency (pesos) whose spot market value has increased. More generally the buyer of a call option always hopes for an increase in the spot rate for the underlying currency, while the seller always hopes that currency will depreciate.

Why would Merrill buy, and Sumitomo sell, a call option? Sumitomo expects pesos to depreciate relative to the dollar and, therefore, believes the option will expire unexercised. Sumitomo accepts the currency risk of peso appreciation because it is a paid premium. Sumitomo sells the option to earn premium income.

The risk of loss that Sumitomo assumes is enormous, and the potential losses huge, if Sumitomo does not actually own 70 million pesos—a case referred to as selling "uncovered" or "naked" call options. Suppose that the market spot race for pesos changes to 3.25 pesos per dollar. As explained above, Merrill exercises the option. Sumitomo will be forced to buy 70 million pesos on the spot market at a cost of $21,538,462.00 and sell them to Merrill for $20,000,000. The exercise results in a loss of over $1.5 million (excluding the premium income earned from selling the call option). The larger the spot market movement in pesos, the larger the losses. A change in the spot rate to 2.75 pesos would result in a loss of almost over $5.5 million (the cost of covering in the spot market, $25,454,545, minus the set exercise amount, $20,000,000).

Conversely, there are a number of possible motivations for Merrill's purchase. First, it may be hedging against the currency risk that pesos will appreciate relative to the dollar in the future. Merrill may have an obligation owed in Mexican pesos that will mature in the future. For example, it may have issued certificates of deposit or other liabilities denominated in pesos.

Second, Merrill might speculated in movements in the dollar-peso spot market. Suppose its forecasts indicate that the peso will appreciate to 3 pesos per dollar within ninety days. Merrill buys a ninety-day call option for 70 million pesos with a strike price of, for instance, 3.50 pesos per dollar. If the spot rate rises above 3.50 pesos per dollar, then Merrill will exercise the option at a cost of $20,000,000. It will immediately re-sell the 70 million pesos (obtained from the exercise of the option) at 3 pesos per dollar for $23,333,333.33—a profit of over $3 million.

Interestingly, Merrill's long position in peso call options in the above scenario can be hedged by short sales of pesos in the spot market. Suppose the peso depreciates to 3.75 pesos per dollar, contrary to Merrill's forecast. The call option is not in the money and will expire unexercised. Merrill "loses" the premium it paid. But, Merrill can easily compensate for this loss by short selling pesos in the spot market. Suppose Merrill had sold 70 million pesos short at a spot rate of 3.55 pesos per dollar-thereby earning $19,718.310. Merrill must cover its short position by buying pesos in the spot market. But, it does so at the depreciated rate of 3.75 pesos per dollar—a cost of $18,666.667. The profit from the short sale is $1,051,643 (the difference between $19,718,310 and $18,666,667), which dwarfs the premium paid for the unexercised option.

A third motivation for Merrill to buy the 70 million peso call option is to speculate in movements in the options market. An option buyer is not obligated to hold the option until it expires. There is an active secondary market for foreign exchange options in which the buyer can sell the option for a price, or premium. The premium, for secondary market transactions in options has two components, intrinsic value and time value.

The intrinsic value of an option is the economic benefit that would be gained if the option were exercised immediately. Suppose Merrill buys a 30-day American-style option for 70 million Mexican pesos with a strike price of 3.50 pesos per dollar. As explained above, the option is in the money if the dollar-peso spot rate is 3.25 pesos per dollar. The call would have an intrinsic value of 3.25 pesos per dollar because it can be exercised at 0.25 pesos per dollar and the pesos can be re-sold on the spot market at 3.25 pesos per dollar. An option that is at- or out-of-the-money has no intrinsic value.

Normally, the premium for this option would not be 0.25 pesos per dollar but rather some higher figure depending on the time value of the option. The time value of a call or put is the amount of the premium that exceeds the intrinsic value. During the period before the option expires, the potential profit associated with exercising the option can increase (or the potential loss can decrease) because, for example, the spot exchange rate may fluctuate or interest rates may change. The longer the time before the expiration of the option, the greater the chance that an event will occur that increases the profitability from exercising the option. Thus, the actual premium in the secondary market will reflect the time value. The time value of every option decays as the expiration date of the option draws near, and it is zero on that date.

As intimated above, a number of factors influence the secondary market price of an option: the spot rate, strike price, time remaining until expiration, volatility of the underlying currency, and interest rates. Of these factors, the most critical is the price of the underlying currency—the spot rate. The delta or hedge ratio measures the relationship of changes in the premium to changes in the spot exchange rates. A delta of 0.50 means that the option premium moves half as much as the spot rate. If pesos move from 3.50 per dollar to 3.25 per dollar, the premium will move by 12 1/2 pesos per dollar. As the spot rate changes, so too does the delta. An option that is deeply in the money has a delta of approximately 1.00, while an option that is deeply out-of-the-money has a delta of roughly zero. (Rarely are these extremes reached.) The delta is a critical figure because it allows traders to identify options that are most responsive to the underlying currencies and thereby make better hedging and speculating decisions.

C. Put Options

Suppose that on December 1 Merrill sells a 30-day American-style put option on 70 million Mexican pesos to Sumitomo with an exercise price of 3.50 pesos per dollar. Sumitomo, of course, pays Merrill a premium for the option. As the buyer of the put, Sumitomo has the right but not the obligation to sell 70 million pesos to Merrill for $20,000,000. Thus, no matter what the dollar-peso exchange rate on the spot market, Sumitomo is guaranteed $20,000,000 for the pesos. Plainly, Sumitomo expects that pesos will depreciate in the spot market so that the put option will enter into the money. Buyers of put options hope that the underlying currency that is the subject of the put depreciates in the spot market whereas sellers of puts hope that this currency appreciates.

Merrill has a different expectation about the future of the dollar-peso spot market. It is obligated to buy pesos from Sumitomo for $20,000,000 but does not think this obligation will materialize because pesos will appreciate in the spot market. If the spot rate for pesos rises to 3.25 pesos per dollar, for example, Sumitomo will be better off selling its pesos on the spot market it will earn $21,538.461. Because Merrill believes that the spot price for pesos will remain the same or appreciate, it is willing to bear the currency risk that Sumitomo seeks to shed. As in the above case in which Sumitomo sells call options, a key motivation for Merrill to sell put options is to earn premium income. The potential risk of loss to Merrill is enormous. The greater the depreciation in the spot rate for pesos, the greater the loss Merrill will incur as it buys pesos pursuant to the option at an expensive strike price and off loads the pesos on the spot market at the depreciated rate.

Similar hedging and speculative motives that cause Merrill to buy calls might lead to buy puts. Suppose that over time Merrill has accumulated a large long position in pesos. However, Merrill expects that the peso will depreciate in the spot market. If Merrill buys peso puts, then it locks in the sale price at the strike price, thereby hedging against the currency risk that pesos will become a less valuable asset relative to the dollar. For instance, consider a 70 million peso put with a strike price of 3.50 pesos per dollar. If the peso depreciates to 3.75 pesos per dollar, then Merrill can exercise the put and sell the pesos for a guaranteed $20,000,000 instead of the spot market value $18,666,666.67.

Merrill might buy peso puts even if it does not have an underlying long position in pesos. For example, it might speculate in the dollar-peso spot market. Or, it might speculate in the options market itself, in which case the points made regarding call option pricing in the secondary market hold true for puts as well. In either event, buying puts would indicate it is speculating that the spot rate will depreciate and that the spot rate will enter into the money.

D. *Herstatt* Risk Yet Again

Under certain circumstances, the problem of *Herstatt* risk is manifest in the market for OTC foreign exchange options. At the outset of an options transaction when a buyer pays a premium, there is no *Herstatt* risk. The premium payment is one-way and not one of two legs of a transaction, thus rendering it different from settlements of payment obligations in a spot, forward, or swap transaction. When an option is sold in the secondary market, again there is no *Herstatt* risk because the new buyer of the option makes a one-way, non-contingent payment to the former buyer of the option.

Herstatt risk exists whenever an option is exercised. At that juncture, the settlement of two payments transactions must occur. The underlying currency which is the subject of the option must be transferred from the seller to the buyer of a call option or from the buyer to the seller of a put option. In exchange for this transfer, a payment must be made in the opposite direction for the cost of the underlying currency (denominated in dollars in the above examples) as per the exercise price. In so far as settlement occurs in different time zones, *Herstatt* risk exists.

. . . .

III. The Relationship Between Currency Risk and Political Risk

NOTE ON CURRENCY RISK AND POLITICAL RISK*

Typically, "currency risk" is viewed as distinct from "political risk." Arguably, however, currency risk is a species of political risk. Indeed, the term "currency risk" can be defined broadly to encompass the range of threats brought about by changes in host nation monetary policy, such as increased exchange controls, government-initiated inflation, or hard currency exchange prohibitions. For example, a change in Vietnamese government policy with regard to hard currency exchanges may prevent an American joint venture rubber tire manufacturing operation from repatriating its profits from Vietnam to the United States. This threat is magnified when market forces, such as natural depreciation in the local currency, further affect the convertibility (and thus the repatriation to the United States) of the venture's profits.

The host country's government also may damage the profitability of the operation by causing inflation. For example, if the local currency in the *situs* country of the direct investment is sufficiently devalued, the conversion of the local currency into hard currency may not yield profits as expected. This type of risk can be classified as either "market risk" or "political risk," as the host country's government-generated inflation is the source of the loss of profits.

In the case of project finance investments—for example, infrastructure projects such as hydroelectric power generation facilities or superhighways—currency risk is a consideration of paramount importance.

> Currency risk is a critical issue in cross-border financings of power projects; even where the economics of the venture are strong, this issue can quickly derail a good prospect. In many countries there may be limitations, both legal and practical, on the ability of ventures to exchange local currency for hard currency. For this reason, the majority of successful international project financings to date have been of natural resource, commodity and petrochemical projects whose output is sold in the export market and thus

---

* This Note was prepared by Christopher C. Matteson, Esq.

generate hard currency directly. Power generation projects present a new horizon; sales of power to private or state-owned utilities within the host country almost certainly will generate local currency, and cross-border financing will be dependent on the ability of the venture to exchange local currency for remittable hard currency.[1]

Currency risk thus plays a major role in investment schemes, particularly whenever a portion of the revenue will be generated locally, in a soft local currency, and the costs associated with the FDI are in a hard currency.

Consider this illustration of the many effects of currency risk in the telecommunications sector in India.

The depreciation of the rupee has set off alarm bells at cellular telecom companies. The fall in the rupee by almost 10 per cent over the last 18 months has resulted in an equal increase in the cost of equipment purchased in dollars forcing some companies to reconsider debt issues abroad. The depreciation is much more than that assumed in project estimates.

The companies are contemplating switching to rupee funds, increasing the internal rate of depreciation in project plans and creating exchange reserves on their balance sheets to mitigate the impact of the depreciating rupee on their projects. "Companies will exchange dollar funds for rupees," predicted Anil Virmani, chief financial officer of Escotel Cellular.

Since equipment costs account for between 30 and 60 per cent — depending on other costs like licence fees and operating costs — of project costs, finance executives are worried that the cost inflation due to currency depreciation will get out of hand. The current rate of depreciation is almost double the figure of 4-5 per cent a year that companies have envisaged in their project plans.

The extent by which the interest costs (including the cost of hedging against depreciation) of these companies will shoot up has not been worked out by the companies yet, but sources estimate that it will go up between five to 10 per cent. "They (the companies) will have to pump in funds for the extra depreciation and cover for future (foreign exchange) risk," one finance executive said.

The companies will also have to hedge for short-term expenses like handset purchases, voice mail systems, software for billing systems and other value-added features. Typically, these expenses are estimated to stand at Rs. 15-20 crore a year and the interest costs (on account for hedging) on this are expected to go up. [A "crore" is the Indian term for ten million. Thus, 15-20 crore are equal to 150-200 million rupees.] . . . . To compound problems, cellular companies cannot take foreign exchange cover for repayments on long-term loans and supplier's credit. Typically, these repayments have a moratorium of four years and hedging instruments for such long tenors is not available in the domestic market. The longest forward cover taken has been . . . for three years.

Sources also predicted that a fallout of the rupee's depreciation will be that basic telecom companies will insist on supplier's credit being disbursed in rupees instead of dollars as is the norm. However, equipment vendors will resist

---

1. Jonathan J. Green, *Managing Risks in International Power Projects*, 672 PLI/COMM.L. & PRAC. COURSE HANDBOOK SERIES 683-84 (1993).

this move since they will have to take the currency risk—a practice they will desist from since they have burnt their fingers in currency crises in South-East Asia.[2]

Thus, the issue of currency risk is a crucial one that can affect an investment in many ways, whether generated by an act of a sovereign government (in the form of currency devaluation) or by market forces (in the form of currency depreciation).

Since the Asian economic crisis began on 2 July 1997 with the devaluation of the Thai baht, many investors in the Asian infrastructure finance market have been forced to re-evaluate their positions. Governments have reduced their requirements for infrastructure construction and expansion.

Some of the biggest infrastructure schemes have already been canceled while sponsors of other projects are seeking to renegotiate terms.....Robin Gibbons, director of corporate and project finance for BZW Asia says: "A number of these schemes were already struggling. I would also expect lending margins, which had become very competitive, to widen...."....[S]ome bold infrastructure projects have been postponed or thrown into doubt by the recent financial crisis. Dr Mahathir Mohamad, the Malaysian prime minister, announced plans [in September, 1997] to delay several large infrastructure projects. These included the M$13.6bn (GBP 2.8bn) Bakun Dam, the northern region international airport in Kedah and KL Linear City, a 2 km long building over the route of a Kuala Lumpur river.[3]

To be sure, many observers argue the long term outlook for infrastructure and other investments in Asia is good. Indeed, the author of the above-quoted passage states that "Asia, in spite of the recent turmoil in financial sectors, remains one of the world's biggest markets for project finance. International bankers expect the region's demand for private sector finds to remain high, even if governments, investors and lenders pause for breath after the recent currency and stock market falls."[4]

These passages illustrate the following point with regard to FDI in general and project finance in particular: currency risk, whether market generated, host-government generated, or a hybrid of both, must be accounted for in the planning stages of an investment. Certainly, insuring against currency risk through various means—such as hedging or the purchase of inconvertibility insurance—is a prerequisite for a successful investment. The investor should have the fortitude to weather situations such as the Asian crisis and remain present for a rebound in markets.[5]

---

2. How the Industry Fares Against the Falling Rupee, Bus. Standard (India) at 4, Nov. 27, 1997, 1997 Westlaw 15064455.

3. Andrew Taylor, *Survey—Asian Infrastructure, Power & Water, Project Finance*, Fin. Times, September 23, 1997, 1997 Westlaw 11055444.

4. *Id.*

5. Although made in the context of portfolio investment, rather than FDI, additional comments of other experts predicting a rosier future for investors can be found, even in the wake (indeed, the midst) of the Asian financial crisis. These comments emphasize that despite the existence of currency risk and its consequences, investors should account for this risk as much as possible while maintaining a long-term outlook.

Kara Tan Bhala, a first vice president and senior portfolio manager at Merrill Lynch & Company, doesn't sound worried about her employment prospects, even though the two finds she manages, Merrill's Emerging Tigers and Dragon funds, saw their size lopped by 50 percent or more in 1997.....Despite the difficulties at the funds she manages, Ms. Tan Bhala has tried to keep a healthy outlook.....[She] said she had been doing some selective stock buying in Thailand and Malaysia..... "A lot of things out there are trading below book value," she said. "As an investor right now you have

IV. Coping with Exchange Controls

Documents Supplement References:

1. *IMF Agreement Article VIII:2(b)*

Sir Joseph Gold, The IMF's Article VIII, Section 2(b) and Scurpulosity, in Yearbook of International Financial & Economic Law 25-27,

45-51 (Joseph J. Norton, Ed.) (1998)

The Problem

Two French authors of great renown were watching the waters of a stream that circumnavigated the rocks the stream encountered. The men of letters fell into a contest to find the most appropriate word for describing this natural process. Finally, they reached agreement on the word "scrupulosity." By this choice, they were recalling the aptness of the classical origin of *scrupulus* and, more important, were extolling the certainty and predictability of what they were observing, without denying that overwhelming forces of nature could bring about the adaptation of riparian channels as time goes by. These qualities resemble ideals the IMF has recognised in the interpretation of obligations under the Articles and in the formulation of policies of the organisation.

... [T]he IMF has not dedicated itself to scrupulosity, as described above, in applying Article VIII, Section 2(b) of the constitutive treaty. The failure of the IMF's mandate under this provision can be attributed to the obstinate unwillingness of the organisation after 1949 to exercise its power of interpretation of the provision. This phenomenon in the experience of the IMF and perhaps in the law and practice of other international organisations is worth probing. The phenomenon can be described as the virtual extinction of a provision, even though it has not lost its rationale or achieved its objective. This result has occurred without amendment of the articles.

Article VIII, Section 2(b) is formulated as follows:

> Exchange contracts which involve the currency of any member and which are contrary to the exchange control regulations of that member maintained or imposed consistently with this Agreement shall be unenforceable in the territories of any member. In addition, members may, by mutual accord, cooperate in measures for the purpose of making the exchange control regulations of either member more effective, provided that such measures and regulations are consistent with this Agreement.

It is easy to conclude that a primary objective of the provision is to effect a change in the principle of many national legal systems that the so-called "revenue" laws of a promulgator do not receive recognition, including enforcement, beyond the territo-

---

to look beyond sentiment and look at value for money. There is more downside in the near term, I think, *but in three years to five years, you will probably see markets double where they are right now.*"
Kenneth N. Gilpin, *Focus on Emerging Markets; Asian Tremors Leave Sector Managers Shaken but Optimistic*, N.Y. TIMES, January 4, 1998, at 7 (emphasis added). *See also, Project Finance Market Seen Strong Despite Political, Commercial Risks*, GLOBAL POWER REP. at 5, Oct. 31, 1997. 1997 WESTLAW 9382014.

ries of the promulgator of such laws. The negotiators of the Articles thought this principle to be outmoded because members of the IMF should cooperate with other members in helping each other to enforce certain revenue laws that were within the province of the IMF. The Articles contained indications that the revenue laws in question were "exchange control regulations" approved by the IMF. The logic of this departure from the past was that various purposes of the IMF would be promoted for the benefit of all members by a new principle. A further consideration was that members had supplied the IMF with resources to help fellow members overcome financial difficulties in the short or medium term and abandon the exchange control regulations that were supposed to meet that objective but were nevertheless detrimental in the longer term to the purposes of the IMF. Guided by this logic, the IMF adopted an authoritative interpretation on 10 June 1949, which described the meaning and effect of the provision as follows:

> 1. Parties entering into exchange contracts involving the currency of any member of the Fund and contrary to exchange control regulations of that member which are maintained or imposed consistently with the Fund Agreement will not receive the assistance of the judicial or administrative authorities of other members in obtaining the performance of such contracts. That is to say, the obligations of such contracts will not be implemented by the judicial or administrative authorities of member countries, for example by decreeing performance of the contracts or by awarding damages for their non-performance.

> 2. By accepting the Fund Agreement members have undertaken to make the principle mentioned above effectively part of their national law. This applies to all members, whether or not they have availed themselves of the transitional arrangements of Article XIV, Section 2.

An obvious result of the foregoing undertaking is that if a party to an exchange contract of the kind referred to in Article VIII, Section 2(b) seeks to enforce such a contract, the tribunal of the member country before which the proceedings are brought will not, on the ground that they are contrary to the public policy (*ordre public*) of the forum, refuse recognition of the exchange control regulations of the other member which are maintained or imposed consistently with the Fund Agreement. It also follows that such contracts will be treated as unenforceable, notwithstanding that, under the private international law of the forum, the law under which the foreign exchange control regulations are maintained or imposed is not the law which governs the exchange contract or its performance.

The mystery is to be resolved is why the IMF has refrained from further authoritative interpretation of the provision notwithstanding the increasing need for explication.

....

Consequences

Tohubohu, an expression derived from Hebrew and signifying a complex of turbulence, anarchy and confusion, describes the consequences of the IMF's failure in the years after 1949 to adopt authoritative interpretation of Article VIII, Section 2(b) even though problems were accumulating.

After noting the existence of Article VIII, Section 2(b), Professor Frédéric-Edouard Klein of the University of Basle has added that "the rest is uncertainty and controversy." It is of interest therefore to discover the reasons why the IMF has not interpreted Article VIII, Section 2(b) beyond the modest clues that can be found in its

Decision No. 446-4 of 10 June 1949. That early decision of the IMF was not the result of any initiative by members. The legal staff had proposed the interpretation of 1949 in the exhilaration of finding in the Articles a provision that abandoned the traditional doctrine that what were called "revenue" laws in some legal systems were limited to territorial application by promulgators and were not entitled to broader enforcement.

The negotiators of the Articles had realised the logic of a new cooperative institution in international monetary matters. What then were the implications of allowing the provision to wither away, not only for the institution itself but also as a development in the practice of international treaty law, particularly in view of the power of final interpretation that had been conferred on the institution? As was noted in 1989:

> [a] consequence of not amending [or, it might have been added, of not interpreting] the provision has certainly been that the courts in some countries have been able, in the absence of authoritative interpretation by the IMF, to reduce the provision almost to extinction.

In the absence of an official explanation of the failure of the IMF to interpret Article VIII, Section 2(b), it is necessary to rely on surmise. An immediate presumption that must be made is that the IMF has deliberately avoided further authoritative interpretation under Article XXIX or its forerunner in order to preserve as much flexibility as possible under the Articles. Authoritative interpretation has often been regarded as close to amendment in legal solemnity. This supposition is not wholly persuasive, however, because it does not explain why the IMF has not resorted to informal interpretation, as it has so often on other matters. The IMF has not concluded, as it has on certain matters, that non-interpretation was intended to give members authority to develop the *corpus juris* of the institution as experience was gained, especially in relation to matters on which the negotiators had not been able to reach sufficient agreement.

The avoidance of interpretation might be understood to reflect a doctrine expressed by [John Maynard] Keynes. As early as April 1943, he declared in his *Proposals for an International Clearing Union* that "[t]here should be the least possible interference with internal policies, and the plan should not wander from the international terrain." Thus, the Articles when drafted defined the IMF's regulatory jurisdiction in terms of the international terrain. If balance of payments difficulties arose notwithstanding the exercise of that jurisdiction, help could be forthcoming from the IMF by making its resources available under its financial jurisdiction. Conditionality, as the *quid pro quo* a member would then have to accept in return for financial help, was not as limited in scope as the IMF's regulatory jurisdiction. When the original system of the Articles collapsed, the principles on which it was based were adapted. The organisation's regulatory jurisdiction became narrower than in the past, but its financial jurisdiction became its main activity. Article VIII, Section 2(b) lapsed into even more profound torpor, because giving the provision greater vitality by interpretation would mean that members would have to assist other members in the pursuit of their international policies and would have to accept reduction of their freedom to choose their domestic policies. As was said in 1984, "[w]e need not be surprised, therefore, that the recapture of sovereignty as a principle for determination of external policies and retention of sovereignty for domestic policies has been observed as the principle for the IMF's role in the revised monetary system."

A more likely explanation of the IMF's non-interpretation of Article VIII, Section 2(b) is that each member has inevitably been forced to adopt its own interpretations in its judicial or political activities. In performing this task a member has had the opportunity to rely on its national legal doctrines, and in this connection to preserve as much as it decently could of its traditional private international law. National courts have also taken advantage of the opportunity to develop the law in directions not specifically related to the Articles. A good example is the judicial reaction to the problem of whether Article 2 of the Uniform Commercial Code in the United States applies to the trading of bank balances denominated in different currencies as transactions in 'goods' within the meaning of the Code. Courts adopting this conclusion have not been deterred by the anomaly of extending to foreign exchange dealings a provision closely associated in its origin with hard goods. Another example of this homage to the past is the struggles of German courts to fit the concept of unenforceability into established German law.

A possible explanation of the IMF's inaction in these days may be the stirrings about enlarging the regulatory jurisdiction of the institution so that it comprehends restrictions on inward or outward movements of capital. These ideas reflect both the enlarged volume of capital on the move and the greater impact this phenomenon has had on the stability of the international monetary system. Opponents of greater jurisdiction may fear that even the collection of information under Article VIII, Section 2(b) may be advance warning of a campaign to invest the IMF with regulatory jurisdiction over capital transactions and correspondingly diminish the discretionary authority of members. Growth in the number of Departments in the structure of the IMF may expand the varieties of advice the Managing Director receives on pressing for or obstructing reforms in relation to international capital transactions. Whatever the explanation may be, the IMF has certainly refrained from instituting a standard procedure by which members would inform the IMF of cases involving monetary law related to the Articles. It has sometimes been protested in defense of this elected ignorance that lengthy and arduous negotiation would be required in order to reach agreement on any new interpretation and then on the national means for giving it efficacy. The argument is feeble in view of the assurance that members have given the IMF that they have taken all steps to enable them to carry out their obligations under the Articles.

As a result, interpretation may require consideration of an increasingly complicated body of decisional law and business practices in which the IMF and its lawyers have not been expert. The officials of member countries who have specialised in the affairs of the IMF may have a similar reluctance to consider proposals of new or modified interpretations of the Articles. Furthermore, private lawyers become reluctant to press members to seek interpretation by the IMF. The following sentence in Decision No. 446-4 ceases to have any practical importance: "The Fund will be pleased to lend its assistance in connection with any problem which may arise in relation to the foregoing interpretation or any other aspect of Article VIII, Section 2(b)." If the IMF were to support requests for interpretation under this sentence, the effect might be to encourage members having different views on a problem of interpretation to transform the interpretative process under the Articles into contests among members as winners or losers in disputes. The original intent, however, was to avoid tournaments and to find the solution in accordance with the Articles that would best promote the interests of the IMF and all its members.

Numerous other reactions may help to explain the virtual disappearance of authoritative interpretation. Lack of interest in legal questions because of the expansion of the economic and financial business of the IMF may be one such explanation. The political and other complications created by the attempt to establish the Interpretation Committee may be another deterrent. The increase in the number of Departments in the structure of the IMF is a deterrent in the sense that more IMF officials may think it necessary or useful to participate in finding solutions for any problems for which interpretation is contemplated. A decline in the influence and activities of the Legal Department may be another explanation for the avoidance of interpretation. Few Executive Directors have had training or experience in the law, for which reason they may tend not to raise legal issues. Executive Directors may wish not to engage the interest of more than the traditional domestic participants (Treasuries and central banks) in the business of the IMF. The cohesion among members thought to be necessary for agreement on authoritative interpretation and domestic effectiveness must not be overlooked. For example, if legal problems related to capital transfers arise, members that are capital exporters may have interests that differ from those of members that are capital importers. The decline of official IMF interpretation may be responsible for the reluctance of litigants and courts to see problems referred to the IMF.

The obsolescence of the provisions on interpretation seems not to have been acknowledged as a problem because of the unwillingness of the IMF to emphasise disunity among members in their understanding of the Articles. The IMF recoiled from consequences such as this because they might undermine the desired impression of an institution based on collaboration among members rather than dictation by the IMF in the form of authoritative interpretation. Another consequence may have been the rejection of interpretation of Article VIII, Section 2(b) as an instrument for the international control of indebtedness. Interpretation might have been seen as favouring either creditors or debtors but not both. The IMF might have feared an impression that the organisation was failing in its duties. To counteract any such suspicion, the staff of the Legal Department may have expressed restrictive understandings of what is meant by interpretation. Again, the difficulty of finding a financial or economic rationale for some foreign exchange restrictions has fostered the view that they must have been imposed for reasons of security under Decision No. 446-4, and so are within the competence of the IMF even though the IMF has held that the IMF is not a suitable forum for discussing military considerations, including those that lead to the imposition of security restrictions.

Although the IMF has avoided straightforward interpretations, it has nevertheless taken decisions by means of a special procedure that obscures their character as interpretations. The procedure has been followed to give effect to the last paragraph of IMF Decision No. 446-4, which was formulated as follows:

> The Fund will be pleased to lend its assistance in connection with any problem which may arise in relation to the foregoing interpretation or any other aspect of Article VIII, Section 2(b). In addition, the Fund is prepared to advise whether particular exchange control regulations are maintained or imposed consistently with the Fund Agreement.

The procedure purports to give effect to the first sentence of the paragraph, but includes other understandings that might be defended by reference to the second sentence. The understandings are set forth in the drafts of letters by the Legal Department in response to written inquiries by the legal advisers of private litigants that ask whether exchange control regulations specified by them in a member's legal instruments were imposed consistently with the Articles. A draft letter explains that the relevant question is whether the regulations are consistent with the Articles at the time it is sought to enforce the contract to which the regulations relate. Therefore, unless the litigant's legal advisers specify otherwise, it is irrelevant to determine whether restrictions no longer in force were consistent with the Articles while in force. No discussion is ventured on the legal issue and its broader legal implications debated among scholars on whether the crucial date as of which to determine consistency is the date of the introduction of the restrictions or the date of attempted enforcement of the contract. The memorandum with which the Legal Department's draft reply is transmitted to the Executive Board for approval announces that the matter will not be placed on the Board's agenda, unless an Executive Director gives notice of a wish for discussion within one week of the availability of the memorandum. In the absence of notice, the draft letter will be understood to be approved by the Executive Board for transmission to the inquirer.

In another example of this procedure, the staff memorandum accompanying the draft response declares that regulations requiring the surrender to the authorities of foreign exchange receipts do not restrict the making of payments and transfers for current international transfers and, as the regulations can be applied without the approval of the IMF, they are consistent with the Articles. This logic can be questioned. If restrictions are not subject to the Articles, it is not obvious that therefore they are consistent with the Articles. If one thinks of trade restrictions, which are not within the IMF's regulatory jurisdiction, it is difficult to declare that therefore they are consistent with the Articles. Similarly, it is said that taxes on remittances that are the result of inward capital transfers are consistent with the Articles if the taxes do not produce multiple currency practices or other practices for which the IMF's approval is required but has not been obtained.

The reply declares that it is based on the current text and implementation of the member's provisions, and that this approach is in accordance with Article VIII, Section 2(b), which prevents the enforcement of a contract that is contrary to exchange control regulations that are maintained or imposed by the member at the time when enforcement is sought. This version, however, is not a correct paraphrase of Article VIII, Section 2(b). The provision does not mention the date as of which it is necessary to take account of exchange control regulations.

The procedure described above is based on the assumption that the problem of consistency with the Articles depends on whether the exchange control regulations to be examined are as they were when the contract was entered into or as they are when enforcement is sought by a contracting party. The IMF chooses the latter alternative, although it is sometimes said that this choice is made because the question is understood to pose the two alternatives described here unless the question is defined in some other way in the inquiry. If the inquiry is specified to relate exclusively to the facts as they were at the time of entry into the contract, the reason may be that under a member's practice, regulations that were inconsistent with the Articles at that date would preclude enforcement of the contract at all subsequent dates, whether the regulations are withdrawn or modified in some other way before enforcement is sought. The rationale of such a practice might be to avoid a backlog of undischarged obligations that would deter the member from undertaking the convertibility of its currency.

David Reid, Foreign Exchange Controls and Repatriation, in Negotiating and Structuring International Commercial Transactions 67-79

(Shelly P. Battram & David N. Goldsweig Eds., 1991)

INTRODUCTION

No seller of goods or provider of services needs to be told that it wants to be paid for its transaction; nor does any company entering into a joint venture overseas require reminding that, if it be so fortunate as to make profits, it may want to remit them back home and if, for whatever reason, it wants to pull out early, it will want repayment of its capital or loans or to continue to receive the license fees or royalties for technology it has supplied. A company can, on paper, look very strong financially; it may have overseas subsidiaries which are very profitable, but what if it cannot get the cash out of those subsidiaries? It could be in considerable cash flow difficulties as a result; it may be very expensive for it to remit the earnings if it is required to purchase the necessary foreign exchange at an unfavorable rate because of a multitiered exchange rate operated by a host country. What about a company['s] executives who are posted abroad and wish to take back to their home country their savings or, possibly, their pension? All these are issues which are related to questions of exchange control on payments and repatriation of investments and their earnings.

BACKGROUND

Exchange controls are a significant tool of a government, enabling it to control the monetary supply and to set priorities by controlling access to foreign exchange. In the purely financial context, unrestricted capital flows can play havoc with a nation's economic sovereignty, can deplete foreign exchange resources and divert national savings.

The regulation of payments from one country to another is not new. For example, in England laws restricting the export of gold and silver were introduced in the early part of the fourteenth century and in the following centuries numerous laws were passed making the export of precious metals illegal without the King's license. In fact, if you look at the history of exchange control in England, the periods without any form of exchange control are relatively short. (Exchange control in the UK was abolished in 1979.)

. . . .

It is helpful when considering the application of exchange controls to consider their purpose. A developed exchange control system is like a wall or barrier surrounding the country and, similar to the import and export of goods, there are gates through which payments may pass controlled by the government (or, more often, by commercial banks on the government's behalf.) The theory is that without the controls, capital needed for domestic purposes could flow out of the country or unwanted capital could flow in. (Switzerland and, at times, Germany have maintained restrictions on capital inflows).

The regime of exchange controls tends to be stricter in developing countries, because of insufficient foreign exchange and heightened concern for protection of the domestic economy, and less strict or non-existent in developed countries. For example, the USA, UK, Germany, Denmark and the Netherlands have no exchange control restrictions and the Member States of European Community were to have abolished by 1st July 1990 exchange controls on a wide variety of cross border payments and transaction between residents of the European Community (with a longer period for Spain and Greece). It should be noted that this does not mean that exchange controls need to have been abolished on payments by an EC residents to a US resident, but it is difficult to see how a Member State can maintain effective exchange controls as regards third countries when there must be no restrictions regarding EC members.

. . . .

COMMON CHARACTERISTICS OF EXCHANGE CONTROLS

Let us consider some common characteristics of exchange controls. The following restrictions may apply to a person resident for exchange control purposes in a particular state, unless the relevant authority grants a permission or license.

1. Surrender of foreign exchange.

    Residents are commonly required to sell all export proceeds in return for local currency usually at the official rate of exchange to the central bank or commercial bank or other authorized person for this purpose.

    Some countries may require the repatriation and surrender of any foreign currency and gold held by a resident.

2. No foreign bank accounts.

    It follows that where the restrictions in paragraph 1 apply, residents cannot hold bank accounts outside the State or bank accounts within the State denominated in a foreign currency.

    Some countries permit a variety of different accounts to be maintained such as:

    (a) Non-resident accounts—These may only be held by non-residents and payments into the account can only be from overseas or with permission from within the State. The account is in effect outside the exchange control borders; it is as if it is overseas.

    (b) External—similar to non-resident accounts, these may be held by diplomats or international organizations.

    (c) Blocked—such as those containing funds payable to non-residents awaiting release of foreign exchange or permission to transfer abroad.

3. No borrowing in foreign currencies.

    Residents may be prohibited from borrowing in foreign currencies.

4. No borrowing from non-residents.

    Residents may be prohibited from borrowing in domestic or foreign currency from non-residents.

5. No purchasing or selling foreign currencies other than through authorized persons.

6. No payment to be made to, or for the credit of, a non-resident.

    Permission may be available for bona fide commercial production of appropriate evidence. In countries with rules based on the United Kingdom's former system of exchange control it is not possible to obtain exchange control permission for payments under guarantees ahead of any demand for payment, because of the contingent nature of a guarantee.

7. No registration of a non-resident as the registered holder of a share of a company.

    Permission might be needed for a non-resident to become the registered holder of shares and also when the non-resident wishes to sell shares. This restricts access to the local capital market.

8. No issue of bearer securities or, if permitted, no delivery to a non-resident.

    This is, presumably, because of the ease with which these can be transferred or exported without detection.

9. Non-residents may be prohibited from borrowing domestically, whether in foreign or domestic currency.

This will affect the operations of an overseas subsidiary or possibly, a joint venture, if it is considered non-resident for exchange control purposes and will restrict access to local capital markets.

10. Restrictions on conversion of currencies at the official exchange rate.

Some countries maintain multiple exchange rates which can be used for different purposes. Usually there will be an official exchange rate in effect subsidized by the central bank or other authority which can be used for only a limited class of transactional. The other exchange rates, such as a commercial rate, may be freely negotiable or otherwise reflect the supply and demand in a limited pool. This can be complex but companies need to be aware of what rate will be applied to any particular transaction they are contemplating and to investigate if forward cover is available.

11. Compensating transactions may be prohibited.

These are where a resident of country X agrees with a resident of country Y to make a particular payment in country X for the person's account on the understanding that the resident of country Y will make a corresponding payment in country Y for the country X resident's account.

It will be seen from the above examples that international transactions would be virtually impossible without specific permissions in every case. Consequently, in order to facilitate dealings, governments have developed general permissions to cover certain categories of transactions and may also have delegated authority to commercial banks and others who may have limited authority to grant certain types of permission.

Penalties for breaching exchange control laws can be severe, with fines sometimes running at several times the sums involved. Under domestic law a contract entered into in breach of the domestic exchange control laws may be illegal and *void* (in which case it may be that no party can enforce or recover under it). Alternatively in some jurisdictions, for example those which follow the UK approach, the exchange control law automatically implies in the contract a condition that the particular obligation will not be performed until exchange control permission is granted. It may also imply an obligation on the part of the resident party to use its best efforts to obtain that permission.

EXCHANGE CONTROLS AND FREEZING OR BLOCKING ORDERS

Freezing or blocking orders such as were introduced...concerning Iraq and Kuwait, and earlier against Libya and Iran, appear to be similar to exchange controls but usually have a different purpose; they are less concerned with conserving exchange resources than with protecting other national interests or maintaining national defenses....[T]hey can unpredictably upset many international commercial transactions.

RECOGNITION OF EXCHANGE CONTROLS

1. Local enforcement in a local court

Bringing an action in a local court against a defendant for enforcement of a transaction against that country's exchange control laws will probably not succeed even if the transaction concerned is governed by a different system of law. In other words, do not assume that by contracting under, say, New York law, a claimant will be able to enforce contract in the court of country X against country X's exchange control laws.

2. Enforcement outside the country whose exchange control laws are breached

There is now a large number of cases where contracts in breach of exchange control laws of a particular country have been considered by courts outside that country.

How these are approached depends on whether or not the IMF Agreement, being the Articles of Agreement of the International Monetary Fund signed in 1944 at Bretton Woods and amended in 1969 and 1978, applies. This is because the IMF Agreement imposes an overriding requirement on the rules of the contract or the forum which would otherwise apply.

Where the IMF Agreement Does Not Apply

Where a claim is brought in an external court against a defendant claiming defense on the basis of exchange control laws, the position may be determined by whether the law governing the contract is the same as that imposing the exchange control or is an external law.

If the governing law is the same as the exchange control law, the exchange control restrictions will probably be recognized, unless, for example, they are penal, discriminatory or contrary to public policy. This is a hazard of contracting under the local system of law and consequently for the exchange controls not to be recognized they have to be extreme. Both the English and the US courts have recognized foreign exchange controls.

If, however, the governing law of the contract is a law different from that imposing the exchange control, then the exchange control will probably be ignored even if this would result in the defendant having to perform an act illegal in its own country. But the English courts will not enforce a contract where the exchange control is imposed by the law of the place where the payment must be made, although the US courts seem to have adapted a more flexible approach by, for example, requiring that performance be moved to a country where payment can be made. Also the English courts may be reluctant to enforce a contract which is intended to violate the laws of a country with which the UK has friendly relations.

Where the IMF Agreement Does Apply

Recognition of exchange controls is different where the IMF Agreement applies. This is because the provisions of Article VIII, Section 2(b) of IMF Agreement superimposes a requirement on the private international law of each Member State.

Article VIII 2(b) provides as follows:

"Exchange contracts which involve the currency of any member and which are contrary to the exchange control regulations of that member maintained or imposed consistently with this Agreement shall be unenforceable in the territories of any member."

This seemingly straightforward sentence has been the subject of much scholarly analysis, and has been considered by the courts in a number of countries with inconsistent results.

The purpose of Article VII 2(b) is to ensure that the courts of the forum will recognize the relevant foreign exchange control regulations even though they might not be part of the governing law or might otherwise under the rules of the forum be ignored for reasons of public policy or similar....

One of the reasons for the confusion caused by the cases is that domestic courts tend to approach the interpretation of treaties differently from domestic statutes.

Usually courts are not allowed to go behind a domestic statute; they must consider it on its face and not necessarily go into its legislative history. For treaties, however, it is permissible to look at the working documents leading to the treaty in order to ascertain its meaning and to achieve its purpose.

... [I]t is worth considering a number of the phrases in Article VIII 2(b) so as to highlight some of the problems and to show the varied approaches adopted in different countries.

(a) "Exchange Contracts" — The narrow interpretation of this phrase catches only contracts to exchange the currency of one country into the currency on another. If this is followed, then it would not cover a wide range of transactions where direct currency exchange is involved.

The broader interpretation is that an exchange contract is one which any way affects a country's exchange resources; for example, if a resident of one country agrees to make a payment in a foreign currency to a non-resident, that resident may have to sell domestic currency to purchase foreign currency, thus using the foreign exchange reserves of the state.

The English courts have adopted both narrow and broad approaches. In one case (*Wilson, Smithett & Cope Ltd v. Terruzzi* [1976] 1 All E.R. 817 C.A.)), an Italian resident failed in his defense on Italian exchange control grounds to pay sterling in London in respect of dealings on the London Metal Exchange. The court held that a broad definition would restrict international trade. Yet the courts in *United City Merchants (Instruments) Limited v. Royal Bank of Canada* [1982] 1 ALL E.R. 720 adopted a different approach. In that case a UK seller and a Peruvian buyer agreed on a price in US dollars for goods to be paid through a letter of credit. The letter of credit was opened for twice value of the goods on the basis that the seller would remit the balance to Peruvian buyer's bank account in the US contrary to Peruvian exchange control. The confirming bank refused payment relying, in part, on Article VIII 2(b). The House of Lords divided the transaction into two, holding the confirming bank liable for the genuine part of the transaction but not for the balance since that was a monetary transaction in disguise.

In contrast the New York court in *Zeevi & Sons Ltd v. Grindlays Bank (Uganda) Ltd.*, 37 N.Y. 2d 220, 333 N.E. 2d 168, 371 N.Y.S. 2d 892 (1975) held that a letter of credit was not an exchange contract and disregarded Ugandan exchange control restrictions, although it is possible to regard the decision as taken on the grounds of public policy, since it was considered that the acts of the Ugandan government, in canceling all payments to Israeli companies, were confiscatory and discriminatory, and taken to avoid liability under a letter of credit validly opened prior to the introduction of exchange control regulation.

....

(b) "Contracts" — If the claim does not involve a contract, then it appears Article VIII 2(b) does not apply. Therefore actions in tort and actions in rem may not be covered.

(c) "Exchange Control Regulations" — This phrase is generally regarded as covering only those laws controlling the movement of currency, property or services in order to protect the exchange resources of a country. Thus it would not usually cover tariffs, trade restrictions or trading with enemy regulations. Nor would it cover exchange controls which are not genuine as such, *i.e.*, not passed with the intention of protecting the economy. It also does not apply to legal tender laws, being those laws requiring settlement of transactions in a particular currency in order to discharge obligations under municipal law.

(d) "Maintained or imposed consistently with this Agreement"—This means that not all exchange control regulations need to be recognized, only these which are consistent with the IMF Agreement not to impose restrictions on payments of current transactions, except in times of currency shortage. "Current transactions" include payments in connection with foreign trade on loans and a moderate amount for amortization of loans.

(e) "Unenforceable"—This is obviously not the same as providing that the contract is illegal but that the courts should not assist in its performance or award damages for a breach. A contract may be unenforceable, but still legally binding. If this is the case, then it may be possible to exercise self-help remedies which do not require assistance of the courts, such as set-off. It also may be possible to sever the unenforceable term and enforce the remainder of the contract.

HOW TO DEAL WITH EXCHANGE CONTROLS

Exchange controls cannot usually be legally avoided; a party selling goods to or investing in a project or providing services to a foreign country may rely on obtaining payment from that country; that is the source of payment and consequently its exchange control laws will affect the ability of the foreign party to obtain payment. There may, however, be a number of ways to organize a transaction or practices which can be followed which may limit or reduce the exposure.

1. Choice of Law and Jurisdiction

Choosing an external system of law and an external forum for disputes may assist in obtaining a judgment against an obligor whose defense is based on an exchange control regulation. This is because the regulation is not part of the law governing the contract or alternatively, because the regulation is not part of the law of the place of performance. This is not foolproof insulation from the defendant's law as Article VIII 2(b) of the IMF Agreement may apply and override the proper law or law of place of performance.

Having obtained a judgment, a plaintiff may be able to enforce it against assets of the defendant outside the country imposing the exchange control but may still be faced by the local exchange control if it attempts to enforce in that country.

2. Exchange Control Consents as Conditions Precedent

Obviously exchange control consents should be obtained as early as possible in a transaction. Usually the grant of exchange control permission will be made as a express condition precedent to, for example, the borrowing of a loan or shipment of goods. It may be prudent for the supplier to limit the scope of its obligations until the necessary consents have been granted and to impose on the overseas purchaser or borrower an obligation to obtain the relevant consent.

3. Scope of Exchange Control Consents

Exchange control consents should cover (a) entry into the contract and (b) performance of all obligations under the contract. In countries which operate several exchange rates, the consent might also cover which exchange rate will apply to the transaction.

In some countries, it is not possible to obtain exchange control consents until after agreements have been signed or, . . . until after the loans have been disbursed. It is wise, however, to obtain advances comfort or advise that the consent will be obtained.

. . . .

4. *Registration of the Transaction and Maintenance of Records*

It is important to ensure that the transaction is properly registered or filed with the appropriate government authorities and that the supplier or investor keep copies of filings, records and other details concerning the investment.

Proper registration may be a requirement to obtaining an exchange control consent at a later date. Also in countries which operate more than one exchange rate, it may be necessary to show which exchange rate was used when funds entered the country.

5. *Requiring the Purchaser to Maintain Foreign Exchange Sources*

It may be possible for the purchaser or borrower to retain all or part of its foreign exchange earnings which can then be used to meet its obligations to overseas contractors or even charged to them by way of security.

This can sometimes be made a requirement of a joint venture or project financing.

6. *Obtaining Currency Undertakings from the Central Bank*

The central bank or authority in charge of allocating foreign exchange may be willing to enter into an undertaking directly with the overseas supplier (usually a lender) to make available the necessary foreign exchange to the domestic obligor, (usually the government or a public body), to grant the necessary permissions to make the payment and to ensure that sufficient foreign exchange is available.

This undertaking creates a direct contractual link between the central bank and the overseas supplier and may itself constitute an exchange contract under Article VIII 2(b) of the IMF Agreement. Considerations as to governing law, jurisdiction and sovereign immunity will still apply.

Regardless of whether or not currency undertaking is obtained, it is important to identify which governmental authority is in charge of allocating foreign exchange to domestic enterprises.

7. *Barter or Obtaining Product in Settlement*

It may be possible for the supplier to receive payment by ways of barter or other payment in kind from the overseas purchaser [*i.e.*, a countertrade arrangement] although the transaction may have to be structured carefully to fall outside the exchange control net, for example, outside the requirement for the overseas purchaser to surrender foreign exchange earned on exports.

. . . .

9. *Export Credit Insurance*

Suppliers should consider obtaining export credit insurance which may cover the risk of exchange controls being imposed or permissions revoked.

. . . .

11. *Investing in Enterprises that Earn Foreign Exchange*

As a general rule, those organizations that earn foreign exchange may be allowed to retain all or portion of it or may have readier access to it. Also, such organizations may have greater influence and be more powerful in countries which experience foreign exchange shortages because of the power conferred by earnings or controlling foreign exchange attributable to the easier access to foreign goods and services. Investing in, or selling to, such organizations may be safer than to others.

12. *Currency Indemnity*

It is sometimes appropriate to obtain currency indemnity from the overseas purchaser or borrower. This normally provides that if it is necessary to convert a foreign currency claim into local currency for the purpose of obtaining a judgment or enforcing it or if there is some other local rule which allows an overseas purchaser or borrower to tender local currency in satisfaction of a claim (*e.g.*, payment into a blocked account), then the overseas person will pay the supplier any additional amounts as are necessary to result in the supplier receiving the full amount in foreign currency contracted for, after converting the local currency into foreign currency. The indemnity should also cover the relevant foreign exchange costs and any premium payable on conversion.

13. *Self-help Remedies*

Suppliers may be able to exercise self-help remedies and thereby avoid the application of exchange control regulations. If a remedy such as set-off can be exercised without resort to the courts, then this can effective in reducing foreign exchange exposure. Companies which export from, and purchase through, a number of different subsidiaries may need to consider consolidating operation operations or assigning debts for set-off purposes.

14. *The Use of Blocked Funds*

What can be done if in spite of all the best precautions, a supplier or investor ends up holding funds in a blocked account at a bank in a foreign country? There are a number of possibilities, including:

(a) Waiting for permission to be granted—usually this depends on the availability of foreign exchange. The funds may or may not be bearing interest.

(b) Using the funds for new investment. The government may allow this but it will be important to ensure that the funds retain their character as funds ultimately eligible for remittance overseas and any governmental permission should expressly recognize this Debt/equity swap plans which are commonly set up under developing country bank debt reschedulings are an example of this.

Also in the case of Nigeria's re-scheduling of uninsured trade debt in the early 1980's, trade creditors who took promissory notes in satisfaction of their claims were able to use them, able to transfer them to others to use, for investment in Nigeria.

(c) Transfer the blocked funds to third parties. There may be an offshore market in blocked funds in which they sold at a discount. The funds are not always technically transferred under these arrangements. Rather, there is an assignment of the debt. Exchange control permission for this transfer may be necessary.

REPATRIATION

Most of what has been said about exchange controls applies to repatriation of overseas investments.

It is, however, worth emphasizing the following:

1. There may be specific rules concerning repatriation, particularly in developing countries. These may require that repatriation permission will not be granted until after a specific period and then, only at a maximum amount or percentage of investment per year....

2. Repatriate promptly. It may be better not to delay repatriation in case later there arises a shortage of foreign exchange or a change in government policy or there becomes a risk of expropriation.

3. It may be possible to purchase repatriation rights from others.

4. Branch operations in foreign countries may reduce the repatriation exposure in that any operations outside the country and held by the company would not be subject to repatriation.....

Banco Do Brasil, S.A. v. A.C. Israel Commodity Co.
12 N.Y.2d 371 (N.Y. Ct. App. 1963)

BURKE, JUDGE.

The action upon which the attachment here challenged is based is brought by appellant as an instrumentality of the Government of Brazil to recover damages for a conspiracy to defraud the Government of Brazil of American dollars by illegally circumventing the foreign exchange regulations of Brazil.

Defendant-respondent, Israel Commodity, a Delaware corporation having its principal place of business in New York, is an importer of Brazilian coffee. The gist of plaintiff's complaint is that Israel conspired with a Brazilian exporter of coffee to pay the exporter American dollars which the exporter could sell in the Brazilian free market for 220 Brazilian cruzeiros each instead of complying with Brazil's foreign exchange regulations which in effect required a forced sale of the dollars paid to the exporter to the Government of Brazil for only 90 cruzeiros. Through this conspiracy, the Brazilian exporter profited by the difference between the amount (in cruzeiros) it would have received for the dollars from the Government of Brazil and the amount it received in the open market in violation of Brazilian law, Israel profited by being able to pay less dollars for the coffee (because the dollars were worth so much more to the seller), and the plaintiff suffered a loss measured by the difference in amount it would have to pay for the same number of dollars in the open market and what it could have paid for them through the "forced sale" had its foreign exchange regulations been obeyed. The evasion was allegedly accomplished through the exporter's forgery of the documents evidencing receipt of the dollars by plaintiff Banco Do Brasil, S. A., and without which the coffee could not have left Brazil.

Plaintiff argues that respondent's participation in the violation of Brazilian exchange control laws affords a ground of recovery because of Article VIII (§ 2, subd. [b]) of the Bretton Woods Agreement, a multilateral treaty to which both this country and Brazil are signatories. The Section provides: "Exchange contracts which involve the currency of any member and which are contrary to the exchange control regulations of that member maintained or imposed consistently with this Agreement shall be unenforceable in the territories of any member." (60 U.S. Stat. 1411.) It is far from clear whether this sale of coffee is covered by subdivision (b) of Section 2. The Section deals with "exchange contracts" which "involve" the "currency" of any member of the International Monetary Fund, "and *   *   * are contrary to the exchange control regulations of that member maintained or imposed consistently with" the agreement. Subdivision (b) of Section 2 has been construed as reaching only "transactions which have as their immediate object 'exchange,' that is, international media of payment" or a contract where the consideration is payable in the currency of the country whose exchange controls are violated. More recently, however, it has been suggested that it applies to "contracts which in any way affect a country's exchange resources." A similar view has been advanced to explain the further textual difficulty existing with respect to whether a sale of coffee in New York for American dollars "involves the currency" of Brazil, the member whose exchange controls were allegedly violated. Again it is suggested that adverse effect on the exchange resources of a member *ipso facto* "involves" the "currency" of that member. We are inclined to view an interpretation of subdivision (b) of Section 2 that sweeps in all contracts affecting any members' exchange resources as doing considerable violence to the text of the Section. It says "involve the currency" of the country whose exchange controls are violated; not "involve the exchange resources." While noting these doubts, we nevertheless prefer to rest this decision on other and clearer grounds.

The sanction provided in subdivision (b) of Section 2 is that contracts covered thereby are to be "unenforceable" in the territory of any member. The clear import of this provision is to insure the avoidance of the affront inherent in any attempt by the courts of one member to render a judgment that would put the losing party in the position of either complying with the judgment and violating the exchange controls of another member or complying with such controls and refusing obedience to the judgment. A further reasonable inference to be drawn from the provision is that the courts of no member should award any recovery for breach of an agreement in violation of the exchange controls of another member. Indeed, the International Monetary Fund itself, in an official interpretation of subdivision (b) of Section 2 issued by the Fund's Executive Directors, construes the Section as meaning that "the obligations of such contracts will not be implemented by the judicial or administrative authorities of member countries, for example, by decreeing performance of the contracts or by awarding damages for their non-performance." (International Monetary Fund Ann. Rep. 82-83 [1949], 14 Fed. Reg. 5208, 5209 [1949].) An obligation to withhold judicial assistance to secure the benefits of such contracts does not imply an obligation to impose tort penalties on those who have fully executed them.

From the viewpoint of the individuals involved, it must be remembered that the Bretton Woods Agreement relates to international law. It imposes obligations among and between States, not individuals. The fact that by virtue of the agreement New York must not "enforce" a contract between individuals which is contrary to the exchange controls of any member, imposes no obligation (under the law of the transaction— New York law *   *   *) on such individuals not to enter into such contracts. While it does mean that they so agree at their peril inasmuch as they may not look to our courts for enforcement, this again is far from implying that one who so agrees commits a tort in New York for which he must respond in damages. It is significant that a proposal to make such an agreement an "offense" was defeated at Bretton Woods.

Lastly, and inseparable from the foregoing, there is a remedial consideration which bars recovery in this case. Plaintiff is an instrumentality of the Government of Brazil and is seeking, by use of an action for conspiracy to defraud, to enforce what is clearly a revenue law. Whatever may be the effect of the Bretton Woods Agreement, . . . "A contract made in a foreign country between citizens thereof and intended by them to be there performed" in that one State does not enforce the revenue laws of another. Nothing in the Bretton Woods Agreement is to the contrary. In fact its use of the unenforceability device for effectuation of its purposes impliedly concedes the unavailability of the more direct method of enforcement at the suit of the aggrieved government. By the second sentence of subdivision (b) of Section 2, further measures to make exchange controls more effective may be agreed upon by the member States. This is a matter for the Federal Government which not only has not entered into such further accords but has not even enacted the enabling provision into law (U.S. Code, tit. 22, § 286h).

Therefore, the order should be affirmed....

CHIEF JUDGE DESMOND, *dissenting*.

The order should be reversed and the warrant of attachment reinstated since the complaint alleges a cause of action within the jurisdiction of the New York State courts.

If there had never been a Bretton Woods Agreement and if this were a suit to enforce in this State the revenue laws of Brazil it would have to be dismissed under the ancient rule most recently restated in *City of Philadelphia v. Cohen*, 11 N.Y.2d 401. But Cohen and its predecessor cases express a public policy which lacks applicability here because of the adherence of the United States to the Bretton Woods Agreement. As we noted in *Perutz v. Bohemian Discount Bank in Liquidation*, 304 N.Y. 533, the membership of our Federal Government in the International Monetary Fund and other Bretton Woods enterprises makes it impossible to say that the currency control laws of other member States are offensive to our public policy. Furthermore, the argument from *City of Philadelphia v. Cohen* . . . and similar decisions assumes erroneously that this is a suit to collect internal taxes assessed by the Brazilian Government. In truth, it is not even an effort to enforce Brazil's currency regulations. This complaint and other papers charge a tortious fraud and conspiracy to deprive plaintiff, an instrumentality of the Brazilian Government, of the dollar proceeds of coffee exports to which proceeds the bank and its government were entitled. This fraud, it is alleged, was accomplished by inserting in coffee shipping permits references to nonexistent exchange contracts and to nonexistent assignments to plaintiff of the foreign exchange proceeds of the coffee exports and by forging the signatures of banking officials and Brazilian officials, all with the purpose of making it appear that there had been compliance with the Brazilian statutes or regulations. The alleged scheme and effect of the conspiracy as charged was to obtain for defendant-respondent coffee in New York at a reduced price, to enable the Brazilian defendants to get more "cruzeiros" per dollar in violation of law and to deprive Brazil of the cruzeiros which it would have received from these coffee sales had the fraud not been committed. According to the complaint and affidavits defendant Israel not only knew of and intended to benefit by the perpetration of this fraud but participated in it in New York by making its purchase agreements here and by here receiving the shipping documents and making payments. The Israel corporation is alleged to have been one of the consignees of some 36,000 bags of coffee exported from Brazil to New York in 1961 without compliance with the Brazilian law and thus to have fraudulently and conspiratorially caused to Brazil damage of nearly $2,000,000. Refusal to entertain this suit does violence to our national policy of cooperation with other Bretton Woods signatories and is not required by anything in our own States policy.

. . . .

Order affirmed, with costs. . . . .

United City Merchants (Investments) Ltd.
V. Royal Bank of Canada

[1982] 2 All E.R. 720 (House of Lords)

Lord Diplock. My Lords, this appeal ... raises two distinct questions of law. ... The first, which I will call the documentary credit point, relates to the mutual rights and obligations of the confirming bank and the beneficiary under a documentary credit. ... The second question, which I will call the Bretton Woods point, ... turns on the construction of the Bretton Woods Agreements Order in Council 1946, SR & O 1946/36 and its application to the particular facts of the instant case.

.... The documentary credit point depends on the contractual relationship between the sellers (or their transferee) and the confirming bank. The Bretton Woods point is about the effect on that relationship of certain special provisions in an agreement between the sellers and the buyers that was collateral to their contract of sale. [The portion of Lord Diplock's opinion on the documentary credit point is omitted. Documentary credits are dealt with in a separate chapter of this Casebook.]

....

A Peruvian company, Vitrorefuerzos SA (the buyer), agreed to buy from the second appellant (the seller) plant for the manufacture of glass fibres (the goods) at a price of $662,086 fob London for shipment to Callao. Payment was to be in London by confirmed irrevocable transferable letter of credit for the invoice price plus freight, payable as to 20% of the invoice price on the opening of the credit, as to 70% of the invoice price and 100% of the freight on presentation of shipping documents and as to the balance of 10% of the invoice price on completion of erection of the plant in Peru.

The buyer arranged with its Peruvian bank, Banco Continental SA (the issuing bank), to issue the necessary credit and the issuing bank appointed the respondent, Royal Bank of Canada (the confirming bank), to advise and confirm on its own behalf the credit to the seller. The confirming bank duly notified the seller on 30 March 1976 of the opening of the confirmed irrevocable transferable letter of credit. So far as concerned the 70% of the invoice price and 100% freight there was nothing that was unusual in its terms. It was expressed to be subject to the Uniform Customs and Practice for Documentary Credits (1974 revision) of the International Chamber of Commerce (the Uniform Customs) and to be available by sight drafts on the issuing bank against delivery, inter alia, of a full set "on board" bills of lading evidencing receipt for shipment of the goods from London to Callao on or before a date in October 1976, which was subsequently extended to 15 December 1976.

The initial payment of 20% of the invoice price was duly made by the confirming bank to the seller. Thereafter, in July 1976, the seller transferred to its own merchant bankers, the first appellant, its interest under the credit as security for advances; but nothing turns on this so far as ... the Bretton Woods point is concerned. In dealing with the relevant law ... I shall accordingly treat the seller as having continued throughout to be the beneficiary of the confirmed credit.

The goods, which had to be manufactured by the seller, were ready for shipment by the beginning of December 1976. It was intended by the loading brokers acting on behalf of Prudential Lines Inc (the carriers) that they should be shipped on a vessel belonging to the carriers (the American Legend) due to arrive at Felixstowe on 10 December 1976. (The substitution of Felixstowe for London as the loading port is immaterial. It was acquiesced in by all parties to the transaction.) The arrival of the American Legend at Felixstowe was canceled and another vessel, the American Accord, was substituted by the loading brokers; but its date of arrival was scheduled for 16 December 1976, one day after the latest date of shipment required by the documentary credit. The goods were in fact loaded on the American Accord on 16 December 1976; but the loading brokers, who also acted as agents for the carriers in issuing bills of lading, issued in the first instance a set of 'received for shipment' bills of lading dated 15 December 1976 and handed them over to the sellers in return for payment of the freight. On presentation of the shipping documents to the confirming bank on 17 December that bank raised various objections to their form, of which the only one that is relevant to the documentary credit point was that the bills of lading did not bear any dated "on board" notation. The bills of lading were returned to the carriers' freight brokers who issued a fresh set bearing the notation, which was untrue: "These goods are actually on board 15th December 1976. E. H. Mundy and Co. (Freight Agents) Ltd. as Agents." The amended bills of lading together with the other documents were represented to the confirming bank on 22 December 1976, but the confirming bank again refused to pay on the ground that they "had information in their possession which suggested that shipment was not effected as it appears in the bill of lading."

.... The seller's original quotation for the sale price of the glass fibre making plant was half the figure that ultimately became the invoice price for the purposes of the documentary credit. The buyer who was desirous of converting Peruvian currency into United States dollars available to it in the United States, a transaction which was contrary to Peruvian exchange control regulations, persuaded the seller to invoice the plant to it at double the real sale price in United States dollars and to agree that it would within ten days after drawing on the documentary credit for each of the three instalments of the invoice price remit one-half of the amount so drawn to the dollar account in Miami, Florida, of an American corporation controlled by the buyer. This the seller agreed to do; and of the first instalment of 20% of the now doubled invoice price of $662,086, which was the only drawing that it succeeded in making under the credit, it transmitted one-half, *viz* $66,208, to the American corporation in Florida. It would have done the same with one-half of the next drawing of 70% of the invoice price payable against shipping documents, if the confirming bank had paid this instalment.

....

The Bretton Woods point arises out of the agreement between the buyers and the seller collateral to the contract of sale of the goods between the same parties that out of the payments in United States dollars received by the sellers under the documentary credit in respect of each instalment of the invoice price of the goods they would transmit to the account of the buyers in America one-half of the United States dollars received.

The Bretton Woods Agreements Order in Council 1946, made under the Bretton Woods Agreements Act 1945, gives the force of law in England to art VIII, s 2(*b*) of the Bretton Woods Agreements, which is in the following terms:

> Exchange contracts which involve the currency of any Member and which are contrary to the exchange control regulations of that member maintained or imposed consistently with this Agreement shall be unenforceable in the territories of any member....

My Lords, I accept as correct the narrow interpretation that was placed on the expression "exchange contracts" in this provision of the Bretton Woods Agreements by the Court of Appeal in *Wilson, Smithett & Cope Ltd v Teruzzi* [1976] I All ER 817, [1976] QB 683. It is confined to contracts to exchange the currency of one country for the currency of another; it does not include contracts entered into in connection with sales of goods which require the conversion by the buyer of one currency into another in order to enable him to pay the purchase price. As was said by Lord Denning MR in his judgment in the *Teruzzi* case, the court in considering the application of the provision should look at the substance of the contracts and not at the form. It should not enforce a contract that is a mere "monetary transaction in disguise."

I also accept as accurate what was said by Lord Denning MR in a subsequent case as to the effect that should be given by English courts to the word "unenforceable." The case, *Batra v Ebrahim* [1977] CA Transcript 197B, is unreported, but the relevant passage from Lord Denning's judgment is helpfully cited by Ackner LJ in his own judgment in the instant case (*see* [1981] 3 All ER 142 at 166, [1982] AC 208 at 241-242). If in the course of the hearing of an action the court becomes aware that the contract on which a party is suing is one that this country has accepted an international obligation to treat as unenforceable, the court must take the point itself, even though the defendant has not pleaded it, and must refuse to lend its aid to enforce the contract. But this does not have the effect of making an exchange contract that is contrary to the exchange control regulations of a member state other than the United Kingdom into a contract that is "illegal" under English law or render acts undertaken in this country in performance of such a contract unlawful. Like a contract of guarantee of which there is no note or memorandum in writing it is unenforceable by the courts and nothing more.

Mocatta J., professing to follow the guidance given in the *Teruzzi* case, took the view that the contract of sale between the buyer and the seller at the inflated invoice price was a monetary transaction in disguise and that, despite the autonomous character of the contract between the seller and the confirming bank under the documentary credit, this too was tarred with the same brush and was a monetary transaction in disguise and therefore one which the court should not enforce. He rejected out of hand what he described as a "rather remarkable submission" that the seller could recover that half of the invoice price which represented the true sale price of the goods, even if they could not recover that other half of the invoice price which they would receive as trustees for the buyers on trust to transmit it to the buyer's American company in Florida. He held that it was impossible to sever the contract constituted by the documentary credit: it was either enforceable in full or not at all.

In refusing to treat the seller's claim under the documentary credit for that part of the invoice price that it was to retain for itself as the sale price of the goods in a different way from that in which he treated its claim to that part of the invoice price which they would receive as trustees for the buyer, I agree with all three members of the Court of Appeal the judge fell into error.

I avoid speaking of "severability," for this expression is appropriate where the task on which the court is engaged is construing the language that the parties have used in a written contract. The question whether and to what extent a contract is unenforceable under the Bretton Woods Agreements Order in Council 1946 because it is a monetary transaction in disguise is *not* a question of construction of the contract but a question of the substance of the transaction to which enforcement of the contract will give effect. If the matter were to be determined simply as a question of construction, the contract between the sellers and the confirming bank constituted by the documentary credit fell altogether outside the Bretton Woods Agreements: it was not a contract to exchange one currency for another currency but a contract to pay currency for documents which included documents of title to goods. On the contrary, the task on which the court is engaged is to penetrate any disguise presented by the actual words the parties have used, to identify any monetary transaction (in the narrow sense of that expression as used in the *Teruzzi* case) which those words were intended to conceal and to refuse to enforce the contract to the extent that to do so would give effect to the monetary transaction.

In the instant case there is no difficulty in identifying the monetary transaction that was sought to be concealed by the actual words used in the documentary credit and in the underlying contract of sale. It was to exchange Peruvian currency provided by the buyer in Peru for U.S. $ 331,043 to be made available to it in Florida; and to do this was contrary to the exchange control regulations of Peru. Payment under the documentary credit by the confirming bank to the seller of that half of the invoice price (*viz* $ 331,043) that the seller would receive as trustee for the buyer on trust to remit it to the account of the buyer's American company in Florida was an essential part of that monetary transaction and therefore unenforceable; but payment of the other half of the invoice price and of the freight was not: the seller would receive that part of the payment under the documentary credit on its own behalf and retain it as the genuine purchase price of goods sold by it to the buyer. I agree with the Court of Appeal that there is nothing in the Bretton Woods Agreements Order in Council 1946 that prevents the payment under the documentary credit being enforceable to this extent.

As regards the first instalment of 20% of the invoice price, this was paid by the confirming bank in full. No enforcement by the court of this payment is needed by the buyers. The confirming bank, if it had known at the time of the monetary transaction by the buyer that was involved, could have successfully resisted payment of one-half of that instalment; but even if it was in possession of such knowledge there was nothing in English law to prevent it from voluntarily paying that half too. As regards the third instalment of 10% of the invoice price, that never fell due within the period of the credit. What is in issue in this appeal is the second instalment of 70% of the invoice price and 100% of the freight which, as I have held under the documentary credit point, fell due on the re-presentation of the documents on 22 December 1976. In my opinion the seller is entitled to judgment for that part of the second instalment which was not a monetary transaction in disguise, that is to say 35% of the invoice price and 100% of the freight, amounting in all to U.S. $ 262,807.49, with interest thereon from 22 December 1976.

. . . .

Appeal allowed.

Part III

Regulatory Challenges

Chapter 9

Regulating Foreign Direct Investment

I. Challenges Posed by FDI

Documents Supplement References:
1. *Restatement Sections 401-403, 414, 421, and 431.*

Claudio Grossman and Daniel D. Bradlow, Are We Being Propelled Towards A People-Centered Transnational Legal Order?

9 American University Journal of International
Law and Policy 1, 2-9, 11-13, 22-25 (1993)

INTRODUCTION

Sovereignty is the fundamental concept around which international law is presently organized. This principle holds that "[e]xcept as limited by international law or treaty, each state is master of its own territory." Consistent with this conception of absolute sovereignty, international law has traditionally been concerned with the relations between co-equal sovereign states. Each sovereign state can only be legally bound by those commitments it willingly makes to other sovereign states, and by those few principles which are viewed as binding on all states. Those issues that arise from the relationship between the state and its citizens, and between those citizens *inter se*, are viewed as part of the domestic affairs of each sovereign state and thus outside the scope of international law.

This theory of international law, founded upon a clear division between domestic and international issues, was reasonable, as long as most human activity took place within clearly defined geographic boundaries; that is, within nation-states. It became less satisfactory as technological and socio-economic developments expanded the range of activities and socio-economic developments expanded the range of activities whose causes or effects transcended national boundaries and increased national interdependence.

The international community responded to these changes by creating international organizations mandated to coordinate specific areas of international relations.

Examples of the organizations include the League of Nations and the International Labour Organisation. These organizations, however, did not alter the basic orientation of international law because they were organized around the fundamental principle of sovereignty. In addition, the organizations lacked the effective powers needed to compel sovereign states to abide by their rules and decisions.

The Second World War provided members of the international community with a powerful and tragic lesson in the dangers inherent in an international legal order based upon a notion of absolute sovereignty. The contemporary international order severely limited the ability of the international community to intervene in the internal affairs of sovereign states. This lesson provided the impetus for the creation of new international organizations. The new organizations were still organized around the principle of sovereignty, but they were given some ability to compel member states to comply with their rules and decisions.

These new organizations included the United Nations, the International Monetary Fund, and the International Bank for Reconstruction and Development. The United Nations was charged with the maintenance of peace and security. Its Charter recognized, without further definition, the existence of human rights that imposed international obligations on all member states. This initial recognition was sufficient to initiate the development of human rights law and the process of international organizational supervision of those rights. The International Monetary Fund (IMF) was mandated to regulate an international monetary order based on the member states' commitment to freely convertible currencies and stable but flexible exchange rates. The International Bank for Reconstruction and Development (World Bank or IBRD) was established to fund the reconstruction of war torn Europe, and to develop the poorer countries of the world. The mandate of the World Bank was to complement private capital and to facilitate the growth of both the borrower's and the world's economy.

The international community's support for international organizations and willingness to place restrictions on state sovereignty was not unlimited. The international community ultimately failed to ratify the creation of a fourth international organization, the International Trade Organization (ITO). The ITO would have regulated most non-monetary aspects of the international economy. The only surviving remnant of the ITO is the General Agreement on Tariffs and Trade (GATT). This intergovernmental agreement establishes the framework for international trade in goods between the contracting parties. [Of course, on 1 January 1995, two years after this article was published, the World Trade Organization (WTO) was born as a result of the 1986-93 Uruguay Round multilateral trade negotiations. The WTO is the modern-day reincarnation of the failed ITO.]

Even though the organizations were originally founded upon the principle of sovereignty, the establishment of the United Nations and the Bretton Woods Institutions constituted a movement away from an international legal order based solely upon absolute sovereignty. Both the United Nations and the IMF created a superstructure which operates above the level of the individual member states, and to which each member state agreed to surrender some aspect of its sovereignty in return for the political, economic or social benefits to be derived from membership in the organization. For example, by joining the United Nations, member states agreed to limit their ability to use force and to submit decisions relating to international peace and security to the U.N. Security Council. They also granted the General Assembly broad authority to discuss publicly issues of international concern.

Similarly, by joining the IMF, member states agreed to surrender some of their control over their exchange rate and their monetary policy. Further, member states agreed to abide by the international monetary rules formulated at the Bretton Woods Conference. The IMF was mandated to monitor compliance with these rules through regular consultations with all member states. The benefits to be derived from compliance include an efficient international payments mechanism, IMF financial support if the country experienced difficulty in meeting its international monetary obligations; and membership in the World Bank, where the country could obtain financing for development projects. World Bank loans, whose covenants restricted the borrower's future conduct or imposed certain reporting requirements on the borrower, also contributed to the erosion of absolute sovereignty.

During the first few decades after World War II, the movement away from sovereignty often was not perceptible. Indeed, in the wake of decolonization, the role of sovereignty in international law appeared to be strengthened by the growing number of nation-states in the world and by their aggressive assertion of the rights of sovereign states. These developments, however, masked a slow but steady diminution in the realities of sovereign power and a growing gap between the legal principle of sovereignty and the factual reality of a world of limited sovereign states.

This gap between theory and reality has manifested itself in two ways. First, there has been a steady increase in the number of activities whose effects spill over national boundaries and in activities which states are unable to regulate independently. Examples of these issues include global environmental issues; nuclear proliferation; financial flows; refugees; transfers of technology; the trade, labor, consumer, and tax consequences of globalized production patterns; and such criminal law problems as drug trafficking and gun control. Since effective resolution of the legal issues that arise from these activities can only occur at the international level, there is a growing body of international law that seeks to either regulate the activities or to coordinate national regulation efforts.

The internationalization of these issues has also affected the traditional separation of powers between the executive and legislative branches of government. In a reality based on the internationalization of an increasing range of issues coupled with the resulting erosion of the distinction between domestic and international issues, the power of the executive, based on its authority in the realm of international affairs, has expanded at the expense of the legislature.

Given that the legislative branch is the branch of government that most directly represents the sentiments of civil society and in which most of the battles for democratization of social life have been fought, this expansion of executive power has assumed an undemocratic character. It creates a substantial obstacle to the participation by the members of civil society in the affairs that most directly affect them. The expansion of executive power is also forcing private actors to adopt a broader definition of their interests and a more cosmopolitan perception of their politic allies.

The second manifestation of the gap between theory and reality, therefore, has been an increase in the number of actors on the international stage. In addition to states, these actors now include national liberation stage movements; business, consumer, environmental, human rights and other non-governmental organizations (NGOs); political parties; and trade unions. These new actors have recognized that without internationalizing their operations their impact will be limited. They have, thus, begun to develop transnational affiliations and the capacity to operate internationally so that they can make their voices heard in a meaningful way.

The most significant example of this phenomenon is the Transnational Corporation (TNC). While TNCs have existed for centuries, their ability to plan and operate on a global basis grew dramatically as the post-World War II era unfolded. Stimulated by new investment opportunities and technological developments, TNCs have developed the ability to produce their goods and services in multiple interconnected locations. This development has encouraged global distribution patterns and transnational strategic planning.

One important effect of these developments is that TNCs have become "de-nationalized" in the sense that they view the world, rather than their home or host states, as their base of operations. The fact that they have multiple production facilities means that TNCs can evade state power and the constraints of national regulatory schemes by moving their operations between their different facilities around that world. Having multiple production facilities also means that those private actors such as trade unions, consumer groups, and environmental organizations, that traditionally interact with TNCs on a country-by-country basis, are being forced to transnationalize so that they can interact with the TNCs in a meaningful way.

This growth in corporate power raises a significant problem for traditional international law. First, it means that whatever the international legal status of states may be, the sovereign has less power, measured in terms of control over human, natural, financial and other resources, than those corporations that it is supposedly regulating. This suggests that in fact the sovereign is no longer "master of its own territory."

The growing power of the TNCs also poses a challenge to the notion that the primary focus of international law should be relations between states. Such a narrow view of international law allows TNCs to evade accountability for their actions at the domestic level by shifting production between different sites. The absence of clear international standards means that they can also avoid regulation at the international level. Thus, TNCs are able to operate in an unregulated manner. This regulatory situation is not beneficial for the TNCs and the multitude of stakeholders in their operations. The absence of an effective regulator complicates the efforts of TNCs to establish universally recognized standards of conduct for the host state-foreign investor relationships.

. . . .

II. The forces for change

A. Technological Changes

In the past fifteen to twenty years, developments in information technologies and telecommunications have revolutionized the world economy and the way in which human beings conduct their day to day affairs. These developments and "globalizing" the international economy and creating transnational linkages between private actors.

Investors can use computer programs to plan their investment strategies and electronic funds transfers to move instantaneously their funds around the world in search of better returns. Engineers working for the same company but in different countries can use computer technologies to work simultaneously on the same design project. Researchers and scholars located around the world can conduct an ongoing international dialogue over electronic mail or E-mail networks. Human rights and other social activists can use facsimiles and E-mail to inform the world of developments in their countries. The global media can then spread this information instantaneously around the world.

While these technological developments open up exciting possibilities for human development, they also significantly diminish state control over such activities. All the activities described above can occur at speeds that make it difficult for state regulators to detect the activity. Even if they can detect the action, regulators experience difficulty in sanctioning the actor. The speed of the transaction impedes the state's ability to trace the action and identify the actor. In addition, the public's relatively easy access to the computer and telecommunication networks that constitute the infrastructure for these new technologies makes it difficult for states to regulate their use. In fact, those states that have sought to limit the public's access to these new technologies or their ability to use these technologies have found that the price in terms of their ability to participate in the international economy is higher than they can afford.

The result of these developments is that private actors can use these technologies not only to neutralize the regulatory efforts of their sovereign states, but also to determine the legitimacy and authority of the current government. Moreover, these technologies enable individuals and groups to develop connections with others outside their sovereign states that may be stronger than the connections felt towards their compatriots. Accordingly, there is a resulting weakening of national consciousness and the inchoate beginnings of a global conscious.

In such an environment, the relevance and efficacy of an international legal order based on sovereign states is open to debate. This international legal order affords no formal recognition to the corporations, industry associations, NGOs and other private actors who, by virtue of their access to these new technologies, play an increasingly active role in international affairs. In addition, the legal order does not reflect the fact that the new technologies have so enhanced the power of private actors relative to the state that, in many cases, it is not feasible to establish sustainable international standards of conduct without the participation of these private actors or without creating an international body that exercises greater power over its member states than states appear to be willing to surrender.

A good example of an area where the desirability of an international regulatory body is clear is the banking industry. As banks now have the ability and the client-driven need to move instantaneously funds around the world, it is no longer possible for each individual nation state to regulate effectively its banks. In the absence of a central bank that has global jurisdiction, the only sustainable regulatory framework is one that has the support of all the participating banks and financial actors. If not, banks can easily avoid the effects of any regulatory framework that they oppose by moving their money and activities to a non-regulated jurisdiction. Essentially, the banks will exercise this option as long as there is one non-participating jurisdiction.

In short, these technological developments have so undermined the concept of sovereignty that, on some issues, effective rule making and enforcement cannot take place, either at the domestic or the international level, without the full participation of interested private actors. Moreover, the globalized nature of these issues suggests the need for a coherent set of rules that will be applicable at both the domestic and the international level.

. . . .

E. Re-conceptualizing International Legal Issues

The deficiencies of the present international legal order based on the *de jure* sovereignty of the nation-state and a relatively clear distinction between international and domestic legal issues are obvious. The nation-state is no longer functionally "the master of its own territory." Some private actors and international organizations have at least as much power as the sovereign state. They are able to use their power to influence the decisions and policies of the individual nation-state in the domestic realm and of the community of states in the international arena. This shift in power is beginning to produce an international civil society, based on shared interests and new loyalties, the members of which are beginning to demand the right to be full participants in the formulation of international rules and decisions.

These developments pose two challenges for international law. First, it needs to recognize and incorporate into its jurisdiction all international actors. The states, international organizations, and private actors such as transnational corporations; trader unions; consumer, environmental, development and human rights NGOs; and private individuals, are now all engaged in the ongoing process of formulating and implementing international legal standards. An international legal process that fails to allow non-state actors to participate fully in the process cannot develop legal norms that are fully responsive to the needs of the international community.

Second, international law must adapt to the reality that the instantaneous transmittal of information around the globe ensures that the impact of all significant social, economic, cultural, and political issues transcend national boundaries. This development transforms all of these issues into either domesticated international issues or internationalized domestic issues in the sense that they simultaneously affect all societies, are influenced by the national debates in each of these societies. Furthermore, this concept reveals that the belief in clear distinction between domestic and international legal issues is fundamentally flawed.

International lawyers cannot meet these challenges by merely redefining international legal issues. Any redefinition that retains the standard distinction between domestic and international issues will be inadequate because it will not incorporate both the domestic and the international dimensions of each issue. Instead we need to develop new legal norms that consider both the domestic and international dimensions of the issues to which they are applicable, as well as new institutional arrangements that accommodate all the participants in the international legal process. This undertaking requires a fundamental re-conceptualization of the norms and institutions of international law. . . . [T]wo of the principles that should shape the new legal process can be identified.

The first of these principles is that of participation. Essentially, all parties that will be directly affected by the decisions and actions taken, regarding any particular issue, should be able to participate in the formulation of those decisions. While the form of participation may vary according to the nature of the issue involved, all affected parties should be assured of meaningful participation in the fora in which decisions are made. A corollary to this principle is that all affected parties should have appropriate access to the information needed to ensure that their participation is meaningful.

The second principle is that all affected parties should be able to hold those who make and implement polices that affect them accountable for their actions. The form of the accountability may vary, but generally a sustainable legal order must provide all those affected by a particular decision with the ability to hold those who make and implement the decision responsible for the consequences of their actions.

Neither of these principles is linked to sovereignty or to the international or domestic nature of an issue. The sole criterion used to identify the parties who should be able to participate in decision making is the nature and the impact of the decision to be taken. Similarly, the criterion used to identify who should be given the ability to hold decisions makers accountable is who is actually affected by the decisions that have been taken and the consequences thereof. The identity of those to be held accountable depends only on who actually has the power to make and implement decisions.

The fact that sovereignty is irrelevant to these two principles means that they will help international legal order that is people-centered, rather than state-centered. This focus creates the possibility for a much more cooperative and rights based legal order than exists under the present state-centered international order. However, a people-centered legal order provides no obstacle to stronger states or social groups interested in making an unjustified intervention in the internal affairs of weaker states or social groups. This in turn creates the risk that a people-centered legal order could result in the centralization of power in the international community.

The new international legal order, therefore, needs a means to distinguish between legitimate international action in solidarity with other members of the global community and the unjustified use of power. The two basic principles offer a good starting point for finding a solution to this problem. Participation establishes the duty of every state or group, that seeks to intervene in the affairs of any other state or group, to obtain authorization for its actions through a decision-making mechanism in which all interested parties will have the right to participate. Accountability establishes the right of the target state or group to hold the intervenors responsible for the consequences of their actions.

II. Multilateral Initiatives to Regulate FDI

A. The Uruguay Round Trims Agreement

Documents Supplement References:

1. *The General Agreement on Tariffs and Trade (GATT) (30 October 1947) (especially Articles I, III, VI, and XI).*

2. *The Uruguay Round Agreement on Trade-Related Investment Measures (TRIMs) (1993).*

3. *United Nations, Draft Code of Conduct on Transnational Corporations (12 June 1990).*

GATT PRESS SUMMARY, NEWS OF THE URUGUAY ROUND, 14-15 (APRIL 5, 1994)

Agreement on Trade Related Aspects of Investment Measures

The agreement recognizes that certain investment measures restrict and distort trade. It provides that no contracting party shall apply any TRIM inconsistent with Articles III (national treatment) and XI (prohibition of quantitative restrictions) of the GATT. To this end, an illustrative list of TRIMs agreed to be inconsistent with these articles is appended to the agreement. The list includes measures which require particular levels of local procurement by an enterprise ("local content requirements") or which restrict the volume or value of imports such an enterprise can purchase or use to an amount related to the level of products it exports ("trade balancing requirements").

The agreement requires mandatory notification of all non-conforming TRIMs and their elimination within two years for developed countries, within five years for developing countries and within seven years for least-developed countries. It estab-

lishes a Committee on TRIMs which will, among other things, monitor the implementation of these commitments. The agreement also provides for consideration, at
a later date, of whether it should be complemented with provisions on investment
and competition policy more broadly.

Robert H. Edwards and Simon N. Lester, Towards a More Comprehensive World Trade Organization Agreement on Trade Related Investment Measures

33 Stanford Journal of International Law
169, 170-80, 187, 195-97, 199, 201-04, 206-13 (1997)

I. INTRODUCTION

Governments have often looked to trade policy as a tool to protect their national
industries from international competition. For hundreds of years, tariffs and quotas
were the primary, if not the sole, forms of protectionist trade policy. Their operation
is fairly simple: Tariffs impose a tax on imported goods, and quotas limit the amount
of imports, according to monetary value or quantity.

After World War II, however, the major industrialized countries concluded that
competing protectionist trade policy regimes were undermining world economic welfare. In response, they agreed to a set of rules, the General Agreement on Tariffs and
Trade (GATT), which limited the use of tariffs, quotas, and other barriers to trade.
Unfortunately, as restrictions were placed on these measures, many governments
found new ways to protect and assist domestic industries, frustrating the purpose of
the Agreement. Governments were particularly fond of subsidies, which give domestic industries an advantage over rivals through direct and indirect financial assistance.

More recently, governments have employed trade related investment measures
(TRIMs) to promote the development of domestic industries. TRIMs are government
measures that require or encourage specific behavior by private investors. For example, a government may require that an investor that manufactures goods in the country purchase a minimum percentage of inputs from domestic sources. This is known
as a "domestic content" requirement. Alternatively, the government may give the investor an incentive to purchase from domestic sources by granting a subsidy for such
a purchase. Such measures are designed to alter the operating environment of foreign
direct investors, and thereby encourage decisions that are beneficial to the host country. The objective of the domestic content requirements and incentives described
above is to promote domestic production to the disadvantage of foreign producers.

Such policies represent a departure from the free market paradigm that ideally
governs investment decisions. In the absence of TRIMs, foreign direct investors rely
on market signals to determine where and how to invest, procure inputs, and sell
products. TRIMs, however, change the factors influencing these decisions. If an investor that would otherwise source its inputs from a more efficient foreign producer
is forced to buy from a domestic company, its cost structure will be altered. [G]overn-
ments' use of TRIMs distorts international trade flows and reduces social welfare in
the host country and in the world economy as a whole.

The primary catalyst for the proliferation of TRIMs has been the massive increase in foreign investment flows.....As FDI has grown, so has the use of TRIMs,
because host countries have increasingly employed TRIMs to extract greater economic benefits from foreign investment.

While initially the GATT's primary focus was to limit the use of tariffs and quotas, it also has attempted to regulate subsidies and TRIMs. The first substantial attempt to restrict the use of subsidies came during negotiations in the Tokyo Round of GATT negotiations (1974-1979). The resulting agreement, the Subsidies Code, proved insufficient. Consequently, GATT members formulated a much stricter and more detailed regulatory regime for subsidies during the Uruguay Round (1986-1993). In contrast to the Tokyo Round Code, the Uruguay Round Subsidies Agreement provides an extensive definition of "subsidy." In addition, the Agreement considerably expands the scope of the GATT's regulatory power over subsidies.

The first attempt to develop a formal agreement regulating TRIMs came in the Uruguay Round, which culminated in the establishment of the World Trade Organization (WTO). This effort may prove to be as unsuccessful as the earlier attempt to regulate subsidies. While the WTO TRIMs Agreement improves upon prior GATT jurisprudence in the area, it is deficient in a number of ways. For example, the Agreement does not prohibit all TRIMs outright — it merely states that certain TRIMs violate Articles III and XI of the GATT, and are therefore prohibited. [GATT Article III contains the famous non-discrimination, or national treatment, principle. In brief, the government of an importing country must treat imported products on a substantively equal basis as quantitative barriers to imports (*e.g.*, quotas), though there are several exceptions. The GATT is reproduced in the *Documents Supplement*.] Moreover, the TRIMs Agreement does not regulate the use of export requirements, one of the most trade-distorting TRIMs. The Agreement recognizes these shortcomings, providing for the WTO Council for Trade in Goods to review the Agreement and propose amendments within five years.

. . . .

II. TRIMS IN THE WORLD ECONOMY

A. Why TRIMs Are Employed by Host Governments

Despite growing multilateral concern about the increased use of TRIMs, there is no exact formula for identifying them. This uncertainty exists in part because the term itself reflects a political judgment that a certain measure reduces economic welfare and should therefore be prohibited. Thus, countries with different policy objectives may disagree as to which measures should be classified as TRIMs. In addition, evaluating the effect of a measure on trade flows is essential to identifying it as a TRIM. However, it is difficult to isolate the effect of a particular measure, because the investment environment in many countries is defined by a variety of measures, only some of which actually affect trade flows.

The United Nations has devised four categories of TRIMs: performance requirements, investment incentives, corporate measures (restrictive business practices), and home-country measures. With respect to regulating TRIMs, this Article will focus on disincentive TRIMs, including performance requirements and what is essentially a subcategory of performance requirements—so called "performance incentives," which are incentives linked in some manner to performance requirements. Incentives not linked to performance are excluded from our proposed scheme for TRIMs regulation. . . . .

Performance requirements are mandates imposed by a government on an investor, compelling the investor to make certain purchasing, sales, or manufacturing decisions. Through export requirements, for example, the government may require an investor to sell a certain amount of its locally produced goods abroad. Another subcategory of performance requirements are the aforementioned performance incentives, in which financial advantages flow to those investors who meet certain performance standards. These financial incentives can be used to induce the same behavior mandated by performance requirements.

Investment incentives are fiscal contributions intended to influence investment location decisions. Governments employ such TRIMs to encourage multinational companies to locate manufacturing and other operations in their countries. Such measures include cash grants and other direct fiscal contributions by the government to the potential investor as well as tax holidays and other measures exempting the investor from otherwise applicable taxes.

Many governments, especially those in the developing world, view government intervention in the economy as an effective means of promoting domestic industry and increasing national income levels. These governments believe that a broad industrial-promotion policy will allow them to shift the terms of trade in their favor so as to increase economic growth rates. TRIMs are often a key ingredient of such policies. A further rationale many developing countries have given for using TRIMs is that the measures are necessary to combat the restrictive business practices employed by transnational corporations.... [P]erformance requirements are important "if there are structural rigidities and biases within multinational enterprises against disrupting established internal patterns of installed capacity and intra-firm trade."

One example of a restrictive business practice is transfer pricing. If the parent corporation is providing inputs to an overseas subsidiary, it may overvalue the products it sells to this entity in order to reduce profits for the subsidiary and raise them for the parent. As a result, the subsidiary in the host country will pay less in taxes, and the parent will be able to repatriate its profits indirectly. Host countries argue that certain TRIMs are simply a response to this practice, designed to ensure that they realize the desired gains from FDI. For example, if the concern is that transnational corporations will repatriate their profits instead of reinvesting them in the host country, an incentive scheme could be designed that provides favorable tax treatment for reinvested earnings.

Economists are divided over whether interventionist policies can actually promote growth. Most believe that the case for intervention is weak and that TRIMs distort international trade flows, thereby reducing the welfare benefits associated with free trade. However, general economic analysis of TRIMs is not highly developed. The difficulties in isolating the effects of specific TRIMs from complex packages of government rules have resulted in a relative paucity of empirical studies on the impact of these measures.....

There are, however, basic arguments for and against TRIMs. The conventional case against TRIMs, and against protectionism in industrial policy in general, has its origins in the concept of comparative advantage and the resulting gains to be derived from trade as developed initially by David Ricardo in the early nineteenth century. Successive generations of economists have elaborated on the basic Ricardian model of comparative advantage, developing ever more complex models of international trade. These economists agree with Ricardo's basic conclusion that both national and global welfare will be maximized when governments allow market forces to direct trade flows.

The theory of comparative advantage holds that a country will always be relatively more efficient at producing certain goods than other countries. Free trade allows countries to specialize in producing the goods for which they have a comparative advantage, and then to exchange these goods for those which other nations produce relatively more efficiently. Specialization will maximize wealth on a global level, even if a particular country could produce all goods more efficiently than its trading partners. Thus, under a free trade system total production and wealth will be maximized. Government intervention will only distort the incentives of private economic actors, causing them to produce in a less efficient manner.

The case for TRIMs, on the other hand, is an argument for government intervention in the market. Advocates of "strategic" trade theory argue that certain nonmarket forces can have a significant impact on trade flows, in a way that the traditional theories of free trade cannot explain. These theorists argue that there are certain strategic sectors in which labor and capital earn higher rents than other sectors, due to advantages such as economies of scale, experience, and innovation. Accordingly, trade measures may be capable of expanding national income even when a country lacks a comparative advantage in those strategic sectors, thus justifying some form of government intervention. Such analyses contrast with neoclassical theory, according to which trade flows are driven solely by comparative advantage and resource endowments, and transactions costs are immaterial. In short, strategic trade theory questions the traditional assumptions that markets are perfectly competitive and trade flows respond frictionlessly to market forces. Government intervention can be an effective way to correct these market imperfections. By intervening, a government may be able to "beat the market"; that is, increase national wealth at a rate that is faster than under normal market conditions.

One example of such government intervention is support for "infant industries." According to the infant industry argument, "developing countries have a *potential* advantage in manufacturing, but new manufacturing industries in developing countries cannot initially compete with well-established manufacturing in developed countries. In order to allow manufacturing to get a toehold, governments should temporarily support new industries until they have grown strong enough to meet international competition." The economic rationale for this intervention is that dynamic increasing returns to scale may eventually be achieved if unit costs are related to cumulative output. Under this scenario, per unit production costs will fall as experience in production increases, enabling the industry's goods to become more competitive. By protecting a domestic industry from foreign competition at the outset, the government gives the industry a chance to gain more experience in production. Without such government intervention, the industry would be too weak to compete with established foreign rivals.

B. Use of TRIMs by Host Governments

Host country governments have used TRIMs both to attract foreign investment and to channel it to meet domestic needs. Investment measures allow governments to define the types of projects desired, screen investment proposals, specify incentives for accepted projects, and impose controls over investors' operations. Because they serve multiple functions, investment measures often contain a mixture of subsidies and controls. For example, the right to receive a subsidy from a government may be linked to achieving certain performance goals. In such a case, an incentive (e.g. a reduction in import duties) may be linked to a performance requirement (e.g. achieving a minimum level of exports). The exact mixture of subsidies and controls depends on a large number of factors, including the objectives of the host government, the economic position of the country, and the characteristics of the industry.

In developing countries with large domestic markets like Brazil, Mexico, and Indonesia, policies have tended to be less liberal, resulting in greater use of performance requirements and less use of investment incentives. Large-market developing countries may be able to pursue such a combination of measures because foreign direct investors are eager to gain access to the domestic markets by setting up production in these countries. Traditionally, these governments have utilized regulations more than incentives, "adopting various measures to channel foreign capital to specific sectors, to exclude foreign investment from other sectors, and in general to exercise control over the investment process." In recent years, however, the policy mix of these large-market countries has shifted towards greater use of the subcategory of performance requirements known as performance incentives.

Other countries' policies tend to be less restrictive, offering more incentives than controls. Such policies are often found in the European Union (E.U.), especially among its smaller members, which hope to attract foreign direct investors seeking to secure a manufacturing base in the Union. Ireland, for example, has pursued less-restrictive policies partly in order to compete with other member states for foreign direct investors attracted by the benefits of the single market.

. . . .

1. Introduction to the Classification of TRIMs

In our taxonomy displayed in Figure 1, we have sought to bring order to the wide array of measures that have been classified and analyzed as TRIMs.

The columns in Figure 1 separate TRIMs based on their impact the profitability of the foreign investment. TRIMs tending to increase the investor's profit, for example by reducing the investor's costs of production (e.g. tax holidays), are placed in the left column and are called "Incentive TRIMs." TRIMs that tend to decrease the profit associated with the investment, for example by requiring the investor to source inputs locally even though the same inputs are available from foreign sources at lower cost, are placed in the right column and are called "Disincentive TRIMs."

The rows divide TRIMs according to their impact on trade flows. Some TRIMs may lead to a decline in imports as compared to the level of imports that would have obtained without the measure. For example, local content requirements mandate that an investor source more inputs locally than the investor would have absent the requirement. Other things being equal, this will result in a decrease in imports into the country applying the TRIM. Other TRIMs may instead lead to an increase in exports from the country applying the measure. For example, export minimums require an investor to export a minimum percentage of its production. Other things being equal, this requirement will result in a higher level of exports from the country applying the minimum than would have obtained otherwise. Other TRIMs may have an uncertain impact on trade flows. For example, it is difficult to predict *ex ante* how a restriction on the remittance of profits may affect trade flows. If profits cannot be remitted, they may be used either to purchase more local goods (which leads to a decline in imports), or to purchase foreign goods as inputs for the manufacturing process (which leads to an increase in imports).

. . . .

III. GATT/WTO REGULATION OF TRIMS

. . . .

D. The WTO TRIMs Agreement

The result of the Uruguay Round TRIMs negotiations was the Agreement on Trade Related Investment Measures, which prohibits WTO member countries from

FIGURE 1. TAXONOMY OF TRADE RELATED INVESTMENT MEASURES
Effects on Investment/Profit

Effects on Trade	Incentive	Disincentive
Reduction of Imports	**I** Sales Tax Exemption on Domestic Machinery	**IV** Local Content Requirements Manufacturing Requirements Prior Import Deposits Trade-Balancing Requirements (e.g. Counter Trade)
Uncertain	**II** Accelerated Depreciation Cash Grants Debt-Equity Swap Programs Dividend Tax Waivers Elimination of Exchange Risk on Foreign Loans Exclusive Licensing Exemption from Registration Taxes Goverment Procurement Preferences Priority Access to Credit Inflation Adjustments in Tax Accounting Liberal Loss-Carry-Forward Provisions Loan Guarantees Non-exemption Guarantees Subsidized Buildings Subsidized Equity Purchases by Government Subsidized Land Subsidized Leasing Subsidized Loans Tariff Exemptions on Imported Machines Tax Credits Tariff Exemptions on Land Tax Holidays and Reductions Tax Sparing Agreements Training Grants Wagon Subsidies	**V** Controls or Taxes on Remitted Dividends Domestic Sales Requirements Foreign Exchange Restrictions Licensing Requirements Limits on Debt-Equity Ratios Limits on Use of Used Equipment Local Equity Requirements Local Labor Requirements Manufacturing Limitations Remittance Restrictions Technology Transfer Requirements
Reduction of Imports	**III** Export Subsidies	**VI** Export Minimums Export Performance Requirements Product Mandate Requirements

applying "any TRIM that is inconsistent with the provisions of Article III or Article XI of GATT 1994." Article 5 of the Agreement requires members to notify the Council for Trade in Goods of all TRIMs currently in use that do not conform to the Agreement, and to eliminate such TRIMs within a certain period of time depending on the country's level of development. Disputes over members' use of TRIMs are to be settled under the normal dispute settlement mechanisms of the WTO.

In many ways, the Agreement is incomplete. Overall, advocates of an entirely new agreement did not gain much ground. Although the Agreement specifies that certain TRIMs are prohibited, it does so only in the context of existing GATT articles. Thus, other trade-distorting TRIMs that arguably violate the intent and spirit of the GATT are still permitted. The Agreement also incorporates traditional GATT exceptions to its requirements—such as Article XII and Article XVIII balance-of-payments exceptions—and grants lengthy transition periods, as long as seven years for the least-developed countries, to eliminate the forbidden practices.

The Annex to the Agreement contains an "illustrative list" of prohibited TRIMs — implemented as either performance requirements or performance incentives — that violate the obligation of national treatment provided for in Article III, Section 4 of the GATT. This list includes:

[TRIMs] which are mandatory or enforceable under domestic law or under administrative rulings, or compliance with which is necessary to obtain an advantage, and which require:

(a) the purchase or use by an enterprise of products of domestic origin or from any domestic source . . . ; or

(b) that an enterprise's purchases or use of imported products be limited to an amount related to the volume or value of local products that it exports.

Thus, the Annex prohibits both local content and trade balancing requirements, under (a) and (b) of paragraph 1, respectively.

The Annex then provides examples of TRIMs that are inconsistent with the obligation in Article XI, Section 1 of the GATT to eliminate quantitative restrictions:

[TRIMs] which are mandatory or enforceable under domestic law or under administrative rulings, or compliance with which is necessary to obtain an advantage, and which restrict:

(a) the importation by an enterprise of products used in or related to its local production, generally or to an amount related to the volume or value of local production that it exports;

(b) the importation by an enterprise of products used in or related to its local production by restricting its access to foreign exchange to an amount related to the foreign exchange inflows attributable to the enterprise; or

(c) the exportation or sale for export by an enterprise of products, whether specified in terms of particular products, in terms of volume or value of products, or in terms of a proportion of volume or value of its local production.

This paragraph applies generally to import restrictions and trade-balancing requirements (subparagraph (a)), trade balancing through foreign-exchange restrictions (subparagraph (b)), and various export restrictions (subparagraph (c)).

As mentioned above, there are important exceptions to these prohibitions on TRIMs. First, Article 4 specifically notes that developing countries may deviate from the TRIMs Agreement when experiencing balance-of-payments difficulties, in accordance with Article XVIII of the GATT. Second, Article 5 allows countries substantial transition periods before fully complying with the Agreement. The length of this period depends on a country's status as developed (two years), developing (five years), or least developed (seven years).

. . . .

IV. DEVELOPING A TAXONOMY FOR TRIMS

The complex nature of investment and trade regulation makes it difficult to develop a definitive list of TRIMs. To date there is no such list, nor is there a widely accepted classification scheme. In order to analyze the impact of TRIMs and evaluate mechanisms for their regulation, it is necessary to develop a workable taxonomy. The task at hand is to group these TRIMs in a manner that will facilitate the development of international norms regarding their use.

A. Identifying TRIMs

Developing a taxonomy for TRIMs requires at least two distinct but interconnected efforts. The first step is to identify and describe TRIMs employed by host governments. The second step involves evaluating the theoretical or actual impact that each measure has on investment and trade flows, and determining which measures require action.

. . . .

B. Classifying TRIMs Based on Their Effect on Profit

TRIMs have varying effects on the potential profit from foreign investment in the host country. Incentive TRIMs (including, *inter alia*, performance incentives) tend to enhance profit by providing preferential treatment to foreign investors in the form of subsidies or other incentives. In contrast, disincentive TRIMs (including, *inter alia*, performance requirements) impose additional costs and can therefore limit profit.

1. Incentive TRIMs

Measures taken by the host government which benefit the investor are defined as incentive TRIMs and are placed under the category of "Incentive" in Figure 1. Tax holidays, loan guarantees, and accelerated depreciation are a few examples. These measures decrease the costs associated with FDI in a particular host country. Accordingly, host country governments often use such measures to attract investment.

However, some incentives or subsidies may not be very appealing to transnational corporations because they are conditioned on the fulfillment of certain requirements. For example, a country may provide for a reduction in import duties (an incentive), if the investor agrees to achieve certain local content requirements (a performance requirement). For the purpose of this Article, these types of measures are labeled "performance incentives." This type of measure imposes a mixture of costs and benefits on the foreign investor, so the effect on profit varies.

2. Disincentive TRIMs

Disincentive TRIMs impose additional costs on the foreign direct investor. Such TRIMs can affect an investor's purchasing, sales, or manufacturing decisions. For example, performance requirements, such as local content requirements, may increase the costs of doing business by requiring a corporation to source locally inputs which could be obtained more cheaply abroad. Other types of disincentive TRIMs restrict repatriation of profits, for example by taxing remitted dividends, limiting debt-equity ratios, and restricting the utilization of used equipments.

C. Classifying TRIMs Based on Their Impact on Trade Flows

The USTR [United States Trade Representative] TRIMs negotiating team [to the Uruguay Round] developed a useful guide for classifying TRIMs based on their effect on trade. Two major groupings from that classification have been adopted here: (1) TRIMs associated with an artificial reduction of imports into the host country; and (2) TRIMs associated with artificial inducement or increase of exports from the host country. We have added a third group to the taxonomy: those TRIMs that have a more tenuous connection to trade flows, making it difficult to predict their trade effects *ex ante*.

TRIMs that artificially reduce imports include local content requirements and foreign exchange restrictions. Local content requirements, for example, mandate that the investor purchase inputs locally that it otherwise might import from another country. TRIMs that artificially increase exports include export requirements and product mandate requirements. An investor subject to an export requirement must export a certain amount or percentage of production. A product mandate requirement, by requiring an investor to manufacture a specific product, may result in an increase in exports if there is insufficient demand in the local market for the mandated product.

The final category involves those TRIMs that have an unpredictable impact on trade flows. Local equity requirements are a good example. They typically mandate that local investors hold a certain percentage ownership of a company created by foreign investment. The impact of a local equity requirement on the management decisions of the foreign direct investor is uncertain because it depends on a large number of variables, including percentage ownership of the local investor and whether the foreign investor favors local companies when sourcing inputs. Moreover, according to the USTR negotiating team submission, "if local equity requirements are overly burdensome, investors may decide to forego an investment, locate elsewhere or not produce certain products in the host country that they would have in the absence of such requirements, thereby changing investment and trade flows."

V. THE FRAMEWORK FOR A NEW AGREEMENT

The framework for a new TRIMs Agreement proposed in this Article is intended to go beyond the existing TRIMs Agreement in two important ways. First, a new taxonomy is offered that divides TRIMs into incentive TRIMs and performance requirements, and then classifies them according to their impact on trade flows. The scheme is useful because it defines the types of measures in the proposed regime, thereby making an agreement easier to reach. Based on this taxonomy, we reach a determination as to which TRIMs have the most distorting effect on international trade flows, and should therefore be prohibited.

Second, our proposed framework addresses a broad range of trade-distorting TRIMs, regardless of their technical compliance with existing articles. The current Agreement, by contrast, merely prohibits certain measures that have been found to violate existing GATT Articles III and XI.

It is important to clarify the full extent of the application of our proposed agreement. First, TRIMs traditionally have referred to conditions imposed by a host country. But these measures also may be imposed on domestic companies, with the same trade-distorting effects. For this reason, our proposal could apply to measures directed at both foreign and domestic investment, unlike the current TRIMs Agreement, which is concerned only with foreign investment.

Because many TRIMs are carried out at the subnational government level, a truly comprehensive TRIMs agreement must address measures taken by subnational as well as national governments. The only reference to subnational TRIMs in the current Agreement is in Article 6 on transparency, which states in paragraph 2 that "[e]ach Member shall notify the Secretariat of the publications in which TRIMs may be found, including those applied by regional and local governments and authorities within their territories." A new TRIMs agreement should expressly regulate these TRIMs, and not merely provide for their identification by member countries. Accordingly, the proposals in this Article are intended to apply to government measures taken at both the national and subnational levels.

A. The GATT Subsidies Agreement as a Model for TRIMs Regulation

. . . .

2. The WTO Subsidies Agreement

The Uruguay Round negotiations produced a more comprehensive regime [than the Tokyo Round Subsidies Code] for regulating subsidies. Unlike the [Tokyo Round] Subsidies Code, this Agreement provides an extensive definition of "subsidy." Moreover, the Agreement expands the scope of the GATT's regulatory power in this area. As in the Tokyo Round Subsidies Code, the Agreement makes clear that not all subsidies are subject to WTO discipline; however, it does prohibit or make actionable a much broader class of subsidies.

The Agreement regulates subsidies by what has become known as the "traffic light" method. Subsidies are divided into three categories: "(1) prohibited, or 'Red Light,' subsidies, (2) permissible but actionable, or 'Yellow Light,' subsidies and (3) nonactionable, or 'Green Light,' subsidies." Prohibited subsidies are forbidden regardless of whether any type of injury is attributable to them. There are two categories of Red Light subsidies: subsidies contingent upon export performance and subsidies contingent upon the use of domestic rather than imported goods. The former category, export subsidies, was included in the Tokyo Round Subsidies Code in substantially the same form, while the latter category, sometimes referred to as "import substitution" subsidies, is new.

Under Article 5, a member that believes it has been harmed by subsidies not formally prohibited as Red Light subsidies can challenge their use in the WTO. Such Yellow Light subsidies will be found illegal if they have "adverse effects" on the complaining country. Adverse effects include injury to the domestic industry of another WTO member, nullification or impairment of benefits accruing to a member, or "serious prejudice" to the interests of another member.

Injury to the domestic industry is defined later in the Agreement as "material injury to a domestic industry, threat of material injury to a domestic industry or material retardation of the establishment of such an industry. An injury determination "shall be based on positive evidence and involve an objective examination of both (a) the volume of subsidized imports and the effect of the subsidized imports on prices in the domestic market for like products and (b) the consequent impact of these imports on the domestic producers of such products."

Adverse effects also arise if a party's benefits as a WTO member have been "nullified or impaired" within the meaning of Article 5 of the Subsidies Agreement. This can occur in two situations. In the standard case, if a country has violated a GATT provision, there will be a rebuttable presumption that benefits have been nullified or impaired. In rare cases, a country may allege that its benefits are being impaired by another country's actions even though those actions are not themselves violations of GATT rules. This type of case is much more difficult for a complainant to prove.

Finally, Article 6 sets out four situations that presumptively lead to serious prejudice: if the total *ad valorem* subsidy exceeds five percent; if the subsidies are used to cover operating losses sustained by a particular industry; if the subsidies cover operating losses sustained by an enterprise, other than one-time measures which provide time for the development of long-term solutions and enable a country to avoid social problems; and direct forgiveness of debt. Subsidies of the type set out in Article 6 are presumed to cause serious prejudice unless the subsidizing member can rebut the presumption by demonstrating that the subsidy has not resulted in any of the effects listed in Article 6, Paragraph 3.

Article 6, Paragraph 3 describes effects-based situations where serious prejudice can be said to exist: (1) when the subsidy displaces or impedes the importation of a like product of another member; (2) when the subsidy impedes the exportation of a like product of another member from a third country market; (3) when the subsidy results in a dramatic price differential between the subsidized product and like products, or causes significant price suppression, price depression, or lost sales in the market of the subsidized product; and (4) when the subsidy increases the world market share of the subsidizing member for a primary product or commodity, and the increase follows a consistent trend over the period during which subsidies have been granted.

Article 8 of the Subsidies Agreement identifies those subsidies that are not actionable, including subsidies that are not specified under Article 2 and those listed under Article 8, Paragraph 2, the "Green Light" category. There are three categories of subsidies explicitly allowed under this Article. First, government aid for research is allowed as long as it covers "not more than 75 per cent of the costs of industrial research or 50 per cent of the costs of pre-competitive development activity, and is limited to the costs of personnel, plant and equipment, technical knowledge, direct overhead costs, and other direct costs. Next, subsidies are permitted to aid disadvantaged regions "pursuant to a general framework of regional development." Finally, government financial assistance may be used to "promote adaptation of existing facilities to new environmental requirements imposed by law ... which result in greater constraints and financial burdens on firms," subject to certain conditions. The principal conditions are that (1) the subsidy at issue is nonrecurring; (2) the subsidy is limited to twenty percent of the cost of adapting to the new law; (3) the subsidy does not cover the cost of replacing and operating the subsidized investment; (4) the subsidy does not cover any manufacturing cost savings that may be achieved; and (5) the subsidy is available to all enterprises that can adopt the newly-required equipment or production processes.

The WTO Subsidies Agreement is well structured, although its implementation remains uncertain. The Agreement properly balances the two conflicting goals described above: regulating the use of trade-distorting subsidies, and preserving the ability of governments to use subsidies to further social and economic policy. Although governments recognize that competing subsidies may undermine world prosperity, there are still many policy objectives for which subsidies can be effective tools.

In achieving this balance, the Agreement takes into account the broad range of effects a particular subsidy may have. At one end of the spectrum are those subsidies that severely distort trade and may or may not fulfill any internationally accepted social or economic goals. At the other end are subsidies designed specifically to promote such goals but which might produce some negative trade effects as well. In the middle are a wide range of subsidies that have varying trade-distorting effects and positive social benefits. The Agreement either prohibits or allows these subsidies based on a determination of whether they impose adverse effects on the host country's trading partners.

Those subsidies that are the most trade distorting — export subsidies and import-substitution subsidies — are singled out as Red Light measures and are strictly prohibited. Because these subsidies are necessarily harmful to foreign trading partners, no social or economic policy goal justifies their use. The Agreement also expressly allows the use of subsidies (Green Light measures) when they are designed to further accepted social or economic goals, such as environmental cleanup, regional development, and research. While Green Light measures will likely include subsidies that are trade distorting, negative effects on trade flows are deemed to be outweighed by their social benefits. Red Light subsidies, however, are prohibited even if it is argued that they are socially beneficial; i.e., Article 3 trumps Article 8.

Lastly, the Subsidies Agreement creates a middle category for all other subsidies. These subsidies were placed in this category because they are potentially harmful to trading partners, but they may also have domestic benefits. They are classified as "actionable," and will be considered to violate the Subsidies Agreement if they are found to have "adverse effects," under the terms described above. The Agreement contemplates no balancing of negative trade effects and domestic benefits once a subsidy in this category is challenged; these subsidies are simply prohibited if they are found to be harmful to a trading partner.

B. Categorizing TRIMs Within a New Agreement

... TRIMs and subsidies have similar purposes, and some TRIMs in fact have a subsidy component. Essentially, governments use both as tools of industrial policy to promote economic growth and as measures to further other social and economic objectives. Because of the similarity between TRIMs and subsidies, it is logical that a new TRIMs regime be based on the WTO Subsidies Agreement.... [T]he TRIMs discussed here are performance requirements and performance incentives, rather than all incentive-based TRIMs.

1. Fitting TRIMs into the Traffic Light Categories

a. Prohibited (Red Light) TRIMs

The taxonomy in Part IV identifies certain TRIMs that have a definite effect on trade flows. These measures may either increase the implementing country's exports or reduce its imports. Because these TRIMs are inherently trade distorting, no domestic social or economic benefits justify their use, and they should therefore be eliminated. The following TRIMs fall under this classification: export performance requirements, product-mandating requirements, trade-balancing requirements, local content requirements, and manufacturing requirements and limitations.

b. Actionable (Yellow Light) TRIMs

Other TRIMs have a less definite effect on trade flows. As our taxonomy makes clear, it is impossible to determine *ex ante* whether certain measures will reduce, increase, or have no effect on trade flows. In order best to address this category of TRIMs, these measures should be considered "actionable" as this term is understood in the Subsidies Agreement, and thus subject to the "adverse effects" test. If an actionable imposes adverse effects on investors, the measure will be prohibited. TRIMs in this category include local equity requirements, licensing requirements, and technology transfer requirements.

c. Permitted (Green Light) TRIMs

The Subsidies Agreement allows subsidies to be used for regional aid, environmental concerns, and research. While it is unlikely that TRIMs will be effective in the last two situations, they may be used to enhance economic development in specific regions. To that end, the Subsidies Agreement provision permitting these subsidies should also apply to TRIMs. As is true in the Subsidies Agreement, TRIMs that fall into the Red Light category in the proposed framework are prohibited regardless of their purpose.

. . . .

3. Exception for Developing Countries

In its original form, the GATT applied to all countries equally. No special exemptions were granted for countries with low income levels. This situation changed, however, as former colonies gained independence in the 1950s and 1960s. As these territories became sovereign nations and joined international treaties like the GATT, their collective voice began to influence rule making in these bodies. In the GATT, one of the first tangible results of this influence was the Generalized System of Preferences, a special exemption which allowed developed countries to grant preferential tariff rates to their less-developed trading partners.

In the Subsidies Agreement, developing countries are eligible for similar "special and differential treatment." Article 27, Paragraph 1 of the Agreement recognizes that "subsidies may play an important role in economic development programmes of developing country Members." Accordingly, the prohibition on export subsidies does not apply to the "least-developed countries," and does not apply to other developing countries for a period of eight years. In the meantime, these subsidies will be judged under the more lenient terms of the "actionable" category described above. Similarly, the prohibition on import substitution subsidies does not apply to least-developed countries for a period of eight years, or to other developing countries for five years. Furthermore, developing countries are exempt from the presumption of serious prejudice set out in paragraphs 1 and 2 of Article 6. Such serious prejudice must instead be demonstrated by "positive evidence."

While the development exception in the Subsidies Agreement is somewhat limited, it is much more explicit than the corresponding exception under Article 4 of the TRIMs Agreement. The latter states that developing country members "shall be free to deviate temporarily from the [TRIMs Agreement] to the extent and in such a manner as Article XVIII of GATT...permit[s] the Member to deviate from the provisions of Articles III and XI of GATT 1994." Article XVIII provides an exception for balance-of-payments difficulties that is potentially very important, because it has been used extensively by developing countries throughout the history of the GATT. In addition, transition periods of two, five, or seven years are allowed under Article 5 of the TRIMs Agreement, depending on the country's economic status.

While granting a wider exception for developing countries may be contrary to the goal of limiting the use of TRIMs, it may be the only way to achieve a more comprehensive agreement than the existing one. Many developing countries use TRIMs extensively and wish to continue doing so. As a result, it may be necessary to include in any proposed agreement the type of transition periods and exemptions granted to developing countries under the GATT in general and the Subsidies Agreement in particular.

....

B. Towards a Multilateral Agreement on Investment (MAI)?

Eric M. Burt, Developing Countries and the Framework for Negotiations on Foreign Direct Investment in the World Trade Organization

12 American University Journal of International
Law and Public Policy1015, 1040-49 (1997)

....

III. The OECD Multilateral Agreement on Investment (MAI)

A. Origins of the MAI

Outside of the GATT/WTO framework, the Organization for Economic Cooperation and Development ("OECD") has dealt extensively with investment issues. Recognizing the tremendous growth and increasing importance of FDI to the international economy, the OECD Ministers established a Negotiating Group in the OECD 1995 Ministerial meeting to begin negotiating a Multilateral Agreement on Investment ("MAI"). The OECD goal is to complete negotiations by the 1998 ministerial meeting and for the Agreement to enter into force by January 1, 1999. [The OECD failed to complete negotiations on the MAI by the end of 1998. Indeed, in April 1998, the OECD announced a six-month pause in negotiations, and neither OECD member countries nor OECD officials would or could commit to a new deadline for completion. Several difficult, contentious issues must be resolved. First, France and Canada insist on a "cultural exception" to ensure that national cultural industries are not dominated by foreign investors. American cultural industries (Hollywood, for instance) are the global leader, and its mega-media and entertainment giants (*e.g.*, Disney) are likely to be against this exception, which might block or restrict their access to lucrative foreign markets, and prevent them from acquiring foreign cultural industry companies. Second, France and some other developed countries insist that foreign investors be held to core labor standards. This position is seen by opponents as disguised protectionism designed to drive up labor costs in other countries and rob those countries of their comparative advantage with respect to certain products. Third, again France and some other developed countries want the United States to renounce the right to sanction foreign firms that invest in countries deemed by the United States to be strategic threats, such as Cuba, Iran, and Libya. Accordingly, the 1996 Helms-Burton Act and 1996 Iran and Libya Sanctions Act would need to be repealed, and the United States would need to foreswear future use of unilateral investment sanctions. The United States, while appearing hypocritical in seeking an MAI that liberalizes trade and investment, on the one hand, but reserving the unilateral sanction mechanism on the other hand, seems unlikely to bow to this

demand. Fourth, the European Union (EU) wants the MAI to contain separate liberalization standards for regional integration organizations. The United States counters
that such an approach would enshrine bilateral discrimination in the MAI. Fifth,
labor and environmental groups are concerned that an MAI would lead to a "race to
the bottom" as governments lower their labor and environmental standards to attract foreign investment. These groups are seen as closet protectionists by proponents
of investment liberalization. Finally, there is a vigorous debate as to whether the
OECD - as opposed to the WTO - is the proper forum for negotiating an MAI. Ideally, the WTO is preferable insofar as its membership is far broader than that of the
OECD. Yet, the WTO's broader membership is precisely what makes it an unwieldy
forum for negotiating an MAI. In sum, as of this writing, no final MAI is on the horizon.] The OECD MAI seeks "high standards" for the liberalization of investment
measures and post-establishment investment protection and an effective dispute settlement mechanism providing for both state-to-state and investor-to-state disputes.
MAI will be a freestanding international treaty with an existence separate from the
other OECD instruments. It will be open for accession to all interested countries,
both OECD members and non-OECD members.

B. The Particulars of the MAI

Although the MAI negotiation is still ongoing, the basic framework of the MAI
is discernable.

1. Definition of Investment

The MAI will define "investment" broadly to enable a comprehensive application of the agreement. The definition will fall somewhere between the classical definition of FDI and the definition of portfolio investment. The objective is to cover all
forms of tangible and intangible investment that create an actual stake in the host
economy.

2. The Main Principles: National Treatment, Most-Favored Nation Treatment, and Transparency

The MAI liberalization provisions for host country investment measures and performance requirements will be based on the principles of national treatment, most-
favored nation treatment (MFN), and transparency, and will apply to both the pre-
and post-establishment stages of investment. Mechanisms for a standstill and roll-
back of investment measures are already in place. The MAI would go much further
than the TRIMs Agreement in prohibiting investment measures and performance requirements because the MAI seeks to eliminate all "investment-distorting" measures
rather than the more limited set of "trade-distorting" measures addressed in the
TRIMs Agreement. At a minimum the MAI will prohibit all of the measures suggested by the United States in the TRIMs negotiations, except perhaps for investment
incentives. Furthermore, while the TRIMs and GATS [Uruguay Round General
Agreement on Trade in Services] Agreements employ a bottom-up approach the MAI
will utilize the more encompassing top-down approach to liberalization of investment measures. Parties to the MAI will be required to liberalize all measures or sectors unless a measure or sector is specifically excluded from the liberalization obligations.

Although the objective of any agreement is to keep exceptions and derogations
to the general obligations at a minimum, the MAI negotiators are discussing certain
standard exceptions to the general obligations of national treatment and MFN treat-

ment. Negotiators are discussing the inclusion of exceptions for reasons of national security, public order, and international peace and security. An exception for the protection of "linguistic and cultural diversity" is also being considered. The Agreement will also allow specific national reservations, listing measures that a State will maintain, although not conforming to the general obligations. In addition, the Negotiating Group is considering whether to allow a temporary derogation from the general obligations for serious balance of payments difficulties. On the whole, the MAI promises to significantly advance the liberalization of investment measures and performance requirements far beyond the limited level of liberalization achieved in the Uruguay Round agreements.

3. Investor/Investment Protection

The MAI provisions on investor and investment protection were among the first agreed to in the negotiating sessions. The MAI will borrow from the standard of treatment for investments provided for in most bilateral investment treaties. The MAI will require "fair and equitable treatment" at least as favorable as required by international law along with "constant protection and security" for investments. Expropriation will be prohibited except if it is "in the public interest, on a nondiscriminatory basis, against payment of prompt, adequate and effective compensation, and in accordance with due process of law." Negotiators are considering whether to include language to cover exchange rate risk on the amount of compensation. The MAI will also contain provisions for compensation under certain circumstances of loss due to strife. Finally, all payments to and profits from an MNE investment will be freely transferable under the MAI at the market rate of exchange. A balance of payments derogation from this free transferability obligation is being considered.

4. Dispute Settlement in the MAI

The MAI will provide for WTO-style state-to-state dispute settlement, with stages for consultation, conciliation, mediation, and, if necessary, binding arbitration by a panel of experts. There is also a consensus to include provisions for investor-to-state dispute settlement in the MAI. Binding investor-to-state arbitration that would empower an arbitration panel to order a change in the host country's laws, however, would raise loss of sovereignty concerns. Some have suggested that a NAFTA-style investor-to-state dispute settlement mechanism may be appropriate to remedy sovereignty concerns. Such a mechanism would allow the investor to recover monetary damages from the host country government but would not empower the arbitration panels to order changes in a host country's laws. The final elements of the MAI's investor-to-state dispute settlement mechanism are still being negotiated, but it is certain that the MAI will provide some sort of investor-to-state arbitration mechanism. The provision for investor-to-state dispute settlement, by itself, will be significant because it offers more than what is currently available under the WTO system.

5. Special Issues: MNE Practices & Developing Country Accession

MAI negotiators are also considering a number of sub-issues and whether and how they should be provided for in the Agreement. Among the additional issues being discussed are provisions for the free movement of personnel, privatization and state enterprise issues, and MNE practices. The issue of restrictive MNE practices is particularly important, considering that the OECD hopes to secure the accession of developing countries to the MAI and the control of restrictive business practices is a primary concern for developing countries. Although the MAI Negotiating Group recognizes that MNE practices can negatively affect investment, the majority of the negotiators believe that it is not appropriate for the MAI to contain provisions on MNE practices.

Nevertheless, the MAI will be open to accession by non-OECD countries, including developing countries. The OECD has undertaken a commitment to actively pursue those non-OECD countries interested in acceding to the Agreement and has theorized that all countries, including developing countries, desiring to attract further direct investment will benefit from accession to the Agreement. After the Agreement enters into force, acceding countries will be required to accept certain "core" conditions of the Agreement. Negotiators, however, are considering whether to allow a transition period or temporary reservations to the obligations for developing countries acceding at this stage.

C. BENEFITS AND LIMITATIONS OF THE MAI

The MAI will become the most comprehensive set of multilateral rules on foreign direct investment in existence. Its provisions go much further than the current multilateral agreements in this area, GATS and TRIMs, in liberalizing investment measures and in providing rules for the protection of investments. The MAI's coverage of "investment-distorting" investment measures will result in the liberalization of a much broader array of measures than the more limited coverage of "trade-distorting" investment measures in the TRIMs Agreement. Furthermore, the Uruguay Round agreements do not deal with issues of expropriation and the free transfer of capital. The MAI's coverage of these issues is, thus, unique to the multilateral economic system. The MAI is a welcome addition to the field.

The Agreement, however, has several shortcomings that will limit its ultimate value to the world economic system. The OECD is an organization comprised primarily of developed countries and tends to view FDI issues from a developed country perspective. [The OECD membership includes the following 29 countries: Australia, Austria, Belgium, Canada, the Czech Republic, Denmark, Finland, France, Germany, Greece, Hungary, Iceland, Ireland, Italy, Japan, Korea, Luxembourg, Mexico, The Netherlands, New Zealand, Norway, Poland, Portugal, Spain, Sweden, Switzerland, Turkey, the United Kingdom, and the United States.] Only these developed country OECD members have been able to participate in the negotiation of the Agreement. Although the MAI will be a free-standing international treaty open to accession of all countries, it is doubtful that the Agreement will secure the accession of many non-OECD countries, especially developing countries, because of the developed-country orientation of the Agreement. The decision of MAI negotiators to exclude provisions regulating the restrictive business practices of MNEs is an additional weakness of the Agreement in its effort to attract developing countries.

The absence of developing country participation in the Agreement will greatly diminish its value to the international economic system. The subjection of developing countries to the liberalization requirements of the MAI would yield much greater benefits to the international economic system. The capital-exporting developed countries, more or less, already maintain relatively few barriers to foreign direct investment. It is the developing countries who maintain substantial barriers to investment and whose participation would, therefore, generate greater benefits through the corresponding liberalization of these barriers.

III. Plurilateral Initiatives on FDI: The OECD Guidelines

Documents Supplement References:

1. OECD Guidelines for
   Multinational Enterprises (21 June 1976, with commentary)

Organization for Economic Co-Operation and Development, Declaration on International Investment and Multinational Enterprises

OECD Press Release A(76)20, 21 June 1976 (reprinted
in 15 International Legal Materials 975 (1976))

[The OECD *Guidelines for Multinational Enterprises* initially was published as the Annex to the Declaration of 21 June 1976. In 1975, the OECD established a Committee on International Investment and Multinational Enterprises (CIME), which is the OECD's principal body for discussing issues pertaining to FDIs and MNCs. The CIME is made up of investment policy officials from OECD member countries, staffed by officials from the OECD Directorate for Financial, Fiscal, and Enterprise Affairs, typically meets twice a year, and normally operates on the basis of consensus. Among its products are the Declaration of 21 June 1976 and the *Commentary on the Guidelines*. Both the *Guidelines* and *Commentary* are reproduced in the *Documents Supplement*. The text of each provision of the *Guidelines* is followed by commentary on that provision.]

THE GOVERNMENTS OF OECD MEMBER COUNTRIES[1]

Considering

That international investment has assumed increased importance in the world economy and has considerably contributed to the development of their countries; that multinational enterprises play an important role in this investment process; that co-operation by Member countries can improve the foreign investment climate, encourage the positive contribution which multinational enterprises can make to economic and social progress, and minimise and resolve difficulties which may arise from their various operations;

That, while continuing endeavours within the OECD may lead to further international arrangements and agreements in this field, it seems appropriate at this stage to intensify their co-operation and consultation on issues relating to international investment and multinational enterprises through inter-related instruments each of which deals with a different aspect of the matter and together constitute a framework within which the OECD will consider these issues:

---

1. The Turkish Government was not in a position to participate in this Declaration.

Declare:

Guidelines I. That they jointly recommend to multinational enterprises
for MNE's   operating in their territories the observance of the *Guidelines* as set
                 forth in the Annex hereto having regard to the considerations and
                 understandings which introduce the *Guidelines* and are an integral
                 part of them. [The *Guidelines* are reproduced in the *Documents
                 Supplement*.]

National II. 1   That Member countries should consistent with their needs to
Treatment   maintain public order, to protect their essential security inter-
                     ests and to fulfil commitments relating to international peace
                     and security, accord to enterprises operating in their territories
                     and owned or controlled directly or indirectly by nationals of
                     another Member country (hereinafter referred to as "Foreign-
                     Controlled Enterprises") treatment under their laws, regula-
                     tions and administrative practices, consistent with interna-
                     tional law and no less favourable than that accorded in like
                     situations to domestic enterprises (hereinafter referred to as
                     "National Treatment").

            2   That Member countries will consider applying "National
                Treatment" in respect of countries other than Member countries.

            3   That Member countries will endeavour to ensure that their
                territorial subdivisions apply "National Treatment".

            4   That this Declaration does not deal with the right of Member
                countries to regulate the entry of foreign investment or the
                conditions of establishment

Inter-   III. 1   That they recognise the need to strengthen their co-operation
national   in the field of international direct investment.

Investment 2   That they thus recognise the need to give due weight to the
Incentives and   interests of Member countries affected by specific laws,
Disincentives   regulations and administrative practices in this field (here-
                    inafter called "measures") providing official incentives and
                    disincentives to international direct investment.

            3   That Member countries will endeavour to make such
                measures as transparent as possible, so that their importance
                and purpose can be ascertained and that information on them
                can be readily available.

*Consultation-*IV. That they are prepared to consult one another on the above matters
Procedures   in conformity with the Decisions of the Council relating to Inter-
                    Governmental Consultation Procedures on the Guidelines for
                    Multinational Enterprises, on National Treatment and on Interna-
                    tional Investment Incentives and Disincentives.

Review   V.   That they will review the above matters within three years with a
                 view to improving the effectiveness of international economic co-
                 operation among Member countries on issues relating to interna-
                 tional investment and multinational enterprises.

IV. Regional Initiatives on FDI: NAFTA Chapter 11

Documents Supplement References:

NAFTA Chapter 11: Investment, Services and Related Matters.

North American Free Trade Agreement, Statement of Administrative Action, Chapter Eleven: Investment

H.R. Doc. No. 159, 103D Cong., 1st Sess. 140-46, 148-49 (4 November 1993)

A.   SUMMARY OF NAFTA PROVISIONS

Chapter Eleven comprises two parts. Part A sets out each government's obligations with respect to investors from other NAFTA countries and their investments in its territory. Part B affords investors the right to seek compensation through international arbitration for a violation of the provisions of Part A....

1. *Section A — Investment*

a. Scope and Coverage

Part A provides four basic protections to "investors of other Parties": nondiscriminatory treatment; freedom from "performance requirements;" free transfer of funds related to an investment; and expropriation only in conformity with international law.

"Investment" is broadly defined in Article 1139, and both existing and future investments are covered. "Investor of a Party" is defined to encompass both firms (including branches) established in a NAFTA country, without distinction as to nationality of ownership, and NAFTA-country nationals. The chapter applies where such firms or nationals make or seek to make investments in another NAFTA country.

The Chapter applies to all governmental measures relating to investment, with the exception of measures governing financial services, which are treated in Chapter Fourteen. Under Article 1112, in the event of any inconsistency between Chapter Eleven and another chapter, the other chapter will prevail.

b. Non-discrimination and Minimum Treatment Standards

Articles 1102 and 1103 set out the basic non-discrimination rules of "national treatment" and "most-favored-nation treatment." These rules require, respectively, each government to treat NAFTA investors and their investments:

- no less favorably than its own investors and their investments, and

- no less favorably than investors of other countries and their investments.

Article 1102 makes clear that the "national treatment" rule prohibits governments from imposing local equity requirements or requiring an investor from another NAFTA country, by reason of its nationality, to sell an investment. Furthermore, Article 1102 provides that the treatment provided by state and provincial governments to investors from other NAFTA countries and their investments must be no less favorable than the most favorable treatment they provide to domestic investors and their investments.

Article 1104 specifies that investors and their investments are to be accorded the better of national or most favored-nation treatment. Article 1105 provides that each country must also accord NAFTA investors treatment in accordance with international law.

c. Performance Requirements

Article 1106 imposes disciplines on seven types of "performance requirements." Under Article 1106, a government may not, as a condition for the establishment or operation of an investment, require a firm to:

- limit its sales in the domestic market by conditioning such sales on exports or foreign exchange earnings;

- buy or use components from a local supplier or accord a preference to domestic goods or services;

- achieve a minimum level of "domestic content;"

- limit its imports to a certain percentage of exports or foreign exchange inflows associated with the investment;

- transfer technology to any domestic entity, except to remedy an alleged violation of competition law;

- export a specified level of goods or services; or

- supply designated regional or world markets solely from its local production.

A government generally may not use the first four of the requirements listed above as a condition for receiving an advantage, such as a tax holiday....

The rules prohibiting performance requirements apply with respect to all investments, whether by non-NAFTA investors, domestic investors, or investors from another NAFTA country. For example, under Article 1106, the Mexican Government may not require a Japanese-owned (or Mexican-owned) firm in its territory to export to the United States.

By virtue of Article 1108(8), NAFTA's disciplines on the second, third and sixth type of performance requirement listed above do not apply to a NAFTA government's export promotion programs or foreign aid activities. In addition, the prohibition against the second, third, fifth and seventh type of performance requirement does not apply in connection with government procurement. Finally, under Article 1106(6), the disciplines on the second and third category of performance requirements do not affect a government's ability to apply nondiscriminatory environmental measures.

d. Management

Article 1107 prohibits NAFTA governments from requiring local firms owned by investors from other NAFTA countries to fill senior management positions with local nationals. A government may require a simple majority of the board of directors to be local nationals, however, as long as the requirement does not materially impair the investor's control over its investment.

e. Reservations and Exceptions

Article 1108 creates a system of limited "reservations" and "grandfathering" to exempt certain laws and regulations that are not in conformity with the non-discrimination, performance requirement and senior management obligations described above.

The NAFTA governments have recorded in their schedules to Annexes I, II, and III a specific "reservation" for all federal-level measures inconsistent with those obligations that they wish to maintain....

(1) Reservations for Existing Measures

Annex I sets out each government's reservations for existing, inconsistent measures at the federal government level. Existing non-conforming measures at the state or provincial level are automatically "grandfathered" for two years. By the end of that period, any such measure must have been listed as a "reservation" in Annex I in order for the exemption to remain in effect. The two-year period was negotiated in order to allow time for the states and the federal government to identify all such measures and to include them in the Annex, if desired.

Existing measures at the local level that are inconsistent with Chapter Eleven rules are automatically "grandfathered" on a permanent basis.

Laws and regulations that are "grandfathered" or listed as a reservation in Annex I are exempt from challenge under the NAFTA, even if they are amended or renewed, so long as they are not made more inconsistent with the Agreement. If a measure is liberalized, however, any such liberalization may not be reversed by a subsequent amendment.

Canada took various reservations in Annex I based on its exceptions under the CFTA [Canada-U.S. Free Trade Agreement]. Such reservations include the right to review direct acquisitions of C$150 million or more, restrictions in the oil and gas sectors, and limitations in connection with the ownership and privatization of certain state enterprises.

Mexico retained the right under Annex I to review large acquisitions. The initial threshold for review, $25 million, will increase to $150 million in the tenth year after entry into force of the Agreement. The $150 million threshold will be adjusted annually for inflation and later for economic growth as well, but the amount can never be higher than the Canadian threshold. Other principal Mexican exceptions in Annex I are reservations on the ownership of land, for cable television, air and land transportation, and retail sales of certain petrochemical products....

For its part, the United States took reservations for existing, non-conforming legislation in respect of such matters as nuclear power, broadcasting, mining, customs brokers and air transportation.

....

(4) Transfers

Article 1109 requires each NAFTA government to permit transfers relating to an investment covered by Chapter Eleven to be made freely and without delay, including transfers of profits, royalties, sales proceeds and other remittances relating to an investment. Further, no government may require its own investors to repatriate profits generated by their investments in another NAFTA country. Exceptions permit a government to prevent transfers under certain laws of general application, such as bankruptcy laws....

(5) Expropriation and Compensation

Under Article 1110, a NAFTA government may not expropriate an investment made by an investor from other NAFTA countries other than for a public purpose, on a non-discriminatory basis and in accordance with due process of law. Compensation must be paid without delay at the fair market value of the expropriated investment, plus any applicable interest, and must be freely realizable and transferable.

(6) Special Formalities

Articles 1111 permits a NAFTA government to adopt or maintain "special formalities" in connection with the establishment of an investment, so long as such requirements do not materially impair the substance of any right accorded by Chapter Eleven. Special formalities include requirements such as typical state incorporation requirements. Article 1111 also permits a government to seek routine information and data from investments covered by the chapter.

(7) Denial of Benefits

Article 1113 describes those circumstances under which a NAFTA government may refuse to apply the protection of Chapter Eleven to firms, or their investments, that otherwise qualify for coverage under the chapter, where the firms are owned or controlled by investors from a non-NAFTA country.

The article preserves the foreign policy prerogative of each government to deny benefits to firms owned or controlled by nationals of a non-NAFTA country with which it does not have diplomatic relations or to which it is applying economic sanctions.

It also permits each government to deny benefits to such firms if they have no substantial business activities in the NAFTA country where they are established. Thus shell companies could be denied benefits but not, for example, firms that maintain their central administration or principal place of business in the territory of, or have a real and continuous link with, the country where they are established. This provision requires the denying government to give prior notification, and to consult, in accordance with Articles 1803 and 2006.

(8) Environmental Measures

Article 1114 affirms that Chapter Eleven does not preclude a NAFTA government from adopting, maintaining or enforcing measures otherwise consistent with the chapter to ensure investment is consistent with its environmental protection goals. The article also provides that no government should waive or relax its environmental measures in order to attract or retain an investment. Derogations from this provision are subject to compulsory consultations if requested by a NAFTA government but are not subject to formal dispute settlement under Chapter 20. The Commission on Environmental Cooperation, created by the supplemental agreement on environmental cooperation, may assist in such consultations.

2. Section B — Investor-State Dispute Settlement

Section B of Chapter Eleven provides a mechanism for an investor to pursue a claim against a host government that it has breached its obligations under Section A.

This mechanism is patterned after the investor-State dispute settlement mechanism of the standard U.S. bilateral investment treaty and permits an investor to submit its claim to binding arbitration under internationally-accepted rules.

a. Nature of Claims

Articles 1116 and 1117 set forth the kinds of claims that may be submitted to arbitration: respectively, allegations of direct injury to an investor, and allegations of indirect injury to an investor caused by injury to a firm in the host country that is owned or controlled by the investor. In both cases, investors may bring claims where the injury results from an alleged breach of Section A....

All claims must be brought within three years....

Article 1138(1) excludes from investor-State dispute settlement decisions to prohibit or limit investment on national security grounds. Read together with Annex 1138(2), Article 1138(2) also excludes from investor-State dispute settlement, and from government-to-government dispute settlement under Chapter Twenty, decisions taken by Canada or Mexico to prohibit or restrict an acquisition under their laws providing for screening of foreign investment.

b. Initiation of Dispute Settlement Proceedings

Article 1118 encourages the settlement of claims through consultation or negotiation. Articles 1119 and 1120 set forth the process leading up to the submission of a dispute to an arbitral panel.

Article 1119 provides that an investor must provide notice of its intention to submit a claim to arbitration at least 90 days before doing so, and specifies the content of such notice. Article 1120 provides that once six months have elapsed from the events giving rise to a claim, the investor may submit the claim for arbitration to:

- the International Centre for the Settlement of Investment Disputes (ICSID), provided both the country of the investor and the host country are parties to the ICSID Convention (neither Canada nor Mexico currently is);

- ICSID's "Additional Facility," in the event one such country is not a party to the Convention; or

- an *ad hoc* arbitral tribunal established under the arbitration rules of the United Nations Commission on International Trade Law (UNCITRAL).

Because the NAFTA will give rise to private rights of action under Mexican law, Annex 1120.1 avoids subjecting the Mexican Government to possible "double exposure" by providing that a claim cannot be submitted to Chapter Eleven arbitration where the same claim has been made before a Mexican court or administrative tribunal.

....

f. Nature of Relief

Under Article 1134, a tribunal may order interim protection measures to preserve existing rights of the disputants, including the preservation of evidence. A tribunal cannot, however, order attachment of assets or enjoin the government from applying any measure that is the subject of the dispute.

Article 1135 limits a final award to money damages or restitution, or a combination of both; awards of restitution must offer the alternative of paying damages. No punitive damages may be awarded.

g. Enforcement of Arbitral Awards

Article 1136 sets forth rules governing enforcement of final awards. Paragraph one restates the traditional rule that an arbitral award has no precedential effect and is binding only on the particular disputants in the matter. Paragraph two obliges a disputant to abide by and comply with the award. Paragraph three provides a disputant the opportunity to seek revision or annulment of the award before enforcement may be sought.

Paragraph four requires each Party to provide for enforcement of an award in its territory. The Federal Arbitration Act (9 U.S.C. 1 *et seq.*) satisfies the requirement for the enforcement of non-ICSID awards in the United States. The Convention on the Settlement of Investment Disputes Act of 1966 (22 U.S.C. 1650, 1650a) provides for the enforcement of ICSID awards.

In the event that a country does not comply with an award, paragraphs five and six provide that the investor's government may request a government-to-government arbitration panel under Article 2008 to consider the matter. The initiation of such proceedings would not prevent the investor from seeking enforcement of the award.

. . . .

V. Bilateral Investment Treaties (BITs)

Documents Supplement References:

1.   *United States Model Bilateral Investment Treaty (BIT) (1998)*

United Nations Centre on Transnational Corporations & International Chamber of Commerce

Bilateral Investment Treaties 1959-1991 iii-iv, 1-3, 7-12 (1992)

PREFACE

Foreign direct investment has come to play an essential role in the world economy. With world-wide flows reaching the level of nearly $225 billion in 1990 for a total world stock of over $1.5 trillion, foreign direct investment is today one of the most important forms of international economic activity, and a main vehicle for channeling financial and trade flows, technology and know-how to virtually all parts of the world. Not surprisingly, the provision of favourable conditions for foreign direct investment through national and international policies and instruments has become a priority for policy-makers and business executives.

Bilateral treaties for the promotion and protection of foreign investment are a prominent feature of current inter-State cooperation on foreign direct investment. Such treaties — which are legally binding on the parties — have been concluded in large numbers mainly between Western countries on the one hand, and developing and Central and Eastern European countries, on the other. Increasingly, however, these treaties are also being concluded between newly industrializing countries and others; developing and Central and Eastern European countries; and between developing countries.

Bilateral investment treaties are normally concluded between a capital exporting country and a capital importing country. In as much as investment may flow in both directions, these treaties are reciprocal. The two parties have the same rights and obligations *vis-a-vis* each other. A traditional capital exporting country may, thus, occasionally be in the position of a capital importing country and vice versa.

The main objective of the capital exporting country is to obtain legal protection for foreign investment under international law and thus reduce as much as possible the non-commercial risks facing foreign investors in host countries. Hence, provisions in bilateral investment treaties are intended to supplement the protection standards afforded by the laws of the host country. These guarantees in an intergovernmental agreement are considered to be of a higher and more reliable nature than those provided for under the domestic laws of the host country which are subject to unilateral modification. Bilateral investment treaties prescribe a wide range of protection standards which cover the most important aspects of the treatment of foreign investors by their host countries. These usually include some of the general principles of customary international law on the treatment of foreign property abroad, such as fair, equitable and non-discriminatory treatment; observance of undertakings — *pacta sunt servanda* — and prompt, adequate and effective compensation in the event of expropriation.

The *capital importing country*, on the other hand, concludes bilateral investment treaties as one measure to attract foreign investment. In that manner, the objectives of the contracting parties complement each other, the overall purpose being the facilitation of foreign direct investment flows by granting a measure of stability and reliability in the relations between foreign investors and their host and home countries. In the absence of a global instrument providing the same level of protection for foreign investors, bilateral treaties are a significant aspect of governmental efforts to establish a favourable climate for foreign direct investment.

CHAPTER I

THE EMERGENCE AND GROWTH OF BILATERAL INVESTMENT TREATIES

Beginning in the late eighteenth century, individual countries concluded bilateral commercial treaties which, while not exclusively devoted to foreign investment, contained provisions affecting the ability of one country's nationals to do business or own property in the territory of the other State. The United States, for example, concluded agreements known as Treaties of Friendship, Commerce and Navigation. Before the First World War, the objective of those treaties, which were signed primarily with European States, was to protect the expansion of trade and shipping. Later, they also sought to encourage United States investment abroad by prescribing the treatment to be given to nationals of the contracting parties regarding the establishment and protection of investments. However, very few developing countries were party to those treaties.

After the Second World War, two new initiatives emerged with respect to the protection of investments abroad. The first initiative was limited to the underwriting by official agencies of political risk insurance. Thus, the United States and Canada as capital exporting countries aimed at the consolidation of political risk insurance by their official investment insurance programmes (such as the Overseas Private Investment Corporation in the United States) by seeking agreement with capital importing countries to accept such insurance in their countries.

The agreements concluded to that effect provided specifically for subrogation of the insurance agency to the rights and claims of the investor and for the settlement of disputes arising out of the agreement with the host country. The United States has concluded over 110 such agreements, and Canada 33.

The post-Second World War period also saw the emergence of another treaty practice, initiated by several European countries, with the negotiation individually with capital importing countries of bilateral treaties for the promotion and protection of foreign investments, otherwise referred to as bilateral investment treaties. The Federal Republic of Germany started this initiative. It concluded its first treaty in 1959 and in 1991 is still ahead in this movement with 77 such treaties concluded. It was followed shortly thereafter by Switzerland, which now has 51 treaties including some 17 economic cooperation agreements that contain substantial sections on investment protection and promotion. France joined during the 1960s and the United Kingdom in the early 1970s. They have recently reached 45 and 47 treaties, respectively. The Netherlands, which also began concluding bilateral investment treaties in the 1960s, follows with 32 treaties, and the Belgium/Luxembourg Economic Union has concluded 29 treaties since the 1960s.

It was in the 1970s and 1980s that the conclusion of bilateral investment treaties developed into a deliberate policy of most capital exporting countries. This policy was in part inspired by an initiative taken by a private international group of prominent lawyers and businessmen named the Association for the Promotion and Protection of Foreign Investment (APPI), in Geneva, to draft a convention for the protection of foreign property, which was later brought by the International Chamber of Commerce to the Organisation for Economic Co-operation and Development (OECD). That text, which became known as the Abs-Shawcross Draft Convention after its principal authors, was, after some revision by the OECD governments, recommended by the OECD Council of Ministers to its member States as a model for the preparation of bilateral agreements. Whilst the draft was never adopted as a convention, bilateral treaties concluded since 1962 have to no small degree been inspired by its contents.

In 1982, the United States joined in the practice and launched its own model. To date, it has signed 13 treaties and is in the process of negotiating an additional nine treaties. As other countries like Japan, Sweden, Denmark, Austria and Italy became major capital exporters, they too signed bilateral investment treaties with recipient countries. Italy has concluded 22 treaties, Sweden 16, Denmark 13 and Austria 10 (see table 2).

Initially, most bilateral investment treaties were concluded between western countries and developing countries, mainly from Africa and Asia and the Pacific regions. Some Central and Eastern European countries, like Romania, began concluding bilateral treaties as early as the 1970s, and others followed during the early 1980s (Bulgaria, Hungary and Yugoslavia). Also some developing countries, particularly in South-East Asia — as their level of economic development rose — began concluding bilateral treaties as part of their efforts to export capital and investment to other developing countries, mainly within the region (for example, Singapore, the Republic of Korea, Malaysia, Sri Lanka and Indonesia). There were also treaties concluded between developing countries and Central European countries (*e.g.*, Romania with Pakistan, Senegal, Egypt, Cameroon, Morocco and Sri Lanka). China joined in this practice in 1982 and has since concluded 28 treaties with Western, developing and Central European countries.

Since 1987, a number of Central and Eastern European countries have begun concluding bilateral investment treaties as part of their efforts to attract foreign investment in the wake of political and economic reforms. To date, Poland has concluded 16 treaties; the former USSR 14; Czechoslovakia 13; and Hungary 18.

Another significant trend in the past few years has been the conclusion of bilateral investment treaties by Latin American countries, such as Argentina, Bolivia and Venezuela. In the past, the countries of that region typically rejected bilateral investment treaties, mainly due to their adherence to the Calvo doctrine. The number of bilateral investment treaties signed by Latin American countries rose from six in the 1960s and two in the 1970s, to 13 in the 1980s and 10 in the 1990s.

Overall, the number of bilateral investment treaties signed has grown steadily from 83 treaties in the 1960s, to 176 in the 1970s, and 377 at the end of 1989. By early 1991, about 440 bilateral investment treaties had been concluded.

CHAPTER II

MAIN FEATURES OF BILATERAL INVESTMENT TREATIES

Most bilateral investment treaties deal with a varying number, or sometimes with all, of the following issues:

- Preamble
- Scope of application of the
- Conditions for the entry of an investment
- Promotion of investment
- General standards of treatment
  * Fair and equitable treatment
  * National treatment
  * Most-favoured-nation treatment
- Standards of treatment on specific issues
  * Operational conditions of the investment
  * Transfer of payments and repatriation of capital
  * Losses due to armed conflict or internal disorder
  * Dispossession of the investor
  * Subrogation
  * Settlement of disputes

A. Preamble

The preamble of bilateral investment treaties normally contains statements of their objective and purpose. They usually underline the contracting States' faith in the private sector and stress the desire to intensify economic cooperation, the creation of favourable conditions for investment by nationals and companies of one State in the territory of the other, and the encouragement of contractual protection for such investment.

B. Scope of application

Bilateral investment treaties contain various revisions that deal with their scope of application, normally in the context of the definition of "investment," "nationals," "companies" and "territory" of the contracting parties, and the duration of the treaty, including the effects it may continue to produce after its extinction. The provisions on these issues have far reaching implications on the extent of the obligations undertaken by the contracting States. Most agreements provide a list of the types of investments covered, normally preceded by a phrase indicating that the list is not exclusive. The list typically includes movable and immovable property, all kinds of property rights, shares, debts, copyrights, industrial property rights, know-how, trademarks, and concessions under public law or under contract for the exploitation of natural resources. Moreover, the definitions used are normally wide enough to cover other types of direct investment involving non-equity resources, sometimes referred to as "new forms of cooperation," such as management, marketing or turnkey contracts which are becoming increasingly important.

C. Entry of an investment

While the definition of investment determines generically what transactions fall under the scope of the treaty, this does not mean in itself that any such transaction will be automatically covered by it. Most bilateral investment treaties state that investments must be made in accordance with the rules and regulations of the host country and are subject to approval. In this manner, the contracting States retain ample discretion to regulate the entry of investment from the other party and to stipulate terms and conditions for its establishment. Under some treaties, however, this discretion is limited by the country's obligation to afford national and/or most-favoured-nation treatment in granting permission to the investments of the other contracting party, but even then the parties retain the right to prescribe exceptions to the application of these standards in specific sectors or matters. Thus, in the treaties concluded by United States so far, permission for establishment is to be granted on the basis of national and most-favoured-nation treatment, with exceptions regarding sectors and matters expressly stipulated therein or in separate protocols, or prescribed in national legislation.

In the national legislation of many countries, including developed market economies, foreign direct investment is prohibited in certain industries, such as public utilities, vital or strategic industries, and medium-size and small industries being developed by local enterprises. In addition to the admission clauses which, by referring to the national laws of the host country, may indirectly limit investments in certain sectors or exclude them from reserved ones, the desire on the part of host countries not to allow certain foreign direct investment is expressed in some investment agreements by stating that foreign direct investment is not to be encouraged or promoted in specified industries or that it will not be granted the treatment accorded to national investors in those industries.

D. Promotion of investment

By virtue of their titles, most bilateral investment treaties are meant to encourage investments as well as to protect them. Indeed, the capital importing country normally negotiates bilateral investment treaties as one of the measures to attract investment. The majority of treaties concluded in the past decade contain a standard promotion clause that stipulates that each contracting party shall create favourable conditions for the establishment of investments of the other contracting party and, subject to its right to exercise powers conferred by its laws, shall admit such investment. Thus, while those treaties generally do not guarantee an absolute right of entry and establishment, there is nevertheless a clear emphasis on facilitating the entry of investments between the contracting parties.

E. General standards of treatment

1. Fair and equitable treatment

Most bilateral investment treaties prescribe fair and equitable treatment for the investments of the contracting parties. This is a general standard of treatment that has been developed under customary international law. While there is still no precise definition of the content of this standard, its inclusion in bilateral investment treaties serves several purposes, not only as a basic standard but also as an auxiliary element for the interpretation of specific provisions of the treaty or in order to fill gaps in the treaty. Although the content of certain standards of traditional international law and their applicability to foreign investment have been questioned by some developing countries, classical international law doctrine and most bilateral investment treaties normally consider certain elements to be part of fair and equitable treatment, such as non-discrimination, the international minimum standard and the duty of protection of foreign property by the host country.

2. National and most-favoured-nation treatment

The principle of national treatment is also a common ingredient of bilateral investment treaties. This principle requires that, for the purpose of the treaty, foreign investors should be treated in the same way as nationals. This clause is usually accompanied by a number of exceptions, either in the treaty itself or in related instruments. Among the most common exceptions to national treatment are those relating to national security and public order, and those concerning the development objectives and priorities of the host country. To achieve those objectives, a few countries have inserted a list of sectors or activities which are excepted from the application of the principle of national treatment.

Most bilateral investment treaties include a most-favourable-treatment clause to the effect that investment shall receive treatment at least as favourable as the host State has undertaken to provide to investments by nationals and companies of another State. Moreover, national and most-favoured-nation treatment are often found in combination in bilateral investment treaties. In this manner, investors can avail themselves of the more favourable of these two standards. In relation to the effects of national and most favourable treatment, questions have sometimes been expressed about the scope of either or both clauses in an investment context. For example, the determination of what is a "similar" enterprise or activity, the meaning of the words "in the same circumstances" or the assessment of the effect of special benefits granted to local investors in specific situations might require some interpretation by the contracting parties.

F. Standards of treatment on specific issues

1. Operational conditions

With respect to the operational aspects of an investment, some specific aspects are left to be determined by the national laws of the contracting States. Thus, bilateral investment treaties are often silent about such matters as performance requirements, the employment of local personnel, the use of credit facilities and disclosure of information. Sometimes, however, treaties may provide for "sympathetic consideration" for entry, sojourn and employment of foreign nationals in connection with investment. Some treaties however, notably those concluded by the United States, provide for treaty rights with respect to a number of operational matters such as, for example, right of entry and sojourn of aliens for the purpose of operating the investment and employment.

In approving investments, host countries sometimes impose performance requirements (often combined with incentives), which compel the enterprise to operate in particular ways, for example, exporting a minimum amount of its production or purchasing a minimum amount of locally produced goods or services. Clauses concerning performance requirements are not an invariable feature of bilateral investment treaties but the treaties signed by the United States do seek to eliminate performance requirements between the contracting parties by including a clause that specifically prohibits [them].

2. Transfer of payments

The provisions on the transfer of payments are considered one of the most important aspects of bilateral investment treaties by both contracting parties. Most bilateral investment treaties maintain in principle that investors should be able to transfer freely and without restrictions all payments relating to their investments, such as income from invested capital, and the proceeds from liquidation of this capital. At the same time, many bilateral treaties also impose certain limitations upon the free transfer of currency, intended to accommodate the concerns of the host country over its balance of payments. Generally, it is added that these restrictions must be in accordance with the host country's obligations to exercise equitably and in good faith the powers conferred by its laws. A number of recent bilateral treaties provide for the phasing out of the repatriation of capital, if this is warranted by the host State's foreign exchange situation.

In addition, some bilateral investment treaties require that the transfer of currency must be effected in freely convertible currency. Some treaties go on to stipulate the formula for calculating the applicable rate of exchange.

3. Losses due to armed conflict or internal disorder

A clause providing for compensation for losses due to armed conflict or internal disorder is a common feature of bilateral investment treaties. While it is not usual in these treaties to prescribe an absolute right to compensation, they guarantee the foreign investor at least the same treatment as that of the nationals of the host country in this area. However, some treaties do provide for more far-reaching right to compensation.

4. Dispossession of the investor

One of the main purposes of bilateral investment treaties is to provide protection to the investor against nationalization, expropriation and other types of dispossession by the Government of the host country. A treaty obligation in this respect, expressed in clear terms according to traditional international law may be particularly important as a means of attracting foreign direct investment. This seems to be borne out by the historical experience of the industrialized countries, both old and new.

Practically all bilateral investment treaties restate the international law principle that a State may expropriate foreign property within its territory, provided that it is for a public purpose, in a non-discriminatory manner, upon payment of compensation, and with judicial review. The formulations of this rule found in bilateral investment treaties reflect various degrees of protection of investors.

A second major question is the standard of compensation that the expropriating State will be obliged to follow in compensating the expropriated investor. Many bilateral investment treaties reflect the so-called Hull Formula stating that such compensation must be "prompt, adequate and effective". The meaning of these words is usually explained in the treaty. Other bilateral investment treaties have used different wordings but with similar effect. Thus, the United States prototype treaty explains what is to be understood by "adequate" compensation: it must be "equivalent" to the *fair market value* of the expropriated investment *immediately before the expropriating action was taken or became known* shall include interest as from the date of expropriation. Under the model treaty of Germany, "compensation shall be equivalent to the value of the investment expropriated immediately before the date of expropriation or nationalization was publicly announced". In the protocol, it is specified that value means market value. The Swiss standard draft uses the Hull formula without specifying the notion of "adequate compensation". The African Asian Legal Consultative Committee (AALCC) Model A stipulates that compensation is to be computed "in accordance with recognized principles of valuation such as fair market value". To sum up, market value is the method most generally used for the valuation of expropriated assets.

As for the modalities of the payment of compensation, many bilateral treaties require that it be "without delay, fully realizable and freely transferable".

5. Subrogation

Subrogation clauses are to be found in practically all bilateral investment treaties. They provide that if investors have received payments from their national investment insurance agencies against "political risks", the home country or its agency succeeds in the rights or claims of the investor against the host State. Subrogation is conceptually to be distinguished from diplomatic protection (also contemplated in bilateral investment treaties as part of the inter-State settlement procedures under the treaty). The former implies essentially a contractual relationship (it is part of the insurance contract) and is normally practised before the courts of the host State.

6. Settlement of disputes

Early bilateral investment treaties were concerned only with settlement of disputes between the contracting parties on the application and interpretation of the treaty. However, a trend towards including provisions on the settlement of disputes between the investor and the host State soon began to emerge and, since the conclusion of the 1965 *Washington Convention on the Settlement of Investment Disputes Between States and Nationals of Other States* (ICSID), clauses concerning dispute settlement in the framework of ICSID have been included in many bilateral investment treaties.

The merit of the Convention is that its clauses are designed to meet the concerns of both developing and developed countries. For that reason, almost all bilateral investment treaties provide for dispute settlement by international arbitration at the initiative of either the investor or the host country. ICSID is the arbitration mechanism chosen for this purpose in a great number of treaties. Other frameworks and mechanisms, such as the International Chamber of Commerce and the Arbitration Rules of the United Nations Commission for International Trade Law (UNCITRAL) are also chosen.

Willingness on the part of a host country to submit investment disputes with investors to impartial international arbitration is often seen (by investors) as a significant encouragement to investment as reflected in the terms of many investment agreements.

United States Department of State, Bureau of Economic and Business Affairs
U.S. Bilateral Investment Treaty (BIT), (released 28 July 1997)

The Bilateral Investment Treaty (BIT) Program supports the key U.S. government economic policy objectives of promoting U.S. exports and enhancing the international competitiveness of U.S. companies.

The BIT program's basic aims are to:

- protect U.S. investment abroad in those countries where U.S. investors' rights are not protected through existing agreements such as our treaties of Friendship, Commerce and Navigation;

- encourage adoption in foreign countries of market-oriented domestic policies that treat private investment fairly; and

- support the development of international law standards consistent with these objectives.

Since 1982, the United States has signed 39 BITs, of which 29 are now in force. We have ongoing negotiations with many countries from all over the world.

The U.S. Government has placed a priority on negotiating BITs with countries undergoing economic reform and where we believe we can have a significant impact on the adoption of liberal policies on the treatment of foreign direct investment. BITs also complement and support our regional initiatives on investment liberalization in the Asia Pacific Economic Cooperation Forum (APEC) and the Free Trade of the Americas initiative. In addition, they lay the policy groundwork for broader multilateral initiatives in the OECD and eventually, the WTO.

U.S. Bilateral Investment Treaties provide U.S. investors with six basic guarantees:

First, our BITs ensure that U.S. companies will be treated as favorably as their competitors.

- investors receive the better of national or most favored nation (MFN) treatment both when they seek to initiate investment and throughout the life of that investment, subject to certain limited and specifically described exceptions listed in annexes or protocols to the treaties.

Second, BITs establish clear limits on the expropriation of investments and ensure that U.S. investors will be fairly compensated.

- Expropriation can occur only in accordance with international law standards that is, for a public purpose, in a nondiscriminatory manner, under due process of law, and accompanied by payment of prompt, adequate, and effective compensation.

Third, BITs guarantee that U.S. investors have the right to transfer funds into and out of the country without delay using a market rate of exchange. This covers all transfers related to an investment, including interest, proceeds from liquidation, repatriated profits and infusions of additional financial resources after the initial investment has been made. Ensuring the right to transfer funds creates a predictable environment guided by market forces.

Fourth, BITs limit the ability of host governments to require U.S. investors to adopt inefficient and trade distorting practices. In particular, performance requirements, such as local content or export quotas, are prohibited.

- This provision may also open up new markets for U.S. producers and increase U.S. exports. U.S. investors protected by BITs can purchase competitive U.S.-produced components without restriction on inputs in their production of various products.

- They can also import other U.S.-produced products for distribution and sale in the local market. And they cannot be forced, as a condition of establishment or operation, to export locally produced goods back to the U.S. market or to third-country markets.

Fifth, BITs give U.S. investors the right to submit an investment dispute with the treaty partner's government to international arbitration. There is no requirement to use that country's domestic courts.

Sixth, BITs give U.S. investors the right to engage the top managerial personnel of their choice, regardless of nationality.

VI. FDI and National Security

Documents Supplement References:

1. *The Exon-Florio Amendment, 50 U.S.C. App. 2170.*

Authorities Relating to Political or Economic Security
Section 721 of the Defense Production Act of 1950, as Amended
("Exon/Florio"), in House Committee on Ways and Means,
105th Congress, 1st Session, Overview and Compilation of U.S. Trade
Statutes 183-84 (Committee Print, 25 June 1997)

Section 721 of the Defense Production Act of 1950, as amended ("Exon/Florio")

The proposed purchase in 1988 of an 80 percent share of Fairchild Semiconductor Corporation by Fujitsu, Ltd. sparked congressional interest concerning takeovers of American firms by foreign companies which raise national security considerations. Section 5021 of the Omnibus Trade and Competitiveness Act of 1988 amended Title VII of the Defense Production Act of 1950 [*codified at 50 U.S.C. App. 2170, and reproduced in the Documents Supplement*] to add provisions (commonly known as "Exon/Florio," the chief congressional sponsors) because of concerns that the federal government lacked specific authority to prevent such acquisitions.

The provisions authorize the President, after he makes certain findings, to take actions for such time as he considers appropriate to suspend or prohibit an acquisition, merger, or takeover of a person engaged in interstate commerce in the United States by or with foreign persons so that such control will not threaten to impair the national security. To activate this authority, the President has to find that there is credible evidence that leads him to believe the foreign interest exercising control might take action that threatens to impair the national security and that other laws do not provide adequate and appropriate authority to protect the national security in the matter. The President has to report the findings to the Congress with a detailed explanation.

In making any decision to exercise the authority under this provision, the President may consider such factors as: (1) domestic production needed for projected national defense requirements; (2) the capability and capacity of domestic industries to meet national defense requirements; and (3) the control of domestic industries and commercial activities by foreign citizens as it affects the capability and capacity of the United States to meet the requirements of national security. The standard of review is "national security;" the provision affects only overseas investment flowing into the United States and is not intended to authorize investigations of investments that could not result in foreign control of persons engaged in interstate commerce nor have any effects on transactions which are outside the realm of national security.

Among the actions available to the President is the ability to suspend a transaction. The President may also seek appropriate relief in the district courts of the United States in order to implement and enforce the provisions, including broad injunctive and equitable relief including, but not limited to, divestment relief.

United States General Accounting Office, Foreign Investment—Foreign Laws and Policies Addressing National Security Concerns
1-13, 20-42, GAO/NSIAD-96-61 (April 1996)

Results in Brief

Japan, France, Germany, and the United Kingdom each have the authority to block investments for national security reasons, as does the United States. However, all five countries have infrequently used this authority in recent years. Some of these countries have established processes for reviewing foreign investment for national security concerns. [As stated in footnote 3 of the report, "national security-related industries include — but are not limited to — companies that have defense contracts or make defense sales."] Japan and France review certain foreign direct investments for national security and other concerns. Germany and the United Kingdom have no general screening authority that explicitly considers national security issues related to foreign investment, but the United Kingdom can consider harm to public interest in its antitrust review process.

U.S. defense company officials we interviewed said they had not pursued defense-related direct investment in Japan, France, Germany, or the United Kingdom because of basic economic factors such as the size of the defense markets in these countries, as well as informal barriers, such as domestic company ownership structures. The officials said that such factors could be more important considerations in some countries than the legal framework. Most countries offer investment incentives, but U.S. defense company officials did not cite these as a major reason for investing.

U.S. defense company officials said they were pursuing access to overseas defense markets through strategies other than foreign direct investment. For example, U.S. defense companies either licensed technology to Japanese companies or made direct sales to Japan. In the three European countries, U.S. companies formed partnerships to compete for particular projects.

Background

International mergers and acquisitions have increased in recent years, returning to the high levels of activity that characterized the late 1980s. Cross-border mergers in Europe in 1994 were almost double the level of 1993 in value terms. U.S. firms were the most active buyers in Europe. Similarly in the United States, foreign companies significantly increased their investment activity. However, Japanese companies decreased their overseas acquisitions in the first half of 1994.

According to the Organization for Economic Cooperation and Development (OECD), total foreign direct investments inflows and outflows among member countries have increased in recent years. [The OECD definition of foreign direct investment is capital invested for the purpose of acquiring a lasting interest in an enterprise and exerting a degree of influence on that enterprise's operation.] OECD reported that inflows grew by almost 60 percent for selected countries while outflows grew by 14 percent in the 1993-94 time period. The growth of inflows is largely attributable to massive inflows into the United States. However, there is a significant variation in flows across individual countries.

....

Defense Industry Activities

In the defense industry, company business activities have been affected by declining defense budgets. France, Germany, the United Kingdom, and the United States have decreased their defense budgets in real terms over recent years. In contrast, Japan's defense budget has been increasing but at a decreasing rate, from a 3.8-percent increase between 1990 and 1991 to a 0.9-percent increase between 1993 and 1994.

....

Given declining defense budgets, most defense firms worldwide are consolidating to improve competitiveness. U.S. defense firms have pursued consolidation within the United States to downsize and reduce overcapacity. To a certain extent, some of the European countries have contracted and restructured their individual defense industries. Germany and the United Kingdom, in particular, have encouraged numerous defense manufacturers to consolidate into unified conglomerates or "national champions." In contrast, French defense companies have consolidated more slowly. Mergers and acquisitions are uncommon in Japan's defense industry, which is restructuring by such means as shifting resources away from defense production into commercial sectors and reducing production lines.

According to the Center for Strategic and Budgetary Assessments, cross-border defense mergers, acquisitions, and joint ventures have been largely intra-European. Transatlantic defense investment activity has been characterized by European acquisitions of U.S. companies rather than U.S. acquisitions of European companies. Few U.S. companies are acquiring Japanese companies. The Center for Strategic and Budgetary Assessments also reports that foreign acquisition occurring in Japan are between companies only marginally engaged in defense work.

....

International Agreements With Provisions Affecting National Security

Agreements among countries have widely recognized the right of sovereign nations to take measures protecting their essential national security interests. For example, article 223 of the Treaty of Rome [which established the European Economic Community] states in part that European member nations may take measures "necessary for the protection of the essential interest of its security which are connected with the production of or trade in arms, munitions and war material." This article essentially allows national governments to suspend European Union free trade and competition rules on the grounds of national security. Also, OECD's main foreign direct investment instruments, the National Treatment Instrument and Codes of Liberalization, recognize that countries can take actions based on essential security or other interests.

In September 1995, OECD began negotiating a multilateral agreement on investment. This agreement is intended to develop high standards for liberalization of foreign direct investment regimes and investment protection and to include effective dispute settlement. Exceptions to the investment principles will be negotiated. According to some experts, one exception will permit each member country to exempt certain industries or sectors from the agreement commitments due to national security concerns.

Broad Authority Exists to Block Investments for National Security Reasons

The Exon-Florio legislation grants the President of the United States the authority to take appropriate action to suspend or prohibit foreign acquisitions, mergers, or takeovers of U.S. businesses that threaten to impair the national security. To exercise this authority, the President must find that (1) credible evidence exists that the foreign interest exercising control might take action that threatens to impair national security and (2) provisions of law, other than the Exon-Florio legislation and the International Emergency Economic Powers Act, do not provide adequate authority to protect the national security. Since the enactment of the legislation in 1988, the President has used this authority once when ordering divestiture of a Chinese company's acquisition of a U.S. aircraft parts company.

Japan, France, Germany, and the United Kingdom do not have laws directly analogous to the Exon-Florio legislation, but nevertheless have broad legislative authority to block foreign investments for reasons of national security or national interest. For example, the Japanese and French laws provide the governments broad powers to block investments that might imperil national security, public order, and public safety. The Japanese government has not invoked this authority in recent years while the French government has restricted nine investments in the past several years. Germany's law also permits restriction of private investment flows in either direction for balance of trade considerations and foreign policy, public order, and national security reasons, but such restrictions have not been used to date. The United Kingdom has never used its broad discretionary power to block foreign investments for national interest. The legal investment frameworks of Japan, France, Germany, and the United Kingdom are discussed in appendixes II, III, IV, and V, respectively.

In the United States, the President designated CFIUS [the Committee on Foreign Investment in the United States, an inter-agency group] as responsible for reviewing foreign investment transactions. Although notifications are voluntary, CFIUS retains the right to review at any time any acquisition not notified to the Committee. The Exon-Florio regulations also permit a CFIUS member to submit a notice of a proposed or completed acquisition for a national security review. A CFIUS determination that there are no national security issues essentially eliminates the risk that the President will at a later time block the transaction or order a divestiture.

Each of the countries we examined has a reviewing mechanism that differs in focus from CFIUS. Japan and France both have a formal process in which foreign investments are reviewed for several reasons, including public order, public safety, and national security. The United Kingdom and Germany have no general screening authority that explicitly considers national security issues related to foreign investment. However, as do many other nations, the United Kingdom and Germany have antitrust screening mechanisms. The United Kingdom, through its antitrust process, may make determinations based on harm to public interest. Germany's antitrust review mechanism does not screen for adverse impact on national security, but antitrust decisions against a merger may be overturned if the merger is considered to be in the public interest.

As shown in table 1, similarities and differences exist among the CFIUS process and selected reviewing mechanisms in Japan and France. For example, CFIUS and the other countries' reviewing entities are similar in that they perform case-by-case evaluations. These reviews have resulted in few denied transactions based on national security concerns. However, significant differences exist among the reviewing mechanisms. Japan and France review foreign investments for national security and other reasons. While transactions are voluntarily notified to CFIUS, the two countries' reviewing mechanisms require mandatory notification for transactions meeting certain criteria. Also, Japan and France have a judicial appeal process, unlike the United States.

Limitations Reported to OECD

All five countries impose some type of sectoral restrictions on foreign direct investment that are notified to OECD. For example, the five countries impose similar restrictions on maritime transport. OECD members also report measures based on public order and essential security interests that are considered limitations to the National Treatment Instrument. [A non-binding agreement stating that OECD member countries will apply the same laws, regulations, and administrative practices to foreign-owned companies as would apply to domestic investors in like situations, and requiring member countries to notify the OECD of all measures that are exceptions to this principle.] Of the five countries, only Germany reported no limitations for essential security interests. Table 2 shows the national treatment limitations that affect defense or national security-related areas in our selected countries.

Economic Conditions and Informal Barriers Influence Investment Decisions

Fundamental economic conditions and informal barriers to doing business in the selected countries can be important determinants of whether U.S. firms pursue foreign direct investment options. Officials at many of the U.S. defense companies we interviewed were not planning to invest abroad because of the relatively small size of the countries' defense markets. They frequently cited basic economic factors and informal barriers, such as high land prices or domestic company ownership structures, as more important to their evaluation of investment options than the legal framework. Furthermore, the officials said that governments offer some incentives to invest, such as tax breaks, but these are not a significant factor in making investment decisions.

Some U.S. defense company officials we interviewed said the size of the defense markets in the four countries often did not justify major equity investments. For example, the German and British defense budgets are declining, which can make it less attractive for U.S companies. Although the Japanese government has one of the larger defense budgets, it has a comparatively smaller equipment acquisition budget. [T]he U.S. defense budget was larger than those of the other countries reviewed.

. . . .

U.S. defense and commercial companies are affected by the business environment overseas. In weighing decisions to invest abroad, U.S. company officials we interviewed said certain economic or social conditions can serve as disincentives. For example, companies established in France and Germany face strict labor practices and

TABLE 1 SELECTED COUNTRIES' FOREIGN INVESTMENT REVIEWING MECHANISM[b]

Characteristics of reviewing mechanisms	United States	Japan	France[c]
Reason for reviewing	National security.	National security, public order, public safety, and economy.	Public order, health, or security; public functions; research, production, or trade in arms, ammunition, explosive powders and substances destined for military use or wartime equipment.
Reviewing body	CFIUS.	Ministry of Finance and Ministry in charge of industry.	Ministry of Economics and Finance, consulting with Ministries of Industry and Defense.
Notification	Voluntary.	Mandatory.	Mandatory.
Review time	Thirty-day review; 45-day investigation; 15-day presidential review for cases investigated.	Thirty days; can be extended up to 5 months	Up to 1 month, unless postponement rights are exercised.
Judicial appeal	No.	Yes.	Yes.
Case-by-case evaluation	Yes.	Yes.	Yes.
Outcomes and time frame	Fifteen cases investigated since 1988; President blocked 1 case.	None since 1992 law revisions.	Eight rejected in 1992–93 and one in 1994 for public order reasons.

[b] Germany and the United Kingdom are not included in the table because neither country has a foreign investment specific review mechanism that can consider national security implications.

[c] The French government changed its foreign investment law in February 1996 to abolish prior authorization of non-European investments meeting certain French franc thresholds. However, prior authorization is still required for all foreign investments in French entities carrying out public functions or activities that may affect public health, order, or security, or for investments involving research, production or trade in arms, ammunition, explosive powders and substances destined for military use or wartime equipment.

Source: GAO *analysis.*

TABLE 2: SELECTED PUBLIC ORDER AND ESSENTIAL SECURITY-RELATED MEASURES RELATED TO OECD

Country	Foreign investment measures based on essential security considerations	Government purchasing measures based on essential security considerations	Other related measures
United States	The Exon-Florio legislation provides the President power to block foriegn acquisitions that threaten to impair national security.	Foreign controlled enterprises may not be granted a contract or subcontract involving classified information except under special arrangements determined on a case-by-case basis.	None.
Japan	Specific investment plans of foreign controlled enterprises could be altered or suspended when national security, public order, or public safety is deemed threatened in such industrial sectors as aircraft, arms, explosives, nuclear energy, and space.	None.	None.
France	National treatment is not applicable to enterprises whose activities are directly or indirectly related to national defense and and armaments. The government reserves the right to apply conditions on the creation, extension, or conduct of business enterprises under foreign control or to obtain guarantees.	Preference is accorded to locally owned firms in procurement for the armed forces with regard to items for military purposes.	None.
Germany	None.	None.	None.
United Kingdom	British Aerospace PLC and Rolls Royce PLC restrict the number of foreign-held shares at any one time to 29.5 percent of the ordinary voting equity. The articles of association also provide citizenship requirements for the directors.	In a limited number of cases, foreign-controlled enterprises may not be granted defense procurement contracts where where overriding security reasons apply.	Certain citizenship requirements for ex-Plessy companies engaged in classified work. VSEL consortium PLC has citizenship requirements for certain executives. There is also a veto over disposal of company assets.

Source: *National Treatment for Foreign Controlled Enterprises*, OECD, 1993.

cannot lay off workers easily. In Japan, obstacles to doing business include labor costs, the tax burden, and high rent and land costs. Such factors make investment expensive and can affect the profit margins of established companies in these countries.

U.S. defense company officials we interviewed indicated company ownership structures can deter foreign direct investment. For example, extensive cross-share-holdings between businesses and large institutions exist in both Germany and Japan, which serve the long-term investment needs of domestic companies and discourage foreign investors. In France, the government has majority ownership of most of the major defense companies and significant influence over other private defense-related companies. Unlike France, the United Kingdom has largely privatized most companies since 1979. However, the British government retains "golden shares," or special consent rights, in certain privatized companies. This may include placing limits on foreign ownership as with British Aerospace PLC and Rolls Royce PLC.

Each of the countries has incentives to offer foreign investors, but these incentives played a limited role in influencing the investment decisions of the U.S. defense company officials we interviewed. Most of the countries offer some form of a tax incentive, low interest loan, or subsidy. Regional incentives exist to attract foreign investors to certain geographic areas. However, none of these investment incentives are defense specific.

Given the defense investment climate and economic conditions, many U.S. defense company officials we interviewed did not view foreign direct investment as an essential part of their strategy. However, some investments have been made. For example, General Electric and the French company, SNECMA, collaborated for over 20 years on the CFM-56 jet engine for commercial aircraft and established an equity joint venture in 1974 to supply propulsion systems. In 1993, BDM International, Inc., invested in the German company, IABG, which conducts aerospace testing and military and environmental studies.

Defense Companies Pursue Other Strategies to Gain Market Access

To gain market access, U.S. defense companies are largely seeking project-by-project business arrangements with European companies or selling in niche markets. These arrangements can be less expensive for U.S. companies to pursue compared to capital intensive equity investments. Some U.S. company officials said that having relationships with European partners is helpful because they offer knowledge of the regulatory environment. Successful partnerships include McDonnell Douglas and Westland Helicopters to produce Apache helicopters for the British Ministry of Defense. E-Systems joined with three German companies in developing the Senior Guardian recognizance program. Motorola, through a French distributor, sells certain electronic products in French niche markets, where the principal French defense electronics manufacturer Thomson-CSF is not present.

In contrast with the European business arrangements, U.S. defense companies export defense products and license technology from the United States rather than make capital investments in Japan. This strategy is more advantageous to pursue because direct investment in Japan is expensive. For example, Hughes Aircraft is licensing its radar technology to a Japanese company for Japan's F-15s. Also, Japan has obtained technology and items from U.S. firms for the FS-X program. The U.S. Department of State had approved over 500 FS-X munitions export licenses by March 1994. Most of these licenses covered hardware for the development and production of the prototype aircraft.

. . . .

Japan's Foreign Exchange and Foreign Trade Control Law (FECL) is the primary law pertaining to foreign direct investment and provides the authority to block or restructure an investment. This law requires prior notification of a proposed invest-ment in certain industries so that the Ministry of Finance and other ministries may review the proposed investment to determine whether the investment might adversely affect national security, public order, public safety, or the Japanese economy. This au-thority, however, has not been used at least since 1992 because (1) foreign investors informally consult with the ministries before formal notification and (2) the min-istries use administrative guidance [i.e., unwritten orders given by Japanese govern-ment officials to firms to implement official policies, based on the broad discretionary power of the Japanese government bureaucracy rather than on specific laws] to affect any potential investments. Indirect barriers and economic conditions, such as the structure of Japan's defense industry and the high cost of doing business in Japan, discourage foreign investment in Japan, rather than Japanese legal restrictions. In-stead of foreign direct investment, U.S. defense companies prefer to license technol-ogy to Japanese companies or export directly to Japan.

. . . .

Legal Framework Exists for Reviewing and Blocking Foreign Investments

As Japan's primary law concerning foreign direct investment, FECL provides that the ministries may advise or order an investor to either restructure or suspend a proposed investment if they determine that the investment may harm national secu-rity, public order, public safety, or the economy. However, the Japanese government has not used this authority at least since FECL was amended in 1992, according to Japanese government officials. Industry observers indicated that the ministries are commonly consulted by companies or their legal representatives to obtain informal approval prior to official notification. Ministry officials stressed that this consultation is optional. Nonetheless, the ministries have the opportunity to influence investment decisions prior to formal notification through these consultations or by administra-tive guidance, according to foreign company representatives and members of acade-mia.

FECL provides a broad definition of foreign direct investment. FECL defines for-eign investment as (1) having at least 10 percent foreign ownership of shares in a company listed on a Japanese stock exchange; (2) having foreign ownership of any shares in an unlisted company; (3) establishing a branch, factory, or other business office in Japan; (4) consenting to change the corporate objectives of a domestic com-pany with one-third or more foreign ownership; or (5) lending certain types of money to domestic companies.

Notification Procedures

FECL and its implementing documents require reporting or notification of all foreign direct investment in Japan. The law provides for ex post facto, or "after the fact," reporting for investments in most industries, which are identified in a public notice. A foreign investor must file a report with the Ministry of Finance and the min-istry with jurisdiction over the industry through the Bank of Japan within 15 days after a transaction occurs. Ministry of International Trade and Industry (MITI) offi-cials stated that the reason for ex post facto reporting was for statistical purposes and in case of an emergency, such as a financial crisis or war.

The law requires prior notification for exceptional cases, in which foreign direct domestic investment is proposed (1) by an investor from a country not listed in the public notice and for which Japan has reciprocity concerns and (2) in an industry not listed in the public notice. The public notice excludes industries relating to national security, public order, or public safety, as well as industries reserved by Japan under the OECD Code of Liberalization of Capital Movements. Failure to notify the ministries can result in jail time and/or a monetary fine.

FECL authorizes the Ministry of Finance and the ministries of jurisdiction to review for national security and economic reasons any proposed investments in industries requiring prior notification. The law provides ministerial review to determine whether the proposed investments might (1) imperil the national security or disturb the maintenance of public order or public safety or (2) adversely and seriously affect the Japanese economy. Sectors that require prior notification include aircraft and aircraft parts, explosives and munitions, atomic power, space development, and certain types of telecommunications.

Japan also requires prior notification of investments in sectors reserved through the OECD Code of Liberalization of Capital Movements. Under the OECD code, Japan reserves the following industries: agriculture, forestry and fisheries; mining; oil; leather and leather products manufacturing; air transport; and maritime transport. A Ministry of Finance official stated that these industries are reviewed mainly for economic reasons, although some are also reviewed for national security reasons.

The Review Process

Ministerial reviews may extend from 30 days to 5 months. The ministries have 30 days to review a proposed investment after a foreign company has notified the ministries of its intent to invest. If the investor has not received a response within that time, the transaction may be completed, according to MITI officials. The ministries may extend the review period for up to 4 months if they believe further inquiry is necessary. A Committee on Foreign Exchange and Other Transactions also may extend the review period an additional month.[1] However, a Finance Ministry official stated that the review period usually is less than 30 days.

FECL and its related documents do not provide criteria to determine whether a proposed investment will pose a national security or economic threat. The ministries review investments on a case-by-case basis and therefore apply no set standards, according to MITI officials. The notification form requires information concerning the percentage of shares to be acquired, the business plan of the investing company, and the reason for the transaction. However, the ministries may consider information related to foreign control, such as the number of foreign board members and the foreign company's reputation, according to Japanese government officials.

Investors may appeal the decision of the ministries. FECL provides for a public hearing if an investor wishes to contest the result of the ministerial review. After the public hearing, an investor may appeal to the Japanese courts to try to overturn a decision.

Economic Factors and Indirect Barriers Inhibit Investment

Economic factors and indirect barriers, rather than Japanese laws, appear to be the primary determinants of foreign investment across sectors. The U.S. company representatives that we interviewed stated that they have encountered no legal barriers to foreign investment in Japan in recent years. An American Chamber of Commerce in Japan report also indicates that legal barriers to investment in Japan have been removed.

The nature of Japan's defense industry acts as a deterrent to foreign investment in that sector. Japan's market for defense items is considered by many observers to be

---

1. The committee is appointed by the Minister of Finance to provide an opinion on direct investment and other matters.

too small to warrant the expense of establishing facilities in Japan. Establishing manufacturing facilities in Japan would be too costly and, according to one U.S. defense company official, would take away from economies of scale achieved at U.S. production facilities. Japan's defense market has primarily one client, the Japan Defense Agency, because the Japanese government basically prohibits exporting defense items to third countries. While the Japan Defense Agency has one of the larger defense budgets in the world, only 18.4 percent was devoted to equipment acquisition in fiscal year 1995. Furthermore, the Japan Defense Agency's preference for domestic procurement of defense items and the prohibition on arms exports increases the acquisition costs because of the high per unit cost of small production runs. As a result, the acquisition budget buys fewer items.

The size and structure of Japanese companies that produce defense items also discourage U.S. defense companies from attempting to purchase a controlling share in these companies. Japan has few companies dedicated solely to defense production. Most of the Japan Defense Agency's defense purchases are from huge Japanese conglomerates, such as Mitsubishi Heavy Industries, Kawasaki Heavy Industries, and Fuji Heavy Industries. However, defense sales provide a small percentage of sales for these companies compared to U.S. defense companies. For example, defense-related sales account for about 13 percent of Mitsubishi Heavy Industries' total sales, even though the company is the Japan Defense Agency's top defense contractor and is ranked as 1 of the top 20 defense companies worldwide. Furthermore, U.S. company officials stated that the size of a "heavy" makes it too expensive to try to buy a controlling portion of one. Some U.S. company officials stated that, even if they wanted to acquire a Japanese company that does defense work, the Japanese government would discourage such action.

Across sectors, business practices, structural barriers, and economic factors are frequently cited as major obstacles to investment. For example, a study commissioned by the American Chamber of Commerce in Japan and the Council of the European Business Community cited selective enforcement of regulations as one of the main barriers to doing business in Japan. Many of the representatives of U.S. defense companies we interviewed, as well as numerous studies, stated that the high cost of doing business in Japan, including labor costs, the tax burden, rent and land costs, and regulatory issues, is a disincentive to investment. Foreign acquisitions of Japanese companies face barriers caused by cross-shareholding — the practice of companies holding shares of each other's stock — and *keiretsu* relationships — groups of affiliated companies in related or unrelated fields that hold each other's shares and may also have financial (such as bank loans) or manufacturer-supplier ties or distributor relationships. Cross-shareholding and *keiretsu* relationships lessen the amount of shares available to buy on the stock market. In addition, cross-shareholding may prevent a foreign company from taking management control of a company, even if the foreign company is the largest individual shareholder. The relationships among *keiretsu* members make it difficult for foreign companies to buy into a member company and also to sell products to members of the *keiretsu*.

Recent bilateral discussions between the U.S. and Japanese governments have addressed some of the barriers to U.S. investment in Japan. The resulting agreement, which was signed in July 1995, detailed actions that the Japanese government has recently taken and outlined criteria for assessing the effectiveness of these actions. In addition, the Japanese government has pledged to promote foreign investment into Japan.

. . . .

Few, if any, U.S. companies have invested in Japan's defense industry, according to U.S. company, industry association, and Japanese government officials we interviewed. U.S. defense company officials have indicated that the decision not to invest in Japanese businesses is not based on Japan's regulatory environment, but on economic reasons. Instead, U.S. companies have realized sales to Japan through exporting from the United States and licensing technology, making the expense of investing in Japan unnecessary. Many U.S. companies have established branch or representative offices to facilitate these activities in Japan but do not have manufacturing facilities. When U.S. firms that have defense contracts in the United States have established either joint ventures or 100 percent-owned subsidiaries in Japan, these firms target the consumer market, not defense.

France

The French foreign investment law requires prior approval of foreign direct investment in sectors that affect public functions, public order, health, security, or aspects of the defense industry, but certain prior authorization requirements were recently liberalized. The French Ministry of Economics and Finance has the authority to block foreign investments made without proper authorization. The Ministry consults with the Ministry of Defense in cases concerning investment in national security-related industries. To date, Ministry officials are unaware of any proposed investments by U.S. companies that were denied on national security grounds in recent years. Nonetheless, few of the major French defense companies are available for U.S. companies to acquire because most are owned by the French government. U.S. companies prefer teaming with French companies on a project-by-project basis to achieve defense sales in France.

....

Legal Framework Exists for Reviewing Foreign Direct Investment

French law requires prior authorization from the French Ministry of Economics and Finance for foreign investments concerning (1) public functions, (2) public order, health, or security, or (3) research, production or trade in arms, ammunition, explosive powders and substances destined for military use or wartime equipment. The Ministry of Economics and Finance has the authority to block foreign investment in these areas made without proper authorization. Ministry of Economics and Finance officials were unaware of any proposed U.S. investments being denied approval in recent years. However, the French government blocked eight transactions by non-U.S. companies in 1992 and 1993 and one in 1994 on public order grounds.

French law defines foreign direct investment as (1) the purchase, establishment, or expansion of a business or branch or (2) any other transactions that enable non-residents to acquire or increase control over a company engaged in industry, commerce, agriculture, finance, or real estate. It also generally defines foreign control as occurring when at least 20 percent of a company's shares are owned by nonresidents or by companies under the control of nonresidents. However, other factors may be considered when determining foreign control, such as whether loans, commercial ties, or licensing arrangements result in additional control by a foreign entity. A company not listed on the stock exchange is considered under foreign control when at least 33.33 percent of its voting rights are owned by nonresidents.

Notification/Authorization Procedures

Foreign investors must notify the French Ministry of Economics and Finance of the intent to invest in sectors relating to government functions; public health, safety, or order, or defense. The government has up to 1 month in which to respond. If the government does not respond, the investment is presumed to be approved, unless the

Ministry of Economics and Finance exercises its right of postponement. Any investor who has failed to file the prior notification or to obtain the required prior authorization is subject to a fine. The Minister of Economics and Finance is able to annul an investment that would have been denied if the procedures had been observed.

Until recently, French law made a distinction between European Union and non-European Union investors in sectors not related to national security, public health, safety, or order. Specifically, European Union investors were not required to obtain prior approval when acquiring a controlling interest in a French company. However, such approval was required for non-European Union investors acquiring a controlling interest in any French company if the assets were worth at least 50 million French francs or had annual sales of at least 500 million French francs. In February 1996, the French government enacted legislation eliminating this prior authorization requirement for non-European investors. Under the new law, all investors are required to submit administrative notification to the French government when the investment is made. This notification is required for statistical purposes and to verify that the transaction has taken place.

The French government's investment approval process is headed by the Ministry of Economics and Finance. However, the Ministry of Economics and Finance consults with the Ministry of Industry on all transactions and with the Ministry of Defense if there is a national security concern. The Ministry of Defense is responsible for monitoring industry structures to ensure that strategic defense-related supplies are not excessively concentrated in foreign-controlled sources, when these sources are less reliable. Typically, sectors relating to national security could include dual-use sectors such as chemicals and electronics, as well as production of weapons. Ministry of Economics and Finance officials were not aware of any recent cases in which the Ministry of Defense advised against approving an acquisition by a foreign investor.

French law does not provide criteria for evaluating a proposed acquisition. Furthermore, if the French government were not in favor of a proposed acquisition, it could negotiate with investors informally. Foreign investors have the right to appeal French government decisions in court, but in practice that right is not exercised. U.S. embassy officials stated that U.S. companies may be reluctant to appeal decisions to avoid the risk of impairing future business ventures in France.

Other Limitations on Foreign Investment

France maintains restrictions on foreign investment activity in certain sectors of the economy. Under the OECD Code of Liberalization of Capital Movements, France reserves the right to restrict foreign investment in air transport, maritime transport, and insurance. In addition, France takes exceptions to the OECD National Treatment Instrument in the following areas: agriculture, air transport, broadcasting, insurance, maritime transport, publishing, road transport, telecommunications, and tourism. In the national security-related sectors, the French government reserves the right to restrict the creation, expansion, or operation of foreign-controlled aerospace companies. Furthermore, foreign-controlled defense companies are not entitled to national treatment in defense procurement by the French government.

Indirect Barriers Hinder Foreign Direct Investment

In general, the approval process for foreign investment is not considered a significant barrier to foreign investment. Officials from the U.S. Embassy in Paris stated that they have not received complaints from U.S. companies since 1990 and that there have been no major investment disputes since 1984. Indirect barriers to investment appear to inhibit foreign investment.

French government ownership of a company can inhibit foreign investment. The French government has majority ownership of most of France's major defense companies. As a result, controlling shares are not available for foreign companies to purchase. French defense companies were included in the 1993 privatization law, but these companies have yet to be privatized. In the event of privatization, French law prohibits the French government from selling more than 20 percent equity to non-European Union investors during the first share offering to the public. Subsequently, private investors may resell their shares to non-European Union investors. After privatization the French government can control a strategically important company through a "golden share." Application of this measure has remained limited, since few of the major French defense companies are privatized.

. . . .

Overcapacity and restrictive labor practices serve as disincentives to foreign investment in French defense companies. Reducing current overcapacity in French defense companies would require massive layoffs. French law provides workers with extensive compensation packages in the event of layoffs. As a result, several U.S. company officials stated that they did not see the possibility of sufficient returns through investing in French defense companies.

Across sectors, cross-shareholding among French corporations and close relationships among French company and government officials can make it difficult for foreign investors to acquire French companies. Often two or more French companies will hold shares of each other's stock, thus providing a pool of stable shareholders. According to a U.S. embassy report, the practice of cross-shareholding arose from the French government owning most large banks and insurance companies in the past. The French government used the banks and insurance companies to invest in other companies as a way of controlling other firms. In addition to cross-shareholding, many French company officials have close personal relationships with government officials. Most top French company and government officials are alumni of the same universities. In addition, many top French company executives sit on each others' board of directors.

. . . .

Teaming Arrangements Are an Alternative to Foreign Direct Investment

U.S. defense companies generally are not interested in investing in France to achieve defense sales. General Electric and SNECMA have collaborated for over 20 years on the CFM-56 jet engine for commercial aircraft, and they formed a joint venture company in 1974 to supply propulsion systems. U.S. firms typically either sell in niche markets in which French firms do not compete or team with French firms on a project-by-project basis to sell to the Ministry of Defense.

U.S. companies benefit from teaming with French defense companies because the chances of selling to the French Ministry of Defense are greater. Since the French government is subsidizing overcapacity in its defense industry, it is unlikely to award prime contracts for major equipment procurement to a foreign contractor. Furthermore, French companies maintain close contacts with Ministry of Defense officials and understand the French defense procurement process.

The Federal Republic of Germany has the legal authority to restrict foreign direct investment in its national security-related industries, but it has no administrative controls, bodies, or practices that overtly monitor, screen, track, or otherwise restrict such investments. Restrictions on foreign ownership are limited to a few nondefenserelated sectors and public monopolies. While U.S. defense company officials identified disincentives to investment in the defense sector, they indicated that they pursue market access to Germany through project-by-project teaming arrangements rather than through mergers or acquisitions.

. . . .

Legal Authority, but No Framework Exists for Restricting Foreign Direct Investment

Germany retains the authority to regulate and/or restrict foreign investment on the basis of national security, but it has never used that authority. The German Foreign Trade Law gives the government the power to restrict foreign direct investment for reasons of national security, public order, foreign policy, and balance of trade considerations. However, to date, the government has never imposed restrictions on foreign direct investment for reasons of national security. The 1956 Treaty of Friendship, Commerce and Navigation between the United States and Germany recognized the German government's authority to take such actions necessary to protect its national security interest. This authority would allow the German government to prohibit foreign direct investment by U.S. firms for national security reasons, but that authority has never been invoked.

Germany has no other administrative controls, bodies, or practices that restrict foreign investment in its national security-related industries. German officials stated that their government neither screens nor tracks foreign direct investment in German national security-related industries. U.S. government analyses concur with this assessment.

The German government's Federal Cartel Office has the authority to review mergers and acquisitions, including foreign direct investment, for violations of German antitrust laws. However, the Cartel Office, an independent government agency that administers German antitrust laws, does not screen for adverse impact to national security. If the Cartel Office prohibited a proposed merger on the grounds it would have a detrimental impact on competition, the Minister of Economics could override the Cartel Office's decision if it deemed the merger to be in the public interest. Public interest can include job preservation or military necessity.

Germany imposes no limitations on national treatment for foreign investors in the national security-related sectors or other sectors. Germany extends national treatment to any foreign firm that establishes itself in Germany, whether or not it is in the national security-related sector. Under German law, any foreign firm registered as a limited liability company (GmbH) or a joint stock company (AG) is regarded as a domestic company. It also imposes no currency or administrative controls on foreign direct investment.

Germany generally allows 100 percent foreign ownership of any company within the country, except for a few sectors. Germany reserves the right to restrict investment in air transport, maritime transport, and broadcasting under the OECD Code of Liberalization of Capital Movements. Germany also takes exceptions to the OECD National Treatment Instrument for foreign investment in air and maritime transport. OECD reported that Germany has no other informal measures that may impede foreign investment.

Germany Lacks a Self-Sufficient Defense Industry to Protect From Foreign Investors

German and U.S. officials stated that historical and economic factors account for Germany's lack of restrictions on foreign investment in its defense industrial sector.

Germany has accepted its dependence on the United States and the other North Atlantic Treaty Organization nations for its national security. Moreover, Germany has always been economically more dependent on outside sources for its supply of strategic minerals and fuels than the United States, according to one Ministry of Finance official.

The post-war German defense industry has also been open to foreign collaboration and investment because it has never been self-sufficient. Germany, unlike the United States or France, does not have a great power status to preserve through protecting a self-sufficient defense industrial base, according to a U.S. government official. A Ministry of Defense official concurred, estimating that about 70 percent of Germany's military weapon systems are made in cooperation with other countries. Furthermore, Germany does not limit foreign direct investment through any defense industrial base policies or economic security policies.

Security and Industrial Base Concerns Raised in Foreign Acquisition

German and U.S. officials know of only one case where national security-related concerns were raised in an unsuccessful attempt to block the acquisition of a German firm by a U.S. defense company. The German government organized a review team headed by the Ministry of Finance to examine the proposed sale's terms and the U.S. company's ties to the U.S. government. Both German and U.S. officials stressed that this was an ad-hoc procedure, on a one-time basis. The Ministry of Defense was one of the first agencies to approve the sale. The Ministry of Defense had been subsidizing the German company at a loss and wanted to privatize it, according to a U.S. defense company official.

The German federal government approved of the sale, but others tried to block it. Members of the Bundestag (Federal Parliament) and German defense companies that were organizing a consortium to buy the company objected on the grounds that the United States would obtain German defense secrets. The French government also objected to a U.S. company testing sensitive technology that the German company and French companies shared through cooperative projects. Furthermore, the state government objected to the potential loss of high-technology jobs within the German state and pressured the federal government to reverse its decision.

In response to these objections, the U.S. company modified its acquisition offer and attained a significant minority share in the German firm. It also worked out arrangements with the federal government to safeguard both sensitive defense data and German jobs. For example, the federal government agreed to establish a Defense Oversight Board consisting of personnel from the Ministry of Defense and the German company to review security procedures and determine whether there are problems with foreign influence and control to be resolved.

Economic Factors and Government Requirements Impede Investment in National Security-Related Industries

U.S. government and company officials we interviewed cited both economic factors and German government requirements as disincentives to invest in Germany's national security-related industries. Germany's high labor costs and tax rates can limit foreign direct investment. Moreover, Germany's strict business regulations give the government authority over both foreign and domestic companies. Companies established in Germany face rigid labor practices; they cannot lay off workers easily and cannot move or alter facilities without government permission. This tight control of the business environment constitutes more of an investment disincentive than any government body or screening practice, according to one U.S. official.

German business relationships and corporate structure also inhibit foreign direct investment. The close and long-term business relationships German firms maintain with their suppliers are difficult for foreign firms to penetrate. In addition, German corporations have interlocking relationships with banks that make it difficult for outsiders to invest. In 1988, banks and insurance companies owned more than 20 percent of Germany's publicly traded companies.

U.S. government and defense company officials cite the unfavorable investment climate in Germany as reasons not to invest. The declining German defense budget and the relatively low rates of return on investment in the shrinking European defense sector are among the most important factors influencing investment decisions.

German export controls, procurement regulations, and classified information security procedures can also pose barriers to investment in the defense sector, according to U.S. defense company officials. German conventional weapon export controls have become particularly strict recently. German procurement regulations are complicated and difficult to understand, according to some U.S. company officials. One German industry representative pointed out, however, that every country has such regulations that give an advantage to the domestic firms most familiar with them.

Germany's classified information security procedures were mentioned as a possible barrier to investment, but these procedures were also characterized as less rigorous in comparison to those of other countries. According to a German official, the Ministry of Economics is not concerned about foreign ownership of German defense companies. The government maintains control of classified materials and information through an "access check" of prospective buyers performed by the Ministry of Economics. In this official's view, these checks present no problems to firms from the North Atlantic Treaty Organization countries.

. . . .

U.S. Defense Companies Use Other Means to Obtain Market Access in Germany

U.S. defense company representatives and embassy officials in Germany stated that U.S. defense firms seek market access through cooperative ventures with German firms on a project-by-project basis rather than pursue longer term direct investment in Germany. Most of the U.S. defense companies we contacted use this approach, including one company that has acquired a small German defense-related firm.

Some company representatives stated that their U.S.-produced goods remain sufficiently competitive to generate sales in niche markets (i.e., fulfill a German demand for subsystems they lack the capability to produce themselves). They stated that to successfully compete, U.S. firms enter partnerships with German firms to allow German participation, gain influence with the German government, and acquire knowledge of the procurement process through their German partners.

United Kingdom

British law provides no legal framework specifically designed to monitor foreign direct investment for national security reasons. However, the U.K government has the authority to block or restructure takeovers of U.K. companies by foreign or domestic companies for national or public interest reasons. The United Kingdom restricts foreign direct investment in certain sectors of the economy, which are registered under the OECD *Code of Liberalization of Capital Movements*. Also, the government retains a special share in key privatized companies, which in some cases limits foreign ownership and also accords certain veto powers to the government. U.S. company officials in the United Kingdom believe that the legal and regulatory climate presents no obstacle to investments and that U.S. defense firms are more likely to enter into teaming relationships with U.K companies rather than engage in mergers or acquisitions.

. . . .

Legal Framework Can Consider National Security Issues

The United Kingdom has no general notification requirements that specifically govern all forms of foreign investment. The Industry Act of 1975 provides the U.K. government with the authority to intervene when the takeover of important manufacturing concerns by nonresidents is against the national interest. The law does not define the term "important." However, manufacturing industries are defined under the Standard Industrial Classification Orders and include defense-related sectors such as ordinance and aerospace equipment manufacturing. The U.K. government has never used the authority provided under this act.

The Fair Trading Act of 1973 provides an anti-competitive review of both foreign and domestic mergers and acquisitions. The act includes provisions permitting review of transactions that meet a certain threshold for adverse effect on competition and the public interest. The Director General of Fair Trading initially performs the review and advises the Secretary of State for Trade and Industry whether the merger or acquisition should be investigated further by the Monopolies and Mergers Commission, an independent body. Under the law, the Secretary of State for Trade and Industry has the authority to block or force divestiture of mergers and acquisitions that the Monopolies and Mergers Commission investigated and found to be against the public interest. A Department of Trade and Industry official said that acquisitions can be blocked for national interest reasons. The Secretary has 6 months after a merger to request that the Monopolies and Mergers Commission investigate the merger. The commission has up to 6 months to investigate the merger, but the Secretary may authorize an additional 3 months. Companies can appeal the Secretary's decision to the judicial system.

The Fair Trading Act broadly defines the term "against the public interest." The law requires that the commission consider such factors as (1) effect on competition in the United Kingdom, (2) consumer interests, (3) development of new products, (4) cost reduction, (5) balancing the distribution of industry and employment, and (6) promotion of competitive activities of U.K. companies abroad. However, the commission is not limited to consideration of these factors.

The Ministry of Defense provides input to the commission when mergers of defense companies are under investigation, regardless of whether the companies are national or foreign-owned, according to a Defense Ministry procurement policy official. The Ministry of Defense's objective is to ensure that the investigation's results do not adversely affect its ability to obtain value for money on procurement or inhibit competition for defense procurement.

Other Limitations on Foreign Investment

The United Kingdom maintains restrictions on foreign investment activity in certain sectors of the economy. Under the OECD *Code of Liberalization of Capital*

Movements, the United Kingdom reserves the right to restrict foreign investment in air transport, broadcasting, and maritime transport. In addition, the United Kingdom reports limitations to the OECD National Treatment Instrument based on public order and essential security considerations in the following areas: investment in aerospace and maritime transport and obtaining government defense procurement contracts. The National Treatment Instrument also lists further measures taken by the United Kingdom affecting corporate structure in certain defense firms.

Government Involvement May Inhibit Foreign Direct Investment in Some U.K. Companies

Company officials we interviewed stated that the legal and regulatory framework in the United Kingdom is not a barrier or disincentive to foreign investment. However, one U.S. company official stated that the involvement of the U.K. government in some U.K. defense companies could inhibit foreign investment. After it privatized three major defense companies, the U.K. government maintained limits on foreign ownership for public order and essential security reasons. This government control and authority is not rooted specifically in law. Instead, this involvement arises from government ownership of a "golden share" established in the articles of incorporation of these companies. This share does not give the U.K. government control over the companies' routine business activities, investment decisions, or appointments. In each case, the articles provide British citizenship requirements for the companies' board of directors. Other limitations are the following:

- The articles of incorporation for British Aerospace PLC limits foreign ownership of voting stocks to 29.5 percent.

- The articles of incorporation of Rolls Royce PLC also limits foreign ownership of voting stocks to 29.5 percent. Furthermore, the U.K. government has the power to veto major disposal of assets.

- The articles of incorporation of VSEL restrict the size of any shareholding interest (domestic or foreign) but also provide the government a veto on major asset disposal decisions. The recent acquisition of VSEL by GEC was accompanied by an amendment to the articles of incorporation of VSEL to allow GEC alone to exceed the 15-percent limitation on individual shareholdings. The U.K. government does not hold a golden share in GEC, but it will continue to hold the VSEL golden share.

....

U.S. Companies Use Approaches to Defense Procurement Other Than Foreign Direct Investment

U.S. defense company officials generally did not see direct investment as an essential part of their strategy to gain access to the U.K. defense market. Rather, companies pursue access through the common practice forming project-by-project teaming arrangements with U.K. companies to gain access to defense procurement contracts. For example, McDonnell Douglas teamed with Westland to win a recent competition to supply the British army with attack helicopters. In another case, Lockheed was awarded a contract to deliver 25 C-130J transport planes to the Royal Air Force. In this instance, Lockheed was the prime contractor and was part of a consortium of 36 U.K. companies that was formed to successfully compete for this procurement.

One U.S. defense company, however, became a U.K. company by incorporating in the United Kingdom. Company representatives indicated that, for business reasons, it was important to adopt a British identity. However, the U.S. company is not investing in a manufacturing facility in the United Kingdom. Furthermore, the U.S. company teams with other U.K firms to compete for contracts. For example, in one case the U.S. company acted as prime contractor, but in another case, a U.K company acted as prime contractor.

Chapter 10

Regulating Multinational Corporate Conduct

I. Corruption and MNCs

Documents Supplement References:

1. OECD *Convention on Combating Bribery of Foreign Public Officials in International Business Transactions (1997), with Commentaries.*

2. *United States Foreign Corrupt Practices Act (FCPA) of 1977, as amended.*

A. Is Corruption Bad?

Kimberly Ann Elliott, Corruption as an International Policy Problem: Overview and Recommendations, in Corruption and the Global Economy

175, 177-190, 192-200, 216-24 (Kimberly Ann Elliott Ed., June 1997)

THE MANY MEANINGS OF CORRUPTION

The challenges facing corruption analysts begin with how to define it. Most people know corruption when they see it. The problem is that different people see it differently. The most commonly specified definition is something along the lines of *the abuse of public office for private gain*. But, the meaning of each of the elements of the definition—abuse, public office, private gain—is subject to debate. And "contention over who gets to decide what those terms mean is [often] the most important political dimension of the [corruption] problem. Ultimately, defining corruption is a social and political process, although certainly some lines may be drawn and some behaviors universally condemned."

What is clearly excluded from this definition is identical behavior that occurs entirely within the private sector. Insider dealing, bribes to secure private contracts, and other practices that might be considered corrupt are ignored in this analysis, not because their economic effects are small, but because the topic is already complex, and it need not be made even more unwieldy. Both the private and public sectors may

715

also at times be plagued by "internal" corruption-theft or fraud that is perpetrated on a firm or public agency by its employees without the involvement of an outside actor. Although graft in the public sector clearly represents "abuse of public office for private gain," it is not a major focus of this analysis, which looks more closely at corruption arising from the interaction between the public and private sectors.

Figure 1 illustrates this nexus, dividing the actors in a country into three groups: private actors, elected politicians, and non-elected public officials identified as bureaucrats and the judiciary. The Figure highlights the fact that sectors often expected to behave autonomously within their separate spheres in fact interact extensively. [T]he key difficulty lies in balancing access and autonomy so that public officials have both the information and independence necessary to promote the public interest.

In this stylization, petty corruption occurs when private actors interact with non-elected government officials, particularly lower-level, administrative bureaucrats. These transactions involve taxes, regulations, licensing requirements, and the discretionary allocation of government benefits such as subsidized housing, scholarships, and jobs. It is at the highest levels of government, where political leaders, the bureaucracy, and the private sector all interact, that grand corruption may occur. This consists of government decisions that typically cannot be made without high level political involvement. Examples include the procurement of big ticket items such as military equipment, civilian aircraft, or infrastructure or broad policy decisions about the allocation of credit or industrial subsidies. Distortions at both levels can arise from either economic influences, such as bribes, or from personal allegiances, such as ties of family, tribe, or friendship.

At times the line dividing the licit and illicit interactions of private agents and politicians becomes blurred, as illustrated so vividly by the debate in the United States over campaign finance reform. [There are] difficulties in distinguishing between bribes and legal campaign contributions and the degree of reciprocity expected. [There are] seven hypothetical situations ranging from a case in which a contributor gives to candidate X because he does not like candidate Y — meaning he is not rewarding X and expects nothing from him — to a case in which the contributor gives to candidate X with the expectation that X will vote a particular way on a particular piece of legislation — meaning full reciprocity is expected. In the latter case, the "distinction between bribe and contribution is close to collapsing." Situations like the latter, especially where contributions to top political leaders or their parties are intended to influence specific decisions, for example on defense procurements, can be labeled grand corruption. In general, however, because of the complexities involved and because campaign finance reform does not lend itself to international coordination, what is often called electoral corruption is largely ignored in this discussion.

The final area of overlap, in Figure 1 is between elected and non-elected government officials. The variety of interactions occurring here prevents the use of a handy shorthand for the illicit activity that might arise. One possibility is "bribe sharing," if politicians pass on proceeds from a bribe in order to influence how legislation is implemented by bureaucrats or vice versa. Similarly, a high-level elected official might share bribe proceeds with lower levels of the bureaucracy in order to fulfill an understanding arising from a bribe. Another possibility is that either bureaucrats or politicians might bribe a judge in order to avoid prosecution or reduce a penalty. Less direct exchanges might also occur, such as appointments of "friendly" judges — even relatives — with the expectation that they will treat the leadership's friends with leniency.

In each of these spheres, lines must be drawn between legitimate and illegitimate interaction. Bribes of public officials fall into the category that is easiest to define be-

Figure 1.
Types of Corruption

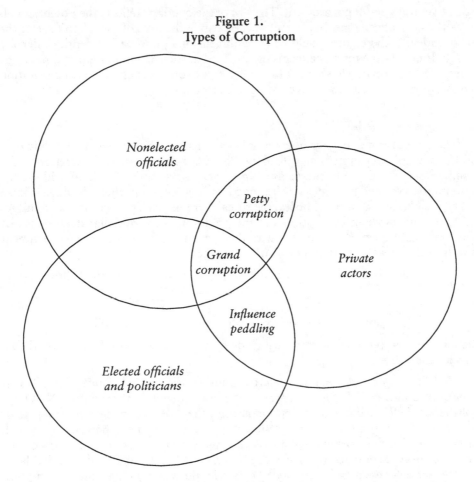

cause they are illegal in most countries and typically involve a direct exchange of money for favors. An illegal transaction involving indirect exchange, perhaps over a period of time, may be more difficult to police and to prosecute in court than a bribe, which is already difficult enough to detect given the secrecy involved. Questionable transactions in which the exchange is indirect and does not run afoul of the law will be the most difficult to discipline. An example of the latter might be the high-level attention given to a trade dispute between the United States and the European Union over bananas, following large campaign contributions by Carl Linder, head of Chiquita Bananas, to both the Democratic and Republican Parties.

In political terms, what is ultimately being sought in all these cases is influence. Each society will, through the process of political give-and-take, draw a line somewhere between licit and illicit public-private interactions. Though the divide may vary across countries and over time, legitimate gifts can usually be distinguished from illegitimate bribes: gifts can be given openly, bribes cannot. Similarly, corporations unsure about where to draw the line should use the "newspaper test": if it would cause discomfort on appearing in tomorrow's newspaper, then don't do it.

Figure 1 illustrates just one possible set of arrangements; many alternative configurations with different implications for the predominant type or volume of corruption are possible. The relative size of the areas of overlap will vary with the relative size of government and the balance of power between the executive and legislative branches of government. The size of the overlaps reflects the potential volume of illicit transactions, but it is not necessarily indicative of the magnitude of the impact. Ideally, the Figure would be three-dimensional, illustrating depth or density as well. It is possible for some forms of corruption, such as influence peddling, to be widespread but relatively shallow in impact, while others such as grand corruption may occur less often and yet have a deeper impact.

Sources of Corruption

The temptation to engage in corrupt behavior may arise whenever a public official has control over something valued by the private sector and the discretion to determine how it will be allocated. And since every government in the world spends money and taxes and regulates its citizens to one degree or another, "[w]hatever size and type of state a country chooses, the threat...remains." But as suggested in Figure 1, the incidence of corruption and the predominant forms that it takes across countries might be expected to vary with the size, structure, and type of government as well as the types of activities in which it engages.

[T]he "basic ingredients of corruption" [are summarized] in the following formula:

$$\text{Corruption} = \text{Monopoly} + \text{Discretion} - \text{Accountability}.$$

The aim here is to use what empirical evidence is available to look for general patterns across countries.

First, a measure of corruption across countries is needed. Since 1995, Transparency International (TI), a Berlin-based non-governmental organization (NGO) established in 1993 to combat corruption around the world, has released rankings of countries according to how corrupt they are perceived to be. The ranking, which starts at zero for the most corrupt and goes to ten for the least corrupt, is based on a survey of surveys compiled by Professor Johann Graf Lambsdorff and is available on the Internet. Because it includes only 54 countries, however, I have added corruption ratings from a second source that covers more than 100 countries.

As for evidence on the sources of corruption, it is difficult to measure bureaucratic discretion across countries. But quantitative indicators of potential monopoly-government size and the importance of industrial policies, trade restrictions, and other state interventions in the economy — are available for many countries. Accountability of public officials, which determines the likelihood that corruption will be punished, is more difficult to measure objectively. But accountability is derived in part from the political structure in which officials operate, and qualitative indicators of relative political openness are also available for a large number of countries.

One simple measure of the role of the state in an economy is its size.... [T]he larger the government, as measured by its share of GDP, the higher the level of expected corruption. A large government share of GDP could indicate a large bureaucracy and a lot of regulation and red tape; it might also be expected that the larger the share of national income that passes through government hands, the greater the opportunities for malfeasance. But, the experiences of Norway and Sweden show that high levels of government spending do not necessarily lead to higher levels of corruption. In fact, for 83 countries for which data are available, there is a strong positive correlation between low levels of corruption and the level of central government expenditure. Moreover, in the 16 most corrupt economies for which data are available, the average share of government expenditure is 21 percent of GDP, well below the 32 percent average for the sample as a whole.

More important than the size of government are the types of activities in which it engages. Most obviously, a government that restricts economic competition — for example, through maintenance of trade restrictions or monopolistic state-owned enterprises — will create economic rents (profits in excess of a normal return in competitive markets) and thus greater incentives and opportunities for rent-seeking corruption. [There is] evidence on the correlation between corruption and the share of state-owned enterprises in nonagricultural GDP and between corruption and the openness of economies as measured by trade shares. Though simple correlations do not demonstrate causality, both coefficients offer at least some support for the hypothesis that more direct government intervention in the economy will tend to produce more corruption. By far the strongest of the correlations however, is the qualitative measure of economic freedom developed by Freedom House, which is a subjective index designed to measure in 66 countries the freedom to hold property, earn a living, operate a business, invest one's earnings, and trade internationally.

Although the level of potential rents created by the government's role in the economy may be an incentive for engaging in corrupt activities, holding public officials accountable for those activities will offset the temptation. Freedom House also gauges governments for the level of political rights and civil liberties permitted and protected. This index captures some elements of transparency (media freedom) and accountability (the degree to which citizens are allowed to express their opinion through protest and the ballot box) that one would expect to find positively correlated with cleaner government. Indeed, [there is] a relatively strong correlation between political openness as measured by Freedom House and lower levels of corruption. This supports Johnston's [the] — conclusion that "combating corruption and encouraging open, competitive politics can be closely allied reform goals."

Other factors that may affect the opportunities for corruption include the stage of economic and political development and how development interacts with cultural tradition. This is not to suggest, as is sometimes argued, that certain cultures are inherently corrupt. Rather, the argument is that broad environmental factors — history and culture — influence the evolution of political and economic institutions, their legitimacy in the eyes of the governed, and the capacity of government to deliver the services demanded of it. Moreover, in times of transition when values, standards, and institutions are undergoing change, countries may become particularly prone to certain forms of corruption.

Table 2 lists countries perceived as more and less corrupt according to the survey of surveys compiled by TI. It is immediately obvious that in the eyes of international business, for whom and by whom these assessments and surveys are compiled, relatively more developed and richer countries are perceived to be less corrupt than poorer ones. It is likely that the differences in relative levels of corruption between developed and developing countries are somewhat overstated because of the way corruption is usually defined and measured in these surveys. Nevertheless, there are a number of reasons that developing countries might be more vulnerable to corruption and that, in turn, corruption might help to keep them poor.

Low wages are frequently cited as a source of corruption. When public sector wages do not even cover subsistence, the petty bureaucrat may be expected to supplement his salary with "tips." This situation recalls the European feudal era when "public" office typically was regarded as private property, with the proceeds of office serving as remuneration for services rendered (usually loyalty to the sovereign).

Table 2
A Partial Profile of Corruption Around the World
(1996 Rankings)

Least corrupt (in descending order)	Most corrupt (in descending order)
New Zealand	Nigeria
Denmark	Pakistan
Sweden	Kenya
Finland	Bangladesh
Canada	+China
Norway	Cameroon
Singapore	Venezuela
Switzerland	Russia/USSR
Netherlands	India
Austria	Indonesia
Ireland	Philippines
United Kingdom	Uganda
Germany	

Note: *As Transparency International makes clear, these rankings should not be interpreted as saying that Nigeria is the most corrupt country in the world. The rankings are subjective assessments of business and others; they do not include all forms of corruption and they cover only 54 countries.*

Poverty is also often accompanied by illiteracy, which may make it easier for relatively more literate bureaucrats to exploit their clients. In addition to inadequate pay and illiteracy, other factors identified in a cross-country study of seven developing countries in East Asia were: inadequate management controls and lack of adequate technology for monitoring, poor recruitment and selection procedures, including nepotism, poor working conditions and facilities, lack of public information, and generally inadequate capacity to meet the demand for government services.

Social attitudes toward government institutions are also important.... [It is] argued that "new [post-colonial] states" were particularly vulnerable to corruption because "the idea of the national interest is weak...[because] the 'state' and its organs were identified with alien rule and were proper objects of plunder," and because corruption is easier to conceal where the rules are unclear, the commitment to them is weak, or the enforcement institutions themselves are weak (the police and judiciary, in particular). It may be that these factors put in motion a vicious cycle whereby initial, supposedly transitional, conditions facilitate corruption that further undermines the state's legitimacy and capacity, and evokes yet more corruption. This could help explain why many "new" states suffer from pervasive corruption 30 years or more after independence.

DOMESTIC ECONOMIC CONSEQUENCES OF CORRUPTION

While positive effects in certain situations have been claimed for corruption, most scholars agree that widespread corruption is detrimental to economic and political development.... [Specifically,] higher levels of corruption may lower total investment (and thus growth) and skew the allocation of government spending, particularly away from public education. Even when relatively contained, corruption can cause inefficiency in the allocation of resources, greater inequities in income distribution, and the loss of savings and investment due to the flight abroad of proceeds from bribes.

CORRUPTION AS A SECOND BEST

Some analysts and observers argue that corruption need not be inimical to economic development. When facing an inept or understaffed bureaucracy or inefficient regulators, corruption may be a rational second-best response. Also, where the rule of law is weak, as in Russia and China today, corruption may serve as an alternative means of contract enforcement. Samuel Huntington said, "In terms of economic growth, the only thing worse than a society with a rigid, over-centralized dishonest bureaucracy is one with a rigid, over-centralized, honest bureaucracy." In this context, bribes are often called "speed money" or "grease" and are viewed not only as reasonable but as enhancing efficiency in situations where red tape or state control of the economy may be strangling economic activity. As suggested below, however, the conditions under which corruption has positive economic effects appear to be fragile.

When the demand for government services exceeds the bureaucracy's ability to keep up, speed money, in the form of a "voluntary tax" or "tip," may be offered to a public official in exchange for faster or more efficient service. This second-best solution has net positive effects for the economy as a whole, however, only if the official is constrained — by limits on discretion or political power or by careful monitoring — from introducing new delays or regulations to increase bribe collections. Empirical evidence suggests the net effects are often negative. The Santhanam Committee found in its investigation of corruption in India many years ago that the "custom of speed money has become one of the most serious causes of delay and inefficiency," because bureaucrats will do nothing until paid off. In Ecuador, under allegedly corrupt ex-President Abdala Bucaram, the processing time for import shipments in the port city of Guayaquil reportedly increased from two days to a month. More broadly, a statistical analysis of more than 60 countries [found] that corruption is negatively correlated with investment even in the presence of large amounts of "red tape" — when corruption in the form of grease money would be expected to be most beneficial.

Corruption may also be a second-best response when a bureaucrat is bribed to ignore official duties that entail enforcement of regulations that are inefficient, duplicative, or simply unnecessary. In this case, there may also be a welfare gain. Edward Banfield offers the example of the New York City construction industry, which at the time was governed by an 843-page building code that required as many as 130 permits from a variety of city departments for large projects. Banfield cites a city commission study that found that most builders typically applied for only the most important permits, often bribed officials to get those permits quickly, and then paid off the police or inspectors to avoid harassment for not having the others. The commission concluded that none of the bribes they investigated "resulted from a builder's effort to get around the requirements of the building code. What was being bought and sold, an official said, was time."

While corruption in particular situations may be efficiency-enhancing, it is difficult to restrict it to only those situations. Because these transactions are usually secret, it is difficult to monitor them to ensure that the public interest is not subverted. In a competitive market with reasonably honest enforcement agencies, especially the judiciary,...[a] "performance rule" might work to ensure generally efficient outcomes. Under this "rule," if the builder does not abide by essential safety regulations and the building collapses, he will go out of business or go to jail and the corrupt inspector will also be punished. With less competition and accountability, however, both parties will be more likely to escape punishment and more tempted to cross the line, skirting regulations or standards to cut costs in ways that affect quality and are not simply timesaving. And when government benefits are allocated, what ensures that a bribe only cuts through red tape and does not divert benefits intended for "worthy," individuals to those with the ability to pay?

MISALLOCATION AND REDISTRIBUTION OF RESOURCES

The supply of bribes is often linked to a desire to influence the creation or distribution of scarce government benefits or of the economic rents that often arise when government intervenes in the economy. Bribes that are extorted by government officials introduce distortions by raising the cost of doing business. Whether extorted or voluntary, the degree of distortion tends to rise with the rank of the official involved and the value of the bribe (or other exchange).

The distinction between bribes that are voluntarily offered or extorted is similar to the distinction, between corruption involving and not involving theft. In the latter case, the official turns over the full cost of the public good or service (for example, a license) to government coffers but is able to extract additional bribes, because he is in a position to withhold the service and in effect create an artificial shortage. In this situation, competition among suppliers of public services might reduce the probability that bribes will be extorted, because the applicant can go to another official. Among those most vulnerable to extorted bribes are firms with high fixed costs and without alternative production locations, producers or brokers of perishable goods, or uneducated taxpayers or other constituents in need of government services. Firms working under contracts with fixed deadlines and penalties for delays will also be vulnerable to bribe demands.

In the case of corruption with theft, the official accepts a bribe in exchange for lowering or waiving the price of the good (for example, by influencing a tax bill), thus depriving the government of its due. "Corruption with theft is obviously more attractive to the buyers" and competition among buyers in this type of case will tend to increase the level of corruption.

Petty corruption generally refers to the routine government transactions typically overseen by middle and lower-level bureaucrats, such as tax payments, allocation of permits, and regulatory enforcement. At higher levels of the bureaucracy and among the political leadership, officials and politicians will tend to control more valuable assets or opportunities and have more discretion in their allocation. At this level, decisions are made regarding major procurements (including airplanes, military equipment, power-generating equipment, and telecommunications infrastructure) and major investment projects (including roads, irrigation projects, and dams). The greater the concentration of political power (*i.e.*, the less accountable that politicians and high-level officials are) the greater the opportunities will be to engage in corrupt behavior.

Certain decisions, such as those concerning government procurement and infrastructure, can only be made at higher levels of government. Even where particular projects respond to social needs, corruption may increase their costs, lower the quality, or lead to inappropriate choices of technology. (The more complex the project, the harder it is to prove that bribery rather than technical specifications determined the award of a contract.) Worse are "white elephant" projects that enrich officials and suppliers but serve little public purpose. A National Public Radio broadcast on corruption in Nigeria cited the construction of four incinerators in Lagos, none of which worked properly and which together represented considerable excess capacity.

Corruption can also reduce the resources available to poor countries by facilitating capital flight or by driving away international donors. It is estimated that $60 billion left Russia between 1992 and 1996, with current capital flight continuing at $12 billion annually, almost all of it illegally. Corruption may also contribute to capital flight because of the desire to hide illicit wealth from scrutiny or repossession, and the more uncertain the political situation, the more likely that the fruits of corruption will be stashed abroad.

The potential impact on aid flows was demonstrated in the Kenyan energy sector, which was suffering from inadequate capacity and regular power failures in 1995. "Donor allergy" had developed from what, one source described as "a slap in the face of the donor community" during construction of the Turkwel Gorge dam several years earlier. The contract was awarded without competitive bidding. In the judgment of a report by the European Community, "the project ended up costing many times its original, already inflated price as a result of kickbacks paid to government officials." In late 1995, the *Financial Times* reported that international donors had not funded any power projects in Kenya for the previous five years.

Finally, decisions on government procurement may lead to less efficient resource allocation when bribery plays a role in the selection of the supplier. If all eligible firms are willing to bribe and have the same information, the most efficient supplier will be able to offer the highest bribe, so that corruption would have no impact on resource allocation. But some firms, including more efficient ones, may choose not to bribe or may be constrained from doing so (as U.S. firms are by the FCPA [Foreign Corrupt Practices Act]). The secrecy surrounding corruption also makes information harder to obtain. Firms that may not be the most efficient but that spend the most time "making friends" may obtain inside information that allows them to learn how much to bid and whom and how much to bribe. Since favoritism is another common form of corruption, favored firms may also collude with officials to raise the price of winning bids while setting aside kickbacks for these cooperative officials.

Even though greater amounts of money will typically be required when individual transactions take place at the higher political and administrative levels, it is not clear that the aggregate effects of grand corruption are necessarily greater than those of petty corruption. The harassment element of petty corruption, in the form of extortion, for example, might be expected to have a broader negative effect on private economic behavior than would grand corruption, which is likely to be limited to fewer sectors. Rampant petty corruption may also be more politically corrosive over time because it affects more people on a regular basis. The point is that although a little bit of high-level corruption may be more damaging to an economy than a little bit of low-level malfeasance, pervasive petty corruption may still be quite harmful. Of course, it is unlikely that petty corruption would become widespread in the absence of corruption at top levels of the government, but one should not underestimate the potential effects of low-level corruption simply because individual cases may involve small sums.

COMPETITION, CREDIBILITY, AND THE SYSTEMIC EFFECTS OF CORRUPTION

When corruption and its consequences cannot be controlled and contained, the credibility of government suffers, the security of property rights erodes, and the level of uncertainty and risk in the economy increases. If public officials cannot be relied upon to deliver on promises when bribed, or if necessary approvals for a project cannot be obtained at reasonable cost because officials at successive layers of bureaucracy demand a piece of the action, then corruption will prejudice economic activity more than if it were controlled and promises were credible.

Shleifer and Vishny analyze corruption markets that are monopolistic, competitive, or made up of independent monopolists. When the market structure is monopolistic, a king, dictator, or ruling party (for example the Communist Party in the old Soviet Union) is able to organize the market and ensure both predictability — it is known who must be bribed and by how much — and security of property rights over government goods or services once the bribes are paid. When the market among public officials is competitive, constituents shop around until they find an honest official and avoid paying a bribe. In the real world, however, a business owner or investor often needs several permits from more than one agency. If the public officials in this case act as independent monopolists, each setting a bribe price with no regard for what the others are doing, the total cost of the bribes will not be known in advance and may escalate to a level where the planned project becomes unprofitable. The problem will be particularly acute if there is free entry into the bribe market; that is, if bureaucrats can create new rules or regulations in order to get in on the action. In this case uncertainty is greater and property rights are not secure. Under these circumstances, economic activity that requires interaction with the government will either move into the informal sector, move abroad (or to another city or region), or in extreme cases, such as in Russia today, "mafias" may move in to provide the protection for property rights and contract enforcement that the government cannot.

As might be expected from Shleifer and Vishny's model, higher levels of corruption have a significant and negative correlation with lower levels of gross domestic investment. [Moreover, such levels seem to have] a large negative impact on foreign direct investment (FDI) to corruption. One problem in interpreting these results arises if corruption is endogenous to economic conditions; that is, the observed lower levels of investment are due to the effects of poverty rather than corruption. In many cases, however, the causality is likely to run in both directions, with corruption and poverty reinforcing one another.

While the negative relationship between corruption and investment may hold in general, some analysts argue that, in countries where the rule of law is weak, corruption may substitute for other forms of contract enforcement and *decrease* uncertainty for investors. China, as it undergoes the transition to a market economy, may benefit in the short run from corruption as a substitute for legal forms of contract enforcement. China in recent years has become the largest recipient of FDI among developing countries, China may be a special case, because of the large proportion of its FDI from overseas Chinese. "[O]verseas Chinese capital apparently is less sensitive to corruption, possibly because [these investors] are better able to use personal connections to substitute for the rule of law..."

In sum, corruption that creates broadly felt negative externalities, such as unsafe infrastructure or environmental degradation, will be more damaging socially and politically than corruption that simply reallocates economic rents arising from government policy or imperfect competition. Most damaging of all, however, is corruption that is pervasive at all levels. Given the difficulties in controlling corruption, it is not likely to be compatible with sustainable long-term economic growth, just as it is not compatible with sustainable democracy.

POLITICAL CONSEQUENCES OF CORRUPTION

Analyses of political corruption in less developed societies, especially those focusing on the operation of patronage machines, sometimes find beneficial effects. In this framework, corruption helps provide a separate, possibly more accessible communication network, soften the interaction between citizens and a government they may not understand, and may even prevent violence. It is also argued that corruption sometimes provides access for groups otherwise excluded from political influence, for example, ethnic Chinese minorities in Thailand and Indonesia. Similarly, an expert on Asian politics argued recently that corruption in China had had some positive economic effects by providing access to marginalized groups, "which has led to the diversification and strengthening of the economy."

Professor Sun Yan concluded, however, that corruption had simultaneously "served to benefit the Mafia and entrenched elites," and that in general "its undemocratic and detrimental nature causes moral decay, social discontent, and political alienation." Johnston also concludes that

> Sometimes corruption appears as an adaptive force, "humanizing" government and enabling citizens to influence policy. More often, corruption allows those with disproportionate money and access to protect and enhance their advantages....

Equally important, as Johnston points out, in some cases "corruption props up institutions and regimes that might otherwise be ready for needed changes."

On the other hand, corruption may be destabilizing in situations where it is used as a club by the "outs" to attack the "ins." Opposition parties may exploit scandals, exaggerating or even inventing evidence of corruption in order to undermine support for reforms that affect their constituents or to gain power so they can get a piece of the action. The seemingly endless rotation of military coups and civilian governments in Nigeria is one example; Ghana during and after Nkrumah is another. Thus, in assessing the impact of corruption on political stability, it is important to distinguish between corruption and scandal.

Corruption may be particularly dangerous and destabilizing during times of transition. During times of rapid change, the institutions that could control corruption may be weak or underdeveloped. Liberalization and deregulation of the economy, while helpful in the long run, may spur corruption in the short run if development of the institutional structure lags. And, if the gains of liberalization seemed to be skewed because of corruption, and corruption is associated with democratization and market capitalism, reforms become more difficult to implement and could even be short-circuited.

DISTORTION OF INTERNATIONAL TRADE AND INVESTMENT

Most public statements about the evils of corruption include a reference to distortion of international competition and trade flows. Former U.S. Trade Representative and Commerce Secretary Michael Kantor called corruption "a virus threatening the health of the international trading system." The United States has a particular interest in the impact of bribery on international transactions because of the perception that the US FCPA presents a significant competitive disadvantage for US firms competing with multinational firms from countries that do not penalize and may even implicitly encourage the use of bribes to win contracts abroad. [The Foreign Corrupt Practices Act is discussed in the Note below.]

The net impact of corruption on trade is not clear, however. Bribes could lead to either an increase or a decrease in the volume of trade, depending on the circumstances. Although corruption may well affect the composition of trade, with regard to products and countries, it is not clear that focusing on corruption is a more effective policy response than focusing on the conditions that give rise to corruption or on the observable policy outcomes that may be influenced by corruption.

CORRUPTION AS AN IMPEDIMENT TO INTERNATIONAL TRADE

The general aims of the international trade rules under the WTO are to remove impediments to trade and, to a lesser degree, investment, and to eliminate discrimination among member countries. Depending on the circumstances, however, corruption may either increase or decrease impediments to trade and investment. Impediments will be increased if corruption is out of control, too costly, or primarily in the form of extortion. Impediments might be lower if corruption is a second-best response to existing barriers or other distortions. Also, many procurement markets, such as aircraft, are sectors with economies of scale and imperfect competition, so corruption may redistribute economic rents but have little effect on global welfare. Moreover, while WTO rules are intended to constrain government trade policies, many instances of corruption subvert government policy. When illicit payments influence the outcome of government policy and lead to the creation of a new trade barrier or an illegal export subsidy, the existing rules will normally be sufficient to address the consequences.

Customs agencies are notorious for corruption in many countries. The net impact, however, is not obvious. Extortion of a shipper by customs officials, who, for example, threaten to allow a shipment of bananas to rot on the dock, could reduce the level of imports if the shipper is unable or unwilling to pay the bribe. But imagine an alternative scenario: suppose the exporter of the bananas offers a bribe if the customs official will lower the duty amount. In that case, rather than reducing trade, corruption might actually increase it (while lowering public revenues). And, since the anecdotal evidence suggests that tax evasion is perhaps the most common motive for bribery, it seems plausible that it might increase trade at the margin. One would also expect that, the more restricted trade is, the more likely that an increase in trade will result from corruption. Either scenario could cause problems for firms prevented from offering bribes — whether from moral sensitivity or by the law. In either case, exporters of homogeneous or highly perishable products would be most vulnerable, those selling specialized and technologically sophisticated products less so.

In developing an appropriate international policy response, the impact on the policy of the countries involved also matters. Does corruption influence the formulation of policy and lead to discrimination against imports or foreign investment? Or does it subvert the government's declared policy and international commitments? In the first case, the injured WTO Member may be able to use existing rules to challenge the discriminatory policy directly. For example, several U.S. steel companies recently asked the Clinton administration to file a complaint with the WTO claiming that South Korean government subsidies to Hanbo Steel, allegedly influenced by bribes to government officials, had distorted world steel markets. In other cases where corruption subverts government policy, and particularly where it deprives the government of customs revenue, the government has an incentive to act, and the problem may reflect inadequate government capacity rather than intent to discriminate.

If corruption affects primarily the allocation of trade flows and not the volume and if any resulting discrimination among suppliers is due primarily to differences in treatment of transnational bribery among exporting countries (rather than the importing government's policy), it might be more appropriate to analyze the problem as a potential export subsidy. As with other export subsidies, which are generally prohibited by the WTO, no exporter gains relative to another if equivalent subsidies are available to all. The prevention of subsidy wars is in fact the major incentive for countries to negotiate agreements to constrain themselves. But in the case of transnational bribery, where a major competitor, the United States, is unilaterally constrained by the FCPA, the incentive for other countries to enact controls is weaker. This has been a major source of concern and frustration for U.S. policymakers and firms.

INTERNATIONAL INITIATIVES TO COMBAT CORRUPTION

Corruption's effects on economic development and political legitimacy spill over a given country's borders, affecting global peace and prosperity. Thus, it is natural that corruption concerns the international community as a whole, just as distortions in international trade and investment flows are also concerns. The most important role of the international community is providing financial and technical support to countries undertaking difficult anti-corruption reforms.

Other international anti-corruption initiatives focus on the role of multinational corporations in offering bribes and the impact on international transactions, particularly government procurement, where the public and private sectors do business directly. Potentially, the most important are the efforts in the OECD to deter and punish transnational bribery. Also [noteworthy] arc the American Convention against Corruption approved by the members of the Organization of American States (OAS), which includes measures to promote cooperation among member states in enforcing anti-corruption laws, and recent efforts by the World Bank and World Trade Organization to restrict the opportunities for corruption in government procurement contracts. Highlighting the need to address both supply and demand, the UN General Assembly approved a resolution in December 1996 calling on members to take "concrete action" against all forms of corruption. The non-binding UN declaration incorporates elements of both the OAS Convention and the OECD recommendations. Some countries have proposed resuming negotiations on a universal anti-corruption treaty under UN auspices, but little progress has been made to date and UN action on this issue remains primarily rhetorical.

Corruption also raises global concerns because of how it facilitates international criminal activity, particularly drug trafficking and money laundering. Money laundering can have significant collateral economic effects and the liberalization of financial markets around the world has contributed to its spiraling growth. Nevertheless, the primary locus of concern is the criminal activity that spawns these activities and, while a reduction in corruption would clearly help, the primary policy responses must still focus on law enforcement, financial market regulation, and drug-addiction treatment.

The Inter-American Convention Against Corruption

One of the striking things about the OAS anti-corruption initiative is the leading role played by several South American countries in advancing the process. The first steps were taken in March 1994 when President Clinton invited heads of state in the Western Hemisphere to a summit to discuss strengthening and consolidating democracy and promoting economic growth in the region. Anti-corruption action was an important American objective for the summit, but President Clinton initially spoke of the need for improved governance in the hemisphere without making explicit mention of corruption. Inclusion of an explicit anti-corruption initiative on the summit agenda was then promoted by Ecuadorian Vice President Alberto Dahik, who was the chairman of the Advisory Council of Transparency International (TI) at the time, and Venezuelan President Rafael Caldera, who attributed the bank failures and financial crisis that struck his country shortly after he took office in 1993 to the corruption of his predecessors.

At the Summit of the Americas held in Miami in December 1994, the leaders of 34 Western Hemisphere countries (all but Cuba) agreed on a "Declaration of Principles" and a "Plan of Action" for strengthening and expanding cooperation and economic integration in the region. The portion of the plan of action that addresses measures to strengthen democracy included an initiative against corruption. Although this initiative listed several steps that countries should consider taking to combat corruption and improve governance, including potentially farreaching institutional reforms, the initial focus was on the provision calling for development within the OAS of "a hemispheric approach to acts of corruption in both the public and private sectors that would include extradition and prosecution of individuals so charged." The leaders also called on "the governments of the world to adopt and enforce measures against bribery in all financial or commercial transactions with the Hemisphere."

The resulting Inter-American Convention against Corruption was adopted 29 March 1996 in Caracas, a little more than a year after it had been proposed. It was signed there by representatives of 21 countries in a special session. The United States signed before the OAS General Assembly in Panama the following June, after the treaty had been thoroughly examined by the U.S. Justice Department. The principal provisions of the convention require adherents to criminally sanction bribery, transnational bribery, and "illicit enrichment," and to cooperate with one another in the investigation and prosecution of acts defined as corrupt in the convention, through extradition and assistance in recovering illicitly acquired property or wealth. The convention also discourages the use of bank secrecy laws as the basis for withholding cooperation from investigations of corruption.

The key provision from the U.S. perspective is Article VIII, which effectively internationalizes the FCPA by requiring parties to the convention to make it a crime to bribe foreign public officials. Article IX requires each member state to "establish under its laws as an offense a significant increase in the assets of a government official that he cannot reasonably explain in relation to his lawful earnings during the performance of his functions." This provision has been depicted as an essential tool in combating a phenomenon cloaked in secrecy and deception. But it was also the most troublesome for U.S. negotiators and prevented the United States from immediately signing the convention in Caracas. Although implementation is subject to the Constitution and fundamental legal principles of each member state, the U.S. Justice Department wanted to ensure that the language did not conflict with the U.S. Constitution and legal tradition that the accused is innocent until proven guilty.

Thus, the focus in the convention is on criminal sanctions and enforcement. Though the scope for an international role is limited, corollary domestic and institutional reforms are still rather weakly dealt with in the convention. Article III refers to "preventive measures" that members "agree to consider ... within their own institutional systems." These measures include standards of conduct for public officials, "mechanisms to enforce these standards," and strengthening government procedures in the areas of hiring, government procurement, and tax collection. Signatories also agree to consider "whistle-blower" protection and "oversight bodies with a view to implementing modern mechanisms for preventing, detecting, punishing, and eradicating corrupt acts." Article III notes the need for "mechanisms to encourage participation by civil society" and NGOs and the "study of further preventive measures that take into account the relationship between equitable compensation and probity in public service." These domestic reforms are crucial if the convention is to be an effective anti-corruption instrument. Unfortunately, there are no follow-up measures specified in the convention to support or monitor the implementation of these reforms.

As of the end of 1996, only a handful of countries had ratified the OAS convention, and the Clinton administration had not yet submitted it to the U.S. Senate.

The Inter-American Convention against Corruption is the first document of its kind, codifying anti-corruption measures in a treaty reached by both developed and developing countries. If the potential is to be realized, however, a number of steps must be taken. First, the United States should set an example by quickly ratifying the convention.

Second, greater attention to other implementation issues is needed.

Controlling the Supply of Bribes: The Organization for Economic Cooperation and Development and the International Chamber of Commerce

The initiatives of the ICC [International Chamber of Commerce] on OECD focus on deterring the use of bribery by multinational enterprises in the course of business operations in foreign countries, allegedly a major source of illicit payments. Like the United Nations, the ICC and OECD initially considered the problem of transnational bribery in the 1970s, following a series of scandals and the passage in the United States of the FCPA. These initial efforts failed to make an impact, but interest has been renewed in the 1990s.

The OECD revived its interest in the corruption issue in 1993 under the prompting of the Clinton administration. In early 1994, the Committee on International Investment and Multinational Enterprises approved a recommendation for submission to the Council that urged members to "take concrete and meaningful steps" against the bribery of foreign officials. The recommendation, which also created a Working Group on Bribery in International Business Transactions, was formally adopted by the OECD Council of Ministers later that spring. This was followed two years later by a second recommendation approved by the Council that called on members to end the tax deductibility of transnational bribes and to consider means of imposing criminal sanctions on such behavior. Neither recommendation is legally binding on members, but both contain provisions for the monitoring and review of actions taken to implement the recommendations. The working group has also been developing "best practice" principles for accounting and auditing procedures to facilitate effective enforcement. Secrecy is an essential component in the bribery transaction, so transparency and thorough record keeping are important tools to control corruption.

The results with respect to national implementation of the recommendations are thus far mixed, however. Recently, the United Kingdom concluded that a 1906 anti-bribery law could be interpreted as covering bribery of foreign officials, though it had not previously been used for that purpose. Japan also not long ago announced that it would take steps to criminally sanction transnational bribery, probably by amending its Law for the Prevention of Unfair Competition, which carries criminal sanctions. The Japanese government expects the measure to be passed and to take effect in April 1998, but concerns have been raised as to whether Japan's Fair Trade Commission will be more effective on this issue than it has been on other fair competition issues in the past.

Regarding the tax deductibility of bribes, only Norway has completely implemented the recommendation; a handful of countries have legislation pending, but most OECD members have not moved to implement the recommendation on tax deductibility. France and Germany have said they cannot eliminate tax deductibility until the criminalization issue is resolved. One OECD member state has taken steps to end tax deductibility for bribes, but only following a criminal conviction for bribery, presumably in the country where it occurs.

The breakthrough in the OECD came in May 1997 when the members agreed to quickly negotiate and promptly implement an international convention to criminal-ize transnational bribery. Although the United States, supported by most other OECD members, had opposed the convention approach because of the legal complexity and delay involved, France and Germany, supported by Japan and Spain, insisted that criminal sanctions be codified in a formal convention. The compromise involved setting tight deadlines for final implementation of treaty provisions. The final convention would be based on the draft principles for criminalization developed by the OECD working group. That text defines the perpetrators and collaborators in acts of bribery, acts that would constitute a criminal violation, how to establish jurisdiction, and how to ensure effective enforcement in light of the different legal and judicial systems among OECD countries. [The final OECD *Convention on Combating Bribery of Foreign Public Officials in International Business Transactions*, reached in 1997, along with the official *Commentaries*, are reproduced in the *Documents Supplement*.]

As the OECD has progressed in its efforts to prevent international corruption, interest in codes of conduct and compliance programs for multinational cooperation has increased. The ICC appointed a committee in 1994 to review its earlier report on transnational bribery, issued in 1977, and to update the recommendations as appropriate. Major contributions of the new report include the strengthened "rules of conduct" for preventing illicit payments and a recommendation to establish a standing committee "to promote widespread use of the rules and to stimulate cooperation between governments and world business." The report, approved by the ICC executive board in March 1996, also calls on governments to make procurement procedures more transparent, to condition government contracts with corporations on their abstaining from bribery, and to implement promptly, the steps recommended by the OECD on this issue.

Targeting Grand Corruption in Government Procurement: The World Bank and the World Trade Organization

The World Bank and most other international and national aid agencies require international competitive bidding when official funds are used in whole or in part to fund government procurement of goods, services, or projects. The World Trade Organization (WTO) also oversees rules on government procurement, but they are incorporated in a multilateral agreement currently subscribed to by only 22 countries (the United States, the 15 countries of the European Community, Canada, Israel, Japan, Norway, South Korea, and Switzerland). The issue currently before the WTO is how to expand the country coverage of rules on transparency and due process in government procurement.

For those procurements where international competitive bidding is appropriate, World Bank guidelines emphasize transparency at all stages of the bidding process, from the public call for bids through the award of contracts. They also provide for the World Bank to review and evaluate bids and award contracts. The Bank may declare a "misprocurement" if procedures are not followed or if it later finds it had received "incomplete, inaccurate, or misleading information" or if corruption influenced the award. In July 1996, the World Bank further tightened its guidelines by removing the constraint that misprocurement due to corrupt practices can only be declared following a decision by a court of law, by revising the standard bidding documents that must be used in Bank-funded procurements to require disclosure of commissions paid to agents or other third-party intermediaries in the bidding process, and by introducing sanctions against borrowing countries and international firms that engage in corrupt practices. The potential sanctions include rejection of contract awards or cancellation of the portion of a loan linked to fraudulent or corrupt practices, and the blacklisting of firms that engage in such practices, either indefinitely or for a specified period of time.

TI has further suggested that the World Bank should encourage the use of corporate codes of conduct by making them a condition for bidding on Bank-funded projects. Some in the World Bank have resisted this proposal, however, because it could reduce competition (because so few firms outside the United States currently have codes), and it would increase the paperwork and red tape, which are already substantial. Those in the bank opposed to the proposal also argue that the offsetting benefits may be few because of the difficulties in ensuring that newly created codes are no more than fig leaves.

Finally, recent changes in how the Bank evaluates its own performance, though adopted for other reasons, could have anti-corruption benefits. Both personal and institutional success previously were measured by the volume of loan approvals. Complaints from NGOs and other groups about the consequences of this approach in relation to the environment, human rights, and other areas contributed to a reassessment of project review and loan approval. More careful analysis of the development impact of proposed projects should reduce the likelihood that "white elephant" projects receive funding approval. The most important way in which the Bank (and other international financial institutions) can contribute to the fight against corruption, however, is through capacity building and promotion of institutional reforms.

Although bribery and nepotism are recognized as anathema for efficient government procurement, most governments *openly* intervene in favor of domestic suppliers for a variety of procurement projects, arguing national security or industrialization goals. The current WTO Government Procurement Agreement (GPA) is primarily intended to reduce the level of explicit discrimination in favor of domestic suppliers and to introduce greater competition into these markets. In addition to listing the government entities and activities subject to its rules, the GPA specifies extensive and detailed bidding procedures regarded by representatives of some countries as excessively complex and burdensome. Although Taiwan and Singapore are currently involved in negotiations on access to the agreement, few additional countries are expected to join any time soon.

Because the membership of the GPA is limited, the United States is seeking an agreement on transparency, openness, and due process in government procurement that would be mandatory for all WTO Members. Under such an agreement, which U.S. negotiators hope would be an interim step to full acceptance of GPA disciplines, WTO Members would not have to reduce home-country preferences or otherwise liberalize their government procurement regimes, but they would have to abide by agreed on procedural rules. A major objective of the proposed rules would be to ensure that when international bids are entertained, the process is not distorted by bribery. At the WTO ministerial meeting in Singapore in December 1996, however, few other countries embraced the US proposal to conclude within a year an agreement on transparency in government procurement. U.S. negotiators were only able to obtain a rather weak call to "establish a working group to conduct a study on transparency in government procurement practices . . . and, based on this study, to develop elements for inclusion in an appropriate agreement. . . ."

B. Is Corruption Cultural?

Joongi Kim and Jong B. Kim, Cultural Differences in the Crusade Against International Bribery: Rice Cake Expenses in Korea and the Foreign Corrupt Practices Act

6 Pacific Rim Law & Policy Journal 549, 561-70 (1997)

III. Cultural Differences and the Example of Rice-Cake Expenses in Korea

A. Origins of "Ttokkap" (Rice-cake expenses)

One of the most serious challenges against international efforts to combat bribery comes from those countries that assert that cultural differences must be respected in any attempt to reach an international consensus against bribery. The practice of giving "*ttokkap*" in Korea offers a representative example of how questionable gifts or payments may be viewed differently. The diversity of opinion surrounding what constitutes impermissible action can be largely attributed to different cultural perceptions.

In Korean "*ttokkap*" literally means rice-cake expenses and traces its origins to payments that were offered to cover for the expenses for buying rice-cakes, a precious food source in earlier times. *Ttokkap* was largely offered for the sake of hospitality or as a natural token of gratitude for deeds done. Through the centuries, the practice of giving gifts or payments such as *ttokkap* has become a customary practice, culturally ingrained into the fabric of Korean society. It was generally given over the major holidays of the year, "*Chusok*" (Korean Thanksgiving) and New Year's Day. Many other countries throughout Asia have similar practices. These innocuous origins notwithstanding, the problem is that over the years *ttokkap* payments have often times degenerated into a means to improperly obtain favors from public officials. From a legal perspective, the challenging question in Korea is whether, and under what circumstances, the payment of *ttokkap* might be considered an illegal bribe.

B. Bribery Under Korean Law

The Korean Criminal Code (*Hyongpop*) criminalizes the receiving and giving of bribes by public officials under Article 129 through Article 133. Officials that receive bribes will be sentenced to less than five years imprisonment or will be disqualified from government service for less than ten years for accepting bribes. Those that promise, give or express an intent to give bribes will be punished under Article 133 and will be sentenced to less than five years imprisonment or less than twenty million won (U.S. $ 25,000) in fines.

More specifically, the main section of the Criminal Code, Article 129, provides that any public official that "receives, demands or promises a bribe *in relation to his official duties* (emphasis added)" will be guilty of bribery. To constitute bribery, therefore, Korean courts will generally seek to ascertain whether two factors have been met. First, the official must receive a payment that must bear a relation to the official's duties. The question is how broadly to interpret the extent of an official's duties. For instance, payments made to an official in charge of the procurement of supplies in order to obtain a favorable tax break would not qualify because the payment does not have a sufficient relation with the official's responsibilities or duties.

The Supreme Court nevertheless affords some flexibility in determining the extent of an official's duties. The court states that the duties need not be those specifically stipulated by law but may include "the entire scope of official duties that one is responsible for according to one's rank." The scope of the duties therefore may include previous or future duties or, due to the division of work, may include duties not personally handled by the official but, for example, those that are still within their sphere of influence.

A second related element that courts will consider is if the payment was given "in consideration for" the official's duties. Payment must thereby be given in return for a favor or as a quid pro quo. Although these are all factors to consider, the Supreme Court has found that in determining whether the payment was "in consideration for" an official's duties, the briber need not specifically request a favor nor does the bribe have to result in action or inaction. According to the Court, the payment, in other words, must amount to illegal compensation or improper profits for the actions of a public official.

Under this statutory framework, the leading Supreme Court case on bribery, decided in 1984, outlined the frequently cited principles involved in the prosecution of bribery. While finding a provincial agriculture official guilty of bribery, the Court first described that the purpose of criminalizing bribery is to maintain the "fairness of official decisions and society's trust in these decisions." The court next added that in punishing bribery the "central protective interest involved is the incorruptibility of official actions." In conclusion, the court stated that the question of bribery does not depend on whether the violation of one's duty actually occurs, whether a favor was requested, or whether the bribe was received before or after an official decision.

C. The Social Courtesy Exception

The Korean Supreme Court has nevertheless acknowledged that a "social courtesy exception" exists under which certain payments or gifts made to officials may not be punishable as a bribe. Under this exception, the courts have focused on the second element in determining bribery. Payments or gifts offered as mere social courtesies were viewed as not being given in consideration for an official's acts, and therefore did not amount to an impermissible bribe. Instances where parties have attempted to use the social courtesy exception often times involve fees associated with meals, drinks and entertainment, and gifts and contributions made in connection with a marriage or funeral ceremony.

The issue of how to determine when a payment or gift might be considered a social courtesy versus an illegal bribe under the law, however, has become a delicate balancing act. The primary emphasis appears to be whether the payment was sufficiently in consideration for action within an official's duties. The courts will also consider whether the monetary payment or favor provided exceeds socially acceptable levels. Some scholars argue that even if a moderate described below, the Supreme Court, however, appears to believe that while the socially acceptable size of the payments will be considered, the primary factor remains whether the payment was in consideration for an official's actions.

In a 1979 case the Supreme Court disagreed with a lower court judgment and found that the social courtesy exception did not apply to the defendant. The Supreme court first noted that in its judgment sufficient evidence existed to find that the payment was part of a request for a favor in return for the duties of the public official from the Ministry of Culture. At the same time, the Supreme Court justices did note the size of the payments and stressed that the two payments that were given to the official were significantly large because they were more than twice that of the public official's base salary of 90,000 won ([approximately] U.S. $ 112.50 [before the Asian economic crisis]). Thus, the payments exceeded socially acceptable levels.

Moreover, in 1984, in perhaps the leading case on the social courtesy exception, the Supreme court found a Ministry of Labor official guilty of bribery for, among other things, being treated to a 70,000 won ([approximately] U.S. $ 88) dinner by a company director. The Court held that sufficient consideration existed because the payor requested a favor within the official's duties. Although the monetary sum involved was meager, this fact alone would not allow the payment to qualify as entertainment falling under the scope of the social courtesy exception. The Court emphasized that the meal was clearly related to the duties of the official and that, in addition to the meal, the official, the Chief of the Foreign Employment Section, received two monetary payments, one before and one after the date of the dinner. Therefore, despite the small sum involved with the dinner, the Court held it amounted to bribery because specific requests were made and overall additional monetary payments were also exchanged.

D. Ttokkap and Current Legal Trends

Ttokkap payments must be examined under the interpretive structure created by the Korean Supreme Court. Under this legal framework, *ttokkap* offered merely as a gift of hospitality during *Ch'usok* and over the New Year's Day holidays has been traditionally viewed as being exempt from criminal punishment in Korea. In essence, the social courtesy exception has been found to encompass the *ttokkap* giving practice. Such *ttokkap* is not considered a bribe because it is not given in return or in consideration for any official acts. Questionable *ttokkap* has avoided consideration as a bribe because frequently it is given merely as a type of insurance, not for immediate or specific benefits but for future favorable consideration. Therefore, when initially given it lacks a nexus with a public official's actions. As for socially acceptable levels of permissible payments, while it varies depending upon the position of the recipient, many believe that payments must exceed ten million won ([approximately] U.S. $12,500) for it to be considered an impermissible payment that would create a sufficient nexus and therefore amount to a bribe.

The practice of giving "rice-cake expenses" has recently received increased scrutiny due to several cases involving high profile figures receiving sums of extraordinary proportions. Prosecutors still have been reluctant to bring cases based merely on *ttokkap* payments. Yet they have demonstrated recently that in certain circumstances they will seek convictions for certain types of payments. These cases have highlighted the issues surrounding the practice of giving *ttokkap*.

In the sensational slush fund scandal involving former President Chun Doo Hwan, Roh Tae Woo and over a dozen chaebol heads, the Korean courts for the first time developed a "comprehensive bribe theory" and found that payments given by these corporate leaders amounted to illicit payments. Many of the payments, which over a several year period ranged by individual from 4 billion won ([approximately] U.S. $ 5 million) to as much as 15 billion won ([approximately] U.S. $ 18.8 million), were given around *Ch'usok* and New Year's Day without any specific requests associated with them or specific consideration in mind was difficult to find, and heretofore would most likely have been considered as permissible *ttokkap*.

The Seoul District court and subsequently the High Court, however, emphasized a multitude of factors to find that taken as a whole the comprehensive nature of the payments amounted to illegal bribes. They cited the vastness of the payments, which in total amounted to 510 billion won ([approximately] U.S. $ 638 million) between the two ex-Presidents, and the continuous nature in which they were given. The defendants challenged that the prosecution failed to provide a sufficient nexus between the payments and any specific acts done by the ex-presidents, but this argument was rejected by the courts.

The judges found that, as the head of the government, the Presidents had such a broad range of power that they could influence practically any decision. The clandestine nature of the payments, which were usually delivered during individual and informal closed meetings at the official residence of the Presidents, was also cited as a contributing factor. Similarly, they stressed that the funds were usually amassed under a complex scheme and laundered from secret corporate funds throughout a conglomerate's network of subsidiaries and related companies. Finally, contradicting the argument that the funds were political donations, most of the funds were not expended for political purposes but were personally retained by the Presidents well after their terms had ended. The High Court also suggested that as elected politicians, even if the payments were considered good will contributions, they were not solicited according to the Law Prohibiting Solicitations of Contributions and therefore must be viewed as illegal bribes. While its review was limited, the Supreme court briefly confirmed that as long as the payments were part of or were directly related to the President's overall duties, then they would be considered bribes. It added that the payments did not have to be given specifically for some consideration.

In sum, although in many instances no specific requests were made with the payments, the courts held that given the comprehensive nature of the payments they amounted to bribes given as general compensation for "preference over other competing companies or at least to avoid any negative consequences." Testimony also existed to the effect that the senior government officials involved in managing the money also believed that the payments were suspect. Therefore, the courts held that sufficient consideration existed between the payments and official acts, and that the levels of the payments far exceeded socially acceptable standards.

Another illustrative case that recently ended deserves attention. Following accusations from a National Assemblyman from the leading minority party, on March 23, 1996, Chang Hak-ro, a presidential secretary in charge of personal matters for the [former] President Kim Young Sam, was arrested for receiving bribes and delivering favors in return. It is interesting to note that in the process of indicting Chang for receiving 621 million won ([approximately] U.S. $ 776,000) in bribes, the Seoul District Public Prosecutor's Office specifically stated that they excluded a total of 2.1 billion won ([approximately] U.S. $ 2.6 million) in additional payments given by various individuals because they were only viewed as "*ttokkap*" or "friendly allowance money." These payments were apparently given without any specific expectation for anything in return and lacked a sufficient nexus. Chang's official duties had little direct relation to any policy making decisions because he acted merely as a personal steward to the President. In addition, prosecutors apparently believed that because the sums were relatively small they were within the socially acceptable standards. Although the *ttokkap* payments were excluded, Chang was nevertheless convicted and sentenced to four years for receiving bribes and ordered to pay a 700 million won confiscatory penalty.

Taken together, these two cases illustrate the continuing difficulties the Korean legal process faces when trying to determine the illegality of *ttokkap* gifts or payments. Although the decision in the slush fund trials marked a notable shift in the prosecution of certain forms of payments, the law still remains uncertain toward seasonal offerings. It should also be noted that the slush fund actions were being undertaken in a highly charged political atmosphere. They were tightly intertwined with the consolidated trial which also involved charges for treason and mutiny. One might easily argue, however, that the payments in the slush fund trial only applied to the peculiar and special circumstances involved in that sensational trial.

C. Regulatory Interests Versus Business Interests?

NOTE ON THE UNITED STATES FOREIGN CORRUPT PRACTICES ACT*

I. When in Rome, Should We Pay the Emperor?

Cross-border business transactions are what the global economy is all about. Yet, whether these transactions are conducted successfully, or at all, depends very much on the business laws and policies of individual countries. American businesses competing for contracts in Asia, the Middle East, Latin America, and Europe invariably encounter stiff competition from foreign competitors. Some of these wily competitors use every possible edge to gain a competitive advantage and seize valuable market share.

One edge available to foreign competitors, but not American firms, is bribery. Bribery of foreign officials, common in many parts of this world and used by many foreign corporations in their normal course of business, is proscribed for Americans. The Foreign Corrupt Practices Act ("FCPA" or "Act") penalizes American entities and individuals for bribing foreign officials. What is the FCPA? How does it operate and what are its ramifications? Most importantly, is it bad for American business?

II. OVERVIEW OF THE FCPA

A. History and Overview of the Act

It is an interesting but little known fact that the FCPA was one of the many legislative responses to the Watergate scandal. Watergate Special Prosecutors discovered the existence of numerous corporate political slush funds that evaded normal accounting controls. Responding to the discovery of such funds the Securities and Exchange Commission (SEC) launched an investigation to determine the extent to which the slush funds upset corporate accounting procedures. The SEC found most slush funds existed to bribe foreign officials to implement policy favorable to American business or award it contracts. The SEC's discovery of hundreds of millions of dollars in foreign bribes shocked and infuriated the American public. Reacting to public indignation and SEC revelations, Congress enacted the FCPA in 1977.

---

* This Note was prepared by Ramsey R. Taylor, Esq., Scribner, Hall & Thompson, Washington, D.C. The views expressed are those of the author. All footnotes have been omitted. This Note does not discuss the *OECD Convention on Combating Bribery of Officials in International Business Transactions*. The reader should refer to the *Documents Supplement* for that *Convention* and the *Commentaries* on it.

The Senate Committee originating the legislation described the Act as an anti-bribery law. Enactment of the FCPA was recommended to bring corrupt practices to a halt and restore public confidence in the integrity of the American business system. The Act is one of the most significant expansions of the federal securities laws since their passage in the New Deal era. Enacted as an amendment to the Securities and Exchange Act of 1934 (1934 Act), the FCPA employs two broad strategies to proscribe bribery of foreign government officials by American companies. First, the Act expressly makes it illegal for any United States entity or agent thereof to bribe a foreign government official or third-party intermediary. Second, the Act imposes strict corporate accounting controls to eliminate off-the-books slush funds.

B. The Prohibition of Bribery

The first strategy is to forbid payments to those with the ability to make decisions financially beneficial to relevant corporations. This part of the FCPA imposes a blanket prohibition on, and criminalizes, foreign corporate bribery. At its simplest, a corporation violates this FCPA provision if a company representative gives something of value to a foreign official with the corrupt intent of securing business. The elements of a violation include a foreign official, an official representative of an American corporation, corrupt intent, and an improper payment.

The FCPA prohibits American corporations from inducing any foreign official to influence any act regarding the obtaining or retention of business for that corporation. The Act prohibits bribing an acting official, an official party member, or any other person who can influence an official decision that will assist an American firm in obtaining or retaining business. The Act defines a foreign official as any officer, employee, or person acting in an official capacity on behalf of any government. Courts have interpreted the definition of a foreign official fairly broadly. Unlike her benefactor, the foreign official who accepts the corrupt payments is not subject to prosecution under the FCPA. The person bribing the foreign official must be a direct corporate representative or someone acting on behalf of the corporation. The corporation is liable for bribery by any officer, director, employee, agent of the corporation, or stockholder acting on behalf of the corporation.

The Act requires the presence of a requisite level of intent in the mind of the corporate representative making the bribe — the intent to improperly obtain business for the corporation. The bribe must be done with the purpose of influencing the official to make a decision favorable to a corporation. Corrupt intent, for purposes of the FCPA, is any intent to influence an official action. The corrupt payment, usually in cash or a similar liquid asset, can actually take any form for purposes of accountability under the Act. Courts have held specifically that a bribe need not be in cash.

C. Requirements of Internal Corporate Accounting

The second strategy to combat bribery by Americans of foreign government officials is to attempt to control corporate bribery through mandatory accounting requirements. These requirements aim to make corporate accounting more transparent. Greater financial disclosure is intended to preclude use of hidden slush funds and make it easier for the SEC and the Department of Justice to spot questionable financial transactions. The established accounting security provisions for public issuers impose mandatory tight internal control of asset accounts. The accounting provisions require those subject to its provisions to keep accurate records and establish strict internal corporate accounting controls. Congress declined to limit application of the Act to businesses acting internationally. All public issuers must comply with the accounting provisions of the Act, or face SEC enforcement action.

The first method to control corporate accounting is through imposing stringent record keeping standards on those subject to the Act. Issuers are required to make and keep books, records, and accounts, which in reasonable detail, accurately and fairly reflect the transactions and dispositions of assets. Reasonable detail is such a level of detail and degree of assurance as would satisfy prudent officials in the conduct of their own affairs.

The second FCPA accounting provision is the requirement for companies to devise and maintain a system of internal accounting controls sufficient to provide reasonable assurances to auditors that all payments are authorized and proper. The Act requires procedures ensuring that: (1) all transactions are authorized; (2) all transactions are recorded in such a way as to comply with Generally Acceptable Accounting Principles (GAAP) maintaining full accountability for the assets; (3) all access to assets is authorized; and, (4) books and records are periodically checked against existing assets to determine any possible discrepancies. The internal controls try to keep rogue agents from bribing corporate officials without corporate authorization, and ensure corporate executives are held criminally accountable for the actions of inferiors.

D. The 1988 Amendments

The FCPA as passed in 1977 drew serious criticism for incorporating vague and ambiguous standards making compliance with the Act difficult for business. Responding to this criticism, Congress amended the FCPA in the Omnibus Trade and Competitiveness Act of 1988. The amendments clarify ambiguities of the original FCPA that had curtailed legitimate business activity Congress did not intend to proscribe. Such ambiguities also had made it difficult for the Department of Justice and SEC to enforce the Act. That is, vague provisions had made violation issues uncertain, which made the Justice Department and SEC reluctant to spend precious prosecution resources on questionable transgressions. Indeed, the Justice Department and SEC initiated only 25-30 anti-bribery cases under the unamended FCPA. The 1988 amendments give enforcement authorities more concrete guidelines for successful prosecutions.

Responding to business concerns about FCPA "overkill," in amending the FCPA Congress introduced affirmative defenses for lawful expenditures and reasonable payments, as well as introducing an exception for payments to officials for routine governmental action (known as "grease payments"). Clarifying standards of behavior, the amendments define what must be done to comply with the accounting provisions and delineate the level of intent necessary to violate the bribery provisions.

1. The Affirmative Defenses

The 1988 amendments add an affirmative defense to the FCPA for payments lawful in foreign countries. Initially, the 1977 FCPA made any gift intended to induce an official to retain or utilize a corporation's services unlawful. This meant that making a legal gift to an official in a foreign jurisdiction exposed the corporation to sanction in the United States. The affirmative defense added in 1988 legalizes actions lawful in foreign jurisdictions making payments or gifts to an official lawful under the written laws and regulations of the foreign country sufficient to provide a defense to making that payment.

The 1988 amendments also include an affirmative defense for legitimate corporate expenditures connected to the promotion and sale of goods. This defense allows payments, originally prohibited under the 1978 FCPA, that are reasonable and *bona fide* expenditures to be made to foreign officials. Reasonable and legitimate expenditures are those genuinely related to sale or promotion of a product. Previously, expenditures related to in-person marketing and sales costs involving foreign officials were legally uncertain. This ambiguity prevented businesses from expending legitimate marketing and sales costs for fear of triggering Department of Justice investigations. Curtailing such expenditures associated with normal business promotion curbed American corporate competitive advantage.

To allow American business to expend costs associated with normal business practice, the amendments incorporate an exemption for a payment, gift, offer, or promise of anything of value that was made, or was a reasonable and *bona fide* expenditure, such as travel and lodging expenses. The payment must be directly related to either the promotion, demonstration or explanation of products or services; or the execution or performance of a contract with a foreign government or agency. This defense allows corporations to conduct promotional seminars, sponsor conferences and provide for product and factory inspection, activities questionable under the 1977 FCPA.

2. The Exception for Routine Governmental Action

The 1988 amendments introduce an exception to the ban on payments to foreign officials, allowing American corporation to make "grease payments." Grease payments are demands, usually from low level officials, for payments to facilitate official duties. Examples of grease payments include giving harbor masters gratuities to process key cargo papers or paying residence, officials tips for providing residency visas. Recognizing that these payments do not involve improper acquisition of business and minimal abuse of government position on the part of foreign officials, Congress legalized such payments.

The 1988 amendments clarify the ambiguities in the definition of what constitutes "routine governmental action." The amendment provides that there is an exception for payments that facilitate routine governmental actions. Acceptable routine governmental actions for purposes of making facilitating payments are defined in the amendment as including such actions as document processing, obtaining permits and similar low-level governmental services. Businesses may make payments to expedite basic services necessary to reside and function in a society. Conversely, payments connected to decisions to award new business, or actions related to the decision making process connected to the award of new business, are specifically exempted from the exception.

3. Amending the Bribery Standard

The 1988 amendments clarify the definition of "bribery" for purposes of criminal and civil liability under the FCPA. The prior standard, which was broader than the domestic criminal bribery standard, prohibited payments made for the purpose of influencing any act or decision of such a person in his official capacity, including a decision to perform his official functions. The amendments narrow the statutory definition of bribery, bringing it in line with the domestic statute. The amendment prohibits all payments intended to influence foreign officials, other than those payments specifically exempted by the facilitating payments exception. The House Conference Committee stated that the SEC and the Department of Justice should not construe the term "influence" so broadly as to prohibit companies from lobbying or otherwise representing their interests.

The 1988 amendments also clarify the level of intent sufficient to constitute *mens rea* for purposes of violating the Act. To find mental culpability, the amendments substituted the word "knowing" in place of the former "knowing or having reason to know of a violation." This amendment removes ambiguities in the 1977 Act which imposed criminal liability for negligent rather than simply purposeful actions. The modified FCPA requires purposeful action, defining a person as knowing if either: (1) the person is "aware" that he or she is engaging in the conduct; or (2) the person has a firm belief that a result is substantially certain to occur. Under the new amendments, to have a mental state sufficient for conviction a person must be aware that a course of action involves or will probably result in bribery. Mere negligence is no longer sufficient to hold an actor intentionally liable under the FCPA.

4. Amendments to the Accounting Standards

Addressing criticism of the accounting provisions, Congress corrected ambiguities and concretely specified corporate requirements for purposes of FCPA compliance. The accounting provisions had drawn criticism for requiring irrelevant disclosures and subjecting business to a strict, yet vague, standard of accountability. The accounting provisions had been further criticized for their excessive scope of applicability, which made every issuer subject to the disclosure requirements, even those with no business overseas. The 1988 amendments address only the materiality standard, requiring a more culpable level of conduct for violations than the original statutory enactment. The strongest criticism of the 1977 FCPA accounting provisions had been directed at the absence of a clear "materiality" standard for holding business accountable. The lack of a clear standard confused businesses regarding the level of supervision they should implement in accounting controls. With no clear statutory guidance defining reasonable compliance, corporations were uncertain of how to cost-effectively comply with the Act. The 1988 FCPA accounting amendments clarified the ambiguities and introduced a more substantive accountability standard.

The 1988 amendments make an entity criminally liable when it knows of a transgression, raising the level of intent necessary for conviction from simple negligence to purposeful action. The 1977 FCPA imposed liability for internal breaches of the FCPA on an ambiguous "should have known" standard. Under this standard a transgressor is accountable for all internal violations of the FCPA accounting provisions that the transgressor "should have known" about. The 1988 amendment changes the "should have known" standard to the more substantive and more culpable "knowing" or "knowing circumvention" or "knowing failure to implement a system of internal accounting controls" consistent with the statutory requirements to constitute violations of the FCPA. The conscious intent requirement replaces the more vague reason to know requirement under the previous code. The culpability of the malefactor, for purposes of conviction, is a higher standard under the 1988 amendments than the 1977 FCPA. Originally mere negligence held an actor criminally liable but the 1988 amendment requires intent or deliberate failure to conform with the Act, sufficient to constitute a violation. The amendments require that the issuer use good faith efforts to the extent reasonable to comply with the FCPA in the system of internal accounting controls. "Reasonable" is defined as the level of detail and degree of assurance that would satisfy prudent officials in the conduct of their own business. The House Senate Conference Committee stated that the Record keeping amendments make simple negligence or mere foolishness insufficient for liability. However, the Committee stressed that ignorance of a breach is not a defense and liability cannot be avoided by engaging in a conscious disregard of the facts.

III. ADMINISTRATIVE AND ENFORCEMENT MECHANISMS

A. Elements for Successful Government Enforcement

How is the FCPA implemented in practice? Obviously, before a pertinent government agency can begin a successful investigation and prosecution under the FCPA, there must be a violation of the Act: a completed bribery crime. For purposes of successful prosecution the government must prove five key elements to meet its burden of proof: (1) an actor; (2) a corrupt *mens rea*, *i.e.*, an evil intent; (3) a payment; (4) a proper recipient of the payment; and, (5) satisfaction of the business purposes test. When it proves all five elements beyond a reasonable doubt, the government will win a criminal conviction under the FCPA.

First, there must be an actor or transgressor who initiates and completes the crime. For purposes of the FCPA, the actor can be any entity acting on behalf of a corporate organization. The FCPA applies to any officer, director, employee, or agent of the firm and any stockholder acting on behalf of the firm making use of the mails or any means or instrumentality of interstate commerce. Individuals and firms may be liable if they aid, abet, counsel, command, induce, procure, or willfully cause another to violate the anti-bribery provisions. Furthermore, liability is imposed if an actor simply conspires to violate those provisions.

The second element the government must prove to successfully prosecute a violation of the FCPA is the presence of the proper mental state or *mens rea* of the crime. To violate the Act, the actor must possess the requisite corrupt intent when committing the crime. The payment made to the official by the actor must be accompanied by intent to induce the recipient to misuse her official position to wrongfully direct business to the payor. The legislative history notes that intent must be corrupt and that the word "corruptly" in the statute connotes an evil motive or purpose.

The FCPA requires the presence of a payment, some manifest compensation, to induce the foreign official to abuse her position. The government needs to prove the existence of consideration between the actor and key official. The FCPA prohibits paying, offering, promising to pay (or authorizing to pay or offer) money or anything of value to a foreign official to influence her decision. Courts have held any transactions of any value are sufficient to constitute a violation of the FCPA. With no payment there can be no bribe and the government may not convict under the statute.

The fourth element the government needs to prove for a successful prosecution is that the corrupt payment was received by a key party. The recipient of the payment must be in an official position or have the means to influence official decisions. The FCPA prohibition on payments extends to a foreign official, a foreign political party or party official, or any candidate for political office. The FCPA defines "foreign official" broadly to include (1) any officer or employee of a foreign government or any department, agency or instrumentality thereof, (2) any person acting in an official capacity for or on behalf of such government or department, agency, or instrumentality thereof, or (3) any person acting in an official capacity for or on behalf of such government or department, agency or instrumentality. It is clear, then, that agents of or intermediaries for a foreign government, as well as full-time foreign government officials, are covered. This makes sense; otherwise the FCPA could be circumvented simply by funneling a bribe to a foreign government official through a third party.

Finally, the prosecution must prove the actor making the corrupt payment possessed the requisite motive for conviction when making that payment. The FCPA prosecution requires proof of the culpable fundamental purpose of the crime; the motive of the crime must satisfy the "Business Purpose Test." The Business Purpose Test requires that payments be made in order to assist the firm in obtaining business or retaining business for or with, or directing business, to any person. The business to be obtained or retained need not be with the actual foreign government or foreign instrumentality.

B. The SEC's Role in FCPA Compliance

Congress gives primary enforcement authority as regards the FCPA to the SEC and Department of Justice. The SEC is responsible for enforcing the accounting requirements of the FCPA by monitoring corporate control over internal accounting. The SEC has promulgated accounting regulations pursuant to the 1934 Act, and it is responsible for enforcing these provisions. The scope of authority granted to the FCPA, to require accounting compliance, includes all companies which must register with the SEC under Section 12 and file reports under Section 15(d) of the 1934 Act. Consequently, all publicly traded corporations fall under the aegis of the accounting provisions, whether or not they engage in foreign business activities.

The SEC brings most of its enforcement actions as injunctive actions under section 21(d) of the 1934 Act. The SEC is empowered to seek injunctions against future violations whenever it appears that any person is violating or about to violate the 1934 Act or regulations or rules thereunder. The SEC may seek a restraining order or a temporary or permanent injunction. The SEC is assiduous in pursuing any violations of the accounting provisions. The SEC uses the FCPA to enjoin any violators who fail to conform with Generally Accepted Accounting Principles (GAAP). The SEC uses the FCPA to prosecute corporations with no foreign business who would not be in a position to engage in bribery of a foreign official. Since the SEC focuses its investigative and prosecutorial resources on violations of GAAP the best way for a corporation to avoid triggering such an investigation is by complying with such principles.

C. The Justice Department's Role in FCPA Enforcement

The second agency Congress charged with enforcing the FCPA is the Department of Justice. The Department of Justice is the agency charged with primary enforcement of the anti-bribery provisions of the FCPA. It is critical for corporate counsel to know what "signals" its client might send that will raise the Justice Department's suspicion, the nature of a Justice Department investigation, and the remedies the Justice Department will seek when prosecuting a suspected transgressor.

1. Initiation of an Investigation

As indicated, the Department of Justice has the authority and responsibility to investigate violations of the bribery provisions of the FCPA. It views the fundamental purpose of the FCPA as elimination of all bribery of foreign government officials. Therefore, it focuses its primary investigatory efforts on conduct potentially connected to such bribery. The Justice Department initiates investigations of suspected bribery when an entity "triggers" the interest of the Department by engaging in conduct fulfilling certain criteria.

The Department of Justice looks for patterns of behavior which signal a violation of the Act. As most Department of Justice trip wires involve discrepancies in corporate financial statements and records, a corporation should structure its records to avoid arousing the Department's interest. However, the corporation should take special care to avoid the following "red flags" that usually trigger an investigation:

- payments of unusually large commission to agents;

- payments to one or more individuals who do not render substantial services;

- payments labeled "miscellaneous expenses," particularly when paid from cash accounts;

- employment of agents with dubious reputations;

- employment of agents with close relationships to a foreign government;

- payments made to third parties or in third countries for no obvious purposes.

The Department of Justice will also initiate investigations upon receiving information from an informer that a violation has occurred. Most such investigations involve situations where a corporation has made payments to a foreign official, and the Justice Department finds out through revelation by the defendant or the third party agent who actually made the bribe.

2. Unique Aspects of the FCPA Investigative Procedure

The Department of Justice follows a fundamentally different procedure when investigating alleged FCPA violations from the procedure used with purely domestic crimes. The presences of foreign governments as a party to the violation effect a sensitive, delicately handled case. Once reasonably assured of an FCPA violation the Department of Justice proceeds with its investigation. It conducts the investigation in a unique approach suited to the unique nature of the FCPA. It conducts the investigation with great sensitivity, because the possible crime involves foreign officials and, therefore, could have disastrous political ramifications for under-sensitive conduct. The Department of Justice intentionally modifies its usual investigative techniques to avoid international political fall-out, and often uses assistance from the Department of State to achieve this goal. At the same time, the political importance of prosecuting major American corporate figures for FCPA violations ought not to be underestimated. A prosecutor's career can be "made" on just one such successful prosecution.

The Department of Justice tries to work with the foreign government to obtain further information and enhance its investigation. In some situations, the Justice Department will make an executive agreement with the foreign government, limited to that specific investigation, obligating the Department and relevant foreign ministry to use best efforts to assist each other in the investigation, any possible prosecutions and protect mutual confidences. These agreements are limited to protecting source confidentiality and other procedural safeguards.

Once ensured that the violation occurred, the Department of Justice withdraws the low profile status of the investigation and reveals information necessary to obtain a successful prosecution. While sensitive to the political nature of the information gathered, the Department of Justice will not withhold information necessary to further its prosecution. It withholds the name of the foreign official who received the bribe only in cases of a plea bargain with the perpetrator, or if there is a strong foreign policy basis for protecting that foreign official.

3. Remedies

When seeking remedies for transgressors, the Department of Justice has several enforcement mechanisms at its disposal. It can seek civil injunctions, criminal convictions, fines and any other relief deemed appropriate under the circumstances. The most common remedy is enjoinment and similar injunctive relief. However, the Department of Justice generally does not initiate such pre-trial and injunctive actions until a thorough investigation of the alleged bribery produces reasonable certainty that the Act did occur. Upon acquisition of evidence sufficient to ensure substantial certainty of a violation of the Act, the Justice Department seeks the injunctive action. Usually, it is successful in obtaining an injunction, a guilty plea or — as occurs in the majority of cases — a plea bargain. Corporate executives, eager to avoid prison time for actions generally committed by subordinates, are usually willing to pay monetary penalties. In this regard, the Department of Justice remedies under the FCPA are similar to remedies available under most federal criminal statutes. At the same time, the pattern raises the familiar concern of white-collar criminals "getting off" for misdeeds that would put poorer defendants behind bars.

4. The Review Procedure

Congress mandates that the Department of Justice create a review procedure for businesses concerned about compliance with the FCPA. The review procedure is available for businesses to review questionable transactions with the appropriate authorities and ensure that those transactions do not transgress the FCPA. The review procedure has not proven a key source of information, as Congress intended it, but rather has been used sparsely. Its effectiveness has been limited by the Justice Department's refusal to implement an opinion record and the hesitancy of business to disclose sensitive information to the agency.

To comply with the review requirement the Department of Justice has issued guidelines establishing the procedure whereby submitted proposals are reviewed regarding potential circumvention of the FCPA. While the legislative purpose of the procedure is to give the business community a set of guidelines to refer to when conducting business in foreign jurisdictions, substantive information is sparse. The Department of Justice refuses to establish an opinion record of past reviews of proposed conduct. It rejects establishing an opinion record because it would be "inconsistent with the function for which opinions are provided, to furnish an indication of the Department's current enforcement policy on a specific factual situation." Furthermore, the Department of Justice says the opinion records would be of limited use because the investigation and prosecution of particular allegations of violation of the FCPA raise such complex enforcement problems abroad as well as difficult issues of jurisdiction and statutory construction that any guidance would be limited to the facts of that particular case and opinion.

Consequently, American business has little administrative guidance to consult when reviewing questionable situations. The review procedure has been used sparingly since implementation, as American firms are not eager to make full disclosure of very proprietary matters to the Department of Justice, especially when such disclosure must be signed by the Chief Executive Officer who then assumes liability. Corporations and executive board members are not eager to assume liability if the review process triggers a Department of Justice investigation. Furthermore, no corporation is likely to announce to the Department of Justice that it plans a business transaction that may be illegal. Companies concerned about disclosing sensitive information to the Department of Justice probably utilize the procedure only if they believe their actions are legal.

D. The Commerce Department and the FCPA

The Department of Commerce has no enforcement role with respect to the FCPA or any legal status interpreting the Act. However, it supplies general guidance to

American exporters who have questions about the FCPA. Discussions with Commerce of specific factual situations, not posed hypothetically, are subject to the following limitations:

- Commerce cannot guarantee that information supplied will be kept confidential;

- Commerce personnel who discuss fact-specific situations will not be subject to deposition or testimony regarding their discussion;

- Materials supplied to Commerce are subject to release under the Freedom of Information Act;

- Because Commerce has no enforcement role, there should be no reliance on advice from commerce; and,

- The situation under discussion should not relate to any matter pending before the Department of Commerce.

E. Sanctions

Sanctions under the FCPA for improperly influencing a foreign official are severe, incorporating both civil and criminal penalties. In cases of plea bargains, the Department of Justice will seek all profits received from business resulting from the improper solicitation as well as an equivalent punitive penalty. The 1988 amendments increase penalties for violations to accompany the higher standards of intent necessary to commit violations of this Act. Specifically, Congress increased the civil penalty for an individual violator from ten thousand to one hundred thousand dollars, but mere negligence is no longer sufficient to find a violation. The following table lists the sanctions for single violations with a comparison of penalty provisions before and after the 1988 amendments. One payoff can invoke several violations of the FCPA so a court may add up the number of violations for purposes of assessing penalties.

Act	1977	1988
Corporate/Issuer Violation	$1 Million	$2 Million
Individual Violation—Civil Penalty	$10,000	$100,000
Individual Violation—Criminal Penalty (prison time)	5 years	5 years

Any fine levied on an individual may not be paid by the corporation employing the individual, either directly or indirectly. Instead, an individual defendant and the corporation are required to pay separately. In other words, indemnification for purposes of civil penalties is not permitted.

F. Practice: Planning to Mitigate FCPA Liability

As suggested, companies seeking to avoid liability under the FCPA should structure business activities to avoid sending the Department of Justice and SEC "signals" that may trigger an investigation. However, avoidance of certain trip wires will generally preclude an investigation. There are a number of precautions a company can take to avoid FCPA liability or mitigate damages, particularly in the selection of agents to do business overseas, in case a future violation is ever found out.

In order to ensure the most advantageous position in the event of Department of Justice investigation, a company should exercise the utmost due diligence possible. A company setting up a system following the guidelines below may be able to convince cynical Department of Justice investigators that it did not intend to violate the Act and, therefore, avoid liability.

A Written Policy: The company should adopt a written policy, distributed to foreign corporate representatives, that emphasizes FCPA compliance. The policy should include basic information about the nature of the FCPA, including its provisions and penalties. The policy should stress that all foreign representatives are to be selected solely on the basis of merit. Corrupt payments to foreign officials by employees or representatives of the company should explicitly be prohibited. Policy should dictate that managers and employees who have access or discretion over company funds certify, on an annual basis compliance with the company policy and the FCPA.

A Written Agreement: The company should utilize written agreements with foreign marketing representatives. These agreements should specifically provide for and be made contingent upon compliance with United States law, particularly the FCPA. The agreement should further state that no part of the agent's compensation is to be used to make any payments, bribes or kickbacks to a third party. The agreement should terminate immediately if any actions of the agent are found to be impermissible under United States law.

One familiar pattern companies use to circumvent the FCPA starts with the company requiring hired agents to sign no-bribery agreements. Local representatives of the company then close their eyes to whatever the agents do, including how agents spend commissions. To avoid being criminally liable in such a situation the company should closely monitor the activities of the agent. Requiring the agent to disclose financial statements, accounting for assets obtained from the company, as well as to disclose statements indicating FCPA compliance will probably convince the Department of Justice that due diligence has been exercised.

A Background Investigation: The company should conduct a thorough background investigation of the agent's reputation in the business community. The efforts of the company to ascertain the reputation of the representative must be thoroughly documented. If the agent has a shady reputation, has been involved in bribery in the past or has an unusually close relationship with government officials, the company should consider utilizing another business agent. If a company does retain an agent with a less than saintly reputation, the company should be extra diligent in documenting demands that the agent comply with the FCPA while in the company's employ.

An Opinion of Counsel: The corporation should retain a local counsel to explore the relevant legal environment and the laws related to the FCPA. The corporation should make itself aware of what local laws apply to the issue of bribery and to what degree the corporation is liable for the actions of the contractor based on the contractor's vicarious liability status. If payments are to be made to officials, allowed under local laws, and subject to the FCPA affirmative defense, opinion of local counsel that the payments are legal should be solicited and thoroughly documented.

An Employee Certification: The employee who retains an agent in a foreign country should certify why the employee chose that agent. The employee should document the search process, evaluation of candidates, and reason for final decision. During the search process, documentation describing position requirements should emphasize to applicants that bribery and improper influence are not acceptable practice.

IV. THE EFFECTS OF THE FCPA ON BUSINESS

Is the FCPA bad for American business? Roughly a quarter century after enactment of the FCPA, this question persists. The Act has engendered a divisive debate, and it is easy to answer by saying "yes and no." In other words, a clear answer remains elusive.

A. The Act Damages American Business

Arguably, American business is harmed seriously by an over-broad FCPA; hence the Act should be suspended, even repealed. This argument hinges on an examination of the international economic ramifications and domestic ramifications of the FCPA, the degree of administrative policy support for the FCPA, and the acceptance in other countries and cultures of bribery as a relatively routine business practice.

1. The FCPA: Millstone on American Business Expansion

The loudest criticisms of the FCPA focus on the detrimental ramifications of the Act. The Act retards the expansion of American business in many of the booming economies of the world. Bribery is part of the culture in many vital foreign markets, and the FCPA detracts from America's competitive advantage when competing for these valuable government procurements. At the present the fastest growing markets in the world are in Asia, in which many economies are notorious for their acceptance of bribery. For the United States to continue its role as the major player in the global economy, it must compete successfully in Asia in particular, where at least three out of every five people in the world live. The ramifications of the FCPA also extend to other emerging and vital markets: the Middle East, Eastern Europe, the Commonwealth of Independent States, and Latin America are all dynamic markets with cultures that accept some bribery. There is striking evidence that the FCPA handcuffs American businesses' ability to market itself in these key regions.

The Indonesian economy is one market in which American business finds itself at a disadvantage because of the FCPA. Indonesia, with roughly 200 million people, is the largest Islamic nation in the world. Until the Asian economic crisis, it boasted one of the fastest growing economies in the world. It is one of the ten emerging markets the United States government has targeted as imperative for promoting American exports and business. Indonesia also has a long-standing reputation for tacit approval of bribery in its commercial system: in the early 1970's, former President Suharto's wife, Tien, was known as "Mrs. Tien Percent" for her role in official corruption. Indeed, allegations of widespread corruption in the Suharto family and regime were a key reason why President Suharto was forced from office in the midst of the Asian economic crisis.

The FCPA has put American companies at a competitive disadvantage for winning contracts in Indonesia. An American lawyer stated he was involved in three cases in which American telecommunications companies had to pass up joining multinational consortiums because of the Act's restrictions. The telecommunications field is considered one of the fastest growing and most critical markets for national economic success in the 21st century, and the United States may be locked out of the huge consumer market because of FCPA restrictions.

The largest market in the world, with more than one billion consumers, is China. More than any other single market in the world, China presents vast potential for business expansion and exploitation. The President of the American Chamber of Commerce has noted that American anti-corruption legislation is an obstacle for American companies wanting to do business in China. Corruption is commonplace, and nearly every firm involved in China has to bribe officials at one level or another to continue doing business. While official Chinese reports claim there is little or no corruption in the People's Republic, reliable sources report the opposite. Interviews with traders and firms involved in China show that a large percentage of western companies deal with the issue of corruption in day-to-day business activities.

The FCPA is criticized as poorly drafted and culturally biased in its prohibition against paying official bribes in places like China. The Act is impractical, unrealistic, and difficult to interpret in the context of doing business with China, because of the inherently different nature of Asian business. It is often difficult to define whether standard business transaction payments in China would be considered legal under American law. For example, a common business transaction in China consists of giving government officials trips abroad. One trader reports that travel costs for officials to "view" products are almost always built into the product sales price. While legitimate business trips may be legal under the FCPA, justified as "a reasonable and *bona fide* business expenditure," American businesses are nervous about condoning such trips when sanctions for FCPA violations are so severe. Opportunities for business, in what will soon be the largest economy in the world, may be lost because of American statutory restrictions dictating morality to a culture predating the United States by 4,000 years.

Expansion in other important Asian markets is similarly hampered for American business by FCPA restrictions. Japan, presently the largest economy in Asia, is known for corruption reaching from the Prime Minister down to local district political leaders. Bids for government construction jobs are routinely rigged for the highest briber, precluding American construction and engineering firms from getting a foothold in the market — unless they wish to breach American federal law. American companies doing business in Malaysia worry that they cannot get contracts because they are not allowed to bribe with other competitors.

Ramifications of the FCPA extend beyond the Asian hemisphere into other expanding markets around the globe. Dow Corning has been locked out of South American markets many times because it has refused to pay the bribes necessary to get the business. In the Middle East corruption is a way of life in some places, with low level officials paid low salaries with the understanding that their income will be supplemented. In Saudi Arabia, the wealthiest Middle Eastern Country, *baksheesh* is an essential element of business and raises the price of every contract from three to fifteen percent depending on the nature of the transaction. To do major business projects in Saudi Arabia, it is essential to be connected, via an agent or middleman, to a member of the royal family, which controls not just government, but business as well. American businesses attempting to comply with the FCPA lose out on business opportunities if they do not do what is "required."

Eastern Europe is yet another critical emerging market for the American business community to penetrate and establish itself in. Official corruption and "mafia" control of business is notorious and United States companies wishing to make in-roads will be met with demands for special compensation. The FCPA may preclude American business from meeting those demands. Thus, the act might curb the spread of business in the new democracies the United States spent forty years trying to free from communism. In Russia bribery is a mandate for business wishing to expand into the local market. In a country where government salary rises lag far behind persistent inflation most bureaucrats are responsive, if not eager, to accept bribes. In a report for President Yeltsin, a research team concluded that the Russian Mafia controlled 70 to 80 percent of all private business and banking activity.

These former communist markets are so important and so lucrative that many firms circumvent the boundaries of the Act to maintain market share. While the Act precludes American firms from paying bribes or paying off mafia-type groups, many American firms in Russia circumvent the intent of the law by hiring a "consultant," which is simply part of the price of doing business. In the meantime, America's strongest regional competitors, the Germans, have no qualms about playing by the local rules. Germans, exploiting geographical advantage and historical business connections, have emerged as a dominant supplier to the East European market. With no FCPA to check contract acquisition, German firms write off bribes as business expenses.

2. Internal Effects of the FCPA

The ramifications of the FCPA are felt in the domestic United States market through curtailed business expansion decisions. When firms decide they cannot compete in some international markets because of the FCPA, they do not expand. Businesses that do not expand do not hire American workers, order more parts or contribute to GNP growth.

Small business employs more Americans than large business, and plays a vital role in the economy, often the quickest to rebound after recessions, buoying recovery. Vital to the lifeblood of the American economy, small business reports that the FCPA sharply curtails plans for expansion. Those small businesses feel the weight of the FCPA on plans to globalize. A recent survey of small businesses indicates that bribery is the number one problem faced by those firms overseas. By implication, small firms are more susceptible to pressures of bribery, being more dependent on one area and single region sales. Demands for bribes accompanied by pressure from the FCPA not to pay preclude planned expansion in many instances. The legal and ethical cost of acquiring contracts, with the potentially disastrous ramifications of Department of Justice intervention, drives the cost of business too high for small business to cost effectively expand in some parts of the world.

To be sure, the FCPA does not always prevent small business in questionable situations from expanding. But, the results of such expansion can be disastrous if the Department of Justice finds a violation. Some small businesses are much more willing than large firms, which are equipped with a staff of lawyers and compliance officers, to be creative and circumvent the parameters of the Act. Indeed, some small businesses struggling to establish themselves overseas simply may have to be more "hungry" for profits, and thus more tolerant of unethical practices, than large companies whose presence they are challenging.

Some firms that see business advantages in expanding to regions where bribery is common enough to make FCPA compliance a liability look for ways to skirt the Act. They can and do try to circumvent the FCPA through use of offshore subsidiaries and well placed "commission agents." However, this common practice dulls American competitive advantage for two reasons. First, using subsidiaries and special agents is costly, driving up the cost of business and consequently cutting profits for American investors. Second, legal costs and overhead are increased as firms utilize more legal resources to ensure that corporate legal exposure under this practice is minimized.

Large firms have also lost competitive advantage and business as a result of the FCPA. In a poll of bigger business exporters, 70 percent of the respondents felt that their export business was adversely affected by enactment of the FCPA. The most common impacts of the FCPA on business was reduction of overseas operations of respondent firms, followed by firms feeling constrained in those overseas dealings by the FCPA. In the one official government study of the impact of the FCPA, the Comptroller General concluded that the Act makes business difficult and has precluded American companies from obtaining lucrative foreign contracts. According to the same report, the United States is one of the few countries to make bribery of foreign officials illegal.

Large business also feels the bite of the FCPA in the increased cost of methods used to manage personnel. In a survey of business exporters, large business management expressed frustration with the FCPA saying "it hits you before you know it, most of the time when you are in a jam already." Business needs to have experienced people on the ground to deal with the practical ramifications of the Act. Therefore, the FCPA draws more experienced and expensive senior personnel from the home office to regional posts who ensure that the corporation complies with the FCPA and are able to deal with any complications. Most international firms expressed the feeling that hiring young people to be involved in overseas operations means the corporation has to deal with zealots and younger people who are more likely to violate FCPA provisions in their desire to succeed and move up the corporate ladder. This has forced firms to locate senior personnel at overseas posts. The senior personnel may be more valuable at corporate headquarters, but the FCPA prompts misallocation of human capital to ensure statutory compliance.

The Act also is criticized for being overly broad in its scope of application. The FCPA may well be one more example of Congress overreacting to a political scandal (Watergate). After all, the FCPA applies to all issuers of stocks, bonds and securities, not just those issuers who transact foreign trade. Many firms who have no international presence must expend valuable resources on compliance with the Act. These resources could be used to further expand and contribute to the economy. The Act has a detrimental effect on the United States' domestic economy; it curtails expansion and wastes resources, costing jobs, business opportunities and chances to mitigate the United States trade deficit.

3. Acceptance of Bribery by America's Trade Competitors

Few other major trading nations have adopted the American policy of outlawing international bribery. Sweden is one of the few countries to join the United States in passing laws making it illegal for their citizens to bribe foreign officials. Many foreign nations encourage, or at least tacitly endorse, official bribery — even providing government incentives for bribery that brings national business. Switzerland and West Germany explicitly allow tax deductions for certain illegal payments. By comparison, the United States Internal Revenue Code specifically prohibits American corporations from deducting bribes as business expenses under the auspices of the FCPA. How serious the other countries are in combating bribery in the future will depend very much on whether they reverse their policy on the tax deductibility of bribes. As long as bribery is legalized as a legitimate business expense for foreign companies, their American counterparts will remain at a competitive disadvantage.

There are foreign countries that do not explicitly endorse bribery in their laws and regulations, but they usually are willing to overlook corporate payments that may be actionable in the United States. England is a case in point. So long as company accounting records show the illicit payments across borders as "business development expenses," or something similar, no company laws are broken. Furthermore, many countries are not so quick to impose domestic constraints on citizen action outside of the home jurisdiction, and are not interested in controlling external corporate behavior. In Britain, for example, not only are there no British laws preventing a British company from bribing officials of other nations, but Her Majesty's government has explicitly stated it is not interested in such foreign behavior. According to Claire Davies, former press officer for the British government's Department of Trade and Industry, "the bribery of a foreign official is a matter for the country that the British company is in at the time of the bribe." In the face of foreign governmental indifference or acceptance of foreign bribery it makes little economic sense for United States businesses to refrain from the common practice consequently losing business.

B. In Support of the FCPA; Addressing Damaging Practices Abroad

The pro-FCPA position states that the actual economic impact of the FCPA is minimal, and the United States pays a very small economic price for prohibiting such a morally reprehensible activity. The FCPA attempts to eradicate an insidious and damaging practice: abuse of official position for personal gain. Bribery and corruption costs hundreds of millions of dollars in development, has brought down political parties and contributed to turmoil in transnational political relations.

1. The Economic and Social Havoc of Corruption

Corruption hurts economies of nations that allow it to flourish. It hurts rational market development, preventing nations from utilizing resources to the fullest. Development is uneven and poor decisions are made regarding allocation of resources because corrupt practices distort decision making. Bribes lead to the selection of incompetent and unscrupulous suppliers of goods and services or may encourage countries to purchase goods and services unsuitable or surplus to their needs. Corruption directly channels aid money out of the countries it is intended for, funneling it to the private bank accounts of those in positions to benefit. One Swiss banking source estimates that more than U.S. $20 billion is held in the country's bank accounts for leaders from African states alone. Growing mal-distribution of resources between "North" and "South" is a cause of transnational political tension. More efficient decision making and resource allocation may narrow the gap between the developed and developing nations of the world, easing political tensions, furthering equitable relations.

Along with damaging development and wasting resources corruption is a detriment to business, a game situation where all players lose. When a market requires that competitors resort to bribery none can be sure of winning the contract, but each must pay so as not to be outdone. As bribers bid against each other, the cost of acquiring the contract rises — but the efficacy of bribery does not. At this point of diminishing returns, the competitors realize they would gain from an agreement outlawing bribes — but the game is too far afoot for this to happen. An agreement would reduce the overhead costs of acquiring business and increase profitability of the venture, yet the possibility of a cheater precludes an agreement.

There are some places in the world where this point of diminishing returns has been reached and competitors have made agreements to refrain from extending gratuities. One example is Beijing, where some companies have made informal arrangements with their competitors. Apparently, Chinese journalists demand "appearance money" to cover press conferences. Several foreign firms decided to try and break this tradition. Led by Hill & Knowlton, a United States public relations group, many public relations firms agreed not to pay the Chinese media for coverage of their clients.

Asia, the fastest growing and largest market in the world has long been known as the land where little could be done without payouts to key officials. However, in defiance of this reputation is the emergence of a trend proscribing the practice across the region. Increasingly, the practice is viewed by government officials and consumers alike as unacceptable and destructive to the national economy. For example, Korea was once notorious for bribery and political patronage. Recently, Korean governments have taken a firm stance against bribery, especially among the higher levels of the bureaucracy. Some observers even report that bribery has been removed as a factor in deal-making and deal-breaking. As Korea moves towards becoming one of the most modern and competitive economies in the world, it is demanding a higher level of ethics from its government and business leaders.

At least until the Asian economic crisis struck, Malaysia had shown an increasing commitment to reduce corruption. Corruption in government procurement had soured relations between it and Great Britain. The government, furious at British companies that bribed Malay officials for sizable infrastructure contracts, declared these companies ineligible to bid on contracts in the foreseeable future. The British government protested the ruling, but the government — seeking to end a damaging practice — did not heed its former Colonial master, and so continued to ban some of Great Britain's largest corporations from participating in its lucrative government procurement market. Whether Malaysia continues on this impressive anti-corruption path, however, remains to be seen.

Bribery threatens more than economic development in some parts of Asia. Democracy and human health can be casualties. Hong Kong won a good name after the establishment of the Independent Commission Against Corruption in 1974. But, in the wake of the handover by Britain of Hong Kong back to China on 1 July 1997, is corruption a threat again in Hong Kong? If so, how might China react? Local government members and activists, such as lawyer Martin Lee, fear China will use corruption as an excuse to suppress democratic institutions — even though China itself may be to blame for some of the corruption in Hong Kong. In Thailand, corruption has led to deadly consequences, costing the lives of many citizens. The toleration of corruption, specifically the alliance between police and owners of fleshpots, has fueled an AIDS epidemic, with around 400,000 Thais infected with AIDS from brothels an honest police force would have shut down. It is estimated that the AIDS rate in Thailand is among the highest in the world, but the sex trade is so lucrative for officials and brothel owners that it is almost impossible to suppress.

Corruption and bribery also threaten political stability, and may reverse civil and humanitarian advances in several new democracies. In the fledgling democracy of South Africa, the former wife of President Nelson Mandela has been implicated in corruption scandals. Allegations of corruption threaten to damage the African National Congress and split it into smaller factions, which may not have the coherence or desire to resist radical calls for retaliation against white South Africa or for nationalization of economic resources. Several prominent officials in the South African government are calling on American businesses that left South Africa, protesting apartheid and now returning, to help the cause of democracy by resisting the offers of those who would throw deals their way for graft.

In Russia, corruption threatens political reform with the alarming potential to return the world to the Cold War era. Russia has become notorious for corruption on a vast scale, with as much as 70-80 percent of business controlled by organized crime. The danger of the rampant style corruption is that it is associated with the economic reform programs of post-Communist Russia and might lead to a political backlash in favor of "clean" nationalists or communists. The nationalists or communists could then suppress democracy in the name of sanitizing the government and eliminating corruption.

In ostensibly "clean" Europe and North America, corruption upsets relations among close political allies. A former Secretary General of NATO, Willy Claes, has been implicated in a scandal involving an Italian helicopter manufacturer. The manufacturer paid a $1.7 million gift to Mr. Claes' political party in Belgium that helped the manufacturer obtain the contract for the $267 million sale. As Mr. Claes was party leader at the time of the payment, calls for his resignation erupted. Corruption reaching into the ranks of NATO, weakening the titular leadership, exacerbates the already difficult job of readjusting NATO to the post cold war world.

Within Europe, recent scandals involving bribes to secure military sales have made headlines. These scandals involved Swedes paying bribes to Indian officials, British paying Saudis, German officials making payments to Turkish officials, and the French spreading payments all over the developing world. With competition for military contracts tight in a Europe emerging from recession, bribery does not build sound political alliances, preventing further solidification of the European Union.

2. St. George and The Dragon: The Just Fight

With evidence that corruption is one of the most important and damaging factors threatening third world development, international opposition to corruption has coalesced in different spots around the world. In developing countries from Thailand to Nigeria, grassroots campaigns against corruption are gaining strength. There is a real recognition that aid projects are hijacked by graft and real economic dislocation is the result of such activities.

One group that has emerged on the international scene assuming an advocacy role in the field of corruption, similar to that of Amnesty International in the field of human rights, is Transparency International ("TI" hereinafter). TI is a Berlin based coalition dedicated to crusading against corruption in international business. This non-profit organization, which has raised funds from various Governments and international corporations, is staffed with veterans of aid, commerce and development organizations all with first-hand knowledge of the devastation that corruption brings.

Peter Eigen, chairman of TI and former senior official with the World Bank, warns that corruption threatens development and the growth of fragile political institutions. Corruption is bad for business and seriously undermines the fledgling democracies of Eastern Europe. TI has focused its efforts on revealing corporate corruption and trying to coordinate a global code of ethical procurement practice, preventing corporations from resorting to unethical methods of contract acquisition. The first success in this program in Ecuador, where tenders for a $600 million government-funded pipeline contract were limited to companies who signed a code of business conduct stating the business will not engage in corporate bribery anywhere in the world. TI intends to persuade governments throughout the developing world to adopt such codes: it will publish lists of governments who do not outlaw bribery and the corporations who bribe.

3. The Fight for a Substantively Meaningful, Truly Multilateral Agreement

Supporters of the FCPA argue that an international version of the Act should be drafted and enforced by all of the major trading countries, as well as all of the major developing countries. International condemnation of bribery would mitigate resource mal-distribution, improving development, alleviating political tensions and rationalizing economic decisions involving international contracts.

There are short and long term benefits to implementing and enforcing an international agreement. The avoidance of bribery of officials, which when it becomes en-

demic is a huge hidden cost for business, and the avoidance of developmental and political tensions are laudable goals in and of themselves. There are also moral benefits
to upholding high standards of ethical conduct. Those opposed to enactment of an
international code cite its detrimental economic effects on American business. They
also claim that enforcement of the act would be weak in an international arena where
success of flagship industries promotes political stability on the home-front.

Those supporting the enactment of a code point to studies that the FCPA has had
no negative economic consequences on American business abroad, and that no objective studies reveal any evidence to the contrary. These supporters argue the decline
of the proportion of American business in parts of the world, such as the Middle
East, is usually attributable to factors other than the FCPA.

Furthermore, there are legal alternatives to bribery that influence official decision
making that are not distortionary to economic decision making or detrimental to
economies and development. These "legal alternatives" would still be available
under a new international code. This legal bribery can also be more effective than
monetary payments in inducing a foreign government to award a contract. Often information (regarding new technology, etc.), prestige, recognition, donations to local
charities and other creative substitutes can be more effective and engender stronger
long term business and community ties than a simple monetary payment. These options, open to United States business, carry few of the detrimental economic and ethical implications of raw bribery.

The United States plans to tie the issue of corruption to international trade.
Mickey Kantor, former United States Trade Representative, has said that the United
States will press other countries to adopt foreign corrupt practice rules within the
World Trade Organization (WTO). His effort is part of an American strategy to
shape the WTO's agenda in the New Millennium. Proposals might include restrictions on membership for WTO Members who do not outlaw corporate bribery.
Other methods of assimilating the FCPA into the WTO include legal concessions
granting contracting parties the right to impose disparate tariffs on nations that condone foreign bribery. It is foreseeable that until the WTO implements such provisions
creating an international FCPA of sorts, the United States might use its authority to
act unilaterally under Section 301 of the Trade Act of 1974, as amended, to punish
countries that allow their nationals to bribe and thereby steal business from American firms.

V. CONCLUSION

The FCPA addresses and attempts to curb an unacceptable practice, bribery.
Bribery involves abuse of public trust and threatens the integrity and foundation of
governments. The economic distortionary effects of corruption are immense, arguably costing some parts of the world decades of retarded development. The cost of
bribery is also political, as it threatens fragile developing democratic institutions
across the globe, and may be immeasurable in terms of lost human lives and retarded
civil liberties. The FCPA codifies the moral American ideal that people should deal
squarely with each other; a statutory "Golden Rule." The United States requires this
behavior of its own citizens, and increasingly demands this from others with whom
it transacts business. To advance the American notion of square dealing and prevent
economic detriment associated with the Act, a truly multilateral FCPA could be enacted. Such an agreement would level the international playing field, promote economic development, mitigate political tensions and move the world to an optimal
economically efficient point.

Unfortunately, not all of the rest of the world echoes the American sentiments on square dealing. Some of America's major trading partners not only allow bribery of foreign officials, but in some cases condone it. Foreign competitors tax deductibility of business expenses, *i.e.*, their bribery of officials, does not leave American firms competing on a level playing field. While studies conflict, American business seems to be handcuffed by the FCPA. Just the costs of compliance — ensuring that the Act is not violated — renders American business less competitive and reduces profits for investors. In an era when national success is linked to economic success, the United States cannot afford to let valuable market opportunities pass. When a sizeable percentage of American jobs creation is linked to exporting goods and services, the United States must make its corporate competitiveness in the transnational market.

The solution: level the playing field. For the moment the FCPA should be suspended. American business should be allowed to compete for foreign contracts in any manner possible. Simultaneously, the United States should pursue efforts to implement a meaningful multilateral agreement outlawing bribery. When such an agreement is in place, and enforced, the FCPA can be "unfrozen" — indeed, it will be the pre-existing legislation that implements the international agreement. But, until then, the moral high ground is too costly for the United States. Jobs, economic development, and market share in an intensely competitive 21st century are too valuable to forgo.

Lamb v. Phillip Morris, Inc.
915 F.2d 1024 (6th Cir. 1990)

RALPH B. GUY, JR., Circuit Judge.

In this antitrust action, plaintiffs Billy Lamb and Carmon Willis appeal from the dismissal of their claims against defendants Phillip Morris, Inc. (Phillip Morris), and B.A.T. Industries, PLC (B.A.T.). Because we find that the act of state doctrine presents no impediment to adjudication of the plaintiffs' antitrust claims, we reverse the district court's dismissal of those claims and remand them for further consideration. Since we find that no private right of action is available under the Foreign Corrupt Practices Act of 1977 (FCPA), 15 U.S.C. §§ ,78dd-1, 78dd-2, we affirm the dismissal of the plaintiffs' FCPA claim.

I.

. . . .

Plaintiffs Lamb and Willis, along with various other Kentucky growers, produce burley tobacco for use in cigarettes and other tobacco products. Defendants Phillip Morris and B.A.T. routinely purchase such tobacco not only from Kentucky markets serviced by the plaintiffs, but also from producers in several foreign countries. Thus, tobacco grown in Kentucky competes directly with tobacco grown abroad, and any purchases from foreign suppliers necessarily reduce the defendants' purchase of domestic tobacco.

On May 14, 1982, a Phillip Morris subsidiary known as C.A. Tabacalera National and a B.A.T. subsidiary known as C.A. Cigarrera Bigott, SUCS. entered into a contract with La Fundacion Del Nino (the Children's Foundation) of Caracas, Venezuela. The agreement was signed on behalf of the Children's Foundation by the organization's president, the wife of the then President of Venezuela. Under the terms of the agreement, the two subsidiaries were to make periodic donations to the Children's Foundation totaling approximately $12.5 million dollars. In exchange, the subsidiaries were to obtain price controls on Venezuelan tobacco, elimination of controls on retail cigarette prices in Venezuela, tax deductions for the donations, and assurances that existing tax rates applicable to tobacco companies would not be increased. According to the plaintiffs' complaint, the defendants have arranged similar contracts in Argentina, Brazil, Costa Rica, Mexico, and Nicaragua.

In the plaintiffs' view, the donations promised by the defendants' subsidiaries amount to unlawful inducements designed and intended to restrain trade. The plaintiffs assert that such arrangements result in artificial depression of tobacco prices to the detriment of domestic tobacco growers, while ensuring lucrative retail prices for tobacco products sold abroad. In this action, the plaintiffs seek redress in the forms of treble damages and injunctive relief principally for the former result-reduction in domestic tobacco prices.

The plaintiffs filed their complaint alleging violations of federal antitrust laws on August 21, 1985, in the United States District Court for the Eastern District of Kentucky. Both defendants promptly moved for dismissal on several grounds. The plaintiffs then sought leave to amend their complaint to add a claim under the FCPA....
[T]he the district court dismissed the plaintiffs' antitrust claims as barred by the act of state doctrine, and dismissed the FCPA claim as an impermissible private action. This appeal follows. [The court's reversal of the district court's dismissal of the antitrust claim is omitted.]

. . . .

III.

Although the Foreign Corrupt Practices Act was enacted more than a decade ago, the question of whether an implied private right of action exists under the FCPA apparently is one of first impression at the federal appellate level. Thus, we must analyze the FCPA, which generally forbids issuers of registered securities and other "domestic concerns" (as well as their agents) to endeavor to influence foreign officials by offering, promising, or giving "anything of value," see 15 U.S.C. §§ 78dd-l(a), 78dd-2(a), to ascertain whether the plaintiffs may assert a private cause of action. The Supreme Court recently explained that:

> In determining whether to infer a private cause of action from a federal statute, our focal point is Congress' intent in enacting the statute. As guides for discerning that intent, we have relied on the four factors set out in *Cort v. Ash,* 422 U.S. 66...(1975), along with other tools of statutory construction. Our focus on congressional intent does not mean that we require evidence that Members of Congress, in enacting the statute, actually had in mind the creation of a private cause of action.... The intent of Congress remains the ultimate issue, however, and "unless this congressional intent can be inferred from the language of the statute, the statutory structure, or some other source, the essential predicate for implication of a private remedy simply does not exist."

Thompson. v. Thompson, 484 U.S. 174, 179...(1988) (citations omitted). Thus, as *Thompson* makes clear, our central focus is on congressional intent... " with an eye toward" the four *Cort* factors: (1) whether the plaintiffs are among "the class for whose especial benefit," the statute was enacted; (2) whether the legislative history suggests congressional intent to prescribe or proscribe a private cause of action; (3) whether "implying such a remedy for the plaintiff would be 'consistent with the underlying purposes of the legislative scheme'"; and (4) whether the cause of action is "'one traditionally relegated to state law, in an area basically the concern of States, so that it would be inappropriate to infer a cause of action.'" *See Chairez v. United States I.N.S,* 790 F.29 544, 546 (6th Cir.1986) (quoting *Cort,* 422 U.S. at 78).

A. "Especial Beneficiaries"

The defendants contend, and we agree, that the FCPA was designed with the assistance of the Securities and Exchange Commission (SEC) to aid federal law enforcement agencies in curbing bribes of foreign officials. According to the Senate report regarding the FCPA, the Senate Committee on Banking, Housing and Urban Affairs initially "ordered reported a bill, S. 3664, which incorporated the SEC's recommendations and a direct prohibition against the payment of overseas bribes by any U.S. business concern." S.REP. NO. 114, 95TH CONG., 1ST SESS. 2, *reprinted in* 1977 U.S. CODE CONG. & ADMIN. NEWS 4098, 4099. As the Senate report indicates, the resulting enactment of the FCPA represents a legislative endeavor to promote confidence in international trading relationships and domestic markets; *see id.* at 3, 1977 U.S. CODE CONG. & ADMIN. NEWS at 4100-01; the authorization of stringent criminal penalties amplifies the foreign policy and law enforcement considerations underlying the FCPA. *See, e.g.,* 15 U.S.C. § 78dd-2(g). The House Conference report refers to the "jurisdictional, enforcement, and diplomatic difficulties" of broadening the FCPA's reach, *see* H.R. CONF. REP. NO. 831, 95th Cong., lst Sess. 14, *reprinted in* 1977 U.S.CODE CONG. & ADMIN. NEWS 4121, 4126, thereby addressing concerns typically of special interest to law enforcement officials. In light of these comments and the general tenor of the FCPA itself, which requires the Attorney General to participate actively in encouraging and supervising compliance with the Act," *see, e.g.,* 15 U.S.C. §§ 78dd-l(e), 78dd-2(f), we find that the FCPA was primarily designed to protect the integrity of American foreign policy and domestic markets, rather than, to prevent the use of foreign resources to reduce production costs. The plaintiffs, as competitors of foreign tobacco growers and suppliers of the defendants, cannot claim the status of intended beneficiaries of the congressional enactment under scrutiny.

B. Congressional Intent Concerning Private Rights of Action

Despite the paucity of authority in the legislative history for their position, the plaintiffs assert that Congress fully intended to permit private rights of action under the FCPA. We disagree. The plaintiffs have identified only one reference in a House report to a private right of action: "The committee intends that courts shall recognize a private cause of action based on this legislation, as they have in cases involving other provisions of the Securities Exchange Act, on behalf of persons who suffer injury as a result of prohibited corporate bribery." H.R. REP. NO. 640, 95TH CONG., 1ST SESS. 10 (1977). Unlike the House, the Senate initially included a provision that expressly conferred a private right of action under the FCPA on competitors. *See* S. 3379, 94th Cong., 2d Sess. § 10, 122 Cong. Rec. 12,605, 12,607 (1976). Significantly, the Senate committee deleted that provision. *See* S.REP. NO. 1031, 94TH CONG., 2D SESS. 13 (1976). The availability of a private right of action apparently was never resolved (or perhaps even raised) at the conference that ultimately produced the compromise bill passed by both houses and signed into law; neither the FCPA as enacted nor the conference report mentions such a cause of action. *See* 15 U.S.C. §§ 78dd-1, 78dd-2; H.R. CONF. REP. NO. 831, 95TH CONG., 1ST SESS., *reprinted in* 1977 U.S. CODE CONG. & ADMIN. NEWS 4121. Because the conference report accompanying the final legislative compromise makes no mention of a private right of action, we infer that Congress intended no such result. Accordingly, we reject the plaintiffs' assertion that one isolated comment in an earlier House report mandates recognition of a private right of action.

C. Consistency with the Legislative Scheme

Recognition of the plaintiffs' proposed private right of action, in our view, would directly contravene the carefully tailored FCPA scheme presently in place. Congress recently expanded the Attorney General's responsibilities to include facilitating compliance with the FCPA. *See* 15 U.S.C. §§ 78dd-l(e), 78dd-2(f). Specifically, the Attorney General must "establish a procedure to provide responses to specific inquiries" by issuers of securities and other domestic concerns regarding "conformance of their conduct with the Department of Justice's [FCPA] enforcement policy...." 15 U.S.C. §§ 78dd-l(e)(1), 78dd-2(f)(1). Moreover, the Attorney General must furnish "timely guidance concerning the Department of Justice's [FCPA] enforcement policy...to potential exporters and small businesses that are unable to obtain specialized counsel on issues pertaining to [FCPA] provisions." 15 U.S.C. §§ 78ddl(e)(4), 78dd-2(f)(4). Because this legislative action clearly evinces a preference for compliance in lieu of prosecution, the introduction of private plaintiffs interested solely in post-violation enforcement, rather than pre-violation compliance, most assuredly would hinder congressional efforts to protect companies and their employees concerned about FCPA liability.

D. Alternative Avenues of Redress

Regulation of bribery directed at foreign officials cannot be characterized as a matter traditionally relegated to state control. In this respect, implying a private right of action under the FCPA — a statutory scheme aimed at activities ordinarily undertaken abroad — would not intrude upon matters of state concern. Nevertheless, the international reach of federal antitrust laws dilutes the plaintiffs' assertion that a private cause of action under the FCPA constitutes the only viable mechanism for redressing anti-competitive behavior on a global scale.... Because the potential for recovery under federal antitrust laws in this case belies the plaintiffs' contention that an implied private right of action under the FCPA is imperative, we attach no significance to the absence of state laws proscribing bribery of foreign officials. More importantly, since none of the *Cort* factors supports the plaintiffs' private right of action theory, we *affirm* the district court's dismissal of the FCPA claim.

II. Human Rights and MNCs

A. Overview

Documents Supplement References:

1. *United Nations, Universal Declaration of Human Rights (adopted 10 December 1948)*

2. *Torture Victim Protection Act of 1991, 28 U.S.C. Section 1350 Note*

3. *Genocide Crime, 18 U.S.C. Section 1091*

4. *International Labor Organization, Tripartite Declaration of Principles Concerning Multinational Enterprises and Social Policy (adopted 16 November 1977)*

NOTE ON THE EXPANDING RESPONSIBILITIES
OF MULTINATIONAL CORPORATIONS *

Introduction[1]

Markets are opening up around the globe. Indeed, the disintegration of the communist world has allowed for a mobility of capital that ignores all of the Cold War boundaries and creates a new world order.

With this movement of capital comes the movement of goods and ideas. Some scholars believe this will lead to a breakdown of cultures and the inevitable decline of the traditional nation-state. This view is by no means universally accepted, but no one can challenge the important role private investors now hold in modern international economic relations.[2] For example, at the beginning of the decade, less than 50 percent of the international capital moving into the developing world was from private sources. By 1996, private investment claimed over 84 percent of that amount.

Doubtless the key player in the "global privatization" phenomenon is the multinational corporation (MNC), also known as the transnational corporation (TNC). The statistics are startling:

- While the 200 largest corporations employ less than three fourths of one percent of the world's work force, they account for 28 percent of world economic activity. The 500 largest corporations account for 70 percent of world trade.

- Foreign Direct Investment (FDI) of corporations in the developing world has expanded rapidly — climbing from $24 billion in 1990 to $93 billion in 1996.

- By the early 1990s, there were almost 37,000 TNCs in the world. In 1990, the worldwide outflow of FDI, which is a measure of the productive capacity of TNCs, totaled $234 billion. In 1992, the stock of FDI had reached $2 trillion. Parent TNCs have generated some 170,000 foreign affiliates, forty-one percent of which are located in developing countries.

- Just one percent of TNCs own approximately one-half of all FDI stock.

As can logically be expected, many scholars, governments, and interest groups are alarmed at the power TNCs have with respect to various social and environmental issues. Their power seems to exceed that of many nation-states.

Of the world's hundred largest economies, fifty-one are not countries but corporations. Corporations are like feudal domains that evolved into nation-

---

* The assistance of Scott McBride, Esq. in preparing this Note is gratefully acknowledged.

1. The introductory section draws on a variety of sources, including Zillah Eisenstein, *Stop Stomping on the Rest of Us: Retrieving Publicness from the Privatization of the Globe*, 4 IND. J. GLOBAL LEGAL STUD. 59, 65 (1996); KENICHI OHMAE, THE END OF THE NATION STATE 15 (1995); Mark L. Movesian, *The Persistent Nation State and the Foreign Sovereign Immunities Act*, 18 CARDOZO L. REV. 1083, 1109(1996); Hillary F. French, *When Foreign Investors Pay for Development*, WORLDWATCH 8, 9 (May 1997); Robert Kaplan, *Was Democracy Just a Moment?*, ATL. MONTHLY, 55, 71 (Dec. 1997); Robert J. Fowler, *International Environmental Standards for Transnational Corporations*, 25 ENVTL. L. 1 (1995).

2. *See* RICHARD BARNET & JOHN CAVANAGH, GLOBAL DREAMS 423 (1995) ("Ford's economy is larger than Saudi Arabia's and Norway's"); THOMAS DONALDSON, THE ETHICS OF INTERNATIONAL BUSINESS 31 (1992) ("[W]ith the exception of a handful of nation-states, multinationals are alone in possessing the size, technology, and economic reach necessary to influence human affairs on a global basis.").

states; they are nothing less than the vanguard of a new Darwinian organization of politics. Because they are in the forefront of real globalization while the overwhelming majority of the world's inhabitants are still rooted in local terrain, corporations will be free for a few decades to leave behind the social and environmental wreckage they create — abruptly closing a factory here in order to open an unsafe facility with a cheaper work force there.[3]

Whereas the majority of the top 100 nation-states are democracies of one form or another subject to at least some extent to the demands of citizens, TNCs are beholden to shareholders scattered across the globe. These shareholders may not care about, or may be unaware of, illegal or heinous atrocities being committed in other lands — possibly with the involvement or tacit complicity of some TNC managers.[4] After all, the traditional view of the essence of the relationship between corporations and their shareholders is that the former is in the business of maximizing the wealth of the latter. Put bluntly, most investors — with some notable exceptions, like the California State Pension Fund — make share purchase decisions based on expected financial rewards in relation to their risk profile, not based on political or social correctness.

To be sure, in theory TNCs are held responsible to the laws governing the host countries in which they operate. While this might be a substantial deterrent in "developed" countries with a rigorous rule of law, the situation in many developing countries is another matter entirely. "MNCs find developing countries desirable because they provide the most efficient production in today's market."[5] Just as American states lowered environmental standards to attract business and investment in the 1940's, 1950s, and 1960's,[6] developing countries are behaving likewise today to draw in international investment. It is no secret that the standards of these countries often "do not conform with international standards for labor or the environment, or when they do conform, they are not enforced."[7] This stark reality accompanies the global "trend toward deregulation of heavily regulated industries and privatization of state-owned enterprises."[8]

This Note discusses the irresponsible actions of several TNCs and then explains the difficulties and inadequacies of voluntary corporate codes of conduct in the absence of an international enforcement organization. The Note considers the gradual enforcement of customary international law in American federal courts through the Alien Tort Claims Act. In so doing, it reveals the process of how the list of crimes condemned by "the law of nations" has grown. It also takes note of a potentially important argument offered by some scholars that federal courts are not authorized

---

3. Robert Kaplan, *Was Democracy Just a Moment?*, ATLANTIC MONTHLY 55, 71 (Dec. 1997) (emphasis added).

4. *See* Elizabeth Glass Geltman & Andrew E. Skroback, *Environmental Activism and the Ethical Investor*, 22 J. CORP. L. 465, 467 (1997) ("While publicly held corporations are generally required to disclose material, non-public information, they are generally not required to disclose their general environmental philosophy."). The same is true for human rights and labor rights standards.

5. Ariadne K. Sacharoff, Note, *Multinationals in Host Countries: Can They Be Held Liable Under the Alien Tort Claims Act for Human Rights Violations?*, 23 BROOK. J. INT'L L. 927, 929 (1998).

6. *See* DANIEL C. ESTY, GREENING THE GATT 22 (1994) (noting how "states sold themselves as attractive sites for new industrial facilities at least in part because they offered low costs, including lax pollution control requirements...this pattern of interstate competition contributed significantly to the drive for national environmental standards in the United States").

7. Sacharoff, *supra*, at 929.

8. Robert W. Hahn, *Achieving Real Regulatory Reform*, U. CHI. LEGAL F. 143 (1997).

under the Constitution to define what actions constitute violations of customary international law for purposes of the Alien Tort Claims Act.

I. EXAMPLES OF IRRESPONSIBLE TNCS

It would be irresponsible, as well as downright wrong, to lump all TNCs together, to try to paint too broad a picture. They are seldom, if ever, entirely sinful or saintly. Some TNCs have proven to be model business partners in the countries in which they have invested.[9] Others have significantly contributed to the destruction of the environment and the violation of numerous human rights.

Because TNCs often are attracted to developing countries with few regulatory restrictions, the resulting inadequacies in health and safety procedures can prove to be volatile. The best known example of this was the 1984 gas leak at Union Carbide Corporation's gas plant in Bhopal, India. Between 2,000 to 3,000 people were killed, and over 200,000 people were injured.[10]

More recently, a case was filed in United States District Court for the Central District of California, *National Coalition Government of the Union of Burma v. Unocal, Inc.*,[11] in which the plaintiffs alleged that the Unocal Corporation was in a joint venture with the controlling Burmese government and assisted the government in engaging in numerous human rights abuses, including torture and forced labor. The decision handed down by the court merely found subject-matter jurisdiction over the some of the claims, so it has yet to be determined by a finder of fact if any of the allegations are true. Plaintiffs alleged that workers on the project used threats of death to force thousands of Karen, Mon, and Tavoyan villagers in Burma to travel to forced labor camps, clear forest in the pipeline region, and build other infrastructure related to the project. At least one plaintiff claimed that he frequently witnessed physical abuse and brutality against other forced labors, including one worker who was beaten until he vomited blood and was then tied to a stake for 15 hours.

Although there are many more reported cases of irresponsible TNC behavior around the globe,[12] the most often cited example, and perhaps most dramatic, con-

---

9. *See United States International Trade Commission, International Trade and the Role of Labor Standards*, Int'l Econ. Rev., *in* Raj Bhala, International Trade Law: Cases and Materials 1305, 1309 (1996) (stating that "overall, labor conditions in U.S.- invested sectors are similar to or better than those in the rest of the economy").

10. Jodi Berlin Ganz, *Heirs Without Assets and Assets Without Heirs: Recovering and Reclaiming Dormant Swiss Bank Accounts*, 20 Fordham Int'l L.J. 1306 (1997). *See also* Neil A.F. Popovic, *In Pursuit of Environmental Human Rights: Commentary on the Draft Declaration of Principles on Human Rights and the Environment*, 27 Colum. Hum. Rts. L. Rev. 487, 488 (1996)(giving a similar account, although with different numbers of those dead and wounded). It should be noted that injured Indians did file a claim in New York (the state where Union Carbide was incorporated), but jurisdiction was rejected under *"forum non conveniens." See* In re Union Carbide Corp. Gas Plant Disaster at Bhopal, India in December, 1984, 601 F. Supp. 1035 (1985). The court believed that the Indian government had sufficient judicial means to enforce the case, and it would have been extremely difficult and expensive to bring the majority of witnesses and plaintiffs to New York.

11. National Coalition Government of the Union of Burma, *et. al.*, v. UNOCAL, Inc., 1997 U.S. Dist. LEXIS 20975 (C.D. Cal., Oct. 29, 1997).

12. *See, e.g.*, Campaign for Labor Rights, *Disney & McDonald's Linked to $0.06/Hour Sweatshop in Vietnam* (March 1997) <http://www.compugraph.com/clr/alerts/ dis001.html> (reporting that a factory in Vietnam which makes toys for Disney and McDonald's forces workers to work 10 hour days, seven days a week in poorly ventilated factories. In February, 1997, 200 workers fell ill and 3 were hospitalized due to prolonged exposure to a chemical solvent that can cause damage to the liver and kidneys); Campaign for Labor Rights, *Soccer Balls: Inflated with Hot Air?*

cerns the activities of Royal Dutch Shell in Nigeria.[13] In the 1950's Shell Oil and the Nigerian government began a joint venture, Shell Nigeria, to find and extract oil in the Ogoni region of the African nation. To this day, Shell continues to pump over 900,000 barrels of oil a day from the ground and remains an extremely important resource to the economy of the country and the government, which still owns fifty-five percent of the corporation.

Shell has succeeded in both destroying a great deal of the environment in the Ogoni region, as well as violating the human rights of hundreds of persons living there. The water pollution problem is so bad that the area has seen an extremely large increase in incidents of organic diseases, such as cancer. Shell spilled approximately 1.6 million gallons of oil in the Niger Delta region between 1982-1992, an amount so large that it constituted forty percent of all of Shell's oil spill worldwide.

In October 1990, protesters organized peaceful demonstrations against Shell's environmental destruction. Shell requested protection from the Mobil Police Force, and the next day 81 protesters were killed and 495 houses were partially or totally destroyed. As a result of this horrifying slaughter, Ogoni village chiefs created an organization, the Movement of the Survival of the Ogoni People (MOSOP), to call for a protection of Ogoni rights and political autonomy.

MOSOP members began protesting peacefully at oil pumps around the country, inciting Shell to again request police aid. Protesters were attacked, yet again, and 35 people were massacred. This time, witnesses allege that Shell did far more than stand idly by and watch. Instead, the claims are that the corporation aided the government by donating helicopters, boats, and jeeps to the police forces that attacked protesters.

The situation grew even worse when, on 10 November 1995, the leader of MOSOP, Ken Saro-Wiwa, was executed along with eight other MOSOP members after being judged in a hearing that was an obvious farce. Despite a unified cry of outrage from the human rights community around the globe, the Nigerian government claimed it was justified in its actions, and it continues to work side by side with Shell to the present day. "Shell Oil does not face any repercussions for its activities in Nigeria, even though these activities violate international law."[14]

(March 1997) <html> (reporting that despite the signing of a Partnership Agreement with UNICEF and the International Labor Organization in which Nike agreed to address the issue of child labor, it continued, as of February 1997, to use child labor in the manufacture of soccer balls in Pakistan and India); Campaign for Labor Rights, *Nike: Buying Silence?* (February 1998) <http://www.compugraph. com/clr/alerts/nike buying silence.html> (reporting that Nike is well known for its abuse of workers around the globe — including in Vietnam); Rain Forest Action Network, *Ecuador President Freezes Texaco Operations*, (March 1997) <http://www.ran.org/ran /ran_campaigns/amazonia/texaco freeze .html> (reporting that the President of Ecuador has suspended Texaco's toxic oil clean up effort because it has failed to meet agreed-upon standards. In 1992, Texaco spilled at least 16.8 millions of gallons of crude oil in the Ecuadorian Amazon and agreed to a clean-up effort only after a $1.5 billion lawsuit was filed in United States federal district court).

13. The following sources were consulted for this description of Shell's activities in Nigeria: Sacharoff, *supra*, at 951-55; Joshua P. Eaton, *The Nigerian Tragedy, Environmental Regulation of Transnational Corporations, and the Human Rights to a Healthy Environment*, 15 B.U. INT'L L.J. 261, 266-68 (1997); Douglas Cassel, Essay, *Corporate Initiative: A Second Human Rights Revolution?* 19 FORDHAM INT'L L.J. 1963, 1971 (1996); Campaign: Ken Saro Wiwa, *The Ken Saro Wiwa Campaign ($HELL ON EARTH)*, (Feb. 25, 1998) <http://www.gem.co.za/ELA/ken.html>.

14. Sacharoff, *supra*, at 955. A suit has been filed against Shell Oil in the Southern District of New York, but apparently as of 20 March 1998, Shell Oil has not responded to the complaint. *See* Wiwa v. Royal Dutch Petroleum Co., No. 96 Civ. 8386 (S.D.N.Y. Nov. 8, 1996).

II. VOLUNTARY CODES OF CONDUCT

As cautioned above, not all TNCs are irresponsible. In fact, some TNCs actually are working to strengthen human rights and environmental movements in developing countries. Foremost among these MNCs is Reebok International.

Reebok first became heavily involved in the human rights movement in 1988 when the company joined with Amnesty International in sponsoring the "Human Rights Now!" international concert tour. That same year, Reebok created the "Reebok Human Rights Award," which is given out annually to a young person who has contributed to the human rights movement. A cynic can retort that Reebok's actions are motivated by public relations, yet Reebok backs up its proclaimed dedication to human rights with corporate "Human Rights Production Standards."[15]

Reebok's standards are examples of what is more commonly known as a "Voluntary Code of Conduct." Several American TNCs have adopted such codes, including household names like Levi Strauss & Co.,[16] Wal-Mart, Liz Claiborne, JC Penney, Phillips-Van Heusen, Starbucks Coffee, Compaq, and GAP, Inc.[17] Several of these Codes are reproduced later in this Chapter. The truth is, however, that many of these corporations acted only after being targeted by the media or facing a threat public boycott. Was then Edward, First Baron Thurlow and Chancellor of England in the early 1600s, correct when he asked rhetorically, "Did you ever expect a corporation to have a conscience when it has no soul to be damned, and no body to be kicked?[18]

Arguably, what matters even more than the reason for the creation of the Codes is that the Codes remain in place and are prove to be effective. Reebok's standards state that the corporation will enforce human rights in the areas of non-discrimination, working hours/overtime, forced/compulsory labor, fair wages, child labor, freedom of association, and the creation of a safe and healthy work environment.[19] To be

---

15. REEBOK, HUMAN RIGHTS PRODUCTION STANDARDS (on file with Raj Bhala); *See also* About Reebok Human Rights, *Reebok & Human Rights,* (Feb. 25, 1998) <http://www. reebok.com/ humanrights/about.html>.

16. *See* Levi STRAUSS & CO. GLOBAL SOURCING & OPERATING GUIDELINES, THE BUSINESS PARTNER TERMS OF ENGAGEMENT AND THE COUNTRY ASSESSMENT GUIDELINES; Barbara A. Frey, *The Legal and Ethical Responsibilities of Transnational Corporations in the Protection of International Human Rights,* 6 MINN. J. GLOBAL TRADE 153, 179 (1997)("Most notable is the Levi Strauss & Co. policy that commits the company not to do business in countries with pervasive violations of basic human rights.")

17. WAL-MART STORES, INC., STANDARDS FOR VENDORS; Liz Claiborne Worker's Rights, *Liz Claiborne Inc.'s Compliance Practices* and *Work Place Code of Conduct,* (Feb. 18, 1998) <http://www.lizclaiborne.com/conduct.html>; The JCPenney Supplier Legal Compliance Program, *Labor Law Compliance, Foreign Sourcing Issues, Supplier Responsibility for Factory Compliance, Our Investigative Procedures* and *Our Policy for Contract Violations,* (Feb. 18, 1998) <http://www.jcpen ney.com/newhome/content/legalcom.htm# para4.html>; PHILLIPS-VAN HEUSEN, GUIDELINES FOR VENDORS; STARBUCKS COFFEE COMPANY, FRAMEWORK FOR CODE OF CONDUCT, , STARBUCKS FRAMEWORK FOR ACTION (1998-99), and STARBUCK'S ENVIRONMENTAL MISSION; Compaq, *1995-1996 Environmental Report: Environmental Policy,* (Feb. 25, 1998) <http://www.compaq. com/ corporate/ehss/95-96rpt/ep.html>; GAP, INC., CODE OF VENDOR CONDUCT and GAP AND THE ENVIRONMENT. *See also* Cassel, *supra,* at 1969.

18. *Quoted in* William S. Laufer, *Integrity, Diligence and the Limits of Good Corporate Citizenship,* 34 AMERICAN BUSINESS LAW JOURNAL 157 (1996).

19. *See* REEBOK, *supra.* Barbara Frey divides corporate codes of conduct into three categories: "vendor standards regarding forced and child labor; standards in support of civil and political rights; and criteria for investment." Frey, *supra,* at 177. These very sensible distinctions are unimportant for the analysis herein, except to show that TNCs vary in their emphases as regards codes.

sure, some TNCs have standards that are far stronger in addressing environmental issues than labor rights. Nonetheless, Reebok's standards are a good example of the current trend toward implementing ethical principles into a corporate mission statement.

A. Other Voluntary Corporate Code Initiatives

During the 1970's and 1980's, approximately 125 American TNCs signed onto a corporate code policy known as the "*Sullivan Principles*." The *Sullivan Principles* were created in response to the near ubiquitous calls for divestment from South Africa because of apartheid. The signatories, including such TNCs as Exxon, Mobil, and IBM, committed themselves to racially non-discriminatory employment, fair wages well above the minimum cost of living, and the use of their corporate influence to help end apartheid in South Africa. The performance of each "Sullivan TNC" was subject to outside audit.

Unfortunately, the *Sullivan Principles* did not succeed in their objectives. In 1987, the author of the *Principles*, Reverend Sullivan, pronounced the system a failure. Of course, the cynic would state that the *Principles* actually succeeded in the underlying purpose for most of the signatories; namely, the TNCs continued to profit from enterprises in South Africa and simultaneously hold the respect of the international business community.

Other organizations have also tried to create workable codes of conduct for multinationals. They, too, have had limited or no success. (Several of these efforts are discussed in another Chapter of this Casebook.) For example, the United Nations tried unsuccessfully for fifteen years to produce a *Code of Conduct for Transnational Corporations*, eventually abandoning the project.

In 1976, the Organization for Economic Cooperation and Development (OECD) introduced labor standards for TNCs. One year later, the International Labor Organization (ILO) adopted similar codes that focused specifically on worker's rights in employment. Both products still are in existence, but each is critically flawed in one common respect: the OECD labor standards and ILO codes pre-suppose an adversarial relationship between a host country government and a TNC. In those cases in which the government actually condones a TNC's behavior, like (allegedly) in the cases of Unocal and Shell, there is no means to enforce the standards. In other words, what to do when a nasty host country government and TNC collude?

The *MacBride Principles*, named after the late founder of Amnesty International, Sean MacBride, were drafted by a United States-based group of advocates to encourage TNCs to respond to the history of discrimination and strife in Northern Ireland. The *Principles* promote employment procedures free from religious biases, as well as a safe and secure workplace. Although there are eighty publicly traded American firms operating in Northern Ireland, only thirty-two were signed onto the *MacBride Principles* as of February 1995. A good percentage of the support of the *Principles* has come from the sixteen American states and more than forty American cities that have enacted the *Principles* as law. Unfortunately, however, "[t]he *MacBride Principles* are not followed by the corporate community, largely because of the lack of public pressure...[s]hareholder resolutions are the main vehicle for these principles' implementation, and all shareholder resolutions failed."[20]

---

20. Frey, *supra*, at 176.

The Clinton Administration has enacted two voluntary corporate code programs of its own. The *Model Business Principles* were enacted in May 1995 "as a substitute for a human rights- linkage to trade with China."[21] The *Model Business Principles* are entirely voluntary and lack an enforcement mechanism.[22] The United States Department of Commerce is responsible for "implementing" the *Principles*. But, as of March 1996 "the Commerce Department's efforts appear to consist mainly for looking for a place to put an information clearinghouse, and working on nomination procedures for the awards it plans to hand out annually to firms exemplifying the *Model Principles*."[23] Notably, neither human rights groups nor business groups have been very supportive of President Clinton's *Principles*.

The second Clinton Administration program comes from the "No Sweat" initiative that the Department of Labor has been enforcing over the last two years. On 14 April 1997, members of the "Apparel Industry Partnership" agreed to a *Code of Conduct* that would prohibit child labor, worker abuse, harassment, and discrimination.[24] This *Code* also recognizes workers' rights of freedom of association and collective bargaining, sets a cap on mandatory overtime, and promotes a safe and healthy environment. The primary difference between this *Code* and the *Model Business Principles* is that the 18 initial signatories also agreed to the creation of independent external monitors "to conduct reviews of company policies and practices." An internal monitoring system also is to be enforced in each company to ensure the *Code* is enforced both domestically and internationally.

Worthy of note is that the MNCs agreeing to the *Apparel Codes of Conduct* are not subject to external monitoring in countries outside of the United States. Thus, as with all other voluntary code of conduct programs, there is no enforcement mechanism to guarantee that corporations follow their claims to corporate responsibility in developing countries.

B. Enforcement Problems

Clearly, the greatest problem with voluntary programs of corporate responsibility is the lack of adequate enforcement mechanisms. True, some corporations, such as Levi Strauss & Co., have chosen to avoid investment in countries with pervasive human rights violations, guided in part by Levi's own corporate code.[25] Unfortunately, there are many examples of corporations with codes that all but ignore the ethical guidelines contained in them.

Is Nike in this category? On the one hand, Nike has an agreement on corporate conduct which Nike asks sub-contractors to sign. On the other hand, Nike has been accused by many of violating human and labor rights standards around the globe. The answer is not yet clear. Consider Guess?, which puts a label on its apparel saying "100% guaranteed sweatshop free." Yet, Guess? has made the National Labor Committee's list of the nine greediest companies and seems to be notorious for using sweatshop labor.[26] The point is that it is difficult to take voluntary compliance pro-

21. Sacharoff, *supra*, at 933.

22. *See Voluntary "Model Business Principles" Issued by the Clinton Administration May 26, 1995*, DAILY REP. FOR EXECUTIVES (BNA), 1995 DER 104 d103, available in LEXIS, Exec Library, DrExec File.

23. Cassel, *supra*, at 1975.

24. *See President Clinton Announces Apparel Industry Partnership Agreement*, White House Press Release (April 14, 1997).

25. *See* Frey, *supra*, at 187.

26. *See* Campaign for Labor Rights, *Guess? Who's Lying*, (Dec. 10, 1997), <http://www.compugraph.com/clr/alerts/guess_whos_lying.html>.

grams seriously if TNCs themselves raise doubts as to whether they take them seriously. Perhaps, in the end, only an external sanction — which may include the condemnation of retail buyers that results in a serious diminution of sales revenue and market share — can work to police multinational corporate conduct.

III. THE ALIEN TORT CLAIMS ACT

As long as developing country governments continue to participate in or tacitly support human rights violations and environmental destruction, TNCs will have the freedom to behave in a socially irresponsible manner — unless they feel constrained by some other force. What are some of the alternative forces? One is the American judicial system. Through the remarkable Alien Tort Claims Act, injured parties of any nationality can bring suit against TNCs that have violated customary international law. This law helps persuade TNCs to uphold standards that might otherwise be merely words on paper.

The Alien Tort Claims Act was enacted as part of the Judiciary Act of 1789 and is codified at Section 1350 of Title 28 of the United States Code. The Act states simply that:

> The district courts shall have original jurisdiction of any civil action by an alien for a tort only, committed in violation of the law of nations or a treaty of the United States.

For over 150 years, the courts did little to acknowledge the existence of this law. Of course, the obvious reason for giving little force to such a statute was there was neither a need nor desire for the courts of one country to punish representatives of the government of another country over the violation of rights of individuals that were, at least in theory, enforceable under international law. To have such a trial would imply (1) there was sufficient reason to believe there would be some means of enforcing the verdict, (2) there was little possibility of retaliation by the governments whose agents were found to be guilty of violating international law, and (3) international law was enforceable in local courts. Only in the midst of the Cold War, following the creation of the United Nations, did the United States federal courts give force to the ATCA.[27] Some of these cases are excerpted later in this Chapter of the Casebook.

Through these cases, the courts have suggested that what qualifies as customary international law may change over time, especially as an increasing number of international treaties and agreements are signed. However, particularly after the *Filartiga* case excerpted below, to be recognized as an international tort under Section 1350, an alleged violation must be definable, obligatory (rather than hortatory), and universally condemned.

Authors Beth Stevens and Michael Ratner go further. In their text, *International Human Rights Litigation in U.S. Courts*, they identify seven acts that appear to be "universally condemned" under international law, in addition to genocide and war crimes.[28] These are (1) slavery, (2) piracy, (3) violations of safe conducts and the rights of ambassadors, (4) racial discrimination, (5) gender violence and discrimination, (6) terrorism (including hijacking and hostage-taking), and (7) systematic violations of human rights.

---

27. *See* BETH STEPHENS & MICHAEL RATNER, INTERNATIONAL HUMAN RIGHTS LITIGATION IN U.S. COURTS 8 (1996) ("[T]he decades following World War II had seen a tremendous growth in human rights norms, with major new human rights agreements drafted by the United Nations and regional human rights bodies.").

28. *See* STEPHENS, *supra*, at 80-94.

What about environmental harm? This is a new and potentially controversial candidate for inclusion as a "universally condemned" act under customary international law. Several scholars have written on the subject,[29] and the entire study of international environmental law is centered around the various treaties and agreements that exist in this field. American courts have been slow to accept this idea of the right to a healthy environment as a universally accepted human right — but this may be changing. The *Beanal* case, excerpted below, discussed the problem, albeit in what may be *dicta*.

Can a TNC be held liable under the ATCA? The answer is yes. In general, applicable federal common law currently recognizes jurisdiction over private actors, like TNCs, in two situations: (1) cases in which the state is involved (*i.e.*, "color of law," partnerships, joint ventures), and (2) cases in which the host country's government is ineffective in finding a remedy for injured parties. Accordingly, in the first situation, if a TNC aids a host country government in encouraging or condoning genocide, slavery, murder, torture, systematic racial discrimination, prolonged arbitrary detention, or other human rights violations, any injured party can file a claim under ATCA and meet the subject matter jurisdiction requirements. TNCs can be held just as accountable as the government, depending on the violation. Possibly, this also is true in the case of extreme environmental destruction.

As for the second situation, suppose a TNC acts on its own, and the host country cannot provide a sufficient judicial remedy for those injured by the TNC's wrongdoing. Then, American federal courts can find jurisdiction over claims involving a small, distinct list of violations of customary international law. This list has been narrowly interpreted to include piracy, slave trading, hijacking, genocide and human rights violations that can be termed "war crimes." Notably, neither inhuman labor conditions nor environmental degradation would creating standing in federal courts if there was no state involvement.

IV. MODERN FEDERALISM ARGUMENTS

There is little dispute that the Supreme Court in the last few years has delegated a great deal of power to the individual states through the Tenth Amendment.[30] A group of influential scholars argues that customary international law, contrary to the holding in *Filartiga*, is *not* part of the federal common law. They contend courts should not apply customary international law as federal law, unless authorized to do so by the federal political branches. They cite recent Supreme Court decisions to buttress their point and suggest the Court agrees with it.

---

29. *See, e.g.*, Neil A.F. Popovic, *In Pursuit of Environmental Human Rights: Commentary on the Draft Declaration of Principles on Human Rights and the Environment*, 27 COLUM. HUM. RTS. L. REV. 487 (1996); Michelle Leighton Schwartz, *International Legal Protection for Victims of Environmental Abuse*, 18 YALE J. INT'L L. 355 (1993); Mark Allan Gray, *The International Crime of Ecocide*, 26 WISC. INT'L J.L. 215 (1996); Joshua P. Eaton, *The Nigerian Tragedy, Environmental Regulation of Transnational Corporations, and the Human Right to a Healthy Environment*, 15 B.U. INT'L J.L. 261 (1997); Dinah Shelton, *Human Rights, Environmental Rights, and the Right of Environment*, 28 STAN J. INT'L L. 103 (1991).

30. *See, e.g.*, Printz v. United States, 117 S. Ct. 2365 (1997) (striking down provisions in the Brady Handgun Violence Prevention Act that required state and local law enforcement officials to conduct background checks on prospective purchasers of handguns); United States v. Lopez, 514 U.S. 549 (1995) (restricting federal regulation of traditional state powers under the Tenth Amendment); Gregory v. Ashcroft, 501 U.S. 452 (1991) (relying on federalism grounds to narrow the scope of the Age Discrimination and Employment Act as applied to appointed state judges).

These scholars, specifically Professors Jack Goldsmith, Curtis Bradley, and Arthur Weisburd, conclude "the Constitution limits states' roles in a few, specifically-defined foreign affairs contexts."[31] Their conclusion rests on two arguments. First, the Executive and Legislative Branches have been granted a good deal of power over foreign affairs by the Constitution, but nowhere is the Judiciary granted the ability to pre-empt state laws that involve foreign affairs (beyond the abilities already provided in the Constitution). In other words, they argue the framers of the Constitution did not intend to give sweeping powers to the federal courts in the areas of foreign affairs. The second argument is one of statutory construction. Professors Goldsmith, Bradley, and Weisburd believe Congress, in passing the Alien Tort Claims Act, never intended for the Judiciary to define independently certain statutory terms beyond the meaning given to those terms at the time the Act was passed.

In support of this approach to federal common law, Professor Goldsmith offers a detailed historic account of the federal common law, customary international law, and the opinions of the Supreme Court on matters of foreign affairs. Although he believes that the courts are correct in applying customary international law through the Alien Tort Claims Act, he states that the court in *Filartiga* was wrong in its analysis of federal jurisdiction over the "law of nations." The *Filartiga* court decided torture was a violation of the law of nations, claiming that customary international law was part of federal common law. Professor Goldsmith believes that the court had no constitutional mandate to make such a decision, and that any broadening of the definition of "law of nations" must be specifically declared by Congressional action. Following *Filartiga*, Congress passed the Torture Victim Protection Act which covers "torture and extra-judicial killing," but goes no further. Professor Goldsmith states that this is the proper means by which the "law of foreign relations" can be expanded, and points out that the Act narrowly limits the scope of the federal prohibition to only those acts that are done under color of foreign law.

Conclusion

Aside from a few countries, TNCs are the most powerful economic and social forces in the global economy. Sadly, some TNCs have abused this power and caused considerable harm to individuals, communities, and the environment. To be sure, some TNCs have adopted voluntary corporate codes to help self-regulate irresponsible business decisions. But, such measures often have been shown to be unpredictable and unreliable indicators of actual corporate behavior.

The ATCA seems to be a more effective tool to require TNCs to abide by certain human rights standards not originally covered by customary international law. However, if Professor Goldsmith and like-minded scholars are correct, the Supreme Court may yet rule that American federal courts do not have the power to interpret customary international law to include and govern any bad acts except those (1) recognized by the common law and Constitution in 1789, and (2) that are specifically mandated by Congress through statutes.

QUESTIONS

1.   A multinational corporation, Biswing, Inc., invests in the small, African country of Northern African Republic (NAR). Biswing manufactures shoes and re-

---

31. Curtis A. Bradley & Jack L. Goldsmith, III, *The Current Illegitimacy of International Human Rights Litigation*. 66 FORDHAM L. REV. 319, 350 (1997) (referring to the list mentioned in Article I, Section 10 of the Constitution).

quires a lot of manual labor to guarantee that all of its orders are filled every month. The NAR government is very pleased that Biswing is in the country and is investing there, because NAR is one of the poorest countries in the world — landlocked and very underdeveloped. Biswing brings some much needed capital into the country and often gets away with whatever it desires. Considering the following scenarios:

1st: One day, Biswing accidentally has a chemical leak from the tanning process of the shoes. The tanning fluid is extremely toxic, and flows into the ground water and nearby lake. Not even a week has passed when villagers living within a mile radius of the plant start getting very sick. By the end of the month, 546 people have died — 300 of these are children. The people cry for justice, but the government stalls the judicial process. Four years later, two villagers who have moved to New York file a complaint in U.S. federal court. Assuming Biswing is incorporated in New York (*i.e.*, *in personam* jurisdiction exists), what is the result?

2nd: The NAR government asks Biswing to assist it in getting a couple of Biswing's employees to talk. Biswing complies and locks the three employees in a room in the basement of the plant for several days. The employees get free, flee to America, and file a claim in New York. Result?

3rd: Biswing decides that costs are too high and begins to hire school- age children. A few of those children fly to New York and file a complaint under ATCA. What is the result if the NAR government openly approved of the children working and even assisted Biswing in finding children? What is the result if Biswing did this without state assistance?

4th: A war breaks out in NAR and Biswing openly sides with the current government. Biswing hires thugs to break into rebel headquarters and murders dozens of families. One little girl escapes and, with the assistance of American missionaries, lands in New York and files her complaint. Result?

5th: Professor Goldsmith's argument, discussed in the Note above, is correct and the Supreme Court rules that federal courts have been far too liberal in broadening of customary international law. Biswing breathes a big sigh of relief and at the next meeting of the Board of Directors, the CEO says "O.K. Boys, we can do any damn thing we want!" He pulls out the cigars and asks for the President of NAR to come into the room. The two start laughing and plotting their next dastardly deed. Within three months, NAR is known as the slave-trading capital of Africa, and Biswing's profits are soaring thanks to the cheapest workforce in the world. Within a year, Biswing is pulling in the profits from various terrorists that it has paid to destroy competitor firms in other African countries. Within two years, Biswing employees have successfully hijacked the majority of trucks being used all around the African continent by competitor shoe manufacturers. Life is good for Biswing. Several injured parties fly to New York and file complaints. Result?

2.   Evaluate the following as a possible *Model Mandatory Minimum Corporate Code of Conduct* ("*Model Code*") for all American multinational corporations.

A multinational corporation, meaning a corporation incorporated in any state of the United States of America with a branch or subsidiary (but not merely a representative office) in another country, will be held in violation of customary international law, and therefore subject to penalty under U.S. federal law, if said corporation is found to violate any of the following principles in a country other than the United States of America:

1. No multinational corporation will practice, encourage, or condone systematic racial discrimination.

2. All multinational corporations will respect the environment of host countries, regulate pollution controls effectively, and commit themselves to comply to all of the environmental laws of host countries.

3. No multinational corporation will practice, encourage, or condone slavery, slave trade, forced or other compulsory labor.

4. No multinational corporation will practice, encourage, or condone prolonged arbitrary detention or the forced disappearance of individuals.

5. No multinational corporation will practice, encourage, or condone genocide, war crimes, or the murder of individuals.

6. No multinational corporation will practice, encourage, or condone the usage of torture or the infliction of cruel, inhuman or degrading treatment upon individuals.

7. All multinational corporations will respect the right of association and the right to organize and bargain collectively. All multinational corporations will seek to assure that no employee is penalized because of his or her non-violent exercise of his right to associate, organize and bargain collectively.

8. All multinational corporations will provide a safe and healthy workplace, and will not expose employees to hazardous conditions. All multinational corporations involved in the manufacture of goods must require that business partners, including sub-contractors, allow the corporation full knowledge of the production facilities used.

All multinational corporations would be required to reasonably enforce the standards listed above. Should a violation of the *Code* be discovered, a multinational corporation would be obligated to find appropriate means to inform shareholders and the public of actions undertaken to correct the violation. A multinational corporation would be held liable under a civil penalty of customary international law, if the alleged violation occurred solely under the guidance of the corporation or while the corporation was acting under color of law, in a joint venture, or in a partnership with violating public officials.

B. What Are the Linkages?

William H. Meyer, Human Rights and MNCs: Theory Versus Quantitative Analysis

18 Human Rights Quarterly 368, 375-82, 386-94, 396-97 (1996)

. . . .

III. THEORIES OF HUMAN RIGHTS AND DEVELOPMENT

Two schools of thought are readily identifiable when it comes to theories of MNCs, development, and rights in the third world. One view is generally pro-MNC.

Highlighting the advantages that multinationals provide for developing countries, it may be termed the "engines of development" school. The more critical or anti-MNC view stresses the negative impact of multinationals on developing nations. This theory may be termed the "Hymer thesis," because it was heavily influenced during its early development by the work of economist Stephen Hymer. Central elements of the Hymer thesis are congruent with, at times almost indistinguishable from, those of dependency theorists.[1] While both views, pro-MNC and anti-MNC, were developed to identify the economic impact of multinationals, and while theorists on both sides rarely refer to human rights as such, their implications for human rights in the third world are easily derived. Competing policy proposals also support each view.

A. The Engines of Development Theory

The pro-MNC view holds that multinationals operating in the third world directly promote economic and social rights, and indirectly support civil and political rights. If there is a positive linkage between economic development and human rights,[2] then to the extent that multinationals promote development, they must also enhance human rights. Kathleen Pritchard singles out socioeconomic rights, such as the rights to unemployment protection and social security, as those rights most likely to be promoted by development. These rights "are expected to depend on the level of economic development."[3] Under this theory, MNCs that promote development by creating jobs, by bringing in new capital and new technology, and by providing employee benefits such as health care necessarily would be promoting economic and social rights.

The possible connection between MNCs and civil or political rights is much less direct. Early theories of development advocated infusions of foreign investment and foreign business into developing countries as a way to promote the expansion of a politically stable, urban middle class. The new middle class would in turn enhance stability and political tolerance in the larger society.[4] Hence, civil and political freedoms (for example, democracy) would expand as third world nations modernized.

After World War II, U.S. foreign policies on aid and investment were based in part on the logic that MNCs are engines for third world development. The Alliance for Progress of the 1960s, the Reagan-Bush Caribbean Basin Initiative, the Baker Plan, the Brady Plan, President Reagan's bilateral investment treaties, and NAFTA all included provisions to open the third world to greater U.S. investment and a larger MNC presence. Washington often has proposed an open environment for direct foreign investment by MNCs as a tool to expand development, increase welfare, and promote democracy in the third world, all at the same time.[5]

---

1. *See, e.g.*, Samir Amin, *Toward an Alternative Strategy for Auto-centered Development*, in TRANSNATIONAL CORPORATIONS AND WORLD ORDER 404 (George Modelski ed., 1979); FERNANDO HENRIQUE CARDOSO & ENZO FALETTO, DEPENDENCY AND DEVELOPMENT IN LATIN AMERICA (1971); Osvaldo Sunkel, *Big Business and "Dependencia,"* in TRANSNATIONAL CORPORATIONS AND WORLD ORDER, *supra*, at 216. [These sources discuss, *inter alia*, dependency theory.]

[For convenience, a few of the footnotes in this excerpt have been omitted, and some of the *supra* references in the footnotes that are reprinted have been altered slightly.]

2. *See* Kathleen Pritchard, *Human Rights and Development: Theory and Data*, in HUMAN RIGHTS AND DEVELOPMENT 329 (David Forsythe ed. 1989).

3. *Id.*

4. DANIEL LERNER, THE PASSING OF TRADITIONAL SOCIETY: MODERNIZING THE MIDDLE EAST (1964). (The politically stable middle class represents the political side of Lerner's "cognitive flexibility" created by modernization.)

5. Office of Public Communication, United States Department of State, *Caribbean Basin Initiative*, GIST, Apr. 1990.

B. The Hymer Thesis

A second view holds that MNCs directly contribute to violations of human rights in developing countries. The most carefully elaborated theoretical support for this position can be found in the work of economist Stephen Hymer.[6] Although Hymer does not use the language of human rights, his work on the organizational structure of multinational corporations provides a strong theoretical grounding for this second view.

Hymer begins with two laws of economic development: the law of increasing size and the law of uneven development. In an often-quoted passage, Hymer describes the first law:

> Since the beginning of the Industrial Revolution, there has been a tendency for the representative firm to increase in size from the workshop to the *factory* to the *national corporation* to the *multi-divisional corporation* to the *multinational corporation*.[7]

Hymer predicted that multi-nationalization would increase greatly in the 1980s. He was correct. Hymer also argues that the first law leads directly to the second law, entailing "the tendency of the system to produce poverty as well as wealth, underdevelopment as well as development."[8] This is due to the very structure of the MNC itself.

Drawing on the work of Alfred Chandler and Fritz Redlich, Hymer identifies three levels of MNC organization.[9] Level III, the lowest level of the MNC, is concerned with day-to-day operations. Level II coordinates managers at Level III. Level I, top management, sets goals and planning for the entire firm, "strategy rather than tactics." This is the level at which one would find French's CID Structures. Hymer offers the United States, specifically New York City, as an example of a Level I location. Furthermore, location theory

> suggests that Level III activities would spread themselves over the globe according to the pull of manpower, markets and raw materials....Level II activities...tend to concentrate in large cities [near Level III]....Level I activities, the general offices, tend to be even more concentrated than Level II activities, for they must be located close to the capital market, the media, and the government.[10]

The organizational structure of MNCs allegedly creates uneven or dual development. The explanation that the ultimate source of this pattern is to be found within the very structure of the MNC itself is Hymer's key contribution to theories of dual development. "It is not technology which creates inequality; rather it is *organization*...."[11] Because "specialization by nationality can be expected within the multinational corporation hierarchy,"[12] it creates "a division of labor based on nationality" at the global level.[13] James Caporaso's work would be a more recent example of

---

6. Stephen Hymer, *The Multinational Corporation and the Law of Uneven Development*, in TRANSNATIONAL CORPORATIONS AND WORLD ORDER, *supra*, at 386.

7. *Id*. at 386.

8. *Id*. at 387.

9. *Id*. at 393 (citing Alfred D. Chandler & Fritz Redlich, *Recent Developments in American Business Administration and Their Conceptualization*, BUS. HIST. REV., Spr. 1961, at 103).

10. *Id*. at 393-94.

11. *Id*. at 395.

12. *Id*. at 396.

13. *Id*.

research that reveals the international structures of corporate/capitalist divisions of labor.[14]

In regard to an international pattern of dual development, Hymer's work on MNCs is consistent with dependency theory. Using the dependency theory categories of center and periphery, one would say that Level III is in the rural periphery of third world nations; Level II is in the urban center of these peripheral third world nations; and Level I is located in the industrialized centers of the West.

Hymer sees in this pattern of dual development a system of international domination by MNCs that leads to a deterioration of human rights in both the civil-political and the socioeconomic spheres. Hymer sees the masses of the third world, amounting to roughly two-thirds of the third world's population, as the group paying the greatest cost to maintain the system, while reaping the fewest benefits. In order to perpetuate their system of domination, multinationals "must keep the excluded two-thirds of the population under control,"[15] which it may do via "family planning or counterinsurgency."[16] U.S. foreign policy, at times, has been built around such counterinsurgency programs in the third world. The Office of Public Safety and the International Police Academy would be only two of the many relevant examples. These programs provided the means of repression used by many Latin American and Asian clients of the United States to violate the human rights of oppressed populations.[17]

In sum, if Hymer is correct, the internal organizational structure of MNCs creates dual development. Dual development creates the need to "control" the masses. In turn, instruments of control can entail repression and curtailment or denials of civil and political rights for the populations of developing countries.

Theorists and policymakers sympathetic to Hymer's view are also skeptical of the alleged socioeconomic benefits for developing countries from MNC investment. They would contest claims from the engines of development school that MNCs promote economic and social rights by creating jobs, providing capital, and importing technology. Empirical studies of many developing countries, especially those in Latin America, have shown that attracting MNCs has, in some instances: eliminated more jobs than they create;[18] absorbed local capital without bringing in external funds, thus harming local entrepreneurs;[19] and provided technology inappropriate to third world needs, hence once again doing more harm than good.[20] If MNCs do more harm than good, then they do not expand socioeconomic rights; instead, they diminish welfare in these areas.

Noam Chomsky, Edward S. Herman, and others have further argued that U.S. foreign aid can produce essentially the same results.[21] By contributing to repressive

---

14. James A. Caporaso, A Changing International Division of Labor (1987).

15. Hymer, *supra*, at 400.

16. *Id.*

17. Lars Schoultz, Human Rights and United States Policy Toward Latin American 168-210 (1981).

18. Ronald Muller, *Poverty is the Product, in* Transnational Corporations and World Order, *supra*, at 245.

19. Joan Edelman Spero, The Politics of International Economic Relations (1990).

20. Robert S. Walters & David H. Blake, The Politics of Global Economic Relations 170 (4th ed. 1992).

21. Noam Chomsky, The Culture of Terrorism (1988); Noam Chomsky, The Political Economy of Human Rights (1979); Noam Chomsky & Edward S. Herman, The Washington Connection and the Third World Fascism (1979).

elements in both the public and private sectors, foreign aid and foreign corporations allegedly create a business climate and a political order that are more conducive to their interests. They are "investing in repression."

Hymer's alternative strategy for third world development is based on policies that move away from MNCs toward a system of regional economic integration. These policy preferences are echoed by the South Commission, chaired by Julius Nyerere, which in its final report favors regional integration and new controls over MNCs through regulation of foreign investment.[22] Theorists and policymakers who advocate "dependency reversal" also tend to caution developing countries against reliance on MNCs in their pursuit of economic development.[23]

C. Testable Hypotheses

These two theoretical views on MNCs and human rights in developing nations lead to a set of empirically testable hypotheses. First, the engines of development school would suggest that MNCs promote human rights, especially socioeconomic rights. Second, the Hymer thesis implies that MNCs in the third world create situations that lead to lower levels of human rights, especially violations of civil and political rights. Third, the null hypothesis must also be kept in mind. It is possible that *both* schools of thought are wrong. MNCs may have *no* discernible relation to human rights in developing countries.

The remainder of this paper presents tests to subject these theories to quantitative evaluations. A series of tests seems to be called for, given the numerous ways in which variables like human rights or MNCs could be transformed into measurable components of operational models. This study seeks a best-case test[24] of the two theories on human rights and development. However, before turning to various types of quantitative human rights indicators and alternate methods for measuring MNC activities, it is necessary first to ask a prior question: Is quantitative study of human rights (in any form) a legitimate scientific enterprise?

IV. QUANTITATIVE STUDIES OF HUMAN RIGHTS

A. Is Quantification Justifiable?

Quantitative study of human rights is especially problematic. Given the nature and importance of this area, quantification often has been criticized as inappropriate. To quantify is necessarily to depersonalize and even dehumanize a topic's content. The supreme value of human rights requires that one always keeps in mind the specific human costs in terms of lives, pain, and suffering that violations of rights entail.[25] Richard P. Claude and Thomas B. Jabine, editors of a special issue of the *Human Rights Quarterly* devoted to quantitative studies, stressed this point when they said that the "essential nature of human rights is qualitative, not quantitative."[26]

---

22. THE SOUTH COMMISSION, THE CHALLENGE TO THE SOUTH 208, 233 (1990); *see also* WALTERS & BLAKE, *supra*, at 193-94.

23. CHARLES DORAN ET AL., NORTH-SOUTH RELATIONS: STUDIES IN DEPENDENCY REVERSAL (1983).

24. A best-case test is one that would most fairly and clearly evaluate claim of the basis of its own arguments. I want to conduct a series of tests that will produce results directly relevant to the empirical claims imbedded in the theories outlined in this paper.

25. Richard P. Claude & Thomas B. Jabine, *Editors' Introduction, Symposium: Statistical Issues in the Field of Human Right*s, 8 HUM. RTS. Q. 551 (1986).

26. *Id.* at 553.

They hasten to add, however, that "it now seems clear that although measurement might not represent the central feature, it must play a role in studying, assessing, and planning for human rights."[27]

Available quantitative data on human rights, while necessary for theoretical and policy reasons, must also be viewed with skepticism given the special problems of reliability and validity for these measures. The data are incomplete and "soft." For example, quantitative numbers on violations of integrity of the person (for example, torture) are usually not released by the governments that are the most egregious violators. There are also questions about political bias among human rights groups that rank nations according to their human rights records.[28] Problems unique to particular variables will be addressed as those variables are introduced into the tests discussed below.

According to Harry Scoble and Laurie Wiseberg, no single adequate measure or scale of human rights has been developed yet. They believe that academic research, therefore, has a "vital role" to play in establishing new measures.[29] Robert J. Goldstein argues that because there is no single universally accepted concept of human rights, it is important to develop many different indicators for the many different types of rights.[30] The tests elaborated in the present study were developed with these considerations in mind.

Claude and Jabine, Goldstein, and Pritchard also made the case that quantitative studies advance theoretical understandings while supporting the policies needed to protect human rights. They lament the fact that: "The search has barely begun for theory supported by data."[31] Goldstein believes that quantification has the potential to: reduce subjectivity; enhance testing, replication, and comparative methodologies; and disprove commonly held assumptions about human rights.[32] Pritchard argues that "quantification is advisable," because human rights is such an "emotional" term.[33] The science of human rights research, however, must remain closely tied to relevant policy issues. Claude and Jabine go on to argue that good quantitative data enhance the likelihood that human rights will be supported through condemnation of violators and through changes in policy to guarantee rights more strongly.[34]

According to these authors, "every technique that can better inform judgement is now needed.... In short, there is an important place for measurement and refined statistical approaches to the subject of internationally defined human rights."[35] Goldstein closes by adding a cautionary note: "What must be avoided is a dependence on

---

27. *Id.* (emphasis added); *see also* HUMAN RIGHTS AND STATISTICS (Richard P. Claude & Thomas B. Jabine eds., 1992).

28. *See, e.g.,* FREEDOM IN THE WORLD: POLITICAL RIGHTS AND CIVIL LIBERTIES (annual surveys produced by Freedom House in New York).

29. Claude & Jabine, *supra*, at 558 (summarizing Harry M. Scoble & Laurie S. Wiseberg, *Problems of Comparative Research on Human Rights*, *in* GLOBAL HUMAN RIGHTS: PUBLIC POLICIES, COMPARATIVE MEASURES, AND NGO STRATEGIES 147, 167 (Ved P. Nanda *et al.* eds., 1981)).

30. Robert Justin Goldstein, *The Limitations of Using Quantitative Data in Studying Human Rights Abuses*, 8 HUM. RTS. Q. 607, 610 (1986).

31. Claude & Jabine, *supra*, at 554-55.

32. Goldstein, *supra*, at 607-08.

33. Pritchard, *supra*, at 331.

34. Claude & Jabine, *supra*, at 556.

35. *Id.* at 554.

Figure 1
Specification of Prior Model

HI:	HR	=	f(development)
H2a:	C/P	=	f(GNP)
H2b:	PQLI	=	f(GNP)
	HR	=	human rights
	C/P	=	rankings of civil liberties and political rights by Freedom House
	GNP	=	gross national product per capita
	PQLI	=	physical quality of life index from the Overseas Development Council

statistics *alone* in an area such as human rights.... What is needed is a combination: statistical information where it is meaningful and reliable, non-statistical information where it is meaningful and reliable, and judgement too."[36]

. . . .

C. Empirical Models

The bulk of prior quantitative studies posited rights as a function of development. These studies used the Freedom House rankings of civil liberties and political rights and the PQLI as benchmarks for "rights," and GNP per capita as the benchmark for development. Figure 1 displays simple specifications of these models.

Hypotheses H1 states that human rights are a function of development. Hypotheses H2a and H2b give form to development as GNP. H2a uses civil-political rankings as benchmarks for civil and political rights. H2b uses the PQLI as an indicator for socioeconomic rights.[37] As noted above, additional variables such as government spending and cultural characteristics were factored into some of the prior models, but these have been omitted from Figure 1.

Figure 2 provides an initial specification of the MNC model. Hypothesis H3 in Figure 2 specifies human rights as a function of development and multinational corporations. Hypothesis H4 uses direct foreign investment (DFI) as a means to quantify MNC presence in developing nations. DFI is the most valid and reliable measure of MNC operations in developing countries. To know where MNCs locate, one must follow a trail of money.

MNCs find their entry into developing countries via investment. DFI is used to establish new plants and operational facilities, to buy into existing plants and operations, or to form joint ventures with local corporations and governments. For Hymer, MNCs and DFI are virtually synonymous. When listing terms used to describe "the beast," he lists "multinational corporations" and "foreign investment" (among oth-

---

36. Goldstein, *supra*, at 626-27.
37. Civil-political (C/P) rights are sometimes also termed first generation rights. Economic and social (or socioeconomic) are sometimes also termed second generation rights.

Figure 2
Specification of the MNC Model

H3:	HR	=	f(development + multinationals)
H4:	HR	=	f(GNP + DFI)
H5a:	C/P	=	f(GNP + DFI)
H5b:	PQLI	=	f(GNP + DFI)
	DFI	=	direct foreign investment

ers) as equivalent terms.[38] DFI as measured in this study refers only to foreign investment by U.S. firms.[39] US investment is by far the most important individual measure of DFI. U.S. multinationals account for as much as 50 percent of total foreign investment in the third world.[40]

Hypotheses H5a and H5b measure human rights through the civil-political indices from Freedom House, and through the PQLI index of socioeconomic rights. Because prior quantitative studies used these same indices, the present study can replicate and verify those prior works, thereby advancing cumulation in quantitative human rights research.

Freedom House's annual surveys include rankings for each nation on seven-point scales of civil liberties and political freedoms. (The present study inverts the original scale, so that a higher score on the Freedom House scale indicates a higher level of human rights.) Critiques of Freedom House's methodology have focused on the alleged "definitional weaknesses . . . vagueness and ambiguity" said to be inherent in any such "impressionistic" approach to rating human rights within nations.[41] Critics also argue that the Freedom House data are "too narrow to provide a framework for general human rights assessment."[42] However, "even [these same] critics view the [Freedom House] data as providing useful quantitative information regarding civil and political rights conditions over a relatively large sample."[43] John McCamant, despite some criticism, notes that the work by Freedom House is "the only attempt so far to produce an overall measure of a country's performance on civil and political rights."[44] Jorge Dominguez, despite reservations, terms the Freedom House rankings as "useful judgements" that "are needed for particular kinds of political assessment."[45] Finally, McCamant endorses the Freedom House data to the extent that the

38. Hymer, *supra*, at 388.

39. Data for total foreign investment in third world nations (US DFI plus non-US DFI) are not generally available. U.S. foreign investment by country serves as the most accurate available indicator of total DFI. US DFI is the single largest source of total DFI.

40. Sheila Page, *Developing Country Attitudes Toward Foreign Investment, in* DEVELOPING WITH FOREIGN INVESTMENT 28 (Vincent Cable & Bishnodat Persaude eds., 1987).

41. John F. McCamant, *A Critique of Present Measures of 'Human Rights Development' and an Alternative, in* GLOBAL HUMAN RIGHTS: PUBLIC POLICIES, COMPARATIVE MEASURES, AND NGO STRATEGIES 130 (Ved P. Nanda *et al.* eds., 1981).

42. JORGE I. DOMINGUEZ, ENHANCING GLOBAL HUMAN RIGHTS 32 (1979).

43. Pritchard, *supra*, at 331.

44. McCamant, *supra*, at 130.

45. DOMINGUEZ, *supra*, at 31-32.

Figure 3
Final Specification of the MNC Model

	H6:	CL	= GNP + DFI + Aid + Debt
H7:	PR	=	GNP + DFI + Aid + Debt
H8:	ILLIT	=	GNP + DFI + Aid + Debt
H9:	INFMOR	=	GNP + DFI + Aid + Debt
H10:	LIFEXP	=	GNP + DFI + Aid + Debt
	Aid	=	U.S. developmental aid
	Debt	=	total foreign debt
	CL	=	civil liberties ranked by Freedom House
	PR	=	political rights ranked by Freedom House
	ILLIT	=	illiteracy rate of adult population
	INFMOR	=	infant mortality per 1000 live births
	LIFEXP	=	life expectancy at age one

"scoring does not have any obvious geographical or ideological bias."[46] Poe and Tate also provide a detailed defense for use of Freedom House data.[47]

Of course, things other than MNCs and development could help determine levels of human rights in developing countries. Figure 3 introduces the final specifications of the MNC model, which include U.S. economic aid and total foreign public debt as additional independent variables. A large body of critical literature argues that U.S. foreign aid often leads to violations of human rights in the third world.[48] A more recent school of thought holds that the third world debt crisis is a source of rights.

violations. Debt burdens force developing countries to accept austerity measures and structural adjustments if they want to qualify for loans from the International Monetary Fund or the World Bank. Critics see the concomitant reductions in spending on welfare programs as the essential equivalent of curtailing economic and social rights. Furthermore, as popular opposition to austerity erupts, the governments of affected nations turn to repression and violations of civil-political rights to restore order.[49]

Figure 3 breaks down the Freedom House rankings into political rights versus civil liberties. It also disaggregates the PQLI into its constituent parts: infant mortality, literacy rates, and life expectancy at age one. Proliferating these numerous speci-

---

46. McCamant, *supra*, at 132.

47. Steven C. Poe & Neal Tate, *Repression of Human Rights to Personal Integrity in the 1980s: A Global Analysis*, 88 AM. POL. SCI. REV. 853, 857 (1994). While there is an almost endless debate in the prior literature over the validity and reliability of indices of rights such as that published by Freedom House and others, I choose not to involve myself in that debate for the purposes of this study. Beyond the reasons listed above, use of indicators such as the PQLI and Freedom House rankings allow for replication and cumulation of quantitative research on human rights.

48. CHOMSKY & HERMAN, *supra*.

49. *See* Jeffrey Sachs, *Making the Brady Plan Work*, 68 FOREIGN AFF. 87, 91-92 (1989); *see also* Sigrun I. Skogly, *Structural Adjustment and Development: Human Rights — An Agenda for Change*, 15 HUM. RTS. Q. 751 (1993); Sigrun I. Skogly, *Human Rights and Economic Efficiency: The Relationship between Social Cost of Adjustment and Human Rights Protection*, in HUMAN RIGHTS IN DEVELOPING COUNTRIES YEARBOOK 1994, at 43 (Peter Baehr *et al.* eds., 1994).

fications of both dependent and independent variables will allow for a series of tests that can evaluate Hypothesis H4 most fairly and most accurately.[50] Controlling for other possible determining variables also helps to ensure that the study does not stipulate spurious relationships among rights, development, and investment.

DFI itself can be divided into alternative indicators: net income versus number of employees. While used in the tests below, these alternate indicators have been left out of Figure 3 for the sake of simplicity and brevity.

Keep in mind also the null hypothesis (HO); it is a logical possibility that DFI is *unrelated* to human rights in developing nations.

This study tests the MNC model over time. Cross-national data on developing countries were drawn from two time periods.[51] The first tests look at the MNC model for the years from 1983 (for the independent variables) to 1985 (for the dependent variables). A second set of tests looks at the same model for the years from 1987 (independent variables) to 1990 (dependent variables).[52] The study assumes a time lag of roughly two to three years between the determinants and the levels of human rights. There is no discussion in the prior literature regarding how long it takes for aid, debt, GNP, or investment to impact upon rights in developing countries.[53]

---

50. *See* CAPORASO, *supra.*

51. Nations in the samples: 1985 sample (N = 52); Algeria, Argentina, Bangladesh, Bolivia, Brazil, Burundi, Chad, Chile, Colombia, Costa Rica, Dominican Republic, Ecuador, El Salvador, Egypt, Ghana, Guatemala, Haiti, Honduras, India, Indonesia, Jamaica, Jordan, Kenya, Liberia, Malawi, Malaysia, Mauritania, Mexico, Morocco, Nicaragua, Niger, Nigeria, Pakistan, Panama, Paraguay, Peru, Rwanda, Senegal, Sierra Leone, Singapore, Somalia, Sudan, Syria, Thailand, Tunisia, Turkey, Uganda, Uruguay, Venezuela, Zaire, Zambia, Zimbabwe.

1990 sample (N = 39): Argentina, Bangladesh, Bolivia, Brazil, Chile, Colombia, Costa Rica, Dominican Republic, Ecuador, El Salvador, Egypt, Ghana, Guatemala, Honduras, India, Indonesia, Jamaica, Kenya, Malaysia, Mexico, Morocco, Nicaragua, Nigeria, Pakistan, Panama, Paraguay, Peru, Singapore, Somalia, Sudan, Syria, Thailand, Tunisia, Turkey, Uruguay, Venezuela, Zaire, Zambia, Zimbabwe.

These samples contain developing nations from all regions of the third world. They also represent slightly less than half of all developing countries. Problems with availability of data preclude taking a random sample that has sufficient size. Data collection began by gathering information on all eighty-eight developing countries for which Freedom House, the Commerce Department, the World Bank, and AID publish data (see sources listed *infra*, note 116). I sought to make the study as inclusive as possible. I performed listwise deletion then eliminated cases with missing data for any of the variables. There are sound statistical reasons for preferring listwise deletion. Furthermore, I chose not to substitute alternative indicators for missing data as has been commonly done in prior studies using multiple regression (see for example, Poe & Tate, *supra*). This process left fifty-two nations for the 1985 data and thirty-nine nations for the 1990 data. While not a random sample, this group or developing countries is large enough and diverse enough to allow for robust testing. Conclusions drawn from these samples therefore apply to the third world as a whole.

52. The sampling for this study was done during 1992-1993, at which time the most recent available data for the combined indicators (dependent variables) was the year 1990. I also went back five years to 1985 data (dependent variables) for a second sample. Comparing results from the 1985 and 1990 data allow us to see if the trends in the data hold up over time. An obvious next step to follow up on this study would be to analyze data for 1995, when they become available. Such a follow-up study would also indicate whether the prior relationships among DFI, rights, GNP, aid, and debt identified here have changed during the post Cold War era.

53. A lag of at least two years would seem necessary to allow the effects of DFI to find their way into a nation's political economy. A lag of more than three years runs the risk of compounding the effects of DFI with too many other extraneous factors (changes in government, etc.).

Figure 4
Equations

H6/E1:	CL	=	$a + B_1 GNP + B_2 DFI + B_3 Aid + B_4 Debt$
H7/E2:	PR	=	$a + B_1 GNP + B_2 DFI + B_3 Aid + B_4 Debt$
H8/E3:	ILLIT	=	$a + B_1 GNP + B_2 DFI + B_3 Aid + B_4 Debt$
H9/E4:	INFMOR	=	$a + B_1 GNP + B_2 DFI + B_3 Aid + B_4 Debt$
H10/E5:	LIFEXP	=	$a + B_1 GNP + B_2 DFI + B_3 Aid + B_4 Debt$
	a	=	intercept
	$B_?$	=	beta (standarized coefficients)

Prior quantitative study of human rights has been limited primarily to correlation analysis. While useful, correlations alone reveal relatively little about the interactions between variables. Bivariate correlations are unable to control for additional factors and, therefore, can lead to spurious conclusions. David L. Banks and Poe and Tate argue that empirical research on rights must move to ordinary least squares methods.[54]

The present study employs multivariate regression,[55] which has the advantage of separating the influence of one determining factor from that of other determinants. Correlation coefficients alone tend to "inflate the importance" of any single independent variable.[56] Multiple regression, on the other hand, allows us to separate out the impact of one independent variable, while holding other determinants constant.

Figure 4 indicates how Equation 1 though Equation 5 further elaborate Hypotheses H6 through H10, the models to be tested. These equations provide the parameters necessary for multiple regression.

V. CONCLUSIONS FROM THE EMPIRICAL DATA

Table 1 contains the parameter estimates for Equation 1 (1985 and 1990) and the parameter estimates for Equation 2 (also 1985 and 1990).[57] Rankings of civil liberties and political rights are compared to levels of GNP per capita, direct foreign investment, U.S. economic aid, and foreign debt.[58] All tables report the standardized

---

54. Poe & Tate, *supra*; David L. Banks, *The Analysis of Human Rights Data Over Time*, 8 Hum. Rts. Q. 654 (1986).

55. The terms multivariate regression and multiple regression are synonymous with multivariate analysis; *see supra*.

56. Michael S. Lewis-Beck, Applied Regression: An Introduction 25 (1980).

57. Parameter estimates are the numerical values given to slope estimates in multiple regression.

58. Data on civil liberties and political rights are from Raymond D. Gastil, Freedom in the World: Political Rights and Civil Liberties 1984-85, at 22-23 (1985) and Freedom House Survey Team, Freedom on the World: Political Rights and Civil Liberties 1990-91, at 454-56 (1991). Data on GNP are measured per capita; Gastil, *supra*, at 14-19; Freedom House Survey Team, *supra*, at 457-59. All data on foreign investment are measured in U.S. dollars or total employees and are from the Bureau of Economic Analysis, U.S. Department of Commerce, U.S. Direct Investment Abroad (1983 and 1987). Data on total public debt, illiteracy, infant mortality, and life expectancy are from World Bank, World Development Reports (1983, 1985, 1987, 1990). Data on total foreign aid in U.S. dollars are from the Agency for International Development, Development and the National Interest (1989).

Table 1
Civil and Political Rights

Indicator	GNP	DFI [measure]	Aid	Debt	R²(adj.)
CL 1985	.27	-.37* [empl.]	.08	.41	.22 (.14)
(N=52)	(1.89)	(2.08)	(.48)	(.69)	
	.29*	-.15* [income]	.08	.27	.14 (.06)
	(1.97)	(.86)	(.55)	(1.56)	
PR 1985	.26	-.41* [empl.]	.07	.12	.22 (.14)
(N=52)	(1.76)	(2.29)	(.44)	(.33)	
	.27	-.09 [income]	.06	.25	.13 (.04)
	(1.72)	(.52)	(.38)	(1.44)	
CL 1990	.31*	-.26 [empl.]	.29*	.17	.24 (.16)
(N=39)	(1.99)	(1.22)	(1.98)	(.60)	
	.36*	-.34 [income]	.28*	.47*	.29 (.20)
	(2.27)	(1.47)	(1.97)	(2.00)	
PR 1990	.38**	-.22 [empl.]	.26	.19	.26 (.18)
(N=39)	(2.47)	(1.06)	(1.80)	(.69)	
	.41**	-.41 [income]	.23	.49*	.32 (.23)
	(2.67)	(1.77)	(1.61)	(2.13)	

* = p<.05
** = p<.01
*** = p<.001

coefficients (beta weights) for the slope estimates.[59] The tables do not contain correlation coefficients.[60] DFI has been measured via total employees, or net income. T-ratios are in parentheses beneath each beta, and variance explained is reported as both R2 and adjusted R2 (adjusted R2 in parentheses).[61] Reading across each line in Tables 1-3 gives us the beta values for each equation, with changing indicators for DFI (employment versus income) from one line to the next. Changing indicators for DFI leads to slight changes in the parameter estimates for the other independent variables (GNP, aid, debt) as well as slight changes in the values for R2. The results are striking, especially if one pays close attention to the directions of the relationships, statistical significance of the estimates (or lack thereof), and the relative importance of the explanatory variables.

The conclusion from Table 1 that has the greatest relevance to theories of human rights and development is the positive relationship between the presence of MNCs and C/P rights in the third world. Foreign investment is *positively* associated with both civil liberties and political freedoms. This positive association is consistent over

---

59. Standardized coefficients are the slope estimates measured in terms of units of standard deviations.

Values for the intercept (constant) in each equation are not reported because there is no intuitive interpretation for those numbers. A given intercept would equal the estimated value for the human rights indicator(s) of a nation with no GNP, no DFI, no aid, and no debt. Obviously, there could not be such a country (hence the non-intuitive nature of intercepts in these data).

60. Correlation coefficients are the same thing as bivariate (or multivariate) correlations.

61. Adjusted for sample size and for the number of independent variables in the model.

time (from 1985 to 1990). It is also consistent across different indicators of DFI. Increased presence of U.S. multinationals goes along with rising levels of civil and political rights across this sample of developing countries, regardless of whether MNC income or MNC employment is used to measure DFI. Furthermore, the positive relationship is statistically significant in the 1985 data when measuring DFI via the numbers of employees working for U.S. MNCs. Lack of significance in the 1990 data cautions against generalizing too far beyond the developing countries in these samples. Still, the beneficial impact of foreign investment on civil-political rights is clear, consistent, and carries theoretical importance.

GNP, U.S. aid, and foreign debt also stand in positive association to first generation rights in the third world. Developing countries with higher levels of development, more economic aid, and heavier debt burdens tend to score better in regard to the C/P rankings. The positive relationship between GNP and C/P rights in Table 1 is consistent with prior quantitative studies of human rights and development. Even when controlling for DFI, increased development is positively correlated to better human rights, thereby increasing our confidence in the reliability of the prior research. Furthermore, the positive associations between development/aid/debt (on the one hand), and civil-political rights (on the other hand) are statistically significant in the more recent (1990) data. Hence it is reasonable to conclude that these relationships characterize all developing nations, including those not contained in these samples.

One advantage of discussing beta weights rather than correlation coefficients is the ability to compare the relative importance of explanatory variables. Betas calculate the changes in a standard deviation of the dependent variables associated with an increase of one standard deviation in an independent variable (while holding the other independent variables constant). Therefore, standardized coefficients can be compared to one another. Table 1 shows that GNP is the determinant with the greatest overall effect on changes in civil and political rights. The absolute values for GNP exceed all other parameter estimates in almost every case (a notable exception is the 1985 DFI employee data). While direct investment by MNCs adds less to the explanatory power of the model than does GNP, it is worth restating and stressing the nature of the association between DFI (both measures) and C/P rights. A positive relationship between investment and civil-political rights is consistent across different indicators of DFI (employees, income) and consistent over time.

The fit of the MNC models to the empirical data is also relatively good, especially when compared to the variance explained by prior studies. R2 values in Table 1 reveal that as much as-one-quarter to one-third of the variance in the C/P indices is associated with the combined variance of the independent variables in the MNC model. The strength of the MNC model is roughly the same or slightly better than that of other quantitative studies when it comes to accounting for C/P rights. However, the MNC model exceeds the explanatory power of prior models when we turn to the areas of economic and social rights.

. . . .

VI. THEORIES OF MNCS AND HUMAN RIGHTS REVISITED

This study sought to establish the possible causal nature of multinational corporations in regard to human rights in developing countries. Two theories of MNCs and human rights, the engines of development thesis and the Hymer thesis, provided a point of departure. MNCs were defined in terms of direct foreign investment, which was measured by two different indicators. MNC investment was found to be *positively* associated with political rights and civil liberties in the third world. En-hanced GNP per capita also has a positive impact upon first generation rights. These relationships were consistent over time, and consistent between the two measures of DFI.

. . . .

The implications . . . suggest that the engines of development school is correct in its assertion that MNCs promote both civil-political rights and socioeconomic wel-fare. The Hymer thesis is incorrect in its claims that MNC investment tends to go along with violations of civil-political rights and lower standards of welfare in devel-oping countries. The best available empirical data provide no support for Hymer's view.

C. The Emerging Case Law

Filartiga v. Pena-Irala
630 F.2D 876 (2d Cir. 1980)

IRVING R. KAUFMAN, Circuit Judge:

Upon ratification of the Constitution, the thirteen former colonies were fused into a single nation, one which, in its relations with foreign states, is bound both to observe and construe the accepted norms of international law, formerly known as the law of nations. Under the Articles of Confederation, the several states had interpreted and applied this body of doctrine as a part of their common law, but with the found-ing of the "more perfect Union" of 1789, the law of nations became preeminently a federal concern.

Implementing the constitutional mandate for national control over foreign rela-tions, the First Congress established original district court jurisdiction over "all causes where an alien sues for a tort only [committed] in violation of the law of na-tions." Judiciary Act of 1789, ch. 20, § 9(b), 1 Stat. 73, 77 (1789), *codified at* 28 U.S.C. § 1350. Construing this rarely-invoked provision, we hold that deliberate tor-ture perpetrated under color of official authority violates universally accepted norms of the international law of human rights, regardless of the nationality of the parties. Thus, whenever an alleged torturer is found and served with process by an alien within our borders, § 1350 provides federal jurisdiction. Accordingly, we reverse the judgment of the district court dismissing the complaint for want of federal jurisdic-tion.

I

The appellants, plaintiffs below, are citizens of the Republic of Paraguay. Dr. Joel Filartiga, a physician, describes himself as a longstanding opponent of the govern-ment of President Alfredo Stroessner, which has held power in Paraguay since 1954. His daughter, Dolly Filartiga, arrived in the United States in 1978 under a visitor's visa, and has since applied for permanent political asylum. The Filartigas brought this action in the Eastern District of New York against Americo Norberto Pena-Irala (Pena), also a citizen of Paraguay, for wrongfully causing the death of Dr. Filartiga's seventeen-year old son, Joelito. . . .

The appellants contend that on March 29, 1976, Joelito Filartiga was kidnapped and tortured to death by Pena, who was then Inspector General of Police in Asuncion

Paraguay. Later that day, the police brought Dolly Filartiga to Pena's home where she was confronted with the body of her brother, which evidenced marks of severe torture. As she fled, horrified, from the house, Pena followed after her shouting, "Here you have what you have been looking for so long and what you deserve. Now shut up." The Filartigas claim that Joelito was tortured and killed in retaliation for his father's political activities and beliefs.

Shortly thereafter, Dr. Filartiga commenced a criminal action in the Paraguayan courts against Pena and the police for the murder of his son. As a result, Dr. Filartiga's attorney was arrested and brought to police headquarters where, shackled to a wall, Pena threatened him with death. This attorney, it is alleged, has since been disbarred without just cause.

During the course of the Paraguayan criminal proceeding, which is apparently still pending after four years, another man, Hugo Duarte, confessed to the murder. Duarte, who was a member of the Pena household, claimed that he had discovered his wife and Joelito in *flagrante delicto*, and that the crime was one of passion. The Filartigas have submitted a photograph of Joelito's corpse showing injuries they believe refute this claim. Dolly Filartiga, moreover, has stated that she will offer evidence of three independent autopsies demonstrating that her brother's death "was the result of professional methods of torture." Despite his confession, Duarte, we are told, has never been convicted or sentenced in connection with the crime.

In July of 1978, Pena sold his house in Paraguay and entered the United States under a visitor's visa. He was accompanied by Juana Bautista Fernandez Villalba, who had lived with him in Paraguay. The couple remained in the United States beyond the term of their visas, and were living in Brooklyn, New York, when Dolly Filartiga, who was then living in Washington, D. C., learned of their presence. Acting on information provided by Dolly the Immigration and Naturalization Service arrested Pena and his companion, both of whom were subsequently ordered deported on April 5, 1979 following a hearing. They had then resided in the United States for more than nine months.

Almost immediately, Dolly caused Pena to be served with a summons and civil complaint at the Brooklyn Navy Yard, where he was being held pending deportation. The complaint alleged that Pena had wrongfully caused Joelito's death by torture and sought compensatory and punitive damages of $10,000,000. The Filartigas also sought to enjoin Pena's deportation to ensure his availability for testimony at trial. The cause of action is stated as arising under "wrongful death statutes; the U. N. Charter; the Universal Declaration on Human Rights; the U. N. Declaration Against Torture; the American Declaration of the Rights and Duties of Man; and other pertinent declarations, documents and practices constituting the customary international law of human rights and the law of nations," as well as 28 U.S.C. § 1350, Article II, sec. 2 and the Supremacy Clause of the U. S. Constitution. Jurisdiction is claimed under the general federal question provision, 28 U.S.C § 1331 and, principally on this appeal, under the Alien Tort Statute, 28 U.S.C. § 1350.

... [T]here has been no suggestion that Pena claims diplomatic immunity from suit. The Filartigas submitted the affidavits of a number of distinguished international legal scholars, who state unanimously that the law of nations prohibits absolutely the use of torture as alleged in the complaint. ...

Judge Nickerson heard argument on the motion to dismiss on May 14, 1979, and on May 15 dismissed the complaint on jurisdictional grounds. The district judge recognized the strength of appellants' argument that official torture violates an emerging norm of customary international law. Nonetheless, he felt constrained by dicta contained in two recent opinions of this Court, *Dreyfus v. von Finck*, 534 F.2d 24 (2d Cir.), *cert. denied*, 429 U.S. 835 (1976); *IIT v. Vencap, Ltd.*, 519 F.2d 1001 (2d Cir. 1975), to construe narrowly "the law of nations," as employed in § 1350, as excluding that law which governs a state's treatment of its own citizens.

. . . .

II

Appellants rest their principal argument in support of federal jurisdiction upon the Alien Tort Statute, 28 U.S.C. § 1350, which provides: "The district courts shall have original jurisdiction of any civil action by an alien for a tort only, committed in violation of the law of nations or a treaty of the United States." Since appellants do not contend that their action arises directly under a treaty of the United States, a threshold question on the jurisdictional issue is whether the conduct alleged violates the law of nations. In light of the universal condemnation of torture in numerous international agreements, and the renunciation of torture as an instrument of official policy by virtually all of the nations of the world (in principle if not in practice), we find that an act of torture committed by a state official against one held in detention violates established norms of the international law of human rights, and hence the law of nations.

The Supreme Court has enumerated the appropriate sources of international law. The law of nations "may be ascertained by consulting the works of jurists, writing professedly on public law; or by the general usage and practice of nations; or by judicial decisions recognizing and enforcing that law." *United States v. Smith*, 18 U.S. (5 Wheat.) 153, 160-61, 5 L.Ed. 57 (1820). In *Smith*, a statute proscribing, "the crime of piracy [on the high seas] as defined by the law of nations," 3 Stat. 510(a) (1819), was held sufficiently determinate in meaning to afford the basis for a death sentence. The *Smith* Court discovered among the works of Lord Bacon, Grotius, Bochard and other commentators a genuine consensus that rendered the crime "sufficiently and constitutionally defined."

The *Paquete Habana*, 175 U.S. 677 (1900), reaffirmed that

> where there is no treaty, and no controlling executive or legislative act or judicial decision, resort must be had to the customs and usages of civilized nations; and, as evidence of these, to the works of jurists and commentators, who by years of labor, research and experience, have made themselves peculiarly well acquainted with the subjects of which they treat. Such works are resorted to by judicial tribunals, not for the speculations of their authors concerning what the law ought to be, but for trustworthy evidence of what the law really is.

Modern international sources confirm the propriety of this approach. [Indeed, the] Court pointed out in footnote 8 of its opinion that "[t]he Statute of the International Court of Justice, Arts. 38 & 59, June 26, 1945, 59 Stat. 1055, 1060 (1945) provides:

Art. 38

1. The Court, whose function is to decide in accordance with international law such disputes as are submitted to it, shall apply:

   (a) international conventions, whether general or particular, establishing rules expressly recognized by the contesting states;

(b) international custom, as evidence of a general practice accepted as law;

(c) the general principles of law recognized by civilized nations;

(d) subject to the provisions of Article 59, judicial decisions and the teachings of the most highly qualified publicists of the various nations, as subsidiary means for the determination of the rules of law.

2. This. provision shall not prejudice the power of the Court to decide a case *ex aequo et bono*, if the parties agree thereto.

Art. 59

The decision of the Court has no binding force except between the parties and in respect of that particular case."

Habana is particularly instructive for present purposes, for it held that the traditional prohibition against seizure of an enemy's coastal fishing vessels during wartime, a standard that began as one of comity only, had ripened over the preceding century into "a settled rule of international law" by "the general assent of civilized nations." Thus it is clear that courts must interpret international law not as it was in 1789, but as it his evolved and exists among the nations of the world today. *See Ware v. Hylton*, 3 U.S. (3 Dall.) 198, 1 L.Ed. 568 (1796) (distinguishing between "ancient" and "modern" law of nations).

The requirement that a rule command the "general assent of civilized nations" to become binding upon them all is a stringent one. Were this not so, the courts of one nation might feel free to impose idiosyncratic legal rules upon others, in the name of applying international law. Thus, in *Banco Nacional de Cuba v. Sabbatino*, 376 U.S. 398 (1964), the Court declined to pass on the validity of the Cuban government's expropriation of a foreign-owned corporation's assets, noting the sharply conflicting views on the issue propounded by the capital-exporting, capital importing, socialist and capitalist nations.

The case at bar presents us with a situation diametrically opposed to the conflicted state of law that confronted the *Sabbatino* Court. Indeed, to paraphrase that Court's statement there are few, if any, issues in international law today on which opinion seems to be so united as the limitations on a state's power to torture persons held in its custody.

The United Nations Charter (a treaty of the United States, *see* 59 Stat. 1033 (1945)) makes it clear that in this modern age a state's treatment of its own citizens is a matter of international concern. It provides:

With a view to the creation of conditions of stability and well-being which are necessary for peaceful and friendly relations among nations...the United Nations shall promote...universal respect for, and observance of, human rights and fundamental freedoms for all without distinctions as to race, sex, language or religion.

Id. Art. 55. And further:

All members pledge themselves to take joint and separate action in cooperation with the Organization for the achievement of the purposes set forth in Article 55.

Id. Art. 56.

While this broad mandate has been held not to be wholly self-executing, this observation alone does not end our inquiry. For although there is no universal agreement as to the precise extent of the "human rights and fundamental freedoms" guaranteed to all by the Charter, there is at present no dissent from the view that the guaranties include, at a bare minimum, the right to be free from torture. This prohibition has become part of customary international law, as evidenced and defined by the Universal Declaration of Human Rights, General Assembly Resolution 217 (III)(A) (Dec. 10, 1948) which states, in the plainest of terms, "no one shall be subjected to torture." The General Assembly has declared that the Charter precepts embodied in this Universal Declaration "constitute basic principles of international law." G.A.Res. 2625 (XXV) (Oct. 24, 1970).

Particularly relevant is the Declaration on the Protection of All Persons from Being Subjected to Torture, General Assembly Resolution 3452, 30 U.N. GAOR Supp. (No. 34) 91, U.N.Doc. A/1034 (1975). The Declaration expressly prohibits any state from permitting the dastardly and totally inhuman act of torture. Torture, in turn, is defined as "any act by which severe pain and suffering, whether physical or mental, is intentionally inflicted by or at the instigation of a public official on a person for such purposes as...intimidating him or other persons." The Declaration goes on to provide that "[w]here it is proved that an act of torture or other cruel, inhuman or degrading treatment or punishment has been committed by or at the instigation of a public official, the victim shall be afforded redress and compensation, in accordance with national law." This Declaration, like the Declaration of Human Rights before it, was adopted without dissent by the General Assembly.

These U.N. declarations are significant because they specify with great precision the obligations of member nations under the Charter. Since their adoption, "[m]embers can no longer contend that they do not know what human rights they promised in the Charter to promote." Moreover, a U.N. Declaration is, according to one authoritative definition, "a formal and solemn instrument, suitable for rare occasions when principles of great and lasting importance are being enunciated." 34 U.N. ESCOR, Supp. (No. 8) 15, U.N. Doc. E/cn.4/1/610 (1962) (memorandum of Office of Legal Affairs, U.N. Secretariat). Accordingly, it has been observed that the Universal Declaration of Human Rights "no longer fits into the dichotomy of 'binding treaty' against 'non-binding pronouncement,' but is rather an authoritative statement of the international community." Thus, a Declaration creates an expectation of adherence, and "insofar as the expectation is gradually justified by State practice, a declaration may by custom become recognized as laying down rules binding upon the States." Indeed, several commentators have concluded that the Universal Declaration has become, *in toto*, a part of binding, customary international law.

Turning to the act of torture, we have little difficulty discerning its universal renunciation in the modern usage and practice of nations. The international consensus surrounding torture has found expression in numerous international treaties and accords. *E.g.*, *American Convention on Human Rights*, Art. 5, OAS Treaty Series No. 36 at 1, OAS Off. Rec. OEA/Ser 4 v/II 23, doc. 21, rev. 2 (English ed., 1975) ("No one shall be subjected to torture or to cruel, inhuman or degrading punishment or treatment"); International Covenant on Civil and Political Rights, U.N. General Assembly Res. 2200 (XXI)A, U.N. Doc. A/6316 (Dec. 16, 1966) (identical language); European Convention for the Protection of Human Rights and Fundamental Freedoms, Art. 3, Council of Europe, European Treaty Series No. 5 (1968), 213 U.N. T.S. 211 (*semble*). The substance of these international agreements is reflected in modern municipal — *i. e.*, national — law as well. Although torture was once a routine concomitant of criminal interrogations in many nations, during the modern and hopefully more enlightened era it has been universally renounced. According to one survey, torture is prohibited, expressly or implicitly, by the constitutions of over fifty-five nations, including both the United States and Paraguay. Our State Department reports a general recognition of this principle:

> There now exists an international consensus that recognizes basic human rights and obligations owed by all governments to their citizens.... There is no doubt that these rights are often violated; but virtually all governments acknowledge their validity.

Department of State, *Country Reports on Human Rights for 1979*, published as Joint Comm. Print, House Comm. on Foreign Affairs, and Senate Comm. on Foreign Relations, 96th Cong. 2d Sess. (Feb. 4, 1980) Introduction at 1. We have been directed to no assertion by any contemporary state of a right to torture its own or another nation's citizens. Indeed, United States diplomatic contacts confirm the universal abhorrence with which torture is viewed:

> In exchanges between United States embassies and all foreign states with which the United States maintains relations, it has been the Department of State's general experience that no government has asserted a right to torture its own nationals. Where reports of torture elicit some credence, a state usually responds by denial or, less frequently, by asserting that the conduct was unauthorized or constituted rough treatment short of torture.

Memorandum of the United States as *Amicus Curiae* at 16 n.34.

Having examined the sources from which customary international law is derived — the usage of nations, judicial opinions and the works of jurists — we conclude that official torture is now prohibited by the law of nations. The prohibition is clear and unambiguous, and admits of no distinction between treatment of aliens and citizens. Accordingly, we must conclude that the dictum in *Dreyfus v. von Finck* supra, 534 F.2d at 31, to the effect that "violations of international law do not occur when the aggrieved parties are nationals of the acting state," is clearly out of tune with the current usage and practice of international law. The treaties and accords cited above, as well as the express foreign policy of our own government, all make it clear that international law confers fundamental rights upon all people vis-a-vis their own governments. While the ultimate scope of those rights will be a subject for continuing refinement and elaboration, we hold that the right to be free from torture is now among them. We therefore turn to the question whether the other requirements for jurisdiction are met.

III

Appellee submits that even if the tort alleged is a violation of modern international law, federal jurisdiction may not be exercised consistent with the dictates of Article III of the Constitution. The claim is without merit. Common law courts of general jurisdiction regularly adjudicate transitory tort claims between individuals over whom they exercise personal jurisdiction, wherever the tort occurred. Moreover, as part of an articulated scheme of federal control over external affairs, Congress provided, in the first Judiciary Act, § 9(b), 1 Stat. 73, 77 (1789), for federal jurisdiction over suits by aliens where principles of international law are in issue. The constitutional basis for the Alien Tort Statute is the law of nations, which has always been part of the federal common law.

It is not extraordinary for a court to adjudicate a tort claim arising outside of its territorial jurisdiction. A state or nation has a legitimate interest in the orderly resolution of disputes among those within its borders, and where the *lex loci delicti commissi* is applied, it is an expression of comity to give effect to the laws of the state where the wrong occurred. Thus, Lord Mansfield in *Mostyn v. Fabrigas*, 1 Cowp. 161 (1774), *quoted in McKenna v. Fisk*, 42 U.S. (1 How.) 241, 248, 11 L.Ed. 117 (1843), said:

> [I]f A becomes indebted to B, or commits a tort upon his person or upon his personal property in Paris, an action in either case may be maintained against A in England, if he is there found.... [A]s to transitory actions, there is not a colour of doubt but that any action which is transitory may be laid in any county in England, though the matter arises beyond the seas.

Mostyn came into our law as the original basis for state court jurisdiction over out-of-state torts, *McKenna v. Fisk, supra,* 42 U.S. (1 How.) 241, 11 L.Ed. 117 (personal injury suits *held* transitory).... Here, where *in personam* jurisdiction has been obtained over the defendant, the parties agree that the acts alleged would violate Paraguayan law, and the policies of the forum are consistent with the foreign law, state court jurisdiction would be proper. Indeed, appellees conceded as much at oral argument.

Recalling that *Mostyn* was freshly decided at the time the Constitution was ratified, we proceed to consider whether the First Congress acted constitutionally in vesting jurisdiction over "foreign suits," alleging torts committed in violation of the law of nations. A case properly "aris[es] under the ... laws of the United States" for Article III purposes if grounded upon statutes enacted by Congress or upon the common law of the United States. The law of nations forms an integral part of the common law, and a review of the history surrounding the adoption of the Constitution demonstrates that it became a part of the common law *of the United States* upon the adoption of the Constitution. Therefore, the enactment of the Alien Tort Statute was authorized by Article III.

During the eighteenth century, it was taken for granted on both sides of the Atlantic that the law of nations forms a part of the common law. 1 Blackstone, Commentaries 263-64 (1st Ed. 1765-69); 4 *id.* at 67. Under the Articles of Confederation, the Pennsylvania Court of Oyer and Terminer at Philadelphia, *per* McKean, Chief Justice, applied the law of nations to the criminal prosecution of the Chevalier de Longchamps for his assault upon the person of the French Consul-General to the United States, noting that "[t]his law, in its full extent, is a part of the law of this state...." *Respublica v. DeLongchamps*, 1 U.S. (1 Dall.) 113, 119, 1 L.Ed. 59 (1784). Thus, a leading commentator has written:

> It is an ancient and a salutary feature of the Anglo-American legal tradition that the Law of Nations is a part of the law of the land to be ascertained and administered, like any other, in the appropriate case. This doctrine was originally conceived and formulated in England in response to the demands of an expanding commerce and under the influence of theories widely accepted in the late sixteenth, the seventeenth and the eighteenth centuries. It was brought to America in the colonial years as part of the legal heritage from England. It was well understood by men of legal learning in America in the eighteenth century when the United Colonies broke away from England to unite effectively, a little later, in the United States of America.

Dickenson, *The Law of Nations as Part of the National Law of the United States*, 101 U.PA. L.REV. 26, 27 (1952).

Indeed, Dickenson goes on to demonstrate that one of the principal defects of the Confederation that our Constitution was intended to remedy was the central government's inability to "cause infractions of treaties or of the law of nations, to be punished." 1 FARRAND, RECORDS OF THE FEDERAL CONVENTION 19 (rev. ed. 1937) (Notes of James Madison). And, in Jefferson's words, the very purpose of the proposed Union was "[t]o make us one nation as to foreign concerns, and keep us distinct in domestic ones."

As ratified, the judiciary article contained no express reference to cases arising under the law of nations. Indeed, the only express reference to that body of law is contained in Article I, sec. 8, cl. 10, which grants to the Congress the power to "define and punish... offenses against the law of nations." Appellees seize upon this circumstance and advance the proposition that the law of nations forms a part of the laws of the United States only to the extent that Congress has acted to define it. This extravagant claim is amply refuted by the numerous decisions applying rules of international law uncodified in any act of Congress. *E. g., Ware v. Hylton*, 3 U.S. (3 Dall.) 198, 1 L.Ed. 568 (1796); *The Paquete Habana, supra,...; Sabbatino, supra....* A similar argument was offered to and rejected by the Supreme Court in *United States v. Smith, supra*, 18 U.S. (5 Wheat.) 153, 158-60, 5 L.Ed. 57 and we reject it today. As John Jay wrote in *The Federalist* No. 3, "Under the national government, treaties and articles of treaties, as well as the laws of nations, will always be expounded in one sense and executed in the same manner, whereas adjudications on the same points and questions in the thirteen states will not always accord or be consistent." Federal jurisdiction over cases involving international law is clear.

Thus, it was hardly a radical initiative for Chief Justice Marshall to state in *The Nereide*, 13 U.S. (9 Cranch) 388, 422, 3 L.Ed. 769 (1815), that in the absence of a congressional enactment, United States courts are "bound by the law of nations, which is a part of the law of the land." These words were echoed in *The Paquete Habana, supra*: "[i]nternational law is part of our law, and must be ascertained and administered by the courts of justice of appropriate jurisdiction, as often as questions of right depending upon it are duly presented for the determination."

The Filartigas urge that 28 U.S.C. § 1350 be treated as an exercise of Congress's power to define offenses against the law of nations. While such a reading is possible, we believe it is sufficient here to construe the Alien Tort Statute, not as granting new rights to aliens, but simply as opening the federal courts for adjudication of the rights already recognized by international law. The statute nonetheless does inform our analysis of Article III, for we recognize that questions of jurisdiction "must be considered part of an organic growth — part of an evolutionary process," and that the history of the judiciary article gives meaning to its pithy phrases. The Framers' overarching concern that control over international affairs be vested in the new national government to safeguard the standing of the United States among the nations of the world therefore reinforces the result we reach today.

Although the Alien Tort Statute has rarely been the basis for jurisdiction during its long history, in light of the foregoing discussion, there can be little doubt that this action is properly brought in federal court. This is undeniably an action by an alien, for a tort only, committed in violation of the law of nations. The paucity of suits successfully maintained under the section is readily attributable to the statute's requirement of alleging a "*violation* of the law of nations" (emphasis supplied) at the jurisdictional threshold. Courts have, accordingly, engaged in a more searching preliminary review of the merits than is required, for example, under the more flexible "arising under" formulation. Thus, the narrowing construction that the Alien Tort Statute has previously received reflects the fact that earlier cases did not involve such well-established, universally recognized norms of international law that are here at issue.

For example, the statute does not confer jurisdiction over an action by a Luxembourgeois international investment trust's suit for fraud, conversion and corporate waste. *IIT v. Vencap*, 519 F.2d 1001, 1015 (1975). In *IIT*, Judge Friendly astutely noted that the mere fact that every nation's municipal law may prohibit theft does not incorporate "the Eighth Commandment, 'Thou Shalt not steal'...[into] the law of nations." It is only where the nations of the world have demonstrated that the wrong is of mutual, and not merely several, concern, by means of express international accords, that a wrong generally recognized becomes an international law violation within the meaning of the statute. Other recent § 1350 cases are similarly distinguishable.

IIT adopted a dictum from *Lopes v. Reederei Richard Schroder*, 225 F.Supp. 292 (E.D.Pa.1963) to the effect that "a violation of the law of nations arises only when there has been 'a violation by one or more individuals of those standards, rules or customs (a) affecting the relationship between states or between an individual and a foreign state and (b) used by those states for their common good and/or in dealings *inter se*." We have no quarrel with this formulation so long as it be understood that the courts are not to prejudge the scope of the issues that the nations of the world may deem important to their interrelationships, and thus to their common good. As one commentator has noted:

> the sphere of domestic jurisdiction is not an irreducible sphere of rights which are somehow inherent, natural, or fundamental. It does not create an impenetrable barrier to the development of international law. Matters of domestic jurisdiction are not those which are unregulated by international law, but those which are left by international law for regulation by States. There are, therefore, no matters which are domestic by their 'nature.' All are susceptible of international legal regulation and may become the subjects of new rules of customary law of treaty obligations.

Preuss, "Article 2, Paragraph 7 of the Charter of the United Nations and Matters of Domestic Jurisdiction," Hague *Receuil* (Extract, 149) at 8, *reprinted in* H. Briggs, *The Law of Nations* 24 (1952). Here, the nations have made it their business, both through international accords and unilateral action, to be concerned with domestic human rights violations of this magnitude. The case before us therefore falls within the *Lopes/IIT* rule.

Since federal jurisdiction may properly be exercised over the Filartigas' claim, the action must be remanded for further proceedings. Appellee Pena, however, advances several additional points that lie beyond the scope of our holding on jurisdiction. Both to emphasize the boundaries of our holding, and to clarify some of the issues reserved for the district court on remand, we will address these contentions briefly.

IV

Pena argues that the customary law of nations, as reflected in treaties and declarations that are not self-executing, should not be applied as rules of decision in this case. In doing so, he confuses the question of federal jurisdiction under the Alien Tort Statute, which requires consideration of the law of nations, with the issue of the choice of law to be applied, which will be addressed at a later stage in the proceedings. The two issues are distinct. Our holding on subject matter jurisdiction decides only whether Congress intended to confer judicial power, and whether it is authorized to do so by Article III. The choice of law inquiry is a much broader one, primarily concerned with fairness, consequently, it looks to wholly different considerations. Should the district court decide that the *Lauritzen* analysis requires it to apply Paraguayan law, our courts will not have occasion to consider what law would govern a suit under the Alien Tort Statute where the challenged conduct is actionable under the law of the forum and the law of nations, but not the law of the jurisdiction in which the tort occurred.

Pena also argues that "[i]f the conduct complained of is alleged to be the act of the Paraguayan government, the suit is barred by the Act of State doctrine. This argument was not advanced below, and is therefore not before us on this appeal. We note in passing, however, that we doubt whether action by a state official violation of the Constitution and laws of the Republic of Paraguay, and wholly unratified by that nation's government, could properly be characterized as an act of state. Paraguay's renunciation of torture as a legitimate instrument of state policy, however, does not strip the tort of its character as an international law violation, if it in fact occurred under color of government authority.

Finally, we have already stated that we do not reach the critical question of *forum non conveniens*, since it was not considered below. In closing, however, we note that the foreign relations implications of this and other issues the district court will be required to adjudicate on remand underscores the wisdom of the First Congress investing jurisdiction over such claims in the federal district courts through the Alien Tort Statute. Questions of this nature are fraught with implications for the nation as a whole, and therefore should not be left to the potentially varying adjudications of the courts of the fifty states.

In the twentieth century the international community has come to recognize the common danger posed by the flagrant disregard of basic human rights and particularly the right to be free of torture. Spurred first by the Great War, and then the Second, civilized nations have banded together to prescribe acceptable norms of international behavior. From the ashes of the Second World War arose the United Nations Organization, amid hopes that an era of peace and cooperation had at last begun. Though many of these aspirations have remained elusive goals, that circumstance cannot diminish the true progress that has been made. In the modern age, humanitarian and practical considerations have combined to lead the nations of the world to recognize that respect for fundamental human rights is in their individual and collective interest. Among the rights universally proclaimed by all nations, as we have noted, is the right to be free of physical torture. Indeed, for purposes of civil liability, the torturer has become — like pirate and slave trader before him — *hostis humani generis*, an enemy of all mankind. Our holding today, giving effect to a jurisdictional provision enacted by our First Congress, is a small but important step in the fulfillment of the ageless dream to free all people from brutal violence.

Tel-Oren v. Libyan Arab Republic

726 F.2D 774 (D.C. Cir. 1984) (concurring opinion of Judge Bork),
cert. denied, 470 U.S. 1003 (1985)

PER CURIAM:

Plaintiffs in this action, mostly Israeli citizens, are survivors and representatives of persons murdered in an armed attack on a civilian bus in Israel in March 1978. They filed suit for compensatory and punitive damages in the District Court, naming as defendants the Libyan Arab Republic, the Palestine Liberation Organization, the Palestine Information Office, the National Association of Arab Americans, and the Palestine Congress of North America.

In their complaint, plaintiffs alleged that defendants were responsible for multiple tortuous acts in violation of the law of nations, treaties of the United States, and criminal laws of the United States, as well as the common law. Jurisdiction was claimed under four separate statutes: 28 U.S.C. § 1831 (federal question jurisdiction); 28 U.S.C. § 1332 (diversity jurisdiction); 28 U.S.C. § 1350 (providing jurisdiction over actions by an alien alleging a tort committed in violation of the law of nations or a treaty of the United States); and the Foreign Sovereign Immunities Act of 1976, 28 U.S.C. §§ 1330, 1602-1611....

The District Court dismissed the action both for lack of subject matter jurisdiction and as barred by the applicable statute of limitations. Plaintiffs appeal the District Court's rulings on two of their claimed jurisdictional bases, 28 U.S.C. §§ 1331, 1350, and on the statute of limitations issue.

We affirm the dismissal of this action. Set out below are separate concurring statements of Judge Edwards, Judge Bork, and Senior Judge Robb, indicating different reasons for affirming the result reached by the District Court.

. . . .

BORK, Circuit Judge, concurring:

This case grows out of an armed attack on a civilian bus in Israel on March 11, 1978. Appellants (plaintiffs below) are sixty-five of the persons seriously injured in the attack and the survivors of twenty-nine of the persons killed. Appellees (defendants below) are the Libyan Arab Republic ("Libya"), the Palestine Liberation Organization ("PLO"), the Palestine Information Office ("PIO"), and the National Association of Arab Americans ("NAAA"). Appellants alleged in their complaint that appellees were responsible for the 1978 attack, and they sought compensatory and punitive damages. Specifically, appellants charged appellees with torts committed in violation of international law and of some treaties and statutes of the United States as well as with commission of and conspiracy to commit various intentional common law torts. Jurisdiction over the common law tort counts is pendent and will fail if the other counts fail.

The district court dismissed the action for lack of subject matter jurisdiction. We agree that the complaint must be dismissed, although our reasons for agreement differ. I believe, as did the district court, that, in the circumstances presented here, appellants have failed to state a cause of action sufficient to support jurisdiction under either of the statutes on which they rely. 28 U.S.C. §§ 1831, 1850. Neither the law of nations nor any of the relevant treaties provides a cause of action that appellants may assert in courts of the United States. Furthermore, we should not, in an area such as this, infer a cause of action not explicitly given. In reaching this latter conclusion, I am guided chiefly by separation of powers principles, which caution courts to avoid potential interference with the political branches' conduct of foreign relations.

I.

According to the complaint, on March 8, 1978, thirteen heavily armed members of the PLO left Lebanon for Israel. They were under instructions from the PLO to seize and hold Israeli civilians in ransom for the release of PLO members incarcerated in Israel jails. If their plans broke down, the terrorists were to kill their hostages.

The complaint's allegations of what happened upon the terrorists' arrival in Israel constitute a tale of horror. Since my analysis does not turn upon the particulars of those events, they need not be described in detail. The thirteen terrorists landed by boat and, after killing an American photographer they encountered on the beach, made their way to the main highway between Haifa and Tel Aviv. There they stopped and seized a civilian bus, a taxi, a passing car, and, later, a second civilian bus taking the passengers hostage. While proceeding toward Tel Aviv with their many hostages gathered in the first bus, the terrorists fired on and killed numerous occupants of passing cars as well as some of their own passengers. They also tortured some of their hostages.

The police finally brought the terrorist-controlled bus to a halt by shooting at the tires and engine of the bus as it passed through a police barricade. The terrorists reacted by shooting a number of their hostages and, eventually, by blowing up the bus with grenades. As a result of the terrorists' actions, twenty-two adults and twelve children were killed, and sixty-three adults and fourteen children were seriously wounded.

Appellants in this case are most of those wounded and the survivors of most of those killed, as well as the guardians and next friends of those wounded minors who may not sue in their own capacity. Appellants alleged in their complaint that appellees are responsible for the deaths and injuries. According to the complaint's allegations, the PLO not only recruited and trained the thirteen terrorists but also planned, financed, supplied, and "claimed responsibility" for the operation. Libya, plaintiffs alleged, trained the PLO instructors who trained the thirteen terrorists, planned, supplied, financed, and "claimed responsibility" for the operation, and gave an official "hero's welcome" to the ship that carried the terrorists to Israel. As for the PIO and the NAAA, the complaint contains only the general allegations that the PIO is an agent and instrumentality of the PLO and that both the PIO and the NAAA helped plan, finance, outfit, and direct the terrorist operation.

Though the complaint sought recovery under five theories of liability, only two need be considered to decide this appeal. Count II charges defendants with tortuous actions in violation of the law of nations. Count III charges defendants with tortuous actions in violation of various treaties of the United States. The district court granted the NAAA's motion to dismiss for lack of jurisdiction. The portion of the district court's inquiry that is relevant here is whether the allegations of Counts II and III sufficed to support jurisdiction under sections 1331 or 1350.

Section 1331 provides: "The district courts shall have original jurisdiction of all civil actions arising under the Constitution, laws, or treaties of the United States." Section 1350 provides: "The district courts shall have original jurisdiction of any civil action by an alien for a tort only, committed in violation of the law of nations or a treaty of the United States." With respect to Count III's allegation of treaty violations, the district court found jurisdiction lacking on the ground that none of the treaties alleged to be violated either expressly or impliedly gave rise to a private right of action. With respect to Count III's allegation that appellees violated the law of nations, the district court held that neither section 1331 nor section 1350 provided jurisdiction. Section 1331 jurisdiction is lacking, the court held, because federal common law, which incorporates the law of nations, cannot be constituted to grant a cause of action without "judicial interference with foreign and international relations." Section 1350 jurisdiction is lacking, the district court held, for the same reason: International human rights law grants no private right of action, and section 1350, like section 1331, must be interpreted narrowly to require such a right in suits for violation of international law.

In this appeal, appellants agree with the district court that, for purposes of the issues raised in this case, the jurisdictional requirements of sections 1331 and 1350 are the same.... Contrary to the holding of the district court, however, they contend that at least some of the treaties they cite in their complaint impliedly provide private rights of action for the claims in Count III and that federal common law provides private rights of action for the claims in Count II. Thus, appellants argue, section 1350 gives jurisdiction over the claims of the alien plaintiffs and section 1331 gives jurisdiction over the claims of all the plaintiffs, including those who are United States citizens.

For the reasons given below, appellants' contentions must be rejected. I first consider separation of powers principles that counsel courts, in a case like this, not to infer any cause of action not expressly granted. I then show that the treaties on which appellants rely create no private causes of action. Turning next to appellants' claim under general principles of international law, I conclude that federal common law does not automatically accord appellants a cause of action and that appellants have not been granted a cause of action by federal statute or by international law itself. Finally, in order to clarify what I believe we should and should not have decided, I discuss the recent decision of the Second Circuit in *Filartiga v. Pena-Irala*, 630 F.2d 876 (2d Cir. 1980), a case having some similarities to this one.

II.

The question in this case is whether appellants have a cause of action in courts of the United States for injuries they suffered in Israel.... [T]he Second Circuit in *Filartiga* assumed, that Congress' grant of jurisdiction also created a cause of action. That seems to me fundamentally wrong and certain to produce pernicious results. For reasons I will develop, it is essential that there be an explicit grant of a cause of action before a private plaintiff be allowed to enforce principles of international law in a federal tribunal. It will be seen below, however, that no body of law expressly grants appellants a cause of action; the relevant inquiry, therefore, is whether a cause of action is to be inferred. That inquiry is guided by general principles that apply whenever a court of the United States is asked to act in a field in which its judgment would necessarily affect the foreign policy interests of the nation.

The Supreme Court explained in *Davis v. Passman*, 442 U.S. 228 (1979), that to ask whether a particular plaintiff has a cause of action is to ask whether he "is a member of the class of litigants that may, as a matter of law, appropriately invoke the power of the court." The Court said that the "question of who may enforce a *statutory* right is fundamentally different from the question of who may enforce a right that is protected by the Constitution." In addressing the question, as the *Davis* opinion itself makes clear, the focus may be at least as much on the character of the issues presented for decision as on the character of the class of litigants seeking an adjudication, and the result of the inquiry might well be that certain claims cannot be litigated at all in certain forums.

This case presents a question not covered by the analyses described by the *Davis* Court for statutory and constitutional causes of action. An analysis of the appropriateness of providing appellants with a cause of action must take into account the concerns that are inherent in and peculiar to the field of international relations. My assessment of those concerns leads me to a conclusion different from that reached in *Davis*, for here there appear to be "special factors counseling hesitation in the absence of affirmative action by Congress." The factors counseling hesitation are constitutional; they derive from principles of separation of powers.

The crucial element of the doctrine of separation of powers in this case is the principle that "[t]he conduct of the foreign relations of our Government is committed by the Constitution to the Executive and Legislative — 'the political' — Departments." *Oetjen v. Central Leather Co.*, 246 U.S. 297, 302, (1918). That principle has been translated into a limitation on judicial power in the international law area principally through the act of state and political question doctrines. Whether or not this case falls within one of these categories, the concerns that underlie them are present and demand recognition here.

"The act of state doctrine in its traditional formulation precludes the courts from inquiring into the validity of the public acts a recognized foreign sovereign power committed within its own territory." *Banco Nacional de Cuba v. Sabbatino*, 376 U.S. 398, 401, (1964). Originally, the doctrine rested primarily on notions of sovereignty and comity. See *Underhill v. Hernandez*, 168 U.S. 250, 252, (1897). In more recent formulations, there has been "a shift in focus from the notions of sovereignty and the dignity of independent nations...to concerns for preserving the 'basic relationships between branches of government in a system of separation of powers,' and not hindering the executive's conduct of foreign policy by judicial review or oversight of foreign acts." *Manningion Mills, Inc. v. Congoleum Corp.*, 595 F.2d 1287, l292 (3d Cir. 1979) (quoting *Sabbatino*, 376 U.S. at 423.

The *Sabbatino* Court explained that, although the Constitution does not compel the act of state doctrine, the doctrine has "'constitutional' underpinnings. It arises out of the basic relationships between branches of government in a system of separation of powers. It concerns the competency of dissimilar institutions to make and implement particular kinds of decisions in the area of international relations." The Court emphasized the separation of powers basis for the doctrine when it observed that the doctrine's "continuing vitality depends on its capacity to reflect the proper distribution of functions between the judicial and political branches of the Government on matters bearing upon foreign affairs." In its principal post-*Sabbatino* act of state case, the Supreme Court again stressed the centrality of separation of powers concerns: "The major underpinning of the act of state doctrine is the policy of foreclosing court adjudications involving the legality of acts of foreign states on their own soil that might embarrass the Executive Branch of our Government in the conduct of our foreign relations." *Alfred Dunhill of London, Inc. v. Cuba*, 425 U.S. 682, 697, (1976). The courts of appeals have likewise emphasized the decisive role played, in applying the doctrine, by the two relevant aspects of separation of powers: the potential for interference with the political branches' functions and the fitness of an issue for judicial resolution.

The same separation of powers principles are reflected in the political question doctrine. The Supreme Court gave that doctrine its modern formulation in *Baker v. Carr*, 369 U.S. 186, 217, (1962):

> Prominent on the surface of any case held to involve a political question is found a textually demonstrable constitutional commitment of the issue to a coordinate political department; or a lack of judicially discoverable and manageable standards for resolving it; or the impossibility of deciding without an initial policy determination of a kind clearly for nonjudicial discretion; or the impossibility of a court's undertaking independent resolution without expressing lack of the respect due coordinate branches of government; or an unusual need for unquestioning adherence to a political decision already made; or the potentiality of embarrassment from multifarious pronouncements by various departments on one question.

Questions touching on the foreign relations of the United States make up what is likely the largest class of questions to which the political question doctrine has been applied. If it were necessary, I might well hold that the political question doctrine bars this lawsuit, since it is arguable, as much of the remainder of this opinion will show, that this case fits several of the categories listed in *Baker v. Carr*. Such a determination is not necessary, however, because many of the same considerations that govern application of the political question doctrine also govern the question of the appropriateness of providing appellants with a cause of action.

Neither is there a need to consider whether the act of state doctrine applies to bar this case from going forward. Although the act of state doctrine might well apply to Libya's alleged role in the 1978 bus attack, it would seem not to apply, in its current formulation, to the alleged acts of the PLO, the PIO, and the NAAA, none of which would seem to be a state under international law. Nevertheless, to the extent the act of state doctrine is based predominantly, if not exclusively, on separation of powers concerns (as it has increasingly come to be), its own rationale might justify extending it to cover the acts of such entities as the PLO where adjudication of the validity of those acts would present problems of judicial competence and of judicial interference with foreign relations. Such an extension would bring the act of state doctrine closer, especially in its flexibility, to the political question doctrine.... Whether the two doctrines should be merged and how, if merged, they would apply to the allegations of appellants' complaint are issues beyond the scope of our inquiry. Instead, those doctrines are drawn upon for what they say about the separation of powers principles that must inform a determination of appellants' litigating their claims in federal court.

Those principles counsel against recognition of a cause of action for appellants if adjudication of their claims would raise substantial problems of judicial interference with nonjudicial functions, such as the conduct of foreign relations. Appellants' complaint requires a determination, either at the jurisdictional stage or at the stage of defining and applying a rule of decision, whether international law has been violated. I am therefore guided in large measure by the Supreme Court's observation in *Sabbatino* that

> the greater the degree of codification or consensus concerning a particular area of international law, the more appropriate it is for the judiciary to render decisions regarding it, since the courts can then focus on the application of an agreed principle to circumstances of fact rather than on the sensitive task of establishing a principle not inconsistent with the national interest or with international justice. It is also evident that some aspects of international law touch more sharply on national nerves than do others; the less important the implications of an issue are for our foreign relations, the weaker the justification for exclusivity in the political branches.

There is no need to decide here under what circumstances considerations such as these might deprive an individual of a cause of action clearly given by a state, by Congress, by a treaty, or by international law. In the absence of such a cause of action, they lead to the conclusion that adjudication of appellants' claims would present grave separation of powers problems. It is therefore inappropriate to recognize a cause of action allowing appellants to bring this suit.

Most important, perhaps, even appellants concede that the incidents described in appellants' complaint are properly understood only when viewed in the context of the continuing conflicts in the Middle East. Indeed, appellants point out that "[o]ne of the primary purposes of the March 11 attack was to sabotage the foreign relations of the United States and its negotiations by destroying the positive efforts made in the Camp David accords." The Camp David accords, of course, were but one of the major efforts made by the United States to resolve the myriad problems behind the series of military and political conflicts that have kept the Middle East at or near the center of American foreign relations for at least the last fifteen years. A judicial pronouncement on the PLO's responsibility for the 1978 bus attack would likely interfere with American diplomacy, which is as actively concerned with the Middle East today as it has ever been.

The potential for interference with foreign relations is not diminished by the PLO's apparent lack of international law status as a state. Nor does it matter whether the Executive Branch officially recognizes, or has direct dealings with, the PLO. The fact remains that the PLO bears significantly upon the foreign relations of the United States. If any indication of that role is needed, it is provided by the official "observer" status that the PLO has been accorded at the United Nations, as well as by the diplomatic relations that the PLO is reported to have with some one hundred countries around the world.

The nature of appellants' international law claims provides a further reason for reluctance to recognize a cause of action for appellants. Adjudication of those claims would require the analysis of international legal principles that are anything but clearly defined and that are the subject of controversy touching "sharply on national nerves." *Banco Nacional de Cuba v. Sabbatino*, 376 U.S. at 428. The *Sabbatino* Court warned against adjudication of such international law issues. Because I believe that judicial pronouncements on the merits of this case should be avoided, I mention only briefly some of the difficulties raised by some of the claims in appellants' complaint.

Appellants would have to argue, if their case were adjudicated, for an exception to the general rule that international law imposes duties only on states and on their agents or officials. *See* L. Henkin, R. Pugh, O. Schachter & H. Smit, *International Law*, 246-47 (1980). . . . If, as would appear, the PLO is not a state, a finding that it should nonetheless be held to the duties imposed by the customary rules of international law governing the conduct of belligerent nations, would not entail merely the application of an agreed principle to new facts. Rather, a finding that because of its governmental aspirations and because of the role it has played in the Middle East conflicts the PLO should be subject to such rules would establish a new principle of international law. Likewise, to interpret various human rights documents as imposing legal duties on nonstates like the PLO would require both entering a new and unsettled area of international law and finding there an exception to international law's general rule.

Another difficulty presented by appellants' complaint is that some of the documents on which they rely as statements of customary principles of international law expressly make the purposes of an action relevant to its unlawfulness. For example, appellants allege that appellees violated the proscription, in article 51 of the Protocol I of the Geneva Conventions of 12 August 1949, on "[a]cts or threats of violence the primary purpose of which is to spread terror among the civilian population." They also allege that appellees violated the proscription on genocide, defined in the Convention on the Prevention and Punishment of the Crime of Genocide, Dec. 9, 1948, 78 U.N.T.S. 277, to mean acts calculated to bring about the physical destruction, in whole or in part, of a national, ethnic, racial, or religious group. Adjudication of these claims would require inquiry into the PLO's intention in planning the 1978 bus attack (assuming the PLO's involvement) and into the organizational goals of the PLO. The dangers of such inquiry into the intentions of the PLO are similar to those attending an inquiry into the intentions of a state. . . .

In addition, appellants' principal claim, that appellees violated customary principles of international law against terrorism, concerns an area of international law in which there is little or no consensus and in which the disagreements concern politically sensitive issues that are especially prominent in the foreign relations problems of the Middle East. Some aspects of terrorism have been the subject of several international conventions, such as those concerning hijacking,...and attacks on internationally protected persons such as diplomats...But no consensus has developed on how properly to define "terrorism" generally. As a consequence, "'[i]nternational law and the rules of warfare as they now exist are inadequate to cope with this new mode of conflict." *Transnational Terrorism: Conventions and Commentary* xv (R. Lillich ed. 1982). "The dismal truth is that the international community has dealt with terrorism ambivalently and ineffectually." Shestack, *Of Private and State Terror — Some Preliminary Observations*, 13 RUTGERS L.J. 453, 463 (1982).

Customary international law may well forbid states from aiding terrorist attacks on neighboring states. Although that principle might apply in a case like this to a state such as Libya (which is not a proper party here), it does not, at least on its face, apply to a nonstate like the PLO. More important, there is less than universal consensus about whether PLO-sponsored attacks on Israel are lawful. One important sign of the lack of consensus about terrorism generally, and about PLO activities in particular, is that accusations of terror are often met not by denial of the fact of responsibility but by a justification for the challenged actions.

Indeed, one of the key documents relied on as evidence of an international law prescription on terrorism, the Declaration on Principles of International Law Concerning Friendly Relations and Co-operation Among States in Accordance with the Charter of the United Nations, G.A. Res. 2625, 25 U.N.GAOR Supp. (No. 28) at 121, U.N.Doc. A/8028 (1970), was said by at least one state at the time of its promulgation not to be applicable to Palestinian terrorist raids into Israel supported by Arab states. 24 U.N.GAOR 297, U.N. Doc. A/C.6/SR. 1160 (1969) (remarks of Mr. El Attrash of Syria). Attempts to secure greater consensus on terrorism have foundered on just such issues as the lawfulness of violent action by groups like the PLO fighting what some states view as "wars of national liberation."

There is, of course, no occasion here to state what international law should be. Nor is there a need to consider whether an extended and discriminating analysis might plausibly maintain that customary international law prohibits the actions alleged in the complaint. It is enough to observe that there is sufficient controversy of a politically sensitive nature about the content of any relevant international legal principles that litigation of appellants' claims, would present, in acute form, many of the problems that the separation of powers principles inherent in the act of state and political question doctrines caution courts to avoid. The lack of clarity in, and absence of consensus about, the legal principles invoked by appellants, together with the political context of the challenged actions and the PLO's impingement upon American foreign relations, lead to the conclusion that appellants' case is not the sort that is appropriate for federal-court adjudication, at least not without an express grant of a cause of action.

I turn next to examine treaties, common law, congressional enactments and customary international law to determine, whether any of these sources of law provides a cause of action for appellants. In light of what has been said, it would require a very clear showing that these other bodies of law grant appellants a cause of action before my concerns about the principles of separation of powers could be overcome. But, as will be seen, there is no clear grant of a cause of action to be found. In truth, the law concerning treaties and customary international law of its own force appears actually to deny appellants any cause of action.

III.

Treaties of the United States, though the law of the land, do not generally create rights that are privately enforceable in courts. *Foster v. Neilson*, 27 U.S. (2 Pet.) 253, 314, 7 L.Ed. 415 (1829), *overruled on other grounds*, *United States v. Pezeheman*, 32 U.S. (7 Pet.) 51, 8 L.Ed. 604 (1883); *Canadian Transport Co. v. United States*, 663 F.2d 1081, 1092 (D.C.Cir. 1980); *Dreyfus v. Von Finck*, 534 F.2d 24, 29-30 (2d Cir.), *cert. denied*, 429 U.S. 835 ... (1976). Absent authorizing legislation, an individual has access to courts for enforcement of a treaty's provisions only when the treaty is self-executing, that is, when it expressly or impliedly provides a private right of action. When no right is explicitly stated, courts look to the treaty as a whole to determine whether it evidences an intent to provide a private right of action.

In Count III of the complaint, appellants alleged that defendants violated the following "treaties of the United States":

—Geneva Convention Relative to the Protection of Civilian Persons in Time of War, Aug. 12, 1949, 6, U.S.T. 3516, T.I.A.S. No. 3365, 75 U.N.T.S. 287;

—Articles 1 and 2 of the Charter of the United Nations, June 26, 1945, 59 Stat. 1031, T.S. No. 993;

—Convention With Respect to the Laws and Customs of War on Land, July 29, 1899, 32 Stat. 1803, T. S. No. 403; Convention Respecting the Laws and Customs of War on Land, Oct. 18, 1907, 36 Stat. 2277, T.S. No. 539 (Hague Conventions);

—Geneva Convention Relative to the Treatment of Prisoners of War, Aug. 12, 1949, 6 U.S.T. 3316, T.I.A.S. 3364, 75 U.N.T.S. 135;

—Convention to Prevent and Punish the Acts of Terrorism Taking the Forms of Crime Against Persons and Related Extortion That Are of International Significance, Feb. 2, 1971, 27 U.S.T. 3949, T.I.A.S. No. 8413 (Organization of American States (OAS) Convention);

—Protocols I and II to the Geneva Conventions of 12 August 1949, June 7, 1977, Diplomatic Conference on Reaffirmation and Development of International Humanitarian Law Applicable in Armed Conflict, reprinted in Italy 16 I.L.M. 1391, 1442 (1977);

—Declaration on Principles of International Law Concerning Friendly Relations and Co-operation Among States in Accordance with the Charter of the United Nations, G.A.Res. 2625, 25 U.N.GAOR Supp. (No. 28) at 121, U.N.Doc. A/8028 (1970);

—Universal Declaration of Human Rights, G.A.Res. 217, U.N. 3 GAOR, U.N. Doc. 1/777 (1948);

—International Covenant on Civil and Political Rights, Annex to G.A. Res. 2200, 21 U.N.GAOR Supp. (No. 16) at 52, U.N. Doc. A/6316 (1966);

—Basic Principles for the Protection of Civilian Populations in Armed Conflicts, G.A. Res. 2675, 25 U.N. GAOR Supp. (No. 28) at 76, U.N.Doc A/8028 (1970);

—Convention on the Prevention and Punishment of the Crime and Genocide, Dec. 9, 1948, 78 U.N.T.S. 277;

—Declaration of the Rights of the Child, G.A.Res. 1386, 14 U.N.GAOR Supp. (No. 16) at 19, U.N. Doc. A/4354 (1959); and

—American Convention on Human Rights, Nov. 22, 1969, O.A.S. Official Records OEA/Ser. K/XVI/1.1, Doc. 65, Rev. 1, Corr. 1, *reprinted in* 9 I.L.M. 101 (1970), 65 AM.J.INT'L L. 679 (1971).

Only the first five of these alleged treaties are treaties currently binding on the United States. *See* Treaties Affairs Staff, Office of the Legal Adviser, Department of State, *Treaties in Force* (1983). Even if the remaining eight are relevant to Count II of the complaint as evidence of principles of international law, they are not treaties of the United States. Since Count III (tortuous actions in violation of the treaties of the United States) purports to state a cause of action distinct from that stated in Count II (tortuous actions in violation of the law of nations), the last eight of the thirteen alleged treaties of the United States can provide no basis for jurisdiction over the claims in Count III under the treaty components of sections 1331 and 1350.

Of the five treaties in force, none provides a private right of action. Three of them — the Geneva Convention for the Protection of Civilian Persons in Time of War, the Geneva Convention Relative to the Treatment of Prisoners of War, and the OAS Convention to Prevent and Punish Acts of Terrorism — expressly call for implementing legislation. A treaty that provides that party states will take measures through their own laws to enforce its proscriptions evidences its intent not to be self-executing. These three treaties are therefore not self-executing. Indeed, with respect to the first Geneva Convention, one court has already so held. *Huynh Thi Anh v. Levi*, 586 F.2d 626, 629 (6th Cir. 1978).

Articles 1 and 2 of the United Nations Charter are likewise not self-executing. They do not speak in terms of individual rights but impose obligations on nations and on the United Nations itself. They address states, calling on them to fulfill in good faith their obligations as members of the United Nations. Sanctions under article 41, the penultimate bulwark of the Charter, are to be taken by states against other states. Articles 1 and 2, moreover, contain general "purposes and principles," some of which state mere aspirations and none of which can sensibly be thought to have been intended to be judicially enforceable at the behest of individuals. These considerations compel the conclusion that articles 1 and 2 of the U.N. Charter were not intended to give individuals the right to enforce them in municipal courts, particularly since appellants have provided no evidence of a contrary intent.

The Hague Conventions similarly cannot be construed to afford individuals the right to judicial enforcement. Although the Conventions contain no language calling for implementing legislation, they have never been regarded as law private parties could enforce. If they were so regarded, the code of behavior the Conventions set out could create perhaps hundreds of thousands or millions of lawsuits by the many individuals, including prisoners of war, who might think their rights under the Hague Conventions violated in the course of any large-scale war. Those lawsuits might be far beyond the capacity of any legal system to resolve at all, much less accurately and fairly; and the courts of a victorious nation might well be less hospitable to such suits against that nation or the members of its armed forces than the courts of a defeated nation might, perforce, have to be. Finally, the prospect of innumerable private suits at the end of a war might be an obstacle to the negotiation of peace and the resumption of normal relations between nations. It is for these reasons that the Conventions are best regarded as addressed to the interests and honor of belligerent nations, not as raising the threat of judicially awarded damages at war's end. The Hague Conventions are not self-executing. The Second Circuit has drawn the same conclusion, *Dreyfus v. Von Finck*, 534 F.2d at 30, and appellants have pointed to no case holding otherwise in the more than three-quarters of a century since the Conventions were adopted.

None of the five treaties relied on by appellants thus even implicitly grants individuals the right to seek damages for violation of their provisions. Appellants have, therefore, failed to state a cause of action for violation of any treaties of the United

States. Count III of their complaint, consequently, does not come within the arising-under jurisdiction of section 1331. Nor does it come within section 1350, because this provision, like section 1331, is merely a jurisdiction-granting statute and not the implementing legislation required by non-self-executing treaties to enable individuals to enforce their provisions. *See Dreyfus v. Von Finck*, 534 F. 2d at 28 (affirming dismissal for lack of cause of action under treaties in suit by alien where jurisdiction expressly based on sections, 1331 and 1350).

IV.

Appellants' argument that they may recover damages for violations of international law is simple. International law, they point out, is part of the common law of the United States. This proposition is unexceptionable. *See, e.g., The Paquete Habana*, 175 U.S. 677 (1900) *United States v. Smith*, 18 U.S. (5 Wheat.) 153, 5 L. Ed. 57 (1820). But appellants then contend that federal common law automatically provides a cause of action for international law violations, as it would for violations of federal common law rights. I cannot accept this conclusion.

Appellants' argument reflects a confusion of two distinct meanings of "common law". That term has long referred to the body of court-made law whose origins can be traced to the medieval English legal system. It has also come to refer generally to law (mostly court-made) not based on a statute or constitution. "Federal common law", in particular, has been used "to refer generally to federal rules of decision where the authority for a federal rule is not explicitly or clearly found in federal statutory or constitutional command." To say that international law is part of federal common law is to say only that it is nonstatutory and nonconstitutional law to be applied, in appropriate cases, in municipal courts. It is not to say that, like the common law of contract and tort, for example, by itself it affords individuals the right to ask for judicial relief.

Thus, the step appellants would have us take — from the phrase "common law" to the implication of a cause of action — is not a simple and automatic one. Neither is it advisable. The considerations of separation of powers rehearsed above provide ample reason for refusing to take — a step that would plunge federal courts into the foreign affairs of the United States.

Appellants, seeking to recover for a violation of international law, might look to federal statutes either for a grant of a cause of action or for evidence that a cause of action exists. These notions may be quickly dismissed. The only plausible candidates are the two jurisdictional statutes relied on by appellants, sections 1331 and 1350 of Title 28 of the United States Code. Neither of those statutes either expressly or impliedly grants a cause of action. Both statutes merely define a class of cases federal courts can hear; they do not themselves even by implication authorize individuals to bring such cases. As the Supreme Court has stated, "[t]he Judicial Code, in vesting jurisdiction in the District Courts, does not create causes of action, but only confers jurisdiction to adjudicate those arising from other sources which satisfy its limiting provisions." *Montana-Dakota Utilities Co. v. Northwestern Public Service Co.*, 341 U.S. 246, 249 (1951). *See also Dreyfus v. Von Finck*, 534 F.2d at 28 (neither 1331 nor 1350 grants a cause of action).

Although the jurisdictional statutes relied on by appellants cannot be read to provide a cause of action, those statutes might conceivably provide evidence of Congress' recognition (as opposed to creation) of one. Appellants do not suggest that section 1331 is evidence of any such recognition, as nothing in its language or history could support such a reading. Rather, appellants focus on section 1350, which is concerned expressly and only with international law (treaties and customary international law) and therefore might suggest that Congress understood, when providing jurisdiction through section 1350, that some individuals would be able to take advantage of that jurisdiction because they had causes of action for torts committed in violation of the law of nations.

The broadest reading of section 1350 as evidence of congressional recognition of such a cause of action is that it merely requires that a plaintiff prove that the actions complained of violated international law. If that jurisdictional prerequisite is met, according to appellants, the plaintiff has a cause of action for tort damages, as he would for any tort. This approach is adopted by the Second Circuit in *Filartiga*....I believe, nonetheless, that this construction of section 1350 must be rejected for several reasons.

First, appellants' broad reading would have to apply equally to actions brought to recover damages for torts committed in violation of treaties, since treaties stand in exactly the same position in section 1350 as principles of customary international law (the law of nations). Such an application would render meaningless, for alien plaintiffs, the well established rule that treaties that provide no cause of action cannot be sued on without (express or implied) federal law authorization.

...[T]he analysis of the Second Circuit in *Filartiga,* would also make all United States treaties effectively self-executing. As appellants here seek evidence of a cause of action to vindicate an asserted international law right that they do not assert itself affords them a private right of action, their claim is indistinguishable, under the language of section 1350, from a claim brought to vindicate rights set forth in a non-self-executing treaty.

In addition, appellants' construction of section 1350 is too sweeping. It would authorize tort suits for the vindication of any international legal right. As demonstrated below, that result would be inconsistent with the severe limitations on individually initiated enforcement inherent in international law itself, and would run counter to constitutional limits on the role of federal courts. Those reasons demand rejection of appellants' construction of section 1350 unless a narrow reading of the provision is incompatible with congressional intent. There is no evidence, however, that Congress intended the result appellants suggest.

What is known of the origins of section 1350 was perhaps best described by Judge Friendly in *IIT v. Vencap, Ltd.*, 519 F.2d 1001, 1015 (2d Cir.1975): "This old but little used section is a kind of legal Lohengrin;...no one seems to know whence it came." Section 1350 was enacted, in almost its current form, as part of the Judiciary Act of 1789, ch. 20, 1 Stat. 73, 77. I have discovered no direct evidence of what Congress had in mind when enacting the provision. The debates over the Judiciary Act in the House — the Senate debates were not recorded — nowhere mention the provision, not even, so far as we are aware, indirectly.

Historical research has not as yet disclosed what section 1350 was intended to accomplish. The fact poses a special problem for courts. A statute whose original meaning is hidden from us and yet which, if its words are read incautiously with modern assumptions in mind, is capable of plunging our nation into foreign conflicts, ought to be approached by the judiciary with great circumspection. It will not do simply to assert that the statutory phrase, the "law of nations," whatever it may have meant in 1789, must be read today as incorporating all the modern rules of international law and giving aliens private causes of action for violations of those rules. It will not do because the result is contrary not only to what we know of the framers' general purposes in this area but contrary as well to the appropriate, indeed the constitutional, role of courts with respect to foreign affairs.

What little relevant historical background is now available to us indicates that those who drafted the Constitution and the Judiciary Act of 1789 wanted to open federal courts to aliens for the purpose of avoiding, not provoking, conflicts with other nations. *The Federalist* No. 80 (A. Hamilton). A broad reading of motion 1350 runs directly contrary to that desire. It is also relevant to a construction of this provision that until quite recently nobody understood it to empower courts to entertain cases like this one or like *Filartiga*. As Justice Frankfurter said in *Romero. v. International Terminal Operating Co.*, 858 U.S. 354, 379 (1959):

> The considerations of history and policy which investigation has illuminated are powerfully reinforced by the deeply felt and traditional reluctance of this Court to expand the jurisdiction of the federal courts through a broad reading of jurisdictional statutes. A reluctance which must be even more forcefully felt when the expansion is proposed, for the first time, eighty-three years after the jurisdiction has been conferred.

In the case of section 1350, the period before the expansion was proposed is more than twice eighty-three years.

Though it is not necessary to the decision of this case, it may be well to suggest what section 1350 may have been enacted to accomplish, if only to meet the charge that my interpretation is not plausible because it would drain the statute of meaning. The phrase "law of nations" has meant various things over time. It is important to remember that in 1789 there was no concept of international human rights; neither was there, under the traditional version of customary international law, any recognition of a right of private parties to recover. Clearly, cases like this and *Filartiga* were beyond the framers' contemplation. That problem is not avoided by observing that the law of nations evolves. It is one thing for a case like *The Paquete Habana* to find that a rule has evolved so that the United States may not seize coastal fishing boats of a nation with which we are at war. It is another thing entirely, a difference in degree so enormous as to be a difference in kind, to find that a rule has evolved against torture by government so that our courts must sit in judgment of the conduct of foreign officials in their own countries with respect to their own citizens. The latter assertion raises prospects of judicial interference with foreign affairs that the former does not. A different question might be presented if section 1350 had been adopted by a modern Congress that made clear its desire that federal courts police the behavior of foreign individuals and governments. But section 1350 does not embody a legislative judgment that is either current or clear and the statute must be read with that in mind.

What kinds of alien tort actions, then might the Congress of 1789 have meant to bring into federal courts? According to Blackstone, a writer certainly familiar to colonial lawyers, "the principal offences against the law of nations, animadverted on as such by the municipal laws of England, [were] of three kinds; 1. Violation of safe-conducts; 2. Infringement of the rights of ambassadors; and 3. Piracy." 4. W. BLACKSTONE, COMMENTARIES 68, 72, *quoted in* 1 W.W. CROSSKEY, POLITICS AND CONSTITUTION IN THE HISTORY OF THE UNITED STATES (1953) ("Crosskey"). One might suppose that these were the kinds of offenses for which Congress wished to provide tort jurisdiction for suits by aliens in order to avoid conflicts with other nations.

The Constitution, of course, gave particular attention to piracy and to the rights of ambassadors. Article I, section 8, links piracy and the law of nations by granting Congress power "to define and punish Piracies and Felonies committed on the high Seas, and Offences against the Law of Nations." And Article III, section 2, gives the

Supreme Court original jurisdiction over "all Cases affecting Ambassadors, other Public Ministers and Consuls." Section 9 of the Judiciary Act of 1789 (now section 1350) gave jurisdiction to district courts, concurrent with that of state courts and circuit courts, over tort suits by aliens for violations of the law of nations. Judiciary Act of 1789, ch. 20, § 9, 1 Stat. 73, 76-77. This may well have envisaged a tort like piracy (a citizen could use diversity jurisdiction).

The idea that section 9 of the original Judiciary Act, now section 1350, was concerned with the rights of ambassadors (and other foreign representatives) is suggested by another provision of the statutes. Section 13 gave the Supreme Court such original and exclusive jurisdiction over all suits *against* ambassadors "as a court of law can have or exercise consistently with the "law of nations" (emphasis added). Judiciary Act of 1789, ch. 20, § 13, 1 Stat. 73, 80-81. That section, however, gave the Court original but not exclusive jurisdiction of "all suits brought by ambassadors other public ministers, or in which a consul, or vice consul, shall be a party" (emphasis added). This appears to tie in to the grant of tort jurisdiction for suits by aliens in what is now section 1350. (Section 1350's use of the broader term "aliens" may merely indicate that the torts of piracy and violations of safe-conduct, which would involve plaintiffs other than ambassadors, were included.)

An intent to protect the rights of ambassadors is also plausible historically. According to Crosskey, the Convention, in assigning to Congress the power to "define and punish...Offences against the Law of Nations" had in mind, aside from piracy, the rights of ambassadors. Crosskey at 459. He draws this conclusion from the notoriety of a case discussed by both Lord Mansfield, of the Court of King's Bench, and by Blackstone. An ambassador of the Czar had been arrested by his English creditors, and, was, in the process "somewhat roughed up before the arrest was accomplished." He demanded of the Queen that his assailants be subjected to "severe 'corporal Punishment.'" English law at the time, however, did not permit punishment severe enough to satisfy the offended ambassador, who protested to Czar Peter. The Czar demanded that the offenders be put to death. As a result, the law was changed, giving the Chief Justice of Queen's Bench, among other members of the "executive" branch, the power to try any offenses against ambassadors, and the Czar was placated. This "slightly ridiculous affair," according to Crosskey, was well-known because of repeated comment upon it. If this was indeed the incident the Convention considered in allocating to Congress the power to "define and punish...Offences against the Law of Nations," it may be that the First Congress, sensitive to the international ramifications of denying ambassadors redress, enacted section 1350 to give ambassadors the option of bringing tort actions in federal courts as well as in state courts.

These thoughts as to the possible original intention underlying section 1350 are admittedly speculative, and those who enacted the law may well have had additional torts in mind. I offer these possibilities merely to show that the statute could have served a useful purpose even if the larger tasks assigned it by *Filartiga*...are rejected. Moreover, if the offenses against the law of nations listed by Blackstone constituted the torts the framers of section 1350 had in mind, then the creation of federal jurisdiction for the redress of aliens' grievances would tend to ease rather than inflame relations with foreign, nations. That result comports with Hamilton's, expressed desire. Whether evidence so slim as to the intended office of the statute provides materials from which courts today may properly make substantive law is a jurisprudential issue with which, given the grounds upon which I would place our decision, I need not grapple today. But when courts go beyond the area in which there is any historical evidence, when they create the substantive rules for topics such as that taken up in *Filartiga* ... then law is made with no legislative guidance whatever. When that is so, it will not do to insist that the judge's duty is to construe the statute in order not to flout the will of Congress. On these topics, we have, at the moment, no evidence what the intention of Congress was. When courts lack such evidence, to "construe" is to legislate, to act in the dark, and hence to do many things that, it is virtually certain, Congress did not intend. Any correspondence between the will of Congress in 1789 and the decisions of the courts in 1984 can then be only accidental. Section 1350 can probably be adequately understood only in the context of the premises and assumptions of a legal culture that no longer exists. Perhaps historical research that is beyond the capacities of appellate judges will lift the darkness that now envelops this topic, but that has not yet occurred, and we should not attempt to anticipate what may or may not become visible.

Congress' understanding of the "law of nations" in 1789 is relevant to a consideration of whether Congress, by enacting section 1350, intended to open the federal courts to the vindication of the violation of any right recognized by international law. Examining the meaning of the "law of nations" at the time does not, contrary to my colleague's charges, "avoid the dictates of *The Paquete Habana*" and "limit the 'law of nations' to its 18th Century definition." The substantive rules of international law may evolve and perhaps courts may apply those new rules, but that does not solve the problem of the existence of a cause of action. If plaintiffs were explicitly provided with a cause of action by the law of nations, as it is currently understood, this court might — subject to considerations of justiciability — be required by section 1350 to entertain their claims. But, as discussed below, international law today does not provide plaintiffs with a cause of action.

Recognition of suits presenting serious problems of interference with foreign relations would conflict with the primary purpose of the adoption of the law of nations by federal law — to promote America's peaceful relations with other nations. See *The Federalist* No. 80 (A. Hamilton).... Adjudication of international disputes of this sort in federal courts, disputes over international violence occurring abroad, would be far more likely to exacerbate tensions with other nations than to promote peaceful relations.

Under the possible meaning I have sketched, section 1350's current function would be quite modest, unless a modern statute, treaty, or executive agreement provided a private cause of action for violations of new international norms which do not themselves contemplate private enforcement. Then, at least, we would have current political judgment about the role appropriate for courts in an area of considerable international sensitivity.

V.

Whether current international law itself gives appellants a cause of action requires more extended discussion. Appellants' claim, in Count II of their complaint, is that appellees have committed the "torts of terror, torture, hostage-taking and genocide," in violation of various customary principles of international law. Such principles become law by virtue of the "general assent of civilized nations." *The Paquete Habana*, 175 U.S. at 694. Unlike treaties and statutes, such law is not authoritatively pronounced by promulgation in a written document but must be found in the "customs and usages of civilized nations" as evidenced by the works of "jurists and commentators." *Id.* at 700, *see* Statute of the International Court of Justice, art. 38, 59 Stat. 1055 (1945), T.S. No. 993. Consequently, any cause of action that might exist, like the precise meaning of the customary principles themselves, must be inferred from the sources that are evidence of and attempt to formulate the legal rules. The district court found, and appellants have not argued to the contrary, that none of the documents appellants have put forth as stating the international legal principles on which they rely expressly state that individuals can bring suit in municipal courts to enforce the specified rights. Moreover, we have been pointed to nothing in their language, structure, or circumstances of promulgation that suggests that any of those documents should be read as implicitly dealing that an individual should be able to sue in municipal courts to enforce the specified rights. In any event, there is no need to review those documents and their origins in further detail, for, as a general rule, international law does not provide a private right of action, and an exception to that rule would have to be demonstrated by clear evidence that civilized nations had generally given their assent to the exception.

International law typically does not authorize individuals to vindicate rights by bringing actions in either international or municipal tribunals. "'Like a general treaty, the law of nations has been held not to be self-executing so as to vest a plaintiff with individual legal rights.'" *Dreyfus v. Von Finck*, 534 F.2d at 31 (quoting *Pauling v. McElroy*, 164 F. Supp. at 393). "[T]he usual method for an individual to seek relief is to exhaust local remedies and then repair to the executive authorities of his own state to persuade them to champion his claim in diplomacy or before an international tribunal." *Banco Nacional de Cuba v. Sabbatino*, 376 U.S. at 422-23.

This general relegation of individuals to a derivative role in the vindication of their legal rights stems from "[t]he traditional view of international law ... that it establishes substantive principles for determining whether one country has wronged another." 376 U.S. at 422. One scholar explained the primary role of states in international law as follows:

> Since the Law of Nations is based on the common consent of individual States, States are the principal subjects of International Law. This means that the Law of Nations is primarily a law for the international, conduct of States, and not of their citizens. As a rule, the subjects of the rights and duties arising from the Law of Nations are States solely and exclusively.

1 L. OPPENHEIM, INTERNATIONAL LAW: A TREATISE 19 (H. Lauterpacht 8th ed. 1955). Even statements of individuals' rights or norms of individual conduct that have earned the universal assent of civilized nations do not become principles of international law unless they are "used by ... states for their common good and/or in dealings *inter se.*" ...

If it is in large part because "the Law of Nations is primarily a law between States" that international law generally relies on an enforcement scheme in which individuals have no direct role, that reliance also reflects recognition of some other important characteristics of international law that distinguish it from municipal law. Chief among these is the limited role of law in the international realm. International law plays a much less pervasive role in the ordering of states' conduct within the international community than does municipal law in the ordering of individuals' conduct within nations. Unlike our nation, for example, the international community could not plausibly be described as governed by laws rather than men. "[I]nternational legal disputes are not as separable from politics as are domestic legal disputes.... " *First National City Bank v. Banco Nacional de Cuba*, 406 U.S. at 775.

International law, unlike municipal law (at least in the United States), is not widely regarded as a tool of first or frequent resort and as the last word in the legitimate resolution of conflicts. Nations rely chiefly on diplomacy and other political tools in their dealings with each other, and these means are frequently incompatible with declarations of legal rights. Diplomacy demands great flexibility and focuses primarily on the future rather than on the past, often requiring states to refrain, for the sake of their future relations, from pronouncing judgment on past conduct. Since states adopt international law to improve their relations with each other, it is hardly surprising in the current world that they should generally retain for themselves control over the ability to invoke it. Nor is it surprising that international law is invoked less often to secure authoritative adjudications than it is to bolster negotiating positions or to acquire public support for foreign-relations policies. "By and large, nations have resisted third-party settlement of their disputes and adjudicative techniques have played a very limited role in their relations." One consequence is that international law has not been extensively developed through judicial decisions. See L. Henkin, R. Pugh, O. Schachter & H. Smit, *supra,* at 88 ("The strongly political character of many international issues accounts for the relative paucity of judicial decisions in contemporary international law.").

This remains true even as international law has become increasingly concerned with individual rights. Some of the rights specified in the documents relied upon by appellants as stating principles of international law recognizing individual rights are clearly not expected to be judicially enforced throughout the world.... Some of the key documents are meant to be statements of ideals and aspirations only; they are, in short, merely precatory.... Some define rights at so high a level of generality or in terms so dependent for their meaning on particular social, economic, and political circumstances that they cannot be construed and applied by courts acting in a traditional adjudicatory manner.... Some expressly oblige states to enact implementing legislation, thus impliedly denying a private cause of action.

It may be doubted that courts should understand documents of this sort as having been assented to as law by all civilized nations since enforcement of the principles enunciated would revolutionize most societies. For that reason, among others, courts should hesitate long before finding violations of a "law of nations" evidenced primarily by the resolutions and declarations of multinational bodies. In any event, many of the rights they declare clearly were not intended for judicial enforcement at the behest of individuals. The express provision in the European Convention for the Protection of Human Rights and Fundamental Freedoms, Nov. 4, 1950, art. 25, 213 U.N.T.S. 221, E.T.S. 5, of an international tribunal to which individuals may bring claims, thus evidencing states' ability to provide private rights of action when they wish to do so, is an extraordinarily exception that highlights the general absence of individual-complaint procedures. Even that exception, moreover, is a far cry from the authorization of ordinary municipal-court enforcement. Current international human rights law, in whatever sense it may be called "law," is doubtless growing. But it remains true that even that branch of international law does not today generally provide a private right of action.

Appellants, therefore, are not granted a private right of action to bring this lawsuit either by a specific international legal right or impliedly by the whole or parts of international law.

VI.

In *Filartiga v. Pena-Irala* 630 F.2d 876 (2d Cir.1980), the Second Circuit, which did not address the issue of the existence of a cause of action, held that section 1350 afforded jurisdiction over a claim brought by Paraguayan citizens against a former Paraguayan official. The plaintiffs, a father and daughter, alleged that the defendant had tortured his son, her brother, in violation of international law's proscription of official torture. To highlight what I believe should be the basis for our holding, it is worth pointing out several significant differences between this case and *Filartiga*.

First, unlike the defendants in this case, the defendant in *Filartiga* was a state official acting in his official capacity. Second, the actions of the defendant in *Filartiga* were in violation of the constitution and laws of his state and were "wholly unratified by that nation's government." Third, the international law rule invoked in *Filartiga* was the proscription of official torture, a principle that is embodied in numerous international conventions and declarations, that is "clear and unambiguous" in its application to the facts in *Filartiga*, and about which there is universal agreement "in the modern usage and practice of nations."

Thus, in *Filartiga* the defendant was clearly the subject of international-law duties, the challenged actions were not attributed to a participant in American foreign relations, and the relevant international law principle was one whose definition was neither disputed nor politically sensitive. None of that can be said about this case. For these reasons, not all of the analysis employed here would apply to deny a cause of action to the plaintiffs in *Filartiga*.

I differ with the *Filartiga* decision however, because the court there did not address the question of whether international law created a cause of action that the private parties before it could enforce in municipal courts. For the reasons given, that inquiry is essential.

Kadic v. Karadzic
70 F.3d 232 (2d Cir. 1995)

JON O. NEWMAN, Chief Judge:

Most Americans would probably be surprised to learn that victim of atrocities committed in Bosnia are suing the leader of the insurgent Bosnian-Serb forces in a United States District Court in Manhattan. Their claims seek to build upon the foundation of this Court's decision in *Filártiga v. Peña Irala*, 630 F.2d 876 (2d Cir.1980), which recognized the important principle that the venerable Alien Tort Act, 28 U.S.C. § 1350 (1988), enacted in 1789 but rarely invoked since then, validly creates federal court jurisdiction for suits alleging torts committed anywhere in the world against aliens in violation of the law of nations. The pending appeals pose additional significant issues as to the scope of the Alien Tort Act: whether some violations of the law of nations may be remedied when committed by those not acting under the authority of a state; if so, whether genocide, war crimes, and crimes against humanity are among the violations that do not require state action; and whether a person, otherwise liable for a violation of the law of nations, is immune from service of process because he is present in the United States as an invitee of the United Nations.

These issues arise on appeals by two groups of plaintiffs-appellants from the November 19, 1994, judgment of the United States District Court for the Southern District of New York (Peter K. Leisure, Judge), dismissing, for lack of subject-matter jurisdiction, their suits against defendant-appellee Radovan Karadžić, President of the self-proclaimed Bosnian-Serb republic of "Srpska." *Doe v. Karadžić* 866 F.Supp. 734 (S.D.N.Y. 1994) (*"Doe"*). For the reasons set forth below, we hold that subject-matter jurisdiction exists, that Karadžić may be found liable for genocide, war crimes, and crimes against humanity in his private capacity and for other violations in his capacity as a state actor, and that he is not immune from service of process. We therefore reverse and remand.

BACKGROUND

The plaintiffs-appellants are Croat and Muslim citizens of the internationally recognized nation of Bosnia-Herzegovina, formerly a republic of Yugoslavia. Their complaints, which we accept as true for purposes of this appeal, allege that they are victims and representatives of victims, of various atrocities, including brutal acts of rape, forced prostitution, forced impregnation, torture, and summary execution, carried out by Bosnian-Serb military forces as part of a genocidal campaign conducted in the course of the Bosnian civil war. Karadžić, formerly a citizen of Yugoslavia and now a citizen of Bosnia-Herzegovina, is the President of a three-man presidency of the self-proclaimed Bosnian-Serb republic within Bosnia-Herzegovina, sometimes referred to as "Srpska," which claims to exercise lawful authority, and does in fact exercise actual control, over large parts of the territory of Bosnia-Herzegovina. In his capacity as President, Karadžić possesses ultimate command authority over the Bosnian-Serb military forces, and the injuries perpetrated upon plaintiffs were committed as part of a pattern of systematic human rights violations that was directed by Karadžić and carried out by the military forces under his command. The complaints allege that Karadžić acted in an official capacity either as the titular head of Srpska or in collaboration with the government of the recognized nation of the former Yugoslavia and its dominant constituent republic, Serbia.

The two groups of plaintiffs asserted causes of action for genocide, rape, forced prostitution and impregnation, torture and other cruel inhuman, and degrading treatment, assault and battery, sex and ethnic inequality, summary execution, and wrongful death. They sought compensatory and punitive damages, attorney's fees, and, in one of the cases, injunctive relief. Plaintiffs grounded subject-matter jurisdiction in the Alien Tort Act, the Torture Victim Protection Act of 1991 ("Torture Victim Act"), ... *codified at* 28 U.S.C. § 1350 note ..., the general federal-question jurisdictional statute, 28 U.S.C. § 1331 ..., and principles of supplemental jurisdiction, 28 U.S.C. § 1367. ...

In early 1993, Karadžić was admitted to the United States on three separate occasions as an invitee of the United Nations. According to affidavits submitted by the plaintiffs, Karadžić was personally served with the summons and complaint in each action during two of these visits while he was physically present in Manhattan. Karadžić admits that he received the summons and complaint in the *Kadic* action, but disputes whether the attempt to serve him personally in the *Doe* action was effective.

. . . .

DISCUSSION

. . . .

I. Subject-Matter Jurisdiction

Appellants allege three statutory bases for the subject-matter jurisdiction of the District Court — the Alien Tort Act, the Torture Victim Act, and the general federal-question jurisdictional statute.

A. The Alien Tort Act

1. General Application to Appellants' claims

The Alien Tort Act provides:

The district courts shall have original jurisdiction of any civil action by an alien for a tort only, committed in violation of the law of nations or a treaty of the United States.

28 U.S.C. § 1350.... Our decision in *Filártiga* established that this statute confers federal subject-matter jurisdiction when the following three conditions are satisfied (1) an alien sues (2) for a tort (3) committed in violation of the law of nations (*i.e.*, international law). The first two requirements are plainly satisfied here, and the only disputed issue is whether plaintiffs have pleaded violations of international law.

Because the Alien Tort Act requires that plaintiffs plead a "violation of the law of nations" at the jurisdictional threshold, this statute requires a more searching review of the merits to establish jurisdiction than is required under the more flexible "arising under" formula of section 1331. Thus, it is not a sufficient basis for jurisdiction to plead merely a colorable violation of the law of nations. There is no federal subject-matter jurisdiction under the Alien Tort Act unless the complaint adequately pleads a violation of the law of nations (or treaty of the United States).

Filártiga established that courts ascertaining the content of the law of nations "must interpret international law not as it was in 1789, but as it has evolved and exists among the nations of the world today." We find the norms of contemporary international law by "'consulting the works of jurists, writing professedly on public law; or by the general usage and practice of nations; or by judicial decisions recognizing and enforcing that law.'" *Filártiga*, F.2d at 880 (quoting *United States v. Smith*, 18 U.S. (5 Wheat.) 153, 160–61 (1820)). If this inquiry discloses that the defendant's alleged conduct violates "well-established, universally recognized norms of international law," as opposed to "idiosyncratic legal rules," then federal jurisdiction exists under the Alien Tort Act.

Karadžić contends that appellants have not alleged violations of the norms of international law because such norms bind only states and persons acting under color of a state's law, not private individuals. In making this contention, Karadžić advances the contradictory positions that he is not a state actor, even as he asserts that he is the President of the self-proclaimed Republic of Srpska. For their part, the Kadic appellants also take somewhat inconsistent positions in pleading defendant's role as President of Srpska, and also contending that "Karadžić is not an official of any government."

Judge Leisure accepted Karadžić's contention that "acts committed by non-state actors do not violate the law of nations," and considered him to be a non-state actor. The Judge appears to have deemed state action required primarily on the basis of cases determining the need for state action as to claims of official torture, without consideration of the substantial body of law, discussed below, that renders private individuals liable for some international law violations.

We do not agree that the law of nations, as understood in the modern era confines its reach to state action. Instead, we hold that certain forms of conduct violate the law of nations whether undertaken by those acting under the auspices of a state or only as private individuals. An early example of the application of the law of nations to the act of private individuals is the prohibition against piracy. In *The Brig Malek Adhel*, 43 U.S. (2 How.) 210, 232, 11 L.Ed. 239 (1844), the Supreme Court observed that pirates were "*hostis humani generis*" (an enemy of all mankind) in part because they acted "without...any pretense of public authority." *See generally* 4 William Blackstone, *Commentaries on the Laws of England* 68.... Later examples are prohibitions against the slave trade and certain war crimes.

The liability of private persons for certain violations of customary international law and the availability of the Alien Tort Act to remedy such violations was early recognized by the Executive Branch in an opinion of Attorney General Bradford in reference to acts of American citizens aiding the French fleet to plunder British property off the coast of Sierra Leone in 1795. The Executive Branch has emphatically restated in this litigation its position that private persons may be found liable under the Alien Tort Act for acts of genocide, war crimes, and other violations of international humanitarian law.

The *Restatement (Third) of the Foreign Relations Law of the United States* (1986) ("*Restatement (Third)* ") proclaims: "Individuals may be held liable for offenses against international law, such as piracy, war crimes, and genocide." The *Restatement* is careful to identify those violations that are actionable when committed by a state, *Restatement (Third)* § 702, and a more limited category of violations of "universal concern," *id.* § 404, partially overlapping with those listed in section 702. Though the immediate focus of section 404 is to identify those offenses for which a state has jurisdiction to punish without regard to territoriality or the nationality of the offenders, the inclusion of piracy and slave trade from an earlier era and aircraft hijacking from the modern era demonstrates that the offenses of "universal concern" include those capable of being committed by non-state actors. Although the jurisdiction authorized by section 404 is usually exercised by application of criminal law, international law also permits states to establish appropriate civil remedies, *id.* § 404 cmt. b, such as the tort actions authorized by the Alien Tort Act. Indeed, the two cases invoking the Alien Tort Act prior to *Filártiga* both applied the civil remedy to private action.

Karadžić disputes the application of the law of nations to any violations committed by private individuals, relying on *Filártiga* and the concurring opinion of Judge Edwards in *Tel-Oren v. Libyan Arab Republic*, 726 F.2d 774, 775 (D.C.Cir.1984), *cert. denied*, 470 U.S. 1003, . . . (1985). *Filártiga* involved an allegation of torture committed by a state official. Relying on the United Nations' Declaration on the Protection of All Persons from Being Subjected to Torture, G.A.Res. 3452, U.N. GAOR, U.N. Doc. A/1034 (1975) (hereinafter "Declaration on Torture"), as a definitive statement of norms of customary international law prohibiting states from permitting torture, we ruled that "*official* torture is now prohibited by the law of nations." *Filártiga*, 630 F.2d at 884 (emphasis added). We had no occasion to consider whether international law violations other than torture are actionable against private individuals, and nothing in *Filártiga* purports to preclude such a result.

Nor did Judge Edwards in his scholarly opinion in *Tel-Oren* reject the application of international law to any private action. On the contrary, citing piracy and slave-trading as early examples, he observed that there exists a "handful of crimes to which the law of nations attributes individual responsibility." Reviewing authorities similar to those consulted in *Filártiga*, he merely concluded that torture — the specific violation alleged in *Tel-Oren* was not within the limited category of violations that do not require state action.

Karadžić also contends that Congress intended the state-action requirement of the Torture Victim Act to apply to actions under the Alien Tort Act. We disagree. Congress enacted the Torture Victim Act to codify the cause of action recognized by this Circuit in *Filártiga*, and to further extend that cause of action to plaintiffs who are U.S. citizens. *See* H.R.Rep. No. 367, 102d Cong., 2d Sess., at 4 (1991), *reprinted in* 1992 U.S.C.C.A.N. 84, 86 (explaining that codification of *Filártiga* was necessary in light of skepticism expressed by Judge Bork's concurring opinion in *Tel-Oren*). At the same time, Congress indicated that the Alien Tort Act "has other important uses and should not be replaced," because

Claims based on torture and summary executions do not exhaust the list of actions that may appropriately be covered [by the Alien Tort Act]. That statute should remain intact to permit suits based on other norms that already exist or may ripen in the future into rules of customary international law.

Id. The scope of the Alien Tort Act remains undiminished by enactment of the Torture Victim Act.

2. Specific Application of Alien Tort Act to Appellants' Claims

In order to determine whether the offenses alleged by the appellants in this litigation are violations of the law of nations that may be the subject of Alien Tort Act claims against a private individual, we must make a particularized examination of these offenses,, mindful of the important precept that "evolving standards of international law govern who is within the [Alien Tort Acts] jurisdictional grant." In making that inquiry, it will be helpful to group the appellants' claims into three categories: (a) genocide, (b) war crimes, and (c) other instances of inflicting death, torture, and degrading treatment.

(a) *Genocide.* In the aftermath of the atrocities committed during the Second World War, the condemnation of genocide as contrary to international law quickly achieved broad acceptance by the community of nations. In 1946, the General Assembly of the United Nations declared that genocide is a crime under international law that is condemned by the civilized world, whether the perpetrators are "private individuals, public officials or statesmen." G.A.Res. 96(I), 1 U.N.GAOR, U.N. Doc. A/64/Add.1, at 188-89 (1946). The General Assembly also affirmed the principles of Article 6 of the Agreement and Charter Establishing the Nuremberg War Crimes Tribunal for punishing "'persecutions on political, racial, or religious grounds,'" regardless of whether the offenders acted "'as individuals or as members of organizations.'"

The Convention on the Prevention and Punishment of the Crime of Genocide, 78 U.N.T.S. 277, *entered into force* Jan. 12, 1951, *for the United States* Feb. 23, 1989 (hereinafter "Convention on Genocide"), provides a more specific articulation of the prohibition of genocide in international law. The Convention, which has been ratified by more than 120 nations, including the United States, defines "genocide" to mean

> any of the following acts committed with intent to destroy, in whole or in part, a national, ethnical, racial or religious group, as such—
>
> (a) Killing members of the group;
>
> (b) Causing serious bodily or mental harm to members of the group;
>
> (c) Deliberately inflicting on the group conditions of life calculated to bring about its physical destruction in whole or in part;
>
> (d) Imposing measures intended to prevent births within the group;
>
> (e) Forcibly transferring children of the group to another group.

Convention on Genocide art. II. Especially pertinent to the pending appeal, the Convention makes clear that "[p]ersons committing genocide...shall be punished, *whether they are constitutionally responsible rulers, public officials or private individuals.*" *Id.* art. IV (emphasis added). These authorities unambiguously reflect that, from its incorporation into international law, the proscription of genocide has applied equally to state and non-state actors.

The applicability of this norm to private individuals is also confirmed by the Genocide Convention Implementation Act of 1987, 18 U.S.C. § 1091, which criminalizes acts of genocide without regard to whether the offender is acting under color of law, *see id.* § 1091(a) ("[w]hoever" commits genocide shall be punished), if the crime is committed within the United States or by a U.S. national, *id.* § 1091(d). Though Congress provided that the Genocide Convention Implementation Act shall not "be construed as creating any substantive or procedural right enforceable by law by any party in any proceeding," *id.* § 1092, the legislative decision not to create a new private remedy does not imply that a private remedy is not already available under the Alien Tort Act. Nothing in the Genocide Convention Implementation Act or its legislative history reveals an intent by Congress to repeal the Alien Tort Act insofar as it applies to genocide, and the two statutes are surely not repugnant to each other. Under these circumstances, it would be improper to construe the Genocide Convention Implementation Act as repealing the Alien Tort Act by implication.

Appellants' allegations that Karadžić personally planned and ordered a campaign of murder, rape, forced impregnation, and other forms of torture designed to destroy the religious and ethnic groups of Bosnian Muslims and Bosnian Croats clearly state a violation of the international law norm proscribing genocide, regardless of whether Karadžić acted under color of law or as a private individual. The District Court has subject-matter jurisdiction over these claims pursuant to the Alien Tort Act.

(b) *War crimes.* Plaintiffs also contend that the acts of murder, rape, torture, and arbitrary detention of civilians, committed in the course of hostilities, violate the law of war. Atrocities of the types alleged here have long been recognized in international law as violations of the law of war. Moreover, international law imposes an affirmative duty on military commanders to take appropriate measures within their power to control troops under their command for the prevention of such atrocities.

After the Second World War, the law of war was codified in the four Geneva Conventions, which have been ratified by more than 180 nations, including the United States. Common article 3, which is substantially identical in each of the four Conventions, applies to "armed conflict[s] not of an international character" and binds "each Party to the conflict...to apply, as a minimum, the following provisions":

Persons taking no active part in the hostilities...shall in all circumstances be treated humanely, without any adverse distinction founded on race, colour, religion or faith, sex, birth or wealth, or any other similar criteria.

To this end, the following acts are and shall remain prohibited at any time and in any place whatsoever with respect to the above-mentioned persons:

(a) violence to life and person, in particular murder of all kinds, mutilation, cruel treatment and torture;

(b) taking of hostages;

(c) outrages upon personal dignity, in particular humiliating and degrading treatment;

(d) the passing of sentences and carrying out of executions without previous judgment pronounced by a regularly constituted court....

Geneva Convention I art. 3(1). Thus, under the law of war as codified in the Geneva Conventions, all "parties" to a conflict — which includes insurgent military groups — are obliged to adhere to these most fundamental requirements of the law of war.

The offenses alleged by the appellants, if proved, would violate the most fundamental norms of the law of war embodied in common article 3, which binds parties to internal conflicts regardless of whether they are recognized nations or roving hordes of insurgents. The liability of private individuals for committing war crimes has been recognized since World War I and was confirmed at Nuremberg after World War II, and remains today an important aspect of international law. The District Court has jurisdiction pursuant to the Alien Tort Act over appellants' claims of war crimes and other violations of international humanitarian law.

(c) *Torture and summary execution.* In *Filártiga*, we held that *official* torture is prohibited by universally accepted norms of international law, and the Torture Victim Act confirms this holding and extends it to cover summary execution. Torture Victim Act §§ 2(a), 3(a). However, torture and summary execution — when not perpetrated in the course of genocide or war crimes — are proscribed by international law only when committed by state officials or under color of law.

In the present case, appellants allege that acts of rape, torture, and summary execution were committed during hostilities by troops under Karadžić's command and with the specific intent of destroying appellants' ethnic-religious groups. Thus, many of the alleged atrocities are already encompassed within the appellants' claims of genocide and war crimes. Of course, at this threshold stage in the proceedings it cannot be known whether appellants will be able to prove the specific intent that is an element of genocide, or prove that each of the alleged torts were committed in the course of an armed conflict, as required to establish war crimes. It suffices to hold at this stage that the alleged atrocities are actionable under the Alien Tort Act, without regard to state action, to the extent that they were committed in pursuit of genocide or war crimes, and otherwise may be pursued against Karadžić to the extent that he is shown to be a state actor. Since the meaning of the state action requirement for purposes of international law violations will likely arise on remand and has already been considered by the District Court, we turn next to that requirement.

3. The State Action Requirement for International Law Violations

In dismissing plaintiffs' complaints for lack of subject-matter jurisdiction, the District Court concluded that the alleged violations required state action and that the "Bosnian-Serb entity" headed by Karadžić does not, meet the definition of a state. Appellants contend that they are entitled to prove that Srpska satisfies the definition of a state for purposes of international law violations and, alternatively, that Karadžić acted in concert with the recognized state of the former Yugoslavia and its constituent republic, Serbia.

(a) *Definition of a state in international law.* The definition of a state is well established in international law:

> Under international law, a state is an entity that has a defined territory and a permanent population, under the control of its own government, and that engages in, or has the capacity to engage in, formal relations with other such entities.

Restatement (Third) § 201.... "[A]ny government, however violent and wrongful in its origin, must be considered a de facto government if it was in the full and actual exercise of sovereignty over a territory and people large enough for a nation." *Ford v. Surget*, 97 U.S. (7 Otto) 594, 620, 24 L.Ed. 1018 (1878) (Clifford, J., concurring).

Although the *Restatement's* definition of statehood requires the *capacity* to engage in formal relations with other states, it does not require recognition by other states. *See Restatement (Third)* § 202 cmt. b ("An entity that satisfies the requirements of § 201 is a state whether or not its statehood is formally recognized by other states."). Recognized states enjoy certain privileges and immunities relevant to judicial proceedings, but an unrecognized state is not a juridical nullity. Our courts have regularly given effect to the "state" action of unrecognized states.

The customary international law human rights, such as the proscription of official torture, applies to states without distinction between recognized and unrecognized states. It would be anomalous indeed if non-recognition by the United States which typically reflects disfavor with a foreign regime — sometimes due to human rights abuses — had the perverse effect of shielding officials of the unrecognized regime from liability for those violations of international norms that apply only to state actors.

Appellants' allegations entitle them to prove that Karadžić's regime satisfies the criteria for a state, for purposes of those international law violations requiring state action. Srpska is alleged to control defined territory, control populations within its power, and to have entered into agreements with other governments. It has a president, a legislature, and its own currency. These circumstances readily appear to satisfy the criteria for a state in all aspects of international law. Moreover, it is likely that the state action concept, where applicable for some violations like "official" torture, requires merely the semblance of official authority. The inquiry, after all, is whether a person purporting to wield official power has exceeded internationally recognized standards of civilized conduct, not whether statehood in all its formal aspects exists.

(b) *Acting in concert with a foreign state*. Appellants also sufficiently alleged that Karadžić acted under color of law insofar as they claimed that he acted in concert with the former Yugoslavia, the statehood of which is not disputed. The "color of law" jurisprudence of 42 U.S.C. § 1983 is a relevant guide to whether a defendant has engaged in official action for purposes of jurisdiction under the Alien Tort Act. A private individual acts under color of law within the meaning of section 1983 when he acts together with state officials or with significant state aid. The appellants are entitled to prove their allegations that Karadžić acted under color of law of Yugoslavia by acting in concert with Yugoslav officials or aid.

B. The Torture Victim Protection Act

The Torture Victim Act, enacted in 1992, provides a cause of action for official torture and extrajudicial killing:

> An individual who, under actual or apparent authority, or color of law, of any foreign nation—
>
> (1) subjects an individual to torture shall, in a civil action, be liable for damages to that individual; or
>
> (2) subjects an individual to extrajudicial killing shall, in a civil action, be liable for damages to the individual's legal representative, or to any person who may be a claimant in an action for wrongful death

The statute also requires that a plaintiff exhaust adequate and available local remedies, imposes a ten-year statute of limitations, and defines the terms "extrajudicial killing" and "torture."

By its plain language, the Torture Victim Act renders liable only those individuals who have committed torture or extrajudicial killing "under actual or apparent authority, or color of law, of any foreign nation." Legislative history confirms that this language was intended to "make[] clear that the plaintiff must establish some governmental involvement in the torture or killing to prove a claim," and that the statute "does not attempt to deal with torture or killing by purely private groups." In construing the terms "actual or apparent authority" and "color of law," courts are instructed to look to principles of agency law and to jurisprudence under 42 U.S.C. § 1983, respectively.

Though the Torture Victim Act creates a cause of action for official torture, this statute, unlike the Alien Tort Act, is not itself a jurisdictional statute. The Torture Victim Act permits the appellants to pursue their claims of official torture under the jurisdiction conferred by the Alien Tort Act and also under the general federal question jurisdiction of section 1331, to which we now turn.

C. Section 1331

The appellants contend that section 1331 provides an independent basis for subject-matter jurisdiction over all claims alleging violations of international law. Relying on the settled proposition that federal common law incorporates international law, *see The Paquete Habana*, 175 U.S. 677, 700...(1900)..., *Filártiga*, 630 F.2d at 886, they reason that causes of action for violations of international law "arise under" the laws of the United States for purposes of jurisdiction under section 1331. Whether that is so is an issue of some uncertainty that need not be decided in this case

In *Tel-Oren*, Judge Edwards expressed the view that section 1331 did not supply jurisdiction for claimed violations of international law unless the plaintiffs could point a remedy granted by the law of nations or argue successfully that such a remedy is implied. The law of nations generally does not create private causes of action to remedy its violations, but leaves to each nation the task of defining the remedies that are available for international law violations. Some district courts, however, have upheld section 1331 jurisdiction for international law violations.

We recognized the possibility of section 1331 jurisdiction in *Filártiga*, 630 F.2d at 887 n. 22, but rested jurisdiction solely on the applicable Alien Tort Act. Since that appears to provide a remedy for the appellants' allegations of violations related to genocide, war crimes, and official torture, and the Torture Victim Act also appears to provide a remedy for their allegations of official torture, their causes of action are statutorily authorized, and, as in *Filártiga*, we need not rule definitively on whether any causes of action not specifically authorized by statute may be implied by international law standards as incorporated into United States law and grounded on section 1331 jurisdiction.

II. Service of Process and Personal Jurisdiction

Appellants aver that Karadžić was personally served with process while he was physically present in the Southern District of New York. In the *Doe* action, the affidavits detail that on February 11, 1993, process servers approached Karadžić in the lobby of the Hotel Intercontinental at Ill East 48th St. in Manhattan, called his name and identified their purpose, and attempted to hand him the complaint from a distance of two feet, that security guards seized the complaint papers, and that the papers fell to the floor. Karadžić submitted an affidavit of a State Department security officer, who generally confirmed the episode, but stated that the process server did not come closer than six feet of the defendant. In the *Kadic* action, the plaintiffs obtained from Judge Owen an order for alternate means of service, directing service by delivering the complaint to a member of defendant's State Department security detail, who was ordered to hand the complaint to the defendant. The security officer's affidavit states that he received the complaint and handed it to Karadžić outside the Russian Embassy in Manhattan. Karadžić's statement confirms that this occurred during his second visit to the United States, sometime between February 27 and March 8, 1993. Appellants also allege that during his visits to New York City, Karadžić stayed at hotels outside the "headquarters district" of the United Nations and engaged in non-United Nations-related activities such as fund-raising.

Fed.R.Civ.P. 4(e)(2) specifically authorizes personal service of a summons and complaint upon an individual physically present within a judicial district of the United States, and such personal service comports with the requirements of due process for the assertion of personal jurisdiction.

Nevertheless, Karadžić maintains that his status as an invitee of the United Nations during his visits to the United States rendered him immune from service of process. He relies on both the Agreement between the United Nations and the United States of America Regarding the Headquarters of the United Nations, *reprinted at* 22 U.S.C. § 287 note (1988) ("Headquarters Agreement"), and a claimed federal common law immunity. We reject both bases for immunity from service.

A. Headquarters Agreement

The Headquarters Agreement provides for immunity from suit only in narrowly defined circumstances. First, "service of legal process...may take place within the headquarters district only with the consent of and under conditions approved by the Secretary-General." *Id.* § 9(a). This provision is of no benefit to Karadžić, because he was not served within the well-defined confines of the "headquarters district," which is bounded by Franklin D. Roosevelt Drive, 1st Avenue, 42nd Street, and 48th Street. Second, certain representatives of members of the United Nations, whether residing inside or outside of the "headquarters district," shall be entitled to the same privileges and immunities as the United States extends to accredited diplomatic envoys. *Id.* § 15. This provision is also of no benefit to Karadžić, since he is not a designated representative of any member of the United Nations.

A third provision of the Headquarters Agreement prohibits federal, state, and local authorities of the United States from "impos[ing] any impediments to transit to or from the headquarters district of...persons invited to the headquarters district by the United Nations...on official business." *Id.* § 11. Karadžić maintains that allowing service of process upon a United Nations invitee who is on official business would violate this section, presumably because it would impose a potential burden — exposure to suit — on the invitee's transit to and from the headquarters district. However, this Court has previously refused "to extend the immunities provided by the Headquarters Agreement beyond those explicitly stated." *See Klinghoffer v. S.N.C. Achille Lauro*, 937 F.2d 44, 48 (2d Cir. 1991). We therefore reject Karadzic's proposed construction of section 11, because it would effectively create an immunity from suit for United Nations invitees where none is provided by the express terms of the Headquarters Agreement.

The parties to the Headquarters Agreement agree with our construction of it. In response to a letter from plaintiffs' attorneys opposing any grant of immunity to Karadžić, a responsible State Department official wrote: "Mr. Karadžić's status during his recent visits to the United States has been solely as an 'invitee' of the United Nations, and as such he enjoys no immunity from the jurisdiction of the courts of the United States." Letter from Michael J. Habib, Director of Eastern European Affairs, U.S. Dept. of State, to Beth Stephens (Mar. 24, 1993) ("Habib Letter"). Counsel for the United Nations has also issued an opinion stating that although the United States must allow United Nations invitees access to the Headquarters District, invitees are not immune from legal process while in the United States at locations outside of the Headquarters District.

B. Federal common law immunity

Karadžić nonetheless invites us to fashion a federal common law immunity for those within a judicial district as a United Nations invitee. He contends that such a rule is necessary to prevent private litigants from inhibiting the United Nations in its ability to consult with invited visitors. Karadžić analogizes his proposed rule to the "government contacts exception" to the District of Columbia's long-arm statute, which has been broadly characterized to mean that "mere entry [into the District of Columbia] by non-residents for the purpose of contacting federal government agencies cannot serve as a basis for in personam jurisdiction." He also points to a similar restriction upon assertion of personal jurisdiction on the basis of the presence of an individual who has entered a jurisdiction in order to attend court or otherwise engage in litigation.

Karadžić also endeavors to find support for a common law immunity in our decision in *Klinghoffer*. Though, as noted above, *Klinghoffer* declined to extend the immunities of the Headquarters Agreement beyond those provided by its express provisions, the decision applied immunity considerations to its construction of New York's long-arm statute, N.Y.Civ.Prac.L. & R. 301..., in deciding whether the Palestine Liberation Organization (PLO) was doing business in the state. *Klinghoffer* construed the concept of "doing business" to cover only those activities of the PLO that were not United Nations-related.

Despite the considerations that guided *Klinghoffer* in its narrowing construction of the general terminology of New York's long-arm statute as applied to United Nations activities, we decline the invitation to create a federal common law immunity as an extension of the precise terms of a carefully crafted treaty that struck the balance between the interest of the United Nations and those of the United States.

Finally, we note that the mere possibility that Karadžić might at some future date be recognized by the United States as the head of state of a friendly nation and might thereby acquire head-of-state immunity does not transform the appellants' claims into a nonjusticiable request for an advisory opinion, as the District Court intimated. Even if such future recognition, determined by the Executive Branch, would create head-of-state immunity, it would be entirely inappropriate for a court to create the functional equivalent of such an immunity based on speculation about what the Executive Branch *might* do in the future.

In sum, if appellants personally served Karadžić with the summons and complaint while he was in New York but outside of the U.N. headquarters district, as they are prepared to prove, he is subject to the personal jurisdiction of the District Court.

III. Justiciability

We recognize that cases of this nature might pose special questions concerning the judiciary's proper role when adjudication might have implications in the conduct of this nation's foreign relations. We do not read *Filártiga* to mean that the federal judiciary must always act in ways that risk significant interference with United States foreign relations. To the contrary, we recognize that suits of this nature can present difficulties that implicate sensitive matters of diplomacy historically reserved to the jurisdiction of the political branches. *See First National Bank v. Banco Nacional de Cuba*, 406 U.S. 759, 767 ... (1972). We therefore proceed to consider whether, even though the jurisdictional threshold is satisfied in the pending cases, other considerations relevant to justiciability weigh against permitting the suits to proceed.

Two nonjurisdictional, prudential doctrines reflect the judiciary's concerns regarding separation of powers: the political question doctrine and the act of state doctrine. It is the "'constitutional' underpinnings" of these doctrines that influenced the concurring opinions of Judge Robb and Judge Bork in *Tel-Oren*. Although we too recognize the potentially detrimental effects of judicial action in cases of this nature, we do not embrace the rather categorical views as to the inappropriateness of judicial action urged by Judges Robb and Bork. Not every case "touching foreign relations" is nonjusticiable, *see Baker v. Carr*, 369 U.S. 186, 211...(1962);..., and judges should not reflexively invoke these doctrines to avoid difficult and somewhat sensitive decisions in the context of human rights. We believe a preferable approach is to weigh carefully the relevant considerations on a case-by-case basis. This will permit the judiciary to act where appropriate in light of the express legislative mandate of the Congress in section 1350, without compromising the primacy of the political branches in foreign affairs.

Karadžić maintains that these suits were properly dismissed because they present nonjusticiable political questions. We disagree. Although these cases present issues that arise in a politically charged context, that does not transform them into cases involving nonjusticiable political questions. "[T]he doctrine 'is one of "political questions," not one of "political cases."'" *Klinghoffer*, 937 F.2d at 49 (quoting Baker, 369 U.S. at 217...).

A nonjusticiable political question would ordinarily involve one or more of the following factors:

> a textually demonstrable constitutional commitment of the issue to a coordinate political department; or [2] a lack of judiciary discoverable and manageable standards for resolving it; or [3] the impossibility of deciding without an initial policy determination of a kind clearly for nonjudicial discretion; or [4] the impossibility of a court's undertaking independent resolution without expressing lack of the respect due coordinate branches of government; or [5] an unusual need for unquestioning adherence to a political decision already made; or [6] the potentiality of embarrassment from multifarious pronouncements by various departments on one question.

Baker v. Carr, 369 U.S. at 217.... With respect to the first three factors, we have noted in a similar context involving a tort suit against the PLO that "[t]he department to whom this issue has been 'constitutionally committed' is none other than our own — the Judiciary." *Klinghoffer*, 937 F.2d at 49. Although the present actions are not based on the common law of torts, as was *Klinghoffer*, our decision in *Filártiga* established that universally recognized norms of international law provide judicially discoverable and manageable standards for adjudicating suits brought under the Alien Tort Act, which obviates any need to make initial policy decisions of the kind normally reserved for nonjudicial discretion. Moreover, the existence of judicially discoverable and manageable standards further undermines the claim that such suits relate to matters that are constitutionally committed to another branch.

The fourth through sixth *Baker* factors appear to be relevant only if judicial resolution of a question would contradict prior decisions taken by a political branch in those limited contexts where such contradiction would seriously interfere with important governmental interests. Disputes implicating foreign policy concerns have the potential to raise political question issues, although, as the Supreme Court has wisely cautioned, "it is 'error to suppose that every case or controversy which touches foreign relations lies beyond judicial cognizance.'"

The act of state doctrine, under which courts generally from judging the acts of a foreign state within its territory, *see Banco Nacional de Cuba v. Sabbatino*, 376 U.S. at 428..., *Underhill v. Hernandez*, 168 U.S. 250, 252,...(1897), might be implicated in some cases arising under section 1350. However, as in *Filártiga*, we doubt that the acts of even a state official, taken in violation of a nation's fundamental law and wholly unratified by that nation's government, could properly be characterized as an act of state.

In the pending appeal, we need have no concern that interference with important governmental interests warrants rejection of appellants' claims. After commencing their action against Karadžić, attorneys for the plaintiffs in *Doe* wrote to the Secretary of State to oppose reported attempts by Karadžić to be granted immunity from suit in the United States; a copy of plaintiffs' complaint was attached to the letter. Far from intervening in the case to urge rejection of the suit on the ground that it presented political questions, the Department responded with a letter indicating that Karadžić was not immune from suit as an invitee of the United Nations. *See* Habib Letter, *supra*. After oral argument in the pending appeals, this Court wrote to the Attorney General to inquire whether the United States wished to offer any further views concerning any of the issues raised. In a "Statement of Interest," signed by the Solicitor General and the State Department's Legal Adviser, the United States has expressly disclaimed any concern that the political question doctrine should be invoked to prevent the litigation of these lawsuits: "Although there might be instances in which federal courts are asked to issue rulings under the Alien Tort Statute or the Torture Victim Protection Act that might raise a political question, this is not one of them." Though even an assertion of the political question doctrine by the Executive Branch, entitled to respectful consideration, would not necessarily preclude adjudication, the Government's reply to our inquiry reinforces our view that adjudication may properly proceed.

As to the act of state doctrine, the doctrine was not asserted in the District Court and is not before us on this appeal. Moreover the appellee has not had the temerity to assert in this Court that the acts he allegedly committed are the officially approved policy of a state. Finally, as noted, we think it would be a rare case in which the act of state doctrine precluded suit under section 1350, *Banco Nacional* was careful to recognize the doctrine "in the absence of...unambiguous agreement regarding controlling legal principles," such as exist in the pending litigation, and applied the doctrine only in a context—expropriation of an alien's property—in which world opinion was sharply divided.

Finally, we note that at this stage of the litigation no party has identified a more suitable forum, and we are aware of none. Though the Statement of the United States suggests the general importance of considering the doctrine of *forum non conveniens*, it seems evident that the courts of the former Yugoslavia, either in Serbia or war-torn Bosnia, are not now available to entertain plaintiffs' claims, even if circumstances concerning the location of witnesses and documents were presented that were sufficient to overcome the plaintiffs' preference for a United States forum.

Conclusion

The judgment of the District Court dismissing appellants' complaints for lack of subject-matter jurisdiction is reversed, and the cases are remanded for further proceedings in accordance with this opinion.

Beanal v. Freeport-McMoran, Inc.

969 F.Supp. 362 (E.D. LA. 1997)

DUVAL, District Judge.

Before the court is a motion to dismiss Plaintiff Tom Beanal's ("Beanal") claims against Freeport-McMoRan, Inc. and Freeport-McMoRan Copper & Gold, Inc. (collectively "Freeport")....Having reviewed the pleadings, the memoranda, and the applicable law, the court finds as follows for the reasons set forth below: (1) Plaintiff has standing to bring claims on his own behalf for cultural genocide of the Amungme tribe, certain human rights violations, and environmental claims, but lacks standing to bring claims on behalf of others for summary execution and disappearances; (2) Plaintiff has failed to state a claim for genocide in violation of the law of nations, pursuant to the Alien Tort Statute; (3) Plaintiff has failed to allege state action as required under the Alien Tort Statute because he failed to allege that Freeport acted under color of Indonesian law; (4) The Torture Victim Protection Act does not supersede or impliedly repeal the causes of action under the Alien Tort Statute for torture and extrajudicial killing committed in violation of the law of nations; (5) The Torture Victim Protection Act does not apply to corporations; and (6) Plaintiff has failed to state a claim for an environmental tort in violation of the law of nations.

The Parties

Plaintiff Tom Beanal ("Beanal") is a resident of Tamika, Irian Jaya within the Republic of Indonesia. He is a leader of the Amungme Tribal Counsel of Lambaga Adat Suku Amungme (LEMASA). He filed suit against Freeport on April 29, 1996, individually and on behalf of all other similarly situated. Plaintiff filed his first amended complaint on May 16, 1996. Since no class has been certified, Beanal is the lone plaintiff at this stage.

Defendants Freeport-McMoRan, Inc. and Freeport-McMoRan Copper & Gold, Inc. are Delaware corporations headquartered in New Orleans, Louisiana. Freeport owns an Indonesia-based subsidiary named P.T. Freeport Indonesia ("PT-FI").

Freeport operates the "Grasberg Mine," an open pit copper, gold and silver mine situated in the Jayawijaya Mountain in Irian Jaya, Indonesia. The mine allegedly encompasses approximately 26,400 square kilometers.

The Complaint

Beanal's first amended complaint alleges that Freeport has committed environmental torts, human rights abuses, and cultural genocide. Beanal states that the court has jurisdiction over this case based on diversity jurisdiction, pursuant to 28 U.S.C. § 1332 ("§ 1332"), The Alien Tort Statute, 28 U.S.C. § 1350 ("§ 1350"), and the Torture Victim Protection Act of 1991, sec. 1, et seq., 28 U.S.C. § 1350 note. Freeport's motion to dismiss focuses solely on the latter basis for jurisdiction under § 1350, and does not mention Plaintiff's diversity based claims. Accordingly, the court does not address those claims for damages and specific relief, if any, based on diversity jurisdiction. Since the prerequisites for diversity jurisdiction appear to have been satisfied and are not contested, this court has subject matter jurisdiction so long as Plaintiff can state at least one claim for relief. The court could exercise supplemental jurisdiction over other claims against Freeport. 28 U.S.C. § 1367.

The court reviews the claims made pursuant to § 1350 to determine if a cause of action exists. The current view of § 1350 is that it grants a federal cause of action as well as a federal forum in which to assert the claim. *Xuncax v. Gramajo*, 886 F.Supp. 162, 179 (D.Mass.1995).... The Fifth Circuit has acknowledged the generally held view that section 1350 is appropriately used by individuals asserting claims for violation of the international law of human rights. *De Sanchez v. Banco Central de Nicaragua*, 770 F.2d 1385, 1396, n. 16 (5th Cir.1985). Freeport appropriately moved to dismiss for failure to state a cause of action, under Rule 12(b)(1). Fed. R. Civ. Proc. 12(b)(1) and (6).

Summary of Freeport's Bases for Dismissal

Freeport asserts numerous reasons for the court to dismiss the claims for human rights violations and the environmental claims. First, Freeport argues that Beanal lacks standing to bring human rights claims in his own behalf or on behalf of others. As to the human rights claims asserted pursuant to the Alien Tort Statute, Freeport argues: (1) The Allen Tort Statute does not provide a private right of action; (2) Freeport is not a state actor; and (3) The TVPA supersedes the Alien Tort Statute for claims of torture and extrajudicial killings. As to the human rights violations asserted under the Torture Victim Protection Act ("TVPA"), Freeport argues that Beanal has failed to state a claim because: (1) The TVPA does not apply to corporations; (2) Beanal has not alleged that Freeport acted under color of foreign law; (3) Beanal failed to exhaust local remedies.

Freeport asserts five bases for dismissal of claims for international environmental torts brought under § 1350: (1) Beanal lacks standing to bring the environmental claims; (2) Beanal has failed to state a claim because environmental practices do not violate the law of nations; (3) The act of state doctrine bars Beanal's claims; (4) The local action doctrine mandates dismissal; and (5) The claims should be dismissed for failure to join an indispensable party, namely, the Republic of Indonesia.

The court discusses each issue in turn.

....

A. STANDING

....

Beanal has standing to assert claims on his own behalf. Beanal does not purport to be an organizational representative. Beanal identifies himself as "a leader of the Amungme Tribal Council Lembaga Musyawarah Adat Suku Amungme ('LEMASA')," but does not appear to be suing on behalf of "LEMASA" since he sued "individually and on behalf of all other similarly situated class members (Indigenous People of Irian Jaya)." Unlike Beanal, LEMASA is not listed as a party and the complaint does not indicate that LEMASA is bringing suit.

Furthermore, Beanal has not alleged facts which would entitle him to bring claims on behalf of a third party. Typically, there are three instances in which third party standing is permissible: (1) where individuals can represent the interests of parties who are unlikely to be able to represent their own interests; (2) where there is a close relationship between the advocate and the third party; and (3) where a statute is challenged as being unconstitutionally over-broad. Beanal has not alleged facts that would entitle him to claim any of these exceptions to the general rule against third party standing.

By definition, claims for disappearance and summary execution are based on harm to a third party. Section 1350 is silent concerning a plaintiffs standing to bring suit based on an injury to another. It is generally assumed that where Congress is silent as to such a detail, federal courts borrow from state law, unless its application would defeat the purpose of the federal statute. In *Xuncax* the court determined who could bring a claim under § 1350 for summary execution and disappearances by following the approach used by other courts in determining the statute of limitations applicable under § 1350. To determine whether to apply federal or state limitations period, the Court must first identify the closest analogies under both federal and state law...." The *Xuncax* court found that the statute most analogous, to § 1350 was the Torture Victim Protection Act, which provides that the victim's "legal representative" or "any person who may be a claimant in an action for wrongful death," may recover based on an extrajudicial killing. The House Report on the TVPA states that "[c]ourts look to state law for guidance as to which parties would be proper wrongful death claimants." H.R.Rep. No. 256, 102nd Cong., 1st, Sess. 87 (1991). This court is also persuaded that the Torture Victim Protection Act is most analogous to § 1350. Accordingly, the court turns to Louisiana law to determine who can bring suit under the Alien Tort Statute.

Louisiana law does not permit the bringing of a wrongful death action by a non-relative of the victim. Louisiana Civil Code Article 2315.2 lists the following surviving relatives of the deceased who may bring a wrongful death action: spouse, children, father, mother, brothers, sisters. La. C.C. Art. 2325.2. The court finds that Beanal, who has not identified himself as a relative of any victim, would be unable to bring a wrongful death action in Louisiana, and therefore lacks the standing to sue on behalf of victims of disappearance or summary execution under § 1350.

To meet the standing requirements under Article III, the Fifth Circuit requires that plaintiff demonstrate two things:

> "[1] First, that he personally has suffered some actual or threatened injury as a result of the putatively illegal conduct of the defendant, and [2] second, a causal connection between the injury and the conduct such that the injury is "likely to be redressed by a favorable decision. The Supreme Court has recognized that injuries to a plaintiff's aesthetic conservational and recreational interests are sufficient to meet the first requirement of Article III standing."

For purposes of determining standing on a motion to dismiss, the court "presumes that general allegations embrace those specific facts that are necessary to support the claim."

In light of Beanal's status as the sole named plaintiff, the court finds that he has standing to bring claims on his own behalf for certain human rights violations, genocide and environmental torts. Beanal alleges in his complaint that he has been personally inured by certain human rights abuses and environmental practices. The court finds that Beanal has standing to assert those claims for which he alleges an individualized injury. Beanal requests a judgment for money damages as well as specific relief, either of which would redress the harm caused by Freeport for its alleged wrongdoing, if any.

Disregarding those allegations which appear to have been made on behalf of other putative class members, the following specific injuries shall be regarded as having been asserted by Plaintiff individually:

(1) Torture, detention, surveillance, destruction of property. Plaintiff may have experienced such practices personally and claims damages for associated injuries.

(2) Purposeful, deliberate, contrived and planned cultural demise of the Amungme culture due to various human rights and environmental vio-

lations. The court permits Beanal to make his claim for "cultural genocide" as a member of the Amungme tribe only.

(3) All alleged environmental violations from various mining practices carried out in and nearby the locality where Plaintiff resides, including: destruction, pollution, alteration, and contamination of natural waterways, as well as surface and ground water sources; deforestation; destruction and alteration of physical surroundings. Plaintiff alleges that he is a resident of Tamika, Irian Jaya, Indonesia, where the Grasberg mine is located, and is a member of an indigenous tribe that inhabits the area. As a local inhabitant, Plaintiff has a palpable interest in the damage Freeport allegedly causes to nearby waterways and water source, soil, and forests, as well as any aesthetic injuries.

B. HUMAN RIGHTS VIOLATIONS

Beanal seeks to redress human rights violations under the Alien Tort Statute and the Torture Victim Protection Act. As noted above, Beanal complains individually of (1) arbitrary arrest and detention (2) torture (3) surveillance, (4) destruction of property, and (5) severe physical pain and suffering. Beanal alleges that Freeport engaged in these abuses through its security guards "in conjunction with third parties."

Based on a liberal construction of his complaint, Plaintiff may have been injured in connection with the following incidents described in the complaint:

(1) Repeated acts of torture have occurred at Freeport security stations and Freeport containers, which conduct includes kicking with military boots, beating with fists, sticks, rifle butts, stones; starvation, standing with heavy weights on the subject's head; shackling of thumbs, wrists and legs;

(2) Security surveillance of Plaintiff and others resulting in fear and mental stress;

(3) Torture victims were forced to stand in Freeport containers in water calf-high which reeked of human feces;

(4) Indigenous people have been detained with their eyes taped shut, thumbs tied, subject to repeated beatings by Freeport security personnel and third parties acting in conjunction with said personnel.

The court must determine whether Beanal has stated a cause of action under the Alien Tort Statute or the Torture Victim Protection Act for any of these alleged injuries.

1. § 1350: The Alien Tort Statute

The Alien Tort Statute provides:

The district courts shall have original jurisdiction of any civil action by an alien for a tort only, committed in violation of the law of nations.

28 U.S.C. § 1350. Beanal has not pled nor argued that a treaty applies. Rather, Beanal asserts that Freeport's conduct violated the law of nations.

Though mostly ignored since its enactment in 1789, § 1350 has more recently been used in connection with international human rights litigation. *Filártiga v. Pena-Irala*, 630 F.2d 876, 887 (2d. Cir.1980). Courts have recognized important precepts which relate to this case, namely, where a private individual asserts a claim against a private actor for violation of the law of nations. First, § 1350 provides a private right of action. *Id.* at 887...; *Kadic v. Karadžić*, 70 F.3d 232, 238 (2d Cir.1995); *Xuncax*, 886 F.Supp. at 179.... Second, an individual found to have violated the law of nations may be held liable under § 1350. *Filártiga* 630 F.2d at 880; *Kadic*, 70 F.3d at 239; *Xuncax* 886 F.Supp. at 179....

To make out a claim under § 1350, three elements must be satisfied: (1) an alien sues (2) for a tort (3) committed in violation of the law of nations. *Kadic*, 70 F.3d at 238.... The first two requirements are satisfied here: Beanal is an alien and has alleged tortious conduct.

The issue before the court, therefore, is to determine whether the alleged conduct sets forth a violation of the law of nations. To do so, the court must determine, first, whether there is an applicable norm of international law and, second, whether it has been violated. To be recognized as an international tort under § 1350, the alleged violation must be definable, obligatory (rather than hortatory), and universally condemned. *Filártiga*, 630 F.2d at 881. In making its determination, a court is guided by the sources from which customary international law is derived, including the usage of nations, judicial opinions and the works of jurists. *Id.* citing *Filártiga*, 630 F.2d at 884; *cf. Carmichael v. United Technologies Corp.*, 835 F.2d 109, 113 (5th Cir.1988). *Filártiga* instructed that the law of nations is dynamic, rather than static: "[C]ourts must interpret international law not as it was in 1789, but as it has evolved and exists among the nations of the world today." In sum, an international tort, *i.e.*, one that violates the law of nations, should satisfy the following requirements:

> (1) no state condones the act in question and there is a recognizable "universal" consensus of prohibition against it; (2) there are sufficient criteria to determine whether a given action amounts to the prohibited act and thus violates the norm; (3)   the prohibition against it is non-derogable and therefore binding at all times upon all actors.

Xuncax, 886 F.Supp. at 184...; *Restatement (Third) of Foreign Relations Law of the United States* §§ 701-702 ("*Restatement*").

Freeport first contends that state action is required to violate international law. Freeport argues that Beanal has failed to allege state action and therefore cannot state a claim for violation of the law of nations. Freeport further maintains that Beanal has failed to allege facts to state a claim for genocide even if the court should find that state action is not a required element of that claim.

The court must determine whether state action is required to state a claim in violation of the law of nations. On this point, the Second Circuit's decision in *Kadic v. Karadžić*, 70 F.3d 232 (2d Cir.1995), is instructive. In *Kadic*, two groups of victims, Croat and Muslim citizens of Bosnia Herzegovina, filed suit against Radovan Karadžić, the self-claimed President of Bosnian-Serb Republic within Bosnia Herzegovina. The plaintiffs complained that they were the victims of various human rights violations, including rape, forced prostitution, forced impregnation, torture, summary execution, genocide, other cruel, inhuman, and degrading treatment, assault and battery, sex and ethnic inequality, and wrongful death. The victims sought relief under the Alien Tort Statute, The Torture Victim Protection Act, and federal question jurisdiction. The district court dismissed the suit for lack of subject matter jurisdiction. The Second Circuit reversed and remanded the case to the district court for further findings as to genocide, war crimes, state action, torture and extrajudicial killing.

In *Kadic*, the Second Circuit held that state action is not required for all international torts. Certain conduct violates the law of nations whether committed by a state or private actor, whereas other conduct only violates the law of nations if committed by a state actor. This court, as guided by the analysis in *Kadic*, reaches the same conclusion. Genocide, for example, violates international law, whether undertaken by a state or non-state actor. The *Restatement* provides that a state has jurisdiction "to define and prescribe punishment for certain offenses recognized by the community of nations as of universal concern," such as piracy, hijacking, genocide, war crimes, and certain acts of terrorism. *Restatement* § 104. So-called "universal jurisdiction" exists over the specified offenses, as a matter of customary law, "as a result of universal condemnation of those activities and general interest in cooperation to suppress them, as reflected in widely accepted international agreements and resolutions of international organizations." *Id.*, comment a. Where a state has universal jurisdiction, it may punish conduct although the state has no links of territoriality or nationality with the offender or victim. Universal jurisdiction includes civil tort actions. *Id.*, comment b. Though the list of offenses specified in section 404 is not static, genocide is the only relevant offense for which universal jurisdiction exists and no state action must be proven.

A broader range of conduct is actionable as violative of the law of nations only when committed by a state actor. *Restatement* section 702 provides:

A state violates international law if, as a matter of state policy, it practices, encourages, or condones

(a) genocide;

(b) slavery or slave trade;

(c) the murder or causing the disappearance of individuals;

(d) torture or other cruel, inhuman, or degrading treatment or punishment;

(e) prolonged arbitrary detention;

(f) systematic racial discrimination; or

(g) a consistent pattern of gross violation of internationally recognized human rights.

As discussed below, some of the acts listed under section 702, *e.g.*, murder and torture, could be actionable without proof of state action if committed as acts of genocide. Standing alone, however, the acts of murder and torture are only actionable by proof of state action.

2. § 1350 Claim Not Requiring State Action: Genocide

Beanal's complaint of genocide is less than crystal clear. One portion of the first amended complaint is entitled "Cultural Genocide," but the word "genocide" does not otherwise appear. Beanal essentially complains that the alleged human rights abuses and environmental violations have resulted in the demise of the culture of the indigenous tribal people.

The court reviews the facts Beanal alleges under the caption "Cultural Genocide":

¶ 41. The Plaintiffs specifically reallege each and every paragraph of the foregoing complaint.

¶ 42. The Plaintiffs allege that the human rights violation and the eco-terrorism engaged in by the defendant corporations have destroyed the rights and culture of the Amungme and other Indigenous tribal people.

¶ 43. Since defendant corporations have commenced their operations, many Amungme people have been displaced and relocated to areas in the lowlands away from their cultural heritage of highland living.

¶ 44. Other Indigenous tribal people, including but not limited to Komora Tribe, have met the same fate.

¶ 45. The egregious human rights and environmental violations, which have terrorized the tribal communities of the Amungme and other Indigenous tribal people, destroyed their natural habitats and caused dislocation of the populations have resulted in the purposeful, deliberate, contrived and planned demise of a culture of indigenous people whose rights were never considered, whose heritage and culture were disregarded and the result of which is ultimately to lead to the cultural demise of unique pristine heritage which is socially, culturally and anthropologically irreplaceable.

Since Plaintiff re-alleges the human rights and environmental practices in connection with the cultural genocide claim, the court may consider whether any of those allegations would be redressable if committed as acts of genocide.

Genocide is an international tort. The crime of genocide was clearly recognized in the aftermath of the Second World War by the United Nations, international conventions, United States law and case law. Article II of the Convention on the Prevention and Punishment of the Crime of Genocide, 78 U.N.T.S. 277, ("Convention on Genocide"), defines the crime of genocide as:

[A]ny of the following acts committed with intent to destroy, in whole or in part, a national, ethnical, racial or religious group, as such

(a) Killing members of the group;

(b) Causing serious bodily or mental harm to the group;

(c) Deliberately inflicting on the group conditions of life calculated to bring about its physical destruction in whole or in part;

(d) Imposing measures intended to prevent births within the group;

(e) Forcibly transferring children of the group to another group.

This definition is generally accepted for purposes of customary law. *Restatement* § 702, comment d. The Convention on Genocide unambiguously applies to all: "[p]ersons committing genocide...shall be punished, whether they are constitutionally responsible rulers, public officials, or private individuals." Convention on Genocide, art. IV. This language squares with the Genocide Convention Implementation Act of 1987, 18 U.S.C. § 1091 (1988), and the *Restatement*, § 702, note d: both non-state actors and state actors may be held liable for genocide.

The application of the definition of genocide to Beanal's complaint causes the court to pause. As mentioned above, Beanal does not allege genocide, but rather "cultural genocide." The court focuses on the allegation that Freeport's conduct has resulted in displacement, relocation and "purposeful, deliberate, contrived and planned demise of a culture of indigenous people." As defined, genocide means the destruction of a "group" not a "culture." The court accepts at face value that as a tribe, the Amungme would constitute a "group." Furthermore, as defined, genocide includes deliberate acts on the group conditions of life "calculated to bring about its physical destruction," but does not purport to include acts which cause "displacement" and "relocation" absent any physical destruction. Finally, the acts of killing and causing serious bodily or mental harm constitute genocide only if they are carried out with the specific intent to destroy the group. The court is unwilling to make leaps of logic necessary to support a claim for genocide on unpled facts. Clearly, Beanal has alleged certain acts, such as torture, which, if committed with the requisite intent, could constitute an act of genocide. The problem is that Beanal has failed to make the core allegation that Freeport is committing genocide on a group of people. If Beanal in fact means that Freeport is destroying the Amungme culture, then he has failed to state a claim for genocide. On the other hand, if Beanal intended to state that Freeport is committing acts with the intent to destroy the Amungme group, *i.e.*, its members, then he has failed to make this allegation sufficiently explicit. The court finds that a claim for genocide is not sufficiently clear and Beanal shall be given the opportunity to make a more definite statement....

3. § 1350 Claims Requiring State Action

Beanal must allege state action in order to state a claim under § 1350 for non-genocide related human rights violations abuses. *Restatement* § 702, *Kadic*, 70 F.3d at 244. International law prohibits states from engaging in certain human rights abuses, including genocide, murder, causing disappearance, torture, cruel and inhuman treatment or punishment, prolonged arbitrary detention and systematic race discrimination. The *Restatement* provides that "a state violates international law, if as a matter of state policy, it practices, encourages or condones" certain proscribed conduct. With the exception of genocide, Plaintiff must allege state action in order to state a claim for any of these violations.

To allege state action, the challenged conduct must be attributable to the state; in other words, it must be official conduct. A state is responsible for any violation of its obligations under international law resulting from action or inaction by "any organ, official, employee, or other agent of a government or of any political subdivision, acting within the scope of authority or under color of such authority."

Freeport does not satisfy the definition of a "state" as that term is defined in international law. *Restatement* § 201.

Under international law, a state is an entity that has a defined territory and a permanent population, under the control of its own government and that engages in, or has the capacity to engage in, formal relations with other such entities.

The fact that Freeport is itself not a "state" does not preclude its liability for violation of the law of nations since state actors, not merely the state itself, can be held liable for such violations. *Restatement* § 207.

The court must determine whether Plaintiff has sufficiently alleged that Freeport's alleged conduct constitutes state action. Preliminarily, the court notes that nowhere in his complaint does Plaintiff allege that Freeport is a state actor, that Freeport was clothed with actual or apparent authority of the Republic of Indonesia, that Freeport aided or abetted official conduct or that Freeport acted under color of Indonesian law. As discussed below, any such terminology is used in the complaint to link the alleged conduct to Freeport, rather than to link Freeport to the Indonesian government. In an effort to liberally construe the complaint, the court probes the allegations to determine if such facts could form a basis for state action.

To determine whether state action has been alleged, the court considers the test contained in *Restatement* section 207 and the "under color of law" jurisprudence of 42 U.S.C. § 1983 ("§ 1983"). *Kadic*, 70 F.3d at 245...; *Restatement* § 207, note 4. It is difficult to discern from his complaint the theory of state action that Beanal seeks to establish. In his memorandum, Beanal argues that the allegations contained in Paragraph 8 of the Amended Complaint satisfy the state action requirement. Plaintiff argues that "the 'symbiotic relationship' among FREEPORT's employees, within its security force, and the Indonesian military" satisfies the requirement that those individuals acted under the "actual apparent authority" of the Republic of Indonesia. Though this argument lends some insight into a Plaintiff's theory of state action, Plaintiff cannot augment his complaint through his opposition memorandum. The facts forming a basis for state action must be discernible from the face of the complaint. The following allegations implicate some governmental involvement:

¶ 8.   The corporate defendants maintain a military presence within its mining operation wherein troops of the Republic of Indonesia are fed, transported, paid and provided equipment from the defendants in order to assist its operations.

¶ 10. ... [Freeport has] systematically engaged in a corporate policy both directly and indirectly through third parties which has resulted in human violations against the Amungme tribal people and other Indigenous tribal people.

¶ 11. ... The Indonesian Government is a major shareholder of the P.T. Freeport Indonesia, an affiliate of the defendants, Freeport, and the defendants' principle source of corporate income.

¶ 12. ... [D]efendants' security guards in conjunction with third parties acting by and through the corporate policy of the defendants have engaged in summary execution, arbitrary arrest and detention, torture, disappearances, surveillance and the destruction of property. Said violations have occurred on FREEPORT buses, within FREEPORT workshops, at FREEPORT security command centers, FREEPORT security stations, FREEPORT private roadways and containers owned by said corporate defendants.

¶ 21. That various human rights reports contain repeated first hand accounts of the brutal human rights violations of the FREEPORT security personnel and/or agents of FREEPORT whose conduct acquiesced to, accepted, adopted and/or ratified by the defendant corporations as of their corporate policy in operation and expanding their FREEPORT concession in Irian Jaya, Indonesia at expense of the local indigenous people.

¶ 22. The Plaintiffs allege that FREEPORT security personnel or third parties supported by defendant corporations were acting under actual or apparent authority of the defendant corporations.

The court analyzes these allegations using the "under color of authority" test contained in the comments to *Restatement* section 207.

In determining whether an act was within the authority of an official or an official body, or was done under color of such authority, (clause (c)), one must consider all the circumstances, including whether the affected parties reasonably considered the action to be official, whether the action was for public purpose or for private gain, and whether the persons acting wore official uniforms or used official equipment.

Restatement § 207, comment d. Applying the considerations noted in the *Restatement* reveals no easy conclusions regarding an allegation of state action. First, it is unclear whether the "affected parties reasonably considered the action to be official."

Beanal does not allege what exactly happened to him, who exactly he thought was involved in the challenged conduct, or whether he considered such person(s) to be engaging in official conduct. Second, it is unclear what purpose such abusive "security" practices could serve. Ostensibly, Freeport is motivated by "private gain", *i.e.*, corporate profit seeking, and the "security" practices and presence of Indonesian military personnel are designed to "assist [Freeport's] operations." The fact that the Indonesian Government funds Freeport does not convert Freeport's alleged practices into official action. Beanal has not alleged that Freeport is carrying out some "public purpose" through its harsh security practices on behalf of the Indonesian government. Beanal does allege that Freeport maintains, *i.e.*, feeds, transports, pays and equips, Indonesian military personnel on the premises. One could draw the inference that the military personnel participated first hand in the challenged conduct, help to create a martial atmosphere or lend an air of authority to Freeport's security practices. These are mere inferences, not allegations. Beanal alleges that the Indonesian military personnel uses equipment supplied by Freeport, not the government and does not indicate whether the military personnel wear official forms. Based on the *Restatement* test for official conduct, some of Plaintiff's allegations point to official action involving Indonesian Government personnel, while other allegations indicate that Freeport engaged in private conduct which occurred in the presence of Indonesian military personnel. Since the foregoing analysis is inconclusive, the court further probes the allegations pertaining state action.

The court considers the "under color of law" jurisprudence of § 1983. In *Kadic*, the Second Circuit declared that plaintiff meet the state action requirement by alleging that defendant "acted in concert with foreign state." In *Carmichael*, the Fifth Circuit stated, without deciding, that a private actor could be liable in tort for violation of international law by conspiring in, aiding or abetting official acts. In determining whether defendant "acted in concert" with a foreign state the court is guided by the "under color of law" jurisprudence applied in § 1983 cases. Section 1983 provides a cause of action against any person who, acting under color of state law, abridges rights created by the Constitution and the law of the United States. Section 1983 grants a remedy for violations of the Fourteenth Amendment of the United States Constitution, which provides, "No State shall...deprive any person of life, liberty, or property, without due process of law." In deciding whether the Fourteenth Amendment has been violated, courts distinguish between private and governmental conduct. By condemning only certain official conduct, these laws exclude a vast range of conduct visited upon victims at the hands of private actors. This dichotomy between private and official conduct is mirrored in international law. *See Restatement* § 207, comment c (A state is responsible under international law only for official acts, but not for acts by private actors.).

A private actor can be found liable under § 1983 for engaging in conduct which constitutes state action. The proper defendants in a § 1983 claim are those who represent the state in some capacity. *Gallagher v. Neil Young Freedom Concert*, 49 F.3d 1442, 1446 (10th Cir.1995). Similarly, in customary international law, a state is liable for official conduct committed by state officials. *Restatement* § 207, comment c, and § 702. The court understands the term "state" as it is used in the *Restatement* to be consistent with that term under § 1983 jurisprudence, *i.e.*, "those who represent the state." Accordingly, to make out his claim Beanal must allege that Freeport engaged in state action in violation of his rights under the international law of human rights.

Corporations can represent the state. Both private individuals and private entities can be state actors and can be held liable under § 1983. Section 1983 does not require that the defendant be an officer of the State. "Private persons jointly engaged with state officials in the challenged action, are acting under color of law for purposes of § 1983 purposes." Section 1983 applies to all persons, including corporations. The *Restatement* does not address who can be sued for human rights violations. Comment h to *Restatement* section 702 provides:

> In general, a state is responsible for officials or official bodies, national or local, even if the acts were not authorized by or known to the responsible national authorities, indeed even if expressly forbidden by law, decree or instruction. The violations of human rights cited in this section, however, are violations of customary international law only if practiced, encouraged, or condoned by the government of a state as official policy.

Section 702 uses the term "state," and the comments refer to "officials or official bodies." This language does not preclude corporate liability. Indeed, the term "official bodies" could cover private entities, rather than individuals, which engage in official conduct. *Carmichael* contemplated such corporate liability for a private actor which conspired in, aided or abetted official torture. Thus, the court finds that a corporation found to be a state actor can be held responsible for human rights abuses which violate international customary law. Having so concluded, the court now considers four tests used to determine whether a private actor has engaged in state action for purposes of § 1983.

The Supreme Court has recognized several circumstances in which a private actor can be held to have acted under color of law within the meaning of § 1983. In *Gallagher*, the Tenth Circuit Court of Appeals summarized the relevant tests:

> The Court has taken a flexible approach to the state action doctrine, applying a variety of tests to the facts of each case. [1] In some instances, the Court has considered whether there is a sufficiently close nexus between the State and the challenged action of the regulated entity so that the action of the latter may be fairly treated as that of the State itself. [2] The Court has also inquired whether the state has so far insinuated itself into a position of interdependence with the private party, that there is a symbiotic relationship between them. [3] In addition the Court has held that if a private party is a willful participant in joint activity with the State or its agents then state action is present. [4] Finally the Court has ruled that a private entity that exercises powers traditionally exclusively reserved to the State is engaged in state action.

The court refers to these four tests as (1) the nexus test, (2) the symbiotic relationship test, (3) the joint action test, and (4) the public function test.

Gallagher concerned the interaction between public officers and private security personnel. In *Gallagher* a group of individuals sued the University of Utah, a concert promoter and a private security corporation under section 1983 for violation of their Fourth Amendment rights. The plaintiffs were subjected to pat-down searches by the private security guards before entering the concert facility. University security officers observed but did not participate in the pat-down searches. After applying the four state action tests mentioned above, the Tenth Circuit Court of Appeals held that (1) the observation of the pat-down searches by university officials failed to provide the required nexus for state action, (2) the incidental benefits derived by the university from the concert were insufficient to satisfy the symbiotic relationship test for state action, and (3) the joint action test for state action was not satisfied due to plaintiffs' failure to present any evidence that the university officers influenced or assisted the conducting of the pat-down searches. The holdings in *Gallagher* are instructive in determining whether a factual predicate for state action exists in Beanal's complaint. Notably, *Gallagher* involved a motion for summary judgment rather than a motion to dismiss, which means that the *Gallagher* court engaged in a more demanding inquiry than is appropriate here.

The Nexus Test

Under the nexus test, a plaintiff must demonstrate that there is a sufficiently close nexus between the government and the challenged conduct such that the conduct may fairly be treated as that of the State itself. Governmental regulation, subsidy, approval of or acquiescence in the private conduct does not make the State responsible for the conduct. To satisfy the nexus test, the state must be significantly involved in or actually participate in the alleged conduct. *Id.* at 1449, ... *D'Amario v. Providence Civic Center Authority*, 783 F.2d 1 (1st Cir.1986).

The *D'Amario* case bears some factual resemblance to this one. In *D'Amario*, both a private concert promoter company and a municipally owned company were found to be state actors who abridged plaintiffs' First Amendment rights. Civic center employees enforced a so-called "no camera" rule at certain performances at the publicly operated Providence Civic Center. Although the "no camera" policy stemmed from the contractual agreement between two private parties, the enforcement of policy by the civic center employees constituted state action under the nexus test.

By contrast, in *Gallagher*, the court found that the observation by public employees of the pat-down searches performed by private security guards did not satisfy the nexus test for state action. The nexus test would be met if appellant could demonstrate that the pat-down searches directly resulted from the University's policies, but the mere presence of police officers did not transform the conduct of private parties into state action. The nexus test requirements of significant involvement and actual participation can be summarized as follows: where public officers enforce violative policies, there is state action; where public officers merely observe the enforcement of violative policies, there is no state action.

Beanal fails to allege facts sufficient to establish state action based on the nexus test. From the complaint it appears that Freeport's security personnel are distinct from the military personnel. Beanal specifically states that the mine is "policed" by Freeport's paramilitary type security personnel. He further alleges, "Additionally, upon information and belief, the corporate defendants maintain a military presence...in order to assist its operations." Beanal does not allege, however, what role those Indonesian troops played in the alleged violative conduct. Put simply, Beanal hasn't alleged whether the military personnel helped enforce Freeport's policies or merely observed Freeport's private security guards engage in the violative conduct. Inferentially, the complaint seeks to link the troops to the violations at hand. To draw that conclusion, however, would require the court to make up facts not alleged in the complaint.

The Symbiotic Relationship Test

State action can be established under the symbiotic relationship test if the state "has so far insinuated itself into a position of interdependence" with a private party that "it must be recognized as a joint participant in the challenged activity." *Burton* [v. Wilmington Parking Authority,], 365 U.S. [715] at 725. To establish a symbiotic relationship, the state and the private entity need be "physically and financially integral."

In *Burton*, the Court held a private restaurant to be a state actor. The Court found that by virtue of leasing its parking garage from a state agency, the restaurant functioned as a "physically and financially integral and, indeed, indispensable part" of the state's operation of its property. The parking structure was located on public property and maintained through public funds; its primary purpose was to lease parking space to commercial lessees.

The symbiotic relationship test from *Burton* is narrowly interpreted. The Court has held that state regulation, state funding, state approval of challenged conduct do not necessarily establish a symbiotic relationship between the state and a private entity. Two salient facts from *Burton* remain critical: that the state profited from the restaurant's discriminatory practices and that the restaurant was an indispensable part of a state project.

In *Gallagher*, the court found no symbiotic relationship existed based on the fact that the pat-down searches took place on University property and the fact that the University profited from the concert. The two entities were not "functionally intertwined," long-term dependence of one on the other was lacking, and the contractual benefits generated by the unconstitutional contract were not "indispensable" to the University's financial success. Payment under government contracts, government grants and tax benefits are insufficient to establish a symbiotic relationship between the government and a private entity.

Beanal's complaint alleges a close link between Freeport and Indonesian government. The complaint alleges that the Indonesian Government is a major shareholder in P.T. Freeport Indonesia, and a principal source of Freeport's corporate income. The complaint also refers to Freeport's "mining concession" throughout the complaint. It appears that the Indonesian government granted Freeport long-term mining rights, although the terms of such agreement are not mentioned in the complaint. There are too few facts alleged upon which to base a symbiotic relationship analysis for purposes of determining whether state action is alleged. A government contract conferring a mining concession and government investment in the operation are insufficient facts, standing alone, to allege a symbiotic relationship between Freeport and the Indonesian government.

The Joint Action Test

State action is present where a private party is a "willful participant in joint action with the State or its agents." As the *Gallagher* court made clear, the joint action test looks to whether the state officials and private parties acted in concert in effecting a particular deprivation of constitutional rights. The Fifth Circuit appears to require some actual participation or cooperation on behalf of the state and private actor in violating complainant's rights. As with the nexus test, state acquiescence or approval of the challenged conduct does not appear sufficient to satisfy the joint action test. Rather, the presence of government officers must have influenced or been an integral part of the challenged conduct. In *Gallagher*, the court found that there was no state action test because there was no evidence that the University shared with the private defendants the common goal to violate plaintiff's constitutional rights by conducting pat-down searches, that the University police influenced the decision to conduct the searches, or that the University played any role in the promotion company's decision to hire the private security company.

Beanal's complaint is insufficient under the joint action test for the reasons discussed with respect to the nexus test. Namely, the complaint fails to state what role, if any, the Indonesian military personnel played in the challenged conduct. In order to state facts sufficient to satisfy the joint action test, there must be some allegation indicating that the troops jointly cooperated in the conduct, jointly participated in the conduct, influenced the conduct or played an integral part in the deprivation of human rights. The complaint merely alleges an Indonesian military presence and obliquely refers to the participation of "third parties" who aided Freeport in the challenged conduct. The court finds that these allegations fail to make out a claim for state action under the joint action test.

The Public Function Test

Finally, state action can exist where a private entity performs a function traditionally the exclusive prerogative of the State. Few public functions have been found to satisfy this test. Among those activities which satisfy the public function test is the operation of a company owned town, *i.e.*, where the "streets, alleys, sewers, stores, residences, and everything else that goes to make a town" are privately owned. The management of a city park is also deemed an exclusive public function.

Again here, Beanal failed to allege facts which would satisfy the state action requirement under the public function test. Beanal alleges that Freeport operates the Grasberg Mine, which encompasses an area of 26,400 square kilometers which site was "policed" by Freeport's security personnel. Beanal further alleges the alleged human rights violations "occurred on FREEPORT buses, within FREEPORT workshops, at FREEPORT security command centers, FREEPORT security stations, FREEPORT private roadways and containers owned by said corporate defendants." It is unclear from the complaint whether Freeport actually operates or owns a town, controls the roads and walkways, residences, markets, etc., or has taken over the functions of regulating local life. The allegations create a picture, nonetheless, of Freeport's vast and draconian control over the Grasberg Mine area.

In sum, Beanal has failed to allege state action. Beanal has failed to allege what role, if any, that Indonesian military personnel played in committing the alleged conduct. More importantly, Beanal has failed to allege facts which would convert Freeport's alleged conduct into official action. State action is required to state a claim for violation of the international law of human rights. The court therefore dismisses without prejudice Beanal's claim for human rights violations under the Alien Tort Statute for failure to state a claim, and grants Plaintiff leave to amend his complaint in order to more specifically allege facts which form the basis for his state action argument, pursuant to Rule 12(e).

Impact of Torture Victim Protection Act on § 1350

The court rejects Freeport's contention that the Torture Victim Protection Act provides the sole cause of action for torture and extrajudicial killing brought under § 1350. The legislative history of the TVPA and recent case law stand for the contrary proposition that the TVPA codifies and expands the remedies available under § 1350. The court has failed to uncover a legislative intent to repeal or limit the kinds of claims redressable under § 1350.

The court focuses on the statutory text, the legislative history and recent case law. The text of the TVPA does not indicate that the statute provides the exclusive set of remedies for torture and extrajudicial killings. Congress unambiguously indicated that the Alien Tort Statute "has other important uses and should not be replaced." H.R. Rep. 367(I), 102nd Cong., 1st Sess. 1991, 1992 U.S.S.C.A.N. 84. In addition to codifying an "unambiguous and modern basis for a cause of action that has been successfully maintained under the existing law," Congress stated:

The TVPA...would enhance the remedy already available under section 1350 in an important respect: while the Alien Tort Claims Act provides a remedy to aliens only, the TVPA would extend a civil remedy also to U.S. citizens who may have been tortured abroad. Official torture and summary executions merit special attention in a statute expressly addressed to those practices. At the same time, claims based on torture or summary executions do not exhaust the list of actions that may appropriately be covered [by] section 1350. That statute should remain intact to permit suits based on other norms that already exist or may ripen in the future into rules of customary international law.

Id. From this passage, it appears that Congress did not intend for the TVPA to impinge on the scope of § 1350 or change the "law of nations." Congress clearly meant for "other norms" and future rules of international customary law to be redressable under § 1350. Congress did not indicate whether the court meant for the TVPA to become the exclusive remedy for torture and extrajudicial killings. Considering that the TVPA "enhances" rather than shrinks the scope of remedies under § 1350, there is no reason to conclude that by enacting the TVPA Congress took away causes of action for torture and extrajudicial killings under § 1350.

The *Kadic* court reached the same conclusion. In *Kadic*, the court reviewed the legislative history and concluded, "The scope of the Alien Tort Statute remains undiminished by enactment of the Torture Victim Protection Act." The court went on to address plaintiff's claims for torture and summary execution § 1350, noting that torture and summary execution are redressable under customary international law.

The court declines to find that TVPA repealed by implication the Alien Tort Statute, either in whole or in part. The doctrine of repeal by implication is disfavored. *Radzanower v. Touche Ross & Co.* 426 U.S. 148, 154...(1976). The Court recognizes certain appropriate circumstances:

There are, however, "two well-settled categories of repeals by implication — (1) where provisions in the two acts are in irreconcilable conflict, the later act to the extent of the conflict constitutes an implied repeal of the earlier one; and (2) if the later act covers the whole subject matter of the earlier one and is clearly intended as a substitute, it will operate similarly as a repeal of the earlier act. But, in either case, the intention of the legislature to repeal must be clear and manifest...." *Posados v. National City Bank*, 296 U.S. 497, 503...(1936).

Id. In applying this test, the court repeats the relevant points discussed above. First, there appears no clear and manifest intent to repeal any portion of § 1350. Second, there is no irreconcilable conflict because the TVPA does not appear to limit any cause of action under § 1350. Recent case law recognizes that a cause of action for extra-judicial killing and torture may lie under § 1350 based on both the TVPA and customary international law. Third, the TVPA was not intended to replace § 1350; the legislature did not change the text of § 1350 or seek to give it a particular meaning. In sum, the TVPA does not supersede or curtail the scope of § 1350 which permits a cause of action by an alien for a tort in violation of the law of nations.

Torture Victim Protection Act

With respect to Beanal's claims brought under the Torture Victim Protection Act, Freeport asserts that Beanal (1) failed to plead the requisite elements of the TVPA, and (2) that the TVPA does not apply to corporations.

The Torture Victim Protection Act provides an explicit cause of action for torture and extrajudicial killing. 28 U.S.C. sec. 1350, note, § 2. The TVPA provides:

(a) Liability — An individual who, under actual or apparent authority, or color of law, of any foreign nation —

   (1) Subjects an individual to torture shall, in a civil action, be liable for damages to that individual; or

   (2) Subjects an individual to judicial killing shall, in a civil action, be liable for damages to the individual's legal representative, or to any person who may be a claimant in an action for wrongful death.

(b) Exhaustion of remedies — A court shall decline to hear a claim under this section if the claimant has not exhausted adequate and available remedies in the place in which the conduct giving rise to the claim occurred.

Id. The terms "torture" and "extrajudicial killing" are defined by the statute. To state a claim under the TVPA, plaintiff must allege (1) that the individual defendant acted under color of law, (2) that defendant subjected an individual to torture or extrajudicial killing, and (3) that plaintiff has exhausted "adequate and available remedies" where the violative conduct occurred. Freeport alleges that Beanal has failed to allege the first and third elements.

By its terms, the TVPA only holds "individuals" liable. The court must determine whether the term "individual" includes a corporation for the purposes of the TVPA. The Fifth Circuit recently iterated the following approach to discern the meaning of a word as used in a statute:

As with any question of statutory meaning, we begin with the language of the statute. In determining a statute's plain meaning, we assume that absent any contrary definition, "Congress intends the words in its enactments to carry their ordinary contemporary, common meaning." *U.S. v. Gray*, 96 F.3d 769, 774 (5th Cir.1996)....The statute is the sole source of congressional intent where the statute is clear and does not demand an absurd result. In the same vein, the Supreme Court stated with respect to interpretation of the Bankruptcy Code: "The plain meaning of legislation should be conclusive, except in rare cases in which the literal application of a statute will produce a result demonstrably at odds with the intention of its drafters. In such cases, the intention of the drafters, rather than the strict language controls." *United States v. Ron Pair Enterprises, Inc.*, 489 U.S. 235, 240-42... (1989), *cited in Jove Engineering, Inc. v. I.R.S.*, 92 F.3d 1539, 1550 (11th Cir.1996).

The text of the TVPA does not define the term "individual." Before resorting to the legislative history, the court notes that the plain meaning of the term "individual" does not typically include a corporation. *Webster's New Collegiate Dictionary* defines "individual" as "a particular being or thing as distinguished from a class, species, or collection...a single human being as contrasted with a social group or institution." Blacks Law Dictionary defines "individual" to mean "a single person as distinguished from a group or class, and also, very commonly, a private or natural person as distinguished from a partnership, corporation, or association...it may, in proper cases, include a corporation." *Black's Law Dictionary* 773 (6th ed.1996), *cited in Jove*, 92 F.3d at 1551. Like the *Jove* court, this court finds that the plain meaning of the term "individual" does not ordinarily include a corporation. *Id.*

A finding that the TVPA does not apply to corporations is not at odds with congressional intent. To give the term "individual" its plain meaning under the TVPA means that the Act does not apply to corporate entities. There is no legislative history as to whether corporations could be held liable under the Act. The House Report accompanying the TVPA bill states, "Only 'individuals', not foreign states, can be sued under the bill." H.R. REP. NO. 367(I), 102ND CONG., 1ST SESS. 1991, 1992 U.S.S.C.A.N.

84....The Senate Report states, The legislation uses the term "individual" to make crystal clear that foreign states or their entities cannot be sued under this bill under any circumstances: "only individuals may be sued." S. REP. NO. 249, 102ND CONG., 1ST SESS.1991....These comments confirm that use of the term "individual" was not inadvertent. Congress purposefully chose the term so as to circumscribe foreign state liability under the Act. Congress does not appear to have had the intent to exclude private corporations from liability under the TVPA. Nevertheless, the Act clearly applies only to "individuals" and this court understands that term to plainly mean natural persons, not corporations. By use of the term "individual" the drafters may have unintentionally excluded corporations from liability under the Act. Even so, this court's interpretation that the TVPA only applies to natural persons is not at odds with the drafters' apparent intentions, and indeed, gives deference to Congress' particular word choice.

The court concludes that because Freeport as a corporation is not an "individual" for purposes of the TVPA, Freeport cannot be held liable under the TVPA. Plaintiff has no cause of action under the TVPA because he cannot satisfy the first element required to state a claim under the Act. The court need not reach the issue of whether Beanal satisfied the exhaustion of remedies requirement.

C. ENVIRONMENTAL CLAIMS

Freeport contends that Plaintiff's environmental claims should be dismissed on at least five different grounds; the court reaches only the first. Plaintiff has failed to state a claim for environmental violations upon which relief can be granted under § 1350 because Freeport's alleged environmental practices do not appear to have violated the law of nations.

As set forth in the complaint, Plaintiff alleges that Freeport's mining operations and drainage practices have resulted in environmental destruction with human costs to the indigenous people. The mine itself has hollowed several mountains, re-routed rivers; stripped forest and increased toxic and non-toxic materials and metals in the river system. Another culprit is discharged water containing tailings from Freeport's mining operations, for it is from this discharge that a stream of environmental and human problems flow, including:

1) pollution, disruption and alteration of natural waterways leading to deforestation;

2) health safety hazards and starvation;

3) degradation of surface and ground water from tailings and solid hazardous waste.

Beanal alleges that the tailings drainage is mismanaged. Beanal further alleges that acid mine drainage is equally devastating, due to resulting sulfide oxidation and leaching, and also inadequately managed. In summary, Plaintiff complains:

Plaintiffs specifically allege that defendant corporations have failed to engage in a zero waste policy, unacceptable enclosed waste management system, have failed to environmental rehabilitation, have failed to engage in an appropriate acid leachate control policy, have failed to adequately monitor the destruction of the natural resources of Irian Jaya and have disregarded and breached its international duty to protect one of the last great natural rain forests and alpine areas in the world.

Id. ¶ 40.

The court next determines whether any of these allegations, if true, amount to a violation of the law of nations. Plaintiff has not alleged that Freeport violated a specific treaty provision. As discussed above, in order to state a claim for violation of the law of nations under § 1350, plaintiff must establish the existence of a cognizable international tort. "These international torts, violations of current customary international law, are characterized by universal consensus in the international community as to their binding status and their content. That is, they are universal, definable, and obligatory international norms." To determine whether such a norm exists, the court may consider the works of jurists, general usage and practice of nations and judicial decisions recognizing and enforcing that law. In this instance, the court reviewed case law, the *Restatement*, and a recent treatise on international environmental law. Having done so, the court discerns no claim of action against Freeport based on an international tort.

As a preliminary matter, courts have recognized that § 1350 may be applicable to international environmental torts. *See Aguinda v. Texaco, Inc.*, 1994 WL 142006 (S.D.N.Y.1994); *Amalon Metals, Inc. v. FMC Corp.*, 775 F.Supp. 668, 670 (S.D.N.Y.1991). Neither of these cases, however, found a cause of action for environmental torts in violation of the law of nations. *Aguinda* referenced the possible application of § 1350 for environmental practices "which might violate international law." That suit was subsequently dismissed on grounds of comity, *forum non conveniens*, and failure to join a necessary party. *Amlon* involved the shipment of allegedly hazardous copper residue to a purchaser in England for metallic reclamation purposes. Among its claims, the purchaser sought recovery in tort under the Alien Tort Statute. The court rejected plaintiff's reliance on the Stockholm principles to support a cause of action under the § 1350 because "those Principles do not set forth any specific proscriptions, but rather refer only in a general sense to the responsibility of nations to insure that activities within their jurisdiction do not cause damage to the environment beyond their borders." This point is well taken with respect to Beanal's complaint.

Beanal has failed to articulate a violation of the international law. Plaintiff states that the allegations support a cause of action based on three international environmental law principles: (1) the Polluter Pays Principle; (2) the Precautionary Principle; and (3) the Proximity Principle. None of the three rises to the level of an international tort. *Principles of International Environmental Law I: Frameworks, Standards and Implementation* 183–18 (Phillipe Sands ed., 1995) (hereinafter "Sands"). Sands includes the three principles mentioned by Plaintiff in a list of general rules and principles "which have broad, if not necessarily universal, support and are frequently endorsed in practice." Also listed are (1) the good-neighborliness and international co-operation principle and (2) the following rule, regarded the cornerstone of international environmental law: "[T]he obligation reflected in Principle 21 of the Stockholm Declaration and Principle 2 of the Rio Declaration, namely that states have sovereignty over their natural resources and the responsibility not to cause environmental damage." Sands concludes:

> Of these general principles and rules only Principle 21/Principle 2 and the good neighborliness/international co-operation principle are sufficiently substantive at this time to be capable of establishing the basis of an international cause of action; that is to say, to give rise to an international customary legal obligation the violation of which would give rise to a legal remedy. The status and effect of the others remains inconclusive, although they may bind as treaty obligations or, in limited circumstances, as customary obligations.

Id.

The three principles relied on by Plaintiff, standing alone, do not constitute international torts for which there is universal consensus in the international community as to their binding status and their content. More to the point, those principles apply to "members of the international community" rather than non-state corporations. Plaintiff alleges that Freeport's environmental practices reflect corporate decisions, rather than state practices. A non-state corporation could be bound to such principles by treaty, but not as a matter of international customary law. Consistent with this conclusion, the *Restatement* mentions only state obligations and liability in the area of environmental law. *Restatement* §§ 601-602.

In sum, Beanal has failed to allege an international environmental tort. The court dismisses Beanal's environmental claims for failure to state a cause of action for violation of international environmental law. Beanal has failed to articulate a substantive claim. In addition, Beanal alleged no facts that would establish, if proven, that Freeport's environmental practices constitute state action. Even assuming for the purposes of this motion that Beanal's allegations are true, Freeport's alleged policies are corporate policies only and, however destructive, do not constitute torts in violation of the law of nations. Having so concluded, the court finds it unnecessary to rule on Freeport's remaining defenses to the environmental allegations lodged against it.

CONCLUSION

For the reasons stated, Beanal's claims brought under § 1350 for cultural genocide, human rights violations and international environmental torts are dismissed without prejudice. Fed. R. Civ. Proc. 12(b)(6). Plaintiff is granted leave to amend his complaint in order to more specifically allege his claims for genocide and human rights violations. Fed. R. Civ. Proc. 12(e).

D. Voluntary Corporate Codes of Conduct

The White House, Clinton Administration
Model Business Principles
(26 May 1995)

Recognizing the positive role of U.S. businesses in upholding and promoting adherence to universal standards of human rights, the [Clinton] Administration encourages all businesses to adopt and implement voluntary codes of conduct for doing business around the world that cover at least the following areas:

1. Provision of a safe and healthy workplace.

2. Fair employment practices, including avoidance of child and forced labor and avoidance of discrimination based on race, gender, national origin or religious beliefs; and respect for the right of association and the right to organize and bargain collectively.

3. Responsible environmental protection and environmental practices.

4. Compliance with U.S. and local laws promoting good business practices, including laws prohibiting illicit payments and ensuring fair competition.

5. Maintenance, through leadership at all levels, of [a] corporate culture that respects free expression consistent with legitimate business concerns, and does not condone political coercion in the workplace; that en-

courages good corporate citizenship and makes [a] positive contribution to the communities in which the company operates; and where ethical conduct is recognized, valued and exemplified by all employees.

In adopting voluntary codes of conduct that reflect these principles, U.S. companies should serve as models, encouraging similar behavior by their partners, suppliers, and subcontractors.

Adoption of codes of conduct reflecting these principles is voluntary. Companies are encouraged to develop their own codes of conduct appropriate to their particular circumstances. Many companies already apply statements or codes that incorporate these principles. Companies should find appropriate means to inform their shareholders and the public of actions undertaken to act in violation of host country or U.S. law. This statement of principles is not intended for legislation.

Reebok International Ltd., Human Rights Production Standards (1998)

A Commitment to Human Rights

Reebok's devotion to human rights worldwide is a hallmark of our corporate culture. As a corporation in an ever-more global economy we will not be indifferent to the standards of our business partners around the world. We believe that the incorporation of internationally recognized human rights standards into our business practice improves worker morale and results in a higher quality working environment and higher quality products. In developing this policy, we have sought to use standards that are fair, that are appropriate to diverse cultures and that encourage workers to take pride in their work.

Human Rights Production Standards

Non-Discrimination

Reebok will seek business partners that do not discriminate in hiring and employment practices on grounds of race, color, national origin, gender, religion, or political or other opinion.

Working Hours/Overtime

Reebok will seek business partners who do not require more than 60 hour work weeks on a regularly scheduled basis, except for appropriately compensated overtime in compliance with local laws, and we will favor business partners who use 48 hour work weeks as their maximum normal requirement.

Forced or Compulsory Labor

Reebok will not work with business partners that use forced or other compulsory labor, including labor that is required as a means of political coercion or as punishment for holding or for peacefully expressing political views, in the manufacture of its products. Reebok will not purchase materials that were produced by forced prison or other compulsory labor and will terminate business relationships with any sources found to utilize such labor.

Fair Wages

Reebok will seek business partners who share our commitment to the betterment of wage and benefit levels that address the basic needs of workers and their families so far as possible and appropriate in light of national practices and conditions. Reebok will not select business partners that pay less than the minimum wage required by local law or that pay less than prevailing local industry practices (whichever is higher).

Child Labor

Reebok will not work with business partners that use child labor. The term "child" generally refers to a person who is less than 14 years of age, or younger than the age for completing compulsory education if that age is higher than 14. In countries where the law defines "child" to include individuals who are older than 14, Reebok will apply that definition.

Freedom of Association

Reebok will seek business partners that share its commitment to the right of employees to establish and join organizations of their own choosing. Reebok will seek to assure that no employee is penalized because of his or her non-violent exercise of this right. Reebok recognizes and respects the right of all employees to organize and bargain collectively.

Safe and Healthy Work Environment

Reebok will seek business partners that strive to assure employees a safe and healthy workplace and that do not expose workers to hazardous conditions.

Application of Standards

Reebok will apply the *Reebok Human Rights Production Standards* in our selection of business partners. Reebok will seek compliance with these standards by our contractors, subcontractors, suppliers and other business partners. To assure proper implementation of this policy, Reebok will seek business partners that allow Reebok full knowledge of the production facilities used and will undertake affirmative measures, such as on-site inspection of production facilities, to implement and monitor these standards. Reebok takes strong objection to the use of force to suppress any of these standards and will take any such actions into account when evaluating facility compliance with these standards.

Phillips Van Heusen, Requirements for Suppliers, Contractors, Business Partners
(October 1997)

A Shared Commitment:

The guidelines you are about to read are of utmost importance to the Phillips-Van Heusen Corporation and to the relationships we form with suppliers, contractors and business partners.

While we place tremendous importance on these relationships, many of which qualify as genuine friendships of long-standing, certain values and standards have always been, and will always remain, paramount. Adherence to these values and standards by the people and companies we do business with is a prerequisite for continuing or establishing relationships with our company.

Indeed, we cannot do businesses with any company that fails to adhere to these ideals.

We believe that by working together to see these standards enforced, our company and its suppliers, contractors and business partners can help achieve a genuine improvement in the lives of working people around the world.

This mission has been a guiding principle of our company for more than a century, and it shall guide us in the future and take precedence over any economic or business concern.

Bruce J. Klatsky

Chairman, President and Chief Executive Officer

Guidelines for Vendors:

While respecting cultural differences and economic variances that reflect the particular countries where we and our vendors do business, our goal is to create, and encourage the creation of, model facilities that not only provide good jobs at fair wages, but which also improve conditions in the community at large. Therefore, we actively seek business associations with those who share our concerns.

- ### Legal Requirements

We expect our vendors to be law abiding citizens and to comply with any and all legal requirements relevant to the conduct of their business. We will seek vendors who respect the legal and moral rights of the employees.

- ### Nondiscrimination

We will not do business with any vendor who discriminates in employment, including hiring, salary, benefits, advancement, discipline, termination or retirement, on the basis of gender, race, religion, age, disability, sexual orientation, nationality or social or ethnic origin.

- ### Child Labor

Employees or our vendors must be over the applicable minimum legal age requirement or be at least 14 years old or older than the age for completing compulsory education in the country of manufacture, whichever is greater. Vendors must observe all legal requirements for the work of authorized minors, particularly those pertaining to hours of work, wages, minimum education and working conditions. We encourage vendors to support night classes and work-study programs, especially for younger workers.

- ### Forced Labor

We will not be associated with any vendor who uses any form of mental or physical coercion. We will not do business with any vendor who utilizes forced labor whether in the form of prison labor, indentured labor, bonded labor or otherwise.

- ### Harassment and Abuse

Vendors must treat employees with respect and dignity. No employee shall be subject to any physical, sexual, psychological or verbal harassment and/or abuse.

- ### Health and Safety

Employers shall provide a safe and healthy work environment to prevent accident and injury to health. Vendors should make a responsible contribution to the health care needs of their employees.

- *Wages and Benefits*

We will only do business with vendors who pay employees, as a floor, at least the minimum wage required by local law or the prevailing industry wage when available, whichever is higher, and who provide all legally mandated benefits.

Employees shall be compensated for overtime hours at the rate established by law in the country of manufacture or, in those countries where such laws do not exist, at a rate at least equal to their regular hourly compensation rate.

- *Hours of Work*

While permitting flexibility in scheduling, we will do business with vendors who do not exceed prevailing [standards and] who appropriately compensate overtime. No employee should be scheduled for more than sixty hours of work per week, and [we] will favor vendors who utilize work weeks of less than sixty hours. Employees should be allowed at least one day off per day week.

- *Freedom of Association*

Employees should be free to join organizations of their own choice. Vendors shall recognize the right of employees to freedom of association and collective bargaining. Employees should not be subject to intimidation or harassment in the exercise of their right to join or to refrain from joining any organization.

- *Environmental Requirements*

We are committed to the environment and will favor vendors who share this commitment. We require our vendors to meet all applicable environmental laws in their countries and to nurture better environments at their facilities and in the communities in which they operate.

- *Commitment to Communities*

We will favor vendors who share our commitment to contribute to the betterment of the communities in which they operate.

PVH has been committed to the enforcement of these standards and has an ongoing approval and monitoring system. Our goal is to engage our suppliers, contractors and business partners in the implementation of these standards. In the past, we have not established business relationships and we have suspended our association with companies that were found to abuse the rights of the employees. We will continue to do so in the future if any of the standards outlined above are violated.

The Phillips-Van Heusen Commitment:

- To conduct all business in keeping with the highest moral, ethical and legal standards.

- To recruit, train and provide career advancement to all associates without regard to gender, race, religion, age, disability, sexual orientation, nationality or social or ethnic origin. Diversity in the workplace will be encouraged. Bigotry, racism and sexual harassment will not be tolerated.

- To maintain a workplace environment that encourages frank and open communications.

- To be concerned with the preservation and improvement of our environment.

- To be ever mindful that our dedication to these standards is absolute and will not be compromised.

Liz Claiborne, Standards of Engagement and Human Rights Policy

(adopted from Apparel Industry Partnership, *Workplace Code of Conduct*) (1998) (posted at visited 18 February 1998)

Liz Claiborne Inc. (LCI) enforces its Standards via the following mechanisms:

- Incorporating worker rights as well as quality control criteria into LCI's factory certification process.

- Scheduled and unscheduled spot inspections by Company representatives.

- Intensified training for sourcing/manufacturing personnel in spotting abuses.

- Mandatory completion of an annual comprehensive human rights questionnaire by all country managers/LCI representatives for every supplier. Questionnaire topics include child labor, wages, benefits, prison labor abuses, discrimination, association rights, health, safety and legal compliance. The questionnaire is revised periodically to reflect new insights and ideas.

Additionally, a significant percentage of our domestic contractors will be audited for wage and hour compliance, as well as other information. We are also providing them with a copy of the U.S. Government's Fair Labor Standards Act. Similar audits have also taken place in certain foreign countries.

- Meetings between the Chairman of LCI and virtually all suppliers to emphasize LCI's commitment to, and expectations with respect to, workers rights.

- Requiring all contract suppliers to post LCI's Standards (in the local language) in common areas of every facility where LCI products are made.

- Encouraging workers to contact LCI local offices directly with reports of violations.

- Working with identified problem contractors to help them meet LCI's standards. Failing that, LCI will warn such contractors and, if necessary, terminate contracts with suppliers who do not improve compliance with LCI standards.

The above mechanisms are based upon a process open to change, as the Company seeks to improve enforcement of its Standards.

Workplace Code of Conduct

Upon joining the Apparel Industry Partnership [AIP], and demonstrating our commitment to its goals, we have adopted the AIP's Workplace Code of Conduct as our own Standards of Engagement and Human Rights policy.

Liz Claiborne Inc. and its subsidiaries are committed to producing high quality products at a good value to our consumer. The Company follows the letter and the spirit of all applicable laws, and maintains a high standard of business ethics and regard for human rights. Moreover, we require sound business ethics from our suppliers. Suppliers must observe all applicable laws of their country, including laws relating to employment, discrimination, the environment, safety and the apparel and apparel-related fields. Suppliers must comply with applicable United States laws relating to the import of products including country of origin labeling, product label-ing and fabric and product testing. If local or industry practices exceed local legal re-quirements, the higher standard applies.

Forced Labor. There shall not be any use of forced labor, whether in the form of prison labor, indentured labor, bonded labor or otherwise.

Child Labor. No person shall be employed at an age younger than 15, or younger than the age for completing compulsory education in the coun-try of manufacture where such age is higher than 15.

Harassment or Abuse. Every employee shall be treated with respect and dig-nity. No employee shall be subject to any physical, sexual, psychological or verbal harassment or abuse.

Nondiscrimination. No person shall be subject to any discrimination in em-ployment including hiring, salary, benefits, advancement, discipline, ter-mination or retirement, on the basis of gender, race, religion, age, disabil-ity, sexual orientation, nationality, political opinion, or social or ethnic origin.

Health and Safety. Employers shall provide a safe and healthy working en-vironment to prevent accidents and injury to health arising out of, linked with, or occurring in the course of work or as a result of the op-eration of employer facilities.

Freedom of Association and Collective Bargaining. Employers shall recog-nize and respect the right of employees to freedom of association and collective bargaining.

Wages and Benefits. Employers recognize that wages are essential to meet-ing employees' basic needs. Employers shall pay employees, as a floor, at least the minimum wage required by local law or the prevailing in-dustry wage, whichever is higher, and shall provide legally mandated benefits.

Hours of Work Except in extraordinary business circumstances, employees shall not be required to work more than the lesser of 60 hours per week or the limits on regular and overtime hours allowed by the law of the country of manufacture. Except in extraordinary circumstances, employees shall be entitled to at least one day of rest in every seven day period.

Overtime Compensation. In addition to their compensation for regular hours of work, employees shall be compensated for overtime hours at such premium rate as is legally required in the country of manufacture or, in these countries where such laws do not exist, at a rate at least equal to their regular hourly compensation rate.

*   *   *

If you believe that these Standards of Engagement are not being upheld or if you have any questions regarding these Standards of Engagement, please contact the Liz Clai-borne country manager. Your identity will be kept in confidence.

Frequently Asked Questions

Many of our consumers want to know more about Liz Claiborne's efforts to encour-age fair and productive working environments. The following are among the most commonly asked questions:

Do workers who manufacture Liz Claiborne's products know their rights?

We require our suppliers to post our "Standards of Engagement," in the appropriate language, in common areas of their facilities. However, we believe we need to do even more.

Liz Claiborne is currently developing a Spanish-language educational video to be screened at some of our contractors' facilities. This workers' rights video will explain our company's policies to the people who manufacture our clothing. It states that, if employees believe our Standards are being violated, they should immediately contact a Liz Claiborne representative who will speak with them on a confidential basis.

How does Liz Claiborne enforce its Standards of Engagement?

Liz Claiborne conducts spot inspections of contractor facilities. We also require our country managers or representatives to fill out annual questionnaires about each contractor's facilities. Topics include child labor, wages, benefits, forced labor abuses and rights of association, as well as health, safety and legal compliance. We are also working with independent monitoring groups — human rights activists and others — to develop a pilot program to scrutinize the conditions on factory floors. Monitors will review facilities' compliance with local laws and our "Standards of Engagement." Liz Claiborne will then investigate each complaint and, if necessary, take steps to correct the problem.

What other steps has Liz Claiborne taken to address the sweatshop issue?

Liz Claiborne has been a pioneer in combating sweatshops. Our general counsel has served as co-chair of the White House *Apparel Industry Partnership*, a Presidential task force formed to make businesses more accountable for workplace conditions. And for the past two years, the U.S. Department of Labor has named Liz Claiborne to its "Trendsetter List" in recognition of our progressive labor policies and practices. To reinforce Liz Claiborne's commitment to humane workplace conditions, our Chief Executive Officer, Paul R. Charron, has personally encouraged virtually all of our contractors to take steps to improve working conditions at their own facilities. This initiative has already led to the construction of an on-site health care clinic at one of our major suppliers' facilities in Guatemala.

Wal-Mart Stores, Inc., Standards for "Vendors" (1998)

Wal-Mart Stores, Inc. ("Wal-Mart") has enjoyed success by adhering to three basic principles since its founding in 1962. The **first principle** is the concept of providing value and service to our customers by offering quality merchandise at low prices every day. Wal-Mart has built the relationship with its customers on this basis, and we believe it is a fundamental reason for the Company's rapid growth and success. The **second principle** is corporate dedication to a partnership between the Company's associates (employees), ownership and management. This concept is extended to Wal-Mart's Vendors who have increased their business as Wal-Mart has grown. The **third principle** is a commitment by Wal-Mart to the communities in which stores and distribution centers are located.

Wal-Mart strives to conduct its business in a manner that reflects these three basic principles and the resultant fundamental values. Each of our Vendors, including our Vendors outside the United States, are expected to conform to those principles and values and to assure compliance in all contracting, subcontracting or other relationships.

Since Wal-Mart believes that the conduct of its Vendors can be transferred to Wal-Mart and affect its reputation. Wal-Mart requires that its Vendors conform to standards of business practices which are consistent with the three principles described above. More specifically, Wal-Mart requires conformity from its Vendors with the following standards, and hereby reserves the right to make periodic, unannounced inspections of Vendor's facilities to satisfy itself of Vendor's compliance with these standards:

1. COMPLIANCE WITH APPLICABLE LAWS

All Vendors shall comply with the legal requirements and standards of their industry under the national laws of the countries in which the Vendors are doing business, including the labor and employment laws of those countries, and any applicable U.S. laws. Should the legal requirements and standards of the industry conflict, Vendors must, at a minimum, be in compliance with the legal requirements of the country in which the products are manufactured. If, however, the industry standards exceed the country's legal requirements, Wal-Mart will favor Vendors who meet such industry standards. Vendors shall comply with all requirements of all applicable governmental agencies. Necessary invoices and required documentation must be provided in compliance with the applicable law. Vendors shall warrant to Wal-Mart that no merchandise sold to Wal-Mart infringes the patents, trademarks or copyrights of others and shall provide to Wal-Mart all necessary for selling merchandise sold to Wal-Mart which is under license from a third party. All merchandise shall be accurately marked or labeled with its country of origin in compliance with applicable laws and including those of the country of manufacture. All shipments of merchandise will be accompanied by the requisite documentation issued by the proper governmental authorities, including but not limited to Form A's, import licenses, quota allocations and visas and shall comply with orderly marketing agreements, voluntary restraint agreements and other such agreements in accordance with applicable law. The commercial invoice shall, in English and in any other language deemed appropriate, accurately describe all the merchandise contained in the shipment, identify the country of origin of each article contained in the shipment, and shall list all payments, whether direct or indirect, to be made for the merchandise, including, but not limited to any assists, selling commissions or royalty payments. Backup documentation, and any Wal-Mart required changes to any documentation, will be provided by Vendors promptly. Failure to supply complete and accurate information may result in cancellation or rejection of the goods.

2. EMPLOYMENT

Wal-Mart is a success because its associates are considered "partners" and a strong level of teamwork has developed within the Company. Wal-Mart expects its "Vendors" to meet the following terms and conditions of employment:

Compensation

"Vendors" shall fairly compensate their employees by providing wages and benefits which are in compliance with the national laws of the countries in which the "Vendors" are doing business or which are consistent with the prevailing local standards in the countries in which the "Vendors" are doing business, if the prevailing local standards are higher. Vendors shall fully comply with the wage and hour provisions of the Fair Labor Standards Act, if applicable, and shall use only subcontractors who comply with this law, if applicable.

Hours of Labor

"Vendors" shall maintain reasonable employee work hours in compliance with local standards and applicable national laws of the countries in which the Vendors are doing business. Employees shall not work more hours in one week than allowable under applicable law, and shall be properly compensated for overtime work. We favor "Vendors" who comply with the statutory requirements for working hours for employees and we will not use suppliers who, on a regularly scheduled basis, require employees to work in excess of the statutory requirements without proper compensation as required by applicable law. Employees should be permitted reasonable days off (which we see as at least one day off to every seven-day period) and leave privileges.

Forced Labor/Prison Labor

Forced or prison labor will not be tolerated by Wal-Mart. Vendors shall maintain employment on a voluntary basis. Wal-Mart will not accept products from Vendors who utilize in any manner forced labor or prison labor in the manufacture or in their contracting, subcontracting or other relationships for the manufacture of their products.

Child Labor

Wal-Mart will not tolerate the use of child labor in the manufacture of products it sells. Wal-Mart will not accept products from Vendors that utilize in any manner child labor in their contracting, subcontracting or other relationships for the manufacture their products. No person shall be employed at an age younger than 15 (or 14 where the law of the country of manufacture allows) or younger than the age for completing compulsory education in the country of manufacture where such age is higher than 15.

Discrimination/Human Rights

Wal-Mart recognizes that cultural differences exist and different standards apply in various countries; however, we believe that all terms and conditions of employment should be based on an individual's ability to do the job, not on the basis of personal characteristics or beliefs. Wal-Mart favors Vendors who have a social and political commitment to basic principles of human rights and who do not discriminate against their employees in hiring practices or any other term or condition of work, on the basis of race, color, national origin, gender, religion, disability, or other similar factors.

3. WORKPLACE ENVIRONMENT

Wal-Mart maintains a safe, clean, healthy and productive environment for its associates and expects the same from its Vendors. Vendors shall furnish employees with safe and healthy working conditions. Factories working on Wal-Mart merchandise shall provide adequate medical facilities, fire exits and safety equipment, well lighted and comfortable workstations, clean restrooms, and adequate living quarters where necessary. Workers should be adequately trained to perform their jobs safely. Wal-Mart will not do business with any "Vendor" that provides an unhealthy or hazardous work environment or which utilizes mental or physical disciplinary practices.

4.   **CONCERN FOR THE ENVIRONMENT**

We believe it is our role to be a leader in protecting our environment. We encourage our customers and associates to always Reduce, Reuse, and Recycle. We also encourage our Vendors to reduce excess packaging and to use recycled and non-toxic materials whenever possible. We will favor Vendors who share our commitment to the environment.

5.   **"BUY AMERICAN" COMMITMENT**

Wal-Mart has a strong commitment to buy as much merchandise made in the United States as feasible. Vendors are encouraged to buy as many materials and components from United States sources as possible and communicate this information to Wal-Mart. Further, Vendors are encouraged to establish U.S. manufacturing operations.

6.   **REGULAR INSPECTION AND CERTIFICATION BY VENDOR**

Vendor shall designate, on a copy of the Wal-Mart Vendor Inspection and Certification Form, one or more of its officers to inspect each of its facilities which produces merchandise sold to Wal-Mart. Such inspections shall be done on at least a quarterly basis to insure compliance with the standards, terms and conditions set forth herein. The Vendor Officer designated to perform such inspections shall certify to Wal-Mart following each inspection (i) that he or she performed such inspection and (ii) that the results reflected on such compliance inspection form are true and correct.

All charges related to the inspection and certification of such facilities shall be paid fully by the Vendor. Vendor shall maintain the completed Inspection and Certification Forms on file at each facility and shall make the forms readily accessible to Wal-Mart, its agents or employees when requested. Any Vendor which fails or refuses to comply with these standards is subject to immediate cancellation of any and all outstanding orders, refusal or return of any shipment, and termination of its business relationship with Wal-Mart.

7.   **RIGHT OF INSPECTION**

To further assure proper implementation of and compliance with the standards set forth herein, Wal-Mart or a third party designated by Wal-Mart will undertake affirmative measures, such as on-site inspection of production facilities, to implement and monitor said standards. Any Vendor which fails or refuses to comply with these standards is subject to immediate cancellation of any and all its outstanding orders, refuse or return any shipment, and otherwise cease doing business with Wal-Mart.

8.   **CONFIDENTIALITY**

Vendor shall not at any time, during or after the term of this Agreement, disclose to others and will not take or use for its own purposes or the purpose of others any trade secrets, confidential information, knowledge, designs, data, know-how, or any other information considered logically as "confidential." Vendor recognizes that this obligation applies not only to technical information, designs and marketing, but also to any business information that Wal-Mart treats as confidential. Any information that is not readily available to the public shall be considered to be a trade secret and confidential. Upon termination of this Agreement, for any cause, Vendor shall return all items belonging to Wal-Mart and all copies of documents containing Wal-Mart's trade secrets, confidential information, knowledge, data or know-how in Vendor's possession or under Vendor's control.

9.   WAL-MART GIFT AND GRATUITY POLICY

Wal-Mart Stores, Inc. has a very strict policy which forbids and prohibits the solicitation, offering or acceptance of any gifts, gratuities or any form of "pay-off" or facilitation fee as a condition of doing business with Wal-Mart; as a form of gratitude, or as an attempt to gain favor or accept merchandise or services at a lesser degree than what was agreed. Wal-Mart believes in delivering and receiving only the total quantity agreed.

Any Vendor, factory or manufacturer who violates such policy by offering or accepting any form of gift or gratuity to any associate, employee, agent or affiliate of Wal-Mart Stores, Inc. will be subject to all loss of existing and future business, regardless of whether the gift or gratuity was accepted. In addition, a Vendor, factory or manufacturer who violates such policy, will be reported to the appropriate governmental authorities of the Vendor's respective and affiliated countries.

Failure to report such information will result in severe action against such Vendor, trading company or factory including but not limited to termination of all existing and future business relationships and monetary damages.

A copy of these Standards for Vendors shall be posted in a location visible to all employees at all facilities that manufacture products for *Wal-Mart Stores, Inc.*

Any person with knowledge of a violation of any of these standards by a Vendor or a Wal-Mart associate should call 1-800-WM-ETHIC (1-800-963-8442) (in countries other than the United States, dial AT&T's U.S.A. Direct Number first) or write to: *Wal-Mart Stores, Inc. Business Ethics Committee, 702 SW 8th St., Bentonville, AR 72716-8095.*

As an officer of_____, a Vendor of Wal-Mart, I have read the principles and terms described in this document and understand my company's business relationship with Wal-Mart is based upon said company being in full compliance with these principles and terms. I further understand that failure by a Vendor to abide by any of the terms and conditions stated herein may result in the immediate cancellation by Wal-Mart of all outstanding orders with that Vendor and refusal by Wal-Mart to continue to do business in any manner with said Vendor. I am signing this statement, as a corporate representative of_____, to acknowledge, accept and agree to abide by the standards, terms and conditions set forth in this Memorandum of Understanding between my company and Wal-Mart. I hereby affirm that all actions, legal and corporate, to make this Agreement binding and enforceable against _____ have been completed.

VENDOR COMPANY NAME,
ADDRESS, TELEPHONE AND FAX NUMBER

_____   Signature: _____
_____
_____   Typed Name: _____
_____   Title: _____

III. The Environment and MNCs

Robert J. Fowler, International Environmental Standards for Transnational Corporations
25 Environmental Law 1-4, 8-30 (1995)

I. Introduction

By the early 1990s, there were almost 37,000 transnational corporations (TNCs) in the world, and their influence on the global economy is enormous. In 1990, the worldwide outflow of foreign direct investment (FDI), which is a measure of the productive capacity of TNCs, totaled $234 billion. In 1992, the stock of FDI had reached $2 trillion. Parent TNCs have generated some 170,000 foreign affiliates, forty-one percent of which are located in developing countries. Nevertheless, the reins remain firmly held in developed countries, where ninety percent of parent TNC are headquartered.

The growth in the number, size, and influence of TNCs has been matter of international concern, particularly to developing countries, for over twenty years. The expansion of TNCs after the Second World War resulted from a number of factors, including spiraling labor costs in developed countries, the increasing importance of economies of scale, improved transportation and communication systems, and rising worldwide consumer demand for new products. By the early 1970s, TNCs had begun to attract considerable interest and concern. Critics of TNCs have argued that their post-war expansion has become increasingly focused on the exploitation of the natural and human resources of developing countries. Ethical issues arising from TNC activities include bribery and corruption, employment and personnel issues, marketing practices, impacts on the economy and development patterns of host countries, environmental and cultural impacts, and political relations with both host and home country governments.

It is also frequently argued that TNCs have grown beyond the control of national governments and operate in a legal and moral vacuum "where individualism has free reign." The notion of corporate nationality may become obsolete in a global economy. The trend towards integrated international production and the resultant reorganization of TNC structures to establish "non-equity" arrangements which allow some control over foreign productive assets contribute to this situation.

Despite the long-held concerns about ethical and other aspects of TNC activity, promotion of FDI has been a recent global political trend. A new international consensus was reached at the seventh United Nations Conference on Trade and Development in 1987 on "structural adjustment," in the form of privatization, deregulation, and liberalization of national economies in return for the easing of the debt burden on developing countries. This has paved the way for a substantial expansion in TNC activities, particularly in the developing world. This expansion has been assisted by recent regional and global free trade agreements, the principal beneficiaries of which may be TNCs.

One result of these initiatives has been a distinct shift away from earlier proposals for the regulation of TNCs. This is indicated most vividly by the United Nations' recent abandonment of its fifteen-year effort to produce a Code of Conduct for Transnational Corporations. Recent policy initiatives at the international level concerning TNCs focus instead on developing guidelines to facilitate FDI, with the principal issues being the development of standards for fair and equitable treatment, national treatment, and most favored nation treatment.

Environmental matters are one exception to this trend. In this area, there appears to be a broad consensus that it is appropriate and desirable to develop standards to guide or direct TNC behavior. A parallel and related recognition has emerged in free trade negotiations, where the proposed global agreement emerging from the Uraguay Round of GATT and regional agreements such as the North American Free Trade Agreement (NAFTA) have been recognized to require specific, additional measures concerning environmental, health, and safety matters. However, considerable uncertainty exists about how to apply environmental standards to TNCs in this new era of free trade, liberalization of national economies, and promotion of FDI. TNCs are key players in terms of development activity, and the perception that they operate in a vacuum between ineffective national laws and non-existent or unenforceable international laws has heightened concerns about the current reach and effectiveness of environmental regulation, particularly where TNCs are operating in developing countries. A considerable amount of attention has been devoted in recent years by TNCs and others to the notion of self-regulation of environmental, health, and safety matters. This may in part reflect a belief that TNCs are beyond any form of regulatory control and should develop their own rules to meet public expectations. It may also constitute an effort by TNCs to anticipate further regulation, either by forestalling it or by being prepared in advance to comply with it.

. . . .

III. ENVIRONMENTAL PERFORMANCE OF TNCS

TNCs operate in a wide range of pollution-intensive and hazardous industries that have products or processes that may harm the environment or negatively impact human health. TNCs are also active in resource development industries, such as mining, petroleum, and agri-business, which can seriously affect environmentally sensitive areas. The general standard of environmental performance of TNCs is therefore a matter of significant international concern. Rather than attempting to catalog various examples of TNC environmental "bad practice," this section identifies the major types of environmental concerns over TNC activities.

Several factors may induce or enable TNCs to evade national controls of environmental, health and safety matters, particularly in developing countries. TNCs possess flexibility, mobility, and leverage which local companies do not enjoy; tend to maintain corporate secrecy about the hazards associated with particular products and processes; and obtain the benefit of legal uncertainties concerning the liability of parent TNCs for their affiliates' activities. In order to assess whether such factors adversely affect the performance of TNCs beyond their home countries, two broad questions are frequently posed. First, have TNCs applied lesser standards to their operations beyond their home base? Second, have TNCs located their operations in countries where lesser standards apply, in order to avoid home country environmental regulation and to attract a competitive advantage? These questions are also addressed in this section.

A. Environmental Concerns

The two TNC activities most commonly identified as raising environmental concerns are the export of hazardous products and the export hazardous processes or technologies. International trade in *products* such as pesticides, pharmaceuticals, toxic chemicals, and hazardous wastes has been an issue for some years especially when it involves sales in developing countries. Both domestic and international measures have been developed to respond to the problems arising from such trade. Domestic measures have included export controls, with particular emphasis upon the concept of prior informed consent. This concept requires a national authority in the importing country to agree before products or technologies which can cause injury to human health or the environment are exported.

TNCs export hazardous *processes* by establishing highly-polluting industries outside home countries, thus creating potential problems pollution control, disposal of hazardous wastes, workers' health and safety, and the risk of major accidents. The accidents at Seveso, Italy; Bhopal, India; and Basel, Switzerland demonstrate the serious consequences that arise when TNCs inadequately manage chemical manufacturing plants.

Problems have also arisen in the primary sector with respect to pollution and hazardous waste management. For example, petroleum exploitation and development in Ecuador allegedly led to the spillage of 17 million gallons of oil from the Trans-Ecuadoran pipeline between 1982 and 1990, and the dumping of 4.3 million gallons of hazardous wastes from flow wells into waterways. Primary industry activities also impact biodiversity and can carry serious consequences for indigenous peoples. Such concerns are particularly pronounced where tropical rain forests have been cleared. In some instances, this has led to pressure on governments and businesses in developed countries to try to halt rain forest development activities in developing countries.

Recent attempts to grapple with the problems of petroleum production in the Ecuadoran Amazon demonstrate the complexities faced by environmentalists in the industralized world. Pressure from environmental groups, particularly in the United States, allegedly fo._   1 the DuPont subsidiary, Conoco, to withdraw from a proposed petroleum pr luction project in that country although it had sought to develop a responsible environmental management plan. Its withdrawal paved the way for other TNCs that were less concerned with environmental and indigenous peoples' concerns to move in without adopting the same safeguards proposed by Conoco and subject to less public scrutiny. This suggests that TNCs face varying degrees of visibility, particularly in their home country, that may affect its level of public accountability with respect to environmental performance.

New areas of concern about the environmental impacts of TNC behavior are also emerging in the 1990s. One of the most significant is the acquisition of intellectual property rights to products derived from plants or animals found in developing countries. A recent example from India concerns, ironically, efforts by an American TNC, W.R. Grace & Co., to develop a biopesticide (to be used in place of chemical pesticides) from the seeds of the neem tree. Indian farmers and environmentalists vociferously oppose allowing Grace to patent the product, partly because of fears that the supply of neem seeds will be reduced in India so that locals will have to purchase the TNC product. The broader charge is that TNCs are raiding and appropriating India's biodiversity. For evidence, critics point to the proposed collaboration by twenty-three foreign TNCs with Indian companies in projects to develop India's genetic resources.

Concerns have also been expressed about the role of pharmaceutical companies in developing countries such as Brazil, where the eighth largest world market in terms of gross receipts is dominated by foreign TNCS. Brazil is under enormous pressure to pass a patent law to protect products manufactured in the country using its biological resources and life forms, even to the extent of facing commercial trade sanctions in the United States should it not do so. At a broader level, the influence of U.S. pharmaceutical companies on the United States' position on the Biodiversity Convention is well-documented and continues to be felt even after the change in Administration. Thus, the economic exploitation of biodiversity by TNCs in developing countries through the growth of new industries such as biotechnology, and the expansion of established industries such as pharmaceuticals and pesticides, presents a whole range of new issues which need to be addressed by policy makers.

B. TNC Double Standards

While TNCs are frequently accused of practicing double standards, "[s]ystematic evidence regarding any differences in the 'cleanliness' of manufacturing technologies employed by multinational corporations in their different countries of operation, and differences between multinational affiliates and local firms, is almost nonexistent." Investigations concerning double standards have focused almost exclusively on the export of processes, particularly those connected with pollution-intensive industries. Little evidence of an equivalent nature exists regarding resource extraction industries.

Some of the earliest research provided extensive evidence in the mid-1980s of TNC double standards with respect to both pollution and worker health and safety. This prompted speculation that industries were fleeing regulation in industrialized countries in order to take advantage of less stringent conditions in the developing world. The existence of double standards was most evident in particularly dirty industries such as asbestos, copper, pesticides, vinyl chloride, and lead smelting. Available evidence on TNC environmental policies and practices, which was gathered primarily in the 1970s, indicates a "dominant pattern of local accommodation" and a tendency to "custom tailoring or adaptation to local policy climates.

The lack of more modern evidence on TNC double standards has been addressed to some extent by two United Nations studies, conducted through the Economic and Social Commission for Asia and the Pacific (ESCAP) and the United Nations Centre for Transnational Corporations (UNCTC). These studies specifically looked at environmental management practices in selected Asian and Pacific countries. The first study found that TNCs adopted lower environmental standards in their operations in the selected developing countries than they did in developed countries. These findings were reinforced in the second study of eight countries in the Asian-Pacific region, which found that in developing countries TNCs frequently based operational standards on locally available environmental technologies and that these standards were generally inferior to those adopted in developed countries. For example, the study found that only twenty-five percent of TNCs surveyed in the pesticide industry in

Thailand adopted "global" environmental standards. More than fifty percent admitted that only local standards were adopted in relation to environmental management. Nevertheless, the evidence of double standards provided in those reports appears almost anecdotal rather than the product of a systematic, comprehensive investigation and must be treated with some caution.

An even more recent study of American TNC practices undertaken by Tufts University, which included investigations in several developing countries, found considerable inconsistency in TNC practices. The non-U.S. operations were sometimes less protective environmentally, but in some cases "were more innovative than the comparable U.S. facility." Some of the factors which the study found led to less protection in facilities outside the United States included lack of enforcement by national or local government; inadequate infrastructure such as waste disposal facilities; presence of a large, temporary work force; difficulty in government agencies obtaining monitoring equipment; and competing priorities such as local health problems, malnutrition, and infant mortality.

However, the Tufts study also highlights significant environmental problems associated with TNC operations in developed countries, including their home countries. This is particularly important given the level of FDI that is still directed by TNCs to developed countries. An indication of such problems is that the number of serious industrial accidents continued to rise in developed countries during the 1980s. While TNCs were involved in less than half of these accidents, the large majority that involved TNCs occurred in their home countries. Although this reflects the existing distribution of industrial output, including FDI, it also serves as a reminder that double standards do not necessarily involve good and bad practices in developed and developing countries, respectively. At times, it may be a case of bad and worse practices.

On the other hand, studies that evidence TNC double standards also indicate that TNCs generally have a better record in relation to environmental, health, and safety concerns than local or state-owned enterprises in developing countries. In part, this is attributed to the superior financial, managerial, and technological resources which TNCs can muster. Since TNCs are larger than local firms, they can more readily absorb the costs of environmental controls and employ more qualified managers and better skilled workers. They are also more likely to be aware of environmental management developments abroad and to have access to and the capacity to transfer modern environmental technology to their operations in developing countries. Furthermore, the larger scale of their operations creates a greater risk of substantial impacts, particularly in the event of a serious accident, and thus may encourage sounder practices than are found in local firms. The Tufts University study found that the greatest influence on TNC environmental, health, and safety decisions in the United States was domestic law and regulation, whereas in Africa it was a concern to avoid high visibility accidents.

While all of these considerations may have induced TNCs to perform above the levels of their local counterparts in developing countries, there still appears to be a gap between local and home country performance which is reflected in a failure to introduce new technologies to affiliated plants in developing countries. The United Nations studies previously referred to found that very limited transfers of environmental technology have occurred in the developing countries which were studied, and they identified a lack of commitment by TNCs to adopting the best available environmental technology in developing countries. Also, it has been alleged that TNCs are engaged in dumping obsolete environmental technologies in developing countries. Thus, it appears that the potential for TNCs to improve, not only their own performance, but also that of local firms with which they deal in developing countries is not sufficiently utilized. In part, this may be due to ongoing concerns about protecting intellectual property rights with respect to new technologies. That TNCs may perform better than their local or state-owned counterparts is hardly exculpatory in relation to the double standards that nevertheless exist, given the very considerable capacity of TNCs to perform at even higher levels which equate with those adopted in their home countries.

It is also frequently argued that TNCs' better performance than local counterparts in developing countries is attributable to the TNCs greater visibility, which in turn leads to more intense scrutiny from the public and shareholders in their home country and from regulators and local communities in the host country. Once again, it appears that such observations are more relevant to potential influences than actual effects. The trend towards public consultation and disclosure by TNCs is uneven and centered on plant operations in TNCs' home countries rather than their operations abroad. The United Nations survey in 1990 made the following observations with respect to the sharing and disclosure of information by TNCs:

> Inadequate information has made it easy for TNCs and governments to allow the location of complex and potentially hazardous industrial facilities in areas where the local population are unaware of the hazards. Without adequate information, no one is able to come up with concrete proof to show that such facilities are indeed hazardous. Information has sometimes been deliberately withheld from communities or even governments to avoid any adverse resistance from the host developing countries. In other cases, TNCs have resisted worst case scenarios when preparing EIAs [environmental impact assessments] for their projects because they are expensive to implement. In effect, they have made their activities appear safe and non-detrimental to the environment.

Despite urgings to the contrary, TNCs appear reluctant to provide better technical information to regulators, especially in developing countries, unless there is a legal obligation to do so. A study by the environmental group, Friends of the Earth, concluded that American TNCs involved in chemical manufacturing in Europe were unwilling to release data on toxic emissions unless they were legally required to do so. Although some TNCs cooperated with the study and indicated support for greater openness, they were clearly in the minority.

It would seem therefore that the level of visibility of TNCs in their operations outside their home countries may be affected by their failure to provide full information concerning these operations. While the better performance of TNCs in developing countries than local or state-owned operators may be explained in part by the greater scrutiny which is directed at TNCs, such performance may be principally related to taking measures to avoid a Bhopal-type accident. It may be possible to encourage even higher levels of environmental performance by TNCs if environmental disclosure requirements applied more rigorously to their operations outside their home countries.

Finally, although TNCs may have practiced double standards in the past, attitudes and practices may be changing significantly. It is asserted with increasing frequency that TNCs are moving voluntarily towards a more uniform approach to environmental, health, and safety practices throughout their operations. The Tufts University study noted that some of the largest TNCs, including Monsanto and DuPont, have become ardent advocates of the concept of pollution prevention and are practicing a new form of environmental stewardship on a self-regulated basis. I highly doubt that the self-regulated approach will suffice to address the past history of double standards. This question and related ones concerning how more uniform environmental health and safety standards might be applied to TNCs are addressed [below].

C. *The Location of TNC Operations to Secure Competitive Advantage*

One other major issue related to TNC environmental performance is whether TNC locational decisions reflect a desire to evade strict environmental regulation in industrialized countries. While most FDI is still directed to developed countries, FDI levels are increasing in developing countries far more rapidly than in developed countries. Also, some evidence shows that growth in pollution-intensive industries in developing countries is out-stripping growth in total industrial production in those countries. FDI has been directed foremost within the manufacturing sector to the chemicals industry — the most pollution-intensive of all manufacturing industries. This has particular implications for developing countries. For example, the ESCAP survey for the United Nations found that the chemicals industry had the highest TNC participation in India, Indonesia, the Philippines and Thailand. A recent study for the World Bank of over forty-three industries in 109 countries found a disproportionately large increase in the presence of dirty industries in developing countries (almost three times as great as the increase in industrialized countries) and concluded that "polluting industry activities are being dispersed internationally and the *dispersion is greatest* in the direction of developing countries."

These findings lend credence to the view first expressed in the 1970s that TNCs may shift manufacturing activities to developing countries with lower environmental, health, and safety standards, or, in other words, may seek out "pollution havens." If this is correct, developing countries might ease or fail to increase domestic environmental controls to prevent polluting industries from migrating; or, alternatively, developed countries might impose import controls on products produced under looser environmental standards elsewhere in order to eliminate an unfair competitive advantage. The latter course has been vigorously opposed by free trade proponents, causing their opponents to argue that relocation of industries and consequential job losses in industrialized countries may well be accelerated by free trade agreements.

However, numerous studies conclude that there is no evidence to prove that differences in environmental regulation between countries have influenced the location of investment by TNCs, other than in a few, specific industries. Some evidence of relocation in developing countries, coupled with plant closures in home countries, has been presented for highly toxic product manufacturing (*e.g.*, asbestos, pesticides, Benzedrine dyes) and heavy metal processing (*e.g.*, copper, zinc, lead). But the general inference from these studies is that other factors have been far more influential than environmental costs in influencing the location decisions of TNCs. These factors include labor intensity, the reflection of natural resource endowments in trade flows, and the possibility that many dirty industries are basic and associated with the early stages of industrialization. In a similar vein, the migration of certain U.S. industries to Mexico (the so-called "maquiladoras," whose production is entirely for the purposes of export and which have led to enormous pollution problems in the U.S.-Mexico border area) has been attributed to factors unrelated to workplace health and safety and pollution control costs. These include "labor wage rates, proximity to the U.S. market and incentives for domestic processing of materials."

It is virtually impossible to argue that environmental costs play no role in the locational decisions of TNCs. The Tufts University study underscores that environmental costs are an increasingly significant factor. Forty percent of American TNC respondents agreed that U.S companies locate in foreign countries because environmental health and safety regulatory systems in those countries are weak. Nevertheless thirty-five percent of respondents disagreed and the balance were either "neutral" or had "no opinion." Perhaps the key is to ask TNCs what they think their competitors would do, rather than what they would do themselves!

Although the debate about locational and competitive issues has some relevance to home country environmental regulation, it does not affect the need for greater accountability by TNCs for their operations in developing countries.

> Whether there is a *wholesale* exodus of hazardous industries fleeing regulation and liability is beside the point. Whether the industrial planners tell interviewers that environmental regulation is a *main* determinant in new site selection is also beside the point. The point is that there is international trade in industrial hazards, increasingly so, and this has predictably grave public health consequences.

The problem is to figure out how to increase TNC accountability in light of the evidence of their increasing involvement in environmentally damaging industries in developing countries and their past practice of applying double standards to their operations. Much of the discussion concerning increased accountability focuses on the issue of how to develop internationally uniform standards with respect to environmental, health, and safety matters for TNCs. The next section explores more fully how such standards might be developed and what types of standards might provide the greatest benefit when applied to TNCs.

IV. DEVELOPING ENVIRONMENTAL STANDARDS FOR TNCS

Frequently, arguments for greater international uniformity of standards for TNCs fail to specify or differentiate between the different kinds of standards that might be applied. A wide range of regulatory measures might readily be described as "environmental standards." One distinction is between product and process standards. Process standards can be further divided into ambient standards, emission or discharge standards, safety and risk standards, and what might be described loosely as "performance standards." An example of performance standards is guidelines for acceptable practices in environmental auditing, environmental accounting, and environmental management programs. Differentiating these various types of environmental standards may be crucial in considering whether and how standards could operate in particular circumstances. In the following discussion, the term "environmental standards" refers to process standards, in particular those which set emission or discharge limits for polluting activities.

Discussions of this topic often also fail to clearly identify the relevant source and regulatory status of environmental standards. In particular they fail to distinguish between standards that are legally enforceable and those that are essentially advisory or voluntary in nature. There are three distinct sources of standards: international law, domestic law, and the voluntary or internal policies of TNCs themselves.

One further distinction is important. There are essentially two ways to force TNCs to apply uniform standards. The first involves international negotiation or harmonization of standards so as to produce a "level playing field" for TNCs, while also enhancing existing levels of environmental protection worldwide. The second method is to directly regulate TNCs to ensure that they apply uniform standards wherever they happen to operate. This approach applies what I will call "choice of standards" rules. These rules determine the source of the particular standards that apply to a TNC in a given situation. Numerous options have been envisaged in this regard, the most frequent rule being to apply the standard of the TNC's "home country." In each of the regulatory contexts discussed below, it is important whether the relevant focus is the development of standards proper or the operation of a "choice of standards" rule.

A. International Law as a Source of Environmental Standards

Considerable support has been expressed in recent years for the development of international environmental standards. For example, Agenda 21, the global action plan for environmental management adopted at the United Nations Conference of Environment and Development in Rio de Janeiro in 1992, states as one of its specific objectives: "[t]o promote, through the gradual development of universally and multilaterally negotiated agreements or instruments, international standards for the protection of the environment that take into account the different situations and capabilities of countries." However, there is a growing body of opinion, which Agenda 21 recognizes, that international environmental standards should not be of a uniform nature.

1. International Environmental Standards — Uniform or Minimum?

Some substantial criticisms have been leveled at the concept of *uniform* international standards, irrespective of whether the standards arise by way of international agreement or through a process of harmonization of national standards. Such uniformity, critics say, could work against sustainable development by forcing inappropriate priorities on developing countries. For example, developing countries do not need "high levels of environmental protection against cancer...at the expense of basic human need[s] such as protection from high infant mortality and rampant malnutrition." Criticisms based on economic analysis suggest that uniform standards would not equalize the international competitive position of TNCs and would not be economically efficient. If TNCs were to face uniform ambient standards, local variables such as the level of industrial activity, its spatial dispersion, and topographical and climate conditions would preclude harmonization of environmental control costs and competitive positions. Similarly, the costs and benefits of emission and discharge standards would vary from one country to another. Differences in national environmental standards can be justified by arguing that the differences reflect geographic, ecological, and demographic variations among countries and hence differing capacities to assimilate pollution.

Environmentalists worry that uniform standards lead inevitably to a lowest common denominator outcome which could threaten environmental gains in some countries, particularly if new free trade rules deem higher standards to be illegal barriers to trade. These concerns have prompted environmentalists to promote new approaches to environmental protection that focus on pollution prevention or waste minimization, rather than the end-of-pipe solutions which environmental standards usually entail.

One response to the arguments against uniform international standards is to challenge the reliance placed on the concept of comparative assimilative capacity. While economists may consider it more efficient for some countries rather than others to host dirty industries and apply less stringent standards, they fail to account for long-term environmental damage. "No country should have the right to degrade the environment irreversibly for future generations in the name of national competitiveness."

A refinement of the concept of uniform international standards is the concept of *minimum* international environmental standards. Under this approach, countries would remain free to adopt more stringent environmental standards if warranted by their particular circumstances. The more stringent standards could include measures designed to promote pollution prevention. This refinement would help prevent the negative effects of downward harmonization, at least to the extent that individual nations would remain free to apply more stringent standards within their own countries without risking the allegation that they are in breach of free-trade rules. Minimum standards, rather than being identical, could operate on a principle of mutual recognition based upon the equivalence of requirements in national laws.

The North American Free Trade Agreement adopts yet another approach by requiring the parties, to the greatest extent possible, to make compatible their respective standards-related measures. Both of these alternatives constitute examples of the harmonization approach, as distinct from direct international regulation, but nevertheless provide interesting alternatives to the uniformity of standards option.

Even critics of uniform international standards agree that such standards are appropriate in two areas: first, with respect to product standards and testing procedures; and second, where there are international externalities in the form of transboundary pollution (including global concerns such as ozone depletion and the greenhouse effect) or damage to or loss of biodiversity which is of worldwide value. Recent developments in international environmental law reflect recognition by the international community of the need for international regulation in these particular areas.

2. Prospects for the Setting of International Environmental Standards

The Tufts University study revealed strong support among TNCs for international standardization of environmental, health, and safety regulations. However, it suggests that standards would have to be perceived as reasonable and enforcement would need to be even among countries in order to provide substantial benefits to TNCs in the form of a "level playing field." Similar findings were reached in a major United Nations survey. "In the only statistical sampling done to date on TNCs and environmental performance, two-thirds of TNCs thought that the UN should work toward standardizing national environmental rules and regulations. A majority also felt that the UN should be active in setting international policy guidelines."

It seems clear that TNCs view the development of international environmental standards as a less desirable process than the standardization or "harmonization" of national environmental standards. Commentators assert that "[a]t the same time as TNCs recognize that better environmental practices will only happen through legislation, most firms take strong public exception to international environmental regulations." Thus, TNCs appear to want a level playing field but are resistant to the use of formal international agreements to achieve this goal. This attitude is attributed to a reluctance to take the lead in proposing international environmental regulations. But a reluctance to lead is not the same as a "strong public exception." The seemingly contradictory positions of TNCs probably reflect a deep-seated resistance to regulation, even where TNCs recognize that beneficial outcomes are likely. TNCs would prefer to see national laws brought more closely into line, perhaps through "soft law" mechanisms which provide guidance to states but do not entail firm obligations, rather than have standards prescribed by international agreement. The extensive promotion of "self-regulation" by corporations and individual TNCs, coupled with some stern resistance even to certain "soft law" measures such as the draft U.N. Code of Conduct for Transnational Corporations, highlights the fragility of any support alleged to exist among TNCs for the development of international environmental standards.

Thus despite the emerging interest in the concept of minimum international environmental standards, and the precedents for international regulation where transboundary or global commons issues are involved, the reality is that the prescription of detailed process standards for environmental, health, and safety matters through legally binding international agreements does not currently appear to have widespread governmental or industry support.

Nevertheless the minimum standards approach has considerable potential and is worthy of further discussion. In particular, some closer attention could be directed to the types of standards which might be best suited to this approach. If prescribed through international agreements which are signed by and bind national governments, it would seem more appropriate for ambient standards, rather than discharge or emissions standards, to be adopted. The few existing examples of international environmental agreements in which standards of a quantifiable nature have been prescribed generally avoid discharge or emissions standards. Instead their effect on TNCs is indirect, and is felt through national legislation designed to implement targets for the reduction or elimination of emissions prescribed for the parties by the relevant agreement. Whichever approach to standards-setting is adopted at the international level, TNCs appear likely to remain beyond the reach of a comprehensive, international regulatory scheme for some time to come.

However, more limited developments in international standards-setting may be envisaged over a shorter time scale. In particular, regional environmental structures and standards may play a significant role in the development of international environmental standards. Some regional organizations, such as the South Pacific Regional Environmental Programme (SPREP), have emerged already for the purpose of developing common approaches to environmental management. Others may arise as part of new trading blocs which might emerge in the new international climate of free trade. The European Union provides an outstanding example of this. The NAFTA Environmental Side Agreement may also provide an important precedent with respect to other, similar regional arrangements which have a free trade basis. However, the capacity of trade related environmental measures to make a positive contribution to environmental protection remains an extremely contentious question. The European Union experience suggests that as economic integration progresses within a region, relevant environmental measures also will evolve in terms of their detail and sophistication. But NAFTA may prove a failure in this regard, and clearly much will depend on the nature of the environmental arrangements which are developed in these kinds of regional trade agreements.

3. Standardization Through the Use of Soft Law Instruments

Some supporters of international regulation also attach considerable importance to the role of soft law instruments, particularly since these may be addressed directly to TNCs, unlike formal international agreements. Rather than place emphasis on legal form, it is argued that the more important consideration is the political commitment of those states who endorse particular instruments. Although soft law instruments impose no firm obligations on signatories, they may provide a basis for incorporation into domestic law and eventually achieve the status of international customary law binding on all countries through resulting changes in state practice and expressed intent. In particular, they provide an avenue for the development of standards in a way which could lead, through their adoption by states, to greater harmonization of domestic standards.

A fundamental difficulty with soft law instruments is that they often constitute a compromise where widespread international consensus has not yet been reached on particular measures. They may not enjoy the support of a large majority of nations and their language may be particularly open-ended or diluted to accommodate differences of opinion.

Nevertheless, soft law instruments now exist in considerable numbers with respect to environmental matters. They constitute therefore a significant avenue for the development of international standards in relation to environment, health, and safety matters.

Another international law approach to obtaining uniform application of environmental standards to TNCs is to incorporate a "choice of standards" rule in international agreements. This would involve specifying the types or sources of environmental standards to be applied specifically to TNCs by signatory states. Such a possibility seems extremely slim, even in the context of a soft law approach, in light of past efforts to produce international guidelines or codes of conduct for TNCs and the current fervor for the promotion of FDI rather than TNC regulation. The draft United Nations Code of Conduct of Transnational Corporations, which was the subject of negotiation for over fifteen years, was formally abandoned in 1992 largely as a result of ongoing resistance by industralized countries and industry organizations to elements of the Code which were perceived to have a regulatory effect. This underlines the limited capacity even of soft law instruments to achieve accountability and responsibility on the part of TNCs, and the depth of the reservations which exist within the international business community concerning any form of international regulation. In any event, the only means of giving effect to a "choice of standards" rule embodied in an international agreement would be by way of domestic legislation, which therefore raises the same issues and considerations that need to be addressed in considering the option of unilateral, domestic action.

While the preceding discussion has focused on the subject of international environmental *standards*, since these have been at the center of the debate concerning regulation of TNC activity, other mechanisms exist which can contribute to environmental management objectives and which may warrant attention at the international level. One example is environmental impact assessment, which now enjoys broad international support in terms of its value as an environmental management tool. Another emerging tool is compulsory environmental information disclosure. The United Nations Centre for Transnational Corporations, prior to its disbandment in 1993, called for uniform principles on information disclosure for TNCs to be developed for consideration in an international agreement. A particular difficulty will be to establish consensus on the nature and purpose of environmental information disclosure requirements, particularly given that there are some significant differences between the United States and European Union approaches to this topic.

B. Domestic Relation of TNCs to Achieve Unifomity of Standards

In the absence of an international approach to the development of environmental standards, it remains open to states to pursue their own approaches with respect to the operations of TNCs who fall within their jurisdiction. Thus, instead of allowing TNCs to operate entirely by reference to the law of the host country, it may be possible to develop domestic rules which determine that similar or uniform standards will apply to TNCs irrespective of whether they are operating in a host or home country. While the development of such "choice of standards" rules will not guarantee international harmonization, it could have a significant effect on the operations of TNCs in at least some countries. This approach can take two forms.

1. Domestic Regulation Through Application of Home Country Standards by the Host Country

First, *host* countries could pass laws requiring TNCs to apply specified standards to their operations. One option frequently advanced is that TNCs should be required to apply home country standards by the relevant host country. This particular approach was recommended, for example, in the ESCAP survey for the United Nations:

> Governments should look into the possibility of revising policies and regulations so that TNCs are bound to adopt the environmental standards of their home countries, while at the same time allowing local firms to be regulated on the basis of local standards...local standards should be gradually upgraded on the basis of a schedule to give local firms time to adjust their operations according to the new standards required and for them to have time to plan out such changes.

However, this approach has been criticized for some of the reasons also advanced against the idea of international uniform standards. In particular, it is suggested that it may lead to inappropriate technology transfer, or to decisions by TNCs to pass over investments in a particular developing country because of the environmental costs involved, even though the proposed activity might be of considerable economic benefit to the country concerned. A practical difficulty with the home country rule is that it would require environmental authorities in the relevant host country to understand and administer differing standards for various TNC facilities, according to their country of origin. This could prove quite impractical. More recently, in the light of free trade advocacy, it has also been argued that such an approach is discriminatory and contrary to the principle of national treatment insofar as it holds TNCs to stricter standards than local or state-owned industries. Whether such measures could be justified as bona fide environmental regulation rather than a protectionist measure under revised free trades is quite doubtful.

Host countries might be able to develop a different "choice of standards" rule which overcomes at least some of these objections. For example, a rule could require TNCs to meet "state of the art" standards with respect to environmental, health and safety matters. But again, this may give rise to problems with respect to inappropriate technology transfer and may seriously discourage FDI in the absence of clear protection for intellectual property rights. Such a standard also could be extremely difficult to administer in practice, even though the concept of "best available technology" is well developed in domestic environmental law.

2. Domestic Regulation Through Extraterritorial Enforcement of Home Country Regulations

The second option with respect to domestic regulation of TNCs is for the *home* country to give extraterritorial effect to its environmental regulations in relation to the operations of its own TNCs abroad. Despite reservations about the legality of this practice under international law, there is some American precedent for this approach in the Foreign Corrupt Practices Act of 1977. Proposals of this kind have been put forward and range from a Foreign Environmental Practices Act, which would extend all relevant domestic standards and regulations to TNC operations abroad, to a more modest proposal that "[h]ome governments could make regulations for their companies that they insist are followed in other countries of operation, for example on standards of testing and labeling of pharmaceutical drugs and on accounting and reporting practices."

Once more, there are criticisms to consider. This approach has been condemned on the grounds that it intrudes excessively into the internal affairs of sovereign states and, particularly in its operation in developing countries, amounts to a new form of "cultural imperialism." There are also some obvious and substantial practical difficulties with the administration and enforcement of domestic standards in a foreign jurisdiction.

An interesting refinement of the home country extraterritoriality approach has been advanced which starts from the position that, for the same reasons that uniform international standards should not be developed, "there should be no attempt by governments to extend home-country environmental norms and standards to the foreign operations of their multinational corporations." Instead, domestic government insurance and finance mechanisms such as the Overseas Private Investment Corporation (OPIC) and the Export Import Bank (Exim Bank) in the United States should develop and apply environmental criteria for FDI which is directed abroad by United States TNCs. As parties to FDI transactions abroad, these federal government bodies have a direct involvement in the relevant projects, unlike other government agencies that might be asked to administer domestic environmental measures abroad. In the case of OPIC, which since 1974 has been required to undertake an environmental assessment of projects it insures, no effort is made to convey the results of the assessment to the host country. Conveying the results could enhance the regulatory efforts of environmental agencies in those countries to where FDI is being directed, and thus lead to a greater likelihood of relatively consistent standards being made applicable to United States TNCs.

3. Regulation Through Import/Export Restrictions

Export and import controls are another domestic means of regulating TNC behavior. Such controls have been embodied in some international agreements dealing with, for example endangered species, ozone-depleting substances, and hazardous wastes. In addition, unilateral domestic controls on exports have also been employed by the United States, for example, particularly to deal with hazardous products such as pesticides or other toxic chemicals. Another option is to impose import restrictions on products that have been produced through inferior environmental protection measures, in order to protect domestic manufacturers and to address global concerns such as tropical deforestation. However, the free-trade movement presents serious difficulties for the proponents of such tragedies, as is reflected in Agenda 21 itself:

> Trade policy measures for environmental purposes should not constitute a means of arbitrary or unjustifiable discrimination or a disguised restriction on international trade. Unilateral actions to deal with environment challenges outside the jurisdiction of the important country should be avoided.

This is a large and separate topic which cannot be addressed here.

C. TNC Self-regulation

Recent surveys have suggested that TNCs are seriously addressing their past deficiencies by undertaking extensive environmental management programs that extend across all their operations. As part of this effort, industry organizations and individual TNCs have contemplated developing voluntary uniform standards. In the case of industry organizations, these measures tend to concentrate on the broader standards of conduct that may be expected of corporations, including TNCS, rather than focusing on ambient or discharge standards of a relatively precise or quantifiable nature. Examples include the International Chamber of Commerce's *Environmental Guidelines for World Business* and *Business Charter for Sustainable Development*, the U.S. and Canadian Chemical Manufacturers' Associations' *Responsible Care* Program, the European Council of Chemical Manufacturers' Federations' *Principles and Guidelines for the Safe Transfer of Technology*, and the Japanese Business Council (Keidomren) *Global Environmental Charter*.

Individual TNCs are also considering the idea of internal standardization of environmental practices, perhaps because they perceive that environmental, health, and safety regulations will become increasingly harmonized in the future anyway. Because applying home country standards encounters all of the objections referred to previously, TNCs have explored other options. One suggestion is for TNCs to work towards "functional equivalence" in their worldwide operations. This is also referred to as "equivalent risk" or a "uniform level of risk." However, insofar as this is essentially a requirement for consistency of approach within a TNC, it seems likely to lead in practice to the application of the home country standards anyway. As yet, TNCs have not adopted this approach in many operations. A further option, which appears to have even less acceptance at present, is for TNCs to volunteer to meet or exceed the highest standards in place in any country in which they operate. Another variation on this idea, also discussed earlier, is to have TNCs meet the current "state of the art" standards with respect to environmental, health, and safety matters. Again, no widespread support for such an approach is discernible among TNCs at present.

The overriding difficulty with all of these possible internal standards, as with industry codes and guidelines, is their voluntary and non-binding character. Even more so than soft law instruments executed by nations, which at least reflect a consensus among some nations that may be reflected in domestic measures from time to time, industry and internal standards offer no mechanisms for ensuring compliance apart from those which exist in any event, such as adverse publicity. Even with the growing evidence of improved attitudes and performance by TNCs with respect to environmental matters, it is an enormous act of faith to trust almost entirely in self-regulation in order to avoid the application of double-standards by TNCs.

V. CONCLUSION

Uncertainty and debate cloud the whole idea of a standards-based approach to TNC regulation. While a few concrete international measures have been developed, more general or comprehensive measures seem unlikely due to TNC opposition and a lack of strong interest in this approach at present on the part of national governments. International environmental standards seem most likely to emerge at first instance in a regional setting, but where these are provided for in trade related agreements, their adequacy and efficacy will be uncertain. Soft law and self-regulatory mechanisms, while reflecting a greater awareness on the part of governments and TNCs of the need for higher levels of environmental performance, offer no guarantees of compliance.

There remains the possibility of domestic regulation, by either the host or home country, which involves the application of a choice of standards rule by the host country or extraterritorial measures by the home country. The arguments against host country measures which are designed to apply foreign standards to TNCs are convincing. Similarly, trade-related measures now face grave uncertainties where these are imposed unilaterally. This leaves only the option of extraterritorial application of domestic requirements by the home country as a possible means of securing better environmental performance from TNCs.

The proposal for the application of domestic environmental standards in an extraterritorial context raises serious concerns of a political, legal, and practical nature. But there may be some more limited contexts in which this approach could operate in a manner that does not blatantly intrude upon foreign sovereignty, meets relevant international and domestic legal standards for judging the validity of extraterritorial legislation, and avoids the practical difficulties with respect to supervision and enforcement.

One mechanism warranting further consideration is an environmental information disclosure requirement, particularly the unique United States community right-to-know process. Its requirements for annual reporting of releases of toxic pollution might be capable of extending to the activities of United States TNCs abroad. A focus on how this approach could be made to work may produce some concrete results in the short term, while the larger debate concerning environmental standards continues.

Joshua P. Eaton, The Nigerian Tragedy, Environmental Regulation of Transnational Corporations, and the Human Right to a Healthy Environment

15 Boston University International Law Journal
262, 264-71, 292-303 (Spring 1997)

II. THE NILE TRAGEDY

Ogoniland, a district in Rivers State in the Niger Delta region of southeastern Nigeria, is a densely populated, 404 square mile strip of land inhabited by approximately 500,000 Ogoni, one of the 250 ethnic groups in Nigeria. In Ogoniland, as in other parts of the Niger Delta region, the communities subsist by fishing the formerly rich waters and farming the formerly arable lands of their region. Unfortunately for the Nigerian people, both those who inhabit oil-producing areas and those who do not, foreign petroleum companies have pervaded the Niger Delta for over thirty-eight years, their noxious products and wastes now polluting virtually all corners of the region. This section identifies the petroleum TNCs operating in Ogoniland and the Niger Delta, details the environmental devastation of that area, discusses the oil industry practices which have caused such devastation, and describes some of the socio-political effects resulting from oil pollution by TNCs in Nigeria.

In 1958, the Royal/Dutch Shell Group (Shell), a TNC held jointly by British and Dutch corporations, first opened oil exploitation operations in Nigeria. The Nigerian government, cognizant of the substantial economic benefits it stood to gain, welcomed Shell to the region. As of 1996, oil revenues accounted for more than three-quarters of Nigerian federal government revenue and over ninety-five percent of Nigeria's export earnings. Almost all Nigerian petroleum is extracted from the tropical Niger Delta region, of which Ogoniland is one of the richest oil-producing areas. Since 1958, Shell has extracted an estimated $30 billion in oil from Ogoniland. Shell conducts its activities in Nigeria under the name Shell Petroleum Development Company of Nigeria (SPCC or Shell), operating a joint venture on behalf of the state-owned Nigerian National Petroleum Corporation (NNPC), which holds fifty-five percent, Shell (thirty percent), Elf Aquitane S.A. of France (ten percent), and Agip S.p.A. of Italy (five percent).

The Nigerian oil industry, dominated by Shell, has maintained a substantial presence in Ogoniland, constructing over 100 oil wells, a petro-chemical complex, two oil refineries, and seven gas flares which burn twenty-four hours a day. The oil industry has "criss-crossed the land with pipelines and divided it with canals."

All of this activity has resulted in what observers have consistently and repeatedly described as the "devastation" of the Ogonis' water, air, and land. In the oil-producing states of the Niger Delta, "both water and soil have become so polluted with oil that fishing, forestry, and agriculture are no longer possible in large areas." In his report for Pronatura, a recent visitor to the Niger Delta region detailed what he found:

> [B]adly-maintained and leaking pipelines, polluted water, fountains of emulsified oil pouring into villagers' fields, pools of sulfur, blowouts, air pollution, canals driven through farmland causing flooding and disruption of fresh water supplies, footpaths blocked by pipelines, drainage problems, polluted wells, inordinate delays in repairing faults and continual noise.

Water pollution by petroleum products constitutes one of the most pressing problems in the Niger Delta region. "In the Niger Delta area, where oil pollution of water is most serious, the effects have often been catastrophic." A film of oil has formed on many water bodies, preventing natural aeration and causing the death of organisms trapped below. Fish, a major source of subsistence for the Ogoni, ingest the oil, becoming unpalatable or even poisonous when eaten. Most Ogoni villages now have no potable water, and piped water does not exist. Potable water must be imported from distant locations at great cost.

Additionally, water pollution in Ogoniland has led to a myriad of health problems for the Ogonis. One villager remarked: "'we have scratches on our body and rashes on our skin any time we go into the water.'" The area has also seen a "phenomenal increase in incidents of organic diseases such as cancer."

The pollution problems suffered by the Ogonis are visibly traceable to the foreign petroleum industry that pervades their land. Nigerian chemistry professor Oladele Osibanjo summed up the pollution problems of the Niger Delta region: "Incessant oil spills of various magnitudes and improper disposal of oil exploration and production wastes according to sound environmental principles have resulted in massive pollution of water and land; destruction of artisanal fishery; and generally adverse socio-economic consequences."

Several TNC practices allow petroleum products to enter and devastate the environment. For example, an extensive network of oil pipelines transports crude oil from the wells to the refineries for processing. These pipelines are poorly maintained and regularly spill large quantities of oil into the environment. SPCC spilt approximately 1.6 million gallons of oil in the Niger Delta region between 1982-1992. These spills constituted forty percent of Shell's oil spills worldwide during the same period.

Uncontrolled releases of oil from wells, known as "blow-outs," contribute to the volumes of crude oil polluting the region. Blow-outs result from lack of maintenance of the wells and want of due care in preventing such catastrophes. At one site "about 2 acres of land has been caked in oil since a blow-out in the 1970s and in the rainy season it pollutes one of the streams...the main source of fresh water in the area." Pollution problems in Ogoniland are further exacerbated by the failure of the foreign oil companies to clean up their oil spills. The Ogonis have reported numerous oil spills which the polluters simply left untouched to pollute the Ogonis' water and crops.

Gas flaring in the Niger Delta region has also led to significant environmental problems. The "continuous flaring of gas in the Niger Delta area over the last forty years or so has contributed significantly to the release of *'Greenhouse gases'* into the atmosphere and not surprisingly to *'Acid-Rain.'*" The Niger Delta communities claim that the acid rain produced by the "gas flaring has destroyed plant and wildlife." Moreover, the inhabitants report that they suffer from respiratory diseases and have become half-deaf from the incessant din of the gas flares.

Solid and liquid toxic waste products either exit refineries through drainpipes which often lead directly into the environment, or are simply dumped where they immediately contaminate the water. "[E]ffluents and emissions are continuously released raw, without treatment or in a few cases with partial, ineffective treatment, into water, land and air." One Nigerian expert reports that the petroleum refineries have "grossly inadequate" waste treatment facilities, and characterizes refinery antipollution devices as ineffective and inefficient.

On January 4, 1993, approximately 300,000 Ogonis gathered in peaceful protest against the environmental devastation of their land, water, and air by SPCC. The protest was led by Ken Saro-Wiwa, a writer, poet, and environmentalist who founded the Movement for the Survival of the Ogoni People (MOSOP). The protesters demanded royalties from the oil taken from their land, better safeguards against pollution, and environmental and social impact studies detailing the cumulative effects of oil pollution in Ogoniland. Continuing protests, some violent, led Shell to suspend its operations in Ogoniland in mid-1993, but it continues to exploit oil resources in other parts of the Niger Delta region.

The protests led SPCC to request assistance from the Nigerian military. The Nigerian military government responded to the Ogoni protests with a vengeance, sending the Rivers State Internal Security Task Force (RSISTF), a special military unit, to seal off Ogoniland and prevent further unrest. In May of 1994, after a mob murdered four Ogoni leaders during a protest, the RSISTF began a "systematic crackdown" in Ogoniland. The RSISTF conducted a series of punitive raids on Ogoni villages. "These raids were characterized by flagrant human rights abuses, including extrajudicial executions, indiscriminate shooting, arbitrary arrests and detention, floggings, rapes, looting, and extortion...." Military operations have also been conducted elsewhere in the Niger Delta region in response to similar community protests. As of September 1996, Ogoniland remained under a strong security force presence and was impossible to visit without government consent.

On May 22, 1994, Ken Saro-Wiwa and eight other MOSOP leaders were arrested for allegedly inciting the murder of four pro-government Ogoni leaders during protests in the town of Gokana. In a trial widely seen as flawed, Saro-Wiwa and the others were found guilty of murder. Two days after the conviction, on November 10, 1995, the Nigerian government executed the nine men to the astonishment and outrage of the international community. Appeals to Shell to use its influence to save the men were in vain, with Shell proclaiming that "[i]t is not for a commercial organization like Shell to interfere in the legal processes of a sovereign state such as Nigeria." As a result of the executions, the United States, Britain, and several other countries withdrew their ambassadors from Nigeria, the World Bank canceled a $100 million loan to Nigeria for a natural gas liquefaction project, and the Commonwealth, an association comprising Britain and its former colonies, ıspended Nigeria from its membership.

The environmentally abusive practices of the oil industry in Nigeria have caused the devastation of an indigenous people's homeland. These events evidence the failure of existing legal regimes which purport to regulate the environmental practices of TNCs....

....

IV. HUMAN RIGHTS AND THE RIGHT TO A HEALTHY ENVIRONMENT

...[What follows is] an overview of the interaction between human rights law and environmental law. It concludes that the time has arrived for formal recognition, by way of an international hard-law convention, of the human right to a healthy environment.

A. *The Assertion of Established Human Rights to Protect the Environment and Victims of Environmental Abuse*

Traditionally, international law has been largely silent concerning the rights of individuals or groups of individuals who suffered from environmental damage. The Stockholm Declaration [of 1972] was the first international law instrument to recognize the relationship between individual human rights and the quality of the environment. The Stockholm Declaration is more formally known as Report of the United Nations Conference on the Human Environment, and is U.N.Doc.a/conf.48/14/rev.1 (1972)] Principle 1 of the Stockholm Declaration states that "[m]an has the fundamental right to freedom, equality and adequate conditions of life, in an environment of a quality that permits a life of dignity and well-being." This principle does not proclaim a fundamental human right to a healthy environment, but implies that basic environmental health is necessary for the free enjoyment and exercise of recognized human rights. Accordingly, environmental degradation may interfere with an individual's traditional human rights to such an extent as to violate those rights.

The assertion of established human rights has proven to be one of the most successful means of using human rights to protect the environment and victims of environmental abuse. In international human rights committees and tribunals, such as the United Nations Human Rights Committee and the European Court of Human Rights, individual petitioners have invoked a myriad of rights which they claimed were violated through poor environmental practices. These rights include the rights to life, privacy, family life, health, food, personal security, an adequate standard of living, suitable working conditions, self-determination, and freedom from apartheid and genocide.

Today, the right to life may form part of *jus cogens* in international human rights law, meaning that it is a right which may not be set aside by treaties. Article 3 of the United Nations Universal Declaration of Human Rights proclaims that "[e]veryone has the right to life, liberty, and security of person." States may have an international duty not only to refrain from activities which threaten the lives and health of individuals, but also to take positive steps to prevent such activities within their respective jurisdictions.

In 1984, the Inter-American Commission on Human Rights accepted a petition submitted on behalf of the Yanomani Indians of Brazil alleging that the Brazilian government had violated their right to life under the American Declaration of the Rights and Duties of Man. There, the government had constructed a highway through the Indians' territory, causing massive environmental harm and bringing to the area many outsiders with contagious diseases to which the Yanomani Indians were not immune. The Commission found that Brazil had violated the Indians' right to life, liberty, and personal security by not taking timely and effective measures to prevent the environmental damage which led to loss of life and cultural identity among the Yanomani.

The United Nations Human Rights Committee, established in 1967 by the International Covenant on Civil and Political Rights, has indicated a willingness to recognize environmental harm as a violation of the right to life contained in Article 6(l) of the Covenant. In one case, residents of Port Hope, Ontario, brought an action before the Committee against the Canadian government for its failure to clean up 200,000 tons of radioactive waste remaining in a nearby dump which had been closed. Although the case was dismissed for failure to exhaust local remedies, the Committee observed that it raised "serious issues, with regard to the obligation of States parties to protect human life."

The European Court of Human Rights (ECHR) has been less willing to recognize that environmental pollution may violate an individual's right to life as contained in Article 2 of the European Convention on Human Rights (European Convention). In the case of *X v. Austria*, the Court narrowly interpreted Article 2, holding that it primarily protects physical life and deprivations of it. Instead, the Court has found that environmental harm may violate an individual's right to respect for her private life and home contained in Article 8 of the European Convention. This right encompasses both a person's intimate life and physical well-being, as well as guaranteeing a certain quality of life. In *Arrondelle v. United Kingdom*, the applicant, who lived between the runway of a British airport and the highway, claimed that the intensity, duration, and frequency of noise badly affected her health in violation of Article 8. The case was deemed admissible by the European Commission on Human Rights, but the parties reached a settlement before the case was decide.

In the *Powell and Rayner Case*, the ECHR considered a claim that noise pollution from Heathrow airport violated the applicants' Article 8 rights to privacy and home life. Although the Court determined that the rights of the applicants had been infringed, it found that the state had a strong economic interest in maintaining an airport which outweighed the rights of the applicants. Also considering noise abatement measures taken by the British government, the Court concluded that the noise pollution did not violate the European Convention.

In 1994, the ECHR heard the case of *López Ostra v. Spain*. The applicant, a Spanish national, alleged that her right to private and family life had been violated by the erection of a water purification and waste treatment plant near her residence. The plant had been constructed improperly and emitted noxious fumes and effluents, forcing the applicant to relocate. The Court held that the consequences of environmental degradation may so affect an individual's well-being as to deprive her of the enjoyment of her private and family life. The Court acknowledged the positive duty of public authorities to take necessary measures to protect these rights. Having failed to do so, Spain was held in violation of Article 8.

B. *The Assertion of Procedural Rights to Protect the Environment and Victims of Environmental Abuse*

In addition to asserting established substantive rights to protect victims of environmental abuse, human rights advocates have invoked certain international procedural "environmental rights." These include: (i) the right of individuals to information concerning a government's activities which may adversely affect the environment, and a corresponding duty of the state to inform individuals directly affected; (ii) the right of individuals to participate in decision-making which concerns the environment, and a corresponding duty of states to facilitate citizen participation; and (iii) the right of individuals to recourse for environmental harm suffered.

These principles are embodied in several international instruments, the most recent of which is Principle 10 of the Rio Declaration, which states:

Environmental issues are best handled with the participation of all concerned citizens, at the relevant level. At the national level, each individual shall have appropriate access to information concerning the environment that is held by public authorities, including information on hazardous materials and activities in their communities, and the opportunity to participate in decision-making processes. States shall facilitate and encourage public awareness and participation by making information widely available. Effective access to judicial and administrative proceedings, including redress and remedy, shall be provided.

[The Rio Declaration, resulting from a June 1992 gathering in Rio de Janeiro of representatives from most of the world's nations and several hundred non-governmental organizations (NGOs), is more formally known as Adoption of Agreements on Environment and Development, U.N. Conference on Environment and Development, and is U.N. Doc. A/conf.151//5/Rev.1 (1992).] Although this is a non-binding, soft-law instrument, these principles may have become embedded in current customary or general international law, and accordingly could create duties for states under international law.

Other international instruments which recognize such procedural rights include the U.N. Convention on Environmental Impact Assessment in a Transboundary Context, the United Nations World Charter for Nature, the International Covenant on Civil and Political Rights, and the European Convention on Human Rights.

While both the assertion of established human rights and the recognition of procedural environmental rights have done much to protect the environment and victims of environmental abuse, these approaches are still limited in their effect. Procedural rights do not guarantee positive environmental results. The existing substantive rights offer only a narrow scope of protection for the environment and individuals suffering from environmental pollution. Under the current regime, environmental harm to individuals cannot constitute a cause of action in and of itself, but must be linked to a substantive right, leaving courts and commissions on the shaky ground of creatively extending rights. These limitations may be most effectively addressed through the formal recognition in international law, through an international hard-law convention, of a substantive human right to a healthy environment.

C. *The Human Right to a Healthy Environment*

Evolving from Principle 1 of the Stockholm Declaration, various formulations of the right to a healthy environment have been included in international instruments. Principle 1 of the Rio Declaration states that "[h]uman beings...are entitled to a healthy and productive life in harmony with nature." Article 24 of the 1981 African Charter on Human and Peoples' Rights recognizes the right of "all peoples...to a general satisfactory environment favorable to their development." In 1988, the Organization of American States added the Protocol of San Salvador to the American Convention on Human Rights. Article 11(l) of the Protocol of San Salvador provides that "[e]veryone shall have the right to live in a healthy environment and to have access to basic public services;" however, an individual right of petition was not granted for this right. Both the 1989 Convention on the Rights of the Child and the 1989 International Labour Organization Convention Concerning Indigenous and Tribal Peoples in Independent Countries emphasize the important link between environmental protection and human rights, yet fall short of proclaiming the right to a healthy environment. In addition to these instruments, nearly a third of the world's constitutions recognize the existence of such a right or create specific environmental duties for the state.

1. Customary and General International Law

While the instruments discussed above evidence a broadening international acceptance of the human right to a healthy environment, it is unlikely that such a right currently exists as a norm of general or customary international law applicable to all states.

In order to establish a norm as one of customary international law, one must show "uniform and consistent state practice engaged in out of a sense of obligation that observance of such a norm is required by international law." Such norms are easily established. The inclusion of the right to a healthy environment in international law instruments and national constitutions provides some evidence of the requisite state practice, but it seems unlikely that this practice could be considered "uniform and consistent." Indeed, state practice in recognizing and implementing the right thus far has been sporadic and generally inconsistent.

In addition to uniform and consistent state practice, the formation of customary international law requires a showing that the state practice is engaged in out of a sense of legal obligation, an element often referred to as *opinio juris*. This is the "element that ties customary international law to the consent of states." Essentially, *opinio juris* is established if there exists sufficient evidence to demonstrate that states believe that the right to a healthy environment currently reflects international law, and that the states recognize such a right because they have an obligatory legal duty to do so. Both international law instruments and state practice indicate that states view the incipient right to a healthy environment as a mere aspiration, not a legal obligation. Accordingly, the right to a healthy environment cannot yet be seen as a norm of customary international law.

Nor can the right to a healthy environment currently be seen as a general principle of international law. Such a principle is deemed to exist if it is "inherent in the nature or the basic concept of the international system." Thus far, states have not treated the right to a healthy environment as a basic or fundamental principle inherent in the nature of their relations. Therefore, the right to a healthy environment does not form part of general international law.

Nevertheless, a multilateral hard-law treaty asserting the existence of the right to a healthy environment may help to establish the right as one of customary international law. While such a treaty would create new affirmative legal duties owed to individuals by the *treaty signatories*, the establishment of the right to a healthy environment in customary international law is essential to the creation of duties owed by *all* states. If the treaty is one which receives widespread ratification, it will substantially reinforce the state practice element of customary international law. Additionally, it will work to speed up the process by which states not parties to the treaty recognize the right to a healthy environment as legally binding and apply it in their internal legal systems. Moreover, the possibility exists that customary international law will be "crystallized" during the treaty-making process as to the human right to a healthy environment.

2. Establishment of the Human Right to a Healthy Environment

The foregoing discussion indicates that there exists no common agreement as to how an international environmental right should be defined. Once the international community agrees upon the necessity for the establishment of such a right, its terminology, scope, and content must be determined. Initially, one should note that the right to a healthy environment has been stated using a myriad of adjectives: clean, balanced, ecologically balanced, protected, livable, suitable, humane, decent, and generally satisfactory. The term "healthy" is broad enough to encompass all of these, yet specific enough to qualify the right in a meaningful way.

In discussing the possible scope and content of the right to a healthy environment, one author suggests:

> The right to a clean environment cannot be interpreted as the right to "an ideal environment." In the world today, a certain degree of pollution is inevitable. The term "clean" should mean a healthy environment, free from dangerous pollution, such as that stemming from radiation or from heavy metal or chemical industries, and free from pollution exceeding the possibility of natural self-purification and endangering consequently the ecological balance and health.

In its most basic formulation, the right to a healthy environment would be violated when, as a result of human activity, natural or artificial substances are released into the environment which pollute the land, water and/or air to an extent that individuals suffer a substantial impairment of the quality of their lives, significant health problem, or death. Additionally, human activities, or the substances they produce, that injure or destroy plants or animals upon which humans depend, would violate the right to a healthy environment. As with all human rights, nuances and interpretive extensions of the right to a healthy environment will develop through adjudication on a case-by-case basis.

Many commentators, including this author, see the protection of the right to a healthy environment as an essential prerequisite to the fulfillment of many other human rights. Individuals living in ecologically devastated or unhealthy environments may be prevented from exercising and enjoying the basic international human rights to which they are entitled. Accordingly, the establishment of the right to a healthy environment in international law will not only work to protect the environment and victims of its abuse, but will help to safeguard those human rights already accepted and revered by the international community.

Unfortunately, despite recent trends recognizing the importance of environmental protection and the human right to a healthy environment, the formation of such a right ultimately depends upon a willingness of states to relinquish sovereignty and establish duties to protect the right. At present, a majority of states are probably unwilling to do so, including the United States, which has refused to sign the Protocol of San Salvador recognizing the right to a healthy environment. Nevertheless, as the world continues to witness instances of environmental devastation which drastically affect the lives and well-being of individuals, support for the right to a healthy environment will grow, eventually culminating in its international recognition as a fundamental human right.

3. International Duties and the Human Right to a Healthy Environment

International human rights law imposes upon states both the duty to abstain from violating human rights worldwide and the positive duty to prevent violations of human rights within their jurisdictions. With the establishment of the human right to a healthy environment in international law, states will have an international law duty to preserve and maintain a healthy environment throughout their respective jurisdictions. In addition,

> [a] state may become responsible for violations by *private actors* if it fails to exercise due diligence to prevent the violations or to respond to them. If a gov-

ernment does not seriously investigate human rights violations committed by private parties, "those parties are aided in a sense by the government, thereby making the State responsible on the international plane."

Accordingly, if the Federal Republic of Nigeria signed an international convention recognizing the right to a healthy environment, or, alternatively, if the right were established in customary international law, Nigeria would have several duties specific to the oil exploitation operations in the Niger Delta region. These would include: (i) abstaining from violating the Niger Delta region's inhabitants' right to a healthy environment through the government's own oil exploitation activities; (ii) taking affirmative steps to create, preserve and maintain a healthy environment in the region; and (iii) preventing violations of the right to a healthy environment by TNCs operating in the region.

Unfortunately, states such as Nigeria might not ratify a convention recognizing the human right to a healthy environment, and customary international law may take some time to develop. Moreover, once Nigeria finally has an international law duty to protect the human right to a healthy environment, it might nevertheless ignore its duty and violate the right as it violates other international human rights today. These concerns make it necessary to apply international human rights duties to private actors as well as to the state.

"All human rights involve correlative duties for individuals, groups, and governments. Professor Ian Brownlie of the University of Oxford notes that "[i]n general, treaties do not create direct... obligations for private individuals, but, if it was the intention of the parties to do this, effect can be given to the intention." Accordingly, an international covenant establishing the human right to a healthy environment should expressly state that it is the duty of everyone, states and private actors alike, to protect that right. Under this formulation a TNC, such as Shell, would have direct international duties if either its home country or its host country signed and ratified the convention. If the TNC's home country, either the country where a TNC is incorporated or where a majority of its shareholders reside, were to ratify the convention, the TNC would have international law duties throughout its areas of operation; if a TNC's host country were to ratify the convention, the TNC would only have international law duties as to its actions within that country....

Efforts to establish the right to a healthy environment should continue, ideally resulting in the incorporation of the right into existing human rights instruments, as well as the adoption of a multilateral hard-law convention expressly recognizing the right and establishing international law duties for states and private entities alike. Such a convention was recommended in the *Report and Final Recommendation of the Congress on a More Efficient International Law on the Environment and Setting Up an International Court* (Rome Conference) held in Rome in April of 1989.

Along with the formal establishment of the right to a healthy environment, the convention must provide for adequate international enforcement mechanisms.... [T]he solution would be to establish an international commission environment, which could accept individual or group petitions alleging violations by states or TNCs of the petitioners' right to a healthy environment, coupled with an international environmental court to adjudicate such disputes.

Chapter 11

Special Transactions and Sectors

I. Technology Transfer

A. Dilemmas for Multinational Corporations and Host Countries

Peter Muchlinski, Multinational Enterprises and the Law
425-47, 449 (1995)

1 The Nature of Technology Transfer

1.1 "Technology" and "Technology Transfer"

....The Draft *TOT Code* [*i.e.*, the draft *International Code of Conduct for Technology Transfer*, discussed below] suggests, in its definition of "technology transfer," that "technology" should be described as "systematic knowledge for the manufacture of a product, for the application of a process or for the rendering of a service and does not extend to the transactions involving the mere sale or lease of goods." This is not particularly enlightening, save for the fact that it clearly excludes goods that are sold or hired from the ambit of "technology." Thus it is the knowledge that goes into the creation and provision of the product or service that is of importance.

Such knowledge should be seen as encompassing both the technical knowledge on which the end product is based and the organizational capacity to convert the relevant productive inputs into the finished item or service, as the case may be. Thus,... "technology" includes not only "knowledge or methods that are necessary to carry on or to improve the existing production and distribution of goods and services," but also "entrepreneurial expertise and professional know-how." The latter two elements may often prove to be the essential competitive advantage possessed by the technology owner. As will be shown below, MNEs [multi-national enterprises] will be in a particularly advantageous position in this regard.

"Technology transfer" is the process by which commercial technology is disseminated. This will take the form of a technology transfer transaction, which may or may not be a legally binding contract, but which will involve the communication, by the transferor, of the relevant knowledge to the recipient. Among the types of transfer transactions that may be used, the draft *TOT Code* has listed the following:

(a) The assignment, sale and licensing of all forms of industrial property, except for trade marks, service marks and trade names when they are not part of transfer of technology transactions;

(b) The provision of know-how and technical expertise in the form of feasibility studies, plans, diagrams, models, instructions, guides, formulae, basic or detailed engineering designs, specifications and equipment for training, services involving technical advisory and managerial personnel, and personnel training;

(c) The provision of technological knowledge necessary for the installation, operation and functioning of plant and equipment, and turnkey projects;

(d) The provision of technological knowledge necessary to acquire, install and use machinery, equipment, intermediate goods and/or raw materials which have been acquired by purchase, lease or other means;

(e) The provision of technological contents of industrial and technical cooperation arrangements.

The list excludes non-commercial technology transfers, such as those found in international cooperation agreements between developed and developing states. Such agreements may relate to infrastructure or agricultural development, or to international cooperation in the fields of research, education, employment or transport.

1.2 The Generation and Use of Technology: the Interests of Technology-exporting and Technology-importing States Compared

The respective interests of technology-exporting and technology-importing states are best understood in the context of the international market for commercial technology. Although technology exists in non-proprietary forms that can be generally accessed, as, for example, in publicly available books or journals, the present concern focuses on proprietary technology, that is technology that is capable of generating a profit for its owner.

The first assumption underlying the market for commercial technology is that such technology should be treated as the private property of its owner and not as a public good capable of general use at little or no cost to its user. Commercial technology is usually commoditized through the application of intellectual property rights, which give the owner a legally determined monopoly over the use and disposal of that right, or by way of protected and restrictive contractual transfer as in the case of non-patentable know-how that is secret. This process of commoditization may help to increase the value of the technology to its owner by creating relative scarcity through legally restricted access to it. However, not all types of useful knowledge are so treated. Thus, knowledge in agriculture, health sciences or services is relatively free from private claims based on intellectual property and should be more freely available.

The generation of commercial technology is closely bound up with the technological infrastructure of a country. This includes the public and private organizations which fund the development and adaptation of technology, the public and private research and development (R&D) organizations that conduct work on new and improved technology, the intermediaries who move the technology around the country and across its borders and the users who apply the technology in their business activities or who are the end consumers of products incorporating the technology in question. Consequently, the states that possess the more developed systems for generating, delivering and using technology are likely to be the leading sources of proprietary technology.

MNEs are strongly influential in the operation of national and international technological infrastructures. They can be found operating at each stage of such a system in the most technologically advanced economies of the world. That this should be so stems from the fact,... that one of the main ownership specific advantages of MNEs is their ability to "produce, acquire, master the understanding of and organise the use of technological assets across national boundaries." Consequently, MNEs are a major force in shaping international markets for technology, particularly on the supply side. Their influence on the demand side is also significant, given that increasing amounts of international technology transfers occur between related enterprises.

With regard to the supply side, the world's major MNEs will seek to control commercial technology markets for maximum gain, exploiting their dominant position in such markets. However, the degree of control exercised by these firms may vary according to the type of technology involved. A distinction has been drawn between markets for "conventional" technology, where the technology is sufficiently distributed for many firms from many countries to be able to supply it, and markets for "high" technology, where the technology can be developed only by a few very large firms with very high R&D spending and where constant innovation is the basis for competitive success. Examples of the former include footwear, textiles, cement, pulp and paper or food processing. Examples of the latter include aerospace, electronics, computers, chemicals and machinery. The supply of technology in "conventional" industries is said to be relatively competitive, given the stable and generally non-proprietary nature of the technology involved. By contrast, in "high" technology areas competitive supply is likely to be restricted. Owners will guard the source of their competitive advantage, making their technology available only on restrictive terms favourable to the earning of a monopoly rent. This tendency may be reinforced because of the absence of viable alternative technology suppliers that could offer competition over the terms and conditions of transfer. However, not all "high" technology markets should be seen as uncompetitive on the supply side. For example, in the newer high technology industries, such as semiconductors or computers, the entry of smaller, innovative firms has stimulated choice in sources of technological supply, making for increased competition in that field, although in the long term concentration can be predicted to occur. Furthermore, as high technology matures into conventional technology, new entrants into the field can be expected. The competitive situation on the supply side of a market for technology is not, therefore, a static phenomenon, and each industrial sector should be analyzed on its own terms.

The demand side of the market will also be conditioned by the nature of the technological infrastructure present in the state where the recipient is situated. Thus a distinction can be made between conditions in technologically advanced recipient states and those in technologically less developed states. Conditions in the former are characterized by an ability to absorb technology effectively through advanced production systems, a highly trained workforce, high demand for the technology concerned and the ability to pay for it. Furthermore, technologically advanced recipients will be in a stronger position to bargain over the terms of supply. Alternative local sources of technology that can compete with the technology on offers from outside are more likely to exist. Furthermore, there exists a greater likelihood that the purchaser will itself be in a strong position to condition the market, as where it is another major corporation operating at the same level of the market as the supplier, or where it is in a quasi-monopolistic position, such as the postal and telecommunications authority of a major advanced country. As will be shown in more detail below, in advanced countries the principal concern is that of ensuring the existence of workable competition even in highly concentrated technology markets. Thus competition law plays a significant role in the regulation of technology transfers to such countries.

By comparison, the absorption of proprietary technology in LDCs [less developed countries] is more problematic. The absence of a sophisticated technological infrastructure has significant consequences for demand conditions. In particular, a high level of dependency on outside suppliers is created due to the lack of alternative, domestically generated, technology. This creates a weak bargaining position which is exacerbated by the relative lack of information about technology caused by the absence of adequate numbers of skilled specialists who could evaluate the technology. In such cases the technology owner is likely to enjoy a monopolistic position in relation to the recipient market and may be able to exact excessive prices and restrictions on the utilization of the imported technology.

Furthermore, as is elaborated in the next section, it is less likely that the technology owner will be able to introduce the technology by means other than direct investment through a controlled subsidiary. In LDCs, the incidence of firms that can act as licensees of advanced technology is much smaller than in developed countries. Consequently, the conditions of technology transfer will be determined by the needs of the MNE as an integrated enterprise. These may be inimical to the interests of the importing state, to the extent that control over technology within the firm is less likely to result in its dissemination to potential competitors, if any, in that state.

During the 1970s, when the debate on technology transfer to LDCs became a significant pillar of the wider call for a New International Economic Order, one issue in particular stood out as encapsulating the inequitable situation of LDCs in the market for technology. This was the issue of whether MNEs could supply "appropriate technology" to LDCs. It was argued that LDCs were disadvantaged in technology markets because the available technology was inappropriate to their real needs. The argument was put on two levels. First, the type of technology that had been generated by MNEs from the developed countries was incapable of utilizing the primary factor endowment of LDCs, namely unskilled labour, as it was geared to capital-intensive forms of production requiring fewer, high-skilled personnel. Thus, in LDCs, MNEs tended to set up production enterprises that had little effect on local skill and employment patterns. Secondly, the types of products made by MNEs were said to be inappropriate to LDC markets. Either they were high-technology products with highly specialized uses that few consumers in LDCs could use, or they were mass consumption items geared towards the wants of Western consumer markets that distorted consumption patterns in LDCs by persuading consumers to spend what little disposable income they had on unnecessary products, such as soft drinks, "junk foods," cigarettes or cosmetics.

The first argument has been challenged on economic grounds, in that there may be no necessary correlation between labour-intensive technologies and welfare in LDCs. In any case, there is considerable evidence showing that much investment by MNEs in LDCs is of a labour-intensive kind that is geared to take advantage of lower labour costs in the production of goods for export markets. The true problem may be that MNEs are uninterested in transferring any but the more mature and labour-intensive technologies to LDCs, given the limitations of local markets for advanced technology goods and processes, and the uneconomic costs of adapting existing proprietary technology to LDC conditions.

The second argument can be opposed on the ground that it is based on a subjective opinion as to what is "appropriate" as a consumer good in an LDC. In a free-market economy, the fact that the demand exists is more important in economic terms than its social implications. Thus, MNEs can be expected to generate demand for their products among those in LDCs who can afford them and/or who can be persuaded to buy them. None the less, despite the weaknesses of the "appropriate technology" argument, it offered an impetus for the reconsideration of policy in this area.

Thus, concerns over the monopolistic tendencies of suppliers in LDC technology markets and the "appropriate technology" argument provided the main justifications for calls for greater regulation of international technology transfers in the interests of LDCs. This gave rise to new kinds of legal regimes, pioneered by the Latin American states, based on specialized technology transfer laws, and to negotiations for an international code of conduct on technology transfer under the auspices of UNCTAD.

2 Technology Transfer by MNEs and Its Legal Effects

There are two principal methods of technology transfer open to the MNE. The first is to license the technology at arm's length to an independent licensee or to a joint venture with a local partner. The second is to transfer the technology internally to a subsidiary. This may involve the licensing of intellectual property rights and/or know-how by the parent to the subsidiary in return for royalty payments, although informal, royalty-free transfers may also take place. The choice of methods will be determined by what will serve to maximize the MNE's income from the technology in question.

The choice is conditioned by a number of factors. Assuming that a suitable licensee, or joint venture partner, exists in the host country, the MNE is more likely to consider licensing the technology, or setting up a joint venture, where the entry barriers, such as the relatively limited size of the market, are too great to make an independent direct investment viable. Indeed, in some cases, a licensing arrangement or a joint venture may be the only legally permissible form of entry. Furthermore, where the firm is a newcomer to international markets and lacks the expertise to undertake direct investment, licensing to a third party or to a joint venture may be preferable. On the other hand, licensing may create too many medium- to long-term costs to be worthwhile. In particular, the MNE must consider whether licensing will increase the risk of deterioration in quality owing to the licensee's misuse of the technology, and whether the licensee will pass on the technology to competitors. Such problems may be diminished by the imposition of restrictive conditions on the licensee in the licensing agreement. However, if the technology concerned is a "core" technology with a long commercial life span, licensing may involve too many risks. In this respect, a joint venture may serve to ensure greater operational control over the use of the technology. However, it may not protect the owner from allowing the other joint venture partner to become familiar with the technology and to use this advantage to set up in competition with the owner. Thus, if the owner has the ability to do so, it may prefer direct investment over licensing, as this permits closer control over the use of the technology and is more likely to preserve its confidential nature.

The transfer of technology by direct investment is more likely in LDCs, given the absence of suitable potential licensees or joint venture partners, and because the MNE can provide the technology as part of a larger "package" that includes capital, management, backup services, access to markets and other associated benefits which are locally in short supply. In such cases, the major question is whether the host state will in fact gain any transfer of the technology out of the firm into the wider local economy. Much will depend on the willingness of the MNE to train more personnel than it needs, the surplus employees being free to apply their experience elsewhere in the local economy. However, MNEs do not appear to make the training of local personnel a major priority, and it is questionable whether there will be sufficient outlets for the application of the skills newly learnt by the local employees of MNEs. If there are, then restrictive covenants in contracts of employment may seek to protect the commercial advantage of the MNE by preventing the use of such skills by former employees for the benefit of competitors.

From the above, it can be seen that the legal structure of the recipient of the technology is a significant matter influencing the extent to which the general diffusion of the technology concerned into the wider local economy is likely to occur. Direct investment through a wholly owned subsidiary is most likely to keep the technology under the control of its owner. The terms of transfer to the subsidiary are likely to restrict the use of the technology for the benefit of the MNE alone, and this aim will be enforced by managerial control from the parent. On the other hand, a joint venture or a licensing agreement may allow the local partner or licensee to gain access to the technology and to diffuse it in the wider economy, provided that the terms of the transfer are not too restrictive. Consequently, one legal issue of relevance to the regulator is whether to restrict investments involving technology transfer to legal forms that are more likely to result in technology diffusion. Hence there may be a preference, in host state law, for joint ventures or licensing arrangements over direct investment.

The second major legal issue that arises in all cases of technology transfer, whether between related or between independent entities, concerns the actual terms of the transfer transaction and the degree to which these affect the likelihood that the technology will be made available to those who could benefit from it. The nature and content of such terms form much of the basis for technology transfer regulation, in both technology-rich and technology-poor countries. Therefore, a brief overview of the most common terms in technology transfer transactions is in order.

3 Restrictive Terms in Technology Transfer Transactions

Technology licenses, whether between the affiliated undertakings of an MNE or between an MNE and a third party, will contain terms that seek to preserve the competitive advantage of the technology owner against abusive exploitation by the technology recipient. While such terms may be unobjectionable where the legitimate interests of the technology owner are being protected, they may also be used by the owner as a means of obtaining an unfair commercial advantage over the recipient through the exploitation of its generally weaker bargaining position. In developed recipient states, such abusive behaviour by the transferor has been dealt with as a competition issue. However, in LDCs, even if commercially legitimate restraints are placed on the recipient, the effect of these on the ability of the host state to absorb and learn from the imported technology, or to use it as a catalyst for economic development, may be too restrictive. Therefore, controls over restrictive terms based on competition law alone may be ineffective as a means of safeguarding the public interests involved.

Restrictive terms in technology transfer transactions may be conveniently classified into two main categories: those that restrict the recipient's commercial policy in respect of the conduct of business involving the transferred technology and those that seek to preserve the exclusive ownership and use of the technology by the transferor.

3.1 Restrictions on the Commercial Policy of the Technology Recipient

Technology transfer agreements will usually include restrictions on the commercial policy of the recipient that are designed to maximize the profit that the transferor can earn from its inventions and know-how. These will concern *inter alia* restrictions on the purchasing, production and marketing policies of the recipient.

Thus, at the level of purchasing policy, transferors may insist on the recipient buying its requirements for raw materials, plant and machinery and other goods or services from the transferor. Such 'tie-ins' may be legitimate where certain inputs, given their quality and characteristics, can only be obtained from the transferor. However, where suitable substitutes are available more cheaply on the open market, such tie-ins are harder to justify on efficiency grounds. Indeed, they may be a means of extracting monopolistic profits from the recipient that go beyond what may be legitimately expected from the mere ownership of the technology. Such manipulations have been condemned under the competition laws of developed countries, although a tying arrangement will not be upset where there are genuine commercial reasons for its existence. From the perspective of an LDC, tying arrangements may create special problems. First, such an arrangement may conceal the true cost of the technology package, in that although the royalty payments imposed on the recipient may be reasonable, they may be enhanced by the overpricing of tied inputs through transfer pricing manipulations. Secondly, tying arrangements may have the further effect of preventing backward economic integration through the growth of local suppliers. Thus local economic development may be inhibited.

The recipient may be restricted further by clauses requiring the production of minimum quantities of product, which may be linked to a minimum royalty requirement, and by clauses setting the duration of the agreement. Where the agreement is of excessive duration this may force the recipient to acquire obsolete technology and prevent it from obtaining technology from alternative suppliers. The agreement may also contain field-of-use restrictions which limit the application of the technology to particular fields only. This may be reasonable as a means of giving the transferor control over the use of its inventions, but competition authorities will not normally tolerate such a restriction where it acts as a disguised method of dividing markets. For an LDC, field-of-use restrictions may prevent the full exploitation of the technology in all the areas where it may be of value as a stimulus to economic development.

At the marketing level, the recipient may be restricted as to the export markets in which it can sell products incorporating the technology in question. The owner will justify such protection on the basis that it ensures an adequate return on the cost of developing the technology. It is an aspect of the monopoly right that is inherent in patented technology, or in the competitive advantage gained by the development of secret know-how. Reasonable territorial restrictions on the business of technology recipients have been accepted under the competition laws of developed states, on the basis that some restriction of intra-brand competition may be necessary to ensure the widest possible dissemination of products incorporating the proprietary technology. On the other hand, LDCs have argued that such restrictions simply inhibit their ability to earn foreign exchange through exports. There is undoubtedly a danger that an integrated MNE will use technology licenses with its subsidiaries to insulate geographical markets. Markets in which high prices prevail may be protected from imports of cheaper products produced in another market by an affiliate, thereby stifling price competition between affiliates. Where the cheaper products originate in an LDC, then some loss to revenue may be predicted as a result of such export restrictions.

A similar restraint on the recipient's commercial freedom may come from price fixing provisions. The transferor may insist that the transferee charges a high price for products incorporating the transferred technology. This may prevent price competition between the transferor and recipient, by protecting the transferor's home market against cheaper imports from the recipient. Where such price controls are imposed on a plant operating in an LDC, the opportunity to earn foreign exchange from exports to higher price areas will be lost.

Although price fixing is generally regarded as a particularly serious anti-competitive practice, in licensing arrangements a degree of price control over the licensee may be justifiable as an aspect of the licensor's monopoly rights that stem from its invention. Given that the licensee is unlikely to license a direct competitor, and that the licensor has an interest in allowing the greatest exploitation of its invention, the licensee may in fact be encouraged to sell at the lowest prices possible. However, in the context of an LDC economy, this argument may not be sufficient to justify restrictions on the earning capacity of the recipient. On the other hand, where the recipient is a wholly owned subsidiary, the ability to control corporate policy may be limited, even under competition principles. It may be necessary to impose export requirements as a condition of entry.

3.2 Restrictions on the Use of Technology on the Part of the Recipient

Restrictions falling under this heading aim at the preservation of the confidential nature of the technology transferred and at the preservation of the owner's competitive advantage stemming from the technology. Thus, it is common to find confidentiality clauses in technology transfer agreements. These are generally unobjectionable, provided they are not of excessive duration, as where the duty continues even though the intellectual property right protecting the technology has run out, or the know-how involved has entered the public domain. Similarly, clauses preventing the recipient from entering into arrangements with competitors of the transferor, from manufacturing competing products or from using competing technology can be justified on the basis of confidentiality. However, in the context of an LDC economy such restraints may inhibit the gaining of experience in the field where the technology is used.

More problematic are clauses that inhibit the acquisition of skill and experience on the part of the recipient as a result of interaction with the technology transferred. This may allow the recipient to compete with the transferor after the expiry of the agreement, a situation that challenges the monopoly of the transferor. To counter this threat, the agreement may prohibit the use of the technology transferred after the expiry of the agreement, or permit use only upon the continued payment of a royalty. This is acceptable where the intellectual property rights involved have not yet expired or the relevant know-how has not entered the public domain. On the other hand, a blanket prohibition on post-term use where such rights have expired, or where the know-how has become public knowledge as a result of the transferor's actions, may be unduly exploitative, as would a requirement to pay further royalties in these circumstances.

In addition the recipient may be prevented from conducting its own research and development work on the transferred technology, or, in the absence of such a prohibition, it may be obliged to transfer any resulting improvements to the transferor on a non-reciprocal basis. Such strong "grant-back" provisions have been condemned under the competition laws of developed countries. For LDCs such clauses would be especially worrying as they would inhibit the learning process that can result from the use of imported technology, and lessen the likelihood of adaptation to local needs.

Thus, restrictive clauses in technology transfer transactions will have significant effects on the manner in which the technology may be used by the recipient. The extent to which the recipient can benefit in the long term from the use of the technology will depend on the limits of contractual freedom granted to the transferor for the exploitation of its innovation. In this the responses of developed and less developed states have differed, and to these we now turn.

4 The Two Principal Models of Technology Transfer Regulation

From the above it can be seen that the priorities of preserving workable competition in technology markets, as espoused by developed recipient states, may not always answer the priorities of ensuring economic development espoused by less developed recipient states. Thus two distinct models for the regulation of technology transfer have emerged from these two groups of states. The developed recipients follow a model that preserves the essential logic of a legally permitted monopoly right in proprietary technology based on intellectual property law and freedom of contract, tempered in its excesses by competition law. By contrast, LDCs have sought to create a regime of technology transfer laws that go beyond the preservation of workable competition and seek to control technology transfers in the interests of development, thereby qualifying the legal effects of private property in innovation. A comparison of these models will now be made.

4.1 The Developed Country Model

Developed recipient countries accept the private property character of commercial technology through their use of patent and trademark laws as the basis for defining the scope of that property. Such rights have been given reciprocal protection between states under international conventions embodying the principles of national treatment, non-discrimination and priority, thereby guaranteeing the same protection of industrial property rights to nationals and to foreign right holders. This reflects the fact that most advanced states are not only purchasers of foreign technology but also exporters in their own right, thereby giving them an interest in the reciprocal protection of intellectual property rights.

As noted above, the principal concerns in this area are related to the preservation of competition in industries where technology is controlled by relatively few owners. This will involve, first, the control of cooperative arrangements and concentrations between competitors that may have an adverse effect on the availability of essential technology to third parties without any compensating technological progress and/or benefits to consumers. Secondly, as already discussed in the previous section, excessive restrictions on the commercial policy and use of technology by a recipient will be regulated. In both cases the aim is to protect the right of the technology owner to profit from its invention or know-how, while at the same time preventing the creation of monopolistic horizontal structures and/or vertical relationships in the market concerned. This balancing of interests is achieved through the use of a "rule of reason" approach whereby the anti-competitive effects of the technology owner's actions are weighed against the beneficial effects on the economy of protecting its proprietary rights in the technology.

. . . .

4.2 The LDC Model

This model is characterized by a reserved attitude to the protection of intellectual property rights coupled with the adoption of specialized technology transfer laws. The model is more complex to explain than that evolved by developed recipient states. This is because it attempts to address issues of economic development against the background of the internationalization of the developed country model of technology transfer regulation, a model that is suitable for the needs of technologically mature and innovative economies, and that places considerably more emphasis on the rights of intellectual property holders than might have been the case when the developed states were themselves undergoing the process of industrialization.

4.2.1 *Reserved approach to the protection of intellectual property rights*

Unlike the technologically advanced countries, LDCs have been less willing to accept uncritically the assumptions behind the international system of intellectual property protection. Since 1961, LDCs have been seeking reform of that system. The process started when, in 1961, Brazil introduced a draft resolution in the Second Committee of UN General Assembly calling for a study of the effects of patents on the transfer of technology. This led, in 1964, to a report by the Secretary-General, entitled 'The role of patents in the transfer of technology to developing countries'. It concluded that reform of the system was unnecessary. Most of the states that replied to the UN questionnaire on which the report was based said that patents provided an aid to their development by promoting technology transfer. Only India, Lebanon and Cuba offered the opposite opinion. However, by the 1970s this approach had changed. In particular, UNCTAD had taken up the issue of technology transfer. In this connection, it undertook several influential studies, including one on the role of patents in technology transfer and one on the role of trademarks in LDCs. Furthermore, in 1974 negotiations were under way to reform the *Paris Convention for the Protection of Industrial Property* under the auspices of the body charged with its administration, the World Intellectual Property Organization (WIPO). These developments resulted in the formulation of a comprehensive critique as to the appropriateness of traditional intellectual property laws as instruments for the transfer of technology to LDCs. The basic arguments concerned the problems associated with patents and trademarks and with the principles underlying the international system of protection.

As regards patents, it was argued that the granting of patent rights in LDCs would have adverse consequences on development in that they would be taken out for reasons that had little to do with the traditional uses of patents. Given that most of the world's patents were owned by foreign firms operating in developed country markets, patent protection in an LDC was not aimed at encouraging local innovation. Instead, the principal reason for taking out such a patent was attributed to the desire of the firm to protect its markets and licensing rights in the LDC concerned, thereby preventing rivals from entering in its place. Thus the patent would give the owner an import monopoly over the market concerned. Furthermore, the patent owner would rarely, if ever, work the patent in the LDC concerned. Thus, the grant of the patent would retard technology transfer not only by closing off competition but also by allowing the owner to neutralize the technology concerned through non-use. The latter problem is not unique to LDCs. The industrial property laws of most states provide for compulsory licensing of patents that are not worked. However, according to the UNCTAD study of 1975 most LDCs did not use their compulsory licensing procedures because of the costs and delays involved. Finally, it was argued that the existence of patent rights could encourage the conclusion of unduly restrictive licensing agreements, which, given the absence of antitrust laws in most LDCs, could not be effectively controlled.

Regarding trademarks, it was argued that while such rights served the useful functions of guaranteeing quality and source, they also created adverse effects in LDC economies. In particular, trademarks tended to be owned by the subsidiaries of foreign MNEs and used to enhance market power either through their promotion by intensive advertising or through licensing to local distributors. These activities would result in considerable social costs as consumers with limited incomes would pay high prices for foreign branded products. Furthermore, local distributors would bear the cost of developing market share without any guarantee of benefiting from the resulting goodwill created towards the marked product. This goodwill would accrue to the foreign trademark owner rather than to the local licensee. In the light of such views certain LDCs adopted laws to control the use of trademarks. Thus Mexico enacted a Law on Inventions and Trademarks in 1976, which required the concurrent use of the local licensee's mark with that of the foreign licensor, in the belief that the good-will generated by the licensee would be associated not only with the foreign mark but also with the local mark. In 1972, under the Generic Names Drug Act, Pakistan banned the use of trademarks in the pharmaceutical industry. This had disastrous re-sults, leading to sales of ineffective counterfeit drugs bearing the permitted generic name and to a black market in branded drugs. This law was repealed in 1976.

Finally, as regards the international system of protection, the LDCs have sought to reform, in particular, the application of the national treatment standard to their national legal regimes. Thus the 1975 UNCTAD study on patents proposed the introduction of preferential treatment for LDCs. This has been justified on the ground that LDCs and developed countries are in an unequal relationship based on the fact that most of the patent rights that stand to benefit from national treatment are held by MNEs from de-veloped countries, and because the few patents that are issued for the nationals of LDCs involve individual inventors, not MNEs, and create distinctive needs for protection. In addition LDCs sought to reform the principle of priority contained in article 4 of the *Paris Convention*. By this principle, any person who has filed an application for a patent in one of the contracting states has a right to claim similar protection as a matter of pri-ority in other contracting states for up to twelve months. The LDCs have argued that this period is too long and acts as a disincentive to invention in LDCs.

All the above arguments have been subjected to forceful criticism. The LDC posi-tion on patents has been doubted by proponents of the developed country approach, who still assert the original justification for patent protection as lying in the provision of incentives for innovation by enterprises. According to Professor Beier, "it is only patent protection which gives enterprises the necessary incentive to file their important inventions abroad and converts an invention into an object of international trade that can be transferred without too great a risk." Such a position lies behind the greater con-trols over *TRIPs* [*Agreement on Trade-Related Aspects of Intellectual Property Rights*] in the Uruguay Round Final Act.... [The *TRIPs Agreement* is treated more fully in courses on International Trade Law or International Intellectual Property Rights.]

However,... a MNE may not require the possession of patent rights to protect its competitive advantage in technology. More significant are its abilities to conduct costly R&D and to integrate patented technology with non-patentable know-how, without which the patented elements of the technology may be useless. Thus the true problem for LDCs is not so much that patents are taken out by foreign firms, but that the major producers of technology tend to possess considerable market power to which the pro-tection of intellectual property is no more than a subsidiary form of protection. This suggests policy responses in other fields of law, especially competition law.

The arguments relating to trademarks have been criticized on the grounds that, in the absence of assured quality in the products of local firms and of effective con-sumer protection legislation, foreign trademarks can act as marks of quality. Fur-thermore, the adverse effects stemming from the link between foreign trademarks and advertising is seen as a purely theoretical argument that cannot support the view that removal of trademark rights will prevent socially inefficient consumption. Fur-thermore,... the commercial functions that trademarks perform may lead to the cre-ation of a marketing infrastructure in LDCs that will facilitate the distribution of goods containing transferred technology.

Finally, the arguments concerning reform of the international system of protec-tion have not led to the hoped for reforms. Given the relatively weak bargaining position of the LDCs this is not surprising. The technologically advanced countries have few incentives to modify a system that suits their needs. However, ... some recognition of the interests of LDCs appears in the Final Act of the Uruguay Round negotiations, in that such countries can postpone the patent protection contained therein for up to ten years, and developed countries are encouraged to ensure adequate technology transfer to LDCs.

There may be some advantages to be gained by LDCs from adhering to a traditional system of intellectual property law. In particular, it may indicate that the state concerned has a favourable attitude to foreign investors who rely on patented technology. It may also avoid the risk of economic retaliation against the LDC on the ground that it does not respect intellectual property rights as provided, for example, under the US [Omnibus] Trade and Competitiveness Act [of] 1988 [*i.e.*, the "Special 301" provision, which is also treated in courses on International Trade Law].

On the other hand, a recent study by the UN Transnational Corporations Management Division (the successor to the UNCTC), into the link between intellectual property protection and foreign investment finds that heightened intellectual property protection provides no clear impetus to investment flows. The issue depends on the industry concerned, the types of intellectual property rights granted and the general level of technological and economic development of the host state. Thus, there remains considerable doubt as to the effect of intellectual property laws on the development process.

4.2.2 Specialized technology transfer laws

As part of the movement for greater control over the process of technology transfer, numerous LDCs began, in the 1970s, to experiment with specialized technology transfer laws.... The main thrust for these developments came from Latin America, with the adoption in 1969 of the *Andean Foreign Investment Code* under Decision 24 of the *Cartagena Agreement*, and the passing of several national laws between 1971 and 1981. Other LDCs from Africa and Asia followed suit, as did a small number of Southern European and formerly socialist Eastern European states. Of developed countries only Japan has used such laws.

The essence of technology transfer laws is the screening of international technology transfer transactions by a national authority with the aim of ensuring that the technology transferred is of use to the national economy and that the terms and conditions of transfer do not amount to an abuse of the transferor's superior bargaining power. Such laws are normally limited to transactions between a foreign transferor and a local recipient. Transactions between related enterprises are not addressed in most statutes, although some laws have contained strict controls over royalty payments for technology transferred between affiliated enterprises, as a means of controlling transfer price manipulations. Indirect transfers between foreign transferors and local recipients effected through a local intermediary, who receives the technology under an approved contract and then transfers it subject to unacceptable terms, may also be covered.

The normal procedure is for the parties to submit either a draft or an executed contract for approval. This may involve a registration of the agreement with the screening authority. The authority will then assess the contract in the light of the legal standards laid down for review. These will concern *inter alia*: an examination of the restrictive clauses imposed on the recipient with a view to identifying prohibited restrictions; the reasonableness of the consideration payable; the costs and benefits of the transaction in relation to the economic and social development of the recipient state; the nature of the technology involved, paying particular attention to its positive effects on local productive capacity and skills development, the ability of the local economy to develop the technology by itself, and the age and effectiveness of the technology; whether the package involves excessive tie-ins and other costs; the extent of any warranties limiting or excluding the transferor's liability for the technology; and the duration of the agreement, which must not be excessive.

Failure to register the agreement for approval may lead to its being nullified. Other sanctions may include fines for the performance of an unapproved transaction, prohibition of payments in favour of the transferor and the denial of fiscal benefits. The approving authority may impose conditions on the parties as the price for approval. This may include amendments to the agreement itself. In particular, the relevant law may require the adoption of local law as the proper law of the agreement, thereby preventing its avoidance through the choice of a foreign law.

Technology transfer laws share many features in common with other areas of law applicable to MNEs. However, they fill a distinct niche in the system of MNE regulation. This can be explained by a comparison of technology transfer laws with related areas of law, in particular with foreign investment screening laws, antitrust laws and foreign exchange and tax laws.

Like foreign investment screening laws, technology transfer laws introduce an administrative review procedure as a condition of entry into the local economy. Indeed, they may complement the foreign investment law of a host state by regulating non-equity forms of entry such as licensing agreements. Secondly, in common with antitrust laws, technology transfer laws regulate restrictive practices in technology transfer agreements. However, unlike antitrust laws, technology transfer laws seek to intervene in the operation of commercial markets in technology and regulate them in favour of the broader national economic interest in economic development. Although the use of antitrust law as an instrument of national or regional industrial policy is often debated, its primary aim is to prevent anti-competitive practices in the market, not to control it. Thirdly, technology transfer laws may be used as an additional means for regulating balance-of-payments issues by controlling the terms on which royalties will be paid for the importation of foreign-owned technology, by regulating tying arrangements involving the importation of inputs from abroad and by controlling the total number of technology transfer transactions that may be permitted at any one time. Similarly, as noted above, such laws may close off a potential conduit for transfer pricing manipulations by MNEs based on royalty remittances.

On the other hand, technology transfer laws pose a clear challenge to the logic of intellectual property laws. First, by regulating the consideration to be paid, they do not accept the legitimacy of allowing the owner of commercial technology to obtain monopoly rents from its application in the recipient state. Secondly, such laws may impose restrictions on the use of the technology by way of performance requirements, and may include limitations on the protection afforded to foreign patents or trademarks. Thirdly, as a consequence of these characteristics, technology transfer laws question the basis of the international system of intellectual property protection in that they reject the principles of national treatment and non-discrimination between foreign and local intellectual property rights, a rejection reinforced by the mandatory requirement of local law as the proper law of the technology transfer transaction. Thus, it is not surprising that such laws have become a target for limitation in the Uruguay Round negotiations....

5 The Draft UNCTAD Code of Conduct on the Transfer of Technology

In order to acquire international legitimacy for the kinds of technology transfer policies outlined in the previous section, LDCs have sought the adoption of an international code on technology transfer (*TOT Code*). This has been done under the auspices of UNCTAD which, ... was active in articulating the LDC perspective on this issue. The participating states have been grouped into three interest groupings for the purpose of negotiating the *TOT Code*. The LDCs formed the Group of 77. They sought a legally binding code, which would cover all forms of technology transfer transactions and give primacy to the recipient state's laws and dispute settlement procedures. The developed market economy countries formed Group B. They sought a voluntary code that would balance the rights and duties of the technology transferor and recipient, and leave the parties free to decide on dispute settlement procedures. The third group, Group D, comprised the former Eastern Bloc states and Mongolia. These states took broadly the same position as the Group of 77, though they did not take a view on the legal character of the code, or on applicable laws and dispute settlement procedures. They stressed the equality of states and the need for non-discrimination in technology transfer transactions. Subsequently, the People's Republic of China joined the Conference as an independent participant, aiming to learn from the experience and to use this in formulating its own technology transfer policy.

The process began with extensive preliminary negotiations between 1976 and 1978 which led to the formulation of a draft negotiating text. Thereupon the UN General Assembly, by its resolution 32/188 of December 1977, decided to convene a UN Conference, under the auspices of UNCTAD, to negotiate a final draft and to take all the necessary decisions for its adoption. The Conference held six sessions between 1978 and 1985. However, no further sessions have taken place, due to deadlock over several crucial issues. It is not proposed to undertake a detailed analysis of the draft *Code*. ... The present concern rests with the reasons behind the above-mentioned deadlock.

The issues that remain to be settled are those where the developed country and LDC models of technology transfer regulation fail to converge. The first of these concerns the regulation of restrictive business practices in technology transfer agreements, covered by chapter 4 of the draft *Code*. The Group B countries wish to control such restrictions on the basis of competition law, and emphasize that only those practices which unreasonably restrain trade should be prohibited. The Group of 77, on the other hand, see such practices as being inherently unfair, being a product of superior bargaining power on the part of the transferor. They favour the prohibition of such restrictions altogether. ... The disagreement stems from the fear of LDCs that a competition based approach will allow the avoidance of the *TOT Code* on the part of the supplier, given that it is not likely to be adopted as a legally enforceable instrument. Further disagreement exists under chapter 4 as to whether different standards should apply to transfers of technology between commonly owned enterprises. The Group B states see no reason for different treatment, limiting control only to those cases where the transaction amounts to an anti-competitive abuse of a dominant position. By contrast the Group of 77 wish to introduce a standard that permits such transactions as long as they do not adversely affect the transfer of technology.

The second major area of disagreement concerns the issues of applicable law and settlement of disputes under chapter 9. The LDCs have advocated a restrictive regime on the choice of law governing technology transfer agreements. They wish to see the law of the recipient country as the mandatory proper law of the contract, thereby avoiding the 'delocalization' of technology transfer agreements. On the contrary, the Group B states favour the preservation of the parties' freedom to choose the proper law provided it has a genuine connection with the transaction. As regards the settlement of disputes, the Group of 77 have opposed an absolute right for the parties to settle their disputes by arbitration. In their view, such a right has to be determined in the light of any rules to the contrary in the law of the technology-importing state. By contrast both the Group B and Group D states have favoured free choice of arbitration. It was on this issue that the Conference broke down in 1981. At the Sixth Session this issue was not discussed and negotiations concentrated exclusively on the choice of law question.

In order to salvage the negotiating process, the Secretary-General of UNCTAD and the President of the Conference have held regular consultations with interested governments. However, significant divergences of opinion have remained on the above-mentioned issues. Indeed, at the eighth session of UNCTAD it was recognized that

> conditions do not currently exist to reach full agreement on all outstanding issues in the draft code of conduct. Should governments indicate, either directly or through the Secretary-General of UNCTAD reporting according to General Assembly resolution 46/214, that there is the convergence of views necessary to reach agreement on all outstanding issues, then the Board should re-engage and continue its work aimed at facilitating agreement on the code.

> ....

6 Concluding Remarks: the Demise of the LDC Challenge to the International System of Technology Transfer?

It is arguable that, in contemporary economic and political conditions, the challenge of the LDCs to the established international technology transfer system is weakening and may have failed. The reasons for this can be seen both at the level of national laws and in the ascendancy of developed country positions in international organizations.

At the national level, specialized technology transfer laws have not delivered the hoped for improvements in access to modern productive technology. For example, in Nigeria the system of technology transfer regulation set up under the National Office of Industrial Property Act 1979 has been largely ignored by foreign and Nigerian businessmen when entering agreements involving the licensing of technology. Thus contracts often contain restrictive clauses that are prohibited under the law. A failure to obtain modern technology has also been noted in relation to the technology transfer provisions in Nigerian petroleum legislation. Indeed, it is arguable that the existence of controls over technology transfer agreements may simply act as a deterrent to the importation of technology in that the incentive for the technology owner to exploit its competitive advantage in the recipient state is reduced.

As a consequence of the relative ineffectiveness of technology transfer controls, developing host states appear increasingly to be modifying, if not abandoning, such controls....

....

Apart from changes in national regimes, attempts at instituting reforms in the international system of intellectual property protection have not been successful. As noted earlier, the proposed reforms of the *Paris Convention* have not come about, the negotiations over the *TOT Code* are stalled and,... a new regime aimed at the strengthening of the international system of intellectual property protection has been put forward as part of the Uruguay Round Final Act. In these circumstances it is hard to envisage the broader development of national or international regimes that place the interests of LDCs in the acquisition of technology above the interests of the owners of commercial technology in protecting its status as private property.... [T]he LDCs themselves appear to be acquiescing to this view.

B. Multilateral Efforts to Protect Intellectual Property Rights: The Uruguay Round Trips Agreement

Documents Supplement References:

1. *Uruguay Round TRIPs Agreement.*

Uruguay Round Trade Agreement, Statement of Administrative Action, Agreement on Trade Related Aspects of Intellectual Property Rights

H.R. Doc. No. 316, 103d Cong., 2d Sess.,"
Vol. 1 981-990 (September 27, 1994)

A. SUMMARY OF PROVISIONS

The *Agreement on Trade-Related Aspects of Intellectual Property Rights (Agreement on TRIPs)* establishes comprehensive standards for the protection of intellectual property and the enforcement of intellectual property rights in WTO member countries. It requires each WTO member country to apply the substantive obligations of the world's most important intellectual property conventions, supplements those conventions with substantial additional protection, and ensures that critical enforcement procedures will be available in each member country to safeguard intellectual property rights. The *Agreement* requires few changes in U.S. law and regulations and does not affect U.S. law or practice relating to parallel importation of products protected by intellectual property rights.

The *Agreement* is organized in seven parts. Part I deals with general principles, Part II provides standards for protection for various forms of intellectual property, copyright and neighboring rights, trademarks, geographical indications, industrial designs, patents, integrated circuit layout designs, and trade secrets. Part III regulates enforcement of intellectual property rights and Part IV deals with procedures for acquiring and maintaining such rights. Finally, the *Agreement* provides for dispute prevention and settlement in Part V, transitional arrangements in Part VI, and institutional and final provisions in Part VII.

1. Compliance with Multilateral Conventions

Article 2 of the *Agreement* requires each WTO member country to give effect to the substantive obligations of the *Paris Convention for the Protection of Industrial Property* (1967). Article 9 provides that member countries must also comply with Articles I through 21 and the appendix of the *Berne Convention for the Protection of Literary and Artistic Works* (1971). The United States is already a party to each of these conventions. The *Agreement* creates no rights or obligations with respect to authors' "moral rights" under Article 6 *bis* of the *Berne Convention*.

2. National Treatment and Most-Favored-Nation Treatment

Article 3 imposes a broad national treatment obligation on each WTO member country with respect to intellectual property protection. It requires each government to give "nationals" from other member countries treatment that is no less favorable than that which it gives to its own nationals with regard to the protection of intellectual property rights. The term "national" is defined by reference to the criteria for eligibility for protection under four relevant international conventions (the *Paris, Berne,* and *Rome Conventions* and the *Treaty on Intellectual Property in Respect of Protection of Integrated Circuits).* Any person or entity that qualifies for protection under these four conventions will be entitled to protection on a national treatment basis by all WTO member countries under the *Agreement on TRIPs.*

The *Agreement* also includes a broad most-favored-nation (MFN) obligation for each WTO member country. This provision requires each country to grant to nationals of other member countries any "advantage, favor, privilege or immunity" given to nationals of any other country with regard to the protection of intellectual property. A footnote to Article 3 makes clear that both the national treatment and MFN clauses generally confer rights with respect to all "matters affecting the availability, acquisition, scope, maintenance and enforcement of intellectual property rights as well as those matters affecting the use of intellectual property rights specifically addressed in this *Agreement.*"

There are a few exceptions to the broad national treatment and MFN clauses. With respect to the rights of performers, producers of sound recordings, or broadcasting organizations, national treatment and MFN rights only cover the rights provided under the *Agreement on TRIPs.* Also, the *Agreement* permits member counties to continue to exercise exceptions to national treatment provided in certain international intellectual property agreements. Benefits from intellectual property agreements that enter into force prior to the *WTO Agreement* need not be extended on an MFN basis, nor do benefits from general agreements concerning judicial assistance or law enforcement. Finally, the procedural provisions of multilateral agreements negotiated under the auspices of the World Intellectual Property Organization, such as the *Patent Cooperation Treaty,* are exempt from these national treatment and MFN obligations.

3. Copyright and Related Rights

After defining the relationship between the *Agreement on TRIPs* and the *Berne Convention,* the *Agreement* reiterates the basic principle of copyright protection — that protection extends only to expression and not to ideas, methods of operation, or mathematical concepts. This principle is embodied in section 102(b) of the U.S. Copyright Act (17 U.S.C. 101 *et. seq.).*

Article 10 of the *Agreement* confirms that all types of computer programs are "literary works" under the *Berne Convention* and requires each WTO country to protect them as such. It also requires copyright protection for compilations of data or other materials that are original by reason of their selection or arrangement.

Article 11 of the *Agreement* requires member countries to provide exclusive rental rights (the right to authorize or to prohibit commercial rental to the public of originals or copies of a work) with respect to at least computer programs and cinematographic works. WTO countries need not provide rental rights in respect of cinematographic works unless rental has led to widespread copying having a materially detrimental effect on the author's exclusive right of reproduction of the work.

Article 12 of the *Agreement* provides minimum standards for the term of protection for copyrighted works. The term of protection for many works is the life of the author plus 50 years, but whenever the term of protection is not linked to the life of a person, Article 12 requires that the term be a minimum of fifty years (except for works of applied art or photographs).

Article 9:2 of the *Berne Convention* now bans the imposition of limitations on, or exceptions to, the reproduction right except when such limits or exceptions do not conflict with a normal exploitation of the work and do not unreasonably prejudice the legitimate interests of the right holder. Article 13 of the *Agreement on TRIPs* widens the scope of this provision to all exclusive rights in copyright and related rights, thus narrowly circumscribing the limitations and exceptions that WTO member countries may impose. This approach is consistent with section 107 of Copyright Act (17 U.S.C. 107) relating to fair use of copyrighted works.

Article 14 requires member countries to provide sound recording producers a fifty-year term of protection and the right to authorize or prohibit the direct or indirect reproduction and commercial rental of their sound recordings. However, a WTO member country that on April 15, 1994, had a system of payment of equitable remuneration to compensate for rental of recordings is permitted to keep that system (only Japan and Switzerland qualify under this exception).

With respect to performers, the *Agreement* requires WTO countries to make it possible for performers to prevent unauthorized fixation, broadcast or reproduction of their live performances. Broadcasting organizations are to be accorded similar rights, although member countries have the option of providing protection consistent with the *Rome Convention* or providing owners of copyright in works broadcasted the right to prevent the same acts. The *Agreement* also makes Article 18 of the *Berne Convention* regarding the protection of existing works explicitly applicable to sound recordings.

4. Trademarks

Article 16 of the *Agreement on TRIPs* sets out certain basic rights that member countries must grant to the holders of a "trademark," as defined in paragraph one of Article 15. For example, the use of identical marks on identical goods and services will be presumed to create a likelihood of confusion and thus to be improper. Additionally, Article 16 requires each member country to apply the provisions of Article 6 *bis* of the *Paris Convention*, concerning the protection of well-known trademarks, to service marks. This *Article* also clarifies the standard for determining whether a trademark is "well-known."

Article 18 of the *Agreement* requires that the initial registration of a trademark must be for a term of not less than seven years and that the registration of a trademark must be renewable indefinitely.

Article 19 applies when a member country requires use of a trademark to maintain its registration. It provides that a trademark can be canceled for non-use only after an uninterrupted period of at least three years of non-use. However, countries must permit a trademark owner to establish the existence of circumstances beyond his control which led to the non-use of the trademark. Valid reasons for non-use as set forth in Article 19, include import restrictions on or other government requirements for goods or services protected by the trademark. Use of a trademark by another person is recognized as use of the trademark for the purpose of maintaining a registration, if such use is controlled by the trademark owner.

Article 20 safeguards the role of a trademark as an indication of the source of the trademarked product or service by prohibiting imposition of special requirements, such as use with another trademark, that could impair this role. Member countries may, however, require the firm or person producing the goods or services to include its trademark along with, but not linked to, the trademark distinguishing the goods or services at issue.

5. Geographical Indications

Articles 22 through 24 provide for the protection of geographical indications for goods. Article 22 requires member countries to provide interested parties a means to prevent the use of product descriptions that mislead the public regarding the geographic origin of a good or that constitute "an act of unfair competition" under Article 10 *bis* of the *Paris Convention*. In addition, member countries must either refuse or invalidate the registration of a trademark that contains a false indication of geographic origin of the product that misleads the public. This Article also prohibits the use of a geographical indication which, although correctly reflecting the origin of the good, nonetheless falsely represents to the public that the good originates in another geographic location.

Article 23 provides additional protection for geographical indications for wines and spirits. A geographical indication for wines or spirits which does not originate in the location indicated may not be used or registered even though the true geographical origin is indicated on the product. "Homonymous geographical indications" remain protected to the extent that they do not falsely represent to the public that a good originates in another geographic location.

Article 24 specifies limited exceptions to Articles 22 and 23. First, if a trademark, which contains a geographical indication identifying wines or spirits, was used in a continuous manner with regard to the same or related goods or services for ten years before April 15, 1994, or in good faith before that date, the prohibition set forth in Article 23 is inapplicable. Secondly, a member country does not have to prevent continued and similar use of a geographical indication used on or in connection with goods or services that was applied for or registered in good faith, or where rights have been acquired through good faith use, before the application of these provisions in that member country, or before the geographical indication is protected in its country of origin. These two provisions permit flexibility in expanding product lines covered by the affected trademark without jeopardizing rights in the trademark. Lastly, member countries may continue to use pre-existing grape varietal names for products of the vine, regardless of whether such names are geographical indications of another member country, provided that as of the date the *WTO Agreement* enters into force, the grape variety in question existed in the country permitting continued use. The principle underlying this provision also applies to the use of a person's own name or the name of his predecessor in business, except where the name is used in such a manner as to mislead the public.

Articles 23 and 24 provide for further negotiations on this subject. The Council on TRIPs, established under Article IV of the *WTO Agreement*, will oversee negotiations on a multilateral system of notification and registration of geographical indications for wines. Member countries will also negotiate on increased protection for individual geographical indications for wines and spirits. In these negotiations, the United States will seek improved protection for names of U.S. spirits that meet the definition of a geographical indication.

6. Industrial Designs

Articles 25 and 26 of the *Agreement* require each member country to provide protection for independently created industrial designs that are new or original and that meet the other conditions specified. Designs that are functional may be excluded from protection. The owner of a protected design must be given the right to prevent others from making or selling, for a commercial purpose, articles that copy or substantially copy the protected design. In addition, each government must provide a term of protection of at least ten years. Article 25 explicitly requires governments to provide protection for textile designs, either under an industrial design law or through copyright to ensure that right owners can obtain protection without delay and unreasonable cost. Protection currently available under U.S. patent and copyright law meets the requirements of these articles.

7. Patents

a. Scope of Patentable Technology

Article 27 requires each WTO country to make patents available for inventions in all fields of technology, provided that the inventions are new, involve an inventive step (*i.e.*, are not obvious) and are capable of industrial application (*i.e.*, are useful). Governments will no longer be able to discriminate in respect to the enjoyment of patent rights based on the area of technology, place of invention, or whether the product is imported or locally made. Member countries may exclude particular inventions from patentability only in a few, narrowly defined cases.

WTO countries must make patent protection available for essentially all fields of technology, including pharmaceuticals, micro-organisms, and non-biological and microbiological processes. While they may deny patent protection for plants, they must provide for the protection of plant varieties either by patents or by an effective *sui generis* system or a combination of these two forms of protection. The United States provides both patent protection and plant breeder's rights. Those member countries that choose to implement a *sui generis* system of protection for plant varieties may adopt a system consistent with the *International Convention for the Protection of New Varieties of Plants (UPOV Convention)*. The *Agreement on TRIPs* calls for the level of protection provided to plants and animals to be reviewed four years after the date of entry into force of the *WTO Agreement*. At that time, the United States will seek improved patent protection for plants and animals.

Special provisions apply to WTO member countries that do not already provide product patent protection for pharmaceutical and agricultural chemical products on the date the *WTO Agreement* enters into force. Each such country must immediately provide an interim system that permits patent applications for these products to be filed. When the application is examined, novelty will be determined as of the date of that filing. If a product is the subject of an application under this interim system, the country in question must provide exclusive marketing rights for a period of five years after the product receives marketing approval, or until a patent is granted or rejected, whichever period is shorter. To qualify for market exclusivity, the product must also be patented in another WTO member country and approved for marketing there.

b. Scope of Patent Rights

Article 28 specifies that a patent must include the right to exclude others from making, using, offering for sale, selling, or importing the product. The *Agreement* permits limited exceptions to the exclusive rights conferred by a patent if certain conditions are met. United States law contains some such exceptions, such as those set out in section 271(e) of the Patent Act (35 U.S.C. 271(e)).

The *Agreement on TRIPs* puts stringent conditions on use of a patented invention without the authorization of the right holder. This includes situations involving use of the invention by the government or use by a third party authorized by the government under a "compulsory" license. These conditions, including special conditions applicable to semiconductor technology, will also apply to compulsory licensing of rights protecting integrated circuit layout designs. Many foreign countries will be required to eliminate provisions that now subject patents to compulsory licenses if the patented invention is not produced locally.

c. Term of Protection

Article 33 requires that the term of protection available for a patent must be at least 20 years from the filing of the application. This provision permits member countries to provide for extensions of patent terms to yield patent terms that extend beyond twenty years measured from the filing date.

d. Burden of Proof

A final provision in the *Agreement's* patent section addresses the allocation of the burden of proof with regard to enforcement of patents covering processes. The provision requires each member country to provide its judicial authorities with the power to order a party accused of infringing a patented process to prove that its product, if identical to the product that would stem from exercise of a patented process, was produced using a different process. The provision should facilitate the ability of a process patent holder to establish infringement.

8. Protection for Integrated Circuit Layout Designs

Articles 35 through 38 of the *Agreement* provide for the protection of semiconductor integrated circuit layout designs at a level fully consistent with the U.S. Semiconductor Chip Protection Act (17 U.S.C. 901, *et seq.*). They include provisions for the protection of a product incorporating a protected layout design and require innocent infringers to pay a reasonable royalty for the sell-off of stock on hand or on order when they receive notice that they are dealing with infringing designs. Article 37 makes the limitations on compulsory licenses in Article 31 applicable to layout designs. These conditions permit compulsory licensing of semiconductor technology only for public non-commercial use or to remedy an anti-competitive practice. Article 38 provides for a minimum ten-year term of protection.

9. Protection of Undisclosed Information

Article 39 requires each member country to provide protection to the holders of undisclosed information (trade secrets) provided the information is secret, has commercial value, and has been subject to reasonable steps to keep it secret. The *Agreement* lists some acts that constitute misappropriation of a trade secret and provides that acquisition of undisclosed information by a third party would in some cases constitute misappropriation.

Article 39 also requires member countries to protect against unfair commercial use of the information they require companies to submit to obtain marketing approval of chemical or pharmaceutical products that utilize new chemical compounds.

....

11. Enforcement Procedures

Part III of the *Agreement* establishes extensive requirements to ensure that intellectual property rights will be effectively enforced both at and inside each member country's borders. Section 1 requires each government to provide fair and transparent enforcement procedures, including by providing intellectual property right holders access to effective judicial procedures for the enforcement of intellectual property rights. If a country provides for administrative enforcement proceedings that result in a civil remedy, Article 49 requires that those procedures conform to principles equivalent in substance to the rules set out in Section 2 for judicial procedures.

Section 2, concerning judicial procedures, requires each member country to provide for preliminary and final injunctive relief, measures to preserve evidence, civil damages, and other remedies in intellectual property enforcement proceedings. The Section also includes safeguards to protect parties from abuse of litigation procedures.

Section 3 requires member countries to establish effective procedures allowing trademark and copyright owners to obtain seizures of counterfeit and pirated goods at the border, subject to certain safeguards. For example, to protect legitimate importers, Article 55 provides that actions concerning whether goods detained at the border are infringing must be initiated within ten working days in most cases and 20 working days in appropriate cases. Such actions may be initiated by the customs authorities or any party other than the defendant in the action. Bonding requirements and improved availability of information on customs actions are important elements of this section.

Section 4 permits member countries to establish border enforcement procedures for rights other than trademark and copyright, subject to certain additional safeguards. For example, if a member country implements the border enforcement provisions of the *Agreement* with respect to patents, integrated circuits, trade secrets, or industrial designs, any allegedly infringing products being detained by customs authorities must be released upon payment of a bond after a specified period of time. The Section also permits customs officials to take action on their own initiative to prevent the importation of infringing goods.

Under Section 5, WTO member governments must provide criminal sanctions to address willful copyright piracy and trademark counterfeiting on a commercial scale. Criminal sanctions may also be provided to address infringement of other intellectual property rights, particularly when the infringement is willful and done on a commercial scale.

. . . .

13. Transparency and Dispute Settlement

Article 63 requires member countries to publish, or at least make publicly available in a national language, all laws, regulations, final judicial decisions, and administrative rulings of general application that pertain to the availability, scope, acquisition, enforcement, or prevention of the abuse of intellectual property rights. They must also publish any agreements they enter into with other WTO governments.

Article 64 makes clear that disputes arising under the *Agreement on TRIPs* are to be settled under the terms of the WTO *Dispute Settlement Understanding*. However, governments may not initiate cases against other WTO countries alleging "nonviolation," nullification, or impairment of benefits under the *Agreement* during the first five years after the *WTO Agreement* goes into effect. During the five-year period, the TRIPs Council may make recommendations to the WTO Ministerial Conference concerning the appropriate scope and procedures for addressing such complaints. Approval of the recommendations or any decision to extend the five-year moratorium on bringing such cases must be made by consensus.

14. Transitional Arrangements

Articles 65 and 66 define when member countries have to meet the obligations of the *Agreement on TRIPs*. All member countries are given a "grace period" of one year after the entry into force of the *WTO Agreement* before having to apply any provisions of the *Agreement on TRIPs*. Any developing country, and some countries that are in the process of changing from centrally-planned to market economies, must implement the national treatment and MFN provisions after the one-year grace period but may delay implementation of all other substantive *TRIPs* provisions for four years after that date. An additional five-year period is available for developing countries to extend product patent protection to technologies that were not formerly eligible for protection. Least-developed country members must apply the national treatment and MFN provisions after the general one-year grace period but may delay implementation of all other *TRIPs* provisions for ten years from that date. The TRIPs Council may grant such countries further extensions under certain circumstances. Use of any of the transitional provisions is subject to a standstill requirement, *i.e.*, any changes made during the relevant transition period cannot result in a lesser degree of consistency with the *Agreement*.

14. Institutional Arrangements and Final Provisions

Article IV of the *WTO Agreement* establishes a Council for TRIPs to oversee the functioning of the *Agreement on TRIPs*....

....

The "final provisions" on application of the *Agreement* provide that no member country will have any obligations in regard to acts that occurred before that country had to apply the *Agreement*, but the government will be bound in respect of all subject matter existing on that date....

Trade Agreements Resulting From the Uruguay Round of Multilateral Trade Negotiations, Hearings Before the House Committee on Ways and Means

103D Cong., 2D Sess. 127-33 (February 1, 1994) (Testimony of Eric H. Smith, Executive Director and General Counsel, International Intellectual Property Alliance (IIPA) on Behalf of the IIPA)

Mr. Chairman and Members of the Committee:

I am Eric Smith, Executive Director and General Counsel of the International Intellectual Property Alliance. We greatly appreciate the opportunity to present the views of the U.S. copyright-based industries on the just concluded *Final Act* embodying the agreement of the 117 members of what soon is expected to become the new World Trade Organization (WTO). In particular, our views will be limited to a discussion of a critical part of final Uruguay Round package, the *Agreement on Trade-Related Aspects of Intellectual Property Rights, Including Trade in Counterfeit Goods*, the so-called *TRIPs Agreement*.

We will also provide our preliminary views on the creation and implementation of a post-Uruguay Round strategy to correct some of the unfortunate deficiencies in the *Agreement* and to ensure the continuation of an aggressive and effective U.S. trade policy to reduce the still massive losses to the U.S. economy, and to U.S. job growth from the scourge of piracy and other unjustifiable barriers to market access affecting these industries.

The IIPA is comprised of eight trade associations that collectively represent the U.S. copyright-based industries — the motion picture, recording, computer software and music and book publishing industries. Our member associations are:

American Film Marketing Association (AFMA);

Association of American Publishers (AAP);

Business Software Alliance (BSA);

Computer and Business Equipment Manufacturers Association (CBEMA);

. . . .

Motion Picture Association of America (MPAA); [and]

. . . .

Recording Industry Association of America (RIAA).

These industries represent the leading edge of the world's high technology, entertainment and publishing industries and are among the fastest growing and largest segments of our economy.

Mr. Chairman, IIPA testified before this Subcommittee in January 1992 following the issuance of the "Dunkel text" [a prior draft of proposed Uruguay Round trade agreements] and again in November 1993 immediately preceding the final round of the just completed negotiations. Our views then were that an acceptable agreement in the GATT would go far to aid in reducing the severe losses suffered by the U.S. from inadequate levels of protection and enforcement of U.S. copyrighted works around the world, but that the Dunkel text contained certain key deficiencies that would allow our trading partners to continue to discriminate against our copyrighted products or fail to take remedial action to end continuing piracy of those products. We highlighted, in particular, the inadequate provisions on national treatment and the long transition periods that could permit the multiplication of losses to our economy until the *Agreement* became legally binding on those countries taking advantage of the transition. IIPA has estimated that the U.S. economy was already losing $15-17 billion in 1992 due to piracy outside this country.

IIPA ASSESSMENT OF THE FINAL TRIPS AGREEMENT

Today we must unfortunately inform the Subcommittee of our grave disappointment that these deficiencies were not corrected in the final *TRIPs Agreement*. While none of our members will seek to oppose the *WTO Agreement*, many of them will not be able to warmly endorse it. However, on careful balance, our members believe that, with the help of a resolute U.S. bilateral trade policy on intellectual property, the impact of the deficiencies in the *TRIPs* and *GATS Agreements* can be mitigated.

Despite this disappointment, the final agreement contains many positive elements. The *Agreement*:

- incorporates the high levels of protection in the *Berne Convention*, in practice ensuring that the over 117 GATT members will join the latest text of Berne;

- covers many of the critical issues faced by our industries as a result of recent changes in technology following the last revision of the *Berne Convention* in 1971 including

  - protection of computer programs as literary works under the Berne Convention;

  - protection for electronic databases;

- provision of an exclusive right to control the rental of computer programs;

- establishes necessary high levels of protection for sound recordings above that secured in existing international conventions including

  - extending the term of protection to a full 50 years;

  - provision of an exclusive right to control rental of sound recordings (with, unfortunately, a "grandfather" provision permitting Japan to continue providing only 1 year of such an exclusive right);

  - provision for the protection of sound recordings in existence prior to the effective date of the *Agreement* in accordance with the same rules covering works protected under the *Berne Convention*;

- ensures that only trade-related economic rights, not "moral rights" are covered and subject to dispute settlement;

- establishes detailed obligations in the area of enforcement including remedies available in civil cases, a requirement of deterrent criminal fines and jail terms in the area of copyright piracy and trademark counterfeiting, and effective border control to prevent imports of infringing product; and

- significantly revises the currently ineffective GATT dispute settlement machinery, ensuring rapid conclusion of cases, preventing the guilty party from blocking sanctions, and making the taking of cross-sectoral retaliation automatic against the guilty party.

The two major flaws in the final *TRIPs Agreement* which were described in some detail in our November 1993 testimony before the Subcommittee detract from these overall well-recognized gains.

1. National Treatment

U.S. negotiators sought in vain to obtain agreement of the European Union to fill the gaps and clarify the ambiguities in the national treatment provisions in the Dunkel text. In his testimony last week before the Subcommittee, Ambassador [Mickey] Kantor [President Clinton's USTR] emphasized that he was "bitterly disappointed by the European Union's intransigence with respect to national treatment and market access for our entertainment industries." Had the EU been willing to cease its discrimination against U.S. rightholders, the chances of worldwide acceptance of the U.S.' improved proposal (known as Article 14 *bis*) would have been vastly increased. However, notwithstanding the failure to eliminate these gaps and ambiguities, IIPA firmly believes that the existing national treatment obligation in Article 3 of the *TRIPs Agreement* does provide national treatment for many classes of U.S. rightholders.

In some cases, however, WTO members will argue that they are free, without violating their international WTO obligations, for example, to discriminate against U.S. record companies by denying them the critical right to control the public performance and broadcasting of their works by digital means while extending that right to their domestic recording companies. As another example, under this national treatment provision, they could also seek to deny to U.S. record companies the proceeds resulting from blank tape levies to provide some, however inadequate, payment to rights owners for the home taping of their recording. This could happen at the same time as the United States extends full national treatment under its recently adopted blank tape levy on digital recordings to that country's recording companies and performers whose recordings are copied here. The U.S. motion picture industry and U.S. artists and performers could continue to be denied appropriate shares of blank tape video levies on the grounds that the *TRIPs* national treatment provision authorizes this continuing discrimination and subsidy to their own industry. In the end, if these efforts by our trading partners are successful, the U.S. stands to lose millions of dollars in royalties justly due its industries and the American jobs that could be created with those funds will never materialize.

2. Overly Long Transition Periods

The *TRIPs Agreement* continues to permit those countries that qualify as "less developed countries" an additional four years beyond July 1, 1996 (the date for all "developed" countries), or until July 1, 2000, before they must bring their domestic legislation and enforcement regimes into full compliance with the obligations in the *Agreement*. The countries in transition to market economies also may benefit from this additional transition period. Countries qualifying as "least developed countries" can take until July 1, 2005, to bring their regimes into compliance.

At present, there are a large number of developing countries that, as a result of inadequate legislation or lax enforcement, cause, collectively, billions of dollars in lost jobs and income to the United States. As the result of an aggressive bilateral program using Special 301, Section 301, the Generalized System of Preferences Program and similar programs, the U.S. Government has succeeded in bringing many of these countries to within months of compliance with the basic obligations in the *TRIPs Agreement*. Countries like Thailand, Turkey, Egypt, South Korea, Indonesia, Brazil, Venezuela, Philippines, India and Poland (all GATT members), to name but a few, together account for close to *$1.8 billion* in losses due to piracy of U.S. copyrights. Were all these countries to take full advantage of their transition period rights under the *Agreement* (and assuming losses remain at the same level as in 1992; though they are likely to increase), the U.S. economy would lose an additional *$7 billion* over that four-year period. This is a staggering blow to these industries and to the U.S. economy as they seek to add the new high-tech and high-wage jobs necessary for this country to be competitive into the next century.

What is plainly apparent is that none of these ten named countries needs or deserves to take an additional four-year period to deal with the problem of copyright piracy. USTR has been negotiating with each of these countries for well over five years already; many have indicated their commitment to significantly reduce piracy in 1994 or are already in breach of existing bilateral commitments to the United States. For any of these countries to take advantage of their rights under the *TRIPs Agreement* would be an outrage that the United States simply must not tolerate. Unfortunately, the *TRIPs Agreement* could condone such action.

In addition to these two major flaws in the text, the final *TRIPs* text also contains a new concession — this time to the *developed* countries — permitting them to have the benefit of a five-year moratorium on the application of the "nullification and impairment" provisions of the *Agreement*. IIPA has always viewed this remedy, which gets at the "spirit" rather than the letter of the obligations in the *Agreement*, as providing key leverage to ensure that our major trading partners cannot undermine the *Agreement* for protectionist reasons. We regret that this concession was made but believe its absence can be compensated for by a clear and unequivocal U.S. trade policy that would result in punishing any country, at the end of the five-year moratorium, for any actions during the moratorium which had the effect of "nullifying or impairing" any benefit in the *Agreement* which the U.S. had bargained for.

THE CONTINUING NEED FOR AN EFFECTIVE BILATERAL TRADE POLICY IN INTELLECTUAL PROPERTY

The IIPA agrees with Ambassador Kantor's testimony that the multilateral disciplines imposed upon WTO members will provide great leverage in ensuring that the levels of protection mandated in the *TRIPs Agreement* are strictly met by our trading partners. For this reason, we have from the beginning supported the effort to include intellectual property disciplines in a new round of trade negotiations. However, the deficiencies of the *TRIPS Agreement* we have noted are severe, and must be addressed by continuing aggressive action by the U.S. government in bilateral or other multilateral fora.

The need to create and maintain open markets for our most productive industries, such as our copyright industries, has been correctly recognized by the Administration as critical to U.S. economic, foreign and security policy, not just to trade policy. It is essential, therefore, that the U.S. ensure that the economic impact resulting from these flaws is minimized.

We are particularly pleased by President Clinton's acknowledgment in his December 15 letter to the Congress notifying it of his intention to enter into the new *Agreement* that "we were unable to overcome our differences with our major trading partners [on the audiovisual quotas in *GATS* and the national treatment issue in *TRIPs*]" but that the U.S. intends to reserve "*all our legal rights* to respond to policies that discriminate in these areas" (emphasis added).

Such "legal rights" must include Section 301 [a highly controversial provision under United States trade law for investigating and possibly taking unilateral action against the acts, policies, or practices of foreign governments that violate United States international legal rights, or are unjustifiable, unreasonable, or discriminatory that burden or restrict United States commerce] and Special 301 [a related provision in United States international trade law for investigating and possibly taking unilateral action against a country violating American intellectual property rights] to which Ambassador Kantor also testified last week. IIPA believes that Section 301 and particularly Special 301 and the GSP, CBI, and ATPA Programs remain fully viable both prior to the effective date of the WTO on July 1, 1995 and after that date. Such initiatives are most important with respect to countries that seek to take advantage of the transition period to delay confronting and resolving their piracy problems and with respect to issues not adequately addressed in this *Agreement*.

IIPA members are still in the process of evaluating and considering trade and non-trade policy options in the intellectual property area to ensure that our trading partners promptly open their markets to U.S. copyrighted works and avoid taking advantage of actual and potential national treatment loopholes in the *TRIPs Agreement*. Similar consideration is being given to dealing with the issue of broadcast and new technology quotas and similar restrictions faced by our audiovisual industry, particularly in the European Union. Finally, consideration must also be given to ensuring that multilateral obligations in the intellectual property area continue to keep pace with technological developments. Clearly, it will not be possible to secure quickly major changes to the *TRIPs Agreement* which may become necessary due to unforeseen technological developments. A continuing and aggressive bilateral program must also be able to safeguard U.S. interests in this event as well.

1. U.S. Trade and Non-Trade Policies Before July 1, 1995

In our judgment, this brief period is a critical one for U.S. policy in the intellectual property area. Because U.S. flexibility on a bilateral level is greatest during this period, we believe that agreements should be secured with as many of our developing trading partners as possible — encouraged by all the "carrots" of U.S. trade and non-trade programs as possible and leveraged by all the bilateral or multilateral "sticks" at our disposal — committing them *not* to take advantage of the transition periods otherwise available to them under the *TRIPs Agreement*. Such commitments can be contained in bilateral IPR, trade, investment or other similar agreements. We should also use this period to engage bilaterally with the EU to seek to resolve the national treatment problems that face our industries there. Of course, to be successful at the latter enterprise will require taking a careful inventory of what the EU member states need from the U.S. and ensuring that it is not provided without a resolution of the national treatment question.

The Special 301 process should not be the only tool available to secure improvements in intellectual property protection. Other avenues, as noted above, such as using the benefits made available to other countries through both trade *and non-trade* programs, should be coordinated and applied by the Administration. Such programs would include not only preferential trade programs, like GSP (which we urge be renewed this year), the CBI and ATPA, trade programs like the Enterprise for the Americas Initiative (EAI) for Latin America and APEC for Asia, but also non-trade incentives, like aid programs, and World (and regional) Bank loans and concessions. All such government programs should be coordinated under an export-oriented trade policy which seeks to maximize the market-opening, anti-piracy objectives of the United States.

2. U.S. Trade and Non-Trade Policies After July 1, 1995

While the procedures under Special 301, including the identification of countries that pose IPR problems to the U.S. under Section 182 and the commencement of investigations against countries named as Priority Foreign Countries, should continue in effect and should be aggressively used by the Administration, remedies available to the U.S. under its bilateral programs — because of the wider coverage of, and bindings in, the WTO — become more limited. [Mr. Smith noted the IIPA's strong agreement "with statements recently made by Administration officials that where the U.S. national interest is demonstrably at stake, the U.S. should not hesitate to take sanctions even in WTO-bound areas if it would be fruitful in ending the conduct which is damaging to those interests."] However, withdrawal of preferential benefits extended to any country under programs like the GSP, CBI and ATPA may still occur for failure to meet IPR criteria established for these programs. Countries that unfairly take advantage of the WTO authorized transition period to continue to steal U.S. intellectual property should also be made vulnerable to removal of other trade and non-trade benefits that they receive from the U.S.

Concerted efforts should be made to encourage our trading partners, in appropriate cases, to join the NAFTA and adhere to the strong IPR text of this *Agreement*. We note in particular that the NAFTA contains a straight-forward national treatment provision of the type the U.S. was unable to achieve in the GATT. [Mr. Smith noted that it was unfortunate that Canada was able to extend its "cultural exemption" in the Canada-U.S. Free Trade Agreement to insulate it from obligations in the IP portion of the NAFTA, including national treatment. Any such implementation of this exemption would, however, he believed be met by immediate U.S. retaliation. He added that the "cultural exemption" applies only to Canada and would not be extended to any other potential NAFTA member.]

IMPLEMENTATION OF THE WTO AGREEMENT

Congress should ensure that it mandates the Administration, through the implementing legislation process, to (a) undertake an inventory of trade and non-trade measures available to the U.S. in both these time periods, (b) continue aggressive use of Special 301, preferential trade programs and all other avenues of trade and non-trade leverage, and (c) interpret the new *WTO Agreement*, including in particular the national treatment language, in a manner strictly favorable to the U.S. position.

....

C. Regional Efforts to Protect Intellectual Property Rights: NAFTA

Documents Supplement References:

1. NAFTA *Chapter Seventeen - Intellectual Property.*

North American Free Trade Agreement, Statement of Administrative Action, Chapter Seventeen: Intellectual Property

H.R. Doc. No. 159, 103D Cong., 1st Sess. 184-88 (November 4, 1993)

A. SUMMARY OF PROVISIONS

Chapter Seventeen establishes comprehensive standards for the protection of intellectual property and the enforcement of intellectual property rights in the three NAFTA countries. It requires each government to apply the substantive provisions of the world's most important intellectual property conventions, supplements those conventions with substantial additional protections, and ensures that critical enforcement procedures will be available in each country to safeguard intellectual property rights. The Agreement requires few changes in U.S. law and regulations and does not affect U.S. law or practice relating to parallel importation of products protected by intellectual property rights.

1. Adherence to Multilateral Conventions

Article 1701 requires each government to give effect to the substantive obligations of several key international agreements providing for the protection of intellectual property. These are Paris, Berne and Geneva conventions [*i.e.*, the 1967 *Paris Convention for the Protection of Industrial Property*, the 1971 *Berne Convention for the Protection of Literary and Artistic Works*, and the 1971 *Geneva Convention for the Protection of Producers of Phonograms Against Unauthorized Duplication of their Phonograms*, respectively] as well as the convention on the protection of plant breeder's rights [*i.e.*, the 1978 or 1991 *International Convention for the Protection of New Varieties of Plants*]. The United States is currently a party to each of these conventions. The NAFTA Agreement, however, confers no rights and imposes no obligations on the United States with respect to Article 6 *bis* of the *Berne Convention* or the rights derived from that [A]rticle. Thus, the U.S. implementation of this provision of the *Convention* is not subject to dispute settlement under the NAFTA.

2. National Treatment

Article 1703 imposes a broad national treatment obligation on the three governments in respect of intellectual property. It requires each country, subject to limited exceptions, to give "nationals" from other NAFTA countries treatment that is "no less favorable" than that it gives to its own nationals with regard to the protection and enforcement of intellectual property rights. In addition, Article 1703 precludes a NAFTA government from conditioning national treatment with respect to the acquisition of rights in copyright or "neighboring rights" on compliance with formalities or conditions, such as first fixation in that country.

[Observe, however, that there are two notable exceptions to the obligation of a NAFTA Party to accord national treatment in its IPR laws to persons from other NAFTA Parties. The first exception concerns the right of a performer to control the secondary use of a sound recording of her original performance. Secondary use may occur through a subsequent public performance or broadcasting. Under Mexican IPR law, the original performer has the right to control secondary use. In contrast, the original performer does not have this right under U.S. law. Rather, secondary use rights are held by the copyright owner, who may or may not be the original performer. Because of the difference in Mexican and U.S. law, Mexico refused to protect the secondary use right of a foreign original performer. That is, Mexico argued it should not have to protect the secondary use right associated with an American performer's original performance in Mexico because the U.S. did not protect the secondary use right relating to a Mexican performer's original performance in the U.S. The result in NAFTA is that the secondary use rights of a U.S. or Canadian original performer with respect to a sound recording are subject to a reciprocity, not national treatment, standard. *See* NAFTA Article 1703:1. Accordingly, Mexico treats an American original performer the same way the U.S. treats a Mexican original performer. A second departure from the national treatment principle concerns the Canadian "cultural industries" exemption. *See* NAFTA Articles 2106-2107; Annex 2106. In effect, Canada can deny national treatment and the minimum level of IPR protection otherwise required by NAFTA to protect its cultural heritage. Obviously, this departure is designed in part for the benefit of Quebec and French-language works and aimed at U.S. films, sound-recordings, and written materials. The U.S. reserved the right to withdraw comparable benefits under NAFTA if Canada exercises the cultural industries exemption. *See* GARY CLYDE HUFBAUER & JEFFREY J. SCHOTT, NAFTA — AN ASSESSMENT 85-90 (1993).]

3. Protection for Literary and Artistic Works

Article 1705, governing copyright protection, confirms that all types of computer programs are "literary works" under the *Berne Convention*, and requires each government to protect them as such. It also requires copyright protection for compilations of data or other material that by reason of the selection or arrangement of the material are original.

Article 1705 also provides that copyright holders must be accorded exclusive rights to authorize or prohibit certain acts in respect of their works, such as importation, communication to the public, and first public distribution. It also requires each government to permit the transfer of rights in literary or artistic works by contract and provides that persons acquiring or holding such rights by virtue of a contract must be able to exercise those rights in their own names and enjoy their benefits.

In addition, Article 1705 requires a minimum [generally, 50-year] term of protection for copyrighted works, including sound recordings, and sharply circumscribes the imposition of limitations on, or exceptions to, the rights provided for in the [A]rticle....

Article 1706 requires NAFTA countries to provide sound recording producers the right to authorize or prohibit the direct or indirect reproduction, importation, commercial rental and first public distribution of their sound recordings.

Article 1707 provides important protection for copyrighted television programming transmitted via encrypted satellite signals. It requires each government to make it a crime for persons to manufacture, sell or distribute equipment designed for unauthorized decoding of such signals. It also requires governments to provide civil penalties for the distribution of satellite signals that have been decoded without authorization.

4. Trademark Protection

Article 1708 sets out certain basic rights that the three governments must grant to the holder of a "trademark," as defined in the [A]rticle. Among these rights is a requirement that there be a presumption that using signs similar or identical to a trademark will result in a likelihood of confusion, and thus that such use may be prevented. [Furthermore, the NAFTA Parties must ensure that trademarks can be registered initially for at least 10 years and renewed for successive terms of at least 10 years. *See* NAFTA Article 1708:7. The Parties are prohibited from adopting compulsory licensing measures (*e.g.*, a law forcing a foreign trademark owner to license its trademark to a local company.)

Article 1706 also requires each country to establish a system for registering trademarks. In addition, each government must apply the provisions of Article 6 *bis* of the *Paris Convention*, concerning the protection of well-known trademarks, to service marks. The [A]rticle also clarifies the standard for determining whether a trademark is "well-known." This [A]rticle safeguards the role of a trademark as an indication of the source of the product or service by prohibiting imposition of special requirements, such as use with another trademark, that could impair that function.

Paragraphs two and three of Article 1712 require NAFTA governments to refuse to register marks that are deceptively misdescriptive in respect of geographic origin regardless of whether the mark has acquired distinctiveness.

5. Patent Protection

Article 1709 improves considerably on the level of patent protection required under existing international agreements. Under the NAFTA, each government must make patents available for inventions in all fields of technology, provided that the inventions are new, useful and "non-obvious." [The minimum patent protection period under Article 1709:12 is 20 years from the date of filing, or 17 years from the date of grant.] Article 1709 allows NAFTA countries to exclude certain limited subject matter from patentability, including some plants and animals that are patentable under U.S. law. [Observe the additional possible exclusions from patentability to protect "*ordre public* or morality," and for biotechnology inventions. *See* NAFTA Article 1709:2, 3(c).]

Article 1709 also requires any NAFTA country that did not offer product patent protection for pharmaceutical or agricultural chemical products before the dates specified in the Agreement to provide such protection, upon request, to any such product if it has been patented by another NAFTA government and is being marketed in the country for the first time. The protection must be granted for the unexpired term of any patent granted by the other NAFTA government.

Article 1709 also imposes strict conditions on the granting of compulsory licenses and provides that the importation of a patented product will satisfy any requirement to "work" a patent in that country. In addition, the [A]rticle requires NAFTA governments to place the burden of proof on the defendant, under certain conditions, in process patent infringement actions. Finally, the NAFTA does not establish, directly or indirectly, any right to engage in parallel importation of patented products among the territories of NAFTA countries.

6. Protection for Integrated Circuit Layout Design

Article 1710 requires NAFTA countries to provide protection for layout designs of semiconductor integrated circuits at a level consistent with current U.S. law. The [A]rticle includes protection for products incorporating a protected layout design, requires "innocent infringers" to pay a royalty on stock on hand or on order when they have notice that they are dealing with infringing designs, prohibits compulsory licensing of layout designs and provides for a minimum 10 year term of protection. [However, Annex 1710.9 gives Mexico four years — *i.e.*, until January 1, 1998 — to satisfy the requirements of Article 1710.]

7. Protection for Trade Secrets

The NAFTA is the first international agreement to include detailed provisions requiring the protection of trade secrets. Article 1711 defines what must be protected as a trade secret, describes the rights that must be provided and, in defining an "act contrary to honest commercial practices," provides an illustrative list of prohibited acts.

Article 1711 also requires NAFTA countries to protect information that they require companies to submit for purposes of obtaining marketing approval of new pharmaceutical or agricultural chemical products. In most cases, NAFTA governments must prohibit other persons from using such information for five years after its submission, unless the person that developed the information consents to its use.

8. Geographical Indications

Article 1712 requires each government to ensure that interested persons can prevent the use of product descriptions or designations that mislead the public regarding the geographic origin of a good or that constitute "an act of unfair competition" under the *Paris Convention*. In addition, each government must either refuse to register or invalidate the registration of a trademark containing a geographic indication that falsely represents to the public the geographic origin of the product. [It appears that under Article 1712:2, an interested person from a non-NAFTA Party can request that a NAFTA Party refuse to register, or invalidate the registration of, a trademark of a person from a NAFTA Party. For example, a French champagne producer could seek to invalidate a Mexican-registered trademark of a U.S. champagne producer, if the French producer can show that the U.S. producer's geographical indication in its trademark misleads the Mexican public.]

Use of generic terms that include a geographic indication may continue under the NAFTA. In addition, governments are precluded from adopting measures that adversely affect a person's right to use its name in connection with its business or that of its predecessor, unless the name is part of a trademark and there is a likelihood of confusion with that mark or use of the name would mislead the public.

9. Industrial Designs

Chapter Seventeen requires each government to provide protection for independently created industrial designs that are new or original and that meet the other conditions specified in Article 1713. [Observe that NAFTA Article 1713:1(a) uses the term "significantly differ" instead of the U.S. "non-obvious" standard. Article 1713:1(b) employs the phrase "technical or functional considerations" rather than the U.S. concept of "ornamentability." In some cases, the NAFTA language could pose difficulties for U.S. rights holders and their lawyers. *See* GARY CLYDE HUF-BAUER & JEFFREY J. SCHOTT, NAFTA — AN ASSESSMENT 85-90 (1993).] The owner of a protected design must have the right to prevent others from making or selling articles for a commercial purpose that copy or substantially copy the protected design. In addition, each government must provide a term of protection of at least ten years. Protection currently available under U.S. patent and copyright law meets the requirements of this [A]rticle.

10. Enforcement Procedures

Chapter Seventeen also establishes extensive requirements to ensure that intellectual property rights will be effectively enforced both at and inside each country's borders. Articles 1714 and 1715 require each government to provide fair and transparent enforcement procedures, including access by intellectual property rights holders to effective judicial proceedings for the enforcement of intellectual property rights. [This requirement is particularly important for U.S. rights holders, many of whom are suspicious of IPR enforcement in Mexico.] If a government provides for administrative enforcement proceedings, Article 1715 requires that they conform in substance to the rules set out in the [A]rticle for judicial procedures.

Article 1716 requires each government to provide for preliminary and final injunctive relief, measures to preserve evidence, civil damages and other remedies in intellectual property enforcement proceedings. The [A]rticle also includes safeguards to protect litigants from abuse of litigation procedures. Under Article 1717, NAFTA governments must provide criminal sanctions to address willful copyright piracy and trademark counterfeiting on a commercial scale.

Article 1718 ensures that NAFTA governments will put in place effective procedures allowing trademark and copyright owners to obtain seizures of pirated and counterfeit goods at the border, subject to certain safeguards. For example, to protect legitimate imports, Article 1718 provides that actions concerning whether goods detained at the border are infringing must be initiated within ten working days in most cases.

The [A]rticle permits NAFTA governments to establish border enforcement procedures for rights other than trademark and copyright, subject to certain additional safeguards. For example, if a government implements the border enforcement provisions of the NAFTA with respect to patents, integrated circuits, trade secrets or industrial designs, any allegedly infringing products being detained by its customs authorities must be released upon payment of a bond after a specified period of time. The [A]rticle also permits customs officials to take action on their own to prevent the importation of infringing goods.

. . . .

12. Protection of Existing Subject Matter

Article 1720 clarifies the application of the NAFTA to acts and rights arising before the effective date of this Agreement for the United States. In general, the Agreement does not apply to acts that occur before the date of application of its provisions for a particular country. This general provision is subject to the qualifications in the remainder of the [A]rticle. For example, in respect of sound recordings and other copyrighted works, the provisions of Article 18 of the *Berne Convention* governs [*sic*] works that have not fallen into the public domain in their country of origin. The obligation under the NAFTA to provide a rental right in regard to Article 1718 provides that actions concerning whether goods detained at the border are infringing must be initiated within ten working days.

II. Countertrade

Documents Supplement Reference:

1. UNCITRAL *Legal Guide on International Countertrade Transactions (1993).*

Pompoliu Verzariu, International Countertrade— A Guide for Managers and Executives

1-2, 4-5 (United States Department of Commerce, August 1992)

An Overview of Current Countertrade Practices

International countertrade is a practice whereby a supplier commits contractually — as a condition of sale — to reciprocate and undertake certain specified commercial initiatives that compensate and benefit the buyer. The ensuing linked cross-border trade exchanges may serve finance, marketing, and public policy objectives of the trading parties. Although the manner in which the reciprocal obligation is fulfilled may vary in different countertrade transactions, the distinctive feature of countertrade arrangements is the performance requirement on which the sale is conditioned.

Assets exchanged in countertrade arrangements may range from physical goods (such as finished goods and commodities) to intangibles (such as technical transfers, commercial rights, and services). The legal arrangements governing these reciprocal asset transfers may range from contracts entailing offsetting import/export transactions to equity participations.

In the 1980s, countertrade transactions were mainly a means of financing trade turnovers and new capital projects in developing countries. In the 1990s, the practice is emerging as a vehicle for modernizing existing production capacity and of ensuring the repatriation of profits from investments in countries beset by external debt problems.

Countertrade practices are practically always influenced by some form of government intervention or scrutiny. They can be mandated by legislation (a rare occurrence now), governed by internal ministerial directives, or subjected to government approval. In addition to being common in the trade of developing countries, countertrade arrangements now represent a reality of doing business with government purchasing agencies in both developed and developing countries when significant dollar value civilian procurements are involved.

Managed or conditioned trade, of which countertrade is an example, has always existed in international commerce. Characteristics of such trade practices are: the type of unilateral action or reciprocity required of suppliers; the preferential treatment granted in return; and the nature of public intervention in the transaction. These factors can sometimes combine to create economic inefficiencies and market distortions, minimizing the dynamics of market forces and introducing noncommercial considerations, especially when countertrade is mandated by governments.

Yet, countertrade practices are a fact of life in today's international trading environment. These practices represent an alternative to no trade in some cases — in particular whenever traditional finance credit is unavailable to support the transaction. In recent years, more than 100 nations, including some developed countries, have required some form of countertrade for at least a portion of their foreign procurements, compared with only 15 countries in 1972. However, enforcement of the practice has not been uniform, stringent, or always successful.

Factors Contributing to Countertrade

Probably the single most important contributing factor to the pressure for compensatory arrangements in international trade is the decreasing ability of many developing countries to adequately finance their import needs through the commercial credit mechanisms that dominated lending in the late 1970s and early 1980s.

Officially supported grants and loans — which represent the bulk of medium- and long-term lending to developing countries — provided about 65 percent of financing to developing countries in 1985-89, compared with only about 35 percent in 1980-82. The trend — away from commercial bank lending and toward official grants and net official loans — persisted in 1989 and 1990 and is expected to continue over the next several years.

This situation has constrained the ability of developing countries to import the capital goods necessary to build new industrial capacity and has curtailed imports of spares and goods that are essential to sustain ongoing production. As a result, many debt-ridden governments view self-liquidating import finance schemes as emergency procedures, opportunistic solutions, or short-term relief to endemic economic problems.

The current situation in Eastern Europe and in the successor states of the former Soviet Union also portends increased pressures by these governments for self-financed deals. Since the advent of *perestroika*, these nations have embarked on a path of economic reform, shifting away from central planning toward individual forms of market-driven economies. Their requirements for huge amounts of foreign funds are constrained, however, by their low creditworthiness and the need to compete for a finite pool of Western capital. The high risk of lending to local borrowers, the potential legal problems related to repossessing assets as a result of insolvency, and the self-financing objectives of the region's governments make countertrade an alternate way for financing imports and for providing a mechanism that could enhance the opportunity for liquidating external debt in case of default.

Increased competition among suppliers in shrinking export markets in many developing countries and compensatory requirements linked to government procurements also have contributed to the spread of countertrade practices. Many Western suppliers, mostly multinational companies, now consider countertrade as a necessary cost of doing business in countries affected by credit constraints — a "second best" arrangement bred by imperfect markets where incremental costs are justified by longer term commercial interests. For these exporters, the practice can represent an undesirable imposition, a necessity dictated by market considerations, a competitive advantage, or an alternative to no trade.

Western suppliers have occasionally volunteered countertrade arrangements in their bid proposals, in the hope of influencing decisions and gaining a competitive edge. Retrofitting or utilizing existing production capacity in developing countries on the basis of countertrade also may be a way for Western firms to diversify their international sources of supply for finished goods or components, if it is cost effective.

Limitations of Countertrade

Countertrade programs enacted by developing countries have fallen short of official expectations. Even though the number of countries using countertrade has increased during the last decade, pressures for such arrangements have vastly exceeded the number of completed transactions. Major reasons for this shortfall are market acceptance problems for the types and volumes of goods offered for countertrade at the asked-for prices, risk adverse attitudes of Western exporters toward countertrade-related commitments, and bureaucratic bottlenecks in developing countries.

Problems in developing countries related to countertrade include the following:

- Policies aimed at short-term solutions that ignore risk and cost sharing with the foreign partner;

- Unpredictable approval processes and regulatory shifts;

- Inflexible attitudes that result when bureaucracies engage in untested programs; and

- Difficulties in insulating foreign exchange earnings from the sale of countertrade goods for import finance purposes. (Developing country central bankers tend to put higher priority on balance of payments over trade finance.)

The ebbing of private lending from industrialized to developing countries through the 1980s has made it difficult for many developing economies to diversify and upgrade standards of production, therefore limiting the choice of counterdeliveries available to Western suppliers.

Sourcing of countertrade goods has also been hampered in many markets by production shortfalls induced by credit-related import restrictions on production feedstocks and spares. In addition, exports and domestic consumption are usually given preference over the provision of goods for countertrade arrangements. As a result of these problems, the odds of any countertrade negotiations resulting in an actual contract have been estimated by some practitioners to be less than 20:1.

The use of countertrade is not appropriate for all exporters or for all types of trade transactions. Countertrade transactions usually involve a substantial allocation of resources by the trading parties and often require suppliers to structure financial packages that are tailored to the needs and limitations of the client. As a result, countertrade arrangements favor firms that rely on established foreign market positions; absorb the countertraded products within their corporate, subcontractor, or end-user networks; have the necessary financial resources or backing; and engage in substantial dollar value transactions with profit margins that can accommodate the incremental costs of such practices.

The costs, risks, and ad hoc nature of countertrade transactions have reduced the number and type of companies that can afford to be active in markets or in projects requiring countertrade arrangements. The limited ability of world markets to absorb surplus goods and products in low demand, at prices that are often inflated, has also constrained the growth of countertrade practices.

Countertrade and the U.S. Government

U.S. agency involvement with compensatory practices is governed by the U.S. Government's arm's length policy on countertrade and offsets, by the statutes that vest authority in the Department of Agriculture to barter government-held agricultural inventories, and by the laws that permit the Department of Defense and the Federal Emergency Management Agency to barter National Defense Stockpile commodities.

U.S. Government Policies

The U.S. Government policy on countertrade was developed in 1983. It has been cited repeatedly by U.S. Government officials but was never issued as a public document. [Section 2205 of the Omnibus Trade and Competitiveness Act of 1988 mandates the establishment of an Interagency Group on Countertrade whose responsibility is, inter alia, to review and evaluate U.S. policy on countertrade and offsets, in light of current trends in international commerce. In Presidential Order 12661 of December 28, 1988, the president named 12 agencies as members of the interagency group. The group is in the process of preparing a public statement that addresses the U.S. Government policy on countertrade and offsets in nonmilitary trade.] The policy prohibits U.S. agencies from promoting countertrade and states that, although the U.S. Government views countertrade as generally contrary to an open free-trading system, it will not oppose participation by U.S. companies in countertrade transactions unless such activity could have a negative impact on national security. Consistent with this policy, U.S. agencies may provide advisory and market intelligence services to U.S. businesses and advise U.S. businesses that countertrade goods are subject to U.S. trade laws, including quotas.

In addition, U.S. agencies are to review applications for government export financing for projects containing countertrade/barter on a case-by-case basis, taking account of the distortions caused by these practices. The policy states that the United States will continue to oppose government-mandated countertrade and should consider raising its concerns about such practices with relevant governments and in multilateral fora. Finally, the policy urges U.S agencies to exercise caution in the use of their barter authority, reserving it for those situations that offer advantages not offered by conventional market operations.

The U.S. Government policy on offsets in military exports was announced by the White House on April 16, 1990. The Statement reads:

Statement by the Press Secretary

The President announced today his Policy on Offsets in Military Exports. This responds to the requirement under the FY [fiscal year] 1989 National Defense Authorization Act, Section 825, 10 U.S.C. Sec. 2505.

The President stated that the United States Government is committed to the principles of free and fair trade. Consequently, the United States Government views certain offsets for military exports as economically inefficient and market distorting.

Mindful of the need to minimize the adverse effects of offsets in military exports, while ensuring that the ability of U.S. firms to compete for military export sales is not undermined, the President has established the following policy:

- *No agency of the U.S. Government shall encourage, enter directly into, or commit U.S. firms to any offset arrangement in connection with the sale of defense goods or services to foreign governments.*

- *U.S. Government funds shall not be used to finance offsets in security assistance transactions except in accordance with currently established policies and procedures.*

- *Nothing in this policy shall prevent agencies of the U.S. Government from fulfilling obligations incurred through international agreements entered into prior to the issuance of this policy.*

- *The decision whether to engage in offsets, and the responsibility for negotiating and implementing offset arrangements, resides with the companies involved.*

- *Any exceptions to this policy must be approved by the President through the National Security Council.*

. . . .

Countertrade and U.S. Export Programs

U.S. Government export programs do not provide special accommodations for cases involving countertrade, nor does the presence of countertrade make a case ineligible for U.S. agency support. The support is, however, predicated on compliance with the agencies' operational standards. They include evaluation of adverse impacts on national security, compliance with U.S. law, reasonable assurance of repayment, and consideration of U.S. Government policy and political interests as these relate to the transaction or to the foreign country.

The Export-Import Bank of the United States (Eximbank) will not provide financing for the countertrade aspect of a transaction or accept countertrade as security, but the U.S. export component is eligible for all types of Eximbank support. Repayment to Eximbank must be in hard (convertible) currency and must not be related to the successful completion of a side contract associated with countertrade. A principal consideration in Eximbank's decision to support a transaction involving countertrade is the net economic impact of the project on U.S. industry. The goal is to ensure that the countertrade element in the proposed project will not have a significant adverse effect on a similar U.S.-produced good.

The Overseas Private Investment Corporation (OPIC)—the U.S. agency that insures private investments against certain political risks in less developed countries, and finances the investment and/or development of eligible projects of U.S. investors in those countries—must refuse to participate in any project involving performance requirements that would adversely affect the trading posture of the United States. However, OPIC has a considerable amount of discretion, under its operational statutes, to evaluate the effect on the United States of the imposition of a performance requirement.

OPIC reviews countertrade practices of the investment projects it assists as part of implementing its performance requirements mandate. Section 231(m) of the Foreign Assistance Act of 1961, as amended, directs OPIC:

to refuse to insure, reinsure, or finance any investment subject to performance requirements which would reduce substantially the positive trade benefits likely to accrue to the United States from the investment.

These trade-related performance requirements involve stipulations imposed by host governments on investments that typically require local sourcing or the export of production associated with the project. OPIC interprets its mandate broadly to encompass investments where approvals are contingent upon government-imposed countertrade agreements—in effect export requirements. To date, no projects with such conditions have been denied assistance on the basis of OPIC's performance requirements criterion, *i.e.*, that the agreements had the potential to reduce substantially the positive U.S. trade benefits of these investments.

The Department of Commerce has been providing advisory assistance on countertrade to U.S. exporters since 1976, as part of its export support programs. In 1990, the Department established a Financial Services and Countertrade Division within the International Trade Administration to comply with the organizational provisions mandated by the Omnibus Trade and Competitiveness Act of 1988 (1988 Trade Act). Responsibilities vested in the division include organizing and disseminating countertrade information and notifying Federal agencies of countertrade opportunities for government-owned surplus commodities. Information on countertrade practices in individual countries is also being provided by Department of Commerce country desk officers and its Foreign Commercial Service, and by State Department officers stationed abroad.

Pompiliu Verzariu and Paula Mitchell, International Countertrade—Individual Country Practices

1-7, 10-11, 17, 25, 31-33 (United States
Department of Commerce, August 1992)

Forms of Compensatory Trade

Definitions of countertrade used by industry or found in the open literature and in government publications are often inconsistent and sometimes used interchangeably with offsets — a range of industrial compensation practices that go beyond linked trade turnovers of goods and services... [The Glossary is excerpted below.] Although both countertrade and offsets are recognized as terms describing business transactions based on reciprocity, [the discussion below] follows the prevalent definition of terms used in industry and in publications that designate countertrade narrowly as a reciprocal exchange of goods and services. Countertrade operations generally serve to alleviate foreign exchange shortages of importers, while offsets serve to advance industrial development objectives.

In its simplest form, countertrade involves contractually linked commercial undertakings of two enterprises in two countries. The structure of countertrade transactions varies according to the characteristics of the projects financed and the types of assets that form the means of repayment. Assets that have been exchanged and have been used to repay exporters include physical goods (*e.g.*, equipment and commodities), services (*e.g.*, transportation and engineering), rights to the use of assets (*e.g.*, technology licenses and leases), and even lien instruments (*e.g.*, debt paper). Repayment offered U.S. exporters has also been in the form of temporary ownership of the exported asset — as in build-operate-transfer arrangements.

Countries with established or rapidly developing industrial bases usually emphasize countertrade arrangements involving transfers of technology and manufacturing production processes. Countries with economies relying on the production of commodities or light industrial goods generally emphasize countertrade arrangements that result primarily in additional exports.

The contractual arrangements under which reciprocal asset transfers occur may also vary according to transaction types — *e.g.*, cashless exchanges of goods of comparable value, parallel import/export transactions each entailing separate financial settlements, and production sharing commitments or equity positions tying the foreign partner to specific export obligations. Most countertrade arrangements have so far involved exchanges of goods and services for other such assets.

Characteristic terms associated with countertrade arrangements are:

- *Countertrade ratio* — The percent of the value of the original export that is offset by counterdeliveries;

- *Disagio* — The subsidy paid as a commission or discount by the original exporter to a broker who assumes responsibility for marketing the counterdeliveries; and

- *Switch* — The trade activities whereby rights to countertrade goods are transferred to third parties.

The side agreement linking the primary and secondary contracts in a countertrade arrangement is alternatively referred to as a "protocol," a "link contract," or a "framework contract."

In a broader sense, countertrade arrangements include government-to-government bilateral trade agreements transferring reciprocal market access privileges (beyond tariff treatment concessions) between two nations. The latter arrangements, in the form of bilateral clearing or bilateral trade agreements, stipulate or facilitate exchanges between two countries under preferential terms. They are intended to integrate economies of particular countries, recognize special political and regional trade relations, or reflect trading interests for raw material resources.

Characteristic terms associated with bilateral clearing arrangements are:

- *Swing* — The margin of credit allowed on a bilateral clearing account beyond which all trade exchanges stop; and

- *Clearing switch* — The *disagio*-driven financial operations whereby bilateral clearing imbalances are monetarized by brokerage networks through final sale of products (usually sourced from the country with the clearing arrear).

There are five main forms of compensatory trade arrangements: offset, barter, buyback (or compensation), counterpurchase, and umbrella countertrade agreements. Each of these is examined in detail in the following paragraphs.

Offsets

Offsets is the umbrella term for a broad range of industrial and commercial compensation practices required as a condition of purchase in commercial or government-to-government sales of either military (*e.g.*, fighter aircraft) or high-cost civilian hardware (*e.g.*, commercial aircraft, overland and satellite telecommunication systems). Both defense and nonmilitary offsets involve overseas production that results in the creation or expansion of industrial capacity in the importer's country. The offset arrangements may include joint responsibility for the execution of a specific production program and for sourcing purchases in the buyer's country, inclusive of subcontractor production.

The compensatory relationships associated with offsets apply to both civilian and defense exports. They are consistent with the definitions in U.S. Executive Branch reports that, in turn, are based on terminology adopted by the U.S. defense sector in the 1960s. The means to implement offsets are:

Coproduction — Overseas production that permits a foreign government(s) or producer(s) to acquire the technical information to manufacture all or part of a U.S.-origin article.

Coproduction related to military exports is based on a government-to-government agreement. It includes government-to-government licensed production and excludes licensed production based on direct commercial arrangements by U.S. manufacturers. Coproduction in nonmilitary exports is based on an agreement contracted directly between exporter and importer.

Licensed Production — Overseas production of a U.S.-origin article based upon transfer of technical information under direct commercial arrangements between a U.S. manufacturer and a foreign government or producer.

Subcontractor Production — Overseas production of a part or component of a U.S.-origin article. The subcontract does not necessarily involve license of technical information and is usually a direct commercial arrangement between the U.S. manufacturer and a foreign producer.

Overseas Investment — Investment arising from the offset agreement, taking the form of capital invested to establish or expand a subsidiary or joint venture in the foreign country.

Technology Transfer — Transfer of technology that occurs as a result of an offset agreement and that may take the form of research and development conducted abroad, technical assistance provided to the subsidiary or joint venture of overseas investment, or other activities under direct commercial arrangement between the U.S. manufacturer and a foreign entity.

Countertrade — In addition to the types of offset defined above, various types of commercial countertrade arrangements may be required as part of offset commitments. They may include barter, buyback, or counterpurchase arrangements which are defined in the next sections.

Offsets associated with military exports are frequently divided into direct and indirect classes.

Direct Offsets — Contractual arrangements that involve goods and services referenced in the sales agreement for military exports.

Indirect Offsets — Contractual arrangements that involve goods and services unrelated to the exports referenced in the sales agreements.

Policies on offsets related to nonmilitary government procurements vary in different countries, ranging from detailed conditions to flexible guidelines. Some public agencies explicitly require offset commitments when requesting bids for civilian procurements. Other countries rely on government guidelines, regulations, or internal directives that make compensatory linkages for nonmilitary government procurements a desirable, if not necessary, prerequisite for bid consideration. (The GATT rules do not apply to defense procurements with clear national security functions.)

The above regulations do not have the force of law and usually leave the formulation of indirect offset initiatives to the bidders. Nevertheless, such directives could be interpreted, because of the involvement of public agencies, as impositions of performance requirements that include practices such as local content....

Barter

Barter is a one-time transaction bound under a single contract that specifies the direct exchange of selected goods or services for another of equivalent value.

Barter is the oldest form of reciprocal trade. No financial transfers are involved in barter transactions. The time interval between exchanges is short and does not usually exceed 12 months. Pure barter arrangements are difficult to implement in international commerce because it may be difficult to reach agreement on how to balance the exchange values of the goods and because the trading parties' needs for each other's goods may not coincide. Assistance by third parties may be necessary, therefore, in disposing of goods and services received in exchange, raising the price of the original exports because of *disagio* fees.

The limited flexibility of barter transactions makes these arrangements a rare occurrence in international commerce. Barter may find application in trade between countries under government-to-government agreements that are dictated by national interests (*e.g.*, the 1983-84 U.S.-Jamaica barter deals that involved exchanges of U.S. Government-owned dairy products for Jamaican bauxite for the U.S. national strategic stockpile.) It may find application as a stop-gap solution in situations where sudden shortages of foreign exchange prevent the preservation of previously established trade levels (*e.g.*, the *ad hoc* barter transactions negotiated between officials from Eastern European countries and officials from republics of the former Soviet Union in the aftermath of the dissolution of the Comecon clearing system).

Brokers may also swap deliveries of equivalent commodities (*e.g.*, petroleum) to each other's clients around the world to save on transportation costs. On occasion, Western suppliers have agreed to accept barter in partial repayment when their developing country customers did not dispose of sufficient foreign exchange to cover the full cost of the import.

Buyback (or Compensation)

Buyback is an agreement whereby the original exporter accepts as full or partial repayment products derived from the original exported product.

Buyback arrangements support the financing of production facilities — *e.g.*, the export of machinery and capital equipment, manufacturing processes, and technology. They may serve to finance turnkey plants or the retrofitting and modernization of existing manufacturing facilities. Buybacks may also be associated with leasing and production sharing arrangements for raw materials (*e.g.*, develop-for-import projects), cooperation agreements that specify long- term industrial and commercial coproduction ventures, and equity ventures. Coproduction and equity ventures that are based on export performance requirements may allow a firm to diversify its supply sources by integrating the venture's goods into the firm's own production or by marketing them through its distribution network.

The length of buyback commitments may be short term (1 year) for product processing arrangements, or medium to long term (5-10 years) for plant construction, investment, and production sharing arrangements. Most buyback arrangements are governed by parallel contracts providing for separate financial settlements for each leg of the linked import/export transactions.

The contractual separation between the two contracts provides flexibility in financing, guarantees, maturity of payments, and deliveries. It also facilitates the transfer for marketing the counter-deliveries from primary exporters to third parties designated by them. Buybacks under production sharing and equity venture arrangements usually entail single contracts specifying, inter alia, the export obligations of the foreign partner. Figure 1 illustrates the model of a buyback transaction.

Counterpurchase

Counterpurchase is an agreement whereby the original exporter accepts as full or partial repayment products unrelated to the original exported product.

Goods that have been offered in the past for counterpurchase have mostly consisted of traditional exports (*e.g.*, agricultural commodities, fertilizers, bulk chemicals, and minerals), goods in surplus or subject to quotas (*e.g.*, industrial and consumer goods, coffee, and textiles), and low technology components. Services have also been occasionally provided to Western firms as repayment (*e.g.*, transportation, engineering, and assembly and processing of imported materials).

Figure 1. Model of a Buyback Transaction

Direct Compensation Contract

	Goods	
Party in	Payment	Party in
country A		country B
	Resultant output	
	Payment	

Counterpurchase arrangements are usually governed by parallel, separate import/export contracts. On occasion, advance purchases by Western exporters have been contractually qualified for countertrade credit to be applied against later sales by the exporter or by his designated parties. When permitted, procedures for acquiring credits are governed by clauses in the countertrade contract and are normally subject to approval and regulations set by government agencies. The transfer (sale) by the exporter of his credits to third parties is occasionally allowed by authorities in some developed countries, but practically never in developing countries. Figure 2 illustrates the model of a counterpurchase transaction.

Figure 2. Model of a Counterpurchase Transaction

Indirect Compensation Contract

Exporter in		Importer in
country A	Goods	country B
	payment	
Internal clearing		Internal clearing
	Goods	
Importer in	Payment	Exporter in
country A or in		country B
third country		

Umbrella Countertrade Agreements

For logistical purposes, and when the projected annual trade turnovers are substantial, counterpurchase transactions may be conducted under an umbrella countertrade agreement that provides for the inclusion of multiple trading parties. Signatories to these agreements are established public and/or private trading parties.

An *evidence account* is an umbrella, agreement contracted between a Western exporter and a government entity in a developing country (*e.g.*, an industrial ministry, or a provincial or state authority). The agreement is designed to facilitate multilateral trade flows when countertrade is a requirement and when trade levels between the two parties are significant and expected to increase. It stipulates trade conditions between the Western company, other independent firms designated by it, and commercial organizations under the jurisdiction of the developing country signatory.

The agreement also requires that the cumulative payment turnovers for the traded goods, not payments of individual transactions, be balanced in an agreed proportion within a specified period of time (typically 1 to 3 years). Trade flows are monitored and financial settlements occur through banks designated by the agreement's signatories.

A *bilateral clearing agreement* is a government-to-government countertrade arrangement whereby two nations agree to exchange a number of products having a specified turnover value over one or more years. The value of the goods traded under the agreement is denominated in accounting units expressed in major currencies — such as clearing U.S. dollars or clearing Swiss francs.

Exporters in each country are paid by designated local banks in domestic currencies. The banks in the importing country then credit the exporting country's account in a clearing currency that can be used only to buy goods in the importing country.

The agreement requires that all trade exchanges stop and not be resumed until a specified trade imbalance value, known as *swing*, is reduced. Trade imbalances have to be settled periodically (*e.g.*, every 3 months) in the currency denominated in the agreement, or converted into cash by *switching* the rights to the trade imbalance to interested third parties at discounted prices.

With the phasing out of the clearing system under which regional trade was practiced among Eastern European countries and the former Soviet Union, and between these countries and other developing nations, clearing trade has decreased substantially in world commerce.

A bilateral *trade protocol* is a government-to-government agreement that governs reciprocal trade between two countries. The contents and purposes of bilateral protocols vary. When governing trade between an industrialized and a developing country, the agreement may prescribe how the governments treat each other's suppliers and may establish a general framework for the development of bilateral relations; or it may set out the terms governing reciprocal trade turnovers of specified commodities (*e.g.*, petroleum) for an equivalent value of industrial goods or technology, or for commitments to build industrial plants.

When governing trade between two developing countries, the agreement typically prescribes a balanced turnover of goods over a particular period of time. Unlike bilateral clearing agreements, each trade transaction is settled through extension of buyer credits to the foreign importers in a convertible currency.

Special Practices

Countertrade has occasionally been tried as a vehicle to gain the release of so-called *blocked currencies* or *blocked funds*. These are usually soft currency funds that cannot be expatriated because of government currency controls and usually represent local earnings by foreign firms or foreign nationals. The unblocking of funds denotes transactions whereby official permission is granted to convert soft into hard currencies and repatriate them in return for some agreed compensatory initiatives by the creditors.

Proceeds from the sale of countertrade goods are sometimes sheltered in offshore *escrow accounts*. By insulating revenues from being routed through developing country foreign trade banks and being subject to the banks' disbursement priorities, offshore escrow accounts ensure timely repayments to Western exporters.

Countertrade arrangements involving escrow accounts need to allow for insufficient cash flows into the escrow accounts. These may arise because of slippages in production or in marketing the goods that generate the escrowed proceeds or by front-loaded imports by the developing country. The method by which the shortfall is redressed must be addressed in the countertrade contract.

Countertrade Practices by Country

Overview

Countertrade and offset requirements are practically always induced by government policies or actions. The propensity of public agencies to involve themselves with countertrade and offsets in nonmilitary trade grew in the 1980s in both developed and developing nations. Official motivations included project financing, increasing export levels, and securing long-term economic or industrial benefits.

In pursuing these aims, countries adopted differing approaches when enacting requirements for reciprocity. Thus, the requirements may be spelled out by public regulations or by internal circulars. They may affect major public procurements or specific categories of imports. They may set guidelines for import/export operations by government agencies and state-owned enterprises or condition approval procedures for private sector transactions.

Countertrade and offset demands in nonmilitary trade are not restricted to developing countries. Despite stated policies that oppose government-mandated reciprocity requirements, several industrialized countries enforce policies that link offset requirements to contract awards for specific civilian government procurements. The practices continue despite an explicit statement in the [Tokyo Round] Government Procurement Code of the General Agreement on Tariffs and Trade (GATT) requesting that code signatories refrain from requiring offsets in nonmilitary trade. [Likewise, Article XVI:(1) of the Uruguay Round Agreement on Government Procurement, which is a plurilateral agreement, states that "[e]ntities shall not, in the qualification and selection of suppliers, products or services, or in the evaluation of tenders and award of contracts, impose, seek or consider offsets." The footnote to this prohibition defines "offsets" as "measures used to encourage local development or improve the balance-of-payments accounts by means of domestic content, licensing of technology, investment requirements, counter-trade or similar requirements." However, Article XVI:(2) of the Agreement authorizes developing countries to negotiate at the time of their accession to the Agreement conditions for the use of offsets.]

These policies are patterned after, and, in most cases, administered by the same public units that also monitor fulfillment of defense offset obligations. Though technically not mandatory, failure on the part of foreign suppliers to respond to public entreaties for countertrade and offsets, whenever these are expected of the bidder, effectively excludes them from civilian government contracts.

Industrialized countries' offset policies generally involve flexible guidelines rather than detailed conditions. Government procurement guidelines issued by the Norwegian Ministry of Industry in 1979 require that the procurement of technically advanced material and services by ministries and subordinate services should — to the extent possible — contribute to the development of Norwegian industry.

Australia has implemented a Partnership for Development Program emphasizing commitments by foreign suppliers to long-term commercial cooperation in research and development as a substitute for traditional offset activities.... Canada ... enforces a so-called *rationalization* policy for public procurements of computers and other office equipment. Under this policy, foreign suppliers are given preferred access to the procurements in exchange for major investments in the country's information technology industry.

Greece introduced its nonmandatory offset policy for all civilian government purchases in the mid-1980s. Offsets are intended to provide project financing, foster Greek industrial development, and act as a conduit for technology transfer.

Austria, which relies on the private sector to implement the government's countertrade policy, links approval of private foreign investments in the automotive industry to technology acquisition. Portugal, Belgium, Turkey, and New Zealand also have adopted offset policies for nonmilitary procurements.

In order to assist domestic exporters with countertrade obligations incurred overseas, many industrialized countries have set up special units tasked with providing advisory assistance. This function is performed by staff within public agencies in the United States, Canada, Belgium, the Netherlands, United Kingdom, and Italy. The French Government has instead supported the formation of a separate countertrade assistance entity in the private sector. The Swedish Government was until 1990 a major stockholder through interests held by the Swedish Investment Bank, in a private sector trading company, Sukab, involved in countertrade.

To further stimulate exports, some industrialized country governments have promoted bilateral trade under framework countertrade-like agreements, such as the Franco-Soviet food-for-oil agreement initialed in 1991.

While public involvement with countertrade and offsets in nonmilitary trade has grown in both developed and developing nations, this [discussion] concerns itself only with countertrade practices of developing countries that are not defense related. The following sections provide summaries of countertrade practices in [various] developing countries....

I. Eastern Europe and the Commonwealth of Independent States

Region Summary

Countertrade practices have traditionally played a significant role in the commerce of Eastern Europe and the former Soviet Union. As a result of the current economic problems in the region, they are expected to grow further in importance—provided bureaucratic bottlenecks and product availability problems can solved. The self-financing aspects of countertrade arrangements appeal to these countries' governments as one alternative for financing trade and investment—especially modernizing and retrofitting existing production capacity.

The demise of the Council of Mutual Economic Assistance (CMEA, the Soviet Union and Eastern European regional clearing system) and hard currency shortages have adversely affected procurements, energy and feedstocks of Eastern European enterprises. This situation, in turn, has affected domestic production levels and has forced the countries to reevaluate import sourcing and targeting of export markets. The economic dislocations associated with the decentralization and reformation of the countries' foreign trade apparatus, the phasing out of government subsidies, the price restructuring, the privatization initiatives, and the shortfalls in material distribution have complicated predictable export flows from the region, whether under traditional trade or countertrade arrangements.

In the newly independent republics of the former Soviet Union, industrial production has also been disrupted by the ongoing shift in control from central government to republics, affecting responsibilities for budgets and flows of primary resources and feedstocks to factories. Major complications in implementing countertrade transactions are caused by declining production levels, by regulatory shifts and enhanced state controls on exportable goods, and by transshipment problems caused by the dismantling of the former transportation structures that have resulted in toll-related negotiations among republics.

In addition to the above problems, the ex-Soviet republics have to cope with their new banking system, now in embryonic stage, which cannot yet muster authority and experience to execute deals. The former Soviet bank of foreign trade, Vnesheconombank, has lost exclusive control over financial affairs and resources as a result of export earnings being channeled through emerging republic-owned banks. The newly created banks are severely undercapitalized and have not yet established their creditworthiness vis-a-vis commercial banks in industrialized countries.

In contrast to the region's obsolescent industries, generally substandard product quality, material shortages, and distribution problems is the pool of skilled labor and excess industrial capacity that Eastern Europe and many of the Soviet republics possess. These assets would suggest that buybacks may emerge as the form of countertrade most likely to be practiced in future years. Buybacks could relate to value-added processing in East European countries or consist of counterdeliveries of finished products and components manufactured in these countries under foreign specifications in plants retrofitted or modernized by foreign technology and equipment. Buybacks may also relate to counterdeliveries of Russian commodities and goods produced under production sharing or joint venture agreements.

. . . .

II. Latin America

Region Summary

The early 1980s saw a proliferation of countertrade decrees in Latin America in response to the region's mounting debt problems. The decrees vested authority for approving countertrade transactions with Western suppliers into special government committees that included representatives from the Central Banks or Ministries of Finance. A major intent of the decrees was to foster exports of nontraditional products. However, practically all countertrade transactions approved during the 1980s involved traditional exports. The committees' case-by-case scrutiny and cumbersome approval procedures contributed to the spotty approval record of countertrade transactions.

As debt-reduction induced by the Brady plan initiative and recent privatization laws have been drawing back billions in flight and new investment capital, the cash infusion is ending a decade-old debt crisis in much of the region. The emphasis on privatizing state-owned firms, on easing of restrictive investment laws, on realigning overinflated currency exchange rates, and the emergence of economic blocs that integrate regional trade on free market principles is reducing the need for financing imports through countertrade.

Countertrade on a government-to-government bilateral basis — effected through the various Latin American regional clearing trade and payments systems — represents a more consistent and larger trade turnover than that conducted with foreign private sector suppliers. Regional clearing trade and payments systems in Latin America include those of the American Integration Association (LAIA, also known under the acronym ALADI), the Central American Common Market (CACM), and the Caribbean Common Market (CARICOM).

The LAIA member countries are Argentina, Bolivia, Brazil, Chile, Colombia, the Dominican Republic, Ecuador, Mexico, Paraguay, Peru, Uruguay, and Venezuela. Members of the CACM clearing system are Costa Rica, El Salvador, Guatemala, Honduras, and Nicaragua.

III. Africa and the Middle East

Region Summary

Government-to-government agreements account for most countertrade transactions in Africa and the Middle East. In most of the countries, countertrade arrangements with suppliers from industrialized countries are sporadic occurrences that require official approval on a case-by-case basis. The reason for the preponderant involvement by governments is that the public sector is the largest participant in the region's economic activity and the largest importer, and that the goods produced by most countries in the region consist of prime commodities and raw materials such as agricultural products, minerals, and petroleum. As these goods represent traditional cash crop exports, the nations find little tangible benefits in countertrading commodities needed to generate hard currency for the countries' balance of payments.

Government procurements in some countries in the region (e.g., Israel and Saudi Arabia) may be subject to offset requirements whereby investment, technology transfers, and other business initiatives that help the development of domestic industries are preferred over countertrade. Regional clearing trade and payments systems in Africa include those of the Economic Community of the Countries of Central Africa (CEEAC), Economic Community of the Great Lakes Countries (CEPGL), Preferential Trade Area Clearing House (PTACH), and West Africa Clearing House (WACH).

The CEEAC member countries are Burundi, Cameroon, the Central African Republic, Chad, Congo, Equatorial Guinea, Gabon, Rwanda, Sao Tome and Principe, and Zaire. Members of the CEPGL clearing system are Burundi, Rwanda, and Zaire. Members of the PTACH clearing system are Burundi, Comoros, Djibouti, Ethiopia, Kenya, Lesotho, Malawi, Mauritius, Rwanda, Somalia, Swaziland, Tanzania, Uganda, Zambia, and Zimbabwe. The WACH countries are Burkina Faso, Gambia, Ghana, Guinea, Guinea-Bissau, Liberia, Mauritania, Nigeria, and Sierra Leone.

....

IV. Asia

Region Summary

Enactment of official countertrade provisions in Asian and Pacific area countries grew rapidly during the 1980s, fostered by such active countertrading countries as

India, Indonesia, and the People's Republic of China. Given the commodity-oriented export structure of most of the countries that enforce countertrade and their narrow industrial base, the most prevalent countertrade practice involved counterpurchase transactions under government procurement arrangements.

The bulk of products exported by the region's countries as countertrade has consisted of agricultural products and manufactured goods. The incidence of countertrade transactions successfully concluded with Western suppliers over the decade was erratic and related mostly to government procurements. The number of these transactions did not match the countries' projections when they enacted their countertrade provisions. The regional clearing trade and payments systems in Asia is known as the Asian Clearing Union (ACU).

The ACU member countries are Bangladesh, Burma (also known as Myanmar), India, Iran, Nepal, Pakistan, and Sri Lanka. Tariff preference agreements in the South Pacific area include the Australia-New Zealand Closer Economic Relations and Trade Agreement (ANZCERTA) and the South Pacific Regional Trade and Economic Cooperation Agreement (SPARTECA). The SPARTECA member countries are Australia, New Zealand, Cook Islands, Fiji, Kiribati, Nauru, Niue, Papua New Guinea, Solomon Islands, Tonga, Tuvalu, Vanuatu, and Western Samoa.

. . . .

Glossary

Additionality. Clause in a countertrade contract prescribing that a primary supplier's countertrade obligation can be fulfilled only by incremental exports above achieved trade levels to traditional markets, or by exports to new markets.

Agio. Premium received by a broker from an exporter for assuming the exporter's countertrade obligations. The commission paid to the broker represents a *disagio* for the exporter.

Anticipatory Countertrade. Advance purchases of goods and services from a customer's country that a supplier undertakes, or causes, in expectation of a future sale linked to countertrade requirements. Such proactive purchases may not receive countertrade credit at the time of the export sale unless prior approval by the host country authorities is secured, tying the two import/export transactions.

Barter. One-time transaction bound under a single contract that specifies the direct exchange of selected goods or services for another of equivalent value.

Bilateral Clearing Agreement. Government-to-government reciprocal trade arrangement whereby two nations agree to a trade turnover of specified value over one or more years. The value of the products traded under the agreement is denominated in accounting units expressed in major currencies—such as clearing U.S. dollars, clearing Swiss francs, etc. Exporters in each country are paid by designated local banks in domestic currencies.

Blocked Currency. Currency that cannot be freely transferred into convertible currencies and expatriated. Usually synonymous with foreign-owned funds or earnings in countries where government exchange regulations prohibit their expatriation.

Build-Operate-Transfer (BOT). Debt and equity financing of a major turnkey project, such as a nuclear power plant. The foreign supplier constructs and then operates the completed plant for profit over a contracted number of years. Until the plant is transferred to local ownership, the revenues derived from its operations serve to service debt and generate returns for the supplier.

Buyback. Agreement whereby the primary supplier accepts as full or partial repayment products derived from the original exported product.

Buyer Credit. Credits granted directly to a foreign buyer (importer) by government credit agencies or commercial banks that enable the buyer to pay the supplier (exporter) for imports. The credits are usually guaranteed by a foreign trade bank in the buyer's country.

Credit for Countertrade/Offsets. Procedure that reduces the size of the countertrade/offset commitment of a primary supplier on the basis of prescribed or approved commercial initiatives that the primary supplier and/or its designated agents undertake. Decisions related to the approval and the amount of countertrade/offset credit to be granted to the primary supplier rests with special government agencies that are responsible for monitoring the supplier's countertrade/offset performance.

Counterpurchase. Agreement whereby the primary supplier accepts as full or partial repayment products unrelated to the original exported product.

Countertrade. As used [herein], a generic name for a reciprocal exchange of goods and services, inclusive of licenses, technical documentation, and equipment.

Countertrade Ratio. Percent of the value of the original export that is offset by counterdeliveries.

Debt Swap. Transaction by which external debt, usually owed a commercial bank in a developed country, is swapped for other assets. Devalued debt paper of developing countries has been swapped among creditor banks wishing to consolidate their debt portfolios. Developing country debt has also been swapped for products exported from the debtor country, for equity investment in the debtor country, or for the promotion of socially useful goals in the debtor country — *i.e.*, education, charity, nature conservation, and environmental protection.

Disagio. Commission or subsidy paid by the primary supplier to a third party, usually a broker, that releases the supplier from countertrade obligations. The premium paid represents an *agio* for the third party who receives it.

Escrow Account. Special bank account into which earnings from sales (*e.g.*, convertible currency proceeds from exports) are accumulated. These revenues are set aside for subsequent acquisition of goods and services from a foreign supplier. The escrowed money, usually interest-bearing, is disbursed by the bank to the foreign supplier under payment terms and against documents specified in the supplier's sale contract.

Evidence Account. Umbrella agreement contracted between a Western supplier and a government agency in a developing country (*e.g.*, an industrial ministry, or a provincial or state authority), which is designed to facilitate reciprocal trade flows. The agreement stipulates trade conditions between the Western firm, other independent firms designated by it, and commercial organizations under the jurisdiction of the developing country signatory. It also requires that the cumulative payment turnovers for the traded goods, not payments of individual transactions, be balanced in an agreed-upon proportion within a specified period of time (typically 1 to 3 years). Trade flows are monitored and financial settlements occur through banks designated by the agreement's signatories.

Export Credit Agency. Public or semipublic agency that provides export credits and guarantees. Examples are the Export-Import Bank of the United States, the Export Development Corporation (EDC) of Canada, the Export-Import Bank of Japan

(JEXIM), and the Export Credits Guarantee Department (ECGD) of the United Kingdom.

Factoring. Discounting of short- and medium-term trade debts. The factor assumes responsibility for the credit, collection, and record-keeping functions for the supplier client.

Forfait Financing. Nonrecourse financing based on discounting of bills of exchange or promissory notes by a financing institution that absorbs the risk of collecting payment from the buyer without recourse to the supplier....

Free-Choice Clause. Clause in a countertrade contract that authorizes the primary supplier or its delegate to place orders for any products manufactured in the primary importer's country, without restrictions as to the sectors or companies that are entitled to receive these orders.

Guaranteed Credits. Credits that are insured under export insurance programs of government and government-supported agencies.

Hard Currency. Currency that has sound value, is generally acceptable at face value internationally, and is convertible in the open market. Also known as convertible currency.

Leasing. Financing under which the customer (or lessee) pays for the use of assets (capital goods and equipment) in regular installments as the asset produces revenues. The supplier of the goods (lessor) may be responsible for the servicing and maintenance of the asset. Sometimes the lessee has the option to purchase the asset at residual value upon termination of the lease term.

Link Contract. [A] generic name for the side document that links the import/export components of a countertrade transaction. The link contract specifies conditions under which a primary supplier irrevocably commits to purchase, or cause to be purchased, goods and/or services from sources designated by the primary buyer. It also prescribes penalties or remedial procedures in case of nonperformance. The document is sometimes referred to as a letter of undertaking, a protocol, a framework contract, or just a countertrade contract.

Offsets. Umbrella term for a broad range of industrial and commercial compensation practices required as a condition of purchase in commercial or government-to-government sales of either military or high-cost civilian hardware. Both defense and nonmilitary offsets may result in the creation or expansion of industrial capacity in the importer's country. The offset arrangements may include overseas co-production, licensed production, subcontractor production, investment, technology transfer, and countertrade initiatives.

Penalty Clause. Clause in a countertrade contract that specifies sanctions against one or both signatories of the contract in the event of nonperformance of contractual obligations.

Performance Bond. Security deposit, such as a bank guarantee or a letter of credit opened by the supplier, that guarantees compliance on the part of the supplier with the terms of the sale contract. The deposit, typically 10 percent of the contract amount, is payable to the buyer as liquidated damages in case the supplier defaults on performance.

Project Financing. Financing by a bank or consortium of a major project with long-term revenue generating potential in which the lender's security is based on the expectation that revenues generated by the project will be sufficient to service debt incurred for the project, and/or a mortgage on the project's assets. Project financing is often referred to as *limited recourse financing* because it does not rely for security on recourse to the assets and revenues of the borrowers.

Promissory Note. Short-term credit instrument consisting of a written promise by the buyer (importer) to pay a specified amount of money to the seller (exporter) on demand or on a given future date. Promissory notes are often negotiable.

Protocol. See Link Contract. The term is also used to specify government-to-government agreements that govern reciprocal trade between two countries. Bilateral government protocols may prescribe how the governments treat each other's suppliers and the general framework for the development of bilateral relations. The protocols also may set out the terms governing reciprocal trade turnovers of specified products such as commodities exchanged for industrial goods. Unlike bilateral clearing agreements, each trade transaction is settled through extension of government credits and guarantees.

Supplier Credit. Credits granted by a supplier, usually through commercial banks, to a foreign buyer under deferred payment terms.

Swing. Margin of credit allowed on a bilateral clearing account beyond which all trade exchanges stop and cannot be resumed until the swing imbalance is reduced.

Switch Trading. Trade activities connected with converting bilateral clearing imbalances into convertible currencies through the sale of the clearing imbalance to switch traders at discounted prices. The switch traders then reduce or eliminate the imbalance through import/export transactions that they arrange. The term is also used to denote nonclearing transactions involving triangular or multiple sales of different goods by various brokers. By a series of trades at discounted prices, a primary exporter can convert into hard currency a soft currency payment or a countertraded product in low demand.

Umbrella Agreements. As used [herein] bilateral trade agreement between public agencies of two countries or a public agency and a foreign private enterprise. Umbrella agreements stipulate conditions for substantial trade turnovers, are reviewed on an annual basis, and provide for the inclusion of multiple trading parties.

Value Added. Labor-dependent difference between the selling price of a finished product and the acquisition price for the raw materials, components, and semifinished parts that went into its manufacture.

. . . .

James C. Nobles, Jr. and Johannes Lang, The UNCITRAL Legal Guide on International Countertrade Transactions: The Foundation For a New Era in countertrade?

30 International Lawyer 739-54 (Winter 1996)

Two basic schools of thought exist with respect to the role of countertrade in international business. The first is that countertrade is a complex, convoluted means of conducting business and should be avoided at all costs. The mere suggestion of countertrade as an element of a transaction is an omen. Proponents of this school of thought believe that countertrade is an antiquated relic in the post-Cold War era when countries can easily trade with hard currency. The opposing school subscribes to the belief that countertrade is, and will be, a part of international trade for the foreseeable future. These international business people not only willingly make countertrade a part of their transactions, in some cases they actively seek out countertrade, using it as a marketing tool to help them promote and sell their products in an increasingly competitive world. This group, which includes some of the largest U.S. multinationals, constantly struggles in an ever-changing world for standard formats around which to build their transactions. It is for this group that the *UNCITRAL Legal Guide on International Countertrade Transactions* (the *Guide*) was written.

The *Guide,* issued by the United Nations Commission on International Trade Law (UNCITRAL) in 1993, provides a much-needed framework for international countertrade. The *Guide's* authors have taken a subject that can be very complex and have developed a methodical, logical approach to address the problems that arise in countertrade. Recognizing that the legal issues involved in countertrade are too varied to be addressed by simple form contracts, the *Guide* departs from the avenue taken by prior works that promote form contracts and standardized solutions to countertrade. Rather, the *Guide* attempts to address the various legal issues in a systematic manner. The *Guide* is undoubtedly the most sophisticated analysis of the legal aspects of international countertrade published to date. Although some provisions of the *Guide* are difficult to follow because of the terminology it uses with respect to particular types of transactions, for the most part, the *Guide* provides clear, concise, and detailed guidance on countertrade transactions.

The *Guide* defines countertrade broadly as "transactions in which one party supplies goods, services, technology or other economic value to the second party, and, in return, the first party purchases from the second party an agreed amount of goods, services, technology or other economic value." The *Guide* notes that *linkage* of transactions is the distinguishing feature of countertrade. The *Guide* specifically includes offsets within its scope. Because offsets are becoming increasingly important in sales of large industrial goods, such as power generation systems and military equipment, the inclusion of offsets greatly expands the *Guide's* applicability and relevance to multinational transactions.

I. The Framework of the *Guide*

The *Guide* recognizes that there are no "canned" solutions to countertrade, but rather the contract terms will and should vary from transaction to transaction. The *Guide* adopts a checklist or road map approach to international countertrade transactions. Instead of seeking to dictate a solution to specific problems (for example, pricing and linkage), the *Guide* illuminates the parameters of the issues that arise in these complex transactions. The *Guide's* methodology is to circumscribe the numerous typical countertrade pitfalls and then provide a range of possible solutions to these pitfalls. In a building block fashion, the *Guide* begins with the real world assumption that countertrade transactions are usually based upon a contract for the supply of goods, with the countertrade aspects of the transactions then being constructed around the original contract.

Although the *Guide* addresses specific countertrade contractual provisions, it does not seek to impose certain forms for countertrade agreements. In fact, the *Guide* discourages standard forms based on the justified suspicion that when standard forms are suggested, the parties to a countertrade transaction will blindly fill in the blanks without due consideration of the unique legal aspects of their specific countertrade transaction. The *Guide's* admonition against standard form contracts is also, perhaps, in recognition that prior attempts to develop standard form countertrade agreements have been, at best, only marginally successful.

Some countertrade practitioners suggest that modern countertrade has moved beyond the categories addressed in the *Guide* (for example, barter, buybacks, and offsets). While it is true that many countertrade transactions, particularly those involving offsets, do not fit within the outlined categories, the *Guide* is perhaps even more relevant in this environment since it is not a "how-to" manual. Virtually all of the specific issues addressed arise repeatedly in countertrade. Those in the countertrade community who have studied the *Guide* generally welcome its somewhat simplistic style of issue identification and resolution, particularly in view of the fact that their transactions are typically mired with complexity.

The *Guide* seeks to circumscribe the boundaries of various countertrade issues by focusing on legal issues. After identifying and explaining the issues, the *Guide* makes recommendations for addressing certain issues. The *Guide* provides three levels of guidance. The highest level of recommendation is denoted by "should."

The intermediate level of recommendation is communicated by the words "advisable" or "desirable." At the lowest level, the *Guide* counsels the parties in terms of "may" or "might." Other cautionary signals used frequently include "utmost caution" and "warning." Perhaps in recognition of the complexities of countertrade, the *Guide* adopts this counseling manner with respect to only a few of the many issues it discusses. The *Guide* would be a more effective tool if its authors had utilized this paternalistic approach more often.

One weakness of the *Guide* is its suggestion that parties can resolve all countertrade issues through negotiation. While in theory this proposition is true, in practice there are many obstacles to negotiated solutions. For example, laws of the various countries involved in the transaction may prevent certain negotiated solutions. Similarly, some enterprises, such as state-owned companies, may be subject to severe restrictions on their operations that prevent them from agreeing to solutions that multinationals readily find acceptable. Finally, businesspeople in emerging markets, particularly those trained in communistic and socialistic economic systems, may not fully appreciate the impact of some of the suggested negotiated solutions to countertrade problems since the *Guide* promotes to a certain extent solutions that would typically be adopted by Western multinational companies.

The *Guide* does not have the force of law, and it is not written with the suggestion that it be adopted by countries as a Countertrade Code. To the contrary, the *Guide* contains little that could be implemented as binding law. Thus, the *Guide* can not be viewed as a "gap filler" to deal with issues unresolved by the negotiators. Rather, the *Guide* seeks to complement existing government laws, including those specifically addressing countertrade. The *Guide* concedes that countertrade is a proper subject of governmental regulation, but does not advocate a specific governmental policy on countertrade except to the extent that it suggests that governments should promote countertrade as an effective tool for certain types of international trade.

The *Guide* focuses only on those legal aspects unique to countertrade. All countries have, of course, rules governing contractual issues, including those specific to international trade. Few legal systems regulate countertrade. Those countries that do have rules governing countertrade rarely regulate the private law contractual aspects of countertrade. Thus, the basic premise of the *Guide* is to provide a framework within which these legal issues may be addressed.

The *Guide* is not drafted from a regional perspective. It does, however, advocate many of the positions that a large Western multinational company might be expected to take in countertrade transactions. In doing so, the Guide's authors have been able to avoid dictating pro-Western, pro-developed country positions on countertrade issues. Instead, the *Guide* adopts methods that have facilitated successful countertrade transactions, as opposed to blindly recommending countertrade approaches that a multinational company would not pursue. On the other hand, the *Guide* cautions the parties that the legal systems of all countries are different, and each system may have its own rules that address many of the issues discussed in the *Guide*.

II. Analysis of Key Chapters

The structure and methods of the *Guide* are best illustrated by a brief review of several of its chapters. These chapters are chosen because either they offer new insight into dealing with issues (countertrade commitment) or they address the *essentialia negotii* (goods, pricing, payment) of a countertrade transaction. Both are always of great importance.

A. Linkage

As recognized by the *Guide,* linkage of cross-border commercial obligations that would ordinarily stand alone is the essence of countertrade. Indeed, the *Guide* breaks new ground in its development of the linkage concept. The *Guide* observes that unlinked countertrade agreements "cannot be distinguished from straightforward independent transactions." Thus, the *Guide* "advises" the parties to include the linkage issue in their negotiations, reach agreement on the linkage issue, and then unambiguously reflect their agreement in the contract documents, regardless of the format which those contracts might take. Several options for linking various components of a transaction are suggested.

In discussing linkage, the *Guide* confuses the concept somewhat by interchanging terminology, thereby making it difficult to follow the discussion. For example, the *Guide* attempts to distinguish between a "link" and "linkage," and "independence" and "interdependence" of obligations. Although the *Guide* appears to distinguish independence and interdependence in the context of specific obligations of the parties, it is not consistent in its use of this terminology.

While the concepts of linkage and interdependence are central themes throughout the *Guide,* the most focused discussion of linkage and interdependence is in the context of remedies for failing to complete a countertrade transaction. The *Guide* rejects outright the concept that all countertrade transactions should be interdependent by stressing that "in general terms...the extent of interdependence will depend on the circumstances and contractual provisions of each case." The *Guide* also notes that there is virtually no legal authority on the concept of interdependence and, thus, advises the parties to specifically address the question of interdependence in their agreements. The *Guide* then provides an in-depth analysis of interdependence in some problematic or conflicting situations in the completion of countertrade transactions, such as the failure to conclude a supply contract, the termination of a supply contract, the failure to pay, and the failure to deliver goods.

B. The Countertrade Commitment

The *Guide* recognizes that one of the leading reasons that countertrade transactions are not consummated is due to the parties' failure to define their respective obligations with specificity. In keeping with its theme of providing a framework for successful countertrade transactions, the *Guide* repeatedly counsels countertraders to make their negotiated solutions as specific and detailed as possible. On the other hand, the *Guide* is pragmatic in that it recognizes that countertrade transactions can be successful even in those situations in which the parties are unable to reach agreement on all aspects of the arrangement from the outset. As experienced countertraders appreciate, uncertainty is almost always present in a countertrade commitment. In fact, one of the primary tasks facing a successful countertrader is to define the commitments on all sides of the transaction with specificity. With this background, the *Guide,* in one of its strongest chapters, sets forth the requirements for successful countertrade commitments.

The *Guide* defines "countertrade commitment" as "the commitment of the parties to enter into a future contract or contracts." Although the *Guide* generally favors binding supply contracts over countertrade commitments, the *Guide* notes that a countertrade commitment may be used when the parties do not simultaneously conclude separate contracts for the entire supply of goods, services, or other things of value in both directions.

Nonetheless, the *Guide* advises caution with respect to countertrade commitments, noting several points that it deems "advisable" with respect to commitments to future action or agreements. In setting forth the considerations that the parties should take into account when deliberating the possibility of entering into a countertrade commitment, the *Guide* strongly encourages the parties to define the terms of future supply contracts with particularity. Further, the parties should define at what stage a countertrade commitment will be deemed to be fulfilled, including the fulfillment period, the rate of fulfillment (fulfillment credits), and the mechanisms for confirming that commitments have been fulfilled (including timing issues). The *Guide* also advises the parties to determine the impact, if any, of any nonconforming purchases upon the countertrade commitment.

The *Guide* notes that under some legal systems contract terms and conditions left open by the parties may be "filled in" by commercial codes or be supplied by a tribunal called upon to adjudicate the transaction. On the other hand, the *Guide* strongly cautions the parties against leaving open terms and conditions for agreement at a later date. The *Guide* also dissuades the parties from letting third parties determine the terms and conditions unless those third parties are independent of the parties to the countertrade transaction and unless the nature and extent of this decision are defined by the parties in advance. In one of the strongest positions taken by the *Guide,* it advises "utmost caution" in leaving a contract term for the later unilateral determination by one of the counterttrade parties.

C. The Goods

One of the major issues in most countertrade transactions is the quantity, quality, and nature of the goods offered in one or more stages of the transaction. The *Guide* addresses many of the issues involved in the supply of goods, noting that these issues are one of the major reasons countertrade transactions fail. Although the *Guide* addresses goods from a general perspective, its focus is on goods supplied in a counterimport transaction. The *Guide* also recognizes that countertrade today involves not only goods, but also services, technology, and investment.

Consistent with its teaching in other areas, the *Guide* advises the parties to conduct due diligence with respect to all aspects of the goods, including their availability, the quantities that can realistically be made available during the relevant periods, and their quality. One of the primary due diligence areas is governmental regulation of items available for countertrade, including the possible requirement for the counterimporter (the original exporter) to obtain import licenses for the goods sold to the counterimporter.

Countertrade goods are often set forth in lists. The *Guide* addresses many common issues involved with the use of lists, including the frequently encountered problem of the listed goods being "unavailable." In the case of unavailable goods, the *Guide* suggests two alternatives. First, to the extent that the listed goods are "unavailable," the purchaser's countertrade commitment could be reduced. Second, the supplier could be liable for liquidated damages if the listed goods cannot be made available. At the same time, the *Guide* suggests that the purchaser be required to designate within a defined period those goods which it will purchase from the list and provide its specifications with respect to those products.

One of the major hindrances to countertrade is the perception among certain companies that only goods of an inferior quality are available for countertrade. Furthermore, exporters are concerned that if they enter into a countertrade transaction under these circumstances, they will have little or no control over the quality of goods they will receive. The *Guide* seeks to deal with this problem by advising countertrade parties to address quality issues at the outset by adopting commercially recognized quality standards and cautioning the parties that the goods may be subject to many different types of commercial standards. The *Guide* also alerts the parties that the countertraded goods may be subject to mandatory regulations or customs of trade usage that prescribe minimum quality standards. Of course, standards may differ depending upon the market. Thus, the *Guide* recommends that the parties be specific as to the quality standard by linking it to a particular country or market.

Once quality standards are set, the goods must be tested to ensure that the standards are met. In an effort to remove the quality control barrier to countertrade, the *Guide* strongly recommends inspection of the countertrade goods before the conclusion of the original supply contract ("pre-contractual quality control") so that the exporter will be assured that the countertrade goods meet its quality criteria.

Several issues that arise in the inspection procedures are discussed, including the question of what weight will be given to the inspector's findings. For example, the inspection report conceivably could directly affect the contractual relationship of parties entering into a supply contract and countertrade agreement. Thus, if the inspection reveals that the goods conform to the agreed criteria, the supply contract and the countertrade agreement could become legally binding.

The *Guide* also identifies several issues commonly encountered in specifying quantities of goods. For example, if the amount of the goods required to be purchased is determined by reference to a set monetary amount and the price of the goods changes, the required quantity changes accordingly. A similar issue arises when a counterimporter is required to purchase a specific monetary amount of goods from a list of goods available for countertrade. If some of those goods are unavailable, the counterimporter may find itself required to purchase goods that it did not originally intend to purchase. The *Guide* suggests that this common problem might be addressed by setting maximum and minimum levels of the listed goods that a party would be required to purchase from a predetermined list.

D. Pricing

Pricing is the "weak point" in countertrade transactions. The reasons are numerous and include the failure or inability of the parties to identify the countertrade goods from the outset, and the length of time between the execution of the countertrade agreement and the fulfillment of that agreement. The *Guide* recognizes these practical pricing problems, but cautions the parties to "specify in the countertrade agreement the price of the goods that will be the subject-matter of the future supply contract" or at least to "provide a method according to which the price will be determined at the time the supply contract is to be concluded." Further, the *Guide* cautions parties to a barter transaction to include pricing of the goods in the barter exchange in order to address trade imbalances as well as other trade issues.

As with other cautionary advice offered by the *Guide*, much of the pricing counseling is directed at the neophyte countertrader. Seasoned countertraders know the importance of pricing in the transactions and realize the many intricacies of pricing issues. Nonetheless, even the experienced countertrader can benefit from reviewing the pricing chapter from time to time, since the pricing issues vary greatly from deal to deal. In this regard, the *Guide* provides an excellent overview of pricing issues that may, or perhaps should, arise in negotiations.

Several options for determining price are critiqued. One common solution is to refer to published or commonly recognized markets or indices. The *Guide* discusses several considerations the parties should evaluate before tying the price to these mechanisms. These considerations include the need to define specific exchanges or markets to which the price is tied as well as the need to include averaging mechanisms to adjust for price fluctuations over the term of the transaction. Another solution is to tie the price to the price offered by a competitor. Again, the *Guide* notes the pitfalls of using this option and suggests alternatives to using competitor pricing as a reference.

Another commonly used pricing method addressed by the *Guide* is a "most favored customer clause." The *Guide* suggests several different ways in which parties might incorporate a most favored customer clause into the countertrade agreement. The *Guide*, notes, for example, that the parties "may wish to indicate the means to be used to identify the most-favored customer," to "specify the date as of which the most-favored-customer price is to be determined," and to detail "any specially discounted prices (preferential prices) offered by the supplier to certain customers that should not be taken into account."

While the *Guide* discourages the parties from agreeing to agree on a price in the future, it does set forth the parameters they might consider in adopting this pricing option. Examples given by the *Guide* include specifying a range within which the negotiated price must fall as well as an agreement that the negotiated price meet certain standards as "competitive," "reasonable," or "world market"; however, following its teaching that the parties must be specific and detailed in their agreements, the *Guide* suggests that the parties define these terms. In one of its strongest positions on countertrade issues, the *Guide* understandably counsels that a countertrade party should exercise "utmost caution" in allowing price to be determined by the other countertrade party.

Consistent with its teaching of identifying countertrade solutions, the *Guide* addresses the need to adjust the pricing of countertrade goods in long-term contracts. The solution that it favors is to tie the price of the countertrade goods to an index. All pricing issues are not, however, so simple that an adjustment in an index will solve the problem, particularly if the issue arises out of currency fluctuations. Thus, the *Guide* suggests the possibility of including a currency clause in the countertrade agreement to tie pricing into currency fluctuations. Because currency issues are complex, this limited discussion may leave the parties unaware of all of the nuances and possibilities that could result from currency fluctuations in countertrade transactions.

E. Payment

The *Guide* focuses the discussion of payment on linking payments in a countertrade transaction so that both parties obtain the benefit of their bargain. As the *Guide* recognizes, linkage is the central issue of all countertrade transactions, and the linking of payment is one of the strongest means to reach a linkage between the different contracts. The *Guide* notes that payment linkage may be driven by two issues. First, linked payments may be used where one of the parties may encounter difficulty in paying in the agreed currency. Second, linked payments are used as security devices to secure other stages of countertrade transactions. Following its theme of exactitude, the *Guide* stresses the need to "agree on the details of the linked payment mechanism in the countertrade agreement." The *Guide* then critiques alternatives to achieving payment linkage including: (a) retention of funds by the importer; (b) blocking of funds; and (c) use of set-off accounts. Each of these alternatives is briefly reviewed to give the reader a flavor of the *Guide's* recommended framework for resolving these payment issues.

1. *Retention of Funds by Importer*

Under the retention of funds approach, the importer purchases goods from the exporter in advance of the fulfillment of a counterexport agreement in order to generate funds to pay for the counterexporter goods. Typically the importer retains the funds from the sale (possibly in a special account) to cover the cost of the export goods. This type of transaction is commonly referred to as an "advance purchase."

In an advance purchase transaction, the importer typically retains the funds until they are sufficient to pay for the goods that the importer desires to sell to the exporter (often plant and equipment). As the *Guide* correctly points out, "[a] consideration as to the acceptability of such an arrangement would be the exporter's confidence that the importer will hold the funds in accordance with the countertrade agreement." Since the funds remain within the importer's control, exporters do not favor this solution because the funds may become subject to claims of the importer's creditors as well as claims of third parties. Nevertheless, if the importer and exporter agree to hold the funds in a special account, they must agree upon the terms and conditions (that is, the timing) of the release of the funds.

2. *Blocking of Funds*

The *Guide* discusses blocking of funds in accordance with the method of using blocked accounts and crossed letters of credit. Both methods permit the importer to retain possession of the counterexport goods until the funds are secured. The *Guide* generally identifies the issues that the parties should consider in using a blocked account, including the question of whether an account of special legal status, such as a trust account or *compte fiduciaire*, should be used. Also strongly encouraged is the use of a block account agreement.

In using the crossed letters of credit technique, the exporter (which ships goods to pay for the counterexport contract) opens an export letter of credit to pay for the export contract. The export letter of credit then serves as a basis for opening a counterexport letter of credit to pay for the counterexport stage of the transaction. The *Guide* advises the parties to address several issues concerning the letters of credit, including the designation of the participating banks, the instructions to be given to the banks for issuance of the letters of credit and application of proceeds, and the documents required to be presented to obtain payment. As is common throughout, the *Guide* fails to note the costs involved in implementing a particular structure (in this case, the letter of credit costs). Similarly, it fails to note the circumstances under which the use of letters of credit might be required (as opposed to other more easily financeable solutions). For example, a Western buyer might be required to post a letter of credit in a countertrade transaction with certain developing countries that require the use of letters of credit in export transactions as a means of exchange control.

3. *Set-Off Account*

The *Guide* contrasts a set-off account with a blocked account by noting that a set-off account is a record-keeping mechanism although it may be administered by a bank. Perhaps as a testament to the wide use of set-off and similar accounts in the Cold War trade era, the *Guide's* discussion of set-off accounts is fairly comprehensive; however, it does not discuss the relationship of set-off to inter-country clearing accounts or to evidence accounts. The *Guide* notes that numerous national laws govern the use of set-off accounts and that contracts establishing the accounts are referred to by a variety of names including the *compte courant, cuenta corriente, and Kontokorrent*.

The *Guide* points out that the basic premise of a set-off account is that payments are not actually made, but instead are set off against each other. The *Guide* cautions the parties that they should consider any controlling laws regarding set-off as well as other issues, including the timing of entries into the set-off account, the imposition of balance limits, and the liquidation of the accounts.

III. Using the *Guide*

A. How to Apply the *Guide*

The *Guide* is not a "how to" manual or road map of countertrade. Those looking to learn countertrade from the *Guide* will face a hopeless task. To the contrary, the *Guide* is more in the nature of a reference tool to be read and re-read by the practitioner in the progressive development of countertrade skills. Even seasoned countertrade experts find something in the *Guide* of use to them, particularly as they put together countertrade transactions new to them.

The *Guide* is a facilitator. It seeks to help countertrade parties structure successful deals by identifying the issues commonly encountered in countertrade transactions. The *Guide* provides various answers to countertrade issues, and it attempts to assist the parties in resolving the multitude of issues through negotiated solutions that are incorporated into the countertrade agreements. For some issues, the *Guide* counsels the parties on those alternatives that are not viable. On the other hand, the *Guide* does not seek to provide solutions to all issues. In many situations, the countertrade parties will realize the *Guide* has only hinted at the real issues, leaving the parties not only to articulate the issues, but also to find the solutions.

The *Guide's* underlying premise is that no country regulates the entire universe of issues that arise in countertrade transactions. Further, even the courts and authorities of those countries that attempt to regulate countertrade do not have much guidance available to them on how to resolve the various issues that may arise. Thus, the *Guide* adopts a self-help method of strongly suggesting to the parties that they reach negotiated solutions to these issues. Through negotiated solutions, the parties can lower the total risks of a transaction.

The *Guide* stresses a theme of reasonableness in transactions. Often countertrade transactions fail because the parties refuse to take reasonable and realistic positions with respect to issues unique to countertrade. The *Guide* explains most of the major issues in traditional countertrade transactions and defines various approaches the parties may take with respect to those issues.

III. Government Procurement

A. The Uruguay Round Plurilateral Agreement on Government Procurement

Documents Supplement References:

1. *Uruguay Round Agreement on Government Procurement (1994).*

GATT PRESS SUMMARY, NEWS OF THE URUGUAY
ROUND 30 (APRIL 5, 1994)

Government Procurement

The Final Act contains a Ministerial Decision to accession procedures to the *Government Procurement Agreement* which is designed to facilitate wider membership of developing countries. It envisages consultations between the existing members and applicant governments. These would be followed by the establishment of accession working parties to examine the offers made by applicant countries (in other words, the public entities whose procurement of good and services will be opened up to international competition) as well as the export opportunities for the applicant country in the markets of existing signatories.

This Ministerial Decision should be distinguished from the negotiations which have led to a new *Agreement on Government Procurement*, whose scope is much broader, and which opens up government procurement worth hundreds of billions of dollars to international competition. These negotiations are not formally part of the Uruguay Round but they have been concluded within the same timescale and for at least some participants their results add an important element to the liberalization of market access achieved in the Round. The Government Procurement negotiations had three objectives: to extend the coverage of the *Agreement* to services (at present it covers only goods); to broaden the application of the *Agreement* by bringing in sub-central levels of government and certain public utilities; and to improve the existing text of the *Agreement*.

Uruguay Round Trade Agreement, Statement of Administrative Action, Agreement on Governemtn Procurement

H.R. Doc. No. 316, 103d Cong., 2d Sess.,
Vol. 1, 1037-42 (September 27, 1994)

A. SUMMARY OF PROVISIONS

The renegotiated *GATT Government Procurement Agreement* (*1996 Code*) represents a substantial improvement over the *1979 Tokyo Round Government Procurement Agreement* (*1979 Code*), which requires central government agencies in member countries to observe non-discriminatory, fair, and transparent procedures when they purchase goods. The *1996 Code* covers the procurement of both goods and services, including construction services, and applies to purchases by sub-central governments and government-owned enterprises, as well as by central governments.

The *1996 Code* requires members to follow significantly improved procurement procedures. It prohibits the use of offsets, unless a country specifically negotiates an exception in its schedule to the agreement. The *1996 Code* also requires the establishment of a domestic bid challenge system to enhance enforcement of the non-discriminatory, transparent, and open procurement procedures mandated by it. Finally, the *1996 Code* introduces added flexibility to accommodate advances in procurement techniques, such as electronic tendering, and to provide for the particular procurement requirements of sub-central governments and government-owned enterprises.

The *1996 Code* allows each signatory to negotiate coverage on a reciprocal, bilateral basis with the other members of the *Code*. The United States concluded comprehensive coverage packages with several countries but will not automatically extend this coverage to all other signatories. Rather, the United States offered to apply the *1996 Code* to our sub- central governments and-government-owned entities only for those countries that were willing to open their government procurement markets in sectors of high priority to the United States. The United States left open the possibility of expanding coverage with other signatories in the future.

Signatories to the *1996 Code* include the following members of the *1979 Code* — Austria, Canada, the member states of the European Union, Finland, Israel, Japan, Norway, Sweden, Switzerland, and the United States — plus one new member, the Republic of Korea. The *1996 Code* will enter into force on January 1, 1996 for all members, except that Korea will delay implementation for one year. The United States will terminate its participation in the *1979 Code* on the entry into force of the *1996 Code*.

1. *Scope and Coverage*

a. Central Government Entities

Subject to limited exceptions, each signatory will apply the *1996 Code's* rules to all central government entities (generally executive branch but in some cases judicial and legislative branches) whenever they purchase goods and services (including construction services) above the *Code* value threshold. Japan, for example, will cover the Diet and all central government ministries. The European Union will apply the *1996 Code* to E.U.-level entities as well as to all central government ministries in E.U. member states.

For the United States, the *1996 Code* will apply to all U.S. executive branch agencies (but not to Congress or the Judiciary), with certain exceptions. The United States will not cover the Federal Aviation Administration since other *Code* signatories were not willing to extend comprehensive coverage to the purchase of air traffic control equipment. Furthermore, the United States will not apply *Code* rules to NASA for bids by Japanese firms in light of Japan's refusal to cover its National Space Development Agency.

b. Sub-central Government Entities and Government-Owned Enterprises

Although the *1996 Code* is drafted so that it can apply to state and provincial procurement and government-owned enterprises, the extent to which such purchases are actually included for particular countries is set out in each government's "schedule" to the agreement, based on the results of negotiations among the signatories. As a result of negotiations with all participants prior to December 15, 1993, and negotiations with the E.U. between December 15, 1993 and April 15, 1994, the United

States offered to apply the *1996 Code* to purchases by specified government entities in 37 states, purchases by federally-owned utilities, and purchases by several sub-central utilities (the Port Authority of New York and New Jersey, the Port of Baltimore, and the New York Power Authority). In return, the United States received commitments by other member countries to open key domestic procurement markets to U.S. suppliers.

As of April 15, 1994, only the E.U., Israel, and Korea had undertaken sufficient commitments with respect to the United States to warrant reciprocal coverage of U.S. sub-central entities and government-owned utilities. The United States has offered to extend coverage of its sub-central government entities and government-owned utilities to other member countries once they meet U.S. market access requirements.

To implement the United States sub-central offer, agreed to as part of the U.S.-E.U. procurement agreement reached on April 13, 1994, the United States will amend its *Code* schedule once the E.U. Council of Ministers approves the agreement.

c. Services

The *1996 Code* covers government purchases of services for the first time. Most countries limited their coverage of services to those sectors in which they were willing to make market access commitments under the *General Agreement on Trade in Services*. The United States offered coverage of services procurement in all but seven services sectors, but only on the basis of reciprocal access from other signatories. Most *Code* members were willing to apply the *1996 Code* to procurement of key services, such as computer, environmental, and value-added telecommunications services.

d. Thresholds

The *1996 Code* applies to purchases by covered entities only above specified amounts, expressed in terms of Special Drawing Rights, or SDRs (one SDR currently equals approximately \$1.40). Except as noted, these are:

Central Government Purchases

- 130,000 SDRs (\$182,000) for goods and services; [and]
- five million SDRs (\$7 million) for construction services.

Sub-central Government Purchases

- 200,000 SDRs (\$280,000) for goods and services, except for the United States and Canada, which will apply a threshold of 355,000 SDRs (\$500,000); [and]
- five million SDRs (\$7 million) for construction services, except for Japan and Korea, which will apply a threshold of 15 million SDRs (\$21 million).

Purchases by Government-Owned Enterprises

- 400,000 SDRs (\$560,000) for goods and services, except that the United States will apply a threshold of \$250,000 for the Federally owned utilities; [and]
- five million SDRs (\$7 million) for construction services, except for Japan and the Republic of Korea, which will apply a threshold of 15 million SDRs (\$21 million).

The United States will apply a threshold of 15 million SDRs for construction services procured by sub-central entities and government-owned enterprises with respect to Korea since that is the threshold to be applied by Korea.

e. Exclusions

During the negotiations, each signatory negotiated the exclusion of certain procurement from the obligations imposed by the *1996 Code*. In the case of the United States, these exclusions carry forward those in the U.S. schedule to the *1979 Code*. These include exclusions for:

- purchases under small or minority-owned business preference programs;

- procurement for national security purposes and certain items purchased by the Department of Defense, including those subject to "Berry Amendment"-type restrictions;

- purchases by the Department of Agriculture for farm support programs and human feeding programs;

- purchases by the Agency for International Development for the purpose of providing foreign assistance (purchases not for the direct benefit or use of AID); and

- procurement by the General Services Administration of Federal Supply Groups 51 and 52 (hand tools and measuring tools) and Federal Supply Class 7340 (cutlery and flatware).

In addition, certain states excluded specified procurement, such as those for construction-grade steel, motor vehicles, coal, and printing services. The U.S. schedule also excludes purchases under state programs promoting the development of distressed areas and business owned by minorities, disabled veterans, and women, as well as "Buy American" restrictions applied to procurement by state and local governments made with Federal grants pursuant to the Federal Transit Act (49 U.S.C. App. 1601 *et seq.*), the Federal Highway Act (23 U.S.C. 101 *et seq.*) and the Airport Improvements Act (49 U.S.C. App. 2201 *et seq.*)

The U.S. schedule also specifically excludes from *1996 Code* coverage set-asides on behalf of small and minority businesses. This exclusion exempts from *Code* rules U.S. and state government procurement programs such as those that give preference to small businesses, business concerns, and private and voluntary organizations owned or controlled by women or socially and economically disadvantaged individuals, historically black colleges and universities, and colleges and universities with substantial Hispanic or Native American enrollment. The President does not have the authority to waive existing or future laws, regulations, procedures, or practices under these programs to allow procurement from *Code* signatories.

Finally, the *Code* does not cover procurement with funds not appropriated by Congress, such as procurement by employee recreation associations or other employee associations.

2. *General Disciplines*

Article I defines the scope of the obligations by reference to procurement by entities included in each country's schedule to the *1996 Code*. Article III requires signatories to accord national treatment with respect to these covered procurements to goods, services, and suppliers from foreign signatories. In a significant improvement over existing *Code* provisions, Article XVI prohibits the use of offsets, such as local content or investment requirements. A developing country may negotiate an exception in its schedule. If it does, however, the schedule may specify precise limitations on the imposition of offsets and offsets can only apply as a condition for bidding, not as a criterion for award. Israel is the only country that negotiated an offsets exception.

3. Procurement Procedures

Articles VI through XV require the use of fair and transparent procedures for procurements covered under the *1996 Code* and include provisions on technical specifications, qualification to bid, publication, selection, time limits, bid documentation and submission, receipt and opening of bids, awarding of contracts, contract negotiation, and limited tendering. Among the improvements in procurement procedures provided by the *1996 Code* is Article XX, which requires each signatory to establish a domestic bid challenge system for covered procurement. Such systems must provide for an independent assessment of alleged violations of the *1996 Code* agreement and should go far in improving domestic enforcement of *Code* obligations.

The *1996 Code's* procedural requirements also depart in a number of respects from those of *1979 Code* in order to accommodate new areas of coverage and to allow for greater efficiencies in procurement. For example, notice and publication procedures for sub-central government entities and government-owned enterprises have been relaxed. For central government entities that publish annual forecasts of upcoming procurements, time limits for receiving tenders may be shorter, in line with changes contemplated in the U.S. *National Performance Review* for purchases by the federal government of "off-the-shelf" products.

Furthermore, Article XXIV:8 recognizes that new technologies are likely to arise in national procurement systems and specifically notes that the *1996 Code* should not become an "unnecessary obstacle" to progress in the use of information technology in government procurement. The United States sought to include language of this nature in order to ensure that it can proceed with its efforts to introduce electronic contract formation into the procurement process.

4. Future Negotiations and Expansion of Membership

Article XXIV:7 provides for negotiations on the expansion of membership and improvement of the *1996 Code* beginning within three years after the entry into force of the agreement. In particular, future negotiations will focus on eliminating remaining discriminatory measures and practices in government procurement and tailoring procedures to take into account electronic bidding. The Committee on Government Procurement, the governing body for the *1996 Code*, is expected to establish an ambitious work program for expanding *Code* membership. Australia, the People's Republic of China, and Taiwan are likely candidates for membership in the near future. In addition, the United States will encourage the Committee to explore transitional mechanisms for increasing transparency and competition in non-signatory procurement markets, particularly in developing countries and economies in transition, as a stepping stone towards eventual *Code* membership.

B. NAFTA Chapter Ten

Documents Supplement Reference:

1. *North American Free Trade Agreement, Chapter Ten—Government Procurement (1993)*

North American Free Trade Agreement,
Statement of Administrative Action,
Chapter Ten: Government Procurement

H.R. Doc. No. 159, 103d Cong., 1st Sess. 134-37 (November 4, 1993)

A. SUMMARY OF NAFTA PROVISIONS

Chapter Ten [instructs] the three NAFTA countries to eliminate "buy national" restrictions on the majority of non-defense-related purchases by their federal governments of goods and services provided by firms in North America. For the United States and Canada, this represents a further elimination of barriers to participation in each other's government procurement markets, building on the [Tokyo Round] GATT Agreement on Government Procurement ("GATT Code") and the [Canada-U.S. Free Trade Agreement, CFTA].

Under the NAFTA, Mexico — which is not a party to the GATT Code — has committed for the first time to eliminate discriminatory government procurement practices. Mexico has made this undertaking solely in respect of U.S. and Canadian firms, goods and services. European, Asian and other competitors do not benefit from Mexico's procurement commitment under the NAFTA.

1. Scope and Coverage

Chapter Ten covers virtually all federal government agencies in the three countries, as well as a significant number of federal government enterprises, often referred to as "parastatals" in this context. The agreement applies not only to procurement of goods, but also, for the first time in an international trade agreement, to procurement of services, including construction services. The entities, goods and services covered by the chapter are specified in Annex 1001. Article 1022 provides that changes in the coverage specified by each Party are permitted only under exceptional circumstances.

a. Covered Entities

Chapter Ten will for the first time give U.S. products and services guaranteed access to procurement by Mexican Government agencies. Chapter Ten also goes beyond the CFTA by extending coverage for goods to additional U.S. and Canadian federal agencies, and to services and construction services purchased at the federal level. Unlike the CFTA, NAFTA will also cover purchases by government-controlled enterprises, including those by Mexican parastatals, whose purchases account for a large percentage of total Mexican government procurement.

As set forth in Annex 1001.2a, the Mexican Government will provide U.S. and Canadian suppliers growing access to purchase contracts by PEMEX, the state-owned petroleum company, and CFE, the Mexican Government's electrical utility. When the NAFTA enters into force, Mexico will immediately open 50 percent of PEMEX and CFE procurement to U.S. and Canadian goods and services, with progressive annual increases through 2002. Thereafter, Mexico's government procurement market in the energy sector will be completely open, subject to limited PEMEX and CFE procurement "set-asides" for Mexican suppliers.

b. Thresholds

Chapter Ten applies to purchases by specified federal government agencies and federal government-controlled enterprises in each NAFTA country above certain U.S. dollar thresholds:

- purchases of goods over $25,000 by federal agencies in the United States from Canadian suppliers or by Canadian federal agencies from U.S. suppliers;

- for other procurements by federal government agencies in the three countries, purchases of goods and services over $50,000 and purchases of construction services over $6.5 million; and

- for federal government-owned enterprises, purchases of goods and services over $250,000 and purchases of construction services over $8 million.

The $25,000 threshold for U.S.-Canada procurements of goods effectively carries forward the threshold in use under the CFTA.

c. Exclusions

The rules of Chapter Ten do not apply to certain kinds of purchases by the U.S. Government, among them:

- purchases under small or minority business set-aside programs;

- procurements for national security purposes and certain items purchased by the Department of Defense, including those subject to "Berry Amendment"-type restrictions;

- purchases by the Department of Agricultural for farm support programs and human feeding programs;

- purchases by the Agency for International Development for the purpose of providing foreign assistance (purchases not for the direct benefit or use of AID); and

- procurements by state and local governments, including procurements funded by federal grants, such as those made pursuant to the Federal Transit Act (49 U.S.C. App. 1601 *et seq.*) and the Federal Aid Highway Act (23 U.S.C. 101 *et seq.*).

The Schedule of the United States contained in the General Notes, Annex 1001.2b specifically excludes from Chapter Ten's coverage set-asides on behalf of small and minority businesses. This exclusion exempts from Chapter Ten's rules U.S. Government procurement programs such as those which give preference to small businesses, business concerns and private and voluntary organizations owned or controlled by women or socially and economically disadvantaged individuals, historically black colleges and universities, and colleges and universities with substantial Hispanic or Native American enrollment. The exclusion is identical to that taken by the U.S. Government under the *GATT Code*. It means that the President does not have the authority to waive existing or future laws, regulations, procedures or practices under these programs to allow procurements by Mexican or Canadian businesses.

2. *General Disciplines*

The general rule of Chapter Ten, set out in Article 1003, is that the three governments must treat goods and services from another NAFTA country — and suppliers of such goods and services — "no less favorably" than domestic goods, services and suppliers with respect to purchases by covered government entities. In addition, under Article 1006, each government is required to ensure that its entities do not consider, seek or impose "offsets" in the evaluation of bids or the award of contracts. "Offsets" are contract conditions that encourage local development or improve the country's balance-of-payments accounts by requiring, for example, local content, the licensing of technology, local investment or countertrade. Article 1007 provides that the purpose and effect of technical specifications should not be to impose unnecessary obstacles to trade.

3. *Procurement Procedures*

Articles 1008 to 1016 set out a series of rules designed to ensure that procurement practices in all three countries are fair, transparent and predictable.

The basic rule, established by Article 1008, is that of non-discrimination in procurement procedures. The NAFTA also requires covered entities to follow procedures similar to those required under the *GATT Code*, with respect to qualification of suppliers, time limits, documentation, award of contracts and other aspects of the procurement process. The United States and Canada already adhere to these procedures. Mexico will be adopting them for the first time under the NAFTA. They will result in significant changes in the way Mexico conducts its procurements.

Article 1014, for example, requires a minimum degree of fairness and competition in the process used to negotiate a procurement, while Article 1015 requires contract awards to be made in accordance with criteria set out in advance. Article 1016 recognizes that each government will sometimes need to deviate from the rule of open competition. But the article requires that "limited tendering" be as competitive as possible and be used only in limited circumstances.

In order to promote fair and open procurement procedures, Article 1017 requires each government to maintain a "bid challenge" mechanism enabling individual suppliers to have the entire bidding process reviewed. Suppliers from other NAFTA countries will have the right to challenge both bid procedures and contract awards, and will be assured that an independent body in each country will review such challenges and recommend action to correct any discrepancies.

---

* This Note was prepared by Heather Anderson, Esq., Cole, Raywid & Braverman, LLP, Washington, D.C. The views expressed are those of the author.

1. International Telecommunications Union, *World Telecommunications Development Report 1996/1997*, Executive Summary.

IV. Telecommunications

NOTE ON FDI AND REGULATION IN THE TELECOMMUNICATIONS SECTOR[*]

Introduction

The telecommunications industry has become a dominant force in the international business community. It is one of the leading service industries in the world, with a value estimated to reach $1 trillion by the end of 1998.[1] It is also the driving force behind the "Second Information Revolution," which will affect the way we think about the world around us. It will make us question "what is real, what is imaginary, and where the borderline between them is — or should be."[2] Telecommunications is more than the ability to place a phone call or subscribe to HBO. It is a global revolution that is altering culture, erasing lines of knowledge dividing the haves and the have-nots, and transforming the way the world views entertainment, exchanges information, and communicates daily.

Most industry experts agree telecommunications has developed beyond traditional sectors of broadcast and telephony. Former Federal Communications Commission (FCC) Chairman Reed Hundt identifies five lanes that may be used to access the information superhighway: (1) broadcast, (2) cable, (3) wired, (4) wireless, and (5) satellite.[3] These are avenues of regulation, however, and need to be explained further. For example, broadcast is a service, while cable, wireline, wireless, and satellite are all technologies used to transmit a service, like broadcast.

Sound confusing? It is, and when you throw in a number of service providers and regulators, you have a hornet's nest that will keep even the most seasoned telecommunications veteran wondering where the industry is going. Thus, it is rare to find generalists in the area of telecommunications. Most telecommunications experts concentrate on a single area of service, or more likely, a single area of technology. This specialization may be necessary to understand the "Babylonian confusion" of abbreviations, acronyms and other jargon that new technology has introduced.[4] But, the telecommunications industry is continuing to develop across traditional lines and is moving in new directions, demanding a general understanding of the entire field of telecommunications.

One of the aims of this Note is to give definition to some (but not all) of these technologies, services, and service providers, and illustrate how they cross over. An in-depth look at every technology and service is too ambitious for the confines of this Note, and would possibly end up being more confusing than helpful. The goal is to show the relationship among the three matrixes of telecommunications: (1) technologies, (2) services, and (3) providers. The matrixes are changing and developing, and it is impossible to pigeon-hole telecommunications into convenient categories. Sometimes, the service drives the technology. More often, technology creates a new service, and providers are constantly searching for ways to supply more services. This "bundling" of services is very popular to consumers, especially

---

2. "The United Nations and Technology for Sustainable Development," speech by Dr. Pekka Tarjanne, Secretary-General, International Telecommunication Union; September 29, 1995.

3. KENNETH C. CREECH, ELECTRONIC MEDIA LAW AND REGULATION 375 (2d ed. 1996).

4. ANTON A. HUURDEMAN, GUIDE TO TELECOMMUNICATIONS TRANSMISSION SYSTEMS xii (Artech House, Inc. 1997).

in developing countries. The challenge facing telecommunications providers, regulators and users, however, continues to be the ever-changing horizon of technology, coupled with the constant cross-over among the technology, service and provider matrixes.

This Note also highlights emerging technologies in the satellite and wireless sectors, in addition to the evolution of the Internet, as a service. These are growth areas in global telecommunications, but they show particular potential for developing countries to participate and compete in the telecommunications industry. Some of the names of these emerging technologies — MMDS, SMA-TV, DBS, DTH — are an alphabet soup of acronyms, which can be very intimidating to business executives and international business lawyers alike. Accordingly, the first section of this Note explains what these acronyms stand for, and what the new technologies offer for developed and developing countries.

Telecommunications is a regulated industry, domestically and internationally. There are several issues that are important to the regulation of telecommunications, including limited radio spectrum, diversity of standards, foreign ownership and competition, universal service requirements, and accounting rates. While it is not possible to discuss all aspects of each of these issues here, some features of these issues arise in the context of regulatory examples below. Moreover, the second part of this Note focuses on the regulatory environment for international telecommunications. This section discusses the roles of the International Telecommunications Union (ITU) and the World Trade Organization (WTO) in helping, or in some cases, hindering the advance of telecommunications. The ITU and the WTO have made huge strides in international spectrum allocation and harmonization, opening new markets to competition, and assisting in the development of telecommunications infrastructures in developing countries. But, critics charge that these organizations are hampered by bureaucracy and the need to achieve majority consensus.[5] The industry may be growing beyond what the ITU and the WTO have been able to supervise, and this growth is spurred by the industry itself. If the ITU and WTO (and arguably the FCC and other developed, domestic regulatory bodies) cannot keep up with technological growth, how can fledgling regulatory bodies in countries like India and Brazil hope to establish a system that meets the challenges of technology?

This question serves as a point of departure for the final sections of the Note. With the exception of China, India and Brazil are two of the largest developing telecommunication markets in the world today. India and Brazil continue to struggle with regulatory and privatization issues. Most industry analysts have pegged India and Brazil for investment and growth, due in part to their enormous populations and potential for development. They are also two markets that have caused significant problems for telecommunications companies and investors.

In India, the desire to provide universal service (basic telecommunications services, like telephones, at an affordable rate to every citizen) is balanced against the need to attract foreign investors who are more interested in high tech business services like satellite phones, fax, and Internet. In Brazil, the demand for advanced services is growing faster than the Brazilian government can accommodate. Wary of for-

5. Cynthia Beltz, *Global Telecommunications Rules: The Race with Technology*, ISSUES IN SCIENCE AND TECHNOLOGY, Mar. 22, 1997

6. "The United Nations and Technology for Sustainable Development," speech by Dr. Pekka Tarjanne, *supra*.

eign telecommunications providers, Brazil is attempting to strike a balance between foreign investors and government control.

To be sure, these sorts of issues are not necessarily unique to India and Brazil. They are representative of many of the issues facing developing telecommunications markets around the world. Hence, India and Brazil are excellent case studies.

Finally, it is the overall goal of this Note to illustrate the double-edged sword of technology for developing countries - and indeed, the rest of the world. On the one side, technology has the power to narrow the "telecommunications development gap," first discovered by Sir Donald Maitland more than ten years ago,[6] by allowing developing countries to learn from the mistakes of developed countries. The economic miracle of the Asian-Pacific region (notwithstanding the Asian economic crisis of the late 1990s) is, in part, attributed to the ability of many countries there to go from manually operated to digital exchanges, bypassing completely the semi-automatic stage of network development.

But, like a precocious child, technology is sometimes an unpredictable and unwelcome challenge, which may prove to be a stumbling block of mountainous proportions for developing countries. As evidenced by the difficulties of the ITU, WTO and developed, domestic regulatory bodies such as the FCC, the challenge lies in the ability of developing countries to create a regulatory body that is flexible, so as to meet the regulatory changes that new and emerging technologies inevitably demand. Additionally, the telecommunications industry currently is led by well-financed companies in the developed world, as well as global consortiums. Who else can provide the financing for multi-billion dollar satellite constellations? Developing countries must find a way to compete in this market, perhaps by providing local, regional, or national services, in conjunction with foreign-backed infrastructure and hardware. In this way, developing countries may find a niche market that will spur growth in their economies and help narrow the telecommunications development gap.

I. THE THREE MATRIXES OF TELECOMMUNICATIONS

To provide some coherent explanation of what telecommunications is today and where it is going, it is important to separate the *technologies*, *services*, and *providers* into three distinct matrixes. Each matrix is described below in greater detail. It is impossible to discuss all technologies, services and providers herein, but it is possible to focus on the general categories of technology, as well as emerging services offered by emerging technology. In particular, the provider matrix is limited to a few providers that are truly global telecommunications services providers. Of course, there are several other providers that are successful in using their dominant positions in domestic markets to pursue a lucrative international market.

It is difficult to illustrate the three matrixes — technology, services, and providers — without some element of cross-over. It is overly simplistic, and indeed inaccurate, to suggest they are totally distinct from one another. But, because some definition is needed initially, consider the matrixes separately. Thereafter, some of the cross-overs are illustrated.

A. The Technology Matrix

"Technology" is the way that a service is transmitted. In this section, four general technologies are discussed: (1) cable, (2) wireline, (3) wireless, and (4) satellite. What becomes really complicated is the cross-over with services, because of a chicken-and-egg dilemma. Does the demand for new and improved services drive technology? Or, does the technology create new and improved services? Technology is increasingly able to offer more services, and services are increasingly available via diverse technologies. Nevertheless, it is the rapid increase in technology that leads to a final discussion of how regulatory agencies can continue to regulate services and providers, domestically and internationally.

1. Cable

There are several reasons why the cable industry has prospered in the United States, and just as many reasons why it has not enjoyed similar success on a global level. What is cable? What can it do? Where is it going?

Cable television is the transmission of video signals over a coaxial cable.[7] Of course, there are also system components consisting of a headend, trunk cable, feeder cable, drop cables and a home terminal,[8] but understanding these terms is not necessary in order to grasp the basic operation of cable. Cable operates over coaxial cable, that is fed directly into a household. Cable television first appeared in the late 1940's in Oregon and Pennsylvania. It proved to be very successful in communities that were located great distances from television stations, which send signals over-the-air via electromagnetic spectrum. Antennas, set on hilltops, received the electromagnetic broadcast signal, which was then sent out via cable to residents, allowing them to receive local broadcasts with better reception. This is one of the reasons cable television has prospered in the United States, namely, significantly better reception than with over-the-air antennas.

But, the cost of laying cable into expansive rural areas meant the growth in the popularity of cable in the United States was slow. Cable is not an economically efficient technology in rural areas. The real benefit of cable is found in a crowded urban area, where tall buildings makes over-the-air reception poor, and the cost of cable is minimized by the number of people living in a confined space. Not all countries are as geographically diverse - or as large - as the United States. Some countries, Uruguay for example, find half of its population living in its capitol city, Montevideo. This country can benefit from the use of cable in delivering broadcast and paid programming, as well as multimedia applications in the future, because cable is an economically efficient technology for its high-density areas. The same is not necessarily true for a country like India, however. India, too, has a large population, but it is spread over a considerable geographic area. Consequently, India has embraced the economically efficient satellite industry, which can cover the entire country without the expense of laying tens of thousands of miles of coaxial cable.

The cost of building and servicing a cable franchise is prohibitive for most start-up companies. The expansive grid of cables required to deliver the quality of programming to the number of households demanding the service in the United States has taken fifty years to build and upgrade, at an enormous cost to cable companies. These companies, of course, pass on this cost to subscribers. The cost of basic cable service per month in America is more than many families around the world earn in a month. Cable is expensive to build, expensive to maintain, and expensive to enjoy.

Governments in developing countries make the valid argument that it is ridiculous to spend money on cable television, which is considered a luxury in most countries, when money can better be spent on basic communications such as fiber optic telephone lines. The cable industry's answer lies in the flexibility of cable technology. Cable does not have to be used exclusively for the delivery of pay-per-view programming. In addition to the traditional use of coaxial cable in Common Antennae Television (CATV or Cable TV), it may be used in the long-distance transmission of analog and digital signals, especially in countries that have not upgraded to fiber-optic wire (discussed below). But, the future for cable, as with most technologies, is its ability to provide multimedia. In the United States, where coaxial cable lines run past 97 percent of homes, cable television providers are researching ways of connecting directly to household personal computers (PCs), and offering an economical avenue to the Internet.

2. Wireline

The difference between cable and wireline technology is not clear to everyone. After all, both are physical lines that enter the home. Both are capable of transmitting audio and visual communications. But, the technical differentiation lies in the make-up of the wire.

Although coaxial cable has a copper element, the copper wires used in telephony are very different. Additionally, much of today's telephone wire in advanced countries is made from fiber optics, which provide nearly unlimited capacity, especially in digital transmissions. Copper wire predominates in developing countries, and some developed countries find it prohibitively expensive to replace extant copper infrastructure with fiber optics. "Copper wire-based cables connect the majority of the worldwide 600 million telephone subscribers with their local telephone exchanges."[9] To be sure, existing copper infrastructures can be upgraded. But, the future of wireline technology lies in the success of fiber optics, and competition from satellite technology makes any serious investment in copper lines economically infeasible.

Fiber-optic technology has revolutionized, and continues to revolutionize, interactive telephony. Its transmission characteristics are far superior to copper lines. Consider the submarine cable field. The development of fiber optic technology means a great increase in capacity, a tremendous reduction in per circuit costs, and an expansion of the variety of services available via submarine cable.[10] Most think of wireline technology in terms of its use in telephone lines, domestic and long distance. But, fiber-optic technology allows wireline to be used to carry video programming, and to data transfer via digital lines. In sum, the future of wireline technology lies in fiber optics, which allow superior quality and almost unlimited capacity, together with variety in service options.

3. Wireless

Wireless technology covers both "radio-relay" and "mobile radio" communications. The distinction is more evident in the discussion of wireless services, which include many services, such as wireless local loop, cellular phones (analog and digital), personal communication systems (PCS), and paging. "Radio-relay" communications refer to a point-to-point service, i.e., two fixed points, like a radio station tower to a radio receiver in your home. "Mobile radio" communications often are radio-relay from a fixed point to a mobile receiver, such as a cellular phone, a pager, or a global positioning system (GPS). The mobile receiver moves with a person or automobile.

Of course, in reality it is more complicated than this. Radio-relay is the basic relay of information via the electromagnetic spectrum. Mobile radio expanded on this concept, concentrating on the direction of the signal (to single or multiple mobile

---

9. HUURDEMAN, *supra,* at 134.
10. Leslie Taylor, *Current Trends in Regulation, in* ISSUES IN TELECOMMUNICATIONS POLICY: A SOURCEBOOK 91 (Jane H. Yurow ed. 1983).

receivers). Satellite technology, discussed below, takes this technology yet another step forward, and into another dimension. But, the basic radio-relay technology used in mobile radio and satellite remains the same. They utilize radio spectrum, and they are often used simultaneously, or in combination with another technology. For example, a television program may leave a television station in Paris, France, via radio-relay or wireline to an earth station, that transmits it (via allocated spectrum) to a satellite, which transmits to a receiving station, which transmits to a home in Abijan, Côte d'Ivoire via radio-relay or wireline technology. In transmitting that program from Paris to Abijan, three or four technologies are used.

Instead of using copper or fiber-optic cable to transmit signals, radio-relay uses the atmosphere as the transmission medium, generating, modulating, amplifying, and directing very high frequencies through the atmosphere. Each modulated, short, electromagnetic wave really is a "packet" containing voice or data. The key is to avoid any interference with other electromagnetic waves that also are being transmitted through the atmosphere. Additionally, the further the wave has to travel, the weaker the signal becomes. "Consequently, radio-relay transmission is limited in two ways: to the direct line of sight between stations and by the attenuation in the atmosphere."[11] Therefore, the use of repeater stations is necessary to amplify the signal over a greater distance.

As the service matrix below illustrates, the use of wireless technology is a boon to developing countries. It offers the same services that cable or fiber-optic wireline technology provide, but typically at a significantly lower cost. The economics are obvious. Copper and fiber optic lines require a great deal of cost to build and install: the cable itself, trenches, switching stations, and submarine systems, all of which is necessary to link the rest of the world to the already large grid of serviced telecommunications users. That is not to say that wireless systems are cheap. There is still the cost of the relay stations, as well as of the individual receivers, for example, handheld telephones - or "handhelds." Nevertheless, the advantages of wireless technology for undeveloped telecommunications markets is indisputable.

Mobile radio, that is, transmission not to a fixed location, but to a person irrespective of their location, can be less expensive than satellite communication "wherever population density and existing public infrastructure... economically justify the deployment of the relevant fixed part of a mobile network."[12] In rural or underdeveloped areas, however, satellite technology may prove more economically viable for mobile communications, as many satellite systems do not require the base stations, and control and switching equipment, needed by mobile radio systems.

4. Satellite

There are great strides being made in all of the technologies discussed above. However, the satellite industry has the potential to revolutionize the concept of "international telecommunications" in a way the others do not have the capability to achieve. One important reason is that satellite communications simultaneously can service a greater area than any other technology, usually at a lower cost to the consumer. But, satellite systems, often called "constellations," are very expensive and risky, and call for an enormous amount of international cooperation and organization.

---

11. HUURDEMAN, *supra*, at 210.
12. HUURDEMAN, *supra*, at 287.

From an engineering perspective, satellite transmission borrows a great deal from radio-relay, especially in terms of frequency — or spectrum usage — to avoid interference. A satellite provides the transmission of a signal between two earth stations using an uplink from the first earth station to the satellite and a downlink back to the second earth station. That, of course, is the elementary explanation. There are other important ingredients in a successful satellite system, including the earth station, the satellite's orbit, launching systems, antennas, transponder capacity, and power supply.

Satellites are not just the newest form of telecommunications technology. They also are the most dynamic and controversial. The first communications satellite was launched in 1957, although it was not until the launch of the SYNCOM satellites in 1963 that the world learned the real potential of satellites to offer common communication services, such as telephone, teletype and fax transmission among, for instance, the United States, Asia, and Africa. Because of the enormous cost of research and development, the satellite industry was launched by government-backed and regulated programs, which are now under pressure to privatize in order to compete on an equal footing with a number of corporate satellite systems.[13] In addition to the traditional government-owned global operators, several regional operators have sprung up. Examples are ARABSAT, AUSSAT, EUTELSAT, AsiaSat, and PanAmSat (the first private global satellite network operator.) These regional providers allow several countries, together with private interests, to pool resources in order to serve a specific region, and thereby satisfy the separate telecommunication needs of each region. The regional providers are an excellent opportunity for poorer countries to be involved with this very important technology. Unfortunately, it is increasingly becoming a status symbol and source of national pride for a country to have its own satellite system (or at least its own satellite) as illustrated by South Korea's intent to launch a low-earth-orbiting (Little Leo) satellite system.

No doubt, satellites will continue to experience the greatest growth among the above technologies. But, each technology will continue to offer certain benefits that may be just right for a particular user. Thus, rather than anticipating that one technology will come to dominate all others, it is more likely that the various technologies will continue to interact with each other, and compliment each other in numerous ways.

Main Criteria for Selecting Specific Transmission Solutions*

Criteria	Copper Line	Optical Fiber	Radio Relay	Mobile Radio	Satellite
Transmission Capacity					
Low and medium	*	*	*	*	*
High		*	*		*
Very High		*			
Distance					
Short	*	*	*	*	

---

13. The Communication Satellite Corporation (COMSAT) was established in 1963 to develop commercial satellites in the United States. COMSAT became the driving force behind the International Telecommunications by Satellite (INTELSAT) consortium of United Nations members. This consortium wanted to expand satellite communications to a global level. INTELSAT, together with INMARSAT (another global network provider of mobile satellite services) is in the process of privatizing. These government-owned and operated services have dominated the commercial satellite industry due to their privileged status throughout the last forty years.

	1	2	3	4	5
Medium		*	*		*
Long	*	*		*	
Very Long		*			*
Geology					
Flat area, soft soil	*	*		*	
Mountainous			*	*	*
Jungle			*	*	*
Marshy and lakes			*	*	*
Oceans		*			*
Geography					
Industrialized area		*		*	
Urban		*	*	*	*
Rural	*		*	*	*
Population Density					
Low, scattered				*	*
Medium		*	*	*	*
High			*	*	*
Infrastructure					
Electricity and roads					
Good	*	*		*	
Bad			*	*	*
Nonexistent				*	*
Right of Way					
Easy to obtain	*	*			
Difficult to obtain			*	*	*
Existing Cable Ducts	*	*			
Existing Radio-Relay Towers			*	*	
Project Implementation					
Standard	*	*			
Short time			*		
Very short time					*
Environment					
Electromagnetic radiation	*				
Earthquake zone			*	*	*
Network					
Fixed Stations	*	*	*		
Stations on flexible sites			*	*	*
Stations at short distances with frequent drop and insert	*	*			
Star topology	*			*	*
Ring topology		*	*		
Lower capacity spurs in high-capacity networks		*	*		
Access from public to cellular networks and interconnection of cells			*		
Minor extensions of copper line networks	*				

	Col 1	Col 2	Col 3	Col 4
Private Customers				
Companies with				
various sites				
In urban areas	*	*	*	
In isolated areas		*	*	*
Pipelines, highways				
New	*		*	
Existing		*	*	
Communication required				
during construction		*	*	*
Special Circumstances				
International events		*	*	*
Emergency at natural				
disaster		*	*	*
Reconstruction after war		*	*	*
Flexible TV studio access		*		*
Operation Mode				
Mobile		*	*	
Dual routing				
Terrestrial	*	*		
Intercontinental	*			*

Table reprinted from Anton A. Huurdeman, *Guide to Telecommunications Transmission Systems* 333-34 (1997).

B. The Service Matrix

What is the difference between a "service" and a "technology"? A "service" is what people want: the ability to "telephone" someone, to receive programming through their radio or television antennas, to receive enhanced video services, and to send or receive data in minutes or even seconds. For example, a broadcast, such as a radio or network television program, historically has been transmitted via electromagnetic spectrum, using radio-relay technology. Today, a broadcast may be delivered through cable, wireless, wireline, or satellite technology.

It is important to maintain the conceptual distinction between services and technology, because new technology constantly assaults the distinction. The Internet is an excellent example. The Internet is a "service." It can be provided to the consumer via cable, fiber optic wire, or satellite. However, the Internet allows the consumer to send and receive video, data and even voice services, so some would label it a "technology." Some services actually are sub-services of a more general service. That is the best way to describe the Internet to someone who insists on putting a label on it. Here, then, is the problem of growing cross-over between services and technology. The Internet is just one service out of many that will cause problems of definition and subsequently, regulation in the future. The following services are categorized by the type of technology that has made them popular, although several technologies may compete to deliver the service. Not every service is mentioned, rather new or developing services are highlighted.

1. Broadcast

In the United States, broadcast always has been a cornerstone of telecommunications. Together with telephony, it has been the focal point of the work of most telecommunications lawyers since the early 1900's. Simplistically speaking, "broadcast" is the delivery and reception of programming via radio and television. What it is today, and what it will be tomorrow, is a much more complex question. Even more complex, is what it is outside the United States.

Different countries define broadcast services in their own way, often imposing different regulations than broadcasters find in the United States. Europe, for example, argues that Direct Broadcast Satellite (DBS), Direct to Home Satellite Systems (DTH), and Digital Audio Radio Service (DARS) should be regulated as broadcast services. (The difference between DBS and DTH is discussed later.) In the United States, DBS and DTH are regulated as paid subscription satellite services and are excused from many of the regulations applicable to broadcast services. The disparity in regulatory treatment based on this service definition is apparent in the WTO Telecommunications schedules that each WTO Member submitted in 1997.

Historically, the technology used to transmit broadcast signals has been radio-relay via the electromagnetic spectrum. This means that anyone with the proper receiver (*e.g.*, a television or radio antenna) can pick up this programming for free. That is the essence of broadcast — free programming to anyone who can receive it. Because of its importance in providing a "universal service," there are specific requirements, as well as special privileges authorized by domestic regulators, like the FCC. Today, there are several technologies that can deliver broadcast signals. Thus, what was once considered the essence of local or domestic communications, now can be transmitted around the world.

In turn, the issue of foreign control over domestic broadcasting is a tense political subject, not only in this country, but worldwide. Every country fears foreign domination of its broadcast services. After all, for many governments, broadcast services are a key way to control the domestic polity - and remain in power. Less ominously, many governments rightly are concerned about the transmission of immoral programming by western broadcast service providers, and about the harmonization of global culture at the expense of local heritages as a result of western-dominated broadcast content. Consequently, foreign ownership restrictions still are placed on broadcasting licenses and, as a service, broadcasting probably enjoys more protection by domestic regulators than any other service (except, perhaps, the legal profession!).

2. High Definition Television (HDTV) or Digital Television (DTV)

High definition television (HDTV) has brought broadcasting back into the regulatory spotlight. HDTV is advanced television that allows viewers to receive theater-quality programming. However, only people with high-definition television sets will be able to receive these signals. To phase out conventional television, without too much burden on those who cannot afford the new service, the FCC has designed a transitional plan that allows for the simultaneous broadcast of digital HDTV and conventional analog signals by setting aside additional spectrum. This spectrum means a shift of previously allocated spectrum, which does not please everyone. HDTV is, therefore, a formidable broadcasting challenge for domestic regulators.

3. Voice Telephony

The term "voice telephony" is used instead of simply "voice" to define this service in a way everyone understands. Today, the transfer of voice can be done in several ways, but most people think of voice service as going to their telephone, placing a call, and talking with someone on the other end in "real time." The service is not in the transfer of words you speak, but the transfer of the sounds and inflection of the voice itself. This may appear obvious, but it is what separates voice from data transmission, like facsimile (fax) or electronic mail (e-mail).

The developments in voice telephony stem from advanced technology. However, voice telephony may suffer via traditional analog transmission due to the necessity of repeater stations and the threat of distortion over long distances. Digital transmission, as a series of on and off coded signals, is not affected by distance, and therefore offers better quality, whether applied to telephone, data or video services. Fiber optic cables have also increased the capacity, efficiency, and cost-effectiveness of wireline telephony.

Voice telephony is considered a basic telecommunications service in most countries, and yet the teledensity level (the number of households with basic telecommunications services) in several developing countries is extremely low. Because teledensity is often shown as a percentage of telephones to people, developing countries with larger populations usually have lower teledensity percentages. India has a teledensity of 1.6, which means only 1.6 people out of 100 have access to a telephone.

Increasingly, voice telephony is provided by wireless and satellite systems, especially to areas that do not already have a wireline (copper or fiber-optic) infrastructure already in place. But, traditionally wireline technology has been the technology of choice for most domestic and long-distance telephony. With more than millions and millions of people registered on waiting lists for telephone connection, the wireline market will remain strong into the next century.[14]

4. Cable Television

In the United States, cable TV has grown from a rural service to a prosperous deliverer of multi-channel programming. Cable companies are no longer confined to the re-transmission of local broadcast channels. They can offer their customers original programming, movies, and religious and children's programming, usually at a premium.

The FCC has vacillated in its regulatory policies regarding cable, beginning with very little interest in the service, moving to franchising standards, two-way capability requirements, and public access channels, to considering deregulation in the wake of competition. Competition in the multi-channel video programming distribution (MVPD) market has increased with the entry of wireless cable (multi-channel, multi-point distribution services, or MMDS, discussed below), satellite master antenna television system operator (SMA-TV), and DBS technologies.

Nevertheless, cable television commands the lion's share of the MVPD market, especially in the United States, where more than 55 million subscribers spend more than $20 billion every year. Because of this dominance of cable into many homes, the cable industry has the opportunity to compete with local telephone companies by teaming up with long-distance telephone carriers to offer telephony and multimedia (*e.g.*, Internet) services.[15] This opportunity only exists in countries where cable has a predominant presence into homes, and may require upgrading of existing cable systems.

---

14. ITU, *World Telecommunications Development Report 1996/1997, supra.*

15. Notwithstanding a rumored alliance with a national cable provider, AT&T announced that any merger between its long-distance service and cable's provision of local telephone services would entail a vast improvement or upgrade of existing cables. *See* Satellite Communications Bar Association, *SkyReport* (Mar. 1998).

16. Mary E. Stanhope, *PCS Markets: The Land of Opportunity*, Cellular & Mobile Int'l, Sept. 1, 1997.

5. *Multi-channel, Multi-point Distribution Service (MMDS)*

Cable television faces competition from wireless and satellite delivery systems that are struggling for footholds in the MVPD market. One of those services is MMDS, or "wireless cable." Instead of receiving cable television through the traditional cable, more than four million subscribers receive signals via microwave transmission from a central radio base station. MMDS is an application of a larger system known as wireless local loop (WLL), which is based on cellular radio systems, and can offer subscribers within a small area (usually 10 km or less) high-quality transmission of voice, video and data signals. The advantages and disadvantages of WLL are similar to cellular, and will vary according to the environment and needs of individuals.

6. *Cellular*

Most people think about cellular phones when asked about mobile technology. There are a lot of other services provided by mobile technology that are used everyday. Paging systems are a good example. Nevertheless, cellular telephones have become a widespread service around the world. Owning a cellular phone is increasingly less akin to owning a Mercedes Benz, but the status symbol associated with a cell phone is one of several benefits of cellular service.[16]

Cellular telephones are small, mobile broadcast stations that receive and transmit signals to a wired telephone plant. The plant has a limited area of transmission, known as a "cell." Many overlapping cells give seamless coverage in larger geographical areas. The benefit of course, is that an individual is not bound to a fixed wire point. Additionally, cellular systems require spectrum, not wireline infrastructure. So, assuming the domestic regulator allocates spectrum free of charge, the cost of the cellular system is remarkably less-expensive than the traditional wireline service. It also means that anyone with the correct receiver can pick up your conversation, although advanced coding techniques have increased privacy.

Analog and digital cellular networks operate simultaneously in most areas. Analog networks currently have the advantage of larger coverage, lower infrastructure and consumer costs. Still, the advantage of digital over analog transmission is evident: better quality, higher capacity, more efficient use of spectrum, better security, and easier integration with data and computer needs.

7. *Personal Communications Services (PCS)*

PCS is the ability to have person-to person communication under one national — or even international — phone number, regardless of whether you are at home, the office, or in your car. To be able to offer coverage to all of these places, numerous microcells are used to link the network, similar to the way cellular service operates.

But, PCS is superior to cellular. PCS operates in a higher frequency, and can offer three or four times the number of channels that cellular can offer. Additionally, its highly-efficient digital technology offers more security with reduced eavesdropping or number cloning, clearer connections with less background noise, and fewer "dropped" calls.

Developing countries have embraced PCS as an alternative to wireline networks, which take years to build and often provide lower quality of service. This is illustrated in the predicted subscriber growth over the next five years: 25% annually in developing countries overall, and 80% annually in India, alone. PCS also offers a quick, low cost entry, and a flexible configuration that can enhance existing wireline networks in several areas.

8. Satellite Master Antenna Television (SMA-TV)

SMA-TV provides video programming to large multi-unit buildings, such as office buildings, apartment complexes, and hotels. Each building has a satellite dish that receives the programming signal and distributes it over a series of wirelines into each individual unit. SMA-TV has proven a viable competitor to cable in areas with high population densities, due in part to the fact that no right-of-way is necessary to build a cable line into the building itself. Individual units now have a consumer choice among program providers wishing to service an entire building. Before SMA-TV and DBS systems, it was usually the decision of the building owner to determine which cable provider had monopoly access to the building. Individual units could choose between whether to subscribe to the monopolist, or take their chances with over-the-air reception of broadcast programming.

9. Direct Broadcast Satellite (DBS) and Direct to Home (DTH)

Video programming provided via satellite has many names, and each country uses a different one. In the United States, the FCC differentiates between DTH, which is all programming provided by satellite, and DBS, which is programming provided via a high-powered satellite and received by a small, home receiver dish.

DTH includes first generation, C-band transmissions, which require large satellite dishes to be mounted near the home. A recent development in DTH is called "DirecPC," which began in 1996. It allows PC users to access the Internet and receive data directly through their home satellite dish.

DBS operates in the Ku-band, and perhaps in the future, via the higher Ka-band. DBS requires smaller, pizza-sized dishes that can be mounted on a home. Improvements in DBS technology include signal compression, which allows more channel capacity per satellite transponder. This means the consumer gets more channels, with a picture and sound that rival laser and compact disc quality. The cost of the hardware, such as the individual receiver dishes, is falling as technology advances, which means that DBS has the potential to compete aggressively with cable in the MVPD market. Additionally, DBS has shown great potential in developing areas that do not enjoy the extensive cable infrastructure that is found in the United States or Europe.

10. Global Mobile Personal Communication by Satellite (GMPCS)

GMPCS is a lot more complicated than the following description — ask any satellite expert. But, for the sake of simplicity "GMPCS" is the ability to roam anywhere in the world and use a singular handheld to phone, fax, e-mail, etc. via satellite delivery. There are several areas around the world that do not have terrestrial cellular coverage, so GMPCS works as a supplement, filling in gaps left by terrestrial networks. Where a gap exists, service is transmitted directly to and from a satellite to the handheld. Dual-mode handsets allow users to select automatically the best available cellular or satellite network.

The ITU has divided GMPCS into different categories. The most commonly referred to are Little LEO's and Big LEO's. ("LEO" stands for "low earth orbiting satellites"). This definition of "GMPCS" is much more expansive than what was originally adopted. Some still consider only Big LEO's to fall under the generic term "GMPCS." After all, little LEO's are satellite systems that operate at a frequency below 1 GH and

---

17. "The Future of the Telecommunications Industry in Asia: Global, Mobile and Personal," Speech by Dr. Henry Chasia, Deputy Secretary-General, ITU, Hong Kong, October 28, 1996

offer narrowband services, like data transmission, paging and global positioning systems. In contrast, big LEO's operate at a higher frequency, between 1 GH and 3 GH and can offer interactive voice service, like the satellite telephones described above.

Private corporations that operate on a multinational basis will be the first to benefit from global communications via GMPCS.[17] GMPCS providers, however, still face national regulatory hurdles in several countries. Many such regulators are concerned about a potential loss of national sovereignty, as well as possible bypass and loss of revenue with GMPCS systems.

11. Multimedia Applications

The future challenge for technology — cable, fiber-optic, radio-relay and satellite alike — is the ability to offer multimedia applications. That is, a package where voice, video, data transmission, and access to computer systems is offered through one technology. That may mean a marriage of technologies, for example, satellite and wireless, or fiber-optic and radio-relay, in order to provide the best possible service.

The Internet is the quintessential multimedia service. It offers the free flow of video, voice and data, while getting around domestic regulations that may apply to each individual service. It is projected that the Internet will continue to be the largest telecommunications service in demand for the future. Yet, many developing countries have not been able to merge onto the information superhighway due to a lack of technological infrastructure.

Each technology has advantages and disadvantages with respect to its competition. But, it is apparent that each technology must find a way to deliver multimedia applications to be a viable force in the telecommunications marketplace in the not-so-distant future. It is up to the service provider to tap the global market and find a way to differentiate and exploit the advantages that one transmission system may have over another.

C. The Provider Matrix

Knowing what the technologies are, and knowing how each technology can provide distinct services is important to understanding telecommunications. Equally important is recognizing who is providing this technology and these services, and what is the impact of their position in international telecommunications.

Because many telecommunications systems are local, regional or national, providers of these services do not have much impact on international service. But increasingly, local service providers are investing in new services and technologies, trying to "hedge their bets," as it were, as to what will become successful in the future. Joint ventures, mergers, and acquisitions are frequently used to implement a cross-service investment strategy, and small, local companies, as well as large multinational corporations (MNCs) are playing the telecommunications game.

It is impossible to list all the players. Some of them are well-known. AT&T, Sprint, and MCI command a large share of the world's long distance phone service, together with other giants like British Telecom (BT), Deutsche Telecom, and Nippon Telegraph and Telephone (NTT). They are the ones that built the infrastructure, the long-distance lines and expensive submarine cables. They are also the ones that direct the world's attention to regulatory policy as regards settlement (or accounting) rates.

Still others are not as well known today, but will potentially become big players, indeed household names, in the near future. Huge satellite networks, such as Iridium, Globalstar, Odyssey, ICO, and Teledesic aim to put global communications truly within the reach of every human on the planet. Some of the names behind these networks are familiar: Motorola, Space Systems/Loral, TRW, Microsoft, and McCraw Communications. Not everyone can afford to build, launch and operate a satellite constellation of 12 (Odyssey) to 924 (Teledesic) satellites. But, there is undoubtedly room for the small communications company to find its niche in this marketplace. More services are needed, more infrastructure needs to be built, more education and technical support is required, and more agreement is needed among countries to set standards and regulations.

II. INTERNATIONAL REGULATION

A. Overview of Some of the Regulatory Problems

Chairman Hundt's five lanes of entry onto the information superhighway represent five main areas of service that the FCC regulates. The problem in recent years, however, is a great deal of cross-over among services, and the emergence of new services that seem to defy traditional definition. The FCC has different rules for different services, and information that is carried over network airwaves is subject to regulations that may not apply to the same information sent via the Internet. Therefore, defining a new service becomes a challenge for the FCC, as well as the private sector. A lot of money is spent in the pursuit of pigeon-holing a service into one category or another.

Additionally, service providers are increasingly entering other fields of communication, investing in services that they may have traditionally competed against. Today, local exchange providers may compete in the long distance market and vice-versa. Cable companies may provide telephone and internet services. The Internet may compete in the long-distance telephone market. And, a consortium of cable providers is trying to enter the field of high-power, direct broadcast satellite (DBS) service. *Primestar Partners* is a consortium of the largest cable television providers in the United States. Its service, *Primestar,* operates at a medium-power frequency, while its DBS competitors, *DirecTV, USSB* and *Echostar* operate at a high-power frequency. *Primestar* currently has a roll-up plan before the FCC and the Department of Justice to use a high-power orbital position that is currently owned by *MCI* and Rupert Murdoch's *NewsCorp. NewsCorp.* also owns several lucrative programming companies, including *FOX Sports.* The FCC and the Department of Justice are studying the competition aspects of the plan. Several programming and DBS competitors challenge the roll-up on antitrust grounds, claiming that the *Primestar* plan allows the powerful cable consortium to corner the market on popular programming, and then determine how that programming will be delivered.

The *Primestar* roll-up is illustrative of how technology has changed the way that services are defined, and how they will be regulated in the future. The old rules do not apply easily to the new services, so domestic regulators will have to redefine the way they view competition. These definitional problems are exaggerated in the in-

---

18. Thomas G. Krattenmaker argues in *Telecommunications Law and Policy* (1994) that the sinking of the *Titanic* led to the Radio Act of 1912. The disaster caused the government to realize the need to clear radio waves of interference in times of emergency, in addition to the need to give preference to certain types of radio transmissions, for example, military operations.

ternational context. Not only do industry representatives disagree with government analyses, but governments disagree with other governments as to which services fall into which categories, and what the rules for those categories ought to be.

In sum, definitions are in a constant state of flux, lines are being redrawn, rules are being rewritten. The question of where the plethora of new services should be placed will continue to be at the heart of a lucrative and heated battle among competitors in the private sector, with domestic and international regulators trying to keep up.

Telecommunications regulation was born out of necessity.[18] In the United States, the Radio Act of 1912 requires everyone seeking to broadcast to obtain a license, and from there, the question of who broadcasts, what, when, and how became a matter of policy and debate. Some of these issues, especially those regarding content control, access for political debate, and educational television, are political issues relevant in the domestic context. Each country regulates its telecommunications industry differently, and policies that the U.S. perceives as fundamental may not mean much to other countries.

There are, however, domestic policies that affect international trade in telecommunications. In the United States, like many countries, foreign interests are limited in ownership of broadcasting licenses. This regulation may appear archaic to many, a throwback to protecting national interests in times of war. But, many still argue that broadcast licenses should be granted to national companies dedicated to national programming. This approach ignores the reality that several broadcasters are only small subsidiaries of larger telecommunications conglomerates, some of them nationally owned, but it is increasingly common to find foreign interests merged with national companies. The MCI-British Telecom (BT) merger is a good example of this, as it represents the largest, most expensive merger at that time. The AT&T-BT arrangement is an even better example. To be sure, antitrust and foreign ownership issues were dissected by the FCC and the Department of Justice before these transactions were allowed.

Nevertheless, many countries maintain strict standards with respect to foreign ownership interests in telecommunications, especially in the field of broadcasting, or content programming. Developing countries may see foreign programming as another form of colonialism, although this sentiment is not confined to developing countries. France has always advocated French programming, and found the idea of opening up broadcasting markets, including DBS, to foreign interests and foreign programming unacceptable.[19] The European Union's (EU) decision not to include broadcast services (including DBS) in their WTO schedule, initially met strong opposition from countries like the United States, which eventually fell in line, along with several other countries in a tit-for-tat exchange, excluding broadcast services from their WTO schedule commitments.

But, statistics support the American initiative to open telecommunications markets to competition, and Europe's protectionist policies may explain why it lags behind the United States in its use of information technology, such as e-mail. "Access to the Internet is, according to reports from the Organization for Economic Cooperation and Development, five times higher in member countries with competitive markets than in those with monopoly providers."[20]

---

19. Beltz, *supra.*
20. Beltz, *supra.*

Perhaps the most contentious and difficult task domestic and international regulators perform is the allocation of radio spectrum. When radio and television broadcasting were the only uses for spectrum, and the amount of spectrum seemed infinite, the FCC had no trouble in granting licenses to just about anyone for just about anything. Today, the FCC requires detailed business plans from licensees, complete with engineering specifications and buildout requirements. The number of services now vying for limited spectrum causes headaches for international and domestic regulators. Internationally, the ITU is the organization responsible for "allocating" spectrum, through member consensus (discussed below). It is impossible within the limits of this Note to detail the problems of spectrum allocation, both practically and legally. Issues regarding spectrum allocation, however, are worthy of independent study, because of their effect on the international telecommunications community.

B. The United States Federal Communications Commission (FCC)

Newly-formed regulatory bodies from around the world often look to the FCC for guidance and example in how telecommunications in their own countries should, or at least could, be regulated. The ITU tries to advise these bodies through multilateral symposiums and policy forums, but many countries find this multilateral approach to be slow and inefficient. Many of the problems in telecommunications happen at lightening speed, often leaving the domestic regulators wondering about what just passed them by. An easier and more efficient approach is to follow the example set by your neighbor, especially if that neighbor has a successful, developed regulatory body.[21] In this manner, these countries benefit from the successes and failures of the FCC.

There are plenty of both. Many industry and regulatory experts hail the FCC as the most efficient, effective, and up-to-date telecommunications regulatory body in the world. They are probably right. But, there are just as many critics arguing the FCC sets a bad example for developing countries. The critics even suggest that actions taken by the FCC end up hurting the American telecommunications industry when it knocks on doors of newly-opened foreign markets.

An excellent example of this argument concerns the auction system the FCC has used in the past to allocate orbital positions and spectrum.[22] The auction system often precludes start-up companies, or companies with limited resources from competing with larger consortiums, regardless of their plans to utilize the spectrum or orbital position. Financially insecure countries may see this practice as a bonanza — a way to "sell" the rights to utilize domestic spectrum, or operate a satellite that has the capability of reaching their country. Why shouldn't developing countries use this practice to raise revenue for their own telecommunications industries, which are in dire need of upgrade and buildout? Wealthy, multinational consortiums certainly can afford it, right? It is difficult, and hypocritical for the FCC to criticize these countries for practicing that in which the FCC has engaged. But, the reality is that global com-

---

21. Frederick Tipson, *Global Telecommunications and Local Politics*, 72 CHI.-KENT L. REV. 583 (1996).

22. In 1996, MCI won a full-CONUS orbital slot, capable of disseminating DBS service across the country, for a sum of $ 682 million, the largest amount of money paid to that date for an orbital position. (This figure does not include the costs of manufacturing, insuring, launching and operating the satellite service.)

23. Anthony M. Rutkowski, *The International Telecommunication Union and the Shaping of Technological Developments*, in ISSUES IN TELECOMMUNICATIONS POLICY: A SOURCEBOOK 52 (Jane H. Yurow ed. 1983).

munications providers cannot afford to pay millions of dollars to each country for the right to offer their service. Such a cost is impossible, and may actually impede foreign investment in a developing country until the price is right. That is not to say that auctions are not a viable way for countries to decide between licensees, but the auction process may, on balance, end up hurting developing countries.

The FCC's history in regulating telecommunications in the United States illustrates the challenges that developing regulatory bodies face with their own industries. Although many of these issues are domestic in context, they are international in consequence. It should not surprise international negotiators, attempting to open broadcast markets around the world, when governments stall over the question of foreign influence in national programming.

C. The International Telecommunications Union (ITU)

It became apparent, early on, that regulating telecommunications domestically does not solve the problem of services that operate over oceans and across national boundaries. It became necessary to harmonize equipment, techniques, and regulations internationally.[23] Officially, the International Telegraph Union and the Radio-Telegraph Union were combined in 1932 to form what we know today as the International Telecommunications Union (ITU), although separate consultative committees on radio communications and telegraph/telephone communications still are maintained.

The ITU is an arena for member states to consult and coordinate details regarding international telecommunications. However, as a specialized agency of the United Nations (U.N.), membership has, in the past, been limited to members of the U.N. Although the ITU regularly allows other countries, in addition to manufacturers and industry representatives, to participate in forums (in a non-voting capacity), critics argue that the ITU should be open to all interested countries and parties. Members of the ITU strive to include developing member states, and have committed $ 360 million in an effort to help these countries expand their telecommunications industries. The ITU also has held consultative conferences in non-traditional sites, like Damascus, Syria.[24]

The ITU is governed by its own Convention, agreed upon by member states and reconsidered, revised, and renewed every seven years at the plenipotentiary conference of all ITU members. This allows the ITU to develop, substantively and jurisdictionally, with the development of technologies and services. There are other institutions and organizations that concern themselves with international telecommunications. The World Trade Organization is just one, and is discussed below. The ITU, however, strives to be as inclusive as possible, and seeks to consider telecommunications from the view of the manufacturer and provider, as well as the user and regulator. This practice earns the ITU a certain amount of respect in the telecommunications industry, although some argue that the ITU could be more effective if it had enforcement powers of its own. Unlike the FCC, the ITU cannot enforce judgements against members, but is "only as strong as the willingness of the sovereign states to abide by its treaties."[25]

There are five primary functions of the ITU: (1) spectrum allocation, (2) promulgation of technical standards, (3) development assistance, (4) research, and (5)

---

24. The 1997 meeting of ITU negotiators was convened in Damascus to drum up support for the GMPCS Memorandum of Understanding (MOU).

25. Bittner, *supra*, at 365.

26. Rutkowski, *supra*, at 56.

information handling. Each element is vital to the coordination and growth of international telecommunications. Any decision or undertaking by the ITU is usually made by a consensus of its members. This process, despite the numerous consultative and administrative conferences, can take a very long time and may not address issues as adequately as individual members may wish. Additionally, many of these functions, including spectrum allocation and promulgation of technical standards, require a relinquishing of sovereign power, in order to coordinate and allocate efficiently spectrum to one party or another at an international level. As contentious and imperfect as this system is, most members recognize it as a much more efficient and practical way to allocate spectrum than entering into numerous bilateral agreements whenever a problem is raised. Indeed, this is why the system works, despite a lack of enforcement authority vested in the ITU.

Supporters and critics alike agree that one of the ITU's most challenging functions is the promulgation of technical and operational standards. These include, but are not limited to "accounting rates and collection charges for various international telecommunication services, system interface specifications, plans for regional and global networks, the technical characteristics of signals and emissions, and the allocation of the radio spectrum to various radio services."[26] Not only does this definition hit a number of politically and economically "hot" topics, but it also suggests how vital this function of the ITU is in order to maintain harmony in a worldwide, integrated system.

The last two functions of the ITU, development assistance and information handling, are somewhat related. The ITU's research and information handling activities benefit anyone interested in the telecommunications industry. The ITU edits, sorts, and disseminates this information, through publications, educational programs and its vast central library, a vital resource for governments, scholars and industry officials. This education and information is equally, if not exceedingly important for developing countries. Annually, more than 300 experts from the ITU participate in field missions, and more that 400 people lead training projects in developing countries. An entire bureau was established by the ITU, often referred to as ITU-D (for development), with a budget through the 1990's for aiding developing nations to expand their telecommunications capabilities. ITU-D promotes and develops regional networks, strengthens technical and administrative services, and develops the human resources required to maintain the networks. Additionally, the ITU negotiates directly with international developing banks to secure funding for network development.

D. The World Trade Organization (WTO)

On 15 February 1997, sixty nine of the Members of the WTO signed a historic agreement, liberalizing trade in telecommunication services. The *Agreement on Basic Telecommunications Services* (*Telecom Agreement*, or *Agreement*) expands on the commitments made by individual members under the Uruguay Round *General Agreement on Trades and Services* (GATS) to include basic telecommunications. Under the auspices of the GATS, forty-four countries (all WTO Members), repre-

---

27. Charles M. Oliver, *WTO Agreement on Basic Telecommunications Services and FCC Implementation*, 15 COMMUNICATIONS LAWYER 13 (Winter 1998).

28. 20 of the original 70 signatories to the WTO Agreement missed a critical November 30, 1997 deadline for informing the WTO that steps had been taken domestically to bring their laws in line with the Agreement. *Telecommunications Reports*, December 8, 1997.

29. Oliver, *supra*, at 14.

senting 99 percent of the basic telecommunications revenues of all Members, committed to opening up markets to foreign ownership and competition.[27]

The statistics are a bit confusing, but the enormity of this decision should be readily apparent. The WTO Members committed to the *Telecom Agreement* represent 79 percent of the world economy, though only 19 percent of the world's population. Many of the important, populous, developing countries that have limited telecommunications sectors are not represented— yet—by the *Agreement*.

The essence of the *Telecom Agreement* is the opening up of what were once the largest monopolies in telecommunications: local public telephone services, domestic long distance services, international public long distance, and satellite services. The ambitious target date for this "big bang" was 5 February 1998, *i.e.*, the *Agreement* took effect one year after it was signed. As it turned out, one year was far too ambitious for some countries. Several WTO Members failed to implement, or even adopt their commitments by the February 1998 deadline.[28]

The real substance of the *Telecom Agreement* lies not in the general statement of obligations, known as the "Reference Paper," but in the nitty-gritty details of individual members' schedules. These schedules define and limit individual commitments to the Agreement. So, although the Agreement is broad in scope, it is restricted in its application due to the number of exceptions taken by individual members in their schedules. Additionally, a note by the WTO Director-General clarifies that "any market-opening commitments are implicitly subject to the availability of radio spectra."[29]

This "subject-to-availability" clause may not mean much in developing markets that have a decent amount of spectrum that is neither allocated nor in demand. However, international companies eyeing the American market may be in for a rude awakening when they go to the FCC and apply for spectrum. The FCC already is considering requests for spectrum, which until recently, have not even been named on the spectrum chart. Moreover, the number of applicants for any one piece of spectrum or orbital position makes it difficult for the FCC to choose among equally qualified service providers, and they often fall back on the much-criticized auction process, giving the spectrum or orbital position to the highest bidder. Of course, the FCC would often prefer that industry leaders work out a plan that allows several providers to share spectrum, but that requires industry agreement which is not always practical.

Certainly, the American market is not the focus for every telecommunications provider. Some even argue that the American market is saturated, and wisely focus their attention on larger, less-developed countries with enormous growth potential. But, many developing countries did not sign the *Telecom Agreement*. Those WTO developing country Members that did tended to make significantly limited commitments, wary of MNCs waiting on their doorsteps. Therefore, the questions being asked by these countries are "what does this *Agreement* mean to us, specifically, and what can the WTO do for us, generally?" These are questions that beg a satisfactory answer.

One answer was suggested in 1995 at an ITU Regulatory Colloquium. The Colloquium considered the impact of a WTO agreement on telecommunications on developing countries. The Colloquium found that participation by developing countries

---

30. International Telecommunications Union, *Trade Agreements on Telecommunications: Regulatory Implications; Report of the Fifth Regulatory Colloquium* 41-42 (Dec. 1995).

31. ITU, *Report of the Fifth Regulatory Colloquium, supra*, at 44.

32. Oliver, *supra*, at 15.

had significantly more benefits than drawbacks, including upgrading of telecommunications regulatory structures, potential benefits of better service, such as telemedicine and education, improved conditions of access to long distance carriers, and importantly, an increased interest and security for international investors.[30] The drawbacks, although slight balanced against the benefits, are worthy of mention. They include the probability of a reduction in hard-currency reserves, due to a drop in international accounting rates, as well as the distinct possibility that a national telecommunications provider, whether it be public or private, may not be able to compete against a much more efficient international provider. However, "developing countries are likely to benefit from embracing the WTO principles of market opening and allowing foreign investment as a way of keeping up investment needed to bring their networks to a level allowing them to compete internationally and attract investment in other economic activities to speed their development."[31]

The WTO *Telecom Agreement* commits governments and their national regulatory bodies to opening domestic markets to competition, under transparent, most-favored nation (MFN) principles. Only governments, however, can seek redress through the WTO's *Understanding on the Rules and Procedures Governing the Settlement of Disputes*. One scholar points out the *Agreement* is meaningful "only to the extent that it can be effectively enforced."[32] The WTO's dispute resolution process is a rigorous and efficient one, including consultations, panel reports, a right of appeal for the losing party, and a right of the winning party to retaliate against the losing party if the losing party does not comply with the results of the panel or appeal. Still, a telecommunications corporation must convince its government to bring an action to the WTO under the *Agreement*.

One scholar predicts the United States is likely to be the biggest litigator, because many large conglomerates with global aspirations reside in the United States.[33] However, the United States may find itself on the other side of the WTO dispute process over the FCC's proposed Benchmark Order, which the European Union, among others, has complained about, saying the FCC is trying to regulate extraterritorially.[34] The FCC already has adopted the International Satellite Service Order and the Foreign Participation Order (and of course, has implemented the Telecommunications Act of 1996, which predicts and predates the final *Telecom Agreement*), in compliance with the WTO commitments offered by the United States. The future impact of the *Agreement* on domestic regulation should prove to be interesting and challenging for the FCC.

E. The ITU, WTO, and the Future

The ITU and WTO have a lot to offer the telecommunications world. The ITU, however, has the benefit of knowing the industry, perhaps better than any other organization. Because it attempts to address both public and private sector concerns, the ITU can help educate the WTO. Some observers recommend future collaborations between the ITU and the WTO, for example, in organizing regional workshops to educate the public and private sectors on emerging telecommunications issues.

Ostensibly, the more global telecommunications becomes, the more need there is for international organizations like the ITU and WTO. However, many argue that

---

33. Oliver, *supra*, at 16.
34. *Bangemann: WTO Case Possible against U.S.*, TELECOMMUNICATIONS REPORT INTERNAT'L, Sept. 12, 1997.

neither the ITU nor WTO has the capability of keeping up with the dynamics of the telecommunications industry. Technology develops too fast, services are created overnight, and there is always a new provider around the corner waiting for a chance to jump into the communications race. Many companies are bypassing the bureaucracy of the ITU and going straight to the market itself, negotiating with individual governments and national regulatory bodies. This is the challenge for those domestic institutions. On the one hand, governments welcome the investment. On the other, it is if they are opening the door of the henhouse and inviting the fox in for coffee.

The solution does not appear to be very easy. As the following case studies of India and Brazil show, each country has different needs and different concerns. Yet, each is faced with the same dilemma: how to regulate a telecommunications industry that is in a constant state of growth and change?

III. DEVELOPING COUNTRY CASE STUDIES

A. India

India is one of the largest, most promising markets for telecommunications growth. It has a population of one billion, and a growing consumer class of 250-300 million courtesy of the expansion of its manufacturing and service sectors. India's middle class is hungry for consumer goods and services, including telecommunications services, which the government is hard-pressed to deliver. To raise India's teledensity to the developing world's average of 6 lines per 100 people, India must install more than 60 million new telephone lines at a cost of over $75 billion.[35] It has become painfully obvious that the Indian government alone cannot meet these investment requirements, and so India has become one of the first Asian countries to invite overseas capital and operational expertise into its telecommunications industry to provide basic local and long-distance networks. But, the story of investment and growth in India does not end there, as many investors and telecommunication corporations lament.

Most Asian governments keep a tight, paternalistic hands on the timetables, formats, and new entrants into their telecommunications markets.[36] They are wary of a "new colonialism" that might be introduced by western telecommunications giants touting paradigms of level playing fields, market access, and cost re-balancing. Many services, such as callback, have met with uncertainty, even contempt.[37] Unlike European telecommunications incumbents, which tend to be large, successful monopolies, Asia's state-owned telecommunications companies often portray themselves as victimized underdogs. This point of view is not surprising, given the number of well-financed MNCs courting these governments for the right to offer services that incumbent companies cannot provide, and in some cases, services that have implications which are not fully understood by government officials. For example, traditional wireline technology and local broadcasting are relatively easy to regulate, because it is easy to know who is using or watching what, and when. Satellite and wireless technology are harder to control and keep track of. Chances are greater that satellite providers will have the ability to offer services to households and businesses, domestic and foreign, without the knowledge or control of regulatory agencies. Addition-

---

35. Aileen A. Pisciotta & Talat Ansari, Kelley Drye & Warren LLP, *Foreign Investment and Finance of Telecommunications in India* (Aug. 1997).

36. Vineeta Shetty, *Playing to Win*, COMMUNICATIONS INTERNAT'L, June 1, 1997.

37. Shetty, *supra*.

ally, the presence of satellites that can cover a whole country is unnerving to many governments, which fear that their presence will compromise national security. Might the satellites, controlled by western MNCs, be used by the governments of these MNCs to snoop? In sum, new technology can bypass government control, and each government fears not just a loss of revenue, but also a loss of sovereignty. However, most Asian governments, including India, also recognize the benefits of new telecommunications technology. They have, at least tentatively, embraced the satellite, as well as the wireless, industries.

The regulatory dilemma is manifest in inconsistent policies and licensing procedures. Coupled with government instability and/or economic uncertainty, the policies frustrate potential investors and providers. One example of this frustration occurred in India, when a former Telecommunications Minister decided to increase the minimum bid price for each service region - after opening the bids for basic service licenses. To complicate matters further, the Minister also limited the number of bids an individual consortium could win.

The structure of government involvement in the telecommunications industry in India is itself complicated. Operation of local and long distance services are the responsibility of the Department of Telecommunications (DoT). Mahanagar Telephone Nigam Ltd. (MTNL) operates as a subsidiary of DoT, and is in charge of all telecommunications in Mumbai (Bombay) and New Delhi, India's two largest metropolitan areas. The government owns 100 percent of DoT, but only two-thirds of MTNL. Another subsidiary of DoT, Videsh Sanchar Nigam Ltd. (VSNL), is responsible for international services. Today, 20 percent of VSNL is privately held. As part of its commitment under the WTO *Telecom Agreement*, India established an independent regulator, the Telecom Regulatory Authority of India (TRAI), which consists of a chairman and two other members, who are responsible for setting standards, tariffs, dispute resolution and consumer protection.[38] The operation, or rather the cooperation, of these entities in the future remains an important factor in determining the performance of India's telecommunications market.

Under the National Telecom Policy (NTP) adopted in 1994, the Indian government made express commitments to opening up its telecommunications market to private investment. The NTP was to end the government monopoly over basic telecommunications. Although private sector participation was encouraged to provide universal basic service to rural areas, the privatization of DoT was indefinitely deferred. By signing the *Telecom Agreement*, DoT also committed to allowing one additional wireline operator to compete with DoT for ten years. There are several limitations on this commitment, however, including resale prohibition and the requirement that all competitors must be facilities-based. Foreign equity participation is limited to 25 percent. India also agreed to consider opening international services to competition in 2004. Slowly and cautiously, India is trying to attract private capital to fund the necessary upgrade and expansion of its telecommunications network.

It is only natural that telecommunications operators want to tout their newer, bigger, and better services to new markets, and it is true that value-added services like cellular are growing every year.[39] However, this view ignores the real need in coun-

---

38. Shetty, *supra*.

39. Cellular revenues are forecasted to quadruple to $123 billion by 2005, according to a Pan-Asian Telecom market report.

40. Sudhir Chowdhary, *Direct-to-home television (DTH): Channelling to Your Home...*, COMPUTERS TODAY, Jan. 1, 1997.

41. Chowdhary, *supra*.

tries like India, where the priority lies in the build out of capacity and the provision of universal service to rural areas. The problems with local and long-distance service are the amount of financing needed, and the slow return of that investment over several years. Instead, telecommunications providers focus their attention on multinational business, much of which is located in developed regions of Asia. This investment promises a quicker and more lucrative return.

Somewhere between the rural home and the multinational corporate consumer is the rising Indian middle class consumer, who is demanding more value-added services from PCS to DTH television. The average cable subscriber in India receives 20-30 channels via cable. With DTH, she can get more.[40] But the risks for a DTH provider in India are great. One analyst cautions that a DTH operator will have to be ready to bear losses in the Indian market for the first five years.[41] But, at least one DTH provider is willing to take that risk, partly because it believes the first entrant will be able to capture 70 percent of the estimated five million DTH subscribers in India by the year 2000. Star TV, and its owner, News Corp. have not found the sailing to be smooth on India's regulatory waters. The multinational giant has faced several disappointments in its attempt to provide DTH service to India.

The variety of needs, from the rural consumer to the MNC, require careful, intelligent regulation. Some investors and providers find the attendant lengthy timetable aggravating at best, and prohibitive at worst, and many experts agree that the implementation of telecommunications reforms in Indian will take years. Regulatory authorities must address a multitude of issues, including a determination as to which services should be competitive, the time frame within which competition should be implemented, the conditions and rules for competitors, conditions for licensing, specific technical and tariff terms of connection, and safeguards against anti-competitive behavior by dominant firms. In these respects, India is no different from other Asian countries. "Each country must achieve its own balance between opening segments of the telecom sector to market forces and ensuring the achievement of such social objectives as the expanded availability of basic services at a reasonable cost."[42]

B. Brazil

Brazil, like India, is in the process of developing its telecommunications market. But, there are vast differences between India's needs and Brazil's needs. Different needs call for different solutions. Brazil has chosen the popular avenue of privatization, which is revolutionizing telecommunications markets the world over. Unlike the United States, most countries in the past left the provision of telecommunications to the public sector. State-owned and operated telecommunications monopolies thrived in many countries, including the United Kingdom, France, Germany, Italy, Denmark, the Netherlands, Hungary, Chile, Venezuela, Mexico, Australia, Hong Kong, Indonesia, and New Zealand, just to name a few. All of these countries have now privatized, or are in the process of privatizing, their state "telcos."

To be sure, the divorce between a government and its telecommunications company is not without a number of difficulties. One of the most obvious is an enormous loss of telecommunications revenue to the government's coffers. So why would a government like Brazil's embark on such a process?

---

42. Chowdhary, *supra*
43. Thomas J. Casey & Simone Wu, *"Telecommunications Privatizations: An Overview,"* 17 HASTINGS INT'L & COMP. L.REV. 781.

Neo-classical economists provide one simple answer. Competition provides the consumer with a more efficient product at a lower cost. The free market is a better manager of public resources than the government. This answer may ring true. But, it ignores the reality that a modern telecommunications infrastructure is essential to overall economic development.[43] Traditionally, government-owned telecommunications facilities that served both public and private needs were viewed as essential to national security. The reality today is that an adequate telecommunications infrastructure is necessary to attract FDI.

Aside from a precious few countries with unique commodity or raw materials endowments for which there are few substitutes in either supply or consumption, there are perhaps no countries lacking a good telecommunications infrastructure, or at least a developing one, that are attractive to international investors. In other words, this infrastructure is just as significant as road, bridges, airports, and sea ports. How can you do business if you cannot communicate? Privatizing state assets, including telecommunications monopolies, is a way to attract financial, technological, and managerial investment needed to bring an antiquated network up to date. Usually, the private sector is in a better position to bring about this development than the public sector, where funds may be in short supply. In turn, investors in privatized telecommunications companies pave the road for investors in other industries.

Some governments see the privatization of their telecommunications markets as a way to raise much-needed funds to support other projects. In Greece, two cellular licenses were awarded to the private sector at a price tag of $320 million. In Venezuela, $1.9 billion was paid for a 40 percent stake in the Venezuelan national telephone company. This creates a win-win situation: consumers get a better product at a lower price, due to competition, and the government earns millions of dollars, while still retaining control over licensing standards and licensee obligations.

Another reason for national privatization concerns the speed of technology. It is apparent that technology is growing faster than the speed at which most government-owned telcos can provide services to consumers. It is often the private sector, especially large business, that demands these new services, and will often look to industry, not government, to provide them. Many governments, worried that their outdated regulations will be circumvented by new technology, would rather offer competitive service licenses, or even equity stakes in their own companies, than be left behind. Each country has a different reason — sometimes a combination of reasons — for privatizing its industries, but it is clear the telecommunications industry presents both a challenge and opportunity for most governments.

"The telecommunications sector presents a unique context for privatization. The industry involves ownership, maintenance, and operation of an extensive physical infrastructure, including customer premises equipment (CPE); public transmission facilities (terrestrial fiber optic, cable, microwave, and satellite); provision of services to end-users; and the development, integration, and implementation of technological advances to improve capabilities and services."[44] Some or all of these responsibilities may be offered up to private interests, whether domestic or foreign. Government may maintain control in some of these areas. Whatever control is maintained by the gov-

---

44. Casey & Wu, *supra*, at 786.

45. Edwin Taylor, *Privatization Scheme for Telecom Sector; Other Recent Developments*, LATIN AMERICAN L. & BUS. REP., Jan. 31, 1997.

46. Aileen A. Pisciotta, Kelley, Drye & Warren, LLP, *Telecommunications Regulation in Brazil*, Feb. 1998 (draft).

ernment, it should announce this intention up front and ensure that its activities are predictable and reasonable. Additionally, any government control of telecommunications operations should not be intertwined with the government's regulatory authority. Independent regulation leads to a transparent, consistent, and reliable system that encourages, rather than frustrates private investment. This separation of regulatory and operational control is vital for the success of the privatization.

Brazil unveiled the second level of its plan to privatize its telecommunications industry in December 1996. One of the government's key decisions at this juncture was to establish a new, independent regulatory agency, called the Agência Nacional de Telecomunicaçoes (ANATEL), modeled after America's FCC.[45] Long before the "General Law" was passed in July 1997, some telecom executives complained the agency is too closely linked to the Ministry of Communications (MOC), with which ANATEL maintains indirect links. In fact, the government retains substantial authority through MOC to make general determinations on the classification of services, as well as case-by-case determinations on the acceptable level of foreign investment and ownership restrictions.[46]

Brazil's privatization process started with a 1995 constitutional amendment, which removed the exclusivity rights originally granted to state-owned companies providing public services. What followed was a three step privatization process beginning with the 1996 "Minimal Law." This Law opened up mobile cellular, satellite, and value added services to private investment. In 1997, the "General Law" was passed, creating ANATEL, which has the authority to issue permits, establish rates and tariffs, set technical standards, and manage radio spectrum. The third step is the actual privatization of TELEBRAS, the state-owned and operated telecommunications provider, and its subsidiary, EMBRATEL, which coordinates long distance and international service. This three step process illustrates the importance that Brazil places on "public," as opposed to value-added, services. The government always has maintained the exclusive right to offer telephony, telegraphy, and other public telecommunications services, while private companies have been allowed to offer "other telecommunications services," such as paging. Even today, there are no license requirements for companies that want to offer value-added services in Brazil.

The most complicated level of this telecommunications reform is the process of privatizing TELEBRAS. The company most likely will be divided into four regional companies covering: Sao Paulo; the south and part of the southeast; the north; and the northeast, including the international operations of EMBRATEL.[47] Each region will be privatized separately, and then immediately opened to competition. The government, however, will retain a "Golden Share" of each privatized company to ensure public interest consideration.[48] As described above, this retention of control by the government is viable as long as the new "private" company is obliged to follow the rules set forth by the "independent" regulator, ANATEL.

In general, multinational executives praise Brazil's new legal regime for telecommunications, despite the fact that the government may determine, if it is in the national interest, that 51 percent of the capital in companies holding licenses and concessions must be controlled by Brazilians.[49] Even more promising is Brazil's

---

47. Pisciotta, Kelley, *Telecommunications Regulation in Brazil, supra.*
48. Pisciotta, Kelley, *Telecommunications Regulation in Brazil, supra.*
49. Taylor, *supra.*
50. *WTO Pact's Implementation Date in Limbo as 20 Countries Miss Approval Deadline,* TELECOMMUNICATIONS REPORTS, Dec. 8, 1997.

commitments under the WTO *Telecom Agreement*. Brazil has committed to liberalizing voice, data, telex, telegraph, fax, wireless, paging, and satellite services — an impressive commitment indeed. There are of course, limitations with respect to non-value-added services. All other services require government licensing, although the hope is that through Brazil's commitment to privatization and reform, this process will be transparent, objective, and consistent. Brazil also took some exceptions to the *Telecom Agreement* for the distribution of radio broadcast programming received directly by consumers. This encompasses broadcast services, DTH, DBS, and DARS, among other services. Additionally, in the satellite field, Brazil took an MFN exemption for direct broadcast services, which means that DTH or DBS providers will have to negotiate bilateral agreements with Brazil, perhaps on the basis of reciprocal treatment.

To date, Brazil has not been able to develop or maintain a telecommunications market that can meet the extraordinary demand of its citizens. For example, despite the high cost of Internet access, Brazil has watched Internet use climb from 60,000 subscribers in 1994 to more than 400,000 in 1996, with demand still rising. The government's three-level plan to reform and privatize is an encouraging step in the right direction, and it lays the legal and regulatory groundwork for the success of private telecommunications investment. However, Brazil is one of twenty WTO Member countries that missed a critical 30 November 1997 deadline for informing the WTO that steps were taken domestically to bring domestic laws into compliance with the *Telecom Agreement*, which officially came into effect on 5 February 1998.[50] Fortunately, Brazil is one of six countries, including the Dominican Republic, Portugal, the Philippines, Ghana, and Romania that have sent "provisional" acceptances in a good-faith effort to implement the *Agreement*. The success of Brazil's privatization and reform is as yet uncertain. But, it is clear that the government is striving to comply with its WTO commitments, and to provide the services its citizens demand. Brazil's future accomplishments will be of great interest to international investors and operators, who have a watchful eye on the world's fifth largest telecommunications market.

Conclusion

The one-year plan to adopt and implement the WTO Telecommunications Agreement, itself a tremendously significant accomplishment, was too ambitious for many countries. The plan did not take into account the vast changes to the organizational, administrative, regulatory, and often political and economical structures of the WTO Members that must fulfill their commitments. Not every country found itself in the established position that the United States held when the Agreement was signed. That is, not every country had an independent, educated regulatory body with vast experience in matters of competition and cutting-edge technologies. Countries like India and Brazil had to start over, almost from scratch, in restructuring regulatory bodies independent from, and yet complimentary to, existing government authorities in the services sector. This process cannot possibly be completed overnight, or even in a year. Sometimes, it is a process that is not completed successfully the first time. As the example of Brazil indicates, it may take more than one attempt to strike a successful balance. Additionally, regulatory bodies today, whether established like

---

51. "The United Nations and Technology for Sustainable Development," speech by Dr. Pekke Tarjanne, Secretary-General, ITU, Symposium at the University of San Francisco to commemorate the Fiftieth Anniversary of the founding of the United Nations in San Francisco.

52. Beltz, *supra*.

the FCC, or emerging, as many are around the world, must deal with the question of new technology and the rapidly changing face of telecommunications, which defies traditional rules of regulation. The lines between services and technologies are being erased, and providers are competing to offer a packed service, bundling a number of desired services into one package in order to attract increasingly educated, cost-conscious consumers. How regulation will keep pace with the industry is a challenge that faces every established and emerging regulatory body.

The WTO and the ITU will continue to hold very important places in the field of international telecommunications, but their roles, like the industry itself, will continue to evolve with the needs of governments, investors, corporate providers and consumers. On the Fiftieth Anniversary of the founding of the United Nations, Dr. Pekka Tarjanne, Secretary-General of the ITU, recognized that one of the ITU's most important roles in the future of developing markets is to educate and inform, especially with respect to emerging technologies, such as Wireless Local Loop (WLL) and GMPCS.[51] Additionally, the increasing presence of truly "global" systems requires careful and far-sighted negotiation and cooperation among members of the ITU, in order to ensure that the providers of these services have an adequate amount of available spectrum. Finally, a uniform set of rules is needed to create a transparent, stable framework for the expansion of global systems. The WTO is in a position to provide such rules.

Despite the historic role, and future potential for organizations like the WTO and ITU, many critics argue that "trends in technology and user demand are breaking down barriers between industries and nations at a pace far faster than formal rulemaking institutions can react."[52] Contrast the advance of the Internet with the negotiations leading to the signing of the WTO Telecommunications Agreement. When the Uruguay Round negotiations began, the World Wide Web and Netscape did not even exist. By the end of the Uruguay Round, in 1993, Microsoft Chairman Bill Gates was announcing that the Internet would be the driving force behind all of Microsoft's future development. In February 1997, when the final WTO Telecommunications Agreement was announced, the *Financial Times* of London reported on the launch of the first toll-quality Internet telephony service, capable of international telephone service at greatly reduced rates.[53] Not only did it take the members of the WTO ten years to agree on a common set of rules, it will take several years, decades even, to interpret and fully implement these rules, notwithstanding the WTO's ambitious one-year implementation deadline — which already has proven to be impossible for many countries.

Technology itself can offer consumers a way around outdated regulation, and often overpriced networks, by presenting new ways to receive the same services. Internet telephony and "callback" technology allow people to bypass expensive long-distance telephone services. Regulatory bodies are left with the difficult job of developing rules at a rate that can keep up with the onslaught of technology. This is the challenge for the world's regulatory bodies and international telecommunications and trade organizations, which must help developing countries identify their interests in telecommunications technology and competition. Only a knowledgeable, thoughtful, and flexible regulatory body, that is capable of as much dynamic growth as the industry itself, will be a part of the solution in the 21st century.

---

53. Beltz, *supra*

Chapter 12

International Antitrust Issues

I. An Overview of United States Antitrust Law

NOTE ON UNITED STATES ANTITRUST LAW*

This Note gives a *brief* overview of antitrust law in the United States. The overview is designed to lay a foundation for understanding the explosion of international antitrust issues. Accordingly, the important American antitrust statutes, as well as the case law arising thereunder, are discussed in this Note. The key statutes are Sections 1 and 2 of the Sherman Antitrust Act, Section 7 of the Clayton Act, the Hart-Scott-Rodino Antitrust Improvements Act, the Webb-Pomerene Act, the Export Trading Company Act of 1982, and the Wilson Tariff Act. The outcome of many of the antitrust cases depends on the burdens of proof; *i.e.*, the initial burden on the defendant often will determine the outcome. Accordingly, the discussion below examines these burdens. To be sure, this Note should not be mistaken for a summary of all relevant antitrust law — it is not. It is designed to highlight antitrust law that may raise concerns for international business lawyers.

Two points are important to keep in mind. First, federal antitrust jurisdiction is split between the Department of Justice ("DOJ") and the Federal Trade Commission[1] ("FTC"). Criminal enforcement of the antitrust laws, *i.e.*, Sections 1 and 2 of the Sherman Act, is brought solely by the DOJ. Second, the enforcement of antitrust law is subject to many considerations including what types of cases the DOJ and FTC decide to pursue, as well as the decisions of private parties to pursue antitrust actions under the antitrust law that the DOJ and FTC choose not to pursue.

THE 1890 SHERMAN ANTITRUST ACT

Section 1

Section 1 of the Sherman Antitrust Act ("Sherman Act") establishes the basic antitrust regime by prohibiting conduct that restrains trade. It is brief:

---

*. This Note was prepared by Doug Dziak, Esq.

1. The Jurisdiction of the FTC and the DOJ antitrust division overlap in all areas except criminal enforcement. *See* 65 Antitrust & Trade Reg. Rep. (BNA) 746 (1993).

Every contract, combination in the form of trust or otherwise, or conspiracy, in restraint of trade or commerce among the several States, or with foreign nations, is declared to be illegal. Every person who shall make any contract or engage in any combination or conspiracy hereby declared to be illegal shall be deemed guilty of a felony, and, on conviction thereof, shall be punished by fine not exceeding $10,000,000 if a corporation, or, if any other person, $350,000, or by imprisonment not exceeding three years, or by both said punishments, in the discretion of the court.[2]

Violations of the Sherman Act may be prosecuted as criminal or civil offenses.[3] The Sherman Act provides criminal fines of up to $10,000,000 for corporations. The Act also provides fines of $350,000 and up to three years' imprisonment for individuals who violate its provisions. In civil actions, a person injured by restricted conduct may be awarded treble damages and attorneys' fees.[4]

Proving a Section 1 Violation

Three elements are necessary to establish a violation of Section 1: (1) the existence of a contract, combination, or conspiracy among two or more separate entities that, (2) unreasonably restrains trade and, (3)affects interstate or foreign commerce.[5]

First, the government or private plaintiff must prove the existence of a contract, combination or conspiracy. The evidence of the unlawful agreement can take the form of an express agreement, which the United States Supreme Court has noted is often difficult to produce,[6] or through circumstantial evidence.[7]

The Supreme Court stated that to sustain a violation under the Sherman Act, evidence that excludes other permissible explanations for behavior, including independent action, must first be ruled out, especially if the alleged conduct is economically irrational.[8] This rationality threshold was used by the Court in *Matsushita Electric Industrial Co. v. Zenith Radio Corp*[9] to reverse a motion for summary judgment filed by the defendants. In *Mastushita*, the Court held that a defendant's actions must present a genuine issue of material fact.[10] The antitrust conduct complained of by the plaintiff must make rational economic sense and be consistent with furthering the defendant's interest.[11] In the absence of evidence of a conspiracy to monopolize, the defendants were entitled to summary judgment.[12] The Court noted that the aggressive price cutting by Japanese television manufacturers was the very essence of competition, and by punishing the Japanese producer's behavior through antitrust laws could chill the very behavior antitrust laws are created to protect.[13]

---

2. 15 U.S.C. § 1.

3. 15 U.S.C. §§ 1-2.

4. 15 U.S.C. § 15.

5. *See e.g.,* Maric v. St. Agnes Hospital Corp., 65 F.3d 310 (2d Cir. 1995).

6. *See* Local Union No. 189, Amalgamated Meat Cutters v. Jewel Tea Co., 381 U.S. 676, 720 (1965).

7. *See, e.g.,* United States v. General Motors, 384 U.S. 127 (1966) (explicit agreement not necessary).

8. *See* Matsushita Electric Industrial Co., Ltd. v. Zenith Radio Corp., 475 U.S. 574 (1986).

9. *475 U.S. 574 (1986).*

10. *See Matsushita Electric Industrial Co.,* 475 U.S. at 585.

11. *See Matsushita Electric Industrial Co.,* 475 U.S. at 585-588.

12. *See Matsushita Electric Industrial Co.,* 475 U.S. at 598.

13. *See Matsushita Electric Industrial Co.,* 475 U.S. at 594.

Second, while the text of the Sherman Act prohibits *every* contract, combination, or conspiracy, the Supreme Court has limited its scope to prohibit only unreasonable restraints of trade or commerce.[14] After all, every contract restrains trade in some way by virtue of the obligations incumbent on the parties, so the statute cannot mean literally what it says.

In *Standard Oil Company of New Jersey v. United States*[15], the Court stated the "standard of reason" analysis under common law was the analysis to determine whether particular acts fell within the Sherman Act. Chief Justice White observed that almost every contract can be construed as restraining trade and commerce.[16] At common law, reasonable contracts were not restrained, therefore, the Court stated the Sherman Act's scope should not include "reasonable" contracts.[17]

The Supreme Court further clarified the reasonableness analysis when interpreting the Sherman Act in *Board of Trade of the City of Chicago v. United States*[18]. As Justice Brandeis explained, a literal reading of the Sherman Act would outlaw the entire body of private contract law because "[e]very agreement concerning trade, every regulation of trade restraints." To bind, to restrain is the very essence of contract law.[19]

Recognizing the tension caused by a strict interpretation of the Sherman Act, Justice Brandeis stated, "[t]he true test of legality is whether the restraint imposed is such as merely regulates and perhaps thereby promotes competition or whether it is such as may suppress or even destroy competition."[20] This language remains the "quintessential expression of the rule of reason."[21]

While Justice Brandeis' language implies there is but one type of analysis appropriate for examining behavior under the Sherman Act, courts actually analyze Section 1 of the Sherman Act using two methods.[22] First, certain contracts, combinations, or restraints are deemed so anti-competitive that the actions are *per se* unlawful. However, the Court has affirmed its reluctance to use the *per se* rule stating, "[p]er se treatment is appropriate once experience with a particular kind of restraint enables the Court to predict with confidence that the rule of reason will condemn it."[23] Agreements that are not anti-competitive are judged based on a "rule of reason" analysis. The rule of reason attempts to determine the anti-competitive effects of conduct vis-a-vis the benefits of such conduct.

The final element of a Sherman Act violation requires the act to affect interstate commerce.[24] The regulatory power of the Sherman Act has the correspondingly broad reach of the Commerce Clause.[25] Thus, acts taking place completely in one State still can fall within the reach of the Sherman Act if they substantially affect interstate commerce.[26]

---

14. *See* Standard Oil Company of New Jersey v. United States, 211 U.S. 1, 50-57 (1911).

15. 211 U.S. 1 (1911).

16. *See Standard Oil Company of New Jersey,* 211 U.S. at 60.

17. *See Standard Oil Company of New Jersey,* 211 U.S. at 61.

18. 246 U.S. 231 (1918).

19. *See* Chicago Board of Trade v. United States, 246 U.S. 231, 238 (1918).

20. *See Chicago Board of Trade,* 246 U.S. at 238.

21. *See* ROBERT BORK, THE ANTITRUST PARADOX: A POLICY AT WAR WITH ITSELF, 43 (1993).

22. *See* ABA SECTION OF ANTITRUST LAW, ANTITRUST LAW DEVELOPMENTS, 40 (4th ed.1997).

23. *See* State Oil Co. v. Khan, 118 S.Ct. 275, 279 (1997).

24. *See, e.g.,* Maric v. St. Agnes Hospital Corp., 65 F.3d 310 (2d Cir. 1995).

25. *See, e.g.,* McLain v. Real Estate Bd. of New Orleans, 444 U.S. 232, 241 (1980).

26. *See, e.g., McLain,* 444 U.S. at 241-242.

Per Se Violations[27]

Definitive rules clarify prohibited behavior. But, the Supreme Court has been reluctant to draw such lines when deciding antitrust cases. The Court will use the *per se* rules only "when they relate to conduct that is manifestly anti-competitive."[28] Price fixing is the classic *per se* antitrust violation.[29] However, the Court was reluctant to develop *per se* rules in early antitrust cases.

After a period of inconsistent cases,[30] the Supreme Court held horizontal price fixing *per se* unlawful under the Sherman Act and ended the reasonableness inquiries of such horizontal price fixing.[31] In *United States v. Socony-Vacuum Oil*,[32] a number of oil companies formed a cooperative designed to maintain spot market prices of gasoline. This price fixing was done in an attempt to decrease the volatility faced by smaller, independent oil refiners during the Great Depression.[33] These smaller, independent refineries, who lacked storage facilities, were vulnerable to boom and bust cycles in the oil market and were forced into "distressed" sales of gasoline.[34] The Court rejected the price stabilization theory for the price fixing carried out by the oil companies. Instead the Court focused on the cartel's ability to increase prices. The Court held that although an agreement might fall short of dominion and control of a market, the fact that such an agreement could influence prices was enough to make such price fixing *per se* unlawful.[35]

After *Socony-Vacuum*, the *per se* prohibition against price fixing was no longer in question, and the need for reasonableness analysis in these price fixing cases was eliminated.[36] Furthermore, courts need not accept a defense based on governmental acquiescence with regard to price fixing.[37] Regardless of whether the government agrees to the price setting, a private plaintiff still can proceed with an antitrust action. This opportunity is especially relevant in international markets where one government may permit or perhaps encourage such behavior, yet the company might be violating United States antitrust law.[38]

---

27. This treatment of what constitutes a *per se* violation of the Sherman Act only examines a few situations to which the Court has attached a *per se* label to alleged violations of the Act. For a more complete treatment of *per se* violations under the Act see ABA SECTION OF ANTITRUST LAW, ANTITRUST LAW DEVELOPMENTS (4th ed. 1997).

28. *See* Continental T.V. v. GTE Sylvania Inc., 433 U.S. 36, 50 (1977).

29. *See* Robert Bork, *The Rule of Reason and the Per Se Concept: Price Fixing and Market Division*, 74 YALE L. J. 1, 2 (1965).

30. *See* Appalachian Coals, Inc. v. United States, 288 U.S. 344 (1933). *But see* United States v. Trenton Potteries Co., 273 U.S. 392 (1927).

31. *See* United States v. Socony-Vacuum Oil Co., Inc. et al., 310 U.S. 150, 223 (1940). *But see* Appalachian Coals v. United States, 288 U.S. 344 (1933). The Court used a "reasonableness standard" to determine if a cartel arrangement created by coal producers to stabilize prices in the wake of the Great Depression was permissible. However, the Court rejected a reasonableness analysis when presented with similar facts in *Socony-Vacuum*.

32. *310 U.S. 150 (1940)*

33. *See* United States v. Socony-Vacuum Oil Co., Inc., 310 U.S. 150, 169 (1940).

34. *See* Socony-Vacuum Oil Co., Inc., 310 U.S. at 171.

35. *See* Socony-Vacuum Oil Co., Inc., 310 U.S. at 224.

36. *See* Socony-Vacuum Oil Co., Inc., 310 U.S. at 225.

37. *See* Socony-Vacuum Oil Co., Inc., 310 U.S. at 225.

38. *See* Hartford Fire Insurance Co. v. California, 509 U.S. 764 (1993) (holding that unless there is a direct conflict between national laws, courts need not engage in comity balancing when deciding to exercise jurisdiction). This case is excerpted below.

The Court has held other arrangements as *per se* violations of the Sherman Act in addition to explicit price fixing. For example, it held certain territorial allocations to be *per se* unlawful. In *Palmer v. BRG of Georgia*,[39] the Court held an agreement that allocated territory between two rival bar review courses in Georgia and surrounding states was a *per se* violation of the Sherman Act.[40] In *Palmer*, the defendants had been competing in the Georgia market for bar review courses, but then entered into an agreement allocating Georgia one bar review course. The party allocating the Georgia territory agreed not to compete outside Georgia against the other bar review course.[41] The Court found this market allocation arrangement a *per se* violation of the Sherman Act, because the agreement stifled competition and raised prices by eliminating competition between the two producers.[42]

Certain boycotts are also *per se* violations of the Sherman Act. For example, in *United States v. General Motors*,[43] the Court held that joint collaborative action to restrict access to the supply of cars to low cost retailers was a *per se* violation of the Sherman Act. General Motors ("GM") attempted to restrict the ability of discount houses to obtain cars through GM dealers and resell them to the public, usually at a savings to the consumer.[44] The Court reasoned that such boycotts were *per se* violations of the Sherman Act, because restricting car supplies to low-cost retailers reduces price competition, causing higher prices to consumers.[45]

Unfortunately, the Supreme Court's analysis has been inconsistent in boycott cases. In *Northwest Wholesale v. Pacific Stationery & Printing Co*,[46] the Court wrote that there is more confusion about the scope and operation of the *per se* rule against group boycotts than in reference to any other aspect of the *per se* doctrine.[47] In *Northwest Wholesale*, the Court rejected the argument that an arrangement between cooperative members to remove a member amounted to a *per se* illegal boycott. It found that not every cooperative activity involving a restraint or exclusion will is a *per se* forbidden boycott, because the likelihood of predominantly anti-competitive consequences is absent in some boycotts.[48] The Court was willing to permit boycotts, as long as its purpose and outcome was not designed solely to eliminate competition — otherwise the boycott would be deemed *per se* unlawful.[49]

Attempts to set retail price floors are *per se* violations illegal under the Sherman Act. In *Dr. Miles Medical Co. v. John D. Park & Sons* Co.,[50] the Court held that such agreements are "injurious to the public interest and void."[51] The Court has limited the application of the *per se* rule in these cases, however, generally requiring a show-

---

39. 498 U.S. 46 (1990).

40. *See* Palmer v. BRG of Georgia, Inc., 498 U.S. 46, 49-50 (1990).

41. *See* Palmer, 498 U.S. at 47.

42. *See* Palmer, 498 U.S. at 49-50.

43. 385 U.S. 127 (1966).

44. *See* U.S. v. General Motors, 384 U.S. 127, 130-139 (1966).

45. *See* General Motors, 384 U.S. at 147.

46. 472 U.S. 284 (1985).

47. *See* Northwest Wholesale v. Pacific Stationery & Printing Co., 472 U.S. 284, 294 (1985).

48. *See* Northwest Wholesale, 472 U.S. at 295. *But see* Klor's, Inc. v. Broadway-Hale Stores, Inc., 359 U.S. 207 (1959)(holding that a group boycott initiated at the request of a retailer's competitor that restricted the supply of goods to a small local merchant was *per se* unlawful under the Sherman Act).

49. *See* Northwest Wholesale, 472 U.S. at 295 (1985).

50. *220 U.S. 373 (1911).*

51. *See* Dr. Miles Medical Co. v. John D. Park & Sons Co., 220 U.S. 373, 384-385 (1911).

ing that there is a presumption of rule of reason analysis in resale price arrangements. Without an explicit agreement from the producer to the distributor, the defendant in such cases usually is entitled to a rule of reason analysis.[52]

Certain tying agreements have also been declared *per se* violations of the Sherman Act. Tying occurs when a party agrees to sell a product "only on the condition that the buyer also purchases a different (or tied) product, or agrees that the buyer will not purchase that product from any other supplier."[53] For example, suppose Toyota required all Toyota car owners to purchase replacement headlights from Toyota. Toyota has tied the sale of replacement headlights to the sale of the car.

But, not all refusals to sell products separately will be construed to restrain competition.[54] Some conduct—conduct promoting efficiency—is permitted because the efficiency theory that the conduct is based on is consistent with the Sherman Act. Of course, if the seller has market power in one of the markets, the arrangement is likely unlawful.[55]

In *Eastman Kodak v. Image Technical Services*,[56] the Supreme Court found Kodak was violating the Sherman Act for tying the service of Kodak copiers to the purchase of original equipment manufacturer replacement ("OEM") parts.[57] Kodak refused to sell replacement parts to independent service organizations ("ISOs"), organizations that would underprice Kodak's service prices, while using the Kodak replacement parts. Finding sufficient evidence of a tying agreement, the Court reversed a motion for summary judgment by the lower courts in Kodak's favor.[58] Kodak argued that because it lacked market power in the market for copy machines, it could not possess market power in the market for replacement parts. The Court rejected Kodak's logic, finding Kodak possessed market power in the parts market. The determination of market power in a tied market is often a determinative factor in such cases.

The Supreme Court, perhaps revealing its general disfavor of the absolutes in antitrust, will change from *per se* analysis to rule of reason analysis when the circumstances no longer suggest *per se* analysis is appropriate. In *State Oil Company v. Khan*,[59] the Court overruled *Albrecht v. Herald Co.*[60] by holding that "vertical maximum price fixing, like the majority of commercial arrangements subject to the antitrust laws, should be evaluated under the rule of reason."[61]

Rule of Reason Analysis

As discussed above, some arrangements are deemed *per se* unlawful and clearly harmful to competition. But, many agreements or arrangements have justifiable business purposes which result in pro-competitive, pro-consumer benefits. Such cases are not treated under the *per se* rule, instead they are examined under a rule of reason analysis.

---

52. *See* Business Electronics v. Sharp Electronics, 485 U.S. 717, 724 (1988).
53. *See, e.g.*, Eastman Kodak Co. v. Image Technical Service, Inc., 504 U.S. 451, 461 (1991).
54. *See* Jefferson Parish Hospital Dist. No. 2 v. Hyde, 466 U.S. 2, 11-12 (1984).
55. *See* Jefferson Parish Hospital, 466 U.S. at 12.
56. 504 U.S. 451 (1991).
57. *See* Eastman Kodak Co., 504 U.S. at 457-458.
58. *See* Eastman Kodak Co., 504 U.S. at 464.
59. *See* State Oil Co. v. Khan, 118 S.Ct. 275 (1997).
60. 390 U.S. 145 (1968).
61. *See* State Oil Co., 118 S.Ct. at 285.

Indeed, the rule of reason analysis is presumptive and the most common analysis used under Section 1.[62] Justice Brandeis described the rational for the rule of reason in *Chicago Board of Trade v. United States.*[63]

> The true test of legality is whether the restraint imposed is such as merely regulates and perhaps thereby promotes competition or whether it is such as may suppress or even destroy competition. To determine that question the court must ordinarily consider the facts peculiar to the business to which the restraint is applied; its condition before and after the restraint was imposed; the nature of the restraint and its effects, actual or probable. The history of the restraint, the evil believed to exist, the reason for adopting the particular remedy, the purpose or end sought to be attained, are all relevant facts. This is not because a good intention will save an otherwise objectionable regulation or the reverse; but because knowledge of intent may help the court to interpret facts and to predict consequences.[64]

However, the Courts has not given a great deal of content to the rule of reason analysis. As a practical matter this void has resulted in the analytical framework, such as it is, being done by lower courts.

In *National Society of Professional Engineers v. United States*[65], the Supreme Court explained "[c]ontrary to its name, the Rule does not open the field of antitrust inquiry to any argument...[i]nstead, it focuses directly on the challenged restraint's impact on competitive conditions."[66] The rule of reason inquiry, then, is whether the challenged agreement is one that promotes competition, or one that suppresses competition.[67] Generally, a party challenging conduct must show some market power by the defendant. One method of showing market power is to define the relevant market in the narrowest terms possible. Thus, the balancing of anticompetitive effects are weighed against the pro-competitive benefits, which the defendant would present in rebuttal to the alleged anti-competitive effects of the agreement. The finder of fact then weighs the evidence to determine if the conduct violates the Section 1.

Section 2

Section 2 of the Sherman Act prohibits monopolization, attempts to monopolize, and conspiracies to monopolize. Section 2 of the Sherman Act is similar to Section 1, but Section 2 governs individual actors and unilateral actions. Section 2 of the Sherman Act reads:

> *Every* person who shall monopolize, or attempt to monopolize, or combine or conspire with any other person or persons, to monopolize any part of the trade or commerce among the several States, or with foreign nations, shall be deemed guilty of a felony, and, on conviction thereof, shall be punished by fine not exceeding $10,000,000 if a corporation, or, if any other person, $350,000, or by imprisonment not exceeding three years, or by both said punishments, in the discretion of the court.[68]

---

62. *See, e.g.,* U.S. v. Brown University, 5 F.3d 658, 688 (3rd Cir. 1993)

63. 246 U.S. 231 (1918).

64. *See* Chicago Board of Trade v. United States, 246 U.S. at 238.

65. *435 U.S. 679 (1978).*

66. *See* National Society of Professional Engineers *v.* United States, 435 U.S. 678, 688 (1978).

67. *See National Society of Professional Engineers*, 435 U.S. at 691.

68. *See* 15 U.S.C. § 2.

Thus, Section 2 of the Sherman Act prohibits monopolization, attempts to monopolize, or conspiracies to monopolize. Section 2, unlike Section 1, does not require multilateral or concerted acts.

The difficulty posed by Section 2 lies in the attempt to strike a balance between encouraging successful business practices, which benefit consumers through lower prices and a wider variety of goods, and punishing business practices, which harm consumers resulting in higher prices and market concentration. The United States Court of Appeals for the Second Circuit acknowledged the dilemma when it noted that if all instances of monopoly power were punished, then the antitrust laws would compel the very sloth they were intended to prevent.[69]

Monopoly Power

The Supreme Court has defined the offense of monopoly power under Section 2 as having two elements: (1) the possession of monopoly power in the relevant market, and (2) the willful acquisition or maintenance of that power as distinguished from growth or development as a consequence of a superior product, business acumen, or historical accident.[70] The first element requires proof that a party has the power to control prices or exclude competition.[71] Significantly, the Court has stated that monopoly power under Section 2 requires something greater than market power under Section 1.[72] Ordinarily, proof of monopoly is inferred from the predominant share of the market.[73] Determination of the proper market for analysis under Section 2 occurs after a factual inquiry into the commercial realities faced by consumers.[74] Not surprisingly, a very important factor is the definition of the relevant market. Once that is defined, the determination of monopoly power depends on the availability of alternative commodities for buyers, and the ability of producers to price above the competitive level for a sustained period.[75]

The second element of monopoly power under Section 2 requires willful acquisition or maintenance of power. This is to be distinguished from growth or development as a consequence of a superior product, business acumen, or historical accident.[76] Often, the very acts that establish a defendant possesses monopoly power will suffice to establish the willful acquisition or maintenance of the power. For example, the Court in *United States v. Grinnell* found the conduct that established Grinnell's monopoly in security and protective services also established their willful acquisition of monopoly power.[77]

But, how ought a court to determine whether monopoly power has been willfully acquired or maintained when such power arises from conduct that is not on its face designed to create monopoly? Developing a test for this second element in such circumstances has remained difficult. Courts have differed in their treatment of the problem. The Supreme Court has given limited guidance by offering factors to con-

69. *See* Berkey Photo, Inc. v. Eastman Kodak Company, 603 F.2d 263, 273 (2d Cir.1979).

70. *See e.g.,* United States v. Grinnell Corp., 384 U.S. 563, 570-571 (1966); Eastman Kodak v. Image Technical Services, 504 U.S. 451, 481 (1992).

71. *See* Eastman Kodak, 504 U.S. at 481.

72. *See* Eastman Kodak, 504 U.S. at 481.

73. *See* Grinnell Corp., 384 U.S. at 571.

74. *See* Eastman Kodak, 504 U.S. at 482.

75. *See* United States v. E.I. du Pont, 351 U.S. 377, 380 (1956).

76. *See* Eastman Kodak, 504 U.S. at 481.

77. *See* Grinnell Corp., 384 U.S. at 576.

sider. It stated that the conduct in question must be viewed in light of the effects on competitors, as well as its impact on consumers.[78] Analyzing the second element, then, depends on the specific circumstances of the facts.[79]

Attempts to Monopolize

Proof of attempted monopolization requires a plaintiff to prove (1) the defendant engaged in predatory or anti-competitive conduct with (2) a specific intent to monopolize and (3) a dangerous probability of achieving monopoly power.[80] The same analysis used in the monopolization cases to measure predatory or anti-competitive conduct is used in attempted monopolization cases.[81] But, unlike monopoly cases, which include a general intent element, attempted monopoly requires a specific intent to monopolize.[82] The specific intent to monopolize is more than an intent to compete vigorously. What is prohibited is conduct which is aimed at destroying competition itself.[83] Thus, courts eschew punishing single-firm actions so as to avoid chilling competition rather than squelching it.[84]

Interestingly, the United States Court of Appeals for the Ninth Circuit tried to blend the "dangerous probability of success" element in its analysis of attempted monopolization with other elements. However, the Supreme Court rejected this attempt to remove "dangerous probability of success" as an element from the attempted monopolization violation. In *Spectrum Sports, Inc. v. McQuillan,*[85] the Court held there must be proof of a dangerous probability of success from a defendant's predatory conduct. Absent such proof of potential success, a defendant cannot violate Section 2 of the Sherman Act.[86]

Conspiracy to Monopolize

Proof of a conspiracy to monopolize requires the plaintiff to show (1) concerted action; (2) an overt act in furtherance of the conspiracy; and (3) specific intent to monopolize.[87] Often the existence of the conspiracy will be proven using the same facts that would prove a violation under the Sherman Act's monopolization criteria.[88]

The same acts necessary in a monopolization or attempted monopolization claim are generally sufficient to provide the overt act necessary to prove conspiracy to monopolize. While a violation requires specific intent, no formal agreement is necessary to constitute an unlawful conspiracy.[89] As in most crimes, the intent can be inferred from the actions of the accused.

---

78. *See* Aspen Skiing Co. v. Aspen Highlands Skiing Corp., 472 U.S. 586, 605 (1985).

79. For a more detailed treatment of the various methodologies courts have used, see ABA SECTION OF ANTITRUST LAW, ANTITRUST LAW DEVELOPMENTS 250-252 (4th ed. 1997).

80. *See* Spectrum Sports, Inc., v. McQuillan, 506 U.S. 447, 456 (1993).

81. *See* ABA SECTION OF ANTITRUST LAW, ANTITRUST LAW DEVELOPMENTS 294 (4th ed. 1997).

82. *See* Spectrum Sports, Inc., 506 U.S. at 456.

83. *See* Spectrum Sports, Inc., 506 U.S. at 458-459.

84. *See* Spectrum Sports, Inc., 506 U.S. at 458.

85. *506 U.S. 447, 459 (1993).*

86. *See* Spectrum Sports, Inc., 506 U.S. at 459.

87. *See, e.g.,* Advanced Health-Care Services v. Radford Community Hospital, 910 F.2d 139, 150 (4th Cir. 1990); Volvo North America Corp. v. Men's Professional Tennis Council, 857 F.2d 55, 74 (2d Cir. 1988).

88. *See, e.g.,* Advanced Health-Care Services, 910 F.2d at 150.

89. *See, e.g.,* American Tobacco Co. v. United States, 328 U.S. 781, 809 (1946).

WILSON TARIFF ACT [90]

The Wilson Tariff Act ("Wilson Act") essentially forbids the same conduct as the Sherman Act.[91] Indeed, courts have construed the two statutes to forbid the same conduct.[92] However, the Wilson Act has an international limitation to it that is apparent from its language:

> Every combination, conspiracy, trust, agreement, or contract is declared to be contrary to public policy, illegal, and void when the same is made by or between two or more persons or corporations, either of whom, as agent or principal is engaged in importing any article from any foreign country into the United States, and when such combination, conspiracy, trust, agreement, or contract is intended to operate in restraint of lawful trade, or free competition in lawful trade or commerce, or to increase the market price in any part of the United States of any article or articles imported or intended to be imported into the United States, or of any manufacture into which such imported article enters or is intended to enter. Every person who shall be engaged in the importation of goods or any commodity from any foreign country in violation of this section, or who shall combine or conspire with another to violate the same, is guilty of a misdemeanor, and on conviction thereof in any court of the United States such person shall be fined in a sum not less than $100 and not exceeding $5000, and shall be further punished by imprisonment, in the discretion of the court, for a term not less than three month nor exceeding twelve months.[93]

Clearly, the language of the Wilson Act is similar to the language of the Sherman Act. However, the Wilson Act, by its language, deals only with importers.

THE CLAYTON ACT[94]

Section 7[95]

Mergers and acquisitions that have the potential to create anti-competitive market conditions are regulated by Section 7 of the Clayton Act. This Section reads in part:

Acquisition by one corporation of stock of another.

> No person engaged in commerce or in any activity affecting commerce shall acquire, directly or indirectly, the whole or any part of the stock or other share capital and no person subject to the jurisdiction of the Federal Trade Commission shall acquire the whole or any part of the assets of another person engaged also in commerce or in any activity affecting commerce, where in any line of commerce or in any activity affecting commerce in any section of the country, the effect of such acquisition may be substantially to lessen competition, or to tend to create a monopoly.

---

90. 15 U.S.C. § 8.

91. *See, e.g.*, Zenith Radio Corp. v Matsushita Electric Industrial Co., Ltd 513 F. Supp 1100, 1162-64. (E.D. Pa. 1981).

92. *See, e.g.*, Western Concrete Structures Co. v. Misui, 760 F.2d 1013, 1019 (1985); In re Japanese Electronic Products Antitrust Litigation, 723 F.2d 238, 252 (1983).

93. 15 U.S.C. § 8.

94. 15 U.S.C. § 18.

95. 15 U.S.C. § 18.

No person shall acquire, directly or indirectly, the whole or any part of the stock or other share capital and no person subject to the jurisdiction of the Federal Trade Commission shall acquire the whole or any part of the assets of one or more persons engaged in commerce or in any activity affecting commerce, where in any line of commerce or in any activity affecting commerce in any section of the country, the effect of such acquisition, of such stocks or assets, or of the use of such stock by the voting or granting of proxies or otherwise, may be substantially to lessen competition, or to tend to create a monopoly.[96]

Horizontal Mergers

Horizontal mergers, the combination of two or more firms that compete in the same market or markets, pose the highest risk of injuring competition. By eliminating competition, a firm may be able to exert market power—that is the ability to maintain prices above the competitive level—in that particular market through the merger. Accordingly, when analyzing a horizontal merger, courts and antitrust enforcement authorities examine several factors, including the market definition and the effect of the merger on competition.

Under Section 7 analysis, a product must be defined by both the product type and geographic location to determine if substitutes are available. The expectation is that substitutes should restrain the power of the merged company to raise prices above the competitive level.[97]

The merger analysis then shifts to examining the effect a merger will have on competition. Certain factors are the focus of attention, such as the merged entity's market share after the merger, and the barriers to entry in the particular industry. No single factor is determinative in deciding if a merger violates Section 7. Furthermore, a merging company can rebut the evidence of lessened competition. For example, the Supreme Court in *United States v. General Dynamics Co.*[98] held that although the government established a *prima facie* violation of Section 7, the defendant successfully rebutted this presumption by showing the merger would not unreasonable restrict competition.[99]

While not statutory law, the DOJ and FTC *Horizontal Merger Guidelines* explain how the government goes about evaluating horizontal mergers and acquisitions. These agencies, charged with the enforcement of Section 7, issued the *Merger Guidelines* to give potential merger or acquisition candidates some degree of predictability in the response of the agencies to possible transactions.[100] The unifying theme of the *Guidelines* is that mergers should not be permitted to create or enhance market power or to facilitate its exercise.[101]

The *Merger Guidelines* describe the process the DOJ and FTC will use in deciding whether to challenge a horizontal merger. First, the agency evaluates the merger

---

96. 15 U.S.C. § 18

97. *See, e.g.,* Brown Shoe Co. v. United States, 370 U.S. 294, 324 (1962).

98. *415 U.S. 486 (1974).*

99. *See* United States v. General Dynamics Co., 415 U.S. 486, 506 (1974).

100. DEPARTMENT OF JUSTICE & FEDERAL TRADE COMMISSION, HORIZONTAL MERGER GUIDELINES § 0 (April 8, 1997).

101. *Merger Guidelines, supra,* at § 0.1. The *Merger Guidelines* provide more detailed descriptions of the analysis the DOJ and FTC will use when deciding whether to challenge a horizontal merger. However, the *Guidelines* do not preclude a private party from attempting to block a merger under Section 7.

to determine if it will increase concentration enough to result in a concentrated market as defined by the agency.[102] Second, the agency will consider the potential adverse effects of the merger by examining the harm to competition.[103] Third, the agency will assess, whether a competing market participant would be timely, likely and sufficient to deter or counteract the anti-competitive effects of the merger.[104] Fourth, the agency will consider efficiency gains that could not be reasonably achieved by the merging parties.[105] Lastly, the agencies will determine, whether, but for the merger, if one of the parties would likely fail.[106]

Vertical Mergers

The Clayton Act also prohibits vertical mergers that would substantially lessen competition. Theoretically, vertical mergers can cause anti-competitive conditions by creating a market in which opportunities to competitors are foreclosed by the merger. However, challenges to vertical mergers are less likely because there is less chance of consumer harm. The *1984 Vertical Merger Guidelines* discuss three circumstances that may cause the DOJ to challenge such mergers. The markets must be highly integrated, entry into one market must be significantly difficult, and the structure of the other market must be so conducive to non-competitive behavior that entry into that market would be affected by the merger.[107]

For example, in *Ford Motor Co. v. United States*,[108] the Supreme Court upheld a divestiture ordered by the lower court, between Ford Motor Company and an independent manufacturer of spark plugs. The Court stated the presence of oligopoly in the automobile industry should not allow the automakers to lessen competition in the aftermarket for replacement parts. The Court reasoned that the tendency of mechanics to use the same parts to replace original manufacturer parts would lessen competition, thereby running afoul of Section 7 of the Clayton Act.[109]

While the Supreme Court's analysis of vertical mergers has been criticized as being theoretically unsound,[110] the DOJ and FTC occasionally will challenge a vertical merger and obtain a consent decree prohibiting certain practices. For example, a

---

102. *Merger Guidelines, supra,* at § 0.1. The agency will usually define a product market by describing a product and the geographic area. The agency will evaluate the market concentration using the Herfindahl-Hirschman Index ("HHI"). The HHI is determined by summing the squares of the individual market shares of all participants. The agency will divide the HHI measurement by placing it into one of three categories. First, if the post-merger HHI is below 1000, the market is considered unconcentrated and is unlikely to require further analysis by the agency. A post-merger HHI between 1000-1800 is considered moderately concentrated and might warrant further examination if the merger causes certain numerical changes to the HHI. A post-merger HHI greater than 1800 is considered highly concentrated and will require a lower threshold change in the HHI. The presumption of a concentrated market can be overcome. *Id.* at §§ 1.5-1.51.

103. *Merger Guidelines, supra,* at § 2.0.

104. *Merger Guidelines, supra,* at § 0.2.

105. *Merger Guidelines, supra,* at § 0.2. The fourth factor was included in the 1992 *Horizontal Merger Guidelines,* which were revised and reissued April 8, 1997.

106. *Merger Guidelines, supra,* at § 0.2. This failing firm defense is available if the merger would result in a market that would be no more concentrated than if the merger would not take place. Thus, a firm claiming this as a defense should not have reasonable alternatives to the merger. *Id.* at § 5.0.

107. *1984 Vertical Merger Guidelines* at § 4.21

108. 405 U.S. 562 (1972).

109. Ford Motor Co. v. United States, 405 U.S. 562, 568 (1972).

110. *See* ABA SECTION OF ANTITRUST LAW, ANTITRUST LAW DEVELOPMENTS 352 (4th ed. 1997).

joint venture between British Telecom and MCI was challenged, and a consent decree was issued, prohibiting the two companies from discriminating against American telecommunications carriers in accessing international telecommunications services.[111]

HART-SCOTT-RODINO ANTITRUST IMPROVEMENTS ACT OF 1976[112]

The Hart-Scott-Rodino Antitrust Improvements Act of 1976 ("HSR Act") requires parties to proposed mergers or acquisitions that meet specific criteria to inform the government of the plans of the merger. The HSR Act provides the government with a procedural device to slow mergers and examine them for potential antitrust problems, if the parties involved meet certain threshold levels. The HSR Act requires the following:

§ 18a. Pre-merger notification and waiting period.

(a) Filing

Except as exempted pursuant to subsection (c) of this section, no person shall acquire, directly or indirectly, any voting securities or assets of any other person, unless both persons (or in the case of a tender offer, the acquiring person) file notification pursuant to rules under subsection (d)(1) of this section and the waiting period described in subsection (b)(1) of this section has expired, if —

(1) the acquiring person, or the person whose voting securities or assets are being acquired, is engaged in commerce or in any activity affecting commerce;

(2)(A) any voting securities or assets of a person engaged in manufacturing which has annual net sales or total assets of $10,000,000 or more are being acquired by any person which has total assets or annual net sales of $100,000,000 or more;

(B) any voting securities or assets of a person not engaged in manufacturing which has total assets of $10,000,000 or more are being acquired by any person which has total assets or annual net sales of $100,000,000 or more; or

(C) any voting securities or assets of a person with annual net sales or total assets of $100,000,000 or more are being acquired by any person with total assets or annual net sales of $10,000,000 or more; and

(3) as a result of such acquisition, the acquiring person would hold —

(A) 15 *per centum* or more of the voting securities or assets of the acquired person, or

(B) an aggregate total amount of the voting securities and assets of the acquired person in excess of $15,000,000. In the case of a tender offer, the person whose voting securities are sought to be acquired by a person required to file notification under this subsection shall file notification pursuant to rules under subsection (d) of this section.

(b) Waiting period; publication; voting securities.

(1) The waiting period required under subsection (a) of this section shall —

---

111. *See* United States v. MCI Communications Corp. & BT Forty- Eight Co., 1994-2 Trade Cases (CCH) ¶ 70,730 (D.C. Cir.)(final judgment).
112. 15 U.S.C. 18a.

(A) begin on the date of the receipt by the Federal Trade Commission and the Assistant Attorney General in charge of the Antitrust Division of the Department of Justice (hereinafter referred to in this section as the "Assistant Attorney General") of —

(i) the completed notification required under subsection (a) of this section, or

(ii) if such notification is not completed, the notification to the extent completed and a statement of the reasons for such noncompliance, from both persons, or, in the case of a tender offer, the acquiring person; and

(B) end on the thirtieth day after the date of such receipt (or in the case of a cash tender offer, the fifteenth day), or on such later date as may be set under subsection (e)(2) or (g)(2) of this section.

(2) The Federal Trade Commission and the Assistant Attorney General may, in individual cases, terminate the waiting period specified in paragraph (1) and allow any person to proceed with any acquisition subject to this section, and promptly shall cause to be published in the Federal Register a notice that neither intends to take any action within such period with respect to such acquisition.

(3) As used in this section

(A) The term "voting securities" means any securities which at present or upon conversion entitle the owner or holder thereof to vote for the election of directors of the issuer or, with respect to unincorporated issuers, persons exercising similar functions.

(B) The amount or percentage of voting securities or assets of a person which are acquired or held by another person shall be determined by aggregating the amount or percentage of such voting securities or assets held or acquired by such other person and each affiliate thereof.

(c) Exempt transactions.

The following classes of transactions are exempt from the requirements of this section —

(1) acquisitions of goods or realty transferred in the ordinary course of business;

(2) acquisitions of bonds, mortgages, deeds of trust, or other obligations which are not voting securities;

(3) acquisitions of voting securities of an issuer at least 50 *per centum* of the voting securities of which are owned by the acquiring person prior to such acquisition;

(4) transfers to or from a Federal agency or a State or political subdivision thereof;

(5) transactions specifically exempted from the antitrust laws by Federal statute;

(6) transactions specifically exempted from the antitrust laws by Federal statute if approved by a Federal agency, if copies of all information and documentary material filed with such agency are contemporaneously filed with the Federal Trade Commission and the Assistant Attorney General;

(7) transactions which require agency approval under section 1467a(e) of title 12, section 1828(c) of title 12, or section 1842 of title 12;

(8) transactions which require agency approval under section 1843 of title 12 or section 1464 of title 12, if copies of all information and documentary material filed with any such agency are contemporaneously filed with the Federal Trade Commission and the Assistant Attorney General at least 30 days prior to consummation of the proposed transaction;

(9) acquisitions, solely for the purpose of investment, of voting securities, if, as a result of such acquisition, the securities acquired or held do not exceed 10 *per centum* of the outstanding voting securities of the issuer;

(10) acquisitions of voting securities, if, as a result of such acquisition, the voting securities acquired do not increase, directly or indirectly, the acquiring person's *per centum* share of outstanding voting securities of the issuer;

(11) acquisitions, solely for the purpose of investment, by any bank, banking association, trust company, investment company, or insurance company, of (A) voting securities pursuant to a plan of reorganization or dissolution; or (B) assets in the ordinary course of its business; and

(12) such other acquisitions, transfers, or transactions, as may be exempted under subsection (d)(2)(B) of this section.

(d) Commission rules.

The Federal Trade Commission, with the concurrence of the Assistant Attorney General and by rule in accordance with section 553 of title 5, consistent with the purposes of this section —

(1) shall require that the notification required under subsection (a) of this section be in such form and contain such documentary material and information relevant to a proposed acquisition as is necessary and appropriate to enable the Federal Trade Commission and the Assistant Attorney General to determine whether such acquisition may, if consummated, violate the antitrust laws; and

(2) may -

(A) define the terms used in this section;

(B) exempt, from the requirements of this section, classes of persons, acquisitions, transfers, or

transactions which are not likely to violate the antitrust laws; and

(C) prescribe such other rules as may be necessary and appropriate to carry out the purposes of this section.

(e) Additional information; waiting period extensions.

(1) The Federal Trade Commission or the Assistant Attorney General may, prior to the expiration of the 30-day waiting period (or in the case of a cash tender offer, the 15-day waiting period) specified in subsection (b)(1) of this section, require the submission of additional information or documentary material relevant to the proposed acquisition, from a person required to file notification with respect to such acquisition under subsection (a) of this section prior to the expiration of the waiting period specified in subsection (b)(1) of this section, or from any officer, director, partner, agent, or employee of such person.

(2) The Federal Trade Commission or the Assistant Attorney General, in its or his discretion, may extend the 30-day waiting period (or in the case of a cash tender offer, the 15-day waiting period) specified in subsection(b)(1) of this section for an additional period of not more than 20 days (or in the case of a cash tender offer, 10 days) after the date on which the Federal Trade Commission or the Assistant Attorney General, as the case may be, receives from any person to whom a request is made under paragraph (1), or in the case of tender offers, the acquiring person, (A) all the information and documentary material required to be submitted pursuant to such a request, or (B) if such request is not fully complied with, the information and documentary material submitted and a statement of the reasons for such noncompliance. Such additional period may be further extended only by the United States district court, upon an application by the Federal Trade Commission or the Assistant Attorney General pursuant to subsection (g)(2) of this section.

(f) Preliminary injunctions; hearings.

If a proceeding is instituted or an action is filed by the Federal Trade Commission, alleging that a proposed acquisition violates section 18 of this title, or section 45 of this title, or an action is filed by the United States, alleging that a proposed acquisition violates such section 18 of this title, or section 1 or 2 of this title, and the Federal Trade Commission or the Assistant Attorney General (1) files a motion for a preliminary injunction against consummation of such acquisition *pendente lite*, and (2) certifies the United States district court for the judicial district within which the respondent resides or carries on business, or in which the action is brought, that it or he believes that the public interest requires relief *pendente lite* pursuant to this subsection, then upon the filing of such motion and certification, the chief judge of such district court shall immediately notify the chief judge of the United States court of appeals for the circuit in which such district court is located, who shall designate a United States district judge to whom such action shall be assigned for all purposes.

(g) Civil penalty; compliance; power of court.

(1) Any person, or any officer, director, or partner thereof, who fails to comply with any provision of this section shall be liable to the United States for a civil penalty of not more than $10,000 for each day during which such person is in violation of this section. Such penalty may be recovered in a civil action brought by the United States.

(2) If any person, or any officer, director, partner, agent, or employee thereof, fails substantially to comply with the notification requirement under subsection (a) of this section or any request for the submission of additional information or documentary material under subsection (e)(1) of this section within the waiting period specified in subsection (b)(1) of this section and as may be extended under subsection (e)(2) of this section, the United States district court -

(A) may order compliance;

(B) shall extend the waiting period specified in subsection (b)(1) of this section and as may have been extended under subsection (e)(2) of this section until there has been substantial compliance, except that, in the case of a tender offer, the court may not extend such waiting period on the basis of a failure, by the person whose stock is sought to be acquired, to comply substantially with such notification requirement or any such request; and

(C) may grant such other equitable relief as the court in its discretion determines necessary or appropriate, upon application of the Federal Trade Commission or the Assistant Attorney General.

(h) Disclosure exemption.

Any information or documentary material filed with the Assistant Attorney General or the Federal Trade Commission pursuant to this section shall be exempt from disclosure under section 552 of title 5, and no such information or documentary material may be made public, except as may be relevant to any administrative or judicial action or proceeding. Nothing in this section is intended to prevent disclosure to either body of Congress or to any duly authorized committee or subcommittee of the Congress.

(i) Construction with other laws.

(1) Any action taken by the Federal Trade Commission or the Assistant Attorney General or any failure of the Federal Trade Commission or the Assistant Attorney General to take any action under this section shall not bar any proceeding or any action with respect to such acquisition at any time under any other section of this Act or any other provision of law.

(2) Nothing contained in this section shall limit the authority of the Assistant Attorney General or the Federal Trade Commission to secure at any time from any person documentary material, oral testimony, or other information under the Antitrust Civil Process Act (15 U.S.C. 1311 et seq.), the Federal Trade Commission Act (15 U.S.C. 41 et seq.), or any other provision of law.

(j) Report to Congress; legislative recommendations.

Beginning not later than January 1, 1978, the Federal Trade Commission, with the concurrence of the Assistant Attorney General, shall annually report to the Congress on the operation of this section. Such report shall include an assessment of the effects of this section, of the effects, purpose, and need for any rules promulgated pursuant thereto, and any recommendations for revisions of this section.[113]

The HSR Act is supplemented by implementing regulations that are contained in the *Code of Federal Regulations*.[114] Merging entities are generally required to file a premerger notification with the DOJ and FTC when the parties meet the following criteria: (1) one of the parties has annual net sales (or revenues) or total assets exceeding $100 million and the other party has annual net sales (or revenues) or total assets exceeding $10 million;[115] and

(2) the price or value of the acquired stock or assets exceeds $15 million or the person obtains greater than 15 percent of the acquired firm's outstanding stock.[116]

The HSR Act creates a mandatory waiting period before an acquisition can be completed. In cash tender offers, the initial statutory waiting period is 15 days after

---

113. 15 U.S.C. § 18a
114. *See* 16 C.F.R. § 801.1.
115. 15 U.S.C. § 18a(a)(2).
116. 15 U.S.C. § 18a(a)(3).

the parties file notification with the government.[117] The regulatory agencies can then pursue an investigation if they so choose by requesting additional information from the merging parties.[118] The DOJ or FTC is able to seek an injunction against a proposed merger that either believes to violate the antitrust laws.[119]

WEBB-POMERENE ACT[120]

The Webb-Pomerene Act allows American exporters a limited antitrust exemption to form and operate associations to engage in collective export sales.[121] The Act reads:

§ 61 Export trade; definitions

The words "export trade" wherever used in this sub-chapter mean solely trade or commerce in goods, wares, or merchandise exported, or in the course of being exported from the United States or any Territory thereof to any foreign nation; but the words "export trade" shall not be deemed to include the production, manufacture, or selling for consumption or for resale, within the United States or any Territory thereof, of such goods, wares, or merchandise, or any act in the course of such production, manufacture, or selling for consumption or for resale.

The words "trade within the United States" wherever used in this sub-chapter mean trade or commerce among the several States or in any Territory of the United States, or in the District of Columbia, or between any such Territory and another, or between any such Territory or Territories and any State or States or the District of Columbia, or between the District of Columbia and any State or States.

The word "association" wherever used in this sub-chapter means any corporation or combination, by contract or otherwise, of two or more persons, partnerships, or corporations.

§ 62 Export trade and antitrust legislation

Nothing contained in the Sherman Act (15 U.S.C. 1 *et seq.*) shall be construed as declaring to be illegal an association entered into for the sole purpose of engaging in export trade and actually engaged solely in such export trade, or an agreement made or act done in the course of export trade by such association, provided such association, agreement, or act is not in restraint of trade within the United States, and is not in restraint of the export trade of any domestic competitor of such association:

Provided, That such association does not, either in the United States or elsewhere, enter into any agreement, understanding, or conspiracy, or do any act which artificially or intentionally enhances or depresses prices within the United States of commodities of the class exported by such association, or which substantially lessens competition within the United States or otherwise restrains trade therein.

---

117. *See* 15 U.S.C. § 18a(b)(1)(A)-(B).
118. *See* 15 U.S.C. § 18a(e)(1).
119. *See* 15 U.S.C. § 18a(f).
120. 15 U.S.C. §§ 61-65.
121. *See* 15 U.S.C. § 62 (1994).

§ 63 Acquisition of stock of export trade corporation

Nothing contained in section 18 of this title shall be construed to forbid the acquisition or ownership by any corporation of the whole or any part of the stock or other capital of any corporation organized solely for the purpose of engaging in export trade, and actually engaged solely in such export trade, unless the effect of such acquisition or ownership may be to restrain trade or substantially lessen competition within the United States.

§ 64 Unfair methods of competition in export trade

The prohibition against "unfair methods of competition" and the remedies provided for enforcing said prohibition contained in the Federal Trade Commission Act (15 U.S.C. 41 *et seq.*) shall be construed as extending to unfair methods of competition used in export trade against competitors engaged in export trade, even though the acts constituting such unfair methods are done without the territorial jurisdiction of the United States.

§ 65 Information required from export trade corporation; powers of Federal Trade Commission

Every association which engages solely in export trade, within thirty days after its creation, shall file with the Federal Trade Commission a verified written statement setting forth the location of its offices or places of business and the names and addresses of all its officers and of all its stockholders or members, and if a corporation, a copy of its certificate or articles of incorporation and bylaws, and if unincorporated, a copy of its articles or contract of association, and on the 1st day of January of each year every association engaged solely in export trade shall make a like statement of the location of its offices or places of business and the names and addresses of all its officers and of all its stockholders or members and of all amendments to and changes in its articles or certificate of incorporation or in its articles or contract of association. It shall also furnish to the Commission such information as the Commission may require as to its organization business, conduct, practices, management, and relation to other associations, corporations, partnerships, and individuals. Any association which shall fail so to do shall not have the benefit of the provisions of sections 62 and 63 of this title, and it shall also forfeit to the United States the sum of $100 for each and every day of the continuance of such failure, which forfeiture shall be payable into the Treasury of the United States, and shall be recoverable in a civil suit in the name of the United States brought in the district where the association has its principal office, or in any district in which it shall do business. It shall be the duty of the various United States attorneys, under the direction of the Attorney General of the United States, to prosecute for the recovery of the forfeiture. The costs and expenses of such prosecution shall be paid out of the appropriation for the expenses of the courts of the United States.

Whenever the Federal Trade Commission shall have reason to believe that an association or any agreement made or act done by such association is in restraint of trade within the United States or in restraint of the export trade of any domestic competitor of such association, or that an association either in the United States or elsewhere has entered into any agreement, understanding, or conspiracy, or done any act which artificially or intentionally enhances or depresses prices within the United States of commodities of the class exported by such association, or which substantially lessens competition within the United States or otherwise restrains trade therein, it shall summon such association, its officers, and agents to appear before it, and thereafter conduct an investigation into the alleged violations of law. Upon investigation, if it shall conclude that the law has been violated, it may make to such association recommendations for the readjustment of its business, in order that it may thereafter maintain its organization and management and conduct its business in accordance with law. If such association fails to comply with the recommendations of the Federal Trade Commission, said Commission shall refer its findings and recommendations to the Attorney General of the United States for such action thereon as he may deem proper.

For the purpose of enforcing these provisions the Federal Trade Commission shall have all the powers, so far as applicable, given it in the Federal Trade Commission Act (15 U.S.C. 41 *et seq.*).

§ 66. Short title

This sub-chapter may be cited as the "Webb-Pomerene Act."

What does the above-quoted language amount to? The Webb-Pomerene Act exempts export association activities, which do not restrain United States commerce or restrain American exporters from entering third markets, from antitrust prosecutions.[122] The exemption is limited to the export of goods, wares, and merchandise. The Webb-Pomerene exemption does not prohibit a foreign antitrust authority from prosecuting the association under foreign antitrust statutes. The export association must file their articles or contract of association, as well as an annual report with the FTC to qualify for the exemption.[123] Unlike the Export Trading Company Act of 1982, discussed below, the Webb-Pomerene Act does not apply to trade in services.[124]

In practice, the combined effects of (1) courts narrowly interpreting the Webb-Pomerene Act and (2) yearly compliance requirements make the Act a relatively unimportant antitrust exemption.[125] While they once accounted for a significant share of American exports, the most available data indicate that Webb-Pomerene exports now account for a fairly negligible share.[126]

EXPORT TRADING COMPANY ACT OF 1982[127]

The Export Trading Company Act of 1982 ("ETCA") created an office within the Department of Commerce to promote and encourage the creation of export trade associations and export trading companies. This new office was to facilitate the flow of information between producers of exportable goods and services and firms offering export trade services.[128] The ETCA allows a party to apply for a certificate of review declaring that the activity does not violate the antitrust laws of the United

---

122. *See* 15 U.S.C. § 62
123. *See* 15 U.S.C. § 65
124. *See* 15 U.S.C. § 4002 (A)(1).
125. *See* SPENCER WEBER WALLER, INTERNATIONAL TRADE AND U.S. ANTITRUST LAW § 6.05(1) (1997).
126. *See* JOHN M. BREEN, EXPORT PRACTICE CUSTOMS AND INTERNATIONAL TRADE LAW 429 (Terence P. Stewart ed., 1994). In the period 1930-1934, Webb-Pomerene exports accounted for 12.2 percent of American exports. By 1976, Webb-Pomerene exports accounted for just 1.5 percent of American exports.
127. 15 U.S.C. §§ 4001-4021.
128. 15 U.S.C. § 4003.

States.[129] If the applicant is successful, the Secretary of Commerce will issue a certificate specifying what export trade activities are covered under the ETCA.[130] The ETCA not only acts as a government pre-approval of certain activities, it also restricts private antitrust remedies.[131] The future viability and usefulness of both Webb-Pomerene associations and export combinations organized under the ETCA has been questioned.[132]

II. Standing

Pfizer, Inc. v. Government of India
434 U.S. 308 (1978)

MR. JUSTICE STEWART delivered the opinion of the Court.

In this case we are asked to decide whether a foreign nation is entitled to sue in our courts for treble damages under the antitrust laws. The respondents are the Government of India, the Imperial Government of Iran, and the Republic of the Philippines. They brought separate actions in Federal District Courts against the petitioners, six pharmaceutical manufacturing companies. The actions were later consolidated for pretrial purposes in the United States District Court for the District of Minnesota. [The Court observed that similar actions were also brought by Spain, South Korea, West Germany, Colombia, Kuwait, and the Republic of Vietnam. Vietnam was a party to this case in the Court of Appeals and was named as a respondent in the petition for *certiorari*. Subsequent to the filing of the petition Vietnam's complaint was dismissed by the District Court on the ground that the United States no longer recognized the Government of Vietnam; the dismissal was affirmed by the Court of Appeals. Vietnam has not participated as a party in this Court. Some of the other suits have been withdrawn and the rest are pending.] The complaints alleged that the petitioners had conspired to restrain and monopolize interstate and foreign trade in the manufacture, distribution, and sale of broad spectrum antibiotics, in violation of §§ 1 and 2 of the Sherman Act, as amended, 15 U. S. C. §§ 1, 2. Among the practices the petitioners allegedly engaged in were price fixing, market division, and fraud upon the United States Patent Office. India and Iran each alleged that it was a "sovereign foreign state with whom the United States of America maintains diplomatic relations"; the Philippines alleged that it was a "sovereign and independent government." Each respondent claimed that as a purchaser of antibiotics it had been damaged in its business or property by the alleged antitrust violations and sought treble damages under § 4 of the Clayton Act, 15 U.S.C. § 15, on its own behalf and on behalf of several cases of foreign purchasers of antibiotics.

---

129. 15 U.S.C. § 4013 (a).

130. 15 U.S.C. § 4013 (b).

131. *See* 15 U.S.C. § 4016(b)(1). Under the ECTA, private parties can sue for injunctive relief, actual damages, the loss of interest on damages, and the cost of the suit. However, the ECTA does not include treble damages.

132. *See* SPENCER WEBER WALLER, INTERNATIONAL TRADE AND U.S. ANTITRUST LAW § 6.05 (3) (1997). Professor Waller suggests using the laws as bargaining chips in future trade negotiations dealing with international cartels.

The petitioners asserted as an affirmative defense to the complaints that the respondents as foreign nations were not "persons" entitled to sue for treble damages under § 4. In response to pretrial motions the District Court held that the respondents were "persons" and refused to dismiss the actions. The trial court certified the question for appeal. The Court of Appeals for the Eighth Circuit affirmed, and adhered to its decision upon rehearing en banc. We granted *certiorari* to resolve an important and novel question in the administration of the antitrust laws.

I

As the Court of Appeals observed, this case "turns on the interpretation of the statute." A treble-damages remedy for persons injured by antitrust violations was first provided in § 7 of the Sherman Act, and was re-enacted in 1914 without substantial change as § 4 of the Clayton Act. Section 4 provides:

> "[A]ny person who shall be injured in his business or property by reason of anything forbidden in the antitrust laws may sue therefor in any district court of the United States in the district in which the defendant resides or is found or has an agent, without respect to the amount in controversy, and shall recover threefold the damages by him sustained, and the cost of suit, including a reasonable attorney's fee."

Thus, whether a foreign nation is entitled to sue for treble damages depends upon whether it is a "person" as that word is used in § 4. There is no statutory provision or legislative history that provides a clear answer; it seems apparent that the question was never considered at the time the Sherman and Clayton Acts were enacted. [The Court observed that Sherman and Clayton Acts each provide that the word "person" "shall be deemed to include corporations and associations existing under or authorized by the laws of either the United States, the laws of any of the Territories, the laws of any State, or the laws of any foreign country." 15 U.S.C. §§ 7, 12. It stated that it is apparent that this definition is inclusive rather than exclusive, and does not by itself imply that a foreign government, any more than a natural person, falls without its bounds.]

The Court has previously noted the broad scope of the remedies provided by the antitrust laws. "The Act is comprehensive in its terms and coverage, protecting all who are made victims of the forbidden practices by whomever they may be perpetrated." *Mandeville Island Farms, Inc. v. American Crystal Sugar Co.*, 334 U. S. 219, 236. And the legislative history of the Sherman Act demonstrates that Congress used the phrase "any person" intending it to have its naturally broad and inclusive meaning. There was no mention in the floor debates of any more restrictive definition. Indeed, during the course of those debates the word "person" was used interchangeably with other terms even broader in connotation. For example, Senator Sherman said that the treble-damages remedy was being given to "any party," and Senator Edmunds, one of the principal draftsmen of the final bill, said that it established "the right of anybody to sue who chooses to sue." 21 Cong. Rec. 2569, 3148 (1890).

In light of the law's expansive remedial purpose, the Court has not taken a technical or semantic approach in determining who is a "person" entitled to sue for treble damages. Instead, it has said that "[t]he purpose, the subject matter, the context, the legislative history, and the executive interpretation of the statute are aids to construction which may indicate" the proper scope of the law. *United States v. Cooper Corp.*, 312 U. S. 600, 605.

II

The respondents in this case possess two attributes that could arguably exclude them from the scope of the sweeping phrase "any person." They are foreign, and they are sovereign nations.

A

As to the first of these attributes, the petitioners argue that, in light of statements made during the debates on the Sherman Act and the general protectionist and chauvinistic attitude evidenced by the same Congress in debating contemporaneous tariff bills, it should be inferred that the Act was intended to protect only American consumers. Yet it is clear that a foreign *corporation* is entitled to sue for treble damages, since the definition of "person" contained in the Sherman and Clayton Acts explicitly includes "corporations and associations existing under or authorized by... the laws of any foreign country." Moreover, the antitrust laws extend to trade "with foreign nations" as well as among the several States of the Union. 15 U.S.C. §§ 1, 2. Clearly, therefore, Congress did not intend to make the treble-damages remedy available only to consumers in our own country.

In addition, the petitioners' argument confuses the ultimate purposes of the antitrust laws with the question of who can invoke their remedies. The fact that Congress' foremost concern in passing the antitrust laws was the protection of Americans does not mean that it intended to deny foreigners a remedy when they are injured by antitrust violations. Treble-damages suits by foreigners who have been victimized by antitrust violations clearly may contribute to the protection of American consumers.

The Court has noted that § 4 has two purposes: to deter violators and deprive them of "'the fruits of their illegality,'" and "to compensate victims of antitrust violations for their injuries." *Illinois Brick Co. v. Illinois*, 431 U.S. 720, 746. To deny a foreign plaintiff injured by an antitrust violation the right to sue would defeat these purposes. It would permit a price fixer or a monopolist to escape full liability for his illegal actions and would deny compensation to certain of his victims, merely because he happens to deal with foreign customers.

Moreover, an exclusion of all foreign plaintiffs would lessen the deterrent effect of treble damages. The conspiracy alleged by the respondents in this case operated domestically as well as internationally. If foreign plaintiffs were not permitted to seek a remedy for their antitrust injuries, persons doing business both in this country and abroad might be tempted to enter into anticompetitive conspiracies affecting American consumers in the expectation that the illegal profits they could safely extort abroad would offset any liability to plaintiffs at home. If, on the other hand, potential antitrust violators must take into account the full costs of their conduct, American consumers are benefitted by the maximum deterrent effect of treble damages upon all potential violators.

B

The second distinguishing characteristic of these respondents is that they are sovereign nations. The petitioners contend that the word "person" was clearly understood by Congress when it passed the Sherman Act to exclude sovereign governments. The word "person," however, is not a term of art with a fixed meaning wherever it is used, nor was it in 1890 when the Sherman Act was passed. Indeed, this Court has expressly noted that use of the word "person" in the Sherman and Clayton Acts did not create a "hard and fast rule of exclusion" of governmental bodies. *United States v. Cooper Corp.*, 312 U.S. at 604-605.

On the two previous occasions that the Court has considered whether a sovereign government is a "person" under the antitrust laws, the mechanical rule urged by the petitioners has been rejected. In *United States v. Cooper Corp.*, the United States sought to maintain a treble-damages action under § 7 of the Sherman Act for injury to its business or property. The Court considered the question whether the United States was a "person" entitled to sue for treble damages as one to be decided not "by a strict construction of the words of the Act, nor by the application of artificial canons of construction," but by analyzing the language of the statute "in the light, not only of the policy, intended to be served by the enactment, but, as well, by all other available aids to construction." *Id.*, at 605. The Court noted that the Sherman Act provides several separate and distinct remedies: criminal prosecutions, injunctions, and seizure of property by the United States on the one hand, and suits for treble damages "granted to redress private injury" on the other. *Id.*, at 607-608. Statements made during the congressional debates on the Sherman and Clayton Acts provided further evidence that Congress affirmatively intended to exclude the United States from the treble-damages remedy. *Id.*, at 611-612. Thus, the Court found that the United States was not a "person" entitled to bring suit for treble damages.

In *Georgia v. Evans*, 316 U.S. 159, decided the very next Term, the question was whether Georgia was entitled to sue for treble damages under § 7 of the Sherman Act. The Court of Appeals, believing that the *Cooper* case controlled, had held that a State, like the Federal Government, was not a "person." This Court reversed, noting that *Cooper* did not hold "that the word 'person,' abstractly considered, could not include a governmental body." 316 U.S., at 161. As in *Cooper*, the Court did not rest its decision upon a bare analysis of the word "person," but relied instead upon the entire statutory context to hold that Georgia was entitled to sue. Unlike the United States, which "had chosen for itself three, potent weapons for enforcing the Act," 316 U.S. at 161, a State had been given no other remedies to enforce the prohibitions of the law. To deprive it also of a suit for damages "would deny all redress to a State, when mulcted by a violator of the Sherman Law, merely because it is a State." *Id.*, at 162-163. Although the legislative history of the Sherman Act did not indicate that Congress ever considered whether a State would be entitled to sue, the Court found no reason to believe that Congress had intended to deprive a State of the remedy made available to all other victims of antitrust violations.

It is clear that in *Georgia v. Evans* the Court rejected the proposition that the word "person" as used in the antitrust laws excludes all sovereign states. And the reasoning of that case leads to the conclusion that a foreign nation, like a domestic State, is entitled to pursue the remedy of treble damages when it has been injured in its business or property by antitrust violations. When a foreign nation enters our commercial markets as a purchaser of goods or services, it can be victimized by anticompetitive practices just as surely as a private person or a domestic State. The antitrust laws provide no alternative remedies for foreign nations as they do for the United States. [The Court observed that while THE CHIEF JUSTICE'S dissent says there are "weapons in the arsenals of foreign nations" sufficient to enable them to counter anticompetitive conduct, such as cartels or boycotts, such a political remedy is hardly available to a foreign nation faced with monopolistic control of the supply of medicines needed for the health and safety of its people.] The words of *Georgia v. Evans* are thus equally applicable here:

> "We can perceive no reason for believing that Congress wanted to deprive a [foreign nation], as purchaser of commodities shipped in [international] commerce, of the civil remedy of treble damages which is available to other purchasers who suffer through violation of the Act.... Nothing in the Act, its his-

tory, or its policy, could justify so restrictive a construction of the word 'person' in § 7.... Such a construction would deny all redress to a [foreign nation], when mulcted by a violator of the Sherman Law, merely because it is a [foreign nation]." 316 U.S. at 162-163.

III

The result we reach does not involve any novel concept of the jurisdiction of the federal courts. This Court has long recognized the rule that a foreign nation is generally entitled to prosecute any civil claim in the courts of the United States upon the same basis as a domestic corporation or individual might do. "To deny him this privilege would manifest a want of comity and friendly feeling." *The Sapphire*, 11 Wall. 164, 167; *Monaco v. Mississippi*, 292 U.S. 313, 323 n.2; *Banco Nacional de Cuba v. Sabbatino*, 376 U.S. 398, 408-409; *see* U.S. Const., Art. III, § 2, cl. 1. To allow a foreign sovereign to sue in our courts for treble damages to the same extent as any other person injured by an antitrust violation is thus no more than a specific application of a long-settled general rule. To exclude foreign nations from the protections of our antitrust laws would, on the other hand, create a conspicuous exception to this rule, an exception that could not be justified in the absence of clear legislative intent.

Finally, the result we reach does not require the Judiciary in any way to interfere in sensitive matters of foreign policy. [The Court stated that in a letter that was presented to the Court of Appeals when it reconsidered this case en banc, the Legal Adviser of the Department of State advised "that the Department of State would not anticipate any foreign policy problems if...foreign governments [were held to be] 'persons' within the meaning of Clayton Act § 4." A copy of this letter is contained in the Memorandum for the United States as *Amicus Curia* in opposition to the petition for a writ of *certiorari* filed in this Court.] It has long been established that only governments recognized by the United States and at peace with us are entitled to access to our courts, and that it is within the exclusive power of the Executive Branch to determine which nations are entitled to sue. *Jones v. United States*, 137 U.S. 202, 212; *Guaranty Trust Co. v. United States*, 304 U.S. 126, 137-138; *Banco Nacional de Cuba v. Sabbatino, supra*, at 408-412. Nothing we decide today qualifies this established rule of complete judicial deference to the Executive Branch.

We hold today only that a foreign nation otherwise entitled to sue in our courts is entitled to sue for treble damages under the antitrust laws to the same extent as any other plaintiff. Neither the fact that the respondents are foreign nor the fact that they are sovereign is reason to deny them the remedy of treble damages Congress afforded to "any person" victimized by violations of the antitrust laws.

Accordingly, the judgment of the Court of Appeals is *Affirmed*.

....

Mr. Chief Justice Burger, with whom MR. JUSTICE POWELL and MR. JUSTICE REHNQUIST join, *dissenting*.

The Court today holds that foreign nations are entitled to bring treble-damages actions in American courts against American suppliers for alleged violations of the antitrust laws; the Court reaches this extraordinary result by holding that for purposes of § 4 of the Clayton Act, foreign sovereigns are "persons," while conceding paradoxically that the question "was never considered at the time the Sherman and Clayton Acts were enacted."

I dissent from this undisguised exercise of legislative power, since I find the result plainly at odds not only with the language of the statute but also with its legislative history and precedents of this Court. The resolution of the delicate and important policy issue of giving more than 150 foreign countries the benefits and remedies enacted to protect American consumers should be left to the Congress and the Executive. Congressional silence over a period of almost a century provides no license for the Court to make this sensitive political decision vastly expanding the scope of the statute Congress enacted.

A

"The starting point in every case involving construction of a statute is the language itself." *Blue Chip Stamps v. Manor Drug Stores*, 421 U.S. 723, 756 (1975)....
.The relevant provisions here are § 1 of the Clayton Act in which the word "person" is defined, and § 4 in which the treble-damages remedy is conferred on those falling within the precisely enumerated categories. Section 1 provides, in relevant part:

> "The word 'person' or 'persons' wherever used in this Act shall be deemed to include corporations and associations existing under or authorized by the laws of either the United States, the laws of any of the Territories, the laws of any State, or the laws of any foreign country."

Section 4 then incorporates this definition by providing:

> "That any person who shall be injured in his business or property by reason of anything forbidden in the antitrust laws may sue therefor in any district court of the United States in the district in which the defendant resides or is found or has an agent, without respect to the amount in controversy, and shall recover threefold the damages by him sustained, and the cost of suit, including a reasonable attorney's fee."

Even on the most expansive reading, these two sections provide not the slightest indication that Congress intended to allow foreign nations to sue Americans for treble damages under our antitrust laws. The very fact that foreign sovereigns were not included within the definition of "person" despite the explicit reference to corporations and associations existing under the "laws of any foreign country" in the same definition ought to be dispositive under established doctrine governing interpretation of statutes. I therefore see no escape from the conclusion that the omission by Congress of foreign nations was deliberate.

The inclusion of foreign *corporations* within the statutory definition in no sense argues for a different characterization of Congress' intent. At the time of the passage of both the Sherman and Clayton Acts, foreign sovereigns, even when acting in their commercial capacities, were immune from suits in the courts of this country under the doctrine of sovereign immunity. *See The Schooner Exchange v. McFaddon*, 7 Cranch 116 (1812); *Ex parte Peru*, 318 U.S. 578 (1943); *Mexico v. Huffman*, 324 U.S. 30 (1945). Foreign corporations, of course, had no such immunity. *See, e.g., Shaw v. Quincy Mining Co.*, 145 U.S. 444, 453 (1892); *In re Hohorst*, 150 U.S. 653, 662-663 (1893). Given that "person" as used in the Clayton and Sherman Acts refers to both antitrust plaintiffs and defendants, the decision of Congress to include foreign corporations while omitting foreign *sovereigns* from the definition most likely reflects this differential susceptibility to suit rather than any intent to benefit foreign consumers or to enlist their help in enforcing our antitrust laws. It would be little short of preposterous to think that Congress in 1890 was concerned about giving such rights to foreign nations, even though it might well decide to do so now.

Respondents' claim that this disparate treatment cannot be justified today when foreign states effectively control many large foreign corporations and when sovereign immunity has been limited by the Foreign Sovereign Immunities Act of 1976, Pub. L. 94-583, 90 Stat. 2891, is not an argument appropriately addressed to or considered by this Court. If revisions in the statute are required to take into account contemporary circumstances, that task is properly one for Congress particularly in light of the sensitive political nature and foreign policy implications of the question.

The Court's reliance on the references to "foreign nations" in §§ 1 and 2 of the Sherman Act and § 1 of the Clayton Act to support an argument that Congress was specifically concerned with foreign commerce and foreign nations in 1890 when the disputed definition was enacted is similarly unavailing. As a threshold matter, congressional concern with the foreign commerce of the United States does not entail either a desire to protect foreign nations or a willingness to allow them to sue Americans for treble damages in our courts. The Webb-Pomerene Act, as amended, 15 U.S.C. § 61 *et seq.*, passed within only a few years of the Clayton Act, indicates that such a concern may instead be served at the *expense* of foreign states and consumers. [The Webb-Pomerene Act exempts certain actions of export associations from the antitrust laws, but the exemption applies only if the association's actions do not restrain trade or affect the price of exported products within the United States, and do not restrain the export trade of any domestic competitor of the association. 15 U.S.C. § 62. Although the Act was subsequently regarded as carving out an exemption from the antitrust laws, the legislative history indicates considerable question at the time whether the conduct of exporters meeting the conditions specified in the Act would have violated the antitrust laws even without the putative exemption. *See* H.R. Rep. No. 50, 65th Cong., 1st Sess., 2 (1917).]

In any event, the relevant language of §§ 1 and 2 of the Sherman Act, as subsequently incorporated in the Clayton Act, does not support respondents' contention. The reference to "commerce...with foreign nations" appeared only in the final draft of the Act as reported by the Senate Judiciary Committee, and replaced language in the numerous earlier drafts of Senator Sherman to the following effect:

> "That all arrangements, contracts, agreements, trusts, or combinations between persons or corporations made with a view or which tend to prevent full and free competition in the production, manufacture, or sale of articles of domestic growth or production, or of the sale of articles *imported* into the United States,...are hereby declared to be against public policy, unlawful and void...." 21 CONG. REC. 2598 (1890) (first draft) (emphasis added).

The focus of this language on protecting *domestic* consumers from anticompetitive practices affecting the *importation* of goods into the United States could not be more clear, nor could the absence of any attention to affording comparable protection for foreign consumers of American exports. The language substituted by the Judiciary Committee — language tracking that appearing in the Commerce Clause — was chosen to mollify the objections of those Senators who felt the proposed statute exceeded Congress' constitutional power to regulate commerce, [and] that language was not intended to work any substantive change in the focus or scope of the Act. To read this language as evidencing an intent to protect foreign nations or foreign consumers simply belies its lineage.

B

The legislative history of the treble-damages remedy gives no more support to the result reached by the Court than does the language of the statute. As five of the eight judges of the Court of Appeals concluded—and indeed as the majority here concedes—"Congress, in passing § 4 of the Clayton Act, 15 U.S.C. § 15, gave no consideration *nor did it have any legislative intent whatsoever, concerning the question of whether foreign governments are 'persons' under the Act*." 550 F.2d 396, 399. The conversion of this silence in 1890 into an affirmative intent in 1978 is indeed startling.

The failure of Congress even to consider the question of granting treble-damages remedies to foreign nations provides the clearest possible argument for leaving the question to the same political process that gave birth to the Sherman and Clayton Acts. To rely on the absence of any *express* congressional intent to exclude foreign nations from taking advantage of the treble-damages remedy is a remarkable innovation in statutory interpretation. It is a strange way to camouflage the unassailable conclusion that the legislative history offers no affirmative support for the result reached today. Further, as this Court observed just last Term, the legislative history of the treble-damages remedy which does exist "indicate[s] that it was conceived of primarily as a remedy for '[t]he people of the, United States as individuals,' especially consumers." *Brunswick Corp. v. Pueblo Bowl-O-Mat, Inc.*, 429 U.S. 477, 486 n.10 (1977), *quoting from* 21 Cong. Rec. 1767-1768 (1890) (remarks of Sen. George). What we so recently saw as primarily a remedy for American consumers is now extended to all the nations of the world-a boon Congress might choose to grant but has not done so.

C

In the absence of any helpful language in the statute or any affirmative legislative history, the Court attempts to base its expansive reading of "person" on Mr. Justice Frankfurter's decision in *Georgia v. Evans*, 316 U.S. 159 (1942), granting the State of Georgia and all other *domestic* States the right to sue for treble damages. I fail to see how that result dictates this one.

In *Georgia v. Evans*, Mr. Justice Frankfurter concluded that absent the right to sue for treble damages, our States would be left without any remedy against violators of the antitrust laws. The Court today analogizes the situation of foreign nations to that of the States in *Evans*, and finds the analogy dispositive. When viewed solely in terms of the remedies specifically provided by the antitrust laws, the plight of domestic States and foreign sovereigns may, in this limited respect, be roughly comparable. But the very limited scope of the inquiry in *Evans* precludes consideration of the manifold and patently obvious respects in which foreign nations and our own domestic States differ-cogent differences bearing on the question under consideration here, though obviously not at all on the Court's inquiry in *Evans*.

First, the disparate treatment of foreign and domestic States is a legitimate source of concern only on the assumption that Congress in passing the Sherman Act intended - or even contemplated - that these two categories of political entities were so essentially alike that they were entitled to the same remedies against anticompetitive conduct. As I have already suggested, this assumption derives no support from either the statutory language or anything in the legislative history. Although our own States were also not the expressly intended beneficiaries of the Act. to deny them the treble-damages remedy would, as Mr. Justice Frankfurter perceived, have the unmistakable result of effectively denying surrogate protection to American citizens in whose behalf the State acts and for whose benefit the Sherman Act was enacted. Thus, while the result in *Evans* is a tolerable taking of certain liberties with the literal language of the statute, the congruence of that result with Congress' purpose can scarcely be doubted. This same logic, however, does not even remotely apply to the situation of foreign nations.

Second, it simply is not the case that absent a treble-damages remedy, foreign nations would be denied any effective means of redress against anticompetitive practices by American corporations. Unlike our own States, whose freedom of action in this regard is constrained by the Commerce and Supremacy Clauses, foreign sovereigns remain free to enact and enforce their own comprehensive antitrust statutes and to impose other more drastic sanctions on offending corporations. One need look no further than the laws of respondents India and the Philippines for evidence that such remedies are possessed by foreign nations. And indeed, *amicus* West Germany has demonstrated that such laws are not mere idle enactments. During the pendency of this action, it notified petitioner Pfizer that a proceeding under German antitrust law was being commenced involving some of the same allegations which are made in the complaint filed by respondents in their treble-damages actions in this country.

While problems of jurisdiction and discovery may render antitrust actions against foreign defendants somewhat more problematic than a suit against a corporation in its own country, the limited experience of the Common Market nations in applying their antitrust laws to foreign corporations suggests that such difficulties are certainly not insoluble and are likely exaggerated. And, as the presently existing treaty between the United States and West Germany indicates, *reciprocal* agreements providing for cooperation in antitrust investigations undertaken by foreign nations are an effective means of mitigating the rigors of discovery in foreign jurisdictions.

Third, it takes little imagination to realize the dramatic and very real differences in terms of coercive economic power and political interests which distinguish our own States from foreign sovereigns. The international price fixing, boycotts, and other current anticompetitive practices undertaken by some Middle Eastern nations are illustrative of the weapons in the arsenals of foreign nations which no domestic State could ever employ. Nor do our domestic States, in any meaningful sense, have the conflicting economic interests or antagonistic ideologies which characterize and enliven the relations among nation states.

Viewed in this light, it is clear that the decision to allow foreign sovereigns to seek treble damages from Americans and to rely on standards of competitive behavior in fixing liability which those very same nations flout in their business relationships with this country is a decision dramatically different from the one Mr. Justice Frankfurter faced in *Evans*. To consider the result reached there as to Georgia determinative of the result here is to substitute a "hard and fast rule of inclusion" for the "hard and fast rule of exclusion" which Justices Frankfurter and Roberts eschewed in *Evans* and *Cooper*, respectively. Only the most mechanical reading of our prior precedent will justify such a result.

Further, the result reached by the Court today confronts us with the anomaly that while the United States Government cannot sue for treble damages under our antitrust laws, other nations are free to engage in the most flagrant kinds of combinations for price fixing, totally at odds with our antitrust concepts, and nevertheless are given the right by the Court to sue American suppliers in American courts for treble damages plus attorneys' fees. It is no answer to say that the United States needs no civil treble-damages remedy since it has reserved for itself the power to pursue criminal remedies against American suppliers for antitrust violations. What that response overlooks is that our criminal antitrust remedies hardly compare with the infinite array of political and commercial weapons available to a foreign nation for use against the United States itself or against American producers and suppliers. This, again, underscores how completely the problem is a matter of policy to be resolved by the political branches without the intrusion of the Judiciary.

D

Finally, the Court's emphasis on the deterrent effects of treble-damages actions by foreign sovereigns also will not withstand critical scrutiny. We acknowledged in *Brunswick Corp. v. Pueblo Bowl-O-Mat, Inc.*, 429 U.S., at 485-486, that while treble damages do play an important role in deterring wrongdoers, "the treble-damages provision...is designed primarily as a remedy." To allow foreign sovereigns who were clearly not the intended beneficiaries of this remedy to nevertheless invoke it reverses this priority of purposes, and does so solely on the basis of this Court's uninformed speculation about some possible beneficial consequences to American consumers of this "maximum deterrent." In areas of far less political delicacy, we have been unwilling to expand the scope of the right to sue under the antitrust laws without express congressional intent to do so. *See, e.g., Hawaii v. Standard Oil Co.*, 405 U.S. 251, 264-265 (1972). [The dissent observed that the Court adverts to a letter from the Legal Adviser of the State Department to the Court of Appeals advising that no foreign policy problems were anticipated from a decision holding foreign governments to be persons within the meaning of § 4 of the Clayton Act. The significance of this communication escapes me. Nothing in the Constitution suggests legislative power may be exercised jointly by the courts and the Department of State.]

For these reasons I dissent from the Court's intrusion into the legislative sphere.

MR. JUSTICE POWELL, *dissenting*.

I join THE CHIEF JUSTICE in his dissent, and add a word to emphasize my difficulty with the Court's decision.

The issue is whether the antitrust laws of this country are to be made available for treble-damages suits against American businesses by the governments of other countries. The Court resolves this issue in favor of such governments by constructing the word "person" in § 4 of the Clayton Act to include "foreign governments." No one argues seriously that this was the intent of Congress in 1890 when the term "person" was included in the Act. Indeed, the Court acknowledges that this "question was never considered at the time the Sherman and Clayton Acts were enacted."

Despite this conclusion as to the absence of any congressional consideration, the inviting possibility of treble damages is extended today by judicial action to the sovereign nations of the world. With minor exceptions, the United States recognizes the governments of all of these nations. We may assume that most of them have no equivalent of our antitrust laws and would be unlikely to afford reciprocal opportunities to the United States to sue and recover damages in their courts.

The Court has resolved a major policy question. As the Acting Solicitor General stated in his Memorandum for the United States as *Amicus Curiae*.

> "Whether foreign sovereigns are 'persons' entitled to sue under Section 4 depends largely upon the general policy reflected in the statute, and the general policy of the United States opening its courts to foreign sovereigns."

I had thought it was accepted doctrine that questions of "general policy" — especially with respect to foreign sovereigns and absent explicit legislative authority-are beyond the province of the Judicial Branch. If the statute truly reflected a general policy that dictated the inclusion of foreign sovereigns, the Court might be justified in reaching today's result. In *Georgia v. Evans*, 316 U.S. 159 (1942), a clear policy to protect the

States of the Union was reflected in the antitrust laws and in the legislative history. The Court could "perceive no reason for believing that Congress wanted to deprive a State, as purchaser of commodities shipped in interstate commerce, of the civil remedy of treble damages which is available to other purchasers who suffer through violation of the Act." *Id.*, at 162.

Unlike the majority, I do not believe the same can be said with respect to foreign sovereigns. It is not only the absence of specific congressional intent to include them. It is that the predicate for the Court's approach in *Georgia v. Evans* is not present in the case before us. The solicitude that we assume Congress has for the welfare of each of the United States, especially when the subject matter of legislation largely has been removed from the competence of the States and has been entrusted to the United States, cannot be assumed with respect to foreign nations. Putting it differently, it was not illogical for the *Evans* Court to include the States within the reach of § 4, but it is a quantum leap to include foreign governments.

A court, without the benefit of legislative hearings that would illuminate the policy considerations if the question were left to Congress, is not competent in my opinion to resolve this question in the best interest of our country. It is regrettable that the Court today finds it necessary to rush to this essentially legislative judgment. [The dissent observed that the Court quotes a letter to the effect that "the Department of State would not anticipate any *foreign policy problems*" if § 4 were held to embrace suits by foreign governments. But resolution of the issue here depends not only upon foreign policy considerations but also upon considerations relevant to the general welfare of the United States. The latter are quite beyond the concern of the Department of State and should be considered by the legislative branch. The international business conducted by American corporations has economic and social ramifications of great importance to our country.]

III. Extraterritorial Jurisdiction

Documents Supplement References:

1. *Restatement Sections 402-403, 415*

2. *United States Department of Justice and Federal Trade Commission, Antitrust Enforcement Guidelines for International Operations (April 1995)*

A. The Classic ALCOA Effects Test

United States v. Aluminum Company of America
148 F.2d 416 (2d Cir. 1945)

L. Hand, Circuit Judge.

This appeal comes to us by virtue of a certificate of the Supreme Court, under the amendment of 1944 to § 29 of 15 U.S.C.A. The action was brought under § 4 of that title, praying the district court to adjudge that the defendant, Aluminum Company of America, was monopolizing interstate and foreign commerce, particularly in the manufacture and sale of "virgin" aluminum ingot, and that it be dissolved; and further to adjudge that company and the defendant, Aluminum Limited, had entered into a conspiracy in restraint of such commerce....

. . . .

I.

"Alcoa's" Monopoly of "Virgin" Ingot.

"Alcoa" is a corporation, organized under the laws of Pennsylvania on September 18, 1888;...It has always been engaged in the production and sale of "ingot" aluminum....It has proliferated into a great number of subsidiaries, created at various times between the years 1900 and 1929, as the business expanded. Aluminum is a chemical element; it is never found in a free state, being always in chemical combination with oxygen. One form of this combination is known as alumina; and for practical purposes the most available material from which alumina can be extracted is an ore, called "bauxite." Aluminum was isolated as a metal more than a century ago, but not until about 1886 did it become commercially practicable to eliminate the oxygen, so that it could be exploited industrially. One, Hall, discovered a process by which this could be done in that year, and got a patent on April 2, 1889, which he assigned to "Alcoa," which thus secured a legal monopoly of the manufacture of the pure aluminum until on April 2, 1906, when this patent expired. Meanwhile Bradley had invented a process by which the smelting could be carried on without the use of external heat, as had theretofore been thought necessary; and for this improvement he too got a patent on February 2, 1892. Bradley's improvement resulted in great economy in manufacture, so that, although after April 2, 1906, anyone could manufacture aluminum by the Hall process, for practical purposes no one could compete with Bradley or with his licensees until February 2, 1909, when Bradley's patent also expired. On October 31, 1903, "Alcoa" and the assignee of the Bradley patent entered into a contract by which "Alcoa" was granted an exclusive license under that patent, in exchange for "Alcoa's" promise to sell to the assignee a stated amount of aluminum at a discount of ten per cent below "Alcoa's" published list price, and always to sell at a discount of five per cent greater than that which "Alcoa" gave to any other jobber. Thus until February 2, 1909, "Alcoa" had either a monopoly of the manufacture of "virgin" aluminum ingot, or the the monopoly of a process which eliminated all competition.

The extraction of aluminum from alumina requires a very large amount of electrical energy, which is ordinarily, though not always, most cheaply obtained from water power. Beginning at least as early as 1895, "Alcoa" secured such power from several companies by contracts, containing in at least three instances, covenants binding the power companies not to sell or let power to anyone else for the manufacture of aluminum. "Alcoa" — either itself or by a subsidiary — also entered into four successive "cartels" with foreign manufacturers of aluminum by which, in exchange for certain limitations upon its import into foreign countries, it secured covenants from the foreign producers, either not to import into the United States at all, or to do so under restrictions, which in some cases involved the fixing of prices. These "cartels" and restrictive covenants and certain other practices were the subject of suit filed by the United States against "Alcoa" on May 16, 1912, in which a decree was entered by consent on June 7, 1912, declaring several of these covenants unlawful and enjoining their performance; and also declaring invalid other restrictive covenants obtained before 1903 relating to the sale of alumina. ("Alcoa" failed at this time to inform the United States of several restrictive covenants in water-power contracts; its justification—which the judge accepted—being that they had been forgotten.) "Alcoa" did not begin to manufacture alumina on its own behalf until the expiration of a dominant patent in 1903....

None of the foregoing facts are in dispute, and the most important question in the case is whether the monopoly in "Alcoa's" production of "virgin" ingot, secured by the two patents until 1909, and in part perpetuated between 1909 and 1912 by the unlawful practices, forbidden by the decree of 1912, continued for the ensuing twenty-eight years; and whether, if it did, it was unlawful under § 2 of the Sherman Act, 15 U.S.C.A. § 2. It is undisputed that throughout this period "Alcoa" continued to be the single producer of "virgin" ingot in the United States; and the plaintiff argues that this without more was enough to make it an unlawful monopoly. It also takes an alternative position: that in any event during this period "Alcoa" consistently pursued unlawful exclusionary practices, which made its dominant position certainly unlawful, even though it would not have been, had it been retained only by "natural growth." Finally, it asserts that many of these practices were of themselves unlawful, as contracts in restraint of trade under § 1 of the Act, 15 U.S.C.A. § 1. "Alcoa's" position is that the fact that it alone continued to make "virgin" ingot in this country did not, and does not, give it a monopoly of the market; that it was always subject to the competition of imported "virgin" ingot, and of what is called "secondary" ingot; and that even if it had not been, its monopoly would not have been retained by unlawful means, but would have been the result of a growth which the Act does not forbid, even when it results in a monopoly....

....

We conclude...that "Alcoa's" control over the ingot market must be reckoned at over ninety per cent; that being the proportion which its production bears to imported "virgin" ingot. If the fraction which it did not supply were the produce of domestic manufacture there could be no doubt that this percentage gave it a monopoly—lawful or unlawful, as the case might be. The producer of so large a proportion of the supply has complete control within certain limits. It is true that, if by raising the price he reduces the amount which can be marketed—as always, or almost always, happens—he may invite the expansion of the small producers who will try to fill the place left open; nevertheless, not only is there an inevitable lag in this, but the large producer is in a strong position to check such competition; and, indeed, if he has retained his old plant and personnel, he can inevitably do so. There are indeed limits to his power; substitutes are available for almost all commodities, and to raise the price enough is to evoke them. Moreover, it is difficult and expensive to keep idle any part of a plant or of personnel; and any drastic contraction of the market will offer increasing temptation to the small producers to expand. But these limitations also exist when a single producer occupies the whole market: even then, his hold will depend upon his moderation in exerting his immediate power.

The case at bar is however different, because, for aught that appears there may well have been a practically unlimited supply of imports as the price of ingot rose. Assuming that there was no agreement between "Alcoa" and foreign producers not to import, they sold what could bear the handicap of the tariff and the cost of transportation. For the period of eighteen years—1920-1937—they sold at times a little above "Alcoa's" prices, at times a little under; but there was substantially no gross difference between what they received and what they would have received, had they sold uniformly at "Alcoa's" prices. While the record is silent, we may therefore assume—the plaintiff having the burden—that, had "Alcoa" raised its prices, more ingot would have been imported. Thus there is a distinction between domestic and foreign competition: the first is limited in quantity, and can increase only by an increase in plant and personnel; the second is of producers who, we must assume, produce much more than they import, and whom a rise in price will presumably induce immediately to divert to the American market what they have been selling elsewhere. It is entirely consistent with the evidence that it was the threat of greater foreign imports which kept "Alcoa's" prices where they were, and prevented it from exploiting its advantage as sole domestic producer; indeed, it is hard to resist the conclusion that potential imports did put a "ceiling" upon those prices. Nevertheless, within the limits afforded by the tariff and the cost of transportation, "Alcoa" was free to raise its prices as it chose, since it was free from domestic competition, save as it drew other metals into the market as substitutes. Was this a monopoly within the meaning of § 2? The judge found that, over the whole half century of its existence, "Alcoa's" profits upon capital invested, after payment of income taxes, had been only about ten per cent.... [I]t would be hard to say that "Alcoa" had made exorbitant profits on ingot.... A profit of ten per cent in such an industry, dependent, in part at any rate, upon continued tariff protection, and subject to the vicissitudes of new demands, to the obsolescence of plant and process—which can never be accurately gauged in advance—to the chance that substitutes may at any moment be discovered which will reduce the demand, and to the other hazards which attend all industry; a profit of ten per cent, so conditioned, could hardly be considered extortionate.

There are however, two answers to any such excuse; and the first is that the profit on ingot was not necessarily the same as the profit of the business as a whole, and that we have no means of allocating its proper share to ingot.....[Second,] the whole issue is irrelevant anyway, for it is no excuse for "monopolizing" a market that the monopoly has not been used to extract from the consumer more than a "fair" profit. The Act has wider purposes. Indeed, even though we disregarded all but economic considerations, it would by no means follow that such concentration of producing power is to be desired, when it has not been used extortionately. Many people believe that possession of unchallenged economic power deadens initiative, discourages thrift and depresses energy; that immunity from competition is a narcotic, and rivalry is a stimulant, to industrial progress; that the spur of constant stress is necessary to counteract an inevitable disposition to let well enough alone. Such people believe that competitors, versed in the craft as no consumer can be, will be quick to detect opportunities for saving and new shifts in production, and be eager to profit by them. In any event the mere fact that a producer, having command of the domestic market, has not been able to make more than a "fair" profit, is no evidence that a "fair" profit could not have been made at lower prices.... True, it might have been thought adequate to condemn only those monopolies which could not show that they had exercised the highest possible ingenuity, had adopted every possible economy, had anticipated every conceivable improvement, stimulated every possible demand. No doubt, that would be one way of dealing with the matter, although it would imply constant scrutiny and constant supervision, such as courts are unable to provide. Be that as it may, that was not the way that Congress chose; it did not condone "good trusts" and condemn "bad" ones; it forbad all. Moreover, in so doing it was not necessarily actuated by economic motives alone. It is possible, because of its indirect social or moral effect, to prefer a system of small producers, each dependent for his success upon his own skill and character, to one in which the great mass of those engaged must accept the direction of a few. These considerations, which we have suggested only as possible purposes of the Act, we think the decisions prove to have been in fact its purposes.

It is settled, at least as to § 1, that there are some contracts restricting competition which are unlawful, no matter how beneficent they may be; no industrial exigency will justify them; they are absolutely forbidden. Chief Justice Taft said as much of contracts dividing a territory among producers, in the often quoted passage of his opinion in the Circuit Court of Appeals in *United States v. Addystone Pipe & Steel*

Co., 6 Cir., 85 F. 271, 291.... The Supreme Court unconditionally condemned all contracts fixing prices in *United States v. Trenton Potteries Co.*, 273 U.S. 392, 397, 398, and whatever doubts may have arisen as to that decision from *Appalachian Coals Inc. v. United States*, 288 U.S. 344,... they were laid by *United States v. Socony-Vacuum Co.*, 310 U.S. 150, 220-224.... It will now scarcely be denied that the same notion originally extended to all contracts—"reasonable," or "unreasonable"— which restrict competition. The decisions in *Standard Oil Co. v. United States*, 221 U.S. 1,... and *American Tobacco Co. v. United States*, 221 U.S. 106,... certainly did change this, and since then it has been accepted law that not all contracts which in fact put an end to existing competition are unlawful. Starting, however, with the authoritative premise that all contracts fixing prices are unconditionally prohibited, the only possible difference between them and a monopoly is that while a monopoly necessarily involves an equal, or even greater, power to fix prices, its mere existence might be thought not to constitute an exercise of that power. That distinction is nevertheless purely formal; it would be valid only so long as the monopoly remained wholly inert; it would disappear as soon as the monopoly began to operate; for, when it did—that is, as soon as it began to sell at all—it must sell at some price and the only price at which it could sell is a price which it itself fixed. Thereafter the power and its exercise must coalesce. Indeed it would be absurd to condemn such contracts unconditionally, and not to extend the condemnation to monopolies; for the contracts are only steps toward that entire control which monopoly confers: they are really partial monopolies.

But we are not left to deductive reasoning. Although in many settings it may be proper to weigh the extent and effect of restrictions in a contract against its industrial or commercial advantages, this is never to be done when the contract is made with intent to set up a monopoly. As much was plainly implied in *Swift & Co. v. United States*, 196 U.S. 375, 396... where the court spoke of monopoly as being the "result" which the law seeks to prevent.... Perhaps, it has been idle to labor the point at length; there can be no doubt that the vice of restrictive contracts and of monopoly is really one, it is the denial to commerce of the supposed protection of competition. To repeat, if the earlier stages are proscribed, when they are parts of a plan, the mere projecting of which condemns them unconditionally, the realization of the plan itself must also be proscribed.

We have been speaking only of the economic reasons which forbid monopoly; but, as we have already implied, there are others, based upon the belief that great industrial consolidations are inherently undesirable, regardless of their economic results. In the debates in Congress Senator Sherman himself... showed that among the purposes of Congress in 1890 was a desire to put an end to great aggregations of capital because of the helplessness of the individual before them..... That Congress is still of the same mind appears in the Surplus Property Act of 1944, 50 U.S.C.A. Appendix § 1611 *et seq.*, and the Small Business Mobilization Act, 50 U.S.C.A. Appendix § 1101 *et seq.* Not only does § 2(d) of the first declare it to be one aim of that statute to "preserve the competitive position of small business concerns," but § 18 is given over to directions designed to "preserve and strengthen" their position.... Throughout the history of these statutes it has been constantly assumed that one of their purposes was to perpetuate and preserve, for its own sake and in spite of possible cost, an organization of industry in small units which can effectively compete with each other. We hold that "Alcoa's" monopoly of ingot was of the kind covered by § 2.

It does not follow because "Alcoa" had such a monopoly, that it "monopolized" the ingot market: it may not have achieved monopoly; monopoly may have been thrust upon it. If it had been a combination of existing smelters which united the whole industry and controlled the production of all aluminum ingot, it would certainly have "monopolized" the market. In several decisions the Supreme Court has decreed the dissolution of such combinations, although they had engaged in no unlawful trade practices.... We may start therefore with the premise that to have combined ninety per cent of the producers of ingot would have been to "monopolize" the ingot market; and, so far as concerns the public interest, it can make no difference whether an existing competition is put an end to, or whether prospective competition is prevented. The Clayton Act itself speaks in that alternative: "to injure, destroy, or prevent competition." § 13(a) 15 U.S.C.A. Nevertheless, it is unquestionably true that from the very outset the courts have at least kept in reserve the possibility that the origin of a monopoly may be critical in determining its legality; and for this they had warrant in some of the congressional debates which accompanied the passage of the Act.... This notion has usually been expressed by saying that size does not determine guilt; that there must be some "exclusion" of competitors; that the growth must be something else than "natural" or "normal"; that there must be a "wrongful intent," or some other specific intent; or that some "unduly" coercive means must be used. At times there has been emphasis upon the use of the active verb "monopolize".... What engendered these compunctions is reasonably plain; persons may unwittingly find themselves in possession of a monopoly, automatically so to say: that is, without having intended either to put an end to existing competition, or to prevent competition from arising when none had existed; they may become monopolists by force of accident. Since the Act makes "monopolizing" a crime, as well as a civil wrong, it would be not only unfair, but presumably contrary to the intent of Congress, to include such instances. A market may, for example, be so limited that it is impossible to produce at all and meet the cost of production except by a plant large enough to supply the whole demand. Or there may be changes in taste or in cost which drive out all but one purveyor. A single producer may be the survivor out of a group of active competitors, merely by virtue of his superior skill, foresight and industry. In such cases a strong argument can be made that, although, the result may expose the public to the evils of monopoly, the Act does not mean to condemn the resultant of those very forces which it is its prime object to foster: finis opus coronat. The successful competitor, having been urged to compete, must not be turned upon when he wins. The most extreme expression of this view is in *United States v. United States Steel Corporation*, 251 U.S. 417,... which Sanford, J., in part repeated in *United States v. International Harvester Corporation*, 274 U.S. 693, 708.... [I]in both instances the corporation had less than two-thirds of the production in its hands, and the language quoted was not necessary to the decision; so that even if it had not later been modified, it has not the authority of an actual decision. But, whatever authority it does have was modified by the gloss of Cardozo, J., in *United States v. Swift & Co.*, 286 U.S. 106,... when he said, "Mere size... is not an offense against the Sherman Act unless magnified to the point at which it amounts to a monopoly... but size carries with it an opportunity for abuse that is not to be ignored when the opportunity is proved to have been utilized in the past." "Alcoa's" size was "magnified" to make it a "monopoly"; indeed, it has never been anything else; and its size, not only offered it an "opportunity for abuse," but it "utilized" its size for "abuse," as can easily be shown.

It would completely misconstrue "Alcoa's" position in 1940 to hold that it was the passive beneficiary of a monopoly, following upon an involuntary elimination of competitors by automatically operative economic forces. Already in 1909, when its last lawful monopoly ended, it sought to strengthen its position by unlawful practices, and these concededly continued until 1912. In that year it had two plants in

New York, at which it produced less than 42 million pounds of ingot; in 1934 it had five plants (the original two, enlarged; one in Tennessee; one in North Carolina; one Washington), and its production had risen to about 327 million pounds, an increase of almost eight-fold. Meanwhile not a pound of ingot had been produced by anyone else in the United States. This increase and this continued and undisturbed control did not fall undesigned into "Alcoa's" lap; obviously it could not have done so. It could only have resulted, as it did result, from a persistent determination to maintain the control, with which it found itself vested in 1912. There were at least one or two abortive attempts to enter the industry, but "Alcoa," effectively anticipated and forestalled all competition, and succeeded in holding the field alone. True, it stimulated demand and opened new uses for the metal, but not without making sure that it could supply what it had evoked. There is no dispute as to this; "Alcoa" avows it as evidence of the skill, energy and initiative with which it has always conducted its business; as a reason why, having won its way by fair means, it should be commended, and not dismembered. We need charge it with no moral derelictions after 1912; we may assume that all it claims for itself is true. The only question is whether it falls within the exception established in favor of those who do not seek, but cannot avoid, the control of a market. It seems to us that that question scarcely survives its statement. It was not inevitable that it should always anticipate increases in the demand for ingot and be prepared to supply them. Nothing compelled it to keep doubling and redoubling its capacity before others entered the field. It insists that it never excluded competitors; but we can think of no more effective exclusion than progressively to embrace each new opportunity as it opened, and to face every newcomer with new capacity already geared into a great organization, having the advantage of experience, trade connections and the elite of personnel. Only in case we interpret "exclusion" as limited to manoeuvres not honestly industrial, but actuated solely by a desire to prevent competition, can such a course, indefatigably pursued, be deemed not "exclusionary." So to limit it would in our judgment emasculate the Act; would permit just such consolidations as it was designed to prevent.

. . . .

We disregard any question of "intent." Relatively early in the history of the Act —1905—Holmes, J., in *Swift & Co. v. United States*, 196 U.S. 375, 396,... explained this aspect of the Act.... Although the primary evil was monopoly, the Act also covered preliminary steps, which, if continued, would lead to it. These may do no harm of themselves; but, if they are initial moves in a plan or scheme which, carried out, will result in monopoly, they are dangerous and the law will nip them in the bud. For this reason conduct falling short of monopoly, is not illegal unless it is part of a plan to monopolize, or to gain such other control of a market as is equally forbidden. To make it so, the plaintiff must prove what in the criminal law is known as a "specific intent;" an intent which goes beyond the mere intent to do the act. By far the greatest part of the fabulous record piled up in the case at bar, was concerned with proving such an intent. The plaintiff was seeking to show that many transactions, neutral on their face, were not in fact necessary to the development of "Alcoa's" business, and had no motive except to exclude others and perpetuate its hold upon the ingot market. Upon that effort success depended in case the plaintiff failed to satisfy the court that it was unnecessary under § 2 to convict "Alcoa" of practices unlawful of themselves. The plaintiff has so satisfied us, and the issue of intent ceases to have any importance; no intent is relevant except that which is relevant to any liability, criminal or civil: *i.e.*, an intent to bring about the forbidden act. Note 59 of *United States v. Socony-Vacuum Oil Co.*, 310 U.S. 150, 226,... on which "Alcoa" appears so much to rely, is in no sense to the contrary. Douglas, J., was answering the defendants' argument that, assuming that a combination had attempted to fix prices, it had never had the power to do so, for there was too much competing oil. His answer was that the plan was unlawful, even if the parties did not have the power to fix prices, provided that they intended to do so; and it was to drive home this that he contrasted the case then before the court with monopoly, where power was a necessary element. In so doing he said: "An intent and a power...are then necessary".....In order to fall within § 2, the monopolist must have both the power to monopolize, and the intent to monopolize. To read the passage as demanding any "specific," intent, makes nonsense of it, for no monopolist monopolizes unconscious of what he is doing. So here, "Alcoa" meant to keep, and did keep, that complete and exclusive hold upon the ingot market with which it started. That was to "monopolize" that market, however innocently it otherwise proceeded. So far as the judgment held that it was not within § 2, it must be reversed.

. . . .

III.

"Limited."

"Limited" was incorporated in Canada on May 31, 1928, to take over those properties of "Alcoa" which were outside the United States.....In exchange for all the properties conveyed, "Limited" issued all its common shares to "Alcoa's" common shareholders in the proportion of one for every three; and it thus resulted that the beneficial ownership remained what it had been, except for the interest of "Alcoa's" preferred shareholders, who were apparently considered amply protected by the properties in the United States. At first there remained some officers common to both companies; but by the middle of 1931, this had ceased, and, formally at any rate, the separation between the two companies was complete. At the conclusion of the transfers a majority, though only a bare majority, of the common shares of "Alcoa" was in the hands of three persons: Andrew W. Mellon, Richard B. Mellon, his brother, and Arthur V. Davis [chairman of the board of Alcoa]. Richard Mellon died in 1933, and Andrew in 1937, and their shares passed to their families; but in January, 1939, the Davises, the officers and directors of "Alcoa" and the Mellon families—eleven individuals in all—collectively still held 48.9 per cent of "Alcoa's" shares, and 48.5 per cent of "Limited's"; and Arthur V. Davis was then the largest shareholder in both companies.

The companies had a number of transactions with each other, upon which the plaintiff relies to prove that they did not deal at arms length, but that "Limited" was organized only as a creature of "Alcoa." As one instance, "Limited" apparently would have been able at times to sell aluminum in the United States at a profit but did not do so, because—the plaintiff argues—they had agreed not to compete. The inference is not strong: to break into a new market protected by a tariff subject to change, particularly a market for long in the possession of a single powerful producer, is a step which an outsider might well hesitate to take.....

There was also some evidence that "Alcoa" took part in the formation of the "Alliance," a foreign "cartel" which we shall describe later. This consists very largely of declarations of Arthur V. Davis, put in his mouth by other witnesses; of a cable of Edward K. Davis [a former vice president of Alcoa] to one of "Limited's" other officers; and of the improbability that the "Alliance" should have been set up without the active cooperation of Arthur V. Davis, especially as he was concededly in Europe and in communication with some foreign producers at about the time that the "Alliance" was first bruited. Edward K. Davis was the originator of the "Alliance"; he gave as his reason for it that he feared that the other foreign producers who had already joined in a "cartel," would shut him out. When these producers came to Canada in 1931 to arrange for the "Alliance," they visited Arthur V. Davis and made an extended visit to "Alcoa's" plants in the East. As anticipatory confirmation that "Alcoa" had had a share in forming the "Alliance," the plaintiff also introduced evidence to show that before 1928 "Alcoa" had already had an understanding with foreigners as to prices. This consisted largely of the statements of what others had said about an agreement to keep their prices the same as "Alcoa's." . . .

The Davises in answer to all this evidence swore that "Limited" had been organized for three reasons, quite different from controlling prices in the United States. First, there was at that time a growing nationalism in the British Empire—where "Alcoa" sold most of its foreign aluminum—which manifested itself in the slogan: "Buy British," and which would be better satisfied, if the properties were owned by a Canadian corporation, even though its shareholders were American. Next, "Alcoa" had neglected its foreign properties—relatively—and they would better prosper under a management, singly devoted to them. Finally, the time was coming when Arthur V. Davis wished to take a less active part in affairs; and there would be embarrassment in choosing between [Roy A.] Hunt [Alcoa's president] and Edward K. Davis, as his successor. Both said that the separation between the companies had been actually as complete as it was in form. Arthur said that, although while in Europe shortly before the "Alliance" was formed, foreign producers had spoken to him, he had then and always referred all their inquiries to his brother. He had discussed little with Edward any questions of policy about "Limited"; they had talked for the most part only about the history, development and future of the properties. He had indeed seen a preliminary draft of the agreement, forming the "Alliance," but not its final form until the time of the trial; and he had had nothing whatever to do with its formation. As for the trip of the foreign producers in the United States, it was purely social; a "good-will" excursion, so to say, in which the relations of "Alcoa" and foreign production was not discussed.

Upon the whole evidence the judge found that by 1935 "Limited" had become altogether free from any connection with "Alcoa," and that "Alcoa" had had no part in forming the "Alliance," or in any effort at any time to limit imports, to fix their price, or to intervene in price fixing "cartels" in Europe—except the early ones. In short, he again felt persuaded by the testimony against any inferences to be drawn from the conceded facts, and from the declarations put in the mouths of the Davises. As before, to do otherwise he would have had to find that both these men had deliberately perjured themselves; and we cannot see that these findings present us with anything different in substance from those on which we have already passed. Considering the interests in "Limited" which Arthur V. Davis and both the Mellons had, it would perhaps have taxed our credulity to the breaking point to believe that they knew nothing about the formation of the "Alliance." Arthur V. Davis did not as far as that; and that he and the Mellons should have put into the hands of Edward K. Davis the whole management of "Limited," does not appear to us to pass the bounds of reasonable entertainment. . . . It was not unreasonable to believe that Arthur V. Davis and the Mellons, seeing that some kind of "cartel" might be an inescapable incident to continuing business abroad, wished in 1931 to keep "Alcoa" as far removed from it as possible.

Even so, the question remains whether "Alcoa" should be charged with the "Alliance" because a majority of its shareholders were also a majority of "Limited's" shareholders; or whether that would be true, even though there were a group, common to both, less than a majority, but large enough for practical purposes to control each. It is quite true that in proportion as courts disregard the fictitious persona of a corporation—as perhaps they are increasingly disposed to do—they must substitute the concept of a group of persons acting in concert. Nevertheless, the group must not be committed legally except in so as far as they have assented as a body, and that assent should be imputed to them only in harmony with the ordinary notions of delegated power. The plaintiff did not prove that in 1931, to say nothing of 1936, there was not a substantial minority in each company made up of those who held no shares in the other; and the existence of the same majority in the two corporations was not enough by itself to identify the two. "Alcoa" would not be bound, unless those who held the majority of its shares had been authorized by the group as a whole to enter into the "Alliance"; and considering the fact that, as we shall show, it was an illegal arrangement, such an authority ought convincingly to appear. It does not appear at all....For these reasons we conclude that "Alcoa" was not a party to the "Alliance," and did not join in any violation of § 1 of the Act, so far as concerned foreign commerce.

Whether "Limited" itself violated that section depends upon the character of the "Alliance." It was a Swiss corporation, created in pursuance of an agreement entered into on July 3, 1931, the signatories to which were a French corporation, two German, one Swiss, a British, and "Limited." The original agreement, or "cartel," provided for the formation of a corporation in Switzerland which should issue shares, to be taken up by the signatories. This corporation was from time to time to fix a quota of production for each share, and each shareholder was to be limited to the quantity measured by the number of it held, but was free to sell at any price it chose. The corporation fixed a price every year at which it would take off any shareholder's hands any part of its quota which it did not sell. No shareholder was to "buy, borrow, fabricate or sell" aluminum produced by anyone not a shareholder except with the consent of the board of governors, but that must not be "unreasonably withheld." Nothing was said as to whether the arrangement extended to sales in the United States; but Article X, known as the "Conversion Clause," provided that any shareholder might exceed his quota to the extent that he converted into aluminum in the United States or Canada any ores delivered to him in either of those countries by persons situated in the United States. This was confessedly put in to allow "Limited" to receive bauxite or alumina from "Alcoa," to smelt it into aluminum and to deliver the aluminum to "Alcoa." Edward K. Davis gave as an explanation of this that "Limited" needed some protection against "Alcoa's" possible refusal to convey Alcoa Power Company, which "Alcoa" had never actually bound itself to transfer. Although in 1931 "Alcoa" had all the producing capacity which it seemed likely to need (and so the event proved, for the clause was never invoked), Davis said that he did not know whether in the future the demand might not outrun that capacity, and whether "Alcoa" might not therefore be tempted to hold onto the Lower Development [a large power development at the source of the Saguenay River in Lake St. John, Canada] unless "Limited" would smelt its alumina. That does indeed seem a somewhat far-fetched reason; but on the other hand it is hard to suppose that "Alcoa" really feared that it could not meet its future needs and meant to lean upon "Limited." The incident may be thought to have a bearing on "Alcoa's" implication in the "Alliance"; but its only substantial importance, so far as we can see, is as showing whether the 1931 agreement was intended to cover the United States. That question arose very shortly after the agreement was made, and Edward K. Davis took the position that the United States was included, relying upon absence of any exception in the general language. His interpretation would seem to have been plainly right, not only for the reason he gave, but because otherwise there would have been no occasion for the "Conversion Clause." However, the other shareholders overruled him, and until 1936, when the new arrangement was made, imports into the United States were not included in the quotas. The issue turned out to be unimportant anyway, for the annual average of imports during the five years was in the neighborhood of only fifteen million pounds.

The agreement of 1936 abandoned the system of unconditional quotas, and substituted a system of royalties. Each shareholder was to have a fixed free quota for every share it held, but as its production exceeded the sum of its quotas, it was to pay a royalty, graduated progressively in proportion to the excess; and these royalties the "Alliance" divided among the shareholders in proportion to their shares. This agreement —unlike the first—did not contain an express promise that the "Alliance" would buy any undisposed of stocks at a fixed price, although perhaps § 3 of Subdivision A, of Part X may have impliedly recognized such an obligation. Probably, during the two years in which the shareholders operated under this agreement, that question did not arise for the demand for aluminum was very active. Nevertheless, we understand from "Limited's" answer to an interrogatory that the last price fixed under the agreement of 1931 was understood to remain in force. Although this agreement, like its predecessor, was silent as to imports into the United States, when that question arose during its preparation, as it did, all the shareholders agreed that such imports should be included in the quotas. The German companies were exempted from royalties—for obvious reasons— and that, it would seem, for practical purposes put them out of the "cartel" for the future, for it was scarcely possible that a German producer would be unable to dispose of all its production, at least within any future period that would be provided for. The shareholders continued this agreement unchanged until the end of March, 1938, by which time it had become plain that, at least for the time being, it was no longer of service to anyone. Nothing was, however, done to end it, although the German shareholders of course became enemies of the French, British and Canadian shareholders in 1939. The "Alliance" itself has apparently never been dissolved; and indeed it appeared on the "Proclaimed List of Blocked Nationals" of September 13, 1944.

Did either the agreement of 1931 or that of 1936 violate § 1 of the Act? The answer does not depend upon whether we shall recognize as a source of liability a liability imposed by another state. On the contrary we are concerned only with whether Congress chose to attach liability to the conduct outside the United States of persons not in allegiance to it. That being so, the only question open is whether Congress intended to impose the liability, and whether our own Constitution permitted it to do so: as a court of the United States, we cannot look beyond our own law. Nevertheless, it is quite true that we are not to read general words, such as those in this Act, without regard to the limitations customarily observed by nations upon the exercise of their powers; limitations which generally correspond to those fixed by the "Conflict of Laws." We should not impute to Congress an intent to punish all whom its courts can catch, for conduct which has no consequences within the United States. On the other hand, it is settled law—as "Limited" itself agrees—that any state may impose liabilities, even upon persons not within its allegiance, for conduct outside its borders that has consequences within its borders which the state reprehends; and these liabilities other states will ordinarily recognize. It may be argued that this Act extends further. Two situations are possible. There may be agreements made beyond our borders not intended to affect imports, which do affect them, or which affect exports. Almost any limitation of the supply of goods in Europe, for example, or in South America, may have repercussions in the United States if there is trade between the two. Yet when one considers the international complications likely to arise from an effort in this country to treat such agreements as unlawful, it is safe to assume that Congress certainly did not intend the Act to cover them. Such agreements may on the other hand intend to include imports into the United States, and yet it may appear that they have had no effect upon them. That situation might be thought to fall within the doctrine that intent may be a substitute for performance in the case of a contract made within the United States; or it might be thought to fall within the doctrine that a statute should not be interpreted to cover acts abroad which have no consequence here. We shall not choose between these alternatives; but for argument we shall assume that the Act does not cover agreements, even though intended to affect imports or exports, unless its performance is shown actually to have had some effect upon them....

Both agreements would clearly have been unlawful, had they been made within the United States; and it follows from what we have just said that both were unlawful, though made abroad, if they were intended to affect imports and did affect them. Since the shareholders almost at once agreed that the agreement of 1931 should not cover imports, we may ignore it and confine our discussion to that of 1936: indeed that we should have to do anyway, since it superseded the earlier agreement. The judge found that it was not the purpose of the agreement to "suppress or restrain the exportation of aluminum to the United States for sale in competition with "Alcoa." By that we understand that he meant that the agreement was not specifically directed to "Alcoa," because it only applied generally to the production of the shareholders. If he meant that it was not expected that the general restriction upon production would have an effect upon imports, we cannot agree, for the change made in 1936 was deliberate and was expressly made to accomplish just that. It would have been an idle gesture, unless the shareholders had supposed that it would, or at least might, have that effect. The first of the conditions which we mentioned was therefore satisfied; the intent was to set up a quota system for imports.

The judge also found that the 1936 agreement did not "materially affect the * * * foreign trade or commerce of the United States"; apparently because the imported ingot was greater in 1936 and 1937 than in earlier years. We cannot accept this finding, based as it was upon the fact that, in 1936, 1937 and the first quarter of 1938, the gross imports of ingot increased. It by no means follows from such an increase that the agreement did not restrict imports; and incidentally it so happens that in those years such inference as is possible at all, leads to the opposite conclusion. It is true that the average imports — including "Alcoa's" — for the years 1932-1935 inclusive were about 15 million pounds, and that for 1936, 1937 and one-fourth of 1938 they were about 33 million pounds; but the average domestic ingot manufacture in the first period was about 96 million and in the second about 262 million; so that the proportion of imports to domestic ingot was about 15.6 per cent for the first period and about 12.6 per cent for the second. We do not mean to infer from this that the quota system of 1936 did in fact restrain imports, as these figures might suggest; but we do mean that nothing is to be inferred from the gross increase of imports. We shall dispose of the matter therefore upon the assumption that, although the shareholders intended to restrict imports, it does not appear whether in fact they did so. Upon our hypothesis the plaintiff would therefore fail, if it carried the burden of proof upon this issue as upon others. We think, however, that, after the intent to affect imports was proved, the burden of proof shifted to "Limited." In the first place a depressant upon production which applies generally may be assumed, ceteris paribus, to distribute its effect evenly upon all markets. Again, when the parties took the trouble specifically to make the depressant apply to a given market, there is reason to suppose that they expected that it would have some effect, which it could have only by lessening what would otherwise have been imported. If the motive they introduced was over-balanced in all instances by motives which induced the shareholders to import, if the United States market became so attractive that the royalties did not count at all and their expectations were in fact defeated, they to whom the facts were more accessible than to the plaintiff ought to prove it, for a *prima facie* case had been made. Moreover, there is an especial propriety in demanding this of "Limited," because it was "Limited" which procured the inclusion in the agreement of 1936 of imports in the quotas.

There remains only the question whether this assumed restriction had any influence upon prices, *Apex Hosiery Co. v. Leader*, 310 U.S. 469.... To that *Socony- Vacuum Oil Co. v. United States*, 310 U.S. 150,... is an entire answer. It will be remembered that, when the defendants in that case protested that the prosecution had not proved that the "distress" gasoline had affected prices, the court answered that was not necessary, because an agreement to withdraw any substantial part of the supply from a market would, if carried out, have some effect upon prices, and was as unlawful as an agreement expressly to fix prices. The underlying doctrine was that all factors which contribute to determine prices, must be kept free to operate unhampered by agreements. For these reasons we think that the agreement of 1936 violated § 1 of the Act.

. . . .

Judgment reversed, and cause remanded for further proceedings not inconsistent with the foregoing.

B. Balancing Tests and the Problem of Comity

Timberlane Lumber Company v. Bank of America National Savings and Trust Association
549 F.2d 597 (9th Cir. 1976) ("Timberlane I")

Choy, Circuit Judge:

Four separate actions, arising from the same series of events, were dismissed by the same district court and are consolidated here on appeal. The principal action is *Timberlane Lumber Co. v. Bank of America* (*Timberlane* action), an antitrust suit alleging violations of sections 1 and 2 of the Sherman Act (15 U.S.C. §§ 1, 2) and the Wilson Tariff Act (15 U.S.C. § 8). This action raises important questions concerning the application of American antitrust laws to activities in another country, including actions of foreign government officials. The district court dismissed the Timberlane action under the act of state doctrine and for lack of subject matter jurisdiction. The other three are diversity tort suits brought by employees of one of the Timberlane plaintiffs for individual injuries allegedly suffered in the course of the extended anti-Timberlane drama. Having dismissed the Timberlane action, the district court dismissed these three suits on the ground of forum non conveniens. We vacate the dismissals of all four actions and remand. [The Court's discussion of the other three actions is omitted.]

I. The Timberlane Action

The basic allegation of the Timberlane plaintiffs is that officials of the Bank of America and others located in both the United States and Honduras conspired to prevent Timberlane, through its Honduras subsidiaries, from milling lumber in Honduras and exporting it to the United States, thus maintaining control of the Honduran lumber export business in the hands of a few select individuals financed and controlled by the Bank. The intent and result of the conspiracy, they contend, was to interfere with the exportation to the United States, including Puerto Rico, of Honduran lumber for sale or use there by the plaintiffs, thus directly and substantially affecting the foreign commerce of the United States.

. . . .

Cast of Characters

There are three affiliated plaintiffs in the Timberlane action. Timberlane Lumber Company is an Oregon partnership principally involved in the purchase and distribution of lumber at wholesale in the Unites States for sale and use. Danli Industrial, S.A., and Maya Lumber Company, S. de R.L., are both Honduras corporations, incorporated and principally owned by the general partners of Timberlane. Danli held contracts to purchase timber in Honduras, and Maya was to conduct the milling operations to produce the lumber for export. (Timberlane, Danli, and Maya will be collectively referred to as "Timberland.")

The primary defendants are Bank of America Corporation (Bank), a California corporation, and its wholly-owned subsidiary, Bank of America National Trust and Savings Association, which operates a branch in Tegucigalpa, Honduras. . . . .

Other defendants have been named, but have not been served. Included in this group . . . are two Honduras corporations, Pedro Casanova e Hijos, S.A., and Importadore Mayorista, S. de R.L., and Michael Casanova, a citizen of Honduras (together referred to as "Casanova"), who together represent one of the two main competitors to Timberlane and its predecessor in the Honduran lumber business.

. . . .

The Timberlane complaint identified two co-conspirators not named as defendants. Jose Lamas, S. de R.L. (Lamas), a Honduran corporation, is the second major competitor in the lumber business. Jose Caminals Gallego (Caminals), a citizen of Spain, is described as an agent or employee of the Bank in Tegucigalpa.

Facts as Alleged

The conspiracy sketched by Timberlane actually started before the plaintiffs entered the scene. The Lima family operated a lumber mill in Honduras, competing with Lamas and Casanova, in both of which the Bank had significant financial interests. The Lima enterprise was also indebted to the Bank. By 1971, however, the Lima business was in financial trouble. Timberlane alleges that driving Lima under was the first step in the conspiracy which eventually crippled Timberlane's efforts, but the particulars do not matter for this appeal. What does matter is that various interests in the Lima assets, including its milling plant, passed to Lima's creditors: Casanova, the Bank, and the group of Lima employees who had not been paid the wages and severance pay due them. Under Honduran law, the employees' claim had priority.

Enter Timberlane, with a long history in the lumber business, in search of alternative sources of lumber for delivery to its distribution system on the East Coast of the United States. After study, it decided to try Honduras. In 1971, Danli was formed, tracts of forest land were acquired, plans for a modern log-processing plant were prepared, and equipment was purchased and assembled for shipment from the United States to Danli in Honduras. Timberlane became aware that the Lima plant might be available and began negotiating for its acquisition. Maya was formed, purchased the Lima employees' interest in the machinery and equipment in January 1972, despite opposition from the conspirators, and re-activated the Lima mill.

Realizing that they were faced with better-financed and more vigorous competition from Timberlane and its Honduran subsidiaries, the defendants and others extended the anti-Lima conspiracy to disrupt Timberlane's efforts. The primary weapons employed by the conspirators were the claim still held by the Bank in the remaining assets of the Lima enterprise under the all-inclusive mortgage Lima had been forced to sign and another claim held by Casanova. Maya made a substantial cash offer for the Bank's interest in an effort to clear its title, but the Bank refused to sell. Instead, the Bank surreptitiously conveyed the mortgage to Casanova for questionable consideration, Casanova paying nothing and agreeing only to pay the Bank a portion of what it collected. Casanova immediately assigned the Bank's claim and its own on similar terms to Caminals, who promptly set out to disrupt the Timberlane operation.

Caminals is characterized as the "front man" in the campaign to drive Timberlane out of Honduras, with the Bank and other defendants intending and carrying responsibility for his actions. Having acquired the claims of Casanova and the Bank, Caminals went to court to enforce them, ignoring throughout Timberlane's offers to purchase or settle them. Under the laws of Honduras, an "embargo" on property is a court-ordered attachment, registered with the Public Registry, which precludes the sale of that property without a court order. Honduran law provides, upon embargo, that the court appoint a judicial officer, called an "interventor" to ensure against any diminution in the value of the property. In order to paralyze the Timberlane operation, Caminals obtained embargoes against Maya and Danli. Acting through the interventor, since accused of being on the payroll of the Bank, guards and troops were used to cripple and, for a time, completely shut down Timberlane's milling operation. The harassment took other forms as well: the conspirators caused the manager of Timberlane's Honduras operations, Gordon Sloan Smith, to be falsely arrested and imprisoned and were responsible for the publication of several defamatory articles about Timberlane in the Honduran press.

As a result of the conspiracy, Timberlane's complaint claimed damages then estimated in excess of $5,000,000. Plaintiffs also allege that there has been a direct and substantial effect on United States foreign commerce, and that defendants intended the results of the conspiracy, including the impact on United States commerce.

Act of State

The classic enunciation of the act of state doctrine is found in *Underhill v. Hernandez*, 168 U.S. 250, 252 (1897):

> Every sovereign State is bound to respect the independence of every other sovereign State, and the courts of one country will not sit in judgment on the acts of government of another done within own territory.

From the beginning, this principle has applied in foreign trade antitrust cases. In *American Banana Co. v. United Fruit Co.*, 213 U.S. 347 (1909), the first such case of significance, the American owner of a banana plantation caught in a border dispute between Panama and Costa Rica claimed that a competitor violated the Sherman Act by persuading the Costa Rican government to seize his lands. The act complained of would have required an adjudication of the legality of the Costa Rican seizure, an action which the Supreme Court said our courts could not challenge. More recently, *see Occidental Petroleum Corp. v. Buttes Gas & Oil Co.*, 331 F.Supp. 92 (C.D.Cal.1971), *affirmed* 461 F.2d 1261 (9th Cir.), *cert. denied*, 409 U.S. 950 (1972), the case mentioned from the bench by the district court here in ruling in favor of the defense motion to dismiss. [The *Occidental* case is excerpted below.]

The defendants argue—as the district court apparently held—that the injuries allegedly suffered by Timberlane resulted from acts of the Honduran government, principally in connection with the enforcement of the security interests in the Maya plant, which American courts cannot review. Such an application of the act of state doctrine seems to us to be erroneous. Even if the *coup de grace* to Timberlane's enterprise in Honduras was applied by official authorities, we do not agree that the doctrine necessarily shelters these defendants or requires dismissal of the Timberlane action.

The leading modern statement of the act of state doctrine appears in *Banco Nacional de Cuba v. Sabbatino*, 376 U.S. 398.... Despite contrary implications in *Underhill* and *American Banana*, the Court concluded that the doctrine was not compelled by the nature of sovereignty, by international law, or by the text of the Constitution. Rather, it derives from the judiciary's concern for its possible interference with the conduct of foreign affairs by the political branches of government:

> The doctrine as formulated in past decisions expresses the strong sense of the Judicial Branch that its engagement in the task of passing on the validity of foreign acts of state may hinder rather than further this country's pursuit of goals both for itself and for the community of nations as a whole in the international sphere.

Id. at 423. The Court recognized that not every case is identical in its potential impact on our relations with other nations. For instance:

> [S]ome aspects of international law touch much more sharply on national nerves than do others; the less important the implications of an issue are for our foreign relations, the weaker the justification for exclusivity in the political branches.

Id. at 428. Thus the Court explicitly rejected "laying down or reaffirming an inflexible and all-encompassing rule." *Id.* Whether forbearance by an American court in a given situation is advisable or appropriate depends upon the "balance of relevant considerations." *Id.*

It is apparent that the doctrine does not bestow a blank-check immunity upon all conduct blessed with some imprimatur of a foreign government.....

A corollary to the act of state doctrine in the foreign trade antitrust field is the often-recognized principle that corporate conduct which is compelled by a foreign sovereign is also protected from antitrust liability, as if it were an act of the state itself.....

On the other hand, mere governmental approval or foreign governmental involvement which the defendants had arranged does not necessarily provide a defense.....

The touchstone of *Sabbatino*—the potential for interference with our foreign relations—is the crucial element in determining whether deference should be accorded in any given case. We wish to avoid "passing on the validity" of foreign acts. Similarly, we do not wish to challenge the sovereignty of another nation, the wisdom of its policy, or the integrity and motivation of its action. On the other hand, repeating the terms of *Sabbatino*, "the less important the implications of an issue are for our foreign relations, the weaker the justification for exclusivity in the political branches."

While we do not wish to impugn or question the nobility of a foreign nation's motivation, we are necessarily interested in the depth and nature of its interest. The *Restatement (Second) of Foreign Relations Law of the United States* § 41 (1965) makes an important distinction on this basis in limiting the deference of American courts:

> [A] court in the United States...will refrain from examining the validity of an act of a foreign state by which that state has exercised its jurisdiction *to give effect to its public interests*. [Emphasis added.]

The "public interest" qualification is intentional and significant in the context of Timberlane's action, as a comment to § 41 makes plain:

> *Comment d. Nature of act of state.* An "act of state" as the term is used in this Title involves the public interests of a state as a state, as distinct from its interest in providing the means of adjudicating disputes or claims that arise within its territory.... A judgment of a court may be an act of state. Usually it is not, because it involves the interests of private litigants or because court adjudication is not the usual way in which the state exercises its jurisdiction to give effect to public interests.

Id. at 127.

On the basis of the foregoing analysis, we conclude that the court below erred in dismissing the instant suit on the authority of *Occidental Petroleum Corp. v. Buttes Gas & Oil Co.,* 331 F.Supp. 92, 108-13 (C.D. Cal.1971), *aff'd,* 461 F.2d 1261 (9th Cir.), *cert. denied,* 409 U.S. 950 (1972). The actions of the Honduran government that are involved here—including the application by its courts and their agents of the Honduran laws concerning security interests and the protection of the underlying property against diminution—are clearly distinguishable from the sovereign decrees laying claim to off-shore waters that were at issue in *Occidental Petroleum.* Here, the allegedly "sovereign" acts of Honduras consisted of judicial proceedings which were initiated by Caminals, a private party and one of the alleged co-conspirators, not by the Honduran government itself. Unlike the *Occidental Petroleum* plaintiffs, Timberlane does not seek to name Honduras or any Honduran officer as a defendant or co-conspirator, nor does it challenge Honduran policy or sovereignty in any fashion that appears on its face to hold any threat to relations between Honduras and the United States. In fact, there is no indication that the actions of the Honduran court and authorities reflected a sovereign decision that Timberlane's efforts should be crippled or that trade with the United States should be restrained. Moreover, and once again unlike the situation in *Occidental Petroleum,* plaintiffs here apparently complain of additional agreements and actions which are totally unrelated to the Honduran government. These separate activities would clearly be unprotected even if procurement of a Honduran act of state were one part of defendants' overall scheme.

Under these circumstances, it is clear that the "act of state" doctrine does not require dismissal of the Timberlane action.

Extraterritorial Reach of the United States Antitrust Laws

There is no doubt that American antitrust laws extend over some conduct in other nations. There was language in the first Supreme Court case in point, *American Banana Co. v. United Fruit Co.,* 213 U.S. 347,... (1909), casting doubt on the extension of the Sherman Act to acts outside United States territory. But subsequent cases have limited *American Banana* to its particular facts, and the Sherman Act—and with it other antitrust laws—has been applied to extraterritorial conduct. *See, e.g., United States v. Aluminum Co. of America,* 148 F.2d 416, (2d Cir. 1945) (the "*Alcoa*" case). The act may encompass the foreign activities of aliens as well as American citizens. *Alcoa, supra;....*

That American law covers some conduct beyond this nation's borders does not mean that it embraces all, however. Extraterritorial application is understandably a matter of concern for the other countries involved. Those nations have sometimes resented and protested, as excessive intrusions into their own spheres, broad assertions of authority by American courts. Our courts have recognized this concern and have, at times, responded to it, even if not always enough to satisfy all the foreign critics. *See Alcoa*, 148 F.2d at 443. In any event, it is evident that at some point the interests of the United States are too weak and the foreign harmony incentive for restraint too strong to justify an extraterritorial assertion of jurisdiction.

What that point is or how it is determined is not defined by international law. Nor does the Sherman Act limit itself. In the domestic field the Sherman Act extends to the full reach of the commerce power. To define it somewhat more modestly in the foreign commerce area courts have generally, and logically, fallen back on a narrower construction of congressional intent, such as expressed in Judge Learned Hand's oft-cited opinion in *Alcoa*, 148 F.2d at 443:

> [T]he only question open is whether Congress intended to impose the liability and whether our own Constitution permitted it to do so: as a court of the United States we cannot look beyond our own law. Nevertheless, it is quite true that we are not to read general words, such as those in this Act, without regard to the limitations customarily observed by nations upon the exercise of their powers; limitations which generally correspond to those fixed by the "Conflict of Laws." We should not impute to Congress an intent to punish all whom its courts can catch, for conduct which has no consequences within the United States.

It is the effect on American foreign commerce which is usually cited to support extraterritorial jurisdiction. *Alcoa* set the course, when Judge Hand declared, *id.*:

> [I]t is settled law . . . that any state may impose liabilities, even upon persons not within its allegiance, for conduct outside its borders that has consequences within its borders which the state reprehends; and these liabilities other states will ordinarily recognize.

Despite its description as "settled law," *Alcoa*'s assertion has been roundly disputed by many foreign commentators as being in conflict with international law, comity, and good judgment. Nonetheless, American courts have firmly concluded that there is some extraterritorial jurisdiction under the Sherman Act.

Even among American courts and commentators, however, there is no consensus on how far the jurisdiction should extend. The district court here concluded that a "direct and substantial effect" on United States foreign commerce was a prerequisite, without stating whether other factors were relevant or considered. . . . .It has been identified and advocated by several commentators. *See, e.g.,* W. Fugate, *Foreign Commerce and the Antitrust Laws* 30, 174 (2d ed. 1973).

Other courts have used different expressions, however.

Different standards have been urged by other commentators. Julian von Kalinowski, advocates a "direct *or* substantial" effect test—"any effect that is not *both* insubstantial and indirect" should support jurisdiction, a view that was adopted by the district court in *Occidental Petroleum v. Buttes Gas & Oil Co.*, 331 F.Supp. 92, 102-03 (C.D.Cal.1971), *affirmed on other grounds*, 461 F.2d 1261 (9th Cir.), *cert. denied*, 409 U.S. 950 (1972). [*See* 1 J. von Kalinowski, *Antitrust Law and Trade Regulation* § 5.02[2], at 5-122.] James Rahl turns away from a flat requirement of effects by concluding that the Sherman Act should reach a restraint either "(1) if it occurs *in the course of* foreign commerce, *or* (2) if it *substantially affects* either foreign or interstate commerce." Rahl, *Foreign Commerce Jurisdiction of the American Antitrust Laws*, 43 ANTITRUST L.J. 521, 523 (1974). In essence, as Dean Rahl observes, "[t]here is no agreed black-letter rule articulating the Sherman Act's commerce coverage" in the international context. *Id.*

Few cases have discussed the nature of the effect required for jurisdiction, perhaps because most of the litigated cases have involved relatively obvious offenses and rather significant and apparent effects on competition within the United States. It is probably in part because the standard has not often been put to a real test that it seems so poorly defined. William Fugate, who has identified the "direct and substantial" standard as the rule, has described the meaning of that phrase as being "quite broad." W. Fugate, *supra*, at 174. What the threshold of significance is, however, has not been identified. Nor is it quite clear what the "direct-indirect" distinction is supposed to mean. It might well be, as was said in the context of transnational securities regulation:

> Although courts have spoken in terms of the *Restatement* and of congressional policy, findings that an American effect was direct, substantial, and foreseeable, or within the scope of congressional intent, have little independent analytic significance. Instead, cases appear to turn on a reconciliation of American and foreign interests in regulating their respective economies and business affairs....

Note, *American Adjudication of Transnational Securities Fraud*, 89 HARV.L. REV. 553, 563 (1976).

Implicit in that observation, as it is in several of the cases and commentaries employing the "effects" test, is the suggestion that factors other than simply the effect on the United States are weighed, and rightly so. As former Attorney General (then Professor) Katzenbach observed, the effect on American commerce is not, by itself, sufficient information on which to base a decision that the United States is the nation primarily interested in the activity causing the effect. "[A]nything that affects the external trade and commerce of the United States also affects the trade and commerce of other nations, and may have far greater consequences for others than for the United States." Katzenbach, *Conflicts on an Unruly Horse*, 65 YALE L.J. 1087, 1150 (1956).

The effects test by itself is incomplete because it fails to consider other nations' interests. Nor does it expressly take into account the full nature of the relationship between the actors and this country. Whether the alleged offender is an American citizen, for instance, may make a big difference; applying American laws to American citizens raises fewer problems than application to foreigners. As was observed in *Pacific Seafarers, Inc. v. Pacific Far East Line, Inc.*, 404 F.2d 804, 815 (1968), *cert. denied*, 393 U.S. 1093(1969):

> If...[American antitrust] policy cannot extend to the full sweep of American foreign commerce because of the international complications involved, then surely the test which determines whether United States law is applicable must focus on the nexis between the parties and their practices and the United States, not on the mechanical circumstances of effect on commodity exports or imports.

American courts have, in fact, often displayed a regard for comity and the prerogatives of other nations and considered their interests as well as other parts of the factual circumstances, even when professing to apply an effects test. To some degree, the requirement for a "substantial" effect may silently incorporate these additional considerations, with "substantial" as a flexible standard that varies with other factors. The intent requirement suggested by *Alcoa* is one example of an attempt to broaden the court's perspective, as is drawing a distinction between American citizens and non-citizens.

The failure to articulate these other elements in addition to the standard effects analysis is costly, however, for it is more likely that they will be overlooked or slighted in interpreting past decisions and reaching new ones. Placing emphasis on the qualification that effects be "substantial" is also risky, for the term has a meaning in the interstate antitrust context which does not encompass all the factors relevant to the foreign trade case.

Indeed, that "substantial effects" element of interstate antitrust analysis may well be responsible for the use of an effects test for foreign commerce. The Sherman Act reaches restraints directly intended to limit the flow of interstate trade or whose sole impact is on interstate commerce, but it also reaches "wholly local business restraints" if the particular restraint "substantially and adversely affects interstate commerce." *Hospital Building*, 425 U.S. at 743.... Such a test is necessary in the interstate context to separate the restraints which fall within the federal ambit under the interstate commerce clause from those which, as purely intrastate burdens, remain the province of the states. Since, however, no comparable constitutional problem exists in defining the scope of congressional power to regulate *foreign* commerce, it may be unwise blindly to apply the "substantiality" test to the international setting. Only respect for the role of the executive and for international notions of comity and fairness limit that constitutional grant.

A tripartite analysis seems to be indicated. As acknowledged above, the antitrust laws require in the first instance that there be *some* effect—actual or intended—on American foreign commerce before the federal courts may legitimately exercise subject matter jurisdiction under those statutes. Second, a greater showing of burden or restraint may be necessary to demonstrate that the effect is sufficiently large to present a cognizable injury to the plaintiffs and, therefore, a civil *violation* of the antitrust laws. Third, there is the additional question which is unique to the international setting of whether the interests of, and links to, the United States—including the magnitude of the effect on American foreign commerce—are sufficiently strong, vis-á-vis those of other nations, to justify an assertion of extraterritorial authority.

It is this final issue which is both obscured by undue reliance on the "substantiality" test and complicated to resolve. An effect on United States commerce, although necessary to the exercise of jurisdiction under the antitrust laws, is alone not a sufficient basis on which to determine whether American authority *should* be asserted in a given case as a matter of international comity and fairness. In some cases, the application of the direct and substantial test in the international context might open the door too widely by sanctioning jurisdiction over an action when these considerations would indicate dismissal. At other times, it may fail in the other direction, dismissing a case for which comity and fairness do not require forbearance, thus closing the jurisdictional door too tightly—for the Sherman Act does reach some restraints which do not have both a direct and substantial effect on the foreign commerce of the United States. A more comprehensive inquiry is necessary. We believe that the field of conflict of laws presents the proper approach, as was suggested, if not specifically employed, in *Alcoa* in expressing the basic limitation on application of American laws:

> [W]e are not to read general words, such as those in this Act, without regard to the limitations customarily observed by nations upon the exercise of their powers; limitations which generally correspond to those fixed by the "Conflict of Laws."

148 F.2d at 443. The same idea is reflected in *Restatement (Second) of Foreign Relations Law of the United States* § 40:

> Where two states have jurisdiction to prescribe and enforce rules of law and the rules they may prescribe require inconsistent conduct upon the part of a

person, each state is required by international law to consider, in good faith, moderating the exercise of its enforcement jurisdiction....

The act of state doctrine discussed earlier demonstrates that the judiciary is sometimes cognizant of the possible foreign implications of its action. Similar awareness should be extended to the general problems of extraterritoriality. Such acuity is especially required in private suits, like this one, for in these cases there is no opportunity for the executive branch to weigh the foreign relations impact, nor any statement implicit in the filing of the suit that that consideration has been outweighed.

What we prefer is an evaluation and balancing of the relevant considerations in each case—in the words of Kingman Brewster, a "jurisdictional rule of reason." Balancing of the foreign interests involved was the approach taken by the Supreme Court in *Continental Ore Co. v. Union Carbide & Carbon Corp.*, 370 U.S. 690 (1962), where the involvement of the Canadian government in the alleged monopolization was held not require dismissal. The Court stressed that there was no indication that the Canadian authorities approved or would have approved of the monopolization, meaning that the Canadian interest, if any, was slight and was outweighed by the American interest in condemning the restraint.

The elements to be weighed include the degree of conflict with foreign law or policy, the nationality or allegiance of the parties and the locations or principal places of business of corporations, the extent to which enforcement by either state can be expected to achieve compliance, the relative significance of effects on the United States as compared with those elsewhere, the extent to which there is explicit purpose to harm or affect American commerce, the foreseeability of such effect, and the relative importance to the violations charged of conduct within the United States as compared with conduct abroad. A court evaluating these factors should identify the potential degree of conflict if American authority is asserted. A difference in law or policy is one likely sore spot, though one which may not always be present. Nationality is another; though foreign governments may have some concern for the treatment of American citizens and business residing there, they primarily care about their own nationals. Having assessed the conflict, the court should then determine whether in the face of it the contacts and interests of the United States are sufficient to support the exercise of extraterritorial jurisdiction.

We conclude, then, that the problem should be approached in three parts: Does the alleged restraint affect, or was it intended to affect, the foreign commerce of the United States? Is it of such a type and magnitude so as to be cognizable as a violation of the Sherman Act? As a matter of international comity and fairness, should the extraterritorial jurisdiction of the United States be asserted to cover it? The district court's judgment found only that the restraint involved in the instant suit did not produce a direct and substantial effect on American foreign commerce. That holding does not satisfy any of these inquiries.

The Sherman Act is not limited to trade restraints which have both a direct and substantial effect on our foreign commerce. Timberlane has alleged that the complained of activities were intended to, and did, affect the export of lumber from Honduras to the United States—the flow of United States foreign commerce, and as such they are within the jurisdiction of the federal courts under the Sherman Act. Moreover, the magnitude of the effect alleged would appear to be sufficient to state a claim.

The comity question is more complicated. From Timberlane's complaint it is evident that there are grounds for concern as to at least a few of the defendants, for some are identified as foreign citizens: Laureano Gutierrez Falla, Michael Casanova and the Casanova firms, of Honduras, and Patrick Byrne, of Canada. Moreover, it is clear that most of the activity took place in Honduras, though the conspiracy may have been directed from San Francisco, and that the most direct economic effect was probably on Honduras. However, there has been no indication of any conflict with the law or policy of the Honduran government, nor any comprehensive analysis of the relative connections and interests of Honduras and the United States. Under these circumstances, the dismissal by the district court cannot be sustained on jurisdictional grounds.

We, therefore, vacate the dismissal and remand the *Timberlane* action. [The remand decision is found at 574 F.Supp. 1453 (N.D. Cal. 1983). That decision was affirmed on appeal, and subsequently the Supreme Court denied *writ of certiorari*. The appellate decision follows.]

Timberlane Lumber Company v. Bank of America National Trust and Savings Association
749 F.2d 1378 (9th Cir. 1984), cert. denied, 472 U.S. 1032 (1985) ("Timberlane II")

Sneed, Circuit Judge:

In this antitrust action, Timberlane Lumber Company (Timberlane) alleged that Bank of America, its officers, and other individuals conspired to prevent Timberlane from milling lumber in Honduras and exporting it to the United States. The suit was consolidated with three independent tort actions brought by Timberlane employees for individual injuries suffered during the alleged illegal conduct. The district court dismissed the antitrust action under the act of state doctrine and for lack of subject matter jurisdiction. The consolidated tort actions were dismissed under the doctrine of *forum non conveniens*.

This case has been before us previously. On that appeal, *Timberlane Lumber Co. v. Bank of America, N.T. & S.A.*, 549 F.2d 597 (9th Cir. 1976) *(Timberlane I)* [excerpted above], we established *a tripartite test* for determining *the extent of federal jurisdiction in cases alleging illegal antitrust behavior abroad*. We then vacated the dismissals and remanded the case for additional discovery in light of the new jurisdictional "rule of reason." After allowing additional discovery, the district court granted Bank of America's motion to dismiss the antitrust action for lack of subject matter jurisdiction. *Timberlane Lumber Co. v. Bank of America National Trust and Savings Association*, 574 F. Supp. 1453 (N.D.Cal. 1983) *(Timberlane II)*. The tort actions were again dismissed on forum non conveniens grounds. Timberlane appeals the dismissal in all respects. We affirm.

I.

Facts and Proceedings Below

Timberlane, an Oregon partnership whose primary business is the purchase and distribution of lumber in the United States, formed a partnership with two Honduran corporations (Danli Industrial, S.A. and Maya Lumber Company, S. de R.L.) that were incorporated and principally owned by the general partners of Timberlane. The partnership sought to develop alternative sources of lumber for delivery to the United States from Honduras. It eventually purchased an interest in an existing but financially unstable lumber mill owned by the Lima family.

Before the Timberlane purchase, ownership of the Lima enterprise had been transferred to a group of Lima employees, Bank of America, and another competing lumber mill, Casanova. Timberlane purchased its interest from the Lima employees, who had priority over the other claims. The other two owners refused to sell their interests to Timberlane. Bank of America's actions in connection with these interests form the basis for the alleged illegal antitrust conduct.

Timberlane alleges that Bank of America refused to sell its share in the Lima enterprise because it wanted to protect its interests in other competing lumber mills by driving Timberlane out of the Honduran lumber market. Thus, Timberlane claims that Bank of America transferred its mortgage to Casanova, a Lima enterprise competitor, for no consideration other than a portion of the proceeds collected. Casanova subsequently assigned both interests to Caminals who allegedly attempted to eliminate the Lima enterprise.

Using Honduran law, Caminals tried to foreclose on the mortgages by placing an "embargo" on all property owned by the Lima enterprise. A Honduran court appointed an "intervenor" to prevent a diminution of the Timberlane assets. Timberlane alleges that through the intervenor, Caminals obtained embargos against Timberlane's partners Maya and Danli. It also claims that Bank of America paid the intervenor to use guards and troops to shut down Timberlane's milling operations. It is in this context that Timberlane's employees alleged that they were falsely arrested and imprisoned. Eventually, all of the claims relating to the mortgage foreclosure were resolved in the Honduran court system.

Timberlane filed this antitrust action seeking more than $5,000,000 in damages from Bank of America and its Honduran subsidiaries. Some of Timberlane's employees also brought individual tort actions. The district court, to repeat, dismissed (1) the antitrust action on the ground that the act of state doctrine prevented the federal courts from entertaining suit, and (2) the tort actions on the basis of *forum non conveniens*.

In *Timberlane I,* we vacated the district court's act of state holding and announced a tripartite test for determining the extent of federal jurisdiction over claims alleging illegal antitrust behavior abroad. Because the case was remanded for additional discovery in light of this new "rule of reason" standard, we also vacated the *forum non conveniens* dismissal.

On remand, the district court allowed additional discovery. Bank of America again filed a motion to dismiss the action for lack of subject matter jurisdiction. The district court treated the motion as one filed under Federal Rule of Civil Procedure 12(b)(1) and dismissed the antitrust claim. It also again dismissed the tort claims on *forum non conveniens* grounds. Timberlane appeals the entirety of the district court's judgment.

II.

Application of *Timberlane I's*

Jurisdictional Rule of Reason

B. *Timberlane I's "jurisdictional rule of reason."*

In *Timberlane I,* 549 F.2d at 615, in describing our tripartite jurisdictional test, we said that the

> "problem [of extraterritorial jurisdiction] should be approached in three parts: Does the alleged restraint affect, or was it intended to affect, the foreign

commerce of the United States? Is it of such a type and magnitude so as to be cognizable as a violation of the Sherman Act. As a matter of international comity and fairness, should the extraterritorial jurisdiction of the United States be asserted to cover it?"

The district court applied *Timberlane's* analysis and, on the basis of its third part, concluded that jurisdiction should not be exercised in this case. Although we agree with the district court's conclusion regarding each part of the *Timberlane I* test, we do not expressly approve all of its analysis. Therefore, we discuss each part of the inquiry as set forth in *Timberlane I*.

1. *"Does the alleged restraint affect, or was it intended to affect, the foreign commerce of the United States?"*

The first part of *Timberlane I's* analysis requires "that there be *some* effect - actual or intended - on American foreign commerce before the federal courts may legitimately exercise subject matter jurisdiction under [the antitrust] statutes." 549 F.2d at 613 (emphasis in original). On appeal, Bank of America does not deny that Timberlane has met this requirement. "[B]y alleging the ability and willingness to supply cognizable markets with lumber that they allege would have been competitive with that already in the marketplace, they have satisfied this prong of the Circuit's test." *Timberlane II*, 574 F.Supp. at 1466.

2. *"Is it of such a type and magnitude so as to be cognizable a a violation of the Sherman Act?"*

Under the second part of *Timberlane I's* analysis, "a greater showing of burden or restraint may be necessary to demonstrate that the effect is sufficiently large to present a cognizable injury to the plaintiffs and, therefore, a civil *violation* of the antitrust laws." 549 F.2d at 613 (emphasis in original). Courts and commentators, however, have had difficulty identifying the nature and extent of proof required to satisfy this part of the inquiry.... It has been suggested that *Timberlane I* requires a showing of a "direct and substantial" effect on the foreign commerce of the United States. In fact, however, no such showing is necessary. The only issue under the second part of the inquiry is whether the magnitude of the effect identified in the first part of the test rises to the level of a civil antitrust violation, *i.e.*, conduct that has a direct and substantial anti-competitive effect.....*Timberlane I's* requirement that the allegation state a claim under the antitrust laws, however, "is a 'practical, case-by-case economic judgment,' not one based on 'abstract or mechanistic formulae,'... and...the barrier raised is not very high." *Timberlane I*, 549 F.2d at 615 n. 35 (citations omitted).

In this case, Timberlane alleges that Bank of America conspired with its Honduran subsidiaries to prevent Timberlane from milling lumber in Honduras and exporting it to the United States. Our review of the complaint reveals that Timberlane has alleged an injury that would state a claim under the antitrust laws against Bank of America. Thus, it satisfies the second part of the analysis.

3. *"As a matter of international comity and fairness, should the extraterritorial jurisdiction of the United States be asserted to cover it?"*

Under the third part of *Timberlane I's* analysis, the district court must determine "whether the interests of, and links to, the United States - including the magnitude of the effect on American foreign commerce - are sufficiently strong, vis-a-vis those of other nations, to justify an assertion of extraterritorial authority." 549 F.2d at 613.

This determination requires that a district court consider seven factors. The district court here found that the undisputed facts required that jurisdiction not be exercised in this case. We agree. To support our conclusion each factor will be examined.

a. *The degree of conflict with foreign law or policy"*

We must determine whether the extra-territorial enforcement of United States antitrust laws creates an actual or potential conflict with the laws and policies of other nations. Timberlane argues that no conflict exists between United States and Honduran law. We disagree. The application of United States antitrust law in this case creates a potential conflict with the Honduran government's effort to foster a particular type of business climate.

Although Honduras does not have antitrust laws as such, it does have definite policies concerning the character of its commercial climate. To promote economic development and efficiency within its relatively undeveloped economy, the Honduran Constitution and Commercial Code guarantee freedom of action. The Code specifically condemns any laws prohibiting agreements (even among competitors) to restrict or divide commercial activity. Under Honduran law, competitors may agree to allocate geographic or market territories, to restrict price or output, to cut off the source of raw materials, or to limit credit financing to obtain enterprises as long as the contracting parties are not de facto monopolists.... It appears that Honduran law intimately regulates private commercial activity in that country. Honduran law also promotes agreements that improve the competitive position of domestic industries in world markets by promoting efficiency and economies of scale.

On balance, we believe that the enforcement of United States antitrust laws in this case would lead to a significant conflict with Honduran law and policy. This conflict, unless outweighed by other factors in the comity analysis, is itself a sufficient reason to decline the exercise of jurisdiction over this dispute.

b. *"The nationality or allegiance of the parties and the locations of principal places of business of corporations"*

Next we should consider the citizenship of the parties and witnesses involved in the alleged illegal conduct. In this case, with only one exception, all of the named parties are United States citizens or nationals. But it is also true that "[a]ll of the crucial percipient witnesses to the incidents were either Honduran citizens or residents." *Timberlane II,* 574 F.Supp. at 1470. We believe, therefore, that the citizenship of the parties weighs slightly in favor of the exercise of jurisdiction.

c. *"The extent to which enforcement by either state can be expected to achieve compliance"*

The weighing of this factor yields no clear answer. Of course, any judgment against Bank of America could easily be enforced in a United States court. Whether such a judgment could be enforced as easily in Honduras is less certain. We believe that the enforcement factor tips slightly in favor of the assertion of jurisdiction in this case.

d. *"The relative significance of effects on the United States as compared with those elsewhere"*

A more definitive answer emerges when we compare the effect of the alleged illegal conduct on the foreign commerce of the United States with its effect abroad. The insignificance of the effect on the foreign commerce of the United States when compared with the substantial effect in Honduras suggests federal jurisdiction should not be exercised.

A comparison of Honduran lumber imports to both United States imports and total United States lumber consumption is instructive. During the years 1970 through 1972, the amount of lumber imported from Honduras expressed as a percentage of total United States lumber imports was as follows:

Year	Volume (Board FT)	Value ($)
1970	0.07%	0.09%
1971	0.02%	0.03%
1972	0.04%	0.05%

During the same years, Honduran lumber imports formed an even smaller percentage of total United States lumber consumption:

Year	Volume (Board FT)
1970	0.011%
1971	0.004%
1972	0.008%

Clearly, Honduran imports have only a minuscule effect on United States lumber markets.

Second, a comparison of the specific sub-markets of "Pine Lumber Dressed" and "Pine Lumber Rough" in no way helps Timberlane's case. Honduran imports of both "Pine Lumber" and "Pine Lumber NES Rough" expressed as a percentage of total pine lumber imports were as follows:

Year	Vollume (Board FT)	Value ($)
1970	3.0%	4.6%
1971	2.8%	3.2%
1972	3.4%	3.5%

Again, these figures represent only an insignificant part of the pine lumber import market. And although we do not have the relevant statistics, we believe that Honduran imports represent an insubstantial part of total United States pine lumber consumption.

The actual effect of Timberlane's potential operations on United States foreign commerce is, therefore, insubstantial, even in the narrow pine lumber market. In comparison, the effects of its activity on the considerably smaller Honduran lumber markets would have been much greater. The bank's actions also affect several other aspects of the Honduran economy such as the number of jobs, the amount of foreign exchange and taxes, and the internal competitive market. We believe that the relative significance of effects in this case weighs strongly against the exercise of jurisdiction.

e. "The extent to which there is explicit purpose to harm or affect American commerce"

We should also consider whether the defendant's actions were intended to harm or affect the commerce of the United States. Our review of the record reveals that Bank of America's acts were directed primarily towards securing a greater return on its investment. Its actions were consistent with Honduran customs and practices. Timberlane has not demonstrated that Bank of America had any particular interest in affecting United States commerce.

f. *"The foreseeability of such effect"*

A court should also consider whether, at the time of the alleged illegal behavior, the defendant should have foreseen an effect on the foreign commerce of the United States. Aside from the fact that American commerce has not been substantially affected, Timberlane has not shown that Bank of America should have foreseen the consequences of its actions. Bank of America simply enforced its mortgage in an attempt to recoup its investment. The effects of this action were merely part of the inevitable consequences that flow from attempting to salvage something from a failing business enterprise. We do not believe that a reasonable investor would have foreseen the minimal effect that has occurred here. This weighs against the exercise of jurisdiction.

g. *"The relative importance to the violations charged of conduct within the United States as compared with conduct abroad"*

Finally, a court should consider the location of the alleged illegal conduct in order to assess the appropriateness of the exercise of extraterritorial jurisdiction. In this case both parties agree that virtually all of the illegal activity occurred in Honduras. This factor clearly weighs against the exercise of jurisdiction.

h. *Resolving the Seven Factor Test*

It follows that all but two of the factors in *Timberlane I's* comity analysis indicate that we should refuse to exercise jurisdiction over this antitrust case. The potential for conflict with Honduran economic policy and commercial law is great. The effect on the foreign commerce of the United States is minimal. The evidence of intent to harm American commerce is altogether lacking. The foreseeablility of the anti-competitive consequences of the allegedly illegal actions is slight. Most of the conduct that must be examined occurred abroad. The factors that favor jurisdiction are the citizenship of the parties and, to a slight extent, the enforcement effectiveness of United States law. We do not believe that this is enough to justify the exercise of federal jurisdiction over this case.

AFFIRMED.

Laker Airways v. Sabena, Belgian World Airlines
731 F.2d 909 (D.C. Cir. 1984)

. . . .

Wilkey, Circuit Judge:

We review today the limits of a federal court's power to conserve its adjudicatory authority over a case properly filed with the court when, instead of actively raising all defensive claims in the federal court, the named defendants initiate suits in foreign tribunals for the sole purpose of terminating the federal court's adjudication of the litigation. Three months after Laker Airways, Ltd. ("Laker") filed an antitrust action in United States District Court for the District of Columbia against several defendants, including domestic, British, and other foreign airlines, the foreign airlines filed suits in the High Court of Justice of the United Kingdom seeking an injunction forbidding Laker from prosecuting its American antitrust action against the foreign defendants. After the High Court of Justice entered interim injunctions against Laker, the Court of Appeal issued a permanent injunction ordering Laker to take action to dismiss its suit against the British airlines. In the meantime, Laker responded by requesting injunctive relief in the United States District Court, arguing that a restraining order was necessary to prevent the remaining American defendants and the additional foreign defendants Laker had named in a subsequent antitrust claim from duplicating the foreign defendants' successful request for an English injunction compelling Laker to dismiss its suit against the defendants.

If these defendants had been permitted to file foreign injunctive actions, the United States District Court would have been effectively stripped of control over the claims-based on United States law-which it was in the process of adjudicating. Faced with no alternative but acquiescence in the termination of this jurisdiction by a foreign court's order, United States District Judge Harold H. Greene granted Laker's motion for a preliminary injunction restraining the remaining defendants from taking part in the foreign action designed to prevent the district court from hearing Laker's antitrust claims.

Two of the defendants enjoined from taking part in the English proceeding, KLM Royal Dutch Airlines ("KLM") and Societe Anonyme Belge d'Exploitation de la Navigation Aerienne ("Sabena") now contend on appeal that the court abused its discretion. Their arguments are essentially two-fold: first, that the injunction tramples Britain's rights to regulate the access of its nationals to judicial remedies; second, that the injunction contravenes the principles of international comity which ordinarily compel deference to foreign judgments and which virtually always proscribe any interference with foreign judicial proceedings.

Our review of the limited available facts strongly suggests that both the United States and Great Britain share concurrent prescriptive jurisdiction over the transactions giving rise to Laker's claim. Ordinarily antisuit injunctions are not properly invoked to preempt parallel proceedings on the same in personam claim in foreign tribunals. However, KLM and Sabena do not qualify under this general rule because the foreign action they seek to join is interdictory and not parallel. It was instituted by the foreign defendants for the sole purpose of terminating the United States claim. The only conceivable benefit that KLM and Sabena would reap if the district court's injunction were overturned would be the right to attack the pending United States action in a foreign court. This would permit the appellants to avoid potential liability under the United States laws to which their business operations and treaty obligations have long subjected them. In these circumstances there is ample precedent justifying the defensive use of an antisuit injunction.

The injunction does not transgress either the principles of international comity or nationality-based prescriptive jurisdiction on which KLM and Sabena rely. Limitations on the application of comity dating from the origins of the doctrine recognize that a domestic forum is not compelled to acquiesce in pre- or postjudgment conduct by litigants which frustrates the significant policies of the domestic forum. Accession to a demand for comity predicated on the coercive effects of a foreign judgment usurping legitimately concurrent prescriptive jurisdiction is unlikely to foster the processes of accommodation and cooperation which form the basis for a genuine system of international comity. Similarly, the mere fact of Laker's British juridical status simply does not erase all other legitimate bases of concurrent jurisdiction, as appellants suggest. Thus, the appellants' arguments that the district court abused its discretion fall well short of their mark.

The claims raised by KLM and Sabena do pose serious issues regarding the Judiciary's role in accommodating the conflicting implementation of concurrent prescriptive jurisdiction. We have necessarily inquired into the source of the conflict facing the courts of the United States and United Kingdom, and probed the extent to which the judicial processes may effectively be employed to resolve conflicts like the present one. Given the inherent limitations on the Judiciary's ability to adjust national priorities in light of directly contradictory foreign policies, there is little the Judiciary may do directly to resolve the conflict. Although the flash point of the controversy has been the antisuit injunctions, the real powder keg is the strongly mandated legislative policies which each national court is bound to implement. Thus, it is unlikely that the underlying controversy would be defused regardless of the action we take today.

Because the principles of comity and concurrent jurisdiction clearly authorize the use of a defensive preliminary injunction designed to permit the United States claim to go forward free of foreign interference, we affirm the decision of the district court.

I. BACKGROUND

This case raises especially troublesome issues on two different fronts. It represents a head-on collision between the diametrically opposed antitrust policies of the United States and United Kingdom, and is perhaps the most pronounced example in recent years of the problems raised by the concurrent jurisdiction held by several states over transactions substantially affecting several states' interests. These problems are all the more intractable because of the vehicles involved in the collision: antisuit injunctions designed to preempt the parties' access to the courts of foreign jurisdictions. The intersection of these issues confronts us with the Herculean task of accommodating conflicting, mutually inconsistent national regulatory policies while minimizing the amount of interference with the judicial processes of other nations that our courts will permit. Resolution of this appeal thus requires a clear grasp of both the underlying factual background of Laker's antitrust claims and the complex sequence of litigation and counterlitigation in which those claims have been asserted by Laker and attacked by the foreign defendants.

A. *Laker's Antitrust Claims*

...Laker Airways, Ltd. was founded as a charter airline in 1966. It began charter operations between the United States and United Kingdom in 1970. As early as 1971 it sought to branch out into scheduled transatlantic air service. Laker hoped to gain a sizeable share of the transatlantic market by offering only basic air passage with little or no in-flight amenities and non-essential services. Flying at a reduced cost would enable Laker to set rates much lower than those then charged by existing transatlantic air carriers.

Laker's potential competitors allegedly resisted the entry of this new carrier, delaying the commencement of Laker's novel economy service for several years. However, by 1977 Laker obtained the necessary authorizations from the United States and British governments and inaugurated its low cost transatlantic airline service between London and New York.

The prices for scheduled transatlantic air service are substantially controlled by the International Air Transport Association ("IATA"), a trade organization of the world's largest air carriers. The IATA meets annually to establish fixed fares for air carriage, which are implemented after authorization by national governments of the individual carriers. Laker's fares were approximately one-third of the competing fares offered by other transatlantic carriers which were predominantly set under the auspices of the IATA. The airline members of IATA allegedly perceived Laker's operations as a threat to their system of cartelized prices. The new competition not only jeopardized the established markets of those carriers operating between the United Kingdom and the United States—such as British Airways and British Caledonian Airways-but also affected the demand for services provided by airlines flying direct routes between points in Continental Europe and the United States—such as Swiss Air Transport ("Swissair"), Lufthansa German Airlines ("Lufthansa"), KLM, and Sabena—since some passengers allegedly found it cheaper to fly through London on Laker Airways, rather than direct on the other European transatlantic carriers. During meetings of the IATA in July and August 1977 the IATA airlines allegedly agreed to set rates at a predatory level to drive Laker out of business.

Notwithstanding this asserted predatory scheme, up until 1981 Laker managed to operate at a profit. At its zenith, Laker was carrying one out of every seven scheduled air passengers between the United States and England.

However, during 1981 Laker's financial condition rapidly deteriorated. In mid 1981 the pound sterling declined precipitously. A large segment of Laker's revenues was in pounds, but most of its debts, such as those on its United States financed fleet of DC-10 aircraft, and expenses were in dollars. Already weakened by the asserted predatory pricing scheme, Laker ran into repayment difficulties. Fearing financial collapse, it sought to have its repayment obligations refinanced.

At this point several airlines allegedly conspired to set even lower predatory prices. In October 1981 Pan American Airlines, Trans World Airlines, and British Airways dropped their fares for their full service flights to equal those charged by Laker for its no-frills service. They also allegedly paid high secret commissions to travel agents to divert potential customers from Laker. These activities further restricted Laker's income, exacerbating its perilous economic condition. At IATA meetings in December 1981 at Geneva, Switzerland, and in January 1982 at Hollywood, Florida, the IATA airlines allegedly laid plans to fix higher fares in the spring and summer of 1982 after Laker had been driven out of business.

IATA members also interfered with Laker's attempt to reschedule its financial obligations. After Laker arranged a refinancing agreement, KLM, Sabena, and other IATA airlines allegedly pressured Laker's lenders to withhold the financing which had previously been promised. As a result of these alleged conspiracies, Laker was forced into liquidation under Jersey law in early February 1982.

B. *Litigation History*

In the aftermath of these asserted conspiracies, Laker, through its liquidator, commenced an action in United States District Court for the District of Columbia to recover for the injuries sustained by the airline as a result of the alleged predatory pricing and unlawful interference with its refinancing arrangements. Laker's complaint filed on 24 November 1982, Civil Action No. 82-3362, alleged two counts: (1) violation of United States antitrust laws, and (2) a common law intentional tort. Named as defendants were four American corporations, Pan American World Airways, Trans World Airlines, McDonnell Douglas Corp., and McDonnell Douglas Finance Corp., as well as four foreign airlines, British Airways, British Caledonian Airways, Lufthansa, and Swissair.

Fearing that Laker would commence a second antitrust action against it, Midland Bank, a British corporation involved in Laker's abortive refinancing attempt, filed a preemptive action in the United Kingdom's High Court of Justice on 29 November 1982 seeking to enjoin Laker from naming it as a defendant in any United States antitrust action. An *ex parte* injunction was issued the same day; this became a more permanent preliminary injunction on 4 February 1983.

Shortly thereafter the four foreign defendants in No. 82-3362 initiated a similar suit in the High Court of Justice. Their writs filed on 21 January 1983 sought (1) a declaration that the four foreign defendants were not engaged in any unlawful combination or conspiracy, and (2) an injunction prohibiting Laker from taking any action in *United States courts* to redress an alleged violation by the defendants *of United States antitrust laws*. The writs specifically sought to compel Laker to dismiss its suit against the foreign defendants in No. 82-3362 and to prohibit Laker from instituting any other proceedings in any non-English forum to redress any alleged violation of English or other laws prohibiting intentional or unlawful commercial injury.

The substantive basis for the requested relief was the alleged inapplicability of United States antitrust laws under the Bermuda II Treaty and the British Protection of Trading Interests Act. Shortly thereafter Justice Parker issued an interlocutory injunction preventing Laker from taking any action in the United States courts or elsewhere to interfere with the proceedings the defendants were commencing in the High Court of Justice.

On 24 January 1983, to avoid being enjoined from continuing to sue the four United States defendants, Laker sought a temporary restraining order from the United States District Court preventing the American defendants from instituting similar preemptive proceedings in England. The order was granted the same day, and later extended pending a hearing on Laker's motion for a preliminary injunction.

Approximately three weeks later, on 15 February 1983, Laker commenced in the district court a second antitrust suit, Civil Action No. 83-0416. Appellants KLM and Sabena were named as defendants. A temporary restraining order was also entered against the appellants, preventing them from taking any action in a foreign court that would have impaired the district court's jurisdiction. This order was extended pending a hearing on Laker's motion for a preliminary injunction.

On 2 March 1983, the British defendants in No. 82-3362 successfully petitioned Justice Parker of the High Court of Justice to grant a second interim injunction against Laker preventing Laker from taking "any further steps" to prosecute its United States claim against the British airlines. Although the injunction was only designed to preserve the status quo pending a ruling by the High Court of Justice on the merits of the British airlines' suit seeking dismissal of No. 82-3362, the injunction prevented Laker from filing any discovery or other motions against British Airways and British Caledonian.

At a hearing held five days later, Laker's motion for a preliminary injunction against the four American defendants, KLM, and Sabena was considered by the United States District Court. By order of 7 March 1983 and memorandum opinion dated 9 March 1983, the district court granted a preliminary injunction. The terms of the injunction were designed only to "protect the jurisdiction of [the district court] over these proceedings" to the extent necessary to preserve "the rights of the plaintiff under the laws of the United States." The injunction prevented the defendants from taking any action before a foreign court or governmental authority that would interfere with the district court's jurisdiction over the matters alleged in the complaint.....

KLM Royal Dutch Airlines and Sabena Belgian World Airlines, joined by amici curiae Swissair and Lufthansa, now appeal the 7 March 1983 order and 9 March 1983 memorandum of the district court which enjoined KLM and Sabena from seeking an injunction against Laker's antitrust suit in the English courts. However, during the pendency of this appeal, the process of litigation and counterlitigation has continued in the United States and English courts.

. . . .

In April and May 1983 Laker continued its efforts to proceed in its United States antitrust actions while defending itself against the proceedings in the High Court of Justice which were designed to terminate its United States claims. On 26 April 1983 Laker issued a summons in the High Court of Justice seeking a dismissal or stay of the suits initiated by Lufthansa and Swissair. Laker also moved in the High Court of Justice for a discharge of the injunction granted on 21 January 1983. In a motion for partial summary judgment filed in the United States District Court, Laker affirmatively challenged the defendants' contentions that the action should be dismissed on *forum non conveniens* grounds. By an opinion and order dated 3 May 1983 the district court granted Laker's motion and held that the principles of *forum non conveniens* did not require that jurisdiction be relinquished.

In a judgment read by Justice Parker on 20 May 1983, the High Court of Justice held that the injunctive relief requested by the British airlines was not justified and terminated claims for relief filed by British Caledonian and British Airways. Justice Parker held that the application of American antitrust laws to companies carrying on business in the United States was not contrary to British sovereignty or the terms of the Bermuda II Treaty, at least while the dormant terms of the British Protection of Trading Interests Act had not been invoked. The judgment did recognize that a determination by the English Secretary of State that Britain's trading interests were negatively implicated by the United States antitrust action could change the result." *However, at this point, before any intervention by the British Executive, the British court was willing to hold that Laker could not be prohibited from proceeding with its antitrust claims against British Airways and British Caledonian.* The original interim injunctions were maintained pending an appeal to the Court of Appeal by British Airways and British Caledonian.

The complexion of the controversy changed dramatically the next month when the British Government invoked the provisions of the British Protection of Trading Interests Act ("Act"). Upon a determination that measures taken to regulate international trade outside the United Kingdom "threaten to damage the trading interests of the United Kingdom," the Act authorizes the English Secretary of State to require that any person conducting business in the United Kingdom disobey all foreign orders and cease all compliance with the foreign judicial or regulatory provisions designated by the Secretary of State. The Act authorizes the Secretary of State to prevent United Kingdom courts from complying with requests for document production issued by foreign tribunals, and forbids enforcement of treble damage awards or antitrust judgments specified by the Secretary of State." On 27 June 1983 the Secretary of State for Trade and Industry cited his powers under the Act and issued an order and general directions prohibiting persons who carry on business in the United Kingdom, with the exception of American air carriers designated under the Bermuda II Treaty, from complying with "United States antitrust measures" in the district court arising out of any (1) "agreement or arrangement (whether legally enforceable or not) to which a UK designated airline is a party," or (2) "any act done by a UK designated airline" that relates to the provision of air carriage under the Bermuda II Treaty."

Laker applied for judicial review of the validity of the order and directions. The Court of Appeal considered this application with the appeals by British Airways and British Caledonian of Justice Parker's judgment of 20 May 1983.

On 26 July 1983 the Court of Appeal announced its judgment that the order and directions were well within the power of the Secretary of State to issue, and hence valid. Because the order and directions of the British Executive prevented the British airline from complying with any requirements imposed by the United States District Court and prohibited the airlines from relying on their own commercial documents located within the United Kingdom to defend themselves against Laker's charges, the Court of Appeal concluded that the United States District Court action was "wholly untriable" and could only result in a "total denial of justice to the British airlines." As a result, the Court of Appeal held that Laker must be permanently enjoined from proceeding with its United States antitrust claims against British Airways and British Caledonian.

After a hearing following judgment, the Court of Appeal granted an injunction (1) restraining Laker from taking any steps against British Airways and British Caledonian in the United States action, and (2) directing Laker to use its best efforts to have British Airways and British Caledonian dismissed from the United States action....

C. Current Appeal in this Court

As the litigation now stands, British Airways and British Caledonian have obtained an injunction by the English Court of Appeal restraining Laker from prosecuting its civil antitrust claim against them. Swissair and Lufthansa have applied for similar relief, but their applications are still pending. However, they are apparently protected by the interim injunctions that prevent Laker from taking any action in United States courts to thwart their 21 January 1983 claim for relief. KLM and Sabena are restrained by the United States District Court from joining the English proceedings.

Supported by *amici curiae* Swissair and Lufthansa, KLM and Sabena challenge the United States District Court's preliminary injunction on appeal to this court. They claim that the injunction was unnecessary to protect the district court's jurisdiction and violates their right to take part in the "parallel" actions commenced in the English courts. Denial of this opportunity, they assert, flouts international principles of comity. Moreover, they charge that the district court ignored Britain's "paramount right" to apply British law to Laker, which is a British subject. Appellants and amici request that we overturn the district court's injunction as a clear abuse of discretion.

II. ANALYSIS

This appeal is the direct result of a clash between two governments asserting jurisdiction to prescribe law over a single series of transactions. The district court's injunction is defended by Laker as necessary to protect the court's jurisdiction. If there is no justification for the court's exercise of jurisdiction, the injunctive relief should necessarily fail. Similarly, if the United Kingdom courts would lack jurisdiction over a claim filed by Sabena and KLM, the district court should be under no obligation to defer to the actions of those foreign tribunals. A true conflict arises only if the national jurisdictions overlap. We must therefore begin our analysis with a review of the recognized bases supporting prescriptive jurisdiction, and then examine whether the alleged facts of this case satisfy those requirements.

A. Bases of Concurrent Prescriptive Jurisdiction
Territoriality and Nationality

1. Overview

Territoriality and nationality are the two fundamental jurisdictional bases on which courts of the United States and United Kingdom rely to assert control over the controversy between Laker and the antitrust defendants.

The prerogative of a nation to control and regulate activities within its boundaries is an essential, definitional element of sovereignty. Every country has a right to dictate laws governing the conduct of its inhabitants. Consequently, the territoriality base of jurisdiction is universally recognized. It is the most pervasive and basic principle underlying the exercise by nations of prescriptive regulatory power. It is the customary basis of the application of law in virtually every country.

.... Territoriality-based jurisdiction thus allows states to regulate the conduct or status of individuals to property physically situated within the territory, even if the effects of the conduct are felt outside the territory. Conversely, conduct outside the territorial boundary which has or is intended to have a substantial effect within the territory may also be regulated by the state.

Just as the locus of the regulated conduct or harm provides a basis of jurisdiction, the identity of the actor may also confer jurisdiction upon a regulating country. The citizenship of an individual or nationality of a corporation has long been a recognized basis which will support the exercise of jurisdiction by a state over persons. Under this head of jurisdiction a state has jurisdiction to prescribe law governing the conduct of its nationals whether the conduct takes place inside or outside the territory of the state.

Because two or more states may have legitimate interests in prescribing governing law over a particular controversy, these jurisdictional bases are not mutually exclusive. For example, when the national of one state causes substantial effects in another state, both states may potentially have jurisdiction to prescribe governing law. Thus, under international law, territoriality and nationality often give rise to concurrent jurisdiction. A court faced with assertions of conflicting or inconsistent prescriptive power under facially concurrent jurisdiction must first examine the sufficiency of jurisdictional contacts under each base of jurisdiction to determine whether either claim of jurisdiction is unfounded. If both claims to jurisdiction are legitimately exercised, avenues of conflict resolution must be considered before jurisdiction to prescribe can go forward.

2. *United States Jurisdictional Base*

The prescriptive application of United States antitrust law to the alleged conspiracies between KLM, Sabena, and the other antitrust defendants is founded upon the harmful effects occurring within the territory of the United States as a direct result of the alleged wrongdoing. Before we examine the nature of those effects and consider whether they support the prescriptive jurisdiction over the claimed conspiracies, we wish to make it clear that this aspect of territorial jurisdiction is entirely consistent with nationally and internationally recognized limits on sovereign authority.

It has long been settled law that a country can regulate conduct occurring outside its territory which causes harmful results within its territory. The traditional example of this principle is that of the transnational homicide: when a malefactor in State *A* shoots a victim across the border in State *B*, State *B* can proscribe the harmful conduct. To take a more likely example, embezzlement or unauthorized access to computerized financial accounts can certainly be controlled by the territory where the accounts are located, even though the thief operates by telephone from a distant territory. Other examples are easily multiplied.

Even if invisible, the radiating consequences of anti-competitive activities cause economic injuries no less tangible than the harmful effects of assassins' bullets or thieves' telephonic impulses. Thus, legislation to protect domestic economic interests can legitimately reach conduct occurring outside the legislating territory intended to damage the protected interests within the territory. As long as the territorial effects are not so inconsequential as to exceed the bounds of reasonableness imposed by international law, prescriptive jurisdiction is legitimately exercised.

The territorial effects doctrine is *not* an *extraterritorial* assertion of jurisdiction. Jurisdiction exists only when significant effects were intended within the prescribing territory. Prescriptive jurisdiction is activated only when there is personal jurisdiction, often referred to as "jurisdiction to adjudicate." A foreign corporation doing business within the United States reasonably expects that its United States operations will be regulated by United States law. The only extraterritoriality about the transactions reached under the territorial effects doctrine is that not all of the causative factors producing the proscribed result may have occurred within the territory. Although some of the business decisions affecting United States operations may be made outside the forum state, the entire transaction is not ordinarily immunized.

Certainly the doctrine of territorial sovereignty is not such an artificial limit on the vindication of legitimate sovereign interests that the injured state confronts the wrong side of a one-way glass, powerless to counteract harmful effects originating outside its boundaries which easily pierce its "sovereign" walls, while its own regulatory efforts are reflected back in its face. Unless one admits that there are certain vital interests that can be affected with impunity by careful selection of the decision-making forum, with the result that a country may be forced to rely entirely on the good offices of a foreign state for vindication of the forum's interests-even when vindication of the forum state's own policies-then availability of territorial effects jurisdiction must be recognized. For these reasons territorial effects jurisdiction has been implemented by several European forums. Indeed, the British have vigorously legislated on this principle in the Protection of Trading Interests Act.

a. *Territorial Contacts Justifying Application of United States Antitrust Law.*

The circumstances of this litigation suggest numerous American interests that would be vindicated if Laker is permitted to proceed with its antitrust claim. Although some of the alleged anticompetitive actions occurred within the United States, most of the conspiratorial acts took place in other countries. This distinction, however, has no overriding significance, since the economic consequences of the alleged actions gravely impair significant American interests. If the only interest involved were that of Laker, a British corporation, then it may very well be that United States jurisdiction to prescribe would not exist. However, Laker is in liquidation. Therefore its interests are only nominal compared to those claiming through it.

A primary objective of antitrust laws is to preserve competition, and thus ultimately protect the interests of American consumers. For decades, a great percentage of passengers on North Atlantic air routes has been United States citizens. The greatest impact of a predatory pricing conspiracy would be to raise fares for United States passengers. No other single nation has nearly the same interest in consumer protection on the particular combination of routes involved in Laker's antitrust claims. Application of antitrust laws would thus directly benefit American consumers.

Because Laker is currently being liquidated, the claims of its creditors are even more directly at stake than consumer interests. Laker is now little more than a corporate conduit through which its assets, including any damages owed Laker, will pass to its creditors. Its antitrust action is primarily an effort to satisfy its creditors, who ultimately bear the brunt of the injury allegedly inflicted upon Laker.

Although the precipitous actions of the British airline defendants prevented the district court from conducting a thorough inquiry into the underlying facts relevant to this aspect of the litigation, the facts indicate that Laker's principal creditors are Americans. Laker's fleet of American manufactured DC-10 aircraft was largely financed by banks and other lending institutions in the United States. Moreover, a substantial portion of its total debt obligations are likely to have been American, since the bulk of the debts and expenses were payable in American dollars. The actions of the alleged conspirators destroyed the ability of Laker to repay these American creditors; any antitrust recovery will therefore benefit these United States interests.

In addition to the protection of American consumers' and creditors' interests, the United States has a substantial interest in regulating the conduct of business within the United States. The landing rights granted to appellants are permits to do business in this country. Foreign airlines fly in the United States on the prerequisite of obeying United States law. They have offices and employees within the United States, and conduct substantial operations here. By engaging in this commercial business they subject themselves to the in persona jurisdiction of the host country's courts. They waive either expressly or implicitly other objections that might otherwise be raised in defense. A major reason for this subjection to business regulation is to place foreign corporations generally in the same position as domestic businesses. Thus, United States creditors are entitled to, and do, rely on their ability to enforce their claims against foreign corporations like the appellants.

This equivalency works in both directions. Foreign corporations are privileged to, and do, rely on United States law. Consequently, creditors rely on the ability of foreign corporations, not only to be sued, but to sue in courts. Creditors expect to recover claims derivatively when foreign corporations possess a claim. Foreign corporations thus have the same obligation as domestic corporations-to sue for benefit of creditors when they are financially troubled and need money for satisfaction of creditors' claims.

The United States has an interest in maintaining open forums for resolution of creditors' claims. Just as the appellants are expected to abide by the United States laws governing those who do business here, so is Laker entitled to the protection of those laws. Permitting Laker to maintain its antitrust suit satisfies the legitimate expectations of Laker and its creditors.

b. *Adequacy of United States Territorial Interests*

It is beyond dispute that these contacts support an exercise of jurisdiction under the Sherman and Clayton Acts. Jurisdiction exists under United States anti-trust laws whenever conduct is intended to, and results in, substantial effects within the United States. Under the conspiracy alleged by Laker, the intent to affect American commerce is obvious. The asserted predatory pricing of fares and interference with refinancing attempts were designed specifically to drive Laker out of business and eventually to raise the fares paid by transatlantic passengers, the bulk of whom are American.

Substantial realization of those intended effects has also been alleged by Laker. Laker was forced into liquidation shortly after its refinancing attempts collapsed. Its creditors have not yet been satisfied. The downward pressure on fares induced by Laker's competition, which previously benefitted transatlantic passengers, has been eliminated. Moreover, providing a forum for Laker's suit would also respect domestic creditors' reliance on the ability of foreign corporations to sue and be sued under the United States laws which ordinarily govern the business operations of foreign corporations within the United States. Thus, significant and long standing American economic interests would be vindicated through a successful antitrust action by Laker.

3. British Jurisdictional Base

Some of the British jurisdictional contacts are territorial. The plaintiff did business on routes between the United States and United Kingdom. A number of the purported conspiratorial acts took place in Great Britain. The conspiracy allegedly caused bankruptcy of a corporation operating in Great Britain.

However, the primary base of jurisdiction is the British *nationality* of the parties involved in the transactions cited in Laker's complaint. Laker itself is incorporated under Jersey law, and is thus a British national for purposes of this litigation. Two of the named defendants, British Airways and British Caledonian, are also incorporated under British law. In addition, the conspiracy may also tangentially implicate the activities of other British entities such as the Bank of England and the Civil Aviation Authority.

Regulating the activities of businesses incorporated within a state is one of the oldest and most established examples of prescriptive jurisdiction. We cannot say that these nationality-based jurisdictional contacts would be insufficient to support British jurisdiction over a claim filed by KLM or Sabena, especially when the conspiracy charged does have territorial contacts with the United Kingdom. Thus, existence of British jurisdiction to prescribe is not seriously challenged by Laker.

4. Concurrent Jurisdiction

The sufficiency of jurisdictional contacts with both the United States and England results in concurrent jurisdiction to prescribe. Both forums may legitimately exercise this power to regulate the events that allegedly transpired as a result of the asserted conspiracy.

Concurrent jurisdiction does not necessarily entail conflicting jurisdiction. The mere existence of dual grounds of prescriptive jurisdiction does not oust either one of the regulating forums. Thus, each forum is ordinarily free to proceed to a judgment.

In the current situation, appellants charge that the district court abused its discretion by forbidding them from joining the "parallel" proceeding in the English courts. They argue that this result is compelled both by principles of comity and by respect for a country's paramount interest in controlling the remedies available to its nationals....

B. Propriety of the Antisuit Injunction

It is well settled that English and American courts have power to control the conduct of persons subject to their jurisdiction to the extent of forbidding them from suing in foreign jurisdictions. However, the fundamental corollary to concurrent jurisdiction must ordinarily be respected: parallel proceedings on the same in personam claim should ordinarily be allowed to proceed simultaneously, at least until a judgment is reached in one which can be pled as res judicata in the other. The mere filing of a suit in one forum does not cut off the preexisting right of an independent forum to regulate matters subject to its prescriptive jurisdiction. For this reason, injunctions restraining litigants from proceeding in courts of independent countries are rarely issued.

A second reason cautioning against exercise of the power is avoiding the impedance of the foreign jurisdiction. Injunctions operate only on the parties within the personal jurisdiction of the courts. However, they effectively restrict the foreign court's ability to exercise its jurisdiction. If the foreign court reacts with a similar injunction, no party may be able to obtain any remedy. Thus, only in the most compelling circumstances does a court have discretion to issue an antisuit injunction.

There are no precise rules governing the appropriateness of antisuit injunctions. The equitable circumstances surrounding each request for an injunction must be carefully examined to determine whether, in light of the principles outlines above, the injunction is required to prevent an irreparable miscarriage of justice. Injunctions are most often necessary to protect the jurisdiction of the enjoining court, or to prevent the litigant's evasion of the important public policies of the forum. We consider the applicability of each category in turn.

1. Protection of Jurisdiction

Courts have a duty to protect their legitimately conferred jurisdiction to the extent necessary to provide full justice to litigants. Thus, when the action of a litigant in another forum threatens to paralyze the jurisdiction of the court, the court may consider the effectiveness and propriety of issuing an injunction against the litigant's participation in the foreign proceedings.

These situations may arise either before or after a judgment has been entered. The policies that guide the exercise of discretion vary slightly in each situation. When the injunction is requested after a previous judgment on the merits, there is little interference with the rule favoring parallel proceedings in matters subject to concurrent jurisdictions. Thus, a court may freely protect the integrity of its judgments by preventing their evasion through vexatious or oppressive relitigation.

However, when a party requests the issuance of an injunction to protect the court's jurisdiction *before* a judgment has been reached, the rules are less clear. Some courts issue the injunction when the parties and issues are identical in both actions, justifying the injunction as necessary to prevent duplicative and, therefore, "vexatious" litigation. However, this rationale is *prima facie* inconsistent with the rule permitting parallel proceedings in concurrent in personam actions. The policies underlying this rule—avoiding hardship to parties and promoting the economies of consolidated litigation-are more properly considered in a motion for dismissal for *forum non conveniens*. They do not outweigh the important principles of comity that compel deference and mutual respect for concurrent foreign proceedings. Thus, the better rule is that duplication of parties and issues alone is not sufficient to justify issuance of an antisuit injunction.

Similarly, the possibility of an "embarrassing race to judgment" or potentially inconsistent adjudications does not outweigh the respect and deference owed to independent foreign proceedings. The parallel proceeding rule applies only until a judgment is reached in one of the actions. After that point, the second forum is usually obliged to respect the prior adjudication of the matter. If the rules regarding enforcement of foreign judgments are followed there will seldom be a case where parties reach inconsistent judgments.

There is little, if any, evidence of court sacrificing procedural or substantive justice in an effort to "race" to a prior judgment. To the extent this slight risk exists it is outweighed by the more imports policies favoring respect for concurrent proceedings. In any event, most forums need not fear that their crucial policies would be trampled if a foreign judgment is reached first, since violation of domestic public policy may justify not enforcing the foreign judgment.

These and other factors relied upon to support issuance of prejudgment protective injunctions in aid of jurisdiction do not usually outweigh the importance of permitting foreign concurrent actions. Thus, although they suggest possible bases favoring the district court's decision to enjoin the appellants, we do not find them controlling.

The logical reciprocal of the parallel proceeding rule proves that there must be circumstances in which an antisuit injunction is necessary to conserve the court's ability to reach a judgment. Just as the parallel proceeding rule counsels against interference with a foreign court's exercise of concurrent jurisdiction, it authorizes the domestic court to resist the attempts of a foreign court to interfere with an in personam action before the domestic court. When the availability of an action in the domestic courts is necessary to a full and fair adjudication of the plaintiff's claims, a court should reserve that forum. Thus, where the foreign proceeding is not following a parallel track but attempts to carve out exclusive jurisdiction over concurrent actions, an injunction may be necessary to avoid the possibility of losing validly invoked jurisdiction. This would be particularly true if the foreign forum did not offer the remedy sought in the domestic forum.

The district court's injunction was clearly proper under these principles. As far as could be determined by the initial pleadings and papers filed, jurisdiction to prescribe was properly exercised. Consequently, the court's ability to render a just and final judgment had to be protected, absent clear evidence that the foreign action could fully consider the litigant's claims.

Appellants characterize the district court's injunction as an improper attempt to reserve to the district court's exclusive jurisdiction an action that should be allowed to proceed simultaneously in parallel forums. Actually, the reverse is true. The English action was initiated for the purpose of reserving exclusive prescriptive jurisdiction to the English courts, even though the English courts do not and can not pretend to offer the plaintiffs here the remedies afforded by the American antitrust laws.

Although concurrently authorized by overlapping principles of prescriptive jurisdiction, the British and American actions are *not* parallel proceedings in the sense the term is normally used. This is not a situation where two courts are proceeding to separate judgments simultaneously under one cause of action. Rather, the sole purpose of the English proceeding is to terminate the American action. The writs filed in the High Court of Justice sought to paralyze or halt the proceedings before the United States District Court.....Appellants conceded at oral argument that they are not interested in concurrent proceedings in the courts of the United Kingdom-they want only the abandonment or dismissal of the American action against them.....

Judge Greene faced the stark choice of either protecting or relinquishing his jurisdiction. Midland Bank had previously obtained a preemptive interim injunction against Laker's naming it as a defendant in a United States antitrust action. Subsequently all of the foreign defendants in No. 82-3362 appeared in the High Court of Justice without notice to either Laker or the United States District Court and obtained interim protection. The remaining defendants, although domestic corporations, had to be restrained from attempting to follow the same path. It was equally clear that appellants also intended to seek English injunctive relief. Due to the lack of any prior notice by the four foreign defendants, the district court was threatened with a potential *fait accompli* by the appellants which would have virtually eliminated the court's effective jurisdiction over Laker's facially valid claim. Given the tensions between the parties, it is likely that the threat worsened every day. Thus, there was nothing improper in the district court's decision to enjoin appellants from seeking to participate in the English proceedings solely designed to rob the court of its jurisdiction.

2. Evasion of Important Public Policies

Antisuit injunctions are also justified when necessary to prevent litigants' evasion of the forum's important public policies. This principle is similar to the rule that a foreign judgment not entitled to full faith and credit under the Constitution will not be enforced within the United States when contrary to the crucial public policies of the forum in which enforcement is requested. Both rules recognize that a state is not required to give effect to foreign judicial proceedings grounded on policies which do violence to its own fundamental interests.

The standard for refusing to enforce judgments on public policy grounds is strict; defendants are rarely able to block judgments on these grounds. Enjoining participation in a foreign lawsuit in order to preempt a potential judgment is a much greater interference with an independent country's judicial processes. It follows that an antisuit injunction will issue to preclude participation in the litigation only when the strongest equitable factors favor its use. Both the importance to the forum of the law allegedly evaded, and the identity of the potentially evading party are relevant.

In this situation, the district court's injunction properly prevented appellants from attempting to escape application of the antitrust laws to their conduct of business here in the United States. KLM and Sabena seek to evade culpability under statutes of admitted economic importance to the United States which are specifically applicable to their activities in the United States, and upon which Laker may have legitimately relied.

Whatever the merits of the British defendants' claims based upon the Bermuda II Treaty, KLM and Sabena have no claim to antitrust immunity under their air service treaties. In fact, far from conferring any immunity, *their treaties contain express language subjecting them to the jurisdiction of the United States over predatory pricing and abuse of monopoly power*. Article Twelve of the United States-Belgium Air Transport Services Agreement provides,

(1) Each Party shall allow prices for air transportation to be established by each designated airline based upon commercial considerations in the marketplace.

Intervention by the Parties shall be limited to:

(a) *prevention of predatory or discriminatory prices or practices;*

(b) *protection of consumers from prices that are unduly high or restrictive because of the abuse of a dominant position; and*

(c) *protection of airlines from prices that are artificially low because of direct or indirect governmental subsidy or support.*

There is similar language in the United States-Netherlands air service agreement and the United States-Germany air service agreement.

.... Significantly, in the face of these express treaty provisions appellants have not asserted before the United States courts any claim to immunity under the air service treaties.

In light of these treaty provisions, we find it offensive that KLM and Sabena attempt to ride on the coattails of the British airlines under the Bermuda II Treaty and the *British* Protection of Trading Interests Act, which were respectively intended to regulate British air carriage and to protect primarily the economic interests of British domestic corporations....

....

3. *Effect of the English Injunctions*

The district court's injunction was within its discretion even though the United Kingdom courts have issued in personam injunctions stopping Laker from proceeding against British Airways and British Caledonian. Long experience derived from this country's federal system teaches that a forum state may, but need not, stay its own proceedings in response to an antisuit injunction against a party before the court. This is consistent with the general rule permitting concurrent proceedings on transitory causes of action. In extreme cases it may even be necessary to issue a counterinjunction to thwart another state's attempt to assert exclusive jurisdiction over a matter legitimately subject to concurrent jurisdiction.

In suits involving states, even the Full Faith and Credit Clause does not compel recognition of an antisuit injunction.... Although one state may exercise its prescriptive jurisdiction to create an "exclusive" remedy for an injury, absent some other overriding constitutional stricture, that exclusivity is never so total as to prevent another sovereign from disregarding a foreign remedy in favor of its own administrative scheme tailored to serve its unique needs.

The same result is reached here *a fortiori*, since the mandatory policies of the Full Faith and Credit Clause do not apply to international assertions of exclusive jurisdiction. The antisuit injunction was a necessary and proper vehicle to protect the United States District Court's jurisdiction and prevent the evasion by KLM and Sabena of important domestic laws governing their conduct of business within the United States.

C. *Paramount Nationality*

We turn now to the appellants' argument that Laker's nationality requires the United States District Court to defer to the injunctions issued by the courts of the United Kingdom.

KLM and Sabena do not dispute the power of the United States District Court to issue the injunction. They contend rather that the district court abused its discretion by issuing an antisuit injunction instead of relinquishing its jurisdiction, staying its proceedings, or adopting some other vehicle of conflict resolution. Appellants are therefore in the contradictory position of supporting the right of English courts to issue an antisuit injunction, but opposing the United States District Court's issuance of the same kind of injunction. The only way appellants can differentiate between the two injunctions is to focus on the nationality of Laker.

. . . .

Appellants attempt to prioritize the authority of the courts to proceed in cases of concurrent jurisdiction by arguing that the nationality of the plaintiff gives the plaintiff's state an inherent advantage which displaces all other jurisdictional bases. They label this principle "paramount nationality," and present this as the theory of conflict resolution to be used when concurrent jurisdiction is present: "assuming that two or more states exercise jurisdiction over Laker's allegations, the state with jurisdiction over its national must have the paramount right to determine whether and, if so, where litigation by that national may go forward."

We are asked to recognize an entirely novel rule. Although a court has power to enjoin its nationals from suing in foreign jurisdictions, it does not follow that the United States courts must recognize an absolute right of the British government to regulate the remedies that the United States may wish to create for British nationals in United States courts. The purported principle of paramount nationality is entirely unknown in national and international law. Territoriality, not nationality, is the customary and preferred base of jurisdiction. Moreover, no rule of international law or national law precludes an exercise of jurisdiction solely because another state has jurisdiction. In fact, international law recognizes that a state with a territorial basis for its prescriptive jurisdiction may establish laws intended to prevent compliance with legislation established under authority of nationality-based jurisdiction.

.... Appellants have not cited any cases where the principle has been followed as a method of choosing between competing claims of jurisdiction, despite the numerous occasions when the principle could have been decisive. As this paucity of case law implies, significant adverse consequences would attend the adoption of this rule, and we decline to do so.

The rationale behind the claim of paramount nationality seems to be that particularly important foreign sovereign prerogatives are infringed when a foreign national sues in domestic courts against the wishes of a foreign state. However, this argument ignores the stronger policy interests of the domestic forum. If a country has a right to regulate the conduct of its nationals, then *a fortiori* it has the power to regulate the activities of its *very governmental organizations*, such as its courts, which it establishes and maintains for the purpose of furthering its own public policies.

United States courts must control the access to their forums. No foreign court can supersede the right and obligation of the United States courts to decide whether Congress has created a remedy for those injured by trade practices adversely affecting United States interests. Our courts are not required to stand by while Britain attempts to close a courthouse door that Congress, under its territorial jurisdiction, has opened to foreign corporations. Under the nationality base of jurisdiction, Britain can punish its corporations for walking through that courthouse door, but it cannot close the American door. Thus, although British courts can sanction their citizens for resorting to United States antitrust remedies, United States courts are not required to cut off the availability of the remedy.

The position advanced by appellant would require United States courts to defer to British policy when there is no statement by Congress that it does not wish the courts to provide the remedy. Appellants' argument that there is no absolute duty to exercise jurisdiction has no merit in this context. It is based on abstention and *forum non conveniens* cases, which in turn are premised on the availability of a second forum that can fully resolve the plaintiff's claims. In this case, the English Court of Appeal has admitted that there is no other forum for Laker's claims.

Besides lacking any basis in national or international law, and besides ignoring important domestic interests, the paramount nationality rule would generate more interference than it would resolve. Legislation based on nationality tends to encourage chauvinism and discrimination without enhancing international comity. The paramount nationality rule would be no exception. Foreign plaintiffs in our courts could routinely face public policy challenges in their domestic courts, while our courts would be required to stay proceedings pending foreign authorization. On the other hand, as the district court noted, United States courts could use corporate nationality as a pretext to interject themselves in foreign proceedings involving United States corporations and subsidiaries.

The paramount nationality rule would also be impractical to administer. It would be difficult or impossible to determine when the nationality of a corporation is sufficiently strong that legitimate territorial contacts should be nullified. There are at least five competing methods of determining nationality of a corporation. Multiple countries could simultaneously assert controlling jurisdiction over one "national" corporation based, for example, on shareholder nationality, state of incorporation, or other corporate links to a particular forum. There would be no paramount nation in this situation. The conflicts associated with concurrent jurisdiction would continue to confront the courts.

Finally, KLM and Sabena are not British nationals. Thus, their claims are fundamentally different from those advanced by British Airways and British Caledonian. Nothing gives KLM or Sabena a supreme right to vindicate the British national interests that may be implicated by Laker's suits. Sabena, at least, is specifically entitled to the protection of United States antitrust laws under its air services agreement. KLM no doubt would expect the same protection. No rule of paramount nationality should free them from obligation under United States antitrust laws and at the same time protect them from other corporations' violations. Contrary to appellants' arguments, Laker's nationality is clearly an insufficient basis to reverse the district court.

D. *International Comity*

Appellants and amici curiae argue strenuously that the district court's injunction violates the crucial principles of comity that regulate and moderate the social and economic intercourse between independent nations. We approach their claims seriously, recognizing that comity serves our international system like the mortar which cements together a brick house. No one would willingly permit the mortar to crumble or be chipped away for fear of compromising the entire structure.

"Comity" summarizes in a brief word a complex and elusive concept-the degree of deference that a domestic forum must pay to the act of a foreign government not otherwise binding on the forum. Since comity varies according to the factual circumstances surrounding each claim for its recognition, the absolute boundaries of the duties it imposes are inherently uncertain. However, the central precept of comity teaches that, when possible, the decisions of foreign tribunals should be given effect in domestic courts, since recognition fosters international cooperation and encourages reciprocity, thereby promoting predictability and stability through satisfaction of mutual expectations. The interests of both forums are advanced-the foreign court because its laws and policies have been vindicated; the domestic country because international cooperation and ties have been strengthened. The rule of law is also encouraged, which benefits all nations.

Comity is a necessary outgrowth of our international system of politically independent, socioeconomically interdependent nation states. As surely as people, products and problems move freely among adjoining countries, so national interests cross territorial borders. But no nation can expect its laws to reach further than its jurisdiction to prescribe, adjudicate, and enforce. Every nation must often rely on other countries to help it achieve its regulatory expectations. Thus, comity compels national courts to act at all times to increase the international legal ties that advance the rule of law within and among nations.

However, there are limitations to the application of comity. When the foreign act is inherently inconsistent with the policies underlying comity, domestic recognition could tend either to legitimize the aberration or to encourage retaliation, undercutting the realization of the goals served by comity. No nation is under an unremitting obligation to enforce foreign interests which are fundamentally prejudicial to those of the domestic forum. Thus, from the earliest times, authorities have recognized that the obligation of comity expires when the strong public policies of the forum are vitiated by the foreign act.....

Opinions vary as to the degree of prejudice to public policy which should be tolerated before comity will not be followed, but by any definition the injunctions of the United Kingdom courts are not entitled to comity. This is because the action before the United Kingdom courts is specifically intended to interfere with and terminate Laker's United States antitrust suit.

The district court's antisuit injunction was purely *defensive* — it seeks only to preserve the district court's ability to arrive at a final judgment adjudicating Laker's claims under United States law. This judgment would neither make any statement nor imply any views about the wisdom of British antitrust policy. In contrast, the English injunction is purely *offensive*-it is not designed to protect English jurisdiction, or to allow English courts to proceed to a judgment on the defendant's potential liability under English anticompetitive law free of foreign interference. Rather, the English injunction seeks only to quash the practical power of the United States courts to adjudicate claims under United States law against defendants admittedly subject to the courts' adjudicatory jurisdiction. The Court of Appeal itself recognized that there is no other forum available for resolution of Laker's claims.

It is often argued before United States courts that the application of United States antitrust laws to foreign nationals violates principles of comity. Those pleas are legitimately considered. In conducting this inquiry, a court must necessarily examine whether the antitrust laws were clearly intended to reach the injury charged in the complaint. If so, allowing the defendant's conduct to go unregulated could amount to an unjustified evasion of United States law injuring significant domestic interests. This is one context in which comity would not be extended to a foreign act. On the other hand, if the anticompetitive aspect of the alleged injury is not appreciable; the contacts with the United States are attenuated; and the actions of foreign governments denote the existence of strong foreign interests, then comity may suggest a lack of Congressional intent to regulate the alleged conduct. In this context, comity may have a strong bearing on whether application of United States antitrust laws should go forward.

However, the appellants' plea to comity is fundamentally different. KLM and Sabena contend that comity compels us to recognize a decision by a *foreign* government that *this court* shall not apply its own laws to corporations doing business in this country. Thus, the violation of public policy vitiating comity is not that the evasion of United States antitrust law might injure United States interests, but rather that United States judicial functions have been usurped, destroying the autonomy of the courts. Under the position advanced by appellants, the United States District Court would no longer be free to rule that comity prevented the United States from exercising prescriptive jurisdiction over the defendants, since that determination would be made as of right by a separate forum.

In this latter context we cannot rule that the district court abused its discretion to protect its jurisdiction. Between the state courts, the Full Faith and Credit Clause has not been held to compel recognition of an antisuit injunction. *A fortiori*, the principles of comity do not prevent proceeding in the face of a foreign injunction.

Comity ordinarily requires that courts of a separate sovereign not interfere with concurrent proceedings based on the same transitory claim, at least until a judgment is reached in one action, allowing res judicata to be pled in defense. The appeal to the recognition of comity by the American court in order to permit the critical issues to be adjudicated in England, which is the plea made by appellants here, thus comes based on a very strange predicate. Since the action seeking to determine Laker's right to recover for anticompetitive injuries was first instituted in the United States, the initial opportunity to exercise comity, if this were called for, was put to the United Kingdom courts. No recognition or acceptance of comity was made in those courts. The appellants' claims of comity now asserted in United States courts come burdened with the failure of the British to recognize comity.

Although reciprocity may no longer be an absolute prerequisite to comity, certainly our law has not departed so far from common sense that it is reversible error for a court not to capitulate to a foreign judgment based on a statute like the British Protection of Trading Interests Act, designed to prevent the court from resolving legitimate claims placed before it. We cannot forget that the foreign injunction which creates an issue of comity or forbearance was generated by the English Executive's deliberate interference with a proceeding which had been ongoing in the American courts for over six months. Deference to the English courts is now asked in a situation in which all the English courts are doing is supporting and acquiescing in the action taken by their executive. There never would have been any situation in which comity or forbearance would have become an issue if some of the defendants involved in the American suit had not gone into the English courts to generate interference with the American courts.

There is simply no visible reason why the British Executive, followed by the British courts, should bar Laker's assertion of a legitimate cause of action in the American courts, except that the British government is intent upon frustrating the antitrust policies of the elective branches of the American government. The effort of the British therefore is not to see that justice is done anywhere, either in the United States or British courts, but to frustrate the enforcement of American law in American courts against companies doing business in America. Absent a clear treaty concluded by the United States Executive Branch, this simply cannot be agreed to by the courts of the United States.

Nothing in the British Executive order and directions suggests that they are entitled to comity. The order and directions purport to counteract United States regulation of international trade outside its territorial jurisdiction. The Protection of Trading Interests Act and the order govern "any person in the United Kingdom who carries on business there." They forbid any person in the United Kingdom from furnishing "any commercial document *in the United Kingdom*," or "any commercial information [apparently *regardless of location*] which relates to the said Department of Justice investigation or the grand jury or the District Court proceedings." Even United States airlines would be swept within these broad directives, but for the directions' specific exclusion of United States carriers.

The English Executive has thus issued an order to every airline in the world doing business in England to refuse to submit to the jurisdiction of the American court and not to submit any documents from England pursuant to an order of the American court. If the exercise of "extraterritorial" jurisdiction under United States antitrust laws can ever be described as arrogant, the order and directions issued by the British Government certainly bear the same characteristic. United States antitrust laws are enforced where there is an impact in the United States, but only after an adjudication in the United States courts of a violation. Here the English Executive has presumed to bar foreigners from complying with orders of an American court before there is an adjudication by a court on the merits of the dispute.

Moreover, since oral argument before this court, the English Secretary of State has interpreted the order and directions to bar the furnishing of any "commercial information," even that located exclusively within United States territory. On the basis of this interpretation the British Government has refused to permit Laker's use of commercial information contained in documents situated in the United States to respond to interrogatories propounded by Trans World Airlines. The orders thus interfere with any attempt by Laker to use any commercial information, *whether located in the United Kingdom or the United States*, to proceed against any of the defendants, *whether British or American.*

This development completely undermines the appellants' strongest argument in favor of the application of comity-namely, that all United States interests protected under the antitrust laws could be adequately enforced through means other than a treble damage suit, such as a civil or criminal action brought by the Government, or a creditors' class action. Since the British Government is refusing to permit Laker to proceed with its suit even insofar as it relates to American defendants, it is clear that it would prevent Laker's participation in any proceeding designed to vindicate United States interests allegedly harmed as a result of injuries suffered by Laker and its customers. Thus, Laker would be hampered in assisting the plaintiffs in any alternative action. Without crucial information provided by the injured party, Laker, any other suit would be procedurally doomed to failure, regardless of its merits. *Therefore, comity can not be extended on the grounds that the British directions protect solely British interests while permitting the United States to vindicate its own policies; the truth, the reality, is far different.*

If we are guided by the ethical imperative that everyone should act as if his actions were universalized, then the actions of the British Executive in this particular matter scarcely meet the standard of Kant. For, if the United States and a few other countries with major airlines enacted and enforced legislation like the Protection of Trading Interests Act, the result would be unfettered chaos brought about by unresolvable conflicts of jurisdiction the world over. If we were to forbid every American airline and every foreign airline doing business in the United States from producing documents in response to the summons of an English court, or a French court, or a German court, and the French and the German governments were to enact and enforce similar legislation, there could be no complete resolution of any legal dispute involving airlines around the world. The operations of the airlines would be snarled in a crisscross of overlapping and tangled restrictions to the extent that no airline could be certain of its legal obligations anywhere. Thus, even the practical consequences that would flow from a grant of comity counsel against deferring to the British injunctions triggered by the Protection of Trading Interests Act.

. . . .

Now a word about the position of our dissenting colleague. We submit that the dissent relies on a skewed view of comity, ignoring the significant prejudice to the administration of justice in our courts under United States laws in order to accommodate the strongly asserted views of the British Executive and Judiciary. However laudatory the impulse to adjust and compromise, we are unable to plunge ahead as the dissent advocates. The path to "the seemly accommodation of ... competing national interests" eked out by the dissent turns comity into quicksand, snares the district court in the very pitfalls which it attempted to avoid, and leads the parties and the district court to a result so vague and ill-defined that it cannot possible solve the problems raised by the actions of the two governments. This position is neither legally tenable nor pragmatically dictated by the extraordinary circumstances of this litigation.

The interpretation of international comity propounded by the dissent is a weak reed indeed under the aggravated facts of this case; it does not rest upon any legal precedent, and ignores the previously recognized limits on the doctrine. The central authority quoted, *Hilton v. Guyot,* recognizes that comity never *obligates* a national forum to ignore "the *rights of its own citizens* or of *other persons who are under the protection of its laws.*" Laker's United States creditors and consumers are entitled to the protection of United States antitrust laws. Furthermore, although not a United States citizen, as a corporation operating within the United States, Laker qualifies as an "other person" entitled to the protection of United States law. Heretofore comity has never been thought to require mandatory deferral to a foreign action primarily intended to cut off these domestic interests.

....

...[H]ere it is the *inaction and silence* of the Executive Branch which is said to shut off the availability of the United States forum. Only a very small percentage of private antitrust actions are graced by the intervention of the Antitrust Division of the Department of Justice. This has never before been a prerequisite to maintaining a private antitrust claim. If we were to hold that the absence of this intervention indicated a weakness in Laker's case, or prevented it from going forward, we would be making new antitrust law indeed—law which would directly contravene the congressional purposes in establishing a private right of action.

There are other weighty reasons why the absence of any current expression of affirmative United States interest should not be fatal to Laker's antitrust action. The American Executive has been in contact with the British Executive seeking to iron out differences under the Bermuda II Treaty. It may very well be that since the State Department is seized with the responsibility for negotiations with the British it has advised the Antitrust Division that it would be inappropriate for that division to take an adversary position in the ongoing private civil suit at this time.

The sensitive status of current negotiations may even preclude the Department of State from actively participating in this litigation. Significantly, the British Government is not involved in this litigation either, presumably confining itself to consultation and to the creation and interpretation of the executive orders giving rise to the controversy. This counsels against inviting the Executive to present the views of the United States on remand. Unless and until the views of the American Executive are made known, the absence of any Executive expression of United States sovereign or other interests should not be a bar to proceeding with Laker's suit, or to the protection of jurisdiction to hear the claim.

....

...[T]he dissent offers no practical guidance about how the district court's jurisdiction can be guaranteed under the microscopic range of discretion apparently contemplated in the "further proceedings aimed at narrowing the injunction." It states only that the injunction could be narrowed to allow KLM and Sabena to "follow" Swissair and Lufthansa in bringing declaratory judgment actions, barring only "countersuit injunctive relief *pendente lite.*" This is no protection at all for the district court. Swissair and Lufthansa do not seek a declaratory judgment that British law does not permit Laker to sue in American courts. If this were the only request made by Swissair and Lufthansa then it might very well be permitted.

Instead, Lufthansa and Swissair seek a declaration that they did not breach English and other laws regulating restrictive practices. The writs specifically exclude any requests for a declaratory judgment concerning whether *United States* antitrust laws are violated. However, *the accompanying request for relief*, which it must be assumed they intend to seek if they succeed in obtaining a favorable declaratory judgment, *is not so limited: it seeks an injunction against any action in United States courts based on United States antitrust laws.* The breadth of the relief requested is all the more unusual since the declaratory aspect of the writs exclude consideration of the United

States antitrust law. By suggesting that KLM and Sabena should be permitted to seek this sort of a declaratory judgment, and, implicitly, obtain the requested relief, the dissent cannot seriously intimate that the district court would effectively protect its jurisdiction.

To the extent the dissent would permit the district court to preserve its jurisdiction under the terms of a more limited injunction along the lines contemplated by the district court's proposal, the net result on the desired remand would not be much different from that reached by the majority. There is nothing in our opinion which prevents KLM and Sabena from reconsidering their position or proposing a modification of the district court's order if anything less than complete frustration of the district court's jurisdiction would satisfy the appellants' objective.

E. *Judicial Reconciliation of Conflicting Assertions of Jurisdiction*

We recognize that the district court's injunction, precipitated as it was by preemptive interim injunctions in the High Court of Justice, unfortunately will not resolve the deadlock currently facing the parties to this litigation. We have searched for some satisfactory avenue, open to an American court, which would permit the frictionless vindication of the interests of both Britain and the United States. However, there is none, for the British legislation defines the British interest solely in terms of preventing realization of United States interests. The laws are therefore contradictory and mutually inconsistent.

1. *Nature of the Conflict*

The conflict faced here is not caused by the courts of the two countries. Rather, its sources are the fundamentally opposed national policies toward prohibition of anticompetitive business activity. These policies originate in the legislative and executive decisions of the respective counties.

Congress has specifically authorized treble damage actions by foreign corporations to redress injuries to United States foreign commerce. Equally significant, congress has designed the private action as a major component in the enforcement mechanism. The treble damage aspect of private recoveries is the centerpiece of that enforcement mechanism.

We find no indication in either the statutory scheme or prior judicial precedent that jurisdiction should not be exercised. Legitimate United States interests in protecting consumers, providing for vindicating creditors' rights, and regulating economic consequences of those doing substantial business in our country are all advanced under the congressionally prescribed scheme. These are more than sufficient jurisdictional contacts under *United States v. Aluminum Co. of America* and subsequent case law to support the exercise of prescriptive jurisdiction in this case. Congress has been aware of the decades-long controversy accompanying the recurrent assertion of jurisdiction over foreign anticompetitive acts and effects in the United States dating back nearly forty years but has, with limited exceptions, not yet chosen to limit the laws' application or disapprove of the consistent statutory interpretation reached by the courts. Thus, aside from the unprecedented foreign challenge to the application of the antitrust laws, there is nothing in either the facts alleged in the complaint or the circumstances of the litigation which suggests jurisdiction should not be exercised in Laker's suit.

The English courts have indicated that they, too, have acted out of the need to implement their mandatory legislative policy, and not out of any ill will towards our courts or the substantive law we are bound to follow. Although the injunctive relief sought by British Airways and British Caledonian set the stage for a direct conflict of jurisdiction, until action by the political branches of the English Government the English courts remained largely acquiescent to Laker's invocation of United States jurisdiction. Justice Parker's well reasoned judgment initially denied the injunctive relief sought by British Airways and British Caledonian. That judgment was rendered even after the district court issued the injunction under appeal here.

However, the government of the United Kingdom is now and has historically been opposed to most aspects of United States antitrust policy insofar as it affects business enterprises based in the United Kingdom. The British Government objects to the scope of the prescriptive jurisdiction invoked to apply the antitrust laws; the substantive content of those laws, which is much more aggressive than British regulation of restrictive practices; and the procedural vehicles used in the litigation of the antitrust laws, including private treble damage actions, and the widespread use of pretrial discovery. These policies have been most recently and forcefully expressed in the Protection of Trading Interests Act.

The nature of the direct conflict between the political-economic policies of the two countries is put into focus by considering whether the British Government would have been likely to attempt to stop Laker from suing in United States courts if Laker brought a suit other than an antitrust action. If Laker had sued the American defendants for fraud, or on a contract claim for failure of performance, the British would not have been at all interested in intervening, irrespective of the financial condition of Laker at the time it brought the suit. The indifference would not lessen whether British Airways and British Caledonian were included in the group sued by Laker in the United States court. It is the hated application of United States antitrust laws to conduct involving British corporations that has triggered the involvement of the British Government, and ultimately, the British courts.

Under the provisions of the Protection of Trading Interests Act, *after Justice Parker refused relief*, the English Secretary of State issued an order and directions prohibiting all those carrying on business in the United Kingdom, with the exception of United States designated air carriers, from complying with United States antitrust measures arising out of the provision of air carriage by United Kingdom designated airlines under the terms of the Bermuda II Treaty. Because these directions reflected the firm conclusion of the British Executive Branch that British trading interests were being threatened by Laker's antitrust claim, they presented an entirely different situation to the Court of Appeal than that which Justice Parker had faced. The restrictions placed on the British airlines by these orders "fundamentally altered" the perceived ability of the Court of Appeal to permit concurrent actions. Because *the directions of the British Executive* blocked British Caledonian and British Airways from complying with Laker's discovery requests, the court concluded that the British airlines could not thereafter adequately defend themselves. According to the Court of Appeal, this rendered Laker's claim "wholly untriable" and was therefore "decisive."

Thus, to a large extent the conflict of jurisdiction is one generated by the political branches of the governments. There is simply no room for accommodation here if the courts of each country faithfully carry out the laws which they are entrusted to enforce. The Master of the Rolls expressed hope that "the courts of the two countries will... never be in conflict. The conflict, if there be conflict, will be purely one between the laws of the two countries, for which neither court is responsible." We echo that hope.

2. *Judicial Interest Balancing*

Even as the political branches of the respective countries have set in motion the legislative policies which have collided in this litigation, they have deprived courts of the ability meaningfully to resolve the problem. The American and English courts are obligated to attempt to reconcile two contradictory laws, each supported by recognized prescriptive jurisdiction, one of which is specifically designed to cancel out the other.

The suggestion has been made that this court should engage in some form of interest balancing, permitting only a "reasonable" assertion of prescriptive jurisdiction to be implemented. However, this approach is unsuitable when courts are forced to choose between a domestic law which is designed to protect domestic interests, and a foreign law which is calculated to thwart the implementation of the domestic law in order to protect foreign interests allegedly threatened by the objectives of the domestic law. Interest balancing in this context is hobbled by two primary problems: (1) there are substantial limitations on the court's ability to conduct a neutral balancing of the competing interests, and (2) the adoption of interest balancing is unlikely to achieve its goal of promoting international comity.

. . . .

3. *Political Compromise*

The district court could capitulate to the British attacking law, at the cost of losing its jurisdiction to implement the substantive policies established by Congress. Alternatively it can act to preserve its jurisdiction, running the risk that counter-injunctions or other sanctions will eventually preclude Laker from achieving any remedy, if it is ultimately entitled to one under United States law. In either case the policies of both countries are likely to be frustrated at the cost of substantial prejudice to the litigants' rights.

We unhesitatingly conclude that United States jurisdiction to prescribe its antitrust laws must go forward and was therefore properly protected by the district court. Despite the contrary assertions of the British government, there is no indication in this case that the limits of international law are exceeded by either country's exercise of prescriptive jurisdiction. But even so, application of national law may go forward despite a conflict with international law. Both Britain and the United States recognize this rule. It follows *a fortiori* that national laws do not evaporate when counteracted by the legislation of another sovereign.

Although, in the interest of amicable relations, we might be tempted to defuse unilaterally the confrontation by jettisoning our jurisdiction, we could not, for this is not our proper judicial role. The problem in this case is essentially a political one, arising from the vast difference in the political-economic theories of the two governments which has existed for many years. Both nations have jurisdiction to prescribe and adjudicate. Both have asserted that jurisdiction. However, this conflict alone does not place the court in a position to initiate a political compromise based on its decision that United States laws should not be enforced when a foreign jurisdiction, contrary to the domestic court's statutory duty, attempts to eradicate the domestic jurisdiction. Judges are not politicians. The courts are not organs of political compromise. It is impossible in this case, with all the good will manifested by the English Justices and ourselves, to negotiate an extraordinarily long arms-length agreement on the respective impact of our countries' policies regulating anti-competitive business practices.

. . . .

Unilateral abandonment by the Judiciary of legitimately prescribed national law in response to foreign counter-legislation would not materially advance the principles of comity and international accommodation which must form the foundation of any international system comprised of coequal nation states. The British Government's invocation of the Protection of Trading Interests Act to foreclose any proceeding in a non-English forum brought to recover damages for trade injuries caused by unlawful conspiracies is a naked attempt exclusively to reserve by confrontation an area of prescriptive jurisdiction shared concurrently by other nations. This assertion of interdictory jurisdiction propels into the courts a controversy whose eventual termination is restricted to two unsatisfactory alternatives: (1) either one state or the other will eventually capitulate, sacrificing its legitimate interests, or (2) a deadlock will occur to the eventual frustration of both the states' and the litigants' interests. The underlying goal of the legislation is apparently to compel the United States to cede its claims to regulate those aspects of its domestic economy deemed objectionable by the United Kingdom. However, the possibility of a cooperative, mutually profitable compromise by all affected countries is greatly restricted. Granting recognition to this form of coercion will only retard the growth of international mechanisms necessary to resolve satisfactorily the problems generated when radically divergent national policies intersect in an area of concurrent jurisdiction.

Rather than legitimizing the interference and stultifying effects that would follow widespread acceptance of interdictory jurisdiction, we prefer to permit Laker's suit, based as it is on well recognized prescriptive jurisdiction, to go forward as free as possible from the interference caused by foreign antisuit injunctions.

III. CONCLUSION

The conflict in jurisdiction we confront today has been precipitated by the attempts of another country to insulate its own business entities from the necessity of complying with legislation of our country designed to protect this country's domestic policies. At the root of the conflict are the fundamentally opposed policies of the United States and Great Britain regarding the desirability, scope, and implementation of legislation controlling anticompetitive and restrictive business practices.

No conceivable judicial disposition of this appeal would remove that underlying conflict. Because of the potential deadlock that appears to be developing, the ultimate question is not *whether* conflicting assertions of national interest must be reconciled, but the *proper forum* of reconciliation. The resources of the Judiciary are inherently limited when faced with an affirmative decision by the political branches of the government to prescribe specific policies. Absent an explicit directive from Congress, this court has neither the authority nor the institutional resources to weigh the policy and political factors that must be evaluated when resolving competing claims of jurisdiction. In contrast, diplomatic and executive channels are, by definition, designed to exchange, negotiate, and reconcile the problems which accompany the realization of national interests within the sphere of international association. These forums should and, we hope, will be utilized to avoid or resolve conflicts caused by contradictory assertions of concurrent prescriptive jurisdiction.

However, in the absence of some emanation from the Executive Branch, Laker's suit may go forward against appellants. Laker seeks to recover for injuries it allegedly sustained as a result of the defendants' conduct in violation of United States antitrust laws. The complaint alleges a conspiracy to drive out of business a corporation permitted by United States treaty to operate within the United States treaty to operate within the United States and conducting substantial business here. If Laker's allegations are proved, the intended and actual effects in the United States are clear since Laker, which was carrying up to one out of every seven transatlantic passengers, was subsequently forced into liquidation. Resolution of Laker's lawsuit would further the interests protected under United States law, since American creditors' interests in open forums, and consumers' interests in free competition may be vindicated.

Under these circumstances, judicial precedent construing the prescriptive jurisdiction of the United States antitrust laws unequivocally holds that the antitrust laws should be applied. That jurisdiction is well within the bounds of reason imposed by international law. Because the factual circumstances of this case made a preliminary injunction imperative to preserve the court's jurisdiction, and because that injunction is not proscribed by the principles of international comity, the district court acted within its discretion.

The decision of the district court is therefore

Affirmed.

Starr, Circuit Judge, *dissenting*:

It is with reluctance that I am constrained to dissent, for there is much in the majority's thorough opinion with which I fully agree. The majority's opinion demonstrates persuasively that the jurisdictional basis for Laker's action in the United States District Court is firmly established under settled principles of United States and international law. Judge Wilkey's scholarly analysis further demonstrates that it is not at all unusual for a court vested with jurisdiction to issue appropriate orders to vindicate that jurisdiction, even when such orders arrest the prosecution of actions in the courts of another sovereign.

But it is my judgment that principles of comity among the courts of the international community counsel strongly against the injunction in the form issued here. The concept of comity of nations, a "blend of courtesy and expedience," was defined by the Supreme Court in *Hilton v. Guyot* as the recognition which one nation allows within its territory to the legislative, executive or judicial acts of another nation, having due regard both to international duty and convenience, and to the rights of its own citizens or of other persons who are under the protection of its laws. 159 U.S. 113, 164 (1895).

The difficulty in applying this open-ended idea stems from the fact that "'[c]omity,' in the legal sense, is neither a matter of absolute obligation, on the one hand, nor of mere courtesy and good will, upon the other." *Id.* at 163-64. Few hard-and-fast rules or talismanic tests are to be found. Nonetheless, it is clear that under appropriate circumstances, United States courts will invoke the principle of comity in recognition of the interests of another sovereign.

In light of these principles, it is important to note that this is, at bottom, a private antitrust action filed in a United States court by a foreign litigant against, among others, four United States corporate defendants. This is plainly not an action informed with a public interest beyond that implicated by any private litigant enforcing admittedly important congressionally granted rights. Not only is the instant action not brought by the United States to vindicate sovereign United States interests, but no evidence has been manifested of any sovereign United States interest in the present suit. For whatever reason, and I do not pretend to powers of divination as to why, the Executive has been silent as to what, if any, public interests are touched by Laker's antitrust suit.

In stark contrast, it is clear beyond cavil that the British Executive is emphatically interested in this suit brought by a British subject in United States courts. This sovereign interest articulated by representatives of Her Majesty's government, premised upon British disaffection for the operation and reach of United States antitrust laws, is one that I cannot in conscience reasonably discount. After all, Laker is a British subject which carried on its operations as a heavily regulated air carrier under United Kingdom law. Its routes to and from the United States were established under the umbrella of the Bermuda II Treaty between the United Kingdom and the United States. The United Kingdom thus possesses a clear governmental interest in the activities of a now defunct but once heavily regulated British concern.

To be sure, Laker's status as a British subject, without more, does not mean that United States courts must unalterably bow to the rulings of British courts in actions filed after the instant suit was in progress. The majority has indeed persuasively demonstrated that no principle of "paramount nationality" is recognized in international law. But I am persuaded that it is not at all incompatible with our oath of office for United States judges to recognize the practical reality that the United Kingdom may in fact ultimately have power to prevent Laker's maintaining any United States antitrust action. And the exercise of such a power should not automatically, without benefit of the views of either the British or United States Executive, be deemed violative of United States public policy.....

....

.... By its terms, the District Court's order quite literally forbids the foreign airlines from entering any court in the world, including courts of their own respective nations, to contest Laker's right to maintain the instant action. This approach, fashioned under the strain of critical moments when it reasonably appeared to the learned trial judge that jurisdiction over important defendants might irrevocably be lost, is simply too broad to sustain, in light of the countervailing considerations of comity among nations.

Thus, I would favor vacating the present injunction and remanding the case to the District Court for consideration of narrowing its order. The District Court might well decide to enjoin KLM and Sabena only from seeking countersuit injunctive relief *pendente lite* in the English courts, thus allowing them to follow the example of Lufthansa and Swissair in bringing declaratory judgment actions. This would allow two or more related actions—Laker's antitrust suit and the foreign defendants' declaratory judgment action in foreign court—to proceed simultaneously, without any direct interference from the other sovereign's courts. This type of injunction seems clearly preferable on comity grounds.

A foreign court would thus be allowed to adjudicate the status of the parties before it under that nation's laws and regulatory provisions, including any applicable aviation treaties. If both the United States and foreign actions proceeded to judgment, choice of law questions would likely be presented in the execution of the judgments and would be considered at that stage of the litigation. However, several developments in this matter could moot this potential conflict, including a negotiated settlement of the inter-governmental dispute over the scope and applicability of United States antitrust laws; a decision against Laker on the merits in the United States District Court; or a judicial decision against the foreign defendants in the foreign court. A narrow injunction would thus preserve the possibility that the ultimate conflict-of-laws questions would be mooted, either through diplomatic channels or a defeat either for Laker or the foreign airlines in their respective actions. The narrower injunction would result in substantially less interference with foreign courts, with no "surrender" of the jurisdiction of the United States over Laker's antitrust claims.

I would further suggest that in the exercise of its sound discretion the District Court invite the Executive to present the views of the United States. Those views might well have an important bearing upon the extent of the sovereign interests of the United States, if any, in this action.

A tempest has been brewing for some time among the nations as to the reach of this country's antitrust laws, and today's decision strikes a strong blow in favor of what will be viewed by many of our friends and allies as a rather parochial American outlook. But whether that blow is well conceived, it is, with all respect, at tension with the orderly operation of our two nations' respective judicial systems. As both the majority and the District Court recognize, it is serious business to issue an injunction against proceedings in a sister nation. This is most keenly true with respect to a nation from which we inherited so much of our legal system....

Hartford Fire Insurance Company v. California
509 U.S. 764 (1993)

Justice Souter announced the judgment of the Court and delivered the opinion of the Court with respect to Parts I, II-A, III, and IV, and an opinion concurring in the judgment with respect to Part II-B. [Justice White, Justice Blackmun, and Justice Stevens join this opinion in its entirety, and The Chief Justice joins Parts I, II-A, III, and IV.]

The Sherman Act makes every contract, combination, or conspiracy in unreasonable restraint of interstate or foreign commerce illegal. 15 U.S.C. § 1. These consolidated cases present questions about the application of that Act to the insurance industry, both here and abroad. The plaintiffs (respondents here) allege that both domestic and foreign defendants (petitioners here) violated the Sherman Act by engaging in various conspiracies to affect the American insurance market. A group of domestic defendants argues that the McCarran-Ferguson Act, as amended, 15 U.S.C. § 1011 *et seq.*, precludes application of the Sherman Act to the conduct alleged; a group of foreign defendants argues that the principle of international comity requires the District Court to refrain from exercising jurisdiction over certain claims against it. We hold that most of the domestic defendants' alleged conduct is not immunized from antitrust liability by the McCarran-Ferguson Act, and that, even assuming it applies, the principle of international comity does not preclude District Court jurisdiction over the foreign conduct alleged.

I

The two petitions before us stem from consolidated litigation comprising the complaints of 19 States and many private plaintiffs alleging that the defendants, members of the insurance industry, conspired in violation of § 1 of the Sherman Act to restrict the terms of coverage of commercial general liability (CGL) insurance available in the United States. Because the cases come to us on motions to dismiss, we take the allegations of the complaints as true.

A

According to the complaints, the object of the conspiracies was to force certain primary insurers (insurers who sell insurance directly to consumers) to change the terms of their standard CGL insurance policies to conform with the policies the defendant insurers wanted to sell. The defendants wanted four changes.

First, CGL insurance has traditionally been sold in the United States on an "occurrence" basis, through a policy obligating the insurer "to pay or defend claims, whenever made, resulting from an accident or 'injurious exposure to conditions' that occurred during the [specific time] period the policy was in effect." In place of this traditional "occurrence" trigger of coverage, the defendants wanted a "claims-made" trigger, obligating the insurer to pay or defend only those claims made during the policy period. Such a policy has the distinct advantage for the insurer that when the policy period ends without a claim having been made, the insurer can be certain that the policy will not expose it to any further liability. Second, the defendants wanted the "claims-made" policy to have a "retroactive date" provision, which would further restrict coverage to claims based on incidents that occurred after a certain date. Such a provision eliminates the risk that an insurer, by issuing a claims-made policy would assume liability arising from incidents that occurred before the policy's effective date, but remained undiscovered or caused no immediate harm. Third, CGL insurance has traditionally covered "sudden and accidental" pollution; the defendants wanted to eliminate that coverage. Finally, CGL insurance has traditionally provided that the insurer would bear the legal costs of defending covered claims against the insured without regard to the policy's stated limits of coverage; the defendants wanted legal defense costs to be counted against the stated limits (providing a "legal defense cost cap").

To understand how the defendants are alleged to have pressured the targeted primary insurers to make these changes, one must be aware of two important features of the insurance industry. First, most primary insurers rely on certain outside support services for the type of insurance coverage they wish to sell. Defendant Insurance Services Office, Inc. (ISO), an association of approximately 1,400 domestic property and casualty insurers (including the primary insurer defendants, Hartford Fire Insurance Company, Allstate Insurance Company, CIGNA Corporation, and Aetna Casualty and Surety Company), is the almost exclusive source of support services in this country for CGL insurance. ISO develops standard policy forms and files or lodges them with each State's insurance regulators; most CGL insurance written in the United States is written on these forms. All of the "traditional" features of CGL insurance relevant to this litigation were embodied in the ISO standard CGL insurance form that had been in use since 1973. . . . For each of its standard policy forms, ISO also supplies actuarial and rating information: it collects, aggregates, interprets, and distributes data on the premiums charged, claims filed and paid, and defense costs expended with respect to each form, and on the basis of these data it predicts future loss trends and calculates advisory premium rates. Most ISO members cannot afford to continue to use a form if ISO withdraws these support services.

Second, primary insurers themselves usually purchase insurance to cover a portion of the risk they assume from the consumer. This so-called "reinsurance" may serve at least two purposes, protecting the primary insurer from catastrophic loss, and allowing the primary insurer to sell more insurance than its own financial capacity might otherwise permit. Thus, "[t]he availability of reinsurance affects the ability and willingness of primary insurers to provide insurance to their customers." Insurers who sell reinsurance themselves often purchase insurance to cover part of the risk they assume from the primary insurer; such "retrocessional reinsurance" does for reinsurers what reinsurance does for primary insurers. Many of the defendants here are reinsurers or reinsurance brokers, or play some other specialized role in the reinsurance business; defendant Reinsurance Association of America (RAA) is a trade association of domestic reinsurers.

B

The prehistory of events claimed to give rise to liability starts in 1977, when ISO began the process of revising its 1973 CGL form. For the, first time, it proposed two CGL forms (1984 ISO CGL forms), one the traditional "occurrence" type, the other "with a new 'claims-made' trigger." The "claims-made" form did not have a retroactive date provision, however, and both 1984 forms covered "'sudden and accidental' pollution" damage and provided for unlimited coverage of legal defense costs by the insurer. Within the ISO, defendant Hartford Fire Insurance Company objected to the proposed 1984 forms; it desired elimination of the "occurrence" form, a retroactive date provision on the "claims-made" form, elimination of sudden and accidental pollution coverage, and a legal defense cost cap. Defendant Allstate Insurance Company also expressed its desire for a retroactive date provision on the "claims-made" form. Majorities in the relevant ISO committees, however, supported the proposed 1984 CGL forms and rejected the changes proposed by Hartford and Allstate. In December 1983, the ISO Board of Directors approved the proper 1984 forms, and ISO filed or lodged the forms with state regulators in March 1984.

Dissatisfied with this state of affairs, the defendants began to take other steps to force a change in the terms of coverage of CGL insurance generally available, steps that, the plaintiffs allege, implemented a series of conspiracies in violation of § 1 of the Sherman Act. The plaintiffs recount these steps as a number of separate episodes corresponding to different claims for relief in their complaints; because it will become important to distinguish among these counts and the acts and defendants associated with them, we will note these correspondences.

The first four Claims for Relief in the California Complaint, and the Second Claim for Relief in the Connecticut Complaint, charge the four domestic primary insurer defendants and varying groups of domestic and foreign reinsurers, brokers, and associations with conspiracies to manipulate the ISO CGL forms. In March 1984, primary insurer Hartford persuaded General Reinsurance Corporation (General Re), the largest American reinsurers, to take steps either to procure desired changes in the ISO CGL forms, or "failing that, [to] 'derail' the entire ISO CGL forms program." General Re took up the matter with its trade association, RAA, which created a special committee that met and agreed to "boycott" the 1984 ISO CGL forms unless a retroactive-date provision was added to the claims-made form, and a pollution exclusion and defense cost cap were added to both forms. RAA then sent a letter to ISO "announc[ing] that its members would not provide reinsurance for coverages written on the 1984 CGL forms," and Hartford and General Re enlisted a domestic reinsurance broker to give a speech to the ISO Board of Directors, in which he stated that no reinsurers would "break ranks" to reinsure the 1984 ISO CGL forms.

The four primary insurer defendants (Hartford, Aetna, CIGNA, and Allstate) also encouraged key actors in the London reinsurance market, an important provider of reinsurance for North American risks, to withhold reinsurance for coverages written on the 1984 ISO CGL forms. As a consequence, many London-based underwriters, syndicates, brokers, and reinsurance companies informed ISO of their intention to withhold reinsurance on the 1984 forms, and at least some of them told ISO that they would withhold reinsurance until ISO incorporated all four desired changes into the ISO CGL forms.

For the first time ever, ISO invited representatives of the domestic and foreign reinsurance markets to speak at an ISO Executive Committee meeting. At that meeting, the reinsurers "presented their agreed upon positions that there would be changes in the CGL forms or no reinsurance." The ISO Executive Committee then voted to include a retroactive-date provision in the claims-made form, and to exclude all pollution coverage from both new forms. (But it neither eliminated the occurrence form, nor added a legal defense cost cap.) The 1984 ISO CGL forms were then withdrawn from the marketplace, and replaced with forms (1986 ISO CGL forms) containing the new provisions. After ISO got regulatory approval of the 1986 forms in most States where approval was needed, it eliminated its support services for the 1973 CGL form, thus rendering it impossible for most ISO members to continue to use the form.

The Fifth Claim for Relief in the California Complaint, and the virtually identical Third Claim for Relief in the Connecticut Complaint, charge a conspiracy among a group of London reinsurers and brokers to coerce primary insurers in the United States to offer CGL coverage only on a claims-made basis. The reinsurers collectively refused to write new reinsurance contracts for, or to renew longstanding contracts with, "primary...insurers unless they were prepared to switch from the occurrence to the claims-made form; they also amended their reinsurance contracts to cover only claims made before a "'sunset date,'" thus eliminating reinsurance for claims made on occurrence policies after that date.

The Sixth Claim for Relief in the California Complaint, and the nearly identical Fourth Claim for Relief in the Connecticut Complaint, charge another conspiracy among a somewhat different group of London reinsurers to withhold reinsurance for pollution coverage. The London reinsurers met and agreed that all reinsurance contracts covering North American casualty risks, including CGL risks, would be written with a complete exclusion for pollution liability coverage. In accordance with this agreement, the parties have in fact excluded pollution liability coverage from CGL reinsurance contracts since at least late 1985.

The Seventh Claim for Relief in the California Complaint, and the closely similar Sixth Claim for Relief in the Connecticut Complaint, charge a group of domestic primary insurers, foreign reinsurers, and the ISO with conspiring to restrain trade in the markets for "excess" and "umbrella" insurance by drafting model forms and policy language for these types of insurance, which are not normally offered on a regulated basis. The ISO Executive Committee eventually released standard language for both "occurrence" and "claims-made" umbrella and excess policies; that language included a retroactive date in the claims-made version, and an absolute pollution exclusion and a legal defense cost cap in both versions.

Finally, the Eighth Claim for Relief in the California Complaint, and its counterpart in the Fifth Claim for Relief in the Connecticut Complaint, charge a group of London and domestic retrocessional reinsurers with conspiring to withhold retrocessional reinsurance for North American seepage, pollution, and property contamination risks. Those retrocessional reinsurers signed, and have implemented, an agreement to use their "'best endeavors'" to ensure that they would provide such reinsurance for North American risks "'only...where the original business includes a seepage and pollution exclusion wherever legal and applicable.'"

C

Nineteen States and a number of private plaintiffs filed 36 complaints against the insurers involved in this course of events, charging that the conspiracies described above violated § 1 of the Sherman Act, 15 U.S.C. § 1. After the actions had been consolidated for litigation in the Northern District of California, the defendants moved to dismiss for failure to state a cause of action, or, in the alternative, for summary judgment. The District Court granted the motions to dismiss. It held that the conduct alleged fell within the grant of antitrust immunity contained in § 2(b) of the McCarran-Ferguson Act, 15 U.S.C. § 1012(b), because it amounted to "the business of insurance" and was "regulated by State Law" within the meaning of that section; none of the conduct, in the District Court's view, amounted to a "boycott" within the meaning of the § 3(b) exception to that grant of immunity. 15 U.S.C. § 1013(b). The District Court also dismissed the three claims that named only certain London-based defendants, invoking international comity and applying the Ninth Circuit's decision in *Timberlane Lumber Co. v. Bank of America, N. T. & S. A.*, 549 F.2d 597 (1976).

The Court of Appeals reversed. Although it held the conduct involved to be "the business of insurance" within the meaning of § 2(b), it concluded that the defendants could not claim McCarran-Ferguson Act antitrust immunity for two independent reasons. First, it held, the foreign reinsurers were beyond the regulatory jurisdiction of the States; because their activities could not be "regulated by State Law" within the meaning of § 2(b), they did not fall within that section's grant of immunity. Although the domestic insurers were "regulated by State Law," the court held, they forfeited their § 2(b) exemption when they conspired with the nonexempt foreign reinsurers. Second, the Court of Appeals held that, even if the conduct alleged fell within the scope of § 2(b), it also fell within the § 3(b) exception for "act[s] of boycott, coercion, or intimidation." Finally, as to the three claims brought solely against foreign defendants, the court applied its *Timberlane* analysis, but concluded that the principle of international comity was no bar to exercising Sherman Act jurisdiction.

We granted *certiorari* in No. 91-1111 to address two narrow questions about the scope of McCarran-Ferguson Act antitrust immunity, and in No. 91-1128 to address the application of the Sherman Act to the foreign conduct at issue. [The Court's discussion of No. 91-1111 is omitted.] We now affirm in part, reverse in part, and remand.

. . . .

III

. . . [W]e take up the question presented by No. 91-1128, whether certain claims against the London reinsurers should have been dismissed as improper applications of the Sherman Act to foreign conduct. The Fifth Claim for Relief in the California Complaint alleges a violation of § 1 of the Sherman Act by certain London reinsurers who conspired to coerce primary insurers in the United States to offer CGL coverage on a claims-made basis, thereby making "occurrence CGL coverage . . . unavailable in the State of California for many risks." The Sixth Claim for Relief in the California Complaint alleges that the London reinsurers violated § 1 by a conspiracy to limit coverage of pollution risks in North America, thereby rendering "pollution liability coverage . . . almost entirely unavailable for the vast majority of casualty insurance purchasers in the State of California." The Eighth Claim for Relief in the California Complaint alleges a further § 1 violation by the London reinsurers who, along with domestic retrocessional reinsurers, conspired to limit coverage of seepage, pollution, and property contamination risks in North America, thereby eliminating such coverage in the State of California.

At the outset, we note that the District Court undoubtedly had jurisdiction of these Sherman Act claims, as the London reinsurers apparently concede . . . . . Although the proposition was perhaps not always free from doubt, see *American Banana Co. v. United Fruit Co.*, 213 U. S. 347 (1909), it is well established by now that the Sherman Act applies to foreign conduct that was meant to produce and did in fact produce some substantial effect in the United States. *See Matsushita Elec. Industrial Co. v. Zenith Radio Corp.*, 475 U. S. 574, 582 (1986); *United States v. Aluminum Co. of America*, 148 F.2d 416, 444 (CA2 1945) (L. Hand, J.); *Restatement (Third) of Foreign Relations Law of the United States* § 415, and Reporters' Note 3 (1987) (hereinafter *Restatement (Third) Foreign Relations Law*). [The *Matsushita* case is excerpted below.] Such is the conduct alleged here: that the London reinsurers engaged in unlawful conspiracies to affect the market for insurance in the United States and that their conduct in fact produced substantial effect. [The Court observed in fn. 23 the following: Under § 402 of the Foreign Trade Antitrust Improvements Act of 1982 (FTAIA), 15 U.S.C. § 6a, the Sherman Act does not apply to conduct involving foreign trade or commerce, other than import trade or import commerce, unless "such conduct has a direct, substantial, and reasonably foreseeable effect" on domestic or import commerce. § 6a(1)(A). The FTAIA was intended to exempt from the Sherman Act export transactions that did not injure the United States economy, and it is unclear how it might apply to the conduct alleged here. Also unclear is whether the Act's "direct, substantial, and reasonably foreseeable effect" standard amends existing law or merely codifies it. We need not address these questions here. Assuming that the FTAIA's standard affects this litigation, and assuming further that that standard differs from the prior law, the conduct alleged plainly meets its requirements.]

According to the London reinsurers, the District Court should have declined to exercise such Jurisdiction under the principle of international comity. [The Court observed in fn. 24 the following about Justice Scalia's dissent, *infra*: Justice Scalia contends that comity concerns figure into the prior analysis whether jurisdiction exists under the Sherman Act. This contention is inconsistent with the general understanding that the Sherman Act covers foreign conduct producing a substantial intended effect in the United States, and that concerns of comity come into play, if at all, only after a court has determined that the acts complained of are subject to Sherman Act jurisdiction. *See United States v. Aluminum Co. of America*, 148 F.2d 416, 444 (CA2 1945) ("[I]t follows from what we have…said that [the agreements at issue] were unlawful [under the Sherman Act], though made abroad, if they were intended to affect imports and did affect them"); *Mannington Mills, Inc. v. Congoleum Corp.*, 595 F.2d 1287, 1294 (CA3 1979) (once court determines that jurisdiction exists under the Sherman Act, question remains whether comity precludes its exercise). But cf. *Timberlane Lumber Co. v. Bank of America, N. T. & S. A.*, 549 F.2d 597, 613 (CA9 1976). In any event, the parties conceded jurisdiction at oral argument, and we see no need to address this contention here.] The Court of Appeals agreed that courts should look to that principle in deciding whether to exercise jurisdiction under the Sherman Act. This availed the London reinsurers nothing, however. To be sure, the Court of Appeals believed that "application of [American] antitrust laws to the London reinsurance market 'would lead to significant conflict with English law and policy,'" and that "[s]uch a conflict, unless outweighed by other factors, would by itself be reason to decline exercise of jurisdiction." But other factors, in the court's view, including the London reinsurers' express purpose to affect United States commerce and the substantial nature of the effect produced, outweighed the supposed conflict and required the exercise of jurisdiction in this litigation.

.... [E]ven assuming that in a proper case a court may decline to exercise Sherman Act jurisdiction over foreign conduct (or, as Justice Scalia would put it, may conclude by the employment of comity analysis in the first instance that there is no jurisdiction), international comity would not counsel against exercising jurisdiction in the circumstances alleged here.

The only substantial question in this litigation is whether "there is in fact a true conflict between domestic and foreign law." *Société Nationale Industrielle Aérospatiale v. United States Dist. Court for Southern Dist. of Iowa*, 482 U.S. 522, 555 (1987) (Blackmun, J., concurring in part and dissenting in part). [This case is excerpted below.] The London reinsurers contend that applying the Act to their conduct would conflict significantly with British law, and the British Government, appearing before us as *amicus curiae*, concurs. They assert that Parliament has established a comprehensive regulatory regime over the London reinsurance market and that the conduct alleged here was perfectly consistent with British law and policy. But this is not to state a conflict. "[T]he fact that conduct is lawful in the state in which it took place will not, of itself, bar application of the United States antitrust laws," even where the foreign state has a strong policy to permit or encourage such conduct. *Restatement (Third) Foreign Relations Law* § 415, Comment *j*. No conflict exists, for these purposes, "where a person subject to regulation by two states can comply with the laws of both." *Restatement (Third) Foreign Relations Law* § 403, Comment *e*. Since the London reinsurers do not argue that British law requires them to act in some fashion prohibited by the law of the United States, or claim that their compliance with the laws of both countries is otherwise impossible, we see no conflict with British law. *See Restatement (Third) Foreign Relations Law* § 403, Comment *e*, § 415, Comment *j*. We have no need in this litigation to address other considerations that might inform a decision to refrain from the exercise of jurisdiction on grounds of international comity.

IV

The judgment of the Court of Appeals is affirmed in part and reversed in part, and the cases are remanded for further proceedings consistent with this opinion.

It is so ordered.

Justice Scalia...delivered a *dissenting* opinion. [Justice O'Connor, Justice Kennedy, and Justice Thomas join this opinion in its entirety, and The Chief Justice joins Part I of this opinion.]

....I dissent from the Court's ruling concerning the extraterritorial application of the Sherman Act....

....

II

Petitioners in No. 91-1128, various British corporations and other British subjects, argue that certain of the claims against them constitute an inappropriate extraterritorial application of the Sherman Act. It is important to distinguish two distinct questions raised by this petition: whether the District Court had jurisdiction, and whether the Sherman Act reaches the extraterritorial conduct alleged here. On the first question, I believe that the District Court had subject-matter jurisdiction over the Sherman Act claims against all the defendants (personal jurisdiction is not contested). Respondents asserted non-frivolous claims under the Sherman Act, and 28 U.S.C. § 1331 vests district courts with subject-matter jurisdiction over cases "arising under" federal statutes. As precedents such as *Lauritzen v. Larsen*, 345 U.S. 571 (1953), make clear, that is sufficient to establish the District Court's jurisdiction over these claims.....

The second question—the extraterritorial reach of the Sherman Act—has nothing to do with the jurisdiction of the courts. It is a question of substantive law turning on whether, in enacting the Sherman Act, Congress asserted regulatory power over the challenged conduct. If a plaintiff fails to prevail on this issue, the court does not dismiss the claim for want of subject-matter jurisdiction—want of power to adjudicate; rather, it decides the claim, ruling on the merits that the plaintiff has failed to state a cause of action under the relevant statute.

There is, however, a type of "jurisdiction" relevant to determining the extraterritorial reach of a statute; it is known as "legislative jurisdiction," or "jurisdiction to prescribe," 1 *Restatement (Third) of Foreign Relations Law of the United States* 235 (1987) (hereinafter *Restatement (Third)*). This refers to "the authority of a state to make its law applicable to persons or activities," and is quite a separate matter from "jurisdiction to adjudicate". There is no doubt, of course, that Congress possesses legislative jurisdiction over the acts alleged in this complaint: Congress has broad power under Article I, § 8, cl. 3, "[t]o regulate Commerce with foreign Nations," and this Court has repeatedly upheld its power to make laws applicable to persons or activities beyond our territorial boundaries where United States interests are affected.

But the question in this litigation is whether, and to what extent, Congress *has* exercised that undoubted legislative jurisdiction in enacting the Sherman Act.

Two canons of statutory construction are relevant in this inquiry. The first is the "longstanding principle of American law 'that legislation of Congress, unless a contrary intent appears, is meant to apply only within the territorial jurisdiction of the United States.'" ... We have, however, found the presumption to be overcome with respect to our antitrust laws; it is now well established that the Sherman Act applies extraterritorially. *See Matsushita Elec. Industrial Co. v. Zenith Radio Corp.*, 475 U.S. 574, 582, n. 6 (1986); *see also United States v. Aluminum Co. of America*, 148 F.2d 416 (CA2 1945).

But if the presumption against extraterritoriality has been overcome or is otherwise inapplicable, a second canon of statutory construction becomes relevant: "[A]n act of congress ought never to be construed to violate the law of nations if any other possible construction remains." *Murray v. Schooner Charming Betsy*, 2 Cranch 64, 118 (1804) (Marshall, C.J.). This canon is "wholly independent" of the presumption against extraterritoriality. It is relevant to determining the substantive reach of a statute because "the law of nations," or customary international law, includes limitations on a nation's exercise of its jurisdiction to prescribe. *See Restatement (Third)* §§ 401-416. Though it clearly has constitutional authority to do so, Congress is generally presumed not to have exceeded those customary international-law limits on jurisdiction to prescribe.

Consistent with that presumption, this and other courts have frequently recognized that, even where the presumption against extraterritoriality does not apply, statutes should not be interpreted to regulate foreign persons or conduct if that regulation would conflict with principles of international law. For example, in *Romero v. International Terminal Operating Co.*, 358 U.S. 354 (1959), the plaintiff, a Spanish sailor who had been injured while working aboard a Spanish-flag and Spanish-owned vessel, filed a Jones Act claim against his Spanish employer. The presumption against extraterritorial application of federal statutes was inapplicable to the case, as the actionable tort had occurred in American waters. The Court nonetheless stated that, "in the absence of a contrary congressional direction," it would apply "principles of choice of law that are consonant with the needs of a general federal maritime law and with due recognition of our self-regarding respect for the relevant interests of foreign nations in the regulation of maritime commerce as part of the legitimate concern of the international community." "The controlling considerations" in this choice-of-law analysis were "the interacting interests of the United States and of foreign countries."

Romero referred to, and followed, the choice-of-law analysis set forth in *Lauritzen v. Larsen*, 345 U.S. 571 (1953).... *Lauritzen* also involved a Jones Act claim brought by a foreign sailor against a foreign employer. The *Lauritzen* Court recognized the basic problem: "If [the Jones Act were] read literally, Congress has conferred an American right of action which requires nothing more than that plaintiff be 'any seaman who shall suffer personal injury in the course of his employment.'" The solution it adopted was to construe the statute "to apply only to areas and transactions in which *American law would be considered operative under prevalent doctrines of international law*." (Emphasis added). To support application of international law to limit the facial breadth of the statute, the Court relied upon — of course — Chief Justice Marshall's statement in *Schooner Charming Betsy*, quoted *supra*. It then set forth "several factors which, alone or in combination, are generally conceded to influence choice of law to govern a tort claim." *See also McCulloch v. Sociedad Nacional de Marineros de Honduras*, 372 U.S. 10, 21-22 (1963) (applying *Schooner Charming Betsy* principle to restrict application of National Labor Relations Act to foreign-flag vessels).

Lauritzen, Romero, and McCulloch were maritime cases, but we have recognized the principle that the scope of generally worded statutes must be construed in light of international law in other areas as well. More specifically, the principle was expressed in *United States v. Aluminum Co. of America*, 148 F.2d 416 (CA2 1945), the decision that established the extraterritorial reach of the Sherman Act. In his opinion for the court, Judge Learned Hand cautioned "we are not to read general words, such as those in [the Sherman] Act, without regard to the limitations customarily observed by nations upon the exercise of their powers; limitations which generally correspond to those fixed by the 'Conflict of Laws.'"

More recent lower court precedent has also tempered the extraterritorial application of the Sherman Act with considerations of "international comity." *See Timberlane Lumber Co. v. Bank of America, N. T. & S. A.*, 549 F.2d 597, 608-615 (CA9 1976); *Laker Airways Limited v. Sabena, Belgian World Airlines*, 731 F.2d 909 (1984). The "comity" they refer to is not the comity of courts, whereby judges decline to exercise jurisdiction over matters more appropriately adjudged elsewhere, but rather what might be termed "prescriptive comity": the respect sovereign nations afford each other by limiting the reach of their laws. That comity is exercised by legislatures when they enact laws, and courts assume it has been exercised when they come to interpreting the scope of laws their legislatures have enacted. It is a traditional component of choice-of-law theory. *See* J. Story, *Commentaries on the Conflict of Laws* § 38 (1834) (distinguishing between the "comity of the courts" and the "comity of nations," and defining the latter as "the true foundation and extent of the obligation of the laws of one nation within the territories of another"). Comity in this sense includes the choice-of-law principles that, "in the absence of contrary congressional direction," are assumed to be incorporated into our substantive laws having extraterritorial reach. *Romero, supra*, at 382-383; *see also Lauritzen, supra*, at 578-579; *Hilton v. Guyot*, 159 U.S. 113, 162-166 (1895). Considering comity in this way is just part of determining whether the Sherman Act prohibits the conduct at issue.

In sum, the practice of using international law to limit the extraterritorial reach of statutes is firmly established in our jurisprudence. In proceeding to apply that practice to the present cases, I shall rely on the *Restatement (Third)* for the relevant principles of international law. Its standards appear fairly supported in the decisions of this Court construing international choice-of-law principles (*Lauritzen, Romero, and McCulloch*) and in the decisions of other federal courts, especially *Timberlane*. Whether the *Restatement* precisely reflects international law in every detail matters little here, as I believe this litigation would be resolved the same way under virtually any conceivable test that takes account of foreign regulatory interests.

Under the *Restatement*, a nation having some "basis" for jurisdiction to prescribe law should nonetheless refrain from exercising that jurisdiction "with respect to a person or activity having connections with another state when the exercise of such jurisdiction is unreasonable." *Restatement (Third)* § 403(1). The "reasonableness" inquiry turns on a number of factors including, but not limited to: "the extent to which the activity takes place within the territory [of the regulating state]," *id.*, § 403(2)(a); "the connections, such as nationality, residence, or economic activity, between the regulating state and the person principally responsible for the activity to be regulated," *id.*, § 403(2)(b); "the character of the activity to be regulated, the importance of regulation to the regulating state, the extent to which other states regulate such activities, and the degree to which the desirability of such regulation is generally accepted," *id.*, § 403(2)(c); "the extent to which another state may have an interest in regulating the activity," *id.*, § 403(2)(g); and "the likelihood of conflict with regulation by another state," *id.*, § 403(2)(h). Rarely would these factors point more clearly against application of United States law. The activity relevant to the counts at issue here took place primarily in the United Kingdom, and the defendants in these counts are British corporations and British subjects having their principal place of business or residence outside the United States. Great Britain has established a comprehensive regulatory scheme governing the London reinsurance markets, and clearly has a heavy "interest in regulating the activity," *id.*, § 403(2)(g). Finally, § 2(b) of the McCarran-Ferguson Act allows state regulatory statutes to override the Sherman Act in the insurance field, subject only to the narrow "boycott" exception set forth in § 3(b)—suggesting that "the importance of regulation to the [United States]," *Restatement (Third)* § 403(2)(c), is slight. Considering these factors, I think it unimaginable that an assertion of legislative jurisdiction by the United States would be considered reasonable, and therefore it is inappropriate to assume, in the absence of statutory indication to the contrary, that Congress has made such an assertion.

It is evident from what I have said that the Court's comity analysis, which proceeds as though the issue is whether the courts should "decline to exercise...jurisdiction," rather than whether the Sherman Act covers this conduct, is simply misdirected. I do not at all agree, moreover, with the Court's conclusion that the issue of the substantive scope of the Sherman Act is not in the cases. To be sure, the parties did not make a clear distinction between adjudicative jurisdiction and the scope of the statute. Parties often do not, as we have observed (and have declined to punish with procedural default) before. It is not realistic, and also not helpful, to pretend that the only really relevant issue in this litigation is not before us. In any event, if one erroneously chooses, as the Court does, to make adjudicative jurisdiction (or, more precisely, abstention) the vehicle for taking account of the needs of prescriptive comity, the Court still gets it wrong. It concludes that no "true conflict" counseling non-application of United States law (or rather, as it thinks, United States judicial jurisdiction) exists unless compliance with United States law would constitute a *violation* of another country's law. That breathtakingly broad proposition, which contradicts the many cases discussed earlier, will bring the Sherman Act and other laws into sharp and unnecessary conflict with the legitimate interests of other countries—particularly our closest trading partners.

In the sense in which the term "conflic[t]" was used in *Lauritzen*, and is generally understood in the field of conflicts of laws, there is clearly a conflict in this litigation. The petitioners here, like the defendant in *Lauritzen*, were not compelled by any foreign law to take their allegedly wrongful actions, but that no more precludes a conflict-of-laws analysis here than it did there. Where applicable foreign and domestic law provide different substantive rules of decision to govern the parties' dispute, a conflict-of-laws analysis is necessary.

Literally the *only* support that the Court adduces for its position is § 403 of the *Restatement (Third)*—or more precisely Comment *e* to that provision, which states:

> "Subsection (3) [which says that a State should defer to another state if that State's interest is clearly greater] applies only when one state requires what another prohibits, or where compliance with the regulations of two states exercising jurisdiction consistently with this section is otherwise impossible. It does not apply where a person subject to regulation by two states can comply with the laws of both...."

The Court has completely misinterpreted this provision. Subsection (3) of § 403 (requiring one State to defer to another in the limited circumstances just described) comes into play only after subsection (1) of § 403 has been complied with—*i.e.*, after it has been determined that the exercise of jurisdiction by *both* of the two States is not "unreasonable." That prior question is answered by applying the factors (*inter alia*) set forth in subsection (2) of § 403, that is, precisely the factors that I have discussed in text and that the Court rejects.

I would reverse the judgment of the Court of Appeals on this issue, and remand to the District Court with instructions to dismiss for failure to state a claim on the three counts at issue in No. 91-1128.

C. Extraterritorial Jurisdiction in Criminal Cases

U.S. v. Nippon Paper Industries Company, Ltd.
109 F.3d 1 (1ST Cir. 1997)

Selya, Circuit Judge.

This case raises an important, hitherto unanswered question. In it, the United States attempts to convict a foreign corporation under the Sherman Act, a federal antitrust statute, alleging that price-fixing activities which took place entirely in Japan are prosecutable because they were intended to have, and did in fact have, substantial effects in this country. The district court, declaring that a criminal antitrust prosecution could not be based on wholly extraterritorial conduct, dismissed the indictment. We reverse.

I. JUST THE FAX

. . . .

In 1995, a federal grand jury handed up an indictment naming as a defendant Nippon Paper Industries Co., Ltd. (NPI), a Japanese manufacturer of facsimile paper. The indictment alleges that in 1990 NPI and certain unnamed coconspirators held a number of meetings in Japan which culminated in an agreement to fix the price of thermal fax paper throughout North America. NPI and other manufacturers who were privy to the scheme purportedly accomplished their objective by selling the paper in Japan to unaffiliated trading houses on condition that the latter charge specified (inflated) prices for the paper when they resold it in North America. The trading houses then shipped and sold the paper to their subsidiaries in the United States who in turn sold it to American consumers at swollen pieces. The indictment further relates that, in 1990 alone, NPI sold thermal fax paper worth approximately $6,100,000 for eventual import into the United States; and that in order to ensure the success of the venture, NPI monitored the paper trail and confirmed that the prices charged to end users were those that it had arranged. These activities, the indictment posits, had a substantial adverse effect on commerce in the United States and unreasonably restrained trade in violation of Section One of the Sherman Act, 15 U.S.C. § 1 (1994).

NPI moved to dismiss because, *inter alia*, if the conduct attributed to NPI occurred at all, it took place entirely in Japan, and, thus, the indictment failed to limn an offense under Section One of the Sherman Act. The government opposed this initiative on two grounds. First, it claimed that the law deserved a less grudging reading and that, properly read, Section One of the Sherman Act applied criminally to wholly foreign conduct as long as that conduct produced substantial and intended effects within the United States. Second, it claimed that the indictment, too, deserved a less grudging reading and that, properly read, the bill alleged a vertical conspiracy in restraint of trade that involved overt acts by certain co-conspirators within the United States. Accepting a restrictive reading of both the statute and the indictment, the district court dismissed the case. This appeal followed.

II. ANALYSIS

We begin—and end—with the overriding legal question. Because this question is one of statutory construction, we review de novo the holding that Section One of the Sherman Act does not cover wholly extraterritorial conduct in the criminal context.

Our analysis proceeds in moieties. We first present the historical context in which this important question arises. We move next to the specifics of the case.

A. *A Historical Perspective.*

Our law has long presumed that "legislation of Congress, unless a contrary intent appears, is meant to apply only within the territorial jurisdiction of the United States." *EEOC v. Arabian American Oil Co.*, 499 U.S. 244 (1991). In this context, the Supreme Court has charged inquiring courts with determining whether Congress has clearly expressed an affirmative desire to apply particular laws to conduct that occurs beyond the borders of the United States.

The earliest Supreme Court case which undertook a comparable task in respect to Section One of the Sherman Act determined that the presumption against extraterritoriality had not been overcome. In *American Banana Co. v. United Fruit Co.*, 213 U.S. 347 (1909), the Court considered the application of the Sherman Act in a civil action concerning conduct which occurred entirely in Central America and which had no discernible effect on imports to the United States. Starting with what Justice Holmes termed "the general and almost universal rule" holding "that the character of an act as lawful or unlawful must be determined wholly by the law of the country where the act is done," *id.* at 356, ... and the ancillary proposition that, in cases of doubt, a statute should be "confined in its operation and effect to the territorial limits over which the lawmaker has general and legitimate power," *id.* at 357, the Court held that the defendant's actions abroad were not proscribed by the Sherman Act.

Our jurisprudence is precedent-based, but it is not static. By 1945, a different court saw a very similar problem in a somewhat softer light. In *United States v. Aluminum Co. of Am.*, 148 F.2d 416 (2d Cir.1945) (*Alcoa*), the Second Circuit, sitting as a court of last resort, *see* 15 U.S.C. § 29 (authorizing designation of a court of appeals as a court of last resort for certain antitrust cases), mulled a civil action brought under Section One against a Canadian corporation for acts committed entirely abroad which, the government averred, had produced substantial anticompetitive effects within the United States. The *Alcoa* court read *American Banana* narrowly; that case, Judge Learned Hand wrote, stood only for the principle that "[w]e should not impute to Congress an intent to punish all whom its courts can catch, for conduct which has no consequences within the United States." *Id.* at 443. But a sovereign ordinarily can impose liability for conduct outside its borders that produces consequences within them, and while considerations of comity argue against applying Section One to situations in which no effect within the United States has been shown— the *American Banana* scenario—the statute, properly interpreted, does proscribe extraterritorial acts which were "intended to affect imports [to the United States] and did affect them." *Id.* at 444. On the facts of *Alcoa*, therefore, the presumption against extraterritoriality had been overcome, and the Sherman Act had been violated.

Any perceived tension between *American Banana* and *Alcoa* was eased by the Supreme Court's most recent exploration of Sherman Act's extraterritorial reach. In *Hartford Fire Ins. Co. v. California*, 509 U.S. 764 (1993), the Justices endorsed *Alcoa*'s core holding, permitting civil antitrust claims under Section One to go forward despite the fact that the actions which allegedly violated Section One occurred entirely on British soil. While noting *American Banana*'s initial disagreement with this proposition, the *Hartford Fire* Court deemed it "well established by now that the Sherman Act applies to foreign conduct that was meant to produce and did, in fact, produce some substantial effect in United States." *Id.* at 796. The conduct alleged, a London-based conspiracy to alter the American insurance market, met that benchmark.

To sum up, the case law now conclusively establishes that civil antitrust actions predicated on wholly foreign conduct which has an intended and substantial effect in the United States come within Section One's jurisdictional reach. In arriving at this conclusion, we take no view of the government's asseveration that the Foreign Trade Antitrust Improvements Act of 1982 (FTAIA), 15 U.S.C. § 6a (1994), makes manifest Congress' intent to apply the Sherman Act extraterritorially. The FTAIA is inelegantly phrased and the court in *Hartford Fire* declined to place any weight on it. *See Hartford Fire*, 509 U.S. at 796 n. 23. We emulate this example and do not rest our ultimate conclusion about Section One's scope upon the FTAIA.

B. *The Merits.*

Were this a civil case, our journey would be complete. But here the United States essays a criminal prosecution for solely extraterritorial conduct rather than a civil action. This is largely uncharted terrain; we are aware of no authority directly on point, and the parties have cited none.

Be that as it may, one datum sticks out like a sore thumb: in both criminal and cases, the claim that Section One applies extraterritorially is based on the same language in the same section of the same statute: "Every contract, combination in the form of trust or otherwise, or conspiracy, in restraint of trade or commerce among the several States, or with foreign nations, is declared to be illegal." 15 U.S.C. § 1. Words may sometimes be chameleons, possessing different shades of meaning in different contexts, but common sense suggests that courts should interpret the same language in the same section of the same statute uniformly, regardless of whether the impetus for interpretation is criminal or civil.

Common sense is usually a good barometer of statutory meaning. Here, however, we need not rely on common sense alone; accepted canons of statutory construction point in the same direction. It is a fundamental interpretive principle that identical words or terms used in different parts of the same act are intended to have the same meaning. This principle—which the Court recently called "the basic canon of statutory construction," *Estate of Cowart v. Nicklos Drilling Co.*, 505 U.S. 469, 479 (1992)—operates not only when particular phrases appear in different sections of the same act, but also when they appear in different paragraphs or sentences of a single section.....It follows, therefore, that if the language upon which the indictment rests were the same as the language upon which civil liability rests but appeared in a different section of the Sherman Act, or in a different part of the same section, we would be under great pressure to follow the lead of the *Hartford Fire* Court and construe the two iterations of the language identically. Where, as here, the tie binds more tightly—that is, the text under consideration is not merely a duplicate appearing somewhere else in the statute, but is the original phrase in the original setting—

the pressure escalates and the case for reading the language in a manner consonant with a prior Supreme Court interpretation is irresistible.

The Supreme Court confronted an analogous situation in *Ratzlaf v. United States*, 510 U.S. 135 (1994). There, the court dealt with a single criminal penalty clause, contained in 31 U.S.C. § 5322(a), which authorized punishment for individuals "willfully violating" a number of separate statutory provisions. The defendant was charged under one of these provisions. After noting that identical terms appearing at multiple places within a single statute customarily have a consistent meaning, the Court said: "We have even stronger cause to construe a *single* formulation, here § 5322(a), the same way each time it is called into play." *Id.* at 143.... The *Ratzlaf* Court proceeded to interpret the phrase "willfully violating" to incorporate the same mens rea requirement that had been read into the phrase when section 5322(a) was applied in other contexts. In so doing the Court quoted with approval our statement in *United States v. Aversa*, 984 F.2d 493, 498 (1st Cir.1993) (*en banc*): "Ascribing various meanings to a single iteration... — reading the word differently for each code section to which it applies — would open Pandora's jar. If courts can render meaning so malleable, the usefulness of a single penalty provision for a group of related code sections will be eviscerated."

Ratzlaf is not our only teaching aid. This court recently confronted a situation that, putting together its successive stages, throws light upon the problem at hand. Having found an ambiguity in the phrase "cost of producing self-employment income," 7 U.S.C. § 2014(d)(9), we deferred to a reasonable administrative regulation interpreting it. *See Strickland v. Commissioner, Me. Dept. of Human Servs.*, 48 F.3d 12, 21 (1st Cir.), *cert. denied*, 116 S.Ct. 145 (1995). In a subsequent suit involving the same parties, we debunked the plaintiffs' contention, advanced in a somewhat different context and in connection with a neoteric legal theory, that the phrase in question had a plain meaning. We explained: "Statutory ambiguity does not flash on and off like a bank of strobe lights at a discotheque, shining brightly at the time of one lawsuit and then vanishing mysteriously in the interlude before the next suit appears." *Strickland v. Commissioner, Me. Dep't of Human Servs.*, 96 F.3d 542, 547 (1st Cir.1996). Read in the ensemble, the *Strickland* opinions stand for the proposition that the same phrase, appearing in the same portion of the same statute, cannot bear divergent interpretations in different litigation contexts.

The shared rationale of the *Ratzlaf* and *Strickland* cases reinforces the basic canon of construction and gives us confidence that we should follow the canon here. The words of Section One have not changed since the *Hartford Fire* Court found that they clearly evince Congress' intent to apply the Sherman Act extraterritorially in civil actions, and it would be disingenuous for us to pretend that the words had lost their clarity simply because this is a criminal proceeding. Thus, unless some special circumstance obtains in this case, there is no principled way in which we can uphold the order of dismissal.

NPI and its *amicus*, the Government of Japan, urge that special reasons exist for measuring Section One's reach differently in a criminal context. We have reviewed their exhortations and found them hollow. We discuss the five most promising theses below. The rest do not require comment.

1. *Lack of Precedent.* NPI and its amicus make much of the fact that this appears to be the first criminal case in which the United States endeavors to extend Section One to wholly foreign conduct. We are not impressed. There is a first time for everything, and the absence of earlier criminal actions is probably more a demonstration of the increasingly

global nature of our economy than proof that Section One cannot cover wholly foreign conduct in the criminal milieu.

Moreover, this argument overstates the lack of precedent. There is, for example, solid authority for applying a state's criminal statute to conduct occurring entirely outside the state's borders. *See Strassheim v. Daily*, 221 U.S. 280, 285 (1911) (Holmes, J.) ("Acts done outside a jurisdiction, but intended to produce and producing detrimental effects within it, justify a State in punishing the cause of the harm as if he had been present at the effect, if the State should succeed in getting him within its power."). It is not much of a stretch to apply this same principle internationally, especially in a shrinking world.

2. ***Difference in Strength of Presumption.*** The lower court and NPI both cite *United States v. Bowman*, 260 U.S. 94 (1922), for the proposition that the presumption against extraterritoriality operates with greater force in the criminal arena than in civil litigation. This misreads the opinion. To be sure, the *Bowman* Court, dealing with a charged conspiracy to defraud, warned that if the criminal law "is to be extended to include those [crimes] committed outside of the strict territorial jurisdiction, it is natural for Congress to say so in the statute, and failure to do so will negative the purpose of Congress in this regard." *Id.* at 98.... But this pronouncement merely restated the presumption against extraterritoriality previously established in civil cases like *American Banana*. The *Bowman* Court nowhere suggested that a different, more resilient presumption arises in criminal cases.

    Nor does *United States v. United States Gypsum Co.*, 438 U.S. 422 (1978), offer aid and succor to NPI. Recognizing that "the behavior proscribed by the [Sherman] Act is often difficult to distinguish from the gray zone of socially acceptable and economically justifiable business conduct," *id.* at 440-41,... the *Gypsum* Court held that criminal intent generally is required to convict under the Act. Although this distinguishes some civil antitrust cases (in which intent need not be proven) from their criminal counterparts, the *Gypsum* Court made it plain that intent need not be shown to prosecute criminally "conduct regarded as *per se* illegal because of its unquestionably anticompetitive effects." *Id.* at 440. This means, of course, that defendants can be convicted of participation in price-fixing conspiracies without any demonstration of a specific criminal intent to violate the antitrust laws. Because the instant case falls within that rubric, *Gypsum* does not help NPI.

    We add that even if *Gypsum* had differentiated between civil and criminal price-fixing cases, NPI's reliance on it would still be problematic. Reduced to bare essence, *Gypsum* focuses on *mens rea*, noting that centuries of Anglo-American legal tradition instruct that criminal liability ordinarily should be premised on malevolent intent, whereas civil liability, to which less stigma and milder consequences commonly attach, often requires a lesser showing of intent. There is simply no comparable tradition or rationale for drawing a criminal/civil distinction with regard to extraterritoriality, and neither NPI nor its amicus have alluded to any case which does so.

3. ***The Restatement.*** NPI and the district court both sing the praises of the *Restatement (Third) of Foreign Relations Law* (1987), claiming that it supports a distinction between civil and criminal cases on the issue of extraterritoriality. The passage to which they pin their hopes states:

> [I]n the case of regulatory statutes that may give rise to both civil and criminal liability, such as the United States antitrust and securities laws, the presence of substantial foreign elements will ordinarily weigh against application of criminal law. In such cases, legislative intent to subject conduct outside the state's territory to its criminal law should be found only on the basis of express statement or clear implication.

Id. at § 403 cmt. f. We believe that this statement merely reaffirms the classic presumption against extraterritoriality—no more, no less. After all, nothing in the text of the *Restatement* proper contradicts the government's interpretation of Section One. *See, e.g., id.* at § 402(1)(c) (explaining that, subject only to a general requirement of reasonableness, a state has jurisdiction to proscribe "conduct outside its territory that has or is intended to have substantial effect within its territory"); *id.* at § 415(2) ("Any agreement in restraint of United States trade that is made outside of the United States...[is] subject to the jurisdiction to prescribe of the United States, if a principal purpose of the conduct or agreement is to interfere with the commerce of the United States, and the agreement or conduct has some effect on that commerce."). [The court noted in fn. 5 "that, by their use of the disjunctive in section 402(1)(c) the drafters of the *Restatement* seem to suggest a more permissive standard then we, and other American courts, *see, e.g., Alcoa,* 148 F.2d at 444, would deem met."] What is more, other comments indicate that a country's decision to prosecute wholly foreign conduct is discretionary. *See, e.g., id.* at § 403 rep. n. 8.

4. *The Rule of Lenity.* The next arrow which NPI yanks from its quiver is the rule of lenity. The rule itself is venerable; it provides that, in the course of interpreting statutes in criminal cases, a reviewing court should resolve ambiguities affecting a statute's scope in the defendant's favor. But the rule of lenity is inapposite unless a statutory ambiguity looms, and a statute is not ambiguous for this purpose simply because some courts or commentators have questioned its proper interpretation. [The Court observed in fn. 6 that "[l]eaving aside the lower court's decision in this case, no reported opinion has questioned the applicability of *Hartford Fire*'s exercise in statutory construction to the precincts patrolled by the criminal law. Nevertheless, *Hartford Fire*'s rendition of the statute has drawn criticism from the academy. *See, e.g.,* Kenneth W. Dam, *Extraterritoriality in an Age of Globalization: The Hartford Fire Case,* 1993 Sup.Ct.Rev. 289, 307-13 (1993)."] *See Reno v. Koray,* 115 S.Ct. 2021 (1995). Rather, "[t]he rule of lenity applies only if, after seizing everything from which aid can be derived, [a court] can make no more than a guess as to what Congress intended." *Reno,* 115 S.Ct. at 2029. Put bluntly, the rule of lenity cannot be used to create ambiguity when the meaning of a law, even if not readily apparent, is, upon inquiry, reasonably clear.

That ends the matter of lenity. In view of the fact that the Supreme Court deems it "well established" that Section One of the Sherman Act applies to wholly foreign conduct, *Hartford Fire,* 509 U.S. at 796, we effectively are foreclosed from trying to tease an ambiguity out of Section One relative to its extraterritorial application. Accordingly, the rule of lenity plays no part in the instant case.

5. *Comity.* International comity is a doctrine that counsels voluntary forbearance when a sovereign which has a legitimate claim to jurisdiction concludes that a second sovereign also has a legitimate claim to jurisdiction under principles of international law. Comity is more an aspiration than a fixed rule, more a matter of grace than a matter of obligation. In all events, its growth in the antitrust sphere has been stunted by *Hartford Fire*, in which the Court suggested that comity concerns would operate to defeat the exercise of jurisdiction only in those few cases in which the law of the foreign sovereign required a defendant to act in a manner incompatible with the Sherman Act or in which full compliance with both statutory schemes was impossible. Accordingly, the *Hartford Fire* Court gave short shrift to the defendants' entreaty that the conduct leading to antitrust liability was perfectly legal in the United Kingdom.

In this case the defendant's comity-based argument is even more attenuated. The conduct with which NPI is charged is illegal under both Japanese and American laws, thereby alleviating any founded concern about NPI being whipsawed between separate sovereigns. And, moreover, to the extent that comity is informed by general principles of reasonableness, *see Restatement (Third) of Foreign Relations Law* § 403, the indictment lodged against NPI is well within the pale. In it, the government charges that the defendant orchestrated a conspiracy with the object of rigging prices in the United States. If the government can prove these charges, we see no tenable reason why principles of comity should shield NPI from prosecution. We live in an age of international commerce, where decisions reached in one corner of the world can reverberate around the globe in less time than it takes to tell the tale. Thus, a ruling in NPI's favor would create perverse incentives for those who would use nefarious means to influence markets in the United States, rewarding them for erecting as many territorial firewalls as possible between cause and effect.

We need go no further. *Hartford Fire* definitively establishes that Section One of the Sherman Act applies to wholly foreign conduct which has an intended and substantial effect in the United States. We are bound to accept that holding. Under settled principles of statutory construction, we also are bound to apply it by interpreting Section One the same way in a criminal case. The combined force of these commitments requires that we accept the government's cardinal argument, reverse the order of the district court, reinstate the indictment, and remand for further proceedings.

Reversed and remanded.

Lynch, Circuit Judge, *concurring.*

The question presented in this case is whether Section One of the Sherman Act authorizes criminal prosecutions of defendants for their actions committed entirely outside the United States. Judicial precedents, culminating with the Supreme Court's decision in *Hartford Fire Insurance Co. v. California*, conclusively establish that Section One's jurisdictional reach extends, in civil actions, to foreign conduct that is meant to produce, and does in fact produce, substantial effects in the United States. The next question to be asked is whether there is any persuasive reason to believe that, with regard to wholly foreign conduct, Section One in the criminal context is not co-extensive with Section One in the civil context.

In answering this second question, courts must be careful to determine whether this construction of Section One's criminal reach conforms with principles of international law. "It has been a maxim of statutory construction since the decision in *Murray v. The Charming Betsy*, 2 Cranch 64, 118 (1804), that 'an act of congress ought never to be construed to violate the law of nations, if any other possible construction remains.'" In the *Alcoa* case, Judge Learned Hand found this canon of construction relevant to determining the substantive reach of the Sherman Act, observing that "we are not to read general words [*i.e.*, Section One]... without regard to the limitations customarily observed by nations upon the exercise of their powers." *United States v. Aluminum Co. of Am.*, 148 F.2d 416, 443 (2d Cir.1945).

The task of construing Section One in this context is not the usual one of determining congressional intent by parsing the language or legislative history of the statute. The broad, general language of the federal antitrust laws and their unilluminating legislative history place a special interpretive responsibility upon the judiciary. The Supreme Court has called the Sherman Act a "charter of freedom" for the courts, with "a generality and adaptability comparable to that found... in constitutional provisions." *Appalachian Coals, Inc. v. United States*, 288 U.S. 344, 359-60 (1933). As Professors Areeda and Turner have said, the federal courts have been invested "with a jurisdiction to create and develop an 'antitrust law' in the manner of the common law courts." I Areeda & Turner, *Antitrust Law* ¶ 106, at 15 (1978). The courts are aided in this task by canons of statutory construction, such as the presumption against violating international law, which, serve as both guides and limits in the absence of more explicit indicia of congressional intent.

Here, we are asked to determine the substantive content of Section One's inexact jurisdictional provision, "commerce... with foreign nations." 15 U.S.C. § 1. Because of the "compunctions against the creation of crimes by judges rather than by legislators," II Areeda & Hovenkamp, *Antitrust Law* ¶ 311b, at 33 (1995 rev. ed.), the constitution-like aspects of the antitrust laws must be handled particularly carefully in criminal prosecutions.

As the antitrust laws give the federal enforcement agencies a relatively blank check, the development of antitrust law has been largely shaped by the cases that the executive branch chooses—or does not choose—to bring. Accordingly it has been said that:

> novel interpretations or great departures have seldom, if ever, occurred in criminal cases, which prosecutors have usually reserved for defendants whose knowing behavior would be generally recognized as appropriate for criminal sanctions.

Id. at 34. This case does present a new interpretation. We are told this is the first instance in which the executive branch has chosen to interpret the criminal provisions of the Sherman Act as reaching conduct wholly committed outside of this country's borders.

Changing economic conditions, as well as different political agendas, mean that antitrust policies may change from administration to administration. The present administration has promulgated new *Antitrust Enforcement Guidelines for International Operations* which "focus primarily on situations in which the Sherman Act will grant jurisdiction and when the United States will exercise that jurisdiction" internationally. Brockbank, *The 1995 International Antitrust Guidelines: The Reach of U.S. Antitrust Law Continues to Expand*, 2 J. INT'L LEGAL STUD. 1, *22 (1996). The new *Guidelines* reflect a stronger enforcement stance than earlier versions of the *Guidelines*, and have been described as a "warning to foreign governments and enterprises that the [antitrust enforcement] Agencies intend to actively pursue restraints on trade occurring abroad that adversely affect American markets or damage American exporting opportunities." *Id.* at 21. The instant case is likely a result of this policy.

It is with this context in mind that we must determine if the exercise of jurisdiction occasioned by the decision of the executive branch of the United States is proper in this case. While courts, including this one, speak of determining congressional intent when interpreting statutes, the meaning of the antitrust laws has emerged through the relationship among all three branches of government. In this criminal case, it is our responsibility to ensure that the executive's interpretation of the Sherman Act does not conflict with other legal principles, including principles of international law.

That question requires examination beyond the language of Section One of the Sherman Act. It is, of course, generally true that, as a principle of statutory interpretation, the same language should be read the same way in all contexts to which the language applies. But this is not invariably true. New content is sometimes ascribed to statutory terms depending upon context. As NPI and the Government of Japan point out, the Supreme Court has held that Section One of the Sherman Act, which defines both criminal and civil violations with one general phrase, "should be construed as including intent as an element" of a criminal violation. *United States v. United States Gypsum Co.*, 438 U.S. 422, 443 (1978). Where Congress intends that our laws conform with international law, and where international law suggests that criminal enforcement and civil enforcement be viewed differently, it is at least conceivable that different content could be ascribed to the same language depending on whether the context is civil or criminal. It is then worth asking about the effect of the international law which Congress presumably also meant to respect.

The content of international law is determined "by reference 'to the customs and usages of civilized nations, and, as evidence of these, to the works of jurists and commentators.'" *Hilao v. Estate of Marcos*, 103 F.3d 789, 794 (9th Cir.1996) (quoting *The Paquete Habana*, 175 U.S. 677, 700 (1900)); *see also Kadic v. Karadzic*, 70 F.3d 232 (2d Cir.1995). The *Restatement (Third) of the Foreign Relations Law of the United States* restates international law, as derived from customary international law and from international agreements to which the United States is a party, as it applies to the United States. The United States courts have treated the *Restatement* as an illuminating outline of central principles of international law. *See Hartford Fire*, 509 U.S. at 799,... (citing *Restatement*); *Hartford Fire*, 509 U.S. at 818 (Scalia, J., dissenting) ("I shall rely on the *Restatement (Third) of Foreign Relations Law* for the relevant principles of international law. Its standards appear fairly supported in the decisions of this Court construing international choice-of-law principles... and in the decisions of other federal courts....").

The *Restatement* articulates principles, derived from international law, for determining when the United States may properly exercise regulatory (or prescriptive) jurisdiction over activities or persons connected with another state. It serves as a useful guide to evaluating the international interests at stake. Sections 402 and 403 articulate general principles. Section 415 applies these principles to "Jurisdiction to Regulate Anti-Competitive Activities."

Restatement Section 402(1)(c) states that "Subject to § 403," a state has jurisdiction to prescribe law to "conduct outside its territory that has or is intended to have substantial effect within its territory." Section 403(1) states that, even when Section 402 has been satisfied, jurisdiction may not be exercised if it is "unreasonable." Section 403(2) lists factors to be evaluated in determining if jurisdiction is reasonable:

> (a) the link of the activity to the territory of the regulating state, *i.e.*, the extent to which the activity takes place within the territory, or has substantial, direct, and foreseeable effect upon or in the territory;

   (b) the connections, such as nationality, residence, or economic activity, between the regulating state and the person principally responsible for the activity to be regulated, or between that state and those whom the regulation is designed to protect;

   (c) the character of the activity to be regulated, the importance of regulation to the regulating state, the extent to which other states regulate such activities, and the degree to which the desirability of such regulation is generally accepted;

   (d) the existence of justified expectations that might be protected or hurt by the regulation,

   (e) the importance of the regulation to the international political, legal, or economic system;

   (f) the extent to which the regulation is consistent with the traditions of the international system;

   (g) the extent to which another state may have an interest in regulating the activity; and

   (h) the likelihood of conflict with regulation by another state.

Comment f to Section 403 states that the principles of Sections 402 and 403 "apply to criminal as well as to civil regulation." But, specifically naming the United States antitrust laws, the comment also says that for statutes that give rise to both types of liability, "the presence of substantial foreign elements will ordinarily weigh against application of criminal law." *Id.* The comment argues that legislative intent to apply these laws criminally should only be found on the basis of "express statement or clear implication." *Id.*

While the majority opinion accurately states that this comment is an expression of the clear statement rule, the comment also implies that there are special concerns associated with the imposition of criminal sanctions on foreign conduct. Indeed, most people recognize a distinction between civil and criminal liability; that the law of nations should do so as well is not surprising. And while *Hartford Fire* and earlier judicial decisions have found that the antitrust laws do apply, in the civil context, to foreign conduct, this antitrust common law is not the express statement of legislative intent that the *Restatement* suggests may be appropriate in the criminal context.

Also relevant to the present inquiry is section 415(2), which states that:

Any agreement in restraint of United States trade that is made outside of the United States, and any conduct or agreement in restraint of such trade that is carried out predominantly outside of the United States, are subject to the jurisdiction to prescribe of the United States, if a principal purpose of the conduct or agreement is to interfere with the commerce of the United States and the agreement or conduct has some effect on that commerce.

Restatement § 415(2). Comment a to Section 415 states that the reasonableness principles articulated in Section 403 must still be satisfied.

Application of these principles to the indictment at issue here leads to the conclusion that the exercise of jurisdiction is reasonable in this case. Here, raising prices in the United States and Canada was not only *a* purpose of the alleged conspiracy, it was *the* purpose, thus satisfying Section 415's "principal purpose" requirement. Moreover, Section 415's requirement of "some effect" on United States markets is amply met here. The indictment alleges that NPI sold $ 6.1 million of fax paper into the United States during 1990, approximately the period covered by the charged conspiracy. In 1990, total sales of fax paper in North America were approximately $100 million. NPI's price increases thus affected a not insignificant share of the United States market.

These same factors weigh heavily in Section 403 reasonableness analysis. Because only North American markets were targeted, the United States' interest in combatting this activity appears to be greater than the Japanese interest, which may only be the general interest of a state in having its industries comport with foreign legal norms. Japan has no interest in protecting Japanese consumers in this case as the were unaffected by the alleged conspiracy. The United States, in contrast, has a strong interest in protecting United States consumers, who were affected by the increase in prices. In this situation, it may be that only the United States has sufficient incentive to pursue the alleged wrongdoers, thereby providing the necessary deterrent to similar anticompetitive behavior. In another case, where the consumers of the situs nation were injured as well, that state's interest in regulating anticompetitive conduct might be stronger than it is here.

Other Section 403 factors also counsel in favor of the exercise of jurisdiction here. The effects on United States markets were foreseeable and direct. The Government Japan acknowledges that antitrust regulation is part of the international legal system, and NPI does not really assert that it has justified expectations that were hurt by the regulation. The only factor counseling against finding that the United States' antitrust laws apply to this conduct is the fact that the situs of the conduct was Japan and that the principals were Japanese corporations. This consideration is inherent in the nature of jurisdiction based on effects of conduct, where the situs of the conduct is, by definition, always a foreign country. This alone does not tip the balance against jurisdiction.

For these reasons, I agree with the majority that the district court erred in dismissing the indictment.

QUESTIONS

1.   In his dissent in *Hartford Insurance*, Justice Scalia argues that legislation enacted by Congress is meant only to apply within the territorial jurisdiction of the United States. In light of the Foreign Trade Antitrust Improvements Act of 1982, has not Congress, by implication, expressly applied American antitrust law to certain conduct outside the United States? Is this inconsistent with Justice Scalia's view?

2.   Would the following agreements violate the Sherman Act as interpreted by Judge Hand in *Alcoa*? Under the Foreign Antitrust Improvements Act of 1982?

    a. An agreement among Japanese aftermarket auto-part manufacturers to fix prices in the United States?

    b. An agreement among Japanese auto-part manufacturers to fix prices in Europe, that affected American auto parts exports?

IV. Discovery Problems and Foreign Blocking Statutes

Documents Supplement References:

1.   *Restatement Section 441*

2. *The United Kingdom Protection of Trading Interests Act 1980*

3. *The Hague Convention on the Taking of Evidence Abroad*

Rio Tinto Zinc Corporation v. Westinghouse Electric Corporation

[1978] 1 All E.R. 434, 461-67

Lord Diplock.

[Several utility companies sued Westinghouse, an American corporation, in Federal District Court in Richmond, Virginia, alleging Westinghouse had breached its contracts with them to supply them with uranium.[1] These contracts established a fixed price for the uranium, allowing for an escalation in the price only in the event of increases in the cost of living. Westinghouse's defense was commercial impracticability based on the existence of an international cartel of uranium producers. This cartel limited the supply of uranium, leading to an artificially high price of the commodity, so Westinghouse could no longer perform its supply obligations at the price fixed in its contracts. Westinghouse alleged that two British companies - the Rio Tinto Zinc (RTZ) companies - were members of the cartel. Westinghouse sued the RTZ companies in Illinois, claiming they had violated United States antitrust laws. But, in the Richmond case, to prove a cartel existed and the RTZ companies were members, Westinghouse needed to obtain discovery in Britain. Upon application by Westinghouse, the Federal District Court in Richmond issued letters rogatory to the High Court in England. The letters rogatory requested oral evidence from individual RTZ officials, and documents from RTZ. A High Court master issued an order giving effect to the letters rogatory. The RTZ companies, and the individual witnesses whose testimony was sought, appealed to have the order set aside. A senior master, and on a subsequent appeal a judge, upheld the order. The RTZ companies and witnesses then appealed to the Court of Appeal in England. The Court of Appeal dismissed this appeal, ordering that the letters rogatory be executed. The Court found that the letters rogatory were not an attempt to obtain impermissible pre-trial discovery, though it modified the discovery request by narrowing the range of documents to be produced. The Court also stated that the RTZ companies, and the individual witnesses, might be able to claim a privilege, such as the privilege from self-incrimination set forth in the Fifth Amendment of the United States Constitution. Not surprisingly, they did assert this privilege successfully. At this point, the United States Department of Justice informed the District Court in Richmond that it required evidence gathered pursuant to the letters rogatory in order to further its grand jury investigation into alleged criminal antitrust violations. The District Court issued an order compelling the RTZ companies and individual witnesses to give evidence under the letters rogatory, but it suggested the matter ought to be decided by a United Kingdom court. The RTZ companies and individual witnesses appealed to the House of Lords against the order of the Court of Appeal that the letters rogatory should be executed. The Attorney General of the United Kingdom intervened to state that Her Majesty's Government regarded it as an infringement on British sovereignty that the United States sought evidence from companies or individuals outside of its jurisdiction in connection with an antitrust investigation.]

---

1. This synopsis of the facts and procedural posture is drawn from *Rio Tinto Zinc Corporation v. Westinghouse Electric Corporation*, [1978] 1 All E.R. 434-36.

My Lords, the jurisdiction and powers of the High Court to make the orders that are the subject of this appeal are to be found in §§ 1 and 2 of the Evidence (Proceedings in Other Jurisdictions) Act 1975, and nowhere else. The 1975 Act was passed, in part (which includes §§ 1, 2 and 3), to enable the United Kingdom to ratify the *Convention on the Taking of Evidence Abroad in Civil or Commercial Matters* done at The Hague on 18th March 1970. Ratification by the United Kingdom took place on 16th July 1976, with certain reservations and declarations. The *Convention* had previously been ratified by the United States of America.

Your Lordships have been invited to construe the 1975 Act in conformity with previous decisions of English courts as to the meaning of different words used in a previous statute, the Foreign Tribunals Evidence Act 1856, which was repealed by the 1975 Act. For my part, I do not think that any assistance is to be gained from those decisions. The jurisdiction of English courts to order persons within its jurisdiction to provide oral or documentary evidence in aid of proceedings in foreign courts has always been exclusively statutory. There is no presumption that Parliament, in repealing one statute and substituting another in different terms, intended to make the minimum changes in the previous law that it is possible to reconcile with the actual wording of the new statute, particularly where, as in the instant case, the new statute is passed to give effect to a new international convention.

So disregarding any previous authorities, I turn to the actual terms of the 1975 Act. Section 1 is the section which confers on the High Court jurisdiction to make an order under the Act; § 2 defines what provisions the court has power to include in such an order; while § 3 deals with the right of witnesses to refuse to give oral or documentary evidence under the order.

Under § 1, three conditions precedent must be fulfilled before the court has jurisdiction to make any order under the Act. First, there must be an application for an order for evidence to be obtained in England and Wales, and secondly, the application must be made pursuant to the request of a court exercising jurisdiction outside England and Wales. The third condition precedent as to which the court must be satisfied is in the following terms:

"(b) that the evidence to which the application relates is to be obtained for the purposes of civil proceedings which either have been instituted before the requesting court or whose institution before that court is contemplated."

My Lords, I would not be inclined to place any narrow interpretation on the phrase "evidence...to be obtained for the purposes of civil proceedings." The 1975 Act applies to civil proceedings pending or contemplated in courts and tribunals of all countries in the world. It is not confined to countries that are parties to the *Hague Convention* of 18th March 1970; nor is it limited to courts of law. It extends to tribunals. These courts and tribunals make use of a wide variety of different systems of procedure and rules of evidence in civil matters. In many of these systems it is not possible to draw a distinction between what would be regarded in England as the actual trial of a civil action and what precedes the trial. I do not think that in relation to those countries the expression "civil proceedings" in § 1(b) can have the restricted meaning of the actual trial or hearing of a civil action; and, if this be so, it cannot bear a more restricted meaning in relation to those countries such as the United States of America where, as in England, it is possible to draw a distinction between the trial and what precedes the trial. In my view, "civil proceedings" includes all the procedural steps taken in the course of the proceedings from their institution up to and including their completion and, if the procedural system of the requesting court provides for the examination of witnesses or the production of documents for the purpose of enabling a party to ascertain whether there exists admissible evidence to support his own case or to contradict that of his opponent, the High Court has jurisdiction to make an order under the 1975 Act. Any limitation on the use of this procedure for the purpose of "fishing" discovery is, in my view, to be found in § 2.

The English court cannot be expected to know the systems of civil procedure of all countries from which request for an order under the 1975 Act may come. It has to be satisfied that the evidence is required for the purpose of civil proceedings in the requesting court but, in the ordinary way in the absence of evidence to the contrary, it should, in my view, be prepared to accept the statement by the requesting court that such is the purpose for which the evidence is required.

The letters of request from the United States District Court for the Eastern District of Virginia ("the letters rogatory") contained in the preamble what on a fair reading is, in my view, an adequate statement to this effect; so the High Court had jurisdiction to make an order. It was not bound to do so, but I think that the court should hesitate long before exercising its discretion in favour of refusing to make an order unless it was satisfied that the application would be regarded as falling within the description of frivolous, vexatious or an abuse of the process of the court.

The letters rogatory requested the oral examination of directors and employees of the two RTZ companies and the production of documents by these companies. The relevant limitations on the power of the court to grant these requests are contained in sub-§§ (3) and (4) of § 2 of the 1975 Act. They read as follows:

"(3) An order under this section shall not require any particular steps to be taken unless they are steps which can be required to be taken by way of obtaining evidence for the purposes of civil proceedings in the court making the order (whether or not proceedings of the same description as those to which the application for the order relates); but this subsection shall not preclude the making of an order requiring a person to give (either orally or in writing). . . [an] oath where this is asked for by the requesting court.

"(4) An order under this section shall not require a person—(a) to state what documents relevant to the proceedings to which the application for the order relates are or have been in his possession, custody or power; or (b) to produce any documents other than particular documents specified in the order as being documents appearing to the court making the order to be, or to be likely to be, in his possession, custody or power."

Subsection (3) applies to both oral and documentary evidence. It is this provision which prohibits the making of an order for the examination of a witness not a party to the action for the purpose of seeking information which, though inadmissible at the trial, appears to be reasonably calculated to lead to the discovery of admissible evidence. This is permitted by [Rule] 26 of the United States Federal Rules of Civil Procedure. Under the procedure of the High Court of England depositions of witnesses, either at home or abroad, may be taken before examiners for use at the trial, but the subject-matter of such depositions is restricted to the evidence admissible at the trial. So the evidence requested in the letters rogatory can only be ordered to the extent that it is confined to evidence which will be admissible at the trial of the action in Virginia.

The difficulty involved in the application of sub-§ (3) to proceedings in the United States courts lies in the fact that the examination for discovery of witnesses who are not parties to the action serves a dual purpose: the ordinary purpose of discovery with the wide line of enquiry which that permits and also the purpose of obtaining in the form of a deposition evidence from the witness which will be admissible at the trial in the event of the witness not being called in person.

Westinghouse and the United States district court judge (Judge Merhige) appear to have done their best to limit the request to evidence admissible at the trial; and, as respects the oral evidence of the named directors and employees of the two RTZ companies, I think that, in the main, they have succeeded. To ask for oral evidence from "such other person who has knowledge of the facts" is obviously excessive, but this has never been part of the order as originally made by Master Creightmore. As regards the named persons, however, Westinghouse was in possession of photostatic copies of documents of considerable probative weight, even if technically inadmissible at the trial in the Virginia proceedings, which linked the two RTZ companies and the named persons with operations of an international cartel of uranium producers and gave strong prima facie grounds for believing that those persons could give admissible evidence about the operations; a belief which has been confirmed by their subsequent claims to privilege against self-incrimination.

The request for the production of documentary evidence by the two RTZ companies must satisfy not only the requirements of sub-§ (3) which exclude fishing discovery, but also the stricter requirements of sub-§ (4). Under the procedure of the High Court of England there is no power to order discovery of documents by a person not a party to the action, but such a person can be required by subpoena duces tecum to produce documents to the court or, where his evidence is taken before an examiner prior to the trial, at such examination. There is a good deal of authority cited by Lord Denning MR in his judgment as to how specific the reference to documents must be in subpoena duces tecum. Classes of documents, provided the description of the class is sufficiently clear, may be required to be produced on subpoena duces tecum.

The requirements of § 2(4)(b), however, are not in my view satisfied by the specification of classes of documents. What is called for is the specification of "particular documents" which I would construe as meaning individual documents separately described.

In the letters rogatory most of the many requests for particular documents are followed by a request for "any memoranda, correspondence or other documents relevant thereto." This is far too wide and these words were struck out wherever they appeared by the Court of Appeal in its order of 26th May 1977. The Court of Appeal were in my view bound by § 2(4)(b) to strike from the master's order the words referred to. However, they did not limit themselves to using a blue pencil. In a number of cases they substituted the phrase "any memoranda, correspondence or other documents referred to therein" (sc in the particular document specified). Quite apart from the fact that although it may be sufficient for a subpoena duces tecum I do not think that this is sufficiently specific to satisfy the requirements of § 2(4)(b), I do not consider that the court had any power to substitute a different category of documents for the category which had been requested by the United States court.

Subject, however, to this minor amendment which in the events that have happened has ceased to be of any significance, I think that the order of the Court of Appeal of 26th May 1977 was right. Accordingly, Westinghouse were entitled to proceed with the examination of witnesses and production of documents under Master Creightmore's order subject to any claim to privilege on which the RTZ companies or the individual witnesses were entitled to rely under § 3(1)(a) or (b) of the 1975 Act. Section 3(1) reads as follows:

"A person shall not be compelled by virtue of an order under section 2 to give any evidence which he could not be compelled to give — (a) in civil proceedings in the part of the United Kingdom in which the court that made the order exercises jurisdiction; or (b) subject to subsection (2) below, in civil proceedings in the country or territory in which the requesting court exercises jurisdiction."

When the examination was held, the RTZ companies claimed privilege under para (a), the individual witnesses under para (b).

The privilege claimed by the RTZ companies under para (a) is a privilege under English law. It arises under § 14 of the Civil Evidence Act 1968, which provides as follows:

"(1) The right of a person in any legal proceedings other than criminal proceedings to refuse to answer any question or produce any document or thing if to do so would tend to expose that person to proceedings for an offence or for the recovery of a penalty — (a) shall apply only as regards criminal offences under the law of any part of the United Kingdom and penalties provided for by such law..."

So far as it relates to offences and penalties provided for by the law of the United Kingdom this provision is declaratory of the common law. Its purpose is to remove the doubt as to whether the privilege against self-incrimination extends to offences and penalties under foreign law, a question on which the previous authorities were not wholly consistent.

The penalty to which the companies claim discovery of documents would tend to expose them is a fine imposed by the Commission of the European Communities under Art. 15 of EEC Council Regulation 17/62, for intentionally or negligently acting in breach of Art. 85 of the EEC Treaty. This article of the treaty prohibits cartels which have as their object or effect the prevention, restriction or distortion of competition within the common market. It is directly applicable in the member states; it forms part of the law of England; so does EEC Council Regulation 17/62. For the reasons given by the Court of Appeal in their judgments of 26th May 1977, I agree that a fine imposed by the commission under the regulation is a "penalty" for the purposes of § 14 of the Civil Evidence Act 1968, and that it is enforced by proceedings for recovery of a penalty under the European Communities (Enforcement of Community Judgments) Order 1972.

The RTZ companies took their claim to privilege under § 3(1)(a) of the 1975 Act before the examiner. It was upheld by MacKenna J and on appeal by the Court of Appeal in their judgment of 11th July 1977. The argument for Westinghouse, rejected by the Court of Appeal, that has been pressed in this House was that whatever risk the RTZ companies ran of having a fine imposed on them by the commission it would be in no wise enhanced by the production in the United States proceedings of documents that constituted evidence of their participation in a cartel prohibited by Art. 85(1) of the EEC Treaty. The argument does not involve the proposition that the companies are not infringing Art. 85(1) of the treaty. On the contrary Westinghouse not only assert that they are but also deny that the cartel could be brought within Art. 85(3) which empowers the commission to declare Art. 85(1) to be inapplicable to cartels which satisfy certain conditions.

My Lords, Art. 89 of the treaty imposes on the commission the duty of seeing to the application of Art. 85, of investigating infringements and of taking steps to remedy the situation. If contrary to their duty the commission fail to act they may be called on to so under Art. 175 by any other institution of the community including the European Parliament, or by any member state, and on continued failure may be proceeded against before the European Court of Justice. It is not for your Lordships to speculate why the commission have hitherto remained quiescent in the matter, nor what might stir them into activity. Under EEC Council Regulation 17/62 they have wide powers of investigation under which they could, if they thought fit, themselves compel the RTZ companies to produce the very documents of which Westinghouse seek to obtain production in the instant proceedings. This may be so, but there is a proverb "let sleeping dogs lie" which may have some application in the international politics of uranium production and enrichment which it would be disingenuous to pretend are not lurking in the background of this case.

I do not think that your Lordships are entitled to dismiss as fanciful the risk that if the documents relating to the cartel were produced at the trial in the Virginia proceedings and came, as they then would, into the public domain, the resulting publicity in this sensitive political field might result in pressure on the commission to take against the RTZ companies speedier and severer action than they might otherwise have done and that such action might well include the imposition of penalties under Art. 15 of EEC Council Regulation 17/62. The Court of Appeal in my opinion were right in upholding the refusal of the two RTZ companies to produce the documents requested in the letter rogatory.

It was submitted that since the RTZ companies were entitled to withhold the documents from production, they had a privilege in English law to require their officers and servants to refuse to answer questions that might lead to the disclosure of the contents of the documents or provide evidence that would tend to expose the companies to a penalty. At common law, as declared in § 14(1) of the Civil Evidence Act 1968, the privilege against self-incrimination was restricted to the incrimination of the person claiming it and not anyone else. There is no trace in the decided cases that it is of wider application; no textbook old or modern suggests the contrary. It is not for your Lordships to manufacture for the purposes of the instant case a new privilege hitherto unknown to the law.

There remains to be considered what effect the recent events that have occurred in relation to the named persons' claim to privilege under § 3(1)(b) of the 1975 Act ought to have on the order of Master Creightmore requiring them to give oral evidence. Their right to claim this "Fifth Amendment" privilege depends on United States federal law, and under the 1975 Act, it was for Judge Merhige to rule on the validity of the claim.

In order to obtain a speedy ruling from him the parties, by mutual consent, departed from the procedure laid down in RSC Ord 70, r 6. In view of the imminence of the trial in Virginia they took short cuts. This has led to some degree of procedural confusion as to the capacity in which Judge Merhige was doing the various things he did. This has led to technical disputes about such matters as to whether and if so at what point the letters rogatory were exhausted and as to the legal nature and effect in England of the orders made by Judge Merhige in Virginia on 18th July 1977 ostensibly under the Organized Crime Control Act 1970, 18 United States Code § 6003. I would not wish to decide this part of the case on mere technical errors of procedure that could be cured by the issue of fresh letters rogatory. In my view the events that happened enable me to base my decision on principles which transcend any irregularities in procedure.

The essential facts are: (1) On 14th June 1977 Judge Merhige upheld the claim of the named persons to Fifth Amendment privilege and ruled that they need not answer any questions save as to their names and addresses. (2) On 15th June 1977 a letter was received by Judge Merhige from the United States Department of Justice stating that the oral evidence of the named persons that was requested in the letters rogatory was required by the department for the purpose of a grand jury investigation into alleged offences against the anti-trust laws of the United States. It contained an assurance that the department would not use the testimony of the named persons as the basis for criminal prosecution of them in the United States. (3) On 16th July 1977 a representative of the Department of Justice appeared before Judge Merhige and asked him, on the strength of the letter, to rule that the named persons were no longer entitled to claim their Fifth Amendment privilege. The judge declined. He confirmed his previous ruling; but added that if an application were to be made to him under 18 United States Code §§ 6002 and 6003 for an order requiring the named persons to give evidence on terms that it could not be used against them in any criminal case, he, Judge Merhige, would feel compelled to rule that they were no longer entitled to refuse to answer the questions. (4) On 18th July 1977, applications were made to Judge Merhige, with the written approval of the United States Attorney General, for orders under §§ 6002 and 6003 in respect of each of the named persons; and on the same day the judge issued orders which ordered each of them to "give testimony or provide other information in response to questions pronounced pursuant to letters rogatory issued by this Court." Whatever their procedural defects I am prepared to treat these orders as a ruling by the United States court under § 3(2) of the 1975 Act, that the Fifth Amendment privilege claimed by the named persons is no longer available to them.

My Lords, it is clear from Judge Merhige's rulings of 14th and 16th June 1977 that so long as the evidence in respect of which Fifth Amendment privilege was claimed was to be used for the purposes of civil proceedings only, it could not in the events that happened be obtained under an order made under §§ 1 and 2 of the 1975 Act. Insofar as the evidence was intended to be used for the purposes of criminal proceedings in the United States, which were not yet instituted but were only at the stage of investigation by a grand jury, § 5(1)(b) of the 1975 Act excludes the jurisdiction of the High Court to make an order requiring the evidence to be given.

The United States is not a party to the civil proceedings in which the letters rogatory have been issued. Those proceedings in the words of the United States Attorney General are "private litigation." The intervention of the Department of Justice to seek an order under §§ 6002 and 6003 in private litigation pending in the United States is, we have been told, unprecedented. It is acknowledged by the United States Attorney General in his letter to be contrary to the firm policy of the department "except in the most extraordinary circumstances."

The extraordinary circumstances listed, in addition to the Attorney General's belief that the testimony sought may well be indispensable to the work of the grand jury, include the following statement:

"These persons are British subjects and we have determined that it is highly unlikely that their testimony could be obtained through existing arrangements for law enforcement cooperation between the United States and the United Kingdom."

This is a reference to the long-standing controversy between Her Majesty's Government and the Government of the United States as to the claim of the latter to have jurisdiction to enforce its own anti-trust laws against British companies not carrying on business in the United States in respect of acts done by them outside the territory of the United States. As your Lordships have been informed by Her Majesty's Attorney-General it has long been the policy of her Majesty's Government to deny this claim. Her Majesty's Government regards as an unacceptable invasion of its own sovereignty the use of the United States courts by the United States Government as a means by which it can investigate activities outside the United States of British companies and individuals which it claims infringe the anti-trust laws of the United States. Section 2 of the Shipping Contracts and Commercial Documents Act 1944 was passed in an attempt to thwart this practice. Past attempts by the United States Government to use the United States courts in this investigatory role have been the subject of diplomatic protests. One such protest was made in respect of the intervention of the Department of Justice in the proceedings in the instant case before Judge Merhige on 16th June 1977.

My Lords, what follows from the essential facts I have recounted is: first that the evidence sought from the named persons could not be obtained by Westinghouse so long as the only purposes for which it was required were civil proceedings; secondly, that it was only when that evidence was called for by the United States Department of Justice for the purposes of an investigation by a grand jury in the United States with a view to discovering whether there were grounds for instituting criminal proceedings against someone that under United States law the named persons would become compellable to give it; thirdly, that the purpose for which the Department of Justice was seeking to obtain the evidence was not one for which it could have been obtained by them under the 1975 Act since no criminal proceedings had yet been instituted; fourthly that the evidence was required for the purpose of investigating the activities outside the United States of British companies and individuals for alleged infringements of anti-trust laws of the United States, a procedure which, as the department knew, Her Majesty's Government regards as an unwarrantable invasion of its sovereignty.

My Lords, I have no hesitation in holding that with the intervention of the Department of Justice and its obtaining of the orders under §§ 6002 and 6003 on the 18th July 1977 the continued enforcement of Master Creightmore's order as respects the oral evidence of the named persons would amount to an abuse of the process of the High Court under the 1975 Act. The letters rogatory issued in the civil proceedings in the Virginia court on Westinghouse's application are manifestly being made use of by the Department of Justice for the ulterior purpose of obtaining evidence for a grand jury investigation which it is debarred from obtaining directly by § 5(1)(b) of the 1975 Act. I do not find it necessary to enquire whether the action taken by the department was in connivance with Westinghouse or against its wishes. If the latter, Westinghouse will not be prejudiced by the order of Master Creightmore being now set aside; for in the absence of the department's intervention the oral evidence of the named persons whose claim to Fifth Amendment privilege was upheld by Judge Merhige before 18th July 1977 could not have been obtained by them under that order.

Since the rest of Master Creightmore's order, which relates to the production of documents by the two RTZ companies, is also spent by reason of their claim to privilege being upheld by this House, I would discharge the whole order as from 18th July 1977.

R. Edward Price, Foreign Blocking Statutes and the GATT: State Sovereignty and the Enforcement of U.S. Economic Laws Abroad

23 George Washington Journal of International
Law and Economics 315, 322-31 (1995)

....

I. INTRODUCTION

Foreign blocking statutes exist largely as a response to attempts by the United States to enforce its antitrust law abroad. Several countries have enacted a variety of such statutes, which often require specific approval of discovery requests by foreign parties, prohibit discovery with respect to certain domestic industries, or block the enforcement of foreign judgments within their country. The application of U.S. law abroad, particularly with its comparatively wide scope of discovery, may be seen as intrusive and in violation of the sovereignty of foreign nations. Foreign blocking statutes, however, are harmful in their own right and may be an overreaction to the problems of U.S. antitrust enforcement abroad. Although foreign governments justify blocking statutes with sovereignty concerns, many of these statutes tend to be legal devices that shield industries from competitive outside forces.

International law traditionally did not allow application of a country's domestic law abroad against foreign nationals. This practice began to change for the United States in the area of antitrust law during the late 1920s. In *United States v. Sisal Sales Corporation*, the Supreme Court allowed jurisdiction over conduct that occurred both inside and outside the territorial boundaries of the United States. Arguably, international law has evolved to allow application of a nation's domestic law abroad where the effects of certain foreign behavior are felt in that nation—an expansion of the so-called jurisdiction to prescribe. These two developments, and the continuing globalization of markets and economic behavior, have yielded a legally complicated, yet rather predictable result: Private businesses in the United States litigate against foreign competitors to enforce rights under aggressive U.S. economic laws, particularly antitrust statutes, that provide for treble damages.

Attempts to enforce aggressive U.S. antitrust laws against anticompetitive behavior abroad have caused some foreign governments to claim that their sovereignty has been violated. To protect this sovereignty from outside incursion, many of these governments enacted blocking statutes to prevent compliance with U.S. discovery orders within their borders. Some countries have also enacted statutes that block the enforcement of certain judgments in their country.

Although sovereignty arguments are frequently used to justify these measures, one should not overlook the economic benefit that blocking statutes confer on industries within the countries that have enacted them: the ability to reap the benefits of sales in U.S. markets, while having the freedom to act on the fringes or outside of U.S. antitrust law with substantial impunity. When cast in these terms, blocking statutes can be seen as a form of protectionism cloaked in legal arguments that invoke sovereign prerogative and comity among nations, but that fail to acknowledge their substantive protectionist motivation and result.

Sovereignty concerns that underlie blocking statutes become less significant when one considers the obstacles U.S. plaintiffs must overcome in order to assert jurisdiction over foreign businesses in U.S. courts. There is a general presumption in the United States that "legislation of Congress, unless a contrary intent appears, is meant to apply only within the territorial jurisdiction of the United States." The Foreign Trade Antitrust Improvements Act explicitly requires a "direct, substantial, and reasonably foreseeable effect" on domestic commerce before extraterritorial jurisdiction may be obtained under the Sherman Act. The extent to which U.S. courts will allow private enforcement of the Sherman Act abroad is also subject to the existence of personal jurisdiction over the defendant and, in some federal circuits, to a jurisdictional "rule of reason" that requires a balancing of several factors. Prudential and separation-of-powers considerations, such as the act of state doctrine, require judicial abstention from adjudicating matters where the conduct of a foreign sovereign is at issue. Additionally, the use of U.S.-style discovery practices, often characterized by other countries as free-wheeling, unsupervised "fishing expeditions" by the parties, is subject to a balancing of the interests at hand. U.S. courts thus consider the interests of foreign sovereigns and international comity to be important in the application of U.S. law to foreign actors.

Even when U.S. litigants can overcome this domestic legal threshold, a blocking statute may erect an impassable barrier, either by preventing the discovery of essential evidence, or by preventing the enforcement of a U.S. judgment. In these instances, sovereignty arguments justifying blocking legislation are substantially weakened because a U.S. court balancing all of the interests involved, including that of international comity, which itself encompasses sovereign equality, has decided that fairness dictates the foreign party's acceptance of U.S. jurisdiction and discovery practices. The foreign government, however, frequently asserts a sovereign prerogative in continuing to protect its domestic industry, even though the industry's involvement in U.S. markets has reached a level encompassed by U.S. law and its sovereign interests were considered by U.S. courts in determining the extent to which evidence might be taken in its country.

Although determinations by U.S. courts should not always be the final arbiters that bind foreign governments vis-à-vis the United States, the persistent shielding of foreign industries from the enforcement of U.S. economic law is not simply an act of sovereignty, but an act of economic protectionism. This conclusion is supported by two distinct trends: the General Agreement on Tariffs and Trade (GATT), including its Uruguay Round agreements, and the trend toward international cooperation in antitrust enforcement. The GATT contains broad language regarding the general prohibition of subsidies. The Uruguay Round bolsters this prohibition with its *Agreement on Subsidies and Countervailing Measures* and more effective dispute resolution measures. A recent trend toward international cooperation in the enforcement of banking, securities, and antitrust law is also relevant to the issue of blocking statutes. This trend highlights the increasing importance of enforcing laws against anticompetitive behavior as world trade and the global economy grow. It also weakens sovereignty arguments that may thwart this enforcement....

II. FOREIGN BLOCKING STATUTES

A. *History*

Statutes that prohibit compliance with foreign discovery orders have been in existence for a large portion of this century. Many of these fall into the category of bank secrecy laws enacted to encourage foreign investment and are thereby distinguished from statutes aimed against the enforcement of U.S. antitrust law. This latter variety of blocking statute arose principally in response to private attempts to enforce

U.S. law in *Uranium Antitrust Litigation*, an antitrust suit brought by Westinghouse Electric against domestic and foreign uranium producers, including those from Canada, Australia, Switzerland, and South Africa, for an alleged conspiracy to fix prices in the uranium market.

When Westinghouse attempted to discover evidence in these countries, the foreign producers' governments reacted by passing blocking statutes, filing diplomatic protests, and appearing as amici curiae to argue against the assertion of jurisdiction for reasons of sovereignty and international comity. Canada's diplomatic protest, filed in response to a possible court order to produce information in violation of its blocking statute, is illustrative of the legal, political, and economic concerns raised by these countries when the United States attempted to enforce its antitrust laws against their companies. It states, in part:

> A situation in which courts of the United States imposed sanctions for failure to produce documents or information located in Canada where such production would violate Canadian laws and regulations would be a matter of serious concern to the Government of Canada because it would subordinate to the procedures of U.S. courts the authority of the Government of Canada to prohibit the disclosure of certain information in Canada relating to the production and marketing of Canadian uranium. Such a failure on the part of courts in the United States to recognize the authority of the Canadian Government to prohibit such disclosure would be contrary to generally accepted principles of international law and would have an adverse impact on relations between the U.S.A. and Canada.
>
> ...[T]he participation of all Canadian uranium producers in certain uranium marketing arrangements was a matter of Canadian Government policy.
>
> ...[T]he policy was adopted following action by the United States Government which effectively closed the large U.S. market to Canadian and other foreign uranium producers, with severe adverse consequences for the Canadian uranium mining industry.... *The Canadian Government ...was convinced that preservation of a viable uranium producing industry was essential to the Canadian national interest....*

This protest displays Canada's sovereign interests in preventing U.S. judicial intervention in the form of sanctions for noncompliance with a discovery order. Indeed, the negative reactions of most governments to such attempts indicate that no international norm currently exists that would allow U.S. discovery practices to cross borders without considering other countries' sovereign prerogative. The last sentence of the quoted portion of this protest, however, betrays the motivation behind the blocking statutes: the preservation of a viable industry, in this instance uranium, threatened by outside forces. Where such forces are simply a function of the market, this type of legislation is known as protectionism. The legal insulation provided by blocking statutes thus functions in a subsidy-like manner because it encourages affected industries to continue to operate as cartels and thereby charge artificially high (or low) prices to maintain their profitability or existence.

B. *Varieties of Blocking Statutes*

Four varieties of blocking statutes have been passed in response to the extraterritorial application of U.S. law. The first of these "prohibit[s] any disclosure of documents or other information in connection with foreign discovery orders, unless the orders are passed through appropriate foreign governmental channels." The second vests authority in a government agency to prohibit domestic compliance with certain foreign discovery orders. The third type of blocking statute contain(s) either automatic prohibitions against disclosure of information regarding particular industries, or grants of administrative discretion to prohibit such disclosures. Representative examples of this type of statute include bank secrecy laws, statutes enacted to prohibit disclosure of information regarding uranium production, and laws forbidding disclosure of information concerning the shipping industry. In almost all cases, these statutes were enacted in response to specific U.S. extraterritorial discovery efforts or investigations that were perceived abroad as threatening a particular foreign industry.

Finally, there is a type of blocking statute that prohibits the enforcement of certain foreign judgments.

All of these statutes in some way thwart the enforcement of U.S. antitrust laws; some, however, are more damaging than others. Those simply requiring litigants to lodge their discovery requests with a central authority in the foreign country may slow the discovery process, but are not an obvious hindrance to the litigation itself. Those vesting an authority with the power to deny discovery requests may have a greater impact, depending on how the power is exercised. Statutes that flatly prohibit disclosure of information regarding certain industries are ipso facto in place to protect those industries from the threat of litigation, and erect the most obvious barriers to U.S. antitrust actions. The protectionist function of this type of blocking statute is apparent. The last category, statutes that block the effect of foreign judgments, has largely the same protectionist result as the third.

The extent to which a given statute hinders parties in the United States from enforcing domestic antitrust laws deeply affects U.S. interests vis-à-vis that statute. It also determines that statute's market-distorting effects and the extent to which one may ultimately argue it is a subsidy-like device for the purposes of the GATT.

C. U.S. Concerns Regarding Foreign Blocking Statutes

Although countries have sovereign interests in protecting information within their borders, such an exercise of governmental power evokes sovereign interests in the United States over its economy and over litigation. As one U.S. circuit court has stated:

The United States admittedly has a "national interest" of its own [,] . . . [that of] making certain that any litigant in its courts is afforded adequate discovery to the end that he may fully present his claim, or defense, as the case may be. Such is an understandable and legitimate interest.

Another U.S. circuit court characterized U.S. antitrust laws as "cornerstones of this nation's economic policies. . . ." The desire to preserve competition and to deter anticompetitive forces, which is essential to a market economy, undoubtedly underlies these sentiments. Further, former U.S. Attorney General Griffin Bell said the following:

When we assert antitrust jurisdiction in United States foreign commerce we are not saying that no other nation may have legitimate interests, nor would we deny that sometimes those interests may conflict with our own. What we do say is that we have seen too often situations in international trade where failure to enforce our law against private antitrust conspiracies formed outside our jurisdiction to affect our markets, would have created gaping immunities from compliance with our law. By applying our antitrust laws to foreign persons who seek to do business in our markets, we are merely saying you are welcome in our markets if you abide by our rules of competitions.

The extent to which this U.S. interest is characterized as "sovereign" provides a legal argument, based on sovereignty over activity with substantial effect within the

United States, that can logically counter the arguments posited by countries with blocking statutes based on sovereignty over documents within their borders.

Any discussion of U.S. interests, or of possible international legal ramifications, regarding foreign blocking statutes should include a consideration of both their demonstrated, practical effects on litigants and their larger macroeconomic effects. The former is an empirical analysis, while the latter invokes the logical economic result of blocking legislation. Both types are examined below.

1. The Effects of Blocking Statutes on Litigants

One legal commentator interviewed several international lawyers who had direct experience with blocking statutes to gain an understanding of their everyday effects on litigants. Interestingly, this commentator concluded that blocking statutes seem to pose problems for foreign defendants as well as domestic plaintiffs. For instance, a blocking statute might deter domestic plaintiffs from seeking preliminary injunctions due to the need for early discovery. Ironically, however, the same statute might also encourage defendants to settle the case quickly; the prospect of sanctions for not producing documents in the United States, on the one hand, and sanctions for otherwise violating the foreign defendant's own blocking statute, on the other, make settlement an attractive option. A blocking statute may also work against defendants who would benefit by producing documents favorable to their position.

Aside from effects on individual parties, blocking statutes simply tend to make litigation more expensive and tedious. The United States certainly has an interest in preventing unneeded complexities and expense in litigation. As the commentator who undertook this study wrote:

> Because blocking statutes have had adverse effects on antitrust litigation in the United States, the United States has an interest in seeing these blocking statutes repealed. Blocking statutes create tensions between the United States and the other country whose resident corporation is a defendant in an antitrust suit brought in the United States.... Moreover, the foreign hostility created by U.S. antitrust decisions can have spillover effects in areas having nothing to do with antitrust law. Finally, while the executive branch can decrease the likelihood that a country will implement its blocking legislation through its exercise of prosecutorial discretion, it cannot control a private litigant's decision to sue.

Another indication of the negative effects of blocking statutes is contained in a report of a statement by Assistant U.S. Attorney General Anne K. Bingaman regarding antitrust enforcement attempts by the U.S. Justice Department:

> "It is absolutely essential to crack the wall of discovery," she declared. The Division currently suffers "a terrible handicap" in prosecuting extraterritorial antitrust violations. Although there are a "shocking" number of cartels, largely in Europe and including one or two American firms, that disrupt competition in world markets, the Division is precluded from discovering relevant documents of foreign firms because of blocking statutes in those countries.

Blocking statutes, then, not only pose increased costs for private litigants, but they also prevent effective enforcement of antitrust laws by public authorities seeking to deter foreign cartels with operations in the United States.

2. The Macroeconomic Effects of Blocking Statutes

Because antitrust laws are in place to prevent anticompetitive economic behavior, which artificially raises prices to the detriment of consumers or lowers them to the detriment of the domestic industry, the extent to which foreign blocking statutes protect such anticompetitive behavior encourages artificial prices contrary to an efficient market. This statement of the negative economic effects of blocking statutes may be rather general, but it is nonetheless useful in examining the macroeconomic effects of blocking statutes.

A recent Canadian Supreme Court case highlights the political and economic problems that blocking statutes can cause. *Hunt v. Lac D'Amiante du Québec Ltée* involved a Quebec provincial blocking statute ostensibly passed to avoid discovery in U.S. antitrust cases, yet applied in this case to domestic Canadian litigation arising in the courts of British Columbia. The defendant in this tort case hid behind Quebec's blocking statute to prevent the discovery of documents in Quebec by a provincial court in British Columbia. The Canadian Supreme Court struck down this domestic application of the provincial blocking statute, asserting it was contrary to Canadian federalism, to the common market that federalism was intended to create, and to principles of comity in general. In its revealing opinion, the Canadian court stated:

> Everybody realizes that the whole point of blocking statutes is not to keep documents in the province, but rather to prevent compliance, and so the success of litigation outside the province that that province finds objectionable. This is no doubt part of sovereign right, but it certainly runs counter to comity. In the political realm it leads to strict retaliatory laws and power struggles. And it discourages international commerce and efficient allocation and conduct of litigation. It has similar effects on the interprovincial level, effects that offend against the basic structure of the Canadian federation.
>
> ....
>
> ....The resultant higher transactional costs for interprovincial transactions constitute an infringement on the unity and efficiency of the Canadian market-place, as well as unfairness to the citizen.

One can logically conclude that the interprovincial effects of blocking statutes in Canada are the same as their international effects from country to country. If the Canadian Supreme Court's premise, that blocking legislation results in higher transaction costs and discourages international commerce, is accepted, then blocking legislation should be viewed no differently than a number of nontariff barriers that arose around the same time in the 1970s. Others have commented on the trade-distorting effects of such barriers. On the benefits of foreign trade and the maladies of nontariff barriers, one writer stated:

> Foreign trade connects national price systems into an international price system. Economics cannot even estimate how much of our present prosperity we owe to the ability to buy abroad what would cost more to produce at home.... The international price system as an information system is indispensable for its efficiency.... [Q]uantitative restriction of imports severely impairs the operation of the price system, and therefore the quantitative estimates of trade under restriction are wholly inadequate.... In this context, the estimates of restricted trade take no account of subsidies, which are at present an almost equally important cause of price distortion in international trade.

This juxtaposition of the Canadian Supreme Court's characterization of blocking statutes and these comments about the deleterious effects of nontariff barriers provides new insight into the way blocking legislation should be considered in the future. It erodes the conception that blocking statutes are simply a way for certain countries to protect documents within their borders. Such statutes also impede types of litigation that these countries find particularly threatening; and to the extent this impediment acts like a subsidy and discourages international trade, it causes distortions in the market efficiencies that set prices worldwide.

Because conflicts over foreign antitrust enforcement have been costly for all parties concerned, there has been a recent trend toward cooperation among countries in enforcement procedures. It is worth noting the value of such cooperation as anecdotal evidence which counters suggestions that antitrust enforcement creates market inefficiencies and diplomatic strife.

This cooperation highlights the need for a different solution that allows for better U.S. antitrust enforcement, but protects notions of sovereignty propounded by the foreign countries affected.... [T]he GATT may serve as a persuasive tool to encourage more cooperation in this area. It may also serve to highlight the undesirable effects of blocking statutes and their function of shielding anticompetitive behavior....

....

V. Substantive Claims:
Conspiracy and Predation

Matsushita Electric Industrial Company, Ltd.
v. Zenith Radio Corporation
475 U.S. 574 (1986)

Justice Powell delivered the opinion of the Court.

This case requires that we again consider the standard district courts must apply when deciding whether to grant summary judgment in an antitrust conspiracy case.

I

....

A

Petitioners, defendants below, are 21 corporations that manufacture or sell "consumer electronic products" (CEPs)—for the most part, television sets. Petitioners include both Japanese manufacturers of CEPs and American firms, controlled by Japanese parents, that sell the Japanese-manufactured products. Respondents, plaintiffs below, are Zenith Radio Corporation (Zenith) and National Union Electric Corporation (NUE). Zenith is an American firm that manufactures and sells television sets. NUE is the corporate successor to Emerson Radio Company, an American firm that manufactured and sold television sets until 1970, when it withdrew from the market after sustaining substantial losses. Zenith and NUE began this lawsuit in 1974, claiming that petitioners had illegally conspired to drive American firms from the American CEP market. According to respondents, the gist of this conspiracy was a "'scheme to raise, fix and maintain artificially *high* prices for television receivers sold by [petitioners] in Japan and, at the same time, to fix and maintain *low* prices for television receivers exported to and sold in the United States.'" These "low prices" were allegedly at levels that produced substantial losses for petitioners. The conspiracy allegedly began as early as 1953, and according to respondents was in full operation by sometime in the late 1960's. Respondents claimed that various portions of this scheme violated §§ 1 and 2 of the Sherman Act, § 2(a) of the Robinson-Patman Act, § 73 of the Wilson Tariff Act, and the Antidumping Act of 1916.

After several years of detailed discovery, petitioners filed motions for summary judgment on all claims against them.....The District Court found the bulk of the evidence on which Zenith and NUE relied inadmissible.

The District Court then turned to petitioners' motions summary judgment. The court found that the admissible evidence did not raise a genuine issue of material fact as to the existence of the alleged conspiracy. At bottom, the court found, respondents' claims rested on the inferences that could be drawn from petitioners' parallel conduct in the Japanese and American markets, and from the effects of that conduct on petitioners' American competitors. After reviewing the evidence... the court found that any inference of conspiracy was unreasonable, because (i) some portions of the evidence suggested that petitioners conspired in ways that did not injure respondents, and (ii) the evidence that bore directly on the alleged price-cutting conspiracy did not rebut the more plausible inference that petitioners were cutting prices to compete in the American market and not to monopolize it. Summary judgment therefore was granted on respondents' claims under § 1 of the Sherman Act and the Wilson Tariff Act. Because the Sherman Act § 2 claims, which alleged that petitioners had combined to monopolize the American CEP market, were functionally indistinguishable from the § 1 claims, the court dismissed them also. Finally, the court found that the Robinson-Patman Act claims depended on the same supposed conspiracy as the Sherman Act claims. Since the court had found no genuine issue of fact as to the conspiracy, it entered judgment in petitioners' favor on those claims as well.

B

The Court of Appeals for the Third Circuit reversed. The court began by examining the District Court's evidentiary rulings, and determined that much of the evidence excluded by the District Court was in fact admissible. These evidentiary rulings are not before us.

On the merits, and based on the newly enlarged record, the court found that the District Court's summary judgment decision was improper. The court acknowledged that "there are legal limitations upon the inferences which may be drawn from circumstantial evidence," but it found that "the legal problem...is different" when "there is direct evidence of concert of action." Here, the court concluded, "there is both direct evidence of certain kinds of concert of action and circumstantial evidence having some tendency to suggest that other kinds of concert of action may have occurred." Thus, the court reasoned, cases concerning the limitations on inferring conspiracy from ambiguous evidence were not dispositive. Turning to the evidence, the court determined that a factfinder reasonably could draw the following conclusions:

1. The Japanese market for CEPs was characterized by oligopolistic behavior, with a small number of producers meeting regularly and exchanging information on price and other matters. This created the opportunity for a stable combination to raise both prices and profits in Japan. American firms could not attack such a combination because the Japanese Government imposed significant barriers to entry.

2. Petitioners had relatively higher fixed costs than their American counterparts, and therefore needed to operate at something approaching full capacity in order to make a profit.

3. Petitioners' plant capacity exceeded the needs of the Japanese market.

4. By formal agreements arranged in cooperation with Japan's Ministry of International Trade and Industry (MITI), petitioners fixed minimum prices for CEPs exported to the American market. The parties refer to these prices as the "check prices," and to the agreements that require them as the "check price agreements."

5. Petitioners agreed to distribute their products in the United States according to a "five company rule": each Japanese producer was permitted to sell only to five American distributors.

6. Petitioners undercut their own check prices by a variety of rebate schemes. Petitioners sought to conceal these rebate schemes both from the United States Customs Service and from MITI, the former to avoid various customs regulations as well as action under the antidumping laws, and the latter to cover up petitioners' violations of the check-price agreements.

Based on inferences from the foregoing conclusions, the Court of Appeals concluded that a reasonable factfinder could find a conspiracy to depress prices in the American market in order to drive out American competitors, which conspiracy was funded by excess profits obtained in the Japanese market. The court apparently did not consider whether it was as plausible to conclude that petitioners' price-cutting behavior was independent and not conspiratorial.

The court found it unnecessary to address petitioners' claim that they could not be held liable under the antitrust laws for conduct that was compelled by a foreign sovereign. The claim, in essence, was that because MITI required petitioners to enter into the check-price agreements, liability could not be premised on those agreements. The court concluded that this case did not present any issue of sovereign compulsion, because the check-price agreements were being used as "evidence of a low export price conspiracy" and not as an independent basis for finding antitrust liability. The court also believed it was unclear that the check prices in fact were mandated by the Japanese Government, notwithstanding a statement to that effect by MITI itself.

We granted *certiorari* to determine (i) whether the Court of Appeals applied the proper standards in evaluating the District Court's decision to grant petitioners' motion for summary judgment, and (ii) whether petitioners could be held liable under the antitrust laws for a conspiracy in part compelled by a foreign sovereign. We reverse on the first issue, but do not reach the second.

II

We begin by emphasizing what respondents' claim is *not*. Respondents cannot recover antitrust damages based solely on an alleged cartelization of the Japanese market, because American antitrust laws do not regulate the competitive conditions of other nations' economies. *United States v. Aluminum Co. of America*, 148 F. 2d 416, 443 (CA2 1945) (L. Hand, J.). Nor can respondents recover damages for any conspiracy by petitioners to charge higher than competitive prices in the American market. Such conduct would indeed violate the Sherman Act, but it could not injure respondents: as petitioners' competitors, respondents stand to gain from any conspiracy to raise the market price in CEPS. Finally, for the same reason, respondents cannot recover for a conspiracy to impose nonprice restraints that have the effect of either raising market price or limiting output. Such restrictions, though harmful to competition, actually *benefit* competitors by making supracompetitive pricing more attractive. Thus, neither petitioners' alleged supracompetitive pricing in Japan, nor the five company rule that limited distribution in this country, nor the check prices insofar as they established minimum prices in this country, can by themselves give respondents a cognizable claim against petitioners for antitrust damages. The Court of Appeals therefore erred to the extent that it found evidence of these alleged conspiracies to be "direct evidence" of a conspiracy that injured respondents.

Respondents nevertheless argue that these supposed conspiracies, if not themselves grounds for recovery of antitrust damages, are circumstantial evidence of another conspiracy that *is* cognizable: a conspiracy to monopolize the American market by means of pricing below the market level. The thrust of respondents' argument is that petitioners used their monopoly profits from the Japanese market to fund a concerted campaign to price predatorily and thereby drive respondents and other American manufacturers of CEPs out of business. Once successful, according to respondents, petitioners would cartelize the American CEP market, restricting output and raising prices above the level that fair competition would produce. The resulting monopoly profits, respondents contend, would more than compensate petitioners for the losses they incurred through years of pricing below market level.

The Court of Appeals found that respondents' allegation of a horizontal conspiracy to engage in predatory pricing, if proved, would be a *per se* violation of § 1 of the Sherman Act. Petitioners did not appeal from that conclusion. The issue in this case thus becomes whether respondents adduced sufficient evidence in support of their theory to survive summary judgment. We therefore examine the principles that govern the summary judgment determination.

III

To survive petitioners' motion for summary judgment, respondents must establish that there is a genuine issue of material fact as to whether petitioners entered into an illegal conspiracy that caused respondents to suffer a cognizable injury. Fed. Rule Civ. Proc. 56(e); *First National Bank of Arizona v. Cities Service Co.*, 391 U.S. 253, 288-289 (1968). This showing has two components. First, respondents must show more than a conspiracy in violation of the antitrust laws; they must show an injury to them resulting from the illegal conduct. Respondents charge petitioners with a whole host of conspiracies in restraint of trade. Except for the alleged conspiracy to monopolize the American market through predatory pricing, these alleged conspiracies could not have caused respondents to suffer an "antitrust injury," *Brunswick Corp. v. Pueblo Bowl-O-Mat, Inc.*, 429 U.S. at 489, because they actually tended to benefit respondents. Therefore, unless, in context, evidence of these "other" conspiracies raises a genuine issue concerning the existence of a predatory pricing conspiracy, that evidence cannot defeat petitioners' summary judgment motion.

Second, the issue of fact must be "genuine." Fed. Rules Civ. Proc. 56(c), (e). When the moving party has carried its burden under Rule 56(c), its opponent must do more than simply show that there is some metaphysical doubt as to the material facts. In the language of the Rule, the nonmoving party must come forward with "specific facts showing that there is a *genuine issue for trial*." Fed. Rule Civ. Proc. 56(e) (emphasis added). Where the record taken as a whole could not lead a rational trier of fact to find for the nonmoving party, there is no "genuine issue for trial." *Cities Service, supra*, at 289.

It follows from these settled principles that if the factual context renders respondents' claim implausible — if the claim is one that simply makes no economic sense —

respondents must come forward with more persuasive evidence to support their claim than would otherwise be necessary. *Cities Service* is instructive. The issue in that case was whether proof of the defendant's refusal to deal with the plaintiff supported an inference that the defendant willingly had joined an illegal boycott. Economic factors strongly suggested that the defendant had no motive to join the alleged conspiracy. The Court acknowledged that, in isolation, the defendant's refusal to deal might well have sufficed to create a triable issue. But the refusal to deal had to be evaluated in its factual context. Since the defendant lacked any rational motive to join the alleged boycott, and since its refusal to deal was consistent with the defendant's independent interest, the refusal to deal could not by itself support a finding of antitrust liability.

Respondents correctly note that "[o]n summary judgment the inferences to be drawn from the underlying facts...must be viewed in the light most favorable to the party opposing the motion." *United States v. Diebold, Inc.*, 369 U.S. 654, 655 (1962). But antitrust law limits the range of permissible inferences from ambiguous evidence in a § 1 case. Thus, in *Monsanto Co. v. Spray-Rite Service Corp.*, 465 U.S. 752 (1984), we held that conduct as consistent with permissible competition as with illegal conspiracy does not, standing alone, support an inference of antitrust conspiracy. To survive a motion for summary judgment or for a directed verdict, a plaintiff seeking damages for a violation of § 1 must present evidence "that tends to exclude the possibility" that the alleged conspirators acted independently. 465 U.S. at 764. Respondents in this case, in other words, must show that the inference of conspiracy is reasonable in light of the competing inferences of independent action or collusive action that could not have harmed respondents.

Petitioners argue that these principles apply fully to case. According to petitioners, the alleged conspiracy is one that is economically irrational and practically infeasible. Consequently, petitioners contend, they had no motive to engage in the alleged predatory pricing conspiracy; indeed, they had a strong motive *not* to conspire in the manner respondents allege. Petitioners argue that, in light of the absence of any apparent motive and the ambiguous nature of the evidence of conspiracy, no trier of fact reasonably could find that the conspiracy with which petitioners are charged actually existed. This argument requires us to consider the nature of the alleged conspiracy and the practical obstacles to its implementation.

IV

A

A predatory pricing conspiracy is by nature speculative. Any agreement to price below the competitive level requires the conspirators to forgo profits that free competition would offer them. The forgone profits may be considered an investment in the future. For the investment to be rational, the conspirators must have a reasonable expectation of recovering, in the form of later monopoly profits, more than the losses suffered. As then-Professor Bork, discussing predatory pricing by a single firm, explained:

"Any realistic theory of predation recognizes that the predator as well as his victims will incur losses during the fighting, but such a theory supposes it may be a rational calculation for the predator to view the losses as an investment in future monopoly profits (where rivals are to be killed) or in future undisturbed profits (where rivals are to be disciplined). The future flow of profits, appropriately discounted, must then exceed the present size of the losses." R. Bork, *The Antitrust Paradox* 145 (1978).

As this explanation shows, the success of such schemes is inherently uncertain: the short-run loss is definite, but the long-run gain depends on successfully neutralizing the competition. Moreover, it is not enough simply to achieve monopoly power, as monopoly pricing may breed quick entry by new competitors eager to share in the excess profits. The success of any predatory scheme depends on *maintaining* monopoly power for long enough both to recoup the predator's losses and to harvest some additional gain. Absent some assurance that the hoped-for monopoly will materialize, *and* that it can be sustained for a significant period of time, "[t]he predator must make a substantial investment with no assurance that it will pay off." Easterbrook, *Predatory Strategies and Counterstrategies*, 48 U. CHI. L. REV. 263, 268 (1981). For this reason, there is a consensus among commentators that predatory pricing schemes are rarely tried, and even more rarely successful.

These observations apply even to predatory pricing by a *single firm* seeking monopoly power. In this case, respondents allege that a large number of firms have conspired over a period of many years to charge below-market prices in order to stifle competition. Such a conspiracy is incalculably more difficult to execute than an analogous plan undertaken by a single predator. The conspirators must allocate the losses to be sustained during the conspiracy's operation, and must also allocate any gains to be realized from its success. Precisely because success is speculative and depends on a willingness to endure losses for an indefinite period, each conspirator has a strong incentive to cheat, letting its partners suffer the losses necessary to destroy the competition while sharing in any gains if the conspiracy succeeds. The necessary allocation is therefore difficult to accomplish. Yet if conspirators cheat to any substantial extent, the conspiracy must fail, because its success depends on depressing the market price for *all* buyers of CEPS. If there are too few goods at the artificially low price to satisfy demand, the would-be victims of the conspiracy can continue to sell at the "real" market price, and the conspirators suffer losses to little purpose.

Finally, if predatory pricing conspiracies are generally unlikely to occur, they are especially so where, as here, the prospects of attaining monopoly power seem slight. In order to recoup their losses, petitioners must obtain enough market power to set higher than competitive prices, and then must sustain those prices long enough to earn in excess profits what they earlier gave up in below-cost prices. Two decades after their conspiracy is alleged to have commenced, petitioners appear to be far from achieving this goal: the two largest shares of the retail market in television sets are held by RCA and respondent Zenith, not by any of petitioners. Moreover, those shares, which together approximate 40% of sales, did not decline appreciably during the 1970's. Petitioners' collective share rose rapidly during this period, from one-fifth or less of the relevant markets to close to 50%. Neither the District Court nor the Court of Appeals found, however, that petitioners' share presently allows them to charge monopoly prices; to the contrary, respondents contend that the conspiracy is ongoing—that petitioners are still artificially *depressing* the market price in order to drive Zenith out of the market. The data in the record strongly suggest that that goal is yet far distant.

The alleged conspiracy's failure to achieve its ends in the two decades of its asserted operation is strong evidence that the conspiracy does not in fact exist. Since the losses in such a conspiracy accrue before the gains, they must be "repaid" with interest. And because the alleged losses have accrued over the course of two decades, the conspirators could well require a correspondingly long time to recoup. Maintaining supracompetitive prices in turn depends on the continued cooperation of the conspirators, on the inability of other would-be competitors to enter the market, and (not incidentally) on the conspirators' ability to escape antitrust liability for their *minimum* price-fixing cartel. Each of these factors weighs more heavily as the time needed to recoup losses grows. If the losses have been substantial — as would likely be necessary in order to drive out the competition — petitioners would most likely have to sustain their cartel for years simply to break even.

Nor does the possibility that petitioners have obtained supracompetitive profits in the Japanese market change this calculation. Whether or not petitioners have the *means* to sustain substantial losses in this country over a long period of time, they have no *motive* to sustain such losses absent some strong likelihood that the alleged conspiracy in this country will eventually pay off. The courts below found no evidence of any such success, and — as indicated above — the facts actually are to the contrary: RCA and Zenith, not any of the petitioners, continue to hold the largest share of the American retail market in color television sets. More important, there is nothing to suggest any relationship between petitioners' profits in Japan and the amount petitioners could expect to gain from a conspiracy to monopolize the American market. In the absence of any such evidence, the possible existence of supracompetitive profits in Japan simply cannot overcome the economic obstacles to the ultimate success of this alleged predatory conspiracy.

B

In *Monsanto*, we emphasized that courts should not permit factfinders to infer conspiracies when such inferences are implausible, because the effect of such practices is often to deter procompetitive conduct. Respondents, petitioners' competitors, seek to hold petitioners liable for damages caused by the alleged conspiracy to cut prices. Moreover, they seek to establish this conspiracy indirectly, through evidence of other combinations (such as the check-price agreements and the five company rule) whose natural tendency is to raise prices, and through evidence of rebates and other price-cutting activities that respondents argue tend to prove a combination to suppress prices. But cutting prices in order to increase business often is the very essence of competition. Thus, mistaken inferences in cases such as this one are especially costly, because they chill the very conduct the antitrust laws are designed to protect. "[W]e must be concerned lest a rule or precedent that authorizes a search for a particular type of undesirable pricing behavior end up by discouraging legitimate price competition." *Barry Wright Corp. v. ITT Grinnell Corp.*, 724 F. 2d 227, 234 (CA1 1983).

In most cases, this concern must be balanced against the desire that illegal conspiracies be identified and punished. That balance is, however, unusually one-sided in cases such as this one. As we earlier explained, predatory pricing schemes require conspirators to suffer losses in order eventually to realize their illegal gains; moreover, the gains depend on a host of uncertainties, making such schemes more likely to fail than to succeed. These economic realities tend to make predatory pricing conspiracies self-deterring: unlike most other conduct that violates the antitrust laws, failed predatory pricing schemes are costly to the conspirators. Finally, unlike predatory pricing by a single firm, *successful* predatory pricing conspiracies involving a large number of firms can be identified and punished once they succeed, since some form of minimum price-fixing agreement would be necessary in order to reap the benefits of predation. Thus, there is little reason to be concerned that by granting summary judgment in cases where the evidence of conspiracy is speculative or ambiguous, courts will encourage such conspiracies.

V

As our discussion in Part IV-A shows, petitioners had no motive to enter into the alleged conspiracy. To the contrary, as presumably rational businesses, petitioners had every incentive *not* to engage in the conduct with which the are charged, for its likely effect would be to generate losses for petitioners with no corresponding gains. The Court of Appeals did not take account of the absence of a plausible motive to enter into the alleged predatory pricing conspiracy. It focused instead on whether there was "direct evidence of concert of action." The Court of Appeals erred in two respects: (i) the "direct evidence" on which the court relied had little, if any, relevance to the alleged predatory pricing conspiracy; and (ii) the court failed to consider the absence of a plausible motive to engage in predatory pricing.

The "direct evidence" on which the court relied was evidence of *other* combinations, not of a predatory pricing conspiracy. Evidence that petitioners conspired to raise prices in Japan provides little, if any, support for respondents' claims: a conspiracy to increase profits in one market does not tend to show a conspiracy to sustain losses in another. Evidence that petitioners agreed to fix *minimum* prices (through the check-price agreements) for the American market actually works in petitioners' favor, because it suggests that petitioners were seeking to place a floor under prices rather than to lower them. The same is true of evidence that petitioners agreed to limit the number of distributors of their products in the American market—the so-called five company rule. That practice may have facilitated a horizontal territorial allocation, but its natural effect would be to raise market prices rather than reduce them. Evidence that tends to support any of these collateral conspiracies thus says little, if anything, about the existence of a conspiracy to charge below-market prices in the American market over a period of two decades.

That being the case, the absence of any plausible motive to engage in the conduct charged is highly relevant to whether a "genuine issue for trial" exists within the meaning of Rule 56(e). Lack of motive bears on the range of permissible conclusions that might be drawn from ambiguous evidence: if petitioners had no rational economic motive to conspire, and if their conduct is consistent with other, equally plausible explanations, the conduct does not give rise to an inference of conspiracy. Here, the conduct in question consists largely of (i) pricing at levels that succeeded in taking business away from respondents, and (ii) arrangements that may have limited petitioners' ability to compete with each other (and thus kept prices from going even lower). This conduct suggests either that petitioners behaved competitively, or that petitioners conspired to *raise* prices. Neither possibility is consistent with an agreement among 21 companies to price below market levels. Moreover, the predatory pricing scheme that this conduct is said to prove is one that makes no practical sense: it calls for petitioners to destroy companies larger and better established than themselves, a goal that remains far distant more than two decades after the conspiracy's birth. Even had they succeeded in obtaining their monopoly, there is nothing in the record to suggest that they could recover the losses they would need to sustain along the way. In sum, in light of the absence of any rational motive to conspire, neither petitioners' pricing practices, nor their conduct in the Japanese market, nor their agreements respecting prices and distribution in the American market, suffice to create a "genuine issue for trial." Fed. Rule Civ. Proc. 56(e).

On remand, the Court of Appeals is free to consider whether there is other evidence that is sufficiently unambiguous to permit a trier of fact to find that petitioners conspired to price predatorily for two decades despite the absence of any apparent motive to do so. The evidence must "ten[d] to exclude the possibility" that petitioners underpriced respondents to compete for business rather than to implement an economically senseless conspiracy. In the absence of such evidence, there is no "genuine issue for trial" under Rule 56(e), and petitioners are entitled to have summary judgment reinstated.

VI

Our decision makes it unnecessary to reach the sovereign compulsion issue. The heart of petitioners' argument on that issue is that MITI, an agency of the Government of Japan, required petitioners to fix minimum prices for export to the United States, and that petitioners are therefore immune from antitrust liability for any scheme of which those minimum prices were an integral part. As we discussed in Part II, respondents could not have suffered a cognizable injury from any action that *raised* prices in the American CEP market. If liable at all, petitioners are liable for conduct that is distinct from the check-price agreements. The sovereign compulsion question that both petitioners and the Solicitor General urge us to decide thus is not presented here.

The decision of the Court of Appeals is reversed, and the case is remanded for further proceedings consistent with this opinion.

It is so ordered.

Justice White, with whom Justice Brennan, Justice Blackmun, and Justice Stevens join, *dissenting.*

It is indeed remarkable that the Court, in the face of the long and careful opinion of the Court of Appeals, reaches the result it does. The Court of Appeals faithfully followed the relevant precedents, including *First National Bank of Arizona v. Cities Service Co.*, 391 U.S. 253 (1968), and *Monsanto Co. v. Spray-Rite Service Corp.*, 465 U.S. 752 (1984), and it kept firmly in mind the principle that proof of a conspiracy should not be fragmented, see *Continental Ore Co. v. Union Carbide & Carbon Corp.*, 370 U.S. 690, 699 (1962). After surveying the massive record, including very significant evidence that the District Court erroneously had excluded, the Court of Appeals concluded that the evidence taken as a whole creates a genuine issue of fact whether petitioners engaged in a conspiracy in violation of §§ 1 and 2 of the Sherman Act and § 2(a) of the Robinson-Patman Act. In my view, the Court of Appeals' opinion more than adequately supports this judgment.

The Court's opinion today, far from identifying reversible error, only muddies the waters. In the first place, the Court makes confusing and inconsistent statements about the appropriate standard for granting summary judgment. Second, the Court makes a number of assumptions that invade the factfinder's province. Third, the Court faults the Third Circuit for nonexistent errors and remands the case although it is plain that respondents' evidence raises genuine issues of material fact.

I

The Court's initial discussion of summary judgment standards appears consistent with settled doctrine. I agree that "[w]here the record taken as a whole could not lead a rational trier of fact to find for the nonmoving party, there is no 'genuine issue for trial.'" I also agree that "'[o]n summary judgment the inferences to be drawn from the underlying facts...must be viewed in the light most favorable to the party opposing the motion.'" But other language in the Court's opinion suggests a departure from traditional summary judgment doctrine. Thus, the Court gives the following critique of the Third Circuit's opinion:

> "[T]he Court of Appeals concluded that a reasonable factfinder could find a conspiracy to depress prices in the American market in order to drive out American competitors, which conspiracy was funded by excess profits obtained in the Japanese market. The court apparently, did not consider whether it was as plausible to conclude that petitioners' price-cutting behavior was independent and not conspiratorial."

In a similar vein, the Court summarizes *Monsanto Co. v. Spray-Rite Service Corp.*, as holding that "courts should not permit factfinders to infer conspiracies when such inferences are implausible..." Such language suggests that a judge hearing a defendant's motion for summary judgment in an antitrust case should go beyond the traditional summary judgment inquiry and decide for himself whether the weight of the evidence favors the plaintiff. *Cities Service* and *Monsanto* do not stand for any such proposition. Each of those cases simply held that a particular piece of evidence standing alone was insufficiently probative to justify sending a case to the jury. These holdings in no way undermine the doctrine that all evidence must be construed in the light most favorable to the party opposing summary judgment.

If the Court intends to give every judge hearing a motion for summary judgment in an antitrust case the job of determining if the evidence makes the inference of conspiracy more probable than not, it is overturning settled law. If the Court does not intend such a pronouncement, it should refrain from using unnecessarily broad and confusing language.

II

In defining what respondents must show in order to recover, the Court makes assumptions that invade the factfinder's province. The Court states with very little discussion that respondents can recover under § 1 of the Sherman Act only if they prove that "petitioners conspired to drive respondents out of the relevant markets by (i) pricing below the level necessary to sell their products, or (ii) pricing below some appropriate measure of cost." This statement is premised on the assumption that "[a]n agreement without these features would either leave respondents in the same position as would market forces or would actually benefit respondents by raising market prices." In making this assumption, the Court ignores the contrary conclusions of respondents' expert DePodwin, whose report in very relevant part was erroneously excluded by the District Court.

The DePodwin Report, on which the Court of Appeals relied along with other material, indicates that respondents were harmed in two ways that are independent of whether petitioners priced their products below "the level necessary to sell their products or...some appropriate measure of cost." First, the Report explains that the price-raising scheme in Japan resulted in lower consumption of petitioners' goods in that country and the exporting of more of petitioners' goods to this country than would have occurred had prices in Japan been at the competitive level. Increasing exports to this country resulted in depressed prices here, which harmed respondents. Second, the DePodwin Report indicates that petitioners exchanged confidential proprietary information and entered into agreements such as the five company rule with the goal of avoiding intragroup competition in the United States market. The Report explains that petitioners' restrictions on intragroup competition caused respondents to lose business that they would not have lost had petitioners competed with one another.

The DePodwin Report alone creates a genuine factual issue regarding the harm to respondents caused by Japanese cartelization and by agreements restricting competition among petitioners in this country. No doubt the Court prefers its own economic theorizing to Dr. DePodwin's, but that is not a reason to deny the factfinder an opportunity to consider Dr. DePodwin's views on how petitioners' alleged collusion harmed respondents.

The Court, in discussing the unlikelihood of a predatory conspiracy, also consistently assumes that petitioners valued profit-maximization over growth. In light of the evidence that petitioners sold their goods in this country at substantial losses over a long period of time, I believe that this is an assumption that should be argued to the factfinder, not decided by the Court.

III

In reversing the Third Circuit's judgment, the Court identifies two alleged errors: "(i) [T]he 'direct evidence' on which the [Court of Appeals] relied had little, if any, relevance to the alleged predatory pricing conspiracy; and (ii) the court failed to consider the absence of a plausible motive to engage in predatory pricing." The Court's position is without substance.

A

The flat claim of error is that the Third Circuit treated evidence regarding price fixing in Japan and the so-called five company rule and check prices as "'direct evidence' of a conspiracy that injured respondents." The passage from the Third Circuit's opinion in which the Court locates this alleged error makes what I consider to be a quite simple and correct observation, namely, that this case is distinguishable from traditional "conscious parallelism" cases, in that there is direct evidence of concert of action among petitioners. The Third Circuit did not, as the Court implies, jump unthinkingly from this observation to the conclusion that evidence regarding the five company rule could support a finding of antitrust injury to respondents. The Third Circuit twice specifically noted that horizontal agreements allocating customers, though illegal, do not ordinarily injure competitors of the agreeing parties. However, after reviewing evidence of cartel activity in Japan, collusive establishment of dumping prices in this country, and long-term, below-cost sales, the Third Circuit held that a factfinder could reasonably conclude that the five company rule was not a simple price-raising device:

> "[A] factfinder might reasonably infer that the allocation of customers in the United States, combined with price-fixing in Japan, was intended to permit concentration of the effects of dumping upon American competitors while eliminating competition among the Japanese manufacturers in either market."

I see nothing erroneous in this reasoning.

B

The Court's second charge of error is that the Third Circuit was not sufficiently skeptical of respondents' allegation that petitioners engaged in predatory pricing conspiracy. But the Third Circuit is not required to engage in academic discussions about predation; it is required to decide whether respondents' evidence creates a genuine issue of material fact. The Third Circuit did its job, and remanding the case so that it can do the same job again is simply pointless.

The Third Circuit indicated that it considers respondents' evidence sufficient to create a genuine factual issue regarding long-term, below-cost sales by petitioners. The Court tries to whittle away at this conclusion by suggesting that the "expert opinion evidence of below-cost pricing has little probative value in comparison with the economic factors...that suggest that such conduct is irrational." But the question is not whether the Court finds respondents' experts persuasive, or prefers the District Court's analysis; it is whether, viewing the evidence in the light most favorable to respondents, a jury or other factfinder could reasonably conclude that petitioners engaged in long-term, below-cost sales. I agree with the Third Circuit that the answer to this question is "yes."

It is misleading for the Court to state that the Court Appeals "did not disturb the District Court's analysis of the factors that substantially undermine the probative value of [evidence in the DePodwin Report respecting below-cost sales]." The Third Circuit held that the exclusion of the portion of the DePodwin Report regarding below-cost pricing was erroneous because "the trial court ignored DePodwin's un-contradicted affidavit that all data relied on in his report were of the type on which experts in his field would reasonably rely." In short, the Third Circuit found DePodwin's affidavit sufficient to create a genuine factual issue regarding the correctness of his conclusion that petitioners sold below cost over a long period of time. Having made this determination, the court saw no need—nor do I—to address the District Court's analysis point by point. The District Court's criticisms of DePodwin's methods are arguments that a factfinder should consider.

IV

Because I believe that the Third Circuit was correct in holding that respondents have demonstrated the existence of genuine issues of material fact, I would affirm the judgment below and remand this case for trial.

VI. Substantive Defenses:
Act of State and Sovereign Immunity

Occidental Petroleum Corporation
v. Buttes Gas & Oil Company
331 F.Supp. 92 (C.D. Cal. 1971), aff'd, 461 F.2d 1261
(9th Cir. 1972), cert. denied, 409 U.S. 950 (1972)

Pregerson, District Judge.

This is a private antitrust suit for treble damages and an injunction, brought by Occidental Petroleum Corporation and its wholly owned subsidiary Occidental of Umm al Qaywayn against the Clayco Petroleum Corporation ("Clayco") and its president, Clayman, and the Buttes Gas and Oil Company ("Buttes") and its officers Boreta and Smith. The complaint charges the defendants with conspiracy in restraint of trade, conspiracy to monopolize, and attempted monopoly, all with respect to "the exploration, development and exploitation of petroleum reserves of the territorial waters of the Trucial States [now known as the United Arab Emirates, or U.A.E.]." The plaintiffs and the defendant corporations are holders of offshore oil concessions granted by two adjacent sheikdoms in the Persian Gulf. Defendants are charged with instigating a presently pending international dispute over sovereign rights to a portion of the Gulf—allegedly covering the richest area of plaintiffs' concession—with the result that plaintiffs have been prevented from enjoying the fruits of their concession.

The Court has before it separate motions to dismiss, urged respectively by Clayco and Clayman on the one hand and by the Buttes defendants on the other. Clayco and Clayman claim lack of personal jurisdiction, improper venue, and defective service of process. The Buttes defendants attack the face of the complaint, raising five substantive grounds allegedly warranting dismissal of the action. The two sets of motions will be considered separately. [The Court's discussion of the Clayco-Clayman motion is omitted.]

. . . .

THE BUTTES DEFENDANTS' MOTION

The Buttes defendants do not contest personal jurisdiction or venue. Rather, they urge dismissal of the complaint and action on the grounds of...failure to state a claim upon which relief may be granted....

Plaintiffs assert that, pursuant to their efforts to develop and exploit the petroleum reserves underlying the offshore waters of the Trucial States in the Persian Gulf, they obtained in 1969 a concession from the Ruler of Umm al Qaywayn, one of the Trucial States, granting plaintiffs the exclusive right to explore for, extract, and sell oil underlying the territorial and offshore waters of Umm al Qaywayn. It was plaintiffs' purpose to import into the United States for refining any oil extracted pursuant to this concession. Owing to the unavailability of the Suez Canal, such importation would be made through Pacific Coast seaports in California. The concession agreement is by its own terms to terminate if oil is not discovered in "commercial quantities" in the concession area within four years of the concession's effective date.

Immediately prior to their obtaining the concession from Umm al Qaywayn, plaintiffs allege, defendants Buttes and Clayco had themselves unsuccessfully attempted to negotiate such a concession. Subsequent to plaintiffs' success with Umm al Qaywayn, Buttes and Clayco allegedly negotiated, in December, 1969, a comparable concession by the Ruler of the Trucial State Sharjah, covering its territorial and offshore waters.

The mainland areas of Sharjah and Umm al Qaywayn are situated contiguously at the southeastern end of the Persian Gulf. Sharjah, moreover, asserts sovereignty to the island of Abu Musa, located 38 miles off the coast of its mainland. Plaintiffs allege that at the time defendants' concession was granted by Sharjah, it claimed a territorial waters domain of three miles, including a belt extending that distance seaward from the low water mark of Abu Musa. The territorial waters perimeter off Abu Musa allegedly constituted a boundary between the Sharjah and Umm al Qaywayn concession areas that was acknowledged by both states. A map indicating this boundary is attached to the complaint, and plaintiffs allege that confirmatory copies of this map were included in the two concession agreements when each was submitted to and approved by the British Foreign Office, pursuant to a treaty still in force between Britain and the Trucial States.

Still friendly in the beginning of 1970, plaintiffs and Buttes agreed to exchange information gleaned from seismic tests to be made of the seabed and subsoil underlying their respective concession areas. The results of plaintiffs' tests indicated the presence of oil in extensive quantities at a point within their alleged concession area nine miles seaward from the low water mark of Abu Musa. Plaintiffs proceeded to prepare to drill in this area, expending several million dollars for that purpose by the time the complaint was filed.

The complaint alleges that after learning in March, 1970 of the apparent richness of plaintiffs' concession area, defendants entered into and acted upon a conspiracy to misappropriate plaintiffs' rights to the oil underlying the Persian Gulf nine miles off Abu Musa. The execution of this conspiracy, as alleged, involved a multi-faceted international intrigue whose detail, relevant to the grounds of the instant motion to dismiss, is set out in the margin in the words of the complaint." Briefly stated, after unsuccessfully submitting to the British Political Agent in the Trucial States a plan whereby Buttes would drill for oil in a portion of the Occidental-Umm al Qaywayn concession area, defendants "induced and procured" the Ruler of Sharjah to claim ownership of the oil-rich portion of plaintiffs' concession area by preparing and submitting to the British Agent a concession amendment and two decrees, one of the latter fraudulently backdated to represent that prior to the granting of plaintiffs' concession by Umm al Qaywayn, Sharjah had claimed territorial waters extending *twelve* miles seaward from the low water mark of its territory, including Abu Musa. These representations did not convince the British Foreign Office, which ordered the Ruler of Sharjah to desist and acknowledged the authority of the Occidental-Umm al Qaywayn concession. Defendants allegedly then enlisted the aid of other sovereigns: they "induced and procured" the National Iranian Oil Company, in May, 1970, to claim Iranian sovereignty over Abu Musa and the waters twelve miles seaward therefrom; and defendants thereafter further "induced and procured" the British Foreign Office to request that plaintiffs refrain from their imminent drilling operations until the claims of Sharjah and of the Iranian Company could be resolved. British ships and aircraft menaced plaintiffs' personnel and equipment on the drilling site, and on June 1, 1970, members of the Royal Navy forcibly boarded plaintiffs' equipment. Two days later the Ruler of Umm al Qaywayn directed plaintiffs not to drill in the disputed area; this order, which had the effect of suspending plaintiffs' intended drilling operations under their concession, was allegedly the consequence of threats of exile and acts of military intimidation by British forces made to the Ruler of Umm al Qaywayn. The threats against the Ruler of Umm al Qaywayn, and his order to plaintiffs, were allegedly "direct consequences, fully intended and expected by the defendants, of the conflicting and fraudulent claims with regard to the island of Abu Musa and its territorial waters, which the defendants had induced and procured." The intended upshot of this intrigue, the complaint alleges, is that following the withdrawal of the British from the Persian Gulf area in 1971 defendants will arrange with the Ruler of Sharjah to extract oil and gas from areas covered by plaintiffs' concession.

To remedy the injury suffered from this conspiracy, the plaintiffs request treble their damages of $100 million—the estimated worth of the oil in the concession area —as well as extensive equitable relief, to wit, an injunction restraining defendants or any persons operating in concert with them from disputing the validity of the Occidental concession as alleged in the complaint, from interfering with plaintiffs' operations in the waters of the Trucial States, and from extracting oil from the area of the Occidental concession; in the alternative to this last demand, plaintiffs request the impressment of a trust for their benefit upon any revenues derived by defendants or those acting for them from any part of the plaintiffs' concession area.

The Buttes defendants...assert that this court lacks jurisdiction of the subject matter of the action under the antitrust laws because the complaint fails to allege a substantial anti-competitive effect upon United States commerce.....[T]he defendants contend that since the complaint attacks activities undertaken to influence governmental conduct, this case is not within the subject matter of the antitrust laws, as interpreted by the Supreme Court in Eastern R. R. Presidents Conference v. Noerr Motor Freight, Inc., 365 U.S. 127 (1961), and United Mine Workers of America v. Pennington, 381 U.S. 657 (1965). [D]efendants [also] argue that because the conspiracy and damage complained of are based upon the conduct of several sovereigns, this court is barred from adjudicating plaintiffs' claims by the act of state doctrine. [The Court's discussion of two other arguments made by the defendants is omitted.]

Effect on American Commerce

The Buttes defendants first contend that jurisdiction of this case requires "a substantial anticompetitive effect on American commerce," and that such an effect has not been demonstrated by the complaint. On this basis the court is urged to dismiss the complaint for want of subject matter jurisdiction.

The trade and commerce allegedly restrained in this case involved plaintiffs' intended extraction and importation of oil from the territorial waters of the Trucial States. It would therefore appear that the case is governed by the standards of jurisdiction applicable to restraints of "foreign commerce."

That *some* effect on our foreign commerce is a prerequisite to jurisdiction is evident from the text of the antitrust statutes here involved. Defendants assert that the effect must be "a substantial anti-competitive" one. They rely on the following language from the 1955 *Report of the Attorney General's National Committee to Study the Antitrust Laws*, at 76:

> We feel that the Sherman Act applies only to those arrangements between Americans alone, or in concert with foreign firms, which have such substantial anti-competitive effects on this country's "trade or commerce...with foreign nations" as to constitute unreasonable restraints.

But this quotation seemingly states the criterion for a Sherman Act *violation*. "Substantial anti-competitive effect" is used, in the above text, to qualify "unreasonable restraints;" and it is only unreasonable restraints that Section 1 of the Sherman Act condemns. *See* Beausang, *The Extraterritorial Jurisdiction of the Sherman Act*, 70 DICK.L. REV. 187, 191 (1966): "An 'effect' is a necessary element of *jurisdiction...* , a direct and substantial 'effect' is necessary for Sherman Act *violations*. The problem arises when the standards of illegality (which might be modified to promote foreign trade) are confused with the jurisdictional feature of the 'effect on foreign commerce'" (emphasis original).

In reviewing the cases, Von Kalinowski notes the confusion evident therein:

> The cases that used the word "affect" have said that a restraint must (1) "directly affect," or (2) "substantially affect," or (3) "directly and substantially affect," or (4) simply "affect" the flow of foreign commerce.

1 J. Von Kalinowski, [*Antitrust and Trade Regulation*] § 5.502[2], at 5-120 [(1969)] (footnotes omitted). He concludes that "[t]he better view would seem to be that any effect that is not both insubstantial and indirect will support federal jurisdiction under Section 1." *Id.* at 5-121-22.

The interference with plaintiffs' business of extracting and importing oil into the United States, alleged in the complaint, is certainly a "direct" effect on our foreign commerce. On this basis, the court is disposed to hold that the complaint alleges a sufficient effect on foreign commerce. Moreover, since the standard urged by defendants is largely coterminous with the scope of proof required to establish plaintiffs' section 1 case on the merits, dismissal now on the grounds that that standard has not been met would be premature. In urging dismissal, defendants stress such factors as the smallness of the Buttes Company in relation to plaintiff Occidental Petroleum Corporation, the confined geographical area of plaintiffs' concession, the presently speculative value of that concession, and the presence in the Persian Gulf of numerous other companies extracting oil for importation into the United States. These are matters that would appear to bear upon proof of plaintiffs' claims of antitrust violations; they cannot serve at this stage to defeat jurisdiction.

....

Foreign Government Action

The final two points of this motion are addressed to the peculiar nature of the conspiracy alleged in this case. As detailed above the defendants are charged, exclusively, with "inducing and procuring" assorted executive acts by foreign states; and it is plainly these acts that allegedly have caused and threatened to cause the damage plaintiffs seek to remedy. The Buttes defendants contend that the foregoing circumstances preclude the court from adjudicating this case. Two doctrines are relied upon: the limitation of antitrust jurisdiction articulated in *Eastern R. R. Presidents Conference v. Noerr Motor Freight, Inc.*, 365 U.S. 127 (1961), and the rule of judicial abstention known as the act of state doctrine. The two rules spring from different considerations.

In *Noerr*, the Supreme Court unanimously decided that "the Sherman Act does not prohibit two or more persons from associating together in an attempt to persuade the legislature or the executive to take particular action with respect to a law that would produce a restraint or a monopoly." 365 U.S. at 136. This interpretation of the Sherman Act was reaffirmed, with further elucidation, in *United Mine Workers of America v. Pennington*, 381 U.S. 657 (1965). Since *Noerr* and *Pennington* construed the Sherman Act with reference to influencing American state and federal officials, the threshold question here is whether the teaching of those cases is applicable when foreign governments are involved.

There is no direct authority on this question. The Buttes defendants, however, contend that *Noerr* was implicitly extended to cover the solicitation of foreign governments, in *Continental Ore Co. v. Union Carbide & Carbon Corp.*, 370 U.S. 690 (1962). *Continental Ore* was an antitrust case in which a subsidiary of Union Carbide had allegedly boycotted the plaintiff in the course of exercising discretionary authority as the purchasing agent of the Canadian government. The Court distinguished *Noerr* on ground that "[r]espondents were engaged in private commercial activity, no element of which involved seeking to procure the passage or enforcement of laws." 370 U.S. at 707. Defendants insist that in distinguishing *Noerr* only on its facts, the Court in *Continental Ore* decided sub silentio that the rule of *Noerr* would have applied had there been solicitation of foreign government action. At least one commentator agrees precisely. However, an at least equally tenable interpretation of *Continental Ore* is that the Court deemed it unnecessary, in view of the facts, to decide the legal question at all.

Examination of the premises underlying Noerr indicates that the case's rationales do not readily fit into a foreign context, such as the facts of this case. One of the roots of the *Noerr* decision was a desire to avoid a construction of the antitrust laws that might trespass upon the First Amendment right of petition. 365 U.S. at 138. The constitutional freedom "to petition the Government" carries limited if indeed any applicability to the petitioning of foreign governments. A second basis of *Noerr* is a concern with insuring that, "[i]n a representative democracy such as this," law-making organs retain access to the opinions of their constituents, unhampered by collateral regulation. 365 U.S. at 137. *Noerr* has been held inapplicable to situations in which this relationship has not been deemed threatened. The persuasion of Middle Eastern states alleged in the present case is a far cry from the political process with which *Noerr* was concerned.

In sum, the interests asserted in this case are dissimilar to those that *Noerr* was concerned with safeguarding; therefore, the wholesale application of that exception to the Sherman Act appears inappropriate. However, other considerations become prominent when acts of foreign governments are brought to bar-considerations reflecting a prudent allocation of competence between the American judiciary and executive in the field of foreign relations. The act of state doctrine is the relevant and dispositive principle on this motion to dismiss.

In *Underhill v. Hernandez*, 168 U.S. 250 (1897), the Supreme Court first definitively held that "the courts of one country will not sit in judgment on the acts of the government of another, done within its own territory." This "classic American statement of the act of state doctrine" was reaffirmed by the court most recently in *Banco Nacional de Cuba v. Sabbatino*, 376 U.S. 398 (1964). In the *Sabbatino* case, the bases of the doctrine were at last explicitly elaborated. The act of state doctrine, it was held, is not required by international law. Nor is it compelled by notions of sovereign authority, although they "do bear upon the wisdom of employing" it. Finally, the doctrine is not required by the Constitution.

> The act of state doctrine does, however, have "constitutional" underpinnings. It arises out of the basic relationships between branches of government in a system of separation of powers. It concerns the competency of dissimilar institutions to make and implement particular kinds of decisions in the area of international relations. The doctrine as formulated in past decisions expresses the strong sense of the Judicial Branch that its engagement in the task of passing on the validity of foreign acts of state may hinder rather than further this country's pursuit of goals both for itself and for the community of nations as a whole in the international sphere. 376 U.S. at 423.

In sum, the doctrine is a reflection of the executive's primary competency in foreign affairs, and an acknowledgment of the fact that in passing upon foreign governmental acts the judiciary may hinder or embarrass the conduct of our foreign relations.

> Consideration of the act of state doctrine's relevance to the present case begins with one of the early act of state cases, *American Banana Co. v. United Fruit Co.*, 160 F. 184 (C.C.S.D.N.Y.), *aff'd*, 166 F. 261 (2^d Cir. 1908), *aff'd*, 213 U.S. 347 (1909). The facts of that case are strikingly similar to those now before the court. A private defendant was sued under the Sherman Act for destruction of plaintiff's fledgling banana business in Panama and Costa Rica. The gravamen of the complaint was that the defendant had instigated and procured Costa Rican soldiers to seize and maintain control of plaintiff's plantation and supplies. The trial court dismissed the complaint, stating, "[i]t is impossible to adjudicate this matter without sitting in judgment on the right of Costa Rica to do what was done...this court has no power to sit in judgment on the validity or legality of the act of any sovereign independent nation." 160 F. at 188. The circuit court of appeals affirmed, using the following language:

> Upon principle and authority, it follows that Costa Rica is entitled to immunity from any investigation of its sovereign acts by this court. The plaintiff, however, asserts that this immunity is only an immunity from suit which has no bearing upon the defendant's liability. But, as we have seen, the immunity is far broader than this. The validity of an act adopted by a sovereign state cannot be inquired into at all—directly or collaterally—by the courts of another state. Relief must be sought in the courts of the former state or through diplomatic channels. 166 F. at 266.

On *certiorari*, the result was the same, Justice Holmes writing:

> The substance of the complaint is that, the plantation being within the *de facto* jurisdiction of Costa Rica, that state took and keeps possession of it by virtue of its sovereign power. But a seizure by a state is not a thing that can be complained of elsewhere in the courts....

and then citing *Underhill v. Hernandez* (as had the two lower courts). 213 U.S. at 357-358.

The significance of the *American Banana* case has been somewhat obscured by virtue of the fact that Justice Holmes's opinion expounds at some length a restrictive view of Sherman Act jurisdiction, based upon the situs of primary conduct. This aspect of the opinion has been distinguished in subsequent international antitrust cases. But...the holding of *American Banana* that has endured is that the act of state doctrine bars a claim for antitrust injury flowing from foreign sovereign acts allegedly induced and procured by the defendant. This holding would appear directly to control the present case.

Plaintiffs say that they do not complain of the acts of foreign states set forth in the complaint, but rather only of defendants' conduct in "catalyzing" those acts. This construction of the case is at odds with plaintiffs' papers in at least two crucial respects. In the first place, plaintiffs have in another phase of this motion dubbed the states involved in the present Persian Gulf controversy as co-conspirators. The implication to be drawn from this allegation is that plaintiffs do question the conduct of those states under the antitrust laws—an inquiry which the act of state doctrine surely bars. Second, the complaint charges that several of Sharjah's acts were violative of international law. This claim, too, is barred from American courts by the act of state doctrine—specifically by the *Sabbatino* decision. Indeed, this portion of plaintiffs' pleading appears designed expressly to avoid the anticipated effect of the doctrine, by invoking an exception to it, which will be discussed shortly.

There is, moreover, a further dimension to this case's implication of foreign acts of state. Because a private antitrust claim requires proof of damage resulting from forbidden conduct, plaintiffs necessarily ask this court to "sit in judgment" upon the sovereign acts pleaded, whether or not the countries involved are considered co-conspirators. That is, to establish their claim as pleaded plaintiffs must prove, *inter alia*, that Sharjah issued a fraudulent territorial waters decree, and that Iran laid claim to the island of Abu Musa at the behest of the defendants. Plaintiffs say they stand ready to prove the former allegation by use of "internal documents." But such inquiries by this court into the authenticity and motivation of the acts of foreign sovereigns would be the very sources of diplomatic friction and complication that the act of state doctrine aims to avert.

Instructive precedent for the present issues is found in *Frazier v. Foreign Bondholders Protective Council*, 283 App. Div. 44, 125 N.Y.S.2d 900 (1953). The plaintiffs there claimed that defendants had induced a breach of contract by Peru (the very theory of the action between the present parties in state court). Judge Botein dealt in the following language with plaintiffs' objections to the interposition of an act of state defense:

> The plaintiffs moved to strike the defenses, urging that they do not seek damages from Peru for its breach of contract but from these private defendants for their own tortious conduct in inducing and procuring Peru to break its contract.....
>
> ....
>
> The plaintiffs' characterization of the defenses as an attempt to immunize a private citizen for wrongdoing to another private citizen must be considered in juxtaposition to the assertion in their brief that such wrongdoing resulted in "an outright and unabashed repudiation" by Peru. Our courts are traditionally loath to resolve such issues.
>
> ....
>
> ....Perhaps our courts should be even more sensitive to the involvements of a sovereign's action when the sovereign is not a party to the action, and the

adjudication as it affects its prestige and dignity partakes of the nature of an ex parte proceeding. 125 N.Y.S.2d at 901, 903, 905.

(On remand, defendants' motion for summary judgment was granted. 133 N.Y.S. 2d 606 (Supp.1954).)

It thus appears *prima facie* that the act of state doctrine precludes further adjudication of the present case. Plaintiffs, however, offer several further arguments against this result. They first contend that the doctrine has been sapped of its vitality and rationale by the so-called "Sabbatino Amendment," 22 U.S.C. § 2370(e) (2) [also known as the "Second Hickenlooper Amendment, which was made in 1965 to the Foreign Assistance Act of 1961].

At issue is the significance of the "Sabbatino Amendment" vis-a-vis the act of state doctrine in general. From the plain wording and history of the legislation, that issue is easy to resolve. The statute prescribes, in relevant part:

> Notwithstanding any other provision of law, no court in the United States shall decline on the ground of the federal act of state doctrine to make a determination on the merits giving effect to the principles of international law in a case in which a claim of title or other right to property is asserted by any party including a foreign state (or a party claiming through such state) based upon (or traced through) a confiscation or other taking after January 1, 1959, by an act of that state in violation of the principles of international law....:
> *Provided,* That this subparagraph shall not be applicable...(2) in any case with respect to which the President determines that application of the act of state doctrine is required in that particular case by the foreign policy interests of the United States and a suggestion to this effect is filed on his behalf in that case with the court.

In intent and in actual effect, then, the statute "reverses"— in the absence of a request by the executive— the specific holding of the *Sabbatino* case, that

> the Judicial Branch will not examine the validity of a taking of property within its own territory by a foreign sovereign government, extant and recognized by this country at the time of suit, in the absence of a treaty or other unambiguous agreement regarding controlling legal principles, even if the complaint alleges that the taking violates customary international law. 376 U.S. at 428.

Congress has thus legislated a judicial "presumption" with respect to the foreign relations demands of a limited category of act of state cases. As a matter of record, even this narrow presumption did not conform to the realities of executive judgment. The executive strenuously opposed the enactment of the legislation, and it became law only as a rider to the Foreign Assistance Act—which is why the provision is called the "Sabbatino *Amendment*." In any event, this exception is by its terms extremely narrow, and in all other cases the act of state doctrine remains the law of the land. The legislation has been strictly construed, and courts have continued to rely upon act of state in cases deemed not precisely fitting the statutory language. Plaintiffs' assertion that the Amendment in effect pulled the rug out from under the act of state doctrine in all cases is groundless.

Indeed, plaintiffs appear to recognize this, for their next argument against the application of the act of state doctrine to this case is that the limited exception created by the statute controls here. Plaintiffs have charged in their complaint that the two territorial waters decrees issued by Sharjah, and the amendment of its contract with Buttes and Clayco, constituted "in effect an attempted confiscation, without compensation, of plaintiffs' vested property rights in the oil and gas to which they were entitled . . . in violation of international law." This pleading is insufficient to invoke the Sabbatino Amendment for several reasons. In the first place, the charge of an attempted confiscation, invalid under international law, has not been directed against the other acts of state—by Sharjah and also by Iran, Umm al Qaywayn, and Great Britain—adjudication of which would form an integral part of plaintiffs' case. Moreover, the portion of the complaint here in issue does not itself fall within the Sabbatino Amendment's ambit, for the simple reason that the complaint refers to an "attempted confiscation," whereas the statute applies only to a "confiscation or other taking." It is clear from a reading of the complaint as a whole that the conduct of Sharjah did not amount to an effective confiscation; rather, plaintiffs were allegedly deprived of the enjoyment of their concession only by the cooperative effect of a number of acts of state, of which Sharjah's claims were not the most efficacious. This is not a situation at which the Sabbatino Amendment was aimed.

Plaintiffs next contend that Sharjah and Umm al Qaywayn do not qualify as "states" under the act of state doctrine, because they have delegated to Britain ultimate authority over their foreign relations. The authority cited by plaintiffs indicates a contrary result. In *Carl Zeiss Stiftung v. V.E.B. Carl Zeiss, Jena*, 293 F.Supp. 892 (S.D.N.Y. 1967), *aff'd*, 433 F.2d 686 (2ᵈ Cir. 1970), the act of state doctrine was held applicable to Wuerttemberg, one of the constituent states of West Germany. After citing cases that had accorded act of state treatment to similar national subdivisions, the district court noted that Wuerttemberg "has had the power to engage in foreign relations with the consent of the Government of West Germany and has done so. *See* Article 32, West German Constitution. . . ." 293 F.Supp. at 910; aff'd, 433 F.2d at 703. Under the holding of the *Zeiss* case and the authority on which it relied, the application of act of which it relied, the application of act of state to the Trucial States would appear to follow a fortiori. Previously recognized as independent sovereigns by Britain, the Trucial States acceded supervision over their foreign relations to the latter only by a series of treaties. While the precise international status of these sheikdoms is at present unique and difficult to characterize, their degree of international personality is obviously greater than that, say, of Wuerttemberg. Bearing in mind especially the foreign affairs roots of the act of state doctrine, the court concludes that the doctrine applies to Sharjah and Umm al Qaywayn.

Nor is this conclusion disturbed, as regards Sharjah, by plaintiffs' assertion that some of the conduct of its Ruler was motivated by "his own personal gain and benefit." *Jimenez v. Aristeguieta*, 311 F.2d 547 (5th Cir. 1962), relied on by plaintiffs, holds only that crimes committed by a chief of state outside or in violation of his official authority are not acts of state. Contrariwise, the complaint clearly indicates that the Ruler of Sharjah acted at all times in his official capacity and on behalf of his state. In these circumstances, as the *Jimenez* case itself holds, the act of state doctrine applies.

Conclusion

. . . . [T]he questioning of sovereign acts by the complaint results in its failure to state a claim upon which relief may be granted. . . . [A]ny misconstruction, in the briefs, of the act of state doctrine's import does not foreclose proper disposition of the motion.

The Buttes defendants' motion to dismiss will be granted for failure to state a claim upon which relief may be granted.

. . . .

International Association of Machinists and Aerospace Workers (IAM) v. The Organization of Petroleum Exporting Countries (OPEC)

649 F.2d 1354 (9th Cir. 1981)

Choy, Circuit Judge:

I. INTRODUCTION

The members of the International Association of Machinists and Aerospace Workers (IAM) were disturbed by the high price of oil and petroleum-derived products in the United States. They believed the actions of the Organization of the Petroleum Exporting Countries, popularly known as OPEC, were the cause of this burden on the American public. Accordingly, IAM sued OPEC and its member nations in December of 1978, alleging that their price-setting activities violated United States anti-trust laws. IAM sought injunctive relief and damages. The district court entered a final judgment in favor of the defendants, holding that it lacked jurisdiction and that IAM had no valid anti-trust claim. We affirm the judgment of the district court on the alternate ground that, under the act of state doctrine, exercise of federal court jurisdiction in this case would be improper.

II. FACTUAL BACKGROUND

IAM is a non-profit labor association. Its members work in petroleum-using industries, and like most Americans, they are consumers of gasoline and other petroleum-derived products. They object to the high and rising cost of such products.

OPEC is an organization of the petroleum-producing and exporting nations of what is sometimes referred to as the Third World. The OPEC nations have organized to obtain the greatest possible economic returns for a special resource which they hope will remove them from the ranks of the underdeveloped and the poverty-plagued. OPEC was formed in 1960 by the defendants Iran, Iraq, Kuwait, Saudi Arabia, and Venezuela. The other defendants, Algeria, Ecuador, Gabon, Indonesia, Libya, Nigeria, Qatar, and the United Arab Emirates, joined thereafter.

The OPEC nations produce and export oil either through government-owned companies or through government participation in private companies. Prior to the formation of OPEC, these diverse and sometimes antagonistic countries were plagued with fluctuating oil prices. Without coordination among them, oil was often in oversupply on the world market resulting in low prices. The OPEC nations realized that self-interest dictated that they "formulate a system to ensure the stabilization of prices by, among other means, the regulation of production, with due regard to the interests of the producing and of the consuming nations, and to the necessity of securing a steady income to the producing countries, an efficient economic and regular supply of this source of energy to consuming nations...." OPEC Resolution of the First Conference, Resolution 1.1(3), September 1960.

OPEC achieves its goals by a system of production limits and royalties which its members unanimously adopt. There is no enforcement arm of OPEC. The force behind OPEC decrees is the collective self-interest of the 13 nations.

After formation of OPEC, it is alleged, the price of crude oil increased tenfold and more. Whether or not a causal relation exists, there is no doubt that the price of oil has risen dramatically in recent years, and that this has become of international concern.

Supporters of OPEC argue that its actions result in fair world prices for oil, and allow OPEC members to achieve a measure of economic and political independence. Without OPEC, they say, in the rush to the marketplace these nations would rapidly deplete their only valuable resource for ridiculously low prices.

Detractors accuse OPEC of price-fixing and worse in its deliberate manipulation of the world market and withholding of a resource which many world citizens have not learned to do without.

In December 1978, IAM brought suit against OPEC and its member nations. IAM's complaint alleged price fixing in violation of the Sherman Act, 15 U.S.C. § 1, and requested treble damages and injunctive relief under the Clayton Act, 15 U.S.C. §§ 15, 16. IAM claimed a deliberate targeting and victimization of the United States market, directly resulting in higher prices for Americans.

The defendants refused to recognize the jurisdiction of the district court, and they did not appear in the proceedings below. Their cause was argued by various amici, with additional information provided by court-appointed experts. The district court ordered a full hearing, noting that the Foreign Sovereign Immunities Act (FSIA) prohibits the entry of a default judgment against a foreign sovereignty "unless the claimant establishes his claim or right to relief by evidence satisfactory to the court." 28 U.S.C. § 1608(e).

. . . .

At the close of the trial, the district judge granted judgment in favor of the defendants. The court held, first, that it lacked jurisdiction over the defendant nations under the Foreign Sovereign Immunities Act. The court further held that even if jurisdiction existed in the first instance, the anti-trust action failed because foreign sovereigns are not persons within the meaning of the Sherman Act and because there was no proximate causal connection between OPEC activities and domestic price increases. The court also decided that default judgment could not properly lie against the non-appearing defendants, and that the defendants had not waived their immunity.

III. DISCUSSION

A. *Sovereign Immunity*

In the international sphere each state is viewed as an independent sovereign, equal in sovereignty to all other states. It is said that an equal holds no power of sovereignty over an equal. Thus the doctrine of sovereign immunity: the courts of one state generally have no jurisdiction to entertain suits against another state. This rule of international law developed by custom among nations. Also by custom, an exception developed for the commercial activities of a state. The former concept of absolute sovereign immunity gave way to a restrictive view. Under the restrictive theory of sovereign immunity, immunity did not exist for commercial activities since they were seen as non-sovereign.

In 1976, Congress enacted the FSIA and declared that the federal courts will apply an objective nature-of-the-fact test in determining whether activity is commercial and thus not immune: "The commercial character of an activity shall be determined by reference to the nature of the course of conduct or particular transaction or act, rather than by reference to its purpose." 28 U.S.C. § 1603(d).

A critical step in characterizing the nature of a given activity is defining exactly what that activity is. The immunity question may be determined by how broadly or narrowly that activity is defined. In this case, IAM insists on a very narrow focus on the specific activity of "price fixing." IAM argues that the FSIA does not give immunity to this activity. Under the FSIA a commercial activity is one which an individual might "customarily carr[y] on for profit." H.R.Rep.No.94-1487, 94th Cong., 2d Sess. 16, *reprinted in* [1976] U.S.CODE CONG. & AD.NEWS 6604, 6615. OPEC's activity, characterized by IAM as making agreements to fix prices, is one which is presumably done for profit; it is thus commercial and immunity does not apply.

The court below defined OPEC's activity in a different way: "[I]t is clear that the nature of the activity engaged in by each of these OPEC member countries is the establishment by a sovereign state of the terms and conditions for the removal of a prime natural resource—to wit, crude oil—from its territory." The trial judge reasoned that, according to international law, the development and control of natural resources is a prime governmental function. The opinion cites several resolutions of the United Nations' General Assembly, which the United States supported, and the United States Constitution, Art. 4, § 3, cl. 2, which treat the control of natural resources as governmental acts.

IAM argues that the district court's analysis strays from the path set forth in the FSIA. The control of natural resources is the purpose behind OPEC's actions, but the act complained of here is a conspiracy to fix prices. The FSIA instructs us to look upon the act itself rather than underlying sovereign motivations.

The district court was understandably troubled by the broader implications of an anti-trust action against the OPEC nations. The importance of the alleged price-fixing activity to the OPEC nations cannot be ignored. Oil revenues represent their only significant source of income. Consideration of their sovereignty cannot be separated from their near total dependence upon oil. We find that these concerns are appropriately addressed by application of the act of state doctrine. While we do not apply the doctrine of sovereign immunity, its elements remain relevant to our discussion of the act of state doctrine.

B. *The Act of State Doctrine*

The act of state doctrine declares that a United States court will not adjudicate a politically sensitive dispute which would require the court to judge the legality of the sovereign act of a foreign state. This doctrine was expressed by the Supreme Court in *Underhill v. Hernandez*, 168 U.S. 250, 252 (1897):

> Every sovereign State is bound to respect the independence of every other sovereign State, and the courts of one country will not sit in judgment on the acts of the government of another done within its own territory.

The doctrine recognizes the institutional limitations of the courts and the peculiar requirements of successful foreign relations. To participate adeptly in the global community, the United States must speak with one voice and pursue a careful and deliberate foreign policy. The political branches of our government are able to consider the competing economic and political considerations and respond to the public will in order to carry on foreign relations in accordance with the best interests of the country as a whole. The courts, in contrast, focus on single disputes and make decisions on the basis of legal principles. The timing of our decisions is largely a result of our caseload and of the random tactical considerations which motivate parties to bring lawsuits and to seek delay or expedition. When the courts engage in piecemeal adjudication of the legality of the sovereign acts of states, they risk disruption of our country's international diplomacy. The executive may utilize protocol, economic sanction, compromise, delay, and persuasion to achieve international objectives. Ill-timed judicial decisions challenging the acts of foreign states could nullify these tools and embarrass the United States in the eyes of the world.

The act of state doctrine is similar to the political question doctrine in domestic law. It requires that the courts defer to the legislative and executive branches when those branches are better equipped to resolve a politically sensitive question. Like the political question doctrine, its applicability is not subject to clear definition. The courts balance various factors to determine whether the doctrine should apply.

While the act of state doctrine has no explicit source in our Constitution or statutes, it does have "constitutional underpinnings." *Banco Nacional de Cuba v. Sabbatino*, 376 U.S. 398 (1964). The Supreme Court has stated that the act of state doctrine

> arises out of the basic relationships between branches of government in a sys-
> tem of separation of powers.... The doctrine as formulated in past decisions
> expresses the strong sense of the Judicial Branch that its engagement in the
> task of passing on the validity of foreign acts of state may hinder rather than
> further this country's pursuit of goals both for itself and for the community of
> nations as a whole in the international sphere. *Id.*

The principle of separation of powers is central to our form of democratic government. Just as the courts have carefully guarded their primary role as interpreters of the Constitution and the laws of the United States, so have they recognized the primary role of the President and Congress in resolution of political conflict and the adoption of foreign policy.

The doctrine of sovereign immunity is similar to the act of state doctrine in that it also represents the need to respect the sovereignty of foreign states. The two doctrines differ, however, in significant respects. The law of sovereign immunity goes to the jurisdiction of the court. The act of state doctrine is not jurisdictional. Rather, it is a prudential doctrine designed to avoid judicial action in sensitive areas. Sovereign immunity is a principle of international law, recognized in the United States by statute. It is the states themselves, as defendants, who may claim sovereign immunity. The act of state doctrine is a domestic legal principle, arising from the peculiar role of American courts. It recognizes not only the sovereignty of foreign states, but also the spheres of power of the co-equal branches of our government. Thus a private litigant may raise the act of state doctrine, even when no sovereign state is a party to the action. *See, e.g., Timberlane Lumber Co. v. Bank of America*, 549 F.2d 597, 606 (9th Cir. 1976). The act of state doctrine is apposite whenever the federal courts must question the legality of the sovereign acts of foreign states.

It has been suggested that the FSIA supersedes the act of state doctrine, or that the amorphous doctrine is limited by modern jurisprudence. We disagree.

Congress in enacting the FSIA recognized the distinction between sovereign immunity and the act of state doctrine. Indeed, because the act of state doctrine addresses concerns central to our system of government, the doctrine must necessarily remain a part of our jurisprudence unless and until such time as a radical change in the role of the courts occurs.

The act of state doctrine is not diluted by the commercial activity exception which limits the doctrine of sovereign immunity. While purely commercial activity may not rise to the level of an act of state, certain seemingly commercial activity will trigger act of state considerations. As the district court noted, OPEC's "price-fixing" activity has a significant sovereign component. While the FSIA ignores the underlying purpose of a state's action, the act of state doctrine does not. This court has stated that the motivations of the sovereign must be examined for a public interest basis.

Timberlane, 549 F.2d at 607. When the state *qua state* acts in the public interest, its sovereignty is asserted. The courts must proceed cautiously to avoid an affront to that sovereignty. Because the act of state doctrine and the doctrine of sovereign immunity address different concerns and apply in different circumstances, we find that the act of state doctrine remains available when such caution is appropriate, regardless of any commercial component of the activity involved.

In addition to the public interest factor, a federal court must heed other indications which call for act of state deference. The doctrine does not suggest a rigid rule of application. In the *Sabbatino* case, the Supreme Court suggested a balancing approach:

> some aspects of international law touch more sharply on national nerves than do others; the less important the implications of an issue are for our foreign relations, the weaker the justification for exclusivity in the political branches. 376 U.S. at 428, 84 S.Ct. at 940.

The decision to deny access to judicial relief is not one we make lightly. In *Timberlane Lumber Co. v. Bank of America*, 549 F.2d 597, 606 (9th Cir. 1976), this court noted that "not every case is identical in its potential impact on our relations with other nations." The "touchstone" or "crucial element" is the potential for interference with our foreign relations. *Timberlane*, 549 F.2d at 607. This court has stated:

> we do not wish to challenge the sovereignty of another nation, the wisdom of its policy, or the integrity and motivation of its action. On the other hand, repeating the terms of *Sabbatino*, "the less important the implications of an issue are for our foreign relations, the weaker the justification for exclusivity in the political branches." *Id*.

There is no question that the availability of oil has become a significant factor in international relations. The growing world energy crisis has been judicially recognized in other cases. The record in this case contains extensive documentation of the involvement of our executive and legislative branches with the oil question. IAM does not dispute that the United States has a grave interest in the petro-politics of the Middle East, or that the foreign policy arms of the executive and legislative branches are intimately involved in this sensitive area. It is clear that OPEC and its activities are carefully considered in the formulation of American foreign policy.

The remedy IAM seeks is an injunction against the OPEC nations. The possibility of insult to the OPEC states and of interference with the efforts of the political branches to seek favorable relations with them is apparent from the very nature of this action and the remedy sought. While the case is formulated as an anti-trust action, the granting of any relief would in effect amount to an order from a domestic court instructing a foreign sovereign to alter its chosen means of allocating and profiting from its own valuable natural resources. On the other hand, should the court hold that OPEC's actions are legal, this "would greatly strengthen the bargaining hand" of the OPEC nations in the event that Congress or the executive chooses to condemn OPEC's actions. *Sabbatino*, 376 U.S. at 432.

A further consideration is the availability of internationally-accepted legal principles which would render the issues appropriate for judicial disposition. As the Supreme Court stated in *Sabbatino*,

> It should be apparent that the greater the degree of codification or consensus concerning a particular area of international law, the more appropriate it is for the judiciary to render decisions regarding it, since the courts can then focus on the application of an agreed principle to circumstances of fact rather

than on the sensitive task of establishing a principle not inconsistent with the national interest or with international justice. 376 U.S. at 428...

While conspiracies in restraint of trade are clearly illegal under domestic law, the record reveals no international consensus condemning cartels, royalties, and production agreements. The United States and other nations have supported the principle of supreme state sovereignty over natural resources. The OPEC nations themselves obviously will not agree that their actions are illegal. We are reluctant to allow judicial interference in an area so void of international consensus. An injunction against OPEC's alleged price-fixing activity would require condemnation of a cartel system which the community of nations has thus far been unwilling to denounce. The admonition in *Sabbatino* that the courts should consider the degree of codification and consensus in the area of law is another indication that judicial action is inappropriate here.

The district court was understandably reluctant to proceed on the complaint below and the act of state doctrine provides sound jurisprudential support for such reluctance. While the act of state doctrine does not compel dismissal as a matter of course, in a case such as this where the controlling issue is the legality of a sovereign act and where the only remedy sought is barred by act of state considerations dismissal is appropriate.

IV. CONCLUSION

The act of state doctrine is applicable in this case. The courts should not enter at the will of litigants into a delicate area of foreign policy which the executive and legislative branches have chosen to approach with restraint. The issue of whether the FSIA allows jurisdiction in this case need not be decided, since a judicial remedy is inappropriate regardless of whether jurisdiction exists. Similarly, we need not reach the issues regarding the indirect-purchaser rule, the extra-territorial application of the Sherman Act, the definition of "person" under the Sherman Act, and the propriety of injunctive relief.

The decision of the district court dismissing this action is *Affirmed*.

VII. Harmonizing International Antitrust Law?

Documents Supplement References:

NAFTA *Chapter 15*

NOTE ON THE KODAK-FUJI CASE

Just how broad is the legal regime established by the General Agreement on Tariffs and Trade (GATT) and World Trade Organization (WTO)? Does it, or should it, for example, reach competition policy issues? Private sector restrictive business practices? Tacit government support for such practices?

These issues were brought to the fore in May 1995. The Eastman Kodak Co., the world's largest producer of photographic film and paper, filed a Section 301 petition claiming that systematic anti-competitive practices committed by the Japanese photographic products industry, most notably Kodak's arch-rival the Fuji Photo Film Co., had effectively locked Kodak out of Japan's consumer photographic film and paper market since the 1970s. The United States Trade Representative (USTR) accepted the petition and commenced an investigation pursuant to Section 301(a) of the Trade Act of 1974, as amended, in July 1995 to determine whether Japan's acts, policies, or practices were unjustifiable (*i.e.*, in violation of, or inconsistent with, the international legal rights of the United States) or unreasonable (*i.e.*, while not in violation of these rights, otherwise unfair or inequitable, such as by denying fair and equitable market opportunities through the toleration of anti-competitive practices). Thus began a highly impolite exchange of charges and counter-charges between Kodak and Fuji, and yet another charged trade dispute between the Clinton Administration and the government of former Prime Minister Ryutaro Hashimoto. The result was a stinging American defeat at the WTO whose considerable proportions have yet to be gauged.

The United States and Japan are the first and second largest markets, respectively, in the world for consumer photographic products. (China is expected to replace Japan by the end of the century.) Ironically, Kodak and Fuji are similar in key respects. They are the industry giants: Kodak has 36 percent of the world film market, and a worldwide operating profit margin between 1975-94 of 13 percent; Fuji has 33 percent of the world market and a 15.5 percent margin. The two companies predominate in different parts of the world, and different niches of the market. Neither company wants to cut prices to pinch the other's market share. In effect, they behave as monopolists or oligopolists, depending on the market.

Kodak trotted out market share statistics to support its petition. In many countries other than Japan, its share of the color-film market is 40 percent or higher. In the EU, for instance, it is 40 percent. Yet in Japan, though it invested $750 million, Kodak has only an 8-9 percent share, whereas Fuji has a 70 percent share. In contrast, Fuji has a 12 percent share of the American market. (Fuji disputed these figures, saying each company has about 10 percent of the other's home market, and pointed out that Kodak holds a 70 percent stake in the United States. It also recalled that in 1993 Kodak brought a successful antidumping action, noted below, in an effort to drive Fuji from the American photographic paper market.) Kodak also observed that more than 50 percent of all film sales in Japan are made by thousands of small photospecialty stores and kiosks. While Kodak is the world's leading brand, it is carried in only 30-50 percent of these retailers. In contrast, retail outlets sell more than 80 percent of all film in the United States, and they carry Fuji, Konica, Agfa, Ilford, and/or 3M alongside Kodak film.

Despite citing market share statistics, Kodak wisely eschewed calling for a specific market share target. It knew the Japanese government regretted acquiescing to a 20 percent target in the semi-conductor dispute during the late 1980s, and thus had refused to guarantee a target in 1995 in its raucous auto trade dispute with the United States. (These disputes are discussed in Chapter 11 of the Casebook.) Kodak simply cried for a level playing field in Japan.

Among the practices chronicled in Kodak's nearly 300 page Section 301 petition were (1) clandestine rebates (in the form of cash payments) to distributors in exchange for not carrying competing products, (2) threats of boycotts against distributors or retailers for selling imported products, (3) resale price maintenance at an artificially high level through meticulous monitoring of distributors and retailers, and (4) horizontal price-fixing through pressure on retailers not to discount their prices of Fuji film and prints. Kodak claimed these practices are made possible by Fuji's stranglehold on the Japanese distribution channels for consumer film and photographic paper. In the United States, Kodak and other film companies sell directly to retailers. But, in Japan 70 percent of photographic products pass to retailers through four main distributors, called *tokuyakuten*. Fuji has exclusive agreements with the *tokuyakuten* that create inseverable financial, operational, and technical, as well as legal, ties — a vertical relationship

—that lock out competitors. In fact, Fuji holds equity in two of the *tokuyakuten*, and in several banks that lend to the *tokuyakuten*. Fuji's control of 430 Japanese photofinishing labs, to which Fuji is the exclusive supplier, also facilitated Fuji's anti-competitive practices. Thus, two-thirds of Japan's 280,000 retailers do not sell imported film, and in 30 years the import share in Japan's film market hardly has changed.

Kodak alleged the Japanese government, particularly the Ministry of International Trade and Industry (MITI) and the Japan Fair Trade Commission (JFTC), knew of and participated in the anti-competitive practices. The JFTC, for instance, issues warnings to stores against price discounts or promotions of non-Fuji products, and fails to enforce Japan's Anti-Monopoly Law against Fuji's practices. MITI stands idly by tolerating these practices. (It is worth keeping in mind that in January 1997 the *Financial Times* reported that the United States Department of Justice declined Fuji's request to investigate Kodak's dubious marketing methods, which are discussed below.) Indeed, MITI and the JFTC, said Kodak, acted deliberately to offset Japan's market-liberalizing commitments in the Kennedy and Tokyo Rounds—particularly the dismantling of the tariff wall that protected Fuji and other Japanese companies.

Kodak tried to woo public opinion in Japan and elsewhere. It said Fuji's government-condoned anti-competitive practices translated into an average Fuji film price in Japan that was at least twice the Fuji film price in the United States. Kodak calculated these practices had cost it $5.6 billion in lost revenue in Japan since 1975, while enabling Fuji to accumulate a $10 billion war chest to support illegal dumping in the United States, EU, and Korea. Kodak said Japanese consumers suffered from unnecessarily high prices, and suggested consumers in other countries would be worse off in the long run if Fuji's dumping drove its competitors out of business and Fuji thereafter charged monopoly prices.

Fuji spit back at Kodak in July 1995 with a 585 page rebuttal entitled *Rewriting History*. Kodak's lackluster performance in Japan is a result of its own marketing blunders, said Fuji. Kodak's products are sold at fewer Japanese stores than are Fuji's products not because Fuji has a lock on distribution, but because Kodak ignored Japan until 1984, when Fuji sponsored the Olympic games in Los Angeles. Thereafter, Kodak concentrated only on major cities such as Tokyo and Osaka, and on large retail stores. (While Kodak has a separate stand-alone corporate entity for Greater China, *i.e.*, China, Hong Kong, and Taiwan, it was not until October 1996 - after the WTO action discussed below was commenced - that Kodak created such an entity for Japan. Until then, its Japanese operations were tossed into its Asia-Pacific Region section.) Indeed, Kodak had not approached the *tokuyakuten* in 20 years.

In contrast, Fuji pointed out that its employees are located throughout Japan, and they visit small shops, providing sales promotional and technical assistance. Fuji cited the case of Asanuma & Co., a Japanese distributor, as an illustration of Kodak's foolish squandering of marketing opportunities. In 1973, Asanuma asked Kodak to supply it directly instead of compelling it to buy through a single importer. Kodak refused. In 1975, Asanuma ceased carrying Kodak products and became a Fuji distributor. (Kodak blamed the Japanese government, saying it forced Kodak to use a single importer.) Fuji highlighted the case of Nihon Ryutsu, a group of Japanese retailers with 800 sales outlets, as an illustration of how Kodak can profit from an open Japanese market when it makes an effort. In August 1995, Kodak signed a co-branding pact with Nihon to sell film carrying both the Kodak name and a Japanese name at half the normal Japanese retail price. (In July 1996, Fuji announced it was buying all of the photofinishing operations of Wal-Mart, the biggest photofinishing service provider in the United States, for about $600 million. Kodak jumped to proclaim the openness of the American market.)

As for the alleged anti-competitive rebates to the *tokuyakuten*, Fuji said these were simply lawful sales promotional aids that amounted to at most 3.1 percent of marginal sales. As for barring the *tokuyakuten* from carrying competitor's products, this charge was a complete fabrication. And, as for cross-shareholding, this arrangement was both common and lawful in Japan. In the United States, Fuji noted, Kodak wholly owned its distribution network.

Fuji called Kodak a self-serving hypocrite. It pointed out it has invested far more in the United States than Kodak's $750 million in Japan: $2 billion overall, about $1 billion of which was to build a facility in Greenwood, S.C. to make film, graphic arts and tape products, photographic paper, and single-use cameras. Yet, Fuji's American market share was no more than 10 percent, whereas Kodak held 70 percent of the American wholesale photofinishing market. Unlike Kodak, Fuji faced tariff barriers: the United States imposes tariffs on color film and color paper imports of about 3.7 percent, whereas such products enter Japan duty-free. Worse yet, at every opportunity Kodak flexes its muscles in its home market, albeit without government collusion, and it might well be a monopolist were it not for the fact that until 1994, it operated under two antitrust consent decrees resulting from its dominance of the American film and photofinishing market. The decrees were lifted only after Kodak argued successfully that the film market is global, not national.

One decree, in place since 1954, barred Kodak from selling film that included photoprocessing costs so as to get a captive market for paper and chemicals, and from entering into the private label market. The other decree, in place since 1921, prohibited Kodak from trying to prevent retailers from selling the products of competitors. In spite of the second decree, Fuji argued, Kodak locked up large portions of the American market by offering retailers up-front payments and rebates, for example, $2.7 million a year to the Army and Air Force Exchange Service (AAFES). As a result, it entered into an exclusivity agreement with AAFES. Kodak also had an exclusivity deal with Eckerd Corp., America's fourth largest outlet for film sales to amateur photographers, with over 1,700 drug stores. Indeed, for over 20 years Eckerd has refused to carry Fuji film. Still another example is Publix, a Florida-based chain of 470 grocery stores that has never carried Fuji film. (Indeed, Kodak seemed oblivious to the hypocrisy of which it was accused. In December 1996—after the WTO case discussed below was commenced—Kodak signed an exclusivity arrangement with America's fifth largest film retailer, Price/Costco Inc., involving a cash payment to Price/Costco and marketing discounts and promotions.) Kodak's reply? All of its exclusivity deals resulted from retailer choice, not coercion by Kodak.

In addition to Fuji's "mirror image" argument, *i.e.*, that Kodak rigged the American market to be at least as anti-competitive as the Japanese market, Fuji aggressively accused Kodak of ignoring Fuji's innovations and Kodak's mismanagement. In 1986, Fuji introduced the first disposable camera. By 1995, that camera accounted for 10 percent of Japan's color film market. In 1989, Fuji introduced a high-speed, high-resolution color film. Consequently, Fuji's market share in Japan jumped from 10 to 40 percent. Not until 1991 did Kodak introduce a competing product, ISO 400. Regarding Kodak's purported $5.6 billion loss figure, Kodak deceptively included expenses associated with several restructuring programs, the spin off of its chemical division, and debt incurred to buy the Sterling Drug Co. Yet, at least by one important yardstick, Kodak really had not done that badly in Japan: in a Japanese amateur photographic market valued in 1994 at $9.7 billion, Kodak's annual revenue exceeded $1 billion, at least $500 million of which came from sales of film and paper.

Kodak was hardly diffident in the face of Fuji's countercharges. In November 1995, it unveiled an 1,100 page, two-volume tome compiling *inter alia* Japanese government memos detailing the extent of that government's alleged measures against Kodak going back to 1964. MITI, for example, promulgated "guidelines" for distributors (1) approving a shortened time period for distributors and retailers to pay their bills to Fuji so as to increase their dependence on Fuji, and (2) recommending rebates to strengthen relationships between domestic companies and distributors. In 1982, the government allowed six domestic industry organizations to form the "All Japan Photo Industry Fair Trade Promotion Council" and draft a code calling for resale price maintenance to ensure average gross profits of at least 8 percent and thwart any attempt by Kodak to gain market share by trying to lower its prices.

In August 1996, Kodak also struck back at Fuji by filing a complaint against it with the JFTC, requesting it to investigate Fuji's anti-competitive practices (but thereby tacitly admitting the JFTC could be part of the solution). In July 1997, the JFTC issued the results of its investigations. First, it found Japan's photographic film and paper market was not inaccessible to foreign companies. While the JFTC's report found seven *tokuyakuten* carried Fuji products exclusively, Fuji had not forced such an arrangement. Moreover, Kodak, Konica, and other Fuji competitors had similar arrangements with other distributors. In brief, there was no distribution bottleneck.

Second, the JFTC found Fuji had not violated Japan's Anti-Monopoly Law. Fuji had not abused its equity stakes in the *tokuyakuten* by impairing their independent business judgement, nor had it provided any financing to them since 1965, and then only on one occasion. Still, the JFTC warned Fuji to continue to behave at arm's length.

Third, the JFTC said Fuji's rebates to distributors, whereby larger rebates were given for higher sales volumes, were lawful, partly because the degree of progressivity of the rebates was mild. Still, the JFTC ordered Fuji to revise its sales incentive system so as to lessen the dependence of distributors on Fuji.

Unsatisfied with the JFTC's work, Kodak called its report a whitewash. The USTR accused the JFTC of being neither strong nor independent, and dubbed its report woefully insufficient. MITI shot back that the USTR's comments were immoderate.

The vituperative arguments aside, the United States would have committed a monstrous political blunder in pursuing a Section 301 investigation, but not a simultaneous WTO case. It had been roundly criticized for failing to take its 1995 auto trade dispute with Japan to the WTO. After all, if the DSU was not used by major trading nations for serious disputes — especially by the nation that had fought hardest in the Uruguay Round for a meaningful multilateral dispute resolution mechanism — but only for small matters between less significant powers, then what good was it? Moreover, this time Section 301 did not force the Japanese to the bargaining table: the Japanese government refused to negotiate under the threat of sanctions. Finally, the Kodak-Fuji dispute seemed to present an opportunity not only for a two-pronged GATT-based attack: (1) a GATT Article XXIII:1(a) violation nullification and impairment argument, namely, violation of the GATT Article III national treatment principle as a result of a legally-condoned restrictive distribution system, and (2) a GATT Article XXIII:1(b) non-violation nullification or impairment argument, namely, that the benefits of Japan's tariff-reduction commitments were undermined not by a GATT violation *per se*, but by Japan's toleration of Fuji's anti-competitive practices.

Accordingly, in June 1996 the United States changed tactics. Pursuant to Section 301, the USTR found the Japanese government had engaged in unreasonable acts, policies, and practices—namely, tolerating a market structure that impeded American exports of consumer photographic materials and denied fair and equitable market access. But, the USTR also found the Japanese government nullified or impaired benefits accruing to the United States under the *Uruguay Round Multilateral Trade Agreements*. Hence, the USTR invoked the DSU as required under Section 301. The USTR found three allies in its DSU TOC3case: Australia indicated its support for the American WTO action, and the EU and Mexico joined the American action as third parties.

In abandoning the Section 301 route, the United States bowed to the reality of late 20th century global production: sanctions targeted at Japan might have had little effect on Fuji, and backfired against another American film company, Polaroid Corp. Following the 1993 dumping accusation brought by Kodak that led to the imposition of antidumping duties on Fuji's imported photographic paper, Fuji shifted production of the paper to the United States from Japanese to Dutch plants. By 1997, it was poised to manufacture color film at its new Greenwood, S.C. facilities. As for Polaroid, it held 70 percent of the Japanese market share for instant film. Thus, it was vulnerable were Japan to retaliate against American imports in response to any American sanctions affecting Japanese imports.

Interestingly, in addition to DSU consultations, the United States sought consultations with Japan under the 1960 GATT Working Party *Decision on Arrangements for Consultations on Restrictive Business Practices*, and the EU later joined this request. The *Decision* calls for consultations, but not dispute settlement, among interested governments on private-sector restrictive business practices with a view to eliminating their harmful trade effects. To be sure, such practices are not regulated under the GATT-WTO regime. Japan did not agree to the request until October 1996, and then only on the condition the United States hold reciprocal talks on restrictive American business practices. As a result, this avenue led nowhere.

During the 60-day consultation period mandated by the DSU before recourse to a WTO panel, two defects in the American position became obvious: jurisdiction and persuasiveness. First, was not the heart of the case about competition policy, an area not yet encompassed by the considerable GATT-WTO regime other than by the 1960 GATT Working Party *Decision*? To be sure, the United States emphasized four government-based culprits: (1) MITI's administrative guidelines for the wholesale distribution of photographic film and paper products, which supported a vertical distribution *keiretsu*, (2) a 1967 Japanese cabinet decision to take countermeasures following tariff reductions and investment liberalization, (3) Japan's Law Pertaining to Adjustment of Business Activities of the Retail Industry for Large Scale Retail Stores (LSRS Law), which regulates the opening times, holidays, and floor space for large retailers, the key stores for Kodak insofar as they are most likely to sell imports, and (4) Japan's Law Against Unjustifiable Premiums and Misleading Representations (Premiums Law), which restricts Kodak's ability to use sales incentives (*e.g.*, premiums and promotional offers such as 2-for-1 offers) to encourage retailers to carry its product, and dictates the content of contracts with retailers. The United States argued that both laws were passed with protectionist intent, and the effect of these laws was to deny Kodak and other foreign companies access to Japanese retailers. At stake, claimed the United States, was GATT Article III:4, and Article XVI of the General Agreement on Trade in Services (GATS).

The argument seemed strong. GATT Article III:4, *inter alia*, says that laws and regulations affecting the internal sale of products may not be applied so as to afford protection to a domestic industry. The United States contended the distribution bottlenecks, plus the LSRS Law, were government-condoned differential treatment adversely affecting the ability of foreign film companies like Kodak to market their goods. A fair point indeed. GATS Article XVI makes it impermissible for a WTO Member to impose treatment on a foreign service provider that is less favorable than called for in that Member's Country Schedule. Further, unless otherwise specified in the Schedule, the Member may not impose a restriction on the number of service operations or the total quantity of service output based on an economic needs test (*e.g.*, whether a community needs the service). The United States contended the LSRS Law was based on an economic needs test, and Japan had failed to carve out an exception in its Schedule, hence the Law ran afoul of GATS Article XVI. Again, a fair point.

But, the defect in the American argument was it could be recast too easily and neatly in antitrust terms — and Japan did just that. In the DSU consultations, the Japanese simply replied that MITI's guidelines, the LSRS Law, and the Premiums Law were antitrust matters outside of the present corpus of international trade rules.

The second defect in the American position apparent during the consultation stage was its persuasiveness with respect to differential treatment. Was it not true that the alleged anti-competitive laws and practices in Japan impacted Fuji's domestic competitors just as badly as Kodak and Fuji's other foreign competitors? For example, Konica, the number two Japanese company, had little success in gaining market share against Fuji, because the LSRS Law kept its products, as well as Kodak's, off store shelves. How, then, could the United States maintain that foreign companies were worse off when it seemed that the Japanese government supported Fuji against all of its competitors regardless of their nationality?

Despite these rather insurmountable defects, the warriors at the USTR pressed on. In August 1996, after consultations with Japan failed, the USTR requested and received a WTO panel. The American complaint focused on market access and dwelled on three allegations: (1) the closed Japanese distribution channels, (2) the unavailability of shelf space in Japanese retail stores for foreign film products, and (3) the effective prohibition on foreign film companies offering price rebates to make their product more attractive. The central thrust of the complaint was nullification or impairment of benefits, namely, the systematic collusive support of MITI and the JFTC for Japanese film companies in order to negate Japan's market-opening commitments in the Kennedy and Tokyo Rounds (*i.e.*, removal of tariffs). There was, however, also a non-violation nullification or impairment argument - that the United States was denied the benefit of prior tariff reduction commitments because of Japan's subsequent implementation of anti-competitive measures. But, it seemed halfhearted and left little room for an evaluation of the practices or official government complicity. Perhaps it was for the better, as the USTR must have sensed it was wandering outside the scope of the GATT-WTO regime and into competition policy.

Moreover, possibly sensing weakness in its GATS claim, though arguing it wanted to expand this claim beyond the LSRS Law, the USTR delayed its plan to ask for a second panel to handle the GATS claim. Accordingly, by September 1996 the USTR had divided the complex case procedurally into three parts: (1) a "goods" side focusing on alleged violation of the national treatment principle in GATT Article III as a result of bottlenecks and collusion in the Japanese distribution system, and the operation of the LSRS Law in regulating large retail stores, (2) a "services" side focusing on alleged violations of GATS Article XVI resulting from the LSRS and Premiums Laws, and (3) consultations under the 1960 Working Party *Decision* regarding Fuji's restrictive business practices. As indicated earlier, the third procedure proved ineffectual.

The WTO panel handling the "goods side" of the case consisted of three distinguished experts hailing from Switzerland, New Zealand, and Brazil. In February 1997, the United States presented a 200 page, single-spaced complaint containing 21 specific claims about Japanese government measures, along with 10 volumes of supporting documents. In April 1997, Japan matched Kodak's submissions pound for pound, giving the panel a total of 20,000 pages of evidence in 20 volumes to peruse. In December 1997, on the eve of the panel's decision, Kodak raised the ante once more. It noted a decline in its American market share to 65 percent between 1994-97, an increase in Fuji's share of 3-4 percent annually, and lamented having to lay off nearly 20,000 workers. If the WTO panel did not rule in America's favor, then Kodak would consider bringing a dumping action against Fuji, contending that Fuji film sold in Japan is 170 percent of the price in the United States. The panel rightly ignored Kodak's indecorous pressure.

The long-awaited outcome came with the interim report in December 1997, and issuance of the final report in January 1998 entitled *Japan—Measures Affecting Consumer Photographic Film and Paper*. The WTO panel accepted Japan's arguments in their entirety, thereby dismissing the American complaint. Japan argued successfully that in its voluminous submission the United States had failed to show Japan implemented non-tariff measures designed to counter its tariff liberalization commitments in order block imports of photographic film and paper. Thus, the Americans simply had not proven either violation or non-violation nullification or impairment. The panel agreed that all of the measures of which the United States complained were transparent and aimed at economic modernization, not protection, and many took the form of non-compulsory administrative guidance. The United States could have factored the measures into its negotiations with the Japanese on tariff cuts.

In specific, with respect to the violation nullification or impairment argument, the WTO accepted Japan's denial of the existence of bars to aggressive price, quality, or promotional competition by foreign companies. Japan had highlighted the lack of a correlation between the size of a retail store in Japan and whether the store carries imported film, and the relaxation of many features of the LSRS Law in recent years. Japan also re-iterated arguments that had been made by Fuji in the Section 301 case, namely, that exclusive single-brand wholesaling arrangements are common in the photographic film and paper industry, including in the United States. Most significantly, the panel was moved by Japan's observation that the United States had failed to cite a single Japanese measure that treated imported photographic film or paper differently from like domestic products.

As for the non-violation nullification or impairment argument, the panel agreed with Japan that many of the liberalization countermeasures mentioned by the United States pre-dated the negotiated duty reductions and were no longer in effect. Indeed, Japan said the tariff concessions at issue came in 1979 and 1994 with the Tokyo and Uruguay Rounds, respectively, and did not involve the Kennedy Round. Yet, all of the measures cited by the United States came after the Tokyo or Uruguay Round. What logic was there, Japan suggested, in a non-violation argument not premised on a government measure implemented after a trade concession? To re-state the American argument was to reveal its implausibility: "Japanese measures adopted between 1964-73 nullified Japanese tariff concessions between 1979-94." It would take a devilishly sinister and uniquely farsighted government in Tokyo to concoct ways to undermine trade concessions planned for 10 years later. It would also stand non-violation theory on its head to entertain seriously this fancy.

Moreover, agreed the panel, the key practice of which the United States complained, exclusive single-brand wholesale distribution, existed in Japan before the Japanese government adopted the measures the United States attacked. What logic was there in a non-violation argument where the alleged competitive problem pre-dated the government measures at issue? In other words, Japan and the panel saw immediately why the American non-violation argument was weak: the chronology of events could not possibly support an Article XXIII:1(b) claim. Related to this point was Japan's suggestion that the American complaint confused market share with market access. In 1971, Kodak held 8 percent of the Japanese film and photographic paper market. In that year, Japan implemented a first round of tariff cuts on these products. By 1979, Kodak's market share rose to 14 percent. In 1979, Japan implemented a second round of tariff cuts. Kodak's market share rose to 18 percent by 1983. Yet, the American complaint ignored Kodak's post-tariff cut increases in market share. It focused entirely on Kodak's post-1983 decline in market share — a decline occurring 10-20 years after the emergence of Japan's allegedly anti-competitive measures. For this decline, indicated Japan, again recalling Fuji's arguments, the blame must lie with Kodak's management.

Finally, Japan persuasively indicated that the American complaint was about competition policy, which cannot be raised under the non-violation provision. After all, if it could, then would there not be a slippery slope leading to all sorts of claims not based squarely in the GATT-WTO regime entering through the back door of non-violation into the regime? This point ought to have resonated with the United States, which in the past has weighed in many times in favor of narrow, legalistic interpretations of the GATT texts, and did so again in the *Shrimp-Turtle* case.

The resounding but predictable American defeat in the *Kodak-Fuji* case illustrates a congenital defect in the DSU. There is no check between the consultation and panel stage to ensure that unreasonable positions taken during consultations are abandoned or thwarted at that point. Such positions not only can linger, but gather momentum — often because of political pressures from large firms seeking to shift blame for a declining foreign market share — and generate an unnecessary and potentially destabilizing panel adjudication.

The defeat also illustrates two cultural defects in American participation at the WTO: bad manners and knee-jerk reactions. The USTR attacked the credibility of the WTO, and accused the panel of sidestepping the real issues and focusing on narrow, technical matters. The USTR vowed to consider as binding commitments representations made by Japan in its WTO submission that (1) its market is open, (2) it pursues distribution policies that encourage imports, (3) it does not tolerate anti-competitive behavior and does enforce the Anti-Monopoly Law, (4) it does not discourage the opening of new large retail stores under the LSRS Law and uses only objective criteria to regulate large retail stores under that Law, and (5) it does not restrict retail price competition under the Premiums Law. The USTR set up an interagency committee to monitor developments in Japan, and if Japan failed to live up to these "commitments," then the USTR would take action leading to sanctions. (Japan replied it would not comply with the committee. To be fair to the USTR, the EU later backed the USTR's pledge to hold Japan to its words.) Several members of Congress demanded unilateral sanctions against Japan, and claiming internationalism works against American interests, mortally wounded President Clinton's bid for renewal of fast-track negotiating authority (discussed below). Kodak's Chairman and Chief Executive Officer called the panel report totally unacceptable, and Kodak's Director of

International Trade Relations, forgetting about the 1996 *Japan Liquor Tax* decision (discussed below), said the WTO put its head in the sand and was institutionally incapable of dealing with Japanese trade barriers. Kodak's law firm accused the WTO of exceeding its mandate and competence: the Secretariat is supposed to assist DSU panels, but the firm said it actually made most of the decisions in the case.

Fortunately, upon reflection, the USTR chose not to appeal. For its part, Japan announced plans to abolish the LSRS Law, and revise the Premiums Law by ending limits on promotional offers between businesses and reducing restrictions on the value of promotions that can be made to consumers. And, in July 1998, Kodak announced its share of the American market for 35 mm film had ceased sliding, and indeed was now growing.

NOTE ON GLOBAL COMPETITION POLICY*

I. INTRODUCTION

This Note is a *brief* overview of the raucous contemporary debate about establishing a multilateral, global competition policy, perhaps under the auspices of the World Trade Organization ("WTO"). As used in this Note, the phrase "competition policy" includes antitrust enforcement, restrictive business practices, merger and acquisition regulatory policy, and the regulation of business practices that may distort or impede trade.

Traditionally, competition law has been the prerogative of each sovereign state. Many differences exist in the levels of development of national competition policies ranging from the most developed countries, which often have well established, functioning competition laws to some of the less developed countries (LDCs), which lack any competition law. Many LDCs are beginning discussions about, or have started the process of, implementing a competition policy. For example, as a result of the economic crisis occurring in Indonesia in 1997-1998, the government of Indonesia agreed, as a condition to receiving financial assistance, to enact competition laws as a condition of receiving International Monetary Fund assistance.

Several variables have led members of business, government and academia to call for the establishment of a more global competition policy. This increased interest in global competition policy is a natural result of the ever-more integrated nature of the global market, the cross-border effects corporations have on countries outside of their "home" country, and the uncertainty faced by businesses as countries increasingly fumble about to apply their competition laws to behavior outside their borders. This renewed interest in establishing a global competition policy is likely to lead to *some* competition policy agreement, however, the shape of such an agreement is still very unclear.

The need for international competition policy arises for several reasons, including the absence of global welfare concerns in the decision making process of most national competition policy, the substitution of competition policy as a barrier to trade, the existence of imperfect markets, and the practical experience that, even in the global market with low trade barriers and many players, the need for competition policy still exists. Different ideas about the role and purpose of competition policy make a unified, multilateral, global competition policy difficult to create in the short-run. However, given the GATT and WTO successes in progressively eliminating explicit trade barriers, the WTO may well be the best forum for developing a multilat-

* The assistance of Doug Dziak, Esq. in preparing this Note is gratefully acknowledged.

eral competition policy, even if such policies do not involve the creation of supranational global competition policy. With goals such as the reducing in the abuse of competition policy as a protectionist device, easing the regulatory burden of global businesses trying to meet different requirements established by several legal regimes, and protecting and enhancing global consumer welfare, the WTO could work to develop a successful multilateral competition policy. This global development is not precluded by the existence of bilateral agreements between countries in the area of competition policy. The WTO might be well served to use the experience of the various bilateral agreements to develop a more globally-based competition policy.

This Note favors the creation of an international competition policy agreement, which includes a positive comity requirement, an information sharing agreement, a notification agreement, and a requirement that countries without competition policy will create such laws over a set period of time. An international competition policy agreement does not need to harmonize completely the competition laws of signatory members. Such an agreement will garner little support and would surely fail.

II. NO MULTILATERAL AGREEMENT ON COMPETITION POLICY CURRENTLY EXISTS

Presently, there is no international multilateral agreement on competition policy, despite the existence of several multilateral and bilateral agreements on competition policy.[1] While the creation of these multilateral and bilateral agreements is attributable to the growing number of regional trade blocs and the increase in global trade,[2] the absence of a global multilateral competition policy is not surprising. The absence of a multilateral agreement is attributable to several factors: the variety of legal regimes governing competition policy;[3] different theories regarding the objective(s) of competition law;[4] and the failure of earlier attempts to establish a global competition policy.[5]

Before beginning an in depth discussion of competition policy it would seem necessary to discuss what competition policy actually regulates. The most common areas of competition policy regulation include horizontal agreements, mergers, vertical market restraints and abuse of dominate position. Horizontal restraints are considered harmful because they involve the setting of prices above the competitive level, either by specific price, market allocation or reductions in output. These practices allow market participants to distort imperfect markets and capture above normal profits. Mergers are often regulated, because they can have the tendency to reduce competition between competitors. The scrutiny a merger receives from regulators usually depends on whether the merger is horizontal (involves direct competitors) or vertical (involves the chain of production and distribution for a product). Horizontal mergers are often given the greatest scrutiny because they eliminate competition in a market and can harm consumer welfare.[6] Vertical market restraints are scrutinized often because they include restrictive behavior between upstream and downstream firms. These relationships can lead to restrictions that effect interbrand com-

---

1. *See* WORLD TRADE ORGANIZATION, ANNUAL REPORT 1997, vol. 1, 32 (1997).
2. *See* WTO ANNUAL REPORT, *supra*, at 31.
3. *See* WTO ANNUAL REPORT, *supra*, at 43-48.
4. *See* WTO ANNUAL REPORT, *supra*, at 38-39.
5. *See* Spencer Weber Waller, *The Internationalization of Antitrust Enforcement*, 77 B.U. L. Rev. 343, 349-52 (1997).
6. *See* U.S. DEPARTMENT OF JUSTICE & FEDERAL TRADE COMMISSION, HORIZONTAL MERGER GUIDELINES (1992) (discussing problems with various types of mergers).

petition, which can harm consumers. Abuse of dominant position arises when a firm uses its market position to maintain, exploit or otherwise abuse their position as a monopolist or dominant market member.[7]

A. Different Legal Regimes Governing Competition Policy

A variety of competition policy regimes exist around the world. Some countries have no competition laws. Other countries are in the process of adopting competition laws, or have just enacted competition laws. Still other countries have well-established competition laws.

Category #1: Countries Without Competition Laws

According to the WTO, 70 countries have enacted competition laws, which meant that many countries have yet to enact such laws.[8] The countries without competition laws are usually less developed countries (LDCs), economies in transition from socialism, or both.[9] Some of the countries without competition laws have permitted significant concentrations of economic power under the assumption that large domestic corporations will act as national champions. However, the lack of competition policy has been counter productive, and may even have harmed the competitive position of some of these countries. Their domestic monopolies have not been exposed to international competition, and thus cannot compete with corporations from other countries that have not been protected from the rigors of free trade and investment. The World Bank, finally recognizing the importance of competitive domestic markets to a robust economy, required Indonesia, as a condition of receiving emergency funding to help stem its 1997 economic crisis, to agree to enact a domestic competition law.[10] Such conditional assistance is based on a theory that competition law is necessary to resolve financial problems: without effective competition law industries that are protected from competition will remain inefficient and uncompetitive in the global economy.[11]

Developing countries without competition law have opposed the WTO's efforts to establish a multilateral agreement on competition policy. Some LDCs recommend the matter be taken up at the regional level instead of multilateral level.[12] These countries worry they lack the necessary bureaucratic resources to implement a multilateral agreement, but avow they are not otherwise attempting to obstruct the negotiation of a global agreement. Indeed, many LDCs are still struggling to implement their obligations under the Uruguay Round and would be unable to shoulder the additional burden of creating a functioning bureaucracy to monitor competition policy, especially given that many would be creating competition policy from scratch.[13] LDCs also worry they may lose control because local monopolies, which theoretically can be controlled by an LDC, may lose market share to larger multinational

---

7. *See* WTO ANNUAL REPORT, *supra*, at 40-42.

8. *See* WTO ANNUAL REPORT, *supra*, at 31. *See also A Brief Overview of Competition Law and Policy in Selected South/South-East Asian Countries*, INT'L BUS. LAW. 447, 448 (Nov. 1997).

9. *See* WTO ANNUAL REPORT, *supra*, at 46-47.

10. *See Trade/Competition Policy Discussion Needs More Emphasis on Accord*, 15 Int'l Trade Rep. (BNA) 392 (Mar. 4, 1998).

11. *See* WTO ANNUAL REPORT, *supra*, at 47.

12. *See Trade/Competition Policy Discussion Needs More Emphasis on Accord*, 15 Int'l Trade Rep. (BNA) 392 (1998).

13. *See* Gary G. Yerkey, *Developing Nations Still Oppose Taking Up Investment, Competition Policy in WTO, Aide Says*, 13 Int'l Trade Rep. (BNA) 1829 (1996).

corporations (MNCs) from developed countries.[14] This concern suggests a deep-seated but often unspoken suspicion harbored by some LDCs, namely, that any multilateral agreement on competition policy would operate to their detriment. Why? Because it would ratify the dominant competitive positions of MNCs from the United States, Western Europe, and Japan, but would inhibit the development of industry giants from LDCs.

To be sure, LDCs are not the only jurisdictions lacking competition laws, and in some jurisdictions, such laws may not be indispensable to economic development. In 1997, Hong Kong's government refused to enact antitrust or competition laws after concluding a non-legislative approach was more appropriate. The government of Hong Kong, noting Hong Kong's economic success despite the absence of such laws, declared that competition laws are not the only way of assuring a free and open market.[15]

Category #2: Countries With Recently Enacted Competition Laws

Many of the countries of Eastern Europe, Latin America, and Asia recently have enacted competition laws. Some of these laws are modeled on competition laws of other countries. For example, many Eastern European countries have drawn on the competition laws of the European Union (EU) and Germany. The competition laws of many Latin American countries are based on the wider competition law experience of the United States, Canada, as well as the EU.[16]

In Asia, competition laws have been enacted in several countries - notably China in 1993, and Taiwan in 1992. Recently, Korea broadly revised its Monopoly Regulation and Fair Trade Act to strengthen its competition law. The Korean revisions are designed to create a more competitive market structure in areas where monopolies and oligopolies have become entrenched, as well as remove some of the distortions created by the Korean *chaebol* business arrangements.[17]

A key issue yet to be resolved with respect to all countries boasting new competition laws is enforcement. (Of course, as discussed below, the issue is relevant even in countries with established competition laws.) Having a good antitrust statute on the books is no guarantee that authorities will be willing or able to enforce it energetically, particularly against entrenched business interests with high political connections. This issue, in turn, raises the more general concern about "crony capitalism" revealed by the Asian crisis that appears to continue to plague many newly industrializing countries.

Category #3: Countries With Established Competition Laws[18]

The United States, EU, and Japan all have long-established competition laws. Given that firms from these areas comprise a substantial amount of the world's commercial activity, it appears inevitable that American, European, and Japanese support is required for the formation of any meaningful global competition policy. Yet, while

---

14. *See* Jayanth Govindan, *Malaysia: Concerns About Competition Policy*, INT'L BUS. LAW. 467 (Nov. 1997).

15. *See Hong Kong Government Rules Out Antitrust and Competition Measures*, 14 Int'l Trade Rep. (BNA) 1966 (Nov. 11, 1997). Hong Kong did adopt or modify measures designed to increase economic efficiency in its domestic markets, thus assuring companies face competition.

16. *See* WTO ANNUAL REPORT, *supra*, at 46.

17. *See* Soon-Sik Ju, *Korea: Major Changes in the Fair Trade Commission*, INT'L BUS. LAW., 463-64 (Nov. 1997).

18. *See* GLOBAL COMPETITION POLICY (Edward M. Graham & J. David Richardson eds., 1997), for a more detailed discussion of the various competition laws of developed countries.

the United States, EU, and Japan share some of the same fundamental objectives in their competition laws — *i.e.*, maintaining healthy rivalries among firms and safeguarding competitive markets — divergent economic and social objectives can cause differences in the manner in which competition laws are actually applied.[19] Not surprisingly, therefore, no consensus has emerged on the objectives of global competition policy, or even on the best forum for pursuing such policies.[20]

Also not surprisingly, the uneven application of competition policy in countries with well established and similar competition laws creates problems.[21] A celebrated example is the merger between Boeing and McDonnell-Douglas. It created significant trade tensions between the United States and EU, because despite the approval of the merger granted by American antitrust authorities,[22] the EU Commission challenged the merger, and ultimately required Boeing to alter its long-term supply contracts with some United States airline companies.[23] Mindful of the interests of Europe's Airbus consortium, the Commission was concerned that the merger would result in dominance of the commercial aerospace industry by Boeing. The failure of the Commission to approve the Boeing merger, combined with the EU threat of large monetary penalties if the merger was consummated without first receiving its approval, lead to intervention in the matter by President Clinton, and nearly resulted in the United States implementing retaliatory economic measures against the EU.[24] Certainly, despite the trade friction created by the Boeing - McDonnell-Douglas merger, the United States and EU normally collaborate on competition policy and enforcement issues. In fact, the case was as much about trade policies, defense concerns, and national industries as it was about antitrust policy.[25] As intimated above, the Commission's resistance to the merger, and the demands it placed on Boeing, surely were based in part on the EU's desire to keep Airbus competitive in the market for commercial jets.

Japan's competition law was enacted in 1947 in the wake of the post-World War II Allied occupation. The Anti-Monopoly Law ("AML") established the Fair Trade Commission of Japan ("JFTC") as an independent commission to police Japanese industry. It was modeled after the United States Federal Trade Commission.[26] The

---

19. *See* WTO ANNUAL REPORT, *supra*, at 39.

20. *Compare* Guy de Jonquieres, *Van Miert Seeks Global Competition Rules Accord*, FIN. TIMES, Jan. 31, 1998, at 1, and Joel Klein, *No Monopoly on Antitrust*, FIN. TIMES, Feb. 13, 1998, at 24; (contrasting the different views of the EU Competition Commissioner and the United States Assistant Attorney General for the Antitrust Division of Department of Justice regarding forum choice and the need for a global competition policy).

21. *See, e.g.*, *U.S. Urges Japan to Hurry Deregulation, Strengthen Japan Fair Trade Commission*, 12 Int'l Trade Rep. (BNA) 2044 (1995) (observing that differences between American and Japanese competition policy reoccur frequently, usually with American companies complaining that Japan's inadequate enforcement of antitrust law acts as a trade barrier to American firms trying to enter the Japanese market). *See also Study Finds U.S. Executives Skeptical of Japan's Commitment to Open Trade*, 14 Int'l Trade Rep. (BNA) 1060 (1997); Joel Klein, *No Monopoly on Antitrust*, FIN. TIMES, Feb. 13, 1998, at 24.

22. *See* Nancy Dunne & Emma Tucker, *Boeing and McDonnell Merger Approved*, FIN. TIMES, July 3, 1997 at 1.

23. *See* Jeff Cole *et al.*, *Boeing-McDonnell Merger Clears Hurdle*, WALL ST. J., July 24, 1997, at A2.

24. *See* Brian Coleman, *Clinton Hints U.S. May Retaliate if EU Tries to Block Boeing-McDonnell Deal*, WALL ST. J., July 18, 1997, at A2.

25. *See, e.g.*, *Peace in Our Time*, THE ECONOMIST, July 26, 1997, at 59-61; Peter Norman, *Franco-German Summit Calls for Airbus Response to US Threat*, FIN. TIMES, Sept. 20, 1997, at 2.

26. *See* Mitsuo Matsushita, *The Antimonopoly Law of Japan*, *in* GLOBAL COMPETITION POLICY, *supra*, at 151.

AML prohibits price fixing, bid rigging, resale price maintenance, and market-restraining mergers and acquisitions.[27] Yet, Japanese enforcement of its competition laws frequently has been criticized,[28] and the United States has asked Japan to enforce its antitrust laws and strengthen the JFTC in an effort to reduce non-tariff barriers to imported products.[29] Criticism reached a near fever-pitch in the highly politicized case initiated by Kodak against Fuji in which Kodak claimed Fuji had conspired to limit Kodak's market penetration in Japan. (The Kodak-Fuji case is discussed in the Note above.) Kodak's cause ultimately was taken up by the United States Trade Representative, which brought an action in the WTO against Japan. Japan prevailed, and the JFTC cleared Fuji of AML violations.

Criticism of Japanese antitrust enforcement sometimes confuses competition law issues with issues of the structural relationships between Japanese companies. These companies tend not to establish relationships to facilitate horizontal price fixing agreements in attempts to limit inter-brand competition. Instead, these industrial groupings, known as *keirestu*, are the means to develop long-term vertical relationships between manufactures and distributors. Unfortunately for foreign importers, however, these somewhat unique vertical arrangements among Japanese companies do not include them, and thus they sometimes operate to foreclose access to the Japanese market. Increased application of competition law likely will have only limited effects on these industrial arrangements, because there is often intense inter-brand competition between *keirestu* groups. Given the structure of the arrangements and the level of competition in the domestic market, such relationships probably are lawful under the AML.[30] In other words, because the *keirestu* are not cartel like in the traditional antitrust sense of fixing horizontal prices, the traditional antitrust remedies probably are not the solution to the complex Japanese/American competition policy problem.[31]

American antitrust policy aims to protect consumer welfare from injuries to the competitive process, and to increase economic efficiency. American antitrust laws were passed in the face of increasing concentrations of wealth and the perceived inability of state antitrust legislation to deal with problems arising from these concentrations. (As discussed earlier in this Chapter, the key American antitrust statutes are the Sherman Act,[32] the Clayton Act,[33] the Federal Trade Commission Act,[34] the Hart-

---

27. *See, e.g.*, Akinori Yamada, *Japan: the Anti-Monopoly Law*, INT'L BUS. LAW. 459 (Nov. 1997).

28. Many criticisms exist regarding Japanese enforcement of competition policy, and one footnote cannot possibly begin to cover this area. Usually, this criticism is tied to American complaints regarding access to the Japanese market. Many consider the lax enforcement of Japanese competition laws to be one factor contributing to the persistent trade imbalance between the United States and Japan. *See* CLYDE V. PRESTOWITZ, JR., TRADING PLACES: HOW WE ARE GIVING OUR FUTURE TO JAPAN AND HOW TO RECLAIM IT 303 (1988); *See also* Eleanor M. Fox, *Toward World Antitrust and Market Access*, 91 AM. J INT'L L.1, 19-23 (1997) (discussing Japanese distributors and glass manufacturers collaborating to restrict access of foreign firms to Japanese market).

29. *See U.S. Urges Japan to Hurry Deregulation, Strengthen Japan Fair Trade Commission*, 12 Int'l Trade Rep. (BNA) 2044 (1995).

30. *See* Mitsuo Matsushita, *The Antimonopoly Law of Japan, in* GLOBAL COMPETITION POLICY, *supra*, at 151.

31. *See* Paul Sheard, *Keirestu, Competition, and Market Access, in* GLOBAL COMPETITION POLICY, *supra*, at 501, 538-541.

32. *See* 15 U.S.C. §§ 1-7.

33. *See* 15 U.S.C. §§ 12-27.

34. *See* 15 U.S.C. §§ 41-58.

Scott-Rodino Antitrust Improvements Act of 1976,[35] and two laws permitting the creation of export cartels, the Webb-Pomerene Act,[36] and the Export Trading Company Act.[37]) While nothing in the statutory language expressly requires federal courts to consider economic efficiency, both courts and enforcement agencies often weigh efficiency concerns when analyzing cases.[38]

One of the complexities associated with enforcement of antitrust laws in the United States is the concurrent jurisdiction between the Department of Justice (DOJ) and Federal Trade Commission (FTC). Unlike competition laws in the EU and many other places, American antitrust law creates a right of action for states and private parties injured by anti-competitive practices.[39] Further complicating American antitrust law is its litigation-based enforcement mechanisms.

The EU's competition law was born out of the creation of the common market and is based upon notions that national boundaries must be eliminated. The EU competition law was part of the treaty, specifically Articles 85 and 86, that established the European Economic Community.[40] The overriding interest is the creation of an integrated market, with attendant interests in related to small and medium sized firms, raising living standards of worse-off EU member States, and "fairness." In other words, EU competition law is driven by the policy goal of establishing market integration and assuring the free movement of goods and services across countries.[41] Relative to the United States, therefore, the EU is less vigorous in enforcement actions against mergers or cartels. After all, were the EU to be vigorous in these respects, it would inhibit the development of pan-European companies and, therefore, a true cross-border market. However, EU competition law is often less tolerant of restrictive business practices than is American antitrust law. It has been argued that the EU ought to re-evaluate its competition rules in light of the success of the integration of Europe, reform its competition laws, and allow member States to enforce competition laws.[42]

This is not to suggest that competition law in the EU is wholly dissimilar from antitrust law in the United States. There are some substantive commonalities and policy,[43] yet key differences such as those mentioned above persist. Professor Fox offers

---

35. *See* 15 U.S.C. § 18a.

36. *See* 15 U.S.C. §§ 61-66.

37. *See* 15 U.S.C. §§ 4001-4021.

38. *See, e.g.*, Continental T.V. v. GTE Sylvania Inc., 433 U.S. 36 (1977). *See generally* DEPARTMENT OF JUSTICE AND FEDERAL TRADE COMMISSION HORIZONTAL MERGER GUIDELINES § 4 (April 8, 1997).

39. *See* Eleanor M. Fox, *US and EU Competition Law: A Comparison, in* GLOBAL COMPETITION POLICY, *supra*, at 339.

40. Treaty Establishing the European Economic Community, Mar. 25 1957, 298 UNTS 11, *amended by* Treaty Establishing the European Community, Feb 7, 1992, O.J. (C224) 1 (1992), [1992] 1 C.M.L.R. 573 (1992).

41. *See* Fox, *US and EU Competition Law: A Comparison, supra*, at 353; Fox, *Toward World Antitrust and Market Access, supra*, at 5. In the United States, the development of a national economy with effects of business throughout the country lead to the federalization of antitrust law through the Sherman Act. Federal antitrust law was enhanced with the enactment of other substantive laws dealing with competition policies including the Clayton Act (15 U.S.C. §§ 12-27) and Federal Trade Commission Act (15 U.S.C. §§ 41-58). However, the passage of these statutes was preceded by political and economic integration, thus distinguishing the American from European experience.

42. *See* Alberto Pera & Mario Todino, *Enforcement of EC Competition Rules: Need for a Reform?, in* 1996 FORDHAM CORP. L. INST. 125, 148 (B. Hawk ed., 1997).

43. *See* Fox, *US and EU Competition Law: A Comparison, supra*, at 339; *see also* Fox, *Toward World Antitrust and Market Access, supra*, at 1.

still another contrast, namely, that different social concerns and economic policies upon which the two laws were founded have led to differences in enforcement policies.

The lack of harmonization between European and American policy and law serves to explain why, at least for the foreseeable future, the formulation of a multilateral competition law regime under the auspices of the WTO is unrealistic. If the United States and EU, which share so much in common generally, conflict despite the presence of similarities in their policies and laws, then there is no reason to believe a global agreement with a large number of variegated countries is reasonable to expect in the near future. Perhaps Professor Fox's caution is the best that can be hoped for: in the United States-EU context, different competition laws cannot simply be pushed into greater harmony, but commonality ought to be maximized.[44]

B. Different Policy Goals of Competition Law

As suggested above, the primary reason behind the different substantive nature and enforcement patterns of competition law stems from the different policy goals underlying that law.[45] There is a wide range of stated fundamental objectives of competition policy, including (1) protecting consumer welfare by preventing the undue exercise of market power, (2) enhancing economic efficiency, (3) facilitating economic liberalization, (4) preserving and encouraging the development of market economies, (5) sponsoring economic pluralism and the dispersion of socio-economic power, (6) ensuring fairness and equity in marketplace transactions, (7) promoting the public interest including concerns related to industrial competitiveness, and (8) protecting opportunities for small and medium business.[46] Some of these objectives overlap with one another; very often they conflict with each other in fundamental ways requiring choices between the objectives. For example, how can enhancing economic efficiency and the protecting of small and medium-sized business be squared, if efficiency is enhanced by large companies that benefit from internal economies of scale? Commercial practices that result in fewer and larger businesses are quite likely to drive smaller players out of a market.

The view that economic efficiency is the central goal of competition policy is generally attributed to the "Chicago School" of legal and economic scholars.[47] The School accepts the incompatibility of certain policy goals, such as protecting small players and increasing overall efficiency. The School posits that antitrust law ought to aim to maximize consumer welfare. This aim is accomplished by improving allocative efficiency (the allocation of goods and services within the economy), without impairing productive efficiency (the best use of an economy's factors of production, i.e., land, labor, physical capital, human capital, and technology), so that net societal welfare is in-

---

44. See Fox, US and EU Competition Law: A Comparison, supra, at 354.

45. Much of the discussion below centers on theories of competition and competition policy, which have developed largely in the United States and EU. This should not be regarded as an attempt to lessen the role that other countries will have in the development of global competition policy. It merely is reflective of the considerable experience of the United States and EU.

46. See WTO ANNUAL REPORT, supra, at 39.

47. This ideology is often attributed to scholars who either attended or have been associated with the University of Chicago's Law School and/or Department of Economics. Of course, the use of economic analysis is not limited to those with a relationship to this University. For an interesting discussion of the development of the "Chicago school" see Richard A. Posner, The Chicago School of Antitrust Analysis, 127 U. PA. L. REV. 925 (1979).

creased or, at a minimum, not reduced.[48] Robert Bork argues this result is obtained when the law preserves, improves, and reinforces the powerful economic mechanisms that compel business to respond to consumers. The use of analytical economic tools to decide competition issues is critical, because these tools provide a starting point to evaluate the application of antitrust law in light of the articulated policy aim.[49]

However, the view that competition policy is concerned solely with economic efficiency is not shared by all scholars—though it remains in vogue with American antitrust authorities. Competition policy analysis can also include other non-economic factors. One such factor is increasing individual and business freedom by reducing restrictions imposed by the few over the welfare of the group. Another is regulating economic concentration, which of course could in the long-run result in significant government intervention to control this concentration. Still another policy aim is market integration, discussed above in the EU context, which is significant both economically and politically.[50]

C. The Failure of Previous Attempts At Developing a Global Competition Policy

Recent discussions at the WTO about global competition policy are not the first time international organizations have considered the matter. The Havana Charter for the International Trade Organization ("ITO") included international rules for the control of restrictive business practices.[51] Along with the international finance arrangements reached in the Bretton Woods Agreement, the Havana Charter, drafted in 1946-48, was an effort at global economic reconstruction in the wake of World War II. The Havana Charter contained language obligating countries to prevent private or public commercial business practices affecting international trade that would restrain competition, limit access to markets, or foster monopolistic control, if the practice would have harmful effects on the expansion of production or trade and interfere with other objectives of the Charter.[52] However, when Congress indicated to President Truman that it would not pass the ITO Charter, the Charter died. The world trading system was left with a "provisional" agreement, the General Agreement on Tariffs and Trade ("GATT"), which contained no competition rules.[53] The ITO's death resulted from several factors, including overly-ambitious provisions combined with a lack of a consensus about what competition norms should be.[54]

The present WTO Members would do well to learn from this history and eschew efforts to draft a multilateral competition policy agreement that fails to account for practical concerns of and differences among the Members. Indeed, while some Mem-

---

48. *See* ROBERT H. BORK, THE ANTITRUST PARADOX: A POLICY AT WAR WITH ITSELF 91 (1993) (explaining that maximization of consumer welfare, through efficient markets, is the sole basis for antitrust decisions. Judge Bork has been an intellectual leader of the "Chicago School."); RICHARD A. POSNER, ANTITRUST LAW: AN ECONOMIC PERSPECTICE (1976).

49. *See* BORK, THE ANTITRUST PARADOX, *supra*, at 116-117.

50. *See* Robert Pitofsky, *The Political Content of Antitrust*, 127 U. PA. L. REV. 1051 (1979).

51. *See* WTO ANNUAL REPORT, *supra* at 33.

52. *See* WTO ANNUAL REPORT, *supra* at 76.

53. *See* ALFRED E. ECKES, OPENING AMERICA'S MARKET: U.S. FOEIGN TRADE POLICY SINCE 1776 225-26 (1995). *See also* Douglas E. Rosenthal & Phedon Nicolaides, *Harmonizing Antitrust: the Less Effective Way to Promote International Competition*, *in* GLOBAL COMPETITON POLICY, *supra*, at 358- 59; WTO ANNUAL REPORT, *supra*, at 33.

54. *See* Rosenthal & Nicolaides, *supra*, at 359.

bers want the WTO to take up competition policy,[55] others urge caution,[56] preferring the use of bilateral and regional forums as stepping stones to a global agreement.[57]

Interestingly, the ITO was not the only — or even the first — failure to achieve an international, harmonized competition law. Efforts were made before World War II at the League of Nations, and also in the post-War period at the United Nations and Organization for Economic Co-operation and Development (OECD). These attempts all failed to produce a binding global agreement,[58] in large part because of an inability to identify commonality in the group objective. Without such common ground, the WTO is likely to experience the same disappointment, and would do well to avoid an extensive, detailed push to establish a supranational antitrust code, such as one based on the Munich Code.[59]

III. A MULTILATERAL AGREEMENT ON COMPETITION POLICY IS NEEDED

The caution urged above with respect to the WTO's work on competition policy should not be taken as an argument against a multilateral agreement. To the contrary, a multilateral agreement on competition law is necessary for several reasons. First, in the global economy, a multilateral competition policy would — or should — account for global welfare, not just the welfare of an individual country or group of countries. Under the present patchwork of national competition laws, account is not always taken of the welfare interests of other countries. Second, in a trading system characterized by reduced tariff barriers as a result of successive negotiating rounds under the GATT-WTO auspices, competition policy, or the lack thereof, might be used as a non-tariff barrier to trade. Last, as business becomes increasingly global, vastly different legal regimes and enforcement policies will slow expansion owing to administrative and bureaucratic delays. Thus, with appropriate caution, the WTO may in the long run prove to be an appropriate forum for hammering out a global competition policy accord.

A. Countries Acting Individually Are Unlikely to Account for Global Welfare

A country pursuing competition policy based only on the welfare of its citizens may select and enforce policies that do not maximize global welfare. This situation occurs where the country captures most or all of the gains, but bears few of the costs, of its policy choice. Consider a country that is able to capture the surplus from an anti-competitive act, but experience little of the corresponding welfare loss. Suppose other countries do not share in the gain, but are injured by the anti-competitive act. What incentive does the first country have to pursue a competition policy that maximizes global welfare? Absent a multilateral agreement, the answer might well be "none." Of course the hidden assumption here is that maximizing global economic welfare is a worthy goal of competition law. This assumption is not without criticism, as indicated earlier.

55. See Fox, *Toward World Antitrust and Market Access, supra,* at 2; *European Commission to Urge WTO to Spearhead World Antitrust Battle,* 13 Int'l Trade Rep. (BNA) 1018 (1996).

56. See Gary G. Yerkey, *U.S. Opposes Plan to Negotiate Agreement in WTO, Officials Say,* 14 Int'l Trade Rep. (BNA) 2034 (1997); Gary G. Yerkey, *Developing Nations Still Oppose Taking Up Investment, Competition Policy in WTO,* Aide Says, 13 Int'l Trade Rep. (BNA) 1829 (1996).

57. See *Klein Cites Antitrust Efforts Within the OECD,* 14 Int'l Trade Rep. (BNA) 1867 (1997).

58. See Waller, *supra,* at 349-352.

59. See International Antitrust Code Working Group, *Draft international Code as a GATT-MTO-Plurilateral Trade Agreement,* 65 Antitrust & Trade Reg. Rep. (BNA) No 1628, S-1 (Aug19, 1993).

For example, if China decides to allow all of its domestic producers of toys to form an export cartel, Chinese producers would capture the benefits of such behavior. However, non-Chinese consumers would be harmed through higher prices and lower quantities of available toys. Thus, a home country is able to capture the pro-competitive benefits for the home market, while exporting the anti-competitive effects. The United States could, of course, attempt to restrict or punish the behavior of the Chinese cartel by exercising extraterritorial antitrust jurisdiction. In *Hartford Fire Insurance Co. v. California,*[60] excerpted earlier in this Chapter, the Supreme Court held that American courts may exercise jurisdiction over foreign conduct that violates the antitrust laws. This ruling is based in part on the Effects Doctrine.[61] The Court also held courts need to weigh the interests of other countries—*i.e.,* consider comity—only if there is a direct conflict between domestic law and foreign law. Thus, in the United States-China example, an American court would need to weigh its decision to exercise jurisdiction against Chinese toy makers only if Chinese law condoned or compelled the creation of the export cartel.[62]

The Chinese cartel example also illustrates the "beggar-thy-neighbor" policies plaguing the competition laws of many countries. Such policies are a significant reason why the WTO decided to examine the role of competition policy in the global economy.[63] Two American laws, the Webb-Pomerene[64] Act and the Export Trading Company Act,[65] permit the formation of export cartels that do not cause anti-competitive effects in the United States or affect domestic exporters. Yet, these cartels could have distortive effects on overseas markets. Of course, nothing prevents foreign antitrust authorities from attacking the cartels under applicable foreign law.

To be sure, not all competition policy decisions rendered by a country reduce overall global welfare. For example, suppose the United States permits a merger that harms only EU producers. Suppose further that the overall efficiency gains of the merger result in a net global welfare gain that is not limited to American producers and consumers. Under a global efficiency-based competition policy model, the merger should proceed on the theory that global welfare has increased.

B. Competition Policy as a Barrier to Trade

With the completion of the Uruguay Round, the formation of the WTO, and the resulting reduction in tariff and many non-tariff barriers, a country's protectionist urges may be satisfied by using competition policy as a non-tariff barrier to protect domestic industries. That is, competition policy is a potential protectionist device countries could use to protect domestic producers. Regulatory barriers to entry, permissive enforcement, or the absence of competition law are manifestations of this device.[66] For example, Japan's permissive regulatory structure regarding its conglomerate corporate struc-

---

60. *See* 590 U.S. 764 (1993).

61. The Effects Doctrine grants a country jurisdiction to prescribe laws with respect to certain conduct, including conduct that is outside its territory that has or is intended to have a substantial effect within its territory. *See* RESTATEMENT (THIRD) OF FOREIGN RELATIONS LAW OF THE UNITED STATES § 402 (1987). *See generally* United States v. Aluminum Co. of America, 148 F.2d 416 (2d Cir. 1945) (finding jurisdiction based on the Effects Doctrine); Hartford Fire Insurance Co. v. California, 509 U.S. 764 (1993) (discussing the Effects Doctrine).

62. *See Hartford, supra,* 509 U.S. at 798-99.

63. *See* 1997 WTO ANNUAL REPORT, *supra,* at 30.

64. *See* 15 U.S.C. §§ 61-66.

65. *See* 15 U.S.C. §§ 4001-4021.

66. *See IEE Calls for International Agreement On Antitrust Policy, Faulting Current Rules,* 14 Int'l Trade Rep. (BNA) 2035 (1995).

tures frequently is cited as a non-tariff barrier to trade related to the enforcement of competition laws.[67] This problem, and a number of other related concerns, were raised by the United States in the Kodak-Fuji case, which is discussed in the preceding Note.

In addition, state monopolies and state trading companies - such as a state-owned telecommunications company—create non-tariff barriers that result from a country's competition policy decisions. These decisions are, to be specific, against privatization of the enterprise in question, and against creation of a competitive market for the goods or services provided by the enterprise.

C. Global Business is Hampered by Multiple Legal Regimes

Recent competitive arrangements in the airline and aerospace industry reveal the slowdown in business activity caused by multiple legal regimes. The dispute and settlement of the Boeing - McDonnell-Douglas merger is one example of multiple legal regimes complicating international business arrangements. Another example of an agreement in the airline industry that has been substantially hampered due to regulatory differences is the alliance between British Airways ("BA") and American Airlines ("AA"). Progress on the alliance came to a standstill after the EU Competition Commissioner Karel Van Miert made extensive demands on BA and AA to obtain the EU's blessing of the alliance. The evaluation of the agreement has lasted, to date, about two years.[68] In the global market, such delays will prevent many agreements from being reached simply because the uncertainty and time commitment of such agreements is too great.

D. WTO Agreements and Initiatives

Following the first ministerial meeting of the WTO in Singapore in December 1995, the WTO established a working group on trade and competition policy to identify areas that should be considered within the WTO framework. The WTO's decision to take up competition policy is a response to problems relating to corporate practices that restrict global trade, which have become increasingly apparent as governments reduce tariffs and more obvious non-tariff barriers pursuant to their obligations under the Uruguay Round agreements.[69] To date, however, the WTO working group has made little progress.

Some procedures for addressing competition policy concerns are set forth in the Uruguay Round agreements. For example, under Article IX of the *General Agreement on Trade in Services* (GATS),[70] a WTO Member may be requested by another Member to enter into consultations that would address business practices of service suppliers that restrain competition. Article VIII of the GATS address monopolies and exclusive service providers. It requires WTO Members to prevent monopoly suppliers from failing to extend most-favored nation (MFN) treatment to suppliers from other Members. The Article also prohibits monopoly suppliers from abusing their power when competing outside the area of their monopoly grant. Article VIII should assist in preventing cross-subsidization from a monopolistic market to a competitive market. As another example, Article 40 of the Uruguay Round *Agreement on Trade-*

---

67. *See, e.g.,* PRESTOWITZ, TRADING PLACES, *supra*, at 272-77.

68. *See Airlines' Accord Nears, Suggests EU Antitrust Chief*, WALL ST. J., Jan. 23, 1998, at A6.

69. *See WTO Cites Need for Competition Rules for Business Practices that Restrict Trade*, 14 Int'l Trade Rep. (BNA) 2221 (1997).

70. *See General Agreement on Trade in Services* (GATS), Dec. 15, 1993, 33 INT'L LEGAL MATERIALS 44 (1994).

Related Aspects of Intellectual Property Rights (TRIPs)[71] contains language explicitly addressing competition policy concerns.

Various proposals have been offered concerning the appropriate development of competition policy within the WTO. The proposals range from little or no involvement to creating a supra-national international competition law enforcement regime.[72] The adoption of the "Munich Code," as the agreement to establish a supranational authority is known, is not very likely to succeed at any time in the future, given the variety of legal regimes and the stages of development in the area of competition law. Similarly, because of the range of bilateral and regional agreements that already have been signed, it is unduly pessimistic to forecast that no competition policy agreement ever will be reached. The bilateral and regional agreements are discussed below.

Arguably, the WTO ought to see a workable competition policy as an evolutionary process. It should focus on fostering work at the bilateral level, and then use these agreements to find commonality in the objectives of competition policy. That is, a global agreement should weave together the common threads found in other competition policy agreements. What are these common threads? That is, what ought a multilateral competition policy agreement contain at a minimum?

First, a timetable for all Members - particularly developing countries - to enact competition policy legislation is needed. The WTO must provide technical assistance to Members that lack the bureaucratic resources to create functioning competition laws. Second, the WTO should include a provision that allows for positive comity. A positive comity provision could reduce instances of extraterritorial application of one Member's law regarding conduct occurring outside that Member's borders by providing an alternative remedy for a Member claiming injury from such conduct. Third, and parallel to this comity provision, any multilateral agreement ought to contain the bedrock international trade law principle, embodied in Article III of GATT, of non-discrimination. Only this principle can ensure that one Member's competition authorities do not favor domestic over foreign interests. Last, a multilateral agreement should contain notification obligations that would at least alert one country's competition enforcement agencies that another country is commencing an investigation that could affect the first country's interests

IV. CURRENT BILATERAL AND REGIONAL COMPETITION POLICY

A. Bilateral Agreements and Initiatives

Several cooperation agreements relating to competition policy already have been negotiated on a bilateral basis. These agreements are usually signed to (1) facilitate the discovery process, (2) assist in the notification of national antitrust authorities that an investigation will occur that could affect another country's interests, (3) minimize conflicts arising out of the extraterritorial application of one country's law to actions occurring within another country's borders, and (4) enhance the coordination of trans-national investigations related to competition law.[73] These agreements should serve as a guide for WTO efforts to establish a global competition policy.

---

71. *See Agreement on Trade-Related Aspects of Intellectual Property Rights*, Dec. 15, 1993, 33 INT'L LEGAL MATERIALS 81 (1994).

72. *See* International Antitrust Code Working Group, *Draft international Code as a GATT-MTO-Plurilateral Trade Agreement*, 65 Antitrust & Trade Reg. Rep. (BNA) No 1628, S-1 (Aug19, 1993).

73. *See* WTO ANNUAL REPORT, *supra*, at 81-2.

United States — Canada

The United States and Canada have a history of bilateral cooperation in competition law. After several decades of cooperation in various cases,[74] the United States and Canada signed a Memorandum of Understanding ("MOU") regarding cooperation with respect to the application of national antitrust laws.[75] The United States-Canadia MOU recognizes that while the two countries have close economic links, situations may arise where there is a conflict of laws or interests. As a result, the United States and Canada agreed to (1) notify and consult when an investigation conducted by one country's antitrust authority likely will affect the interests of the other country, (2) notify when one country expects to take action limiting the other country's access to information, (3) consider the other country's interest when enforcing competition laws, (4) eliminate or minimize conflicts between the parties, and (5) inform the other country regarding the commencement of private antitrust suits. The MOU is supplemented by a treaty on mutual assistance in criminal enforcement.[76] As a result, the United States and Canada have cooperated on antitrust investigations, including an antitrust criminal investigation of the thermal fax paper market in which Canadian law enforcement assisted American law enforcement by executing search warrants in Canada to obtain evidence.

United States — Germany

The United States and Germany signed an agreement relating to mutual cooperation regarding restrictive business practices in 1976.[77] The agreement pledges (1) cooperation between antitrust authorities in connection with investigations and proceedings, (2) cooperation in activities related to preventing and ending restrictive business practices, while simultaneously working in international organizations of which both countries are members, (3) agreeing to sharing certain information, and (4) information gathering assistance.

United States — Australia

The United States signed a mutual antitrust enforcement assistance agreement with Australia in 1997, under the auspices of the International Antitrust Enforcement Assistance Act of 1994 ("IAEAA").[78] The IAEAA grants the Attorney General of the United States, and the Federal Trade Commission, the authority to assist a foreign antitrust authority after negotiating an antitrust mutual assistance agreement. The IAEAA limits certain types of information that may be made available to foreign antitrust authorities under such an agreement. The Act places information furnished under Section 7A of the Clayton Act,[79] some evidence resulting from grand jury proceedings,[80] and evidence that is exempt on national security grounds[81] outside the reach of a mutual assistance agreement.

---

74. *See* Waller, *supra*, at 363.

75. *See Memorandum of Understanding as to Notification, Consultation and Cooperation with Respect to the Application of National Antitrust Laws*, Mar. 9, 1984, U.S.-Can., 23 INT'L LEGAL MATERIALS 275 (1984).

76. *See Treaty on Mutual Legal Assistance in Criminal Matters*, Mar. 18, 1985, U.S-Can., 24 INT'L LEGAL MATERIALS 1092 (1985).

77. *See Federal Republic of Germany-United States: Agreement Relating to Mutual Cooperation Regarding Restrictive Business Practices*, Sept. 11, 1976, F.R.G.-U.S., 15 INT'L LEGAL MATERIALS 1282 (1976).

78. *See* 15 U.S.C. §§ 6201-6212.

79. *See* 15 U.S.C. § 18a.

80. *See* 15 U.S.C. § 6204(2).

81. *See* 15 U.S.C. § 6204(3).

The IAEAA, and subsequent agreement with Australia, are designed to allow the United States and its foreign government partners to assist and cooperate with one another in obtaining and providing antitrust evidence that may help enforcement authorities to determine if there has been a violation of applicable antitrust laws. In the United States-Australia pact, the countries also agreed to inform each other when either country is about to start an investigation that may affect important interests of the other country.[82] This agreement is the first under the IAEAA, and it remains to be seen whether the agreement and Act actually increase antitrust enforcement cooperation.

United States — European Union

The United States and European Community (EC)[83] entered into an agreement in 1991 to increase antitrust cooperation and coordinate enforcement.[84] The agreement between the United States and EC includes articles on (1) notification of enforcement activities that may affect the interests of the other country, (2) facilitation of the exchange of information, (3) cooperation and coordination of enforcement activities, and (4) confidentiality for information provided to the other country under the agreement. Perhaps most significantly, there is an article mandating the application of positive comity, that is, requiring (within the bounds of each country's laws) comity considerations The positive comity requirement of the agreement allows one country to ask the other to apply its competition laws, although the application of such law may be discretionary. This could help reduce the necessity of extraterritorial application of one country's competition law for conduct that takes place entirely in the other country's jurisdiction.[85]

France — Germany

While the United States is active in signing bilateral antitrust agreements, other countries also have signed agreements related to competition. For example, France and Germany agreed to cooperate in the policing of restrictive business practices that effect the interests of the two countries.[86] Their agreement obligates both government to assist in proceedings and investigations carried out by their respective competition authorities, and to share information on restrictive business practices that may adversely affect the markets of both countries.

B. Regional Agreements

The EU

As mentioned earlier, the Treaty of Rome, which established the EC, includes an agreement on competition policy. One of the most important principles of the Treaty of

---

82. *See Agreement between the Government of the United States of America and the Government of Australia on Mutual Antitrust Enforcement Assistance*, available at <http://www.usdoj.gov/atr/international/usaus7.htm>.

83. The terms European Union ("EU"), created by the signing of the Treaty on European Union at Maastrict , the Netherlands, in 1992, which became effective in November 1993, and the European Economic Community ("EEC"), now simply the European Community ("EC"), established by the Treaty of Rome, are used synonymously. The two institutions are not identical, but for the purposes of this Note, the distinction between the EC and the EU does not alter the analysis of the EC's experience in competition policy, which is geared toward integrating the European States.

84. *See Agreement Regarding the Application of their Competition Laws*, Sept. 23, 1991, U.S. - E.C., 30 INT'L LEGAL MATERIALS 1491 (1991).

85. *See* Waller, *supra*, at 369.

86. *See Agreement Concerning Cooperation on Restrictive Business Practices*, May 28 1984, Fr.-F.R.G., 26 INT'L LEGAL MATERIALS 531.

Rome was the prevention of beggar-thy-neighbor policies by EU member States. The need to integrate Europe simply reflected the need to avoid the rivalries that had led to two world wars in less than half a century, *i.e.*, creating a common market would be a guarantor against future conflict. Thus, the creation and development of EU competition law must be understood as a tool to implement the broader vision of a united Europe.[87]

Articles 85 and 86 of the Treaty of Rome establish the competition law of the EU member States. Merger regulation was added to the competition law of the EU in 1989.[88] As a result of Articles 85 and 86, agreements and concerted practices that distort competition among the member States, as well as enterprises abusing their dominant position, are prohibited.[89] The EU has been able to develop a set of competition laws that co-exist with the laws of its member States. However, if the laws of a member State conflict or are inconsistent with EU law, then EU law is supreme.[90]

Also as suggested earlier, one important distinction between the American and European experiences concerns different enforcement procedures. Enforcement of EU competition law is based wholly upon parties notifying the European Commission. The Commission then decides whether the conduct at issue significantly restricts competition or serves the needs and interests of the community.[91] The European approach contrasts with the American enforcement mechanism, which is litigation driven by the government, private parties, or both. The pattern of American enforcement also reflects the unique and almost total reliance on concepts of economic welfare as the primary policy aim to be served by antitrust law.[92] The European pattern, by contrast, bespeaks the partly political aim of creating a single market dominated by pan-European companies.

NAFTA

The North American Free Trade Agreement ("NAFTA"), which entered into force in the United States, Canada, and Mexico on 1 January 1994, includes provisions on competition policy. These provisions are set forth in NAFTA Chapter 15, which is entitled "Competition Policy, Monopolies and State Enterprises." Article 1501 states:

1. Each Party shall adopt or maintain measures to proscribe anti-competitive business conduct and take appropriate action with respect thereto, recognizing that such measures will enhance the fulfillment of the objective of this Agreement. To this end the Parties shall consult from time to time about the effectiveness of measures undertaken by each party.[93]

NAFTA requires the parties ensure, through regulatory control, administrative supervision, and other measures that monopolies act within certain bounds of conduct.[94] Chapter 15 also addresses monopolies and state enterprises by allowing the NAFTA Parties to designate monopolies and create state enterprises.[95]

---

87. *See* Waller, *supra*, at 353-55.

88. *See* Fox, *US and EU Competition Law: A Comparison, supra*, at 348.

89. *See* Fox, *Toward World Antitrust and Market Access, supra*, at 6-7 (1997); WTO ANNUAL REPORT, *supra*, at 82-83.

90. *See* Waller, *supra*, at 369.

91. *See* Waller, *supra*, at 354-55.

92. *See, e.g.*, State Oil Co. v. Khan, 118 S.Ct. 275, 282 (1997).

93. *North American Free Trade Agreement*, Dec. 17, 1992, Can.- Mex.-U.S., Art. 1501, 32 INT'L LEGAL MATERIALS 605, 663 (1993).

94. *See* NAFTA Art. 1502.

95. *See* NAFTA Art. 1503.

NAFTA Chapter 15 has been rightly criticized as weak. It does not attempt to harmonize competition laws among the Parties. Nor does it place the existence and enforcement of competition policy on the same level as other provisions in NAFTA. If a Party fails to enact or maintain competition laws, then the remaining Parties have no recourse to the dispute settlement mechanism established by NAFTA.[96]

QUESTIONS

1.   What forum(s) is (are) most likely to solve global competition policy problems? The extraterritorial application of national antitrust laws? Agreements between the most developed countries? Agreements developed within the auspices of regional trade blocs such as the EU and NAFTA? The WTO?

2.   Would the ownership by a foreign sovereign of a firm that engages in conduct that violated United States antitrust laws preclude the exercise of American antitrust jurisdiction in light of the Act of State doctrine?

3.   In the 1990s, the Department of Justice announced that it would enforce United States antitrust laws against conduct occurring overseas that restrains American exports, whether or not there is direct harm to American consumers. Is such a statement consistent with recent Supreme Court decisions? With United States obligations under GATT?

---

96. *See* NAFTA Art. 1501(3).

Appendix

1998 World Development Indicators
Table 1.1 Quality of Life

Source: WorldBank. Reprinted with permission.

	Life expectancy at birth		Prevalence of child malnutrition	Sanitation	Safe water	Adult illiteracy rate		Commercial energy use
	Male years 1996	Female years 1996	% of children under 5 1990–96	% of population with access 1995	% of population with access 1995	% of people 15 and above Male 1995	% of people 15 and above Female 1995	kg of oil equivalent per capita 1995
Albania	69	75	..	..	..	..	..	314
Algeria	68	72	10	..	..	26	51	866
Angola	45	48	35	16	32	..	..	89
Argentina	69	77	2	89	64	4	4	1,525
Armenia	69	76	..	..	..	..	..	444
Australia	75	81	..	90	95	..	..	5,215
Austria	74	80	..	100	..	..	..	3,279
Azerbaijan	65	74	10	..	..	..	..	1,735
Bangladesh	57	59	68	35	79	51	74	67
Belarus	63	74	..	100	..	..	..	2,305
Belgium	73	80	..	100	..	..	..	5,167
Benin	52	57	24	20	50	51	74	20
Bolivia	59	63	16	44	60	10	24	396
Bosnia and Herzegovina	..	53	..	..	..	..	..	364
Botswana	50	53	27	55	70	20	40	383
Brazil	63	71	7	41	72	17	17	772
Bulgaria	67	75	..	99	..	..	..	2,724
Burkina Faso	45	47	33	18	78	71	91	16
Burundi	45	48	38	..	13	51	78	23
Cambodia	52	55	38	..	..	20	47	52
Cameroon	55	58	15	40	41	25	48	117
Canada	76	82	..	85	100	..	..	7,879
Central African Republic	46	51	23	..	18	32	48	29
Chad	47	50	..	21	24	38	65	16
Chile	72	78	1	83	..	5	5	1,065

(continued)

Country								
China	68	71	16	21	90	10	27	707
Hong Kong, China	76	81	..	..	..	4	12	2,212
Colombia	67	73	8	63	76	9	9	655
Congo, Dem. Rep.	51	54	34	..	..	13	32	47
Congo, Rep.	49	54	24	9	47	17	33	139
Costa Rica	75	79	2	..	..	5	5	584
Côte d'Ivoire	53	55	24	..	72	50	70	97
Croatia	68	77	..	54	96	..	..	1,435
Cuba	74	78	8	68	93	4	5	949
Czech Republic	70	77	1	66	..	..	..	3,776
Denmark	73	78	..	100	100	..	..	3,918
Dominican Republic	69	73	6	78	71	18	18	486
Ecuador	67	73	17	64	70	8	12	553
Egypt, Arab Rep.	64	67	9	11	64	36	61	596
El Salvador	66	72	11	68	55	27	30	410
Eritrea	54	56	41	..	..	..	..	..
Estonia	63	76	..	..	..	..	..	3,454
Ethiopia	48	51	48	10	27	55	75	21
Finland	73	81	..	100	100	..	..	5,613
France	74	82	..	96	100	..	..	4,150
Gabon	53	57	15	76	67	26	47	587
Gambia, The	51	55	17	37	76	47	75	55
Georgia	69	77	..	..	..	..	..	342
Germany	73	80	..	100	..	..	..	4,156
Ghana	57	61	27	27	56	24	47	92
Greece	75	81	..	96	..	..	..	2,266
Guatemala	64	69	33	66	60	38	51	206
Guinea	46	47	24	70	62	50	78	64
Guinea-Bissau	42	45	23	20	23	32	58	37
Haiti	54	57	28	24	28	52	58	50
Honduras	65	69	18	62	65	27	27	236
Hungary	65	75	..	94	..	..	..	2,454
India	62	63	66	29	81	35	62	260
Indonesia	63	67	40	51	62	10	22	442
Iran, Islamic Rep.	69	70	16	..	..	22	34	1,374
Iraq	60	63	12	87	44	29	55	1,206

	Life expectancy at birth		Prevalence of child malnutrition	Sanitation	Safe water	Adult illiteracy rate		Commercial energy use
	Male years 1996	Female years 1996	% of children under 5 1990–96	% of population with access 1995	% of population with access 1995	% of people 15 and above Male 1995	% of people 15 and above Female 1995	kg of oil equivalent per capita 1995
Ireland	74	79	..	100	..	..	..	3,196
Israel	75	79	..	70	99	..	..	3,003
Italy	75	81	..	100	..	..	..	2,821
Jamaica	72	77	10	74	70	19	11	1,191
Japan	77	83	3	85	89	..	..	3,964
Jordan	69	72	10	100	..	7	21	1,031
Kazakhstan	60	70	1	..	..	..	..	3,337
Kenya	57	60	23	77	53	14	30	109
Korea, Dem. Rep.	61	65	..	100	100	1	3	1,113
Korea, Rep.	69	76	..	100	89	1	3	3,225
Kuwait	74	79	6	100	..	18	25	9,381
Kyrgyz Republic	62	71	..	53	75	..	..	513
Lao PDR	52	54	40	19	39	31	56	40
Latvia	63	76	..	..	..	..	..	1,471
Lebanon	68	71	9	..	..	10	20	1,120
Lesotho	57	60	21	6	52	19	38	..
Libya	66	70	5	..	90	12	37	3,129
Lithuania	65	76	..	..	..	..	..	2,291
Macedonia, FYR	70	74	..	..	..	..	..	1,308
Madagascar	57	60	32	3	29	..	..	36
Malawi	43	43	28	53	45	28	58	38
Malaysia	70	74	23	91	88	11	22	1,655
Mali	48	52	31	31	37	61	77	21
Mauritania	52	55	48	..	..	50	74	102
Mauritius	68	75	15	100	98	13	21	388
Mexico	69	75	14	66	83	8	13	1,456
Moldova	64	71	..	50	..	..	..	963

(continued)								
Mongolia	64	67	12	..	..	..	..	1,045
Morocco	64	68	10	40	52	43	69	311
Mozambique	44	46	47	21	32	42	77	38
Myanmar	58	61	31	41	38	11	22	50
Namibia	55	57	26	34	..	..	..	..
Nepal	57	57	49	20	48	59	86	33
Netherlands	75	80	..	100	100	..	..	4,741
New Zealand	73	79	..	..	..	..	..	4,290
Nicaragua	65	70	24	31	61	35	33	265
Niger	44	49	43	15	53	79	93	37
Nigeria	51	55	35	36	39	33	53	165
Norway	75	81	..	100	..	..	..	5,439
Oman	69	73	14	79	..	..	..	1,880
Pakistan	62	65	40	30	60	50	76	243
Panama	72	76	7	87	83	9	10	678
Papua New Guinea	57	58	30	22	28	19	37	232
Paraguay	68	74	4	30	..	7	9	308
Peru	66	71	11	44	60	6	17	421
Philippines	64	68	30	..	..	5	6	307
Poland	68	77	..	100	..	..	..	2,448
Portugal	72	79	..	100	..	..	..	1,939
Puerto Rico	71	80	..	..	..	..	..	1,993
Romania	65	73	6	49	..	..	..	1,941
Russian Federation	60	73	3	..	..	..	..	4,079
Rwanda	39	42	29	..	..	30	48	33
Saudi Arabia	69	71	..	86	93	29	50	4,360
Senegal	49	52	22	58	50	57	77	104
Sierra Leone	35	38	29	11	34	55	82	72
Singapore	74	79	14	97	100	4	14	7,162
Slovak Republic	69	77	..	51	..	..	..	3,272
Slovenia	71	78	..	90	..	..	..	2,806
South Africa	62	68	9	46	70	18	18	2,405
Spain	73	81	..	100	99	..	..	2,639

	Life expectancy at birth		Prevalence of child malnutrition	Sanitation	Safe water	Adult illiteracy rate		Commercial energy use
	Male years 1996	Female years 1996	% of children under 5 1990–96	% of population with access 1995	% of population with access 1995	% of people 15 and above Male 1995	% of people 15 and above Female 1995	kg of oil equivalent per capita 1995
Sri Lanka	71	75	38	..	..	7	13	136
Sudan	53	56	34	22	50	42	65	65
Sweden	76	82	..	100	..	..	..	5,736
Switzerland	75	82	..	100	100	..	..	3,571
Syrian Arab Republic	66	71	..	78	85	14	44	1,001
Tajikistan	66	72	..	62	..	..	..	563
Tanzania	49	52	29	86	49	21	43	32
Thailand	67	72	13	70	81	4	8	878
Togo	49	52	25	22	..	33	63	45
Trinidad and Tobago	70	75	7	56	82	1	3	5,381
Tunisia	69	71	9	..	..	21	45	591
Turkey	66	71	10	94	92	8	28	1,009
Turkmenistan	62	69	..	60	85	..	..	3,047
Uganda	43	43	26	57	34	26	50	22
Ukraine	62	73	..	49	97	..	..	3,136
United Arab Emirates	74	76	7	95	98	21	20	11,567
United Kingdom	74	80	..	96	100	..	..	3,786
United States	74	80	..	85	90	..	..	7,905
Uruguay	70	77	4	82	83	3	2	639
Uzbekistan	66	72	4	18	..	..	..	2,043
Venezuela	70	76	5	58	79	8	10	2,158
Vietnam	66	70	45	21	36	4	9	104
West Bank and Gaza	..	..	..	..	..	..	..	..
Yemen, Rep.	54	54	30	51	52	..	..	192
Yugoslavia, FR (Serb./Mont.)	70	75	..	100	..	..	..	1,125
Zambia	44	45	29	23	43	14	29	145
Zimbabwe	55	57	16	58	74	10	20	424

World	65 w	69 w		47 w	78 w	21 w	38 w	1,474 w
Low income	62	64	..	28	76	24	45	393
Excl. China & India	55	58	..	36	51	36	55	132
Middle income	65	71	..	60	..	14	22	1,488
Lower middle income	64	70	..	58	76	14	25	1,426
Upper middle income	66	73	..	64	76	13	16	1,633
Low & middle income	63	67	..	37	76	21	39	762
East Asia & Pacific	67	70	..	29	84	9	24	657
Europe & Central Asia	64	73	..	..	..	..	..	2,690
Latin America & Carib.	66	73	..	57	73	12	15	969
Middle East & N. Africa	66	68	..	..	..	28	50	1,178
South Asia	61	63	..	30	78	38	64	231
Sub-Saharan Africa	51	54	..	37	45	34	53	238
High income	74	81	..	92	..	[a]	[a]	5,123

a. UNESCO estimates illiteracy to be less than 5 percent.

Index